Betty Crocker

cookbook

heart health edition

Wiley Publishing, Inc.

Dear Friends,

Take heart! The best news about heart disease is that many of the risks are within your power to change. The experts agree: Incorporating simple healthy habits can help protect you against heart disease. In fact, the connection between what you eat, your exercise habits, and the other things you do to stay healthy is stronger than ever.

Since heart disease is the number one killer of American women, Betty Crocker is proud to partner with WomenHeart, a national organization whose mission is to improve the quality of life and health care for the 8 million women in this country living with heart disease. In support of this, Betty Crocker has made a donation directly to WomenHeart.

This Betty Crocker Cookbook with its Heart Health section can help you in your daily quest to lead a heart-healthy life. It's bursting with the best for your heart: the most up-to-date information from cardiologists, nutrition information and tips and fitness hints, along with a collection of easy recipes and terrific meal ideas to help you where it counts the most—in your kitchen.

You will love the fact that everything you need to know in the kitchen is all right here. And you can rest assured that the 50+ years of experience from America's Most Trusted Kitchens...tested recipes, the latest comprehensive information and beautiful photography are all wrapped together in this special edition, just for you!

Betty Crocker

Although heart disease still has a reputation of being a man's disease, the truth is that it kills one in four women. One of WomenHeart's goals is to ensure that every woman receives early detection, accurate diagnosis and proper treatment for her heart. We're pleased to join forces with Betty Crocker to spread the message about women's heart awareness, to encourage women to take action to lower their risk factors for heart disease, and to promote the Red Dress, the national symbol of women and heart disease. The Red Dress inspires women everywhere to protect their heart health. Read on for more information about WomenHeart, and ways you can incorporate heart-healthy habits into your own life.

WomenHeart

Playing the Game of Heart Health

Keeping our hearts healthy is like playing a card game: though we begin with whatever we're dealt, the game's outcome is greatly influenced by the skills we use and the choices we make—and perhaps, a little luck. You'll find that at every stage of the game, there's a lot you can do to keep your heart its healthiest. **While only 20 percent are risks you cannot control, a whopping 80 percent are risks you *can* control.**

Your Trump Card: Your Heart

Although it's only about the size of your fist, your heart is a very powerful, hardworking muscle. With every beat, it pumps blood at a rate of about five quarts per minute throughout your body. In a single day, your heart will beat more than 100,000 times, and pump about 2,000 gallons of blood.

Your heart, along with your lungs, is the vital center of your **circulatory system,** which is the network of tubes, called **blood vessels**, that carries blood throughout your body. Blood travels from the heart to the lungs, where it picks up oxygen. Then it passes through the heart again, through blood vessels called **arteries**, to deliver the oxygen and other nutrients to all your body's cells.

From there, the deoxygenated blood is carried by another set of blood vessels, the **veins**, to the heart and lungs. Blood also carries waste products from your cells to your liver and kidneys, which filter them out. After the veins return the blood to the heart, it circulates back to the lungs to pick up oxygen, beginning the cycle all over.

Your pumping heart propels the blood throughout this complex system—and with each beat, the blood travels far. To give you an idea of how hard your heart works, imagine that all your blood vessels were laid end-to-end. They'd stretch for 60,000 miles—long enough to circle the world twice!

Know Your Cards: Major Risk Factors for Heart Disease

Though heart disease is a major killer, tremendous progress in fighting it is being made. In fact, the death rate from coronary heart disease declined by 33 percent from 1994 to 2004. Part of that success is recognizing the risk factors that make heart disease more likely, and working to reduce those risks.

The Factors (20 Percent) You Can't Change:

- Increased Age
- Gender
- Family History

The Large Proportion (80 Percent) You Can Change:

- Smoking
- Overweight or Obesity
- High Blood Pressure
- High Blood Cholesterol
- Inactive Lifestyle
- Diet
- Having Diabetes
- Stress
- Depression

The 20 Percent Hand You're Dealt: Risk Factors You Can't Change

Some risk factors are simply a matter of circumstance—you don't have any control over them. But knowing about them can help you make decisions that can influence your health. The factors include:

Increased Age. Men over age forty-five and women over age fifty-five are at greater risk of developing coronary heart disease than are younger people.

Gender. At least until menopause, women have a lower risk of heart disease than men. This gender difference may be due to the effects of the female hormone estrogen. After menopause, when natural estrogen levels wane, the differences lessen. By age seventy, men's and women's risk of cardiovascular disease (CVD) are about equal.

Family History. If one or both of your parents or grandparents had heart problems at an early age, the likelihood of your developing heart disease is greater than that of people with no family history of the disease. African-Americans and Hispanics have a higher incidence of heart disease than do whites; in fact, heart disease and stroke are the number one and number three killers of Hispanics/Latinos and African-Americans as well as whites.

Diseases of the Heart

When you consider that your heart is part of such an exquisitely tuned, complex system, it's amazing more things don't go wrong. Many of us go through our lives without any problems with our hearts—but others aren't so lucky. In fact, one in three Americans have some form of **cardiovascular disease** (CVD), the catch-all term for diseases of the heart and blood vessels. CVD is our nation's number one killer, causing close to 40 percent of all deaths in 2003. Here is a quick introduction to the most common cardiovascular diseases in the United States:

Coronary Heart Disease (CHD). This is the most common heart disease affecting Americans—and is the cause of one out of every five deaths each year. CHD is sometimes called "coronary artery disease," because it begins in the coronary arteries, those that lead to the heart. If these arteries become clogged with plaques—deposits containing a waxy substance called **cholesterol**—it becomes harder for the blood to get to the heart. Without treatment, the plaques can build up, making the artery walls thicker and less flexible. This is called **arteriosclerosis** (hardening of the arteries), or atherosclerosis.

Plaque-clogged coronary arteries inhibit the flow of oxygen-rich blood to the heart. A warning signal that the heart isn't getting enough oxygen is **angina pectoris,** a disease characterized by brief attacks of pain, pressure or burning in the chest. Angina attacks are painful, but they usually only last a few minutes. The only good that can come from angina pectoris is if the person heeds the body's warning and seeks medical treatment.

If plaques keep building up in a coronary artery, they can eventually burst or tear, causing a blood clot to form. The clot can clog the artery completely, cutting off blood flow to the heart. The affected parts of the heart muscle start to die, resulting in a **heart attack**. A heart attack can be disabling or life-threatening, depending on how much heart muscle is irreversibly damaged and how quickly treatment can be started. About 1.2 million Americans suffer heart attacks each year.

Stroke. Some experts refer to a stroke as a "brain attack," because it occurs when blood flow to part of the brain is reduced, depriving it of the oxygen it needs. Strokes often occur when part of a blood clot travels through the bloodstream and gets lodged in a blood vessel that brings blood to the brain. Some strokes occur when the arteries serving the brain

Don't Delay, Get Help Right Away! Know the Signs of Heart Attack and Stroke

A heart attack occurs when one or more of the heart's arteries is blocked. The blood supply to the heart muscle is severely reduced or stopped; if the blood supply is cut off for more than a few minutes, the heart's muscle cells suffer permanent injury or die. Depending on how much of the heart is damaged, this can kill or disable someone.

Heart attack and stroke are life-threatening emergencies, so **every second counts**. If you notice any of the warning signs below, dial 9-1-1 immediately. Today there are new, clot-busting medications and treatments available that can stop some heart attacks and strokes while they are happening, saving lives and reducing disabilities.

Not all the signs below will occur in every heart attack or stroke. They may go away for a while and then return.

Signs of Heart Attack

Some heart attacks are sudden and intense—no one is in any doubt about what's happening with these "movie heart attacks." More often, though, heart attacks start slowly, with only mild pain or discomfort. The person affected may wait too long before getting help because he or she isn't sure what's wrong. Know the signs:

- **Chest pain.** Most heart attacks involve pain in the center of the chest; it lasts more than a few minutes or it may go away and come back. It can feel like uncomfortable pressure, burning, squeezing or fullness.
- **Discomfort in other areas of the upper body.** Symptoms may also include pain or discomfort in one or both arms, the back, neck, jaw or stomach.
- **Shortness of breath.** This feeling often accompanies chest pain, but it can occur beforehand.
- **Other signs:** Breaking out in a cold sweat, nausea or lightheadedness.
- **Symptoms for women:** Women are somewhat more likely than men to experience back, neck or jaw pain, shortness of breath and/or nausea and vomiting as a symptom of heart attack.

The American Heart Association and the National Heart, Lung and Blood Institute have launched the "Act in Time" campaign to increase awareness of heart attack symptoms and the importance of calling 9-1-1 immediately. Their motto: Don't delay, get help right away!

Signs of Stroke

A stroke occurs when a blood vessel that brings oxygen and nutrients to the brain bursts or is clogged by a blood clot or other particle. Because of this blockage or rupture, part of the brain doesn't get the blood and oxygen it needs. When the nerve cells in the affected area of the brain are deprived of oxygen, they die within minutes.

These are the warning signs of stroke, as identified by the American Stroke Association:

- Sudden numbness or weakness of the face, arm or leg, especially on one side of the body
- Sudden confusion, trouble speaking or trouble understanding speech
- Sudden trouble seeing out of one or both eyes
- Sudden trouble walking, feeling of dizziness, a loss of balance or coordination
- Sudden, severe headaches with no known cause

If you or someone you're with has one or more of these signs, call 9-1-1 immediately. **Check the time so you know when the first symptoms appeared.** For the most common type of stroke, a clot-busting drug can reduce long-term disability if it's administered within three hours of the start of symptoms.

become clogged and hardened by fatty deposits, or are damaged by high blood pressure. Another type of stroke, called a **hemorrhagic stroke,** is caused by bleeding in the brain.

Whatever its cause, a stroke can be devastating. The affected part of the brain can become injured or can even shut down, resulting in paralysis, numbness or speech defects. Strokes can also be fatal: Of the half-million Americans who have a stroke each year, about one quarter do not survive. Luckily, new treatments and promising research continue to improve the odds.

High Blood Pressure (Hypertension). When the force of a heartbeat pushes blood into your arteries, it exerts pressure on the walls of your blood vessels: Picture it like water flowing through a garden hose. Some pressure is needed to keep the blood flowing, but if the blood vessels are constricted for any reason, the pressure rises—just as the force of water increases if you squeeze the hose. Hypertension is like keeping the faucet turned up too much: the increased workload strains your heart, and your blood vessels, just like the hose, get damaged over time.

It's estimated that nearly one out of three Americans has high blood pressure. Because the disease rarely causes symptoms that can be felt, many of them don't know it. But the consequences of letting this "silent killer" go untreated are serious. Having high blood pressure greatly increases your chances of developing heart failure, stroke and kidney failure—especially if you have other risk factors, such as obesity, smoking, diabetes or high cholesterol. That's why your blood pressure is checked at every doctor visit—and why, if it's high, it's so important to keep it under control. Staying on top of your treatment for high blood pressure—which usually involves managing your weight, exercise and medications—can help prevent problems from developing.

The Lipids (Fats) in Your Blood. When you have your cholesterol measured by a blood test, you'll get a **total cholesterol reading:** the amount of cholesterol circulating in your blood. Most cholesterol is made in the body, though the amount is influenced by the amounts and kinds of fats we eat. A high total cholesterol reading, of course, is a risk factor for heart disease—but alone, it doesn't tell the whole story. That's why your cholesterol test includes a **lipid profile,** an analysis of the fats (lipids) present in your blood. Besides total cholesterol, a lipid profile will report your level of **triglycerides (TG)**—a transportable form of fat. While triglycerides are used as a source of energy by the body, persistently high blood triglyceride levels add to your risk of developing coronary heart disease.

Since your blood is mostly water—and water and fat don't mix—these lipids need to attach to proteins in order to travel through the blood. The combination of lipids and proteins is called a **lipoprotein**. Determining the levels of certain types of lipoproteins in your blood can provide important clues about your heart health. Your lipid profile will likely include measures of:

High-Density Lipoprotein (HDL), or "good" cholesterol. HDL carries cholesterol to the liver where it is broken down and removed from the body. The higher your HDL, the lower your risk of cholesterol building up in your arteries, and the lower your risk of developing coronary heart disease.

Low-Density Lipoprotein (LDL), or "bad" cholesterol. LDL carries cholesterol through the bloodstream to your cells. The higher your LDL, the higher your risk of cholesterol building up in your arteries, and the greater your risk of developing coronary heart disease.

Risk Factors You Can Change

When it comes to heart disease, ***about 80 percent of the factors that increase your risk are within your power to change. How you decide to live your life now can make a major difference in what happens to your heart later.*** What's more, since many of the risk factors are interrelated, reducing one risk factor can improve your heart health in other areas. Begin exercising regularly, for example, and you're likely to lower your blood pressure, reduce your weight and improve your cholesterol profile. You can make a powerful difference! Here are some of the most important things you can do:

1. Quit Smoking

While every vital organ of your body suffers when you smoke, it is especially hard on your heart. Depending on how often cigarette smokers light up, they double, triple or even quadruple their risks of heart disease compared to nonsmokers.

Smoking hurts your heart by damaging artery walls and promoting the buildup of fatty deposits within those arteries' walls. It also increases the tendency of blood to clot, setting the stage for a heart attack or a stroke. With every puff you take, nicotine (the chemical most responsible for making smoking so addictive) increases blood pressure and heart rate, and it causes the coronary arteries to constrict, adding to the stress on your heart.

The good news about smoking-related heart disease is that it's preventable: Quit now, and your health risks start to drop right away. Many of the 1.2 million ex-smokers who quit each year do it with the help of nicotine-containing patches, gum, nasal sprays or inhalers that help ease the symptoms of nicotine withdrawal. Nicotine-containing patches and gum are available without a prescription. Your doctor can also put you in touch with organizations for group support, problem-solving and counseling.

2. Aim for a Healthy Weight

Being overweight strains your heart—it has to pump more blood to reach a greater amount of body tissue. Extra pounds increase your risk of developing high blood pressure and high cholesterol, as well as diabetes. The more you weigh, the greater your risk: **People who are considered "obese"**—they weigh more than 20 percent over their ideal weight—**double their risk of developing heart disease**.

Because excess weight is linked to so many problems, *reaching or maintaining a healthy weight can have a major impact.* In fact, few other changes in your life will have such a dramatic, positive effect on your health. Improvements you may realize by reaching a healthy weight:

- Added energy
- Reduced blood pressure, if it's high
- Better control of your glucose, if you have diabetes
- Lower blood cholesterol levels
- Reduced risk of coronary heart disease, stroke and cancers

How can you tell if your weight is healthy? Health experts prefer to use an accurate measurement that takes both weight and height into account: your **body mass index**, or BMI.

The 10-Percent Solution

If you're overweight, losing just a few pounds may seem like a drop in the bucket, but from your heart's point of view, it's a major improvement. Studies show that a weight loss of just 5 to 10 percent of body weight can significantly lower your blood pressure, improve cholesterol readings and, if you are diabetic, improve your ability to control your diabetes.

What does 5 to 10 percent amount to? If you weigh 160 pounds now, it's a weight loss of just eight to sixteen pounds.

DETERMINING YOUR BODY MASS INDEX (BMI)

Body mass index, or BMI, is the measurement of choice for many physicians and researchers studying obesity. BMI uses a mathematical formula that takes into account both a person's height and weight. BMI equals a person's weight in kilograms divided by height in meters squared (BMI=kg/m^2).

The table below has already done the math and metric conversions. To use the table, find the appropriate height in the left-hand column. Move across the row to the given weight. The number at the top of the column is the BMI for that height and weight.

Health experts define a BMI of 19 to 24 as normal. That means if your BMI falls within these boundaries, your weight is probably at a healthy level, and there's no health advantage to changing it. If your BMI is between 25 and 29, you're considered "overweight"; if it's 30 or above, you are in the "obese" category. The higher your BMI within these ranges, the greater your risk of heart problems and other weight-related health issues—and the more you'll benefit from losing weight!

	Normal						Overweight					Obese		
BMI (kg/m^2)	19	20	21	22	23	24	25	26	27	28	29	30	35	40
Height (in.)	Weight (lb.)													
58	91	96	100	105	110	115	119	124	129	134	138	143	167	191
59	94	99	104	109	114	119	124	128	133	138	143	148	173	198
60	97	102	107	112	118	123	128	133	138	143	148	153	179	204
61	100	106	111	116	122	127	132	137	143	148	153	158	185	211
62	104	109	115	120	126	131	136	142	147	153	158	164	191	218
63	107	113	118	124	130	135	141	146	152	158	163	169	197	225
64	110	116	122	128	134	140	145	151	157	163	169	174	204	232
65	114	120	126	132	138	144	150	156	162	168	174	180	210	240
66	118	124	130	136	142	148	155	161	167	173	179	186	216	247
67	121	127	134	140	146	153	159	166	172	178	185	191	223	255
68	125	131	138	144	151	158	164	171	177	184	190	197	230	262
69	128	135	142	149	155	162	169	176	182	189	196	203	236	270
70	132	139	146	153	160	167	174	181	188	195	202	207	243	278
71	136	143	150	157	165	172	179	186	193	200	208	215	250	286
72	140	147	154	162	169	177	184	191	199	206	213	221	258	294
73	144	151	159	166	174	182	189	197	204	212	219	227	265	302
74	148	155	163	171	179	186	194	202	210	218	225	233	272	311
75	152	160	168	176	184	192	200	208	216	224	232	240	279	319
76	156	164	172	180	189	197	205	213	221	230	238	246	287	328

Body weight in pounds according to height and body mass index.

PEAR OR APPLE?

Carrying excess fat is a known health risk, but *where* you carry it on your body matters, too. Studies show that people with "apple" shapes—those who tend to accumulate fat around their waists—have an increased risk of coronary heart disease, high blood pressure, stroke, diabetes and even some cancers, when compared with their "pear"-shaped counterparts—those who tend to carry fat around their hips and thighs. This connection between weight and body shape leads some health experts to feel that taking a waist measurement is important to assess health risks.

To determine whether you're carrying too much fat around your middle, place a tape measure around your waist just above your hipbones. A reading of more than forty inches in a man, or thirty-five inches in a woman, is considered a health risk—especially if your BMI places you in the "overweight" range or above.

HEALTHY WAYS TO LOSE

As tempting as it sounds to "lose ten pounds in one week" (as some diet programs boast), most experts agree that slow, steady weight loss—about one to two pounds per week—is the safest and most effective strategy. The best diet, in fact, isn't a diet that you "go on" or "go off," but a way of living your life more healthfully. If you work at making changes gradually, you'll allow yourself the time to adopt new ways of thinking that result in new behaviors and improved, sustainable habits.

Another reason to avoid crash diets is that they are so hard to stay on: no one can tolerate feeling constantly hungry and deprived for long. A crash diet also makes it harder for you to keep weight off; the diet makes your body believe it is starving, and it reacts by slowing the rate at which you burn calories. Crash dieters almost always regain the weight they lost, and often gain even more.

The best strategies for losing weight include increasing your level of activity. Exercise helps people lose weight more easily and keep it off longer than if they were merely adjusting their diets. Other key factors in successful weight loss include: setting realistic goals; keeping a food and/or exercise diary; rewarding yourself for weight loss accomplishments; acknowledging and accepting setbacks; and enlisting the support of families and friends, support groups or organized weight-loss programs. Your health-care provider can help you find a weight-loss strategy that works for you.

HEART-WISE FAST FOOD

Compare the amount of calories, fat and cholesterol in a typical fast-food lunch:

	Calories	Fat (g)	Sat Fat (g)	Cholesterol (mg)
Super-sized cheeseburger:	730	40	19	75
Medium vanilla shake:	550	13	8	50
Medium French fries:	380	20	4	0
Totals:	1,660	73	31	125

With a better-for-you, heart-healthier fast-food lunch:

	Calories	Fat (g)	Sat Fat (g)	Cholesterol (mg)
Hamburger:	260	9	3.5	30
Side salad:	20	0	0	0
Low fat Italian dressing:	60	2.5	0	0
1 carton low-fat (1%) milk:	100	2.5	1.5	10
Totals:	440	14	5	40

Besides keeping your fat, saturated fat, cholesterol and calories down, heart-healthy meals give you more fiber, vitamins and minerals than do conventional fast-food meals. When you have information and a watchful eye, you are well equipped to make wise choices.

3. Get Moving!

The benefits of exercise really sound too good to be true, don't they? "Lose weight!" "Have more energy!" "Cut your risk of heart disease in half!" In fact, exercise is so important to good health that the lack of it—a sedentary lifestyle—is considered a major risk factor for coronary heart disease. Unfortunately, most Americans—over 60 percent of us—don't get the exercise we need, and that's bad news for our hearts. By staying sedentary, we *double* our risks of developing heart disease.

Why is exercise so important? Your heart is made of muscle—and like any muscle, it benefits from a good workout. Regular activity makes your heart a more efficient pump, and it helps lower your blood pressure and blood cholesterol levels—all while boosting your levels of "good" HDL cholesterol. Regular activity also helps you lose weight and keep it off, which decreases your heart-disease risks even more.

TO GET STARTED

Before you get started, the American Heart Association recommends that men over the age of fifty and women aged fifty-five or older who have previously been sedentary should check with their physician to make sure it is safe to start an exercise program.

To keep your heart healthy, begin by exerting yourself just a little more than usual—and do it regularly. Many health guidelines suggest a goal of sixty minutes of activity, most days of the week. That might seem like a lot if you're inactive now, but, to begin, any activity is better than none. Housework, gardening and yard work qualify, especially if you approach them with zest.

You can ease into an exercise routine by first aiming for thirty minutes of daily activity, then working your way up. If you can't spare a block of time, start with smaller sessions that can be squeezed into your day. You might try a fifteen-minute brisk morning walk and another walk at lunchtime, for example. Gradually increase the frequency and intensity of your activity as your fitness improves.

IT'S NEVER TOO LATE

Pioneering work at Tufts University School of Nutrition, in Massachusetts, proves that you're never too old to benefit from exercise. In their landmark study, researchers introduced strength-training techniques to a group of six nursing home residents whose average age was ninety years. At the beginning of the study, most were so frail they needed help getting out of a chair, and used walkers or canes to get around. But within two months of a supervised weight-lifting program, the residents had more than doubled their strength, on average—and their performance on walking and balance tests improved dramatically. Two of the residents even got rid of their canes!

4. Stay in Charge

Perhaps the most important way you can reduce your risk of heart disease is to take an active role in managing your health. That means treating your body with respect and love by giving it the nutritious foods, exercise and regular rest it needs. It also means staying in touch with your doctor for regular checkups, and recognizing that you are the most important member of your health-care team.

If you have any of the risk factors such as arteriosclerosis, high cholesterol or diabetes, staying in charge of your health is even more important. Even if you take medications for these conditions, taking risk-reducing steps, such as eating a nutritious diet and getting regular exercise, can make these medications more effective and possibly allow you to reduce your dosage level.

5. Eat Heart-ily

Eating healthy isn't complicated—and it doesn't mean giving up your favorite foods, feeling deprived or having to eat "special" meals. In fact, a heart-healthy diet is good for virtually everyone, whether they have heart disease or not! See "Eat to Your Heart's Content," pages xiv to xxiii, for the key components of heart-healthy eating.

Stack the Deck in Your Favor

Eating a variety of foods in moderation, getting regular exercise, staying on top of your health—each one of these healthy lifestyle decisions is like adding another valuable card to your hand. Each one makes an impact in reducing your risk of heart disease—and they all work together to keep you healthy and feeling great.

Taking steps to improve your health can have a trickle-down effect on the rest of your life: Once you start, you'll find that other positive changes will be easier to make. Think of someone you know who has made a big change for the better in his or her health recently. Chances are, that person made other healthy moves along the way—becoming a regular mall walker, say, after losing a few pounds. Positive changes have a way of building on each other—and they can for you, too.

Stress and Your Heart

Think of how your heart pounds when you're nervous or anxious; being "stressed out" certainly feels like it's straining your heart. Studies show that extreme stress—especially when triggered by events over which we have little control, such as the death of a loved one—take a toll on our hearts. Heart attacks occur more often in the six months following a traumatic life event than they do in the six months prior to the event.

While you can't make your life stress-free, you *can* make a big difference by changing the way you react in stressful situations. This is especially important if you have a "Type A" personality: aggressive, competitive and easily frustrated by setbacks. If you feel overwhelmed by the stress in your life, talk with your doctor, who can recommend stress-management techniques, such as yoga, relaxation exercises, meditation and biofeedback. Other techniques:

- **Get plenty of rest** so you're better able to handle what life throws you.
- **Get regular exercise:** it will lift your spirits, boost your energy and help you sleep more soundly.
- **Focus on the present,** rather than spending too much time reliving past events or dreading the future.
- **Talk about your concerns** and seek support from someone you're close to.

Women and Heart Disease

Heart disease—not breast cancer—is *the* number one health risk for women. More and more women are becoming aware of this fact, yet many do not know much about their own personal risk. *Do you?*

Unlike a cold or the flu, heart disease doesn't just happen. It can take years to develop—often quietly and without notice. In fact, symptoms may not be apparent until well after menopause.

A woman's symptoms for heart disease and a heart attack can be very different than a man's. By not recognizing trouble, many women may put off seeking help.

It's important to note that women who have heart attacks and strokes may experience a wide variety and combination of symptoms listed on page v. Women are more likely than men to experience back, neck or jaw pain, shortness of breath and/or nausea and vomitting as a symptom of heart attack.

Pay attention to what your body is telling you and particularly if the symptoms are new, persistent or you find they are getting worse, don't delay calling for help. Better safe than sorry when it comes to a potential heart attack.

Facts about Women and Heart Disease

- Heart disease is the leading cause of death of American women (six times more than breast cancer)
- 13% of women age 45 and over have had a heart attack (435,000 American women have a heart attack each year)
- More women than men die of heart disease each year
- Women are less likely than men to receive beta-blockers, ACE inhibitors or even aspirin after a heart attack
- Women comprise only 25% of participants in all heart-related research studies

THE REAL STORY ABOUT WOMEN AND HEART DISEASE

Myth	Reality
Heart disease is a man's problem.	It's a woman's problem, too. One in three women has some form of cardiovascular disease.
Heart disease occurs later in life.	Atherosclerosis, the buildup of plaque inside artery walls and a factor in heart disease, can begin in childhood.
You can rely on your health-care provider to identify heart disease risks.	Take the initiative to discuss your interests and concerns about heart health. Some health-care providers do not recognize heart disease as a significant threat to women and may not be aware of the differences in symptoms between men and women.
Heart disease in men is the same as heart disease in women.	Research suggests that women may have less obvious changes in blood vessels. Changes may occur more in small vessels, making disease harder to diagnose and resulting in treatment delays.
Men and women have similar symptoms when experiencing a heart attack.	Symptoms often are different for women.
There's little you can do reduce your risk for heart disease.	Women can lower their risk significantly through healthy lifestyle habits.

WomenHeart

WomenHeart was founded in 1998 by three women who had heart attacks in their 40s. They had faced many obstacles, including misdiagnosis and social isolation, and were amazed that the issue seemed invisible within the health community.

Today, WomenHeart is the only national patient-centered advocacy organization that provides support and education to women across America. Their website **www.womenheart.org** provides free information and membership, resources, support and encouragement. The site features:

- Up-to-date information about heart disease and its treatments, mental health concerns, alternative therapies, food and fitness
- Heart News: current heart-health articles
- A bulletin board where members can communicate with other women
- Stories from women living with heart disease
- A monthly e-mail newsletter
- Health tips on topics from weight loss to quitting smoking to exercise-oriented vacations

The Heart Truth Campaign

The Heart Truth is that heart disease is the #1 killer of American women. In fact, one in four women dies of heart disease. But heart disease can also lead to disability and a significantly decreased quality of life. The campaign, sponsored by WomenHeart and the National Heart, Lung and Blood Institute (NHLBI), tells women that heart health starts with you. Talk to your doctor, find out your risk and take action today to lower it.

Unfortunately, most women don't know *The Heart Truth* and don't take their risk seriously—or personally. Although awareness among women has increased—from 34 percent in 2000 to 57 percent in 2006—most fail to make the connection between risk factors, such as high blood pressure and high cholesterol, and their own chance of developing heart disease.

The centerpiece of *The Heart Truth* is the Red Dress, which was introduced as the national symbol for women and heart disease awareness in 2002 by NHLBI. The Red Dress reminds women of the need to protect their heart health and inspires them to take action.

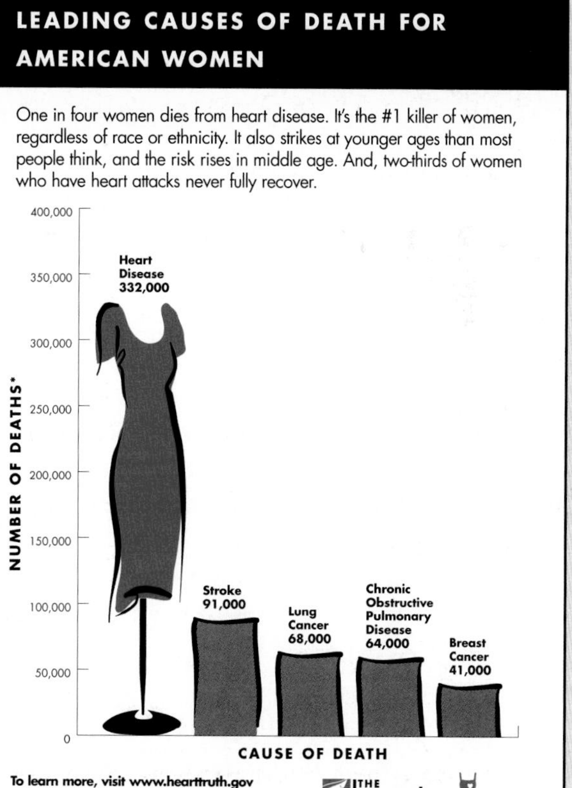

Eat to Your Heart's Content

The 2005 *Dietary Guidelines for Americans*, the most recent recommendations from the U.S. Department of Health and Human Services and Agriculture, reflect science and medicine's current thinking on nutrition and health. They are designed to help you make sound food choices so you get enough, but not too much, of the nutrients you need to stay healthy. They outline a way of eating that is inherently heart-smart: moderate in calories, and based mostly on foods of plant origin rather than animal foods.

The *Dietary Guidelines* recommend we:

- Eat a variety of vegetables and fruits every day.
- Eat a variety of whole grains every day.
- Keep fat intake moderate. Consume mostly unsaturated fats and limit saturated fats, trans fatty acids and cholesterol.
- Adjust our calorie intake to help reach or maintain a healthy body weight.
- Choose beverages and foods that decrease our intake of sugars.
- Use less salt in the foods we prepare and eat.
- Drink alcoholic beverages only in moderation, if at all.

These guidelines will benefit not only your heart, but can also help you reduce your chance of developing cancer, diabetes and digestive disorders. In addition, you'll feel and look better, and you'll have more energy to enjoy your life. The following sections take a look at the key components of a healthy diet in more detail.

Top Foods for a Healthy Heart

Increasing these foods in your diet now may pay off big in helping prevent heart disease later on:

1. ***Fruits and vegetables.*** The brighter, more colorful, greater variety you choose, the better. They are a treasure trove of vitamins and phytonutrients.
2. ***Whole grains.*** Their crunchy, nutty, hearty flavor makes them a treat at any meal. Their fiber, vitamins, minerals and phytonutrients make them a bonus for your heart. Aim for at least three servings of whole grains a day.
3. ***Olive and canola oil.*** They are rich in monounsaturated fat, a type of fat that can benefit cholesterol levels. Substitute them for other fats used in cooking and baking.
4. ***Fish.*** Eat at least twice a week. The Omega-3 fat in fish may slow plaque formation inside arteries, lower blood pressure and positively affect heart rhythm.
5. ***Nuts.*** The type of fat in nuts, plus their fiber, vitamins and minerals are heroes on the heart front. Substitute nuts for less healthful snacks and ingredients. *Note:* Simply adding nuts into your diet tacks on calories: One small handful = about 200 calories.
6. ***Soy.*** If part of a low-fat diet, it may help reduce heart disease risk. Soy is a low-saturated fat, cholesterol-free source of protein. Look for soy milk, soy nuts or tofu as ways to incorporate soy in your diet.

7. ***Legumes.*** Like soy, black beans, kidney beans, pinto or any type of beans can help lower harmful cholesterol levels when they are part of a low-fat diet.

Fruits and Vegetables

Fruits and vegetables provide many nutrients and health benefits. Evidence indicates that eating a diet rich in many veggies and fruits can lower the risk of heart disease. The Dietary Guidelines recommend most Americans eat at least 2 cups of fruit and at least 2 1/2 cups of vegetables every day. Though research continues to uncover the benefits of eating a vegetable- and fruit-rich diet, most Americans just don't get the recommended number of fruits and vegetables, missing out on the great taste and health benefits they provide. Here are just a few of the benefits:

- ***Folic acid.*** Even its name, which sounds like "foliage," is a clue that vegetables, especially leafy green ones, are excellent sources of this important B vitamin. (It's also found in fruits—especially citrus—legumes and other plant foods, as well as in fortified cereals.) Folic acid has long been known to be important in protecting against birth defects.
- ***Phytonutrients.*** These beneficial substances, found in plant foods, help strengthen our bodies' defenses against heart disease and cancer. Some phytonutrients that are attracting attention as possible heart-disease fighters are the carotenoids, vegetables like carrots that are high in beta-carotene (see "Color Them Healthy," page xvi).
- ***Antioxidants.*** These substances may help prevent cholesterol from damaging arteries by preventing "bad" LDL cholesterol from changing to a form that's readily absorbed by arterial cells. Antioxidants include vitamin C, vitamin E and beta-carotene—all found in many fruits and vegetables.
- ***Fiber.*** Fruits and vegetables are good sources of both soluble and insoluble fiber, making them an important weapon against heart disease and other illnesses. Since much of the fiber is contained in the skins of fruits and vegetables, do not peel edible skins.
- ***Fewer calories.*** Even though they'll fill you up as well as take up lots of room on your plate, fresh fruits and vegetables won't set you back much on a calorie count. On average, a half-cup serving of vegetables provides just 25 calories; fresh fruit provides 60. And, with very few exceptions (avocados, coconuts) fresh produce is fat-free.

Ways to Add Vegetables and Fruits to Your Diet

Try these surefire tips to increase your intake of heart-healthy fruits and vegetables:

- Snack on cut-up carrots, celery, cucumbers, radishes, bell peppers and baby tomatoes. Wash and prepare a big batch at the beginning of the week to have on hand, or buy packages of baby carrots, soy nuts or other ready-to-eat vegetables.
- Prepare a smoothie incorporating chopped fresh fruit, ice and a little fat-free plain yogurt.
- Eat your cereal with fruit for an energizing breakfast or snack.

- Start meals with a vegetable-based soup such as minestrone or tomato soup, or with a green salad.
- Sprinkle fresh berries or sliced citrus fruit onto your salad.
- Use salsa as a dip for vegetables and as a topping for baked potatoes or burgers.
- Load your sandwiches with sliced tomatoes, lettuce, onions, roasted peppers or other vegetables.
- Stir frozen chopped spinach, onion-pepper blends, green beans, shredded carrots or zucchini into soups, stews and casseroles.
- Toss pasta with cooked chopped vegetables (or their frozen equivalents) before topping with sauce.
- Eat fresh fruit for dessert.

COLOR THEM HEALTHY

Eat a colorful abundance of fruits and vegetables each day; the pigments that give produce its beautiful colors are the phytonutrients that can help prevent diseases. There is a whole palate of reasons to eat "a rainbow a day":

- ***Red:*** tomatoes, watermelon and pink grapefruit are colored by lycopene, a heart-healthy antioxidant. Cooking makes lycopene more available to the body, so enjoy tomato sauces and tomato soup, keeping an eye on sodium.
- ***Orange:*** carrots, cantaloupes, mangoes, winter squash and sweet potatoes help protect the body's cells against oxidative damage and may help prevent heart disease and cancer.
- ***Red and purple:*** grapes, blueberries, blackberries, strawberries and red cabbage contain anthocyanins, which have antioxidant properties.
- ***Yellow and green:*** spinach, collards, turnip greens, corn, green peas and honeydew melon contain lutein and zeaxanthin, both of which may help prevent macular degeneration, a disease of the eye.
- ***Green:*** broccoli, cabbage and kale contain sulforaphane and indoles, substances that may help fight certain cancers.

Fiber

Protecting your heart doesn't always mean you have to eat less. Nutrition experts wish Americans would eat much more of one nutrient: **fiber**. Fiber is simply the part of plant foods that the body cannot digest. There are two main types, each with important health benefits:

- ***Insoluble fiber*** doesn't dissolve in water. It helps add bulk to stools and keeps the bowels moving regularly. It's found primarily in whole-grain cereals and bread, bran and in the skins of fruits and vegetables.
- ***Soluble fiber*** can dissolve in water. It helps lower cholesterol in the blood. In the small intestine, where most of our food is digested, soluble fiber combines with water to form a gel. The gel binds with cholesterol particles, preventing them from being absorbed, and ushers them out of the body. Studies show that regularly consuming soluble-fiber rich foods, including ready-to-eat whole-grain oat cereal, oatmeal and oat bran, as well as barley, can help reduce blood cholesterol levels.

Since most fiber-rich foods contain both types of fiber, the benefits multiply when you eat them regularly. Foods rich in any type of fiber can also help you control your weight because they're digested more slowly, which may help you feel satisfied longer. For all these reasons, many health organizations, including the American Heart Association, recommend we get at least 25 grams of fiber daily in our diets. Unfortunately, most of us average less than half that: about 12 grams.

Finding Whole-Grain Foods

While plenty of foods may sound fiber-rich—"Cracked-Wheat Bread," or "Seven-Grain Crackers," for example—they may not contain much, if any, whole-grain ingredients. Here are some quick tips for finding true whole-grain foods:

- **Scan the ingredients.** Whole-grain foods list a whole grain—wheat, oats, corn or rice—as the first ingredient. The words "whole" or "whole-grain" appear before the grain's name, e.g., "whole-grain oats."
- **Look for a "whole grain" seal or logo** included on the package of some whole-grain foods.
- **Check for a health statement.** Foods containing a high percentage of whole grains are permitted to make the following claim on their labels: "Diets rich in whole-grain food and other plant foods that are low in total fat, saturated fat and cholesterol may reduce the risk of heart disease and certain cancers."

It's easy to boost the fiber in your diet. Following the *Dietary Guidelines for Americans*, page xiv, will put you on the right track; that eating plan is based primarily on fiber-rich plant foods: whole grains, vegetables and fruits, and legumes (beans and peas). To boost your intake of whole grains, eat at least half of your grain-based foods each day from whole-grain sources.

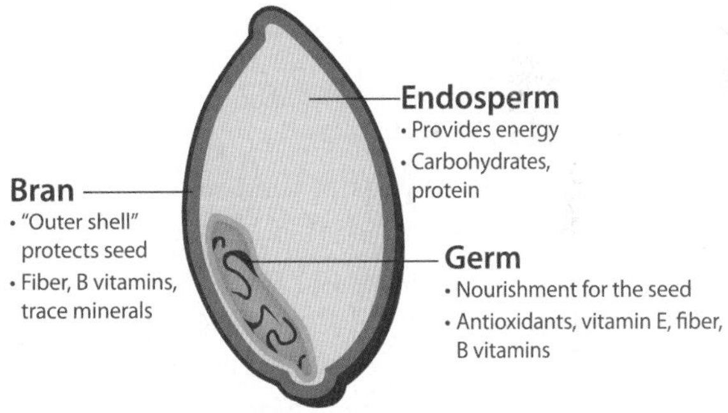

Endosperm
- Provides energy
- Carbohydrates, protein

Bran
- "Outer shell" protects seed
- Fiber, B vitamins, trace minerals

Germ
- Nourishment for the seed
- Antioxidants, vitamin E, fiber, B vitamins

Whole Grains

A whole grain is the entire seed of a grass plant and contains all parts of the grain kernel (see image): the fiber-rich outer coating of bran; the energy-dense middle layer, called the endosperm; and the nutrient-packed germ.

Because whole-grain foods include all parts of the grain, they include all the grain's nutrients, too. Foods made with refined grains lack the nutritious bran and germ components—and even if the grains are enriched later, only some of these nutrients are restored. By choosing the "whole" food, you get the whole package of health benefits.

Remember, if one of the pieces of the grain is missing, it's not whole-grain.

Of course, you can also cook with whole grains, which include quinoa, kasha, wheat berries, amaranth, brown rice, corn, oats, barley and wild rice. Look through the Grain section on pages 337 to 345. Try the Creamy Quinoa Primavera, the Kasha and Bow-Tie Pilaf or the Wheat Berry Salad.

Know the Fat Facts

The fats we eat make food more satisfying and delicious; for example, just think of what dressing does for a salad. Having some fat in our diets helps us feel "filled up" longer. And fat performs vital functions in the body, too, supplying it with essential fatty acids and fat-soluble vitamins, maintaining the integrity of all your body's cells and playing a key role in your immune and nervous systems. Some types of liquid fats (like canola oil) may even help reduce your risk of heart disease.

But most Americans consume too much saturated fat and trans fats and not enough of the heart-healthy mono- and polyunsaturated fats. (The American Heart Association recommends getting less than 7 percent of calories from saturated fats. Currently, our saturated fat consumption averages 11 percent of the calories we eat.) Because diets high in saturated and trans fats are associated with the development of high blood cholesterol, obesity and diabetes—all known risk factors for heart disease—many experts believe our penchant for fat is a major reason why heart disease is so prevalent in this country.

What's more, while some fat is essential for everyone, eating lots of fat (any kind!) can be fattening. At 9 calories per gram, fat contains more than twice the calories of the other types of food we eat: protein and carbohydrates both contain 4 calories/ gram. That's key to understanding why many Americans are overweight. If you're trying to lose weight, cutting the fat in your diet is one of the easiest ways to cut calories. A good goal: *Limit your calories from fat to no more than 35 percent of total calories.*

How Much Fat Should I Eat Every Day?

To estimate how many total grams of fat to aim for, multiply your daily calorie level by 30 percent and divide by 9. For example, if you need 2,000 calories per day, 2,000 calories × .3 = 600 calories. 600 calories ÷ 9 calories per gram of fat = 67 grams.

Cholesterol is a waxy substance used by the body to make hormones and bile acids. Cholesterol is a component in all our cells. It's so vital, our bodies manufacture all we need, but we also get it from eating meat, poultry, eggs and dairy products.

When there's too much cholesterol in your blood, it builds up on the walls of your arteries, setting the stage for coronary heart disease. Compared with saturated and trans fats, the cholesterol we eat doesn't have as much of an effect on our blood cholesterol levels: most of us compensate for the excess cholesterol in our diets by manufacturing less of it in our bodies. Nonetheless, it's important to stay on top of your cholesterol intake, especially when you consider that most cholesterol-rich animal foods also contain saturated fat. *The American Heart Association recommends healthy Americans limit their intake of cholesterol to less than 300 milligrams (mg) per day.*

FAT FACTS TABLE

The foods we eat contain several different types of fats; each causes different reactions in the body. The following table lists the most important fats in our diets, along with experts' recommendations on their consumption:

Type of Fat	Suggested Level (% of Total Calories)	Effect on Heart Disease	Risk
Saturated	Less than 7%	Found in high-fat animal products, cocoa butter, shortening and certain nuts. Solid at room temperature, this fat increases your LDL "bad" cholesterol. **Eating less saturated fat is the most important step you can take to lower your blood cholesterol.**	Increases
Trans	Less than 1%	Created when hydrogen is added to liquid oil and turned into a solid fat. Found in shortening, stick margarine (stick margarine is more hydrogenated than soft tub margarine), baked goods like doughnuts, muffins and French fries. Increases your LDL "bad" cholesterol and may decrease HDL "good" cholesterol. Food labels now include trans fat information in the "Nutrition Facts" statement.	Increases
Monounsaturated	Up to 15%	A "good" fat found in olive oil, canola oil, peanuts, avocados and almonds. Experts believe the bulk of the fats we eat should be monounsaturated.	Decreases
Polyunsaturated	Up to 10%	A class of "good" fats found in vegetable oils such as corn, sunflower and their products, and in many nuts. Known to reduce LDLs—a plus—but may also reduce heart-protective HDLs at the same time.	Decreases
Omega-3 Fatty Acids	0.8%	A type of polyunsaturated fat found in cold-water fish like salmon and sardines; it remains liquid even at very cold temperatures. Other sources: vegetable oils like canola and soybean, flaxseed and walnuts. Populations with diets that include significant amounts of fish regularly have lower rates of heart disease than do populations with diets that feature other kinds of meats.	Decreases

Fishing for Omega-3s

While fish is the richest source of long-chain Omega-3 fatty acids, you don't have to be a fish lover to benefit. Some plant foods contain another type of Omega-3 fatty acid, called alpha-linolenic acid, which may also have similar, heart-healthy benefits. Flaxseeds and walnuts, along with the oils made from them, are concentrated sources. Soybean and canola oils are also good sources, and they are the major contributors of Omega-3s in the American diet. Some supermarkets sell eggs that contain Omega-3s; if you can find them, try using them in your favorite recipes.

Be Good to Your Heart with Smart Fats

The good news: Replacing some saturated-fat foods with poly- and monounsaturated fat foods will help improve your ratio of "protective" cholesterol to "harmful" cholesterol.

To reduce the saturated fat in your diet, and increase the mono-unsaturated fat, think "liquid": use oils instead of butter and shortening. Since all the fats we eat are a combination of different types, even oils have some saturated fat, and some have more than others. The best oils for you include canola, soybean, olive, sunflower and corn. Oils high in saturated fat include coconut, palm and cottonseed.

Here are some ways to add monounsaturated (good) fats to your diet:

- Snack on walnuts, soy nuts, almonds and peanuts or add nuts to salads and stir-fries.
- Sauté and bake with canola or olive oil.
- Snack on small amounts of avocados and olives or top salads and casseroles with them.
- Eat fatty fish once or twice a week, especially salmon, herring, mackerel, sardines, bluefish, pompano and albacore tuna.
- Replace some of the flour in baked goods with ground flaxseed (tablespoon for tablespoon) to increase good Omega-3 fatty acids. One teaspoon of ground flaxseed per day in a muffin, cookie or other baked good provides heart-protective benefits.

Here are some simple ways to lower your overall fat and saturated fat:

- ***Eat smaller portions.*** As portions grow, so do calories and fat. Skip the super-size meals and choose normal-size servings. Fill up on fruits and vegetables if you are still hungry.
- ***Trim visible fat*** from meat and remove skin from chicken and turkey before eating.
- ***Cook lean.*** Use cooking sprays instead of fat in nonstick pans. Also, broil, bake, roast, grill, poach, steam, stew or microwave foods whenever possible.
- ***Select lean chicken, turkey, fish and meat.*** Light-meat chicken and turkey are naturally low in fat, especially if you remove the skin. Most fish is also very lean.
- ***Go meatless a couple of times each week.*** Limiting the amount of meat and poultry you eat can help reduce saturated fat, while increasing fiber and complex carbohydrates. Instead of meat, try dishes made with dried beans and peas, grains, vegetables and fruits.
- ***Choose reduced-fat mayonnaise, salad dressings and sour cream.*** The amount of fat in creamy dressings can add up fast, so use reduced-fat whenever possible.
- ***Use fat-free or reduced-fat dairy products.*** Drink fat-free (skim) milk and use plain nonfat yogurt, cottage cheese, cheese, pudding and ice cream.
- ***Go easy on butter, margarine and cream sauces.*** Use canola oil, trans fat-free margarine or butter in baking and cream sauces only once in a great while.

- ***Cut back on "hidden" fats and trans fats*** in foods like potato or other chips, French fries, high-fat cheeses and in baked goods such as doughnuts, muffins and cookies. Instead, eat lower-fat microwave popcorn, whole-grain tortilla chips, pretzels and other lower-fat snacks.
- ***Be a label reader.*** Nutrition labels tell you how much fat, saturated fat and trans fats each food contains.
- ***Indulge in fresh fruits and vegetables.*** Evidence indicates that eating a diet rich in many veggies and fruits can lower the risk of heart disease.

A Tricky Card: Salt

If you have high blood pressure, or if it runs in your family, reducing the sodium in your diet by cutting down on salt may help. While our bodies only need about 500 milligrams (mg) of sodium per day, the average American consumes about 5,000 mg.

For many people, all that salt isn't a problem; our kidneys divert the excess salt to be excreted in the urine and sweat. But some who are "salt-sensitive" may find that their bodies can't handle any excess salt. It causes them to retain water, increasing their blood volume and placing additional strain on their hearts. Eating a low-salt diet—plus losing excess weight and getting regular exercise—can fight this process.

Since there's no easy way to tell if you're salt-sensitive, many health experts consider it safe and reasonable for everyone to keep their salt intake moderate. The American Heart Association suggests we limit our sodium intake to less than 2,300 mg per day, about the amount in one teaspoon of salt. One great way to cut salt is to eat more fresh foods—preferably home-cooked—and sprinkle salt on only at the table (tasting the food first to see if it needs it, of course). Look for reduced-sodium and low-sodium versions of your favorite foods; there are many.

Instead of Salt, Sprinkle On:

Lemon juice

Vinegar (try herbal varieties, sherry or rice wine vinegar or balsamic vinegar)

Chopped fresh or dried herbs

Salt-free seasoning blends

Grated lemon, lime or orange zest

Chopped fresh chile peppers

Sautéed chopped onions, garlic and/or minced fresh ginger root

A Helpful Card: A DASH of Good News

Can diet really make a difference in managing high blood pressure? Findings from the recent DASH Study (Dietary Approaches to Stop Hypertension) indicate it can. When people ate more fruits, vegetables and low-fat dairy products—and less saturated fat—than a typical American diet, their blood pressures dropped significantly. In some cases, the effects were similar to those achieved by taking medications! A later study found the DASH diet was even more effective if salt was also reduced: the less sodium was consumed, the more blood pressures dropped.

Even if you don't have high blood pressure, DASH is a heart-healthy way to eat; other studies have found the diet can help lower LDL ("bad") cholesterol levels, too. For more information about the DASH diet, check out the National Heart, Lung, and Blood Institute's Web site at www.nhlbi.nih.gov.

A (Moderate) Toast to Alcohol

You've probably heard that a daily drink or two is good for your heart. Indeed, several studies suggest that light to moderate drinkers have a lower risk of heart disease, and perhaps a lower risk of death following heart attacks, than do teetotalers. Moderate amounts may even protect against certain types of strokes. When taken in moderation, alcohol seems to exert its heart-healthy effects by boosting blood levels of HDL ("good") cholesterol, as well as reducing the tendency of blood to clot.

These benefits must be considered within the context of how alcohol addiction can damage lives. Further, excessive amounts of alcohol can raise your blood pressure—that's why most health experts agree: If you're not a drinker now, don't start just to protect your heart. There are so many other ways to lower your heart-disease risks, it's not worth it.

If you do drink, keep your intake moderate: no more than two drinks daily for men, and one for women. One "drink" equals 12 ounces of beer, or 4 to 5 ounces of wine or 1 1/2 ounces (three tablespoons) 80-proof spirits. The recommendations for women are lower because they tend to be smaller and to metabolize alcohol more slowly than men. People ages sixty-five or over should halve those amounts, since they don't metabolize alcohol as efficiently as younger people. The kind of drink isn't as important as how you enjoy it: Drink your alcohol with food to help slow its absorption—and take time to savor the pleasure it adds to the meal. Spread your drinks throughout the week, rather than consuming large amounts at one sitting and abstaining on other days.

Everything in Moderation

By now, you're familiar with the components of a heart-healthy way of eating, but equally important is making sure you're eating an amount that's right for you. In our food-abundant society, where eating opportunities are plentiful and portions are often "super-sized," it's easy to lose track of what "eating in moderation" means. Many health experts believe that eating too much is at the heart of our country's obesity epidemic.

Daily Calories: What's Your Number?

This formula will help you estimate the number of calories you need to hold your current weight steady. If you want to lose weight, eat fewer calories or increase your activity level.

Multiply your current weight by one of the activity factors:

1. If you're sedentary (inactive most of the time): Multiply by 12
2. If you're moderately active (exercise a few times a week): Multiply by 14
3. If you're very active (participate regularly in heavy exercise): Multiply by 16 to 18

Example:
For a sedentary woman who weighs 140 pounds:
140 (pounds) × 12 (activity factor) = 1,680 calories/day
To maintain her current weight, she will need to take in about 1,680 calories per day.

How much should you eat? You can determine the calories your body needs daily with the formula above; individuals' results will vary, depending on how active people are. The formula will give you a rough estimate, but be sure to consult with your doctor or a registered dietitian to find a calorie range that's best for you.

Fighting "Portion Distortion"

Americans are eating more calories than they did a decade ago, and one reason is that portions are larger. According to a recent study, most marketplace food portions are much bigger—sometimes two to eight times larger—than normal. Consider that a typical bowl of spaghetti in an Italian restaurant is about three cups, or six standard servings. With the advent of mega-sized meals, jumbo muffins and extra-big drink cups, it's easy to lose touch with what normal portions look like.

Use this chart to help you visualize the correct portion sizes of the foods you eat most often. To begin, measure your portions—soon you'll be able to "eyeball" them accurately.

1 teaspoon	=	About the size of your fingertip (tip to middle joint)
1 tablespoon	=	About the size of your thumb tip (tip to middle joint)
1/2 cup	=	A fruit or vegetable that fits into the palm of your hand—about the size of a tennis ball
1 ounce nuts	=	Fits into the cupped palm of a child's hand
1 cup	=	About the size of a woman's fist; cereal that fills half of a standard cereal bowl
1 ounce	=	About the size of a standard slice of processed cheese or 2 dominoes
3 ounces meat	=	About the size of a deck of cards or a cassette audiotape

Heart-Smart Snacks

Consider these great heart-healthy snacks:

1. Whole-grain granola bars, fruit-and-grain bars, cereal snack mixes, ready-to-eat cereal and light popcorn. Remember, with whole grains, "three are key!" Select three or more servings of whole-grain foods each day.
2. Fresh fruits and vegetables provide important nutrients and antioxidants. Keep baby carrots, celery sticks, salsa, frozen grapes, bananas, apples, kiwifruit or other favorites on hand.
3. Cereal and yogurt together are a nutritious combination. Choose a high-fiber, whole-grain cereal and a light yogurt. Try layering the two for a parfait!
4. Reduced-fat peanuts or roasted soy nuts are great for munching. For variety, mix them with low-fat popcorn, whole-grain cereal or sprinkle them with your favorite savory herb blends.
5. Dried plums, cranberries, apricots, dates and raisins are the ultimate convenience food, and they contain important vitamins. Stretch them by mixing with pretzels, low-fat popcorn or ready-to-eat cereal.
6. Yogurt smoothies with fruit can be a delicious treat as well as an excellent source of calcium, vitamins and other important nutrients. Simply put your favorite light yogurt and cut-up fresh fruit in the blender, whirl and enjoy!
7. Sandwiches made with lean turkey, beef, ham, tuna or low-fat cheese and whole-grain bread work well for more substantial snacks. Load them up with your favorite raw veggies for a hearty mini-meal.
8. String cheese, mozzarella cheese slices or chunks, or other low-fat cheeses, eaten with or without fresh fruit, provide calcium. To minimize the amount of saturated fat, choose the low-fat or nonfat versions.
9. Tortilla chips, bagel chips and pretzels come in many varieties. Dip them in roasted vegetable dip, guacamole or salsa. Or, enjoy them with low-fat cheese or peanut butter.
10. Reduced-fat crackers, cookies and breads, especially animal, graham, rye crackers, oyster crackers, saltines, matzo, ginger snaps, molasses cookies, bread sticks and flatbread.

Add in Activity

Physical activity is pivotal to a healthy heart. Yet, few women get enough exercise each day to benefit their heart. The ripple effect is significant. Too little physical activity can double your risk for heart disease.

How Much Is Enough?

Having a healthy lifestyle and being successful at weight loss or maintenance includes being physically active. The American Heart Association recommends at least thirty minutes of moderate-intensity activity on most, ideally all, days of the week. If you can't fit in thirty minutes at a time, break it up by doing ten- or fifteen-minute mini workouts. Any way that you can be more active counts. The point is to move more throughout the day. Consider these simple ways to fit in exercise:

Aerobic Exercise. The best exercises for strengthening your heart are **aerobic** activities—those that involve continuous, rhythmic use of your muscles. These include:

Walking briskly (3–4 mph)	Jumping rope
Swimming	Jogging or running
Cycling	Dancing

Choosing an activity you enjoy will help you stick with it longer. Your workout should be intense enough to feel like you're working, but not so strenuous that you can't pass "the talk test": you should always be able to have a conversation with someone during the activity (except swimming, of course). In fact, having an exercise buddy is a great way to get and stay motivated.

To further support your success, try to work out at the same time each day so that it becomes a regular part of your life. Consider thinking about it as the one meeting in your day you *cannot* miss. Prevent boredom by varying your activities: ride your bike on one day, walk briskly around in a shopping mall on another. And don't be too hard on yourself if you miss a day or two. Instead, acknowledge that we all have lapses—and get right back into your routine the following day.

Get the Kids Moving, Too! When kids are physically active every day, they reap the same physical, psychological and social benefits you do. To achieve and maintain a good level of heart and lung fitness, the American Heart Association recommends:

- Children age two and older participate in at least thirty minutes of fun, *moderate-intensity* activities every day.
- Children age two and older participate in at least thirty minutes of *vigorous* physical activities at least three to four days per week.

Be a Role Model: Adopt an active lifestyle yourself, and provide your children with opportunities to have fun being active and growing strong. It's the best way to help kids develop a life-long exercise habit. It doesn't have to be fancy: Get everyone out for a game of tag, go for a bike ride, toss a baseball, kick a soccer or football ball around or take a walk together. Get moving and have fun with your kids!

Live Today with Tomorrow in Mind

It's true: you *can* significantly influence your health. Take advantage of that power. Find out what you can about your heart's health, enjoy the good taste of good foods, the energy you get from physical activity and the happiness that comes from knowing you are doing your best.

Family-Pleasing Recipes that are Heart-Healthy

It's great to have some fast recipes to revamp your family's eating habits in a—well—heart beat. These takes on burgers, fries and more prove you don't have to give up your favorite foods to eat in a way that's good for your heart. Add them to the weekly repertoire, then flip past to find dozens more heart-healthy recipes that appear in every chapter of your *Betty Crocker Cookbook*—from main dishes to desserts.

Creamy Mango Smoothies

PREP TIME: 10 Minutes **START TO FINISH:** 10 Minutes ■
6 SERVINGS (1 CUP EACH)

Rich and creamy, fruit smoothies are great any time of day. They're filling, and full of heart-healthy vitamins and minerals. If mango isn't your thing, try the strawberry variation, or use fresh pineapple or peaches.

2 mangoes, seed removed, peeled and chopped (2 cups)
2 cups mango sorbet
2 containers (6 oz each) French vanilla low-fat yogurt
1½ cups fat-free (skim) milk or soymilk

In blender, place all ingredients. Cover; blend on high speed until smooth.

1 SERVING: CALORIES 200 (CALORIES FROM FAT 10); TOTAL FAT 1g (SATURATED FAT 0.5g, TRANS FAT 0g); CHOLESTEROL 0mg; SODIUM 75mg; TOTAL CARBOHYDRATE 43g (DIETARY FIBER 1g, SUGARS 36g); PROTEIN 5g **% DAILY VALUE:** VITAMIN A 15%; VITAMIN C 30%; CALCIUM 20%; IRON 0% **EXCHANGES:** 1 FRUIT, 1½ OTHER CARBOHYDRATE, ½ SKIM MILK **CARBOHYDRATE CHOICES:** 3

STRAWBERRY SMOOTHIES Substitute 2 cups fresh (hulled) strawberries for the mangoes and 2 cups strawberry sorbet for the mango sorbet.

Sweet Potato Wedges

PREP: 10 Minutes **BAKE:** 30 Minutes ■ **4 SERVINGS**

Serve oven-baked "fries" with your favorite main dish. Using sweet potatoes gives you a big dose of vitamin A!

4 medium sweet potatoes (1½ lb), cut lengthwise into ½-inch wedges
2 tablespoons canola or soybean oil
½ teaspoon salt
¼ teaspoon pepper

1. Heat oven to 450°F. Brush jelly roll pan, 15½ × 10½ × 1 inch, with canola or soybean oil.

2. Toss potatoes with 2 tablespoons oil in large bowl. Sprinkle with salt and pepper. Spread potatoes in single layer in pan.

3. Bake uncovered 25 to 30 minutes, turning occasionally, until potatoes are golden brown and tender when pierced with fork.

1 SERVING: CALORIES 180 (CALORIES FROM FAT 60); TOTAL FAT 7g (SATURATED FAT 0.5g, TRANS FAT 0g, OMEGA-3 0.5g); CHOLESTEROL 0mg; SODIUM 310mg; TOTAL CARBOHYDRATE 28g (DIETARY FIBER 3g); PROTEIN 2g **% DAILY VALUE:** VITAMIN A 340%; VITAMIN C 25%; CALCIUM 4%; IRON 2%; FOLIC ACID 6% **EXCHANGES:** 1 STARCH, 1 OTHER CARBOHYDRATE, 1 FAT **CARBOHYDRATE CHOICES:** 2

Creamy Mango Smoothies ▸

Loaded Potatoes

PREP: 12 Minutes **COOK:** 4 Minutes **STAND:** 4 Minutes ■ **4 SERVINGS**

This yummy main dish combines your favorite foods in a great-tasting way. By using low-fat sour cream and cheese and adding mushrooms and onions, you are lowering the fat and calories and adding important nutrients like fiber, vitamins, calcium and iron.

4 medium unpeeled red potatoes
1 package (8 oz) sliced fresh mushrooms (3 cups)
¾ cup chopped fully cooked ham
8 medium green onions, sliced (½ cup)
⅛ teaspoon ground red pepper (cayenne)
½ cup reduced-fat sour cream
½ cup shredded reduced-fat sharp Cheddar cheese (2 oz)

1. Pierce potatoes with fork. Arrange potatoes about 1 inch apart in circle on microwavable paper towel in microwave oven. Microwave uncovered on High 8 to 10 minutes or until tender. (Or bake potatoes in 375°F oven 1 to 1½ hours.) Let potatoes stand until cool enough to handle.

2. While potatoes are cooking, spray 4-quart Dutch oven with cooking spray; heat over medium-high heat. Cook mushrooms in Dutch oven 1 minute, stirring frequently; reduce heat to medium. Cover and cook 3 minutes; remove from heat. Stir in ham, green onions and red pepper. Cover and let stand 4 minutes.

3. Split baked potatoes lengthwise in half; fluff with fork. Spread 1 tablespoon of the sour cream over each potato half. Top with ham mixture and cheese.

1 SERVING: CALORIES 250 (CALORIES FROM FAT 50); TOTAL FAT 6g (SATURATED FAT 2.5g, TRANS FAT 0g, OMEGA-3 0g); CHOLESTEROL 30mg; SODIUM 560mg; TOTAL CARBOHYDRATE 34g (DIETARY FIBER 5g); PROTEIN 16g
% DAILY VALUE: VITAMIN A 10%; VITAMIN C 20%; CALCIUM 20%; IRON 20%; FOLIC ACID 10%
EXCHANGES: 2 STARCH, 1 VEGETABLE, 1 VERY LEAN MEAT
CARBOHYDRATE CHOICES: 2

Broccoli-Cheese Soup

PREP: 10 Minutes **COOK:** 13 Minutes ■ **6 SERVINGS (1 CUP EACH)**

What better way to "eat your veggies" than in this creamy cheese soup? Does someone in your family not usually eat broccoli? Try this—you may be pleasantly surprised!

1 tablespoon canola or soybean oil
1 medium onion, chopped (½ cup)
1 tablespoon all-purpose flour
1 teaspoon salt
3 cups soy milk or fat-free (skim) milk
2 teaspoons cornstarch
1½ cups shredded reduced-fat sharp Cheddar cheese (6 oz)
3 cups bite-size fresh or frozen (thawed) broccoli flowerets
1 cup low-fat popped popcorn, if desired

1. Heat oil in 3-quart saucepan over medium heat. Stir in onion, flour and salt. Cook 2 to 3 minutes, stirring constantly, until onion is soft.

2. Stir soy milk and cornstarch in small bowl with wire whisk until smooth. Gradually stir into onion mixture. Cook 5 to 6 minutes, stirring frequently, until thick and bubbly.

3. Stir in cheese. Cook about 3 minutes, stirring frequently, until cheese is melted. Stir in broccoli. Cook about 1 minute or until hot, stirring occasionally. If desired, top this creamy cheese soup with popcorn.

1 SERVING: CALORIES 140 (CALORIES FROM FAT 40); TOTAL FAT 4.5g (SATURATED FAT 1.5g, TRANS FAT 0g, OMEGA-3 0g); CHOLESTEROL 5mg; SODIUM 730mg; TOTAL CARBOHYDRATE 14g (DIETARY FIBER 2g); PROTEIN 10g
% DAILY VALUE: VITAMIN A 20%; VITAMIN C 35%; CALCIUM 35%; IRON 6%; FOLIC ACID 10%
EXCHANGES: ½ SKIM MILK, 1 VEGETABLE, ½ HIGH-FAT MEAT, ½ FAT
CARBOHYDRATE CHOICES: 1

Spicy Chicken Drumsticks

PREP: 20 Minutes **BAKE:** 45 Minutes ■ **5 SERVINGS**

Crispy, crunchy chicken doesn't have to be deep-fried to be delicious! To keep saturated fat low, bake, broil, braise, grill or steam—all forms of cooking without adding extra fat.

2 pounds chicken drumsticks
⅓ cup all-purpose flour
⅓ cup yellow whole-grain cornmeal
½ teaspoon ground cumin
½ teaspoon chili powder
¼ teaspoon salt
⅓ cup buttermilk
¼ teaspoon red pepper sauce
Cooking spray

1. Heat oven to 400°F. Spray rectangular pan, 13 × 9 × 2 inches, with cooking spray. Remove skin and fat from chicken.

2. Mix flour, cornmeal, cumin, chili powder and salt in heavy-duty resealable plastic food-storage bag. Mix buttermilk and pepper sauce in medium bowl. Dip chicken into buttermilk mixture, then place in bag. Seal bag and shake until evenly coated. Place chicken in pan; spray chicken lightly with cooking spray.

3. Bake uncovered 40 to 45 minutes or until juice of chicken is no longer pink when centers of thickest pieces are cut.

1 SERVING: CALORIES 190 (CALORIES FROM FAT 35); TOTAL FAT 4g (SATURATED FAT 1.5g, TRANS FAT 0g, OMEGA-3 0g); CHOLESTEROL 85mg; SODIUM 190mg; TOTAL CARBOHYDRATE 15g (DIETARY FIBER 0g); PROTEIN 23g
% DAILY VALUE: VITAMIN A 4%; VITAMIN C 0%; CALCIUM 4%; IRON 15%; FOLIC ACID 8%
EXCHANGES: 1 STARCH, 3 VERY LEAN MEAT
CARBOHYDRATE CHOICES: 1

Broiled Dijon Burgers

PREP: 10 Minutes **BROIL:** 12 Minutes ■ **6 SERVINGS**

Even small changes can make a big difference, so use whole grains whenever you can, like in these hamburger buns. Using fat-free egg gives the burgers an added boost of protein without adding any extra fat.

¼ cup fat-free cholesterol-free egg product or 2 egg whites
2 tablespoons fat-free (skim) milk
2 teaspoons Dijon mustard or horseradish sauce
¼ teaspoon salt
⅛ teaspoon pepper
1 cup soft bread crumbs (about 2 slices bread)
1 small onion, finely chopped (¼ cup)
1 lb extra-lean ground beef
6 whole-grain hamburger buns, split and toasted

1. Set oven control to broil. Spray broiler pan rack with cooking spray.

2. Mix egg product, milk, mustard, salt and pepper in medium bowl. Stir in bread crumbs and onion. Stir in beef. Shape mixture into 6 patties, each about ½ inch thick. Place patties on rack in broiler pan.

3. Broil with tops of patties about 5 inches from heat 6 minutes. Turn, broil until meat thermometer inserted in center reads 160°F, about 4 to 6 minutes longer. Serve patties in buns.

1 SERVING: CALORIES 260 (CALORIES FROM FAT 70); TOTAL FAT 8g (SATURATED FAT 3g, TRANS FAT 1g, OMEGA-3 0g); CHOLESTEROL 45mg; SODIUM 470mg; TOTAL CARBOHYDRATE 26g (DIETARY FIBER 3g); PROTEIN 21g **% DAILY VALUE:** VITAMIN A 2%; VITAMIN C 0%; CALCIUM 6%; IRON 20%; FOLIC ACID 10%
EXCHANGES: 2 STARCH, 2½ VERY LEAN MEAT
CARBOHYDRATE CHOICES: 2

Broiled Dijon Burgers ▶

Rush-Hour Tuna Melts

PREP: 10 Minutes **START TO FINISH:** 20 Minutes ■

4 SERVINGS (2 SANDWICHES EACH)

Because they're made with tuna, fat-free mayo and lower-fat cheese, these extraordinary sandwiches are a terrific heart-healthy option. Kids are more likely to eat what they help make, so get them involved in planning and preparing healthy meals.

1 can (6 oz) solid white tuna in water, drained, flaked
¾ cup chopped celery
2 tablespoons finely chopped onion
½ teaspoon grated lemon peel, if desired
⅓ cup reduced-fat mayonnaise or salad dressing
4 whole wheat English muffins, split, lightly toasted
8 slices tomato
1 cup shredded reduced-fat Cheddar or Monterey Jack cheese (4 oz)

1. Heat oven to 350°F. In medium bowl, mix tuna, celery, onion, lemon peel and mayonnaise.

2. Spread about 3 tablespoons tuna mixture on each English muffin half. Top each with tomato slice; sprinkle with cheese. Place on ungreased cookie sheet.

3. Bake 8 to 10 minutes or until cheese is melted and sandwiches are thoroughly heated.

1 SANDWICH: CALORIES 310 (CALORIES FROM FAT 90); TOTAL FAT 10g (SATURATED FAT 2.5g, TRANS FAT 0g); CHOLESTEROL 25mg; SODIUM 950mg; TOTAL CARBOHYDRATE 31g (DIETARY FIBER 5g); PROTEIN 22g
% DAILY VALUE: VITAMIN A 10%; VITAMIN C 4%; CALCIUM 40%; IRON 15%;
EXCHANGES: 1½ STARCH, ½ OTHER CARBOHYDRATE, 2½ LEAN MEAT, ½ FAT
CARBOHYDRATE CHOICES: 2

Potato-Topped Turkey and Green Bean Bake

PREP: 15 Minutes **BAKE:** 25 Minutes **STAND:** 5 Minutes ■

8 SERVINGS

Hearty casseroles are often high in fat and calories, but not this one! Veggies, turkey and fat-free soup make it an ideal (and tasty) choice for lunch or dinner. Plus, it's high in calcium and iron.

1 lb lean ground turkey
1 medium onion, chopped (½ cup)
½ teaspoon garlic powder
¾ to 1 teaspoon dried thyme leaves
⅔ cup fat-free (skim) milk
2 packages (9 oz each) frozen French-style green beans, thawed, drained
1 can (10¾ oz) condensed 98% fat-free cream of mushroom soup
1 can (8 oz) sliced water chestnuts, drained
1 jar (4 ½ oz) sliced mushrooms, drained
1 bag (16 oz) frozen seasoned potato nuggets

1. Heat oven to 450°F. Spray rectangular baking dish, 13 × 9 × 2 inches, with cooking spray.

2. Spray 10-inch nonstick skillet with cooking spray. Cook turkey, onion, garlic powder and thyme in skillet over medium-high heat until turkey is no longer pink. Stir in milk, green beans, soup, water chestnuts and mushrooms. Heat to boiling. Pour turkey mixture into baking dish. Top with potato nuggets.

3. Bake 20 to 25 minutes or until hot and bubbly. Let stand 5 minutes before serving.

1 SERVING: CALORIES 290 (CALORIES FROM FAT 90); TOTAL FAT 11g (SATURATED FAT 4g, TRANS FAT 2g, OMEGA-3 0g); CHOLESTEROL 40mg; SODIUM 840mg; TOTAL CARBOHYDRATE 31g (DIETARY FIBER 5g); PROTEIN 17g
% DAILY VALUE: VITAMIN A 10%; VITAMIN C 8%; CALCIUM 10%; IRON 15%; FOLIC ACID 8%
EXCHANGES: 2 STARCH, 1½ LEAN MEAT, ½ FAT
CARBOHYDRATE CHOICES: 2

Chewy Chocolate-Oat Bars

PREP: 20 Minutes **BAKE:** 25 Minutes **COOL:** 1 Hour 30 Minutes ■ **16 BARS**

Who doesn't love the taste of chocolate and oats together? These delicious bars are a great way to "sneak" heart-healthy whole grains into your family's snacks. They're perfect for packing into lunch boxes or anytime.

- ½ cup semisweet chocolate chips
- ⅓ cup fat-free sweetened condensed milk (from 14-oz can)
- 1 cup whole wheat flour
- ½ cup old-fashioned or quick-cooking oats
- ½ teaspoon baking powder
- ½ teaspoon baking soda
- ¼ teaspoon salt
- ¾ cup packed brown sugar
- ¼ cup canola or soybean oil
- 1 teaspoon vanilla
- ¼ cup fat-free cholesterol-free egg product or 1 egg
- 2 tablespoons old-fashioned or quick-cooking oats
- 2 teaspoons butter, softened

1. Heat chocolate chips and milk in 1-quart heavy saucepan over low heat, stirring frequently, until chocolate is melted and mixture is smooth; set aside. Heat oven to 350°F. Spray square pan, 8 × 8 × 2 or 9 × 9 × 2 inches, with cooking spray.

2. Mix flour, ½ cup oats, the baking powder, baking soda and salt in large bowl; set aside. Stir brown sugar, oil, vanilla and egg product in medium bowl with fork until smooth; stir into flour mixture until blended. Reserve ½ cup dough in small bowl for topping.

3. Pat remaining dough in pan (spray fingers with cooking spray or lightly flour if dough is sticky). Spread chocolate mixture over dough. Add 2 tablespoons oats and the butter to reserved dough; mix with pastry blender or fork until crumbly. Drop small spoonfuls of oat mixture evenly over chocolate mixture.

4. Bake 20 to 25 minutes or until top is golden and firm. Cool completely, about 1½ hours. For bars, cut into 4 rows by 4 rows.

1 COOKIE: CALORIES 160 (CALORIES FROM FAT 50); TOTAL FAT 6g (SATURATED FAT 1.5g, TRANS FAT 0g, OMEGA-3 0g); CHOLESTEROL 0mg; SODIUM 115mg; TOTAL CARBOHYDRATE 25g (DIETARY FIBER 2g); PROTEIN 3g
% DAILY VALUE: VITAMIN A 0%; VITAMIN C 0%; CALCIUM 4%; IRON 4%; FOLIC ACID 0%
EXCHANGES: 1 STARCH, ½ OTHER CARBOHYDRATE, 1 FAT
CARBOHYDRATE CHOICES: 1½

Peach and Blueberry Crisp with Crunchy Topping

PREP: 20 Minutes **BAKE:** 30 Minutes ■ **6 SERVINGS**

Eating heart healthy doesn't mean totally giving up desserts. The cereal and nuts topping in this crisp gives you the same great taste and crunch as a typical fruit crisp with much less fat and calories. Plus, you're getting a serving of fruit.

- 4 medium peaches, peeled and sliced (2¾ cups)
- 1 cup fresh or frozen (thawed and drained) blueberries
- 2 tablespoons packed brown sugar
- 2 tablespoons orange juice
- 1 teaspoon ground cinnamon
- ¼ teaspoon ground nutmeg
- 1 cup Honey Nut Clusters® cereal, slightly crushed
- ⅓ cup chopped pecans
- ¾ cup frozen (thawed) fat-free whipped topping

1. Heat oven to 375°F. Spray bottom and sides of square baking dish, 8 × 8 × 2 inches, or rectangular baking dish, 11 × 7 × 1½ inches, with cooking spray.

2. Place peaches and blueberries in baking dish. Mix brown sugar, orange juice, cinnamon and nutmeg in small bowl; drizzle over fruit.

3. Bake 15 minutes. Sprinkle with crushed cereal and pecans. Bake 10 to 15 minutes longer or until peaches are tender when pierced with a fork. Serve warm or cold with whipped topping.

1 SERVING: CALORIES 160 (CALORIES FROM FAT 45); TOTAL FAT 5g (SATURATED FAT 0.5g, TRANS FAT 0g, OMEGA 3 0g); CHOLESTEROL 0mg; SODIUM 50mg; TOTAL CARBOHYDRATE 27g (DIETARY FIBER 4g); PROTEIN 2g
% DAILY VALUE: VITAMIN A 2%; VITAMIN C 8%; CALCIUM 2%; IRON 8%; FOLIC ACID 6%
EXCHANGES: 1 STARCH, 1 FRUIT, 1 FAT
CARBOHYDRATE CHOICES: 2

Heart-Healthy Recipes in This Book

Every chapter of *Betty Crocker's Cookbook* has a selection of heart-healthy recipes that you and your family can enjoy. It's not surprising that the chapters on Vegetarian cooking and Rice, Grains, Beans & Pasta are bursting with heart-healthy recipes, but there are also lots of ideas in other chapters, such as Casseroles & Slow-Cooker, Meats, Soups, Sandwiches & Pizzas and 20 Minutes or Less. Even in categories that may be considered taboo—such as Eggs & Cheese and Desserts—there are options that fit a heart-healthy plan. So, dive in and enjoy these good-for-you meals every day.

Check here for a chapter-by-chapter review of heart-healthy recipes.

Appetizers & Beverages

Guacamole
Hummus
Spicy Thai Chicken Wings
Baked Coconut Shrimp
Sautéed Olives
Lighter Chex® Party Mix
Popcorn
Hot Spiced Cider
Strawberry Smoothie
Lemonade
Colada Cooler Punch

Breads

Bran Muffins
Blueberry Muffins
Banana Muffins
Banana Bread
Blueberry-Banana Bread
Zucchini Bread
Dumplings
Lighter Waffles
Corn Bread
Cinnamon-Raisin-Walnut Wheat Bread
Honey–Whole Wheat Bread
Sunflower-Herb Whole Wheat Bread
Sourdough Bread
Focaccia
Ciabatta Stirata
Four-Grain Batter Bread
Whole Wheat Batter Bread
Fresh Herb Batter Bread
Garlic Bread

Cakes & Pies

Jeweled Fruitcake
Angel Food Cake
Lemon Filling
Raspberry Filling
Impossibly Easy Pumpkin Pie

Casseroles & Slow-Cooker

Lighter Chicken Tetrazzini
Lighter Easy Bacon Cheeseburger Lasagna
Lighter Creamy Seafood Lasagna
Spaghetti Pie
Cheesy Pizza Casserole
Lighter Fiesta Taco Casserole
Lighter Cheesy Barbecue Beef Casserole
Lighter Wild Rice and Beef Casserole
Tuna-Pasta Casserole
Mixed Roasted Vegetables and Pasta
Slow-Cooker Turkey Breast with Wild Rice Stuffing
Italian Turkey-Rice Dinner
French Dip Sandwiches
Pulled Jerk Pork Sandwiches
Pork Chop Supper
Chicken Chow Mein
Family Favorite Chili
Potato and Double-Corn Chowder
Vegetable-Beef-Barley Soup
Winter Vegetable Stew

Cookies & Candies

Butterscotch Brownies
Lighter Cream Cheese Brownies
Pumpkin-Spice Bars
Date Bars
Lighter Oatmeal-Raisin Cookies
Chocolate Drop Cookies
Chocolate Crinkles
Gingersnaps
Hazelnut Biscotti
Gingerbread Cookies
Mocha Cookies
Chocolate Fudge
Divinity

Desserts

Baked Apples
Hot Fudge Sundae Cake
Rice Pudding
Meringue Shell
Lemonade Sorbet
Glossy Chocolate Sauce
Caramel Sauce
Lemon Sauce
Orange Sauce
Raspberry Sauce

Eggs & Cheese

French Omelet
Lighter Savory Italian Frittata
Lighter Ham and Swiss Pizza

Vegetables & Fruit

Vegetarian

20 Minutes or Less

Betty Crocker COOKBOOK

Everything You Need to Know to Cook Today

Wiley Publishing, Inc.

Published by Wiley Publishing, Inc., Hoboken, NJ

For general information on our other products and services or to obtain technical support, please contact our Customer Care Department within the U.S. at 800-762-2974, outside the U.S. at 317-572-3993, or fax 317-572-4002.

Wiley also publishes its books in a variety of electronic formats. Some content that appears in print may not be available in electronic books. For more information about Wiley products, visit our Web site at www.wiley.com.

Library of Congress Cataloging-in-Publication Data is available upon request.

ISBN: 978-0-470-17163-9 (special edition)

Manufactured in China

10 9 8 7 6 5 4 3 2 1

Tenth Edition

Photo on page x: Corbis; photo on page xiv: Corbis/Digital Stock; photo on page xv: Photodisc; photo on page xviii: Photodisc, Inc.

GENERAL MILLS

Publisher, Cookbooks: Maggie Gilbert/Lynn Vettel

Manager, Cookbook Publishing: Lois Tlusty

Editors: Cheri Olerud and Lori Fox

Recipe Development and Testing: Betty Crocker Kitchens

Photography and Food Styling: General Mills Photography Studios and Image Library

WILEY PUBLISHING, INC.

Publisher: Natalie Chapman

Executive Editor: Anne Ficklen

Editor: Kristi Hart and Adam Kowit

Production Editor: Shannon Egan and Leslie Anglin

Cover Design: Paul Dinovo and Suzanne Sunwoo

Interior Design and Layout: Laura Ierardi, Holly Wittenberg, Mauna Eichner and Lee Fukui

Photography Art Direction: Becky Landes

Manufacturing Manager: Kevin Watt

The Betty Crocker Kitchens seal guarantees success in your kitchen. Every recipe has been tested in America's Most Trusted Kitchens™ to meet our high standards of reliability, easy preparation and great taste.

Contents

Dear Friends,

The 10th edition of Betty Crocker's Cookbook is bursting with the best—the best recipes, the best photos and the best ideas for how you cook today.

Whether you're just getting started or are comfortable in the kitchen, you want to have a reliable resource for helpful, up-to-date information and to be inspired by great recipes that work time after time. That's just what you'll find in this edition; Betty Crocker is here to help you express your creativity through cooking and baking.

Updated and revised for today's lifestyles, you will love the fact that everything you could ever need to know in the kitchen is all right here. For example, more recipes for busy schedules, healthy eating and vegetarian eating have been added to help you enjoy the way we're eating today. Plus, the best from all of the other editions is included too—over 50 years of experience from America's Most Trusted Kitchens . . . tested recipes, all the latest information and beautiful photography!

And you'll find a wonderful bonus. For a limited time, you will have access to the free online Betty Crocker holiday planner that will help you navigate your way through this busy holiday season. Visit www.wiley.com/go/bettycrockerplanner and let Betty Crocker guide you through the holidays with ease and confidence. Please hurry; this special offer will only be available through January 31, 2006.

We hope this newest edition will become a good friend, helping to encourage and guide you in making great meals and creating lasting memories for family and friends.

Warmly,

Betty Crocker

CHAPTER 1
Getting Started

Measuring Ingredients

GRADUATED NESTING MEASURING CUPS

Look for these nests of metal or plastic cups, which usually increase in size from 1/4 cup to 1 cup. Some sets also include 1/8 (2 tablespoons), 2/3, 3/4 and 2 cups. Reach for them when measuring dry ingredients like flour, sugar and oats, as well as solid fats like butter, margarine and shortening. Do not use these cups for liquids because amounts will not be accurate; recipes are developed using glass measuring cups for liquids (see Glass Measuring Cups, right).

- *For flour, granulated and powdered sugars and Bisquick® Mix,* spoon the ingredient lightly into the cup, then level it off with the straight edge of a metal spatula or knife. Today's flours are presifted before packaging, so sifting again isn't necessary. You can skip sifting powdered sugar before measuring unless you see some lumps.
- *For cereal, dry bread crumbs and oats,* pour into the cup then level off with the straight edge of a metal spatula or knife.
- *For shredded cheese, chopped nuts, coconut and soft bread crumbs,* spoon into the cup and pat down very lightly.
- *For butter, margarine, shortening and brown sugar,* spoon into the cup and pack down firmly with a spatula or spoon.

GRADUATED MEASURING SPOONS

Look for sets of metal or plastic spoons that range in size from 1/4 teaspoon to 1 tablespoon. Some sets contain a 1/8 teaspoon and a 3/4 teaspoon. Use spoons to measure liquids and dry ingredients. If you cook and bake often, consider stocking up with two sets, one for dry ingredients and another for wet ingredients.

- *For thin liquids,* pour into the spoon until full.
- *For thick liquids and dry ingredients,* pour or scoop into the spoon until full, then level off with the straight edge of a metal spatula or knife.

GLASS MEASURING CUPS

These glass or plastic cups for measuring liquids come in 1-, 2-, 4- and 8-cup sizes, some with both conventional and metric markings. To get an accurate reading, place the measuring cup on a flat surface and read the measurement at eye level. For even easier measuring, look for angled plastic measuring cups; they let you read the measurement quickly from the top of the cup. Before measuring sticky liquids like honey, molasses or corn syrup, lightly spray the inside of the cup with cooking spray or wipe lightly with vegetable oil—no sticking!

MEASURING CUPS AND SPOONS

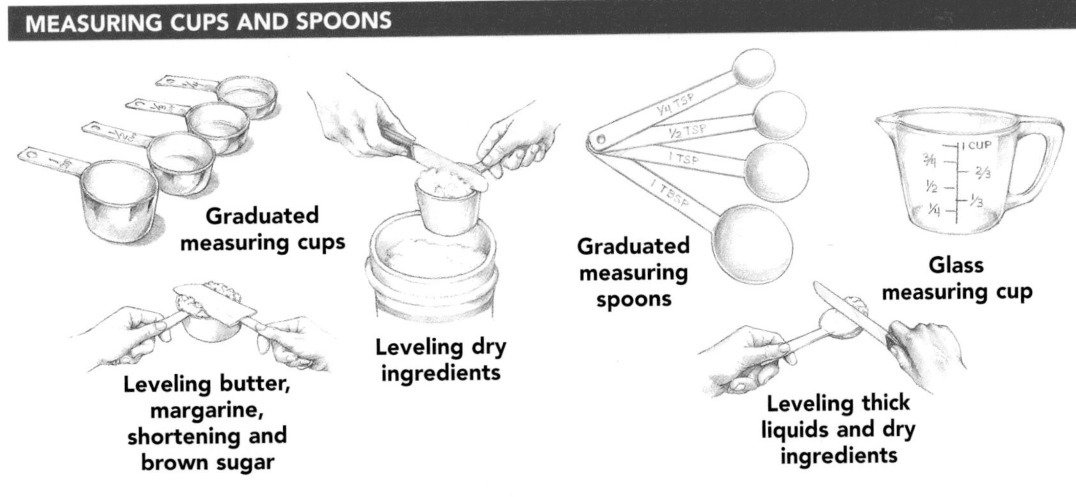

Mixing Ingredients

What's the difference between blending and stirring, beating and whipping, or folding and cutting in? What's a wire whisk used for? Here's your chance to become an instant expert.

MIXING TERMS

Beat: Combine ingredients vigorously with a spoon, fork, wire whisk, electric mixer or hand beater until smooth. Whenever an electric mixer is needed, we've included the mixer speed.

Blend: Combine ingredients with a spoon, wire whisk or rubber spatula until very smooth, or combine ingredients in a blender or food processor.

Cut In: To work butter, margarine or shortening into dry ingredients. As you cut in the fat, it will begin to clump with the dry ingredients. Use a pastry blender, lifting it up and down with a rocking motion, until the particles are the desired size, usually coarse or fine crumbs or the size of a pea. If you don't have a pastry blender, hold a table knife in each hand and pull them through the ingredients in opposite directions, or use your fingertips, working quickly so the heat of your fingers doesn't soften the fat.

Fold: Gently combine ingredients without decreasing their volume. For example, folding dry ingredients into beaten egg whites for angel food cake or folding liqueur into whipped cream, while keeping all the air in. To fold, use a rubber spatula to cut down vertically through the mixture. Next, slide the spatula across the bottom of the bowl and up the other side, carrying some of the mixture from the bottom up and over the surface. Repeat, turning the bowl one-fourth turn after each folding motion.

Mix: Combine ingredients in any way that distributes them evenly.

Process: Use a blender, food processor or mini-chopper to liquefy, blend, chop, grind or knead food.

Stir: Combine ingredients with a circular or figure-8 motion until thoroughly blended.

Whip: Beat ingredients to add air and increase volume until ingredients are light and fluffy. For example, whipping cream or egg whites.

MIXING TOOLS

Hand Beater: Also called a rotary beater. Use for lightly beating eggs, sauces and salad dressings as well as some batters.

Pastry Blender: Use to cut solid fat into flour for pie crusts and doughs for biscuits and scones by lifting the pastry blender up and down with a rocking motion.

Rubber or Silicone Spatulas: Also called scrapers. These are indispensable for many tasks, from folding to mixing, blending and stirring. Consider keeping several spatulas on hand, in both flat and spoon shapes in small, medium and large sizes. They're heatproof so are great for mixing hot foods in saucepans and skillets.

Spoon: Handy for general all-purpose mixing and stirring. Wooden spoons are sturdy enough for stirring thick batters and doughs, and their handles stay cool when stirring hot mixtures on the range. Reach for long-handled spoons when stirring large amounts and slotted metal spoons for removing solids from liquid mixtures.

Wire Whisk: Great for beating eggs, egg whites and thin batters and for stirring puddings, sauces and gravies to help prevent or remove lumps.

Knives

The right tools make cooking easier, and a good set of knives is essential. Visit a department store or a kitchen-supply store to see the various brands and let a knowledgeable salesperson help you pick them out. High-quality knives last a lifetime, so invest in the best knives you can afford.

The best knives are made from high-carbon stainless-steel blades that are riveted in the handle. High-carbon stainless steel resists corrosion and discoloration, and the blades sharpen easily. Before you buy, pick up the knives to make sure they feel balanced and comfortable in your hand.

Keep knives sharpened for the best performance and safety. Always wash knives by hand because dishwasher detergents are too harsh and may damage them over time. The following set of knives is perfect for almost all cooking needs:

Bread Knife (8-inch blade): A serrated blade used for slicing breads, bagels and tomatoes.

Carving Knife (10-inch blade): A long, thin blade used for carving meat and poultry.

Chef's Knife (8- or 10-inch blade): An elongated, wedge-shaped blade used for chopping, dicing and mincing foods.

Paring Knife (3- to 4-inch blade): A short blade used for peeling vegetables and fruits and cutting small amounts of foods.

Utility Knife (6-inch blade): A thin blade used for slicing foods such as sandwiches, fruits, cheeses, cakes, bars and other soft foods.

Electric Mixing Appliances

Many handy small appliances are available to help you save time preparing foods—they will quickly become your best friends in the kitchen.

Blender: Use to liquefy or blend mixtures or chop small amounts of nuts, herbs or bread crumbs. Most batters and doughs are too thick for a blender.

Blender, Handheld: Also called *immersion blenders.* Use to liquefy or blend mixtures in bowls or pots (even while they're cooking!). Since this portable model is much smaller and less-powerful than a regular blender, it may not work as well for some blending tasks.

Electric Mixer: There are two types of electric mixers: handheld and stand. A handheld mixer was used for recipes in this book that specify an electric mixer.

- **Handheld Mixer:** The motor in a handheld mixer isn't as powerful as the one in a stand mixer. A handheld mixer is great for beating eggs, whipping cream and mixing all but the thickest mixtures such as stiff cookie dough or yeast dough.
- **Stand Mixer:** Has a more powerful motor than the handheld mixer. Since the mixer is attached to a stand, your hands are free while it mixes. It often comes with added attachments, including a dough hook.

Food Processor: Use to blend, puree, chop, slice, dice, grind, pulverize and shred many foods. Larger-capacity food processors can mix and knead dough.

Mini-Chopper: Use to chop small amounts of vegetables, nuts and herbs or mix small amounts of sauces and dips.

HELPFUL HOW-TO'S

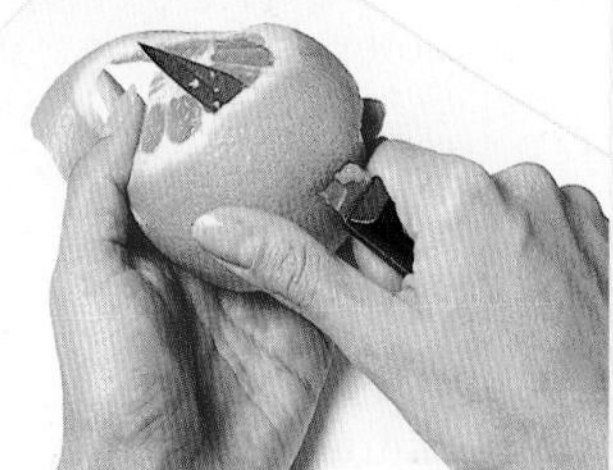

Peel: Cut off outer covering with a paring knife or vegetable peeler, or remove with fingers.

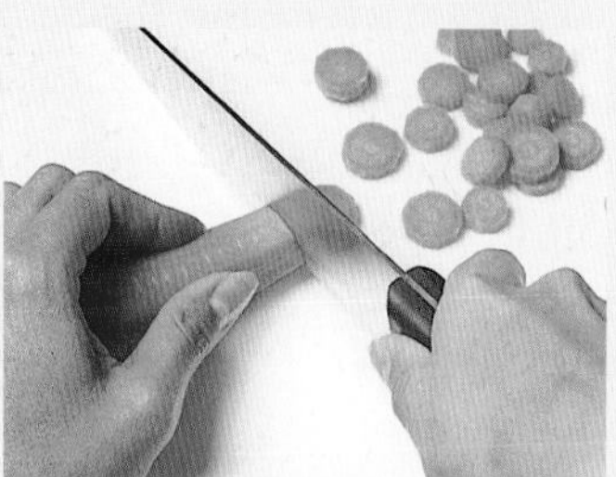

Slice: Cut into flat pieces of the same size.

Julienne: Cut into long, thin slices. Stack slices, then cut into matchlike sticks.

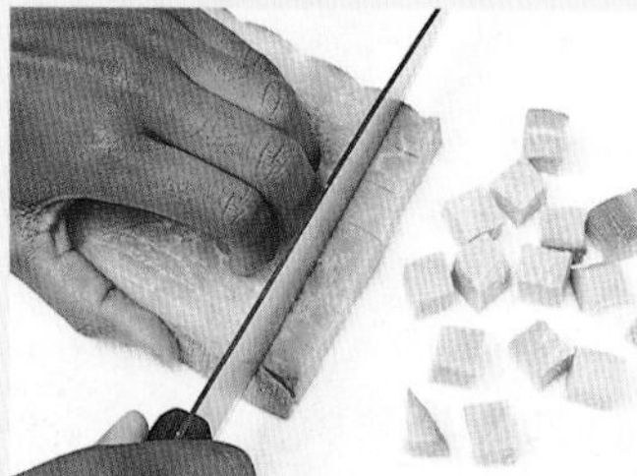

Cube or Dice: Cut food into strips that are the same size on all sides, then cut across strips into 1/2-inch or larger pieces to cube or 1/4-inch pieces to dice.

Chop: Using a chef's knife, cut into pieces of irregular size. Coarsely chop or finely chop as the recipe specifies.

Snip: Cut into very small pieces with kitchen scissors.

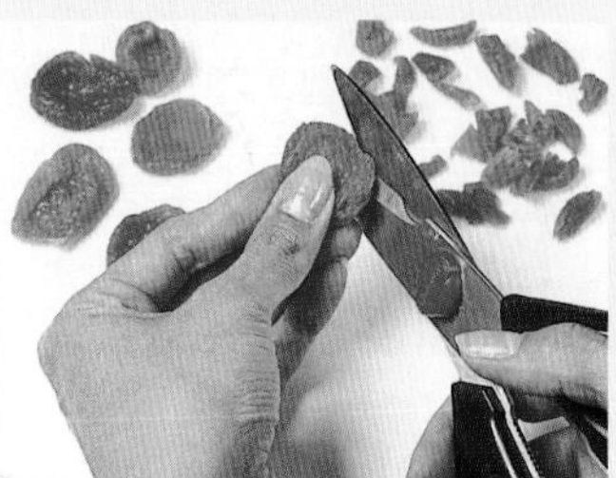

Cut Up: Cut into small pieces of irregular sizes with kitchen scissors or a knife.

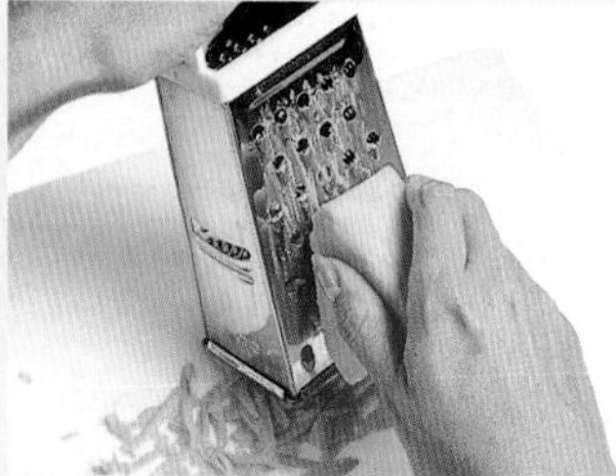

Shred: Push food across a shredder, making narrow or fine strips. Or slice food very thinly with a chef's or utility knife.

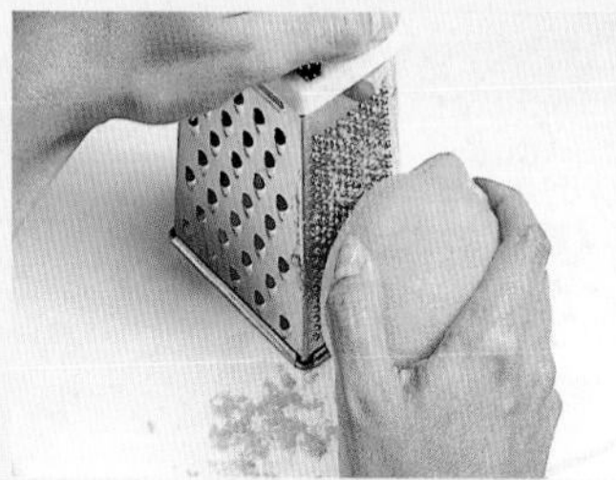

Grate: Rub food across the smallest holes of a grater to make tiny particles.

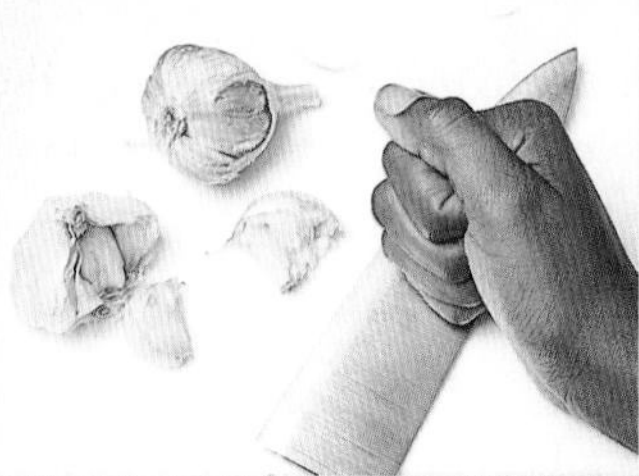

Crush: Press with side of a knife blade or use a meat mallet, mortar and pestle or rolling pin to smash food into small pieces.

Simmer: Cook food in liquid kept just below the boiling point while bubbles rise slowly and break just below the surface.

Boil: Heat liquid or cook food at a temperature that causes bubbles to rise continuously and break on the surface.

HELPFUL HOW-TO'S *(continued)*

Cutting Citrus Fruit Sections: With a table knife or paring knife, loosen membrane from both sides of one section of peeled fruit, then remove the section.

Peeling and Cutting Up Pineapple: Twist the crown off; cut pineapple lengthwise into fourths. Cut off rind, remove core from center. Cut pineapple into chunks, removing any spots of rind.

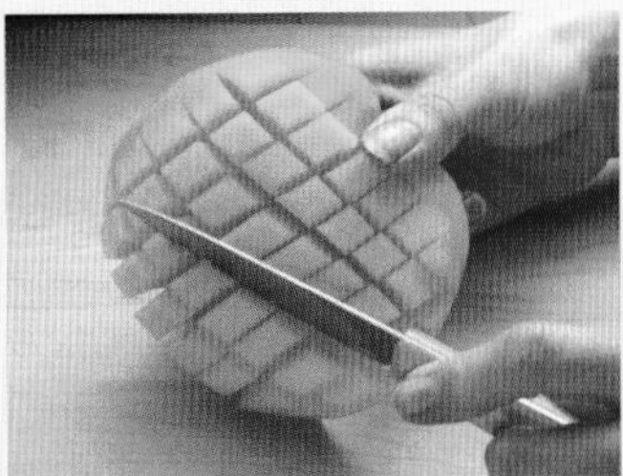

Cutting Mango: Cut lengthwise into two pieces, cutting as close to seed as possible. Make lengthwise and crosswise cuts, 1/2 inch apart, in mango flesh to form a crisscross pattern. Turn each mango half inside out, and scrape off the pieces.

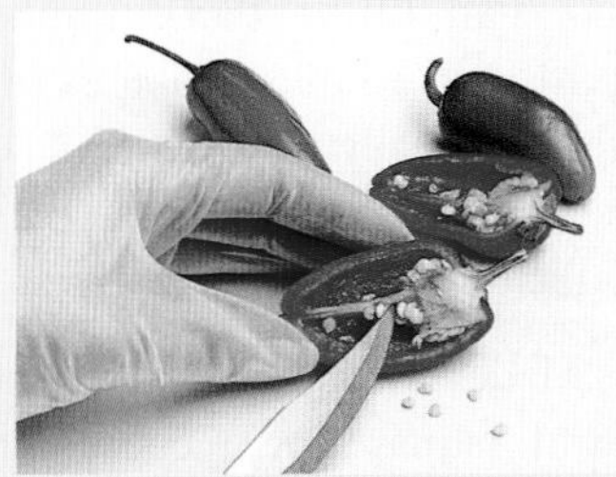

Seeding Chilies: Wearing plastic gloves, cut off stem of chili, cut chili lengthwise in half and scrape out seeds.

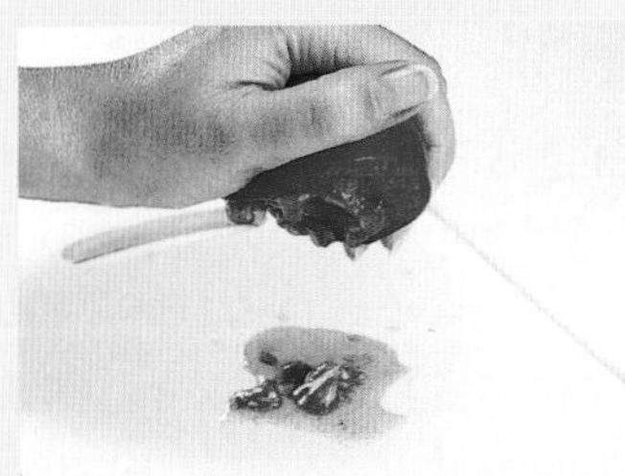

Seeding Tomatoes: Cut tomato crosswise in half. Gently squeeze halves to remove seeds.

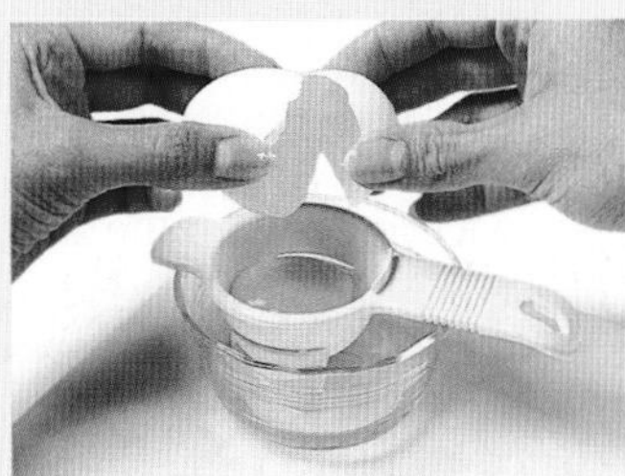

Separating Eggs: Place egg separator over small bowl. Crack open an egg, letting yolk fall into center of separator and the egg white slip through the slots into the bowl.

Pots and Pans

Buying pots, pans and skillets is a wise investment, so shop around and buy the best quality you can afford. Expect prices to vary widely, based upon the materials, thickness and weight. The best heat conductors are copper and aluminum, so buying pans made of one or both of these materials makes good cooking sense. Consider nonstick coating too. Avoid buying uncoated aluminum pans, though, as aluminum can react with acidic foods, causing off-flavors in food and discoloring of the pans.

Look for good, all-purpose cookware that conducts heat well, such as:

- Stainless-steel pans with copper bottoms
- Stainless-steel pans with aluminum or copper sandwiched between the steel on the bottom of the pan (also called clad pans)
- Anodized aluminum pans (electrolytically coated to protect the surface making it dull versus shiny)
- Solid copper pans conduct heat well but are very expensive

FOR COOKING

Dutch Oven, Stockpot: Bigger pots, usually 4-quart size or larger. Perfect for cooking soups, stews and pastas.

Saucepans: Come in a range of sizes from 1- to 3-quart and should have tight-fitting lids; some have a nonstick finish. Use to cook or reheat food on a stove-top.

Skillet, Frying Pan, Sauté Pan: Use to fry or cook almost any kind of food on a stove-top. Usually identified by size such as 8-, 10- or 12-inch, or by capacity such as 3-, 4- or 5-quart; they have a long handle. Although they often can be used interchangeably, some have sloping sides, others have straight sides, and they often vary in depth and capacity.

Specialty Pans: Although not necessary for most recipes, specialty pans can make cooking some foods much easier. Crepe pans, griddles, grill pans, omelet pans and woks are a few to look for.

FOR BAKING

For the recipes in this book, a *pan* refers to a metal pan and a *baking dish* refers to a heat-resistant glass dish. If dark nonstick or glass baking pans are substituted for metal pans, follow the manufacturer's directions, which may recommend reducing the baking temperature by 25°F.

Angel Food Cake Pan (Tube Pan): Round metal pan (10-inch) with a hollow tube in the middle. The bottom is usually removable, making it easier to remove the cake from the pan. Use for angel food, chiffon and sponge cakes.

Baking Dishes: Made of heat-resistant glass and usually round, square or rectangular. Although they can be used to bake cakes and other desserts, they are perfect for lasagna and other main dishes.

Baking Pans: Metal pans that come in a variety of shapes and sizes and are often used for cakes and other desserts.

Casserole: Covered or uncovered glass or ceramic cookware for baking and serving food—all in the same dish.

Cookie Sheet: Flat and rectangular baking sheet that may be open on one or more sides. The open sides allow for good air circulation in the oven when baking cookies, biscuits, scones and shortcakes.

Custard Cups: Small, deep, individual bowl-shaped dishes (6- and 10-ounce) with a flat bottom. They're heatproof, making them perfect for baking individual custards.

Fluted Tube Cake Pan: Fluted, round metal (12-cup) pan with a center tube.

SILICONE BAKEWARE

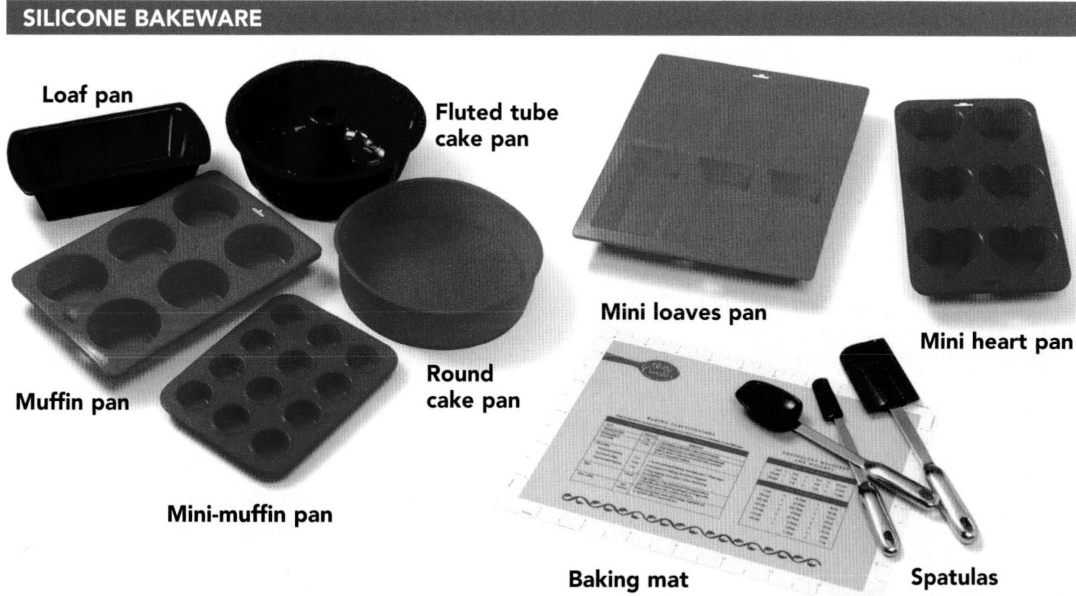

Muffin Cups (Muffin Pan): One pan with 6 or 12 individual cups for baking muffins or cupcakes. The cups range in size from small (or miniature) to jumbo.

Pie Pan: Round metal pan (usually shiny) with a flared side, especially designed for baking pies.

Pie Plate: Round, heat-resistant glass plate with a flared side, especially designed for baking pies.

Pizza Pan: Round metal pan with no sides, low sides or high sides (deep-dish) for baking pizza. Some are perforated to help crisp the crust.

Popover Pan: One pan with 6 deep cups, especially designed for baking popovers.

Silicone Bakeware: Nonstick, flexible bakeware made from a plastic-like material that is safe to use in the oven, microwave, dishwasher and freezer. Available in baking mats (for cookies), fluted tube cake pans, regular cake pans, loaf pans and muffin pans as well as specialty shapes like mini loaves pan, mini fluted tube cake pan and mini heart pan.

Soufflé Dish: Round, open dish with high sides and smooth interior, especially designed for making soufflés.

Springform Pan: Round, deep pan (8-, 9-, 10- or 11-inch) with a removable side. Perfect for cheesecakes and desserts that should not be turned upside down to remove them from the pan. Just release the side and serve (no need to remove the cake from the bottom of the pan).

Tart Pan: Round, shallow pan (10- or 11-inch) with a removable bottom.

Cooking Terms Glossary

Cooking has its own language, its own vocabulary of terms and definitions. Learn it and you'll soon be speaking like a culinary pro! Although this list is not meant to be a complete one, it introduces you to the most common terms if you're a beginning cook, or will refresh your memory if you're an experienced one.

Al dente: Describes the doneness of pasta that's cooked until tender yet firm or somewhat chewy to the bite.

Bake: To cook food in an oven with dry heat. Bake food uncovered for a dry and/or crisp top (breads, cakes, cookies, chicken) or covered to keep things moist (vegetable mixtures, casseroles, stews).

Baste: To spoon, brush or use a bulb baster to add liquid or fats over the surface of food (pan juices over turkey) during cooking to keep food moist.

Batter: Uncooked mixture of flour, eggs, liquid and other ingredients. Batter is thin enough to be spooned or poured (pancakes, muffins).

Blanch: To place food into boiling water for a brief time to preserve color, texture and nutritional value or to remove skin (vegetables, fruits, nuts).

Boil: To heat liquid or cook food at a temperature that causes bubbles to rise continuously and break on the surface. See also Helpful How-To's, page 8.

Bread: To coat a food (chicken, fish, vegetables) by dipping into a liquid (beaten egg, milk), then into bread crumbs, cracker crumbs or cornmeal before frying or baking. See also **Coat.**

Broil: To cook food a measured distance directly under the heat source.

Brown: To cook quickly over high heat, causing the surface of the food to turn brown while keeping the inside moist.

Caramelize Sugar: To melt sugar slowly over low heat until it becomes golden brown in color with a syrupy consistency. Or to sprinkle granulated or brown sugar on top of a food, then use a kitchen torch or place under a broiler until the sugar is melted and caramelized.

Chill: Place food in the refrigerator until it's thoroughly cold.

Chop: Cut food into coarse or fine pieces of irregular shapes, using a knife, food processor or food chopper. See also Helpful How-To's, page 8.

Coat: Cover food evenly with batter, crumbs or flour. See also **Bread.**

Cool: Allow hot food to stand at room temperature until it reaches a desired temperature. Foods placed on a wire rack cool more quickly. Stirring occasionally also helps mixtures cool more quickly and evenly.

Core: To remove the center of a fruit (apple, pear, pineapple). Cores contain small seeds or are woody.

Cover: Place a cover, lid, plastic wrap or foil over a container of food.

Crisp-tender: Describes the doneness of cooked vegetables when they keep some of their crisp texture.

Crush: Press with side of knife blade or use meat mallet, mortar and pestle or rolling pin to smash into small pieces. See also Helpful How-To's, page 8.

Cube: Cut food into squares, 1/2 inch or larger, so it's the same size on all sides, using a knife. See also Helpful How-To's, page 8.

Cut Up: Cut food into small pieces of irregular sizes, using kitchen scissors or knife. Or to cut a large food into smaller pieces (whole chicken into pieces). See also Helpful How-To's, page 8.

Dash: Less than 1/8 teaspoon of an ingredient.

Deep-fry or French-fry: To cook in hot fat that's deep enough to cover and float the food being fried. Sometimes foods are cooked in a shallow amount of oil (about 1 inch). See also **Fry, Panbroil, Panfry, Sauté.**

Deglaze: After a food is panfried, excess fat is removed from the skillet, then a small amount of liquid (broth, water, wine) is added and stirred to loosen the flavorful browned bits of food in the skillet. This mixture is used as a base for gravy and sauce.

Dice: Cut food into 1/4-inch squares, using a knife, so the food is the same size on all sides. See also Helpful How-To's, page 8.

Dip: To moisten or coat a food by submerging into a liquid mixture to cover it completely (dipping onion rings into batter; dipping bread into the egg mixture for French toast).

Dissolve: Stir a dry ingredient (such as flavored gelatin) into a liquid ingredient (boiling water) until the dry ingredient disappears.

Dot: Drop small pieces of an ingredient (butter or margarine) randomly over food (sliced apples in an apple pie).

Dough: A stiff but pliable mixture of flour, liquid and other ingredients (often including a leavening).

Dough can be dropped from a spoon (cookies), rolled (pie crust) or kneaded (bread).

Drain: Pour off liquid by putting the food into a strainer or colander. To drain fat from meat, place the strainer in a disposable container; if saving the liquid, place the strainer in a bowl or other container.

Drizzle: Pour in a thin stream from a spoon, a squeeze bottle with a tip or a liquid measuring cup in an uneven pattern over food (glaze over cake or cookies).

Dust: Sprinkle lightly with flour, granulated sugar, powdered sugar or baking cocoa (dusting coffee cake with powdered sugar).

Flake: Break lightly into small, flat pieces using a fork (cooked fish).

Flute: Squeeze the edge of a pastry with your fingers, making a decorative edge.

Fry: Cook in hot fat over medium to high heat. See also **Deep-fry or French fry, Panbroil, Panfry, Sauté.**

Garnish: Decorate food with small amounts of other foods that have a distinctive color, flavor or texture (fresh herbs, fresh berries, chocolate curls).

Glaze: Brush, spread or drizzle an ingredient (jam or jelly, melted chocolate) on hot or cold food, giving it a thin, glossy coating.

Grate: Rub a hard-textured food (chocolate, citrus peel, Parmesan cheese) across the smallest holes of a grater to make tiny particles. See also Helpful How-To's, page 8.

Grease: Rub the bottom and sides of a pan with shortening, using pastry brush, waxed paper or paper towel. Or spray with cooking spray. Greasing pans prevents food from sticking during baking (cakes, muffins, some casseroles). Don't use butter or margarine for greasing unless specified in a recipe, because foods may stick.

Grease and flour: After greasing a pan with shortening, sprinkle it with a small amount of flour and shake the pan to distribute it evenly. Then, turn the pan upside down and tap the bottom to remove excess flour. Grease and flour pans to prevent sticking during baking.

Grill: See Grilling chapter, pages 261–284.

Heat oven: Turn the oven control(s) to the desired temperature, allowing the oven to heat thoroughly before adding food. Heating, also called *preheating,* takes about 10 minutes for most ovens.

Hull: Remove the stem and leaves from strawberries with a knife or huller.

Husk: To peel off the leaves and silk from fresh ears of corn.

Julienne: Cut into long, thin slices. Stack slices, then cut into matchlike sticks. See also Helpful How-To's, page 8.

Knead: Work dough on a floured surface into a smooth, springy mass, using your hands or an electric mixer with a dough hook. Kneading, which can take up to 10 minutes by hand, develops the gluten in flour and gives an even texture and a smooth, rounded top. See How to Make Yeast Dough, page 82. Biscuit and scone doughs are lightly kneaded about ten times before being rolled or patted out.

Marinate: Let food stand in a marinade—a savory, acidic liquid—in a glass or plastic container for several hours to add flavor. Don't marinate in metal containers because acidic ingredients react with metal to give food an off-flavor. Refrigerate food while it marinates.

Melt: Turn a solid (chocolate, butter) into a liquid or semiliquid by heating.

Microwave: Cook, reheat or thaw food in a microwave oven. See Microwave Cooking and Heating, pages 40–41.

Mince: Cut food into very fine pieces—smaller than chopped, but bigger than crushed—with a knife.

Mix: Combine ingredients evenly, using any method.

Panbroil: Cook meat or other food quickly in an ungreased or lightly greased skillet. See also **Deep-fry or French fry, Fry, Panfry, Sauté.**

Panfry: Fry meat or other food in a skillet, using varying amounts of fat and usually pouring off the fat from the meat during cooking. See also **Deep-fry, Fry, Panbroil, Sauté.**

Peel: Cut off outer covering with a paring knife or vegetable peeler, or remove with fingers. See also Helpful How-To's, page 8.

Poach: Cook food, such as eggs or fish, in a simmering liquid just below the boiling point.

Pound: Flatten boneless cuts of chicken and meat, using a meat mallet or the flat side of a meat pounder, until they're a uniform thickness. Also to tenderize meat by breaking up connective tissue. See How to Flatten Chicken Breasts, page 327.

Puree: Mash or blend food until it's smooth, using a blender or food processor or forcing the food through a sieve.

Reduce: Boil liquid, uncovered, to reduce its volume to either thicken a mixture, or intensify the flavor of the remaining liquid.

Reduce heat: Lower the heat on the stove-top or in the oven so that a food continues to cook slowly and evenly without burning or scorching.

Refrigerate: Place food in the refrigerator to chill or store it.

Roast: Cook meat, poultry or vegetables uncovered in the dry heat of the oven. Meat and poultry are often placed on a rack in a shallow pan without adding liquid; vegetables are usually tossed with oil and are spread in a single layer on a baking pan.

Roll: Flatten dough into a thin, even layer, using a rolling pin (cookies, pie crust). Also to shape balls of cookie dough.

Roll up: Roll a flat food that's spread with a filling—or with the filling placed at one end—beginning at one end until it is log-shaped (caramel rolls, enchilada).

Sauté: Cook food over medium-high heat in a small amount of fat, frequently tossing or turning. See also **Deep-fry or French fry, Fry, Panbroil, Panfry.**

Scald: Heat liquid to just below the boiling point and tiny bubbles form at the edge. A thin skin will form on the top of scalded milk.

Score: Cut shallow lines (1/4 inch deep), diamonds or triangles through the surface of meat, duck or bread to decorate, tenderize or let fat drain away as foods cook or bake.

Sear: Brown meat, fish or seafood quickly on all sides over high heat to seal in the juices.

Season: Add flavor with salt, pepper, herbs, spices or seasoning mixes.

Shred: Push food across a shredding surface to make narrow or fine strips, or to slice very thinly with a knife. See also Helpful How-To's, page 8.

Simmer: Cook in liquid just below the boiling point while bubbles rise slowly and break just below the surface. See also Helpful How-To's, page 8.

Skim: Remove fat or foam from a soup, broth, stock or stew, using a spoon, ladle or skimmer (a flat utensil with holes in it).

Slice: Cut into flat pieces of about the same size (bread, meat).

Snip: Cut into very small pieces with kitchen scissors. See also Helpful How-To's, page 8.

Soft Peaks: Egg whites or whipping cream beaten until the peaks curl when you lift the beaters from the bowl. See also **Stiff Peaks.**

Soften: Let cold food (butter, margarine, cream cheese) stand at room temperature, or microwave on Low power setting, until no longer hard.

Soy: See Soy Products, page 497.

Steam: Cook food by placing it in a steamer basket, which may be metal or bamboo, over a small amount of boiling or simmering water in a covered pan. Steaming helps food retain its flavor, shape, color, texture and nutritional value. See also Fresh Vegetable Cooking chart, page 480.

Stew: Cook slowly in a covered pot, pan or casserole in a small amount of liquid for a long time (beef stew).

Stiff Peaks: Egg whites or whipping cream beaten until peaks stand up straight when you lift the beaters from the bowl. See also **Soft Peaks.**

Stir-fry: Cook small, similar-size pieces of food in a small amount of hot oil in a wok or skillet over high heat while stirring constantly.

Strain: Pour a mixture or liquid through a fine strainer or sieve to remove larger particles.

Tear: Break into pieces with your fingers (lettuce for a salad, bread slices for soft bread crumbs).

Toast: Brown lightly in a toaster, oven, broiler or skillet (bread, coconut, nuts).

Toss: Gently combine ingredients by lifting and dropping them using two utensils (salads).

Whip: Beat ingredients using electric mixer to add air and increase volume until the ingredients are light and fluffy (whipping cream, egg whites).

Zest (Peel): The outside colored layer, or peel, of citrus fruits that contains aromatic oils and flavor. Also to remove the outside layer of citrus fruits in fine strips, using a knife, citrus zester or vegetable peeler. Remove only the colored outer skin, not the bitter white inner membrane.

Ingredients Glossary

Starting with the right ingredients is the secret of every successful cook. Check this list to find the ingredients you'll need for the recipes in this cookbook, as well as other common ingredients.

Baking Powder: Leavening mixture made from baking soda, an acid and a moisture absorber. Double-acting baking powder makes doughs rise twice: once when mixed with moist ingredients and once during baking. Not interchangeable with baking soda.

Baking Soda: Leavening also known as *bicarbonate of soda.* Must be mixed with an acid ingredient such as lemon juice, buttermilk, sour cream, yogurt, molasses or brown sugar in order to make doughs rise. Not interchangeable with baking powder.

Balsamic Vinegar: Created in the area of Modena, Italy, this vinegar is made from the juice of white Trebbiano grapes. The molasses color and intense, sweet flavor result from aging the vinegar in wood barrels.

Bisquick® Mix: A convenience baking mix made from flour, shortening, baking powder and salt. Use for biscuits, muffins, other quick breads, cakes, cookies and some main dishes. Look for a reduced-fat variety too.

Bouillon/Broth/Stock: The liquid made from cooking vegetables, meat, poultry, fish or seafood that's used to make soups and sauces. Stocks are more intensely flavored than broths and are usually strained before using. Supermarkets carry canned beef, chicken and vegetable broths and dehydrated bouillon cubes, granules and pastes.

Capers: Unopened flower buds of a Mediterranean plant that range in size from a peppercorn to a pea. Their sharp, tangy flavor is described as a cross between olives and citrus fruit. Look for them, packed in vinegar brine, in the same aisle as the olives and pickles. Use capers to flavor salad dressings, sauces and condiments.

Cheese: See Natural Cheese chart, pages 231–232.

Chilies: More than 200 varieties of fresh and dried chilies used in cooking around the world. They're available in many colors, sizes and degrees of heat. Chilies range in length from 1/4 inch to 12 inches, with smaller chilies usually being hotter. Rehydrate dried chilies in warm water for at least 30 minutes before using. The ribs and seeds contain most of the heat-containing oils and are hotter than the flesh. Since these

CHILIES & PEPPERS

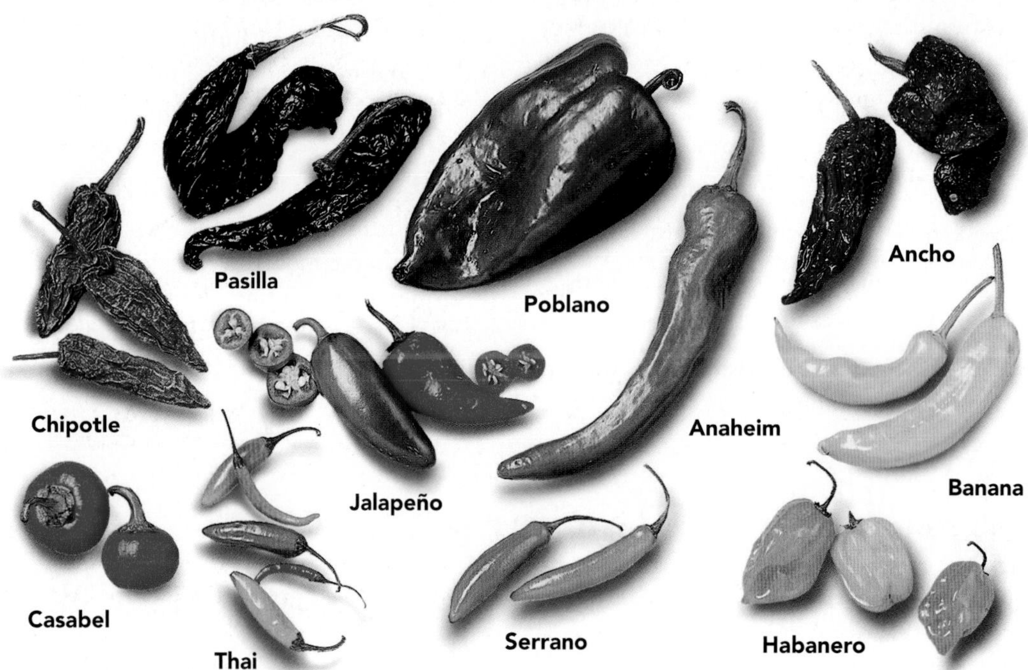

oils can irritate and burn your eyes, nose and skin, always wear plastic or rubber gloves when handling chilies, and wash your hands thoroughly with warm, soapy water when done. Don't cut chilies under running water because the irritating oils can become airborne, irritating your lungs and eyes. See Helpful How-To's Seed Chilies, page 9.

- **Anaheim chilies:** Available fresh or dried, these slim chilies come in various shades of green, are between 5 and 8 inches long and are mildly hot. They're occasionally stuffed and can be bought in cans as "mild green chilies." They're named for the California city that opened a chili pepper cannery.
- **Ancho chilies:** Dried, ripened poblano chilies.
- **Cascabel chilies:** Medium hot, with a distinctive nutty flavor. Dark-blood-red in color, they're plum-shaped and about 1 1/2 inches in diameter. *Cascabel,* meaning "little round bell" or "rattle" in Spanish, chilies are named for the sound they make when shaken. These chilies are also known as *chili bola.*
- **Chili de arbol:** Extremely hot, long, slender red chili in both fresh and dried forms.
- **Chipotle chilies:** Smoked, dried jalapeño chilies. Can be purchased loose in the dried form, pickled or canned in adobo sauce. Chipotle chilies are often used in sauces.
- **Fresno chilies:** Tapered chilies that are light green when young, red when mature. Similar to Anaheim chilies but with all the heat of a jalapeño. Fresno chilies are often used in guacamole.
- **Habanero chilies:** Orange when ripe; available fresh and dried. They look like little lanterns and are considered one of the hottest chilies of them all. Handle with extra care so the oils don't burn you.
- **Hungarian wax chilies:** Large yellow chilies, which are mild to medium hot and come up to 5 inches long. Also known as *banana peppers* or *yellow wax chilies.* They're often pickled.
- **Jalapeño chilies:** Jade-green or red chilies, 2 to 3 inches long, that pack a wallop of heat.

If you're looking for the hottest ones, choose to go for the smallest ones. They're called *escabeche* when pickled and *chipotle* when dried and smoked. Jalapeños are a favorite for nachos, salsas and other sauces.

- **Pasilla chilies:** Long, slender, dried chilies that are medium to very hot with a rich flavor.
- **Pequin chilies:** Tiny red to dark-red dried chilies with searing heat—so use them very sparingly. Handle with extra care so the oils don't burn you.
- **Poblano chilies:** Dark green and slightly flat with a pointed tip, these are mild to hot. Best known for their use in *chiles rellenos*. When dried, they're called *ancho chilies*.
- **Serrano chilies:** Among the hottest chilies, these range from bright green to scarlet. Look for them fresh, canned, dried, pickled and packed in oil with carrots, onions and other vegetables.
- **Thai chilies:** Narrow, thin chilies ranging in color from bright lime green to orange and bright red. They're the source of intense heat that gives a kick to Thai dishes.

Chocolate: Cocoa beans are shelled, roasted and ground to make a thick paste called *chocolate liquor,* which is the base for all chocolate. Cocoa butter is the fat or oil from the cocoa bean. Chocolate liquor is processed to make:

- **Baking cocoa:** Dried chocolate liquor, with the cocoa butter removed, is ground into unsweetened cocoa. Baking cocoa isn't a direct substitute for cocoa drink mixes that contain added milk powder and sugar.
- **Semisweet, bittersweet, sweet and milk chocolate:** Contain from 10 to 35 percent chocolate liquor, varying amounts of cocoa butter, sugar and, for some, milk and flavorings. Available in bars and chips for baking or eating. Since all chocolate is not the same and quality varies, be sure to follow package directions when melting.
- **Unsweetened chocolate:** Contains 50 to 58 percent cocoa butter. Bitter in flavor, it's used primarily in baking.
- **White chocolate:** Is not true chocolate because it doesn't contain any cocoa or chocolate liquor, so doesn't taste chocolaty. Made from cocoa butter, sugar, milk solids and vanilla. Often called *white baking chips* or *vanilla baking bar.*

Coconut: The firm, creamy-white meat of the coconut, the fruit of the coconut palm. It's available shredded or flaked. Shredded coconut is very moist and is used mainly for baking. Flaked coconut, used mainly for decorating, is cut into small pieces and is much drier than shredded coconut.

Coffee: Use brewed coffee or instant coffee granules as an ingredient. See also Brewing Coffee, page 59.

Corn Syrup: Clear, thick liquid made from corn sugar mixed with acid. It's one sweetener that doesn't crystallize and works well for pecan pie, cooked frostings, fruit sauces and jams. Dark and light corn syrups are interchangeable unless one is specifically called for in a recipe.

Cornstarch: A thickener for soups, sauces and desserts that comes from a portion of the corn kernel. Very finely ground, cornstarch makes clear sauces, not opaque sauces like those thickened with wheat flour. To substitute all-purpose flour in a sauce, use half as much cornstarch.

Cream: The smooth, rich dairy product that separates from whole milk and floats to the top, leaving almost fat-free milk at the bottom. Cream is sold in light (also labeled *whipping cream*), heavy (also labeled *heavy whipping cream*) and ultra-pasteurized forms. Heavy whipping cream is higher in fat than light cream. Cream is churned to make butter and buttermilk; it's also pasteurized and processed into several forms:

- **Half-and-half:** A blend of milk and cream containing 10 to 12 percent butterfat. It won't whip, but you can use it in place of light or heavy cream in many recipes.
- **Heavy whipping cream:** The richest cream available in the United States, it has 36 to 40 percent butterfat. It doubles in volume when whipped.

- **Light whipping cream:** The most common form contains 30 to 36 percent butterfat. It doubles in volume when whipped.
- **Sour cream:** Commercially cultured with lactic acid to give it a tangy flavor. Regular sour cream is 18 to 20 percent butterfat. Light sour cream is made from half-and-half and can be substituted for regular sour cream in most recipes. Fat-free sour cream has all the fat removed and may not work well in all recipes that call for regular sour cream.
- **Ultra-pasteurized whipping cream:** Heavy cream that has been heated briefly to kill microorganisms that cause milk products to sour. It has a longer shelf life than regular cream, but it doesn't whip as well and has a slightly cooked flavor. Contains 36 to 40 percent butterfat.

Cream of Tartar: After wine is made, acids left in wine barrels are processed into cream of tartar. Add cream of tartar to egg whites before beating for more stability and volume. You'll also find it in most baking powders as an acid ingredient, helping to make baked goods rise.

Eggs: See Egg Basics, page 219.

Fats and Oils: Fats and oils add richness and flavor to food. In cooking, they improve browning, help hold ingredients together, tenderize baked goods and are used for frying. Fats vary in texture and flavor. The recipes in this book call for a variety of fats because of their specific cooking and baking characteristics.

- **Butter:** A saturated fat made from cream that must be at least 80 percent butterfat by USDA standards. It has a creamy, dairy flavor and melt-in-your-mouth texture. Butter is sold in lightly salted and unsalted sticks. Unsalted butter is also called *sweet butter* because it has no added salt. Lightly salted and unsalted butter are interchangeable without adjusting the salt in the recipe. Butter also comes whipped in tubs and as butter-flavored granules. Use only sticks for baking; whipped butter will give a different texture because of the air beaten into it. Many recipes in this book call for butter or margarine when either can be used. If only butter can be used, recipes will state not to use margarine or vegetable-oil spreads (because they will burn).
- **Butter-margarine blends:** Available in sticks and tubs, blends usually are a combination of 60 percent margarine and 40 percent butter and are interchangeable with butter or margarine. Use only the sticks for baking.
- **Lard:** A saturated fat made from rendered and refined pork fat, lard is not used as much now as in the past. Lard makes very tender, flaky biscuits and pastry.
- **Margarine:** An unsaturated butter substitute made with at least 80 percent fat by weight and flavoring from dairy products. Most margarines contain vegetable oils made from soybeans, cottonseed and corn. The texture and flavor of margarine varies among brands. It's sold in sticks and in tubs as soft spreads. Great as a table spread, as well as for cooking and baking. Use only the sticks for baking.
- **Reduced-calorie or light butter or margarine:** Water and air have been added to these products, and they contain at least 20 percent less fat than regular butter or margarine. Do not use for baking or cooking.
- **Oils for cooking:** Low in saturated fats and containing no cholesterol, these liquid fats are delicate to bland in flavor and are treated to withstand high-temperature cooking and long storage. These oils include
  - **Cooking spray:** Available in regular (unflavored), butter and olive oil varieties. Regular spray is used to spray cooking and baking pans to prevent food from sticking. To cook the low-fat way, spray any type directly on the food.
  - **Olive oil:** Olive oil naturally contains no cholesterol, but it does contain fat. It may contribute to heart health, since it has the highest amount of monounsaturated fat of any vegetable oil. You'll find it's classified

in several ways, including extra-virgin, virgin, olive oil and light olive oil.

- **Vegetable oil:** A blend of oils from various vegetables, such as corn, cottonseed, peanut, safflower, canola and soybean. Use for all cooking and baking.

- **Shortening:** Vegetable oils that are hydrogenated so they'll be solid at room temperature. Shortening is especially good for making flaky, tender pastry and for greasing baking pans. Use butter-flavored and regular shortening interchangeably. Sold in sticks and cans.
- **Vegetable-oil spreads:** Margarine products with less than 80 percent fat (vegetable oil) by weight usually are labeled as vegetable-oil spreads. Use the sticks for all-purpose cooking. Those containing more than 65 percent fat are even fine for baking, so check the label. But the vegetable-oil spreads sold in tubs can't be used for baking because they contain too much water. Look for them as liquids, too, in squeezable bottles. They're great for topping veggies, popcorn or basting, but not for baking.

Flour: The primary ingredient in breads, cakes, cookies and quick breads.

- **All-purpose flour:** Selected wheats blended for all kinds of baking. Available both bleached and unbleached.
- **Bread flour:** Made from wheat higher in gluten-forming protein, which gives more structure and volume to bread, than all-purpose flour. It's the best for making bread-machine breads and other yeast breads. It isn't recommended for cakes, cookies, pastries or quick breads, because they will be less flaky and tender.
- **Cake flour:** Milled from soft wheat, it makes tender, fine-textured cakes.
- **Quick-mixing flour:** Enriched, all-purpose flour that's granular and processed to blend easily with liquid to make gravies and sauces.
- **Rye flour:** Milled from rye grain and low in gluten-forming protein, it is usually combined with wheat flour to increase gluten-forming capabilities.
- **Self-rising flour:** A convenience flour made from a blend of hard and soft wheats that includes baking powder and salt. For best results, don't substitute self-rising flour for other kinds, unless directed in a recipe, because it will throw the leavening and salt proportions out of balance.
- **Whole wheat flour:** Ground from the entire wheat kernel, whole wheat flour gives breads and other baked goods a nutty flavor and dense texture. Stone-ground whole wheat flour has a coarser texture than roller-milled whole wheat flour. Graham flour is a slightly different grind of whole wheat flour but can be used interchangeably with whole wheat flour. Store whole wheat flour in the freezer or refrigerator to keep the fat in the wheat germ from becoming rancid. Always bring flour to room temperature before using.

Garlic: Plump, pungent, egg-size bulbs made up of individual cloves and encased in papery skin. Is in the same family as chives, leeks, onions and shallots. Available in many forms: fresh, peeled and in jars, as a paste, as juice, dried, powdered and flaked. Ideal for seasoning a broad range of dishes from many cuisines.

Gelatin: A colorless, tasteless and odorless powder that thickens when dissolved with hot liquid and then sets when refrigerated. Gelatin is pure protein, processed from beef and veal bones, cartilage, tendons and other tissue. Both plain and sweetened flavors are available.

Gingerroot: Plump tubers with knobby branches. Side branches have a milder tangy ginger flavor than the main root, which can have a hot bite. Grate unpeeled gingerroot, or peel then chop or slice, to season foods such as stir-fries, sauces and baked goods. Wrap tightly in plastic and store in the refrigerator.

Herbs: See pages 422–426.

Honey: A natural sweetener produced by bees. Honey adds distinctive flavor to salads, salad dressings, dips, sauces, beverages and baked goods. Honey can contain spores of *clostridium botulinum,* which can cause infection in infants.

So do not feed honey to children less than 1 year old—it's safe for persons 1 year of age and older. Store honey at room temperature; if refrigerated, it will crystallize more easily and quickly. To make crystallized honey liquid again, heat a saucepan of water to boiling, remove from the heat and place the container of honey in the hot water until the crystals disappear. Or liquefy it fast in the microwave; see Microwave Cooking and Heating, pages 40–41.

Leavening: Ingredients that cause baked goods to rise and develop lighter textures. See also **Baking Powder, Baking Soda, Yeast.**

Legumes: See Legumes Basics, page 346.

Maple Syrup: Golden-brown to amber-colored sweetener made by boiling down the sap of sugar maple trees. Use as a topping and as an ingredient. Refrigerate after opening. Maple-flavored syrup usually is corn syrup combined with a little pure maple syrup. Pancake syrups usually are corn syrup with added maple flavoring.

Mayonnaise/Salad Dressing: This smooth, rich mixture is made from egg yolks, vinegar and seasonings and is beaten to keep its creamy texture during storage. Look for it in jars in regular, light, low-fat and fat-free versions. Salad dressing is similar to mayonnaise, but it's lower in fat because it's made with a starch thickener, vinegar, eggs and sweetener. You can substitute salad dressing for mayonnaise in salads or spreads—but not in hot or cooked dishes, unless the recipe was developed for salad dressing. (Salad dressing may separate when heated.)

Milk: Refers to cow's milk in the recipes in this book.

- **Buttermilk:** Thick, smooth liquid made by culturing skim or part-skim milk with lactic acid bacteria. Adds a tangy flavor to baked goods. Originally, this milk was the liquid left after churning butter, so that's why it's called *buttermilk.*
- **Evaporated milk:** Whole milk with more than half of the water removed before the mixture is homogenized. Evaporated milk is a little thicker than whole milk and has a slightly "cooked" taste. Use it in recipes calling for evaporated milk, or mix with an equal amount of water to replace whole milk. Do not use it as a substitute for sweetened condensed milk in recipes.
- **Fat-free (skim) milk:** Contains virtually no fat.
- **1 percent low-fat milk:** Has 99 percent of milk fat removed.
- **2 percent reduced-fat milk:** Has 98 percent of milk fat removed.
- **Sweetened condensed milk:** Made when about half of the water is removed from whole milk and sweetener is added. Recipes using sweetened condensed milk include bars, candies and pies. Do not substitute it in recipes calling for evaporated milk.
- **Whole or regular milk:** Has at least 3.5 percent milk fat.

Mushrooms: Belonging to the fungus family, mushrooms come both fresh and dried in many shapes, colors and flavors. Check the following list for some of the most common varieties to look for. Cleaning mushrooms is easy: Cut a thin slice from the bottom of the stem. Gently wipe with a cloth or soft brush or rinse quickly with cold water, then pat dry with paper towels. Rehyrdrate dried mushrooms in warm water for at least 30 minutes before using. See also Mushrooms, page 472.

- **Chanterelle:** Bright yellow to orange trumpet-shaped mushrooms usually available dried or canned. Their flavor is nutty and delicate, and their texture, slightly chewy.
- **Crimini:** Also known as the Italian brown mushroom, they're darker in color and stronger in flavor than white mushrooms.
- **Enoki:** Slightly crunchy mushrooms with tiny caps and long, edible stems; grown in clusters. Use as a garnish, toss in salads or tuck in sandwiches.

- **Morel:** A wild mushroom with a rich, earthy flavor that looks like a little cone-shaped sponge. Simply cook in butter or stir into sauces. Look for fresh morels in the produce section from April to June; dried morels, which have a stronger, smokier flavor, are available year-round.
- **Oyster:** Some of the most graceful mushrooms, with shell-shaped cap ranging in color from bluish gray to off-white.
- **Porcini:** Also known as *cèpes,* these wild mushrooms are prized for their strong, woodsy flavor. Although available fresh, the dried version is more common.
- **Portabella:** Also spelled portobello. Large portabella mushrooms have a flat cap and open veins. Due to their meaty texture, they're often grilled and served as a meat substitute. Baby portabella mushrooms are more tender and can be used like white mushrooms.
- **Shiitake:** Known for its meaty flavor and texture, it has a dark brown umbrella-shaped cap and tan gills. The stems are usually woody and should be discarded.
- **White:** The most popular mushroom, sometimes called "button." Creamy white with a rounded cap, it ranges in size from small to jumbo for stuffing.

Mustard: Comes from mustard greens, known for their sharp-tasting seeds and calcium-rich leaves. A quick way to add pungent flavor to foods.

- **Ground mustard:** Finely ground dried mustard seed.
- **Mustard seed:** Whole seeds used for pickling and to season savory dishes.
- **Mustard:** Yellow mustard (also called *American mustard*) is made from mild white mustard seed mixed with sugar, vinegar and seasonings. Dijon mustard, from Dijon, France, is made from brown mustard seed mixed with wine, unfermented grape juice and seasonings.

Look for other varieties at your supermarket or local gourmet or cooking shop.

Organic: Recently, organic foods have grown in prominence. Technically, they are all foods grown without the use of synthetic pesticides or chemical fertilizers. The USDA organic standards also prohibit the use of antibiotics, artificial (or synthetic) flavors, hormones, preservatives, synthetic colors, as well as ingredients that are irradiated or genetically engineered.

Pasta: See Pasta, page 351.

Pesto: A pasta sauce traditionally made by blending fresh basil, pine nuts, Parmesan cheese, garlic and olive oil until smooth. Make it fresh (see Basil Pesto, page 405), or look for it in the refrigerator case or in the pasta-sauce section of your supermarket.

Phyllo (Filo): Paper-thin pastry sheets whose name comes from the Greek word for *leaf.* It's the pastry favored for many Greek and Middle Eastern main dishes and sweets. Look for phyllo sheets in your grocer's freezer and refrigerator sections. The secret of working with phyllo is "Do it fast!" And be sure to cover the extra sheets with waxed paper and a damp kitchen towel so they don't dry out.

Pine Nuts: Small white nuts from several varieties of pine trees. Also known as *pinon* and *pignoli.* Often used in Mediterranean and Mexican dishes. With their high fat content, these nuts turn rancid quickly, so store them in the refrigerator to preserve their flavor.

Puff Pastry: Dozens of layers of chilled butter rolled between sheets of pastry dough. During baking, the moisture in the butter creates steam, causing the dough to puff and separate into thin layers. Use puff pastry for making napoleons, palmiers and other layered desserts. Check your grocer's freezer case for ready-to-use puff pastry sheets and shells.

Red Pepper Sauce: Condiment made from hot chili peppers and cured in either salt or vinegar brine. Many varieties and levels of hotness are available.

Rice: See Grains Basics, page 337.

Roasted Bell Peppers: Sweet red or other color bell peppers that have been roasted and packed in jars with water, salt and citric acid or vinegar. Popular for appetizers, soups and main dishes.

Salad Dressing: See **Mayonnaise.** Also refers to commercially made dressings like ranch and Italian, with the flavor always included when called for in recipes. Look for commercial dressing in both refrigerated and non-refrigerated grocery aisles.

Salsa: A Mexican sauce of tomatoes, onions, green chilies and sometimes cilantro and vinegar. Make it at home (see Salsa, page 416), or buy it fresh, canned or bottled. Green salsa, or *salsa verde,* is made with tomatillos. Also, refers to any sauce of fresh chopped fruits and/or vegetables.

Scallions: Look much like their cousin, the green onion (immature onion). True scallions are milder in flavor than green onions but can be used interchangeably.

Shallots: Onions with multiple cloves that look like garlic. The papery skin that covers the bulbs ranges in color from beige to purple and should be removed. Shallots are milder than onions in flavor but are interchangeable.

Soy Sauce: Chinese and Japanese specialty used in Asian cooking and as a condiment. A dark-brown sauce made from soybeans, wheat, yeast and salt. A low-sodium variety is available.

Sugar: Sweetener produced from sugar beets or cane sugar. Available in several forms:

- **Brown:** Brown sugar, also called *golden sugar,* is made by mixing white sugar with molasses. Look for it in light and dark varieties; dark brown sugar has more molasses added and a stronger flavor. To keep brown sugar soft, store it in a closed container or resealable plastic food-storage bag. If it hardens, add a slice of apple or a slice of fresh bread, it should be soft in a day or two.
- **Coarse:** Also called *decorating* or *pearl sugar,* this large-grained granulated sugar is used for decorating baked goods. Look for coarse sugar near the cake-decorating supplies.
- **Granulated:** White, granular sugar that should be used when recipes call for just "sugar." It's available in boxes and bags, as well as in cubes and 1-teaspoon packets. Superfine sugar is a finer grind and more difficult to find—but it's worth keeping on hand. It dissolves quickly, so it's perfect for using in iced drinks. It's the sugar of choice by baking aficionados, especially for making meringues and frosting.
- **Molasses:** Dark thick syrup from the sugar refining process. Molasses is available in light (mild-flavor) and dark (full-flavor) varieties. Light and dark molasses is interchangeable unless one is specifically called for in a recipe.
- **Powdered:** Also known as *confectioners' sugar,* powdered sugar is granulated sugar that has been processed to a fine powder. Great for frostings and to dust or coat cookies and cakes.
- **Artificial sweeteners:** A variety of products are available. Many are not recommended for baking because the flavor may become bitter—check the labels.

Sun-Dried Tomatoes: Ripe tomatoes that have been dried, making them chewy and sweet with an intense tomato flavor. Available dried or in jars packed in oil with or without herbs. Rehydrate dried tomatoes in warm water for at least 30 minutes before using.

Tofu: Tofu, also called *bean curd,* is curdled soy milk manufactured in a process similar to cheese making. It's rich in high-quality protein, low in saturated fat and contains no cholesterol. Naturally bland and almost flavorless, tofu acts like a sponge, soaking up any flavor it's mixed with. Use tofu in stir-fries, casseroles, soups and stews. See Tofu and Tempeh, page 495.

Tomatillos: Easily mistaken for small green tomatoes, tomatillos grow in a brown paper husk that's removed before use. Citrusy in flavor, tomatillos are used in salsas and Mexican sauces.

Tortillas: Made from ground wheat (flour tortilla) or corn (corn tortilla), tortillas can be eaten plain or as a "wrap" around both hot and cold fillings. The fresh version comes in many flavors as well as a fat-free version. Look for fried taco salad bowls and shells, too.

Truffles: This European fungus that grows wild near the roots of trees is one of the world's most expensive foods. They are located by specially trained dogs and pigs, which use their keen sense of smell to sniff them out. Truffles are roundish in shape, with thick, wrinkled skin and pungent flavor. Excellent in sauces and omelets and as a garnish. Available fresh, canned and as a paste in a tube.

Worcestershire Sauce: Common condiment made from a blend of ingredients: garlic, soy sauce, tamarind, onions, molasses, lime, anchovies, vinegar and other seasonings. White Worcestershire sauce is also available. This sauce gets its name from Worcester, England, where it was first bottled—but the English actually developed it in India.

Yeast: Leavening whose fermentation is the heart and soul of yeast bread. The combination of warmth, food (sugar) and liquid causes yeast to release carbon dioxide bubbles that cause dough to rise. Yeast is very sensitive; too much heat will kill it, and cold will prevent it from growing. Always use yeast before its expiration date.

- **Bread machine yeast:** A finely granulated strain of yeast that works exceptionally well in bread machines.
- **Compressed fresh (cake) yeast:** A small square of fresh, moist yeast found in the dairy case. It's highly perishable, so store in the refrigerator and use within 2 weeks or by the expiration date. One cake of yeast is equal to one envelope of dry yeast. This yeast isn't as popular as dry yeast, so it's often more difficult to find.
- **Quick active dry yeast:** Dehydrated yeast that allows bread to rise in less time than regular yeast. Quick active dry yeast can be used interchangeably with bread machine yeast.
- **Regular active dry yeast:** Dehydrated yeast that can be used in most yeast bread recipes. To use in bread machines, you may need to increase the amount to 1 teaspoon for each 3/4 teaspoon of bread machine yeast.

The "Magic" of Microwaves

What would we do without microwaves? They let us cook foods faster than we ever thought possible. They help us clean up quicker, too, because we have fewer dishes to wash. And they let us heat up leftovers, fast and fresh. Follow the manufacturer's operating instructions for your microwave and information on microwavable utensils. Plus, here are some basics of microwaving that are great to remember.

Food Density: Porous foods, such as breads and cakes, cook quickly. Dense foods, such as potatoes, need longer cooking.

Food Temperature: The colder the food, the longer the cooking time. Foods tested for this book were taken from their normal storage areas—freezer, refrigerator or cupboard shelf.

Food Volume: Increase the cooking time if you increase the amount of food.

Moisture, Sugar, Fat: Foods containing these ingredients cook or heat quickly—so watch them carefully!

Shapes: Round or doughnut-shaped foods or foods in round or ring-shaped containers cook most evenly. Watch foods with uneven shapes more closely during cooking.

Sizes: Small pieces of food cook faster than large ones. Be sure to cut pieces about the same size so they'll cook more evenly and be done at the same time.

Standing Time: Allows foods to finish cooking or distribute heat more evenly.

MICROWAVE TIPS AND TECHNIQUES

Try these techniques to speed up heating, cook food evenly and to make some foods look better when microwaved:

- *Add color* by coating uncooked food with crumbs or brushing with a sauce or glaze before microwaving.
- *For even cooking,* arrange food in a circle with thickest parts to the outside.
- *Cover food* with a lid or plastic wrap. Turn back a corner or 1/4-inch edge of wrap to vent steam for faster cooking. Use waxed paper or microwavable paper towels to prevent spattering.
- If the food is very moist (such as batters), put it on an *upside-down dish* so the bottom center cooks better.
- *Check food at the minimum time* to avoid overcooking. Cook longer if necessary.
- *Stir food* from the outer edge to the center, so food cooks faster and more evenly.
- *If food can't be stirred* and your microwave doesn't have a turntable, rotate the dish 1/2 or 1/4 turn to help the food cook more evenly.
- *Turn some foods over* after part of the cooking time for more even cooking.

MICROWAVE TESTING FOR THIS BOOK

Recipes with microwave directions were tested in countertop microwaves with 700 to 800 watts. If your microwave has a rating of less than 700 watts, lengthen the cooking time; if more than 800 watts, shorten the cooking time.

Cooking at Higher Altitudes—with Success!

If you live at elevations of 3,500 feet or higher, you have some unique cooking challenges. Air pressure is lower, so water has a lower boiling point and liquids evaporate faster. That means recipes for both conventional and microwave cooking need to be adjusted so they'll turn out right every time. Unfortunately, no set of rules applies to all recipes, so sometimes, trial and error is the best way. Here are some guidelines for success:

- Boiling foods such as pasta, rice and vegetables will take longer.
- When microwaving, you may need to add more water and cook foods longer. It all depends on the type and amount of food, the water content of the food and the elevation you're cooking at.
- Cooking meat in boiling liquid or steam takes longer, sometimes as much as 50 to 100 percent. Cooking large meat cuts, such as roasts and turkeys, in the oven also takes longer. Create your own guidelines by using a meat thermometer and writing down how long meats take to cook.
- Most baked goods made with baking powder or baking soda (but not yeast) can be improved with one or more of the following changes:
  - Increase the temperature by 25°F.
  - Increase the liquid.
  - Decrease the baking powder or baking soda.
  - Decrease the sugar and/or use a larger pan.
  - Decrease the fat in very rich recipes, such as pound cakes. Quick breads and cookies usually don't need as many adjustments.
- Yeast bread dough rises faster at high altitudes and can easily overrise. Let dough rise for a shorter time (just until it doubles in size). Flour dries out more quickly at high altitudes, too, so use the minimum amount in the recipe, or decrease the amount by 1/4 to 1/2 cup.
- If you're using a mix, look for specific directions right on the package.
- Because water evaporates faster at higher altitudes, boiled candy, cooked frostings and other sugar mixtures concentrate faster. Watch the recipe closely during cooking so it doesn't scorch. You also may want to reduce the recipe temperature by 2°F for every 1,000 feet of elevation. Or use the cold water test for candy (see How to Test Candy, page 188).
- Deep-fried foods can be too brown on the outside but undercooked on the inside. So that both the outside and inside of food are done at the same time, reduce the temperature of the oil by 3°F for every 1,000 feet of elevation and increase the frying time, if necessary.

HIGH-ALTITUDE EXPERTS

If you're new to high-altitude cooking, call your local U.S. Department of Agriculture (USDA) Extension Service office, listed in the phone book under "County Government," for answers to your questions. Or write to Colorado State University, Department of Food Science and Human Nutrition Cooperative Extension, Fort Collins, CO 80523-1571. Check your library and local bookstores for high-altitude cookbooks.

Home Canning

Think how proud you'll be to serve some jewel-toned jelly, scarlet tomatoes or golden peaches that you've just "put up" (that is, canned yourself) with produce from your garden or local farmers' market. Home canning isn't hard—and the results are certainly worthwhile. Just pick the right canning method, depending on the food, so it will stay safe and won't spoil.

To destroy spoilage organisms such as molds, yeast and bacteria, food must be processed for a *long enough time* at *a high enough temperature.* But the only way to destroy *clostridium botulinum* is by using a pressure canner and following the instructions carefully. If *clostridium botulinum* survives and grows in a sealed jar of food, it can produce a poisonous toxin, which if eaten—even in small amounts—may be fatal.

The amount of acid in the food you're canning determines which canning method's the best to use:

- A **pressure canner** is a large heavy pot with a rack for holding canning jars and has a tight-fitting lid with a vent petcock and a dial or weighted pressure gauge and safety fuse. It's important to only use this type of canner for low-acid foods, such as meat, poultry, seafood and vegetables.
- A **boiling-water canner** is a large kettle with a lid and a rack to hold canning jars. This method is recommended for all acid foods, such as fruits, tomatoes with added acid, jams, jellies and pickled vegetables.
- The **open-kettle** method of canning, which uses no lid, is not recommended because temperatures never get hot enough to kill bacteria.

If you are unsure about the safety of certain home-canned foods, boiling the food for 10 minutes at altitudes below 1,000 feet will destroy these toxins. Boil an extra minute for every 1,000 feet of additional elevation.

STAYING UP-TO-DATE WITH HOME CANNING

For current information about safe home canning, contact:

- National Center for Home Food Preservation at:
  http://www.uga.edu/nchfp/how/can.home.html
- The USDA Complete Guide to Home Canning
  Publication SF 006
  IFAS Publications
  University of Florida
  P.O. Box 110011
  Gainesville, FL 32611
  E-mail: cmh@gnv.ifas.ufl.edu
  Phone: 352-392-1764
  FAX: 352-392-2628
- The University of Georgia
  328 Hoke Smith Annex
  Athens, GA 30602-4356
  FAX: 706-583-0670
- Local USDA Extension Service office listed in the phone book under "County Government."

Food Safety—The Basics

America's food supply is one of the safest in the world. The reason is simple: Farmers, ranchers, food processors, supermarkets and restaurants follow strict rules and regulations to get food to you. But after you take the food out of the grocery store, it's up to you to keep it safe.

Why be concerned about food safety? Because most illnesses reported from "bad food" can be prevented. They're caused by bacterial contamination, which usually results from not handling and storing food correctly in our homes, supermarkets and restaurants. Microorganisms are always around. They're on us and on animals, in the air and water and on raw food. Some bacteria are great to have, like those that create cheese or ferment beer. But other bacteria cause foods to spoil and some even cause food poisoning.

TEMPERATURE REALLY MATTERS

The main difference between bacteria that causes food to spoil and those that can poison food is the temperature at which they survive and grow. Bacteria that spoils can grow at refrigerator temperatures (below 40°F) and usually make food look or smell bad. When this happens, throw it out! Food-poisoning bacteria *don't* grow at refrigerator temperatures. The best growing temperature for these microorganisms is around 100°F, though the actual temperature varies with the particular organism and may range from 40°F to 140°F, or the *danger zone* (the temperature range most bacteria grow and multiply in). These are pathogens, the type of bacteria that if eaten may lead to illness, disease or even death.

To prevent these bacteria from becoming harmful, they must be stopped from multiplying. Pathogenic bacteria are among the most important organisms to control because of the illness they cause in humans. *The majority are invisible attackers; you can't see, smell or even taste them.*

If contaminated food is eaten, people most often get sick within 4 to 48 hours, and it's not always easy to tell if the symptoms are from a case of flu or food poisoning. Call a doctor or go to a hospital immediately if symptoms are severe such as vomiting, diarrhea, fever or cramps, or if the victim is very young, elderly, pregnant, has a weakened immune system or is already ill.

FOUR GOLDEN RULES FOR FOOD SAFETY

Proper cleaning, cooking and refrigeration can control most food-poisoning bacteria. It's under your control—just follow these four golden rules when preparing food:

1. Keep everything in the kitchen **clean.**
2. Keep hot foods **hot.**
3. Keep cold foods **cold.**
4. Don't **cross-contaminate.** See Avoiding Cross-contaminating, page 30.

Keep It Clean

Wash Your Hands

Your mother was right! Proper hand washing can eliminate nearly half of all cases of foodborne illness. Experts recommend washing hands thoroughly with soap and water for at least 20 seconds before handling food. How long is 20 seconds? About how long it takes to recite the alphabet or sing "Happy Birthday."

- Before handling food and utensils and serving and eating food.
- After handling food, especially raw meat, poultry, fish, shellfish and eggs.
- Between jobs like cutting up raw chicken and making a salad.
- After using the bathroom, blowing your nose, changing diapers, touching pets, and handling garbage, dirty dishes, hair, dirty laundry, cigarettes and phones.
- If you have any kind of skin cut or infection on your hands, wear protective plastic or rubber gloves.

- If you sneeze or cough while preparing food, turn your face away and cover your mouth and nose with a tissue; wash your hands afterward.

Cleaning Basics

- Wash all utensils and surfaces with hot, soapy water after contact with raw meat, poultry, fish or seafood.
- Use paper towels when working with—and cleaning up after working with—raw poultry, meat, fish or seafood.
- Clean countertops, appliances, utensils and dishes with hot, soapy water or other cleaners, like those labeled "antibacterial."
- Clean refrigerator surfaces regularly with hot, soapy water.
- Wash the meat and crisper drawers of the refrigerator often, and keep containers for storing food in the refrigerator very clean.
- Sort through perishable foods each week. When it's past its prime, toss it out.
- Wash sponges and dish cloths often in hot water in the washing machine, and for added safety, sanitize them three times a week by soaking them in a mixture of 3/4 cup bleach to 1 gallon (4 quarts) water.
- Keep pets out of the kitchen and away from food.

Cutting Board Checklist

- Hard plastic or glass cutting boards are less porous than wooden boards, so they're the safest for cutting raw poultry, meat, fish and seafood. Check out the thin, flexible silicone or plastic cutting boards and disposable cutting sheets—they're great for cutting and transferring foods.
- Consider buying two cutting boards—one for raw poultry, meat, fish or seafood and a second for other foods.
- Do not use wooden cutting boards for raw poultry, meat, fish or seafood. Wooden cutting boards can be used for foods like fresh produce, bread, nuts and dried fruit.

STAY UP-TO-DATE WITH FOOD SAFETY

For current information about safe food handling and foodborne illness, contact:

- USDA Meat and Poultry Hotline, 1-888-674-6854
- U.S. Food and Drug Administration's Center for Food Safety and Applied Nutrition Automated Outreach and Information Center, 888-723-3366
- FSIS Food Safety Education Staff
Maildrop 5268
5601 Sunnyside Avenue
Beltsville, MD 20705
- Browse the following government Web sites:
  - Gateway to Government Food Safety: http://www.foodsafety.gov
  - FDA/Center for Food Safety and Applied Nutrition: http://www.cfsan.fda.gov
  - USDA/FDA Foodborne Illness Education Information Center: http://www.nal.usda.gov/foodsafety
- Your local health department listed in the government pages of the phone book.

- After each use, wash cutting boards with hot, soapy water; if the board is dishwasher safe, run it through the dishwasher (some plastic cutting boards may warp in the dishwasher). For added safety, sanitize with a mixture of 1 teaspoon chlorine bleach to 1 quart (4 cups) of water. Cover the entire board with the solution and let stand 2 to 3 minutes; rinse thoroughly and air-dry or pat dry with paper towels.
- When a cutting board gets deep scratches and cuts, toss it out!

Keeping Hot Foods Hot

- Bacteria thrive at room temperature or in lukewarm food. Hot foods can't be left at room temperature for more than 2 hours, including prep time. Keeping hot foods hot means keeping them at 140°F or higher.
- Don't partially cook perishable foods, then set them aside or refrigerate to finish cooking later. During cooking, the food may not reach a temperature high enough to destroy bacteria. Foods can be partially cooked in the microwave or parboiled only if the cooking process will continue immediately, such as in grilling.
- No need to worry about the safety of your slow cooker. Harmful bacteria are killed by the direct heat from the pot, the lengthy cooking times and the steam created within the covered pot. See also Slow Cooker Food Safety, page 153.
- Roast meat or poultry at 325°F or above. Lower temperatures can start bacterial growth before cooking is done. Cook meat and poultry completely, following the "doneness" times and temperatures recommended in this book. Use a dial or digital thermometer to make sure meat and poultry are done. See Thermometers, page 31.
- Keep cooked food hot, or refrigerate it until ready to serve. This includes carryout foods, too.
- Reheat leftovers, stirring often, until "steaming" hot (165°F). Using a cover while reheating helps leftovers get hot in the center and retains moisture. Heat soups, sauces and gravies to a rolling boil then boil for 1 minute, stirring constantly, before serving.

PITCH IT OUT!

Do not taste leftover food that looks or smells strange to see if it's okay. When in doubt, throw it out!

Keeping Cold Foods Cold

- Bacteria thrive at room temperature, so don't allow cold foods to stand at room temperature for more than 2 hours, including prep time. Keeping cold foods cold means keeping them at 40°F or lower.
- The most perishable foods are eggs, milk, seafood, fish, meat and poultry or the dishes that contain them, like cream pies or seafood salad. When you shop, put perishables in the cart last. Put packages that can leak into plastic bags to prevent them from dripping on other foods in your cart.
- Take perishable foods straight home, and refrigerate them immediately. If your grocery store is longer than 30 minutes away, bring a cooler containing freezer packs or ice to bring perishable groceries home in. Making even short stops on the way home during hot weather can cause perishable groceries in a hot car to reach unsafe temperatures very quickly.
- Buy food labeled "keep refrigerated" only if they are in a refrigerated case and are cold to the touch. Follow the "keep refrigerated," "safe handling" and "use by" labels on these products; this includes carryout foods, too.
- Select frozen foods that are frozen solid without lots of ice crystals or frost on the package. These are signs that food may have thawed and then refrozen.

- Foods will chill faster if you keep space between them when stocking your refrigerator and freezer. It also helps to divide large amounts into smaller amounts and to store foods in shallow containers.
- Buy an appliance thermometer for all refrigerators and freezers. Refrigerators should run between 35°F and 40°F, and the freezer at 0°F or colder.
- If your electrical power goes out, keep the refrigerator and freezer doors closed to protect food. Refrigerated foods are safe for 4 to 6 hours. Foods in a fully stocked freezer are safe up to two days, but if half-full, for only 24 hours.
- When cleaning your refrigerator or freezer, pack perishables in a cooler with freezer packs or filled with ice.
- Never thaw foods at room temperature—thaw only in the refrigerator or microwave following manufacturer's directions. If you thaw foods in the microwave, cook them immediately.

Avoiding Cross-Contaminating

Cross-contamination happens when cooked or ready-to-eat foods pick up bacteria from other foods, hands, cutting boards and utensils. The general rule is to always keep raw meat, poultry, fish, shellfish and eggs away from other foods. Avoid cross-contamination with these steps:

- Don't chop fresh produce or any food that won't be fully cooked on a cutting board that was used for raw poultry, meat, fish or seafood without cleaning it first as directed in Cutting Board Checklist, pages 28–29. Wash any knives or utensils that were used in hot, soapy water, too.
- Don't put cooked food on an unwashed plate that was used for raw meat, poultry, fish or seafood.
- Keep raw poultry, meat, fish or seafood separate from cooked and ready-to-eat foods in your grocery cart.
- Prevent leaks by repacking leaky packages and thawing foods in the refrigerator on a tray with sides that's large enough to catch all the juices.
- Wash sinks and sink mats with hot, soapy water if they've come in contact with raw poultry, meat, fish or seafood.

KEEPING FOOD SAFE

Canned Foods: Choose cans and jars of food that are in perfect condition—not cans that are leaking, bulging or badly dented or jars with cracks or loose or bulging lids. If you are in doubt about a can of food, don't taste it! Return it to your grocer, and report it to your local health department.

Eggs: Store uncooked "do-ahead" recipes with raw eggs in the refrigerator only for up to 24 hours before cooking. Even though it may be tempting, don't eat unbaked cookie dough or cake batter containing raw eggs.

Foods made with cooked eggs—cheesecakes, cream fillings, custards, quiches and potato salads—must be served hot or cold, depending on the recipe. Refrigerate leftovers immediately after serving. See also Handling and Storing Eggs Safely, page 219, and Cooking Eggs, page 220.

Raw eggs give some dishes, such as frosting, mousse and traditional Caesar salad, a unique texture. When making these recipes, don't use raw eggs in the shell; use only pasteurized egg products and substitutes found in the dairy or freezer case. It's also fine to use reconstituted dried eggs or egg whites. Some processors sell eggs that are pasteurized in the shell, but they're not available nationwide.

Fruits and Vegetables: Before eating, wash all fresh fruits and vegetables with cold running water, using a scrub brush if necessary.

Ground Meat: Don't eat or taste raw ground meat—it's simply not safe. Since the grinding process exposes more of the meat to bacteria, be sure to cook all ground meat thoroughly before eating. Make sure ground-beef dishes like burgers and meat loaf are completely cooked until a meat thermometer inserted in the center of the thickest portion reaches 160°F.

Ham: Most hams are fully cooked, but others need cooking. With so many varieties of hams, it can be confusing, so check the label. If you have any doubts, cook it until a meat thermometer inserted in the center of the thickest portion reaches 160°F.

Luncheon Meats and Hot Dogs: Keep refrigerated, and use within two weeks. If the liquid in a package of hot dogs is cloudy, throw it out. Although hot dogs are fully cooked, reheat them until they're steaming hot all the way through.

Marinades: Marinate foods in the refrigerator in a heavy plastic food-storage bag or nonmetal dish—not at room temperature. For safety's sake, toss out leftover marinade that has had contact with raw meat, poultry, fish or seafood. Or, heat it to a rolling boil then boil at least 1 minute, stirring constantly, before serving. An even better option is to set aside some of the marinade before marinating, then cover and refrigerate it until ready to use.

Milk: Keep all fresh milk products refrigerated. You can store unopened evaporated milk and nonfat dry milk in the cupboard up to several months. Since whole dry milk contains fat, which can become rancid, keep it in the refrigerator and use it within a few weeks. Don't drink unpasteurized milk or milk products because they can contain bacteria.

Poultry: Cook all poultry products according to the directions. Ground poultry, like ground beef, is susceptible to bacterial contamination and must be cooked to 165°F in the center of the thickest portion. See also Poultry Basics, page 315, for thawing, roasting and stuffing safety.

THE FACTS ON FOOD THERMOMETERS

Food thermometers are indispensable friends in the kitchen. In the Betty Crocker Kitchens, they are used to do several things:

- Indicate when foods have reached a safe internal temperature
- Indicate when candy mixtures have cooked long enough
- Prevent overcooking

Many kinds of thermometers are available today; look for them in gourmet kitchen shops and in the cook's tools section in department stores and specialty supermarkets. The most common thermometers include

THERMOMETERS

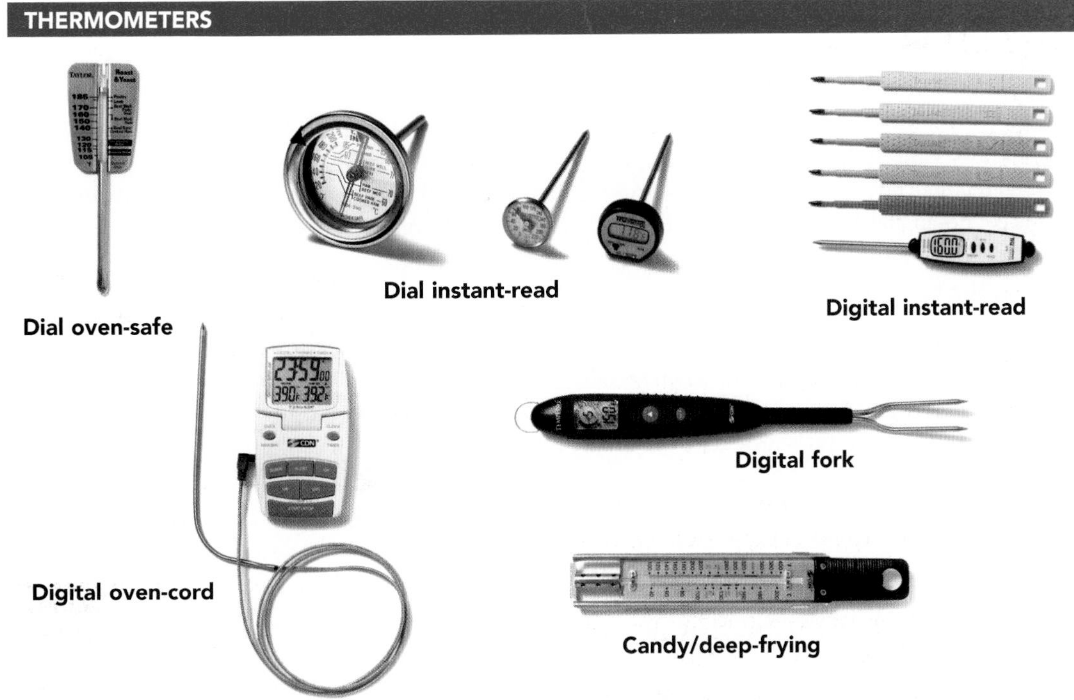

Dial oven-safe

Dial instant-read

Digital instant-read

Digital fork

Digital oven-cord

Candy/deep-frying

Candy/Deep-Frying: Great to use when making candy, cooked frostings and when frying foods in a large amount of oil. They are immersed in the candy mixture or oil during cooking and have markings including the candy-making stages (page 31) and marks for deep-frying.

Dial Instant-Read: Not designed to stay in food during cooking. Can be used for roasts, poultry, casseroles and stuffing. Insert it 2 to 2 1/2 inches deep into thick and thin foods to get a temperature reading; it takes only 15 to 20 seconds. For thin foods, insert it into the side instead of the top.

Dial Oven-Safe: Also called *meat, poultry* or *roast thermometer.* Can be used in roasts, poultry, casseroles and stuffing, staying in the oven while food is cooking. Insert it 2 to 2 1/2 inches deep into food to get a temperature reading. Not recommended for thin foods.

Digital Instant-Read: Not designed to stay in food during cooking. Insert it 1/2 inch deep into thick and thin foods to get a temperature reading; it takes only about 10 seconds. This is the perfect choice to test burgers.

Digital Oven-Cord: Can be used for roasts, poultry, casseroles and stuffing. A metal probe is attached to a long, stay-cool cord that plugs into a magnetic-backed digital unit that can be placed on the oven door, oven surface or countertop. If using for grilled foods, do not attach the unit to the grill lid, because the lid gets too hot. The probe is inserted into the food and can stay there during cooking. The desired temperature is set in advance, and an alarm sounds when the temperature is reached. Although mainly for oven use, they can also be used to check foods on the stove.

Disposable Temperature Indicator: A single-use thermometer that changes color when specific temperature ranges are reached. Follow manufacturer's directions and use only with the foods listed in the directions.

Fork: Not designed to stay in food during cooking. Can be used in most foods. Insert tines equally at least 1/4 inch deep in thickest part of food to get a temperature reading; it takes 2 to 10 seconds.

Pop-Up: Turkeys often come with a thermometer that pops up when the turkey is done. However, the USDA recommends double-checking the temperature in several spots with another type of food thermometer.

How Accurate Are Food Thermometers?

The good news is that most digital and dial thermometers are accurate to within plus or minus 1°F to 2°F. To check your thermometer, heat 2 cups water in a 1-quart saucepan until boiling. Immerse the stem of the thermometer 2 inches into the boiling water. The thermometer should read 212°F after 30 seconds. Check thermometers once or twice a year for accuracy.

PACKING PICNICS AND LUNCHES SAFELY

- Keep lunches cold and safe in insulated lunch bags or small cooler with a freezer-pack, frozen juice box or frozen small plastic bottle of water. Keep the bag or cooler out of the sun. Refrigerate perishable foods carried in an uninsulated lunch bag.
- Wash thermal containers and rinse with boiling water after each use. Be sure hot foods are boiling when poured into these containers.
- Wash fruits and vegetables before packing.
- Chill picnic food before packing in a freezer-pack or ice-filled cooler. Because beverage coolers will be opened more frequently, use one cooler for beverages and one for perishable foods.
- Tightly wrap raw meat, poultry, fish and seafood to keep them from dripping onto other foods. Better yet, pack them in a separate cooler. Bring along a bottle of instant hand sanitizer, antibacterial moistened towelettes or a bottle filled with soapy water for washing hands and surfaces after handling raw poultry, meat, fish or seafood.
- At restaurants or potlucks, salad bars and buffets should look clean. Make sure cold foods are cold and hot foods are steaming.

STORING FOOD IN THE REFRIGERATOR AND FREEZER—SAFELY

Follow these safety tips and the storage times in the Refrigerator and Freezer Food Storage chart, pages 43–44, to keep refrigerated and frozen foods safe. For extra security, use an appliance thermometer and check it often to make sure appliances are maintaining proper temperatures.

In the Refrigerator

- Refrigerator temperatures should be between 35°F and 40°F. When you add large amounts of room-temperature or warm foods, adjust the temperature to a colder setting. Readjust to the normal setting after about 8 hours.
- Before putting food in the refrigerator, cover it or close the original containers tightly to prevent the food from drying out or transferring odors from one food to another. Store produce and strong-flavored foods in tightly covered containers or plastic bags.
- Keep foods in the refrigerator until just before you're ready to use them.

In the Freezer

- Freezer temperatures should be 0°F or lower.
- Wrap food in products labeled for freezer use if possible. If you can't find freezer paper or plastic containers recommended for the freezer, use regular containers with tight-fitting lids or wrap tightly in heavy-duty foil.
- Label and date all packages and containers.
- To prevent freezer burn, remove as much air from packages as possible.
- Store purchased frozen foods in their original packages.
- Follow the first-in first-out rule. Use foods that have been in the freezer the longest before using other foods.
- Always thaw frozen meats, poultry and seafood in the refrigerator—never at room temperature. Allow about 5 hours per pound of frozen food. Or thaw food in your microwave following the manufacturer's directions, then cook immediately.
- To maintain the best flavor and texture of frozen food, follow the times given in the chart. If you keep frozen foods slightly longer, they still will be safe to eat.

Refrigerated and Frozen Food Tips

Baked Products: Cool them completely, then wrap in airtight packaging for freezing. Allow frostings to set at room temperature, or freeze frosted baked goods uncovered *before* packaging to set them, then wrap and freeze.

- **Breads:** Refrigerate bread only during hot, humid weather. To thaw frozen bread, loosen the wrap and let it stand at room temperature for 2 to 3 hours.
- **Cakes:** Refrigerate cakes with custard filling; do not freeze these cakes, because the filling can separate. *Cakes filled and frosted with plain sweetened whipped cream can be frozen.* To thaw frozen unfrosted cakes, loosen the wrap and let stand at room temperature for 2 to 3 hours. To thaw frozen frosted cakes, loosen the wrap and place overnight in the refrigerator.
- **Cheesecakes:** Thaw frozen cheesecakes in their wrapping in the refrigerator for 4 to 6 hours.
- **Cookies:** Place delicate frosted or decorated cookies in single layers in freezer containers, and cover with waxed paper before stacking another layer; freeze. Thaw most cookies in their covered container at room temperature for 1 to 2 hours. To thaw crisp cookies, remove from the container.
- **Pies:** Many freeze well, but avoid freezing custard, cream, and unbaked pumpkin pies. They will separate and become watery.
  - **Frozen unbaked fruit pies:** Unwrap and carefully cut slits in the top crust. Bake at 425°F for 15 minutes. Reduce the oven temperature to 375°F and bake 30 to 45

minutes longer or until the crust is golden brown and juice begins to bubble through the slits.

- **Frozen baked fruit and pecan pies:** Unwrap and thaw at room temperature until completely thawed. Or unwrap and thaw at room temperature 1 hour, then heat in the oven at 375°F for 35 to 40 minutes or until warm.
- **Frozen baked pumpkin pies:** Unwrap and thaw in the refrigerator.

Dairy Products: Check packages for the use-by or sell-by date, and refrigerate in their original containers. The refrigeration time in the Refrigerator and Freezer Food Storage chart, pages 43–44, is for *opened* products.

- **Cream Cheese and Hard Cheese:** If hard cheese is moldy, trim 1/2 inch from the affected area and rewrap cheese tightly. Thaw frozen cheeses, wrapped, in the refrigerator. Because the texture becomes crumbly, use cheese that has been frozen only in baked goods such as casseroles, egg dishes, lasagna and pizza.
- **Ice Cream, Sorbet, Frozen Yogurt:** Freeze in the original containers. To reduce ice crystals, place foil or plastic wrap directly on the surface and re-cover with lids. For best quality, do not thaw and refreeze.
- **Whipped Cream:** It's true! You can freeze both unsweetened and sweetened whipped cream. Drop or pipe small mounds of whipped cream onto a waxed paper–lined cookie sheet; freeze, then place in an airtight container. To thaw, let stand about 15 minutes at room temperature.

Eggs: See How to Handle and Store Eggs Safely, page 219.

Meat Products: Check packages for the use-by or sell-by date. If meat is wrapped in white butcher paper, unwrap it and repackage tightly in moisture- and vapor-resistant materials such as plastic wrap, foil or plastic freezer bags.

Rewrapping meat packaged in clear plastic wrap isn't necessary, but you may want to put it a plastic bag in case the original packaging leaks. To freeze, wrap packages with heavy-duty foil or freezer wrap or place in freezer bags.

Nutrition Glossary

Nutritionists, health experts, and food package labels often use several terms, such as *complex carbohydrates, saturated fat, unsaturated fat* and *trans-fatty acids.* Here's a basic explanation of some of the most common ones:

Carbohydrate: A key source for our energy needs. Sugars are simple carbohydrates; starches, including breads, cereals and pastas, are complex carbohydrates.

Cholesterol: Dietary cholesterol is a fatlike substance found only in animal-based foods. There are different types of dietary cholesterol, including HDLs (high-density lipoproteins, known as "the good cholesterol") that may help protect against heart disease and LDLs (low-density lipoproteins, known as "the bad cholesterol") that may contribute to heart disease. Blood cholesterol is made by our bodies and helps our hormones function properly.

Dietary Fiber: Technically a complex carbohydrate. Fiber is the part of plant-based foods that isn't broken down or used by our bodies. There are two types of fiber: soluble and insoluble. Soluble fiber, which helps lower blood cholesterol levels, is found in foods like oats, beans and strawberries. Insoluble fiber, which helps keep bowel functions regular, is found in foods like whole wheat breads and cereals, apples and cabbage.

Fat: A powerful energy source. Dietary fat provides more than twice the amount of energy supplied by carbohydrates or proteins. It's also a source of essential nutrients. Health organization recommendations for fat intake vary, but they range between 20 and 35 percent of total daily calories. Body fat insulates and protects body organs.

- **Saturated:** Found primarily in animal-based foods. This fat is solid at room temperature. Diets high in saturated fats have been linked to higher levels of blood cholesterol, a risk factor for heart disease.
- **Unsaturated:** Found mostly in plant-based foods. This fat is usually liquid at room temperature. Unsaturated fats may be monounsaturated or polyunsaturated.

Minerals: Elements other than carbon, hydrogen, oxygen and nitrogen that are nutritionally essential in very small amounts. Minerals are inorganic elements, like calcium and iron, found in foods and water.

Nutrients: Substances necessary for life that build, repair and maintain body cells. Nutrients include protein, carbohydrate, fat, water, vitamins and minerals.

Protein: Provides energy and structural support of body cells. Protein, made from building blocks of amino acids, is important for growth.

Trans-Fatty Acids: Fats produced when hydrogen is added to liquid vegetable oil, turning it into a solid fat. Found in shortening, stick margarine, doughnuts and other baked goods.

Vitamins: Essential for controlling body functions. Vitamins are found in small amounts in many foods. Vitamins include vitamin A, B vitamins (such as thiamin, niacin, riboflavin), vitamin C and folic acid.

Steps to a Healthier You

The new food guidance system from the United States Department of Agriculture (USDA), called MyPyramid, emphasizes a personalized approach to improving diet and lifestyle and reinforces current consensus among experts for how Americans should be eating. It replaces the familiar Food Guide Pyramid graphic that illustrated healthy eating. MyPyramid provides a toolbox for healthy eating, including physical activity, smart food choices in every food group, and the importance of calories and the recommended dietary guidelines for Americans. Dietary guidelines provide the recommended number of servings from each food group in order to maintain a balanced and healthy diet. To help us build a healthy lifestyle, MyPyramid illustrates:

- **Personalization.** Recommendations on the kinds and amounts of food to eat each day are based on age, gender and activity level.
- **Moderation.** Six color bands narrow from top to bottom with the wider base indicating foods that should be selected more often and the tip indicating those to be selected less often.
- **Proportionality.** Different widths of the colored food bands suggest how much food should be selected from each food group.
- **Variety.** Six color bands represent the five food groups of the Pyramid plus oils. The food groups are: Grains, Vegetables, Fruits, Milk and Meat & Beans.
- **Gradual Improvement.** The slogan, "Steps to a Healthier You," suggests that individuals can benefit from taking small steps to improve their diet and lifestyle.
- **Physical Activity.** A drawing of a person climbing the steps of the Pyramid is a visual reminder of the importance of daily physical activity.

To see the Pyramid graphic and learn more, visit www.MyPyramid.gov for a personalized approach to a healthier lifestyle.

Entertaining with Ease

SETTING THE TABLE

Remember setting the table when you were a kid? If those early lessons are a bit hazy or if you're teaching someone the basics, here's a quick refresher course:

- Be sure to allow plenty of room for each place at the table.
- Place the knives, forks and spoons 1 inch from the edge of the table. Put the pieces that will be used first farthest from the plate, so flatware is used from the outside toward the plate. The forks are to the left of the plate and the knife (with the blade toward the plate) and then the spoons to the right.
- Set dessert flatware with the other flatware, or bring it to the table with the dessert. If you want to leave it on the table throughout the meal, place above the dinner plate or next to the other flatware closest to the plate.
- Put bread and butter plates above the forks. Put the butter knife horizontally or vertically on the rim or toward the edge of the plate.
- Place salads served with the main course to the left of the forks.
- Arrange glasses above the knife. Water glasses go at the tip of the knife, with beverage and/or wine glasses to the right of the water glass.
- If you're serving coffee or tea at the table, put the cup slightly above and to the right of the spoons.
- Napkins can go in the center of the dinner plate, to the left of the forks or in another creative spot at each place setting. There are lots of clever ways to fold napkins; check your local library or bookstore for ideas.
- Before dessert, clear the table of all serving dishes, plates, glasses, salt and pepper shakers and flatware that won't be used for dessert.
- Have fun! Whether you're serving a weekday meal or holiday dinner, create a welcoming table with colorful place mats, a bowl of fruit for a simple centerpiece or your cherished china and silver.

CRYSTAL-CLEAR VASES AND CARAFES

Do your vases and carafes have water rings and stains from other liquids that are hard to clean? Just reach for some denture cleanser tablets! Put one or two tablets in the vase or carafe, and fill with warm water. The water turns blue or green, depending on the brand of tablet, and starts to fizz vigorously. The fizzing action dissolves stains in just minutes. When the water turns clear again, rinse and dry. If you still have some stubborn spots, just repeat the process with another tablet.

SAMPLE TABLE SETTING

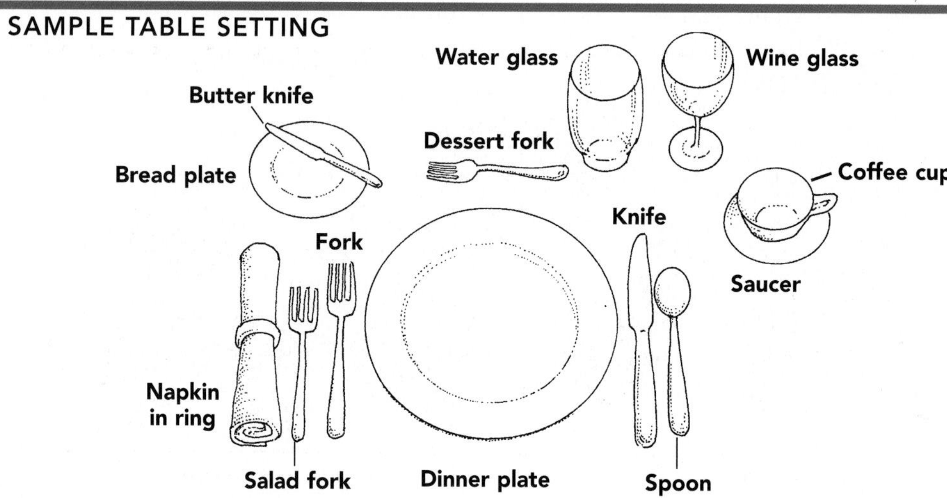

COME FOR A BUFFET!

A buffet is a marvelous way to throw a party, and perfect for many occasions. Foods can be casual or elegant—and many can be made ahead of time. And since the guests serve themselves, you'll have more time to spend with them.

Setting the Buffet Table

Buffets are fun and very flexible! Let guests pick up food, beverages and flatware from the buffet tables, then find a place to sit. Or, set tables with glasses and flatware ahead of time. For a more elegant party, cover the tables with cloths and use place cards if you wish. If you aren't planning table seating, use real plates or very sturdy paper or plastic plates, plus individual eating trays, too, if you have them. To make eating easier for your guests, plan a menu around foods that don't need to be cut with a knife.

- Set up the buffet where it will be most convenient: on kitchen center island or counter, the dining room table, a sideboard, a picnic table, two card tables placed together or a desk.
- Make sure the traffic can move easily around the serving area.
- Place the table in the center of the room, so guests can help themselves from all sides of the table. If there is a large group, set up identical serving lines on opposite sides of the table. Or place the table against a wall to save space while leaving three sides open for serving.
- Be sure guests know where the line starts. Arrange the food in order, so they can serve themselves without backtracking. Put the plates first, then the main course and vegetables, followed by salad, condiments, bread, flatware and napkins.
- While guests finish the main course, clear the buffet table and arrange the dessert, dessert plates and flatware on the buffet table or on a side table.

Buffets, the Safe Way!

- Serve food at buffets in small dishes. Instead of adding fresh food to a dish that already has had food on it, wash the dish or use a different one.
- Keep hot foods hot (at least 140°F) with a slow cooker, fondue pot, chafing dish or warming tray. Warming units heated by canned cooking fuel are safe to use, but units heated with candles don't get hot enough to keep foods safe.
- Keep cold foods cold (below 40°F) on the buffet table by setting dishes in crushed ice.
- Refrigerate salads made with seafood, poultry or meat. Chill both the food and the dish before serving.
- Hot or cold foods should not stand at room temperature for more than 2 hours. If you're not sure how long it's been sitting out, toss it out.
- Store leftovers in the refrigerator for the amount of time recommended in the Refrigerator and Freezer Food Storage chart, pages 43–44.

SAMPLE CASUAL BUFFET

ENTERTAINING WITH CONFIDENCE

What's the secret to successful parties? Naturally, good company and good food. But that's not all. Planning and preparing as much ahead of time as possible is a great idea so you can enjoy the party too! Whether your party is for four or forty, here are some never-fail tips for making it fun, fabulous and a big success.

- If you don't have a special occasion for getting friends or family together, make one up! Create a theme party around the football season kick-off, trying out new recipes, carving pumpkins or a celebration such as Cinco de Mayo.
- Write a guest list. Think about combining personalities, as interesting parties often include people with different backgrounds. Introduce your guests as soon as they arrive, or for a large group, try name tags with "getting-to-know-you" information such as an unusual hobby or best vacation.
- Invite guests ten days to two weeks ahead of time for casual events and two or more weeks for more formal events. Send out written invitations for a formal event, or just call or e-mail guests for casual get-togethers.
- Be specific in your invitation about time, food and dress. For example, "Come for a dress-up dessert party on New Year's Eve at 11 p.m." or "Come to a football party and pig roast on Saturday the 14th at 2 p.m. It'll be outside, so dress for the weather."
- Plan to have enough food and beverages so you won't run out. Be sure to have nonalcoholic beverages on hand.
- Choose foods you're comfortable making. Fill in with foods from a favorite restaurant or deli, or ask people to bring something. See Menu Planning Basics, right.
- Prepare as much of the food ahead of time as possible, so you spend more time with your guests and less time in the kitchen.
- Planning a large get-together? Make it easier on yourself: Hire a neighborhood kid or your own children to help with serving and cleanup.

SERVING A CROWD?

Use the Amounts of Food for a Crowd chart, page 39, to help you figure out how much food to make for a crowd.

MENU PLANNING BASICS

Styles of entertaining have changed. Traditional, formal occasions are less frequent and are being replaced by casual gatherings, spur-of-the-moment get-togethers and potlucks. These changes have made meal planning and enjoying the company of friends and family more carefree and fun! The following tips can take some of the guesswork out of planning meals for weekday dinners or any gathering:

- **Choose from the hundreds of recipes in this book** to create meals fitting any occasion, or mix and match recipes with deli or take out-restaurant foods when time is short.
- **Make a list.** Grocery lists make shopping faster and more economical by cutting down on those last-minute dashes to pick up missing items. Before going shopping, make a quick check of what you already have on hand.
- **Keep your eating patterns and preferences in mind.** Why not have two meals plus snacks rather than three meals a day or eat a heavier meal at noon instead of in the evening? Or how about a special family night that features a vegetarian, ethnic or other type of dinner with a theme?
- **Plan the main course first** and then fill in with other foods that go well with your main course.
- **Make sure flavors go together instead of competing with each other.** Balance out a strongly flavored main dish with a milder-flavored side dish; serve a subtle main dish with a boldly flavored side dish. If the meal has been on the heavier side, choose a lighter dessert; if the meal was a bit lighter, plan an indulgent and rich dessert.
- **Involve your senses—sight, taste, smell and touch.** Keep flavors, textures, colors, shapes

and temperatures in mind. For example, serve spicy with mild; creamy with crisp; white or brown with red, yellow or green; tiny pieces with big chunks; and hot dishes with cold.

- **Use seasonings, sauces, condiments, salsas, relishes and marinades** to jazz up plain foods like grilled chicken or fish, cooked pasta or steamed vegetables.

AMOUNTS OF FOOD FOR A CROWD

Check this chart to figure out how much food to make for a crowd up to 48 servings. Also consider the time of day, weather and number of dishes being served. Plan on one drink per hour per guest; if it's very warm, plan on two.

Food Item	Per Serving	12 Servings	24 Servings	48 Servings
Cakes, 13 × 9", 12-cup Ring or 9" Layer	1/16 cake	1 cake	2 cakes	3 cakes
Cheese Slices	1 ounce	1 pound	2 pounds	4 pounds
Chicken Salad				
Side Dish	1/2 cup	1 1/2 quarts	3 quarts	1 1/2 gallons
Main Dish	1 cup	3 quarts	1 1/2 gallons	3 gallons
Chips	1 ounce	12 ounces	1 1/2 pounds	3 pounds
Coffee				
Brewed	3/4 cup water	9 cups water	18 cups water	36 cups water
Ground Coffee	1 to 2 level tablespoons	1 1/2 cups	3 cups	5 cups
Cookies	2	2 dozen	4 dozen	8 dozen
Crackers	4 crackers	8 ounces	1 pound	2 pounds
Dip	2 tablespoons	1 1/2 cups	3 cups	1 1/2 quarts
Fruit or Vegetable Dippers	4 pieces	4 dozen	8 dozen	16 dozen
Ice	4 ounces	3 pounds	6 pounds	12 pounds
Ice Cream	1/2 cup	2 quarts	1 gallon	2 gallons
Iced Tea, prepared	1 cup	3 quarts	1 1/2 gallons	3 gallons
Meat Cold Cuts	2 1/2 ounces	2 pounds	4 pounds	8 pounds
Meat, Poultry and Fish (boneless)	1/4 pound	3 pounds	6 pounds	12 pounds
Meat, Poultry and Shellfish (bone-in, unshelled)	3/4 pound	9 pounds	18 pounds	36 pounds
Mineral Water	8 ounces	3 quarts	6 quarts	12 quarts
Potato Salad, Baked Beans or Coleslaw	1/2 cup	1 1/2 quarts	3 quarts	1 1/2 gallons
Punch	1/2 cup	1 1/2 quarts	3 quarts	1 1/2 gallons
Rolls	1 1/2 rolls	2 dozen	3 dozen	6 dozen
Salad Dressing	2 tablespoons	1 1/2 cups	3 cups	1 1/2 quarts
Tossed Salad	1 1/2 cups	4 1/2 quarts	9 quarts	4 1/2 gallons
Tea				
Brewed	3/4 cup water	9 cups water	18 cups water	36 cups water
Loose Tea	1 teaspoon	1/4 cup	1/2 cup	1 cup
Tea Bags	1 bag	12 bags	24 bags	48 bags

MICROWAVE COOKING AND HEATING

Your microwave is great for cooking, warming and softening many favorite foods—in minutes. Check this chart for suggested cooking powers and times.

Food, Utensil and Tips	Power Level	Amount	Time
Bacon, thinly sliced (cook) Place on plate or bacon rack lined with paper towels. Place paper towels between layers; cover with paper towel. Microwave until crisp.	High (100%)	1 slice 2 slices 4 slices 6 slices 8 slices	30 seconds to 1 1/2 minutes 1 to 2 minutes 2 to 3 minutes 3 to 5 minutes 4 to 6 minutes
Brown Sugar, hard (soften) Place in glass bowl; cover with damp paper towel, then plastic wrap. Repeat heating once or twice.	High (100%)	1 to 3 cups	1 minute; let stand 2 minutes
Butter or Margarine (melt) Remove foil wrapper. Place in glass bowl or measuring cup; cover with microwavable paper towel.	High (100%)	1 to 8 tablespoons 1/2 to 1 cup	30 to 50 seconds 60 to 75 seconds
Butter or Margarine (soften) Remove foil wrapper. Place in glass bowl or measuring cup, uncovered.	High (100%)	1 to 8 tablespoons 1/2 to 1 cup	10 to 20 seconds 15 to 30 seconds
Caramels (melt) 4-cup glass measuring cup, uncovered	High (100%)	1 bag (14 oz) unwrapped caramels mixed with 2 to 4 tablespoons milk or water	2 to 3 minutes, stirring once or twice
Chocolate, Baking (unsweetened or semisweet) (melt) Place unwrapped squares in microwavable glass dish or measuring cup, uncovered.	Medium (50%)	1 to 3 oz	1 1/2 to 2 1/2 minutes
Chocolate Chips (melt) Place in microwavable glass bowl or glass measuring cup, uncovered. Chips will not change shape.	Medium (50%)	1/2 to 1 cup	2 to 3 minutes
Coconut (toast) Place in 2-cup glass measuring cup or pie plate, uncovered. Stir every 30 seconds.	High (100%)	1/4 to 1/2 cup 1 cup	1 1/2 to 2 minutes 2 to 3 minutes
Cream Cheese (soften) Remove foil wrapper or cover. Place in microwavable glass bowl or leave in plastic tub, uncovered.	Medium (50%)	3-oz package 8-oz package 8-oz tub	45 to 60 seconds 1 to 1 1/2 minutes 45 to 60 seconds
Dried Fruit (soften) Place in 2-cup glass measuring cup; add 1/2 teaspoon water for each 1/2 cup fruit. Cover with plastic wrap, turning back a corner or 1/4-inch edge to vent steam.	High (100%)	1/4 to 1/2 cup 1/2 to 1 cup	30 to 45 seconds 45 to 60 seconds; let stand 2 minutes

(continues)

MICROWAVE COOKING AND HEATING *(continued)*

Food, Utensil and Tips	Power Level	Amount	Time
Fruit, Frozen (thaw) Leave in plastic bag or pouch or transfer to microwavable glass bowl; thaw until most of ice is gone, stirring or rearranging twice.	Medium (50%)	16-oz bag	3 to 5 minutes
Fruit, Refrigerated (warm) Place on floor of microwave.	High (100%)	1 medium 2 medium	15 seconds 20 to 30 seconds; let stand 2 minutes
Honey (dissolve crystals) In jar with lid removed, uncovered. Stir every 20 to 30 seconds or until crystals dissolve.	High (100%)	1/2 to 1 cup	45 seconds to 1 1/2 minutes
Ice Cream (soften) In original container; remove any foil. Let stand 2 to 3 minutes.	Low (10%)	1/2 gallon	2 to 3 minutes
Muffins or Rolls (small to medium) (heat) Place on plate, napkin or napkin-lined basket, uncovered.	High (100%)	1 2 3 4	5 to 10 seconds 10 to 15 seconds 12 to 20 seconds 20 to 30 seconds
Muffins (large to jumbo) (heat) Place on plate or napkin, uncovered. Let stand 1 minute.	High (100%)	1 2 3 4	10 to 20 seconds 20 to 30 seconds 30 to 40 seconds 40 to 50 seconds
Nuts, Chopped (toast) Place in glass measuring cup, uncovered; add 1/4 teaspoon vegetable oil for each 1/4 cup nuts. Stir every 30 seconds until light brown.	High (100%)	1/4 to 1/2 cup 1/2 to 1 cup	2 1/2 to 3 1/2 minutes 3 to 4 minutes
Snacks (crisp popcorn, pretzels, corn chips or potato chips) Place in paper-towel-lined basket, uncovered.	High (100%)	2 cups 4 cups	20 to 40 seconds 40 to 60 seconds
Syrup (heat) Place in glass measuring cup or pitcher, uncovered. Stir every 30 seconds.	High (100%)	1/2 cup 1 cup	30 to 45 seconds 45 to 60 seconds
Water (boil) In glass measuring cup.	High (100%)	1 cup	2 to 3 minutes

PLANNING FRUIT AND VEGETABLE PLATTERS

Use this handy chart to figure out how much produce to buy to make fruit and vegetable platters.

Fruits	Approximate Yield
Cantaloupe, 4-pound	36 chunks
Grapes, 1 pound seedless	12 to 15 clusters
Honeydew, 2-pound	36 chunks
Pineapple, 3- to 4-pound	40 chunks
Strawberries, 1-pound large	20 to 25 berries

Vegetables	Approximate Yield
Asparagus, 1 pound	30 to 45 spears
Bell pepper, 1 large	24 strips, $3\frac{1}{2} \times \frac{1}{4}$"
Broccoli or cauliflower, 2 pounds	32 flowerets, $1\frac{1}{4}$"
Carrots, 1 pound	65 sticks, $3 \times \frac{1}{2}$"
Celery, 4 medium stalks	33 sticks, $4 \times \frac{1}{2}$"
Cucumbers, 2 large	45 sticks, $4 \times \frac{3}{4}$"
Mushrooms, 1 pound	20 medium
Pea pods, 4 ounces	30 pea pods
Zucchini, 3 medium	35 slices, $\frac{1}{2}$"

Salad Greens	Bite-Size Pieces
Boston lettuce, $\frac{1}{2}$-pound head	6 cups
Iceberg lettuce, $1\frac{1}{2}$-pound head	12 cups
Leaf lettuce, 1-pound bunch	8 cups
Romaine, $1\frac{1}{2}$-pound bunch	12 cups
Spinach, $\frac{3}{4}$-pound bunch	8 cups

REFRIGERATOR AND FREEZER FOOD STORAGE

Check this chart for general recommended guidelines on how long to refrigerate and freeze food. To keep the flavor and quality of the food, remember to wrap and seal it properly.

Foods	Refrigerator (34°F to 40°F)	Freezer (0°F or below)
BAKED PRODUCTS		
Breads—coffee cakes, muffins, quick breads and yeast breads	5 to 7 days	2 to 3 months
Cakes—unfrosted and frosted	3 to 5 days	Unfrosted—3 to 4 months Frosted—2 to 3 months
Cheesecakes—baked	3 to 5 days	4 to 5 months
Cookies—baked	Only if stated in recipe	Unfrosted—no longer than 12 months Frosted—no longer than 3 months
Pies—unbaked or baked fruit pies, baked pecan and baked pumpkin pies	Baked pumpkin pies, 3 to 5 days. Store fresh fruit or baked fruit pies and baked pecan pies loosely covered at room temperature no longer than 3 days.	Unbaked fruit pies—2 to 3 months Baked fruit pies—3 to 4 months
Pie Shells—unbaked or baked	Store in freezer	Unbaked shells—no longer than 2 months Baked shells—no longer than 4 months
DAIRY PRODUCTS		
Cheese		
Cottage and ricotta	1 to 10 days	Not recommended
Cream	No longer than 2 weeks	No longer than 2 months
Hard	3 to 4 weeks	6 to 8 weeks
Ice Cream, Sorbet and Frozen yogurt	Freeze only	2 to 4 months
EGGS		
Raw		
Whole in shell	3 weeks	Not recommended
Yolks, whites	2 to 4 days. Cover yolks with cold water.	See Handling and Storing Eggs Safely, page 219.
Cooked		
Whole in shell	1 week	Not recommended
Yolks, whites	1 week	Not recommended
Fats and Oils		
BUTTER	No longer than 2 weeks	No longer than 4 months
Margarine and Spread	No longer than 1 month	No longer than 2 months
Mayonnaise and Salad Dressing	No longer than 6 months	Not recommended
MEATS		
Uncooked		
Chops	3 to 5 days	4 to 6 months
Ground	1 to 2 days	3 to 4 months
Roasts and Steaks	3 to 5 days	6 to 12 months
Cooked	3 to 4 days	2 to 3 months

(continues)

REFRIGERATOR AND FREEZER FOOD STORAGE *(continued)*

Foods	Refrigerator (34°F to 40°F)	Freezer (0°F or below)
MEATS (continued)		
Processed		
Cold cuts	Opened—3 to 5 days	Not recommended
	Unopened—2 weeks	Not recommended
Cured bacon	5 to 7 days	No longer than 1 month
Ham		
Canned, unopened	6 to 9 months	Not recommended
Whole or half, fully cooked	5 to 7 days	1 to 2 months
Slices, fully cooked	3 to 4 days	1 to 2 months
Hot dogs	Opened—1 week	1 to 2 months
	Unopened—2 weeks	1 to 2 months
MILK PRODUCTS		
Buttermilk	No longer than 1 week	Not recommended
Cream, half-and-half and whipping	No longer than 5 days	Not recommended
Cream, whipped	1 or 2 days	No longer than 3 months
Regular milk—whole, 2%, 1% and fat-free (skim)	No longer than 5 days	No longer than 1 month
Sour Cream	No longer than 1 week	Not recommended
Yogurt	No longer than 3 weeks	No longer than 1 month
POULTRY		
Uncooked		
Whole (including game birds, ducks and geese)	1 to 2 days	No longer than 12 months
Cut up	1 to 2 days	No longer than 9 months
Giblets	1 to 2 days	No longer than 3 months
Cooked	3 to 4 days	4 months
SEAFOOD		
Fin Fish		
Uncooked full-flavor fish (mackerel, salmon, trout, tuna, etc.)	1 to 2 days	3 to 6 months
Uncooked mild-flavor fish (cod, flounder, grouper, halibut, orange roughy, snapper, etc.)	1 to 2 days	3 to 6 months
Cooked and breaded fish	Store in freezer	2 to 3 months
Shellfish		
Uncooked	1 to 2 days	3 to 4 months
Cooked	3 to 4 days	1 to 2 months

CHAPTER 2

Appetizers & Beverages

Appetizers & Beverages

Appetizers

Beverages

LOW-FAT = *3g or less, except main dishes with 10g or less* FAST = *Ready in 20 minutes or less* BREAD MACHINE = *Bread machine directions* SLOW COOKER = *Slow cooker directions* LIGHTER = *25% fewer calories or grams of fat*

◀ **Grilled Antipasti Platter with Lemon Aioli (page 55)**

Appetizers by Many Names

Small bites of food called *appetizers* seem to be more popular than ever. Dip them, spread them out or roll them up. Serve them at informal get-togethers, elegant cocktail parties, as a first course at a seated dinner party, or just as casual TV snacks. Look for them under many names:

Canapé: Small pieces of toast, bread, crackers or baked pastry topped with various cheeses, shrimp or some type of spread. They can be hot or cold, simple or elaborate.

Crudité: Raw veggies cut into slices, sticks or pieces, usually served with a dip.

Dips and Dunks: Not too thin or too thick, these tasty mixtures are perfect for dipping chips, crudités and fruit.

Finger Food: No forks, spoons or knives—just fingers will do! Crostini (page 56) and Southwestern Spiced Party Nuts (page 57) are examples.

First Course: One or two appetizers served as a course during a sit-down meal. Instead of a traditional appetizer, the first course could be a small serving of a main dish like Fettuccine Alfredo (page 363) or soup.

Hors d'oeuvre: In French, *hors d'oeuvre* means "outside the work." Bite-size foods eaten apart from the regular meal, often with cocktails.

Spreads: Unlike dips, spreads are thick, so a knife is needed to spread them on bread or hearty crackers.

Creamy Fruit Dip FAST

PREP: 5 min ■ **1 1/2 CUPS DIP**

- 1 package (8 oz) cream cheese, softened
- 1 jar (7 oz) marshmallow creme
- 1 tablespoon milk

In medium bowl, beat all ingredients with electric mixer on medium speed until smooth and creamy.

2 TABLESPOONS: CAL. 125 (CAL. FROM FAT 65); FAT 7g (SAT. FAT 4g); CHOL. 20mg; SODIUM 65mg; CARBS. 14g (FIBER 0g); PRO. 2g
% DAILY VALUE: VIT. A 4%; VIT. C 0%; CALC. 2%; IRON 0%
EXCHANGES: 1 STARCH, 1 FAT
CARB. CHOICES: 1

CREAMY CINNAMON FRUIT DIP Add 1/4 teaspoon ground cinnamon.

CREAMY GINGERED FRUIT DIP Add 2 tablespoons finely chopped crystallized ginger.

Creamy Fruit Dip

Guacamole LOW-FAT

PREP: 20 min **CHILL:** 1 hr ■ **ABOUT 2 3/4 CUPS DIP**

Guacamole comes from the Mexican-Spanish word ahucamolli *meaning avocado sauce. Choosing the right avocados is the secret. Look for ripe ones that yield to gentle pressure but are still just slightly firm. If avocados are too firm, let them stand at room temperature in a closed paper bag until they ripen.*

- 2 jalapeño chilies*
- 2 ripe large avocados
- 2 tablespoons lime or lemon juice
- 2 tablespoons finely chopped cilantro
- 1/2 teaspoon salt
- Dash of pepper
- 1 clove garlic, finely chopped
- 2 medium tomatoes, finely chopped (1 1/2 cups)
- 1 medium onion, chopped (1/2 cup)
- Tortilla chips, if desired

1. Remove stems, seeds and membranes from chilies; chop chilies (page 9). Cut avocados lengthwise in half; remove pit and peel. In medium glass or plastic bowl, mash avocados with fork.

2. Stir in chilies and remaining ingredients except tortilla chips until well mixed.

3. Cover and refrigerate 1 hour to blend flavors. Serve with tortilla chips.

**2 tablespoons canned chopped green chiles can be substituted for the jalapeño chilies.*

1 TABLESPOON: CAL. 10 (CAL. FROM FAT 10); FAT 1g (SAT. FAT 0g); CHOL. 0mg; SODIUM 30mg; CARBS. 1g (FIBER 1g); PRO. 0g
% DAILY VALUE: VIT. A 0%; VIT. C 4%; CALC. 0%; IRON 0%
EXCHANGES: ONE SERVING IS FREE **CARB. CHOICES:** 0

LIGHTER "GUACAMOLE"

For 0 grams of fat and 5 calories per serving, substitute 1 can (14.5 oz) 50%-less-sodium cut asparagus spears, drained and then blended or processed in food processor until smooth, for the avocados. Stir in 1/4 cup fat-free mayonnaise.

Hummus FAST LOW-FAT

PREP: 5 min ■ **ABOUT 1 1/3 CUPS SPREAD**

- 1 can (15 to 16 oz) garbanzo beans, drained
- 1/4 cup olive or vegetable oil
- 1 clove garlic, cut in half
- 2 tablespoons lemon juice
- 1/2 teaspoon salt
- Chopped fresh parsley
- Pita bread wedges, crackers or raw vegetables, if desired

1. In blender or food processor, place beans, oil, garlic, lemon juice and salt. Cover and blend on high speed, stopping blender occasionally to scrape sides if necessary, until uniform consistency.

2. Spoon into serving dish. Garnish with parsley. Serve with pita bread wedges.

1 TABLESPOON: CAL. 60 (CAL. FROM FAT 25); FAT 3g (SAT. FAT 0g); CHOL. 0mg; SODIUM 85mg; CARBS. 6g (FIBER 2g); PRO. 2g
% DAILY VALUE: VIT. A 0%; VIT. C 0%; CALC. 0%; IRON 2%
EXCHANGES: 1 VEGETABLE, 1/2 FAT **CARB. CHOICES:** 1/2

CUMIN-PEPPER HUMMUS Add 1/4 teaspoon ground cumin with the salt. Omit parsley. Sprinkle with coarsely ground pepper.

SUN-DRIED TOMATO HUMMUS Stir 1/3 cup chopped drained sun-dried tomatoes (packed in oil) into blended mixture.

ENTERTAINING WITH APPETIZERS

If you're hosting a party, you can either make all your appetizers or get a little help at the deli or supermarket by picking up crackers, cheeses, dips, spreads, meatballs and cut-up fruits and veggies.

Serving an appetizer buffet instead of a sit-down dinner is a fun option. Plan it just as you would a regular meal with a mix of hot and cold, mild and spicy, colors and textures. See Menu Planning Basics, pages 38–39.

Host a bring-your-favorite-appetizer party. Make one or two appetizers yourself, and provide beverages. Ask guests to bring the recipes to exchange, too!

Spinach Dip

PREP: 15 min **CHILL:** 4 hr ■ **ABOUT $3^1/_2$ CUPS DIP**

- 1 box (9 oz) frozen chopped spinach, thawed
- 1 cup mayonnaise or salad dressing
- 1 cup sour cream
- 1 package (1.4 oz) vegetable soup and recipe mix
- 1 can (8 oz) water chestnuts, drained and chopped
- 1 medium green onion, chopped (1 tablespoon)
- 1 round uncut loaf bread (about 1 lb), if desired

1. Squeeze thawed spinach to drain; spread on paper towels and pat dry. In large bowl, stir spinach, mayonnaise, sour cream, soup mix (dry), water chestnuts and onion until well mixed. Cover and refrigerate at least 4 hours to blend flavors and soften soup mix.

2. Cut 1- to 2-inch slice off top of bread loaf; hollow out loaf, leaving 1/2- to 1-inch shell of bread on side and bottom. Reserve scooped-out bread and top of loaf; cut or tear into pieces to use for dipping. Spoon spinach dip into hollowed-out loaf. Arrange bread pieces around loaf.

1 TABLESPOON: CAL. 40 (CAL. FROM FAT 35); FAT 4g (SAT. FAT 1g); CHOL. 5mg; SODIUM 80mg; CARBS. 1g (FIBER 0g); PRO. 0g
% DAILY VALUE: VIT. A 6%; VIT. C 2%; CALC. 0%; IRON 0%
EXCHANGES: 1 FAT **CARB. CHOICES:** 0

LIGHTER SPINACH DIP

For 2 grams of fat and 30 calories per serving, use reduced-fat mayonnaise and sour cream.

Layered Mexican Snack Platter FAST

PREP: 20 min ■ **16 SERVINGS**

- 1 can (16 oz) refried beans
- 2 tablespoons salsa, chili sauce or ketchup
- $1^1/_2$ cups sour cream
- 1 cup Guacamole (page 46) or purchased guacamole
- 1 cup shredded Cheddar cheese (4 oz)
- 2 medium green onions, chopped (2 tablespoons)
- Tortilla chips, if desired

1. In small bowl, stir refried beans and salsa until well mixed. Spread in thin layer on 12- or 13-inch serving plate or pizza pan.

2. Spread sour cream over beans, leaving about 1-inch border of beans around edge. Spread guacamole over sour cream, leaving border of sour cream showing.

3. Sprinkle cheese over guacamole. Sprinkle onions over cheese. Serve immediately, or cover with plastic wrap and refrigerate until ready to serve. Serve with tortilla chips.

1 SERVING: CAL. 125 (CAL. FROM FAT 80); FAT 9g (SAT. FAT 5g); CHOL. 25mg; SODIUM 220mg; CARBS. 7g (FIBER 2g); PRO. 4g
% DAILY VALUE: VIT. A 6%; VIT. C 14%; CALC. 6%; IRON 4%
EXCHANGES: 1/2 STARCH, 1/2 MEDIUM-FAT MEAT, 1 FAT
CARB. CHOICES: 1/2

LIGHTER LAYERED MEXICAN SNACK PLATTER

For 3 grams of fat and 75 calories per serving, use fat-free refried beans, fat-free sour cream and reduced-fat Cheddar cheese.

Curried Cheese Spread

FAST

PREP: 15 min ■ **2 CUPS SPREAD**

- 1 package (8 oz) cream cheese, softened
- 1 cup shredded Havarti or Monterey Jack cheese (4 oz)
- 1 teaspoon curry powder
- 1/8 teaspoon ground red pepper (cayenne)
- 1/8 teaspoon garlic powder
- 2 tablespoons mango chutney
- 1 teaspoon chopped fresh cilantro
- 1 tablespoon sliced almonds, toasted (page 215)
- Assorted crackers or fresh vegetables, if desired

1. In medium bowl, beat cream cheese, Havarti cheese, curry powder, red pepper and garlic powder with electric mixer on medium speed until smooth and well blended.

2. Spread cheese mixture in 6-inch circle, about 1/2 inch thick, on 8-inch serving plate. Spread chutney over cheese. Sprinkle with cilantro and almonds.

3. Serve spread on crackers or vegetables.

2 TABLESPOONS: CAL. 90 (CAL. FROM FAT 70); FAT 8g (SAT. FAT 5g); CHOL. 25mg; SODIUM 95mg; CARBS. 1g (FIBER 0g); PRO. 3g
% DAILY VALUE: VIT. A 6%; VIT. C 0%; CALC. 4%; IRON 0%
EXCHANGES: 1/2 HIGH-FAT MEAT, 1 FAT **CARB. CHOICES:** 0

LIGHTER CURRIED CHEESE SPREAD

For 4 grams of fat and 55 calories per serving, use reduced-fat cream cheese (Neufchâtel) and substitute reduced-fat Cheddar cheese for the Havarti cheese.

Cheese Ball

PREP: 20 min **STAND:** 30 min **CHILL:** 10 hr ■ **16 SERVINGS**

- 2 packages (8 oz each) cream cheese
- 3/4 cup crumbled blue cheese (4 oz)
- 1 cup shredded sharp Cheddar cheese (4 oz)
- 1 small onion, finely chopped (1/4 cup)
- 1 tablespoon Worcestershire sauce
- 1/2 cup chopped fresh parsley
- Assorted crackers, if desired

1. Place cheeses in medium bowl; let stand at room temperature about 30 minutes or until softened.

2. Beat onion and Worcestershire sauce into cheeses with electric mixer on low speed until mixed. Beat on medium speed 1 to 2 minutes, scraping bowl frequently, until fluffy. Cover and refrigerate at least 8 hours until firm enough to shape into a ball.

3. Shape cheese mixture into 1 large ball. Roll in parsley; place on serving plate. Cover and refrigerate about 2 hours or until firm. Serve with crackers.

1 SERVING: CAL. 160 (CAL. FROM FAT 125); FAT 14g (SAT. FAT 9g); CHOL. 45mg; SODIUM 240mg; CARBS. 2g (FIBER 0g); PRO. 6g
% DAILY VALUE: VIT. A 14%; VIT. C 4%; CALC. 10%; IRON 2%
EXCHANGES: 1 HIGH-FAT MEAT, 1 FAT **CARB. CHOICES:** 0

LIGHTER CHEESE BALL

For 3 grams of fat and 65 calories per serving, use fat-free cream cheese and reduced-fat Cheddar cheese.

Curried Cheese Spread ▶

Smoked Salmon Cheesecake

PREP: 30 min **BAKE:** 50 min **COOL:** 1 hr **CHILL:** 2 hr ■ **36 SERVINGS**

Add a bold splash of color to this savory cheesecake with red caviar, chopped red bell pepper or chopped seeded tomatoes. This makes a fabulous appetizer, especially since it can be made up to 48 hours ahead of time.

Buttery Cracker Crust

1 cup crushed buttery crackers (about 24 crackers)
3 tablespoons butter or margarine, melted

Cheesecake

2 packages (8 oz each) cream cheese, softened
1/4 cup whipping (heavy) cream
2 large eggs
1/4 teaspoon salt
1 1/2 cups shredded Gouda cheese (6 oz)
4 medium green onions, sliced (1/4 cup)
1 package (4.5 oz) smoked salmon, flaked
2 medium green onions, sliced (2 tablespoons), if desired
2 tablespoons red caviar, if desired
Pumpernickel crackers, if desired

1. Heat oven to 375°F. In small bowl, stir crust ingredients until well mixed. Press evenly in bottom of 9-inch springform pan. Bake about 8 minutes or until golden brown.

2. Reduce oven temperature to 325°F. In large bowl, beat cream cheese with electric mixer on medium speed until smooth. Add whipping cream, eggs and salt; beat until smooth. Stir in Gouda cheese, green onions and salmon until well mixed. Spoon evenly over crust in pan.

3. Bake 45 to 50 minutes or until center is set. Run knife around edge of cheesecake to loosen. Cool completely at room temperature, about 1 hour. Cover and refrigerate at least 2 hours but no longer than 48 hours.

4. Remove side of pan. Place cheesecake on serving platter. Top with 2 tablespoons green onions and caviar. Cut into wedges. Serve with crackers.

1 SERVING: CAL. 90 (CAL. FROM FAT 70); FAT 8g (SAT. FAT 5g); CHOL. 35mg; SODIUM 150mg; CARBS. 2g (FIBER 0g); PRO. 3g
% DAILY VALUE: VIT. A 6%; VIT. C 0%; CALC. 4%; IRON 2%
EXCHANGES: 1/2 MEDIUM-FAT MEAT, 1 FAT **CARB. CHOICES:** 0

Brie in Puff Pastry with Cranberry Sauce

PREP: 30 min **BAKE:** 25 min **COOL:** 30 min ■ **12 SERVINGS**

Cranberry Sauce

1 cup fresh cranberries
6 tablespoons packed brown sugar
1 tablespoon orange juice
1/2 teaspoon grated orange peel

Brie in Pastry

1 tablespoon butter or margarine
1/3 cup sliced almonds
1 frozen puff pastry sheet (from 17.3-oz package), thawed
1 round (14 to 15 oz) Brie cheese
1 large egg, beaten
Assorted crackers or sliced fresh fruit, if desired

1. In 1-quart saucepan, stir cranberries, brown sugar and orange juice until well mixed. Heat to boiling, stirring frequently; reduce heat. Simmer uncovered 15 to 20 minutes, stirring frequently, until mixture thickens and cranberries are tender. Stir in orange peel; remove from heat.

2. In 8-inch skillet, melt butter over medium heat. Cook almonds in butter, stirring frequently, until golden brown; remove from heat.

3. Heat oven to 400°F. Spray cookie sheet with cooking spray. Roll pastry into 16 × 9-inch rectangle on lightly floured surface; cut out one 8 1/2-inch circle and one 7-inch circle.

4. Place cheese round on center of large circle. Spoon cranberry sauce and almonds over cheese. Bring pastry up and press around side of cheese. Brush top edge of pastry with egg. Place 7-inch circle on top, pressing around edge to seal. Brush top and side of pastry with egg. Cut decorations from remaining pastry and arrange on top; brush with egg. Place on cookie sheet.

5. Bake 20 to 25 minutes or until golden brown. Cool on cookie sheet on wire rack 30 minutes before serving. Serve with crackers.

1 SERVING: CAL. 275 (CAL. FROM FAT 170); FAT 19g (SAT. FAT 9g); CHOL. 70mg; SODIUM 270mg; CARBS. 17g (FIBER 1g); PRO. 9g
% DAILY VALUE: VIT. A 6%; VIT. C 0%; CALC. 8%; IRON 6%
EXCHANGES: 1 STARCH, 1 HIGH-FAT MEAT, 2 FAT
CARB. CHOICES: 1

Hot Artichoke Dip

PREP: 10 min **BAKE:** 25 min ■ **ABOUT 1 1/2 CUPS DIP**

To save time, mix ingredients in a microwavable casserole. Cover with plastic wrap, folding one edge or corner back 1/4 inch to vent steam. Microwave on Medium-High (70%) for 4 to 5 minutes, stirring after 2 minutes, until hot.

1/2 cup mayonnaise or salad dressing
1/2 cup grated Parmesan cheese
4 medium green onions, chopped (1/4 cup)
1 can (about 14 oz) artichoke hearts, drained and coarsely chopped
Crackers or cocktail rye bread, if desired

1. Heat oven to 350°F.

2. In small bowl, stir mayonnaise and cheese until well mixed. Stir in onions and artichoke hearts. Spoon into ungreased 1-quart casserole.

3. Cover and bake 20 to 25 minutes or until hot. Serve warm with crackers.

1 TABLESPOON: CAL. 50 (CAL. FROM FAT 35); FAT 4g (SAT. FAT 1g); CHOL. 5mg; SODIUM 115mg; CARBS. 2g (FIBER 1g); PRO. 2g
% DAILY VALUE: VIT. A 0%; VIT. C 2%; CALC. 4%; IRON 2%
EXCHANGES: 1 FAT **CARB. CHOICES:** 0

LIGHTER HOT ARTICHOKE DIP

For 1 gram of fat and 20 calories per serving, use 1/3 cup plain fat-free yogurt and 3 tablespoons reduced-fat mayonnaise for the 1/2 cup mayonnaise.

HOT ARTICHOKE-SPINACH DIP Increase mayonnaise and Parmesan cheese to 1 cup each. Stir in 1 box (9 oz) frozen chopped spinach, thawed (squeeze thawed spinach to drain; spread on paper towels and pat dry). Spoon into ungreased 1-quart casserole. Bake as directed.

Hot Crab Dip

PREP: 15 min **BAKE:** 20 min ■ **ABOUT 2 1/2 CUPS DIP**

1 package (8 oz) cream cheese, softened
1/4 cup grated Parmesan cheese
1/4 cup mayonnaise or salad dressing
1/4 cup dry white wine or apple juice
2 teaspoons sugar
1 teaspoon ground mustard
4 medium green onions, thinly sliced (1/4 cup)
1 clove garlic, finely chopped
1 can (6 oz) crabmeat, drained, cartilage removed and flaked
1/3 cup sliced almonds, toasted (page 215)
Assorted crackers or sliced raw vegetables, if desired

1. Heat oven to 375°F.

2. In medium bowl, stir all ingredients except crabmeat, almonds and crackers until well blended. Stir in crabmeat.

3. Spread crabmeat mixture in ungreased 9-inch pie plate or shallow 1-quart casserole. Sprinkle with almonds.

4. Bake uncovered 15 to 20 minutes or until hot and bubbly. Serve with crackers.

1 TABLESPOON: CAL. 50 (CAL. FROM FAT 35); FAT 4g (SAT. FAT 2g); CHOL. 10mg; SODIUM 50mg; CARBS. 1g (FIBER 0g); PRO. 2g
% DAILY VALUE: VIT. A 2%; VIT. C 0%; CALC. 2%; IRON 0%
EXCHANGES: 1 FAT **CARB. CHOICES:** 0

LIGHTER HOT CRAB DIP

For 1 gram of fat and 20 calories per serving, use fat-free cream cheese and fat-free mayonnaise. Omit almonds.

Pizza Dip ▶

Pizza Dip FAST

PREP: 10 min **BROIL:** 2 min ■ **16 SERVINGS**

Assemble this dip on an ovenproof plate up to one day ahead of time; cover tightly with plastic wrap and store in the refrigerator. Broil as directed.

1 package (8 oz) cream cheese, softened
1/2 cup pizza sauce
2 cloves garlic, finely chopped
1/2 cup chopped pepperoni
1 can (2.25 oz) sliced ripe olives, drained
1/3 cup finely diced red bell pepper
5 medium green onions, sliced (1/3 cup)
1/2 cup shredded mozzarella cheese (2 oz)
1/4 cup shredded fresh basil leaves
Hard breadsticks or tortilla chips, if desired

1. Set oven control to broil. In small bowl, stir cream cheese, pizza sauce and garlic until well mixed. Spread in thin layer on 12- or 13- inch ovenproof serving plate. Top with pepperoni, olives, bell pepper and green onions. Sprinkle with mozzarella cheese.

2. Broil with top 4 inches from heat 1 to 2 minutes or until mozzarella cheese is melted. Sprinkle with basil. Serve immediately with breadsticks.

1 SERVING: CAL. 90 (CAL. FROM FAT 70); FAT 8g (SAT. FAT 4g); CHOL. 20mg; SODIUM 200mg; CARBS. 2g (FIBER 0g); PRO. 3g
% DAILY VALUE: VIT. A 10%; VIT. C 6%; CALC. 4%; IRON 2%
EXCHANGES: 1/2 HIGH-FAT MEAT, 1 FAT **CARB. CHOICES:** 0

Buffalo Chicken Wings

PREP: 20 min **BAKE:** 32 min ■ **2 DOZEN APPETIZERS**

12 chicken wings (about 2 lb)
2 tablespoons butter or margarine, melted
1/2 cup all-purpose flour
1/2 teaspoon salt
1/4 teaspoon pepper
1 cup barbecue sauce
1 tablespoon red pepper sauce
1/2 teaspoon Cajun seasoning
1/4 teaspoon ground cumin
1 bottle (8 oz) blue cheese dressing, if desired
Celery, carrot and zucchini sticks, if desired

1. Heat oven to 425°F. Cut each chicken wing at joints to make 3 pieces; discard tip. Cut off and discard excess skin.

2. In 13 × 9-inch pan, melt butter in oven. In large heavy-duty resealable plastic bag, mix flour, salt and pepper. Add chicken; seal bag tightly. Shake until chicken is completely coated with flour mixture. Place chicken in pan.

3. Bake uncovered 20 minutes. Stir barbecue sauce, pepper sauce, Cajun seasoning and cumin in small bowl until well mixed. Turn chicken. Pour sauce mixture over chicken; toss until evenly coated with sauce.

4. Bake uncovered 10 to 12 minutes longer or until light golden brown on outside and juice of chicken is clear when thickest part is cut to bone (180°F). Serve with dressing and celery sticks.

1 APPETIZER: CAL. 80 (CAL. FROM FAT 35); FAT 4g (SAT. FAT 2g); CHOL. 15mg; SODIUM 180mg; CARBS. 6g (FIBER 0g); PRO. 5g
% DAILY VALUE: VIT. A 2%; VIT. C 0%; CALC. 0%; IRON 2%
EXCHANGES: 1 MEDIUM-FAT MEAT **CARB. CHOICES:** 1/2

HOW TO CUT CHICKEN WINGS

Cut each chicken wing at joints to make 3 pieces; discard tip. Cut off excess skin; discard.

Spicy Thai Chicken Wings

LOW-FAT

PREP: 25 min **CHILL:** 1 hr **BAKE:** 50 min ■ **40 APPETIZERS**

You can make and bake these zesty wings up to 24 hours ahead. Cover with foil and refrigerate. To reheat, place the covered pan in the oven at 350°F for 20 to 25 minutes or until the wings are heated through.

20 chicken wings (about 4 lb)
1/4 cup dry sherry*
1/4 cup oyster sauce**
1/4 cup honey
3 tablespoons chopped fresh cilantro
2 tablespoons chili sauce
2 tablespoons grated lime peel
4 medium green onions, chopped (1/4 cup)
3 cloves garlic, finely chopped

1. Cut each chicken wing at joints to make 3 pieces; discard tip. Cut off and discard excess skin.

2. In resealable heavy-duty plastic food-storage bag or large glass bowl, stir remaining ingredients until well mixed. Add chicken to marinade. Seal bag; turn to coat. Refrigerate at least 1 hour but no longer than 24 hours, turning once.

3. Heat oven to 375°F. Place chicken in ungreased 15 × 10 × 1-inch pan. Bake uncovered 30 minutes, stirring frequently. Bake about 20 minutes longer or until juice of chicken is clear when thickest part is cut to bone (180°F).

**1/4 cup chicken broth can be substituted for the sherry.*

***2 tablespoons soy sauce can be substituted for the oyster sauce.*

1 APPETIZER: CAL. 60 (CAL. FROM FAT 25); FAT 3g (SAT. FAT 1g); CHOL. 15mg; SODIUM 70mg; CARBS. 2g (FIBER 0g); PRO. 5g
% DAILY VALUE: VIT. A 0%; VIT. C 0%; CALC. 0%; IRON 2%
EXCHANGES: 1/2 HIGH-FAT MEAT **CARB. CHOICES:** 0

Chicken Satay with Peanut Sauce

PREP: 15 min **MARINATE:** 2 hr **BROIL:** 9 min ■ **4 SERVINGS**

3 tablespoons lime juice
1 teaspoon curry powder
2 teaspoons honey
1/2 teaspoon ground coriander
1/2 teaspoon ground cumin
1/8 teaspoon salt
2 cloves garlic, finely chopped
1 lb boneless skinless chicken breast halves, cut into 1-inch cubes
Peanut Sauce (page 405)
1 medium red bell pepper, cut into 1 1/4-inch pieces
4 medium green onions, cut into 2-inch pieces

1. In small bowl, stir lime juice, curry powder, honey, coriander, cumin, salt and garlic until well mixed. Place chicken in resealable plastic food-storage bag or shallow glass or plastic dish. Pour lime-juice mixture over chicken; stir chicken to coat with lime-juice mixture. Cover and refrigerate 2 hours, stirring occasionally.

2. Make Peanut Sauce.

3. Set oven control to broil. Spray rack in broiler pan with cooking spray. Remove chicken from marinade; reserve marinade. Thread chicken, 1 bell pepper piece and 2 onion pieces on each of eight 8-inch skewers,* leaving space between each piece. Place skewers on rack in broiler pan.

4. Broil with tops about 3 inches from heat 4 minutes. Turn; brush with marinade. Broil 4 to 5 minutes longer or until chicken is no longer pink in center. Discard any remaining marinade. Serve with sauce.

**If using bamboo skewers, soak in water at least 30 minutes before using to prevent burning.*

1 SERVING: CAL. 360 (CAL. FROM FAT 180); FAT 20g (SAT. FAT 4g); CHOL. 70mg; SODIUM 290mg; CARBS. (FIBER 3g); PRO. 34g
% DAILY VALUE: VIT. A 30%; VIT. C 0%; CALC. 4%; IRON 10%
EXCHANGES: 1/2 OTHER CARBOHYDRATES, 5 LEAN MEAT, 3 1/2 FAT
CARB. CHOICES: 1/2

Spicy Lemon Shrimp with Basil Mayonnaise FAST

PREP: 10 min **BROIL:** 5 min ■ **ABOUT 24 APPETIZERS**

This lovely restaurant-style appetizer can be made ahead of time. The shrimp can marinate in the lemon mixture up to 3 hours in the refrigerator before broiling. Make the basil mayonnaise up to a day ahead, and store covered in the refrigerator.

1 tablespoon grated lemon peel
3 tablespoons lemon juice
3/4 teaspoon crushed red pepper
1/2 teaspoon salt
2 cloves garlic, finely chopped
3 tablespoons olive or vegetable oil
1 lb uncooked peeled deveined large shrimp, thawed if frozen and tails peeled
1/2 cup loosely packed fresh basil leaves
1/2 cup mayonnaise or salad dressing

1. Set oven control to broil. In medium glass or plastic bowl, stir lemon peel, lemon juice, red pepper, salt, garlic and 1 tablespoon of the oil until well mixed. Add shrimp; toss to coat.

2. Spread shrimp in ungreased 15 × 10 × 1-inch pan. Broil with tops 2 to 3 inches from heat 3 to 5 minutes or until shrimp are pink and firm.

3. In food processor, place basil and remaining 2 tablespoons oil. Cover and process until basil is chopped. Add mayonnaise; cover and process until smooth. Serve shrimp with mayonnaise.

1 APPETIZER: CAL. 55 (CAL. FROM FAT 45); FAT 5g (SAT. FAT 1g); CHOL. 30mg; SODIUM 105mg; CARBS. 0g (FIBER 0g); PRO. 3g
% DAILY VALUE: VIT. A 2%; VIT. C 0%; CALC. 0%; IRON 2%
EXCHANGES: 1/2 LEAN MEAT, 1/2 FAT **CARB. CHOICES:** 0

Baked Coconut Shrimp

LOW-FAT

PREP: 30 min **BAKE:** 8 min ■ **ABOUT 40 SHRIMP**

Apricot Sauce

3/4 cup apricot preserves
1 tablespoon lime juice
1/2 teaspoon ground mustard

Shrimp

1/4 cup all-purpose flour
2 tablespoons packed brown sugar
1/4 teaspoon salt
Dash of ground red pepper (cayenne)
1 large egg
1 tablespoon lime juice
1 cup shredded coconut
1 lb uncooked peeled deveined small shrimp (about 40), thawed if frozen and tails peeled
2 tablespoons butter or margarine, melted

1. In 1-quart saucepan, stir all sauce ingredients until well mixed. Cook over low heat, stirring occasionally, just until preserves are melted. Refrigerate while making shrimp.

2. Heat oven to 425°F. Spray rack in broiler pan with cooking spray.

3. In shallow bowl, stir flour, brown sugar, salt and red pepper until well mixed. In another shallow bowl, beat egg and lime juice with fork. In third shallow bowl, place coconut.

4. Coat each shrimp with flour mixture. Dip each side of shrimp into egg mixture. Coat well with coconut. Place on rack in broiler pan. Drizzle with butter.

5. Bake 7 to 8 minutes or until shrimp are pink and firm and coating is beginning to brown. Serve with sauce.

1 SHRIMP: CAL. 55 (CAL. FROM FAT 20); FAT 2g (SAT. FAT 1g); CHOL. 25mg; SODIUM 45mg; CARBS. 7g (FIBER 0g); PRO. 2g
% DAILY VALUE: VIT. A 0%; VIT. C 0%; CALC. 0%; IRON 2%
EXCHANGES: 1/2 FRUIT, 1/2 FAT **CARB. CHOICES:** 1/2

Crab Cakes

PREP: 15 min **COOK:** 10 min ■ **6 SERVINGS**

What a classic—golden brown outside, moist and full of crabmeat inside! Crab cakes are also wonderful served as a main course—allow two per person.

- 1/3 cup mayonnaise or salad dressing
- 1 large egg
- 1 1/4 cups soft bread crumbs (about 2 slices bread)
- 1 teaspoon ground mustard
- 1/4 teaspoon salt
- 1/4 teaspoon ground red pepper (cayenne), if desired
- 1/8 teaspoon pepper
- 2 medium green onions, chopped (2 tablespoons)
- 3 cans (6 oz each) crabmeat, well drained, cartilage removed and flaked
- 1/4 cup dry bread crumbs
- 2 tablespoons vegetable oil

1. In medium bowl, mix mayonnaise and egg with wire whisk. Stir in remaining ingredients except oil and dry bread crumbs. Shape mixture into 6 patties, about 3 inches in diameter (mixture will be moist). Coat each patty with dry bread crumbs.

2. In 12-inch nonstick skillet, heat oil over medium heat. Cook patties in oil about 10 minutes, gently turning once, until golden brown and hot in center. Reduce heat if crab cakes become brown too quickly.

◄ **Crab Cakes**

1 SERVING: CAL. 330 (CAL. FROM FAT 160); FAT 18g (SAT. FAT 3g); CHOL. 120mg; SODIUM 690mg; CARBS. 20g (FIBER 1g); PRO. 22g
% DAILY VALUE: VIT. A 2%; VIT. C 2%; CALC. 16%; IRON 14%
EXCHANGES: 1 STARCH, 3 LEAN MEAT, 2 FAT **CARB. CHOICES:** 1

Cheesy Potato Skins

PREP: 15 min **BAKE:** 1 hr 15 min **BROIL:** 11 min ■ **8 SERVINGS**

- 4 large baking potatoes (about 2 lb)
- 2 tablespoons butter or margarine, melted
- 1 cup shredded Colby-Monterey Jack cheese (4 oz)
- 1/2 cup sour cream
- 8 medium green onions, sliced (1/2 cup)

1. Heat oven to 375°F. Prick potatoes with fork. Bake potatoes 1 hour to 1 hour 15 minutes or until tender. Let stand until cool enough to handle.

2. Cut potatoes lengthwise into fourths; carefully scoop out pulp, leaving 1/4-inch shells. Refrigerate potato pulp for another use.

3. Set oven control to broil. Place potato shells, skin sides down, on rack in broiler pan. Brush with butter.

4. Broil with tops 4 to 5 inches from heat 8 to 10 minutes or until crisp and brown. Sprinkle cheese over potato shells. Broil about 30 seconds longer or until cheese is melted. Serve hot with sour cream and green onions.

1 SERVING: CAL. 160 (CAL. FROM FAT 90); FAT 10g (SAT. FAT 6g); CHOL. 30mg; SODIUM 120mg; CARBS. 12g (FIBER 2g); PRO. 5g
% DAILY VALUE: VIT. A 8%; VIT. C 8%; CALC. 10%; IRON 6%
EXCHANGES: 1 STARCH, 2 FAT **CARB. CHOICES:** 1

LIGHTER CHEESY POTATO SKINS

For 5 grams of fat and 115 calories per serving, decrease cheese to 1/2 cup; use fat-free sour cream.

Quesadillas FAST

PREP: 10 min **BAKE:** 5 min ■ **18 APPETIZERS**

- 2 cups shredded Colby or Cheddar cheese (8 oz)
- 6 flour tortillas (8 to 10 inch)
- 1 small tomato, chopped (1/2 cup)
- 4 medium green onions, chopped (1/4 cup)
- 2 tablespoons canned chopped green chiles
- Chopped fresh cilantro or parsley

1. Heat oven to 350°F.

2. Sprinkle 1/3 cup of the cheese evenly over half of each tortilla. Top cheese with remaining ingredients. Fold tortilla over filling. Place on ungreased cookie sheet.

3. Bake about 5 minutes or until hot and cheese is melted. Cut each into 3 or 4 wedges, beginning cuts from center of folded side.

1 APPETIZER: CAL. 95 (CAL. FROM FAT 45); FAT 5g (SAT. FAT 3g); CHOL. 15mg; SODIUM 150mg; CARBS. 9g (FIBER 1g); PRO. 4g
% DAILY VALUE: VIT. A 42%; VIT. C 2%; CALC. 10%; IRON 4%
EXCHANGES: 1/2 STARCH, 1 FAT **CARB. CHOICES:** 1/2

LIGHTER QUESADILLAS

For 1 gram of fat and 45 calories per serving, use reduced-fat cheese and tortillas.

Grilled Antipasti Platter with Lemon Aioli

PREP: 35 min **CHILL:** 1 hr **GRILL:** 15 min ■ **10 SERVINGS**

Lemon Aioli

1 cup mayonnaise or salad dressing
1 teaspoon grated lemon peel
2 tablespoons fresh lemon juice
1 to 2 cloves garlic, finely chopped

Antipasti

1 medium zucchini, cut into 4-inch sticks
1 medium yellow summer squash or crookneck squash, cut into 4-inch sticks
1 medium red bell pepper, cut into 2-inch pieces
2 cups cherry tomatoes
1 cup small whole mushrooms
1 medium red onion, cut into 1/2-inch wedges
2 tablespoons olive or vegetable oil
1 teaspoon salt
20 thin slices hard salami (about 1/4 lb)
1/2 lb mozzarella cheese, cut into 1/2-inch cubes

1. In small bowl, stir all aioli ingredients until well mixed. Cover and refrigerate at least 1 hour before serving.

2. Heat coals or gas grill for direct heat (page 262).

3. In large bowl, toss vegetables with oil and salt. Heat grill basket (grill "wok") on grill until hot. Add vegetables to grill basket. Cover and grill vegetables 6 to 10 minutes, shaking basket or stirring vegetables occasionally, until vegetables are crisp-tender and lightly charred.

4. Arrange salami around edge of large serving platter. Mound grilled vegetables onto center of serving platter. Sprinkle cheese cubes over vegetables. Serve with aioli for dipping.

1 SERVING: CAL. 320 (CAL. FROM FAT 250); FAT 28g (SAT. FAT 7g); CHOL. 35mg; SODIUM 670mg; CARBS. 7g (FIBER 2g); PRO. 10g
% DAILY VALUE: VIT. A 26%; VIT. C 30%; CALC. 18%; IRON 4%
EXCHANGES: 1 VEGETABLE, 1 HIGH-FAT MEAT, 4 FAT
CARB. CHOICES: 1/2

COLD ANTIPASTI PLATTER WITH LEMON AIOLI Omit grilling step. Add 1 cup pitted whole ripe olives and 10 pepperoncini peppers (bottled Italian peppers), drained, with the cheese cubes.

Sautéed Olives

PREP: 20 min **COOK:** 9 min ■ **20 SERVINGS (6 OLIVES EACH)**

2 tablespoons olive or vegetable oil
2 tablespoons chopped fresh parsley
1 medium green onion, chopped (1 tablespoon)
1 teaspoon crushed red pepper
2 cloves garlic, finely chopped
1 cup Kalamata olives (8 oz), drained and pitted
1 cup Greek green olives (8 oz), drained and pitted
1 cup Gaeta olives (8 oz), drained and pitted

1. In 10-inch skillet, heat oil over medium heat. Cook parsley, green onion, red pepper and garlic in oil about 4 minutes, stirring frequently, until garlic just begins to become golden brown.

2. Stir in olives. Cover and cook about 5 minutes, stirring occasionally, until olives are tender and skins begin to wrinkle. Serve warm or cold.

1 SERVING: CAL. 40 (CAL. FROM FAT 35); FAT 4g (SAT. FAT 1g); CHOL. 0mg; SODIUM 420mg; CARBS. 1g (FIBER 0g); PRO. 0g
% DAILY VALUE: VIT. A 2%; VIT. C 0%; CALC. 2%; IRON 2%
EXCHANGES: 1 FAT **CARB. CHOICES:** 0

Crostini

PREP: 15 min **BAKE:** 8 min ■ **12 APPETIZERS**

Crostini *is Italian for "little toasts." They're crunchy appetizing bites often topped with a variety of savory foods. Here's one favorite that features fresh tomatoes, basil and mozzarella. Try this one, then have fun experimenting with different spreads and toppings.*

- 12 slices Italian bread, 1/2 inch thick
- 1/4 cup olive or vegetable oil
- 1 large tomato, chopped (1 cup)
- 3 tablespoons chopped fresh basil leaves
- 1 tablespoon large capers or chopped ripe olives
- 1/2 teaspoon salt
- 1/2 teaspoon pepper
- 12 slices (1 oz each) mozzarella cheese

1. Heat oven to 375°F.

2. On ungreased cookie sheet, place bread slices. Drizzle 1 teaspoon oil over each bread slice.

3. In small bowl, mix tomato, basil, capers, salt and pepper. Spread half of the tomato mixture over bread slices; top each with cheese slice. Spread remaining tomato mixture over cheese.

4. Bake about 8 minutes or until bread is hot and cheese is melted. Serve hot.

1 APPETIZER: CAL. 175 (CAL. FROM FAT 90); FAT 10g (SAT. FAT 4g); CHOL. 15mg; SODIUM 380mg; CARBS. 12g (FIBER 1g); PRO. 10g
% DAILY VALUE: VIT. A 6%; VIT. C 2%; CALC. 22%; IRON 4%
EXCHANGES: 1 STARCH, 1 HIGH-FAT MEAT **CARB. CHOICES:** 1

Roasted Garlic

PREP: 10 min **BAKE:** 50 min ■ **2 TO 8 SERVINGS**

Roasting garlic turns it into a sweet and delicious appetizing spread. Garlic bulbs *(heads of garlic) are made up of as many as 15 sections called cloves.*

- 1 to 4 bulbs garlic
- 2 teaspoons olive or vegetable oil for each garlic bulb
- Salt and pepper to taste
- Sliced French bread, if desired

1. Heat oven to 350°F.

2. Carefully peel paperlike skin from around each bulb of garlic, leaving just enough to hold garlic cloves together. Cut 1/4- to 1/2-inch slice from top of each bulb to expose cloves. Place cut side up on 12-inch square of foil. Prepare garlic bulbs for roasting, see below.

3. Drizzle 2 teaspoons oil over each bulb. Sprinkle with salt and pepper. Wrap securely in foil. Place in pie plate or shallow baking pan.

4. Bake 45 to 50 minutes or until garlic is tender when pierced with toothpick or fork. Let stand until cool enough to handle. To serve, gently squeeze soft garlic out of cloves. Spread garlic on bread.

1 SERVING: CAL. 75 (CAL. FROM FAT 45); FAT 5g (SAT. FAT 1g); CHOL. 0mg; SODIUM 300mg; CARBS. 6g (FIBER 0g); PRO. 1g
% DAILY VALUE: VIT. A 0%; VIT. C 4; CALC. 2; IRON 2
EXCHANGES: 1 VEGETABLE, 1 FAT **CARB. CHOICES:** 1/2

HOW TO PREPARE GARLIC FOR ROASTING

To prepare garlic for roasting, carefully peel paperlike skin from around each bulb of garlic, leaving just enough to hold garlic cloves together. Cut 1/4- to 1/2-inch slice from top of each bulb to expose cloves. Place cut side up on 12-inch square of foil.

Cinnamon-Sugared Nuts

PREP: 10 min **BAKE:** 30 min ■ **2 CUPS NUTS**

- 1 tablespoon slightly beaten large egg white
- 2 cups pecan halves, unblanched whole almonds or walnut halves
- 1/4 cup sugar
- 2 teaspoons ground cinnamon
- 1/4 teaspoon ground nutmeg
- 1/4 teaspoon ground cloves

1. Heat oven to 300°F.

2. In medium bowl, stir egg white and nuts until nuts are coated and sticky.

3. In small bowl, stir remaining ingredients until well mixed; sprinkle over nuts. Stir until nuts are completely coated. In ungreased 15 × 10 × 1-inch pan, spread nuts in single layer.

4. Bake uncovered about 30 minutes or until toasted. Serve slightly warm or cool completely, about 1 hour. Store in airtight container at room temperature up to 3 weeks.

1/4 CUP: CAL. 225 (CAL. FROM FAT 17); FAT 19 (SAT. FAT 2); CHOL. 0g; SODIUM 5mg; CARBS. 11 (FIBER 3); PRO. 3
% DAILY VALUE: VIT. A 0%; VIT. C 0%; CALC. 2%; IRON 4%
EXCHANGES: 1 STARCH, 3 FAT **CARB. CHOICES:** 1

Southwestern Spiced Party Nuts FAST

PREP: 10 min **BAKE:** 10 min ■ **2 1/4 CUPS NUTS**

- 1 can (9.5 to 11.5 oz) salted mixed nuts
- 1 tablespoon butter or margarine, melted
- 2 teaspoons chili powder
- 1/2 teaspoon garlic powder
- 1/2 teaspoon onion powder
- 1/4 teaspoon ground cinnamon
- 1/4 teaspoon ground red pepper (cayenne)
- 2 tablespoons sugar

◀ **Southwestern Spiced Party Nuts**

1. Heat oven to 300°F.

2. In medium bowl, mix nuts and butter until nuts are coated. In small bowl, mix remaining ingredients except sugar; sprinkle over nuts. Stir until nuts are completely coated. Spread in single layer in 15 × 10 × 1-inch pan.

3. Bake uncovered about 10 minutes or until nuts are toasted. Return to medium bowl.

4. While nuts are still hot, sprinkle with sugar and toss to coat. Serve warm, or cool completely, about 1 hour. Store in airtight container at room temperature up to 3 weeks.

1/4 CUP: CAL. 255 (CAL. FROM FAT 190); FAT 21g (SAT. FAT 4g); CHOL. 5mg; SODIUM 240mg; CARBS. 11g (FIBER 3g); PRO. 6g
% DAILY VALUE: VIT. A 4%; VIT. C 0%; CALC. 4%; IRON 6%
EXCHANGES: 1 STARCH, 1/2 HIGH-FAT MEAT, 3 FAT
CARB. CHOICES: 1

Nachos FAST

PREP: 5 min **BAKE:** 4 min ■ **4 SERVINGS**

- 28 tortilla chips
- 1 cup shredded Monterey Jack or Cheddar cheese (4 oz)
- 1/4 cup canned chopped mild green chiles, if desired
- 1/4 cup salsa

1. Heat oven to 400°F. Line cookie sheet with foil.

2. Place tortilla chips on cookie sheet. Sprinkle with cheese and chiles.

3. Bake about 4 minutes or until cheese is melted. Top with salsa. Serve hot.

1 SERVING: CAL. 175 (CAL. FROM FAT 110); FAT 12g (SAT. FAT 6g); CHOL. 25mg; SODIUM 300mg; CARBS. 9g (FIBER 1g); PRO. 8g
% DAILY VALUE: VIT. A 8%; VIT. C 2%; CALC. 22%; IRON 4%
EXCHANGES: 1/2 STARCH, 1 HIGH-FAT MEAT, 1 FAT
CARB. CHOICES: 1/2

CHICKEN NACHOS Sprinkle 1 cup shredded cooked chicken over tortilla chips. Sprinkle with cheese, chiles and 1/4 cup sliced ripe olives. Bake as directed. Top with 1/3 cup sour cream and salsa.

Original Chex® Party Mix

PREP: 20 min **BAKE:** 1 hr ▪ **ABOUT 12 CUPS SNACK**

- 6 tablespoons butter or margarine
- 2 tablespoons Worcestershire sauce
- 1 1/2 teaspoons seasoned salt
- 3/4 teaspoon garlic powder
- 1/2 teaspoon onion powder
- 3 cups Corn Chex® cereal
- 3 cups Rice Chex® cereal
- 3 cups Wheat Chex® cereal
- 1 cup mixed nuts
- 1 cup pretzels
- 1 cup garlic-flavor bite-size bagel chips or regular-size bagel chips, broken into 1-inch pieces

1. Heat oven to 250°F.

2. In large roasting pan, melt butter in oven. Stir in Worcestershire sauce, seasoned salt, garlic powder and onion powder. Gradually stir in remaining ingredients until evenly coated.

3. Bake 1 hour, stirring every 15 minutes. Spread on paper towels to cool. Store in airtight container.

1/2 CUP: CAL. 140 (CAL. FROM FAT 65); FAT 7g (SAT. FAT 1g); CHOL. 10mg; SODIUM 320mg; CARBS. 16g (FIBER 1g); PRO. 3g
% DAILY VALUE: VIT. A 6%; VIT. C 2%; CALC. 4%; IRON 24%
EXCHANGES: 1 STARCH, 1 FAT **CARB. CHOICES:** 1

LIGHTER CHEX® PARTY MIX

For 2 grams of fat and 80 calories per serving, decrease butter to 3 tablespoons. Omit mixed nuts; use fat-free bagel chips.

Oven Caramel Corn

PREP: 20 min **BAKE:** 1 hr **COOL:** 30 min ▪ **ABOUT 15 CUPS SNACK**

- 15 cups popped popcorn
- 1 cup packed brown sugar
- 1/2 cup butter or margarine
- 1/4 cup light corn syrup
- 1/2 teaspoon salt
- 1/2 teaspoon baking soda

1. Heat oven to 200°F.

2. Remove any unpopped kernels from popcorn. Place popcorn in very large roasting pan or very large bowl, or divide popcorn between 2 ungreased 13 × 9-inch pans.

3. In 2-quart saucepan, heat brown sugar, butter, corn syrup and salt over medium heat, stirring occasionally, until bubbly around edges. Continue cooking 5 minutes without stirring; remove from heat. Stir in baking soda until foamy.

4. Pour sugar mixture over popcorn; toss until evenly coated. If using bowl, transfer mixture to 2 ungreased 13 × 9-inch pans.

5. Bake 1 hour, stirring every 15 minutes. Spread on foil or cooking parchment paper. Cool completely, about 30 minutes. Store tightly covered.

1 CUP: CAL. 200 (CAL. FROM FAT 100); FAT 11g (SAT. FAT 5g); CHOL. 15mg; SODIUM 170mg; CARBS. 25g (FIBER 1g); PRO. 1g
% DAILY VALUE: VIT. A 4%; VIT. C 0%; CALC. 2%; IRON 2%
EXCHANGES: 1/2 STARCH, 1 OTHER CARB., 2 FAT
CARB. CHOICES: 1 1/2

NUTTY OVEN CARAMEL CORN Decrease popcorn to 12 cups. Add 3 cups walnut halves, pecan halves or unblanched whole almonds.

Popcorn FAST

PREP: 5 min **COOK:** 5 min ▪ **ABOUT 12 CUPS POPCORN**

- 1/2 cup unpopped popcorn (not microwave popcorn)
- 1/4 cup vegetable oil
- Salt, if desired

1. In 4-quart Dutch oven, add popcorn and oil. Tilt Dutch oven to spread popcorn evenly. Cover and cook over medium-high heat until 1 kernel pops; remove from heat. Let stand 1 minute, then return to heat.

2. Cook, shaking pan occasionally, until popcorn stops popping. Immediately pour into serving bowl. Sprinkle with salt; toss until evenly coated. Serve warm.

1 CUP: CAL. 110 (CAL. FROM FAT 80); FAT 9g (SAT. FAT 1g); CHOL. 0mg; SODIUM 0mg; CARBS. 6g (FIBER 1g); PRO. 1g
% DAILY VALUE: VIT. A 0%; VIT. C 0%; CALC. 0%; IRON 0%
EXCHANGES: 1/2 STARCH, 1 1/2 FAT **CARB. CHOICES:** 1/2

Beverage Basics

What can beat a glass of cool lemonade on a sultry summer day or a cup of steaming hot coffee on a frosty morning? But beverages do more than quench our thirst. They also add sparkle to a party, warmth to a cozy get-together and color and tantalizing flavor to any meal. Stir up a beverage from any of the recipes here, or pick a favorite from the incredible selection of ready-to-drink beverages at your supermarket.

BREWING COFFEE

1. Choose the correct grind for your coffeemaker:
   - Automatic drip coffeemaker: medium grind
   - Espresso maker: fine grind
   - Percolator: coarse grind
   - Plunger or French press pot: coarse grind
2. Use fresh cold water for best flavor.
3. As soon as coffee finishes brewing, serve it immediately, or within 15 minutes. The longer coffee stays in contact with heat, the more harsh and bitter it becomes. If you're not drinking it right away, pour it into an insulated container.

COFFEE BREWING STRENGTH

(PER SERVING)*

Strength of Brew	Ground Coffee	Water
Regular	1 level tablespoon	3/4 cup (6 ounces)
Strong	2 level tablespoons	3/4 cup (6 ounces)

**Best general recommendation*

IT'S ALL IN THE ROASTING!

Each coffee-growing region of the world produces beans with its own distinctive characteristics, giving you with dozens of coffee types as well as exclusive specialty brands to choose from. Roasting brings out the flavor in the bean and determines the richness, mellowness and smoothness of the coffee. The longer the bean is roasted, the darker and stronger-flavored the coffee. Beans may be roasted with or without added flavorings such as vanilla or hazelnut. Sample them all until you find your favorite! Below are the main roasts.

- **American** is the lightest roast with a caramel-like flavor and no oil on the beans.
- **French and Italian** are very dark roasts with pungent aromatic flavors and a large amount of oil on the beans. The bold, strong flavor is preferred for espresso and espresso-based coffee drinks.
- **Full City** is a dark roast with no traces of oil on the bean surface. Flavors range from caramel to chocolate-like with some hints of a dark roast flavor.

DECAFFEINATED COFFEE

Caffeine is a stimulant found in regular coffee that can make many people jittery and shaky. Decaffeinated coffee comes to the rescue!

Caffeine is removed by either a solvent or water process, both causing the loss of some aroma and flavor. The solvent process is faster, less expensive and leaves more flavor. But if you prefer your coffee without solvent residues, choose water-processed decaf.

TEA

Enjoying a cup of tea is steeped in tradition, from the formal afternoon tea of the English to the tea ceremony of the Japanese. Next to water, tea is the most commonly consumed beverage in the world.

There are three main types of tea, characterized by their processing methods:

- **Black tea's** color and aroma develop as the leaves ferment or oxidize during processing. Black tea contains the most caffeine, about 50 to 65 percent of the amount in coffee.

Some familiar varieties are Darjeeling, Assam and Ceylon orange pekoe.

- **Green tea** is pale green in color with a light, fresh flavor. One popular green tea is gunpowder, which get its name because it's rolled in little balls that "explode" when they come in contact with water. Lung Ching is also very popular.
- **Oolong tea** is a cross between green and black teas that's partially fermented. You'll also recognize it as "Chinese restaurant tea." Imperial oolong is prized for its honey flavor, while Formosa Oolong tastes a little like peaches.

From black, green and Oolong tea, there are literally thousands of varieties, including:

- **Blended tea:** A combination of teas such as English breakfast and Earl Grey.
- **Decaffeinated tea:** Almost all the caffeine is removed during processing.
- **Herb tea:** Really not a tea at all, because it doesn't contain tea leaves. It's actually a blend of dried fruits, herbs, flowers and spices in many flavors such as lemon, orange and peppermint.

BREWING GREAT BLACK OR OOLONG TEA

Brewing that perfect pot of tea is as easy as 1, 2, 3!

1. Start with a spotlessly clean teapot. Warm the pot by filling it with very hot water; drain just before adding the tea.
2. Bring fresh, cold water to a full boil in your teakettle.
3. Add tea to the warm teapot: Use about 1 teaspoon of loose tea or 1 tea bag for each 3/4 cup of water. Pour the boiling water over the tea, and let it steep for 3 to 5 minutes to bring out the full flavor. Judge the strength of the tea by tasting it—not by its color. Stir the tea once to blend evenly. Remove the tea bags or infuser, or strain the tea as you pour. If you prefer weaker tea, add hot water after brewing the tea. Serve tea with milk or cream, lemon and sugar, and enjoy!

BREWING GREEN TEA

Green tea is brewed differently from other types of tea. Brew green tea using very hot water, about 170°F to 190°F, not boiling water. If you've already boiled the water, let it stand about 3 minutes before brewing green tea. Stir once to blend evenly.

MAKING CRYSTAL-CLEAR ICED TEA

For clear iced tea, follow these guidelines:

1. Brew a pot of tea, using double the amount of tea.
2. Remove the tea bags or strain out the tea leaves while pouring it into ice-filled glasses or a pitcher.
3. If you're making tea in advance, let it cool to room temperature before putting it in the refrigerator so it doesn't get cloudy.

Because bacteria can multiply during brewing, making sun tea isn't recommended.

TEA EQUIPMENT

To brew a soothing cup of tea, you need only a few simple pieces of equipment:

- **Infuser:** Use an infuser to hold loose tea leaves. Look for them in all shapes and sizes.
- **Tea strainer:** A strainer comes in handy when you brew with loose tea leaves without an infuser. Hold it over the cup to catch the leaves as you pour in the tea.
- **Teapot:** Choose one made of glass, china or earthenware. China pots should have a solid, even glaze inside and out, and the lid should stay on all pots while pouring.
- **Tea Press:** A small glass pitcher with a plunger or a press that lets you brew tea using loose tea leaves. Just add very hot or boiling water and let steep. Then press the plunger to the bottom and pour out the tea (leaves stay in the pot!).

Chai FAST

PREP: 10 min ■ **4 SERVINGS**

2 cups water
1/4 cup loose Darjeeling tea leaves or 5 tea bags black tea
2 cups whole or 2% milk
1/8 teaspoon ground cardamom
2 whole cloves, crushed
2 to 4 black peppercorns, crushed
Pinch of ground cinnamon
1/4 cup sweetened condensed milk or 4 teaspoons sugar

1. In 2-quart saucepan, heat water to a rapid boil over medium-high heat; reduce heat to low. Add tea leaves; simmer 2 to 4 minutes to blend flavors. (If using tea bags, remove and discard.)

2. Stir in remaining ingredients except sweetened condensed milk. Heat to boiling, but do not let milk boil over.

3. Stir in sweetened condensed milk. Strain through strainer into cups.

1 SERVING: CAL. 140 (CAL. FROM FAT 55); FAT 6g (SAT. FAT 4g); CHOL. 25mg; SODIUM 85mg; CARBS. 16g (FIBER 0g); PRO. 6g
% DAILY VALUE: VIT. A 4%; VIT. C 2%; CALC. 20%; IRON 0%
EXCHANGES: 1 MILK, 1 FAT **CARB. CHOICES:** 1

Hot Chocolate FAST

PREP: 5 min **COOK:** 15 min ■ **6 SERVINGS**

3 oz unsweetened baking chocolate
1 1/2 cups water
1/3 cup sugar
Dash of salt
4 1/2 cups milk

1. In 1 1/2-quart saucepan, heat chocolate and water over medium heat, stirring constantly, until chocolate is melted and mixture is smooth.

2. Stir in sugar and salt. Heat to boiling; reduce heat. Simmer uncovered 4 minutes, stirring constantly. Stir in milk. Heat just until hot (do not boil because skin will form on top).

3. Beat with hand beater until foamy, or stir until smooth. Serve immediately.

1 SERVING: CAL. 220 (CAL. FROM FAT 100); FAT 11g (SAT. FAT 7g); CHOL. 15mg; SODIUM 150mg; CARBS. 24g (FIBER 2g); PRO. 8g
% DAILY VALUE: VIT. A 8%; VIT. C 0%; CALC. 22%; IRON 6%
EXCHANGES: 1 OTHER CARB., 1 SKIM MILK, 1 1/2 FAT
CARB. CHOICES: 1 1/2

LIGHTER HOT CHOCOLATE

For 1 gram of fat and 120 calories per serving, substitute 1/3 cup baking cocoa for the chocolate; use fat-free (skim) milk. Mix cocoa, sugar and salt in saucepan; stir in water. Continue as directed in Step 2.

DOUBLE-CHOCOLATE HOT CHOCOLATE Substitute chocolate milk for regular milk.

Hot Spiced Cider

PREP: 5 min **COOK:** 20 min ■ **6 SERVINGS**

6 cups apple cider
1/2 teaspoon whole cloves
1/4 teaspoon ground nutmeg
3 sticks cinnamon

1. In 3-quart saucepan, heat all ingredients to boiling over medium-high heat; reduce heat. Simmer uncovered 10 minutes.

2. Strain cider mixture through strainer into hot-beverage carafe or pitcher to remove cloves and cinnamon if desired. Serve hot.

1 SERVING: CAL. 115 (CAL. FROM FAT 0); FAT 0g (SAT. FAT 0g); CHOL. 0mg; SODIUM 5mg; CARBS. 29g (FIBER 0g); PRO. 0g
% DAILY VALUE: VIT. A 2%; VIT. C 2%; CALC. 2%; IRON 4%
EXCHANGES: 2 FRUIT **CARB. CHOICES:** 2

HOT-BUTTERED-RUM SPICED CIDER Make as directed. For each serving, place 1 tablespoon butter (do not use margarine or vegetable oil spreads), 1 tablespoon packed brown sugar and 2 tablespoons rum in mug. Fill with hot cider.

Chai ▶

Chocolate Milk Shake

FAST

PREP: 10 min ▪ **2 SERVINGS**

3/4 cup milk
1/4 cup chocolate-flavored syrup
3 scoops (1/2 cup each) vanilla ice cream

1. In blender, place milk and syrup. Cover and blend on high speed 2 seconds.

2. Add ice cream. Cover and blend on low speed about 5 seconds or until smooth. Pour into glasses. Serve immediately.

1 SERVING: CAL. 350 (CAL. FROM FAT 115); FAT 13g (SAT. FAT 8g); CHOL. 50mg; SODIUM 150mg; CARBS. 52g (FIBER 2g); PRO. 7g
% DAILY VALUE: VIT. A 12%; VIT. C 2%; CALC. 24%; IRON 4%
EXCHANGES: 2 1/2 OTHER CARB., 1 MILK, 2 1/2 FAT
CARB. CHOICES: 3 1/2

LIGHTER CHOCOLATE MILK SHAKE

For 1 gram of fat and 285 calories per serving, use fat-free (skim) milk; substitute fat-free frozen yogurt for the ice cream.

BERRY MILK SHAKE Substitute strawberry or cherry topping or frozen strawberries or raspberries in syrup, thawed and undrained, for the chocolate-flavored syrup.

CHOCOLATE MALT Add 1 tablespoon natural-flavor or chocolate-flavor malted milk powder before blending.

> **WARM THEM UP!**
>
> Hot cider, hot chocolate and hot punch make great drinks, especially on cold days, Keep them hot in thermal carafes, slow cookers, fondue pots and chafing dishes. If you don't have any of these, serve hot beverages from a saucepan right from the stove.

Eggnog

PREP: 35 min **CHILL:** 2 hr ▪ **10 SERVINGS**

The holidays seem to get even more festive with a cup of nog. For safety's-sake, make eggnog with a cooked egg custard rather than with uncooked eggs.

Soft Custard

3 large eggs, slightly beaten
1/3 cup granulated sugar
Dash of salt
2 1/2 cups milk
1 teaspoon vanilla

Eggnog

1 cup whipping (heavy) cream
2 tablespoons powdered sugar
1/2 teaspoon vanilla
1/2 cup light rum
1 or 2 drops yellow food color, if desired
Ground nutmeg

1. In heavy 2-quart saucepan, stir eggs, granulated sugar and salt until well mixed. Gradually stir in milk. Cook over medium heat 10 to 15 minutes, stirring constantly, until mixture just coats a metal spoon; remove from heat. Stir in 1 teaspoon vanilla. Place saucepan in cold water until custard is cool. (If custard curdles, beat vigorously with hand beater until smooth.) Cover and refrigerate at least 2 hours but no longer than 24 hours.

2. Just before serving, in chilled medium bowl, beat whipping cream, powdered sugar and 1/2 teaspoon vanilla with electric mixer on high speed until stiff. Gently stir 1 cup of the whipped cream, the rum and food color into custard.

3. Pour custard mixture into small punch bowl. Drop remaining whipped cream in mounds onto custard mixture. Sprinkle with nutmeg. Serve immediately. Store covered in refrigerator up to 2 days.

1 SERVING: CAL. 155 (CAL. FROM FAT 90); FAT 10g (SAT. FAT 6g); CHOL. 95mg; SODIUM 100mg; CARBS. 12g (FIBER 0g); PRO. 4g
% DAILY VALUE: VIT. A 10%; VIT. C 0%; CALC. 10%; IRON 0%
EXCHANGES: 1 SKIM MILK, 1 1/2 FAT **CARB. CHOICES:** 1

LIGHTER EGGNOG

For 3 grams of fat and 120 calories per serving, in the Soft Custard, substitute 2 eggs plus 2 egg whites for the 3 eggs and 2 1/4 cups fat-free (skim) milk for the milk. In the Eggnog, substitute 2 cups frozen (thawed) reduced-fat whipped topping for the beaten whipping cream, powdered sugar and vanilla.

Orange Smoothie

FAST LOW-FAT

PREP: 5 min ■ **4 SERVINGS**

- 1 quart (4 cups) vanilla frozen yogurt or ice cream, slightly softened
- 1/2 cup frozen (thawed) orange juice concentrate
- 1/4 cup milk
- Orange slices, if desired

1. In blender, place frozen yogurt, orange juice concentrate and milk. Cover and blend on medium speed about 45 seconds, stopping blender occasionally to scrape sides, until thick and smooth.

2. Pour blended mixture into glasses. Garnish with orange slices.

1 SERVING (ABOUT 1 CUP): CAL. 260 (CAL. FROM FAT 20); FAT 2g (SAT. FAT 2g); CHOL. 10mg; SODIUM 120mg; CARBS. 51g (FIBER 0g); PRO. 10g **% DAILY VALUE:** VIT. A 6%; VIT. C 84%; CALC. 32%; IRON 2% **EXCHANGES:** 2 1/2 FRUIT, 1 SKIM MILK **CARB. CHOICES:** 3 1/2

Strawberry Smoothie

FAST LOW-FAT

PREP: 5 min ■ **4 SERVINGS**

- 1 pint (2 cups) strawberries
- 1 cup milk
- 2 containers (6 oz each) strawberry yogurt (1 1/3 cups)

1. Reserve 4 strawberries for garnish. Cut out the hull, or "cap," from remaining strawberries.

2. In blender, place strawberries, milk and yogurt. Cover and blend on high speed about 30 seconds or until smooth.

3. Pour mixture into 4 glasses. Garnish each with reserved strawberry.

1 SERVING (ABOUT 1 CUP): CAL. 140 (CAL. FROM FAT 20); FAT 2g (SAT. FAT 1g); CHOL. 10mg; SODIUM 80mg; CARBS. 24g (FIBER 2g); PRO. 6g **% DAILY VALUE:** VIT. A 4%; VIT. C 70%; CALC. 20%; IRON 2% **EXCHANGES:** 1 FRUIT, 1 SKIM MILK **CARB. CHOICES:** 1 1/2

STRAWBERRY-BANANA SMOOTHIE Substitute 1 medium banana, cut into chunks, for 1 cup of the strawberries.

Lemonade

FAST

PREP: 10 min ■ **6 SERVINGS**

To maximize the amount of juice from a lemon, roll a room-temperature lemon back and forth on a counter with the palm of your hand, pressing down firmly.

- 3 cups water
- 1 cup lemon juice (about 4 lemons)
- 1/2 cup sugar
- Lemon or orange slices, if desired
- Fresh mint leaves, if desired

1. In large pitcher, stir water, lemon juice and sugar until sugar is dissolved.

2. Serve lemonade over ice. Garnish with lemon slices and mint.

1 SERVING: CAL. 75 (CAL. FROM FAT 0); FAT 0g (SAT. FAT 0g); CHOL. 0mg; SODIUM 10mg; CARBS. 19g (FIBER 0g); PRO. 0g **% DAILY VALUE:** VIT. A 0%; VIT. C 16%; CALC. 0%; IRON 0% **EXCHANGES:** 1 FRUIT **CARB. CHOICES:** 1

LIMEADE Substitute 1 cup lime juice (about 10 limes) for the lemon juice; increase sugar to 3/4 cup. Garnish with lime slices and strawberries if desired.

Colada Cooler Punch

FAST

PREP: 10 min ■ **24 SERVINGS**

- 2 cans (12 oz each) frozen piña colada mix concentrate, thawed
- 2 cans (12 oz each) frozen white grape juice, thawed
- 6 cups cold water
- 12 cups (about 3 liters) lemon-lime soda pop, chilled
- Lemon and lime slices

1. In 4-quart container, stir piña colada and juice concentrates until well mixed. Stir in water; refrigerate.

2. Just before serving, pour piña colada mixture into punch bowl. Add soda pop and lemon and lime slices; gently stir. Pour over ice in glasses.

1 SERVING: CAL. 160 (CAL. FROM FAT 0); FAT 0g (SAT. FAT 0g); CHOL. 0mg; SODIUM 15mg; CARBS. 40g (FIBER 0g); PRO. 0g **% DAILY VALUE:** VIT. A 0%; VIT. C 44%; CALC. 0%; IRON 0% **EXCHANGES:** 2 1/2 FRUIT **CARB. CHOICES:** 2 1/2

Lemon-Strawberry Punch

FAST

PREP: 10 min ▪ **32 SERVINGS**

- 3 cans (6 oz each) frozen lemonade concentrate, thawed
- 1 box (10 oz) frozen strawberries in light syrup, thawed and undrained
- 1 bottle (1 liter) ginger ale

1. In 4-quart container, stir lemonade concentrate and 9 cans water until well mixed.

2. Pour lemonade into punch bowl. Stir in strawberries.

3. Just before serving, add ginger ale and ice; gently stir.

1 SERVING: CAL. 50 (CAL. FROM FAT 0); FAT 0g (SAT. FAT 0g); CHOL. 0mg; SODIUM 5mg; CARBS. 13g (FIBER 0g); PRO. 0g
% DAILY VALUE: VIT. A 0%; VIT. C 10%; CALC. 0%; IRON 0%
EXCHANGES: 1 FRUIT **CARB. CHOICES:** 1

FLOATING ISLAND PUNCH Just before serving, add lemon sherbet by spoonfuls or in small balls from ice-cream scoop to punch in punch bowl.

Lemon-Strawberry Punch

Frozen Strawberry Margaritas

FAST

PREP: 10 min **FREEZE:** 24 hr ▪ **10 SERVINGS**

- 1 can (6 oz) frozen limeade concentrate, thawed
- 1 box (10 oz) frozen strawberries in light syrup, thawed and undrained
- 3 cups cold water
- 3/4 cup tequila
- 1 bottle (1 liter) lemon-lime soda pop, chilled

1. In blender, place limeade concentrate and strawberries. Cover and blend on high speed until smooth. Add water and tequila. Cover and blend on high speed until well blended. Pour into 2-quart plastic container. Cover and freeze 24 hours or until slushy.

2. To serve, place 2/3 cup slush in each glass and fill with 1/3 cup soda pop; stir.

1 SERVING: CAL. 120 (CAL. FROM FAT 0); FAT 0g (SAT. FAT 0g); CHOL. 0mg; SODIUM 15mg; CARBS. 31g (FIBER 1g); PRO. 0g
% DAILY VALUE: VIT. A 0%; VIT. C 24%; CALC. 0%; IRON 0%
EXCHANGES: 2 FRUIT **CARB. CHOICES:** 2

FROZEN RASPBERRY MARGARITAS Substitute 1 box (10 oz) frozen raspberries in light syrup, thawed and undrained, for the strawberries.

Sangria

FAST

PREP: 10 min ▪ **8 SERVINGS**

- 2/3 cup lemon juice
- 1/3 cup orange juice
- 1/4 cup sugar
- 1 bottle (750 ml) dry red wine or nonalcoholic red wine
- Lemon and orange slices, if desired

1. Pour juices into a half-gallon glass pitcher. Add sugar and stir until dissolved.

2. Stir in wine. Add ice if desired. Garnish with lemon and orange slices.

1 SERVING: CAL. 95 (CAL. FROM FAT 0); FAT 0g (SAT. FAT 0g); CHOL. 0mg; SODIUM 10mg; CARBS. 10g (FIBER 0g); PRO. 0g
% DAILY VALUE: VIT. A 0%; VIT. C 14%; CALC. 0%; IRON 2%
EXCHANGES: 1 FRUIT, 1 FAT **CARB. CHOICES:** 1/2

CHAPTER 3

Breads

Quick Breads

Yeast Breads

LOW-FAT = *3g or less, except main dishes with 10g or less* FAST = *Ready in 20 minutes or less* BREAD MACHINE = *Bread machine directions* SLOW COOKER = *Slow cooker directions* LIGHTER = *25% fewer calories or grams of fat*

◀ **Raspberry-White Chocolate Scones (page 75)**

Easy Quick Breads

Quick breads are quick and easy to make because they are leavened with baking powder or baking soda rather than slower-acting yeast. So breads rise properly, be sure to use only fresh baking powder and baking soda—check the container for the expiration date.

PANS AND PAN PREPARATION

When baking loaves of quick breads, choosing the right pan, and preparing it properly, can make a big difference. Here are a few tips followed in the Betty Crocker Kitchens.

- For breads with golden brown color and tender crusts, use shiny pans and cookie sheets, which reflect the heat and avoid over-browning.
- Dark pans or pans with dark nonstick coating absorb heat easier than shiny pans, so baked goods may brown more quickly. Check your manufacturer's use and care instructions. Some suggest reducing the oven temperature by 25°F, and others recommend not greasing the pan at all or using cooking spray.
- If you're using insulated pans, you may need to increase the baking time slightly.
- When making muffins and quick bread loaves, usually only the bottoms of the pan are greased so that the batter doesn't form a lip (overhanging or hard, dry edges) during baking.

MIXING QUICK BREADS

Mix the batter as each recipe suggests. Some batters are mixed until smooth, others until the ingredients are just moistened. If mixed too much, they become tough.

For butter or margarine, the stick form is recommended. Vegetable-oil spread sticks that have at least 65 percent fat can be used, but the batter consistency may be thinner.

Vegetable-oil spreads with less than 65 percent fat, reduced-fat butter or any tub or whipped product are not recommended for quick breads. Because these products contain more water and less fat, the breads will be tough and wet or gummy.

SPECIALTY MUFFIN BAKING GUIDELINES

Convert your favorite 12-muffin recipe to mini or jumbo muffins or to regular or jumbo muffin tops using the directions below.

- The bake times vary up to 10 minutes from the suggested minimum to the maximum; check at the minimum time to see if muffins are done, then check every minute or two until done.
- Muffin batters with large pieces of nuts, fruit or chocolate work better as medium or jumbo muffins because the pieces are too big for mini muffins. For mini muffins, use miniature chips and small pieces of fruit and nuts.
- Pans for baking muffin tops often have a dark nonstick surface; check the manufacturer's instructions to see if reducing the oven temperature by 25°F is recommended.

Muffin Size	Muffin Cup Size	Oven Temperature	Bake Time	Yield
MUFFINS				
Mini	1 3/4 × 1 inch (small)	400°F	10 to 17 minutes	24
Jumbo	3 1/2 × 1 3/4 inches (large)	375°F	25 to 35 minutes	4
MUFFIN TOPS				
Regular	2 3/4 × 3/8 inch	400°F	8 to 10 minutes	18
Jumbo	4 × 1/2 inch	400°F	15 to 20 minutes	6

Bran Muffins

PREP: 10 min **BAKE:** 25 min ▪ **12 MUFFINS**

These hearty muffins freeze perfectly for up to three months. Use resealable plastic freezer bags or freezer containers. Reheat muffins in the microwave (see Microwave Cooking and Heating Guidelines, pages 40–41).

- 1 1/4 cups Fiber One® cereal, crushed, or 2 cups bran cereal flakes, crushed*
- 1 1/3 cups milk
- 1/2 cup raisins, if desired
- 1/2 teaspoon vanilla
- 1/4 cup vegetable oil
- 1 large egg
- 1 1/4 cups all-purpose flour**
- 1/2 cup packed brown sugar
- 3 teaspoons baking powder
- 1/4 teaspoon salt
- 1/4 teaspoon ground cinnamon, if desired

1. Heat oven to 400°F. Grease bottoms only of 12 medium muffin cups with shortening, spray with cooking spray or line with paper baking cups.

2. In medium bowl, stir cereal, milk, raisins and vanilla until well mixed. Let stand about 5 minutes or until cereal has softened. Beat in oil and egg with fork.

3. In another medium bowl, stir remaining ingredients until well mixed; stir into cereal mixture just until moistened. Divide batter evenly among muffin cups.

4. Bake 20 to 25 minutes or until toothpick inserted in center comes out clean. If baked in greased pan, let stand about 5 minutes in pan, then remove from pan to wire rack; if baked in paper baking cups, immediately remove from pan to wire rack. Serve warm if desired.

**To crush cereal, place in plastic bag or between sheets of waxed paper or plastic wrap and crush with rolling pin. Or crush in blender or food processor.*

***If using self-rising flour, decrease baking powder to 1 teaspoon and omit salt.*

1 MUFFIN: CAL. 160 (CAL. FROM FAT 55); FAT 6g (SAT. FAT 1g); CHOL. 20mg; SODIUM 220mg; CARBS. 25g (FIBER 3g); PRO. 3g
% DAILY VALUE: VIT. A 2%; VIT. C 0%; CALC. 12%; IRON 10%
EXCHANGES: 1 1/2 STARCH, 1 FAT
CARB. CHOICES: 1 1/2

DATE-BRAN MUFFINS Stir in 1 cup chopped dates with remaining ingredients in Step 3. Bake as directed.

MUFFIN CURES

The Best Muffins Are . . .

- Golden brown (for light-colored batters)
- Slightly rounded with bumpy tops
- Tender and light
- Even-textured with medium, round holes
- Moist inside
- Easy to remove from the pan

What Happened	Why
Pale muffins	• oven too cool
Peaked and smooth tops	• too much mixing
Tough and heavy	• too much flour • too much mixing
Uneven texture with long holes or tunnels	• too much mixing
Dry	• too much flour • oven too hot • baked too long
Stick to pan	• pan not properly greased
Dark crust but center not done	• oven too hot

Blueberry Muffins

PREP: 10 min **BAKE:** 25 min **STAND:** 5 min ■
12 MUFFINS

- 3/4 cup milk
- 1/4 cup vegetable oil
- 1 large egg
- 2 cups all-purpose flour*
- 1/2 cup sugar
- 2 teaspoons baking powder
- 1/2 teaspoon salt
- 1 cup fresh, canned (drained) or frozen blueberries

1. Heat oven to 400°F. Grease bottoms only of 12 medium muffin cups with shortening, spray with cooking spray or line with paper baking cups.

2. In large bowl, beat milk, oil and egg with fork or wire whisk until well mixed. Stir in flour, sugar, baking powder and salt all at once just until flour is moistened (batter will be lumpy). Fold in blueberries. Divide batter evenly among muffin cups.

3. Bake 20 to 25 minutes or until golden brown. If baked in greased pan, let stand about 5 minutes in pan, then remove from pan to wire rack; if baked in paper baking cups, immediately remove from pan to wire rack. Serve warm if desired.

**If using self-rising flour, omit baking powder and salt.*

1 MUFFIN: CAL. 185 (CAL. FROM FAT 55); FAT 6g (SAT. FAT 1g); CHOL. 20mg; SODIUM 190mg; CARBS. 27g (FIBER 1g); PRO. 3g
% DAILY VALUE: VIT. A 2%; VIT. C 0%; CALC. 6%; IRON 6%
EXCHANGES: 1 STARCH, 1 FRUIT, 1 FAT
CARB. CHOICES: 2

APPLE-CINNAMON MUFFINS Omit blueberries. Beat in 1 cup chopped peeled apple (about 1 medium) with the milk. Stir in 1/2 teaspoon ground cinnamon with the flour. Bake 25 to 30 minutes.

BANANA MUFFINS Omit blueberries. Decrease milk to 1/3 cup. Beat in 1 cup mashed very ripe bananas (2 medium) with the milk. Use packed brown sugar for the sugar.

CHOCOLATE CHIP MUFFINS Omit blueberries. Fold 1 cup miniature semisweet chocolate chips into batter.

CRANBERRY-ORANGE MUFFINS Omit blueberries. Beat in 1 tablespoon grated orange peel with the milk. Fold 1 cup coarsely chopped cranberries into batter.

STREUSEL-TOPPED BLUEBERRY MUFFINS Make muffin batter as directed. In medium bowl, mix 1/4 cup all-purpose flour, 1/4 cup packed brown sugar and 1/4 teaspoon ground cinnamon. Cut in 2 tablespoons firm butter or margarine, using pastry blender (or pulling 2 table knives through ingredients in opposite directions), until crumbly. Divide batter evenly among muffin cups. Sprinkle each with about 1 tablespoon streusel.

LEARN WITH Betty — MUFFINS

These muffins have peaked, smooth tops because the batter was overmixed.

These muffins are slightly rounded with bumpy tops; there are no problems.

These muffins are dry with rough-looking tops because flour was overmeasured, oven was too hot and muffins were baked too long.

Blueberry-Banana and Cranberry-Orange Muffins (page 67)

Banana Bread LOW-FAT

PREP: 15 min **BAKE:** 1 hr **COOL:** 2 hr 10 min ▪ **2 LOAVES, 24 SLICES EACH**

Don't throw away those bananas that are turning brown and soft. Turn them into banana bread.

- $1^1/_4$ cups sugar
- $^1/_2$ cup butter or margarine, softened
- 2 large eggs
- $1^1/_2$ cups mashed very ripe bananas (3 medium)
- $^1/_2$ cup buttermilk
- 1 teaspoon vanilla
- $2^1/_2$ cups all-purpose flour*
- 1 teaspoon baking soda
- 1 teaspoon salt
- 1 cup chopped nuts, if desired

1. Move oven rack to low position so that tops of pans will be in center of oven. Heat oven to 350°F. Grease bottoms only of two 8 × 4-inch loaf pans or one 9 × 5-inch loaf pan with shortening or spray with cooking spray.

2. In large bowl, stir sugar and butter until well mixed. Stir in eggs until well mixed. Stir in bananas, buttermilk and vanilla; beat with spoon until smooth. Stir in flour, baking soda and salt just until moistened. Stir in nuts. Divide batter evenly between 8-inch pans or pour into 9-inch pan.

3. Bake 8-inch loaves about 1 hour, 9-inch loaf about 1 hour 15 minutes, or until toothpick inserted in center comes out clean. Cool 10 minutes in pans on wire rack.

4. Loosen sides of loaves from pans; remove from pans and place top side up on wire rack. Cool completely, about 2 hours, before slicing. Wrap tightly and store at room temperature up to 4 days, or refrigerate up to 10 days.

**If using self-rising flour, omit baking soda and salt.*

1 SLICE: CAL. 70 (CAL. FROM FAT 20); FAT 2g (SAT. FAT 1g); CHOL. 15mg; SODIUM 95mg; CARBS. 12g (FIBER 0g); PRO. 1g
% DAILY VALUE: VIT. A 2%; VIT. C 0%; CALC. 0%; IRON 2%
EXCHANGES: 1/2 STARCH, 1/2 FRUIT **CARB. CHOICES:** 1

BLUEBERRY-BANANA BREAD Omit nuts. Stir 1 cup fresh or frozen blueberries into batter.

QUICK BREAD LOAF TIPS

- For fruit or nut breads, grease only the bottoms of the loaf pans to give the loaves a gently rounded top and avoid overhanging edges.
- Chop or shred fruits, vegetables or nuts before you start making the batter. If you begin mixing the batter and then stop to chop, the batter may get too stiff.
- Mix quick breads by hand, because it's easy to overmix the batter with an electric mixer.
- During baking, large, lengthwise cracks occasionally form on top of the loaf. Don't worry; this is normal and doesn't affect the quality.
- Before slicing loaves, cool them completely so they don't crumble. For the easiest slicing loaves, cover tightly and store for 24 hours before cutting. Cut with a sharp, thin-bladed knife, using a light sawing motion.
- After cooling completely (about 2 hours), wrap loaves tightly and store at room temperature up to 4 days, refrigerate up to 10 days or freeze up to 3 months.

QUICK BREAD LOAF CURES

The Best Quick Bread Loaf Has . . .

Golden brown rounded top

Lengthwise crack (or split) along the top

Thin, tender crust

Moist texture with small even holes

Fruits and/or nuts evenly distributed

What Happened	Why
Didn't rise	• too much mixing • check expiration date on leavening
Tough	• too much mixing • not enough fat
Tunnels	• too much mixing
Rims around the edges	• sides of pan were greased
Compact	• too much flour • too little leavening
Crumbly	• not cooled completely; cut too soon after baking

MINI NUT BREAD LOAVES BAKING GUIDELINES

Mini loaves make gifts! Bake batters in miniature loaf pans, muffin pans or small cake molds in special shapes. To determine how much batter a pan will hold, fill it to the top with water, then pour the water into a measuring cup. Check the chart to see how much batter you should use for the size of your pan. Let the baked breads cool for a few minutes, then loosen the edges with a table knife or metal spatula and carefully remove from the pans. Cool completely on a wire rack.

Approximate Pan Size	Amount of Batter	Approximate Bake Time at 350°F
1/3 cup	1/4 cup	15 to 20 minutes
1/2 cup	1/3 cup	15 to 20 minutes
2/3 to 3/4 cup	1/2 cup	25 to 35 minutes
1 cup	3/4 cup	35 to 40 minutes

Zucchini Bread

PREP: 15 min **BAKE:** 1 hr **COOL:** 2 hr 10 min ▪
2 LOAVES, 24 SLICES EACH

- 3 cups shredded zucchini (2 to 3 medium)
- 1 2/3 cups sugar
- 2/3 cup vegetable oil
- 2 teaspoons vanilla
- 4 large eggs
- 3 cups all-purpose* or whole wheat flour
- 2 teaspoons baking soda
- 1 teaspoon salt
- 1 teaspoon ground cinnamon
- 1/2 teaspoon ground cloves
- 1/2 teaspoon baking powder
- 1/2 cup coarsely chopped nuts
- 1/2 cup raisins, if desired

1. Move oven rack to low position so that tops of pans will be in center of oven. Heat oven to 350°F. Grease bottoms only of two 8 × 4-inch loaf pans or one 9 × 5-inch loaf pan with shortening or spray with cooking spray.

2. In large bowl, stir zucchini, sugar, oil, vanilla and eggs until well mixed. Stir in remaining ingredients except nuts and raisins. Stir in nuts and raisins. Divide batter evenly between 8-inch pans or pour into 9-inch pan.

3. Bake 8-inch loaves 50 to 60 minutes, 9-inch loaf 1 hour 10 minutes to 1 hour 20 minutes, or until toothpick inserted in center comes out clean. Cool 10 minutes in pans on wire rack.

4. Loosen sides of loaves from pans; remove from pans and place top side up on wire rack. Cool completely, about 2 hours, before slicing. Wrap tightly and store at room temperature up to 4 days, or refrigerate up to 10 days.

**If using self-rising flour, omit baking soda, salt and baking powder.*

1 SLICE: CAL. 95 (CAL. FROM FAT 35); FAT 4g (SAT. FAT 1g); CHOL. 15mg; SODIUM 110mg; CARBS. 13g (FIBER 0g); PRO. 2g
% DAILY VALUE: VIT. A 2%; VIT. C 0%; CALC. 0%; IRON 2%
EXCHANGES: 1/2 STARCH, 1 VEGETABLE, 1/2 FAT
CARB. CHOICES: 1

CRANBERRY BREAD Omit zucchini, cinnamon, cloves and raisins. Stir in 1/2 cup milk and 2 teaspoons grated orange peel with the oil. Stir 3 cups fresh or frozen (thawed and drained) cranberries into batter. Bake 1 hour to 1 hour 10 minutes.

PUMPKIN BREAD Substitute 1 can (15 oz) pumpkin (not pumpkin pie mix) for the zucchini.

Sour Cream Coffee Cake

PREP: 30 min **BAKE:** 1 hr **COOL:** 30 min ■
16 SERVINGS

Brown Sugar Filling

1/2 cup packed brown sugar
1/2 cup finely chopped nuts
1 1/2 teaspoons ground cinnamon

Coffee Cake

3 cups all-purpose* or whole wheat flour
1 1/2 teaspoons baking powder
1 1/2 teaspoons baking soda
3/4 teaspoon salt
1 1/2 cups granulated sugar
3/4 cup butter or margarine, softened
1 1/2 teaspoons vanilla
3 large eggs
1 1/2 cups sour cream

Glaze

1/2 cup powdered sugar
1/4 teaspoon vanilla
2 to 3 teaspoons milk

1. Heat oven to 350°F. Grease bottom and side of 10 × 4-inch angel food cake pan (tube pan), 12-cup fluted tube cake pan or two 9 × 5-inch loaf pans with shortening or spray with cooking spray.

2. In small bowl, stir all filling ingredients until well mixed; set aside. In large bowl, stir flour, baking powder, baking soda and salt until well mixed; set aside.

3. In another large bowl, beat granulated sugar, butter, 1 1/2 teaspoons vanilla and eggs with electric mixer on medium speed 2 minutes, scraping bowl occasionally. Beat about one-fourth of the flour mixture and sour cream at a time alternately into sugar mixture on low speed until blended.

4. For angel food or fluted tube cake pan, spread one-third of the batter (about 2 cups) in pan, then sprinkle with one-third of the filling; repeat twice. For loaf pans, spread one-fourth of the batter (about 1 1/2 cups) in each pan, then sprinkle each with one-fourth of the filling; repeat once.

5. Bake angel food or fluted tube cake pan about 1 hour, loaf pans about 45 minutes, or until toothpick inserted near center comes out clean. Cool 10 minutes in pan on wire rack. Remove from pan to wire rack. Cool 20 minutes. In small bowl, stir all glaze ingredients until smooth and thin enough to drizzle. Drizzle glaze over coffee cake. Serve warm or cool.

**If using self-rising flour, omit baking powder, baking soda and salt.*

1 SLICE: CAL. 355 (CAL. FROM FAT 145); FAT 16g (SAT. FAT 9g); CHOL. 75mg; SODIUM 360mg; CARBS. 49g (FIBER 1g); PRO. 5g
% DAILY VALUE: VIT. A 10%; VIT. C 0%; CALC. 6%; IRON 8%
EXCHANGES: 2 STARCH, 1 OTHER CARB., 3 FAT
CARB. CHOICES: 3

BISCUITS TIPS

- One secret to making flaky biscuits is thoroughly blending or "cutting in" the shortening and dry ingredients. A pastry blender, which breaks the shortening into little lumps, works great for cutting in. If you don't have one, you can pull two table knives in opposite directions through the flour and shortening or use a fork.
- For evenly browned, picture-perfect biscuits, roll or pat the dough to an even thickness. See photo in How to Make Biscuits below.
- Dip the biscuit cutter in flour for each biscuit to cut cleanly through the dough without sticking, pushing the cutter straight down through the dough. If you twist as you cut, the biscuits will be uneven. Cut the biscuits as close together as possible.
- If you don't have a biscuit cutter, use the end of an opened 6-ounce juice can or other narrow can or glass, or use cookie cutters for fun shapes. Dip in flour before cutting.
- After cutting as many biscuits as possible, lightly press—don't knead—the scraps of dough together. Roll or pat the remaining dough to 1/2-inch thickness and cut. These biscuits will look slightly uneven.

BISCUIT CURES

The Best Baking Powder Biscuits Are . . .

Light golden brown

High with fairly smooth, level tops

Tender and light

Flaky and slightly moist inside

What Happened	Why
Not high	• too little baking powder • too much mixing • oven too hot
Dark bottom crust	• oven rack placed too low in oven • oven too hot
Tough	• too little shortening • too much mixing or handling • too much flour
Not flaky	• too little shortening • too much mixing • not kneaded enough

HOW TO MAKE BISCUITS

1. Cut shortening into flour mixture until the mixture looks like fine crumbs.

2. Stir in milk until dough leaves side of bowl (dough will be soft and sticky).

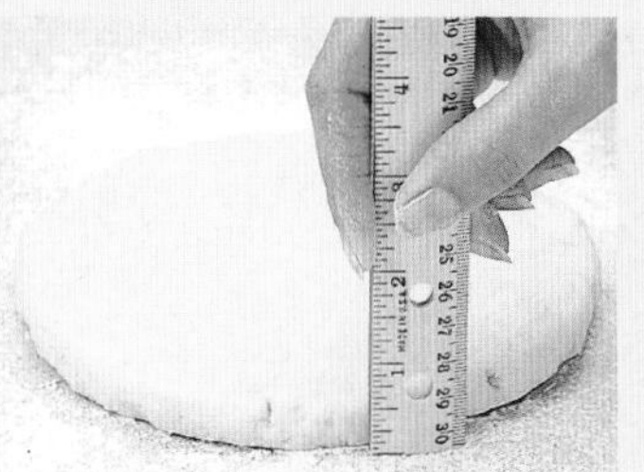

3. Roll or pat the dough 1/2 inch thick. Cut dough with a cutter that has been dipped in flour.

Baking Powder Biscuits

PREP: 10 min **BAKE:** 12 min ▪ **12 BISCUITS**

Plain biscuits hot out of the oven are delicious, but try one of the variations. Split the Sausage Biscuits, add a slice of cheese and you have a delicious handheld breakfast sandwich!

- 2 cups all-purpose flour*
- 1 tablespoon sugar
- 3 teaspoons baking powder
- 1 teaspoon salt
- 1/2 cup shortening
- 3/4 cup milk

1. Heat oven to 450°F.

2. In medium bowl, mix flour, sugar, baking powder and salt. Cut in shortening, using pastry blender (or pulling 2 table knives through ingredients in opposite directions), until mixture looks like fine crumbs. Stir in milk until dough leaves side of bowl (dough will be soft and sticky).

3. Place dough on lightly floured surface. Knead lightly 10 times. Roll or pat 1/2 inch thick. Cut with floured 2- to 2 1/4-inch round cutter. Place on ungreased cookie sheet about 1 inch apart for crusty sides, touching for soft sides.

4. Bake 10 to 12 minutes or until golden brown. Immediately remove from cookie sheet. Serve warm.

**If using self-rising flour, omit baking powder and salt.*

1 BISCUIT: CAL. 160 (CAL. FROM FAT 80); FAT 9g (SAT. FAT 2g); CHOL. 0mg; SODIUM 330mg; CARBS. 18g (FIBER 1g); PRO. 3g
% DAILY VALUE: VIT. A 0%; VIT. C 0%; CALC. 8%; IRON 6%
EXCHANGES: 1 STARCH, 2 FAT **CARB. CHOICES:** 1

BUTTERMILK BISCUITS Decrease baking powder to 2 teaspoons; add 1/4 teaspoon baking soda with the sugar. Substitute buttermilk for the milk. (If buttermilk is thick, using slightly more than 3/4 cup may be necessary.)

DROP BISCUITS Grease cookie sheet with shortening. Increase milk to 1 cup. Drop dough by 12 spoonfuls about 2 inches apart onto cookie sheet.

PESTO BISCUITS Decrease shortening to 1/3 cup, salt to 1/2 teaspoon and milk to 1/2 cup. Cut 1/4 cup Basil Pesto (page 405) or purchased basil pesto into flour mixture with the shortening. Sprinkle with grated Parmesan cheese before baking if desired.

SAUSAGE BISCUITS Decrease shortening to 1/3 cup and salt to 1/4 teaspoon. In 10-inch skillet, cook 1/2 lb bulk pork sausage over medium heat, stirring occasionally, until no longer pink; drain, cool slightly and crumble. Stir sausage into flour-shortening mixture before adding milk.

Easy Garlic-Cheese Biscuits FAST

PREP: 10 min **BAKE:** 10 min ▪ **10 TO 12 BISCUITS**

These biscuits are so yummy, you'll even find them on restaurant menus. Betty Crocker consumers often ask for this recipe.

- 2 cups Original Bisquick® mix
- 2/3 cup milk
- 1/2 cup shredded Cheddar cheese (2 oz)
- 1/4 cup butter or margarine, melted
- 1/4 teaspoon garlic powder

1. Heat oven to 450°F.

2. In medium bowl, stir Bisquick mix, milk and cheese with wire whisk or fork until soft dough forms; beat vigorously 30 seconds. On ungreased cookie sheet, drop dough by 10 to 12 spoonfuls about 2 inches apart.

3. Bake 8 to 10 minutes or until golden brown. In small bowl, stir butter and garlic powder until well mixed; brush on warm biscuits before removing from cookie sheet. Serve warm.

◀ **Easy Garlic-Cheese Biscuits**

1 BISCUIT: CAL. 165 (CAL. FROM FAT 90); FAT 10g (SAT. FAT 5g); CHOL. 20mg; SODIUM 410mg; CARBS. 15g (FIBER 0g); PRO. 4g **% DAILY VALUE:** VIT. A 4%; VIT. C 0%; CALC. 8%; IRON 4% **EXCHANGES:** 1 STARCH, 2 FAT **CARB. CHOICES:** 1

LIGHTER EASY GARLIC-CHEESE BISCUITS

For 2 grams of fat and 105 calories per serving, use Reduced Fat Bisquick® mix, fat-free (skim) milk and reduced-fat Cheddar cheese. Increase garlic powder to 1/2 teaspoon; stir in with the Bisquick mix. Omit butter. Spray warm biscuits with butter-flavored cooking spray if desired.

EASY HERBED-CHEESE BISCUITS Stir in 3/4 teaspoon dried dill weed, dried rosemary leaves, crumbled, or Italian seasoning with the Bisquick mix.

Scones

PREP: 15 min **BAKE:** 16 min ▪ **8 SCONES**

Scone comes from a Scot word (probably schoonbrot *or* sconbrot*) meaning "fine white breads." They're simple to make and resemble biscuits, except they're often sweeter, buttery, richer and more tender. If you have a pizza cutter, use it to cut the scones before and after baking.*

- 1 3/4 cups all-purpose flour*
- 3 tablespoons sugar
- 2 1/2 teaspoons baking powder
- 1/2 teaspoon salt
- 1/3 cup firm butter or margarine
- 1 large egg, beaten
- 1/2 teaspoon vanilla
- 4 to 6 tablespoons whipping (heavy) cream
- Additional whipping (heavy) cream
- White coarse sugar crystals (decorating sugar) or granulated sugar

1. Heat oven to 400°F.

2. In large bowl, mix flour, 3 tablespoons sugar, the baking powder and salt. Cut in butter, using pastry blender (or pulling 2 table knives through ingredients in opposite directions), until mixture looks like fine crumbs. Stir in egg, vanilla and just enough of the 4 to 6 tablespoons whipping cream so dough leaves side of bowl.

3. Place dough on lightly floured surface; gently roll in flour to coat. Knead lightly 10 times. On ungreased cookie sheet, roll or pat dough into 8-inch circle. Cut into 8 wedges with sharp knife that has been dipped in flour, but do not separate wedges. Brush with additional whipping cream; sprinkle with sugar crystals.

4. Bake 14 to 16 minutes or until light golden brown. Immediately remove from cookie sheet; carefully separate wedges. Serve warm.

**If using self-rising flour, omit baking powder and salt.*

1 SCONE: CAL. 225 (CAL. FROM FAT 100); FAT 11g (SAT. FAT 7g); CHOL. 55mg; SODIUM 360mg; CARBS. 27g (FIBER 1g); PRO. 4g
% DAILY VALUE: VIT. A 8%; VIT. C 0%; CALC. 10%; IRON 8%
EXCHANGES: 1 STARCH, 1 OTHER CARB., 2 FAT **CARB. CHOICES:** 2

CHOCOLATE CHIP SCONES Stir in 1/2 cup miniature semisweet chocolate chips with the egg, vanilla and whipping cream.

CURRANT SCONES Stir in 1/2 cup currants or raisins with the egg, vanilla and whipping cream.

RASPBERRY-WHITE CHOCOLATE SCONES Substitute almond extract for the vanilla; increase whipping cream to 1/2 cup. Stir in 3/4 cup frozen unsweetened raspberries (do not thaw) and 2/3 cup white baking chips with the egg, almond extract and whipping cream. Omit kneading step; pat dough into 8-inch circle on ungreased cookie sheet. Continue as directed, except bake 18 to 23 minutes.

Dumplings

PREP: 10 min **COOK:** 20 min ▪ **10 DUMPLINGS**

These dumplings are similar to biscuits except they are cooked on top of simmering stew. Drop them on top of Beef Stew (pages 430–431) or Burgundy Stew (pages 162–163).

1 1/2 cups all-purpose flour*
1 tablespoon parsley flakes, if desired
2 teaspoons baking powder
1/2 teaspoon salt
3 tablespoons shortening
3/4 cup milk

1. In medium bowl, mix flour, parsley, baking powder and salt. Cut in shortening, using pastry blender (or pulling 2 table knives through ingredients in opposite directions), until mixture looks like fine crumbs. Stir in milk.

2. Drop dough by 10 spoonfuls onto hot meat or vegetables in boiling stew (do not drop directly into liquid or dumplings may become soggy). Cook uncovered 10 minutes. Cover and cook 10 minutes longer.

**If using self-rising flour, omit baking powder and salt.*

1 DUMPLING: CAL. 105 (CAL. FROM FAT 35); FAT 4g (SAT. FAT 1g); CHOL. 0mg; SODIUM 220mg; CARBS. 15g (FIBER 1g); PRO. 3g
% DAILY VALUE: VIT. A 0%; VIT. C 0%; CALC. 8%; IRON 4%
EXCHANGES: 1 STARCH, 1/2 FAT **CARB. CHOICES:** 1

HERB DUMPLINGS Substitute 2 teaspoons chopped fresh herbs or 1 teaspoon dried herbs (such as basil, sage or thyme leaves or celery seed) for the parsley.

Popovers LOW-FAT

PREP: 10 min **BAKE:** 35 min ▪ **6 POPOVERS**

Popovers earn their name from their tendency to pop up high out of their baking cups in the oven. They're delicious fresh out of the oven but also can be baked ahead and reheated. After baking the popovers, pierce each with the point of a knife to let the steam out, and cool completely on a wire rack. When it's time to eat, just reheat on an ungreased cookie sheet at 350°F for 5 minutes.

2 large eggs
1 cup all-purpose flour*
1 cup milk
1/2 teaspoon salt

1. Heat oven to 450°F. Generously grease 6-cup popover pan with shortening. Heat popover pan in oven 5 minutes.

2. Meanwhile, in medium bowl, beat eggs slightly with fork or wire whisk. Beat in remaining ingredients just until smooth (do not overbeat or popovers may not puff as high). Fill cups about half full.

3. Bake 20 minutes.

4. Reduce oven temperature to 325°F. Bake 10 to 15 minutes longer or until deep golden brown. Immediately remove from cups. Serve hot.

**Do not use self-rising flour.*

1 POPOVER: CAL. 120 (CAL. FROM FAT 25); FAT 3g (SAT. FAT 1g); CHOL. 75mg; SODIUM 240mg; CARBS. 18g (FIBER 1g); PRO. 6g
% DAILY VALUE: VIT. A 4%; VIT. C 0%; CALC. 6%; IRON 6%
EXCHANGES: 1 STARCH, 1 FAT **CARB. CHOICES:** 1

PANCAKE, WAFFLE AND FRENCH TOAST TIPS

- Mix pancake batter in a 4- or 8-cup glass measuring cup with a handle and spout, then just pour it out onto the griddle or waffle iron.
- Serve immediately, or keep warm in a single layer on a wire rack or paper towel–lined cookie sheet in a 200°F oven. If you stack them, they'll become soggy.

Pancakes

PREP: 5 min **COOK:** 10 min ▪ **NINE 4-INCH PANCAKES**

1 large egg
1 cup all-purpose* or whole wheat flour
3/4 cup milk
1 tablespoon sugar
2 tablespoons vegetable oil
3 teaspoons baking powder
1/4 teaspoon salt

1. In medium bowl, beat egg with hand beater until fluffy. Beat in remaining ingredients just until smooth. For thinner pancakes, stir in additional 1 to 2 tablespoons milk.

2. Heat griddle or skillet over medium heat or to 375°F. (To test griddle, sprinkle with a few drops of water. If bubbles jump around, heat is just right.) Grease griddle with vegetable oil if necessary (or spray with cooking spray before heating).

3. For each pancake, use slightly less than 1/4 cup batter. Cook pancakes until bubbly on top, puffed and dry around edges. Turn and cook other sides until golden brown.

**If using self-rising flour, omit baking powder and salt.*

HOW TO DETERMINE WHEN TO TURN PANCAKES

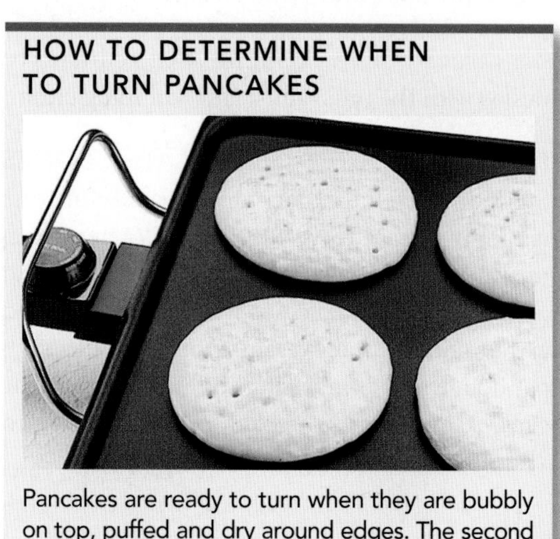

Pancakes are ready to turn when they are bubbly on top, puffed and dry around edges. The second side never browns as easily as the first.

1 PANCAKE: CAL. 110 (CAL. FROM FAT 45); FAT 5g (SAT. FAT 1g); CHOL. 25mg; SODIUM 250mg; CARBS. 13g (FIBER 0g); PRO. 3g
% DAILY VALUE: VIT. A 2%; VIT. C 0%; CALC. 12%; IRON 4%
EXCHANGES: 1 STARCH, 1/2 FAT **CARB. CHOICES:** 1

BERRY PANCAKES Stir 1/2 cup fresh or frozen (thawed and well drained) blackberries, blueberries or raspberries into batter.

BUTTERMILK PANCAKES Substitute 1 cup buttermilk for the 3/4 cup milk. Decrease baking powder to 1 teaspoon. Add 1/2 teaspoon baking soda.

Puffy Oven Pancake

PREP: 10 min **BAKE:** 30 min ▪ **2 TO 4 SERVINGS**

More like a popover than a pancake, this oven pancake puffs up high around the edges when it's done. Serve it quickly, before it sinks.

- 2 tablespoons butter or margarine
- 2 large eggs
- 1/2 cup all-purpose flour*
- 1/2 cup milk
- 1/4 teaspoon salt
- Lemon juice and powdered sugar or cut-up fruit, if desired

1. Heat oven to 400°F. In 9-inch pie plate, melt butter in oven; brush butter over bottom and side of pie plate.

2. In medium bowl, beat eggs slightly with wire whisk or hand beater. Beat in flour, milk and salt just until mixed (do not overbeat or pancake may not puff). Pour into pie plate.

3. Bake 25 to 30 minutes or until puffy and deep golden brown. Serve immediately sprinkled with lemon juice and powdered sugar or topped with fruit.

**Do not use self-rising flour.*

1 SERVING: CAL. 315 (CAL. FROM FAT 160); FAT 18g (SAT. FAT 10g); CHOL. 245mg; SODIUM 460mg; CARBS. 27g (FIBER 1g); PRO. 12g
% DAILY VALUE: VIT. A 16%; VIT. C 0%; CALC. 10%; IRON 12%
EXCHANGES: 2 STARCH, 1 LEAN MEAT, 2 FAT **CARB. CHOICES:** 2

APPLE OVEN PANCAKE Make Puffy Oven Pancake as directed—except sprinkle 2 tablespoons packed brown sugar and 1/4 teaspoon ground cinnamon evenly over melted butter in pie plate. Arrange 1 cup thinly sliced peeled baking apple (1 medium) over sugar. Pour batter over apple. Bake 30 to 35 minutes. Immediately loosen edge of pancake and turn upside down onto heatproof serving plate.

DOUBLE OVEN PANCAKE Melt 1/3 cup butter or margarine in 13 × 9-inch pan. Use 4 large eggs, 1 cup all-purpose flour, 1 cup milk and 1/4 teaspoon salt.

Puffy Oven Pancake

Crepes

PREP: 10 min **COOK:** 25 min ■ **12 CREPES**

Crepe *is French for "pancake," and is much thinner than a regular pancake.*

- 1 1/2 cups all-purpose flour*
- 1 tablespoon sugar
- 1/2 teaspoon baking powder
- 1/2 teaspoon salt
- 2 cups milk
- 2 tablespoons butter or margarine, melted
- 1/2 teaspoon vanilla
- 2 large eggs
- Butter, margarine or shortening
- Applesauce, sweetened berries, jelly or jam, if desired
- Powdered sugar, if desired

1. In medium bowl, mix flour, sugar, baking powder and salt. Stir in milk, 2 tablespoons butter, the vanilla and eggs. Beat with hand beater until smooth.

2. Lightly butter 6- to 8-inch skillet or crepe pan. Heat over medium heat until bubbly.

3. For each crepe, pour slightly less than 1/4 cup batter into skillet. Immediately rotate skillet until thin layer of batter covers bottom. Cook until light brown. Run wide spatula around edge to loosen; turn and cook other side until light brown. Repeat with remaining batter, buttering skillet as needed.

4. Stack crepes, placing waxed paper between each; keep covered. Spread applesauce, sweetened berries, jelly or jam thinly over each warm crepe; roll up. (Be sure to fill crepes so when rolled the more attractive side is on the outside.) Sprinkle with powdered sugar. Unfilled crepes can stacked with plastic wrap between each, then wrapped airtight and frozen up to 2 months.

**If using self-rising flour, omit baking powder and salt.*

1 CREPE: CAL. 150 (CAL. FROM FAT 70); FAT 8g (SAT. FAT 4g); CHOL. 55mg; SODIUM 190mg; CARBS. 15g (FIBER 0g); PRO. 4g
% DAILY VALUE: VIT. A 6%; VIT. C 0%; CALC. 6%; IRON 4%
EXCHANGES: 1 STARCH, 1 1/2 FAT **CARB. CHOICES:** 1

Waffles

PREP: 5 min **BAKE:** 5 min per waffle ■ **SIX 7-INCH ROUND WAFFLES**

Waffle irons use different amounts of batter, so you may end up with more or less than six waffles from this recipe.

- 2 large eggs
- 2 cups all-purpose* or whole wheat flour
- 1 3/4 cups milk
- 1/2 cup vegetable oil, melted butter or margarine
- 1 tablespoon sugar
- 4 teaspoons baking powder
- 1/4 teaspoon salt
- Fresh berries, if desired

1. Heat waffle iron. (Waffle irons without a nonstick coating may need to be brushed with vegetable oil or sprayed with cooking spray before batter for each waffle is added.)

2. In large bowl, beat eggs with wire whisk or hand beater until fluffy. Beat in remaining ingredients except berries just until smooth.

3. Pour slightly less than 3/4 cup batter onto center of hot waffle iron. (Check manufacturer's directions for recommended amount of batter.) Close lid of waffle iron.

4. Bake about 5 minutes or until steaming stops. Carefully remove waffle. Serve immediately. Top with fresh berries. Repeat with remaining batter.

**If using self-rising flour, omit baking powder and salt.*

1 WAFFLE: CAL. 380 (CAL. FROM FAT 200); FAT 22g (SAT. FAT 4g); CHOL. 75mg; SODIUM 480mg; CARBS. 38g (FIBER 1g); PRO. 9g
% DAILY VALUE: VIT. A 4%; VIT. C 0%; CALC. 28%; IRON 14%
EXCHANGES: 2 1/2 STARCH, 4 FAT **CARB. CHOICES:** 2 1/2

LIGHTER WAFFLES

For 7 grams of fat and 255 calories per serving, substitute 1/2 cup fat-free cholesterol free egg product for the eggs, use fat-free (skim) milk and decrease oil to 3 tablespoons.

French Toast LOW-FAT

PREP: 5 min **COOK:** 16 min ▪ **8 SLICES**

3 large eggs
3/4 cup milk
1 tablespoon sugar
1/4 teaspoon vanilla
1/8 teaspoon salt
8 slices sandwich bread or 1-inch-thick slices French bread

1. In medium bowl, beat eggs, milk, sugar, vanilla and salt with wire whisk or hand beater until well mixed. Pour into shallow bowl.

2. Heat griddle or skillet over medium heat or to 375°F. (To test griddle, sprinkle a few drops of water. If bubbles jump around, heat is just right.) Grease griddle with vegetable oil if necessary (or spray with cooking spray before heating).

3. Dip bread into egg mixture. Place on griddle. Cook about 4 minutes on each side or until golden brown.

1 SLICE: CAL. 110 (CAL. FROM FAT 25); FAT 3g (SAT. FAT 1g); CHOL. 80mg; SODIUM 210mg; CARBS. 15g (FIBER 1g); PRO. 5g
% DAILY VALUE: VIT. A 2%; VIT. C 0%; CALC. 6%; IRON 6%
EXCHANGES: 1 STARCH, 1/2 FAT **CARB. CHOICES:** 1

LIGHTER FRENCH TOAST

For 2 grams of fat and 95 calories per serving, substitute 1 egg and 2 egg whites for the 3 eggs and use 2/3 cup fat-free (skim) milk. Increase vanilla to 1/2 teaspoon.

OVEN FRENCH TOAST Heat oven to 500°F. Generously butter 15 × 10 × 1-inch pan. Heat pan in oven 1 minute; remove from oven. Arrange dipped bread in hot pan. Drizzle any remaining egg mixture over bread. Bake 5 to 8 minutes or until bottoms are golden brown; turn bread. Bake 2 to 4 minutes longer or until golden brown.

Corn Bread

PREP: 10 min **BAKE:** 25 min ▪ **12 SERVINGS**

There are many versions of corn bread. This one, sometimes called Yankee Corn Bread, is sweeter than the Southern Buttermilk Corn Bread recipe (page 80).

1 cup milk
1/4 cup butter or margarine, melted
1 large egg
1 1/4 cups yellow, white or blue cornmeal
1 cup all-purpose flour*
1/2 cup sugar
1 tablespoon baking powder
1/2 teaspoon salt

1. Heat oven to 400°F. Grease bottom and side of 9-inch round pan or 8-inch square pan with shortening or spray with cooking spray.

2. In large bowl, beat milk, butter and egg with hand beater or wire whisk. Stir in remaining ingredients all at once just until flour is moistened (batter will be lumpy). Pour into pan.

3. Bake 20 to 25 minutes or until golden brown and toothpick inserted in center comes out clean. Serve warm if desired.

**If using self-rising flour, omit baking powder and salt.*

1 SERVING: CAL. 175 (CAL. FROM FAT 45); FAT 5g (SAT. FAT 3g); CHOL. 30mg; SODIUM 260mg; CARBS. 29g (FIBER 1g); PRO. 4g
% DAILY VALUE: VIT. A 4%; VIT. C 0%; CALC. 10%; IRON 6%
EXCHANGES: 1 STARCH, 1 OTHER CARB., 1 FAT **CARB. CHOICES:** 2

CORN MUFFINS Grease bottoms only of 12 medium muffin cups with shortening or line with paper baking cups. Fill cups about 3/4 full.

Southern Buttermilk Corn Bread

PREP: 10 min **BAKE:** 30 min ■ **12 SERVINGS**

*Many Southerners like to bake their corn bread in a heavy black cast-iron skillet. First they coat the skillet with shortening. Then they preheat it in the oven until piping hot. As they pour in the batter, it bubbles and sizzles, forming a crispy crust on the bottom as it bakes.**

1 1/2 cups yellow, white or blue cornmeal
1/2 cup all-purpose flour**
1 1/2 cups buttermilk
1/4 cup vegetable oil or shortening
2 teaspoons baking powder
1 teaspoon sugar
1 teaspoon salt
1/2 teaspoon baking soda
2 large eggs

1. Heat oven to 450°F. Grease bottom and side of 9-inch round pan, 8-inch square pan or 10-inch ovenproof skillet with shortening or spray with cooking spray.

2. In large bowl, stir all ingredients until well mixed. Beat vigorously 30 seconds. Pour into pan.

3. Bake round or square pan 25 to 30 minutes, skillet about 20 minutes, or until golden brown and toothpick inserted in center comes out clean. Serve warm.

**This method has not been tested in the Betty Crocker Kitchens.*

***If using self-rising flour, decrease baking powder to 1 teaspoon and omit salt.*

1 SERVING: CAL. 145 (CAL. FROM FAT 55); FAT 6g (SAT. FAT 1g); CHOL. 35mg; SODIUM 370mg; CARBS. 19g (FIBER 1g); PRO. 4g
% DAILY VALUE: VIT. A 2%; VIT. C 0%; CALC. 8%; IRON 6%
EXCHANGES: 1 STARCH, 1 FAT **CARB. CHOICES:** 1

CHEESY MEXICAN CORN BREAD Decrease buttermilk to 1 cup. Stir in 1 can (8.5 oz) cream-style corn, 1 can (4.5 oz) chopped green chiles, well drained, 1/2 cup shredded Monterey Jack or Cheddar cheese (2 oz) and 1 teaspoon chili powder.

CORN STICKS Grease 18 corn stick pans with shortening. Fill about 7/8 full. Bake 12 to 15 minutes. Makes 18 corn sticks.

◀ **Southern Buttermilk Corn Bread**

Yeast Bread Basics

Who can resist the aroma of fresh-baked bread? Its wafting smell just says "home." And it's easier to make than you might think, even if you're new to baking. Making yeast breads isn't hard; they just take time for rising—but the results are worth the wait. From artisan-style Asiago Bread (page 85) to Caramel Sticky Rolls (page 95), in this chapter you'll find—and learn to make—breads that rise to any occasion.

CHOOSING THE RIGHT PAN

For well-browned crusts, use noninsulated pans and cookie sheets. Cookie sheets without a rim or sides also will allow better heat circulation, so the breads baked on them will brown better. If you're using pans with a dark nonstick coating, watch the bread carefully so it doesn't get too brown. Check the manufacturer's directions for oven temperature; sometimes reducing it by 25°F is recommended.

For dinner rolls and sweet rolls with tender, golden brown crusts, use shiny cookie sheets and muffin cups, which reflect heat.

YEAST BREAD INGREDIENTS

What does it take to make bread? Flour, yeast, water, salt and sugar are the most common bread ingredients, but there is more to the story.

All-Purpose Flour: All-purpose flour is the most widely used flour. The amount of protein in flour varies with the wheat crop; the moisture content can vary, too. That's why most recipes for kneaded dough give a range of amount of flour. See also Flour, page 19.

Bread Flour: Bread flour is made from a special blend of wheats higher in protein than the wheat used in all-purpose flour. Protein produces gluten, which gives structure and volume to yeast breads. Bread flour is ideal to use in bread machines as well as for all yeast breads. See also Flour, page 19.

Yeast: Yeast is a living organism that converts its food to alcohol and carbon dioxide. It's the carbon dioxide bubbles that make dough rise. Yeast is very sensitive—too much heat will kill it, and too much cold will prevent it from growing. Check the expiration date on the yeast package before using it.

Most of the recipes in this chapter follow the quick-mix method: mixing the yeast with part of the flour, then beating in very warm liquid (120°F to 130°F). Some recipes, however, turn out better if you use the traditional method of dissolving the yeast in warm water (105°F to 115°F).

If you're using quick active dry yeast, rising times may be shorter. Check the package directions for the best results.

For best results, be sure to use the temperatures for liquids given in each recipe. See also Yeast, page 23.

Liquids: Water and milk are usually used in yeast breads. Water gives bread a crisper crust; milk provides a velvety texture and added nutrients.

Sweeteners: Sugar, honey and molasses provide "food" for the yeast to help it grow, add flavor and help brown the crust. Don't use artificial sweeteners because they won't "feed" the yeast.

Salt: Salt is a flavoring needed to control the growth of the yeast and prevent the dough from rising too much, which can cause the bread to collapse. If you reduce the salt in a recipe, both rising times will need to be decreased too.

Fat: Butter, margarine, shortening and vegetable oil make bread tender. In addition to tenderness, butter and margarine add flavor.

Eggs: Eggs are sometimes added for flavor, richness and color.

HOW TO MAKE YEAST DOUGH

1. After the first addition of flour has been beaten in, the dough will be very soft and fall in "sheets" off a rubber spatula.

2. The second addition of flour makes dough stiff enough to knead. Mix in only enough flour so dough leaves the side of the bowl and is easy to handle.

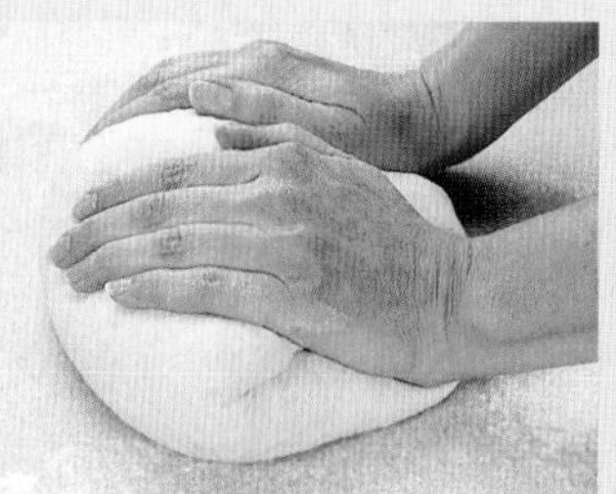

3. To knead, fold dough toward you. With heels of your hands, push dough away from you with a short rocking motion. Move dough a quarter turn; repeat. Dough will feel springy and smooth.

4. Place dough in a large bowl greased with shortening, turning dough to grease all sides.

5. Dough should rise until double in size. Press fingertips about 1/2 inch into dough. If indentations remain, dough has risen enough.

6. Gently push fist into dough to deflate. This releases large air bubbles to produce a finer texture in traditional loaves.

HOW TO SHAPE TRADITIONAL YEAST BREAD LOAVES

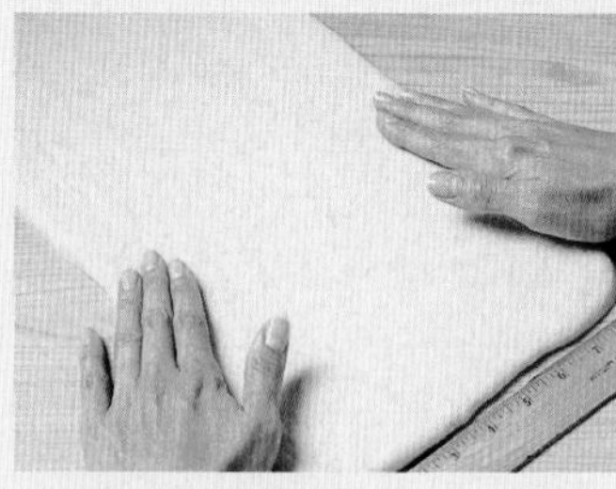

1. Flatten dough with hands or rolling pin into 18 × 9-inch rectangle.

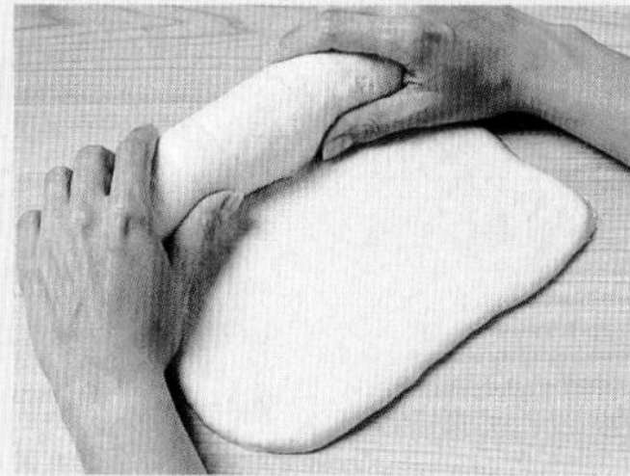

2. Tightly roll dough up toward you, beginning at a 9-inch side.

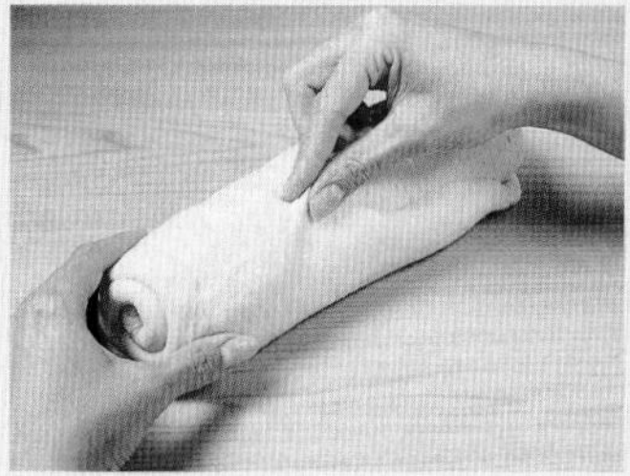

3. Pinch edge of dough into roll to seal.

YEAST BREAD CURES

The Best Yeast Breads and Rolls Are . . .

High and evenly shaped
Uniformly golden or dark brown
Even in texture with no large air holes

What Happened	Why
Not high	• water too hot for yeast • too little flour • not kneaded enough • rising time too short • pan too large
Coarse texture	• rising time too long • too little flour • not kneaded enough • oven too cool
Dry and crumbly	• too much flour • not kneaded enough
Large air pockets	• dough not rolled tightly when loaf was shaped
Yeasty flavor	• rising time too long • temperature too high during rising time

Classic White Bread LOW-FAT

PREP: 35 min **RISE:** 1 hr 50 min **BAKE:** 30 min ■
2 LOAVES, 16 SLICES EACH

6 to 7 cups all-purpose* or bread flour
3 tablespoons sugar
1 tablespoon salt
2 tablespoons shortening
2 packages regular or quick active dry yeast ($4^1/_2$ teaspoons)
$2^1/_4$ cups very warm water (120°F to 130°F)
2 tablespoons butter or margarine, melted, if desired

1. In large bowl, stir $3^1/_2$ cups of the flour, the sugar, salt, shortening and yeast until well mixed. Add warm water. Beat with electric mixer on low speed 1 minute, scraping bowl frequently. Beat on medium speed 1 minute, scraping bowl frequently. Stir in enough remaining flour, 1 cup at a time, to make dough easy to handle.

2. Place dough on lightly floured surface. Knead about 10 minutes or until dough is smooth and springy. Grease large bowl with shortening. Place dough in bowl, turning dough to grease all sides. Cover bowl loosely with plastic wrap and let rise in warm place 40 to 60 minutes or until dough has doubled in size. Dough is ready if indentation remains when touched.

3. Grease bottoms and sides of two 8 × 4-inch or 9 × 5-inch loaf pans with shortening or spray with cooking spray.

4. Gently push fist into dough to deflate. Divide dough in half. Flatten each half with hands or rolling pin into 18 × 9-inch rectangle on lightly floured surface. Roll dough up tightly, beginning at 9-inch side. Press with thumbs to seal after each turn. Pinch edge of dough into roll to seal. Pinch each end of roll to seal. Fold ends under loaf. (See How to Shape Traditional Yeast Bread Loaves, page 82.) Place seam side down in pan. Brush loaves lightly with butter. Cover loosely with plastic wrap and let rise in warm place 35 to 50 minutes or until dough has doubled in size.

5. Move oven rack to low position so that tops of pans will be in center of oven. Heat oven to 425°F.

6. Bake 25 to 30 minutes or until loaves are deep golden brown and sound hollow when tapped. Remove from pans to wire rack. Brush loaves with butter; cool.

**If using self-rising flour, omit salt.*

1 SLICE: CAL. 95 (CAL. FROM FAT 10); FAT 1g (SAT. FAT 0g); CHOL. 0mg; SODIUM 220mg; CARBS. 20g (FIBER 1g); PRO. 3g
% DAILY VALUE: VIT. A 0%; VIT. C 0%; CALC. 0%; IRON 6%
EXCHANGES: 1 STARCH **CARB. CHOICES:** 1

French Bread

PREP: 25 min **RISE:** 3 hr 15 min **CHILL:** 4 hr
BAKE: 20 min ▪ **2 LOAVES, 16 SLICES EACH**

The traditional flavor and texture of French bread is developed by making a sponge and by refrigerating the shaped loaves before baking. A sponge is a bread-dough mixture made in the first step with the yeast and some of the flour and water. Spraying the loaves with water and adding a water pan to the oven help make a crunchy crust. For the most delicious French Bread, serve it the same day you bake it.

- 1 1/2 cups all-purpose flour*
- 1 package regular active dry yeast (2 1/4 teaspoons)
- 1 cup very warm water (120°F to 130°F)
- 1 teaspoon salt
- 1 1/3 to 1 2/3 cups bread flour

1. In large bowl, mix all-purpose flour and yeast. Add warm water. Beat with wire whisk or electric mixer on low speed 1 minute, scraping bowl frequently, until batter is very smooth. Cover tightly with plastic wrap and let stand about 1 hour or until bubbly.

2. Stir in salt and enough bread flour, 1/2 cup at a time, until a soft dough forms. Place dough on lightly floured surface. Knead 5 to 10 minutes or until dough is smooth and springy (dough will be soft). Grease large bowl with shortening. Place dough in bowl, turning dough to grease all sides. Cover bowl loosely with plastic wrap and let rise in warm place 1 hour to 1 hour 15 minutes or until dough has doubled in size. Dough is ready if indentation remains when touched.

3. Grease uninsulated cookie sheet with shortening or spray with cooking spray. Place dough on lightly floured surface, forming it into an oval-shaped mound. Sprinkle top of dough with flour. Press straight down with a straight-edged knife lengthwise on dough to divide it into 2 equal parts (the parts will be elongated in shape). Gently shape each part into a narrow loaf, about 16 inches long, stretching the top of the loaf slightly to make it smooth. Place loaves, smooth sides up, about 4 inches apart on cookie sheet.

4. Cover loaves loosely, but airtight, with plastic wrap. (Loaves will expand slightly in the refrigerator.) Refrigerate at least 4 hours but no longer than 24 hours. (This step can be omitted, but refrigerating develops the flavor and texture of the bread. If omitted, continue with next step.)

5. Uncover loaves and spray with cool water; let loaves rise in warm place about 1 hour or until refrigerated loaves have come to room temperature.

6. Place 8-inch or 9-inch square pan on bottom rack of oven; add hot water to pan until about 1/2 inch from the top. Heat oven to 475°F.

7. Carefully cut 1/4-inch-deep slashes diagonally across loaves at 2-inch intervals with sharp serrated knife. Spray loaves with cool water. Place loaves in oven and spray again.

8. Reduce oven temperature to 450°F. Bake 18 to 20 minutes or until loaves are deep golden with crisp crust and sound hollow when tapped. Remove from cookie sheet to wire rack; cool.

**Do not use self-rising flour.*

1 SLICE: CAL. 40 (CAL. FROM FAT 0); FAT 0g (SAT. FAT 0g); CHOL. 0mg; SODIUM 75mg; CARBS. 9g (FIBER 0g); PRO. 1g
% DAILY VALUE: VIT. A 0%; VIT. C 0%; CALC. 0%; IRON 2%
EXCHANGES: 1/2 STARCH **CARB. CHOICES:** 1/2

MISTING AND CREATING STEAM

Like a crispy crust on your loaf of bread? It's easy—just create moisture in the oven. Using a spray bottle with a fine spray, mist the loaf with water a few times during the first 10 minutes of baking. This slows down the formation of the top crust, so the loaf will rise higher as it bakes and form a crisp crust. Or add moisture by placing a metal pan with hot water in the oven underneath the bread. As the water evaporates, it dries the surface of the bread, forming a crisp crust.

Asiago Bread LOW-FAT

PREP: 25 min **STAND:** 1 hr 15 min **RISE:** 2 hr
BAKE: 35 min ■ **1 LARGE LOAF, 24 SLICES**

This large, flour-dusted loaf is fun to serve! When you slice it, you'll find cheese-lined pockets scattered throughout.

- 3 1/2 to 3 3/4 cups bread flour
- 1 teaspoon sugar
- 1 package regular or quick active dry yeast (2 1/4 teaspoons)
- 1 1/4 cups very warm water (120°F to 130°F)
- 2 tablespoons olive or vegetable oil
- 2 teaspoons dried rosemary or thyme leaves, if desired
- 1 teaspoon salt
- 1 1/4 cups diced Asiago, Swiss or other firm cheese

1. In large bowl, mix 1 1/2 cups of the flour, the sugar and yeast. Add warm water. Beat with wire whisk or electric mixer on low speed 1 minute, scraping bowl frequently. Cover tightly with plastic wrap and let stand about 1 hour or until bubbly.

2. Stir in oil, rosemary and salt. Stir in enough remaining flour, 1/2 cup at a time, until a soft, smooth dough forms. Let stand 15 minutes.

3. Place dough on lightly floured surface. Knead 5 to 10 minutes or until dough is smooth and springy. Knead in 1 cup of the cheese. Grease large bowl with shortening. Place dough in bowl, turning dough to grease all sides. Cover bowl tightly with plastic wrap and let rise in warm place 45 to 60 minutes or until dough has doubled in size. Dough is ready if indentation remains when touched.

4. Lightly grease uninsulated cookie sheet with shortening or spray with cooking spray. Place dough on lightly floured surface. Gently shape into football-shaped loaf, about 12 inches long, by stretching sides of dough downward to make a smooth top. Place loaf with smooth side up on cookie sheet. Coat loaf generously with flour. Cover loosely with plastic wrap and let rise in warm place 45 to 60 minutes or until dough has almost doubled in size.

5. Place 8-inch or 9-inch square pan on bottom rack of oven; add hot water to pan until about 1/2 inch from the top. Heat oven to 450°F.

6. Spray loaf with cool water; sprinkle with flour. Carefully cut 1/2-inch-deep slash lengthwise down center of loaf with sharp serrated knife. Sprinkle remaining 1/4 cup cheese into slash.

7. Bake 10 minutes. Reduce oven temperature to 400°F. Bake 20 to 25 minutes longer or until loaf is deep golden and sounds hollow when tapped. Remove from cookie sheet to wire rack; cool.

1 SLICE: CAL. 105 (CAL. FROM FAT 25); FAT 3g (SAT. FAT 1g); CHOL. 5mg; SODIUM 115mg; CARBS. 16g (FIBER 1g); PRO. 4g
% DAILY VALUE: VIT. A 0%; VIT. C 0%; CALC. 6%; IRON 6%
EXCHANGES: 1 STARCH, 1/2 FAT **CARB. CHOICES:** 1

BAKING STONES AND TILES

Breads baked in professional ovens are often placed directly on heavy stones to create a crisp, brown crust. Duplicate a similar crust at home by using a bread stone, pizza stone or unglazed baking tiles available in cookware shops. Heat the stone or tiles according to manufacturer's directions. Sprinkle cornmeal over the stone. Carefully slide the shaped dough—not dough in a bread pan—directly onto the hot stone by sliding it from a cookie sheet or wooden paddle called a *pelle*. Using a pelle or 2 large spatulas, slide the bread out of the oven onto a cookie sheet, being careful not to touch the hot stone. Let the stone cool in the oven before removing it.

Cinnamon-Raisin-Walnut Wheat Bread

PREP: 25 min **STAND:** 15 min **RISE:** 2 hr **BAKE:** 40 min
▪ **1 LARGE LOAF, 24 SLICES**

- 2 cups whole wheat flour
- 1 package regular or quick active dry yeast (2 1/4 teaspoons)
- 2 cups very warm water (120°F to 130°F)
- 2 tablespoons packed brown sugar
- 2 tablespoons olive or vegetable oil
- 2 teaspoons ground cinnamon
- 2 teaspoons salt
- 2 to 2 1/2 cups bread flour
- 1 cup coarsely chopped walnuts
- 1 cup raisins
- Cornmeal

1. In large bowl, mix whole wheat flour and yeast. Add warm water. Beat with wire whisk or electric mixer on low speed 1 minute, scraping bowl frequently. Cover tightly with plastic wrap and let stand 15 minutes.

2. Stir in brown sugar, oil, cinnamon, salt and 1 cup of the bread flour; beat until smooth. Stir in enough remaining bread flour, 1/2 cup at a time, until a soft, smooth dough forms.

3. Place dough on lightly floured surface. Knead 5 to 10 minutes or until dough is smooth and springy. Knead in walnuts and raisins. Grease large bowl with shortening. Place dough in bowl, turning dough to grease all sides. Cover bowl loosely with plastic wrap and let rise in warm place about 1 hour or until dough has doubled in size. Dough is ready if indentation remains when touched.

4. Grease uninsulated cookie sheet with shortening or spray with cooking spray; sprinkle with cornmeal. Place dough on lightly floured surface. Gently shape into an even, round ball, without releasing all of the bubbles in the dough. Stretch sides of dough downward to make a smooth top. Place loaf with smooth side up on cookie sheet. Spray loaf with cool water. Cover loosely with plastic wrap and let rise in warm place 45 to 60 minutes or until dough has almost doubled in size.

5. Heat oven to 375°F. Spray loaf with cool water. Carefully cut 1/4-inch-deep slashes in tic-tac-toe pattern on top of loaf with sharp serrated knife.

6. Place in oven; spray with cool water. Bake 35 to 40 minutes or until loaf is dark brown and sounds hollow when tapped. Remove from cookie sheet to wire rack; cool.

1 SLICE: CAL. 150 (CAL. FROM FAT 45); FAT 5g (SAT. FAT 1g); CHOL. 0mg; SODIUM 200mg; CARBS. 24g (FIBER 2g); PRO. 4g
% DAILY VALUE: VIT. A 0%; VIT. C 0%; CALC. 2%; IRON 8%
EXCHANGES: 1 STARCH, 1/2 OTHER CARB., 1/2 FAT
CARB. CHOICES: 1 1/2

APPLE-PECAN BREAD Substitute chopped dried apples for the raisins and chopped pecans for the walnuts.

FRUIT AND ALMOND BREAD Omit cinnamon. Substitute diced dried fruit for the raisins and chopped almonds for the walnuts.

◀ **Cinnamon-Raisin-Walnut Wheat Bread**

Honey–Whole Wheat Bread LOW-FAT

PREP: 35 min **RISE:** 1 hr 50 min **BAKE:** 45 min ■
2 LOAVES, 16 SLICES EACH

3 cups whole wheat flour
1/3 cup honey
1/4 cup shortening
3 teaspoons salt
2 packages regular or quick active dry yeast (4 1/2 teaspoons)
2 1/4 cups very warm water (120°F to 130°F)
3 to 4 cups all-purpose* or bread flour
Butter or margarine, melted, if desired

1. In large bowl, beat whole wheat flour, honey, shortening, salt and yeast with electric mixer on low speed until well mixed. Add warm water. Beat with electric mixer on low speed 1 minute, scraping bowl frequently. Beat on medium speed 1 minute, scraping bowl frequently. Stir in enough all-purpose flour, 1 cup at a time, to make dough easy to handle.

2. Place dough on lightly floured surface. Knead about 10 minutes or until dough is smooth and springy. Grease large bowl with shortening. Place dough in bowl, turning dough to grease all sides. Cover bowl loosely with plastic wrap and let rise in warm place 40 to 60 minutes or until dough has doubled in size. Dough is ready if indentation remains when touched.

3. Grease bottoms and sides of two 8 × 4-inch or 9 × 5-inch loaf pans with shortening or spray with cooking spray.

4. Gently push fist into dough to deflate. Divide dough in half. Flatten each half with hands or rolling pin into 18 × 9-inch rectangle on lightly floured surface. Roll dough up tightly, beginning at 9-inch side. Press with thumbs to seal after each turn. Pinch edge of dough into roll to seal. Pinch each end of roll to seal. Fold ends under loaf. (See How to Shape Traditional Yeast Bread Loaves, page 82.) Place seam side down in pan. Brush loaves lightly with butter. Cover loosely with plastic wrap and let rise in warm place 35 to 50 minutes or until dough has doubled in size.

5. Move oven rack to low position so that tops of pans will be in center of oven. Heat oven to 375°F.

6. Bake 40 to 45 minutes or until loaves are deep golden brown and sound hollow when tapped. Remove from pans to wire rack. Brush loaves with butter; cool.

**If using self-rising flour, decrease salt to 1 teaspoon.*

1 SLICE: CAL. 100 (CAL. FROM FAT 20); FAT 2g (SAT. FAT 0g); CHOL. 0mg; SODIUM 220mg; CARBS. 22g (FIBER 2g); PRO. 3g
% DAILY VALUE: VIT. A 0%; VIT. C 0%; CALC. 0%; IRON 6%
EXCHANGES: 1 1/2 STARCH **CARB. CHOICES:** 1 1/2

SUNFLOWER-HERB WHOLE WHEAT BREAD

Add 1 tablespoon dried basil leaves and 2 teaspoons dried thyme leaves with the salt. Stir in 1 cup unsalted sunflower nuts with the all-purpose flour.

CUTTING BREAD

- Place loaf on a cutting board. Slice with a serrated bread knife or an electric knife.
- If bread is very fresh or still warm, turn it on its side to avoid squashing the top.
- Cut round loaves into wedges, or cut slices into fingers or fun shapes with cookie cutters.
- Make Bread Stuffing (pages 317–318) from the leftover pieces.

Rich Egg Bread LOW-FAT

PREP: 30 min **RISE:** 2 hr **BAKE:** 35 min ▪ **1 LOAF, 16 SLICES**

- 3 to 3 1/4 cups all-purpose* or bread flour
- 1/4 cup sugar
- 1 1/2 teaspoons salt
- 1 package regular or quick active dry yeast (2 1/4 teaspoons)
- 1 cup very warm water (120°F to 130°F)
- 2 tablespoons vegetable oil
- 1 large egg
- Butter or margarine, melted, if desired

1. In large bowl, mix 1 1/2 cups of the flour, the sugar, salt and yeast. Add warm water and oil. Beat with electric mixer on low speed 1 minute, scraping bowl frequently. Beat on medium speed 1 minute, scraping bowl frequently. Add egg; beat until smooth. Stir in enough remaining flour to make dough easy to handle.

2. Place dough on lightly floured surface. Knead about 10 minutes or until dough is smooth and springy. Grease large bowl with shortening. Place dough in bowl, turning dough to grease all sides. (At this point, dough can be refrigerated up to 24 hours.) Cover bowl loosely with plastic wrap and let rise in warm place about 1 hour or until dough has doubled in size. Dough is ready if indentation remains when touched.

3. Grease bottom and sides of 9 × 5-inch or 8 × 4-inch loaf pan with shortening or spray with cooking spray. Gently push fist into dough to deflate. Flatten dough with hands or rolling pin into 18 × 9-inch rectangle. Roll up tightly, beginning at 9-inch side. Pinch edge of dough into roll to seal. Pinch each end of roll to seal. Fold ends under loaf. (See How to Shape Traditional Yeast Bread Loaves, page 82.) Place loaf, seam side down, in pan. Cover loosely with plastic wrap lightly sprayed with cooking spray and let rise in warm place about 1 hour or until dough has doubled in size.

4. Move oven rack to low position so that top of pan will be in center of oven. Heat oven to 375°F. Bake 30 to 35 minutes or until loaf is deep golden brown and sounds hollow when tapped. Remove from pan to wire rack. Brush loaf with butter; cool.

**If using self-rising flour, omit salt.*

1 SLICE: CAL. 110 (CAL. FROM FAT 20); FAT 2g (SAT. FAT 0g); CHOL. 15mg; SODIUM 230mg; CARBS. 21g (FIBER 1g); PRO. 3g
% DAILY VALUE: VIT. A 0%; VIT. C 0%; CALC. 0%; IRON 6%
EXCHANGES: 1 1/2 STARCH **CARB. CHOICES:** 1 1/2

BREAD MACHINE DIRECTIONS

Use ingredients listed in recipe—except use 3 1/4 cups bread flour and room-temperature water. Measure carefully, placing all ingredients except butter in bread machine pan in the order recommended by the manufacturer. Select Dough/Manual cycle; do not use delay cycle. Remove dough from pan. Continue with Step 3 for shaping, rising and baking. Rising time may be shorter because dough will be warm when removed from bread machine.

CHALLAH BRAID Make dough as directed in recipe. Lightly grease cookie sheet with shortening or spray with cooking spray. After pushing fist into dough, divide into 3 equal parts. Roll each part into 14-inch rope. Place ropes close together on cookie sheet. Braid ropes gently and loosely, starting in middle; do not stretch. Pinch ends; tuck ends under braid securely. Brush with vegetable oil. Cover loosely with plastic wrap and let rise in warm place 40 to 50 minutes or until dough has doubled in size. Heat oven to 375°F. In small bowl, mix 1 egg yolk and 2 tablespoons water; brush over braid. Sprinkle with poppy seed, if desired. Bake 25 to 30 minutes or until golden brown.

HOW TO BRAID CHALLAH

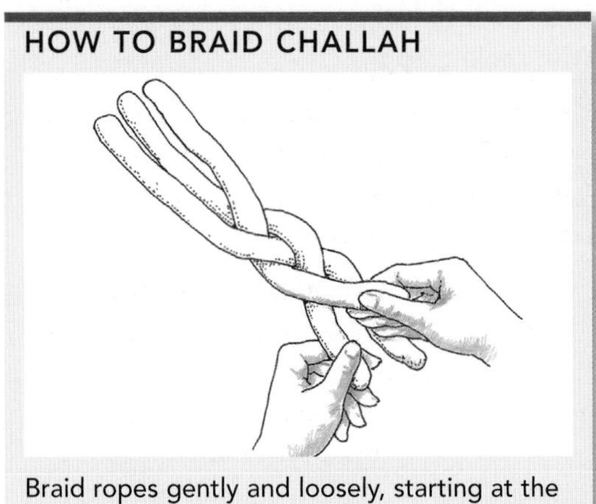

Braid ropes gently and loosely, starting at the middle; do not stretch.

Sourdough Bread LOW-FAT

PREP: 30 min **STAND:** 4 to 5 days **RISE:** 2 hr 15 min
BAKE: 45 min **COOL:** 1 hr ■ **2 LOAVES, 16 SLICES EACH**

1 cup Sourdough Starter
2 1/2 cups all-purpose or bread flour*
2 cups warm water (105°F to 115°F)
3 3/4 to 4 1/4 cups all-purpose or bread flour*
3 tablespoons sugar
1 teaspoon salt
3 tablespoons vegetable oil

1. In 3-quart glass bowl, mix Sourdough Starter, 2 1/2 cups flour and warm water with wooden spoon until smooth. Cover and let stand in warm, draft-free place 8 hours.

2. Add 3 3/4 cups flour, the sugar, salt and oil to mixture in bowl. Stir with wooden spoon until dough is smooth and flour is completely absorbed. (Dough should be just firm enough to gather into ball. If necessary, add remaining 1/2 cup flour gradually, stirring until all flour is absorbed.)

3. On heavily floured surface, knead dough about 10 minutes or until smooth and springy. Grease large bowl with shortening. Place dough in bowl, turning to grease all sides. Cover and let rise in warm place about 1 hour 30 minutes or until dough has doubled in size. Dough is ready if indentation remains when touched.

4. Grease large cookie sheet with shortening. Gently push fist into dough several times to remove air bubbles. Divide dough in half. Shape each half into a round, slightly flat loaf. Do not tear dough by pulling. Place loaves on opposite corners on cookie sheet. Make three 1/4-inch-deep slashes in top of each loaf with sharp knife. Cover and let rise about 45 minutes or until dough has doubled in size.

5. Heat oven to 375°F. Brush loaves with cold water. Place in middle of oven. Bake 35 to 45 minutes, brushing occasionally with water, until loaves sound hollow when tapped. Remove from cookie sheet to wire rack. Cool completely, about 1 hour.

Sourdough Starter

1 teaspoon regular active dry yeast
1/4 cup warm water (105°F to 115°F)
3/4 cup milk
1 cup all-purpose flour*

1. In 3-quart glass bowl, dissolve yeast in warm water. Stir in milk. Gradually stir in flour; beat until smooth. Cover with towel or cheesecloth; let stand in warm, draft-free place (80°F to 85°F) about 24 hours or until starter begins to ferment (bubbles will appear on surface of starter). If starter has not begun fermentation after 24 hours, discard and begin again. If fermentation has begun, stir well; cover tightly with plastic wrap and return to warm, draft-free place. Let starter stand 2 to 3 days or until foamy.

2. When starter has become foamy, stir well; pour into 1-quart crock or glass jar with tight-fitting cover. Store in refrigerator. Starter is ready to use when a clear liquid has risen to top. Stir before using. Use 1 cup starter in recipe; reserve remaining starter. To remaining starter, add 3/4 cup milk and 3/4 cup flour. Store covered at room temperature about 12 hours or until bubbles appear; refrigerate.

3. Use starter regularly, every week or so. If the volume of the breads you bake begins to decrease, dissolve 1 teaspoon active dry yeast in 1/4 cup warm water. Stir in 1/2 cup milk, 3/4 cup flour and the remaining starter.

**Do not use self-rising flour in this recipe.*

1 SLICE: CAL. 110 (CAL. FROM FAT 25); FAT 2.5g (SAT. FAT 0g); CHOL. 0mg; SODIUM 220mg; CARBS. 20g (FIBER 0g); PRO. 3g
% DAILY VALUE: VIT. A 0%; VIT. C 0%; CALC. 0%; IRON 6%
EXCHANGES: 1 1/2 STARCH **CARB. CHOICES:** 1

FASTER DOUGH RISING

To help yeast dough rise a little faster, place the covered bowl on a wire rack over a bowl of very warm water. Or let dough rise in the microwave: Fill a measuring cup with water and microwave until the water boils. Place the bowl of dough in the microwave with the steaming water.

Focaccia LOW-FAT

PREP: 30 min **RISE:** 1 hr **BAKE:** 20 min ▪
2 BREADS, 12 SLICES EACH

Serve slices with a bit of olive oil and shredded Parmesan cheese for dipping.

- 2 1/2 to 3 cups all-purpose* or bread flour
- 2 tablespoons chopped fresh or 1 tablespoon dried rosemary leaves, crumbled
- 1 tablespoon sugar
- 1 teaspoon salt
- 1 package regular or quick active dry yeast (2 1/4 teaspoons)
- 3 tablespoons olive or vegetable oil
- 1 cup very warm water (120°F to 130°F)
- 2 tablespoons olive or vegetable oil
- 1/4 cup grated Parmesan cheese

1. In large bowl, mix 1 cup of the flour, the rosemary, sugar, salt and yeast. Add 3 tablespoons oil and the warm water. Beat with electric mixer on medium speed 3 minutes, scraping bowl frequently. Stir in enough remaining flour until dough is soft and leaves sides of bowl.

2. Place dough on lightly floured surface. Knead 5 to 8 minutes or until dough is smooth and springy. Grease large bowl with shortening. Place dough in bowl, turning dough to grease all sides. Cover bowl loosely with plastic wrap and let rise in warm place about 30 minutes or until dough has almost doubled in size. Dough is ready if indentation remains when touched.

3. Grease 2 cookie sheets or 12-inch pizza pans with small amount of oil or spray with cooking spray.

4. Gently push fist into dough to deflate. Divide dough in half. Shape each half into a flattened 10-inch round on cookie sheet. Cover loosely with plastic wrap lightly sprayed with cooking spray and let rise in warm place about 30 minutes or until dough has doubled in size.

5. Heat oven to 400°F. Gently make 1/2-inch deep depressions about 2 inches apart in dough with fingers. Carefully brush with 2 tablespoons oil; sprinkle with cheese. Bake 15 to 20 minutes or until golden brown. Serve warm or cool.

**Do not use self-rising flour.*

1 SLICE: CAL. 80 (CAL. FROM FAT 25); FAT 3g (SAT. FAT 1g); CHOL. 0mg; SODIUM 120mg; CARBS. 12g (FIBER 0g); PRO. 2g
% DAILY VALUE: VIT. A 0%; VIT. C 0%; CALC. 2%; IRON 4%
EXCHANGES: 1 STARCH **CARB. CHOICES:** 1

CARAMELIZED ONION FOCACCIA Make dough as directed in recipe—except omit rosemary, 2 tablespoons oil and Parmesan cheese. Make onion topping: In nonstick 10-inch skillet, heat 1/3 cup olive or vegetable oil over medium heat. Stir in 4 cups thinly sliced onions (4 medium onions) and 4 cloves garlic, finely chopped, to coat with oil. Cook uncovered 10 minutes, stirring every 3 to 4 minutes. Reduce heat to medium-low. Cook 30 to 40 minutes longer, stirring well every 5 minutes, until onions are light golden brown. (Onions will shrink during cooking.) Continue as directed in recipe—except do not brush dough with oil; after second rising, carefully spread onion mixture over breads. Bake as directed.

BREADSTICKS Make dough as directed in recipe—except omit 2 tablespoons oil. After kneading, cover loosely with plastic wrap and let rest 30 minutes. Grease 2 cookie sheets with shortening or spray with cooking spray; sprinkle with cornmeal if desired. Divide dough into 12 equal pieces. Roll and shape each piece into 12-inch rope, sprinkling with flour if dough is too sticky. Place 1/2 inch apart on cookie sheets. Sprinkle with grated Parmesan cheese or coarse salt if desired. Cover loosely with plastic wrap and let rise in warm place about 20 minutes or until dough has almost doubled in size. Heat oven to 425°F. Bake 10 to 12 minutes or until golden brown.

HOW TO MAKE DEPRESSIONS IN FOCACCIA DOUGH

Gently make 1/2-inch deep depressions about 2 inches apart in dough with fingers.

Ciabatta Stirata

Ciabatta Stirata LOW-FAT

PREP: 25 min **RISE:** 1 hr 50 min **BAKE:** 35 min ■
2 LOAVES, 16 SLICES EACH

The word ciabatta *means "slipper," and* stirata *stands for "pulled and pressed."*

- 2 packages regular active dry yeast (4 1/2 teaspoons)
- 1 1/2 cups very warm water (115°F to 120°F)
- 3 to 3 1/4 cups bread flour or all-purpose flour
- 1 teaspoon salt
- 1/2 teaspoon sugar
- 1 tablespoon olive or vegetable oil

1. In small bowl, dissolve yeast in warm water. Let stand about 5 minutes, stirring occasionally, until yeast comes to top of water. Meanwhile, in large bowl, mix 3 cups of the flour, the salt and sugar.

2. Stir yeast mixture into flour mixture, using wooden spoon, until flour is moistened. Stir in oil. Shape dough into a ball, using hands. (Dough should be soft and slightly sticky. If dough is too wet, work in small amounts of flour until dough holds together.)

3. Place dough on lightly floured surface. Knead 10 to 12 minutes or until dough is smooth and springy. Grease large bowl with shortening; lightly flour. Place dough in bowl, turning dough to coat all sides. Cover and let rise in warm place about 40 minutes or until dough has doubled in size. Dough is ready if indentation remains when touched.

4. Gently push fist into dough to deflate. Place dough on lightly floured surface. Divide dough in half; shape each half into a ball. Cover and let rise on surface about 40 minutes or until dough has doubled in size.

5. Grease 2 large cookie sheets with shortening; lightly flour (or spray with cooking spray; do not flour). Stretch 1 ball of dough into 18 × 6-inch rectangle by pulling edges away from each other. (If dough is sticky, dust lightly with flour while stretching.) Place diagonally on cookie sheet. Gently flatten dough with fingers until about 1/2 inch thick. Repeat with remaining dough. Cover and let rise about 30 minutes or until dough has doubled in size. (Top will be uneven and bumpy.)

6. Heat oven to 375°F. Dust loaves lightly with flour. Bake 25 to 35 minutes or until loaves are golden brown and sound hollow when tapped. (If necessary, cover and refrigerate 1 loaf while the other loaf bakes.) Remove from cookie sheets to wire racks; cool.

1 SLICE: CAL. 55 (CAL. FROM FAT 10); FAT 1g (SAT. FAT 0g); CHOL. 0mg; SODIUM 75mg; CARBS. 10g (FIBER 0g); PRO. 2g
% DAILY VALUE: VIT. A 0%; VIT. C 0%; CALC. 0%; IRON 4%
EXCHANGES: 1/2 STARCH **CARB. CHOICES:** 1/2

Dinner Rolls

PREP: 30 min **RISE:** 1 hr 30 min **BAKE:** 15 min ▪
15 ROLLS

- 3 1/2 to 3 3/4 cups all-purpose flour* or bread flour
- 1/4 cup sugar
- 1/4 cup butter or margarine, softened
- 1 teaspoon salt
- 1 package regular or quick active dry yeast (2 1/4 teaspoons)
- 1/2 cup very warm water (120°F to 130°F)
- 1/2 cup very warm milk (120°F to 130°F)
- 1 large egg
- Butter or margarine, melted, if desired

1. In large bowl, stir 2 cups of the flour, the sugar, 1/4 cup butter, salt and yeast until well mixed. Add warm water, warm milk and egg. Beat with electric mixer on low speed 1 minute, scraping bowl frequently. Beat on medium speed 1 minute, scraping bowl frequently. Stir in enough remaining flour to make dough easy to handle.

2. Place dough on lightly floured surface. Knead about 5 minutes or until dough is smooth and springy. Grease large bowl with shortening. Place dough in bowl, turning dough to grease all sides. Cover bowl loosely with plastic wrap and let rise in warm place about 1 hour or until dough has doubled in size. Dough is ready if indentation remains when touched.

3. Grease bottom and sides of 13 × 9-inch pan with shortening or spray with cooking spray.

4. Gently push fist into dough to deflate. Divide dough into 15 equal pieces. Shape each piece into a ball; place in pan. Brush with butter. Cover loosely with plastic wrap and let rise in warm place about 30 minutes or until dough has doubled in size.

5. Heat oven to 375°F. Bake 12 to 15 minutes or until golden brown. Serve warm or cool.

**If using self-rising flour, omit salt.*

1 ROLL: CAL. 150 (CAL. FROM FAT 35); FAT 4g (SAT. FAT 2g); CHOL. 25mg; SODIUM 190mg; CARBS. 26g (FIBER 1g); PRO. 4g
% DAILY VALUE: VIT. A 2%; VIT. C 0%; CALC. 2%; IRON 8%
EXCHANGES: 2 STARCH **CARB. CHOICES:** 2

BREAD MACHINE DIRECTIONS

Use ingredients listed in recipe—except use 3 1/4 cups bread flour, 2 tablespoons softened butter, 3 teaspoons yeast and 1 cup room-temperature water for the warm water; omit milk. Measure carefully, placing all ingredients except melted butter in bread machine pan in the order recommended by the manufacturer. Select Dough/Manual cycle; do not use delay cycle. Remove dough from pan. Continue as directed in recipe for shaping, rising and baking. Rising time may be shorter because dough will be warm when removed from bread machine.

DO-AHEAD DINNER ROLLS After placing rolls in pan, cover tightly with foil and refrigerate 4 to 24 hours. Before baking, remove from refrigerator; remove foil and cover loosely with plastic wrap. Let rise in warm place about 2 hours or until dough has doubled in size. If some rising has occurred in the refrigerator, rising time may be less than 2 hours. Bake as directed.

CLOVERLEAF ROLLS Grease bottoms and sides of 24 medium muffin cups with shortening or spray with cooking spray. Make dough as directed in recipe—except after pushing fist into dough, divide dough into 72 equal pieces. (To divide, cut dough in half, then continue cutting pieces in half until there are 72 pieces.) Shape each piece into a ball. Place 3 balls in each muffin cup. Brush with butter. Cover loosely with plastic wrap and let rise in warm place about 30 minutes or until dough has doubled in size. Bake as directed. 24 rolls.

CRESCENT ROLLS Grease cookie sheet with shortening or spray with cooking spray. Make dough as directed in recipe—except after pushing fist into dough, cut dough in half. Roll each half into 12-inch circle on floured surface. Spread with softened butter. Cut each circle into 16 wedges. Roll up each wedge, beginning at rounded edge. Place rolls, with points underneath, on cookie sheet and curve slightly. Brush with butter. Cover loosely with plastic wrap and let rise in warm place about 30 minutes or until dough has doubled in size. Bake as directed. 32 rolls.

HOW TO SHAPE DINNER ROLLS

Shape each piece of dough into a ball; place in pan.

HOW TO SHAPE CLOVERLEAF ROLLS

Shape each piece of dough into a ball. Place 3 balls in each muffin cup.

HOW TO SHAPE CRESCENT ROLLS

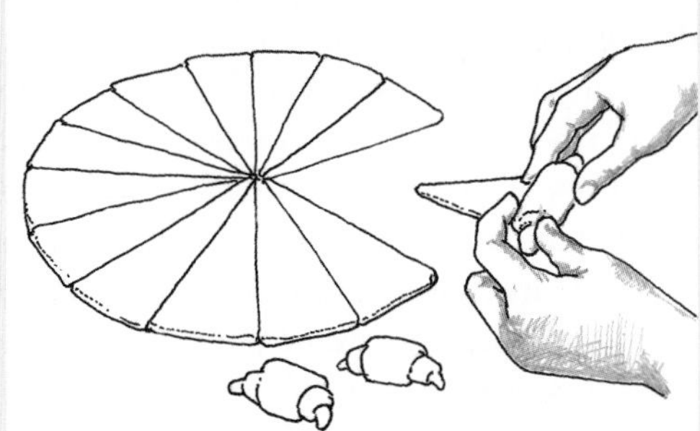

Cut each circle into 16 wedges. Roll up each wedge, beginning at rounded edge. Place rolls, with points underneath, on cookie sheet and curve slightly.

BREAD MACHINE TIPS

Enjoy the old-fashioned aroma and goodness of home-baked bread the fun and easy way—use an electric bread machine! Here are some tips to help you make the best bread-machine bread.

- Read the entire manual, especially the tips and hints.
- Add ingredients in the order listed by the manufacturer.
- Carefully measure ingredients with standard measuring cups and spoons. Even little variations can dramatically affect the finished loaf.
- Use room temperature ingredients, except for refrigerated items like milk, sour cream and eggs.
- For best results, use bread machine yeast; its finer granulation disperses more thoroughly during mixing and kneading.
- Checking the progress is tempting, but peek only during mixing and kneading. Opening the machine during rising or baking can cause the loaf to collapse.
- When using the delay cycle, be sure the yeast doesn't come in contact with liquid or wet ingredients. Don't use the delay cycle with recipes using eggs, fresh dairy products (except butter or margarine), honey, meats or fresh fruits and vegetables, because bacteria can grow during the cycle.
- If you get the urge to experiment by changing the ingredients, make just one change at a time so you can see the result.
- For consistent results, keep your bread machine in the same place, away from drafts or where heat and humidity fluctuate widely. Keep the area around your bread machine open for good ventilation.

Make-Ahead Potato Roll Dough

PREP: 30 min **CHILL:** 8 hr ▪ **YIELD WILL VARY DEPENDING ON TYPE OF ROLLS MADE.**

- 1 package regular active dry yeast ($2^1/_4$ teaspoons)
- $1^1/_2$ cups warm water (105°F to 115°F)
- 1 cup lukewarm unseasoned mashed potatoes
- $^2/_3$ cup sugar
- $^2/_3$ cup butter or margarine, softened
- $1^1/_2$ teaspoons salt
- 2 large eggs
- 7 to $7^1/_2$ cups all-purpose flour*

1. In large bowl, dissolve yeast in warm water. Stir in potatoes, sugar, butter, salt, eggs and 3 cups of the flour. Beat with electric mixer on low speed 1 minute or until smooth. Beat on medium speed 1 minute, scraping bowl frequently. Stir in enough remaining flour to make dough easy to handle.

2. Place dough on lightly floured surface; gently roll in flour to coat. Knead about 5 minutes or until dough is smooth and springy. Grease large bowl with shortening. Place dough in bowl, turning dough to grease all sides. Cover bowl tightly with plastic wrap and refrigerate at least 8 hours but no longer than 5 days.

3. Gently push fist into dough to deflate. Divide dough into 4 equal pieces. Use one-fourth of the dough for any Dinner Roll recipe below.

**Do not use self-rising flour.*

Note: Nutrition information is not possible to calculate because of recipe variables.

MAKE-AHEAD WHOLE WHEAT POTATO ROLL DOUGH Substitute 3 to 4 cups whole wheat flour for the second addition of all-purpose flour.

BROWN-AND-SERVE ROLLS Shape potato roll dough as directed in any roll recipe below. Cover and let rise in warm place 1 hour. Heat oven to 275°F. Bake 20 minutes (do not allow to brown). Remove from pans; cool to room temperature. Wrap in foil. Store in refrigerator up to 8 days or in freezer up to 2 months. At serving time, heat oven to 400°F. Bake 8 to 12 minutes or until brown.

COCKTAIL BUNS Make only $^1/_2$ of recipe. Grease cookie sheet with shortening or spray with cooking spray. Shape dough into 1-inch balls. Place 1 inch apart on cookie sheet. In small bowl, beat 1 egg yolk and 1 tablespoon water with fork. Brush tops of balls with egg mixture. Sprinkle with poppy seed or sesame seed. Cover and let rise in warm place about 1 hour or until dough has doubled in size. Heat oven to 400°F. Bake about 15 minutes or until golden brown. 4 dozen buns.

CRESCENT ROLLS Grease cookie sheet with shortening or spray with cooking spray. Roll one-fourth of potato roll dough into 12-inch circle about $^1/_4$ inch thick on well-floured surface. Spread with softened butter or margarine. Cut circle into 16 wedges. Roll up each wedge, beginning at rounded edge, stretching dough as it is rolled. Place rolls, with points underneath, on cookie sheet and curve slightly. Brush with softened butter or margarine. Cover and let rise in warm place about 1 hour or until dough has doubled in size. Heat oven to 400°F. Bake 15 minutes. 16 rolls.

FOUR-LEAF CLOVERS Grease bottom and sides of 8 to 10 medium muffin cups with shortening or spray with cooking spray. Shape one-fourth of potato roll dough into 2-inch balls. Place 1 ball in each muffin cup. With kitchen scissors, snip each ball completely in half, then into fourths. Brush with softened butter or margarine. Cover and let rise in warm place about 1 hour or until dough has doubled in size. Heat oven to 400°F. Bake 15 to 20 minutes. 8 to 10 rolls.

Caramel Sticky Rolls

PREP: 40 min **RISE:** 2 hr **BAKE:** 35 min ■ **15 ROLLS**

Rolls

3 1/2 to 4 cups all-purpose* or bread flour
1/3 cup granulated sugar
1 teaspoon salt
2 packages regular or quick active dry yeast (4 1/2 teaspoons)
1 cup very warm milk (120°F to 130°F)
1/4 cup butter or margarine, softened
1 large egg

Caramel Topping

1 cup packed brown sugar
1/2 cup butter or stick margarine, softened
1/4 cup corn syrup
1 cup pecan halves (4 oz), if desired

Filling

1/2 cup chopped pecans or raisins, if desired
1/4 cup granulated or packed brown sugar
1 teaspoon ground cinnamon
2 tablespoons butter or stick margarine, softened

1. In large bowl, mix 2 cups of the flour, 1/3 cup granulated sugar, the salt and yeast. Add warm milk, 1/4 cup butter and egg. Beat with electric mixer on low speed 1 minute, scraping bowl frequently. Beat on medium speed 1 minute, scraping bowl frequently. Stir in enough remaining flour to make dough easy to handle.

2. Place dough on lightly floured surface. Knead about 5 minutes or until dough is smooth and springy. Grease large bowl with shortening. Place dough in bowl, turning dough to grease all sides. Cover bowl loosely with plastic wrap and let rise in warm place about 1 hour 30 minutes or until dough has doubled in size. Dough is ready if indentation remains when touched.

3. In 2-quart saucepan, heat brown sugar and 1/2 cup butter to boiling, stirring constantly; remove from heat. Stir in corn syrup. Pour into ungreased 13 × 9-inch pan. Sprinkle with pecan halves.

4. In small bowl, mix all filling ingredients except 2 tablespoons butter; set aside.

5. Gently push fist into dough to deflate. Flatten dough with hands or rolling pin into 15 × 10-inch rectangle on lightly floured surface. Spread with 2 tablespoons butter; sprinkle with filling. Roll rectangle up tightly, beginning at 15-inch side. Pinch edge of dough into roll to seal. Stretch and shape until even. Cut roll into fifteen 1-inch slices with dental floss or a sharp serrated knife. Place slightly apart in pan. Cover loosely with plastic wrap and let rise in warm place about 30 minutes or until dough has doubled in size.

6. Heat oven to 350°F. Bake 30 to 35 minutes or until golden brown. Let stand 2 to 3 minutes. Place heatproof tray or serving plate upside down onto pan; immediately turn tray and pan over. Let pan remain 1 minute so caramel can drizzle over rolls; remove pan. Serve warm.

**If using self-rising flour, omit salt.*

1 ROLL: CAL. 335 (CAL. FROM FAT 110); FAT 12g (SAT. FAT 7g); CHOL. 45mg; SODIUM 250mg; CARBS. 51g (FIBER 1g); PRO. 5g
% DAILY VALUE: VIT. A 8%; VIT. C 0%; CALC. 4%; IRON 10%
EXCHANGES: 2 STARCH, 1 1/2 OTHER CARB., 2 FAT
CARB. CHOICES: 3 1/2

LIGHTER CARAMEL STICKY ROLLS

For 4 grams of fat and 255 calories per serving, make recipe as directed—except omit Caramel Topping and pecan halves. Line pan with foil; spray with cooking spray. Drizzle 1 cup caramel ice-cream topping over foil (heat topping slightly if it is stiff). Continue as directed in steps 4, 5, 6 and 7—except omit chopped pecans from Filling.

BREAD MACHINE DIRECTIONS

Use ingredients listed in recipe—except use 3 1/2 cups bread flour, 1 1/2 teaspoons yeast and 1 cup room-temperature water for the warm milk. Measure carefully, placing all ingredients for Rolls in bread machine pan in the order recommended by the manufacturer. Select Dough/Manual cycle; do not use Delay cycle. Remove dough from pan. Continue as directed in Step 3 for shaping, rising and baking. Rising time may be shorter because dough will be warm when removed from bread machine.

DO-AHEAD CARAMEL STICKY ROLLS After placing slices in pan, cover tightly with plastic wrap or foil and refrigerate 4 to 24 hours. Before baking, remove from refrigerator; remove plastic wrap or foil and cover loosely with plastic wrap. Let rise in warm place about 2 hours or until dough has doubled in size. If some rising has occurred in the refrigerator, rising time may be less than 2 hours. Bake as directed.

CINNAMON ROLLS Omit Caramel Topping and pecan halves. Grease bottom and sides of 13 × 9-inch pan with shortening or spray with cooking spray. Place dough slices in pan. Let rise and bake as directed in steps 4, 5, 6 and 7—except do not turn pan upside down. Remove rolls from pan to wire rack. Cool 10 minutes. Drizzle rolls with Vanilla Glaze (page 71) if desired.

HOW TO CUT CARAMEL STICKY ROLL DOUGH INTO EVEN SLICES

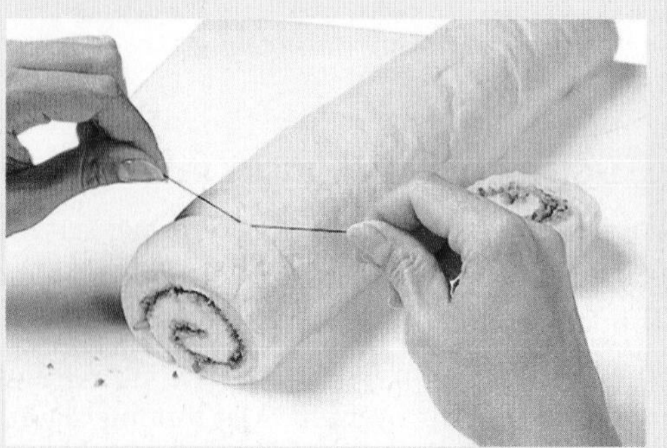

To cut even slices, place a piece of dental floss or heavy thread under the roll, bring ends of floss up and crisscross at top of roll, then pull ends in opposite directions. Or cut with a sharp serrated knife.

MAKING SIGNATURE BREAD CRUSTS

Just before baking, give your bread one of these professional finishing touches:

- *For a shiny crust,* brush the top of the bread with an egg or egg white beaten with a little water. If desired, sprinkle with poppy, caraway or sesame seed or rolled oats.
- *For a softer, deep golden brown crust,* brush with softened butter or margarine.
- *For a crisp crust,* brush or spray lightly with water.
- *For a soft, tender crust,* brush with milk.
- *After brushing the top of the loaf,* slash the top of the loaf with a sharp serrated knife, cutting about 1/4 inch deep, once down the center of the loaf or diagonally across the loaf a few times.

Four-Grain Batter Bread

LOW-FAT

PREP: 15 min **RISE:** 30 min **BAKE:** 25 min ▪
2 LOAVES, 16 SLICES EACH

Homemade bread doesn't get much easier than this! It's called batter bread because the dough is soft and doesn't require kneading. Just mix it, put it in the pan, let it rise and bake.

- Cornmeal
- 4 1/2 to 4 3/4 cups all-purpose* or bread flour
- 2 tablespoons sugar
- 1 teaspoon salt
- 1/4 teaspoon baking soda
- 2 packages regular or quick active dry yeast (4 1/2 teaspoons)
- 2 cups milk
- 1/2 cup water
- 1/2 cup whole wheat flour
- 1/2 cup wheat germ
- 1/2 cup quick-cooking oats

1. Grease bottoms and sides of two 8 × 4-inch loaf pans with shortening or spray with cooking spray; sprinkle with cornmeal.

2. In large bowl, mix 3 1/2 cups of the all-purpose flour, the sugar, salt, baking soda and yeast. In 1-quart saucepan, heat milk and water over medium heat, stirring occasionally, until very warm (120°F to 130°F). Add milk mixture to flour mixture. Beat with electric mixer on low speed until moistened. Beat on medium speed 3 minutes, scraping bowl occasionally.

3. Stir in whole wheat flour, wheat germ, oats and enough remaining all-purpose flour to make a stiff batter. Divide batter evenly between pans. Round tops of loaves by patting with floured hands. Sprinkle with cornmeal. Cover loosely with plastic wrap and let rise in warm place about 30 minutes or until batter is about 1 inch below tops of pans.

4. Heat oven to 400°F.

5. Bake about 25 minutes or until tops of loaves are light brown. Remove from pans to wire rack; cool.

**If using self-rising flour, omit salt and baking soda.*

1 SLICE: CAL. 95 (CAL. FROM FAT 10); FAT 1g (SAT. FAT 0g); CHOL. 0mg; SODIUM 90mg; CARBS. 19g (FIBER 1g); PRO. 4g
% DAILY VALUE: VIT. A 0%; VIT. C 0%; CALC. 2%; IRON 6%
EXCHANGES: 1 STARCH **CARB. CHOICES:** 1

WHOLE WHEAT BATTER BREAD Increase whole wheat flour to 2 cups. Omit wheat germ and oats. Stir in 1 cup raisins with the second addition of all-purpose flour.

Four-Grain Batter Bread ▶

Fresh Herb Batter Bread

LOW-FAT

PREP: 10 min **RISE:** 40 min **BAKE:** 45 min ▪ **1 LOAF, 20 SLICES**

- 3 cups all-purpose flour*
- 1 tablespoon sugar
- 1 teaspoon salt
- 1 package regular or quick active dry yeast (2 1/4 teaspoons)
- 1 1/4 cups very warm water (120°F to 130°F)
- 2 tablespoons chopped fresh parsley
- 2 tablespoons shortening
- 1 1/2 teaspoons chopped fresh or 1/2 teaspoon dried rosemary leaves
- 1/2 teaspoon chopped fresh or 1/4 teaspoon dried thyme leaves
- Butter or margarine, softened, if desired

1. Grease bottom and sides of 8 × 4-inch or 9 × 5-inch loaf pan with shortening or spray with cooking spray.

2. In large bowl, mix 2 cups of the flour, the sugar, salt and yeast. Add warm water, parsley, shortening, rosemary and thyme. Beat with electric mixer on low speed 1 minute, scraping bowl frequently. Beat on medium speed 1 minute, scraping bowl frequently. Stir in remaining 1 cup flour until smooth.

3. Spread batter evenly in pan. Round top of loaf by patting with floured hands. Cover loosely with plastic wrap lightly sprayed with cooking spray and let rise in warm place about 40 minutes or until dough has doubled in size.

4. Heat oven to 375°F.

5. Bake 40 to 45 minutes or until loaf sounds hollow when tapped. Immediately remove from pan to wire rack. Brush top of loaf with butter; sprinkle with additional chopped fresh herbs if desired. Cool.

**If using self-rising flour, omit salt.*

1 SLICE: CAL. 75 (CAL. FROM FAT 10); FAT 1g (SAT. FAT 0g); CHOL. 0mg; SODIUM 120mg; CARBS. 15g (FIBER 1g); PRO. 2g
% DAILY VALUE: VIT. A 0%; VIT. C 0%; CALC. 0%; IRON 4%
EXCHANGES: 1 STARCH **CARB. CHOICES:** 1

Garlic Bread

LOW-FAT

PREP: 10 min **BAKE:** 20 min ▪ **18 SLICES**

- 1 clove garlic, finely chopped, or 1/4 teaspoon garlic powder
- 1/3 cup butter or margarine, softened
- 1 loaf (1 lb) French bread, cut into 1-inch slices

1. Heat oven to 400°F.

2. In small bowl, stir garlic and butter until well mixed.

3. Spread butter mixture over 1 side of each bread slice. Reassemble loaf; wrap securely in heavy-duty foil.

4. Bake 15 to 20 minutes or until hot.

1 SLICE: CAL. 55 (CAL. FROM FAT 10); FAT 1g (SAT. FAT 0g); CHOL. 0mg; SODIUM 95mg; CARBS. 10g (FIBER 0g); PRO. 1g
% DAILY VALUE: VIT. A 0%; VIT. C 0%; CALC. 0%; IRON 4%
EXCHANGES: 1/2 STARCH **CARB. CHOICES:** 1/2

HERB-CHEESE BREAD Omit garlic. Mix 2 teaspoons chopped fresh parsley, 1/2 teaspoon dried oregano leaves, 2 tablespoons grated Parmesan cheese and 1/8 teaspoon garlic salt with the butter.

ONION BREAD Omit garlic if desired. Mix 2 tablespoons finely chopped onion or chives with the butter.

SEEDED BREAD Omit garlic is desired. Mix 1 teaspoon celery seed, poppy seed, dill seed or sesame seed with the butter.

CHAPTER 4

Cakes & Pies

Cakes

Pies & Pastry

LOW-FAT = *3g or less, except main dishes with 10g or less* FAST = *Ready in 20 minutes or less* BREAD MACHINE = *Bread machine directions* SLOW COOKER = *Slow cooker directions* LIGHTER = *25% fewer calories or grams of fat*

◄ **Starlight Yellow Cake (page 106) and Tropical Tres Leches Cake (page 107)**

Cake Basics

When it's time to celebrate, think cake! Whether the occasion's an anniversary, a birthday, a wedding, or perhaps a family reunion picnic, there's a cake in this collection that's perfect. There are classics like Angel Food and Pound, favorites like Banana and Carrot and fashionable newcomers like Molten Chocolate Cakes and Tres Leches Cake. And best of all, these recipes take the guesswork out of baking cakes and put the confidence in. So bake up a cake from our treasure trove of recipes, then stand back and wait for the compliments!

PICKING THE RIGHT PAN

- Use the size of pan called for in a recipe. To determine a pan's size, measure the length and width from inside edge to inside edge. If it's too big, your cake will be flat and dry; too small and it will form a peak or overflow the pan.
- Use shiny pans, which reflect heat, for tender, light brown crusts.
- Dark pans or pans with dark nonstick coating absorb heat easier than shiny pans, so baked goods may brown more quickly. Manufacturers may suggest reducing the oven temperature by 25°F to compensate for this.
- Fill cake pans half full. To determine how much batter novelty pans (heart or star shape, for example) can hold, fill the pan with water, then measure the water; use half that amount of batter. Extra batter? Make cupcakes!
- If you have only one 12-cup muffin pan, cover and refrigerate the remaining batter while the first batch of muffins is baking. Then bake the rest of the batter, adding 1 or 2 minutes to the bake time.

MIXING CAKES

Mixing the batter with the recommended ingredients and techniques helps to turn out a great cake time after time. Here are a few tips for sweet success:

- Cake recipes in this cookbook were tested with electric handheld mixers. If you're using a heavy-duty stand mixer, be sure to follow the manufacturer's directions for the speed setting because overmixing the batter causes tunnels or a sunken center.
- The stick form of butter or margarine is recommended. You may use vegetable-oil spread sticks that have at least 65 percent fat, but the batter consistency may be thinner.
- Vegetable-oil spreads with less than 65 percent fat, reduced-fat butter or any tub of whipped product are not recommended when making cakes. Because they contain more water and less fat, cakes will be tough and wet or gummy.

STORING CAKES

Follow these tips so your cake keeps fresh and delicious until the last piece is eaten.

- Unfrosted cakes: Cool completely before covering and storing to keep the top from becoming sticky.
- Cakes with a creamy powdered sugar frosting: Place in a cake taker or loosely cover with foil, plastic wrap or waxed paper. Store at room temperature.
- Cakes with White Mountain Frosting (page 117), or any egg white-based frostings: Best when served the same day you make them. When stored longer, meringue frostings tend to weep where they touch the cake. To help

lessen this effect, store leftovers in a cake taker with the lid placed on loosely or under a large upside-down bowl with a knife slipped under the edge so air can get in.

- Cakes with whipped cream toppings, cream fillings or cream cheese frostings: Place in a "cake taker" or loosely cover with foil or plastic wrap and refrigerate 3 to 5 days.
- Cakes with very moist ingredients like chopped apples, applesauce, shredded carrots or zucchini, mashed bananas or pumpkin: Refrigerate, especially during humid weather or in humid climates. If stored at room temperature, mold can grow quickly.

HOW TO SPLIT CAKE LAYERS

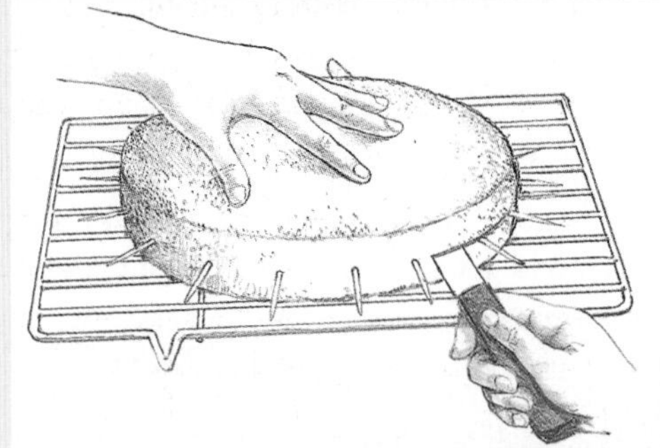

▲ **1.** Mark middle points around side of layer with toothpicks. Using picks as a guide, cut through the layer with a long, thin, sharp knife.

or

2. Split layer by pulling a piece of dental floss or heavy thread horizontally through the middle of the layer, moving floss in a back-and-forth motion. ▼

Shortening Cakes

Shortening cakes are made with butter, margarine or shortening, flour, eggs, a liquid and baking powder or baking soda.

BAKING SHORTENING CAKES

- Place oven rack in the middle position. Place pans in the center of the rack. Arrange round cake pans so they don't touch, leaving at least 1 inch of space between pans and sides of the oven. When making a recipe that uses three round pans, refrigerate batter in third pan if not all pans will fit in the oven at one time; bake third pan separately.
- Grease and flour pans as recommended in each recipe. Greasing with solid vegetable shortening is recommended. Butter, margarine and vegetable oil are not recommended for greasing.

COOLING AND REMOVING SHORTENING CAKES

- Cool cakes that will not be removed from the pan or pans on a wire rack until completely cool.
- Cool cakes that will be inverted, like round, fluted or tube pan cakes, in their pans on wire racks for 5 to 10 minutes.
- To remove a cake from the pan, insert a knife between the cake and the pan and slide it around the side to loosen the edge. Put a wire rack on top of the cake. Holding both the rack and the pan firmly, flip them over and lift the pan off the cake. Flip again onto another rack so the cake can cool top side up. Cool completely on wire racks.

CAKE CURES

The Best Shortening Cakes Are . . .

High, golden brown

Slightly rounded, smooth top

Fine-grained, even textured, not crumbly

Soft, velvety, slightly moist, light, tender

What Happened	Why
Pale	• too little sugar • baking time too short
Does not rise properly	• too much liquid • too much fat • pan too large • oven too cool
Peaked or cracked on top	• too much flour • oven too hot
Rim around edge	• pan sprayed with cooking spray
Coarse grained	• too much shortening
Crumbly	• too much shortening • too much sugar • underbeaten • too little egg (use large eggs)
Dry	• too much baking powder • baking time too long • too little liquid
Heavy, too moist	• too much liquid • too much shortening • too little flour
Batter overflows	• too much batter in pan • pan too small • too much leavening
Sticks to pan	• pan not greased enough • pan greased with oil (okay if not removing cake from pan) • cake left in pan too long before being removed

Chocolate Cake

PREP: 20 min **BAKE:** 45 min **COOL:** 1 hr 10 min ■ **12 SERVINGS**

2 1/4 cups all-purpose* or 2 1/2 cups cake flour
1 2/3 cups sugar
3/4 cup butter or margarine, softened
2/3 cup baking cocoa
1 1/4 cups water
1 1/4 teaspoons baking soda
1 teaspoon salt
1 teaspoon vanilla
1/4 teaspoon baking powder
2 large eggs
Fudge Frosting (page 115) or White Mountain Frosting (page 117), if desired

1. Heat oven to 350°F. Grease bottom and sides of one 13 × 9-inch pan, two 9-inch round pans or three 8-inch round pans with shortening; lightly flour.

2. In large bowl, beat all ingredients except frosting with electric mixer on low speed 30 seconds, scraping bowl constantly. Beat on high speed 3 minutes, scraping bowl occasionally. Pour into pan(s).

3. Bake 13 × 9-inch pan 40 to 45 minutes, round pans 30 to 35 minutes, or until toothpick inserted in center comes out clean. Cool rectangle in pan on wire rack. Cool rounds 10 minutes; remove from pans to wire rack. Cool completely, about 1 hour.

4. Frost 13 × 9-inch cake or fill and frost round layers with Fudge Frosting.

**Do not use self-rising flour.*

1 SERVING: CAL. 325 (CAL. FROM FAT 115); FAT 13g (SAT. FAT 8g); CHOL. 65mg; SODIUM 430mg; CARBS. 48g (FIBER 2g); PRO. 5g
% DAILY VALUE: VIT. A 10%; VIT. C 0%; CALC. 2%; IRON 10%
EXCHANGES: 2 STARCH, 1 OTHER CARB., 2 1/2 FAT
CARB. CHOICES: 3

German Chocolate Cake

PREP: 30 min **BAKE:** 40 min **COOL:** 1 hr 10 min ▪ **12 SERVINGS**

Samuel German, an employee of the Baker's chocolate factory, developed a sweet chocolate in 1852. Over a hundred years later, in 1957, a reader of a Dallas newspaper submitted her recipe for this now-famous three-tiered cake recipe with coconut-pecan frosting. Sales of sweet chocolate soared, and the rest is delicious history!

- 4 oz sweet baking chocolate
- 1/2 cup water
- 2 1/4 cups all-purpose* or 2 1/2 cups cake flour
- 1 teaspoon baking soda
- 1 teaspoon salt
- 2 cups sugar
- 1 cup butter or margarine, softened
- 4 large eggs
- 1 teaspoon vanilla
- 1 cup buttermilk
- Coconut-Pecan Filling and Topping (page 119), if desired

1. Heat oven to 350°F. Grease bottom and side of three 8-inch or 9-inch round pans with shortening. Line bottoms of pans with waxed paper or cooking parchment paper.

2. In 1-quart saucepan, heat chocolate and water over low heat, stirring frequently, until chocolate is completely melted; cool.

3. In medium bowl, mix flour, baking soda and salt; set aside. In another medium bowl, beat sugar and butter with electric mixer on high speed until light and fluffy. Separate eggs; reserve egg whites. Beat egg yolks, one at a time, into sugar mixture. Beat in chocolate and vanilla on low speed. Beat flour mixture into sugar mixture alternately with buttermilk on low speed, beating just until smooth after each addition.

4. Wash and dry mixer beaters. In small bowl, beat eggs whites on high speed until stiff; fold into batter. Pour into pans. Refrigerate batter in third pan if not all pans will fit in oven at one time; bake third pan separately.

5. Bake 8-inch pans 35 to 40 minutes, 9-inch pans 30 to 35 minutes, or until toothpick inserted in center comes out clean. Cool 10 minutes; remove from pans to wire rack. Remove waxed paper. Cool completely, about 1 hour.

6. Fill layers and frost top of cake with Coconut-Pecan Filling and Topping, leaving side of cake unfrosted. Store covered in refrigerator.

**Do not use self-rising flour.*

1 SERVING: CAL. 435 (CAL. FROM FAT 180); FAT 20g (SAT. FAT 12g); CHOL. 115mg; SODIUM 440mg; CARBS. 58g (FIBER 1g); PRO. 6g
% DAILY VALUE: VIT. A 14%; VIT. C 0%; CALC. 4%; IRON 8%
EXCHANGES: 2 STARCH, 2 OTHER CARB., 3 1/2 FAT
CARB. CHOICES: 4

Chocolate Snack Cake

PREP: 10 min **BAKE:** 35 min **COOL:** 15 min ▪ **9 SERVINGS**

You can leave your mixer in the cupboard when making this simple one-layer cake. Just stir it up with a spoon, bake it and enjoy it warm.

- 1 1/2 cups all-purpose flour*
- 1 cup sugar
- 1/4 cup baking cocoa
- 1 teaspoon baking soda
- 1/2 teaspoon salt
- 1/3 cup vegetable oil
- 1 teaspoon white or cider vinegar
- 1/2 teaspoon vanilla
- 1 cup cold water
- Ice cream or whipped cream, if desired

1. Heat oven to 350°F. Grease bottom and side of 9-inch round pan or 8-inch square pan with shortening; lightly flour.

2. In medium bowl, mix flour, sugar, cocoa, baking soda and salt. In small bowl, stir oil, vinegar and vanilla until well mixed. Vigorously stir oil mixture and water into flour mixture about 1 minute or until well blended. Immediately pour into pan.

3. Bake 30 to 35 minutes or until toothpick inserted in center comes out clean. Cool 15 minutes. Serve warm or cool with ice cream.

**Do not use self-rising flour.*

1 SERVING: CAL. 250 (CAL. FROM FAT 80); FAT 9g (SAT. FAT 1g); CHOL. 0mg; SODIUM 270mg; CARBS. 39g (FIBER 1g); PRO. 3g
% DAILY VALUE: VIT. A 0%; VIT. C 0%; CALC. 0%; IRON 6%
EXCHANGES: 1 STARCH, 1 1/2 OTHER CARB., 2 FAT
CARB. CHOICES: 2 1/2

CHOCOLATE CHIP SNACK CAKE Make cake as directed and pour into pan. Sprinkle with 1/3 cup miniature semisweet chocolate chips and 3 tablespoons sugar. Bake as directed.

Chocolate Snack Cake ▲

Date–Chocolate Chip Cake

PREP: 20 min **BAKE:** 55 min **COOL:** 2 hr 15 min ■ **12 SERVINGS**

Dates

1 1/4 cups boiling water
1 cup chopped dates
1 teaspoon baking soda

Chocolate Chip Topping

1/2 cup semisweet chocolate chips
1/4 cup packed brown sugar
1/4 cup all-purpose flour
1 tablespoon butter or margarine, softened

Cake

1 3/4 cups all-purpose flour*
1/2 cup granulated sugar
1/2 cup packed brown sugar
2/3 cup vegetable oil
1 teaspoon baking soda
1 teaspoon vanilla
1/2 teaspoon salt
2 eggs

1. In large bowl, pour boiling water on dates. Stir in 1 teaspoon baking soda. Cool about 15 minutes or until lukewarm.

2. In small bowl, mix all topping ingredients; set aside.

3. Heat oven to 350°F. Stir all cake ingredients into date mixture. Pour into ungreased 9-inch square pan. Sprinkle with topping.

4. Bake 50 to 55 minutes or until toothpick inserted in center comes out clean. Cool completely, about 2 hours.

**If using self-rising flour, omit the baking soda and salt in the cake.*

1 SERVING: CAL. 380 (CAL. FROM FAT 155); FAT 17g (SAT. FAT 5g); CHOL. 40mg; SODIUM 340mg; CARBS. 53g (FIBER 2g); PRO. 4g
% DAILY VALUE: VIT. A 2%; VIT. C 0%; CALC. 2%; IRON 10%
EXCHANGES: 1 STARCH, 1/2 FRUIT, 2 OTHER CARB., 3 1/2 FAT
CARB. CHOICES: 3 1/2

Molten Chocolate Cakes

PREP: 20 min **BAKE:** 14 min **STAND:** 3 min ▪
6 SERVINGS

Serve these cakes while they're still warm. Cut into them and a delicious rich chocolate center flows out. They make the ideal company dessert!

Baking cocoa
6 oz semisweet baking chocolate, chopped
1/2 cup plus 2 tablespoons butter or margarine
3 large whole eggs
3 large egg yolks
1 1/2 cups powdered sugar
1/2 cup all-purpose flour*
Additional powdered sugar, if desired

1. Heat oven to 450°F. Grease bottoms and sides of six 6-ounce custard cups with shortening; dust with cocoa.

2. In 2-quart saucepan, melt chocolate and butter over low heat, stirring frequently. Cool slightly.

3. In large bowl, beat whole eggs and egg yolks with wire whisk or hand beater until well blended. Beat in 1 1/2 cups powdered sugar. Beat in melted chocolate mixture and flour. Divide batter evenly among custard cups.** Place cups on cookie sheet with sides.

4. Bake 12 to 14 minutes or until sides are set and centers are still soft (tops will be puffed and cracked). Let stand 3 minutes. Run small knife or metal spatula along sides of cakes to loosen. Immediately place heatproof serving plate upside down onto each cup; turn plate and cup over and remove cup. Sprinkle with additional powdered sugar. Serve warm.

**Do not use self-rising flour.*

***Batter can be made up to 24 hours ahead. After pouring batter into custard cups, cover with plastic wrap and refrigerate up to 24 hours. You may need to bake the cakes 1 to 2 minutes longer.*

Note: Be sure to grease the custard cups with shortening, dust the cups with cocoa and bake the cakes at the correct oven temperature for the right time. These steps are critical to the success of this recipe. If the centers are too cakelike in texture, bake a few minutes less the next time; if they're too soft, bake a minute or two longer.

1 SERVING: CAL. 550 (CAL. FROM FAT 295); FAT 33g (SAT. FAT 19g); CHOL. 265mg; SODIUM 170mg; CARBS. 56g (FIBER 2g); PRO. 7g
% DAILY VALUE: VIT. A 20%; VIT. C 0%; CALC. 4%; IRON 10%
EXCHANGES: 2 STARCH, 2 OTHER CARB., 6 FAT
CARB. CHOICES: 4

LEARN WITH Betty — MOLTEN CHOCOLATE CAKES

These cakes are too runny because they were not baked long enough.

These cakes have a flowing chocolate center; there are no problems.

These cakes are completely cooked through because they were baked too long.

Silver White Cake

PREP: 10 min **BAKE:** 45 min **COOL:** 1 hr 10 min ■
12 SERVINGS

- $2^1/_4$ cups all-purpose* or $2^1/_2$ cups cake flour
- $1^2/_3$ cups sugar
- $^2/_3$ cup shortening
- $1^1/_4$ cups milk
- $3^1/_2$ teaspoons baking powder
- 1 teaspoon salt
- 1 teaspoon vanilla or almond extract
- 5 large egg whites
- White Mountain Frosting (page 117) or Chocolate Buttercream Frosting (page 115), if desired

1. Heat oven to 350°F. Grease bottom and sides of one 13 × 9-inch pan, two 9-inch round pans or three 8-inch round pans with shortening; lightly flour.

2. In large bowl, beat all ingredients except egg whites and frosting with electric mixer on low speed 30 seconds, scraping bowl constantly. Beat on high speed 2 minutes, scraping bowl occasionally.

3. Beat in egg whites on high speed 2 minutes, scraping bowl occasionally. Pour into pan(s).

4. Bake 13 × 9-inch pan 40 to 45 minutes, 9-inch pans 30 to 35 minutes, 8-inch pans 23 to 28 minutes, or until toothpick inserted in center comes out clean or until cake springs back when touched lightly in center. Cool rectangle in pan on wire rack. Cool rounds 10 minutes; remove from pans to wire rack. Cool completely, about 1 hour.

5. Frost 13 × 9-inch cake or fill and frost round layers with White Mountain Frosting.

**Do not use self-rising flour.*

1 SERVING: CAL. 320 (CAL. FROM FAT 110); FAT 12g (SAT. FAT 3g); CHOL. 0mg; SODIUM 370mg; CARBS. 47g (FIBER 1g); PRO. 5g
% DAILY VALUE: VIT. A 0%; VIT. C 0%; CALC. 10%; IRON 0%
EXCHANGES: 2 STARCH, 1 OTHER CARB., 2 FAT **CARB. CHOICES:** 3

CHOCOLATE CHIP CAKE Fold $^1/_2$ cup miniature or finely chopped regular semisweet chocolate chips into batter.

COCONUT-LEMON CAKE Spread rectangle or fill layers with Lemon Filling (page 120). Frost with White Mountain Frosting (page 117). Sprinkle cake with about 1 cup flaked or shredded coconut.

MARBLE CAKE Before pouring batter into pan(s), remove $1^3/_4$ cups of the batter; reserve. Pour remaining batter into pan(s). Stir 3 tablespoons baking cocoa and $^1/_8$ teaspoon baking soda into reserved batter. Drop chocolate batter by tablespoonfuls randomly onto white batter. Cut through batters with knife for marbled design. Bake and cool as directed in Step 4.

Starlight Yellow Cake

PREP: 10 min **BAKE:** 40 min **COOL:** 1 hr 10 min ■ **12 SERVINGS**

- 2 1/4 cups all-purpose flour*
- 1 1/2 cups sugar
- 1/2 cup butter or margarine, softened
- 1 1/4 cups milk
- 3 1/2 teaspoons baking powder
- 1 teaspoon salt
- 1 teaspoon vanilla
- 3 large eggs
- Chocolate Buttercream Frosting (page 115) or Peanut Butter Buttercream Frosting (page 116), if desired

1. Heat oven to 350°F. Grease bottom and sides of one 13 × 9-inch pan, two 9-inch round pans or three 8-inch round pans with shortening; lightly flour.

2. In large bowl, beat all ingredients except frosting with electric mixer on low speed 30 seconds, scraping bowl constantly. Beat on high speed 3 minutes, scraping bowl occasionally. Pour into pan(s).

3. Bake 13 × 9-inch pan 35 to 40 minutes, 9-inch pans 25 to 30 minutes, 8-inch pans 30 to 35 minutes, or until toothpick inserted in center comes out clean or until cake springs back when touched lightly in center. Cool rectangle in pan on wire rack. Cool rounds 10 minutes; remove from pans to wire rack. Cool completely, about 1 hour.

4. Frost 13 × 9-inch cake or fill and frost round layers with Chocolate Buttercream Frosting.

**If using self-rising flour, omit baking powder and salt.*

1 SERVING: CAL. 285 (CAL. FROM FAT 90); FAT 10g (SAT. FAT 6g); CHOL. 75mg; SODIUM 420mg; CARBS. 44g (FIBER 1g); PRO. 5g
% DAILY VALUE: VIT. A 8%; VIT. C 0%; CALC. 12%; IRON 8%
EXCHANGES: 2 STARCH, 1 OTHER CARB., 1 1/2 FAT
CARB. CHOICES: 3

PEANUT BUTTER CAKE Substitute peanut butter for the butter. Frost with Fudge Frosting (page 115) if desired.

◀ **Peanut Butter Cake with Creamy Cocoa Frosting**

Tres Leches Cake

PREP: 30 min **BAKE:** 40 min **STAND:** 5 min **CHILL:** 3 hr ■ **15 SERVINGS**

In Spanish, tres leches *means "three milks."*

- Starlight Yellow Cake (page 106)
- 1 cup whipping (heavy) cream
- 1 cup whole milk
- 1 can (14 oz) sweetened condensed milk
- 1/3 cup rum or 1 tablespoon rum extract plus enough water to measure 1/3 cup
- 1 cup whipping (heavy) cream
- 2 tablespoons rum or 1 teaspoon rum extract
- 1/2 teaspoon vanilla
- 1/2 cup chopped pecans, toasted (page 215)

1. Heat oven to 350°F. Grease bottom only of 13 × 9-inch pan with shortening. Make Starlight Yellow Cake. Pour batter into pan. Bake 35 to 40 minutes or until toothpick inserted in center comes out clear or until cake springs back when touched lightly in center. Let stand 5 minutes.

2. Pierce top of hot cake every 1/2 inch with long-tined fork, wiping fork occasionally to reduce sticking. In large bowl, stir 1 cup whipping cream, the whole milk, sweetened condensed milk and 1/3 cup rum until well mixed. Carefully pour milk mixture evenly over top of cake. Cover and refrigerate about 3 hours or until chilled and most of milk mixture has been absorbed into cake (surface of cake will be moist.)

3. In chilled large bowl, beat 1 cup whipping cream, 2 tablespoons rum and the vanilla with electric mixer on high speed until soft peaks form. Frost cake with whipped cream mixture. Sprinkle with pecans. Store covered in refrigerator.

1 SERVING: CAL. 475 (CAL. FROM FAT 215); FAT 24g (SAT. FAT 13g); CHOL. 110mg; SODIUM 400mg; CARBS. 57g (FIBER 1g); PRO. 8g
% DAILY VALUE: VIT. A 16%; VIT. C 0%; CALC. 24%; IRON 6%.
EXCHANGES: 2 STARCH, 2 OTHER CARB., 4 1/2 FAT **CARB. CHOICES:** 4

TROPICAL TRES LECHES CAKE Make cake as directed through Step 3—except omit pecans. Sprinkle with 1 cup flaked coconut, toasted (page 215) and 1/2 cup chopped macadamia nuts, toasted (page 215).

Pound Cake

PREP: 20 min **BAKE:** 1 hr 20 min **COOL:** 2 hr 20 min ■ **24 SERVINGS**

- 3 cups all-purpose flour*
- 1 teaspoon baking powder
- 1/4 teaspoon salt
- 2 1/2 cups granulated sugar
- 1 cup butter or margarine, softened
- 1 teaspoon vanilla or almond extract
- 5 large eggs
- 1 cup milk or evaporated milk
- Powdered sugar, if desired

1. Heat oven to 350°F. Grease bottom, side and tube of 10 × 4-inch angel food cake pan (tube pan), 12-cup fluted tube cake pan or two 9 × 5-inch loaf pans with shortening; lightly flour.

2. In medium bowl, mix flour, baking powder and salt; set aside. In large bowl, beat granulated sugar, butter, vanilla and eggs with electric mixer on low speed 30 seconds, scraping bowl constantly. Beat on high speed 5 minutes, scraping bowl occasionally. Beat flour mixture into sugar mixture alternately with milk on low speed, beating just until smooth after each addition. Pour into pan(s).

3. Bake angel food or fluted tube cake pan 1 hour 10 minutes to 1 hour 20 minutes, loaf pans 55 to 60 minutes, or until toothpick inserted in center comes out clean. Cool 20 minutes; remove from pan(s) to wire rack. Cool completely, about 2 hours. Sprinkle with powdered sugar.

**Do not use self-rising flour.*

1 SERVING: CAL. 225 (CAL. FROM FAT 80); FAT 9g (SAT. FAT 5g); CHOL. 65mg; SODIUM 115mg; CARBS. 33g (FIBER 0g); PRO. 3g
% DAILY VALUE: VIT. A 8%; VIT. C 0%; CALC. 2%; IRON 4%
EXCHANGES: 1 STARCH, 1 OTHER CARB., 2 FAT **CARB. CHOICES:** 2

LEMON-POPPY SEED POUND CAKE Substitute 1 teaspoon lemon extract for the vanilla. Fold 1 tablespoon grated lemon peel and 1/4 cup poppy seed into batter.

Sour Cream Spice Cake

PREP: 20 min **BAKE:** 45 min **COOL:** 1 hr ▪ **16 SERVINGS**

2 1/4 cups all-purpose flour*
1 1/2 cups packed brown sugar
1 cup raisins, chopped
1 cup sour cream
1/2 cup chopped walnuts
1/4 cup butter or margarine, softened
1/4 cup shortening
1/2 cup water
2 teaspoons ground cinnamon
1 1/4 teaspoons baking soda
1 teaspoon baking powder
3/4 teaspoon ground cloves
1/2 teaspoon salt
1/2 teaspoon ground nutmeg
2 large eggs
Browned Butter Buttercream Frosting (page 116), if desired

1. Heat oven to 350°F. Grease bottom and sides of one 13 × 9-inch pan or two 8-inch or 9-inch round pans with shortening; lightly flour.

2. In large bowl, beat all ingredients except frosting with electric mixer on low speed 30 seconds, scraping bowl constantly. Beat on high speed 3 minutes, scraping bowl occasionally. Pour into pan(s).

3. Bake 13 × 9-inch pan 40 to 45 minutes, round pans 30 to 35 minutes, or until toothpick inserted in center comes out clean. Cool completely, about 1 hour.

4. Frost 13 × 9-inch cake or fill and frost round layers with Browned Butter Buttercream Frosting.

**If using self-rising flour, decrease baking soda to 3/4 teaspoon and omit baking powder and salt.*

1 SERVING: CAL. 295 (CAL. FROM FAT 110); FAT 12g (SAT. FAT 5g); CHOL. 45mg; SODIUM 50mg; CARBS. 43g (FIBER 1g); PRO. 4g
% DAILY VALUE: VIT. A 4%; VIT. C 0%; CALC. 6%; IRON 10%
EXCHANGES: 1 STARCH, 2 OTHER CARB., 2 FAT **CARB. CHOICES:** 3

Rhubarb Spice Cake

PREP: 25 min **BAKE:** 50 min **COOL:** 1 hr ▪ **16 SERVINGS**

2 cups all-purpose flour*
1 1/2 cups sugar
1/2 cup vegetable oil
1/3 cup water
1 1/4 teaspoons baking soda
1 teaspoon salt
1 teaspoon ground cinnamon
1 teaspoon ground cloves
1 teaspoon ground nutmeg
1 teaspoon vanilla
3 large eggs
1 3/4 cups finely chopped fresh rhubarb
1 cup chopped nuts
Sweetened Whipped Cream (page 217), if desired

1. Heat oven to 350°F. Grease bottom and sides of 13 × 9-inch pan with shortening; lightly flour.

▲ **Rhubarb Spice Cake**

2. In large bowl, beat flour, 1 1/4 of the cups sugar and remaining ingredients except rhubarb nuts and Sweetened Whipped Cream with electric mixer on low speed 1 minute, scraping bowl constantly. Beat on medium speed 2 minutes, scraping bowl occasionally. Stir in rhubarb. Pour into pan. Sprinkle with nuts and remaining 1/4 cup sugar.

3. Bake 45 to 50 minutes or until toothpick inserted in center comes out clean. Cool completely, about 1 hour. Serve with Sweetened Whipped Cream.

**If using self-rising flour, omit baking soda and salt.*

1 SERVING: CAL. 260 (CAL. FROM FAT 115); FAT 13g (SAT. FAT 2g); CHOL. 40mg; SODIUM 260mg; CARBS. 32g (FIBER 1g); PRO. 4g
% DAILY VALUE: VIT. A 0%; VIT. C 0%; CALC. 4%; IRON 6%
EXCHANGES: 1 STARCH, 1 OTHER CARB., 3 FAT **CARB. CHOICES:** 2

Carrot Cake

PREP: 20 min **BAKE:** 45 min **COOL:** 1 hr 10 min ■ **12 SERVINGS**

- 1 1/2 cups sugar
- 1 cup vegetable oil
- 3 large eggs
- 2 cups all-purpose flour*
- 2 teaspoons ground cinnamon
- 1 teaspoon baking soda
- 1 teaspoon vanilla
- 1/2 teaspoon salt
- 3 cups shredded carrots (5 medium)
- 1 cup coarsely chopped nuts
- Cream Cheese Frosting (page 116), if desired

1. Heat oven to 350°F. Grease bottom and sides of one 13 × 9-inch pan or two 8-inch or 9-inch round pans with shortening; lightly flour.

2. In large bowl, beat sugar, oil and eggs with electric mixer on low speed about 30 seconds or until blended. Add flour, cinnamon, baking soda, vanilla and salt; beat on low speed 1 minute. Stir in carrots and nuts. Pour into pan(s).

3. Bake 13 × 9-inch pan 40 to 45 minutes, round pans 30 to 35 minutes, or until toothpick inserted in center comes out clean. Cool rectangle in pan on wire rack. Cool rounds 10 minutes; remove from pans to wire rack. Cool completely, about 1 hour.

4. Frost 13 × 9-inch cake or fill and frost round layers with Cream Cheese Frosting. Store covered in refrigerator.

**If using self-rising flour, omit baking soda and salt.*

1 SERVING: CAL. 440 (CAL. FROM FAT 235); FAT 26g (SAT. FAT 4g); CHOL. 55mg; SODIUM 230mg; CARBS. 46g (FIBER 2g); PRO. 5g
% DAILY VALUE: VIT. A 44%; VIT. C 2%; CALC. 2%; IRON 8%
EXCHANGES: 2 STARCH, 1 OTHER CARB., 5 FAT **CARB. CHOICES:** 3

LIGHTER CARROT CAKE

For 10 grams of fat and 280 calories per serving, substitute 1/2 cup unsweetened applesauce for 1/2 cup of the oil and 1 egg plus 4 egg whites for the eggs. Omit nuts.

APPLE CAKE Substitute 3 cups peeled, chopped tart apples (3 medium) for the carrots.

PINEAPPLE-CARROT CAKE Add 1 can (8 oz) crushed pineapple, drained, and 1/2 cup flaked or shredded coconut with the carrots.

ZUCCHINI CAKE Substitute 3 cups shredded zucchini (about 1 1/2 medium) for the carrots.

Banana Cake

PREP: 15 min **BAKE:** 50 min **COOL:** 1 hr 10 min ▪ **12 SERVINGS**

- $2^1/_2$ cups all-purpose flour*
- $1^1/_2$ cups mashed ripe bananas (3 medium)
- $1^1/_4$ cups sugar
- $^1/_2$ cup butter or margarine, softened
- $^1/_2$ cup buttermilk
- $1^1/_2$ teaspoons baking soda
- 1 teaspoon salt
- 1 teaspoon baking powder
- 2 large eggs
- $^2/_3$ cup chopped nuts
- Cream Cheese Frosting (page 116), if desired

1. Heat oven to 350°F. Grease bottom and sides of 13 × 9-inch pan or two 8-inch or 9-inch round pans with shortening; lightly flour.

2. In large bowl, beat all ingredients except nuts and frosting with electric mixer on low speed 30 seconds, scraping bowl constantly. Beat on high speed 3 minutes, scraping bowl occasionally. Stir in nuts. Pour into pan(s).

3. Bake 13 × 9-inch pan 45 to 50 minutes, round pans 40 to 45 minutes, or until toothpick inserted in center comes out clean. Cool rectangle in pan on wire rack. Cool rounds 10 minutes; remove from pans to wire rack. Cool completely, about 1 hour.

4. Frost 13 × 9-inch cake or fill and frost round layers with Cream Cheese Frosting.

**Do not use self-rising flour.*

1 SERVING: CAL. 330 (CAL. FROM FAT 115); FAT 13g (SAT. FAT 6g); CHOL. 55mg; SODIUM 470mg; CARBS. 49g (FIBER 2g); PRO. 5g
% DAILY VALUE: VIT. A 6%; VIT. C 2%; CALC. 4%; IRON 8%
EXCHANGES: 2 STARCH, 1 OTHER CARB., $2^1/_2$ FAT **CARB. CHOICES:** 3

APPLESAUCE CAKE Substitute $1^1/_2$ cups unsweetened applesauce for the bananas and $^1/_2$ cup water for the buttermilk. Add $1^1/_2$ teaspoons pumpkin pie spice; decrease baking powder to $^3/_4$ teaspoon. Stir in 1 cup raisins with the nuts. Frost with Maple-Nut Buttercream Frosting (page 116) or Cream Cheese Frosting (page 116).

Jeweled Fruitcake

PREP: 15 min **BAKE:** 1 hr 45 min **COOL:** 24 hr ▪ **32 SERVINGS**

- 2 cups dried apricots (11 oz)
- 2 cups pitted dates (12 oz)
- $1^1/_2$ cups nuts (8 oz)
- 1 cup red and green candied pineapple (7 oz), chopped
- 1 cup red and green maraschino cherries (12 oz), drained
- $^3/_4$ cup all-purpose flour*
- $^3/_4$ cup sugar
- $^1/_2$ teaspoon baking powder
- $^1/_2$ teaspoon salt
- $1^1/_2$ teaspoons vanilla
- 3 large eggs
- Light corn syrup, if desired

1. Heat oven to 300°F. Line 9 × 5-inch or 8 × 4-inch loaf pan with foil; grease foil with shortening.

2. In large bowl, stir all ingredients except corn syrup until well mixed. Spread in pan.

3. Bake about 1 hour 45 minutes or until toothpick inserted in center comes out clean. If necessary, cover with foil during last 30 minutes of baking to prevent excessive browning.

4. Remove fruitcake from pan (with foil) to wire rack. For a glossy top, immediately brush with corn syrup. Allow loaves to cool completely and become firm before cutting, about 24 hours. Wrap tightly and store in refrigerator no longer than 2 months.

**If using self-rising flour, omit baking powder and salt.*

1 SERVING: CAL. 200 (CAL. FROM FAT 55); FAT 6g (SAT. FAT 1g); CHOL. 20mg; SODIUM 100mg; CARBS. 35g (FIBER 3g); PRO. 2g
% DAILY VALUE: VIT. A 8%; VIT. C 0%; CALC. 2%; IRON 4%
EXCHANGES: 1 STARCH, 1 FRUIT, 1 FAT **CARB. CHOICES:** 2

MINI JEWELED FRUITCAKE LOAVES Generously grease bottoms and sides of 8 miniature loaf pans, $4^1/_2 \times 2^3/_4 \times 1^1/_4$ inches, with shortening, or line with foil and grease with shortening. Divide batter evenly among pans (about 1 cup each). Bake about 1 hour or until toothpick inserted in center comes out clean. Remove from pans to wire rack. Allow loaves to cool completely and become firm before cutting, about 24 hours. 8 mini loaves.

Foam Cakes

Foam cakes like angel food, sponge and chiffon depend on beaten egg whites for their light and airy texture, but they do differ.

- Angel food cakes have no added leavening (like baking powder), no shortening and no egg yolks. They have a high proportion of beaten egg whites to flour. See Angel Food Cake, page 112.
- Chiffon cakes are a cross between foam and shortening cakes because they're made with leavening, vegetable oil or shortening and egg yolks, as well as beaten whites. See Lemon Chiffon Cake, page 113.
- Sponge cakes use both egg whites and yolks and sometimes a little leavening, but like angel food cakes, they don't contain shortening.

MIXING FOAM CAKES

The secret for making spectacular high and light foam cakes each time? Start with a clean, dry bowl and beaters so the egg whites will beat properly. Even a speck of fat from an egg yolk will keep them from whipping up.

BAKING FOAM CAKES

Don't grease and flour pans for foam cakes unless directed to in the recipe. During baking, the batter has to cling to and climb up the side and tube of the pan.

If you're using an angel food cake pan (tube pan), move the oven rack to the lowest position so the cake will bake completely without getting too brown on top.

FOAM CAKE CURES

The Best Foam Cakes Are . . .

High, golden brown with rounded tops and cracks in surface
Soft, moist and delicate
Angel Food—feathery and fine-textured
Chiffon—springy and medium-textured
Sponge—springy and fine-textured

What Happened	Why
Low and compact	• underbeaten or extremely overbeaten egg whites (use medium speeds on powerful stand mixers) • overfolded batter • incorrect cooling (not cooled upside down) • underbaked
Coarse	• underfolded batter
Tough	• underbeaten egg whites • overfolded batter

Angel Food Cake

PREP: 20 min **BAKE:** 35 min **COOL:** 2 hr ■
12 SERVINGS

Make some Lemon Curd or Lime Curd (page 421) with the leftover yolks.

- 1 1/2 cups powdered sugar
- 1 cup cake flour
- 1 1/2 cups large egg whites (about 12)
- 1 1/2 teaspoons cream of tartar
- 1 cup granulated sugar
- 1 1/2 teaspoons vanilla
- 1/2 teaspoon almond extract
- 1/4 teaspoon salt
- Vanilla Glaze (page 118) or Chocolate Glaze (page 118), if desired

1. Move oven rack to lowest position. Heat oven to 375°F.

2. In medium bowl, mix powdered sugar and flour; set aside. In large bowl, beat egg whites and cream of tartar with electric mixer on medium speed until foamy. Beat in granulated sugar, 2 tablespoons at a time, on high speed, adding vanilla, almond extract and salt with the last addition of sugar. Continue beating until stiff and glossy. Do not underbeat.

3. Sprinkle powdered sugar–flour mixture, 1/4 cup at a time, over egg white mixture, folding in with rubber spatula just until sugar-flour mixture disappears. Push batter into ungreased 10 × 4-inch angel food cake pan (tube pan). Cut gently through batter with metal spatula or knife to break air pockets.

4. Bake 30 to 35 minutes or until cracks feel dry and top springs back when touched lightly. Immediately turn pan upside down onto heatproof funnel or bottle. Let hang about 2 hours or until cake is completely cool. Loosen side of cake with knife or long metal spatula; remove from pan.

5. Spread or drizzle Vanilla Glaze over top of cake.

1 SERVING: CAL. 180 (CAL. FROM FAT 0); FAT 0g (SAT. FAT 0g); CHOL. 0mg; SODIUM 100mg; CARBS. 40g (FIBER 0g); PRO. 4g
% DAILY VALUE: VIT. A 0%; VIT. C 0%; CALC. 0%; IRON 4%
EXCHANGES: 1 1/2 STARCH, 1 OTHER CARB.
CARB. CHOICES: 2 1/2

CHOCOLATE CONFETTI ANGEL FOOD CAKE Stir 2 oz grated semisweet baking chocolate into powdered sugar and flour in Step 2. Continue as directed.

HOW TO MAKE ANGEL FOOD CAKES

Beat egg whites and sugar until stiff and glossy.

To fold sugar-flour mixture into beaten egg white mixture, use a rubber spatula to cut down vertically through center of egg whites, across the bottom of the bowl and up the side, turning the egg whites over. Rotate bowl one-fourth turn and repeat. Continue folding in this way just until ingredients are blended.

Use a metal spatula to cut through batter, pushing batter gently against side of pan and tube, to break large air pockets.

Lemon Chiffon Cake

PREP: 20 min **BAKE:** 1 hr 15 min **COOL:** 2 hr ■
12 SERVINGS

Here's a cake that serves up the best of both worlds—the lightness of angel food and the richness of a layer cake.

- 2 cups all-purpose* or $2^1/_4$ cups cake flour
- $1^1/_2$ cups sugar
- 3 teaspoons baking powder
- 1 teaspoon salt
- $^3/_4$ cup cold water
- $^1/_2$ cup vegetable oil
- 2 teaspoons vanilla
- 1 tablespoon grated lemon peel
- 7 large egg yolks (with all-purpose flour) or 5 large egg yolks (with cake flour)
- 1 cup large egg whites (about 8)
- $^1/_2$ teaspoon cream of tartar
- Lemon Glaze (page 118), if desired

1. Move oven rack to lowest position. Heat oven to 325°F.

2. In large bowl, mix flour, sugar, baking powder and salt. Beat in water, oil, vanilla, lemon peel and egg yolks with electric mixer on low speed until smooth.

3. Wash and dry mixer beaters. In large bowl, beat egg whites and cream of tartar with electric mixer on high speed until stiff peaks form. Gradually pour egg yolk mixture over beaten egg whites, folding in with rubber spatula just until blended. Pour into ungreased 10 × 4-inch angel food cake pan (tube pan).

4. Bake about 1 hour 15 minutes or until top springs back when touched lightly. Immediately turn pan upside down onto heatproof funnel or bottle. Let hang about 2 hours or until cake is completely cool. Loosen side of cake with knife or long metal spatula; remove from pan.

5. Spread Lemon Glaze over top of cake, allowing some to drizzle down side.

**If using self-rising flour, omit baking powder and salt.*

1 SERVING: CAL. 300 (CAL. FROM FAT 110); FAT 12g (SAT. FAT 2g); CHOL. 125mg; SODIUM 360mg; CARBS. 42g (FIBER 1g); PRO. 6g
% DAILY VALUE: VIT. A 4%; VIT. C 0%; CALC. 8%; IRON 8%
EXCHANGES: 2 STARCH, 1 OTHER CARB., 1 FAT **CARB. CHOICES:** 3

ORANGE CHIFFON CAKE Omit vanilla. Substitute 2 tablespoons grated orange peel for the lemon peel.

HOW TO COOL A FOAM CAKE

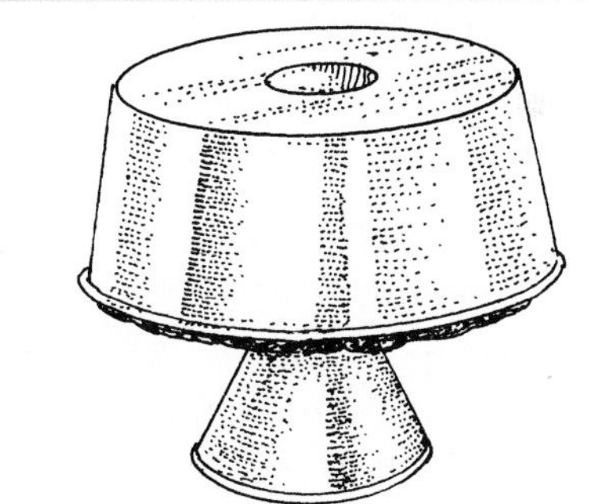

Immediately turn pan upside down onto heatproof bottle or funnel (plastic funnel can be wrapped with foil to make heatproof).

CUTTING CAKES

Layer Cakes: Use a long, thin, sharp knife.

Angel Food, Chiffon, Pound Cakes: Use a long serrated knife in a sawing motion, or use an electric knife.

Fruitcake: Use a long, thin, sharp knife or electric knife. Fruitcakes are easier to cut after standing at least 24 hours. If frosting sticks to the knife, dip knife in hot water and wipe with a damp paper towel after cutting each slice.

Tips for Frosting

- Frosting should be soft enough to spread without running down the sides. If frosting is too stiff, it will pull and tear the cake surface, adding crumbs to the frosting. If frosting is too thin, add more powdered sugar, a couple of tablespoons at a time; if too thick, add a few drops of water or milk.
- Butter and margarine in the stick form are the best for making frostings. Vegetable-oil spreads, tub margarine and tub or whipped butter are not recommended because they contain more water and/or air and less fat, so frostings made with them turn out too soft. Also, ingredients like chocolate don't always melt or mix well with them.
- For the easiest frosting, use a flexible metal spatula. Use a light touch when frosting a cake to help prevent cake layers from sliding and from squishing out the filling from between layers.

HOW TO FROST A TWO-LAYER CAKE

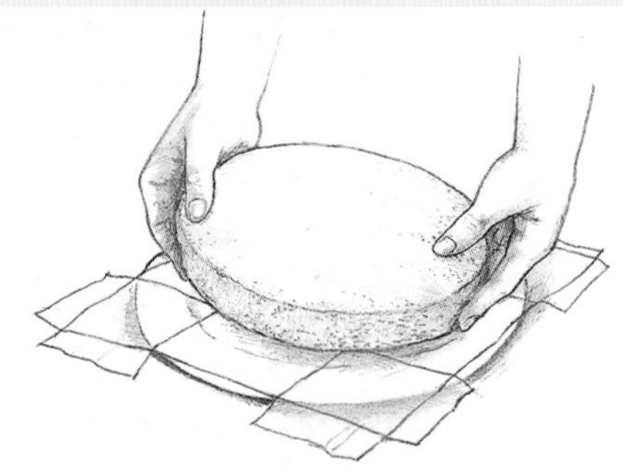

1. Brush any loose crumbs from cooled cake layers. Place 4 strips of waxed paper around edge of plate. Place the first layer, rounded side down, on plate.

2. Spread about 1/3 to 1/2 cup frosting over the top of first layer to within about 1/4 inch of edge.

3. Place second cake layer, rounded side up, on frosted first layer. Coat side of cake with a very thin layer of frosting to seal in crumbs.

4. Frost side of cake in swirls, making a rim about 1/4 inch high above the top of the cake. Spread remaining frosting on top, just to the built-up rim. Carefully remove waxed paper strips.

Fudge Frosting

PREP: 5 min **COOK:** 5 min **COOL:** 45 min ■
8 SERVINGS, ABOUT 3 1/2 CUPS FROSTING

- 2 cups granulated sugar
- 1 cup baking cocoa
- 1 cup milk
- 1/2 cup butter or margarine
- 1/4 cup light corn syrup
- 1/4 teaspoon salt
- 2 1/2 to 3 cups powdered sugar
- 2 teaspoons vanilla

1. In 3-quart saucepan, mix granulated sugar and cocoa. Stir in milk, butter, corn syrup and salt. Heat to boiling, stirring frequently. Boil 3 minutes, stirring occasionally. Cool 45 minutes.

2. Beat in powdered sugar and vanilla with spoon until smooth. Frosts 8- or 9-inch two-layer cake or 13 × 9-inch cake.

1 SERVING: CAL. 360 (CAL. FROM FAT 80); FAT 9g (SAT. FAT 6g); CHOL. 25mg; SODIUM 120mg; CARBS. 71g (FIBER 2g); PRO. 2g
% DAILY VALUE: VIT. A 6%; VIT. C 0%; CALC. 4%; IRON 2%
EXCHANGES: 4 1/2 OTHER CARB., 1/2 FAT **CARB. CHOICES:** 4 1/2

Chocolate Buttercream Frosting FAST

PREP: 15 min ■ **12 SERVINGS, ABOUT 2 CUPS FROSTING**

- 3 cups powdered sugar
- 1/3 cup butter or margarine, softened
- 2 teaspoons vanilla
- 3 oz unsweetened baking chocolate, melted and cooled
- 3 to 4 tablespoons milk

1. In medium bowl, beat powdered sugar and butter with spoon or electric mixer on low speed until blended. Stir in vanilla and chocolate.

2. Gradually beat in just enough milk to make frosting smooth and spreadable. If frosting is too thick, beat in more milk, a few drops at a time. If frosting becomes too thin, beat in a small amount of powdered sugar. Frosts 13 × 9-inch cake generously, or fills and frosts an 8- or 9-inch two-layer cake.

Note: To fill and frost an 8-inch three-layer cake, use a 1-pound box of powdered sugar (4 1/2 cups), 1/2 cup butter or margarine, softened, 1 tablespoon vanilla, 4 oz chocolate and about 1/4 cup milk.

1 SERVING: CAL. 235 (CAL. FROM FAT 80); FAT 9g (SAT. FAT 6g); CHOL. 15mg; SODIUM 35mg; CARBS. 37g (FIBER 1g); PRO. 1g
% DAILY VALUE: VIT. A 4%; VIT. C 0%; CALC. 0%; IRON 2%
EXCHANGES: 1/2 STARCH, 2 OTHER CARB., 1 1/2 FAT
CARB. CHOICES: 2 1/2

CREAMY COCOA FROSTING Substitute 1/3 cup baking cocoa for the chocolate.

MOCHA FROSTING Add 2 1/2 teaspoons instant coffee (dry) with the powdered sugar.

WHITE CHOCOLATE FROSTING Substitute 3/4 cup (3 oz) white baking chips, melted and cooled, for the chocolate.

Vanilla Buttercream Frosting FAST

PREP: 10 min ■ **12 SERVINGS, ABOUT 1 3/4 CUPS FROSTING**

- 3 cups powdered sugar
- 1/3 cup butter or margarine, softened
- 1 1/2 teaspoons vanilla
- 1 to 2 tablespoons milk

1. In medium bowl, mix powdered sugar and butter with spoon or electric mixer on low speed. Stir in vanilla and 1 tablespoon of the milk.

2. Gradually beat in just enough remaining milk to make frosting smooth and spreadable. If frosting is too thick, beat in more milk, a few drops at a time. If frosting becomes too thin, beat in a small amount of powdered sugar. Frosts 13 × 9-inch cake generously, or fills and frosts an 8- or 9-inch two-layer cake.

Note: To fill and frost an 8-inch three-layer cake, use a 1-pound box of powdered sugar (4 1/2 cups), 1/2 cup butter or margarine, softened, 2 teaspoons vanilla and about 3 tablespoons milk.

1 SERVING: CAL. 165 (CAL. FROM FAT 45); FAT 5g (SAT. FAT 3g); CHOL. 15mg; SODIUM 35mg; CARBS. 30g (FIBER 0g); PRO. 0g
% DAILY VALUE: VIT. A 4%; VIT. C 0%; CALC. 0%; IRON 0%
EXCHANGES: 2 OTHER CARB., 1 FAT **CARB. CHOICES:** 2

BROWNED BUTTER BUTTERCREAM FROSTING In 1-quart saucepan, heat 1/3 cup butter (do not use margarine or spreads) over medium heat just until light brown. Watch carefully because butter can brown and then burn quickly. Cool butter. Use browned butter instead of softened butter in recipe.

LEMON BUTTERCREAM FROSTING Omit vanilla. Substitute lemon juice for the milk. Stir in 1/2 teaspoon grated lemon peel.

MAPLE-NUT BUTTERCREAM FROSTING Omit vanilla. Substitute 1/2 cup maple-flavored syrup for the milk. Stir in 1/4 cup finely chopped nuts.

ORANGE BUTTERCREAM FROSTING Omit vanilla. Substitute orange juice for the milk. Stir in 2 teaspoons grated orange peel.

PEANUT BUTTER BUTTERCREAM FROSTING Substitute peanut butter for the butter. Increase milk to 1/4 cup, adding more if necessary, a few drops at a time.

Cream Cheese Frosting FAST

PREP: 10 min ■ **12 SERVINGS, ABOUT 2 1/2 CUPS FROSTING**

This is the perfect frosting for carrot cake and spice or applesauce cakes. Be sure to refrigerate the frosted cake (or any extra frosting), because the cream cheese will spoil if it's left out at room temperature.

- 1 package (8 oz) cream cheese, softened
- 1/4 cup butter or margarine, softened
- 2 to 3 teaspoons milk
- 1 teaspoon vanilla
- 4 cups powdered sugar

1. In medium bowl, beat cream cheese, butter, milk and vanilla with electric mixer on low speed until smooth.

2. Gradually beat in powdered sugar, 1 cup at a time, on low speed until smooth and spreadable. Frosts 13 × 9-inch cake generously, or fills and frosts an 8- or 9-inch two-layer cake. Store frosted cake or any remaining frosting covered in refrigerator.

1 SERVING: CAL. 260 (CAL. FROM FAT 90); FAT 10g (SAT. FAT 7g); CHOL. 30mg; SODIUM 80mg; CARBS. 40g (FIBER 0g); PRO. 2g
% DAILY VALUE: VIT. A 8%; VIT. C 0%; CALC. 2%; IRON 0%
EXCHANGES: 1 STARCH, 1 1/2 OTHER CARB., 2 FAT
CARB. CHOICES: 2 1/2

CHOCOLATE CREAM CHEESE FROSTING Add 2 oz unsweetened baking chocolate, melted and cooled, with the butter.

Caramel Frosting

PREP: 10 min **COOK:** 10 min **COOL:** 30 min ■ **12 SERVINGS, ABOUT 2 CUPS FROSTING**

- 1/2 cup butter or margarine
- 1 cup packed brown sugar
- 1/4 cup milk
- 2 cups powdered sugar

1. In 2-quart saucepan, melt butter over medium heat. Stir in brown sugar. Heat to boiling, stirring constantly; reduce heat to low. Boil and stir 2 minutes. Stir in milk. Heat to boiling; remove from heat. Cool to lukewarm, about 30 minutes.

2. Gradually stir in powdered sugar. Place saucepan of frosting in bowl of cold water. Beat with spoon until smooth and spreadable. If frosting becomes too stiff, stir in additional milk, 1 teaspoon at a time, or heat over low heat, stirring constantly. Frosts 13 × 9-inch cake generously, or fills and frosts an 8- or 9-inch two-layer cake.

1 SERVING: CAL. 225 (CAL. FROM FAT 70); FAT 8g (SAT. FAT 5g); CHOL. 20mg; SODIUM 60mg; CARBS. 38g (FIBER 0g); PRO. 0g
% DAILY VALUE: VIT. A 6%; VIT. C 0%; CALC. 2%; IRON 2%
EXCHANGES: 2 1/2 OTHER CARB., 1 1/2 FAT **CARB. CHOICES:** 2 1/2

White Mountain Frosting

LOW-FAT

PREP: 25 min **COOK:** 10 min ■ **12 SERVINGS, ABOUT 3 CUPS FROSTING**

This fluffy white frosting is so-named because its large white peaks hold up long after it's beaten.

- 2 large egg whites
- 1/2 cup sugar
- 1/4 cup light corn syrup
- 2 tablespoons water
- 1 teaspoon vanilla

1. In medium bowl, beat egg whites with electric mixer on high speed just until stiff peaks form.

2. In 1-quart saucepan, stir sugar, corn syrup and water until well mixed. Cover and heat to rolling boil over medium heat. Uncover and boil 4 to 8 minutes, without stirring, to 242°F on candy thermometer or until small amount of mixture dropped into cup of very cold water forms a firm ball that holds its shape until pressed. For an accurate temperature reading, tilt the saucepan slightly so mixture is deep enough for thermometer.

3. Pour hot syrup very slowly in thin stream into egg whites, beating constantly on medium speed. Add vanilla. Beat on high speed about 10 minutes or until stiff peaks form. Frosts 13 × 9-inch cake generously, or fills and frosts an 8- or 9-inch two-layer cake.

1 SERVING: CAL. 60 (CAL. FROM FAT 0); FAT 0g (SAT. FAT 0g); CHOL. 0mg; SODIUM 15mg; CARBS. 14g (FIBER 0g); PRO. 1g
% DAILY VALUE: VIT. A 0%; VIT. C 0%; CALC. 0%; IRON 0%
EXCHANGES: 1 OTHER CARB. **CARB. CHOICES:** 1

BUTTERSCOTCH FROSTING Substitute packed brown sugar for the granulated sugar. Decrease vanilla to 1/2 teaspoon.

CHERRY-NUT FROSTING Stir in 1/4 cup cut-up candied cherries, 1/4 cup chopped nuts and, if desired, 6 to 8 drops red food color.

PEPPERMINT FROSTING Stir in 1/3 cup coarsely crushed hard peppermint candies or 1/2 teaspoon peppermint extract.

Chocolate Glaze FAST

PREP: 5 min **COOK:** 5 min **COOL:** 10 min ■
12 SERVINGS, ABOUT 1/2 CUP GLAZE

This chocolate glaze recipe can easily be doubled.

- 1/2 cup semisweet chocolate chips
- 2 tablespoons butter or margarine
- 2 tablespoons corn syrup
- 1 to 2 teaspoons hot water

1. In 1-quart saucepan, heat chocolate chips, butter and corn syrup over low heat, stirring frequently, until chocolate chips are melted. Cool about 10 minutes.

2. Stir in hot water, 1 teaspoon at a time, until consistency of thick syrup. Glazes one 12-cup bundt cake, 10-inch angel food or chiffon cake or top of an 8- or 9-inch layer cake.

1 SERVING: CAL. 65 (CAL. FROM FAT 35); FAT 4g (SAT. FAT 2g); CHOL. 5mg; SODIUM 20mg; CARBS. 7g (FIBER 0g); PRO. 0g
% DAILY VALUE: VIT. A 2%; VIT. C 0%; CALC. 0%; IRON 0%
EXCHANGES: 1/2 OTHER CARB., 1 FAT **CARB. CHOICES:** 1/2

MILK CHOCOLATE GLAZE Substitute milk chocolate chips for the semisweet chocolate chips.

MINT CHOCOLATE GLAZE Substitute mint chocolate chips for the semisweet chocolate chips.

WHITE CHOCOLATE GLAZE Substitute white baking chips for the semisweet chocolate chips.

HOW TO GLAZE CAKES

Pour or drizzle glaze over top of flat cakes; spread with spatula or back of spoon, letting some glaze drizzle down side. For fluted tube cakes, spoon glaze over top, letting glaze drizzle down side and center.

Vanilla Glaze FAST

PREP: 5 min ■ **12 SERVINGS, ABOUT 1 CUP GLAZE**

- 1/3 cup butter or margarine
- 2 cups powdered sugar
- 1 1/2 teaspoons regular vanilla or clear vanilla
- 2 to 4 tablespoons hot water

1. In 1 1/2-quart saucepan, melt butter over low heat; remove from heat. Stir in powdered sugar and vanilla.

2. Stir in hot water, 1 tablespoon at a time, until smooth and consistency of thick syrup. Glazes one 12-cup bundt cake, 10-inch angel food or chiffon cake or top of an 8- or 9-inch layer cake.

1 SERVING: CAL. 125 (CAL. FROM FAT 45); FAT 5g (SAT. FAT 3g); CHOL. 15mg; SODIUM 35mg; CARBS. 20g (FIBER 0g); PRO. 0g
% DAILY VALUE: VIT. A 4%; VIT. C 0%; CALC. 0%; IRON 0%
EXCHANGES: 1 1/2 OTHER CARB., 1 FAT **CARB. CHOICES:** 1

LEMON GLAZE Stir 1/2 teaspoon grated lemon peel into melted butter. Substitute lemon juice for the vanilla and hot water.

ORANGE GLAZE Stir 1/2 teaspoon grated orange peel into melted butter. Substitute orange juice for the vanilla and hot water.

DRIZZLE IT!

Making beautiful drizzles of glaze is easy. Drizzle glaze from the tip of a flatware teaspoon; or pour glaze into a resealable plastic food-storage bag, snip off a tiny corner and gently squeeze the bag, moving it back and forth over the top of the cake. Want a thicker drizzle? Just make the hole bigger.

Chocolate Ganache

PREP: 5 min **COOK:** 5 min **STAND:** 5 min ▪
12 SERVINGS, ABOUT 1 1/4 CUPS GANACHE

Ganache is a very rich chocolate glaze made with semisweet chocolate and heavy cream. If you glaze the cake on a cooling rack with waxed paper underneath the rack, the ganache will drip over the side of the cake and the extra drips will fall onto the waxed paper. When the ganache hardens, just slide the cake onto your serving plate—easily and neatly.

2/3 cup whipping (heavy) cream
6 oz semisweet baking chocolate, chopped

1. In 1-quart saucepan, heat whipping cream over low heat until hot but not boiling; remove from heat.

2. Stir in chocolate until melted. Let stand about 5 minutes. Ganache is ready to use when it mounds slightly when dropped from a spoon. It will become firmer the longer it cools.

3. Pour ganache carefully onto top center of cake; spread with large spatula so it flows evenly over top and down to cover side of cake. Glazes 13 × 9-inch cake or top and side of 8- or 9-inch two-layer cake.

1 SERVING: CAL. 105 (CAL. FROM FAT 70); FAT 8g (SAT. FAT 5g); CHOL. 15mg; SODIUM 5mg; CARBS. 9g (FIBER 1g); PRO. 1g
% DAILY VALUE: VIT. A 2%; VIT. C 0%; CALC. 0%; IRON 2%
EXCHANGES: 1/2 OTHER CARB., 1 1/2 FAT **CARB. CHOICES:** 1/2

Coconut-Pecan Filling and Topping

PREP: 10 min **COOK:** 12 min **COOL:** 30 min ▪
12 SERVINGS, 2 3/4 CUPS FILLING

Although this filling is traditionally used for German Chocolate Cake (page 102), it is also delicious on other cakes. Frost layer cakes only between the layers and on top, leaving the sides unfrosted.

1 cup granulated sugar or packed brown sugar
1/2 cup butter or margarine
1 cup evaporated milk
1 teaspoon vanilla
3 large egg yolks
1 1/3 cups flaked coconut
1 cup chopped pecans

1. In 2-quart saucepan, stir sugar, butter, milk, vanilla and egg yolks until well mixed. Cook over medium heat about 12 minutes, stirring frequently, until thick and bubbly.

2. Stir in coconut and pecans. Cool about 30 minutes, beating occasionally with spoon, until spreadable. Fills and frosts top of an 8- or 9-inch two- or three-layer cake.

1 SERVING: CAL. 275 (CAL. FROM FAT 170); FAT 19g (SAT. FAT 9g); CHOL. 75mg; SODIUM 100mg; CARBS. 23g (FIBER 1g); PRO. 3g
% DAILY VALUE: VIT. A 10%; VIT. C 0%; CALC. 6%; IRON 2%
EXCHANGES: 1 STARCH, 1/2 OTHER CARB., 3 1/2 FAT
CARB. CHOICES: 1 1/2

Lemon Filling LOW-FAT

PREP: 5 min **COOK:** 10 min **CHILL:** 2 hr ▪
12 SERVINGS, ABOUT 1¼ CUPS FILLING

Grating the peel from a lemon is easier when the lemon is whole, so grate first, then squeeze out the juice.

- ¾ cup sugar
- 3 tablespoons cornstarch
- ¼ teaspoon salt
- ⅔ cup water
- 1 tablespoon butter or margarine
- 1 teaspoon grated lemon peel
- ¼ cup lemon juice
- 2 drops yellow food color, if desired

1. In 1½-quart saucepan, mix sugar, cornstarch and salt. Gradually stir in water. Cook over medium heat, stirring constantly, until mixture thickens and boils. Boil and stir 1 minute; remove from heat.

2. Stir in butter and lemon peel until butter is melted. Gradually stir in lemon juice and food color. Press plastic wrap on filling to prevent a tough layer from forming on top. Refrigerate about 2 hours or until set. Store cakes or pastries filled with Lemon Filling covered in the refrigerator.

1 SERVING: CAL. 70 (CAL. FROM FAT 10); FAT 1g (SAT. FAT 1g); CHOL. 5mg; SODIUM 55mg; CARBS. 15g (FIBER 0g); PRO. 0g
% DAILY VALUE: VIT. A 0%; VIT. C 0%; CALC. 0%; IRON 0%
EXCHANGES: 1 OTHER CARB. **CARB. CHOICES:** 1

Raspberry Filling LOW-FAT

PREP: 5 min **COOK:** 10 min **COOL:** 30 min ▪
12 SERVINGS, ABOUT ⅔ CUP FILLING

- 1 box (10 oz) frozen raspberries in light syrup, thawed
- 2 tablespoons sugar
- 1 tablespoon cornstarch

1. Drain raspberries, reserving ⅓ cup syrup. In 1-quart saucepan, mix sugar and cornstarch. Stir in reserved raspberry syrup.

2. Heat sugar mixture over medium-low heat, stirring constantly, until mixture thickens and boils. Boil and stir 1 minute.

3. Stir raspberries into sugar mixture. Cool completely, about 30 minutes.

1 SERVING: CAL. 20 (CAL. FROM FAT 0); FAT 0g (SAT. FAT 0g); CHOL. 0mg; SODIUM 0mg; CARBS. 5g (FIBER 1g); PRO. 0g
% DAILY VALUE: VIT. A 0%; VIT. C 2%; CALC. 0%; IRON 0%
EXCHANGES: 1 SERVING IS FREE **CARB. CHOICES:** 0

STRAWBERRY FILLING Substitute 1 box (10 oz) frozen strawberries in light syrup, thawed, for the raspberries.

Pie and Pastry Basics

Everyone loves a slice of homemade pie! Serve it warm, right out of the pie plate with a scoop of ice cream. Contrary to what beginner cooks might think, pies are easy to make—especially with the recipes and tips found here, plus a little practice.

PICKING THE RIGHT PAN

- For tender, flaky crusts, choose heat-resistant glass pie plates or aluminum pie pans with a dull (anodized) finish. Shiny pie pans are not recommended because they reflect heat, causing a soggy bottom crust.
- Pastry and crusts have enough fat in them that pie plates and pans usually don't need to be greased.
- Nonstick pie pans can cause an unfilled one-crust pie crust to shrink excessively during baking. To hold the pastry in place, fold it over the edge of the pie plate and press firmly.

BAKING PIES AND PASTRY

Pies are baked at higher temperatures (375°F to 425°F) than cakes so that the rich pastry dries and becomes flaky and golden brown and the filling cooks all the way through.

To prevent pie crust and pastry edges from getting too brown, cover them with an edge protector ring or with foil (see Preventing Excessive Browning of Pastry Edges, page 122). Bake as directed; remove the foil 15 minutes before the end of the bake time so the edges will brown.

PASTRY CURES

The Best Pastry Is . . .

Golden brown and blistered on top

Crisp, brown undercrust

Tender, cuts easily and holds its shape when served

Flaky and crisp

What Happened	Why
Pale color	• baked in shiny pan instead of in dull pan • underbaked
Pastry looks smooth	• dough was handled too much
Bottom crust is soggy	• baked in shiny pan instead of dull pan • oven temperature too low
Tough	• too much water • too much flour • dough was mixed and handled too much
Too tender; falls apart	• too little water • too much shortening
Dry and mealy, not flaky	• shortening was cut in too finely • too little water

HOW TO PREVENT EXCESSIVE BROWNING OF PASTRY EDGES

▲ **1.** Cover edge of pie with a 2- to 3-inch strip of aluminum foil, gently molding foil to edge of pie.

2. Fold a 12-inch square of foil into fourths; cut the open corner to round it off, making a 12-inch circle of foil. Cut a 3-inch strip from the rounded edge; discard center of foil circle. Unfold foil strip, and gently mold to edge of pie. ▼

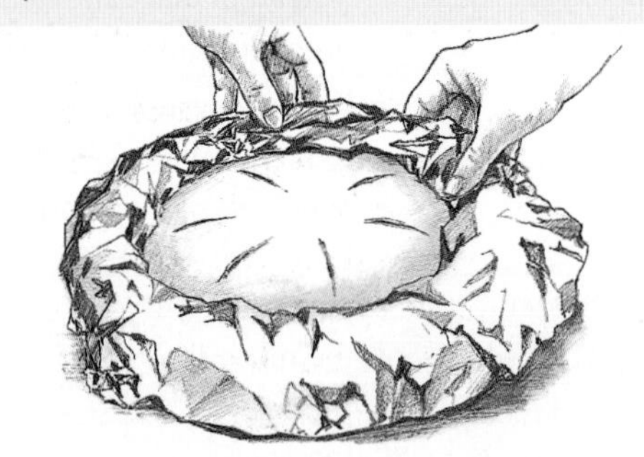

NO MORE PUFFED-UP CRUSTS

To prevent an unfilled one-crust pie crust from puffing up during baking, prick the unbaked pastry in the pie plate all over with a fork to let steam escape. When baking a pie filling in an unbaked one-crust, don't prick it because fillings like custard, pecan or pumpkin will seep under the crust during baking.

FREEZING PIE CRUSTS

- *To freeze unbaked or baked crusts,* place in the freezer until completely frozen. Once frozen, wrap crusts in foil or place in resealable plastic freezer bags.
- *Freeze unbaked crusts* up to two months and baked crusts up to four months.
- *To bake frozen unbaked crusts,* bake them right after taking them out of the freezer. No thawing needed!
- *To thaw baked pie crusts,* unwrap and let stand at room temperature, or heat in the oven at 350°F for about 6 minutes.

FREEZING PIES

- *Many pies can be frozen.* Pecan and pumpkin pies need to be baked before freezing; fruit pies can be frozen unbaked or baked.
- *Creams, custards and pies with meringue toppings can't be frozen* because they break down and become watery.
- *Cool baked pies completely before freezing.* Place pies in the freezer uncovered. When completely frozen, wrap tightly in foil or place in a resealable plastic freezer bag. Freeze baked pies up to four months, unbaked pies up to three months.
- *To serve unbaked frozen pies:* Unwrap and bake frozen pie at 475°F for 15 minutes; reduce oven temperature to 375°F and bake for 45 minutes longer or until center is bubbly.
- *To serve baked frozen pies:* Unwrap and bake frozen pie at 325°F for 45 minutes or until thawed and warm.

Pastry for Pies and Tarts

PREP: 20 min **CHILL:** 45 min ■ **ONE OR TWO 9-INCH CRUSTS (8 SERVINGS)**

Making that perfect pastry is as easy as 1, 2, 3! For more help, check out the information on page 125 and the pictures on page 126.

One-Crust Pie (9-inch)

1 cup all-purpose* or unbleached flour
1/2 teaspoon salt
1/3 cup plus 1 tablespoon shortening
2 to 3 tablespoons cold water

Two-Crust Pie (9-inch)

2 cups all-purpose* or unbleached flour
1 teaspoon salt
2/3 cup plus 2 tablespoons shortening
4 to 6 tablespoons cold water

1. In medium bowl, mix flour and salt. Cut in shortening, using pastry blender (or pulling 2 table knives through ingredients in opposite directions), until particles are size of small peas. Sprinkle with cold water, 1 tablespoon at a time, tossing with fork until all flour is moistened and pastry almost leaves side of bowl (1 to 2 teaspoons more water can be added if necessary).

2. Gather pastry into a ball. Shape into flattened round on lightly floured surface. (For Two-Crust Pie, divide pastry in half and shape into 2 rounds.) Wrap flattened round of pastry in plastic wrap and refrigerate about 45 minutes or until dough is firm and cold, yet pliable. This allows the shortening to become slightly firm, which helps make the baked pastry more flaky. If refrigerated longer, let pastry soften slightly before rolling.

3. Roll pastry on lightly floured surface, using floured rolling pin, into circle 2 inches larger than upside-down 9-inch glass pie plate or 3 inches larger than 10- or 11-inch tart pan. Fold pastry into fourths and place in pie plate; or roll pastry loosely around rolling pin and transfer to pie plate. Unfold or unroll pastry and ease into plate, pressing firmly against bottom and side and being careful not to stretch pastry, which will cause it to shrink when baked. Continue with directions on page 124 for One-Crust Pie or Two-Crust Pie.

**If using self-rising flour, omit salt. Pie crusts made with self-rising flour differ in flavor and texture from those made with all-purpose flour.*

1 SERVING (USING ONE CRUST)): CAL. 145 (CAL. FROM FAT 90); FAT 10g (SAT. FAT 3g); CHOL. 0mg; SODIUM 150mg; CARBS. 12g (FIBER 0g); PRO. 2g **% DAILY VALUE:** VIT. A 0%; VIT. C 0%; CALC. 0%; IRON 4% **EXCHANGES:** 1 STARCH, 1 1/2 FAT **CARB. CHOICES:** 1

FOOD PROCESSOR DIRECTIONS Measure 2 tablespoons water for One-Crust Pie or 4 tablespoons water for Two-Crust Pie into liquid measuring cup; set aside. Place shortening, flour and salt in food processor. Cover and process, using quick on-and-off motions, until mixture is crumbly. With food processor running, pour water all at once through feed tube just until dough leaves side of bowl (dough should not form a ball). Continue as directed in Step 2.

BUTTER CRUST For a richer crust to use with dessert pies, you can substitute butter for half of the shortening. For 9-inch One-Crust Pie, use 3 tablespoons each butter and shortening; for 9-inch Two-Crust Pie, use 1/3 cup plus 1 tablespoon each butter and shortening.

BAKED TART SHELLS

Make pastry as directed for One-Crust Pie (page 124)—except roll pastry into 13-inch circle. Cut into eight 4 1/2-inch circles, rerolling pastry scraps if necessary.

Heat oven to 475°F. Fit circles over backs of medium muffin cups or 6-ounce custard cups, making pleats so pastry will fit closely. (If using individual pie pans or tart pans, cut pastry circles 1 inch larger than upside-down pans; fit into pans.) Prick pastry thoroughly with fork to prevent puffing. Place on cookie sheet.

Bake 8 to 10 minutes or until light brown. Cool before removing from cups. Fill each shell with 1/3 to 1/2 cup of your favorite filling, pudding, fresh fruit or ice cream.

ONE-CRUST PIE

Unbaked (for one-crust pies baked with a filling, such as pumpkin, pecan or custard pie): *For pie,* trim overhanging edge of pastry 1 inch from rim of pie plate. Fold and roll pastry under, even with plate; flute (see Pastry Edges, page 126). *For tart,* trim overhanging edge of pastry even with top of tart pan. Fill and bake as directed in pie or tart recipe, or partially bake crust before adding filling as directed in next paragraph.

Partially Baked To prevent pie crust from becoming soggy, partially bake pastry before adding filling: Heat oven to 425°F. Carefully line pastry with a double thickness of foil, gently pressing foil to bottom and side of pastry. Let foil extend over edge to prevent excessive browning. Bake 10 minutes; carefully remove foil and bake 2 to 4 minutes longer or until pastry *just begins* to brown and has become set. If crust bubbles, gently push bubbles down with back of spoon. Fill and bake as directed in pie or tart recipe, adjusting oven temperature if necessary.

Baked (for one-crust pies baked completely before filling is added, such as coconut cream or lemon meringue pie): Heat oven to 475°F. *For pie,* trim overhanging edge of pastry 1 inch from rim of pie plate. Fold and roll pastry under, even with plate; flute (see Pastry Edges, page 126). *For tart,* trim overhanging edge of pastry even with top of tart pan. Prick bottom and side of pastry thoroughly with fork. Bake 8 to 10 minutes or until light brown; cool on wire rack.

TWO-CRUST PIE

Spoon desired filling into pastry-lined 9-inch glass pie plate. Trim overhanging edge of bottom pastry 1/2 inch from rim of plate. Roll other round of pastry. (Make Lattice Pie Top, page 126, if desired.) Fold top pastry into fourths and cut slits so steam can escape, or cut slits in pastry and roll pastry loosely around rolling pin.

Place pastry over filling and unfold or unroll. Trim overhanging edge of top pastry 1 inch from rim of plate. Fold and roll top edge under lower edge, pressing on rim to seal; flute (see Pastry Edges, page 126). Bake as directed in pie recipe.

REFRIGERATING PIE CRUST DOUGH

The recipe for Pastry for Pies and Tarts (page 123) recommends refrigerating the dough 45 minutes after it's been made. This short break firms the shortening, relaxes the gluten in the flour and lets the water absorb evenly throughout the dough. It also makes the dough easy to roll and results in a tender, flaky crust.

HOW TO MAKE PASTRY

1. Cut shortening into flour and salt, using pastry blender, until particles are the size of small peas.

2. Sprinkle with cold water and toss with fork until all flour is moistened and pastry almost leaves side of bowl.

3. Roll pastry from center to outside edge in all directions. To keep edge from getting too thin, use less pressure on the rolling pin.

4. If edge of pastry splits, patch it with a small piece of pastry. Occasionally lift pastry to make sure it is not sticking.

5. Fold pastry into fourths; place in pie plate with point in center. Unfold; ease into plate, avoiding stretching pastry, which causes it to shrink when baked.

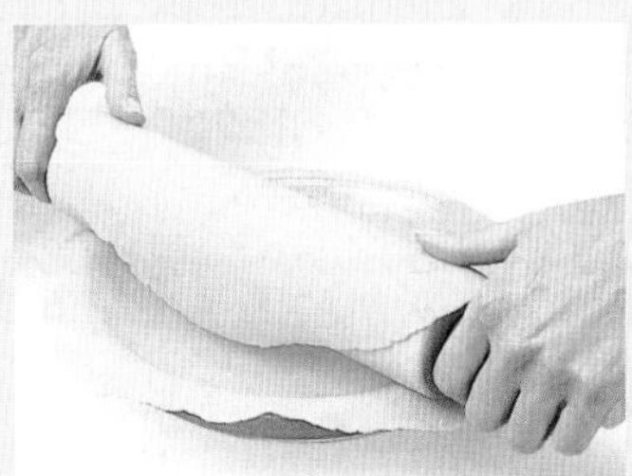

6. Or instead of folding pastry into fourths, roll it loosely around rolling pin and transfer to pie plate. Unroll pastry; ease into plate.

7. For two-crust pie, cut slits or design in top pastry before folding. Carefully place pastry over filling, using method number 5 or 6 above. Let top pastry overhang 1 inch beyond edge of pie plate.

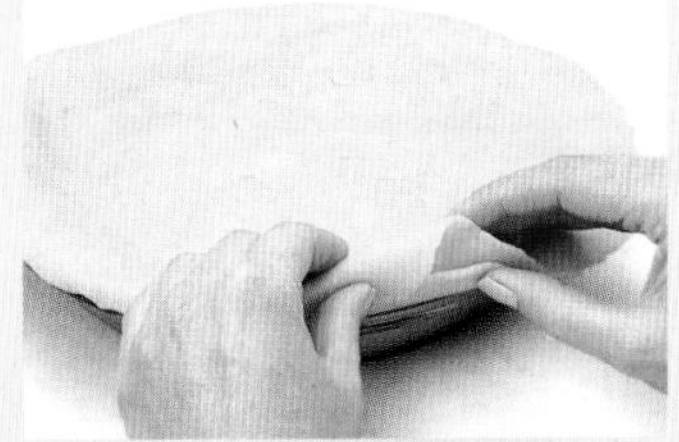

8. Fold and roll overhanging pastry under edge of bottom pastry, pressing to seal.

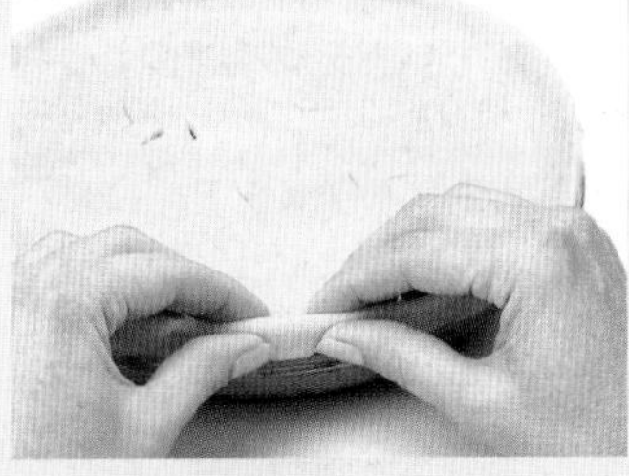

9. Form a stand-up rim of even thickness on edge of pie plate, continuing to press edges together. This seals pastry and makes fluting easier. See also How to Make Pastry Edges, page 126.

LATTICE PIE TOP

1. Make pastry as directed for Two-Crust Pie, page 124, except trim overhanging edge of bottom pastry 1 inch from rim of plate. After rolling pastry for top crust, cut into strips about 1/2 inch wide. (Use a pastry wheel to cut decorative strips.)
2. For Classic Lattice Top, place 5 to 7 strips (depending on size of pie) across filling in pie plate. Weave a cross-strip through center by first folding back every other strip of the first 5 to 7 strips. Continue weaving, folding back alternate strips before adding each cross-strip, until lattice is complete.
3. For Easy Lattice Top, place second half of strips crosswise across first strips instead of weaving. Trim ends of strips.
4. Fold trimmed edge of bottom crust over ends of strips, forming a high stand-up rim. A lattice-top fruit pie is more likely to bubble over than a traditional two-crust pie, but a high rim helps. Seal and flute. See also How to Make Pastry Edges, below. Bake as directed in pie recipe.

HOW TO MAKE A LATTICE PIE TOP

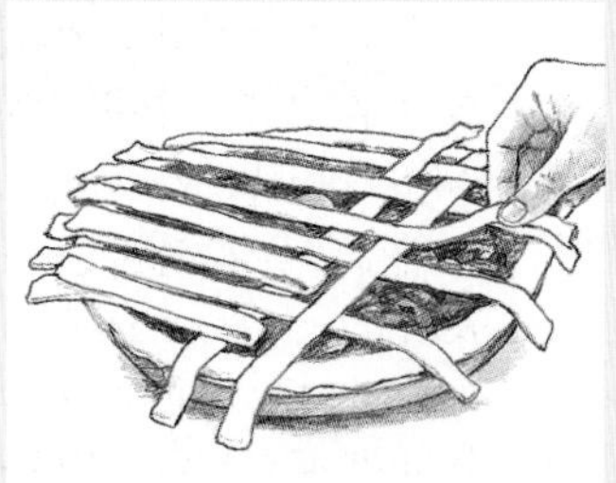

◀ **Classic Lattice Top:** Place 5 to 7 strips of pastry across filling. Fold back alternate strips before adding cross-strips.

Easy Lattice Top: Place 5 to 7 strips of pastry across filling. Place cross-strips over tops of first strips instead of weaving. ▶

HOW TO MAKE PASTRY EDGES

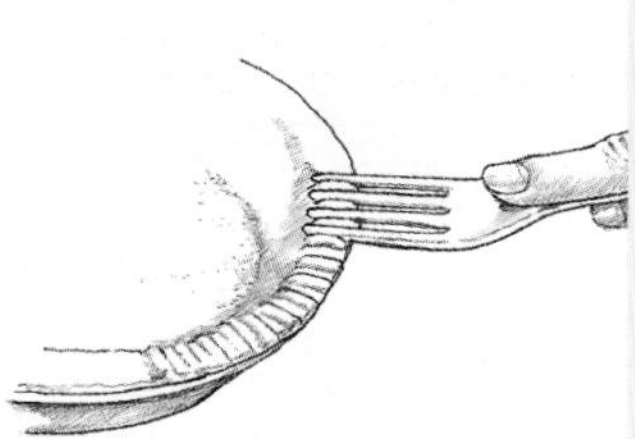

Fork Edge: Flatten pastry evenly on rim of pie plate. Firmly press tines of fork around edge. To prevent sticking, occasionally dip fork into flour.

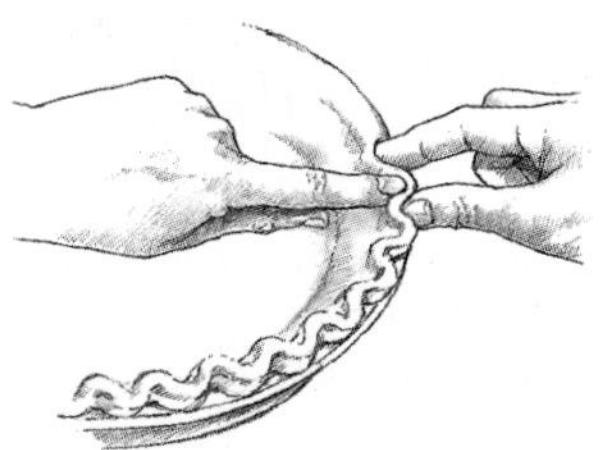

Pinch Edge: Place index finger on inside of pastry rim and thumb and index finger (or knuckles) on outside. Pinch pastry into V shape along edge. Pinch again to sharpen points.

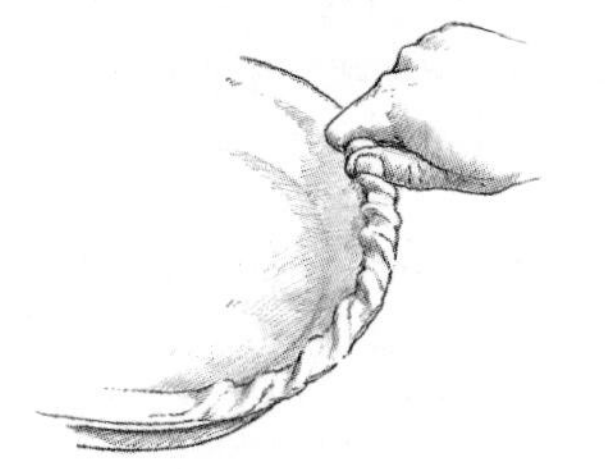

Rope Edge: Place side of thumb on pastry rim at an angle. Pinch pastry by pressing the knuckle of your index finger down into pastry toward thumb.

Easy Buttermilk Pastry

FAST

PREP: 15 min ■ **TWO 9-INCH CRUSTS (8 SERVINGS)**

This pastry is a dream to work with because it's extra easy to roll and handle, and the baked crust is very flaky. It makes enough pastry for a two-crust pie.

- 2 cups all-purpose flour*
- 1 teaspoon salt
- 2/3 cup shortening
- 3 tablespoons butter or margarine
- 2 teaspoons vegetable oil
- 1/3 cup buttermilk

1. In medium bowl, mix flour and salt. Cut in shortening and butter, using pastry blender (or pulling 2 table knives through ingredients in opposite directions), until particles are size of small peas.

2. Mix in oil and buttermilk with fork until all flour is moistened and pastry leaves side of bowl. Divide in half; shape each half into a ball. If making one-crust pie, wrap second ball of pastry and freeze for later use.

3. Roll pastry as directed for One-Crust Pie or Two-Crust Pie recipes (page 124). Fill and bake as directed in pie recipe. Or for pie crust that is baked before filling is added, heat oven to 475°F. Prick bottom and side of pastry thoroughly with fork. Bake 8 to 10 minutes or until light brown; cool on wire rack.

**If using self-rising flour, omit salt. Pie crusts made with self-rising flour differ in flavor and texture from those made with all-purpose flour.*

1 SERVING (USING ONE CRUST): CAL. 155 (CAL. FROM FAT 100); FAT 11g (SAT. FAT 3.5g); CHOL. 5mg; SODIUM 160mg; CARBS. 12g (FIBER 0g); PRO. 2g **% DAILY VALUE:** VIT. A 2%; VIT. C 0%; CALC. 0%; IRON 4% **EXCHANGES:** 1 STARCH, 2 FAT **CARB. CHOICES:** 1

Press-in-the-Pan Oil Pastry

FAST

PREP: 15 min ■ **ONE 9-INCH CRUST (8 SERVINGS)**

No rolling is needed for this crust! Use it for pies that have only a bottom crust. Try it for Pumpkin Pie (page 135) as well as for pie crusts that are baked before being filled.

- 1 1/3 cups all-purpose* or unbleached flour
- 1/2 teaspoon salt
- 1/3 cup vegetable oil
- 2 tablespoons cold water

1. In medium bowl, stir flour, salt and oil until all flour is moistened. Sprinkle with cold water, 1 tablespoon at a time, tossing with fork until all water is absorbed.

2. Gather pastry into a ball. Press in bottom and up side of 9-inch glass pie plate; flute (see How to Make Pastry Edges, page 126).

3. Fill and bake as directed in pie recipe. Or to bake before filling is added, heat oven to 475°F. Prick bottom and side of pastry thoroughly with fork. Bake 10 to 12 minutes or until light brown; cool on wire rack.

**If using self-rising flour, omit salt.*

1 SERVING: CAL. 155 (CAL. FROM FAT 80); FAT 9g (SAT. FAT 1g); CHOL. 0mg; SODIUM 150mg; CARBS. 16g (FIBER 1g); PRO. 2g **% DAILY VALUE:** VIT. A 0%; VIT. C 0%; CALC. 0%; IRON 4% **EXCHANGES:** 1 STARCH, 1 1/2 FAT **CARB. CHOICES:** 1

Press-in-the-Pan Tart Pastry

FAST

PREP: 10 min **BAKE:** 12 min ■ **ONE 11-INCH CRUST (8 SERVINGS)**

- 1 1/4 cups all-purpose flour*
- 1/2 cup butter or margarine, softened
- 2 tablespoons packed brown sugar
- 1 large egg

1. Heat oven to 400°F.

2. In medium bowl, stir all ingredients until dough forms. Press firmly and evenly against bottom and side of ungreased 11-inch tart pan.

3. Bake 10 to 12 minutes or until light brown; cool. Fill as directed in tart recipe.

**Do not use self-rising flour.*

1 SERVING: CAL. 195 (CAL. FROM FAT 110); FAT 12g (SAT. FAT 7g); CHOL. 55mg; SODIUM 85mg; CARBS. 18g (FIBER 1g); PRO. 3g
% DAILY VALUE: VIT. A 10%; VIT. C 0%; CALC. 0%; IRON 6%
EXCHANGES: 1 STARCH, 2 1/2 FAT **CARB. CHOICES:** 1

Graham Cracker Crust

FAST

PREP: 10 min **BAKE:** 10 min ■ **ONE 9-INCH CRUST (8 SERVINGS)**

- 1 1/2 cups finely crushed regular or cinnamon graham crackers (about 20 squares)
- 1/3 cup butter or margarine, melted
- 3 tablespoons sugar

1. Heat oven to 350°F.

2. In medium bowl, stir all ingredients until well mixed. Reserve 3 tablespoons crumb mixture for garnishing top of pie before serving, if desired. Press remaining mixture firmly against bottom and side of 9-inch glass pie plate.

3. Bake about 10 minutes or until light brown; cool. Fill as directed in pie recipe.

1 SERVING: CAL. 135 (CAL. FROM FAT 70); FAT 8g (SAT. FAT 5g); CHOL. 20mg; SODIUM 140mg; CARBS. 16g (FIBER 0g); PRO. 1g
% DAILY VALUE: VIT. A 6%; VIT. C 0%; CALC. 0%; IRON 2%
EXCHANGES: 1 STARCH, 1 1/2 FAT **CARB. CHOICES:** 1

COOKIE CRUMB CRUST Substitute 1 1/2 cups finely crushed chocolate or vanilla wafer cookies or gingersnaps for the graham crackers. Decrease butter to 1/4 cup; omit sugar.

SHOWSTOPPING TOP CRUSTS

Adding a gourmet touch is simple when you use one of these methods before baking:

Shiny crust: Brush crust with milk.

Sugary crust: Brush crust lightly with water or egg white beaten until foamy; sprinkle with granulated sugar or white coarse sugar crystals (decorating sugar).

Glazed crust: Brush crust lightly with a beaten egg or an egg yolk mixed with a little water.

These pie crusts may brown more quickly. If this happens, put a sheet of foil loosely on top of the pie to slow the browning.

Glaze for baked pie crust: In small bowl, stir together 1/2 cup powdered sugar, 2 to 3 teaspoons milk, orange juice or lemon juice and, if desired, 2 teaspoons grated orange peel or lemon peel. Brush or drizzle over warm baked pie, not letting glaze run over the edge of the pie.

Apple Pie

PREP: 30 min **BAKE:** 50 min **COOL:** 2 hr ■ **8 SERVINGS**

Nothing's quite like the smiles you'll see when you bring this pie out of the oven. You have so many good varieties of apples to choose from that you're bound to find at least one of them in your market, during every season. To help you choose, go to our Picking Apples chart on page 218.

Pastry for Two-Crust Pie (page 124) or Easy Buttermilk Pastry (page 127)
1/2 cup sugar
1/4 cup all-purpose flour
3/4 teaspoon ground cinnamon
1/4 teaspoon ground nutmeg
Dash of salt
6 cups thinly sliced peeled tart apples (6 medium)
2 tablespoons firm butter or margarine, if desired
2 teaspoons water
1 tablespoon sugar

1. Heat oven to 425°F. Make pastry.

2. In large bowl, mix 1/2 cup sugar, the flour, cinnamon, nutmeg and salt. Stir in apples. Spoon into pastry-lined pie plate. Cut butter into small pieces; sprinkle over apples. Cover with top pastry that has slits cut in it; seal and flute.

3. Brush top crust with 2 teaspoons water; sprinkle with 1 tablespoon sugar. Cover edge with 2- to 3-inch strip of foil to prevent excessive browning (page 122); remove foil during last 15 minutes of baking.

4. Bake 40 to 50 minutes or until crust is golden brown and juice begins to bubble through slits in crust. Cool on wire rack at least 2 hours.

1 SERVING: CAL. 420 (CAL. FROM FAT 190); FAT 21g (SAT. FAT 7g); CHOL. 10mg; SODIUM 330mg; CARBS. 53g (FIBER 3g); PRO. 4g
% DAILY VALUE: VIT. A 0%; VIT. C 2%; CALC. 0%; IRON 10%
EXCHANGES: 1 1/2 STARCH, 2 FRUIT, 4 FAT **CARB. CHOICES:** 3 1/2

FRENCH APPLE PIE Heat oven to 400°F. Make Pastry for One-Crust Pie (page 124). Spoon apple mixture into pastry-lined pie plate. Omit butter, 2 teaspoons water and 1 tablespoon sugar. Sprinkle apple mixture with Crumb Topping. In small bowl, mix 1 cup all-purpose flour, 1/2 cup packed brown sugar and 1/2 cup firm butter or margarine with fork until crumbly. Cover topping with foil during last 10 to 15 minutes of baking, if necessary, to prevent it from becoming too brown. Bake pie 35 to 40 minutes or until golden brown. Serve warm.

Country Apple Tart

PREP: 40 min **BAKE:** 35 min **COOL:** 1 hr ■ **8 SERVINGS**

No pie plate required! The pie filling is partially wrapped in a pastry crust and baked on a cookie sheet.

Pastry for One-Crust Pie (page 124) or Easy Buttermilk Pastry (page 127)
2/3 cup packed brown sugar
1/3 cup all-purpose flour
4 cups thinly sliced peeled tart apples (4 medium)
1 tablespoon butter or margarine
Granulated sugar, if desired

1. Heat oven to 425°F. Make pastry as directed—except roll pastry into 13-inch circle. Place on ungreased large cookie sheet. Cover with plastic wrap to keep pastry moist while making filling.

2. In large bowl, mix brown sugar and flour. Stir in apples. Mound apple mixture on center of pastry to within 3 inches of edge. Cut butter into small pieces; sprinkle over apples. Fold edge of pastry over apples, making pleats so it lays flat on apples (pastry will not cover apples in center.) Sprinkle pastry with sugar.

3. Bake 30 to 35 minutes or until crust is light golden brown. To prevent excessive browning, cover center of pie with 5-inch square of foil during last 10 to 15 minutes of baking. (See page 122.) Cool on cookie sheet on wire rack 1 hour, or serve warm if desired.

1 SERVING: CAL. 285 (CAL. FROM FAT 110); FAT 12g (SAT. FAT 4g); CHOL. 5mg; SODIUM 165mg; CARBS. 43g (FIBER 1g); PRO. 3g
% DAILY VALUE: VIT. A 0%; VIT. C 2%; CALC. 2%; IRON 8%
EXCHANGES: 1 STARCH, 1 FRUIT, 1 OTHER CARB., 2 FAT
CARB. CHOICES: 3

Blueberry Pie

PREP: 30 min **BAKE:** 45 min **COOL:** 2 hr ▪ **8 SERVINGS**

Pastry for Two-Crust Pie (page 124) or Easy Buttermilk Pastry (page 127)
3/4 cup sugar
1/2 cup all-purpose flour
1/2 teaspoon ground cinnamon, if desired
6 cups blueberries
1 tablespoon lemon juice
1 tablespoon butter or margarine, if desired

1. Heat oven to 425°F. Make pastry.

2. In large bowl, mix sugar, flour and cinnamon. Stir in blueberries. Spoon into pastry-lined pie plate. Sprinkle any remaining sugar mixture over blueberry mixture. Sprinkle with lemon juice. Cut butter into small pieces; sprinkle over blueberries. Cover with top pastry that has slits cut in it; seal and flute. Cover edge with 2- to 3-inch strip of foil to prevent excessive browning (page 122); remove foil during last 15 minutes of baking.

3. Bake 35 to 45 minutes or until crust is golden brown and juice begins to bubble through slits in crust. Cool on wire rack at least 2 hours.

1 SERVING: CAL. 415 (CAL. FROM FAT 170); FAT 19g (SAT. FAT 5g); CHOL. 0mg; SODIUM 270mg; CARBS. 57g (FIBER 4g); PRO. 4g
% DAILY VALUE: VIT. A 0%; VIT. C 10%; CALC. 0%; IRON 10%
EXCHANGES: 1 STARCH, 1 FRUIT, 2 OTHER CARB., 3 1/2 FAT
CARB. CHOICES: 4

BLACKBERRY, BOYSENBERRY, LOGANBERRY OR RASPBERRY PIE Increase sugar to 1 cup. Substitute fresh berries for the blueberries; omit lemon juice.

BLUEBERRY-PEACH PIE Substitute 2 1/2 cups sliced fresh peaches for 4 cups of the blueberries; omit lemon juice. Place blueberries in pastry-lined pie plate; sprinkle with half of the sugar mixture. Top with peaches; sprinkle with remaining sugar mixture. Cover with top pastry; continue as directed in Step 2.

QUICK BLUEBERRY PIE Substitute 6 cups drained canned blueberries or unsweetened frozen (thawed and drained) blueberries for the fresh blueberries.

LEARN WITH *Betty* — PASTRY DOUGH

This pastry dough is too dry to stick together and will not roll because not enough water was added.

There are no problems with this pastry dough; it is neither too dry nor too wet and will roll easily.

This pastry dough is too wet and sticky to roll because too much water was added.

Cherry Pie

PREP: 40 min **BAKE:** 45 min **COOL:** 2 hr ▪ **8 SERVINGS**

There are two types of cherries—sweet and sour. Sour cherries, also called pie cherries, tart cherries *or* tart red cherries *make wonderful pies. Sweet cherries are great for eating fresh, but not for pies. Top the pie with a lattice crust (page 126) and dazzle everyone!*

- Pastry for Two-Crust Pie (page 124) or Easy Buttermilk Pastry (page 127)
- 1 1/3 cups sugar
- 1/2 cup all-purpose flour
- 6 cups sour cherries, pitted
- 2 tablespoons butter or margarine, if desired

1. Heat oven to 425°F. Make pastry.

2. In large bowl, mix sugar and flour. Stir in cherries. Spoon into pastry-lined pie plate. Cut butter into small pieces; sprinkle over cherries. Cover with top pastry that has slits cut in it; seal and flute. Cover edge with 2- to 3-inch strip of foil to prevent excessive browning (page 122); remove foil during last 15 minutes of baking.

3. Bake 35 to 45 minutes or until crust is golden brown and juice begins to bubble through slits in crust. Cool on wire rack at least 2 hours.

1 SERVING: CAL. 535 (CAL. FROM FAT 190); FAT 21g (SAT. FAT 6g); CHOL. 0mg; SODIUM 300mg; CARBS. 80g (FIBER 3g); PRO. 5g
% DAILY VALUE: VIT. A 2%; VIT. C 6%; CALC. 2%; IRON 12%
EXCHANGES: 2 STARCH, 1 FRUIT, 2 OTHER CARB., 4 FAT
CARB. CHOICES: 5

QUICK CHERRY PIE Substitute 6 cups frozen unsweetened pitted red tart cherries, thawed and drained, or 3 cans (14.5 oz each) pitted red tart cherries, drained, for the fresh cherries.

Peach Pie

PREP: 45 min **BAKE:** 45 min **COOL:** 2 hr ▪ **8 SERVINGS**

- Pastry for Two-Crust Pie (page 124) or Easy Buttermilk Pastry (page 127)
- 2/3 cup sugar
- 1/3 cup all-purpose flour
- 1/4 teaspoon ground cinnamon
- 6 cups sliced peaches (6 to 8 medium)
- 1 teaspoon lemon juice
- 1 tablespoon butter or margarine, if desired

1. Heat oven to 425°F. Make pastry.

2. In large bowl, mix sugar, flour and cinnamon. Stir in peaches and lemon juice. Spoon into pastry-lined pie plate. Cut butter into small pieces; sprinkle over peaches. Cover with top pastry that has slits cut in it; seal and flute. Cover edge with 2- to 3-inch strip of foil to prevent excessive browning (page 122); remove foil during last 15 minutes of baking.

3. Bake about 45 minutes or until crust is golden brown and juice begins to bubble through slits in crust. Cool on wire rack at least 2 hours.

1 SERVING: CAL. 435 (CAL. FROM FAT 180); FAT 20g (SAT. FAT 5g); CHOL. 0mg; SODIUM 300mg; CARBS. 59g (FIBER 3g); PRO. 5g
% DAILY VALUE: VIT. A 6%; VIT. C 6%; CALC. 0%; IRON 10%
EXCHANGES: 2 STARCH, 1 FRUIT, 1 OTHER CARB., 3 FAT
CARB. CHOICES: 4

APRICOT PIE Substitute 6 cups fresh apricot halves for the peaches.

QUICK PEACH PIE Substitute 6 cups frozen sliced peaches, partially thawed and drained, for the fresh peaches.

◀ **Cherry Pie**

Rhubarb Pie

PREP: 35 min **BAKE:** 55 min **COOL:** 2 hr ▪ **8 SERVINGS**

Rhubarb is very tart, so there's a lot of sugar in this pie. If you are using young rhubarb picked early in the season, the lower amount of sugar probably will be enough. Older rhubarb needs more sugar.

- Pastry for Two-Crust Pie (page 124) or Easy Buttermilk Pastry (page 127)
- 2 to 2 1/3 cups sugar
- 2/3 cup all-purpose flour
- 1 teaspoon grated orange peel, if desired
- 6 cups 1/2-inch pieces rhubarb
- 1 tablespoon butter or margarine, if desired

1. Heat oven to 425°F. Make pastry.

2. In large bowl, mix sugar, flour and orange peel. Stir in rhubarb. Spoon into pastry-lined pie plate. Cut butter into small pieces; sprinkle over rhubarb. Cover with top pastry that has slits cut in it; seal and flute. Cover edge with 2- to 3-inch strip of foil to prevent excessive browning (page 122); remove foil during last 15 minutes of baking.

3. Bake about 55 minutes or until crust is golden brown and juice begins to bubble through slits in crust. Cool on wire rack at least 2 hours.

1 SERVING: CAL. 535 (CAL. FROM FAT 180); FAT 20g (SAT. FAT 5g); CHOL. 0mg; SODIUM 300mg; CARBS. 84g (FIBER 2g); PRO. 5g
% DAILY VALUE: VIT. A 0%; VIT. C 4%; CALC. 18%; IRON 12%
EXCHANGES: 2 STARCH, 1 FRUIT, 2 1/2 OTHER CARB., 3 FAT
CARB. CHOICES: 5 1/2

QUICK RHUBARB PIE Substitute 2 bags (16 oz each) frozen unsweetened rhubarb, completely thawed and drained, for the fresh rhubarb.

STRAWBERRY-RHUBARB PIE Substitute 3 cups sliced strawberries for 3 cups of the rhubarb. Use 2 cups sugar.

Mixed-Berry Crumble Tart

PREP: 40 min **BAKE:** 45 min ▪ **8 SERVINGS**

- Pastry for One-Crust Pie (page 124)
- 1 1/2 cups sliced fresh strawberries
- 1 1/2 cups fresh blueberries
- 1 cup fresh raspberries
- 2/3 cup sugar
- 2 tablespoons cornstarch
- 3/4 cup all-purpose flour
- 1/2 cup sugar
- 1 teaspoon grated orange peel
- 1/3 cup butter or margarine, melted

1. Heat oven to 425° F. Make pastry as directed—except roll into 13-inch circle. Fold pastry into fourths and place in 10- or 11-inch tart pan; unfold and press against bottom and side of pan. Trim overhanging edge of pastry even with top of pan.

2. In large bowl, gently toss berries with 2/3 cup sugar and the cornstarch. Spoon into pastry-lined pan.

3. In small bowl, stir flour, 1/2 cup sugar, the orange peel and butter with fork until crumbly. Sprinkle evenly over berries.

4. Bake 35 to 45 minutes or until fruit bubbles in center. Serve warm.

1 SERVING: CAL. 415 (CAL. FROM FAT 160); FAT 18g (SAT. FAT 7g); CHOL. 20mg; SODIUM 200mg; CARBS. 60g (FIBER 3g); PRO. 3g
% DAILY VALUE: VIT. A 6%; VIT. C 20%; CALC. 2%; IRON 8%
EXCHANGES: 1 STARCH, 3 FRUIT, 3 1/2 FAT **CARB. CHOICES:** 4

Banana Cream Pie

PREP: 30 min **BAKE:** 10 min **COOK:** 15 min **CHILL:** 2 hr ▪ **8 SERVINGS**

- Pastry for One-Crust Pie (page 124), Easy Buttermilk Pastry (page 127) or Press-in-the-Pan Oil Pastry (page 127)
- 4 large egg yolks
- 2/3 cup sugar
- 1/4 cup cornstarch
- 1/2 teaspoon salt
- 3 cups milk
- 2 tablespoons butter or margarine, softened
- 2 teaspoons vanilla
- 2 large bananas
- 1 cup Sweetened Whipped Cream (page 217)

1. Bake pastry for Baked One-Crust Pie.

2. In medium bowl, beat egg yolks with fork; set aside. In 2-quart saucepan, mix sugar, cornstarch and salt. Gradually stir in milk. Cook over medium heat, stirring constantly, until mixture thickens and boils. Boil and stir 1 minute.

3. Immediately stir at least half of the hot mixture gradually into egg yolks, then stir back into hot mixture in saucepan. Boil and stir 1 minute; remove from heat. Stir in butter and vanilla; cool filling slightly. Slice bananas into pie crust; pour warm filling over bananas. Press plastic wrap on filling to prevent a tough layer from forming on top. Refrigerate at least 2 hours until set.

4. Remove plastic wrap. Top pie with Sweetened Whipped Cream. Cover and refrigerate cooled pie until serving. Store covered in refrigerator.

1 SERVING: CAL. 415 (CAL. FROM FAT 200); FAT 22g (SAT. FAT 9g); CHOL. 135mg; SODIUM 370mg; CARBS. 46g (FIBER 1g); PRO. 7g **% DAILY VALUE:** VIT. A 12%; VIT. C 2%; CALC. 14%; IRON 6% **EXCHANGES:** 1 STARCH, 1 FRUIT, 1/2 OTHER CARB., 1/2 MILK, 4 1/2 FAT **CARB. CHOICES:** 3

CHOCOLATE CREAM PIE Increase sugar to 1 1/2 cups and cornstarch to 1/3 cup; omit butter and bananas. Stir in 2 oz unsweetened baking chocolate, cut up, after stirring in milk in Step 2.

CHOCOLATE-BANANA CREAM PIE Make Chocolate Cream Pie. Cool filling slightly. Slice 2 large bananas into pie crust; pour warm filling over bananas. Continue as directed in Step 3. Garnish finished pie with banana slices if desired.

COCONUT CREAM PIE Omit bananas. Stir in 3/4 cup flaked coconut with butter and vanilla. After topping pie with Sweetened Whipped Cream, sprinkle with additional 1/4 cup flaked coconut.

Mixed-Berry Crumble Tart ▶

Lemon Meringue Pie

PREP: 50 min **BAKE:** 25 min **COOL:** 2 hr 30 min ▪ **8 SERVINGS**

This delicious pie needs only three eggs—the yolks go into the filling, the whites make the meringue. To speed up the beating, let the egg whites warm up to room temperature (30 minutes or less). To prevent the baked meringue from weeping, seal the meringue to the edge of the crust as you pile it on top.

- Pastry for One-Crust Pie (page 124), Easy Buttermilk Pastry (page 127) or Press-in-Pan Oil Pastry (page 127)
- Meringue for 9-Inch Pie (page 212)
- 3 large egg yolks (reserve egg whites for meringue)
- 1 1/2 cups sugar
- 1/3 cup plus 1 tablespoon cornstarch
- 1 1/2 cups water
- 3 tablespoons butter or margarine
- 2 teaspoons grated lemon peel
- 1/2 cup lemon juice
- 2 drops yellow food color, if desired

1. Bake pastry for Baked One-Crust Pie.

2. Heat oven to 350°F. Complete Step 2 of Meringue for 9-Inch Pie.

3. While sugar mixture for meringue is cooling, in small bowl, beat egg yolks with fork; set aside. In 2-quart saucepan, mix sugar and cornstarch. Gradually stir in water. Cook over medium heat, stirring constantly, until mixture thickens and boils. Boil and stir 1 minute.

4. Immediately stir at least half of the hot mixture into egg yolks, then stir back into hot mixture in saucepan. Boil and stir 2 minutes or until very thick; remove from heat.** Stir in butter, lemon peel, lemon juice and food color. Press plastic wrap on filling to prevent a tough layer from forming on top.

5. Complete Step 3 of meringue recipe. Pour hot lemon filling into pie crust. Spoon meringue onto hot lemon filling. Spread over filling, carefully sealing meringue to edge of crust to prevent shrinking or weeping.

6. Bake about 15 minutes or until meringue is light brown. Cool away from draft 2 hours. Refrigerate cooled pie until serving. Store covered in refrigerator.*

**This pie is best served the day it is made. If refrigerated more than 1 day, the filling may become soft.*

***Do not boil less than 2 minutes or filling may stay too soft or become runny.*

1 SERVING: CAL. 455 (CAL. FROM FAT 155); FAT 17g (SAT. FAT 7g); CHOL. 95mg; SODIUM 250mg; CARBS. 70g (FIBER 1g); PRO. 5g
% DAILY VALUE: VIT. A 6%; VIT. C 2%; CALC. 2%; IRON 6%
EXCHANGES: 2 STARCH, 2 1/2 OTHER CARB., 3 FAT
CARB. CHOICES: 4 1/2

Key Lime Pie

PREP: 20 min **BAKE:** 15 min **COOL:** 15 min **CHILL:** 2 hr ▪ **8 SERVINGS**

Key limes, found in the Florida Keys, are smaller and rounder than the more familiar Persian limes and can be difficult to find. The good news is that bottled Key lime juice is available in most large supermarkets.

- Graham Cracker Crust (page 128)
- 4 large egg yolks
- 1 can (14 oz) sweetened condensed milk
- 1/2 cup fresh or bottled Key lime juice or regular lime juice
- 1 or 2 drops green food color, if desired
- 1 1/2 cups Sweetened Whipped Cream (page 217)

1. Make Graham Cracker Crust as directed—except do not bake.

2. Heat oven to 375°F.

3. In medium bowl, beat egg yolks, milk, lime juice and food color with electric mixer on medium speed about 1 minute or until well blended. Pour into unbaked crust.

4. Bake 14 to 16 minutes or until center is set. Cool on wire rack 15 minutes. Cover and refrigerate until chilled, at least 2 hours but no longer than 3 days. Spread with Sweetened Whipped Cream. Store covered in refrigerator.

1 SERVING: CAL. 420 (CAL. FROM FAT 205); FAT 23g (SAT. FAT 10g); CHOL. 145mg; SODIUM 165mg; CARBS. 47g (FIBER 0g); PRO. 6g
% DAILY VALUE: VIT. A 10%; VIT. C 8%; CALC. 16%; IRON 4%
EXCHANGES: 2 STARCH, 1 FRUIT, 4 1/2 FAT **CARB. CHOICES:** 3

Pumpkin Pie

PREP: 20 min **BAKE:** 1 hr 14 min **COOL:** 2 hr ▪ **8 SERVINGS**

Be sure to use canned pumpkin, not pumpkin pie mix, in this recipe. The mix has sugar and spices already in it, so if you have purchased the pumpkin pie mix, follow the directions on that label. Or if you like, use 1½ cups cooked fresh pumpkin.

- Pastry for One-Crust Pie (page 124), Easy Buttermilk Pastry (page 127) or Press-in-the-Pan Oil Pastry (page 127)
- 2 large eggs
- ½ cup sugar
- 1 teaspoon ground cinnamon
- ½ teaspoon salt
- ½ teaspoon ground ginger
- ⅛ teaspoon ground cloves
- 1 can (15 oz) pumpkin (not pumpkin pie mix)
- 1 can (12 oz) evaporated milk
- Sweetened Whipped Cream (page 217), if desired

1. Heat oven to 425°F. Make pastry for Unbaked One-Crust Pie. (If making Press-in-the-Pan Oil Pastry, continue with Step 2 instead of partially baking crust.) After fluting edge of pastry in pie plate, carefully line pastry with a double thickness of foil, gently pressing foil to bottom and side of pastry. Let foil extend over edge to prevent excessive browning. Bake 10 minutes; carefully remove foil and bake 2 to 4 minutes longer or until pastry *just begins* to brown and has become set. If crust bubbles, gently push bubbles down with back of spoon.

2. In medium bowl, beat eggs slightly with wire whisk or hand beater. Beat in remaining ingredients except whipped cream.

3. Cover edge of pie crust with 2- to 3-inch strip of foil to prevent excessive browning (page 122); remove foil during last 15 minutes of baking. To prevent spilling filling, place pie plate on oven rack. Pour filling into hot pie crust.

4. Bake 15 minutes. Reduce oven temperature to 350°F. Bake about 45 minutes longer or until knife inserted in center comes out clean. Cool on wire rack 2 hours. Serve with Sweetened Whipped Cream. After cooling, pie can remain at room temperature up to an additional 4 hours, then should be covered and refrigerated.

1 SERVING: CAL. 295 (CAL. FROM FAT 135); FAT 15g (SAT. FAT 5g); CHOL. 65mg; SODIUM 360mg; CARBS. 33g (FIBER 2g); PRO. 7g
% DAILY VALUE: VIT. A 100%; VIT. C 2%; CALC. 14%; IRON 10%
EXCHANGES: 1 STARCH, 1 FRUIT, 3 FAT **CARB. CHOICES:** 2

PRALINE PUMPKIN PIE Make pie as directed—except decrease second bake time to 35 minutes. Mix ⅓ cup packed brown sugar, ⅓ cup chopped pecans and 1 tablespoon butter or margarine, softened. Sprinkle over pie. Bake about 10 minutes longer or until knife inserted in center comes out clean.

◀ **Key Lime Pie**

Impossibly Easy Pumpkin Pie

PREP: 10 min **BAKE:** 40 min **COOL:** 2 hr ■ **8 SERVINGS**

This pie is "impossibly" easy because you don't need to make pie crust. Just mix all the ingredients up in a bowl and watch. A light crust magically forms as the pie bakes.

- 1 cup canned pumpkin (not pumpkin pie mix)
- 1/2 cup Original Bisquick® mix or Reduced Fat Bisquick® mix
- 1/2 cup sugar
- 1 cup evaporated milk
- 1 tablespoon butter or margarine, softened
- 1 1/2 teaspoons pumpkin pie spice
- 1 teaspoon vanilla
- 2 large eggs
- Sweetened Whipped Cream (page 217), if desired

1. Heat oven to 350°F. Grease 9-inch glass pie plate with shortening.

2. In large bowl, stir all ingredients except whipped cream with fork or wire whisk until blended. To prevent spilling, place pie plate on oven rack. Pour filling into pie plate.

3. Bake 35 to 40 minutes or until knife inserted in center comes out clean. Cool on wire rack 2 hours. Serve with Sweetened Whipped Cream. After cooling, pie can remain at room temperature up to an additional 4 hours, then should be covered and refrigerated. Store pie covered in refrigerator.

1 SERVING: CAL. 165 (CAL. FROM FAT 55); FAT 6g (SAT. FAT 3g); CHOL. 65mg; SODIUM 170mg; CARBS. 23g (FIBER 1g); PRO. 5g
% DAILY VALUE: VIT. A 98%; VIT. C 0%; CALC. 10%; IRON 4%
EXCHANGES: 1 STARCH, 1 VEGETABLE, 1 FAT **CARB. CHOICES:** 1 1/2

Custard Pie

PREP: 15 min **BAKE:** 49 min **COOL:** 2 hr ■ **8 SERVINGS**

For a richer filling, use half-and-half instead of milk.

- Pastry for One-Crust Pie (page 124) or Easy Buttermilk Pastry (page 127)
- 4 large eggs
- 2/3 cup sugar
- 2 2/3 cups milk
- 1 teaspoon vanilla
- 1/2 teaspoon salt
- 1/4 teaspoon ground nutmeg

1. Heat oven to 425°F. Make pastry for Unbaked One-Crust Pie. After fluting edge of pastry in pie plate, carefully line pastry with a double thickness of foil, gently pressing foil to bottom and side of pastry. Let foil extend over edge to prevent excessive browning. Bake 10 minutes; carefully remove foil and bake 2 to 4 minutes longer or until pastry *just begins* to brown and has become set. If crust bubbles, gently push bubbles down with back of spoon.

2. Increase oven temperature to 450°F. In medium bowl, beat eggs slightly with wire whisk or hand beater. Beat in remaining ingredients.

3. Cover edge of pie crust with 2- to 3-inch strip of foil to prevent excessive browning (page 122); remove foil during last 15 minutes of baking. To prevent spilling filling, place pie plate on oven rack. Pour filling into hot pie crust.

4. Bake 20 minutes. Reduce oven temperature to 350°F. Bake 10 to 15 minutes longer or until knife inserted halfway between center and edge comes out clean. Cool on wire rack 2 hours. After cooling, pie can remain at room temperature up to an additional 4 hours, then should be covered and refrigerated.

1 SERVING: CAL. 275 (CAL. FROM FAT 125); FAT 14g (SAT. FAT 4g); CHOL. 110mg; SODIUM 350mg; CARBS. 31g (FIBER 0g); PRO. 6g
% DAILY VALUE: VIT. A 4%; VIT. C 0%; CALC. 8%; IRON 6%
EXCHANGES: 2 STARCH, 2 1/2 FAT **CARB. CHOICES:** 2

Pecan Pie

PREP: 20 min **BAKE:** 50 min ■ **8 SERVINGS**

- Pastry for One-Crust Pie (page 124), Easy Buttermilk Pastry (page 127) or Press-in-the-Pan Oil Pastry (page 127)
- 2/3 cup sugar
- 1/3 cup butter or margarine, melted
- 1 cup corn syrup
- 1/2 teaspoon salt
- 3 large eggs
- 1 cup pecan halves or broken pecans

1. Heat oven to 375°F. Make pastry for Unbaked One-Crust Pie.

2. In medium bowl, beat sugar, butter, corn syrup, salt and eggs with wire whisk or hand beater until well blended. Stir in pecans. Pour into pastry-lined pie plate.

3. Bake 40 to 50 minutes or until center is set. Serve warm or cold.

1 SERVING: CAL. 540 (CAL. FROM FAT 270); FAT 30g (SAT. FAT 9g); CHOL. 100mg; SODIUM 420mg; CARBS. 62g (FIBER 1g); PRO. 5g
% DAILY VALUE: VIT. A 8%; VIT. C 0%; CALC. 2%; IRON 6%
EXCHANGES: 2 STARCH, 2 OTHER CARB., 6 FAT **CARB. CHOICES:** 4

KENTUCKY PECAN PIE Add 2 tablespoons bourbon with the corn syrup. Stir in 1 bag (6 oz) semisweet chocolate chips (1 cup) with the pecans.

Classic French Silk Pie

PREP: 30 min **BAKE/COOL:** 30 min **CHILL:** 2 hr ■ **10 SERVINGS**

Using an egg substitute, which is pasteurized, eliminates the risk of salmonella that can be contracted from raw eggs.

- Pastry for One-Crust Pie (page 124) or Easy Buttermilk Pastry (page 127)
- 1 cup sugar
- 3/4 cup butter, softened*
- 1 1/2 teaspoons vanilla
- 3 oz unsweetened baking chocolate, melted and cooled
- 3/4 cup fat-free cholesterol-free egg product
- 1 1/2 cups Sweetened Whipped Cream (page 217)
- Chocolate curls, if desired

1. Bake pastry for Baked One-Crust Pie. Cool completely.

2. In medium bowl, beat sugar and butter with electric mixer on medium speed until light and fluffy. Beat in vanilla and chocolate. Gradually beat in egg product on high speed or until light and fluffy (about 3 minutes). Pour into pie crust. Refrigerate until set, at least 2 hours but no longer than 24 hours.

3. Spread with Sweetened Whipped Cream. Garnish with chocolate curls. Store covered in refrigerator.

**Do not use margarine or vegetable-oil spreads because filling will be curdled instead of smooth and creamy.*

1 SERVING: CAL. 415 (CAL. FROM FAT 260); FAT 29g (SAT. FAT 15g); CHOL. 35mg; SODIUM 250mg; CARBS. 35g (FIBER 2g); PRO. 4g
% DAILY VALUE: VIT. A 12%; VIT. C 0%; CALC. 2%; IRON 8%
EXCHANGES: 1 STARCH, 1 OTHER CARB., 6 FAT **CARB. CHOICES:** 2

MOCHA FRENCH SILK PIE Beat in 1 1/2 teaspoons instant coffee (dry) with the chocolate.

USING A PASTRY CLOTH AND STOCKINET

Roll out pastry the nonstick way! Use a pastry cloth and a rolling pin cover, called a *stockinet*. Look for -them in specialty cookware stores (or use a lint-free kitchen towel instead of a pastry cloth). Here's how:

Secure a pastry cloth or lint-free kitchen towel around a large cutting board (at least 12 × 12 inches) with masking tape. Place stockinet on rolling pin. Rub flour into both the cloth and stockinet; this prevents sticking, but won't add flour into the pastry.

Also check cookware stores for round boards with a removable, elasticized linen cover marked with circles for various crust dimensions. Roll as directed in How to Make Pastry, page 125. If the pastry begins to stick, rub a little more flour on the cloth and stockinet.

Grasshopper Pie

PREP: 30 min **CHILL:** 4 hr 20 min ▪ **8 SERVINGS**

Named after a favorite after-dinner drink, this pie is flavored with crème de menthe and crème de cacao.

Cookie Crumb Crust (page 128)
1/2 cup milk
32 large marshmallows
1/4 cup green or white crème de menthe
3 tablespoons white crème de cacao
1 1/2 cups whipping (heavy) cream
Few drops of green food color, if desired
Grated semisweet baking chocolate, if desired

1. Bake crust as directed, using chocolate wafer cookies. Reserve about 2 tablespoons crumbs to sprinkle over top of pie if desired.

2. In 3-quart saucepan, heat milk and marshmallows over low heat, stirring constantly, just until marshmallows are melted. Refrigerate about 20 minutes, stirring occasionally, until mixture mounds slightly when dropped from a spoon. (If mixture becomes too thick, place saucepan in bowl of warm water and stir mixture until proper consistency.)

3. Gradually stir in crème de menthe and crème de cacao.

4. In chilled medium bowl, beat whipping cream with electric mixer on high speed until stiff. Fold marshmallow mixture into whipped cream. Fold in food color. Spread in crust. Sprinkle with reserved cookie crumbs or grated chocolate. Refrigerate about 4 hours or until set. Store covered in refrigerator.

1 SERVING: CAL. 400 (CAL. FROM FAT 205); FAT 23g (SAT. FAT 13g); CHOL. 60mg; SODIUM 200mg; CARBS. 45g (FIBER 1g); PRO. 3g
% DAILY VALUE: VIT. A 14%; VIT. C 0%; CALC. 6%; IRON 4%
EXCHANGES: 1 STARCH, 2 OTHER CARB., 4 1/2 FAT
CARB. CHOICES: 3

CAFÉ LATTE PIE Substitute water for the milk; add 1 tablespoon instant coffee (dry) with the water. Substitute coffee liqueur for the crème de menthe and Irish whiskey for the crème de cacao.

IRISH CREAM PIE Substitute 1/3 cup Irish cream liqueur for the crème de menthe and white crème de cacao.

Café Latte Pie ▶

CHAPTER 5

Casseroles & Slow-Cooker

Casseroles

Slow Cooker

Chart

LOW-FAT = *3g or less, except main dishes with 10g or less* FAST = *Ready in 20 minutes or less* BREAD MACHINE = *Bread machine directions* SLOW COOKER = *Slow cooker directions* LIGHTER = *25% fewer calories or grams of fat*

◀ **Fiesta Taco Casserole (page 147)**

Casserole Basics

A casserole, or "hot dish," is comfort food at its best. It can be layered or mixed, have a flaky crust or be topped with mashed potatoes or buttery crumbs. What better way to share a meal with family and friends? Read on for guidelines on dishing up casseroles.

PICKING THE RIGHT DISH

Usually, you'll find casserole dishes made of heat-resistant glass. But they can also be made of ceramic, enamel-coated cast iron and ovenproof clay. Look for ones with lids, as many have them.

CASSEROLE DISH SUBSTITUTIONS

When you want to substitute one dish for another, check this list for equivalents.

Baking dish or pan	Casserole
8-inch square	2 quarts
9-inch square	$2^1/_2$ quarts
11 × 7 inch	2 quarts
13 × 9 inch	3 quarts

FREEZING CASSEROLES

Casseroles are the perfect make-ahead meal. They usually freeze well and are easy to reheat following these guidelines:

- Casseroles can be frozen unbaked or baked. If possible, thaw overnight in the refrigerator. When baking a frozen casserole, the center of the mixture should reach 160°F. Start checking the center at 1 hour; if not yet 160°F, continue baking, checking every 10 to 15 minutes.
- Casseroles made with potatoes, rice or pasta lose some of their texture and tend to get mushier when frozen.
- If you're planning to thaw or reheat a casserole in the microwave, make it in a microwavable dish.
- To avoid putting all of your casserole dishes in the freezer, line the dish with heavy-duty foil before adding the casserole mixture. Once frozen, remove the foil and casserole from the dish and wrap tightly. To bake, remove foil and put the casserole back in the dish. Or freeze casseroles in disposable cookware.
- Cool baked casseroles or casserole leftovers completely before freezing. Wrap tightly with foil or place in containers with tight-fitting lids to prevent freezer burn.
- Label casseroles with contents, date and cooking instructions; freeze up to 3 months.

TOTING CASSEROLES

When you're taking a casserole meal-to-go, follow these guidelines:

- Consider buying an insulated casserole tote. Some totes offer dual thermal/cold packs for keeping hot foods hot and cold foods cold.
- For casseroles and baking dishes with lids, attach rubber bands around the handles and lid to secure the lid. No lid? Cover tightly with foil.
- For dishes with a holder or basket, use it to secure the dish.
- Wrap the casserole in a towel or in newspaper to insulate, and put in a cooler, box or other container that will stay flat and secure in your car.
- For food-safety reasons, don't let perishable hot foods stand out more than 2 hours. Be sure to include transport time and serving time in those 2 hours.

Chicken Tetrazzini

PREP: 20 min **BAKE:** 30 min ▪ **6 SERVINGS**

1 package (7 oz) spaghetti, broken into thirds
1/4 cup butter or margarine
1/4 cup all-purpose flour
1/2 teaspoon salt
1/4 teaspoon pepper
1 cup chicken broth
1 cup whipping (heavy) cream
2 tablespoons dry sherry or water
2 cups cubed cooked chicken or turkey
1 jar (4.5 oz) sliced mushrooms, drained
1/2 cup grated Parmesan cheese

1. Heat oven to 350°F.

2. Cook and drain spaghetti as directed on package.

3. Meanwhile, in 2-quart saucepan, melt butter over low heat. Stir in flour, salt and pepper. Cook, stirring constantly, until mixture is smooth and bubbly; remove from heat. Stir in broth and whipping cream. Heat to boiling, stirring constantly. Boil and stir 1 minute.

4. Stir spaghetti, sherry, chicken and mushrooms into sauce. Pour spaghetti mixture into ungreased 2-quart casserole. Sprinkle with cheese.

5. Bake uncovered about 30 minutes or until bubbly in center.

1 SERVING: CAL. 470 (CAL. FROM FAT 245); FAT 27g (SAT. FAT 15g); CHOL. 110mg; SODIUM 610mg; CARBS. 33g (FIBER 2g); PRO. 24g
% DAILY VALUE: VIT. A 18%; VIT. C 0%; CALC. 14%; IRON 14%
EXCHANGES: 2 STARCH, 2 MEDIUM-FAT MEAT, 3 FAT, 1/2 SKIM MILK
CARB. CHOICES: 2

LIGHTER CHICKEN TETRAZZINI

For 10 grams of fat and 320 calories per serving, decrease butter to 2 tablespoons and Parmesan cheese to 1/4 cup; substitute fat-free (skim) milk for the whipping cream.

Santa Fe Chicken Tortellini Casserole

PREP: 15 min **BAKE:** 35 min ▪ **6 SERVINGS**

Those broken chips at the bottom of the chip bag are perfect for topping off this tasty Southwestern casserole. Or crush whole chips in a resealable plastic food-storage bag with a rolling pin.

1 package (9 oz) refrigerated cheese-filled tortellini
3 tablespoons olive or vegetable oil
2 cups broccoli flowerets
1 medium onion, chopped (1/2 cup)
1 medium red bell pepper, chopped (1 cup)
3 tablespoons all-purpose flour
3/4 cup milk
3/4 cup chicken broth
1 teaspoon ground cumin
4 cups cut-up cooked chicken
3/4 cup shredded Monterey Jack cheese (3 oz)
1/2 cup shredded Colby cheese (2 oz)
1/2 cup crushed tortilla chips, if desired

1. Heat oven to 325°F. Spray 3-quart casserole with cooking spray.

2. Cook and drain tortellini as directed on package.

Chicken Tetrazzini

3. Meanwhile, in 10-inch skillet, heat 1 tablespoon of the oil over medium-high heat. Cook broccoli, onion and bell pepper in oil about 3 minutes, stirring frequently, until crisp-tender. Remove broccoli mixture from skillet.

4. In same skillet, cook flour and remaining 2 tablespoons oil over low heat, stirring constantly, until smooth. Stir in milk, broth and cumin. Heat to boiling over medium heat, stirring constantly; remove from heat. Stir in chicken, Monterey Jack cheese, tortellini and broccoli mixture. Spoon into casserole.

5. Bake uncovered 30 minutes. Sprinkle with Colby cheese and tortilla chips. Bake 5 minutes longer or until casserole is hot in center and cheese is melted.

1 SERVING: CAL. 440 (CAL. FROM FAT 225); FAT 25g (SAT. FAT 9g); CHOL. 140mg; SODIUM 390mg; CARBS. 16g (FIBER 2g); PRO. 38g **% DAILY VALUE:** VIT. A 38%; VIT. C 50%; CALC. 28%; IRON 14% **EXCHANGES:** 1 STARCH, 5 MEDIUM-FAT MEAT **CARB. CHOICES:** 1

Spinach Fettuccine Casserole with Chicken and Bacon

PREP: 20 min **BAKE:** 30 min ■ **4 SERVINGS**

- 1 package (9 oz) refrigerated spinach fettuccine
- 3 tablespoons butter or margarine
- 3 tablespoons all-purpose flour
- 1 can (14 oz) chicken broth
- 1/2 cup half-and-half
- 1 1/2 cups cubed cooked chicken
- 1/2 cup oil-packed sun-dried tomatoes, drained and cut into thin strips
- 2 slices bacon, crisply cooked and crumbled (2 tablespoons)
- 3 tablespoons shredded Parmesan cheese

1. Heat oven to 350°F. Spray 8-inch square baking dish with cooking spray.

2. Cook and drain fettuccine as directed on package.

3. Meanwhile, in 2-quart saucepan, melt butter over medium heat. Stir in flour. Gradually stir in broth. Heat to boiling, stirring constantly; remove from heat. Stir in half-and-half.

4. Stir chicken, tomatoes and bacon into sauce. Add fettuccine; toss gently to mix well. Spoon into baking dish. Sprinkle with cheese.

5. Bake uncovered about 30 minutes or until hot in center.

1 SERVING: CAL. 540 (CAL. FROM FAT 215); FAT 24g (SAT. FAT 11g); CHOL. 140mg; SODIUM 720mg; CARBS. 51g (FIBER 3g); PRO. 30g **% DAILY VALUE:** VIT. A 16%; VIT. C 12%; CALC. 14%; IRON 24% **EXCHANGES:** 3 STARCH, 1 VEGETABLE, 3 MEDIUM-FAT MEAT, 1 FAT **CARB. CHOICES:** 3 1/2

Picadillo Chicken Paella

PREP: 15 min **BAKE:** 1 hr 5 min ■ **4 SERVINGS**

Serve supper as they do in southern Spain with this festive paella, some crusty French bread and lemon or mango sorbet for dessert.

- 1 cup uncooked regular long-grain rice
- 1/2 lb smoked chorizo sausage, sliced
- 1/4 cup raisins
- 1 can (14.5 oz) stewed tomatoes, undrained
- 1 can (14 oz) chicken broth
- 1/2 teaspoon ground turmeric
- 4 chicken legs, skin removed if desired
- 4 chicken thighs, skin removed if desired
- 1/4 teaspoon seasoned salt
- 1/4 teaspoon paprika
- 1 cup frozen green peas, thawed

1. Heat oven to 375°F. Spray 13 × 9-inch glass baking dish with cooking spray.

2. In baking dish, mix uncooked rice, sausage, raisins, tomatoes, broth and turmeric. Arrange chicken on top; press into rice mixture. Sprinkle chicken with seasoned salt and paprika.

3. Cover and bake 30 minutes. Uncover and bake about 30 minutes longer or until liquid is absorbed and juice of chicken is clear when thickest part is cut to bone (180°F). Stir in peas. Bake uncovered 5 minutes.

1 SERVING: CAL. 790 (CAL. FROM FAT 340); FAT 38g (SAT. FAT 13g); CHOL. 155mg; SODIUM 1620mg; CARBS. 61g (FIBER 4g); PRO. 52g **% DAILY VALUE:** VIT. A 10%; VIT. C 12%; CALC. 8%; IRON 32% **EXCHANGES:** 4 STARCH, 3 MEDIUM-FAT MEAT **CARB. CHOICES:** 4

Italian Sausage Lasagna

PREP: 1 hr 10 min **BAKE:** 45 min **STAND:** 15 min ■ **8 SERVINGS**

Here's a great recipe to make ahead. Cover the unbaked lasagna with foil and refrigerate up to 24 hours or freeze up to 2 months. Bake covered for 45 minutes, then uncover and bake 15 to 20 minutes longer (35 to 45 minutes if frozen). Check the center and bake a little longer if necessary until it's hot and bubbly.

- 1 lb bulk Italian sausage or lean (at least 80%) ground beef
- 1 medium onion, chopped (1/2 cup)
- 1 clove garlic, finely chopped
- 3 tablespoons chopped fresh parsley
- 1 tablespoon chopped fresh or 1 teaspoon dried basil leaves
- 1 teaspoon sugar
- 1 can (14.5 oz) whole tomatoes, undrained
- 1 can (15 oz) tomato sauce
- 8 uncooked lasagna noodles
- 1 container (15 oz) ricotta cheese or small curd creamed cottage cheese (2 cups)
- 1/2 cup grated Parmesan cheese
- 1 tablespoon chopped fresh or 1 1/2 teaspoons dried oregano leaves
- 2 cups shredded mozzarella cheese (8 oz)

1. In 10-inch skillet, cook sausage, onion and garlic over medium heat 8 to 10 minutes, stirring occasionally, until sausage is no longer pink; drain.

2. Stir in 2 tablespoons of the parsley, the basil, sugar, tomatoes and tomato sauce, breaking up tomatoes with a fork or snipping with kitchen scissors. Heat to boiling, stirring occasionally; reduce heat. Simmer uncovered about 45 minutes or until slightly thickened.

3. Heat oven to 350°F. Cook and drain noodles as directed on package.

4. Meanwhile, in small bowl, mix ricotta cheese, 1/4 cup of the Parmesan cheese, the oregano and remaining 1 tablespoon parsley.

5. In ungreased 13 × 9-inch glass baking dish, spread half of the sausage mixture (about 2 cups). Top with 4 noodles. Spread half of the cheese mixture (about 1 cup) over noodles. Sprinkle with half of the mozzarella cheese. Repeat layers, ending with mozzarella. Sprinkle with remaining 1/4 cup Parmesan cheese.

6. Cover and bake 30 minutes. Uncover and bake about 15 minutes longer or until hot and bubbly. Let stand 15 minutes before cutting.

1 SERVING: CAL. 430 (CAL. FROM FAT 200); FAT 22g (SAT. FAT 11g); CHOL. 70mg; SODIUM 1,110mg; CARBS. 28g (FIBER 2g); PRO. 29g
% DAILY VALUE: VIT. A 20%; VIT. C 14%; CALC. 48%; IRON 16%
EXCHANGES: 2 STARCH, 3 MEDIUM-FAT MEAT, 1 FAT
CARB. CHOICES: 2

EASY ITALIAN SAUSAGE LASAGNA Substitute 4 cups (from two 26- to 28-oz jars) tomato pasta sauce with meat for the first 8 ingredients. Omit steps 1 and 2.

Easy Bacon Cheeseburger Lasagna

PREP: 30 min **CHILL:** 2 hr **BAKE:** 1 hr 15 min **STAND:** 10 min ■ **8 SERVINGS**

If you like your cheeseburgers with all the extras, top each serving of this lasagna with chopped tomatoes and shredded lettuce.

- 1 1/2 lb lean (at least 80%) ground beef
- 2 medium onions, chopped (1 cup)
- 1/4 teaspoon salt
- 1/8 teaspoon pepper
- 2 cans (15 oz each) chunky tomato sauce
- 1 cup water
- 1 large egg
- 1 container (15 oz) ricotta cheese
- 1 cup shredded Swiss cheese (4 oz)
- 1/4 cup chopped fresh parsley
- 8 slices bacon, crisply cooked and crumbled (1/2 cup)
- 12 uncooked lasagna noodles
- 2 cups shredded Cheddar cheese (8 oz)

1. Spray 13 × 9-inch glass baking dish with cooking spray. In 12-inch skillet, cook beef, onions, salt and pepper over medium-high heat 5 to 7 minutes, stirring occasionally, until beef is brown; drain. Stir in tomato sauce and water. Heat to boiling; reduce heat to medium-low. Simmer uncovered 10 minutes.

2. In medium bowl, beat egg with fork. Stir in ricotta cheese, Swiss cheese, parsley and 1/4 cup of the bacon.

3. Spread about 1 cup of the beef mixture in baking dish. Top with 4 uncooked noodles. Spread half of the ricotta mixture, 2 cups beef mixture and 3/4 cup of the Cheddar cheese over noodles. Repeat layers once, starting with 4 noodles. Top with remaining noodles, beef mixture, Cheddar cheese and bacon. Spray 15-inch length of foil with cooking spray. Cover lasagna with foil, sprayed side down. Refrigerate at least 2 hours but no longer than 24 hours.

4. Heat oven to 350°F. Bake covered 45 minutes. Uncover and bake about 30 minutes longer or until bubbly and golden brown. Cover and let stand 10 minutes before cutting.

1 SERVING: CAL. 605 (CAL. FROM FAT 290); FAT 32g (SAT. FAT 16g); CHOL. 140mg; SODIUM 1150mg; CARBS. 37g (FIBER 3g); PRO. 42g **% DAILY VALUE:** VIT. A 36%; VIT. C 14%; CALC. 46%; IRON 22% **EXCHANGES:** 2 STARCH, 1 VEGETABLE, 5 MEDIUM-FAT MEAT, 1 FAT **CARB. CHOICES:** 2 1/2

LIGHTER EASY BACON CHEESEBURGER LASAGNA

For 7 grams of fat and 420 calories per serving, substitute ground turkey breast for the ground beef, 1/4 cup fat-free cholesterol-free egg product for the egg and reduced-fat mozzarella cheese for the Swiss cheese. Use fat-free ricotta cheese. Decrease bacon to 4 slices. Substitute 1 1/2 cups reduced-fat Cheddar cheese for the 2 cups regular Cheddar cheese.

DOUBLE-BATCH IT!

Make an extra casserole or pan of lasagna to pop in the oven another time. For specific directions, see Freezing Casseroles, page 139.

Easy Bacon Cheeseburger Lasagna ▶

Creamy Seafood Lasagna

PREP: 20 min **BAKE:** 45 min **STAND:** 15 min ■ **8 SERVINGS**

- 9 uncooked lasagna noodles
- 1/4 cup butter or margarine
- 1 medium onion, finely chopped (1/2 cup)
- 2 cloves garlic, finely chopped
- 1/4 cup all-purpose flour
- 2 cups half-and-half
- 1 cup chicken broth
- 1/3 cup dry sherry or chicken broth
- 1/2 teaspoon salt
- 1/4 teaspoon pepper
- 1 container (15 oz) ricotta cheese
- 1/2 cup grated Parmesan cheese
- 1 egg, slightly beaten
- 1/4 cup chopped fresh parsley
- 2 packages (8 oz each) frozen salad-style imitation crabmeat, thawed, drained and chopped
- 2 packages (4 oz each) frozen cooked salad shrimp, thawed and drained
- 3 cups shredded mozzarella cheese (12 oz)
- 1 tablespoon chopped fresh parsley, if desired

1. Heat oven to 350°F. Cook noodles as directed on package.

2. Meanwhile, in 3-quart saucepan, melt butter over medium heat. Cook onion and garlic in butter 2 to 3 minutes, stirring occasionally, until onion is crisp-tender. Stir in flour; cook and stir until bubbly. Gradually stir in half-and-half, broth, sherry, salt and pepper. Heat to boiling, stirring constantly. Boil and stir 1 minute. Remove from heat and set aside.

3. In medium bowl, mix ricotta cheese, Parmesan cheese, egg and 1/4 cup parsley; set aside.

4. Drain noodles. In ungreased 13 × 9-inch (3-quart) glass baking dish, spread 3/4 cup of the sauce. Top with 3 noodles. Spread half of the crabmeat and shrimp over noodles; spread with 3/4 cup of the sauce. Sprinkle with 1 cup of the mozzarella cheese; top with 3 noodles. Spread ricotta mixture over noodles; spread with 3/4 cup of the sauce. Sprinkle with 1 cup of the mozzarella cheese; top with 3 noodles. Spread with remaining crabmeat, shrimp and sauce. Sprinkle with remaining 1 cup mozzarella cheese.

5. Bake uncovered 40 to 45 minutes or until cheese is light golden brown. Let stand 15 minutes before cutting. Sprinkle with 1 tablespoon parsley.

1 SERVING: CAL. 340 (CAL. FROM FAT 80); FAT 9g (SAT. FAT 3.5g); CHOL. 50mg; SODIUM 850mg; CARBS. 44g (FIBER 2g); PRO. 23g
% DAILY VALUE: VIT. A 15%; VIT. C 4%; CALC. 35%; IRON 15%
EXCHANGES: 2 STARCH, 3 1/2 MEDIUM-FAT MEAT, 1/2 FAT
CARB. CHOICES: 3

LIGHTER CREAMY SEAFOOD LASAGNA

For 11 grams of fat and 430 calories per serving, decrease butter to 2 tablespoons; use fat-free half-and-half, fat-free ricotta cheese, reduced-fat Parmesan cheese and reduced-fat mozzarella cheese.

Creamy Seafood Lasagna ▶

Manicotti

PREP: 40 min **BAKE:** 55 min ■ **7 SERVINGS**

- 14 uncooked manicotti shells
- 1 lb lean (at least 80%) ground beef
- 1 large onion, chopped (1 cup)
- 2 large cloves garlic, finely chopped
- 1 jar (26 to 30 oz) tomato pasta sauce (any variety)*
- 2 boxes (9 oz each) frozen chopped spinach, thawed
- 2 cups small curd cottage cheese
- 1 can (8 oz) mushroom pieces and stems, drained
- 1/3 cup grated Parmesan cheese
- 1/4 teaspoon ground nutmeg
- 1/4 teaspoon pepper
- 2 cups shredded mozzarella cheese (8 oz)
- 2 tablespoons grated Parmesan cheese

1. Cook and drain manicotti as directed on package using minimum cooking time (cooking for the minimum time helps prevent the shells from tearing while filling).

2. Meanwhile, in 10-inch skillet, cook beef, onion and garlic over medium heat 8 to 10 minutes, stirring occasionally, until beef is brown; drain. Stir in pasta sauce.

3. Heat oven to 350°F. Spray 13 × 9-inch glass baking dish with cooking spray.

4. Squeeze thawed spinach to drain; spread on paper towels and pat dry. In medium bowl, mix spinach, cottage cheese, mushrooms, 1/3 cup Parmesan cheese, the nutmeg and pepper.

5. In baking dish, spread 1 cup of the beef mixture. Fill manicotti shells with spinach mixture. Place shells on beef mixture in dish. Pour remaining beef mixture evenly over shells, covering shells completely. Sprinkle with mozzarella cheese and 2 tablespoons Parmesan cheese.

6. Cover and bake 30 minutes. Uncover and bake 20 to 25 minutes longer or until hot and bubbly.

**One recipe Italian Tomato Sauce (page 406) can be substituted for the pasta sauce.*

1 SERVING: CAL. 580 (CAL. FROM FAT 200); FAT 22g (SAT. FAT 10g); CHOL. 60mg; SODIUM 1,260mg; CARBS. 55g (FIBER 5g); PRO. 40g
% DAILY VALUE: VIT. A 100%; VIT. C 0%; CALC. 45%; IRON 20%
EXCHANGES: 3 1/2 STARCH, 1 VEGETABLE, 4 MEDIUM-FAT MEAT
CARB. CHOICES: 3 1/2

Manicotti ▶

Spaghetti Pie

PREP: 10 min **COOK:** 16 min **BAKE:** 45 min **STAND:** 5 min ▪ **6 SERVINGS**

If you hold uncooked spaghetti together in a bundle, 4 ounces is about as big around as the size of a quarter.

- 4 oz uncooked spaghetti
- 1/2 lb lean (at least 80%) ground beef
- 1 small green bell pepper, chopped (1/2 cup)
- 1 small onion, chopped (1/4 cup)
- 1 jar (14 oz) tomato pasta sauce (any variety)
- 1 teaspoon chili powder
- 1/2 teaspoon salt
- 1/4 teaspoon pepper
- 2 large eggs
- 1 cup small curd cottage cheese
- 1/2 cup shredded mozzarella cheese (2 oz)

1. Heat oven to 375°F. Spray 10-inch glass pie plate with cooking spray. Cook and drain spaghetti as directed on package.

2. Meanwhile, in 10-inch skillet, cook beef, bell pepper and onion over medium heat 8 to 10 minutes, stirring occasionally, until beef is brown; drain. Stir in pasta sauce, chili powder, salt and pepper. Cook 5 to 6 minutes, stirring occasionally, until sauce is thickened.

3. Place spaghetti in pie plate; gently press on bottom and 1 inch up side of pie plate.

4. In small bowl, stir eggs and cottage cheese until well mixed; spread evenly over spaghetti. Spoon beef mixture over cottage cheese mixture. Sprinkle with mozzarella cheese.

5. Bake 35 to 45 minutes or until center is set. Let stand 5 minutes before cutting.

1 SERVING: CAL. 320 (CAL. FROM FAT 115); FAT 13g (SAT. FAT 5g); CHOL. 100mg; SODIUM 760mg; CARBS. 30 (FIBER 2g); PRO. 22g
% DAILY VALUE: VIT. A 12%; VIT. C 18%; CALC. 12%; IRON 12%
EXCHANGES: 2 STARCH, 2 MEDIUM-FAT MEAT **CARB. CHOICES:** 2

Cheesy Pizza Casserole

PREP: 15 min **BAKE:** 35 min ▪ **6 SERVINGS**

- 3 cups uncooked rigatoni pasta (9 oz)
- 1/2 lb lean (at least 80%) ground beef
- 1/4 cup sliced ripe olives
- 1 jar (4.5 oz) mushroom pieces and stems, drained
- 1 jar (26 to 28 oz) tomato pasta sauce (any variety)
- 1 cup shredded mozzarella cheese (4 oz)

1. Heat oven to 350°F. Cook and drain pasta as directed on package.

2. Meanwhile, in 10-inch skillet, cook beef over medium heat 8 to 10 minutes, stirring occasionally, until brown; drain. In ungreased 2 1/2-quart casserole, mix pasta, beef and remaining ingredients except cheese.

3. Cover and bake about 30 minutes or until hot and bubbly. Sprinkle with cheese. Bake uncovered about 5 minutes longer or until cheese is melted.

1 SERVING: CAL. 430 (CAL. FROM FAT 115); FAT 13g (SAT. FAT 5g); CHOL. 35mg; SODIUM 850mg; CARBS. 58g (FIBER 4g); PRO. 20g
% DAILY VALUE: VIT. A 18%; VIT. C 14%; CALC. 18%; IRON 20%
EXCHANGES: 4 STARCH, 1 1/2 MEDIUM-FAT MEAT
CARB. CHOICES: 4

POTLUCK PANS

If you want to share your favorite casserole but not your dishes, try disposables!

Disposable cookware is handy for toting casseroles to a potluck, to an under-the-weather friend or to welcome home new parents. It lets you bake, microwave, freeze and serve all in the same dish. Look for it in the supermarket aisle with the foil and plastic wraps.

Fiesta Taco Casserole

PREP: 15 min **BAKE:** 30 min ▪ **4 SERVINGS**

1 lb lean (at least 80%) ground beef
1 can (15 to 16 oz) spicy chili beans in sauce, undrained
1 cup salsa
2 cups coarsely broken tortilla chips
3/4 cup sour cream
4 medium green onions, sliced (1/4 cup)
1 medium tomato, chopped (3/4 cup)
1 cup shredded Cheddar or Monterey Jack cheese (4 oz)
Tortilla chips, if desired
Shredded lettuce, if desired
Salsa, if desired

1. Heat oven to 350°F. In 10-inch skillet, cook beef over medium heat 8 to 10 minutes, stirring occasionally, until brown; drain. Stir in beans and 1 cup salsa. Heat to boiling, stirring occasionally.

2. In ungreased 2-quart casserole, place broken tortilla chips. Top with beef mixture. Spread with sour cream. Sprinkle with onions, tomato and cheese.

3. Bake uncovered 20 to 30 minutes or until hot and bubbly. Arrange tortilla chips around edge of casserole. Serve with lettuce and salsa.

1 SERVING (ABOUT 1 1/4 CUPS): CAL. 620 (CAL. FROM FAT 340); FAT 38g (SAT. FAT 18g); CHOL. 120mg; SODIUM 1430mg; CARBS. 34g (FIBER 7g); PRO. 37g **% DAILY VALUE:** VIT. A 35%; VIT. C 0%; CALC. 25%; IRON 30% **EXCHANGES:** 2 STARCH, 1 VEGETABLE, 4 MEDIUM-FAT MEAT, 3 FAT **CARB. CHOICES:** 2

LIGHTER FIESTA TACO CASSEROLE

For 13 grams of fat and 345 calories per serving, substitute ground turkey breast for the ground beef; use reduced-fat sour cream and reduced-fat Cheddar cheese.

EASY CASSEROLE CLEANUP

For quick casserole cleanup, line the casserole with heavy-duty foil, and spray with cooking spray before filling and baking.

Cheesy Barbecue Beef Casserole

PREP: 20 min **BAKE:** 40 min ▪ **6 SERVINGS**

3 cups uncooked ziti pasta (10 oz)
1 lb lean (at least 80%) ground beef
1 medium onion, chopped (1/2 cup)
1 cup barbecue sauce
1 cup shredded mozzarella cheese (4 oz)
1/4 cup chopped fresh parsley, if desired
1 cup milk
1 1/2 cups shredded Cheddar cheese (6 oz)

1. Heat oven to 350°F. Spray 2-quart casserole with cooking spray.

2. Cook and drain pasta as directed on package.

3. Meanwhile, in 10-inch skillet, cook beef and onion over medium-high heat 5 to 7 minutes, stirring occasionally, until beef is brown; drain.

4. Return drained pasta to saucepan. Stir in beef mixture and remaining ingredients except 1/2 cup of the Cheddar cheese. Spoon into casserole. Sprinkle with remaining 1/2 cup Cheddar cheese.

5. Bake uncovered 30 to 40 minutes or until hot in center.

1 SERVING: CAL. 570 (CAL. FROM FAT 205); FAT 23g (SAT. FAT 12g); CHOL. 90mg; SODIUM 750mg; CARBS. 56g (FIBER 2g); PRO. 35g **% DAILY VALUE:** VIT. A 14%; VIT. C 2%; CALC. 36%; IRON 22% **EXCHANGES:** 4 STARCH, 3 MEDIUM-FAT MEAT, 1/2 FAT **CARB. CHOICES:** 4

LIGHTER CHEESY BARBECUE BEEF CASSEROLE

For 6 grams of fat and 450 calories per serving, substitute ground turkey breast for the ground beef. Use fat-free (skim) milk. Substitute 1 cup reduced-fat Cheddar cheese for the 1 1/2 cups regular Cheddar cheese.

Wild Rice and Beef Casserole

PREP: 5 min **COOK:** 10 min **BAKE:** 40 min ▪ **4 SERVINGS**

1 lb lean (at least 80%) ground beef
1 package (6.2 oz) fast-cooking long-grain and wild rice mix
1 can (10.75 oz) condensed tomato soup
1/4 cup milk
1/4 teaspoon pepper
1 cup shredded Cheddar cheese (4 oz)

1. Heat oven to 350°F. Spray 2-quart casserole with cooking spray.

2. In 10-inch skillet, cook beef over medium heat 8 to 10 minutes, stirring occasionally, until brown; drain.

3. Meanwhile, make rice mix as directed on package—except omit butter. Stir rice mixture, soup, milk and pepper into beef. Spoon into casserole.

4. Cover and bake 30 minutes. Sprinkle with cheese. Bake uncovered 5 to 10 minutes longer or until cheese is melted and mixture is hot.

1 SERVING: CAL. 445 (CAL. FROM FAT 215); FAT 24g (SAT. FAT 11g); CHOL. 105mg; SODIUM 860mg; CARBS. 24g; (FIBER 1g); PRO. 33g
% DAILY VALUE: VIT. A 14%; VIT. C 8%; CALC. 18%; IRON 20%
EXCHANGES: 1 1/2 STARCH, 4 MEDIUM-FAT MEAT, 1/2 FAT
CARB. CHOICES: 1 1/2

LIGHTER WILD RICE AND BEEF CASSEROLE

For 10 grams of fat and 320 calories per serving, substitute ground turkey breast for the ground beef and use reduced-fat Cheddar cheese.

Corn Bread–Topped Sausage Pie

PREP: 15 min **COOK:** 12 min **BAKE:** 25 min ▪ **6 SERVINGS**

Sausage Pie

1 lb bulk Italian sausage
1 medium onion, chopped (1/2 cup)
1 small bell pepper, chopped (1/2 cup)
2 cloves garlic, finely chopped
1 can (15 oz) tomato sauce
1 box (9 oz) frozen whole kernel corn, thawed
1 jar (4.5 oz) sliced mushrooms, drained

Corn Bread Topping

2/3 cup cornmeal
1/3 cup all-purpose flour
1/2 cup milk
1 tablespoon sugar
2 tablespoons vegetable oil
2 teaspoons baking powder
1/4 teaspoon salt
1 large egg
1/4 cup shredded Monterey Jack cheese with jalapeño peppers (1 oz)

1. Heat oven to 400°F.

2. In 10-inch skillet, cook sausage, onion, bell pepper and garlic over medium heat 8 to 10 minutes, stirring frequently, until sausage is no longer pink; drain. Stir in tomato sauce, corn and mushrooms. Heat to boiling; remove from heat.

◀ **Corn Bread–Topped Sausage Pie**

3. In medium bowl, stir all topping ingredients except cheese. Beat vigorously with spoon 30 seconds. Stir in cheese.

4. Spoon sausage mixture into ungreased 2-quart casserole. Pour topping over hot sausage mixture, spreading evenly.

5. Bake uncovered 20 to 25 minutes or until topping is golden brown.

1 SERVING: CAL. 430 (CAL. FROM FAT 200); FAT 22g (SAT. FAT 7g); CHOL. 85mg; SODIUM 1320mg; CARBS. 39g (FIBER 4g); PRO. 19g **% DAILY VALUE:** VIT. A 16%; VIT. C 20%; CALC. 18%; IRON 16% **EXCHANGES:** 2 STARCH, 2 VEGETABLE, 1 HIGH-FAT MEAT, 2 1/2 FAT **CARB. CHOICES:** 2 1/2

Shrimp and Pea Pod Casserole

PREP: 5 min **COOK:** 15 min **BAKE:** 25 min ■ **6 SERVINGS**

Sugar snap pea pods are a hybrid pea, crossing the English pea and the flat snow pea. Because they're primarily available in the spring and fall, frozen are used for convenience. Feel free to substitute fresh sugar snaps (cooked and drained) for frozen.

- 3 cups uncooked penne pasta (9 oz)
- 1/2 cup butter or margarine
- 2 cups sliced fresh mushrooms (5 oz)
- 2 cloves garlic, finely chopped
- 1/2 cup all-purpose flour
- 1/2 teaspoon salt
- 1/4 teaspoon pepper
- 2 cups milk
- 2 tablespoons sherry or dry white wine, if desired
- 1 can (14 oz) chicken broth
- 3/4 cup shredded Fontina or Swiss cheese (3 oz)
- 1 lb cooked peeled deveined medium shrimp, thawed if frozen
- 2 cups frozen sugar snap pea pods (from 1-lb bag), thawed and drained
- 1/4 cup finely shredded Parmesan cheese
- 1/4 cup sliced almonds

1. Heat oven to 350°F. Spray 13 × 9-inch glass baking dish with cooking spray.

2. Cook and drain pasta as directed on package.

3. Meanwhile, in 4-quart saucepan or Dutch oven, melt butter over low heat. Cook mushrooms and garlic in butter, stirring occasionally, until mushrooms are tender. Stir in flour, salt and pepper. Cook over medium heat, stirring constantly, until mixture is smooth and bubbly. Gradually stir in milk, sherry and broth until smooth. Heat to boiling, stirring constantly. Stir in Fontina cheese until melted; remove from heat.

4. Stir pasta, shrimp and pea pods into mushroom mixture. Pour into baking dish. Sprinkle with Parmesan cheese and almonds.

5. Bake uncovered 20 to 25 minutes or until cheese is golden brown.

1 SERVING: CAL. 590 (CAL. FROM FAT 245); FAT 27g (SAT. FAT 15g); CHOL. 215mg; SODIUM 990mg; CARBS. 51g (FIBER 4g); PRO. 35g **% DAILY VALUE:** VIT. A 26%; VIT. C 20%; CALC. 30%; IRON 34% **EXCHANGES:** 3 STARCH, 1 VEGETABLE, 3 1/2 MEDIUM-FAT MEAT, 1 1/2 FAT **CARB. CHOICES:** 3 1/2

Shrimp and Pea Pod Casserole

Tuna-Pasta Casserole

PREP: 20 min **BAKE:** 30 min ■ **6 SERVINGS**

Casserole

- 1 1/4 cups uncooked medium pasta shells or elbow macaroni (3 to 4 oz)
- 2 tablespoons butter or margarine
- 2 tablespoons all-purpose flour
- 3/4 teaspoon salt
- 2 cups milk
- 1 cup shredded sharp process American or Cheddar cheese (4 oz)
- 2 cups broccoli flowerets, cooked until crisp-tender and drained*
- 2 cans (6 oz each) tuna in water, drained

Crumb Topping**

- 2/3 cup dry bread crumbs
- 1 tablespoon butter or margarine, melted

1. Heat oven to 350°F.

2. Cook and drain pasta as directed on package.

3. Meanwhile, in 1 1/2-quart saucepan, melt butter over low heat. Stir in flour and salt. Cook over medium heat, stirring constantly, until smooth and bubbly; remove from heat. Gradually stir in milk. Heat to boiling, stirring constantly. Boil and stir 1 minute. Stir in cheese until melted.

4. Stir in pasta, broccoli and tuna; mix well. Spoon into ungreased 2-quart casserole. Cover and bake about 25 minutes or until hot and bubbly.

5. Meanwhile, in small bowl, mix topping ingredients. Sprinkle topping over casserole. Bake uncovered about 5 minutes longer or until topping is toasted.

**1 cup uncooked frozen (thawed) green peas can be substituted for the broccoli.*

***2/3 cup crushed potato chips can be substituted for the Crumb Topping.*

1 SERVING: CAL. 375 (CAL. FROM FAT 125); FAT 14g (SAT. FAT 8g); CHOL. 55mg; SODIUM 910mg; CARBS. 38g (FIBER 2g); PRO. 25g **% DAILY VALUE:** VIT. A 24%; VIT. C 10%; CALC. 24%; IRON 16% **EXCHANGES:** 2 STARCH, 1 VEGETABLE, 2 MEDIUM-FAT MEAT, 1 FAT **CARB. CHOICES:** 2 1/2

SALMON-PASTA CASSEROLE Substitute 1 can (14.75 oz) red or pink salmon, drained, skin and bones removed and salmon flaked, for the tuna.

Macaroni and Cheese

PREP: 25 min **BAKE:** 25 min ■ **4 SERVINGS**

Add surprise to your mac & cheese—mix up your cheeses! Try Jarlsberg, smoked Gouda or white Cheddar for all or half of the sharp Cheddar. Stir in crumbled cooked bacon and 1/2 to 1 cup of Caramelized Onions (page 459) for a hearty, richly flavored twist.

- 2 cups uncooked elbow macaroni (7 oz)
- 1/4 cup butter or margarine
- 1/4 cup all-purpose flour
- 1/2 teaspoon salt
- 1/4 teaspoon pepper
- 1/4 teaspoon ground mustard
- 1/4 teaspoon Worcestershire sauce
- 2 cups milk
- 2 cups shredded sharp Cheddar cheese (8 oz)

1. Heat oven to 350°F.

2. Cook and drain macaroni as directed on package.

3. Meanwhile, in 3-quart saucepan, melt butter over low heat. Stir in flour, salt, pepper, mustard and Worcestershire sauce. Cook over low heat, stirring constantly, until mixture is smooth and bubbly; remove from heat. Stir in milk. Heat to boiling, stirring constantly. Boil and stir 1 minute; remove from heat. Stir in cheese until melted.

4. Gently stir macaroni into cheese sauce. Pour into ungreased 2-quart casserole.

5. Bake uncovered 20 to 25 minutes or until bubbly.

1 SERVING (ABOUT 1 CUP): CAL. 610 (CAL. FROM FAT 305); FAT 34g (SAT. FAT 21g); CHOL. 100mg; SODIUM 790mg; CARBS. 51g (FIBER 2g); PRO. 26g **% DAILY VALUE:** VIT. A 28%; VIT. C 0%; CALC. 46%; IRON 14% **EXCHANGES:** 2 1/2 STARCH, 1 MILK, 1 1/2 HIGH-FAT MEAT, 4 FAT **CARB. CHOICES:** 3 1/2

LIGHTER MACARONI AND CHEESE

For 10 grams of fat and 390 calories per serving, decrease butter to 2 tablespoons. Use fat-free (skim) milk and substitute 1 1/2 cups reduced-fat Cheddar cheese (6 oz) for the 2 cups regular sharp Cheddar cheese.

Mixed Roasted Vegetables and Pasta

PREP: 25 min **BAKE:** 45 min ■ **6 SERVINGS**

1 medium green or yellow bell pepper, cut into 1-inch pieces
1 medium red bell pepper, cut into 1-inch pieces
1 medium onion, cut into 8 wedges and separated
2 medium zucchini, cut into 1-inch pieces
8 oz whole mushrooms
1/3 cup chopped fresh or 2 tablespoons dried basil leaves
3 tablespoons olive or vegetable oil
2 tablespoons red wine vinegar
2 teaspoons Italian seasoning
1/2 teaspoon salt
1/4 teaspoon pepper
2 cups uncooked cavatappi or gemelli pasta
2 medium tomatoes, seeded and cut into 2-inch pieces
1 bag (8 oz) shredded Italian-style four-cheese blend (2 cups)

1. Heat oven to 450°F.

2. In 15 × 10 × 1-inch pan or shallow 3-quart casserole, place bell peppers, onion, zucchini and mushrooms. Sprinkle evenly with basil.

3. In small bowl, mix oil, vinegar, Italian seasoning, salt and pepper; drizzle evenly over vegetables. Bake uncovered 25 to 30 minutes.

4. Meanwhile, cook and drain pasta as directed on package.

5. Reduce oven temperature to 350°F. Add tomatoes and pasta to vegetable mixture; toss to coat. Sprinkle with cheese. Bake uncovered about 15 minutes longer or until vegetables are tender and cheese is melted.

1 SERVING: CAL. 360 (CAL. FROM FAT 125); FAT 14g (SAT. FAT 5g); CHOL. 20mg; SODIUM 410mg; CARBS. 40g (FIBER 4g); PRO. 18g
% DAILY VALUE: VIT. A 50%; VIT. C 60%; CALC. 30%; IRON 16%
EXCHANGES: 2 STARCH, 2 VEGETABLE, 1 HIGH-FAT MEAT, 1 FAT
CARB. CHOICES: 2 1/2

Mixed Roasted Vegetables and Pasta ▶

Slow Cooker Basics

If you haven't yet discovered the wonderful world of using a slow cooker, now's the time. It's a carefree way to fix it, forget it, then come home to supper. For best results, follow these guidelines used in the Betty Crocker Kitchens.

TYPES AND SIZES OF SLOW COOKERS

Slow cookers come with a variety of options and features. Before you begin using your cooker, become familiar with how your model works.

Continuous: The majority of slow cookers sold are continuous cookers. The food cooks continuously by using a very low wattage. The heating coils, located in the outer metal shell of the cooker, remain on constantly to heat the crockery liner. Continuous slow cookers have two or three fixed settings: Low (about 200°F), High (about 300°F) and in some models, auto, which shifts from High to Low automatically. Often the ceramic liners are removable. All recipes in this book were tested using continuous slow cookers.

Intermittent: Intermittent cookers have a heating element in the base and a separate cooking container that is placed on the base. The heat cycles on and off to maintain a constant temperature. Also, some intermittent cookers have a dial with numbers or temperatures rather than Low, Medium and High settings. *Note: The recipes in this cookbook have not been tested in an intermittent cooker. If you have an intermittent cooker, follow the manufacturer's instructions for layering ingredients and selecting a temperature.*

Size: The most common sizes of slow cookers are 1-, 3 1/2-, 4-, 5- and 6-quart. One-quart cookers work well for dips and spreads; 6-quart cookers are great for large cuts of meats and crowd-size recipes. For best results, use the slow cooker size recommended in the recipe. Slow cookers tend to work most efficiently when they are between two-thirds and three-fourths full of food.

SLOW COOKER TIPS

For successful slow cooker meals, follow these guidelines:

- **Spray the inside** of your slow cooker with cooking spray for easy cleanup.
- **Rotate meats halfway through cooking** for even cooking. Food in the bottom of the slow cooker is often moister from being in the cooking liquid, and meat, like ribs, roasts and chicken, will fall off the bones sooner.
- **Root vegetables,** like potatoes and carrots, take longer to cook, so cut them into smaller pieces and put at the bottom of the cooker.
- **Remove skin** from poultry and excess fat from meats before cooking to help prevent a grease layer from forming.
- **Cook and drain** ground meats before adding to the slow cooker.
- **Brown meats and poultry** in a skillet before adding to the slow cooker to add extra flavor and color to the finished dish.
- **Use dried herb leaves** instead of ground because they retain their flavor better during long cook times.
- **Ground red pepper** (cayenne) and red pepper sauce can become bitter. Use small amounts, tasting during the last hour of cooking before adding more.

WATCHING THE CLOCK

Slow cookers require little or no clock watching. Usually, you can make the recipe, turn it on and forget about it until you're ready to eat. Here are some timely tips:

- **A Low setting** is frequently used because longer cooking times fit well into workday schedules. Fast-forward the cooking time by turning the slow cooker to High for 1 hour, which equals 2 hours on Low.

- **Smaller isn't always faster.** Baby-cut carrots, for example, take longer to cook than some other veggies, so checking for doneness is important.
- **Most cooked food can be held up to an hour** on the Low heat setting without overcooking. Some recipes, such as dips and spreads, can be kept on Low for up to two hours. Be sure to stir occasionally if needed.
- **Don't peek!** Removing the cover lets heat escape, adding 15 to 20 minutes to the cooking time. If you can't wait to see inside, try spinning the cover until the condensation and steam clears.

ADDING INGREDIENTS

When it comes to making slow cooker meals, the phrase "save the best for last" often applies. To get the most flavor, try these helpful hints:

- **Develop flavors in the juices** by removing the lid and cooking on the High setting for the last 20 to 30 minutes. This evaporates the water so flavors become more concentrated.
- **Stir in fresh herbs** during the last hour of cooking so they stay flavorful. Some herbs, like oregano and basil, lose flavor with an extended cooking time.
- **Fish and seafood** fall apart during long hours of cooking, and some seafood, like shrimp, become tough. Add these ingredients during the last hour of cooking.
- **Add tender vegetables,** like fresh tomatoes, mushrooms and zucchini, during the last 30 minutes of cooking so they don't become overcooked and mushy.
- **Frozen vegetables** that have been thawed will keep their bright color and crisp-tender texture by adding them during the last 30 minutes of cooking.
- **Dairy products,** like milk, sour cream and cheese, tend to curdle. To help prevent curdling, add them during the last 30 minutes of cooking.

SLOW COOKER FOOD SAFETY

When using a slow cooker, keep the following list of food safety guidelines in mind:

- **Keep all perishable foods** refrigerated until you make the recipe. The slow cooker may take several hours to reach a safe, bacteria-killing temperature. Constant refrigeration assures that bacteria, which multiply rapidly at room temperature, won't get a "head start" during the first few hours of cooking.
- **Thaw frozen** meats and poultry completely before adding to the slow cooker.
- **Cook and drain ground meat** before adding to the slow cooker.
- **Brown poultry and meats** just before adding to the slow cooker. Bacteria can survive and grow if the food is browned the night before and then refrigerated.
- **Use the highest setting** for the first hour of cooking time, if possible. Then lower the slow cooker to the setting specified in the recipe. However, it's safe to cook food on Low the entire time—if you're leaving for work, for example, and preparation time is limited.
- **Cook raw poultry and meats** for a minimum of 3 hours for thorough cooking.
- **Whole chickens and meat loaf** should not be cooked in a slow cooker because the temperature of the middle of the chicken, near the bone, or the center of the meat loaf, can't reach a safe temperature quickly enough.
- **Cut meats and vegetables** into the sizes specified in the recipe, and layer or assemble the ingredients as directed in the cooking method for accurate cooking times and doneness.
- **Remove leftovers** and refrigerate or freeze as soon as you are finished eating. Don't use slow cookers as a storage container.
- **Reheat leftovers** on the stove-top or in the microwave oven rather than in the slow cooker. Heat the cooked food until thoroughly hot and then put into a preheated slow cooker to keep hot for serving.

HIGH ALTITUDE TIPS FOR SLOW COOKERS

Cooking at altitudes at or above 3,500 feet presents a certain challenge, and slow cooking is no exception. Because no set rules apply to all recipes, trial and error is often the best way to make improvements.

- **Longer cooking** is necessary for most foods, particularly meats cooked in boiling liquid. Meats may take twice as long as specified to become tender. To shorten the cooking time, try cooking meats on the High setting instead of on Low.
- **Cut vegetables** into smaller pieces than the recipe suggests to help them cook more quickly.
- **Call your local USDA** (United States Department of Agriculture) Extension Service office, listed in the phone book under "County Government," with questions about slow cooking at high altitudes.

TOP IT!

For more texture and a little extra flavor, sprinkle the top of your slow cooker meal with chopped fresh herbs, grated cheese, crushed croutons or corn chips, chopped tomatoes or sliced green onions just before serving.

Slow Cooker Turkey Breast with Wild Rice Stuffing

LOW-FAT

PREP: 15 min **COOK:** 9 hr ▪ **10 SERVINGS**

4 cups cooked wild rice
3/4 cup finely chopped onion
1/2 cup dried cranberries
1/3 cup slivered almonds
2 medium peeled or unpeeled cooking apples, coarsely chopped (2 cups)
4- to 5-lb boneless whole turkey breast, thawed if frozen

1. In large bowl, mix all ingredients except turkey.

2. In 3 1/2- to 6-quart slow cooker, place turkey. Place wild rice mixture around edge of cooker.

3. Cover and cook on Low heat setting 8 to 9 hours.

1 SERVING: CAL. 290 (CAL. FROM FAT 35); FAT 4g (SAT. FAT 1g); CHOL. 95mg; SODIUM 65mg; CARBS. 25g (FIBER 3g); PRO. 38g
% DAILY VALUE: VIT. A 0%; VIT. C 2%; CALC. 2%; IRON 12%
EXCHANGES: 1 1/2 STARCH, 4 1/2 VERY LEAN MEAT
CARB. CHOICES: 1 1/2

Italian Turkey-Rice Dinner

PREP: 20 min **COOK:** 8 hr ▪ **4 SERVINGS**

Get a head-start on this dinner—Cut up the vegetables as early as two days ahead, if you wish. Store in a resealable plastic food-storage bag in the fridge until you're ready to make the recipe.

- 3 medium carrots, shredded (2 cups)
- 2 medium stalks celery, sliced (1 cup)
- 1 small red bell pepper, chopped (1/2 cup)
- 1/2 teaspoon dried basil leaves
- 1/3 cup water
- 4 turkey thighs (8 to 12 oz each), skin removed
- 1 teaspoon salt
- 1/4 teaspoon pepper
- 1/2 cup uncooked regular long-grain rice
- 1 teaspoon dried oregano leaves
- 1/2 cup shredded Italian-style six-cheese blend or mozzarella cheese (2 oz)

1. In 3 1/2- to 4-quart slow cooker, mix carrots, celery, bell pepper, basil and water. Sprinkle turkey with salt and pepper; place on vegetable mixture.

2. Cover and cook on Low heat setting 6 to 7 hours.

3. Remove turkey from cooker. Stir rice and oregano into vegetable mixture; return turkey to cooker. Cover and cook on Low heat setting about 1 hour or until rice is tender.

4. Remove turkey from cooker. Stir cheese into rice mixture until melted. Serve with turkey.

1 SERVING: CAL. 475 (CAL. FROM FAT 110); FAT 12g (SAT. FAT 5g); CHOL. 230mg; SODIUM 860mg; CARBS. 27g (FIBER 3g); PRO. 65g **% DAILY VALUE:** VIT. A 100%; VIT. C 34%; CALC. 16%; IRON 36% **EXCHANGES:** 1 1/2 STARCH, 1 VEGETABLE, 8 VERY LEAN MEAT, 1 FAT **CARB. CHOICES:** 2

Herbed Beef Roast ▶

Herbed Beef Roast LOW-FAT

PREP: 15 min **COOK:** 8 hr ▪ **12 SERVINGS**

Serve this flavorful roast with Horseradish Mashed Potatoes (page 464). If you have any leftovers, make hot beef sandwiches.

- 3-lb beef boneless tip roast
- 1 teaspoon mixed dried herb leaves (such as marjoram, basil and oregano)
- 1 teaspoon salt
- 1/2 teaspoon pepper
- 2 cloves garlic, finely chopped
- 1 cup balsamic or red wine vinegar

1. If beef roast comes in netting or is tied, do not remove. Spray 12-inch skillet with cooking spray; heat over medium-high heat. Cook beef in skillet about 5 minutes, turning occasionally, until brown on all sides. Sprinkle with herbs, salt and pepper.

2. In 4- to 5-quart slow cooker, place garlic. Place beef on garlic. Pour vinegar over beef.

3. Cover and cook on Low heat setting 6 to 8 hours. Remove netting or strings from beef.

1 SERVING: CAL. 170 (CAL. FROM FAT 70); FAT 8g (SAT. FAT 3g); CHOL. 60mg; SODIUM 250mg; CARBS. 1g (FIBER 0g); PRO. 23g **% DAILY VALUE:** VIT. A 2%; VIT. C 0%; CALC. 0%; IRON 12% **EXCHANGES:** 3 LEAN MEAT **CARB. CHOICES:** 0

Spiced Corned Beef Brisket with Horseradish Sour Cream

PREP: 5 min **COOK:** 9 hr ■ **8 SERVINGS**

Even if it's not St. Patrick's Day, cook up this traditional Irish dinner of corned beef brisket. Your slow cooker makes it simple! Serve with boiled small red potatoes and steamed green cabbage.

1 large sweet onion (Bermuda, Maui or Spanish), sliced
3- to 3 1/2-lb well-trimmed corned beef brisket
3/4 teaspoon crushed red pepper
1 cup reduced-sodium chicken broth
1 tablespoon Worcestershire sauce
1/2 cup sour cream
1 tablespoon cream-style horseradish
2 tablespoons chopped fresh parsley

1. In 5- to 6-quart slow cooker, place onion. Remove beef from package; discard liquid and seasoning packet. Thoroughly rinse beef. Place beef on onion; sprinkle with red pepper. In small bowl, mix broth and Worcestershire sauce; pour over beef.

2. Cover and cook on Low heat setting 8 to 9 hours.

3. In small bowl, stir sour cream, horseradish and parsley until well mixed. Serve with beef and onion.

1 SERVING: CAL. 340 (CAL. FROM FAT 235); FAT 26g (SAT. FAT 9g); CHOL. 130mg; SODIUM 1460mg; CARBS. 3g (FIBER 0g); PRO. 23g
% DAILY VALUE: VIT. A 6%; VIT. C 2%; CALC. 2%; IRON 14%
EXCHANGES: 3 1/2 HIGH-FAT MEAT **CARB. CHOICES:** 0

French Dip Sandwiches

PREP: 5 min **COOK:** 8 hr ■ **10 SANDWICHES**

Easy does it! Make this recipe a day before serving, and store in the fridge overnight. Reheat the beef mixture in a large saucepan on the stovetop and then place in the slow cooker on the Low heat setting for a couple of hours.

3-lb beef boneless chuck roast
1 1/2 cups water
1/3 cup soy sauce
1 teaspoon dried rosemary leaves
1 teaspoon dried thyme leaves
1 clove garlic, finely chopped
1 dried bay leaf
3 or 4 peppercorns
2 loaves (1 lb each) French bread

1. If beef roast comes in netting or is tied, do not remove. In 3 1/2- to 4-quart slow cooker, place beef. In small bowl, mix remaining ingredients except bread; pour over beef.

2. Cover and cook on Low heat setting 7 to 8 hours.

3. Skim fat from surface of juices in cooker; discard bay leaf and peppercorns. Remove beef from cooker; place on cutting board. Remove netting or strings from beef. Cut beef into thin slices. Cut each loaf of bread into 5 pieces, about 4 inches long; cut horizontally in half. Fill bread with beef. Serve with broth for dipping.

1 SANDWICH: CAL. 400 (CAL. FROM FAT 115); FAT 13g (SAT. FAT 4g); CHOL. 50mg; SODIUM 1050mg; CARBS. 46g (FIBER 2g); PRO. 25g
% DAILY VALUE: VIT. A 0%; VIT. C 0%; CALC. 8%; IRON 26%
EXCHANGES: 3 STARCH, 2 MEDIUM-FAT MEAT **CARB. CHOICES:** 3

Porketta Pot Roast

PREP: 15 min **COOK:** 10 hr ■ **8 TO 10 SERVINGS**

- 3-lb pork boneless shoulder roast
- 2 teaspoons Italian seasoning
- 1 1/2 teaspoons fennel seed, crushed
- 3/4 teaspoon salt
- 1/2 teaspoon celery seed
- 3 medium parsnips, peeled and cut into 3/4-inch pieces (3 cups)
- 2 medium sweet potatoes, peeled and cut into 3/4-inch pieces (3 cups)
- 12 cloves garlic, peeled and cut in half
- 1 1/2 cups water

1. If pork roast comes in netting or is tied, do not remove. In small bowl, mix Italian seasoning, fennel seed, salt and celery seed. Pat seasoning mixture evenly onto pork.

2. Heat 12-inch nonstick skillet over medium-high heat. Cook pork in skillet 5 to 10 minutes, turning several times, until brown.

3. In 4- to 5-quart slow cooker, place parsnips, sweet potatoes and garlic. Pour water over vegetables. Place pork on vegetables.

4. Cover and cook on Low heat setting 9 to 10 hours.

5. Remove pork from cooker; place on cutting board. Remove netting or strings from pork. Cut pork across grain into slices; serve with vegetables and juices.

1 SERVING: CAL. 350 (CAL. FROM FAT 180); FAT 20g (SAT. FAT 7g); CHOL. 90mg; SODIUM 290mg; CARBS. 16g (FIBER 3g); PRO. 26g
% DAILY VALUE: VIT. A 86%; VIT. C 10%; CALC. 6%; IRON 8%
EXCHANGES: 1 STARCH, 3 MEDIUM-FAT MEAT, 1 FAT
CARB. CHOICES: 1

◀ **Pulled Jerk Pork Sandwiches**

Pulled Jerk Pork Sandwiches

PREP: 5 min **COOK:** 10 hr 45 min ■ **8 SERVINGS**

Pulled pork, a favorite style of southern and some southeastern barbecues, refers to the method of preparing the cooked pork by pulling it apart with your fingers or two forks.

- 2 1/2-lb pork boneless shoulder
- 1 tablespoon Jamaican jerk seasoning (dry)
- 1/4 teaspoon dried thyme leaves
- 1 medium onion, chopped (1/2 cup)
- 1 cup cola
- 2 cups barbecue sauce
- 8 sandwich buns or flour tortillas (8 to 10 inch)

1. If pork comes in netting or is tied, do not remove. Spray 3 1/2- to 6-quart slow cooker with cooking spray. Rub jerk seasoning over pork; sprinkle with thyme. Place pork in cooker. Sprinkle with onion. Pour cola over pork.

2. Cover and cook on Low heat setting 8 to 10 hours.

3. Remove pork from cooker; place on cutting board. Remove juices from cooker and reserve. Remove netting or strings from pork. Use 2 forks to pull pork into shreds. Return pork to cooker. Stir in barbecue sauce and 1/2 cup of the reserved juices. Increase heat setting to High. Cover and cook 30 to 45 minutes or until heated through.

4. Spoon pork onto buns. In 2-quart saucepan, heat remaining juices to boiling; serve with sandwiches for dipping if desired.

1 SERVING: CAL. 420 (CAL. FROM FAT 125); FAT 14g (SAT. FAT 5g); CHOL. 65mg; SODIUM 900mg; CARBS. 48g (FIBER 2g); PRO. 25g
% DAILY VALUE: VIT. A 4%; VIT. C 2%; CALC. 10%; IRON 16%
EXCHANGES: 2 STARCH, 1 OTHER CARB., 3 LEAN MEAT, 1 FAT
CARB. CHOICES: 3

Caribbean Spiced Ribs

PREP: 15 min **COOK:** 10 hr ■ **6 SERVINGS**

Busy day? Put these ribs in your slow cooker and let them simmer while you're away. Stop at the deli and pick up some coleslaw and corn muffins on your way home. Then just finish cooking the ribs in the barbecue sauce for any easy barbecue supper.

3 lb pork loin back ribs
2 tablespoons instant minced onion
1 teaspoon ground mustard
1 teaspoon crushed red pepper
1/2 teaspoon ground allspice
1/2 teaspoon ground cinnamon
1/2 teaspoon garlic powder
1 medium onion, sliced
1/2 cup water
1 1/2 cups barbecue sauce

1. Spray inside of 5- to 6-quart slow cooker with cooking spray.

2. In small bowl, mix instant minced onion, mustard, red pepper, allspice, cinnamon and garlic powder. Rub mixture into ribs. Cut ribs into 4-inch pieces. Layer ribs and sliced onion in slow cooker. Pour water over ribs.

3. Cover and cook on Low heat setting 8 to 9 hours.

4. Remove ribs from cooker; drain and discard liquid from cooker. Pour barbecue sauce into shallow bowl; dip ribs into sauce. Place ribs in cooker. Pour any remaining sauce over ribs. Cover and cook on Low heat setting 1 hour.

1 SERVING: CAL. 525 (CAL. FROM FAT 295); FAT 33g (SAT. FAT 12g); CHOL. 130mg; SODIUM 730mg; CARBS. 25g (FIBER 1g); PRO. 32g
% DAILY VALUE: VIT. A 2%; VIT. C 4%; CALC. 8%; IRON 14%
EXCHANGES: 1 1/2 OTHER CARB., 4 HIGH-FAT MEAT, 1 FAT
CARB. CHOICES: 1 1/2

Spanish Chicken

PREP: 15 min **COOK:** 8 hr ■ **6 SERVINGS**

1 3/4 lb boneless skinless chicken breasts, cut into 1-inch pieces
1 lb turkey Italian sausages, cut into 1-inch pieces
1 large red bell pepper, chopped (1 1/2 cups)
1 large onion, chopped (1 cup)
2 cloves garlic, finely chopped
1 teaspoon dried oregano leaves
1/2 to 1 teaspoon crushed red pepper
1 can (28 oz) diced tomatoes, undrained
1 can (6 oz) tomato paste
1 can (14 oz) artichoke heart quarters, drained
1 can (4 oz) sliced ripe olives, drained
3 cups hot cooked rice (page 375)

1. In 3 1/2- to 4-quart slow cooker, mix all ingredients except artichoke hearts, olives and rice.

2. Cover and cook on Low heat setting 6 to 8 hours.

3. Stir in artichoke hearts and olives; heat through. Serve with rice.

1 SERVING: CAL. 465 (CAL. FROM FAT 125); FAT 14g (SAT. FAT 4g); CHOL. 120mg; SODIUM 1860mg; CARBS. 46g (FIBER 8g); PRO. 47g
% DAILY VALUE: VIT. A 36%; VIT. C 76%; CALC. 14%; IRON 30%
EXCHANGES: 3 STARCH, 5 VERY LEAN MEAT, 1 FAT
CARB. CHOICES: 3

Spicy Chicken in Peanut Sauce

Spicy Chicken in Peanut Sauce

PREP: 15 min **COOK:** 8 hr ■ **4 SERVINGS**

Pass small bowls of dry-roasted peanuts and chopped fresh cilantro to sprinkle over the chicken, and serve with wedges of warm pita bread.

- 1 tablespoon olive or vegetable oil
- 8 large chicken thighs (about 3 lb), skin removed
- 1 large onion, chopped (1 cup)
- 2 cans (14.5 oz each) diced tomatoes with green chilies, undrained
- 1 can (14.5 oz) crushed tomatoes, undrained
- 2 tablespoons honey
- 1 1/2 teaspoons ground cumin
- 1 teaspoon ground cinnamon
- 1/3 cup creamy peanut butter
- 2 cups hot cooked couscous

1. In 12-inch nonstick skillet, heat oil over medium-high heat. Cook chicken in oil about 4 minutes, turning once, until brown.

2. In 4- to-5-quart slow cooker, mix onion, diced and crushed tomatoes, honey, cumin and cinnamon. Add chicken. Spoon tomato mixture over chicken.

3. Cover and cook on Low heat setting 7 to 8 hours.

4. Stir in peanut butter until melted and well blended. Serve chicken and sauce over couscous.

1 SERVING: CAL. 670 (CAL. FROM FAT 290); FAT 32g (SAT. FAT 8g); CHOL. 115mg; SODIUM 890mg; CARBS. 51g (FIBER 7g); PRO. 51g
% DAILY VALUE: VIT. A 24%; VIT. C 32%; CALC. 16%; IRON 32%
EXCHANGES: 3 STARCH, 6 LEAN MEAT, 1 VEGETABLE, 1 1/2 FAT
CARB. CHOICES: 3 1/2

Mexicali Round Steak

PREP: 15 min **COOK:** 9 hr ■ **6 SERVINGS**

One cup of fresh cilantro used in this recipe might seem like a lot, but cooked for a long time, its becomes very mild, blending in the overall flavor of the dish.

- $1\frac{1}{2}$ lb beef boneless round steak
- 1 cup frozen whole kernel corn, thawed
- 1 cup chopped fresh cilantro
- $\frac{1}{2}$ cup beef broth
- 3 medium stalks celery, thinly sliced ($1\frac{1}{2}$ cups)
- 1 large onion, sliced
- 1 jar (20 oz) salsa
- 1 can (15 oz) black beans, rinsed and drained
- 1 cup shredded Monterey Jack cheese with jalapeño peppers (4 oz)

1. Remove fat from beef. Cut beef into 6 serving pieces. In $3\frac{1}{2}$- to 6-quart slow cooker, place beef. In large bowl, mix remaining ingredients except cheese; pour over beef.

2. Cover and cook on Low heat setting 8 to 9 hours.

3. Sprinkle cheese over beef mixture.

1 SERVING: CAL. 430 (CAL. FROM FAT 170); FAT 19g (SAT. FAT 9g); CHOL. 85mg; SODIUM 910mg; CARBS. 30g (FIBER 7g); PRO. 35g
% DAILY VALUE: VIT. A 24%; VIT. C 14%; CALC. 22%; IRON 30%
EXCHANGES: 2 STARCH, 4 LEAN MEAT, 1/2 FAT **CARB. CHOICES:** 2

Slow Cooker Roast Beef Hash LOW-FAT

PREP: 15 min **COOK:** 9 hr ■ **6 SERVINGS**

- 1 large onion, chopped (1 cup)
- 2 lb beef top round steak, cut into $\frac{1}{2}$-inch cubes
- $\frac{1}{2}$ teaspoon salt
- $\frac{1}{2}$ teaspoon pepper
- 1 envelope (0.87 to 1.2 ounces) brown gravy mix
- 1 cup water
- $3\frac{1}{2}$ cups frozen potatoes O'Brien with onions and peppers (from 28-oz bag)
- 1 cup frozen green peas (from 1-lb bag)

1. In $3\frac{1}{2}$- to 4-quart slow cooker, layer onion, beef, salt, pepper and gravy mix (dry). Pour water over all.

2. Cover and cook on Low heat setting 8 to 9 hours. Meanwhile, thaw potatoes in refrigerator.

3. About 30 minutes before serving, stir thawed potatoes and frozen peas into beef mixture. Increase heat setting to High. Cover and cook 25 to 30 minutes or until potatoes and peas are tender.

1 SERVING: CAL. 275 (CAL. FROM FAT 45); FAT 5g (SAT. FAT 2g); CHOL. 80mg; SODIUM 510mg; CARBS. 24g (FIBER 3g); PRO. 34g
% DAILY VALUE: VIT. A 4%; VIT. C 14%; CALC. 2%; IRON 22%
EXCHANGES: 1 1/2 STARCH, 4 VERY LEAN MEAT, 1/2 FAT
CARB. CHOICES: 1 1/2

Pork Chop Supper

PREP: 15 min **COOK:** 7 hr 15 min ■ **6 SERVINGS**

- 6 pork loin or rib chops, 1/2 inch thick
- 6 medium new potatoes (about 1 1/2 lb), cut into eighths
- 1 can (10.75 oz) condensed cream of mushroom soup
- 1 can (4 oz) mushroom pieces and stems, drained
- 2 tablespoons dry white wine or chicken broth
- 1/4 teaspoon dried thyme leaves
- 1/2 teaspoon garlic powder
- 1/2 teaspoon Worcestershire sauce
- 3 tablespoons all-purpose flour
- 1 tablespoon diced pimientos (from 2-oz jar)
- 1 box (9 oz) frozen green peas, rinsed and drained

1. Heat 10-inch nonstick skillet over medium-high heat. Cook pork chops in skillet 2 to 4 minutes, turning once, until brown.

2. In 3 1/2- to 6-quart slow cooker, place potatoes. In medium bowl, mix soup, mushrooms, wine, thyme, garlic powder, Worcestershire sauce and flour. Spoon half of the soup mixture over potatoes. Place pork on potatoes; cover with remaining soup mixture.

3. Cover and cook on Low heat setting 6 to 7 hours.

4. Remove pork from cooker; keep warm. Stir pimientos and peas into cooker. Cover and cook on Low heat setting about 15 minutes or until peas are tender. Serve with pork.

1 SERVING: CAL. 340 (CAL. FROM FAT 100); FAT 11g (SAT. FAT 4g); CHOL. 65mg; SODIUM 520mg; CARBS. 32g (FIBER 6g); PRO. 28g
% DAILY VALUE: VIT. A 6%; VIT. C 16%; CALC. 6%; IRON 20%
EXCHANGES: 2 STARCH, 3 1/2 LEAN MEAT **CARB. CHOICES:** 2

Chicken Stroganoff Pot Pie

PREP: 20 min **COOK:** 5 hr 10 min ■ **4 SERVINGS**

A bag of frozen stew vegetables—potatoes, carrots, onions and peas—cuts down chopping for this pot pie. The size of the vegetable pieces varies from brand to brand, but all will be done by the end of the cooking time. Fluffy biscuit dumplings top it all off.

- 1 envelope (0.87 to 1.2 oz) chicken gravy mix
- 1 can (10.5 oz) condensed chicken broth
- 1 lb boneless skinless chicken breasts, cut into 1-inch pieces
- 1 bag (16 oz) frozen stew vegetables, thawed and drained
- 1 jar (4.5 oz) sliced mushrooms, drained
- 1/2 cup sour cream
- 1 tablespoon all-purpose flour
- 1 1/2 cups Original or Reduced Fat Bisquick® mix
- 4 medium green onions, chopped (1/4 cup)
- 1/2 cup milk
- 1 cup frozen green peas, thawed

1. In 3 1/2- to 5-quart slow cooker, stir gravy mix and broth until smooth. Stir in chicken, stew vegetables and mushrooms.

2. Cover and cook on Low heat setting 4 to 5 hours.

3. In small bowl, stir sour cream and flour until well mixed. Stir sour cream mixture into chicken mixture. Increase heat setting to High. Cover and cook 20 minutes.

4. In medium bowl, mix Bisquick® mix and onions; stir in milk just until moistened. Stir in peas. Drop dough by rounded tablespoonfuls onto chicken-vegetable mixture.

5. Cover and cook on High heat setting 45 to 50 minutes or until toothpick inserted in center of topping comes out clean. Serve immediately.

1 SERVING: CAL. 530 (CAL. FROM FAT 155); FAT 17g (SAT. FAT 7g); CHOL. 90mg; SODIUM 1770mg; CARBS. 54g (FIBER 4g); PRO. 40g
% DAILY VALUE: VIT. A 100%; VIT. C 12%; CALC. 22%; IRON 26%
EXCHANGES: 3 STARCH, 1 VEGETABLE, 4 LEAN MEAT
CARB. CHOICES: 3 1/2

Chicken Chow Mein

Chicken Chow Mein

LOW-FAT

PREP: 10 min **COOK:** 8 hr 15 min ■ **4 SERVINGS**

Serve this all-in-one meal with orange or apple slices, grapes or melon cubes. Pick up a package of fortune cookies for dessert, and share your good fortunes!

- 8 boneless skinless chicken thighs (about 1 1/2 lb)
- 1 tablespoon vegetable oil
- 2 medium carrots, sliced diagonally (1 cup)
- 2 medium stalks celery, coarsely chopped (1 cup)
- 1 medium onion, chopped (1/2 cup)
- 2 cloves garlic, finely chopped
- 1 can (8 oz) sliced water chestnuts, drained
- 1 cup chicken broth
- 2 tablespoons soy sauce
- 1/2 teaspoon finely chopped gingerroot
- 2 tablespoons cornstarch
- 3 tablespoons cold water
- 1 cup sliced fresh mushrooms (3 oz)
- 1 cup snow (Chinese) pea pods
- Chow mein noodles, if desired

1. Remove fat from chicken. Cut chicken into 1-inch pieces. In 10-inch skillet, heat oil over medium-high heat. Cook chicken in oil about 5 minutes, turning once, until brown.

2. In 3 1/2- to 6-quart slow cooker, place carrots, celery, onion, garlic and water chestnuts. Add chicken. In small bowl, mix broth, soy sauce and gingerroot; pour over chicken.

3. Cover and cook on Low heat setting 6 to 8 hours.

4. In small bowl, mix cornstarch and water until smooth; stir into chicken mixture. Stir in mushrooms and pea pods. Increase heat setting to High. Cover and cook 15 minutes. Serve over noodles.

1 SERVING: CAL. 255 (CAL. FROM FAT 80); FAT 9g (SAT. FAT 2g); CHOL. 60mg; SODIUM 810mg; CARBS. 19g (FIBER 4g); PRO. 25g
% DAILY VALUE: VIT. A 100%; VIT. C 14%; CALC. 6%; IRON 16%
EXCHANGES: 3 VEGETABLE, 3 LEAN MEAT, 1/2 FAT
CARB. CHOICES: 1

Burgundy Stew with Herb Dumplings

LOW-FAT

PREP: 25 min **COOK:** 10 hr 35 min ■ **8 SERVINGS**

To prevent dumplings from becoming soggy on the bottom, drop the dough onto the stew pieces rather than directly into the liquid. The dumplings will steam rather than settle into the liquid and become soggy. Also, be sure the stew is piping hot, so the dumplings will start to cook from the steam right away and become fluffy.

Stew

- 2 lb beef boneless bottom or top round, tip or chuck steak, cut into 1-inch pieces
- 4 medium carrots, cut into 1/4-inch slices (2 cups)
- 2 medium stalks celery, sliced (1 cup)
- 2 medium onions, sliced
- 1 can (14.5 oz) diced tomatoes, undrained
- 1 can (8 oz) sliced mushrooms, drained
- 3/4 cup dry red wine or beef broth
- 1 1/2 teaspoons salt
- 1 teaspoon dried thyme leaves
- 1 teaspoon ground mustard
- 1/4 teaspoon pepper
- 1/4 cup water
- 3 tablespoons all-purpose flour

Herb Dumplings

$1^1/_2$ cups Original Bisquick® mix
$^1/_2$ teaspoon dried thyme leaves
$^1/_4$ teaspoon dried sage leaves, crumbled
$^1/_2$ cup milk

1. In $3^1/_2$- to 6-quart slow cooker, mix all stew ingredients except water and flour.

2. Cover and cook on Low heat setting 8 to 10 hours (or High heat setting 4 to 5 hours).

3. In small bowl, stir water and flour until well mixed; gradually stir into beef mixture. Cover.

4. For dumplings, in medium bowl, mix Bisquick® mix, thyme and sage. Stir in milk just until Bisquick® mix is moistened. Drop dough by spoonfuls onto hot beef mixture. Increase heat setting to High. Cover and cook 25 to 35 minutes or until toothpick inserted in center of dumplings comes out clean.

1 SERVING: CAL. 275 (CAL. FROM FAT 65); FAT 7g (SAT. FAT 2g); CHOL. 60mg; SODIUM 1010mg; CARBS. 26g (FIBER 3g); PRO. 27g
% DAILY VALUE: VIT. A 50%; VIT. C 10%; CALC. 10%; IRON 20%
EXCHANGES: 1 STARCH, 2 VEGETABLE, $2^1/_2$ LEAN MEAT
CARB. CHOICES: 2

Italian Chicken-Lentil Soup

LOW-FAT

PREP: 15 min **COOK:** 6 hr 15 min ■ **6 SERVINGS**

1 lb boneless skinless chicken thighs
1 medium onion, chopped ($^1/_2$ cup)
1 medium zucchini, chopped (2 cups)
4 medium carrots, sliced (2 cups)
1 cup dried lentils (8 oz), sorted and rinsed
$4^1/_2$ cups chicken broth
$^1/_2$ teaspoon salt
$^1/_4$ teaspoon pepper
1 cup sliced mushrooms (3 oz)
1 can (28 oz) diced tomatoes, undrained
$^1/_4$ cup chopped fresh or 1 tablespoon dried basil leaves
Shredded Parmesan cheese, if desired

1. Remove fat from chicken. In $3^1/_2$- to 6-quart slow cooker, mix remaining ingredients except mushrooms, tomatoes, basil and cheese. Add chicken.

2. Cover and cook on Low heat setting 5 to 6 hours.

3. Remove chicken from cooker; place on cutting board. Use 2 forks to pull chicken into shreds. Return chicken to cooker. Stir in mushrooms and tomatoes. Cover and cook on Low heat setting about 15 minutes or until heated through. Sprinkle with basil. Serve with cheese.

1 SERVING: CAL. 255 (CAL. FROM FAT 35); FAT 4g (SAT. FAT 1g); CHOL. 30mg; SODIUM 1200mg; CARBS. 35g (FIBER 12g); PRO. 31g
% DAILY VALUE: VIT. A 100%; VIT. C 24%; CALC. 10%; IRON 32%
EXCHANGES: 2 STARCH, 1 VEGETABLE, $2^1/_2$ VERY LEAN MEAT
CARB. CHOICES: 2

▲ **Italian Chicken Lentil Soup**

Family-Favorite Chili

PREP: 20 min **COOK:** 8 hr 20 min ▪ **8 SERVINGS**

Start this chili with hot cooked ground beef. It's safer, because getting cold, uncooked ground beef to a safe temperature in a slow cooker takes too long. It also eliminates the extra fat and liquid that would accumulate during cooking.

- 2 lb lean (at least 80%) ground beef
- 1 large onion, chopped (1 cup)
- 2 cloves garlic, finely chopped
- 1 can (28 oz) diced tomatoes, undrained
- 1 can (15 oz) tomato sauce
- 2 tablespoons chili powder
- 1 1/2 teaspoons ground cumin
- 1/2 teaspoon salt
- 1/2 teaspoon pepper
- 1 can (15 to 16 oz) kidney or pinto beans, rinsed and drained
- Shredded Cheddar cheese, if desired

1. In 12-inch skillet, cook beef over medium heat 8 to 10 minutes, stirring occasionally, until brown; drain.

2. In 3 1/2- to 6-quart slow cooker, mix beef and remaining ingredients except beans and cheese.

3. Cover and cook on Low heat setting 6 to 8 hours (or High heat setting 3 to 4 hours).

4. Stir in beans. Increase heat setting to High. Cover and cook 15 to 20 minutes or until slightly thickened. Sprinkle with cheese.

1 SERVING: CAL. 305 (CAL. FROM FAT 125); FAT 14g (SAT. FAT 5g); CHOL. 70mg; SODIUM 800mg; CARBS. 22g (FIBER 6g); PRO. 29g **% DAILY VALUE:** VIT. A 28%; VIT. C 20%; CALC. 6%; IRON 30% **EXCHANGES:** 1 STARCH, 1 VEGETABLE, 3 1/2 LEAN MEAT **CARB. CHOICES:** 1 1/2

Easy Bean and Kielbasa Soup

PREP: 15 min **COOK:** 10 hr 15 min ▪ **8 SERVINGS**

If your mornings are rushed, slice the sausage and chop the vegetables the night before and store in resealable plastic food-storage bags in the refrigerator.

- 1/2 package (20-oz size) 15- or 16-dried bean soup mix, sorted and rinsed
- 1 package (16 oz) smoked kielbasa sausage, cut lengthwise in half, then cut crosswise into slices
- 5 cans (14 oz each) chicken broth
- 4 medium carrots, chopped (2 cups)
- 3 medium stalks celery, chopped (1 1/2 cups)
- 1 large onion, chopped (1 cup)
- 2 tablespoons tomato paste
- 1/2 teaspoon salt
- 1 teaspoon dried thyme leaves
- 1/2 teaspoon pepper
- 1 can (14.5 oz) diced tomatoes, undrained

1. In 5- to 6-quart slow cooker, mix all ingredients except tomatoes.

2. Cover and cook on Low heat setting 8 to 10 hours.

3. Stir in tomatoes. Increase heat setting to High. Cover and cook about 15 minutes or until hot.

1 SERVING: CAL. 375 (CAL. FROM FAT 160); FAT 18g (SAT. FAT 6g); CHOL. 35mg; SODIUM 2020mg; CARBS. 35g (FIBER 6g); PRO. 18g **% DAILY VALUE:** VIT. A 100%; VIT. C 14%; CALC. 6%; IRON 16% **EXCHANGES:** 2 STARCH, 1 VEGETABLE, 1 1/2 HIGH-FAT MEAT, 1 FAT **CARB. CHOICES:** 2

Potato and Double-Corn Chowder LOW-FAT

PREP: 15 min **COOK:** 8 hr ■ **6 SERVINGS**

The bacon adds that good smoky flavor to this chowder, but it does lose its crispness when added at the beginning. If you like the crisp texture, stir it in at the end of cooking instead.

- 1 bag (16 oz) frozen hash brown potatoes, thawed (4 cups)
- 1 can (15.25 oz) whole kernel corn, undrained
- 1 can (14.75 oz) cream-style corn
- 1 can (12 oz) evaporated milk
- 1 medium onion, chopped (1/2 cup)
- 8 slices bacon, crisply cooked and crumbled (1/2 cup)
- 1/2 teaspoon salt
- 1/2 teaspoon Worcestershire sauce
- 1/4 teaspoon pepper
- Chopped fresh parsley, if desired

1. In 3 1/2- to 6-quart slow cooker, mix all ingredients except parsley.

2. Cover and cook on Low heat setting 6 to 8 hours (or High heat setting 3 to 4 hours) to develop flavors.

3. Sprinkle each serving with parsley.

1 SERVING: CAL. 315 (CAL. FROM FAT 70); FAT 8g (SAT. FAT 3g); CHOL. 15mg; SODIUM 730mg; CARBS. 55g (FIBER 5g); PROTEIN 11g **% DAILY VALUE:** VIT. A 6%; VIT. C 18%; CALC. 18%; IRON 10% **EXCHANGES:** 3 1/2 STARCH, 1 FAT **CARB. CHOICES:** 3 1/2

TURKEY, POTATO AND DOUBLE-CORN CHOWDER Cook as directed in steps 1 and 2. Increase heat setting to High. Stir in 3 cups cut-up cooked turkey or chicken. Cover and cook 15 to 20 minutes longer.

Vegetable-Beef-Barley Soup LOW-FAT

PREP: 20 min **COOK:** 9 hr ■ **10 SERVINGS**

Top this soup with a handful of herb-flavored croutons and a little grated Parmesan cheese.

- 1 1/2 lb beef stew meat
- 1 small bell pepper, chopped (1/2 cup)
- 3/4 cup chopped onion
- 3/4 cup 1-inch pieces fresh or frozen (thawed) green beans
- 2/3 cup uncooked barley
- 2/3 cup fresh or frozen (thawed) whole kernel corn
- 1 1/2 cups water
- 1 teaspoon salt
- 1 teaspoon chopped fresh or 1/2 teaspoon dried thyme leaves
- 1/4 teaspoon pepper
- 2 cans (14 oz each) beef broth
- 2 cans (14.5 oz each) diced tomatoes with roasted garlic, undrained
- 1 can (8 oz) tomato sauce

1. In 4- to 5-quart slow cooker, mix all ingredients.

2. Cover and cook on Low heat setting 8 to 9 hours.

1 SERVING: CAL. 225 (CAL. FROM FAT 70); FAT 8g (SAT. FAT 3g); CHOL. 40mg; SODIUM 870mg; CARBS. 20g (FIBER 4g); PROTEIN 18g **% DAILY VALUE:** VIT. A 8%; VIT. C 16%; CALC. 4%; IRON 16% **EXCHANGES:** 1 STARCH, 1 VEGETABLE, 2 LEAN MEAT **CARB. CHOICES:** 1

Winter Vegetable Stew

LOW-FAT

PREP: 20 min **COOK:** 10 hr 20 min ▪ **8 SERVINGS**

Parsnips, a root vegetable that looks like creamy white carrots, have a slightly sweet flavor. If you don't have any on hand, use carrots instead.

- 1 can (28 oz) Italian-style (plum) tomatoes
- 4 medium red potatoes, cut into 1/2-inch pieces
- 4 medium stalks celery, cut into 1/2-inch pieces (2 cups)
- 3 medium carrots, cut into 1/2-inch pieces (1 1/2 cups)
- 2 medium parsnips, peeled and cut into 1/2-inch pieces
- 2 medium leeks, cut into 1/2-inch pieces
- 1 can (14 oz) chicken broth
- 1/2 teaspoon dried thyme leaves
- 1/2 teaspoon dried rosemary leaves
- 1/2 teaspoon salt
- 3 tablespoons cornstarch
- 3 tablespoons cold water

1. Drain tomatoes, reserving liquid. Cut up tomatoes. In 4- to 5-quart slow cooker, mix tomatoes, tomato liquid and remaining ingredients except cornstarch and water.

2. Cover and cook on Low heat setting 8 to 10 hours.

3. In small bowl, mix cornstarch and water; gradually stir into stew until blended. Increase heat setting to High. Cover and cook about 20 minutes, stirring occasionally, until thickened.

1 SERVING: CAL. 135 (CAL. FROM FAT 0); FAT 0g (SAT. FAT 0g); CHOL. 0mg; SODIUM 570mg; CARBS. 30g (FIBER 5g); PRO. 4g
% DAILY VALUE: VIT. A 94%; VIT. C 22%; CALC. 8%; IRON 1%
EXCHANGES: 5 VEGETABLE **CARB. CHOICES:** 2

Winter Vegetable Stew ▶

CHAPTER 6

Cookies & Candies

Cookies

Candies

LOW-FAT = *3g or less, except main dishes with 10g or less* FAST = *Ready in 20 minutes or less* BREAD MACHINE = *Bread machine directions* SLOW COOKER = *Slow cooker directions* LIGHTER = *25% fewer calories or grams of fat*

◀ **White Chocolate Chunk–Macadamia Cookies (page 176)**

Cookie and Bar Basics

Who doesn't like homemade cookies, especially when they're just out of the oven? They're fun to eat, easy to tote and guaranteed to please any crowd. Take a moment to review the basics of the various ingredients, mixing techniques and baking know-how. Then bake up a pan of rich chocolate brownies, roll out some sugar cookies or slice up a roll of refrigerator dough—and enjoy!

INGREDIENTS

Cocoa

When recipes call for "cocoa," use unsweetened baking cocoa, not hot chocolate mix products that are sweetened and have additional ingredients. Two types of baking cocoa are available: **nonalkalized** (regular) and **alkalized** ("Dutch" or "European"). Alkalized cocoa goes through a "Dutching" process to neutralize natural acids found in cocoa. The result is a darker cocoa with a mellower chocolate flavor than regular cocoa. The two types of cocoa can be used interchangeably, but baked goods made with Dutch cocoa will be darker in color and a bit milder in flavor.

Flour

Bleached or unbleached all-purpose flour is usually the best to use for cookies and bars. Whole wheat flour may be substituted for one-third to one-half the amount of all-purpose flour; if you use more, the cookies will be too dry. Bread flour isn't recommended because cookies and bars can become tough; and cake flour isn't recommended because cookies become too delicate and fragile and may fall apart. Use self-rising flour only when recipe directions call for it. For more information on specific types of flour and measuring flour, see Flour on page 19.

Oats

Quick-cooking and old-fashioned oats are interchangeable unless recipes call for a specific type. Instant oatmeal products are not the same as quick-cooking and should not be used for baking.

Fats and Oils

Fats add tenderness and flavor to cookies and bars, but not all fats are equal. Butter and margarine are recommended for cookies and bars. Because vegetable-oil spreads with less than 65 percent fat, reduced-calorie or low-fat butter or margarine and tub products contain more water than butter or margarine, cookies made with them will be soft, puffy, tough and will dry out quickly. For more information on specific types of fat, see Fat on page 18.

Softening Butter or Margarine

Most cookie recipes call for softened butter or margarine. But how soft is it supposed to be, and how can you tell when it's soft enough? Let butter soften at room temperature for 30 to 45 minutes. You can also soften it in the microwave;

LEARN WITH Betty — SOFTENING BUTTER

Butter Perfectly Softened

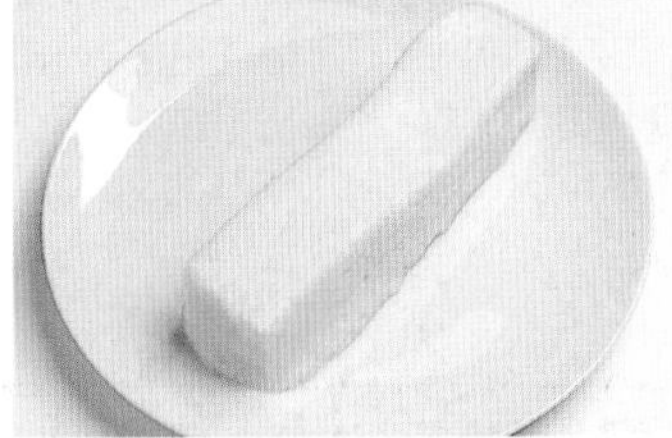

Butter Too Soft

Butter Partially Melted

see Microwave Cooking and Heating chart, page 40. Perfectly softened butter should give gently to pressure (you should be able to leave a fingerprint and slight indentation on the stick), but it shouldn't be soft in appearance. Butter that is too soft or is partially melted results in dough that is too soft, causing cookies to spread too much as they bake.

Sugars

In addition to adding sweetness to cookies and bars, sweeteners also help brown and add tenderness to baked goods.

Most recipes call for granulated white sugar, brown sugar or both, but other types of sweeteners like honey or maple syrup are called for in specific recipes. The higher the sugar-to-flour ratio in a recipe, the more tender and crisp the cookies will be.

Leavening

Cookies usually call for baking soda or baking powder, which are not interchangeable. For more information, see also Baking Powder, page 15, and Baking Soda, page 15.

Eggs

Eggs add richness, moisture and structure to cookies and bars. But too many eggs can make cookies crumbly. All the recipes in this book have been tested with large-size eggs. Egg product substitutes, made of egg whites, can be substituted for whole eggs, but cookies and bars made with them may be puffy and drier.

Liquids

Liquids like water, fruit juice, cream and milk tend to make cookies crisper by causing them to spread more and bar cookies higher, lighter and more cake-like. Add only as much liquid as the recipe calls for.

Nuts, Peanuts and Almond Brickle Chips

When nuts are called for in a recipe, you can substitute any variety of nut or peanuts instead. Use only fresh-tasting nuts in cookies and bars; if they have an off-flavor, throw them out. Nuts can easily become rancid, giving them an unpleasant, strong flavor that can ruin the taste of your cookies. To prevent rancidity, store nuts and peanuts tightly covered in your refrigerator up to 1 year or freezer for up to 2 years. Do not freeze cashews because they can become soggy.

Almond brickle baking chips can also become rancid. To prevent rancidity, store them in the refrigerator up to 1 month or freezer up to 6 months. Always taste these ingredients before adding to a recipe; if they don't taste fresh, throw them out.

PICKING THE RIGHT PANS

Cookie Sheets

Choosing the right cookie sheet makes cookies sweeter by the dozen! There are many types to choose from, including insulated, nonstick and dark surface. Keeping at least three or four cookie sheets on-hand is a great idea. When one batch of cookies is finished baking, another is ready to go!

Choose sheets that are at least 2 inches narrower and shorter than the inside dimensions of your oven, so heat can circulate around them. The sheet may be open on one, two or three sides. If the sheet has four sides, cookies may not brown as evenly during baking.

Shiny smooth-surface or textured aluminum cookie sheets are recommended for baking cookies. These sheets reflect heat, letting cookies bake evenly and brown properly. The recipes in this book were tested using shiny aluminum cookie sheets.

Insulated cookie sheets help prevent cookies from turning too dark on the bottom. Cookies baked on these sheets may take longer to bake, centers may be soft-set, the bottoms will be light colored and cookies may not brown as much overall. Cookies may be difficult to remove from these sheets because the cookie bottom is more tender.

Nonstick and dark surface cookie sheets may result in cookies smaller in diameter and more rounded. The tops and especially the bottoms will be more browned, and the bottoms may be hard. Check cookies at the minimum bake time so they don't get too brown or burn. Follow the manufacturer's directions; some recommend reducing the oven temperature by 25°F.

Baking Pans for Bars

To bake the best bars, choose shiny metal pans in the exact size called for in the recipe. Bars baked in pans that are too big become hard and overcooked, and those baked in pans that are too small can be doughy in the center and hard on the edges. Shiny metal pans reflect the heat away from the bars, preventing the crust from getting too brown and hard. Follow manufacturer's directions when using dark, nonstick and glass baking pans; they may recommend reducing the oven temperature by 25°F or checking for doneness 3 to 5 minutes before the minimum bake time given in the recipe.

GREASING COOKIE SHEETS AND BAKING PANS

- Grease aluminum cookie sheets and baking pans with shortening or cooking spray only when a recipe calls for it. Manufacturers of nonstick baking pans do not recommend using cooking spray because it can form a residue that can't be removed; use only shortening. Greasing with butter, margarine or oil isn't recommended for any type of baking pan because the area between the cookies will burn during baking.
- Or instead of greasing, line cookie sheets with cooking parchment paper or a silicone baking mat.

CUTTING BARS

Pans can sometimes get scratched when bars are cut with a metal knife, so try a plastic knife next time. In fact, a plastic knife works best for cutting brownies and soft, sticky bars such as Lemon Bars (page 174).

MIXING COOKIES AND BARS

An electric mixer or spoon can be used for mixing the sugar, fats and liquids in most of the recipes in this book. When the recipes were tested, there were no significant differences in the appearance or texture of baked cookies mixed with an electric mixer or a spoon. The sugars, fats and liquids usually are beaten together first until well mixed. Flour and other dry ingredients are almost always stirred in by hand to avoid overmixing the dough, which can result in tougher cookies.

STORING UNBAKED COOKIE DOUGH

- Unbaked cookie dough can be tightly covered and refrigerated up to 3 days before baking. If the dough is too stiff to work with, let it stand up to two hours at room temperature until it's easy to work with.
- Most unbaked cookie doughs can be frozen up to 6 months. Do not freeze meringue, macaroon mixtures or any dough using beaten egg whites because the egg whites break down during freezing and the cookies won't bake properly. To freeze, wrap batches of unbaked cookie dough in waxed paper, plastic wrap or foil, then put in resealable plastic freezer bags or containers. Dough can also be shaped into rolls, rectangles or individual cookies before freezing. Freeze rolls and rectangles as directed above. Freeze individual drops of cookie dough on cookie sheets; when dough is completely frozen, put pieces in resealable plastic

freezer bags or containers; label and freeze. Before baking, thaw frozen dough in the refrigerator at least eight hours. If the thawed dough is too stiff to work with, let it stand up to two hours at room temperature until it's easy to work with.

BAKING COOKIES AND BARS

- Scoop cookie dough onto completely cooled cookie sheets. Cookies will spread too much if put on a hot or warm cookie sheet.
- Make all cookies same size so they bake evenly.
- See Baking Pans for Bars, page 169.
- Bake cookies and bars on the middle oven rack. For even baking, baking one sheet at a time is recommended. To bake two sheets at once, position oven racks as close to the middle as possible, and switch sheets halfway through baking so cookies bake more evenly.
- Check cookies and bars at the minimum bake time listed in the recipe because they can overbake quickly becoming too brown or burn.
- Remove from the cookie sheet and cool as directed.
- Remove cookies from a cookie sheet using a flat, thin turner (also called a *metal spatula*).
- Cool bars and brownies in the pan on a wire rack.

Baking a Test Cookie

If you're new to cookie baking or trying a new recipe, bake one test cookie as directed in the recipe. This is a great way to make adjustments before baking a whole sheet of cookies.

- **If the cookie spreads too much,** add 1 to 2 tablespoons of flour to the dough, or refrigerate the dough 1 to 2 hours before baking.
- **If it's too dry,** add 1 to 2 tablespoons of milk to the dough.

REMOVING STUCK COOKIES

If cookies were left to cool too long on the cookie sheet and are difficult to remove without breaking them, here's what to do. Put the cookies back in the oven for 1 to 2 minutes to warm them, and then remove them from the sheet; they should come off easily.

STORING COOKIES AND BARS

Here's a great tip to remember: Store crisp cookies with other crisp ones; soft cookies with other soft ones; chewy cookies with other chewy ones. Never store crisp and chewy or soft cookies together in the same container or the crisp cookies will become soft.

- Store crisp cookies at room temperature in a loosely covered container.
- Store chewy and soft cookies at room temperature in resealable plastic food-storage bags or tightly covered container.
- Let frosted or decorated cookies set or harden before storing; store them between layers of waxed paper, plastic wrap or foil.
- Store different flavors of cookies in separate containers, or they will pick up the flavors of the other cookies. For example, if delicate buttery cookies are stored in the same jar as spicy gingersnaps, they'll all soon taste like ginger.
- Most bars can be stored tightly covered, but check the recipe for sure; some may need to be loosely covered and others need to be refrigerated.
- To freeze cookies and bars, tightly wrap and label; freeze unfrosted cookies up to 12 months and frosted cookies up to 3 months. Do not freeze meringue, custard-filled or cream-filled cookies. Put delicate frosted or decorated cookies in single layers in freezer containers and cover with waxed paper before adding another layer; freeze. Thaw most cookies, covered, in the container at room temperature for 1 to 2 hours. For crisp cookies, remove from the container to thaw.

Butterscotch Brownies

LOW-FAT

PREP: 15 min **BAKE:** 25 min **COOL:** 5 min ■ **16 BROWNIES**

When completely cooled, dress up the rich, chewy bars with a sprinkle of powdered sugar or a drizzle of Chocolate Glaze (page 118) or Vanilla Glaze (page 118).

1/4 cup butter or margarine
1 cup packed brown sugar
1 teaspoon vanilla
2 tablespoons milk
1 large egg
1 cup all-purpose flour*
1/2 cup chopped nuts, if desired
1 teaspoon baking powder
1/2 teaspoon salt

1. Heat oven to 350°F. Grease bottom and sides of 8-inch square pan with shortening.

2. In 1 1/2-quart saucepan, melt butter over low heat; remove from heat. Stir in brown sugar, vanilla, milk and egg. Stir in remaining ingredients. Spread in pan.

3. Bake about 25 minutes or until golden brown. Cool 5 minutes in pan on wire rack. For brownies, cut into 4 rows by 4 rows while warm.

**If using self-rising flour, omit baking powder and salt.*

1 BROWNIE: CAL. 110 (CAL. FROM FAT 25); FAT 3g (SAT. FAT 1g); CHOL. 15mg; SODIUM 130mg; CARBS. 20g (FIBER 0g); PROTEIN 1g **% DAILY VALUE:** VIT. A 2%; VIT. C 0%; CALC. 2%; IRON 4% **EXCHANGES:** 1 OTHER CARB., 1 FAT **CARB. CHOICES:** 1

QUICK PAN CLEANUP!

Line baking pans with foil for super-quick cleanup and easier cutting. To line baking pans with foil, turn pan upside down. Tear off a piece of foil longer than the pan, and shape the foil around the pan; remove foil. Flip the pan over, and gently fit the shaped foil into the pan. When the bars or brownies are cool, just lift them out of the pan by the foil "handles," peel back the foil and cut the bars as directed.

Salted Nut Bars

PREP: 20 min **BAKE:** 20 min ■ **32 BARS**

Love sweet and salty together? Then this yummy and easy-to-put-together bar cookie is made just for you.

1 1/2 cups all-purpose flour*
3/4 cup packed brown sugar
1/4 teaspoon salt
1/2 cup butter or margarine, softened
2 cups salted mixed nuts or peanuts
1 cup butterscotch-flavored chips
1/2 cup light corn syrup
2 tablespoons butter or margarine

1. Heat oven to 350°F. In medium bowl, mix flour, brown sugar and salt. Cut in 1/2 cup butter, using pastry blender (or pulling 2 table knives through ingredients in opposite directions), until evenly mixed.

2. In bottom of ungreased 13 × 9-inch pan, press dough evenly. Bake 15 minutes; cool slightly.

3. Cut up any large nuts. Sprinkle nuts evenly over crust. In 1-quart saucepan, heat remaining ingredients over low heat, stirring occasionally, just until chips are melted. Drizzle butterscotch mixture evenly over nuts. Bake 5 minutes. For bars, cut into 8 rows by 4 rows while warm for easiest cutting.

**If using self-rising flour, omit salt.*

1 BAR: CAL. 150 (CAL. FROM FAT 80); FAT 9g (SAT. FAT 3g); CHOL. 10mg; SODIUM 110mg; CARB. 15g (FIBER 0g); PRO. 2g **% DAILY VALUE:** VIT. A 2%; VIT. C 0%; CALC. 0%; IRON 4% **EXCHANGES:** 1 OTHER CARB., 2 FAT **CARB. CHOICES:** 1

Chocolate Brownies

PREP: 25 min **BAKE:** 45 min **COOL:** 2 hr ■
16 BROWNIES

- 2/3 cup butter or margarine
- 5 oz unsweetened baking chocolate, cut into pieces
- 1 3/4 cups sugar
- 2 teaspoons vanilla
- 3 large eggs
- 1 cup all-purpose flour*
- 1 cup chopped walnuts
- Chocolate Buttercream Frosting (page 115), if desired

1. Heat oven to 350°F. Grease bottom and sides of 9-inch square pan with shortening.

2. In 1-quart saucepan, melt butter and chocolate over low heat, stirring constantly. Cool 5 minutes.

3. In medium bowl, beat sugar, vanilla and eggs with electric mixer on high speed 5 minutes. Beat in chocolate mixture on low speed, scraping bowl occasionally. Beat in flour just until blended, scraping bowl occasionally. Stir in walnuts. Spread in pan.

▲ Chocolate Brownie Pie

4. Bake 40 to 45 minutes or just until brownies begin to pull away from sides of pan. Cool completely in pan on wire rack, about 2 hours. Frost with Chocolate Buttercream Frosting. For brownies, cut into 4 rows by 4 rows.

**Do not use self-rising flour.*

1 BROWNIE: CAL. 295 (CAL. FROM FAT 160); FAT 18g (SAT. FAT 8g); CHOL. 60mg; SODIUM 65mg; CARBS. 31g (FIBER 2g); PRO. 4g
% DAILY VALUE: VIT. A 6%; VIT. C 0%; CALC. 2%; IRON 6%
EXCHANGES: 1 STARCH, 1 OTHER CARB., 3 1/2 FAT
CARB. CHOICES: 2

CHOCOLATE BROWNIE PIE Grease bottom and side of pie plate, 10 × 1 1/2 inches, with shortening. Spread batter in pie plate. Bake 35 to 40 minutes or until center is set. Cool completely in pan on wire rack. Cut into wedges. Omit frosting. Serve with ice cream and Hot Fudge Sauce (page 214) if desired. 12 servings.

CHOCOLATE–PEANUT BUTTER BROWNIES Substitute 1/3 cup crunchy peanut butter for 1/3 cup of the butter. Omit walnuts. Before baking, unwrap 16 one-inch chocolate-covered peanut butter cup candies; arrange on top of the batter. Press candies down so tops of cups are even with top of batter.

Cream Cheese Brownies

PREP: 25 min **BAKE:** 50 min **COOL:** 2 hr ■
48 BROWNIES

Cream Cheese Filling

- 2 packages (8 oz each) cream cheese, softened
- 1/2 cup sugar
- 2 teaspoons vanilla
- 1 large egg

Brownies

- 1 cup butter or margarine
- 4 oz unsweetened baking chocolate
- 2 cups sugar
- 2 teaspoons vanilla
- 4 large eggs
- 1 1/2 cups all-purpose flour*
- 1/2 teaspoon salt
- 1 cup coarsely chopped nuts

1. Heat oven to 350°F. Grease bottom and sides of 13 × 9-inch pan with shortening.

2. In medium bowl, beat all filling ingredients with electric mixer on medium speed until smooth; set aside.

3. In 1-quart saucepan, melt butter and chocolate over low heat, stirring frequently. Remove from heat; cool 5 minutes.

4. In large bowl, beat chocolate mixture, sugar, vanilla and eggs with electric mixer on medium speed 1 minute, scraping bowl occasionally. Beat in flour and salt on low speed 30 seconds, scraping bowl occasionally. Beat on medium speed 1 minute. Stir in nuts. Spread 1 3/4 cups of the batter in pan. Spread filling over batter. Drop remaining batter in mounds randomly over filling; carefully spread to cover cream cheese layer.

5. Bake 45 to 50 minutes or until toothpick inserted in center comes out clean. Cool completely in pan on wire rack, about 2 hours. For brownies, cut into 8 rows by 6 rows. Store covered in refrigerator.

**If using self-rising flour, omit salt.*

1 BROWNIE: CAL. 165 (CAL. FROM FAT 100); FAT 11g (SAT. FAT 6g); CHOL. 45mg; SODIUM 85mg; CARBS. 15g (FIBER 1g); PRO. 2g
% DAILY VALUE: VIT. A 6%; VIT. C 0%; CALC. 2%; IRON 2%
EXCHANGES: 1 STARCH, 2 FAT **CARB. CHOICES:** 1

Toffee Bars

LIGHTER CREAM CHEESE BROWNIES

For 6 grams of fat and 120 calories per serving, use softened reduced-fat cream cheese (Neufchâtel), in the Cream Cheese Filling. For brownies, substitute 1/2 cup unsweetened applesauce for 1/2 cup of the butter and 2 eggs plus 4 egg whites for the 4 eggs. Decrease nuts to 1/2 cup.

Toffee Bars

PREP: 20 min **BAKE:** 30 min **COOL:** 30 min ▪ **32 BARS**

1 cup butter or margarine, softened
1 cup packed brown sugar
1 teaspoon vanilla
1 large egg yolk
2 cups all-purpose flour*
1/4 teaspoon salt
2/3 cup milk chocolate chips or 3 bars (1.55 oz each) milk chocolate, broken into small pieces
1/2 cup chopped nuts

1. Heat oven to 350°F.

2. In large bowl, stir butter, brown sugar, vanilla and egg yolk until well mixed. Stir in flour and salt. Press dough in ungreased 13 × 9-inch pan.

3. Bake 25 to 30 minutes or until very light brown (crust will be soft). Immediately sprinkle chocolate chips over hot crust. Let stand about 5 minutes or until soft; spread evenly. Sprinkle with nuts. Cool 30 minutes in pan on wire rack. To cut into bars easily, cut into 8 rows by 4 rows while still warm.

**If using self-rising flour, omit salt.*

1 BAR: CAL. 135 (CAL. FROM FAT 70); FAT 8g (SAT. FAT 4g); CHOL. 25mg; SODIUM 65mg; CARBS. 15g (FIBER 1g); PRO. 1g
% DAILY VALUE: VIT. A 4%; VIT. C 0%; CALC. 2%; IRON 2%
EXCHANGES: 1 OTHER CARB., 1 1/2 FAT **CARB. CHOICES:** 1

DOUBLE-TOFFEE BARS Stir in 1/2 cup almond brickle chips with the flour and salt.

Lemon Bars

PREP: 10 min **BAKE:** 50 min **COOL:** 1 hr ▪ **25 BARS**

The one-half-inch sides of the crust prevent the filling from sticking to the side of the pan.

1 cup all-purpose flour*
1/2 cup butter or margarine, softened
1/4 cup powdered sugar
1 cup granulated sugar
2 teaspoons grated lemon peel, if desired
2 tablespoons lemon juice
1/2 teaspoon baking powder
1/4 teaspoon salt
2 large eggs
Additional powdered sugar

1. Heat oven to 350°F.

2. In medium bowl, mix flour, butter and 1/4 cup powdered sugar with spoon. Press in ungreased 8-inch or 9-inch square pan, building up 1/2-inch edges. Bake crust 20 minutes; remove from oven.

3. In medium bowl, beat remaining ingredients except additional powdered sugar with electric mixer on high speed about 3 minutes or until light and fluffy. Pour over hot crust.

4. Bake 25 to 30 minutes or until no indentation remains when touched lightly in center. Cool completely in pan on wire rack, about 1 hour. Dust with powdered sugar. For bars, cut into 5 rows by 5 rows.

**Self-rising flour can be used.*

1 BAR: CAL. 95 (CAL. FROM FAT 35); FAT 4g (SAT. FAT 2g); CHOL. 25mg; SODIUM 65mg; CARBS. 14g (FIBER 0g); PRO. 1g
% DAILY VALUE: VIT. A 2%; VIT. C 0%; CALC. 0%; IRON 2%
EXCHANGES: 1 OTHER CARB., 1 FAT **CARB. CHOICES:** 1

LEMON-COCONUT BARS Stir 1/2 cup flaked coconut into egg mixture in Step 3.

Pumpkin-Spice Bars

PREP: 15 min **BAKE:** 30 min **COOL:** 2 hr ▪ **49 BARS**

Check labels carefully when buying canned pumpkin. Two types are available: plain pumpkin, which isn't sweetened and doesn't have any flavoring added, and pumpkin pie mix, which contains sugar and spices.

Bars
4 large eggs
2 cups granulated sugar
1 cup vegetable oil
1 can (15 oz) pumpkin (not pumpkin pie mix)
2 cups all-purpose flour*
2 teaspoons baking powder
2 teaspoons ground cinnamon
1 teaspoon baking soda
1/2 teaspoon salt
1/2 teaspoon ground ginger
1/4 teaspoon ground cloves
1 cup raisins, if desired

Cream Cheese Frosting
1 package (3 oz) cream cheese, softened
1/3 cup butter or margarine, softened
1 teaspoon vanilla
2 cups powdered sugar
1/2 cup chopped walnuts, if desired

◀ **Lemon Bars and Date Bars (pages 174–175)**

1. Heat oven to 350°F. Lightly grease bottom and sides of 15 × 10 × 1-inch pan with shortening.

2. In large bowl, beat eggs, granulated sugar, oil and pumpkin until smooth. Stir in flour, baking powder, cinnamon, baking soda, salt, ginger and cloves. Stir in raisins. Spread in pan.

3. Bake 25 to 30 minutes or until light brown. Cool completely in pan on wire rack, about 2 hours.

4. In medium bowl, beat cream cheese, butter and vanilla with electric mixer on low speed until smooth. Gradually beat in powdered sugar, 1 cup at a time, on low speed until smooth and spreadable. Frost bars. Sprinkle with walnuts. For bars, cut into 7 rows by 7 rows. Store covered in refrigerator.

**If using self-rising flour, omit baking powder, baking soda and salt.*

1 BAR: CAL. 140 (CAL. FROM FAT 65); FAT 7g (SAT. FAT 2g); CHOL. 25mg; SODIUM 90mg; CARBS. 18g (FIBER 0g); PRO. 1g
% DAILY VALUE: VIT. A 28%; VIT. C 0%; CALC. 2%; IRON 2%
EXCHANGES: 1 OTHER CARB., 1 1/2 FAT **CARB. CHOICES:** 1

FROSTING BARS

An "offset metal spatula" (or spreader) is a handy tool for frosting bars. Instead of being perfectly straight, the spatula part has a bend in it near the handle, making it ergonomically friendly and very easy to frost bars in pans. This gem comes in different lengths, is inexpensive and can be found in large department stores and specialty cookware stores.

Date Bars

PREP: 30 min **BAKE:** 30 min **COOL:** 5 min ■ **36 BARS**

Date Filling

3 cups cut-up pitted dates (1 lb)
1/4 cup granulated sugar
1 1/2 cups water

Bars

1 cup packed brown sugar
1 cup butter or margarine, softened
1 3/4 cups all-purpose* or whole wheat flour
1 1/2 cups quick-cooking oats
1/2 teaspoon salt
1/2 teaspoon baking soda

1. In 2-quart saucepan, cook all filling ingredients over low heat about 10 minutes, stirring constantly, until thickened. Cool 5 minutes.

2. Heat oven to 400°F. Grease bottom and sides of 13 × 9-inch pan with shortening.

3. In large bowl, stir brown sugar and butter until well mixed. Stir in flour, oats, salt and baking soda until crumbly. Press half of the crumb mixture evenly in bottom of pan. Spread with filling. Top with remaining crumb mixture; press lightly.

4. Bake 25 to 30 minutes or until light brown. Cool 5 minutes in pan on wire rack. For bars, cut into 6 rows by 6 rows while warm.

**If using self-rising flour, omit salt and baking soda.*

1 BAR: CAL. 145 (CAL. FROM FAT 45); FAT 5g (SAT. FAT 3g); CHOL. 15mg; SODIUM 90mg; CARBS. 25g (FIBER 2g); PRO. 2g
% DAILY VALUE: VIT. A 4%; VIT. C 0%; CALC. 0%; IRON 4%
EXCHANGES: 1 STARCH, 1/2 OTHER CARB., 1 FAT
CARB. CHOICES: 1 1/2

FIG BARS Substitute 3 cups cut-up pitted dried figs for the dates.

Chocolate Chip Cookies

PREP: 10 min **BAKE:** 8 to 10 min per sheet
COOL: 2 min ■ **ABOUT 4 DOZEN COOKIES**

- 3/4 cup granulated sugar
- 3/4 cup packed brown sugar
- 1 cup butter or margarine, softened
- 1 teaspoon vanilla
- 1 large egg
- 2 1/4 cups all-purpose flour*
- 1 teaspoon baking soda
- 1/2 teaspoon salt
- 1 cup coarsely chopped nuts
- 1 bag (12 oz) semisweet chocolate chips (2 cups)

1. Heat oven to 375°F.

2. In large bowl, beat sugars, butter, vanilla and egg with electric mixer on medium speed, or mix with spoon. Stir in flour, baking soda and salt (dough will be stiff). Stir in nuts and chocolate chips.

3. On ungreased cookie sheet, drop dough by rounded tablespoonfuls about 2 inches apart.

4. Bake 8 to 10 minutes or until light brown (centers will be soft). Cool 1 to 2 minutes; remove from cookie sheet to wire rack.

**If using self-rising flour, omit baking soda and salt.*

1 COOKIE: CAL. 135 (CAL. FROM FAT 70); FAT 8g (SAT. FAT 4g); CHOL. 15mg; SODIUM 80mg; CARBS. 16g (FIBER 1g); PRO. 1g
% DAILY VALUE: VIT. A 2%; VIT. C 0%; CALC. 2%; IRON 4%
EXCHANGES: 1 Other Carb., 1 1/2 FAT **CARB. CHOICES:** 1

LIGHTER CHOCOLATE CHIP COOKIES
For 5 grams of fat and 90 calories per serving, decrease butter to 3/4 cup and omit nuts. Substitute 1 cup miniature semisweet chocolate chips for the 12-oz bag of chocolate chips.

CANDY COOKIES Substitute 2 cups candy-coated chocolate candies for the chocolate chips.

CHOCOLATE CHIP BARS Press dough in ungreased 13 × 9-inch pan. Bake 15 to 20 minutes or until golden brown. Cool in pan on wire rack. 48 bars.

JUMBO CHOCOLATE CHIP COOKIES Drop dough by 1/4 cupfuls or #16 cookie/ice-cream scoop about 3 inches apart onto ungreased cookie sheet. Bake 12 to 15 minutes or until edges are set (centers will be soft). Cool 1 to 2 minutes; remove from cookie sheet to wire rack. 1 1/2 dozen cookies.

White Chocolate Chunk–Macadamia Cookies

PREP: 10 min **BAKE:** 10 to 12 min per sheet
COOL: 2 min ■ **ABOUT 2 1/2 DOZEN COOKIES**

Bake up a batch of these gourmet cookie-shop favorites and get ready for rich and buttery treats that are crispy on the outside and chewy in the center.

LEARN WITH Betty — DIFFERENCES IN CHOCOLATE CHIP COOKIES

This cookie is flat because the butter was too soft or partially melted, flour was undermeasured or the cookie sheet was too hot.

This cookie is slightly rounded and evenly golden brown; there are no problems.

This cookie didn't change shape and is hard because too much flour was used.

1 cup packed brown sugar
1/2 cup granulated sugar
1/2 cup butter or margarine, softened
1/2 cup shortening
1 teaspoon vanilla
1 large egg
2 1/4 cups all-purpose flour*
1 teaspoon baking soda
1/4 teaspoon salt
1 package (6 oz) white baking bars (white chocolate), cut into 1/4- to 1/2-inch chunks
1 jar (3.5 oz) macadamia nuts, coarsely chopped

1. Heat oven to 350°F.

2. In large bowl, beat sugars, butter, shortening, vanilla and egg with electric mixer on medium speed until light and fluffy, or mix with spoon. Stir in flour, baking soda and salt (dough will be stiff). Stir in white baking bar chunks and nuts.

3. On ungreased cookie sheet, drop dough by rounded tablespoonfuls about 2 inches apart.

4. Bake 10 to 12 minutes or until light brown. Cool 1 to 2 minutes; remove from cookie sheet to wire rack.

**Do not use self-rising flour.*

1 COOKIE: CAL. 185 (CAL. FROM FAT 100); FAT 11g (SAT. FAT 4g); CHOL. 15mg; SODIUM 100mg; CARBS. 21g (FIBER 1g); PRO. 2g
% DAILY VALUE: VIT. A 2%; VIT. C 0%; CALC. 2%; IRON 4%
EXCHANGES: 1 STARCH, 1/2 OTHER CARB., 2 FAT **CARB. CHOICES:** 1 1/2

SCOOPING OUT THE DOUGH!

A spring-handled cookie or ice-cream scoop makes quick work of forming cookie dough and making cookies the same size. They come in various sizes referred to by number—the larger the number, the smaller the scoop. Because not all manufacturers make scoops the same size, measure the volume of the scoop with water first. Use the size of scoop that drops the amount of dough called for in a recipe. Some common scoop sizes are:

1 level tablespoon = #70 scoop
1/4 cup = #16 scoop

Oatmeal-Raisin Cookies

PREP: 15 min **BAKE:** 9 to 11 min per sheet ▪ **ABOUT 3 DOZEN COOKIES**

Quick-cooking and old-fashioned rolled oats are interchangeable unless recipes call for a specific type. Instant oatmeal products are not the same as quick-cooking or old-fashioned oats and should not be used for baking—you will get gummy or mushy results.

2/3 cup granulated sugar
2/3 cup packed brown sugar
1/2 cup butter or margarine, softened
1/2 cup shortening
1 teaspoon baking soda
1 teaspoon ground cinnamon
1 teaspoon vanilla
1/2 teaspoon baking powder
1/2 teaspoon salt
2 large eggs
3 cups quick-cooking or old-fashioned oats
1 cup all-purpose flour*
1 cup raisins, chopped nuts or semisweet chocolate chips, if desired

1. Heat oven to 375°F.

2. In large bowl, beat all ingredients except oats, flour and raisins with electric mixer on medium speed, or mix with spoon. Stir in oats, flour and raisins.

3. On ungreased cookie sheet, drop dough by rounded tablespoonfuls about 2 inches apart.

4. Bake 9 to 11 minutes or until light brown. Immediately remove from cookie sheet to wire rack.

**If using self-rising flour, omit baking soda, baking powder and salt.*

1 COOKIE: CAL. 120 (CAL. FROM FAT 55); FAT 6g (SAT. FAT 2g); CHOL. 20mg; SODIUM 95mg; CARBS. 15g (FIBER 1g); PRO. 2g
% DAILY VALUE: VIT. A 2%; VIT. C 0%; CALC. 0%; IRON 2%
EXCHANGES: 1 STARCH, 1 FAT **CARB. CHOICES:** 1

LIGHTER OATMEAL-RAISIN COOKIES

For 3 grams of fat and 95 calories per serving, substitute unsweetened applesauce for the shortening and 1/2 cup fat-free cholesterol-free egg product for the eggs. Increase cinnamon and vanilla to 1 1/2 teaspoons each.

Chocolate Drop Cookies

PREP: 25 min **BAKE:** 8 to 10 min per sheet
COOL: 30 min ▪ **ABOUT 3 DOZEN COOKIES**

Save preparation time—use your microwave to melt the chocolate for the cookie dough and the chocolate and butter for the frosting.

Cookies

1 cup granulated sugar
1/2 cup butter or margarine, softened
1/3 cup buttermilk
1 teaspoon vanilla
1 large egg
2 oz unsweetened baking chocolate, melted and cooled
1 3/4 cups all-purpose flour*
1/2 teaspoon baking soda
1/2 teaspoon salt
1 cup chopped nuts

Chocolate Frosting

2 oz unsweetened baking chocolate
2 tablespoons butter or margarine
2 cups powdered sugar
3 tablespoons hot water

1. Heat oven to 400°F. Grease cookie sheet with shortening or spray with cooking spray.

2. In large bowl, beat granulated sugar, 1/2 cup butter, the buttermilk, vanilla, egg and melted chocolate with electric mixer on medium speed, or mix with spoon. Stir in flour, baking soda and salt. Stir in nuts.

3. On cookie sheet, drop dough by rounded tablespoonfuls about 2 inches apart.

4. Bake 8 to 10 minutes or until almost no indentation remains when touched in center. Immediately remove from cookie sheet to wire rack. Cool completely, about 30 minutes.

5. In 2-quart saucepan, melt 2 ounces chocolate and 2 tablespoons butter over low heat, stirring occasionally; remove from heat. Stir in powdered sugar and hot water until smooth. (If frosting is too thick, add more water, 1 teaspoon at a time. If frosting is too thin, add more powdered sugar, 1 tablespoon at a time.) Frost cookies.

**If using self-rising flour, omit baking soda and salt.*

1 COOKIE: CAL. 140 (CAL. FROM FAT 65); FAT 7g (SAT. FAT 3g); CHOL. 15mg; SODIUM 75mg; CARBS. 18g (FIBER 1g); PRO. 2g
% DAILY VALUE: VIT. A 2%; VIT. C 0%; CALC. 0%; IRON 2%
EXCHANGES: 1 STARCH, 1 1/2 FAT **CARB. CHOICES:** 1

LEARN WITH Betty — MELTING CHOCOLATE

This melted chocolate is smooth and creamy; there are no problems.

This melted chocolate has seized, forming a dull, grainy, solid mass because it was melted over too high a heat or a very small amount of liquid was added.

To make seized chocolate smooth and creamy again, stir in or beat in with wire whisk at least 1 tablespoon water, melted butter, vegetable oil or melted vegetable shortening. Heat over very low heat, if necessary, stirring constantly.

Chocolate Crinkles LOW-FAT

PREP: 20 min **CHILL:** 3 hr **BAKE:** 10 to 12 min per sheet ▪ **ABOUT 6 DOZEN COOKIES**

- 2 cups granulated sugar
- 1/2 cup vegetable oil
- 2 teaspoons vanilla
- 4 oz unsweetened baking chocolate, melted and cooled
- 4 large eggs
- 2 cups all-purpose flour*
- 2 teaspoons baking powder
- 1/2 teaspoon salt
- 1 cup powdered sugar

1. In large bowl, stir granulated sugar, oil, vanilla and chocolate until well mixed. Stir in eggs, one at a time. Stir in flour, baking powder and salt. Cover and refrigerate at least 3 hours.

2. Heat oven to 350°F. Grease cookie sheet with shortening or spray with cooking spray.

3. Drop dough by teaspoonfuls into powdered sugar; roll around to coat. Shape into balls. On cookie sheet, place balls about 2 inches apart.

4. Bake 10 to 12 minutes or until almost no indentation remains when touched. Immediately remove from cookie sheet to wire rack.

**If using self-rising flour, omit baking powder and salt.*

1 COOKIE: CAL. 70 (CAL. FROM FAT 25); FAT 3g (SAT. FAT 1g); CHOL. 10mg; SODIUM 35mg; CARBS. 10g (FIBER 0g); PRO. 1g
% DAILY VALUE: VIT. A 0%; VIT. C 0%; CALC. 0%; IRON 2%
EXCHANGES: 1/2 STARCH, 1/2 FAT **CARB. CHOICES:** 1/2

Soft Molasses Cookies

PREP: 10 min **BAKE:** 9 to 11 min per sheet **COOL:** 2 min ▪ **ABOUT 4 DOZEN COOKIES**

- 1 cup sugar
- 3/4 cup sour cream
- 1/2 cup butter or margarine, softened
- 1/2 cup shortening
- 1/2 cup molasses
- 1 large egg
- 3 cups all-purpose flour*
- 1 1/2 teaspoons baking soda
- 1 teaspoon ground cinnamon
- 1 teaspoon ground ginger
- 1/2 teaspoon salt

1. Heat oven to 375°F.

2. In large bowl, beat sugar, sour cream, butter, shortening, molasses and egg with electric mixer on medium speed, or mix with spoon. Stir in remaining ingredients.

3. On ungreased cookie sheet, drop dough by rounded tablespoonfuls about 2 inches apart.

4. Bake 9 to 11 minutes or until almost no indentation remains when touched in center. Cool 1 to 2 minutes; remove from cookie sheet to wire rack. Sprinkle with additional sugar while warm.

**If using self-rising flour, omit baking soda and salt.*

1 COOKIE: CAL. 95 (CAL. FROM FAT 45); FAT 5g (SAT. FAT 2g); CHOL. 10mg; SODIUM 80mg; CARBS. 10g (FIBER 0g); PRO. 1g
% DAILY VALUE: VIT. A 2%; VIT. C 0%; CALC. 0%; IRON 2%
EXCHANGES: 1/2 STARCH, 1 FAT **CARB. CHOICES:** 1/2

SOFT MOLASSES COOKIES WITH VANILLA FROSTING Bake and cool cookies as directed in Step 4, except omit sugar. In large bowl, stir 3 cups powdered sugar, 1/3 cup butter or margarine, softened, 1 1/2 teaspoons vanilla and 2 to 3 tablespoons milk until smooth and spreadable. Frost cookies.

◀ **Soft Molasses Cookies with Vanilla Frosting**

Gingersnaps LOW-FAT

PREP: 15 min **BAKE:** 10 to 12 min per sheet ▪ **ABOUT 4 DOZEN COOKIES**

After baking, these spicy cookies have a crackly and sugary top. Serve them with ice cream, fresh fruit, sorbet or coffee.

1 cup packed brown sugar
3/4 cup shortening
1/4 cup molasses
1 large egg
2 1/4 cups all-purpose flour*
2 teaspoons baking soda
1 teaspoon ground cinnamon
1 teaspoon ground ginger
1/2 teaspoon ground cloves
1/4 teaspoon salt
Granulated sugar

1. Heat oven to 375°F. Lightly grease cookie sheet with shortening or spray with cooking spray.

2. In large bowl, beat brown sugar, shortening, molasses and egg with electric mixer on medium speed, or mix with spoon. Stir in remaining ingredients except granulated sugar.

3. Shape dough by rounded teaspoonfuls into balls. Dip tops into granulated sugar. On cookie sheet, place balls, sugared sides up, about 3 inches apart.

4. Bake 10 to 12 minutes or just until set. Immediately remove from cookie sheet to wire rack.

**If using self-rising flour, decrease baking soda to 1 teaspoon and omit salt.*

1 COOKIE: CAL. 75 (CAL. FROM FAT 25); FAT 3g (SAT. FAT 1g); CHOL. 5mg; SODIUM 70mg; CARBS.11g (FIBER 0g); PRO. 1g
% DAILY VALUE: VIT. A 0%; VIT. C 0%; CALC. 0%; IRON 2%
EXCHANGES: 1 OTHER CARB., 1/2 FAT **CARB. CHOICES:** 1

Peanut Butter Cookies

PREP: 15 min **BAKE:** 9 to 10 min per sheet **COOL:** 5 min ▪ **ABOUT 2 1/2 DOZEN COOKIES**

1/2 cup granulated sugar
1/2 cup packed brown sugar
1/2 cup peanut butter
1/4 cup shortening
1/4 cup butter or margarine, softened
1 large egg
1 1/4 cups all-purpose flour*
3/4 teaspoon baking soda
1/2 teaspoon baking powder
1/4 teaspoon salt
Additional granulated sugar

1. Heat oven to 375°F.

2. In large bowl, beat 1/2 cup granulated sugar, the brown sugar, peanut butter, shortening, butter and egg with electric mixer on medium speed, or mix with spoon. Stir in flour, baking soda, baking powder and salt.

3. Shape dough into 1 1/4-inch balls. On ungreased cookie sheet, place balls about 3 inches apart. Flatten in crisscross pattern with fork dipped in additional granulated sugar.

4. Bake 9 to 10 minutes or until light brown. Cool 5 minutes; remove from cookie sheet to wire rack.

**If using self-rising flour, omit baking soda, baking powder and salt.*

1 COOKIE: CAL. 115 (CAL. FROM FAT 55); FAT 6g (SAT. FAT 2g); CHOL. 10mg; SODIUM 95mg; CARBS. 13g (FIBER 0g); PRO. 2g
% DAILY VALUE: VIT. A 0%; VIT. C 0%; CALC. 0%; IRON 2%
EXCHANGES: 1 STARCH, 1 FAT **CARB. CHOICES:** 1

RICH PEANUT BUTTER CHIP COOKIES

Omit 1/2 cup granulated sugar; increase packed brown sugar to 1 cup. Omit shortening; increase butter or margarine, softened, to 1/2 cup. After stirring in flour, baking soda, baking powder and salt, stir in 1 cup peanut butter chips. Shape dough into balls as directed. Dip tops of balls into sugar, but do not flatten. Bake as directed.

Snickerdoodles

PREP: 10 min **BAKE:** 8 to 10 min per sheet ▪ **ABOUT 4 DOZEN COOKIES**

This favorite, whimsically named cookie originated in New England in the 1800s. It's traditionally rolled in cinnamon-sugar before baking.

- 1 1/2 cups sugar
- 1/2 cup butter or margarine, softened
- 1/2 cup shortening
- 2 large eggs
- 2 3/4 cups all-purpose flour*
- 2 teaspoons cream of tartar
- 1 teaspoon baking soda
- 1/4 teaspoon salt
- 1/4 cup sugar
- 2 teaspoons ground cinnamon

1. Heat oven to 400°F.

2. In large bowl, beat 1 1/2 cups sugar, the butter, shortening and eggs with electric mixer on medium speed, or mix with spoon. Stir in flour, cream of tartar, baking soda and salt.

3. Shape dough into 1 1/4-inch balls. In small bowl, mix 1/4 cup sugar and the cinnamon. Roll balls in cinnamon-sugar mixture. On ungreased cookie sheet, place balls 2 inches apart.

4. Bake 8 to 10 minutes or until set. Immediately remove from cookie sheet to wire rack.

**If using self-rising flour, omit cream of tartar, baking soda and salt.*

1 COOKIE: CAL. 90 (CAL. FROM FAT 35); FAT 4g (SAT. FAT 2g); CHOL. 15mg; SODIUM 55mg; CARBS. 13g (FIBER 0g); PRO. 1g
% DAILY VALUE: VIT. A 2%; VIT. C 0%; CALC. 0%; IRON 2%
EXCHANGES: 1 OTHER CARB., 1 FAT **CARB. CHOICES:** 1

Brown Sugar Refrigerator Cookies LOW-FAT

PREP: 20 min **CHILL:** 2 hr **BAKE:** 6 to 8 min per sheet **COOL:** 2 min ▪ **ABOUT 6 DOZEN COOKIES**

You can call these refrigerator or freezer cookies. Freeze the tightly wrapped cookie dough for up to two months, then slice and bake when you want. Just add 1 or 2 minutes to the baking time when the dough comes straight from the freezer.

- 1 cup packed brown sugar
- 1 cup butter or margarine, softened
- 1 teaspoon vanilla
- 1 large egg
- 3 cups all-purpose flour*
- 1 1/2 teaspoons ground cinnamon
- 1/2 teaspoon baking soda
- 1/2 teaspoon salt
- 1/3 cup chopped nuts

1. In large bowl, beat brown sugar, butter, vanilla and egg with electric mixer on medium speed, or mix with spoon. Stir in remaining ingredients except nuts. Stir in nuts.

2. Shape dough into 10 × 3-inch rectangle on plastic wrap. Wrap and refrigerate about 2 hours or until firm but no longer than 24 hours.

3. Heat oven to 375°F.

4. Cut rectangle into 1/8-inch slices. On ungreased cookie sheet, place slices 2 inches apart.

5. Bake 6 to 8 minutes or until light brown. Cool 1 to 2 minutes; remove from cookie sheet to wire rack.

**If using self-rising flour, omit baking soda and salt.*

1 COOKIE: CAL. 60 (CAL. FROM FAT 25); FAT 3g (SAT. FAT 2g); CHOL. 10mg; SODIUM 45mg; CARBS. 7g (FIBER 0g); PRO. 1g
% DAILY VALUE: VIT. A 2%; VIT. C 0%; CALC. 0%; IRON 2%
EXCHANGES: 1/2 STARCH, 1/2 FAT **CARB. CHOICES:** 1/2

Russian Tea Cakes

PREP: 20 min **BAKE:** 10 to 12 min per sheet
COOL: 10 min ▪ **ABOUT 4 DOZEN COOKIES**

1 cup butter or margarine, softened
1/2 cup powdered sugar
1 teaspoon vanilla
2 1/4 cups all-purpose flour*
3/4 cup finely chopped nuts
1/4 teaspoon salt
Additional powdered sugar

1. Heat oven to 400°F.

2. In large bowl, stir butter, 1/2 cup powdered sugar and the vanilla until well mixed. Stir in flour, nuts and salt until dough holds together.

3. Shape dough into 1-inch balls. On ungreased cookie sheet, place balls about 1 inch apart.

4. Bake 10 to 12 minutes or until set but not brown. Immediately remove from cookie sheet to wire rack; cool 5 minutes.

5. Place additional powdered sugar in small bowl. Roll warm cookies in powdered sugar; cool on wire rack 5 minutes. Roll in powdered sugar again.

**Do not use self-rising flour.*

1 COOKIE: CAL. 75 (CAL. FROM FAT 45); FAT 5g (SAT. FAT 2g); CHOL. 10mg; SODIUM 40mg; CARBS. 7g (FIBER 0g); PRO. 1g
% DAILY VALUE: VIT. A 2%; VIT. C 0%; CALC. 0%; IRON 2%
EXCHANGES: 1/2 STARCH, 1 FAT **CARB. CHOICES:** 1/2

LEMON TEA CAKES Add 1/4 cup crushed lemon drop candies with the butter, powdered sugar and vanilla in Step 2.

PEPPERMINT TEA CAKES Add 1/4 cup crushed hard peppermint candies with the butter, powdered sugar and vanilla in Step 2.

◀ **Thumbprint Cookies and Lemon-Almond Thumbprint Cookies**

Thumbprint Cookies

PREP: 30 min **BAKE:** 10 min per sheet ▪
ABOUT 3 DOZEN COOKIES

1/4 cup packed brown sugar
1/4 cup shortening
1/4 cup butter or margarine, softened
1/2 teaspoon vanilla
1 large egg yolk
1 cup all-purpose flour*
1/4 teaspoon salt
1 large egg white
1 cup finely chopped nuts
About 6 tablespoons jelly or jam (any flavor)

1. Heat oven to 350°F.

2. In medium bowl, beat brown sugar, shortening, butter, vanilla and egg yolk with electric mixer on medium speed, or mix with spoon. Stir in flour and salt.

3. Shape dough into 1-inch balls. In small bowl, beat egg white slightly with fork. Place nuts in small bowl. Dip each ball into egg white, then roll in nuts. On ungreased cookie sheet, place balls about 1 inch apart. Press thumb into center of each cookie to make indentation, but do not press all the way to the cookie sheet.

4. Bake about 10 minutes or until light brown. Quickly remake indentations with end of wooden spoon if necessary. Immediately remove from cookie sheet to wire rack. Fill each thumbprint with about 1/2 teaspoon of the jelly.

**If using self-rising flour, omit salt.*

1 COOKIE: CAL. 70 (CAL. FROM FAT 35); FAT 4g (SAT. FAT 1g); CHOL. 10mg; SODIUM 30mg; CARBS. 7g (FIBER 0g); PRO. 1g
% DAILY VALUE: VIT. A 0%; VIT. C 0%; CALC. 0%; IRON 2%
EXCHANGES: 1/2 STARCH, 1/2 FAT **CARB. CHOICES:** 1/2

LEMON-ALMOND THUMBPRINT COOKIES Roll balls of dough into finely chopped slivered almonds. Fill indentations with Lemon Curd (page 421) or purchased lemon curd instead of the jelly.

Shortbread Cookies

PREP: 20 min **BAKE:** 20 min per sheet ■ **ABOUT 2 DOZEN 1 1/2-INCH COOKIES**

Serve these buttery cookies plain, or dip the edges in melted chocolate and then in chopped nuts.

- 3/4 cup butter or margarine, softened
- 1/4 cup sugar
- 2 cups all-purpose flour*

1. Heat oven to 350°F.

2. In large bowl, stir butter and sugar until well mixed. Stir in flour. (If dough is crumbly, mix in 1 to 2 tablespoons more butter or margarine, softened.)

3. Roll dough 1/2 inch thick on lightly floured surface. Cut into small shapes with knife or use cookie cutters. On ungreased cookie sheet, place shapes 1/2 inch apart.

4. Bake about 20 minutes or until set. Immediately remove from cookie sheet to wire rack.

**Do not use self-rising flour.*

1 COOKIE: CAL. 100 (CAL. FROM FAT 55); FAT 6g (SAT. FAT 4g); CHOL. 15mg; SODIUM 40mg; CARBS. 10g (FIBER 0g); PRO. 1g
% DAILY VALUE: VIT. A 4%; VIT. C 0%; CALC. 0%; IRON 2%
EXCHANGES: 1/2 STARCH, 1 FAT **CARB. CHOICES:** 1/2

PECAN SHORTBREAD COOKIES Stir in 1/2 cup chopped pecans, toasted if desired, with the flour.

Soft No-Roll Sugar Cookies

PREP: 20 min **CHILL:** 2 hr **BAKE:** 13 to 15 min per sheet ■ **ABOUT 3 1/2 DOZEN COOKIES**

- 1 cup granulated sugar
- 1 cup powdered sugar
- 1 cup butter or margarine, softened
- 3/4 cup vegetable oil
- 2 tablespoons milk
- 1 tablespoon vanilla
- 2 large eggs
- 4 1/4 cups all-purpose flour*
- 1 teaspoon baking soda
- 1 teaspoon cream of tartar
- 1/2 teaspoon salt
- 1/2 cup granulated sugar

1. In large bowl, beat 1 cup granulated sugar, the powdered sugar, butter, oil, milk, vanilla and eggs with electric mixer on medium speed, or mix with spoon. Stir in flour, baking soda, cream of tartar and salt. Cover and refrigerate about 2 hours or until firm.

2. Heat oven to 350°F.

3. Shape dough into 1 1/2-inch balls. Place 1/2 cup granulated sugar in small bowl. Roll balls in sugar. On ungreased cookie sheet, place balls about 3 inches apart. Press bottom of drinking glass on each ball until about 1/4 inch thick. Sprinkle each cookie with a little additional sugar.

4. Bake 13 to 15 minutes or until set and edges just begin to turn brown. Immediately remove from cookie sheet to wire rack.

**Do not use self-rising flour.*

1 COOKIE: CAL. 170 (CAL. FROM FAT 80); FAT 9g (SAT. FAT 3g); CHOL. 20mg; SODIUM 90mg; CARBS. 20g (FIBER 0g); PRO. 2g
% DAILY VALUE: VIT. A 4%; VIT. C 0%; CALC. 0%; IRON 4%
EXCHANGES: 1 STARCH, 1/2 OTHER CARB., 1 1/2 FAT
CARB. CHOICES: 1

Hazelnut Biscotti

PREP: 25 min **BAKE:** 1 hr 5 min **COOL:** 20 min per sheet ■ **40 COOKIES**

- 1 cup hazelnuts (filberts), coarsely chopped
- 1 cup sugar
- 1/2 cup butter or margarine, softened
- 1 teaspoon almond extract
- 1 teaspoon vanilla
- 2 large eggs
- 3 1/2 cups all-purpose flour*
- 1 teaspoon baking powder
- 1/2 teaspoon baking soda

1. Heat oven to 350°F. Spread hazelnuts in ungreased shallow pan. Bake uncovered about 10 minutes, stirring occasionally, until golden brown; cool.

2. In large bowl, beat sugar, butter, almond extract, vanilla and eggs with electric mixer on medium speed, or mix with spoon. Stir in flour, baking powder and baking soda. Stir in hazelnuts. Place dough on lightly floured surface. Gently knead 2 to 3 minutes or until dough holds together and hazelnuts are evenly distributed.

3. Divide dough in half. On one side of ungreased cookie sheet, shape half of dough into 10 × 3-inch rectangle, rounding edges slightly. Repeat with remaining dough on same cookie sheet.

4. Bake about 25 minutes or until center is firm to the touch. Cool on cookie sheet 15 minutes; move to cutting board. Cut each rectangle crosswise into 1/2-inch slices, using sharp knife.

5. Place 20 slices, cut sides down, on ungreased cookie sheet. Bake about 15 minutes or until crisp and light brown. Immediately remove from cookie sheet to wire rack; cool. Cool cookie sheet 5 minutes; repeat with remaining slices.

**Do not use self-rising flour.*

1 COOKIE: CAL. 100 (CAL. FROM FAT 35); FAT 4g (SAT. FAT 2g); CHOL. 15mg; SODIUM 45mg; CARBS. 14g (FIBER 0g); PRO. 2g
% DAILY VALUE: VIT. A 2%; VIT. C 0%; CALC. 2%; IRON 4%
EXCHANGES: 1 STARCH, 1/2 FAT **CARB. CHOICES:** 1

ALMOND BISCOTTI Substitute 1 cup slivered almonds for the hazelnuts.

Buttery Spritz **LOW-FAT**

PREP: 25 min **BAKE:** 6 to 9 min per sheet ■ **ABOUT 5 DOZEN COOKIES**

- 1 cup butter, softened*
- 1/2 cup sugar
- 2 1/4 cups all-purpose flour**
- 1 teaspoon almond extract or vanilla
- 1/2 teaspoon salt
- 1 large egg
- Few drops of red or green food color, if desired

1. Heat oven to 400°F.

2. In large bowl, beat butter and sugar with electric mixer on medium speed, or mix with spoon. Stir in remaining ingredients.

3. Place dough in cookie press. On ungreased cookie sheet, form desired shapes.

◀ **Hazelnut Biscotti**

4. Bake 6 to 9 minutes or until set but not brown. Immediately remove from cookie sheet to wire rack.

**Do not use margarine or vegetable oil spreads.*

***Do not use self-rising flour.*

1 COOKIE: CAL. 50 (CAL. FROM FAT 25); FAT 3g (SAT. FAT 2g); CHOL. 10mg; SODIUM 40mg; CARBS. 5g (FIBER 0g); PRO. 1g
% DAILY VALUE: VIT. A 2%; VIT. C 0%; CALC. 0%; IRON 0%
EXCHANGES: 1/2 OTHER CARB., 1/2 FAT **CARB. CHOICES:** 0

CHOCOLATE BUTTERY SPRITZ Stir 2 oz unsweetened baking chocolate, melted and cooled, into butter-sugar mixture.

Sugar Cookies LOW-FAT

PREP: 25 min **CHILL:** 2 hr **BAKE:** 7 to 8 min per sheet
■ **ABOUT 5 DOZEN 2-INCH COOKIES**

1 1/2 cups powdered sugar
1 cup butter or margarine, softened
1 teaspoon vanilla
1/2 teaspoon almond extract
1 large egg
2 1/2 cups all-purpose flour*
1 teaspoon baking soda
1 teaspoon cream of tartar
Granulated sugar

1. In large bowl, beat powdered sugar, butter, vanilla, almond extract and egg with electric mixer on medium speed, or mix with spoon. Stir in flour, baking soda and cream of tartar. Cover and refrigerate at least 2 hours.

2. Heat oven to 375°F. Lightly grease cookie sheet with shortening or spray with cooking spray.

3. Divide dough in half. Roll each half 1/4 inch thick on lightly floured surface. Cut into desired shapes with 2- to 2 1/2-inch cookie cutters. Sprinkle with granulated sugar. On cookie sheet, place cutouts about 2 inches apart.

4. Bake 7 to 8 minutes or until edges are light brown. Remove from cookie sheet to wire rack.

**If using self-rising flour, omit baking soda and cream of tartar.*

1 COOKIE: CAL. 65 (CAL. FROM FAT 25); FAT 3g (SAT. FAT 2g); CHOL. 10mg; SODIUM 45mg; CARBS. 8g (FIBER 0g); PRO. 1g
% DAILY VALUE: VIT. A 2%; VIT. C 0%; CALC. 0%; IRON 0%
EXCHANGES: 1/2 STARCH, 1/2 FAT **CARB. CHOICES:** 1/2

DECORATED SUGAR COOKIES Omit granulated sugar. Frost cooled cookies with Vanilla Buttercream Frosting (page 116) or tinted with food color if desired. Decorate with colored sugar, small candies, candied fruit or nuts if desired.

PAINTBRUSH SUGAR COOKIES Omit granulated sugar. Cut rolled dough into desired shapes with cookie cutters. (Cut no more than 12 cookies at a time to keep them from drying out.) Mix 1 egg yolk and 1/4 teaspoon water. Divide mixture among several custard cups. Tint each with different food color to make bright colors. (If paint thickens while standing, stir in a few drops water.) Paint designs on cookies with small paintbrushes. Bake as directed in Step 4.

Gingerbread Cookies

LOW-FAT

PREP: 25 min **CHILL:** 2 hr **BAKE:** 10 to 12 min per sheet **COOL:** 30 min ■ **ABOUT 2 1/2 DOZEN 2 1/2-INCH COOKIES**

'Tis the season—and it's time to bake cookies! These traditional ones, shaped and decorated as gingerbread men, have been delighting children (and decorating trees) for centuries. Of course, cut them out in any shape you wish.

1 cup packed brown sugar
1/3 cup shortening
1 1/2 cups dark molasses
2/3 cup cold water
7 cups all-purpose flour*
2 teaspoons baking soda
2 teaspoons ground ginger
1 teaspoon ground allspice
1 teaspoon ground cinnamon
1 teaspoon ground cloves
1/2 teaspoon salt

1. In large bowl, beat brown sugar, shortening, molasses and water with electric mixer on medium speed, or mix with spoon. Stir in remaining ingredients. Cover and refrigerate at least 2 hours.

2. Heat oven to 350°F. Grease cookie sheet lightly with shortening or spray with cooking spray.

3. Roll dough 1/4 inch thick on floured surface. Cut with floured gingerbread boy or girl cookie cutters or other shaped cutter. On cookie sheet, place cutouts about 2 inches apart.

4. Bake 10 to 12 minutes or until no indentation remains when touched. Immediately remove from cookie sheet to wire rack. Cool completely, about 30 minutes. Decorate with colored frosting, colored sugar and candies if desired.

**If using self-rising flour, omit baking soda and salt.*

1 COOKIE: CAL. 195 (CAL. FROM FAT 25); FAT 3g (SAT. FAT 1g); CHOL. 0mg; SODIUM 135mg; CARBS. 41g (FIBER 1g); PRO. 3g
% DAILY VALUE: VIT. A 0%; VIT. C 0%; CALC. 4%; IRON 12%
EXCHANGES: 1 STARCH, 1 1/2 OTHER CARB., 1/2 FAT
CARB. CHOICES: 3

Mocha Cookies

PREP: 25 min **CHILL:** 1 hr **BAKE:** 7 min per sheet **COOL:** 30 min ■ **ABOUT 2 1/2 DOZEN**

Cookies

1 large egg
2 tablespoons instant coffee crystals
1 cup granulated sugar
1/2 cup butter or margarine, softened
1 1/2 teaspoons vanilla
1 1/2 cups all-purpose flour*
1/2 cup baking cocoa
1/4 teaspoon baking powder
1/4 teaspoon baking soda
1/4 teaspoon salt

Caramel Drizzle

1 3/4 cups powdered sugar
1/4 cup caramel topping
1/2 teaspoon vanilla
About 2 tablespoons milk

1. In medium bowl, beat egg and coffee crystals with electric mixer on medium speed until crystals dissolve. Add granulated sugar, butter and 1 1/2 teaspoons vanilla. Beat on medium speed until light and fluffy. Stir in remaining cookie ingredients. Cover and refrigerate at least 1 hour until chilled.

2. Heat oven to 375°F. Roll dough 1/8 inch thick on lightly floured surface. Cut with 2 1/2-inch cookie cutters. On ungreased cookie sheet, place dough about 1 inch apart. Bake about 7 minutes or until set. Cool 1 minute; remove from cookie sheet to wire rack. Cool completely, about 30 minutes.

3. In small bowl, mix powdered sugar, caramel topping and vanilla until crumbly. Stir in just enough milk until smooth and thin enough to drizzle. Drizzle over cookies.

**If using self-rising flour, omit baking powder, baking soda and salt.*

1 COOKIE: CAL. 120 (CAL. FROM FAT 30); FAT 3.5g (SAT. FAT 1.5g); CHOL. 15mg; SODIUM 65mg; CARB. 21g (FIBER 0g); PRO. 1g
% DAILY VALUE: VIT. A 2%; VIT. C 0%; CALC. 0%; IRON 2%
EXCHANGES: 1 1/2 OTHER CARB., 1/2 FAT **CARB. CHOICES:** 1 1/2

Candy Basics

We all need a sweet indulgence from time to time. How about truffles, fudge, caramels or toffee? There's nothing like homemade candy! And the best part—thanks to these great tips, candy making just got easier than ever.

PICKING THE RIGHT PAN

The perfect-sized pan can make or ruin a batch of candy. Choose it carefully.

- Use the exact size of saucepan specified; if it's too large or too small, it will affect the cooking time.
- Use the exact size of pan specified so the candy is the right thickness, sets up properly and has the desired texture.
- Grease the pan with butter or margarine or line it with foil, so you'll be able to remove candy easily the minute it's done.

MIXING, COOKING AND COOLING

From picking the right recipe and ingredients to watching the weather, candy making is indeed a science—but one that's easy to master with a little practice.

- Use only full-fat butter or margarine so candies set up properly and have the desired texture. Do not use vegetable-oil spreads, reduced-calorie, reduced-fat or tub products.
- Many candy recipes include buttering the side of the saucepan; this prevents crystals from forming, which would result in grainy candy.
- Don't double the recipe—make two batches instead. Increasing the amount of ingredients changes the cooking time.
- Pay attention to the weather. A cool, dry day is best for making candy. Candy, especially Divinity, won't turn out when made on a humid day (60 percent or higher humidity).
- Follow the recipe carefully. Many candy recipes say not to stir the candy mixture while it cools down before the final step of being beaten or stirred. Stirring during cooling can cause the mixture to crystallize, and the candy will be grainy.

CANDY DONENESS

Using an accurate candy thermometer tells you when candy mixtures have reached the correct temperature. Here are a few tips:

- Check the accuracy of your thermometer by putting it in water and then boiling the water. The thermometer should read 212°F. If the reading is higher or lower, make the adjustment when making candy.
- If you live above 3,500 feet, check an altitude table to find out the boiling point in your area, then adjust the cooking time if necessary.
- To get an accurate reading, be sure the thermometer stands upright in the candy mixture. The bulb, or tip, of the thermometer shouldn't rest on the bottom of the pan. Read the thermometer at eye level. Watch the temperature closely—after 200°F, it goes up very quickly.
- If you don't have a thermometer, use the cold-water test. With a clean spoon, drop a small amount of candy mixture into a cupful of very cold water. Test the hardness as directed in the Candy Cooking Test chart on page 188. If the candy doesn't pass the test, keep cooking.

CANDY COOKING TESTS

Hardness	Temperature	Cold-Water Test
Thread	230°F to 233°F	Fine, thin, 2-inch thread falls off spoon when removed from hot mixture
Soft ball	234°F to 240°F	Forms a soft ball that flattens between fingers
Firm ball	242°F to 248°F	Forms a firm ball that holds its shape until pressed
Hard ball	250°F to 268°F	Forms a hard ball that holds its shape but is pliable
Soft crack	270°F to 290°F	Separates into hard but pliable threads
Hard crack	300°F to 310°F	Separates into hard, brittle threads that break easily

HOW TO TEST CANDY

Thread stage: Fine, thin, 2-inch thread falls off spoon when removed from hot mixture.

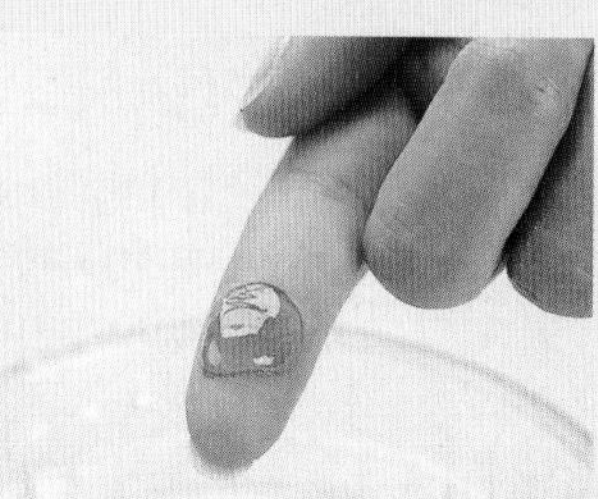

Soft ball stage: Forms a soft ball that flattens between fingers.

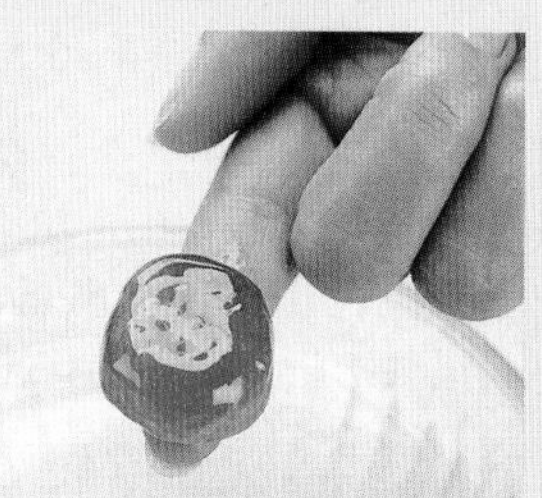

Firm ball stage: Forms a firm ball that holds its shape until pressed.

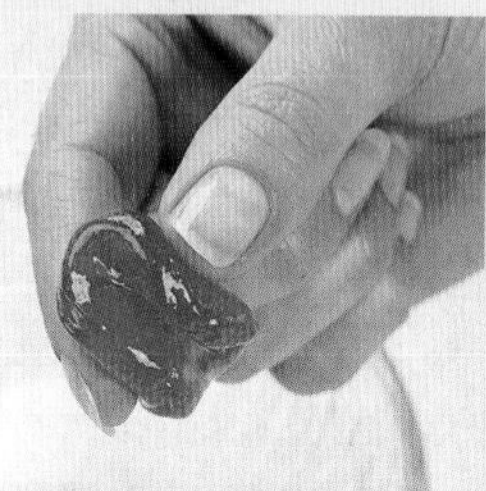

Hard ball stage: Forms a hard ball that holds its shape but is still pliable.

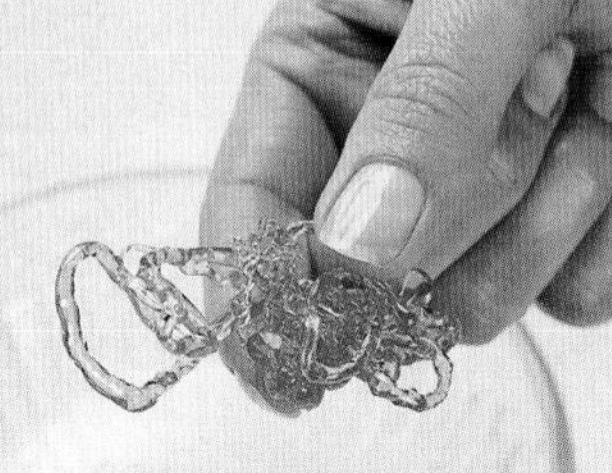

Soft crack stage: Separates into hard but pliable threads.

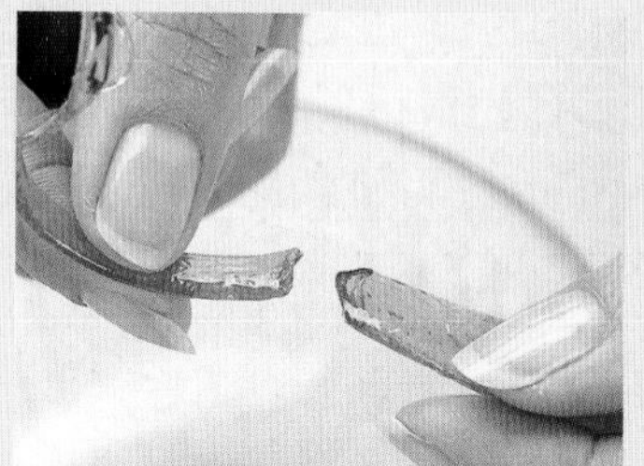

Hard crack stage: Separates into hard, brittle threads that break easily.

Chocolate Fudge LOW-FAT

PREP: 10 min **COOK:** 25 min **COOL:** 1 hr **STAND:** 1 hr ■ **64 CANDIES**

- 4 cups sugar
- 1 1/3 cups milk or half-and-half
- 1/4 cup corn syrup
- 1/4 teaspoon salt
- 4 oz unsweetened baking chocolate or 2/3 cup baking cocoa
- 1/4 cup butter or margarine
- 2 teaspoons vanilla
- 1 cup coarsely chopped nuts, if desired

1. Grease bottom and sides of 8-inch square pan with butter.

2. In 3-quart saucepan, cook sugar, milk, corn syrup, salt and chocolate over medium heat, stirring constantly, until chocolate is melted and sugar is dissolved. Cook, about 25 minutes, stirring occasionally, to 234°F on candy thermometer or until small amount of mixture dropped into cup of very cold water forms a soft ball that flattens when removed from water; remove from heat. Stir in butter.

3. Cool mixture without stirring to 120°F, about 1 hour. (Bottom of saucepan will be lukewarm.) Add vanilla. Beat vigorously and continuously with wooden spoon 5 to 10 minutes or until mixture is thick and no longer glossy. (Mixture will hold its shape when dropped from a spoon.)

4. Quickly stir in nuts. Spread in pan. Let stand about 1 hour or until firm. Cut into 1-inch squares.

1 CANDY: CAL. 75 (CAL. FROM FAT 20); FAT 2g (SAT. FAT 1g); CHOL. 5mg; SODIUM 20mg; CARBS. 14g (FIBER 0g); PRO. 0g
% DAILY VALUE: VIT. A 0%; VIT. C 0%; CALC. 0%; IRON 0%
EXCHANGES: 1 OTHER CARB., 1/2 FAT **CARB. CHOICES:** 1

PENUCHE Substitute 2 cups packed brown sugar for 2 cups of the granulated sugar; omit chocolate.

Super-Easy Fudge LOW-FAT

PREP: 10 min **CHILL:** 1 hr 30 min ■ **64 CANDIES**

For a deeper, richer chocolate flavor, be sure to add the unsweetened baking chocolate.

- 1 can (14 oz) sweetened condensed milk
- 1 bag (12 oz) semisweet chocolate chips (2 cups)
- 1 oz unsweetened baking chocolate, if desired
- 1 1/2 cups chopped nuts, if desired
- 1 teaspoon vanilla

1. Grease bottom and sides of 8-inch square pan with butter.

2. In 2-quart saucepan, heat milk, chocolate chips and unsweetened chocolate over low heat, stirring constantly, until chocolate is melted and mixture is smooth; remove from heat.

3. Quickly stir in nuts and vanilla. Spread in pan. Refrigerate about 1 hour 30 minutes or until firm. Cut into 1-inch squares.

1 CANDY: CAL. 55 (CAL. FROM FAT 20); FAT 2g (SAT. FAT 1g); CHOL. 0mg; SODIUM 10mg; CARBS. 8g (FIBER 0g); PRO. 1g
% DAILY VALUE: VIT. A 0%; VIT. C 0%; CALC. 2%; IRON 0%
EXCHANGES: 1/2 STARCH, 1/2 FAT **CARB. CHOICES:** 1/2

STORING CANDY

Store candy tightly covered at room temperature for up to 2 weeks, unless a recipe specifies otherwise. Or wrap candy tightly and freeze for up to 6 months. To thaw, let the candy stand covered in their containers at room temperature for 1 to 2 hours before serving.

Luscious Chocolate Truffles

Luscious Chocolate Truffles

PREP: 20 min **CHILL:** 25 min **FREEZE:** 30 min
STAND: 30 min ■ **ABOUT 24 CANDIES**

These truffles are as good as any you can buy! And best of all, you can say you've made them yourself. The shortening helps set the chocolate coating so it doesn't melt.

- 1 bag (12 oz) semisweet chocolate chips (2 cups)*
- 2 tablespoons butter or margarine
- 1/4 cup whipping (heavy) cream
- 2 tablespoons liqueur (almond, cherry, coffee, hazelnut, Irish cream, orange, raspberry, etc.), if desired
- 1 tablespoon shortening
- Finely chopped nuts, if desired
- 1/4 cup powdered sugar, if desired
- 1/2 teaspoon milk, if desired

1. Line cookie sheet with foil.

2. In heavy 2-quart saucepan, melt 1 cup of the chocolate chips over low heat, stirring constantly; remove from heat. Stir in butter. Stir in whipping cream and liqueur. Refrigerate 10 to 15 minutes, stirring frequently, just until thick enough to hold a shape.

3. On cookie sheet, drop mixture by teaspoonfuls. Shape into balls. (If mixture is too sticky, refrigerate until firm enough to shape.) Freeze 30 minutes.

4. In 1-quart saucepan, heat shortening and remaining 1 cup chocolate chips over low heat, stirring constantly, until chocolate is melted and mixture is smooth; remove from heat. Using fork, dip truffles, one at a time, into chocolate. Return to foil-covered cookie sheet. Immediately sprinkle some of the truffles with nuts. Refrigerate about 10 minutes or until coating is set.

5. In small bowl, stir powdered sugar and milk until smooth; drizzle over some of the truffles. Refrigerate just until set. Store in airtight container in refrigerator. Serve truffles at room temperature by removing from refrigerator about 30 minutes before serving.

**1 cup milk chocolate chips can be substituted for the 1 cup of semisweet chocolate chips melted in Step 2.*

1 TRUFFLE: CAL. 90 (CAL. FROM FAT 60); FAT 7g (SAT. FAT 4g); CHOL. 5mg; SODIUM 10mg; CARBS. 9g (FIBER 0g); PRO. 0g
% DAILY VALUE: VIT. A 0%; VIT. C 0%; CALC. 0%; IRON 2%
EXCHANGES: 1/2 OTHER CARB., 1 1/2 FAT **CARB. CHOICES:** 1/2

TOFFEE TRUFFLES Stir 3 tablespoons chopped chocolate-covered English toffee candy into whipping cream mixture.

WHITE CHOCOLATE–CHOCOLATE TRUFFLES Stir 3 tablespoons chopped white baking bar (white chocolate) into whipping cream mixture.

Caramels

PREP: 5 min **COOK:** 40 min **COOL:** 2 hr ■ **64 CANDIES**

Cut little rectangles of waxed paper ahead of time, so when you're ready to wrap, you're ready to go! Here's another secret—cutting the caramels with a kitchen scissors is quicker and easier than using a knife.

- 2 cups sugar
- 1/2 cup butter or margarine
- 2 cups whipping (heavy) cream
- 3/4 cup light corn syrup

1. Grease bottom and sides of 8-inch or 9-inch square glass baking dish with butter.

2. In heavy 3-quart saucepan, heat all ingredients to boiling over medium heat, stirring constantly. Boil uncovered about 35 minutes, stirring frequently, to 245°F on candy thermometer or until small amount of mixture dropped into cup of very cold water forms a firm ball that holds its shape until pressed. Immediately spread in baking dish. Cool completely, about 2 hours.

3. Cut into 1-inch squares. Wrap individually in waxed paper or plastic wrap; store wrapped candies in airtight container.

1 CANDY: CAL. 70 (CAL. FROM FAT 35); FAT 4g (SAT. FAT 2g); CHOL. 10mg; SODIUM 15mg; CARBS. 9g (FIBER 0g); PRO. 0g
% DAILY VALUE: VIT. A 2%; VIT. C 0%; CALC. 0%; IRON 0%
EXCHANGES: 1/2 OTHER CARB., 1 FAT **CARB. CHOICES:** 1/2

CHOCOLATE CARAMELS Heat 2 oz unsweetened baking chocolate with the sugar mixture.

Peanut Brittle

PREP: 15 min **COOK:** 40 min **COOL:** 1 hr ■
ABOUT 6 DOZEN CANDIES

- 1 1/2 teaspoons baking soda
- 1 teaspoon water
- 1 teaspoon vanilla
- 1 1/2 cups sugar
- 1 cup water
- 1 cup light corn syrup
- 3 tablespoons butter or margarine
- 1 lb unsalted raw Spanish peanuts (3 cups)

1. Heat oven to 200°F. Grease two 15 1/2 × 12-inch cookie sheets with butter;

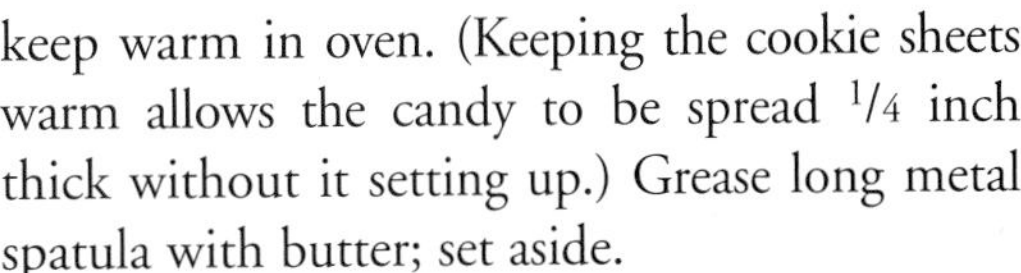

keep warm in oven. (Keeping the cookie sheets warm allows the candy to be spread 1/4 inch thick without it setting up.) Grease long metal spatula with butter; set aside.

2. In small bowl, mix baking soda, 1 teaspoon water and the vanilla; set aside. In 3-quart saucepan, mix sugar, 1 cup water and the corn syrup. Cook over medium heat about 25 minutes, stirring occasionally, to 240°F on candy thermometer or until small amount of mixture dropped into cup of very cold water forms a soft ball that flattens when removed from water.

3. Stir in butter and peanuts. Cook over medium heat about 13 minutes, stirring constantly, to 300°F or until small amount of mixture dropped into cup of very cold water separates into hard, brittle threads. (Watch carefully so mixture does not burn.) Immediately remove from heat. Quickly stir in baking soda mixture until light and foamy.

4. Pour half of the candy mixture onto each cookie sheet and quickly spread about 1/4 inch thick with buttered spatula. Cool completely, at least 1 hour. Break into pieces. Store in airtight container up to 2 weeks.

1 CANDY: CAL. 80 (CAL. FROM FAT 35); FAT 4g (SAT. FAT 1g); CHOL. 0mg; SODIUM 35mg; CARBS. 9g (FIBER 0g); PRO. 2g
% DAILY VALUE: VIT. A 0%; VIT. C 0%; CALC. 0%; IRON 0%
EXCHANGES: 1/2 STARCH, 1 FAT **CARB. CHOICES:** 1/2

TO MICROWAVE Prepare cookie sheets as directed. Omit all water. In 8-cup microwavable measure, mix sugar, corn syrup and peanuts. Microwave uncovered on High 10 to 12 minutes, stirring every 5 minutes, until peanuts are light brown. Stir in vanilla and butter thoroughly. Microwave uncovered on High 4 to 6 minutes to 300°F on microwave candy thermometer or until small amount of mixture dropped into cup of very cold water separates into hard, brittle threads. Quickly stir in baking soda until mixture is light and foamy. Continue as directed in Step 4.

▲ **From top to bottom: Divinity (page 192), Peanut Brittle (above) and Caramels (pages 190–191)**

Toffee

PREP: 15 min **COOK:** 18 min **STAND:** 1 hr ▪
ABOUT 36 PIECES

Packaging gifts for the holidays can be as fun as making them. Wrap coffee tins with holiday paper or foil. Fill with Toffee, separating layers with colored tissue paper or waxed paper.

1 cup sugar
1 cup butter or margarine
1/4 cup water
1/2 cup semisweet chocolate chips
1/2 cup finely chopped pecans

1. In heavy 2-quart saucepan, heat sugar, butter and water to boiling, stirring constantly; reduce heat to medium. Cook about 13 minutes, stirring constantly, to 300°F on candy thermometer or until small amount of mixture dropped into cup of very cold water separates into hard, brittle threads. (Watch carefully so mixture does not burn.)

2. Immediately pour toffee onto ungreased large cookie sheet. If necessary, quickly spread mixture to 1/4-inch thickness. Sprinkle with chocolate chips; let stand about 1 minute or until chips are completely softened. Spread softened chocolate evenly over toffee. Sprinkle with pecans.

3. Let stand at room temperature about 1 hour, or refrigerate if desired, until firm. Break into bite-size pieces. Store in airtight container.

1 CANDY: CAL. 90 (CAL. FROM FAT 65); FAT 7g (SAT. FAT 4g); CHOL. 15mg; SODIUM 35mg; CARBS. 7g (FIBER 0g); PRO. 0g
% DAILY VALUE: VIT. A 4%; VIT. C 0%; CALC. 0%; IRON 0%
EXCHANGES: 1/2 OTHER CARB., 1 1/2 FAT **CARB. CHOICES:** 1/2

Pralines

PREP: 15 min **COOK:** 20 min **COOL:** 1 hr **STAND:** 2 hr ▪
ABOUT 18 CANDIES

Pronounced prah-leen *or* pray-leen, *this confection originated in Louisiana, where pecans are in ample supply.*

2 cups packed light brown sugar
1 cup granulated sugar
1 1/4 cups milk
1/4 cup light corn syrup
1/8 teaspoon salt
1 teaspoon vanilla
1 1/2 cups pecan halves (5 1/2 oz)

1. In heavy 3-quart saucepan, heat sugars, milk, corn syrup and salt to boiling, stirring constantly. Reduce heat to medium. Cook uncovered about 15 minutes, without stirring, to 236°F on candy thermometer or until small amount of mixture dropped into cup of very cold water forms a soft ball that flattens when removed from water. Cool about 1 hour, without stirring, until saucepan is cool to the touch.

2. Add vanilla and pecan halves. Beat with spoon about 1 minute or until mixture is slightly thickened and just coats pecans but does not lose its gloss. On waxed paper, drop mixture by spoonfuls, dividing pecans equally. Let stand uncovered 1 to 2 hours or until candies are firm and no longer glossy.

3. Wrap candies individually in waxed paper or plastic wrap. Store in airtight container.

1 CANDY: CAL. 230 (CAL. FROM FAT 65); FAT 7g (SAT. FAT 1g); CHOL. 0mg; SODIUM 40mg; CARBS. 40g (FIBER 1g); PRO. 1g
% DAILY VALUE: VIT. A 0%; VIT. C 0%; CALC. 4%; IRON 4%
EXCHANGES: 3 OTHER CARB., 1 FAT **CARB. CHOICES:** 2 1/2

Divinity LOW-FAT

PREP: 20 min **COOK:** 35 min **STAND:** 12 hr ▪
ABOUT 40 CANDIES

Divinity is truly divine! Beating it to the right stage is the secret. Check out the tips at the end of this recipe.

2 2/3 cups sugar
2/3 cup light corn syrup
1/2 cup water
2 large egg whites
1 teaspoon vanilla
1 or 2 drops food color, if desired
2/3 cup coarsely chopped nuts, if desired

1. In 2-quart saucepan, cook sugar, corn syrup and water (use 1 tablespoon less water on humid days) over low heat, stirring constantly, until sugar is dissolved. Cook about 20 minutes, without stirring, to 260°F on candy thermometer or until small amount of mixture dropped into cup of very cold water forms a hard ball that holds its shape but is pliable.

2. In medium bowl, beat egg whites with electric mixer on high speed until stiff peaks form. (For best results, use electric stand mixer, not a portable handheld mixer because beating time is about 6 to 10 minutes and mixture is thick.) Gently transfer egg whites to large bowl. Continue beating constantly on medium speed while pouring hot syrup in a thin stream into egg whites. Add vanilla and food color. Beat, scraping bowl occasionally, until mixture holds its shape and becomes slightly dull. (If mixture becomes too stiff for mixer, continue beating with wooden spoon.)* Stir in nuts.

3. On waxed paper, quickly drop heaping teaspoonfuls of mixture from buttered spoon. Let stand uncovered at room temperature at least 4 hours but no longer than 12 hours until candies feel firm and are dry to the touch. Store in airtight container.

**Drop a spoonful of the Divinity mixture onto waxed paper. If it stays in a mound, it has been beaten long enough. If the mixture flattens out, beat another 30 seconds and then check again. If the mixture is too stiff to spoon, beat in a few drops of hot water at a time until it is a softer consistency. If you make this candy on a humid day, you'll have to beat it a little longer to make it mound up.*

1 CANDY: CAL. 70 (CAL. FROM FAT 0); FAT 0g (SAT. FAT 0g); CHOL. 0mg; SODIUM 10mg; CARBS. 15g (FIBER 0g); PRO. 0g
% DAILY VALUE: VIT. A 0%; VIT. C 0%; CALC. 0%; IRON 0%
EXCHANGES: 1 OTHER CARB. **CARB. CHOICES:** 1

Crunchy Peanut Clusters

PREP: 15 min **STAND:** 1 hr ■ **ABOUT 6 1/2 DOZEN CANDIES**

Almond bark, the common name for vanilla-flavored candy coating, confectionery coating or summer coating, is mainly used for candy making. The most common types of candy coating you'll find in grocery stores are vanilla and chocolate; specialty stores, such as cake decorating shops, may carry coating in pastel colors.

- 1 package (24 oz) vanilla-flavored candy coating (almond bark)
- 2/3 cup creamy peanut butter
- 4 cups Cheerios® cereal
- 2 cups miniature marshmallows
- 2 cups dry-roasted peanuts

1. In 4-quart saucepan, melt candy coating over medium heat, stirring frequently. Stir in peanut butter until mixture is smooth. Add remaining ingredients; stirring until completely coated.

2. On waxed paper or cookie sheet, drop mixture by heaping teaspoonfuls. Let stand about 1 hour or until firm. Store tightly covered.

1 CANDY: CAL. 100 (CAL. FROM FAT 55); FAT 6g (SAT. FAT 2g); CHOL. 0mg; SODIUM 50mg; CARBS. 10g (FIBER 1g); PRO. 2g
% DAILY VALUE: VIT. A 0%; VIT. C 0%; CALC. 2%; IRON 2%
EXCHANGES: 1/2 STARCH, 1 FAT **CARB. CHOICES:** 1/2

Rum Balls LOW-FAT

PREP: 20 min **CHILL:** 5 days ▪ **ABOUT 5 DOZEN CANDIES**

1 package (9 oz) thin chocolate wafer cookies, finely crushed (2 1/3 cups)
2 cups finely chopped almonds, pecans or walnuts
2 cups powdered sugar
1/4 cup light rum
1/4 cup light corn syrup
Additional powdered sugar

1. In large bowl, mix crushed cookies, almonds and 2 cups powdered sugar. Stir in rum and corn syrup.

2. Shape mixture into 1-inch balls. Roll in additional powdered sugar. Cover tightly and refrigerate at least 5 days before serving to blend flavors.

1 CANDY: CAL. 65 (CAL. FROM FAT 25); FAT 3g (SAT. FAT 0g); CHOL. 0mg; SODIUM 25mg; CARBS. 10g (FIBER 1g); PRO. 1g
% DAILY VALUE: VIT. A 0%; VIT. C 0%; CALC. 0%; IRON 2%
EXCHANGES: 1/2 STARCH, 1/2 FAT **CARB. CHOICES:** 1/2

BOURBON BALLS Substitute 1/4 cup bourbon for the rum.

BRANDY BALLS Substitute 1/4 cup brandy for the rum.

Peppermint Bark

PREP: 15 min **STAND:** 1 hr ▪ **ABOUT 16 CANDIES**

Candy coating varies depending on the brand—the white color varies, and when melted, some are thinner than others. Make a note of the brand you prefer to work with and watch carefully while melting.

1 package (16 oz) vanilla-flavored candy coating (almond bark), broken into pieces
24 hard peppermint candies

1. Cover cookie sheet with waxed paper, foil or cooking parchment paper. In 8-cup microwavable measure or 2-quart microwavable casserole, place candy coating. Microwave uncovered on High 2 to 3 minutes, stirring every 30 seconds, until almost melted. Stir until smooth.

2. Place peppermint candies in heavy plastic bag; crush with rolling pin or bottom of small heavy saucepan. Pour crushed candies into wire strainer. Shake strainer over melted coating until all of the tiniest candy pieces fall into the coating; reserve the larger candy pieces. Stir coating to mix evenly.

3. On cookie sheet, spread coating evenly. Sprinkle evenly with remaining candy pieces. Let stand about 1 hour or until cool and hardened. Break into pieces.

1 CANDY: CAL. 190 (CAL. FROM FAT 80); FAT 9g (SAT. FAT 6g); CHOL. 0mg; SODIUM 30mg; CARB. 24g (FIBER 0g); PRO. 2g
% DAILY VALUE: VIT. A 0%; VIT. C 0%; CALC. 6%; IRON 0%
EXCHANGES: 1 1/2 OTHER CARB., 2 FAT **CARB. CHOICES:** 1 1/2

CRANBERRY-ALMOND BARK Omit peppermint candies. Stir 1/2 cup each dried cranberries and chopped almonds into melted coating.

MOCHA HAZELNUT LATTE BARK Omit peppermint candies. Stir 1/2 cup each chocolate-covered coffee beans and chopped hazelnuts into melted coating.

RED AND GREEN CANDY BARK Substitute red and green ring-shaped hard candies for the peppermint candies.

SANTA'S BARK Omit peppermint candies. Stir 1/2 cup each red and green plain or mint candy-coated chocolate candies into melted coating.

TROPICAL BARK Omit peppermint candies. Stir 1/2 cup each chopped candied pineapple and macadamia nuts into melted coating.

CHAPTER 7
Desserts

LOW-FAT = *3g or less, except main dishes with 10g or less* FAST = *Ready in 20 minutes or less* BREAD MACHINE = *Bread machine directions* SLOW COOKER = *Slow cooker directions* LIGHTER = *25% fewer calories or grams of fat*

◀ **Apple Crisp (page 196)**

Dessert Basics

Everybody loves dessert! And here's a whole collection of tempting ones—from old-fashioned favorites like strawberry shortcake to comforting desserts like peach cobbler, gingerbread and bread pudding. You'll even find recipes for restaurant specialties like cheesecake, chocolate mousse and crème brûlée. Make one for supper tonight!

DESSERT DRESS-UPS

Easier to make than you think, these "dress-ups" add pizzazz to any dessert.

Garnishes

- Chocolate curls or shavings, see page 210
- Crushed Peanut Brittle, page 191, or Toffee, page 192
- Sliced or whole fresh berries
- Honey-roasted or sweetened nuts
- Ice cream
- Candy or chocolate decorations (available in the supermarket near cake mixes and frostings)
- Purchased cookies like pirouettes (plain or chocolate dipped) and shortbread
- Sliced or diced fruit like kiwifruit, peach, starfruit or mango
- Brush rim of dessert bowls with water or light corn syrup, then dip rim in colored decorating sugar or white coarse sugar crystals
- Ground cinnamon, baking cocoa or powdered sugar (put a small amount of one of these choices in a small sifter, and tap to sprinkle over desserts or plates)
- Toasted coconut or nuts
- Whipped cream (sweetened or flavored), page 217

Sauce Art

Plate painting is a fun way to create a designer look. Pick a dessert sauce from this chapter like Butterscotch, Caramel, Glossy Chocolate, Lemon, Orange or Raspberry Sauce (pages 215–216), or use a purchased sauce and start painting.

Start by pouring sauce into a plastic squeeze bottle (like a honey bottle) or small resealable plastic food-storage bag (snip off a tiny corner), then gently squeeze sauce onto dessert plates to create one of the following designs:

Note: If sauce is too thick, heat in the microwave just until thin enough to drizzle.

Hearts: Drop pools of two contrasting sauces, alternating colors, to form a ring on dessert plate. Drop dime-size dots of a contrasting sauce on every other pool. Draw the tip of a knife or toothpick through the centers of the dime-size dots in a circle to make heart shapes.

Herringbone: Spoon sauce evenly onto dessert plate. Draw three stripes of a contrasting sauce across the first sauce at 1-inch intervals. Draw the tip of a knife or toothpick through the stripes in alternating directions.

Spiderweb: Draw a small ring of sauce in the center of dessert plate. Make a larger ring around the smaller ring, about 1 inch apart, then add a third and larger ring. Starting at the center and moving to the outside ring, draw the tip of a knife or toothpick through the sauce rings toward the outside edge of the plate; repeat, making a web design.

Spirals: Draw a spiral with the sauce starting in the center of dessert plate to within 1/2 inch of the rim. Draw mini spirals evenly spaced on the plate rim.

Apple Crisp

PREP: 20 min **BAKE:** 30 min ■ **6 SERVINGS**

Leftover apple crisp makes a great breakfast treat. Serve it with a dollop of plain yogurt.

- 4 medium tart cooking apples (Greening, Rome, Granny Smith), sliced (4 cups)
- 3/4 cup packed brown sugar
- 1/2 cup all-purpose flour*
- 1/2 cup quick-cooking or old-fashioned oats
- 1/3 cup butter or margarine, softened
- 3/4 teaspoon ground cinnamon
- 3/4 teaspoon ground nutmeg
- Cream or ice cream, if desired

1. Heat oven to 375°F. Grease bottom and sides of 8-inch square pan with shortening.

2. Spread apples in pan. In medium bowl, stir remaining ingredients except cream until well mixed; sprinkle over apples.

3. Bake about 30 minutes or until topping is golden brown and apples are tender when pierced with a fork. Serve warm with cream.

**Self-rising flour can be used.*

1 SERVING: CAL. 310 (CAL. FROM FAT 100); FAT 11g (SAT. FAT 7g); CHOL. 25mg; SODIUM 80mg; CARBS. 52g (FIBER 3g); PRO. 2g
% DAILY VALUE: VIT. A 8%; VIT. C 2%; CALC. 4%; IRON 8%
EXCHANGES: 1 STARCH, 1 FRUIT, 1 1/2 OTHER CARB., 2 FAT
CARB. CHOICES: 3 1/2

BLUEBERRY CRISP Substitute 4 cups fresh or frozen (thawed and drained) blueberries for the apples.

CHERRY CRISP Substitute 1 can (21 oz) cherry pie filling for the apples.

RHUBARB CRISP Substitute 4 cups cut-up rhubarb for the apples. Sprinkle 1/3 cup granulated sugar over rhubarb; stir to combine. Continue as directed in step 2. If rhubarb is frozen, thaw and drain.

Apple Dumplings

PREP: 55 min **BAKE:** 40 min ■ **6 DUMPLINGS**

Cooking apples are a "must" for yummy dumplings because they hold their shape during baking. Different varieties vary by region and by season. If you can't find those suggested here, check the Picking Apples chart on page 218.

- Pastry for Two-Crust Pie (page 124)
- 6 cooking apples (Golden Delicious, Braeburn, Rome), about 3 inches in diameter
- 3 tablespoons raisins, if desired
- 3 tablespoons chopped nuts, if desired
- 1/2 cup sugar
- 1 cup water
- 1/2 cup corn syrup
- 2 tablespoons butter or margarine
- 1/4 teaspoon ground cinnamon
- Cream or Sweetened Whipped Cream (page 217), if desired

1. Heat oven to 425°F.

2. Make pastry as directed—except roll two-thirds of the pastry into 14-inch square; cut into four 7-inch squares. Roll remaining pastry into 14 × 7-inch rectangle; cut into two 7-inch squares. Peel and core apples. Place apple on each square.

3. In small bowl, mix raisins and nuts. Fill apples with raisin mixture. Moisten corners of pastry squares. Bring 2 opposite corners up over apple and pinch together. Repeat with remaining corners, and pinch edges of pastry to seal. Place dumplings in ungreased 13 × 9-inch glass baking dish.

4. In 2-quart saucepan, heat sugar, water, corn syrup, butter and cinnamon to boiling, stirring occasionally. Boil 3 minutes. Carefully pour around dumplings.

5. Bake about 40 minutes, spooning syrup over dumplings 2 or 3 times, until crust is golden and apples are tender when pierced with a small knife or toothpick. Serve warm or cool with cream.

1 SERVING: CAL. 660 (CAL. FROM FAT 290); FAT 32g (SAT. FAT 9g); CHOL. 10mg; SODIUM 450mg; CARBS. 88g (FIBER 4g); PRO. 5g
% DAILY VALUE: VIT. A 4%; VIT. C 4%; CALC. 0%; IRON 10%
EXCHANGES: 2 STARCH, 2 FRUIT, 2 OTHER CARB., 6 FAT
CARB. CHOICES: 6

LIGHTER APPLE DUMPLINGS

For 5 grams of fat and 320 calories per serving, omit Pastry for Two-Crust Pie. Cut stack of 6 sheets frozen (thawed) phyllo (18 × 4 inches) into 14-inch square. Discard remaining strips of phyllo. Cover squares with damp towel to prevent them from drying out. Make 3 stacks of 2 sheets each, spraying each lightly with butter-flavored cooking spray. Fold each stack in half; spray top. Cut stacks in half. Place apple on each square. Omit nuts. Continue as directed in Step 3.

HOW TO SEAL APPLE DUMPLING PASTRY

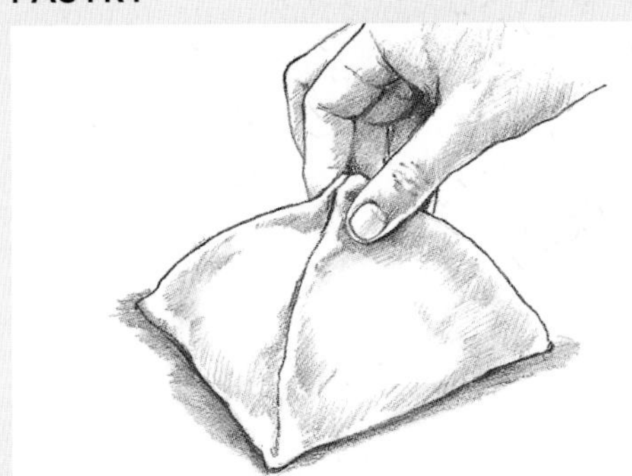

Moisten corners of pastry squares. Bring 2 opposite corners up over apple and pinch together. Repeat with remaining corners, and pinch edges of pastry to seal.

Baked Apples

PREP: 10 min **BAKE:** 40 min ■ **4 SERVINGS**

- 4 large unpeeled tart cooking apples (Rome, Granny Smith, Greening)
- 2 to 4 tablespoons granulated or packed brown sugar
- 4 teaspoons butter or margarine
- 1/2 teaspoon ground cinnamon

1. Heat oven to 375°F.

2. Core apples to within 1/2 inch of bottom. Peel 1-inch strip of skin from around middle of each apple, or peel upper half of each apple to prevent splitting. Place apples in ungreased glass baking dish.

3. Place 1 teaspoon to 1 tablespoon sugar, 1 teaspoon butter and 1/8 teaspoon cinnamon in center of each apple. Sprinkle with additional cinnamon. Pour water into baking dish until 1/4 inch deep.

4. Bake 30 to 40 minutes or until apples are tender when pierced with a fork. (Time will vary depending on size and variety of apple.) Spoon syrup in dish over apples several times during baking if desired.

1 SERVING: CAL. 175 (CAL. FROM FAT 45); FAT 5g (SAT. FAT 3g); CHOL. 10mg; SODIUM 25mg; CARBS. 39g (FIBER 6g); PRO. 0g
% DAILY VALUE: VIT. A 6%; VIT. C 10%; CALC. 2%; IRON 2%
EXCHANGES: 2 FRUIT, 1/2 OTHER CARB., 1/2 FAT
CARB. CHOICES: 2 1/2

MICROWAVING BAKED APPLES

You can make baked apples in minutes in your microwave oven. Just prepare the apples as directed, and place each one in a 10-ounce custard cup or individual microwavable casserole. Do not add water to the cups. Microwave uncovered on High 5 to 10 minutes, rotating cups 1/2 turn after 3 minutes, until apples are tender when pierced with a fork.

Fresh Peach Cobbler

PREP: 25 min **COOK:** 6 min **BAKE:** 30 min ▪
6 SERVINGS

Cobblers are a homey way to use fruit in season. Short on time? Try the blueberry variation—there's no peeling or pitting!

- 1/2 cup sugar
- 1 tablespoon cornstarch
- 1/4 teaspoon ground cinnamon
- 4 cups sliced fresh peaches (6 medium)*
- 1 teaspoon lemon juice
- 1 cup all-purpose flour**
- 1 tablespoon sugar
- 1 1/2 teaspoons baking powder
- 1/2 teaspoon salt
- 3 tablespoons firm butter or margarine
- 1/2 cup milk
- 2 tablespoons sugar, if desired
- Sweetened Whipped Cream (page 217), if desired

1. Heat oven to 400°F.

2. In 2-quart saucepan, mix 1/2 cup sugar, the cornstarch and cinnamon. Stir in peaches and lemon juice. Cook over medium-high heat 4 to 5 minutes, stirring constantly, until mixture thickens and boils. Boil and stir 1 minute. Pour into ungreased 2-quart casserole; keep peach mixture hot in oven.

3. In medium bowl, mix flour, 1 tablespoon sugar, the baking powder and salt. Cut in butter, using pastry blender (or pulling 2 table knives through ingredients in opposite directions), until mixture looks like fine crumbs. Stir in milk. Drop dough by 6 spoonfuls onto hot peach mixture. Sprinkle 2 tablespoons sugar over dough.

4. Bake 25 to 30 minutes or until topping is golden brown. Serve warm with Sweetened Whipped Cream.

**4 cups frozen sliced peaches (from two 1-lb bags), thawed and drained, can be substituted for the fresh peaches.*

***If using self-rising flour, omit baking powder and salt.*

1 SERVING: CAL. 260 (CAL. FROM FAT 55); FAT 6g (SAT. FAT 4g); CHOL. 15mg; SODIUM 370mg; CARBS. 48g; (FIBER 3g); PROTEIN 4g
% DAILY VALUE: VIT. A 8%; VIT. C 4%; CALC. 10%; IRON 6%
EXCHANGES: 1 1/2 STARCH, 1 1/2 FRUIT, 1 FAT **CARB. CHOICES:** 3

FRESH BLUEBERRY COBBLER Substitute 4 cups blueberries for the peaches. Omit cinnamon.

FRESH CHERRY COBBLER Substitute 4 cups pitted red tart cherries for the peaches. Increase sugar in cherry mixture to 1 1/4 cups and cornstarch to 3 tablespoons. Substitute 1/4 teaspoon almond extract for the lemon juice.

Fresh Peach Cobbler ▶

Pineapple Upside-Down Cake

PREP: 15 min **BAKE:** 50 min **COOL:** 15 min ■ **9 SERVINGS**

1/4 cup butter or margarine
2/3 cup packed brown sugar
1 can (20 oz) sliced or crushed pineapple in juice, drained
Maraschino cherries without stems, if desired
1 1/3 cups all-purpose flour*
1 cup granulated sugar
1/3 cup shortening
3/4 cup milk
1 1/2 teaspoons baking powder
1/2 teaspoon salt
1 large egg
Sweetened Whipped Cream (page 217), if desired

1. Heat oven to 350°F.

2. In 10-inch ovenproof skillet or 9-inch square pan, melt butter in oven. Sprinkle brown sugar over butter. Arrange pineapple on brown sugar, cutting one or more slices into pieces if necessary. Place cherry in center of each pineapple slice.

3. In large bowl, beat remaining ingredients except whipped cream with electric mixer on low speed 30 seconds, scraping bowl constantly. Beat on high speed 3 minutes, scraping bowl occasionally. Pour over pineapple.

4. Bake skillet 45 to 50 minutes, square pan 50 to 55 minutes, or until toothpick inserted in center comes out clean.

5. Immediately place heatproof plate upside down onto skillet or pan; turn plate and skillet or pan over. Let skillet or pan remain over cake a few minutes so brown sugar topping can drizzle over cake. Cool 15 minutes. Serve warm with Sweetened Whipped Cream.

**If using self-rising flour, omit baking powder and salt.*

1 SERVING: CAL. 390 (CAL. FROM FAT 125); FAT 14g (SAT. FAT 6g); CHOL. 40mg; SODIUM 270mg; CARBS. 63g (FIBER 1g); PRO. 4g
% DAILY VALUE: VIT. A 6%; VIT. C 4%; CALC. 10%; IRON 8%
EXCHANGES: 1 STARCH, 1 FRUIT, 2 OTHER CARB., 3 FAT
CARB. CHOICES: 4

Strawberry Shortcakes

PREP: 15 min **STAND:** 1 hr **BAKE:** 35 min **COOL:** 10 min ■ **6 SERVINGS**

2 pints strawberries (4 cups), sliced
1/2 cup sugar
2 cups all-purpose flour*
1/2 cup sugar
3 teaspoons baking powder
1/2 teaspoon salt
1/2 cup firm butter or margarine
2/3 cup milk
1 large egg, slightly beaten
Sweetened Whipped Cream (page 217), if desired

1. In large bowl, stir strawberries and 1/2 cup sugar until well mixed. Let stand about 1 hour so strawberries will become juicy.

2. Heat oven to 375°F. Grease bottom and side of 8-inch or 9-inch round pan; lightly flour.

3. In medium bowl, mix flour, 1/2 cup sugar, the baking powder and salt. Cut in butter, using pastry blender (or pulling 2 table knives through ingredients in opposite directions), until mixture looks like coarse crumbs. Stir in milk and egg just until blended. Spoon into pan; spread evenly.

4. Bake 30 to 35 minutes or until toothpick inserted in center comes out clean. Cool 10 minutes.

5. Place serving plate upside down on pan; turn plate and pan over and remove pan. Cut shortcake into wedges. If desired, split shortcakes horizontally in half while hot. Fill and top each wedge with strawberries and Sweetened Whipped Cream.

**If using self-rising flour, omit baking powder and salt.*

1 SERVING: CAL. 375 (CAL. FROM FAT 115); FAT 13g (SAT. FAT 3g); CHOL. 5mg; SODIUM 650mg; CARBS. 62g (FIBER 3g); PRO. 6g
% DAILY VALUE: VIT. A 2%; VIT. C 96%; CALC. 18%; IRON 14%
EXCHANGES: NOT RECOMMENDED **CARB. CHOICES:** 5

DROP SHORTCAKES Heat oven to 425°F. Make dough as directed; drop dough by 8 spoonfuls about 2 inches apart onto ungreased cookie sheet. Bake 12 to 14 minutes or until golden brown.

Gingerbread

PREP: 10 min **BAKE:** 55 min ▪ **9 SERVINGS**

- 2 1/3 cups all-purpose flour*
- 1/2 cup shortening
- 1/3 cup sugar
- 1 cup molasses
- 3/4 cup hot water
- 1 teaspoon baking soda
- 1 teaspoon ground ginger
- 1 teaspoon ground cinnamon
- 3/4 teaspoon salt
- 1 large egg
- Lemon Sauce (page 216), if desired
- Sweetened Whipped Cream (page 217), if desired

1. Heat oven to 325°F. Grease bottom and sides of 9-inch square pan with shortening; lightly flour.

2. In large bowl, beat all ingredients except Lemon Sauce and Sweetened Whipped Cream with electric mixer on low speed 30 seconds, scraping bowl constantly. Beat on medium speed 3 minutes, scraping bowl occasionally. Pour into pan.

3. Bake 50 to 55 minutes or until toothpick inserted in center comes out clean. Serve warm with Lemon Sauce and Sweetened Whipped Cream.

**Do not use self-rising flour.*

1 SERVING: CAL. 350 (CAL. FROM FAT 110); FAT 12g (SAT. FAT 3g); CHOL. 25mg; SODIUM 360mg; CARBS. 58g (FIBER 1g); PRO. 4g
% DAILY VALUE: VIT. A 0%; VIT. C 0%; CALC. 8%; IRON 18%
EXCHANGES: 1 STARCH, 3 OTHER CARB., 2 FAT **CARB. CHOICES:** 4

Hot Fudge Sundae Cake

PREP: 20 min **BAKE:** 40 min **COOL:** 10 min ▪ **9 SERVINGS**

This homey dessert, also known as pudding cake, *separates into two layers as it bakes; one turns into a yummy fudge sauce and the other a moist cake. Serve it warm topped with ice cream.*

- 1 cup all-purpose flour*
- 3/4 cup granulated sugar
- 2 tablespoons baking cocoa
- 2 teaspoons baking powder
- 1/4 teaspoon salt
- 1/2 cup milk
- 2 tablespoons vegetable oil
- 1 teaspoon vanilla
- 1 cup chopped nuts, if desired
- 1 cup packed brown sugar
- 1/4 cup baking cocoa
- 1 3/4 cups very hot water
- Ice cream, if desired

1. Heat oven to 350°F.

2. In ungreased 9-inch square pan, mix flour, granulated sugar, 2 tablespoons cocoa, the baking powder and salt. Mix in milk, oil and vanilla with fork until smooth. Stir in nuts. Spread in pan.

3. Sprinkle brown sugar and 1/4 cup cocoa over batter. Pour water evenly over batter.

4. Bake about 40 minutes or until top is dry. Cool 10 minutes.

5. Spoon warm cake into dessert dishes. Top with ice cream. Spoon sauce from pan onto each serving.

**If using self-rising flour, omit baking powder and salt.*

1 SERVING: CAL. 195 (CAL. FROM FAT 70); FAT 8g (SAT. FAT 4g); CHOL. 120mg; SODIUM 135mg; CARBS. 26g (FIBER 2g); PRO. 7g
% DAILY VALUE: VIT. A 8%; VIT. C 0%; CALC. 6%; IRON 6%
EXCHANGES: 2 STARCH, 1 FAT **CARB. CHOICES:** 2

Chocolate Mousse Brownie Dessert

PREP: 20 min **BAKE:** 45 min **COOL:** 2 hr ■
12 TO 16 SERVINGS

This heavenly dessert can also be baked in a 10-inch springform pan. Bake about 65 minutes. For easier cutting, use a wet knife and cut with a straight up-and-down motion.

- 3/4 cup whipping (heavy) cream
- 1 bag (6 oz) semisweet chocolate chips (1 cup)
- 1 package (1 lb 3.8 oz) fudge brownie mix
- Water, oil and eggs called for on brownie mix package
- 3 large eggs
- 1/3 cup sugar
- Sweetened Whipped Cream, if desired

1. Heat oven to 350°F. Grease bottom only of 13 × 9-inch pan with shortening.

2. In 2-quart saucepan, heat whipping cream and chocolate chips over low heat, stirring frequently, until chocolate is melted and mixture is smooth. Cool about 20 minutes.

3. Meanwhile, make brownie mix as directed on package, using water, oil and eggs. Spread batter in pan.

4. In small bowl, beat 3 eggs and sugar, using wire whisk or hand beater, until foamy. Stir into whipping cream mixture. Pour evenly over brownie batter.

5. Bake about 45 minutes or until topping is set. Cool completely, about 2 hours.

6. Serve at room temperature, or cover tightly and refrigerate until chilled. Top each serving with Sweetened Whipped Cream. Store covered in refrigerator.

1 SERVING: CAL. 450 (CAL. FROM FAT 200); FAT 23g (SAT. FAT 8g); CHOL. 105mg; SODIUM 200mg; CARB. 55g (FIBER 3g); PRO. 5g
% DAILY VALUE: VIT. A 6%; VIT. C 0%; CALC. 6%; IRON 15%
EXCHANGES: 1 1/2 STARCH, 2 OTHER CARB., 4 1/2 FAT
CARB. CHOICES: 3 1/2

Turtle Cheesecake

PREP: 30 min **BAKE:** 50 min **COOL:** 1 hr **CHILL:** 2 hr ■
12 SERVINGS

- 1 1/2 cups finely crushed vanilla wafer cookies (about 40 cookies)
- 1/4 cup butter or margarine, melted
- 2 packages (8 oz each) cream cheese, softened
- 1/2 cup sugar
- 2 teaspoons vanilla
- 2 large eggs
- 1/4 cup hot fudge topping
- 1 cup caramel topping
- 1/2 cup coarsely chopped pecans

1. Heat oven to 350°F. In medium bowl, mix cookie crumbs and butter. Press firmly against bottom and side of 9-inch glass pie plate.

2. In large bowl, beat cream cheese, sugar, vanilla and eggs with electric mixer on low speed until smooth. Pour half of the mixture into pie plate.

3. Add hot fudge topping to remaining cream cheese mixture in bowl; beat on low speed until smooth. Spoon over vanilla mixture in pie plate. Swirl mixtures slightly with tip of knife.

4. Bake 40 to 50 minutes or until center is set. (Do not insert knife into cheesecake because the hole may cause cheesecake to crack as it cools.) Cool at room temperature 1 hour. Refrigerate at least 2 hours until chilled. Serve with caramel topping and pecans. Store covered in refrigerator.

1 SERVING: CAL. 390 (CAL. FROM FAT 210); FAT 24g (SAT. FAT 12g); CHOL. 85mg; SODIUM 310mg; CARB. 39g (FIBER 1g); PRO. 6g
% DAILY VALUE: VIT. A 15%; VIT. C 0%; CALC. 6%; IRON 6%
EXCHANGES: 1 1/2 STARCH, 1 OTHER CARB., 4 1/2 FAT
CARB. CHOICES: 2 1/2

New York Cheesecake

PREP: 45 min **BAKE:** 1 hr 15 min **COOL:** 1 hr
CHILL: 12 hr ▪ **16 TO 20 SERVINGS**

This rich and smooth cheesecake, made with cream cheese, is usually associated with the style of cheesecake popularized by Jewish delicatessens in New York City in the early- to mid-1900s. One quintessential recipe originated at Lindy's, a restaurant on Broadway in Manhattan's Times Square, which made their cheesecake not only popular with the theatre crowd, but also famous worldwide.

Crust

1 cup all-purpose flour*
1/2 cup butter or margarine, softened
1/4 cup sugar
1 large egg yolk

Cheesecake

5 packages (8 oz each) cream cheese, softened
1 3/4 cups sugar
3 tablespoons all-purpose flour*
1 tablespoon grated orange peel, if desired
1 tablespoon grated lemon peel, if desired
1/4 teaspoon salt
5 large eggs
2 large egg yolks
1 cup whipping (heavy) cream
1/3 cup slivered almonds, toasted (page 215), or fresh fruit, if desired

1. Heat oven to 400°F. Lightly grease 9-inch springform pan with shortening; remove bottom. In medium bowl, mix all crust ingredients with fork until dough forms; gather into a ball. Press one-third of the dough evenly on bottom of pan. Place on cookie sheet. Bake 8 to 10 minutes or until light golden brown; cool. Assemble bottom and side of pan; secure side. Press remaining dough 2 inches up side of pan.

2. Heat oven to 475°F.

3. In large bowl, beat cream cheese, 1 3/4 cups sugar, 3 tablespoons flour, the orange peel, lemon peel and salt with electric mixer on medium speed about 1 minute or until smooth. Beat in eggs, egg yolks and 1/4 cup of the whipping cream on low speed until well blended. Pour into crust.

4. Bake 15 minutes.

5. Reduce oven temperature to 200°F. Bake 1 hour longer. Cheesecake may not appear to be done, but if a small area in the center seems soft, it will become firm as cheesecake cools. (Do not insert a knife to test for doneness because the hole could cause cheesecake to crack.) Turn off oven; leave cheesecake in oven 30 minutes longer. Remove from oven and cool in pan on wire rack away from drafts 30 minutes.

6. Without releasing or removing side of pan, run metal spatula carefully along side of cheesecake to loosen. Refrigerate uncovered about 3 hours or until chilled; cover and continue refrigerating at least 9 hours but no longer than 48 hours.

New York Cheesecake ▶

7. Run metal spatula along side of cheesecake to loosen again. Remove side of pan; leave cheesecake on pan bottom to serve. In chilled small bowl, beat remaining 3/4 cup whipping cream with electric mixer on high speed until stiff. Spread whipped cream over top of cheesecake. Decorate with almonds. Store covered in refrigerator.

**Do not use self-rising flour in this recipe.*

1 SERVING: CAL. 515 (CAL. FROM FAT 340); FAT 38g (SAT. FAT 23g); CHOL. 215mg; SODIUM 310mg; CARBS. 35g (FIBER 0g); PRO. 9g
% DAILY VALUE: VIT. A 30%; VIT. C 0%; CALC. 8%; IRON 8%
EXCHANGES: 2 STARCH, 1/2 HIGH-FAT MEAT, 7 FAT
CARB. CHOICES: 2

LIGHTER NEW YORK CHEESECAKE

For 19 grams of fat and 330 calories per serving, omit Crust. Move oven rack to lowest position. Heat oven to 425°F. Lightly grease side only of 9-inch springform pan with shortening. Mix 3/4 cup graham cracker crumbs, 2 tablespoons margarine, melted, and 2 tablespoons sugar; press evenly in bottom of pan. Use reduced-fat cream cheese (Neufchâtel); increase flour to 1/4 cup. Substitute 1 1/4 cups fat-free cholesterol-free egg product for the 5 eggs. Omit 1/4 cup whipping cream. Continue as directed in Steps 4 through 6. Omit 3/4 cup whipping cream and almonds. Serve with fresh fruit if desired.

CHOCOLATE CHIP NEW YORK CHEESECAKE

Fold 1 cup miniature semisweet chocolate chips (3 oz) into cheese mixture before pouring into crust.

CHEESECAKE TIPS

Creating great cheesecake isn't difficult—but it's essential you follow your recipe, step by step. Here are a few general tips to keep in mind:

- To check the doneness for most cheesecakes, touch the top of the cheesecake lightly or gently shake the pan. It may not appear to be done, but if a small area in the center jiggles slightly or seems soft, it will become firm as the cheesecake cools. Do not insert a knife to test for doneness because the hole could cause the cheesecake to crack.
- After baking a cheesecake, some recipes may tell you to turn the oven off and let the cheesecake stand in the oven for at least 30 minutes or to remove it from the oven and let it cool at room temperature for a certain length of time before refrigerating. Follow recipe directions for best results.
- Refrigerate the baked cheesecake uncovered 2 to 3 hours or until chilled, then cover. Covering warm cheesecake may cause moisture to drip onto the top of the cake.
- If the cheesecake has a side crust, after it has cooled for 30 minutes, run a metal spatula or table knife along the side of the crust to loosen it from the pan (if the pan has a removable side, don't remove or release it yet). Loosening the crust keeps the cheesecake from pulling away, which may cause the cheesecake to crack. Do this again before removing the side of the pan.
- To cut cheesecake, dip the knife into water and clean it off after every cut.

Bread Pudding with Whiskey Sauce

Bread Pudding with Whiskey Sauce

PREP: 25 min **STAND:** 20 min **BAKE:** 1 hr 5 min **COOL:** 30 min ▪ **12 SERVINGS**

Firm breads make the best bread pudding because the cut pieces hold up to all of the liquid ingredients without becoming mushy. Although firm bread is best, avoid artisan or rustic breads with a very crisp or hard crust.

Bread Pudding

4 large eggs
1 large egg yolk
3/4 cup sugar
2 1/2 cups milk
2 1/2 cups whipping (heavy) cream
1 tablespoon vanilla
1 teaspoon ground cinnamon
12 oz French or other firm bread, cut into 1/2-inch slices, then cut into 1 1/2-inch pieces (10 cups)
1/2 cup raisins, if desired
2 tablespoons sugar
1/2 teaspoon ground cinnamon
2 tablespoons butter or margarine, melted

Whiskey Sauce

1/2 cup butter or margarine
2 tablespoons water
1 large egg
1 cup sugar
2 tablespoons whiskey or bourbon or 1 teaspoon brandy extract

1. Heat oven to 325°F. Grease bottom and sides of 13 × 9-inch glass baking dish with shortening or spray with cooking spray.

2. In large bowl, beat 4 whole eggs, 1 egg yolk and 3/4 cup sugar with wire whisk until well blended. Beat in milk, whipping cream, vanilla and 1 teaspoon cinnamon until well blended. Stir in 7 cups of the bread pieces and the raisins. Let stand 20 minutes. Pour into baking dish. Lightly press remaining 3 cups bread pieces on top of mixture in baking dish.

3. In small bowl, stir 2 tablespoons sugar and 1/2 teaspoon cinnamon until well blended. Brush top of bread mixture with melted 2 tablespoons butter; sprinkle with cinnamon-sugar. Bake uncovered 55 to 65 minutes or until top is puffed and light golden brown (center will jiggle slightly). Cool 30 minutes.

4. Meanwhile, in 1-quart saucepan, melt 1/2 cup butter over low heat; do not allow to simmer. Remove from heat; cool 10 minutes. Mix water and 1 egg in small bowl; stir into butter until blended. Stir in 1 cup sugar. Cook over medium-low heat, stirring constantly, until sugar is dissolved and mixture begins to boil; remove from heat. Stir in whiskey. Cool at least 10 minutes before serving.

5. Serve sauce over warm bread pudding. Store remaining dessert and sauce covered in refrigerator.

1 SERVING: CAL. 500 (CAL. FROM FAT 270); FAT 30g (SAT. FAT 17g); CHOL. 190mg; SODIUM 300mg; CARBS. 50g (FIBER 1g); PRO. 8g
% DAILY VALUE: VIT. A 22%; VIT. C 0%; CALC. 14%; IRON 6%
EXCHANGES: 1 1/2 STARCH, 1 1/2 OTHER CARB., 1/2 MILK, 5 1/2 FAT
CARB. CHOICES: 3

LIGHTER BREAD PUDDING WITH WHISKEY SAUCE

For 7 grams of fat and 300 calories per serving, substitute 4 cups fat-free (skim) milk and 1 cup half-and-half for the milk and whipping cream. Substitute 2 eggs and 1/2 cup fat-free cholesterol-free egg product for the 4 eggs and 1 egg yolk. Instead of Whiskey Sauce, stir 1 tablespoon bourbon into 1 cup fat-free caramel topping; heat if desired.

Tiramisu

PREP: 35 min **CHILL:** 7 hr ■ **8 SERVINGS**

Mascarpone is a sinfully rich double or triple cream cheese that originated in the Lombardy region of Italy. It has a delicate, buttery flavor with just a hint of sweetness. Look for it in the cheese case in large supermarkets, specialty cheese shops or gourmet food stores.

- 6 large egg yolks
- 3/4 cup sugar
- 2/3 cup milk
- 1 lb mascarpone cheese or 2 packages (8 oz each) cream cheese, softened
- 1 1/4 cups whipping (heavy) cream
- 1/2 teaspoon vanilla
- 1/4 cup brewed espresso or very strong coffee, chilled
- 2 tablespoons rum*
- 2 packages (3 oz each) ladyfingers**
- 1 1/2 teaspoons baking cocoa

1. In 2-quart saucepan, beat egg yolks and sugar with wire whisk until well mixed. Beat in milk. Heat to boiling over medium heat, stirring constantly; reduce heat to low. Boil and stir 1 minute; remove from heat. Pour into medium bowl; place plastic wrap directly onto surface of custard mixture. Refrigerate about 1 hour or until chilled.

◀ **Tiramisu**

2. Add cheese to custard mixture. Beat with electric mixer on medium speed until smooth; set aside.

3. In chilled medium bowl, beat whipping cream and vanilla with electric mixer on high speed until stiff; set aside. In small bowl, mix espresso and rum.

4. Separate ladyfingers horizontally; brush with espresso mixture (do not soak). In ungreased 11 × 7-inch glass baking dish, arrange half of the ladyfingers in single layer. Spread half of the cheese mixture over ladyfingers; spread with half of the whipped cream. Repeat layers with remaining ladyfingers, cheese mixture and whipped cream. Sprinkle with cocoa. Refrigerate at least 4 to 6 hours to develop flavors but no longer than 24 hours. Store covered in refrigerator.

**1/8 teaspoon rum extract mixed with 2 tablespoons water can be substituted for the rum.*

***2 packages frozen (thawed) pound cake (10.75-oz each) can be substituted for the ladyfingers. Place each pound cake on its side; carefully cut each into 3 lengthwise slices (to total 6 slices). Brush each slice with espresso mixture (do not soak). Arrange 3 slices crosswise in baking dish. Layer as directed in step 4, adding remaining 3 slices.*

1 SERVING: CAL. 535 (CAL. FROM FAT 340); FAT 38g (SAT. FAT 22g); CHOL. 270mg; SODIUM 260mg; Carb. 40g (FIBER 1g); PRO. 9g
% DAILY VALUE: VIT. A 32%; VIT. C 0%; CALC. 12%; IRON 10%
EXCHANGES: NOT RECOMMENDED **CARB. CHOICES:** 2 1/2

LADYFINGERS

Ladyfingers are light and airy little sponge cakes served with ice cream or pudding and an essential ingredient in desserts like charlottes or tiramisu. These commercially produced small, oval-shaped cakes can be found in the bakery department or freezer section of the supermarket. If they are not available, you can substitute a 1/2-inch slice of packaged pound cake (from an 8 × 4-inch loaf) for each ladyfinger (unless recipe states otherwise).You'll need twelve slices of pound cake to substitute for a 3-ounce package of ladyfingers.

English Trifle

PREP: 30 min **COOK:** 20 min **CHILL:** 3 hr ▪ **10 SERVINGS**

Prepare this trifle in a pretty glass serving bowl to show off the beautiful layers of cake, fruit and cream.

- 1/2 cup sugar
- 3 tablespoons cornstarch
- 1/4 teaspoon salt
- 3 cups milk
- 1/2 cup dry sherry or other dry white wine or white grape juice
- 3 large egg yolks, beaten
- 3 tablespoons butter or margarine
- 1 tablespoon vanilla
- 2 packages (3 oz each) ladyfingers (24 ladyfingers)
- 1/2 cup strawberry preserves
- 1 pint strawberries (2 cups), sliced, or 1 box (10 oz) frozen sliced strawberries, thawed and drained
- 1 cup whipping (heavy) cream
- 2 tablespoons sugar
- 2 tablespoons slivered almonds, toasted (page 215)

1. In 3-quart saucepan, mix 1/2 cup sugar, the cornstarch and salt. Gradually stir in milk and sherry. Heat to boiling over medium heat, stirring constantly. Boil and stir 1 minute.

2. Gradually stir at least half of the hot mixture into egg yolks, then stir back into hot mixture in saucepan. Boil and stir 1 minute; remove from heat. Stir in butter and vanilla. Cover and refrigerate about 3 hours or until chilled but not firm.

3. Split ladyfingers horizontally in half. Spread cut sides with preserves. In 2-quart serving bowl, layer one-fourth of the ladyfingers, cut sides up, half of the strawberries and half of the pudding; repeat layers. Arrange remaining ladyfingers around edge of bowl in upright position with cut sides toward center. (It may be necessary to gently ease ladyfingers down into pudding about 1 inch so they remain upright.)

4. In chilled medium bowl, beat whipping cream and 2 tablespoons sugar with electric mixer on high speed until stiff. Spread over dessert. Sprinkle with almonds. Cover and refrigerate until serving. Store covered in refrigerator.

1 SERVING: Cal, 375 (CAL. FROM FAT 155); FAT 17g (SAT. FAT 9g); CHOL. 110mg; SODIUM 180mg; CARB. 50g (FIBER 1g); PRO. 6g **% DAILY VALUE:** VIT. A 14%; VIT. C 34%; CALC. 12%; IRON 6% **EXCHANGES:** 2 STARCH, 1 FRUIT, 3 1/2 FAT **CARB. CHOICES:** 3

LIGHTER ENGLISH TRIFLE

For 5 grams of fat and 265 calories per serving, use 1/4 cup fat-free (skim) milk, substitute fat-free cholesterol free egg product for the egg yolks and decrease butter to 1 tablespoon. Omit whipping cream and 2 tablespoons sugar; substitute 2 cups fat-free frozen (thawed) whipped topping.

Crème Brûlée

PREP: 20 min **BAKE:** 40 min **COOL:** 2 hr **CHILL:** 4 hr ▪ **4 SERVINGS**

- 6 large egg yolks
- 2 cups whipping (heavy) cream
- 1/3 cup sugar
- 1 teaspoon vanilla
- Boiling water
- 8 teaspoons sugar

1. Heat oven to 350°F.

2. In small bowl, slightly beat egg yolks with wire whisk. In large bowl, stir whipping cream, 1/3 cup sugar and the vanilla until well mixed. Add egg yolks to cream mixture; beat with wire whisk until evenly colored and well blended.

3. In 13 × 9-inch pan, place four 6-ounce ceramic ramekins.* Pour cream mixture evenly into ramekins.

4. Carefully place pan with ramekins in oven. Pour enough boiling water into pan, being careful not to splash water into ramekins, until water covers two-thirds of the height of the ramekins.

5. Bake 30 to 40 minutes or until top is light golden brown and sides are set (centers will be jiggly).

6. Carefully transfer ramekins to wire rack, using tongs or grasping tops of ramekins with pot holder. Cool 2 hours or until room temperature. Cover tightly with plastic wrap and refrigerate until chilled, at least 4 hours but no longer than 2 days.

7. Uncover ramekins; gently blot any condensation on custards with paper towel. Sprinkle 2 teaspoons sugar over each custard. Holding kitchen torch 3 to 4 inches from custard, caramelize sugar on each custard by heating with torch about 2 minutes, moving flame continuously over sugar in circular motion, until sugar is melted and light golden brown. (To caramelize sugar in the broiler, see Broiler Method below.) Serve immediately, or refrigerate up to 8 hours before serving.

Broiler Method: Sprinkle 2 teaspoons brown sugar over each chilled custard. Place ramekins in 15 × 10 × 1-inch pan or on cookie sheet with sides. Broil with tops 4 to 6 inches from heat 5 to 6 minutes or until sugar is melted and forms a glaze. (If served immediately rather than refrigerated, custard will be softer than if sugar had been caramelized with kitchen torch.)

**Do not use glass custard cups or glass pie plates; they cannot withstand the heat from the kitchen torch or broiler and may break.*

1 SERVING: CAL. 550 (CAL. FROM FAT 405); FAT 45g (SAT. FAT 25g); CHOL. 450mg; SODIUM 50mg; CARBS. 29g (FIBER 0g); PRO. 7g
% DAILY VALUE: VIT. A 36%; VIT. C 0%; CALC. 12%; IRON 4%
EXCHANGES: 2 OTHER CARB., 1 HIGH-FAT MEAT, 7 1/2 FAT
CARB. CHOICES: 2

Crème Brûlée ▶

HOW TO CARAMELIZE SUGAR USING A KITCHEN TORCH

1. Sprinkle 2 teaspoons sugar over each custard.

2. Holding kitchen torch 3 to 4 inches from custard, caramelize sugar on each custard by heating with torch about 2 minutes, moving flame continuously over sugar in circular motion. The sugar is partially melted at this point.

3. Keep moving flame continuously over sugar in circular motion until sugar is melted and light golden brown.

Panna Cotta

Panna Cotta

PREP: 5 min **STAND:** 10 min **COOK:** 7 min **CHILL:** 4 hr ■ **4 SERVINGS**

Italian for "cooked cream," panna cotta is an unbaked egg-free custard with a silky, light texture. If you don't want to unmold the ramekins, pour the custard into four small parfait glasses instead, making sure to leave room at the top for the sauce.

2 cups half-and-half
1 1/2 teaspoons unflavored gelatin
1/4 cup sugar
1 teaspoon vanilla
Dash of salt
Raspberry Sauce (page 216), if desired

1. Pour half-and-half into 1 1/2-quart saucepan. Sprinkle gelatin evenly over cold half-and-half. Let stand 10 minutes.

2. Heat half-and-half mixture over medium-high heat 5 to 7 minutes, stirring constantly, until gelatin is dissolved and mixture is just beginning to simmer (do not allow to boil). Remove from heat.

3. Stir in sugar, vanilla and salt until sugar is dissolved.

4. Pour mixture into four 1/2-cup ramekins or 6-ounce custard cups. Cover with plastic wrap and refrigerate about 4 hours or until set.

5. When ready to serve, run thin knife around edge of each panna cotta. Dip bottom of each ramekin into bowl of very hot water for 5 seconds. Immediately place serving plate upside down onto each ramekin; turn plate and ramekin over and remove ramekin. Serve with Raspberry Sauce.

1 SERVING: CAL. 210 (CAL. FROM FAT 130); FAT 14g (SAT. FAT 9g); CHOL. 45mg; SODIUM 125mg; CARBS. 18g (FIBER 0g); PRO. 4g
% DAILY VALUE: VIT. A 8%; VIT. C 0%; CALC. 15%; IRON 0%
EXCHANGES: 1 OTHER CARB, 1/2 HIGH-FAT MEAT, 2 FAT
CARB. CHOICES: 1

Baked Custard

PREP: 15 min **BAKE:** 45 min **COOL:** 30 min ■ **6 SERVINGS**

3 large eggs, slightly beaten
1/3 cup sugar
1 teaspoon vanilla
Dash of salt
2 1/2 cups very warm milk (120°F to 130°F)
Ground nutmeg

1. Heat oven to 350°F.

2. In medium bowl, beat eggs, sugar, vanilla and salt with wire whisk or fork. Gradually stir in milk. Pour into six 6-ounce custard cups. Sprinkle with nutmeg.

3. Place cups in 13 × 9-inch pan on oven rack. Pour very hot water into pan to within 1/2 inch of tops of cups (see box, below).

4. Bake about 45 minutes or until knife inserted halfway between center and edge comes out clean. Remove cups from water. Cool about 30 minutes. Unmold and serve warm, or refrigerate and unmold before serving. Store covered in refrigerator.

1 SERVING: CAL. 135 (CAL. FROM FAT 45); FAT 5g (SAT. FAT 2g); CHOL. 115mg; SODIUM 120mg; CARBS. 16g (FIBER 0g); PRO. 7g
% DAILY VALUE: VIT. A 6%; VIT. C 0%; CALC. 14%; IRON 2%
EXCHANGES: 1 MILK, 1 FAT **CARB. CHOICES:** 1

CARAMEL CUSTARD (CRÈME CARAMEL)
Before making custard, in heavy 1-quart saucepan, heat 1/2 cup sugar over low heat 10 to 15 minutes, stirring constantly with wooden spoon, until sugar is melted and golden brown (sugar becomes very hot and could melt a plastic spoon). Immediately divide syrup among six 6-ounce custard cups before it hardens in saucepan; carefully tilt cups to coat bottoms (syrup will be extremely hot). Let syrup harden in cups about 10 minutes. Make custard as directed in Step 2; pour over syrup in cups. Bake as directed in Steps 3 and 4. Cool completely; cover and refrigerate until serving or up to 48 hours.

To unmold, carefully loosen side of custard with knife or small spatula. Place dessert dish on top of cup and, holding tightly, turn dish and cup upside down. Shake cup gently to loosen custard. Caramel syrup will drizzle over custard, forming a sauce.

BAKING IN A WATER BATH

Why is custard or crème brûlée baked in a pan of water? The water bath method helps custard bake gently and evenly. Without the hot water, the edges of the custard cook too quickly. Put the custard cups in the empty pan, put the pan in the oven, then carefully pour hot water into the pan. When the custards are done, remove the cups from the water or they will keep cooking.

Rice Pudding LOW-FAT

PREP: 30 min **BAKE:** 45 min **STAND:** 15 min ■ **8 SERVINGS**

Leftover cooked rice can be used in this recipe instead of cooking the rice. Use 1 1/2 cups cooked rice, and increase the bake time by about 5 minutes because the rice will be cold.

1/2 cup uncooked regular long-grain rice
1 cup water
2 large eggs or 4 large egg yolks
1/2 cup sugar
1/2 cup raisins or chopped dried apricots
2 1/2 cups milk
1 teaspoon vanilla
1/4 teaspoon salt
Ground cinnamon or nutmeg
Raspberry Sauce (page 216) or Sweetened Whipped Cream (page 217), if desired

1. In 1 1/2-quart saucepan, heat rice and water to boiling, stirring once or twice; reduce heat to low. Cover and simmer 14 minutes (do not lift cover or stir). All water should be absorbed; if not, drain excess water.

2. Heat oven to 325°F.

3. In ungreased 1 1/2-quart casserole, beat eggs with wire whisk or fork. Stir in sugar, raisins, milk, vanilla, salt and hot rice. Sprinkle with cinnamon.

4. Bake uncovered 45 minutes, stirring every 15 minutes. Top of pudding will be very wet and not set (overbaking may cause pudding to curdle).

5. Stir well; let stand 15 minutes. Enough liquid will be absorbed while standing to make pudding creamy. Serve warm, or cover and refrigerate about 3 hours or until chilled. Serve with Raspberry Sauce. Store covered in refrigerator.

1 SERVING: CAL. 185 (CAL. FROM FAT 25); FAT 3g (SAT. FAT 1g); CHOL. 60mg; SODIUM 130mg; CARBS. 34g (FIBER 1g); PRO. 5g
% DAILY VALUE: VIT. A 4%; VIT. C 0%; CALC. 10%; IRON 4%
EXCHANGES: 2 STARCH, 1/2 FAT **CARB. CHOICES:** 2

Chocolate Mousse

PREP: 20 min **CHILL:** 2 hr ■ **8 SERVINGS**

Its name means froth or foam, describing the light airy appearance of a mousse. For a special touch, garnish with fresh fruit or chocolate curls.

- 4 large egg yolks
- 1/4 cup sugar
- 1 cup whipping (heavy) cream
- 8 oz semisweet baking chocolate, chopped
- 1 1/2 cups whipping (heavy) cream

1. In small bowl, beat egg yolks with electric mixer on high speed about 3 minutes or until thickened and lemon colored. Gradually beat in sugar.

2. In 2-quart saucepan, heat 1 cup whipping cream over medium heat just until hot.

3. Gradually stir at least half of the hot cream into egg yolk mixture, then stir back into hot cream in saucepan. Cook over low heat about 5 minutes, stirring constantly, until mixture thickens (do not boil).

4. Stir in chocolate until melted. Cover and refrigerate about 2 hours, stirring occasionally, just until chilled.

5. In chilled medium bowl, beat 1 1/2 cups whipping cream on high speed until stiff. Fold chocolate mixture into whipped cream. Pipe or spoon mixture into dessert dishes or stemmed glasses. Refrigerate until serving. Store covered in refrigerator.

1 SERVING: CAL. 425 (CAL. FROM FAT 305); FAT 34g (SAT. FAT 20g); CHOL. 190mg; SODIUM 30mg; CARBS. 26g (FIBER 2g); PRO. 4g
% DAILY VALUE: VIT. A 20%; VIT. C 0%; CALC. 6%; IRON 6%
EXCHANGES: 1 STARCH, 1 OTHER CARB., 6 1/2 FAT
CARB. CHOICES: 2

LIGHTER CHOCOLATE MOUSSE

For 14 grams of fat and 255 calories per serving, substitute 2 eggs for the 4 egg yolks, half-and-half for the 1 cup whipping cream and 3 cups frozen (thawed) fat-free whipped topping for the whipped 1 1/2 cups whipping cream.

CHOCOLATE CURLS AND SHAVINGS

To make chocolate curls for garnishing desserts, pull a swivel-bladed vegetable peeler or thin, sharp knife across a block of milk chocolate, using long, thin strokes. The curls will be easier to make if the chocolate is slightly warm (let it stand in a warm place for about 15 minutes before cutting). Semisweet chocolate will make smaller curls. Use a toothpick to lift the curls and arrange them on a frosted cake, pie or dessert. Make chocolate shavings the same way by using shorter strokes.

Vanilla Pudding

PREP: 10 min **COOK:** 10 min **CHILL:** 1 hr ■ **4 SERVINGS**

- 1/3 cup sugar
- 2 tablespoons cornstarch
- 1/8 teaspoon salt
- 2 cups milk
- 2 large egg yolks, slightly beaten
- 2 tablespoons butter or margarine, softened
- 2 teaspoons vanilla

1. In 2-quart saucepan, mix sugar, cornstarch and salt. Gradually stir in milk. Cook over medium heat, stirring constantly, until mixture thickens and boils. Boil and stir 1 minute.

2. Gradually stir at least half of the hot mixture into egg yolks, then stir back into hot mixture in saucepan. Boil and stir 1 minute; remove from heat. Stir in butter and vanilla.

3. Pour pudding into dessert dishes. Cover and refrigerate about 1 hour or until chilled. Store covered in refrigerator.

1 SERVING: CAL. 225 (CAL. FROM FAT 100); FAT 11g (SAT. FAT 6g); CHOL. 130mg; SODIUM 180mg; CARBS. 26g (FIBER 0g); PRO. 6g
% DAILY VALUE: VIT. A 12%; VIT. C 0%; CALC. 16%; IRON 2%
EXCHANGES: 1 1/2 OTHER CARB., 1 MILK, 2 FAT **CARB. CHOICES:** 2

BUTTERSCOTCH PUDDING Substitute 2/3 cup packed brown sugar for the granulated sugar; decrease vanilla to 1 teaspoon.

CHOCOLATE PUDDING Increase sugar to 1/2 cup; stir 1/3 cup baking cocoa into sugar mixture. Omit butter.

TIPS FOR MERINGUES

Meringue, a mixture of egg white, sugar and air, can make a melt-in-your-mouth soft topping for Lemon Meringue Pie (page 134) or a hard, crispy Meringue Shell (page 213) to cradle cream fillings, fruit or ice cream. Follow these tips and you'll soon be making successful meringues every time.

- *Pick a cool, dry day to make meringue.* If it's humid or rainy, the sugar in the meringue absorbs moisture from the air, making the meringue sticky and spongy. Beads, or drops, of sugar syrup may also form on its surface.
- *Start with cold eggs* because they separate more easily. Separate eggs carefully; even a speck of yolk in the whites will keep the whites from whipping up. To prevent contamination from the outside of the shell, don't pass the egg yolk back and forth between the shell halves. Instead, use an egg separator; see Separating Eggs, page 9.
- *Let egg whites stand at room temperature* for 30 minutes, so the egg whites will really fluff up during beating. Or put the whites in a microwavable bowl and microwave uncovered on High for about 10 seconds per egg white to bring them to room temperature. If you heat them too long, they'll cook through.
- *Start with a clean, dry bowl and beaters* so egg whites will beat properly.
- *Beat sugar in gradually,* about 1 tablespoon at a time, so that the meringue will be smooth and not gritty. Continue beating until the meringue stands in stiff, glossy peaks when you lift the beaters out of the mixture. See Stiff Peaks, page 22.

Soft Meringue

- *Spread meringue over the hot pie filling* right up to the crust all the way around so that it will seal. If the meringue is sealed, it helps to prevent it from shrinking or weeping liquid after baking.
- *Cool the pie in a draft-free spot* to prevent the meringue from shrinking as it cools.

Hard Meringue

- *Be sure to bake a hard meringue shell* until it's completely dry to prevent it from becoming soft and gummy.
- *Cool hard meringue shells in the oven,* with the heat turned off, for as long as the recipe suggests so they become dry and crisp.
- *To keep hard meringue shells crisp,* store them in a container with a tight-fitting lid.
- *Fill hard meringue shells just before serving* so they don't absorb moisture from the filling and become chewy, unless the recipe gives other directions.

Meringue for 9-Inch Pie

LOW-FAT

PREP: 20 min ▪ **8 SERVINGS**

Here's a foolproof meringue, thanks to a very simple yet special method. The sugar is cooked with cornstarch and water until thickened, which provides stability to the egg whites during beating and baking. The resulting meringue clings to the pie filling, doesn't shrink and cuts beautifully. It's well worth the small bit of extra time!

- 1/2 cup sugar
- 4 teaspoons cornstarch
- 1/2 cup cold water
- 4 large egg whites
- 1/8 teaspoon salt

1. Heat oven to 350°F.

2. In 1-quart saucepan, mix sugar and cornstarch. Stir in water. Cook over medium heat, stirring constantly, until mixture thickens and boils. Boil and stir 1 minute; remove from heat. Cool completely while making filling for pie recipe. (To cool more quickly, place in freezer about 10 minutes.)

3. In large bowl, beat egg whites and salt with electric mixer on high speed just until soft peaks begin to form. Very gradually beat in sugar mixture until stiff peaks form.

4. Spoon meringue onto hot pie filling. Spread over filling, carefully sealing meringue to edge of crust to prevent shrinking. Bake about 15 minutes or until meringue is light brown. Cool away from drafts.

1 SERVING: CAL. 65 (CAL. FROM FAT 0); FAT 0g (SAT. FAT 0g); CHOL. 0mg; SODIUM 65mg; CARBS. 14g (FIBER 0g); PRO. 2g
% DAILY VALUE: VIT. A 0%; VIT. C 0%; CALC. 0%; IRON 0%
EXCHANGES: 1 OTHER CARB. **CARB. CHOICES:** 1

HOW TO SPREAD MERINGUE OVER PIE

Spoon meringue onto hot pie filling. Spread over filling, carefully sealing meringue to edge of crust to prevent shrinking.

HOW TO SHAPE MERINGUE SHELL

Shape meringue with back of spoon into desired shape, building up side.

Meringue Shell LOW-FAT

PREP: 15 min **BAKE:** 1 hr 30 min **COOL:** 3 hr ▪ **8 SERVINGS**

A meringue shell bakes up crisp yet melts in your mouth when you bite into it.

- 3 large egg whites
- 1/4 teaspoon cream of tartar
- 3/4 cup sugar

1. Heat oven to 275°F. Line cookie sheet with cooking parchment paper or heavy brown paper.

2. In medium bowl, beat egg whites and cream of tartar with electric mixer on high speed until foamy. Beat in sugar, 1 tablespoon at a time; continue beating until stiff peaks form and mixture is glossy. Do not underbeat. On cookie sheet, shape meringue into 9-inch circle with back of spoon, building up side.

3. Bake 1 hour 30 minutes. Turn off oven; leave meringue in oven with door closed 1 hour. Finish cooling at room temperature, about 2 hours.

1 SERVING: CAL. 80 (CAL. FROM FAT 0); FAT 0g (SAT. FAT 0g); CHOL. 0mg; SODIUM 20mg; CARBS. 19g (FIBER 0g); PRO. 1g **% DAILY VALUE:** VIT. A 0%; VIT. C 0%; CALC. 0%; IRON 0% **EXCHANGES:** 1 STARCH **CARB. CHOICES:** 1

INDIVIDUAL MERINGUES Drop meringue by 1/3 cupfuls onto paper-lined cookie sheet. Shape into circles, building up sides. Bake 1 hour. Turn off oven; leave meringues in oven with door closed 1 hour. Finish cooling at room temperature, about 2 hours. Fill with ice cream and drizzle with Hot Fudge Sauce (page 214) or Butterscotch Sauce (page 216). 8 to 10 meringues.

Vanilla Ice Cream

PREP: 10 min **COOK:** 10 min **CHILL:** 3 hr **FREEZE:** Time will vary ▪ **1 QUART ICE CREAM**

- 3 large egg yolks, slightly beaten
- 1/2 cup sugar
- 1 cup milk
- 1/4 teaspoon salt
- 2 cups whipping (heavy) cream
- 1 tablespoon vanilla

1. In 2-quart saucepan, stir egg yolks, sugar, milk and salt until well mixed. Cook just to boiling over medium heat, stirring constantly (do not boil).

2. Pour milk mixture into chilled bowl. Refrigerate uncovered 2 to 3 hours, stirring occasionally, until room temperature. At this point, mixture can be refrigerated up to 24 hours before completing recipe if desired.

3. Stir whipping cream and vanilla into milk mixture. Pour into 1-quart ice-cream freezer and freeze according to manufacturer's directions.

1 SERVING (1/2 CUP): CAL. 265 (CAL. FROM FAT 190); FAT 21g (SAT. FAT 13g); CHOL. 150mg; SODIUM 110mg; CARBS. 16g (FIBER 0g); PRO. 3g **% DAILY VALUE:** VIT. A 16%; VIT. C 0%; CALC. 8%; IRON 0% **EXCHANGES:** 1 STARCH, 4 FAT **CARB. CHOICES:** 1

CHOCOLATE ICE CREAM Increase sugar to 1 cup. Beat 2 oz unsweetened baking chocolate, melted and cooled, into milk mixture before cooking. Decrease vanilla to 1 teaspoon.

FRESH PEACH ICE CREAM Decrease vanilla to 1 teaspoon. Mash 4 or 5 peaches and an additional 1/2 cup sugar with potato masher or in food processor until slightly chunky (not pureed) to make 2 cups; stir into milk mixture after adding vanilla.

FRESH STRAWBERRY ICE CREAM Decrease vanilla to 1 teaspoon. Mash 1 pint (2 cups) strawberries and an additional 1/2 cup sugar with potato masher or in food processor until slightly chunky (not pureed); stir into milk mixture after adding vanilla. Stir in a few drops of red food color if desired.

Lemonade Sorbet LOW-FAT

PREP: 10 min **FREEZE:** 4 hr ▪ **4 SERVINGS**

- 1 1/2 cups cold water
- 1 cup frozen (thawed) lemonade concentrate (from 12-oz can)
- 3 tablespoons honey
- Lemon slices, if desired
- Blueberries, if desired

1. In blender or food processor, place water, lemonade concentrate and honey. Cover and blend on low speed until smooth. Pour into 8-inch square glass baking dish.

2. Freeze about 4 hours until firm, stirring several times to keep mixture smooth. Garnish with lemon slices and blueberries.

1 SERVING: CAL. 185 (CAL. FROM FAT 0); FAT 0g (SAT. FAT 0g); CHOL. 0mg; SODIUM 5mg; CARBS. 47g (FIBER 0g); PRO. 0g
% DAILY VALUE: VIT. A 0%; VIT. C 22%; CALC. 0%; IRON 2%
EXCHANGES: 1 FRUIT, 2 OTHER CARB. **CARB. CHOICES:** 3

LIMEADE SORBET Substitute limeade concentrate for the lemonade concentrate.

◄ **Lemonade Sorbet**

Hot Fudge Sauce LOW-FAT

PREP: 5 min **COOK:** 5 min **COOL:** 30 min ▪
3 CUPS SAUCE

Pour this lavish sauce over your favorite ice cream. Then top it off with colored sprinkles, chopped toffee candy bars, chopped nuts, miniature chocolate chips or cherries—the list is endless!

- 1 can (12 oz) evaporated milk
- 1 bag (12 oz) semisweet chocolate chips (2 cups)
- 1/2 cup sugar
- 1 tablespoon butter or margarine
- 1 teaspoon vanilla

1. In 2-quart saucepan, heat milk, chocolate chips and sugar to boiling over medium heat, stirring constantly; remove from heat.

2. Stir in butter and vanilla until mixture is smooth and creamy. Cool about 30 minutes or until sauce begins to thicken. Serve warm. Store remaining sauce covered in refrigerator up to 4 weeks. Sauce becomes firm when refrigerated; heat slightly before serving (sauce will become thin if overheated).

1 TABLESPOON: CAL. 60 (CAL. FROM FAT 25); FAT 3g (SAT. FAT 2g); CHOL. 0mg; SODIUM 10mg; CARBS. 7g (FIBER 0g); PRO. 1g
% DAILY VALUE: VIT. A 0%; VIT. C 0%; CALC. 2%; IRON 0%
EXCHANGES: 1/2 STARCH, 1/2 FAT **CARB. CHOICES:** 1/2

Glossy Chocolate Sauce

FAST **LOW-FAT**

PREP: 15 min ■ **ABOUT $1^1/_2$ CUP SAUCE**

- $1^1/_2$ cups light corn syrup
- 3 oz unsweetened baking chocolate, cut into pieces
- 1 tablespoon butter or margarine
- $^3/_4$ teaspoon vanilla

1. In 1-quart saucepan, heat corn syrup and chocolate over low heat, stirring frequently, until chocolate is melted; remove from heat.

2. Stir in butter and vanilla. Serve warm or cold. Store covered in refrigerator up to 10 days. Reheat slightly before serving if desired.

1 TABLESPOON: CAL. 90 (CAL. FROM FAT 25); FAT 3g (SAT. FAT 2g); CHOL. 0mg; SODIUM 30mg; CARBS. 17g (FIBER 1g); PRO. 0g
% DAILY VALUE: VIT. A 0%; VIT. C 0%; CALC. 0%; IRON 0%
EXCHANGES: 1 OTHER CARB., 1/2 FAT **CARB. CHOICES:** 1

Caramel Sauce

LOW-FAT

PREP: 5 min **COOK:** 10 min **COOL:** 30 min ■ **$2^1/_2$ CUPS SAUCE**

- 1 cup light corn syrup
- $1^1/_4$ cups packed brown sugar
- $^1/_4$ cup butter or margarine
- 1 cup whipping (heavy) cream

1. In 2-quart saucepan, heat corn syrup, brown sugar and butter to boiling over low heat, stirring constantly. Boil 5 minutes, stirring occasionally.

2. Stir in whipping cream; heat to boiling. Cool about 30 minutes. Serve warm. Store covered in refrigerator up to 2 months. Reheat slightly before serving if desired.

1 TABLESPOON: CAL. 80 (CAL. FROM FAT 25); FAT 3g (SAT. FAT 2g); CHOL. 10mg; SODIUM 20mg; CARBS. 13g (FIBER 0g); PRO. 0g
% DAILY VALUE: VIT. A 2%; VIT. C 0%; CALC. 0%; IRON 0%
EXCHANGES: 1 OTHER CARB., 1/2 FAT **CARB. CHOICES:** 1

TOASTING NUTS, COCONUT AND SESAME SEED

Toasting brings out wonderful flavor! But watch carefully to be sure the food doesn't burn. It's ready when the color changes and you can smell that nice toasted aroma. Remove food immediately from the hot pan or skillet so it doesn't continue to toast and become too dark or scorch.

Stove-top Method: Sprinkle nuts, coconut or sesame seed in an ungreased heavy skillet.

Nuts	Cook over medium heat 5 to 7 minutes, stirring frequently until nuts begin to brown, then stirring constantly until nuts are light brown.
Coconut	Cook over medium-low heat 6 to 14 minutes, stirring frequently until browning begins, then stirring constantly until golden brown.
Sesame seed	Cook over medium-low heat 5 to 7 minutes, stirring frequently until browning begins, then stirring constantly until golden brown.

Oven Method: Heat oven to 350°F; spread nuts, coconut or sesame seed in an ungreased shallow pan.

Nuts	Bake uncovered 6 to 10 minutes, stirring occasionally, until nuts are light brown.
Coconut	Bake uncovered 5 to 7 minutes, stirring occasionally, until golden brown.
Sesame seed	Bake 8 to 10 minutes, stirring occasionally, until golden brown.

Microwave Method

Nuts	Place 1/2 teaspoon vegetable oil and 1/2 cup nuts in 1- or 2-cup glass measuring cup. Microwave uncovered on High 2 minutes 30 seconds to 3 minute 30 seconds, stirring every 30 seconds, until light brown.
Coconut	Spread 1/2 cup in a microwavable pie plate. Microwave uncovered on High 1 minute 30 seconds to 2 minutes, stirring every 30 seconds, until golden brown.

Butterscotch Sauce

PREP: 10 min **COOK:** 5 min **COOL:** 20 min ■ **ABOUT 1 3/4 CUPS SAUCE**

- 1/2 cup granulated sugar
- 1/2 cup packed brown sugar
- 6 tablespoons butter or margarine
- 1/2 cup whipping (heavy) cream
- 1/2 cup light corn syrup
- 1/2 teaspoon salt
- 1 teaspoon vanilla

1. In 2-quart saucepan, stir all ingredients except vanilla. Cook over low heat, stirring constantly, until butter is melted and sugars are dissolved.

2. Increase heat to medium. Heat to boiling, stirring constantly. Boil gently 5 minutes, stirring occasionally; remove from heat. Cool 20 minutes.

3. Stir in vanilla. Serve sauce warm or cool. Store covered in refrigerator up to 10 days. Sauce becomes firm when refrigerated; heat slightly before serving (sauce will become thin if overheated).

1 TABLESPOON: CAL. 85 (CAL. FROM FAT 35); FAT 4g (SAT. FAT 2g); CHOL. 10mg; SODIUM 70mg; CARBS. 12g (FIBER 0g); PRO. 0g
% DAILY VALUE: VIT. A 2%; VIT. C 0%; CALC. 0%; IRON 0%
EXCHANGES: 1 OTHER CARB., 1/2 FAT **CARB. CHOICES:** 1

Lemon Sauce FAST LOW-FAT

PREP: 5 min **COOK:** 10 min ■ **1 1/4 CUPS SAUCE**

- 1/2 cup sugar
- 2 tablespoons cornstarch
- 3/4 cup water
- 1 tablespoon grated lemon peel
- 1/4 cup lemon juice
- 2 tablespoons butter or margarine

1. In 1-quart saucepan, mix sugar and cornstarch. Gradually stir in water. Cook over medium heat, stirring constantly, until mixture thickens and boils. Boil and stir 1 minute; remove from heat.

2. Stir in remaining ingredients. Serve warm or cool. Store covered in refrigerator up to 10 days.

1 TABLESPOON: CAL. 35 (CAL. FROM FAT 10); FAT 1g (SAT. FAT 1g); CHOL. 5mg; SODIUM 10mg; CARBS. 6g (FIBER 0g); PRO. 0g
% DAILY VALUE: VIT. A 0%; VIT. C 2%; CALC. 0%; IRON 0%
EXCHANGES: 1/2 FRUIT **CARB. CHOICES:** 1/2

Orange Sauce LOW-FAT

PREP: 10 min **COOK:** 15 min ■ **ABOUT 2 1/3 CUPS SAUCE**

- 1 cup sugar
- 2 tablespoons cornstarch
- 1 tablespoon all-purpose flour
- 1/4 teaspoon salt
- 1 1/4 cups orange juice
- 1/2 cup water
- 1/4 cup lemon juice
- 1 tablespoon butter or margarine
- 1 teaspoon grated orange peel
- 1 teaspoon grated lemon peel

1. In 1 1/2 quart saucepan, mix sugar, cornstarch, flour and salt. Gradually stir in orange juice, water and lemon juice. Cook over medium heat, stirring constantly, until mixture thickens and boils. Boil and stir 3 minutes; remove from heat.

2. Stir in remaining ingredients. Serve warm. Store covered in refrigerator.

1 TABLESPOON: CAL. 35 (CAL. FROM FAT 0); FAT 0g (SAT. FAT 0g); CHOL. 0mg; SODIUM 20mg; CARBS. 7g (FIBER 0g); PRO. 0g
% DAILY VALUE: VIT. A 0%; VIT. C 4%; CALC. 0%; IRON 0%
EXCHANGES: 1/2 FRUIT **CARB. CHOICES:** 1/2

Raspberry Sauce FAST LOW-FAT

PREP: 5 min **COOK:** 5 min ■ **ABOUT 1 CUP SAUCE**

- 3 tablespoons sugar
- 2 teaspoons cornstarch
- 1/3 cup water
- 1 box (10 oz) frozen raspberries in syrup, thawed and undrained

1. In 1-quart saucepan, mix sugar and cornstarch. Stir in water and raspberries. Cook over medium heat, stirring constantly, until mixture thickens and boils. Boil and stir 1 minute.

2. Strain sauce through a strainer into bowl to remove seeds if desired. Serve sauce warm or cool. Store covered in refrigerator up to 10 days.

1 TABLESPOON: CAL. 30 (CAL. FROM FAT 0); FAT 0g (SAT. FAT 0g); CHOL. 0mg; SODIUM 0mg; CARBS. 7g (FIBER 1g); PRO. 0g
% DAILY VALUE: VIT. A 0%; VIT. C 4%; CALC. 0%; IRON 0%
EXCHANGES: 1/2 FRUIT **CARB. CHOICES:** 1/2

Sweetened Whipped Cream FAST

PREP: 5 min ■ **2 CUPS WHIPPED CREAM***

Always start with cream right from the fridge, and chill your bowl and beaters in the freezer or refrigerator for 10 to 20 minutes or until cold to the touch. If you don't have time to chill the bowl and beaters, the cream will still whip, but it may take longer, especially if your kitchen is warm.

- 1 cup whipping (heavy) cream*
- 2 tablespoons granulated or powdered sugar
- 1 teaspoon vanilla

In chilled medium bowl, beat all ingredients with electric mixer on high speed until soft peaks form.

**For 1 1/2 cups whipped cream, use 3/4 cup whipping (heavy) cream, 2 tablespoons sugar and 1 teaspoon vanilla. For 1 cup whipped cream, use 1/2 cup whipping (heavy) cream, 1 tablespoon sugar and 1/2 teaspoon vanilla.*

2 TABLESPOONS: CAL. 55 (CAL. FROM FAT 45); FAT 5g (SAT. FAT 3g); CHOL. 15mg; SODIUM 5mg; CARBS. 2g (FIBER 0g); PROTEIN 0g
% DAILY VALUE: VIT. A 4%; VIT. C 0%; CALC. 0%; IRON 0%
EXCHANGES: 1 FAT **CARB. CHOICES:** 0

FLAVORED SWEETENED WHIPPED CREAM

In chilled medium bowl, beat 1 cup whipping (heavy) cream, 3 tablespoons granulated or powdered sugar and **one** of the following ingredients with electric mixer on high speed until soft peaks form.

- 1 teaspoon grated lemon or orange peel
- 1/2 teaspoon ground cinnamon
- 1/2 teaspoon ground ginger
- 1/2 teaspoon ground nutmeg
- 1/2 teaspoon almond extract
- 1/2 teaspoon peppermint extract
- 1/2 teaspoon rum extract
- 1/4 teaspoon maple extract

Freezing Sweetened Whipped Cream: Place waxed paper or foil on cookie sheet. Drop whipped cream by spoonfuls onto waxed paper. Freeze uncovered at least 2 hours. Place frozen mounds of whipped cream in a freezer container. Cover tightly and freeze no longer than 2 months.

LEARN WITH Betty — BEATING WHIPPING CREAM

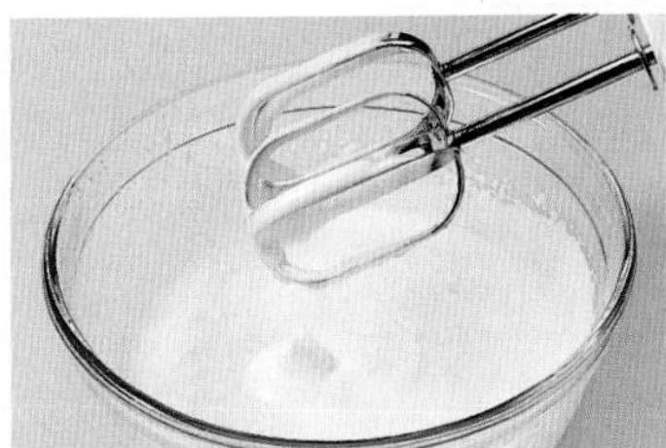

This whipped cream was not beaten long enough to form soft peaks and is best used as a dessert topping. It is too soft to be used in desserts that must set up and become firm enough to cut into serving pieces.

This whipped cream was beaten long enough to form soft peaks. It can be used as a dessert topping and is stiff enough to be used in dessert recipes that call for the cream to be beaten "until soft peaks form."

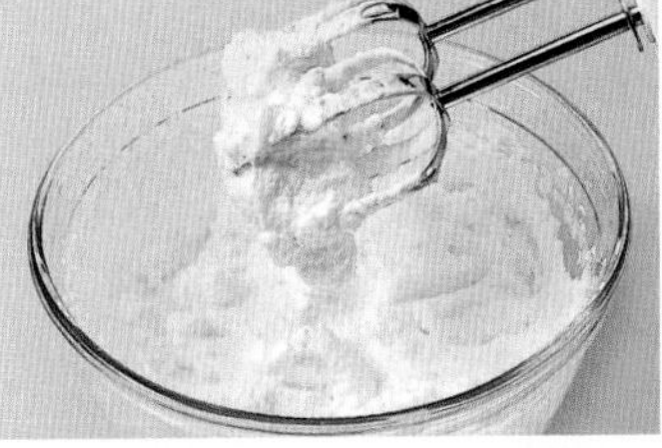

This whipped cream was beaten too long and has begun to curdle and separate. Continued beating will turn it into butter. We do not recommend using this in recipes, but it may be used as a dessert topping if you don't mind the appearance.

PICKING APPLES

This chart lists some of the most common apple varieties and their characteristics. Varieties may vary in flavor and texture according to the season.

Variety	Flavor	Texture	Eating and Salads	Baking	Pies	Sauce
Braeburn	Sweet-Tart	Crisp	X	X	X	X
Cortland	Slightly Tart	Slightly Crisp	X	X	X	X
Crispin/Mutsu	Sweet	Crisp	X	X	X	X
Fireside	Slightly Sweet	Slightly Crisp	X			
Fuji	Sweet	Crisp	X			
Gala	Sweet	Crisp	X			X
Ginger Gold	Sweet	Crisp	X			
Golden Delicious	Sweet	Crisp	X	X	X	X
Granny Smith	Tart	Crisp	X	X	X	X
Haralson	Tart	Crisp	X	X	X	X
Honeycrisp	Sweet	Crisp	X	X		X
Honey Gold	Sweet	Slightly Crisp	X		X	
Ida Red	Slightly Tart	Slightly Crisp		X	X	X
Jonagold	Sweet-Tart	Crisp	X	X	X	X
Jonamac	Sweet-Tart	Tender	X			X
Jonathan	Slightly Tart	Tender	X		X	X
McIntosh	Sweet-Tart	Tender	X			X
Newtown Pippin	Slightly Tart	Crisp	X	X	X	X
Northern Spy	Slightly Tart	Crisp		X	X	X
Paula Red	Slightly Tart	Slightly Crisp	X		X	X
Prairie Spy	Slightly Sweet	Crisp	X	X	X	X
Red Delicious	Sweet	Crisp	X			
Regent	Sweet	Crisp	X		X	
Rome	Slightly Tart	Slightly Crisp		X	X	X
Winesap	Slightly Tart	Crisp	X			

CHAPTER 8

Eggs & Cheese

Eggs

Egg Basics, 219

Cooking Eggs, 220

Cheese

Cheese Basics, 229

Charts

LOW-FAT = *3g or less, except main dishes with 10g or less* FAST = *Ready in 20 minutes or less* BREAD MACHINE = *Bread machine directions* SLOW COOKER = *Slow cooker directions* LIGHTER = *25% fewer calories or grams of fat*

◀ **Hash Brown Potato and Egg Bake (page 235)**

Egg Basics

Eggs are powerful! They're a perfect combination of nutrition and versatility. Packed inside each egg are protein, vitamins, minerals, cholesterol, a little fat and not much sodium. All of this and only 80 calories. In cooking, one or two incredible eggs give structure, bind ingredients together, create lightness and add richness and texture. On top of that, eggs are just plain good eating! Whether you scramble, poach or fry them with a little salt and pepper or whip them into an impressive soufflé, eggs are great to keep on-hand.

HANDLING AND STORING EGGS SAFELY

Store, handle and cook eggs safely by following these guidelines. They'll help keep your food safe from the growth of salmonella or other harmful bacteria.

- *Buy eggs only from the refrigerated case,* and refrigerate them as soon as you get home.
- *Look for eggs with clean, uncracked shells.* Before buying eggs, open the carton and gently move each egg to be sure it hasn't cracked and stuck to the carton. If an egg cracks on the way home, throw it away.
- *Don't wash eggs before storing or using* because washing is a routine part of commercial egg processing.
- *Store eggs in their carton on a shelf,* not the door, so they stay cold and don't absorb odors. Don't store eggs in the egg storage container provided with your refrigerator.
- *Wash hands, utensils, equipment and work area* with hot, soapy water before and after handling raw eggs or recipes made with raw eggs.
- *Egg whites can stand safely at room temperature for up to 30 minutes* before using in recipes that call for beating the whites, like meringue. Room-temperature egg whites, rather than cold egg whites, beat up more quickly and easily and reach their fullest volume.
- *Refrigerate raw eggs and cooked eggs* (including colored eggs). Check the expiration date on the egg carton. Refrigerate:
    - Hard-cooked eggs up to 1 week
    - Raw egg whites up to 4 days in a tightly covered container
    - Unbroken egg yolks up to 2 days, covered with a small amount of water in a tightly covered container.

BUYING EGGS

Eggs are sold by size: pee-wee, small, medium, large, extra-large and jumbo. The most widely available are medium, large and extra-large. Both white- and brown-shell eggs are available, although demand is highest for white eggs. Both types are identical in nutritional content and cooking performance.

Any size of egg can be scrambled, fried, poached or cooked in the shell, but in most other recipes—and always in baked goods—use large eggs. The recipes in this book were tested with large eggs.

Cooking Eggs

Avoid eating raw eggs and foods containing raw eggs. This includes those familiar homemade favorites like ice cream, eggnog, mayonnaise and unbaked cookie dough. Of course these foods are fine if you cook the mixture first or use pasteurized egg products. Eating store-bought versions of these foods are safe to eat because they contain pasteurized eggs; pasteurization destroys salmonella bacteria.

Cook eggs until both the yolk and white are firm, not runny, to prevent contracting salmonella from raw or undercooked eggs. Eggs and mixtures containing eggs are safe to eat when the temperature reaches 160°F in the center. The recipes in this book were tested to meet this requirement.

Serve cooked eggs and dishes containing eggs immediately. Refrigerate leftovers as soon as possible, and use them within two days.

If you're making a "do-ahead" recipe with eggs, refrigerate the unbaked mixture no longer than 24 hours before baking.

GUIDELINES FOR COOKING EGGS

Type	Other Ingredients	Directions	Success Tips
Baked (Shirred)	Butter or margarine, softened	Heat oven to 325°F. Grease custard cups with butter. Carefully break 1 egg into each cup. Sprinkle with salt and pepper. Top each with 1 tablespoon milk or half-and-half. Dot with butter. Bake 15 to 18 minutes or until whites and yolks are firm, not runny.	Instead of dotting with butter, sprinkle egg with 1 tablespoon shredded Cheddar or grated Parmesan cheese if desired.
Fried	Butter, margarine or bacon fat	For 1 or 2 servings, in 7- to 8-inch omelet pan or skillet, melt 1 teaspoon to 2 tablespoons butter over medium-high heat until hot. Break and slip eggs into pan. Immediately reduce heat to low. Cook 5 to 7 minutes, spooning butter over eggs, until whites are set, a film forms over the top and whites and yolks are firm, not runny.	**Lighter Fried Eggs:** Omit butter, margarine or bacon fat; use a nonstick skillet. Cook eggs over low heat about 1 minute or until edges turn white. Add 2 teaspoons water for each egg. Cover and cook about 5 minutes longer or until a film forms over the top and whites and yolks are firm, not runny.
Hard-Cooked	Cold water at least 1 inch above egg(s) placed in single layer.	In saucepan, cover and heat to boiling. Remove from heat; let stand covered 15 minutes. Drain. Immediately place eggs in cold water with ice cubes or run cold water over eggs until completely cooled. To remove shell, crackle it by tapping gently all over; roll between hands to loosen. Peel, starting at large end.	If shell is hard to peel, hold egg in cold water while peeling.
Poached	2 to 3 inches water	In skillet or saucepan, heat water to boiling; reduce to simmering. Break cold eggs, one at a time, into custard cup or saucer. Holding dish close to water's surface, carefully slip eggs into water. Cook 3 to 5 minutes or until whites and yolks are firm, not runny. Remove with slotted spoon.	• Use a large enough pan so eggs do not touch while cooking. • Substitute chicken or beef broth for the water if desired.
Soft-Cooked		Not recommended; soft-cooked eggs do not reach 160°F, the temperature required to kill harmful bacteria.	

Scrambled Eggs FAST

PREP: 5 min **COOK:** 10 min ▪ **4 SERVINGS**

- 6 large eggs
- 1/3 cup water, milk or half-and-half
- 1/4 teaspoon salt
- 1/8 teaspoon pepper, if desired
- 1 tablespoon butter or margarine

1. In medium bowl, beat eggs, water, salt and pepper thoroughly with fork or wire whisk until well mixed.

2. In 10-inch skillet, heat butter over medium heat just until butter begins to sizzle. Pour egg mixture into skillet.

3. As mixture begins to set at bottom and side, gently lift cooked portions with spatula so that thin, uncooked portion can flow to bottom. Avoid constant stirring. Cook 3 to 4 minutes or until eggs are thickened throughout but still moist.

1 SERVING: CAL. 140 (CAL. FROM FAT 100); FAT 11g (SAT. FAT 5g); CHOL. 325mg; SODIUM 260mg; CARBS. 1g (FIBER 0g); PRO. 9g
% DAILY VALUE: VIT. A 10%; VIT. C 0%; CALC. 4%; IRON 4%
EXCHANGES: 1 MEDIUM-FAT MEAT, 1 FAT **CARB. CHOICES:** 0

MEXICAN SCRAMBLED EGGS In 10-inch skillet, cook 1/2 lb chorizo sausage links, cut lengthwise in half and then sliced, 1 small green or red bell pepper, chopped (1/2 cup), and 1 medium onion, chopped (1/2 cup), over medium-high heat about 5 minutes, stirring frequently, until sausage is no longer pink; drain. Add sausage mixture to eggs before cooking the last 3 to 4 minutes in Step 3. Serve egg mixture wrapped in flour tortillas and topped with salsa, shredded cheese and sour cream, if desired.

LEARN WITH Betty — SCRAMBLED EGGS

These eggs are too wet and runny because they were not cooked long enough.

These eggs are fluffy, soft and tender; there are no problems.

These eggs are dry and crumbly because they were overcooked and stirred too frequently.

Potato, Bacon and Egg Scramble FAST

PREP: 10 min **COOK:** 10 min ▪ **5 SERVINGS**

1 lb small red potatoes (6 or 7), cubed
6 large eggs
1/3 cup milk
1/4 teaspoon salt
1/8 teaspoon pepper
2 tablespoons butter or margarine
4 medium green onions, sliced (1/4 cup)
5 slices bacon, crisply cooked and crumbled

1. In 2-quart saucepan, heat 1 inch water to boiling. Add potatoes. Cover and heat to boiling; reduce heat to medium-low. Cook covered 6 to 8 minutes or until potatoes are tender; drain.

2. In medium bowl, beat eggs, milk, salt and pepper with fork or wire whisk until well mixed; set aside.

3. In 10-inch skillet, melt butter over medium-high heat. Cook potatoes in butter 3 to 5 minutes, turning occasionally, until light brown. Stir in onions. Cook 1 minute, stirring constantly.

4. Pour egg mixture into skillet with potatoes and onions. As mixture begins to set at bottom and side, gently lift cooked portions with spatula so that thin, uncooked portion can flow to bottom. Avoid constant stirring. Cook 3 to 4 minutes or until eggs are thickened throughout but still moist. Sprinkle with bacon.

1 SERVING: CAL. 255 (CAL. FROM FAT 135); FAT 15g (SAT. FAT 6g); CHOL. 275mg; SODIUM 340mg; CARBS. 20g (FIBER 2g); PRO. 12g
% DAILY VALUE: VIT. A 12%; VIT. C 14%; CALC. 8%; IRON 16%
EXCHANGES: 1 STARCH, 1 VEGETABLE, 1 HIGH-FAT MEAT, 1 FAT
CARB. CHOICES: 1

▲ **Brunch Eggs on English Muffins**

Brunch Eggs on English Muffins

PREP: 10 min **COOK:** 15 min ▪ **4 SERVINGS**

1 teaspoon butter or margarine
2 teaspoons all-purpose flour
1/2 cup milk
1/4 cup shredded Cheddar cheese (1 oz)
2 teaspoons grated Parmesan cheese
1 teaspoon chopped fresh or 1/4 teaspoon dried basil leaves
Dash of ground red pepper (cayenne)
2 English muffins, split
4 thin slices fully cooked Canadian-style bacon (2 oz)
8 large eggs, beaten
Freshly ground pepper

1. In 1-quart nonstick saucepan, melt butter over low heat. Stir in flour; remove from heat. Gradually stir in milk. Heat to boiling, stirring constantly. Boil and stir 1 minute; remove from heat. Stir in cheeses, basil and red pepper; keep warm.

2. Toast English muffins. In 10-inch nonstick skillet, cook bacon over medium heat until brown on both sides. Remove from skillet; keep warm.

3. Heat same skillet over medium heat. Pour eggs into skillet. As mixture begins to set at bottom and side, gently lift cooked portions with spatula so that thin, uncooked portion can flow to bottom. Avoid constant stirring. Cook 3 to 4 minutes or until eggs are thickened throughout but still moist.

4. Place 1 slice bacon on each muffin half. Top with eggs. Spoon about 2 tablespoons sauce over eggs. Sprinkle with pepper.

1 SERVING: CAL. 255 (CAL. FROM FAT 145); FAT 16g (SAT. FAT 6g); CHOL. 440mg; SODIUM 520mg; CARBS. 17g (FIBER 1g); PRO. 21g; **% DAILY VALUE:** VIT. A 14%; VIT. C 0%; CALC. 18%; IRON 12% **EXCHANGES:** 1/2 STARCH, 3 MEDIUM-FAT MEAT **CARB. CHOICES:** 1

French Omelet FAST

PREP: 10 min ■ **1 SERVING**

Serving an omelet on a warm plate is a nice touch. Right before starting to cook, just rinse the serving plate with hot water to warm it, then dry it thoroughly.

2 teaspoons butter or margarine
2 large eggs, beaten

1. In 8-inch skillet or omelet pan, heat butter over medium-high heat just until butter is hot and sizzling. As butter melts, tilt pan to coat bottom.

2. Quickly pour eggs into pan. While rapidly sliding pan back and forth over heat, quickly stir with spatula to spread eggs continuously over bottom of pan as they thicken. Let stand over heat a few seconds to lightly brown bottom of omelet. Do not overcook; omelet will continue to cook after folding.

3. To remove from skillet, first run spatula under one edge of omelet, folding about one-third of it to the center. Transfer to plate by tilting skillet, letting flat, unfolded edge of omelet slide out onto plate. Using edge of skillet as a guide, flip folded edge of omelet over the flat portion on the plate.

1 SERVING: CAL. 215 (CAL. FROM FAT 160); FAT 18g (SAT. FAT 8g); CHOL. 445mg; SODIUM 170mg; CARBS. 1g (FIBER 0g); PRO. 13g **% DAILY VALUE:** VIT. A 16%; VIT. C 0%; CALC. 4%; IRON 6% **EXCHANGES:** 2 MEDIUM-FAT MEAT, 1 1/2 FAT **CARB. CHOICES:** 0

LIGHTER FRENCH OMELET

For 8 grams of fat and 130 calories per serving, substitute 1/2 cup fat-free cholesterol-free egg product for the eggs.

CHEESE OMELET Before folding omelet, sprinkle with 1/4 cup shredded Cheddar, Monterey Jack or Swiss cheese or 1/4 cup crumbled blue cheese.

DENVER OMELET Before adding eggs to pan, cook 2 tablespoons chopped fully cooked ham, 1 tablespoon finely chopped bell pepper and 1 tablespoon finely chopped onion in butter about 2 minutes, stirring frequently. Continue as directed in Step 2.

HAM AND CHEESE OMELET Before folding omelet, sprinkle with 2 tablespoons shredded Cheddar, Monterey Jack or Swiss cheese and 2 tablespoons finely chopped fully cooked smoked ham or deli ham slices.

HOW TO MAKE A FRENCH OMELET

▲ **1.** To remove from skillet, first run spatula under one edge of omelet, folding about one-third of it to the center.

2. Transfer to plate by tilting skillet, letting flat, unfolded edge of omelet slide out onto plate. Using edge of skillet as a guide, flip folded edge of omelet over the flat portion on the plate. ▼

Salmon and Cream Cheese Omelet FAST

PREP: 5 min **COOK:** 10 min **STAND:** 2 min ▪ **4 SERVINGS**

Omelets make a quick supper! Serve with biscuits and a salad or fresh fruit.

- 4 teaspoons butter or margarine
- 8 large eggs, beaten
- 1/2 cup soft cream cheese with chives and onion
- 1 cup flaked smoked salmon
- Chopped fresh chives, if desired

1. In 8-inch omelet pan or skillet, heat 2 teaspoons of the butter over medium-high heat until butter is hot and sizzling.

2. Pour half of the beaten eggs (about 1 cup) into pan. As eggs begin to set at bottom and side, gently lift cooked portions with spatula so that thin, uncooked portion can flow to bottom. Avoid constant stirring. Cook 3 to 4 minutes or until eggs are thickened throughout but still moist.

3. Spoon 1/4 cup of the cream cheese in dollops evenly over omelet; sprinkle with 1/2 cup of the salmon. Tilt skillet and slip spatula under omelet to loosen. Remove from heat. Fold omelet in half; let stand 2 minutes. Transfer to serving plate; keep warm.

4. Repeat with remaining ingredients to make second omelet. Cut each omelet crosswise in half to serve; sprinkle with chives.

1 SERVING: CAL. 290 (CAL. FROM FAT 200); FAT 22g (SAT. FAT 10g); CHOL. 460mg; SODIUM 470mg; CARBS. 3g (FIBER 0g); PRO. 20g **% DAILY VALUE:** VIT. A 20%; VIT. C 0%; CALC. 6%; IRON 10% **EXCHANGES:** 3 HIGH-FAT MEAT **CARB. CHOICES:** 0

Puffy Omelet

PREP: 15 min **BAKE:** 15 min ▪ **2 SERVINGS**

- 4 large eggs, separated
- 1/4 cup water
- 1/4 teaspoon salt
- 1/8 teaspoon pepper
- 1 tablespoon butter or margarine
- Italian Tomato Sauce (page 404), salsa or tomato pasta sauce, heated, if desired

1. Heat oven to 325°F.

2. In medium bowl, beat egg whites, water and salt with electric mixer on high speed until stiff but not dry. In small bowl, beat egg yolks and pepper on high speed about 3 minutes or until very thick and lemon colored. Fold egg yolks into egg whites.

3. In 10-inch ovenproof skillet, melt butter over medium heat. As butter melts, tilt skillet to coat bottom. Pour egg mixture into skillet. Gently level surface; reduce heat to low. Cook about 5 minutes or until puffy and bottom is light brown. (Carefully lift omelet at edge to see color.)

4. Bake uncovered 12 to 15 minutes or until knife inserted in center comes out clean.

5. Tilt skillet and slip pancake turner or metal spatula under omelet to loosen. Fold omelet in half, being careful not to break it. Slip onto warm serving plate. Serve with Italian Tomato Sauce.

1 SERVING: CAL. 200 (CAL. FROM FAT 145); FAT 16g (SAT. FAT 7g); CHOL. 440mg; SODIUM 460mg; CARBS. 1g (FIBER 0g); PRO. 13g **% DAILY VALUE:** VIT. A 16%; VIT. C 0%; CALC. 4%; IRON 6% **EXCHANGES:** 2 MEDIUM-FAT MEAT, 1 FAT **CARB. CHOICES:** 0

Savory Italian Frittata

LOW-FAT

PREP: 10 min **COOK:** 16 min ▪ **6 SERVINGS**

- 8 large eggs
- 1 tablespoon chopped fresh or 1/2 teaspoon dried basil leaves
- 1 tablespoon chopped fresh or 1/2 teaspoon dried mint leaves
- 1 tablespoon chopped fresh or 1/2 teaspoon dried sage leaves
- 1 tablespoon freshly grated Parmesan cheese
- 1/2 teaspoon salt
- 1/8 teaspoon pepper
- 1/4 cup diced fully cooked ham or prosciutto (2 oz)
- 1 tablespoon butter or margarine
- 1 small onion, finely chopped (1/4 cup)

1. In medium bowl, beat all ingredients except ham, butter and onion thoroughly with fork or wire whisk until well mixed. Stir in ham.

2. In 10-inch nonstick skillet, melt butter over medium-high heat. Cook onion in butter 4 to 5 minutes, stirring frequently, until crisp-tender; reduce heat to medium-low.

3. Pour egg mixture into skillet. Cover and cook 9 to 11 minutes or until eggs are set around edge and light brown on bottom. Cut into wedges.

1 SERVING: CAL. 140 (CAL. FROM FAT 90); FAT 10g (SAT. FAT 4g); CHOL. 290mg; SODIUM 390mg; CARBS. 2g (FIBER 0g); PRO. 10g
% DAILY VALUE: VIT. A 10%; VIT. C 0%; CALC. 6%; IRON 6%
EXCHANGES: 1 1/2 MEDIUM-FAT MEAT, 1/2 FAT **CARB. CHOICES:** 0

LIGHTER SAVORY ITALIAN FRITTATA

For 3 grams of fat and 80 calories per serving, substitute 2 cups fat-free cholesterol-free egg product for the eggs. Use fully cooked turkey ham.

Ham, Vegetable and Cheese Frittata

PREP: 15 min **COOK:** 15 min ▪ **4 SERVINGS**

- 1 tablespoon butter or margarine
- 1/2 cup thinly sliced red bell pepper
- 1/2 cup thinly sliced onion
- 1/2 cup chopped zucchini
- 1 cup chopped cooked ham
- 4 large eggs
- 1/4 cup milk
- 1/4 teaspoon salt
- Dash of pepper
- 1 medium roma (plum) tomato, sliced
- 1/4 cup shredded Italian-style cheese blend (1 oz)
- 1 tablespoon sliced fresh basil leaves, if desired

1. In 10-inch nonstick skillet, melt butter over medium heat. Cook bell pepper, onion, zucchini and ham in butter 3 to 4 minutes, stirring occasionally, until vegetables are crisp-tender and ham is starting to brown.

2. Meanwhile, in small bowl, beat eggs, milk, salt and pepper with fork or wire whisk until well mixed.

3. Pour egg mixture over ham mixture. Cook over medium heat 6 to 8 minutes, stirring gently, until eggs are almost set. Reduce heat to low. Top with tomato slices and cheese. Cover and cook 2 to 3 minutes or until cheese is melted and eggs are completely set. Sprinkle with basil. Cut into wedges.

1 SERVING: CAL. 205 (CAL. FROM FAT 115); FAT 13g (SAT. FAT 5g); CHOL. 245mg; SODIUM 780mg; CARBS. 5g (FIBER 1g); PRO. 17g
% DAILY VALUE: VIT. A 26%; VIT. C 22%; CALC. 10%; IRON 6%
EXCHANGES: 1 VEGETABLE, 2 MEDIUM-FAT MEAT, 1/2 FAT
CARB. CHOICES: 0

◀ **Ham, Vegetable and Cheese Frittata**

Eggs Benedict

PREP: 30 min ■ **6 SERVINGS**

As one story goes, Delmonico's Restaurant in New York was the birthplace of this classic brunch dish. Years ago regular patrons, Mr. and Mrs. LeGrand Benedict, complained of nothing new on the lunch menu. Following Mrs. Benedict's suggestions, the chef created this now-famous international dish, naming it after them.

- Hollandaise Sauce (page 410)
- 3 English muffins
- 3 tablespoons butter or margarine, softened
- 1 teaspoon butter or margarine
- 6 thin slices Canadian-style bacon or fully cooked ham
- 6 Poached Eggs
- Paprika, if desired

1. Make Hollandaise Sauce; keep warm.

2. Split English muffins; toast. Spread each muffin half with some of the 3 tablespoons butter; keep warm.

3. In 10-inch skillet, melt 1 teaspoon butter over medium heat. Cook bacon in butter until light brown on both sides; keep warm.

4. Make Poached Eggs.

5. Place 1 slice bacon on each muffin half. Top with egg. Spoon warm Hollandaise Sauce over eggs. Sprinkle with paprika.

1 SERVING: CAL. 415 (CAL. FROM FAT 295); FAT 33g (SAT. FAT 17g); CHOL. 400mg; SODIUM 670mg; CARBS. 14g (FIBER 1g); PRO. 15g
% DAILY VALUE: VIT. A 26%; VIT. C 0%; CALC. 10%; IRON 10%
EXCHANGES: 1 STARCH, 1 1/2 HIGH-FAT MEAT, 4 FAT
CARB. CHOICES: 1

HOW TO POACH EGGS

Break each egg into custard cup or saucer. Holding dish close to water's surface, carefully slip eggs into water.

Huevos Rancheros

PREP: 45 min **COOK:** 15 min ■ **6 SERVINGS**

Huevos rancheros—Spanish for "rancher's eggs"—originated as "eggs ranchera." Today, it's commonly known as ranch-style or country-style eggs. It's a hearty combination of fried eggs, sausage, salsa and tortillas. When buying tortillas, check for freshness by making sure edges are not dry or cracked.

- 1 1/4 cups Salsa (page 416) or purchased salsa
- 1/2 lb bulk chorizo or pork sausage
- Vegetable oil
- 6 corn tortillas (6 or 7 inch)
- 6 Fried Eggs (page 220)
- 1 1/2 cups shredded Cheddar cheese (6 oz)

1. Make Salsa.

2. In 8-inch skillet, cook sausage over medium heat 8 to 10 minutes, stirring occasionally, until no longer pink; drain. Remove from skillet; keep warm.

3. In same skillet, heat 1/8 inch oil over medium heat just until hot. Cook 1 tortilla at a time in oil about 1 minute, turning once, until crisp; drain.

4. In 1-quart saucepan, heat Salsa, stirring occasionally, until hot.

5. Make Fried Eggs.

6. Spread 1 tablespoon Salsa over each tortilla to soften. Place egg on each tortilla. Top with salsa, sausage, additional salsa and cheese.

1 SERVING: CAL. 465 (CAL. FROM FAT 295); FAT 33g (SAT. FAT 14g); CHOL. 275mg; SODIUM 1,010mg; CARBS. 17g (FIBER 2g); PRO. 25g
% DAILY VALUE: VIT. A 32%; VIT. C 6%; CALC. 24%; IRON 12%
EXCHANGES: 1 STARCH, 3 HIGH-FAT MEAT, 2 FAT
CARB. CHOICES: 1

Eggs with Kielbasa FAST

PREP: 5 min **COOK:** 11 min ▪ **4 SERVINGS**

Kielbasa is a smoked Polish sausage that's usually made from pork, although beef may be added. It comes in a horseshoe-shaped ring that's about 1 1/2 inches in diameter.

- 2 teaspoons vegetable oil
- 1/2 lb fully cooked kielbasa sausage, cut lengthwise in half, then cut crosswise into slices
- 1 large onion, sliced
- 1 medium green bell pepper, thinly sliced
- 8 large eggs
- 1/2 cup milk
- 1/4 teaspoon salt
- 1/8 to 1/4 teaspoon pepper

1. In 10-inch skillet, heat oil over medium heat. Cook kielbasa, onion and bell pepper in oil about 5 minutes, stirring occasionally, until vegetables are tender.

2. Meanwhile, in medium bowl, beat eggs, milk, salt and pepper with fork or wire whisk until blended.

3. Pour egg mixture over kielbasa mixture. As mixture begins to set at bottom and side, gently lift cooked portions with spatula so that thin, uncooked portion can flow to bottom. Avoid constant stirring. Cook 4 to 5 minutes or until eggs are thickened throughout but still moist.

1 SERVING: CAL. 385 (CAL. FROM FAT 260); FAT 29g (SAT. FAT 10g); CHOL. 460mg; SODIUM 820mg; CARBS. 10g (FIBER 1g); PRO. 21g
% DAILY VALUE: VIT. A 16%; VIT. C 24%; CALC. 10%; IRON 10%
EXCHANGES: 1/2 STARCH, 3 HIGH-FAT MEAT, 1 FAT
CARB. CHOICES: 1/2

Breakfast Tacos FAST

PREP: 15 min **COOK:** 5 min ▪ **6 SERVINGS**

- 4 large eggs
- 1/4 teaspoon garlic salt
- 1/4 teaspoon pepper
- 1/4 cup chopped green bell pepper
- 4 medium green onions, chopped (1/4 cup)
- 1 tablespoon butter or margarine
- 1/2 cup shredded Monterey Jack cheese with jalapeño peppers (2 oz)
- 6 taco shells
- 1 cup shredded lettuce
- 1 small avocado, sliced (about 3/4 cup)
- 1/4 cup thick-and-chunky salsa

1. In small bowl, beat eggs, garlic salt and pepper thoroughly with fork or wire whisk. Stir in bell pepper and onions.

2. In 8-inch skillet, melt butter over medium heat. Pour egg mixture into skillet.

3. As mixture begins to set at bottom and side, gently lift cooked portions with spatula so that thin, uncooked portions can flow to bottom. Avoid constant stirring. Cook 3 to 4 minutes or until eggs are thickened throughout. Gently stir in cheese.

4. Heat taco shells as directed on package. Place lettuce in taco shells. Spoon eggs onto lettuce. Top with avocado and salsa.

1 SERVING: CAL. 235 (CAL. FROM FAT 145); FAT 16g (SAT. FAT 4g); CHOL. 155mg; SODIUM 250mg; CARBS. 13g; (FIBER 3g); PRO. 8g
% DAILY VALUE: VIT. A 12%; VIT. C 10%; CALC. 12%; IRON 8%
EXCHANGES: 1 STARCH, 1 HIGH-FAT MEAT, 1 FAT **CARB. CHOICES:** 1

◀ **Breakfast Tacos**

Deviled Eggs FAST

PREP: 15 min ▪ **12 SERVINGS**

Very fresh eggs are difficult to peel. So plan ahead, purchase eggs a week earlier so they'll peel easily. Another trick is to peel eggs under cold running water. To prevent eggs from tipping on the serving plate, cut a thin slice from the bottom of each egg white half before filling.

- 6 Hard-Cooked Eggs (page 220)
- 3 tablespoons mayonnaise, salad dressing or half-and-half
- 1/2 teaspoon ground mustard
- 1/8 teaspoon salt
- 1/8 teaspoon pepper

1. Peel eggs. Cut lengthwise in half. Slip out yolks into small bowl; mash with fork.

2. Stir mayonnaise, mustard, salt and pepper into yolks. Fill whites with egg yolk mixture, heaping it lightly. Cover and refrigerate up to 24 hours.

1 SERVING: CAL. 55 (CAL. FROM FAT 45); FAT 5g (SAT. FAT 1g); CHOL. 110mg; SODIUM 80mg; CARBS. 0g (FIBER 0g); PRO. 3g
% DAILY VALUE: VIT. A 4%; VIT. C 0%; CALC. 0%; IRON 2%
EXCHANGES: 1/2 HIGH-FAT MEAT **CARB. CHOICES:** 0

LIGHTER DEVILED EGGS

For 1 gram of fat and 25 calories per serving, mash only 6 yolk halves in step 1 (reserve remaining yolks for another use or discard). Use fat-free mayonnaise. Stir in 1/3 cup finely chopped zucchini.

DENVER DEVILED EGGS Mix 1 tablespoon each finely chopped red bell pepper, green bell pepper and fully cooked ham into egg yolk mixture.

DEVILED EGGS WITH OLIVES Omit mustard. Mix 1/4 cup finely chopped ripe or pimento-stuffed olives and 1/4 teaspoon curry powder into egg yolk mixture.

ZESTY DEVILED EGGS Mix 1 to 2 tablespoons chopped fresh parsley and 1 teaspoon prepared horseradish into egg yolk mixture.

▲ **Deviled Eggs, Denver Deviled Eggs, Deviled Eggs with Olives and Zesty Deviled Eggs**

LEARN WITH Betty — HARD COOKED EGGS

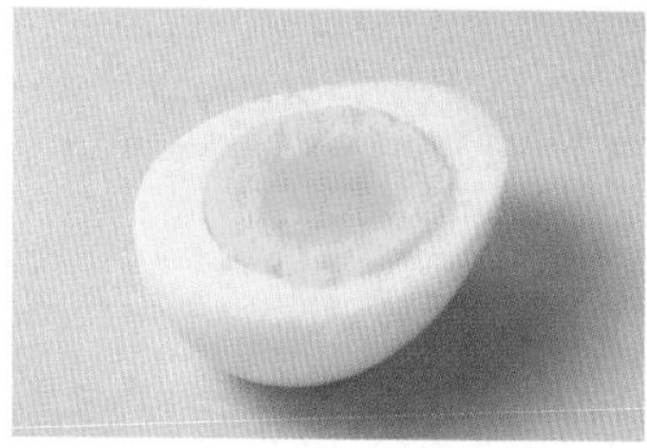

These eggs were not cooked long enough; the center isn't completely cooked.

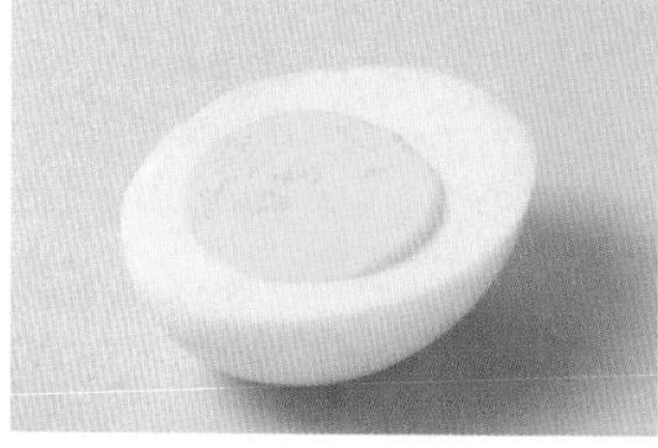

The center of these eggs is completely cooked; there are no problems.

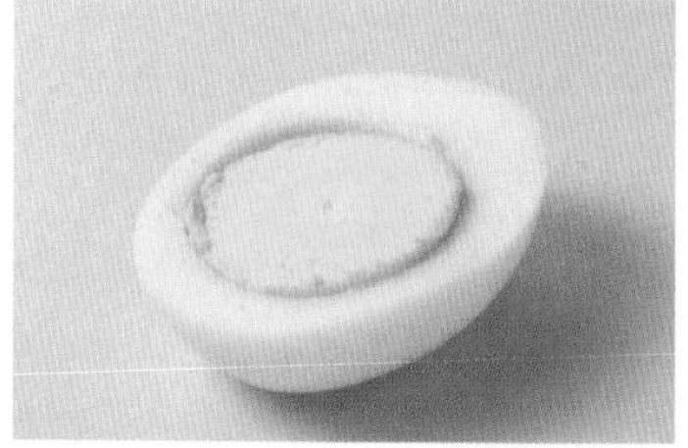

These eggs were overcooked, forming a green or gray ring around the yolk.

Cheese Basics

Explore the wonderful world of cheeses! Discover the many varieties of domestic, imported and artisanal cheeses with all of their different flavors, textures, colors and shapes. And delight in the excitement they'll add to your cooking and eating pleasure.

Legend has it that cheese was "discovered" 4,000 years ago when an Arabian merchant crossing the desert was pleased to find that the milk he'd carried all day in a pouch had transformed into dinner—thin, watery whey and thick curds. To his surprise, it tasted delicious. Although cheese making is more scientific today, the process is similar.

The method used to process milk accounts for the major differences among cheeses, along with their fat contents. All cheeses fall into three broad categories: natural, processed and pasteurized process.

KINDS OF CHEESE

Natural cheeses are either unripened or ripened. Unripened cheeses are made by coagulating milk proteins with acid; examples include cottage cheese and cream cheese. Ripened cheeses are made by coagulating milk proteins with enzymes and culture acids; examples include Cheddar and Parmesan. Due to the extensive variety of natural cheeses, they are categorized by hardness. Check the Natural Cheeses chart on page 231.

Processed cheeses are made by heating one or more natural cheeses and adding emulsifying salts. Processed cheeses contain more moisture than natural cheeses.

Pasteurized process cheeses are those processed using heat and include American cheese, cheese spreads and cheese foods.

ARTISANAL CHEESE

These cheeses are truly a labor of love! They're handcrafted in small batches by artisan cheesemakers in individually owned or small regional companies. To the delight of cheese lovers everywhere, their products are now showing up in cheese cases around the country. Some of these cheeses have unique ingredient combinations like dried cranberries and wild rice. Others are made from the milk of cows grazing on specialized grasses; still others use distinctive processing methods. But all have that same unique ingredient—the artisans' passion for making cheese!

STORING CHEESE

- Soft cheeses like cottage, cream, mascarpone and ricotta are high in moisture, making them more perishable than firmer cheeses. Refrigerate tightly covered and use by the package expiration date.
- Store semisoft, firm and hard cheeses tightly wrapped in waxed paper, foil or plastic wrap in the refrigerator 4 to 8 weeks.
- Store hard cheeses, like Parmesan and Asiago in grated or shredded form, in sealed containers in the refrigerator up to 2 weeks or freeze up to 3 months. If frozen, use directly from freezer.
- Shredded cheeses lose moisture and develop mold easier than solid pieces. Wrap leftover shredded cheese and use within 2 days.
- Store very strong smelling cheeses like blue and Limburger separately and double-wrapped in airtight containers so they don't impart aromas and flavors to other cheeses and foods.
- Freezing hard cheese causes the texture to become crumbly, so cheese that has been frozen is best used as a topping or filling for melting, as an ingredient in casseroles or filled pasta or to sprinkle on hot or cold foods. Freeze cheese in airtight containers up to 2 months.

MOLDY CHEESE

If cheese develops surface mold, cut off about 1/2 inch from each affected side; the remaining cheese should be used within a week. If mold appears on blue cheese (besides the natural blue veining) or on soft cheese like cottage cheese, throw it out. Reduce the chances of mold growth by changing the wrapping each time the cheese is used.

CREATING A CHEESE TRAY

Cheese trays are a flavorful adventure. Serve them as an appetizer platter, a separate meal course or, as in the European tradition—as dessert. With hundreds of domestic and imported cheeses to choose from, you'll discover that creating a beautiful platter is easy. Here's how:

- Choose three to five varieties of cheese with contrasting flavors, from mild to medium to strong, and with textures from creamy to hard. For example, select Brie, blue, Havarti, Jarlsberg, sharp Cheddar and Parmesan. See the Natural Cheeses chart, page 231, for ideas. The combinations are endless!
- Plan on 2 to 3 ounces of cheese per person.
- Most cheeses taste best when served at room temperature. Take cheese out of the refrigerator, cover it and let it stand for 30 minutes to 1 hour before serving. There's one exception; soft cheeses like mascarpone and queso blanco should be removed from the refrigerator just before serving.
- Labeling each type of cheese is a great touch and helps everyone remember favorites.
- Provide a separate serving knife or cheese cutters for each cheese.
- Complement the cheese with fresh and dried fruits, nuts, olives, crackers and breads.

COOKING WITH CHEESE

When melting cheese into a sauce, shred or grate it first for quick melting and even blending. Keep the heat turned down to low, add the cheese as the last ingredient and heat the mixture only long enough to melt.

When melting cheese on top of baked dishes, follow recipe directions or add during the last 10 to 15 minutes of baking time to avoid overbrowning or burning the cheese.

NATURAL CHEESES

Type	Description	Best Use
VERY HARD (GRATING)		
Asiago	Mild when young; nutty and semisharp when aged	Serve as a table cheese for pasta, potatoes, rice, salads, vegetables; grated melts best
Parmesan	Sharp, savory, salty; intensifies with age	Salads, cooked dishes, casseroles, pizza; serve as a table cheese
Romano	Sharp, robust; similar to but richer than Parmesan	Pasta, soups, salads, pizza, egg dishes, stuffings, savory pastries; grated melts best
HARD		
Cheddar	Rich, nutty, from mild to full-bodied bite	Party trays, sandwiches, burgers, pasta, sauces, egg dishes; melts very well
Edam	Mild, slightly salty, nutty	Sandwiches, snacks, salads, soups; shredded melts best
Gouda	Mellow, rich caramel	Sandwiches, snacks, salads, soups; shredded melts best
Gruyère	Mellow and buttery with a nutlike flavor	Fondues, baked dishes, onion soup; excellent melting cheese
Jarlsberg	Slightly sweet, nutty	Baked dishes, sandwiches, snacks
Kasseri	Slightly tart with hints of olive and sweetness	Pasta, snacks
Swiss	Mild, very fruity, mouth-tingling tang	Sandwiches, egg dishes, breads, vegetables; shredded melts best
SEMISOFT		
Blue	Rich, robust, salty with a lingering tanginess	Vegetable, fruit and pasta salads; grilled meats; spreads; dressings; dips; crumbled melts best
Brick	From mild and sweet to savory with a spicy tang	Sandwiches, casseroles; shredded melts best
Colby	Mild to mellow; lightly sweet to sharp and tangy	Sandwiches, sauces, casseroles, snacks; grated melts best
Curds	Mild and milky, rubbery	Snacks
Feta	Very sharp, salty	Greek dishes, salads, hot and cold pasta dishes, egg dishes; melts best in sauces
Fontina	Delicate, nutty with a hint of honey	Sandwiches, snacks, baked dishes; melts very well
Gorgonzola	Robust and spicy	Salads, pasta, soufflés, spreads, dressings, dips; crumbled melts best
Havarti	Buttery, mild yet tangy	Sandwiches, baked potatoes, egg dishes, salads; shredded melts best
Monterey Jack	Mild and slightly zesty; nutty with age	Sandwiches, burgers, salads, Mexican-style dishes; shredded and sliced melt best
Mozzarella (low-moisture, part-skim)	Delicate, mild, milky and stringy	Salads, sandwiches, appetizers, pizza, snacks; shredded and sliced melt best

(continues)

NATURAL CHEESES *(continued)*

Type	Description	Best Use
SEMISOFT		
Muenster	Mild to mellow and buttery	Sandwiches, salads, Mexican-style dishes, snacks; shredded melts best
Port du Salut	Nutty, almost meaty	Sandwiches, snacks; melts best in sauces
Provolone	Creamy, firm, slightly smoky	Sandwiches, pizza, fillings, salads; shredded melts best
Queso Blanco	Slightly salty, fresh and milky	Soups, salads, stuffings, snacks; softens and holds shape when heated but doesn't melt
Reblochon	Mild with flavor of fresh-crushed walnuts	Snacks
Roquefort	Rich, melt-in-your-mouth texture with a clean, sharp, lingering tang	Vegetable, fruit and pasta salads; grilled meats; spreads; dressings; dips
Stilton	Rich, spicy with a blended flavor of blue and Cheddar cheeses	Salads, snacks
Tilsit	Slightly sharp, becoming more pungent with age	Baked dishes, salads, snacks
SOFT		
Boursin	Mild, rich, often seasoned with herbs or pepper	Spreads
Brie	Rich and buttery	Party trays, sandwiches, snacks; softens and flows when heated
Camembert	Creamy, mild to pungent with mushroom undertones	Party trays, sandwiches, snacks; softens and flows when heated
Cottage, dry or creamed	Mild and milky	Baked dishes, salads
Cream	Rich, slightly tangy	Baked dishes, cheesecakes, salads, snacks, spreads; melts best in sauces
Farmer	Mild, fresh with a faintly sour tinge	Baked dishes
Fresh Mozzarella	Delicate, milky flavor	Salads, sandwiches, appetizers, pizza
Limburger	Very strong, robust, strong-smelling	Appetizers, snacks; sliced melts best
Mascarpone	Very soft, mild, sweet, butterlike	Fillings, toppings, dips, spreads, sauces; melts best in sauces
Montrachet (Bûcheron, Chèvre); made from goat's milk	Creamy, fresh, mildly tangy	Appetizers, baked dishes, sauces
Neufchâtel	Mild, rich with a hint of salt	Baked dishes, cheesecakes, salads, snacks, spreads
Ricotta	Mild, slightly sweet	Fillings, stuffings, spreads, cheesecakes

CHEESE

VERY HARD AND HARD CHEESES

VERY HARD

Asiago

Parmesan

Romano

HARD

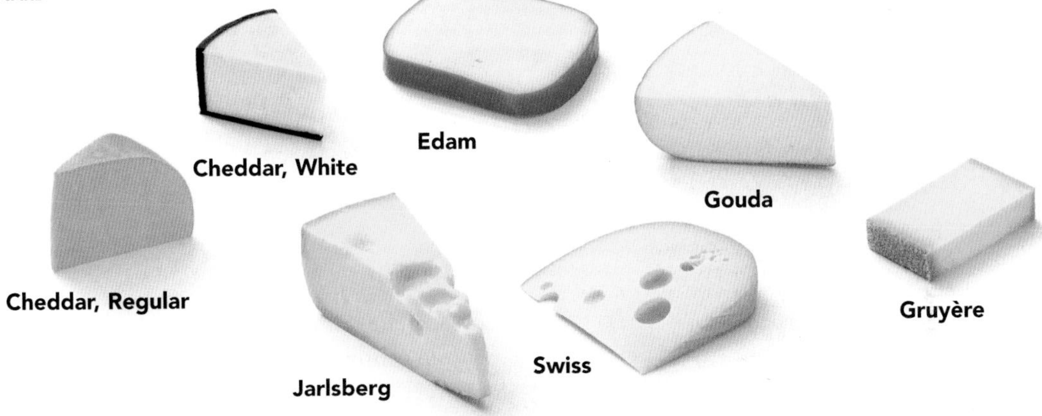

Cheddar, White

Edam

Gouda

Cheddar, Regular

Jarlsberg

Swiss

Gruyère

SEMISOFT CHEESES

Blue

Brick

Colby

Curds

Feta

Fontina

Gorgonzola

Havarti

Monterey Jack

Mozzarella (low-moisture, part skim)

Muenster

Port du Salut

Provolone

Queso Blanco

Reblochon

Stilton

Tilsit

CHEESE *(continued)*

SOFT CHEESES

- Boursin
- Brie
- Camembert
- Cottage, creamed
- Chevrè (goat) cheese
- Cream cheese
- Farmer
- Fresh mozzarella
- Limburger
- Mascarpone
- Montrachet
- Ricotta

Quiche Lorraine

PREP: 25 min **BAKE:** 1 hr 4 min **STAND:** 10 min ▪ **6 SERVINGS**

Hands down, this is one of the best quiches you'll ever taste! The velvety-smooth filling is rich and flavorful, and prebaking the crust makes it crisp and flaky—not soggy.

- Pastry for 9-Inch One-Crust Pie (page 123)
- 8 slices bacon, crisply cooked and crumbled (1/2 cup)
- 1 cup shredded Swiss cheese (4 oz)
- 1/3 cup finely chopped onion
- 4 large eggs
- 2 cups whipping (heavy) cream or half-and-half
- 1/4 teaspoon salt
- 1/4 teaspoon pepper
- 1/8 teaspoon ground red pepper (cayenne)

1. Heat oven to 425°F. Make pastry; after folding pastry into fourths, place in 9-inch quiche dish or pie plate. Unfold and ease into dish, pressing firmly against bottom and side.

2. Carefully line pastry with a double thickness of foil, gently pressing foil to bottom and side of pastry. Let foil extend over edge to prevent excessive browning. Bake 10 minutes; carefully remove foil and bake 2 to 4 minutes longer or until pastry just begins to brown and has become set. If crust bubbles, gently push bubbles down with back of spoon.

3. Sprinkle bacon, cheese and onion in pie crust. In large bowl, beat eggs slightly with fork or wire whisk. Beat in remaining ingredients. Pour into pie crust.

4. Reduce oven temperature to 325°F. Bake 45 to 50 minutes or until knife inserted in center comes out clean. Let stand 10 minutes before serving.

1 SERVING: CAL. 600 (CAL. FROM FAT 460); FAT 51g (SAT. FAT 25g); CHOL. 255mg; SODIUM 550mg; CARBS. 20g (FIBER 1g); PRO. 16g
% DAILY VALUE: VIT. A 24%; VIT. C 0%; CALC. 26%; IRON 8%
EXCHANGES: 1 STARCH, 1 1/2 HIGH-FAT MEAT, 1 VEGETABLE, 8 FAT **CARB. CHOICES:** 1

SEAFOOD QUICHE Substitute 1 cup chopped cooked crabmeat (patted dry), shrimp, seafood sticks (imitation crabmeat) or salmon for the bacon. Use 1/3 cup finely chopped green onions; increase salt to 1/2 teaspoon.

Ham and Cheddar Strata

PREP: 15 min **BAKE:** 1 hr 10 min **STAND:** 10 min ■
8 SERVINGS

Make this strata ahead of time. Follow the directions through Step 3, then cover and refrigerate up to 24 hours.

12 slices bread
2 cups cut-up fully cooked smoked ham (about 10 oz)
2 cups shredded Cheddar cheese (8 oz)
8 medium green onions, sliced (1/2 cup)
6 large eggs
2 cups milk
1 teaspoon ground mustard
1/4 teaspoon red pepper sauce
Paprika

1. Heat oven to 300°F. Spray 13 × 9-inch glass baking dish with cooking spray.

2. Trim crusts from bread. Arrange 6 slices bread in baking dish. Layer ham, cheese and onions on bread in dish. Cut remaining bread slices diagonally in half; arrange on onions.

3. In medium bowl, beat eggs, milk, mustard and pepper sauce with fork or wire whisk; pour evenly over bread. Sprinkle with paprika.

4. Bake uncovered 1 hour to 1 hour 10 minutes or until center is set and bread is golden brown. Let stand 10 minutes before cutting.

1 SERVING: CAL. 345 (CAL. FROM FAT 170); FAT 19g (SAT. FAT 9g); CHOL. 215mg; SODIUM 930mg; CARBS. 20g (FIBER 1g); PRO. 24g
% DAILY VALUE: VIT. A 14%; VIT. C 2%; CALC. 28%; IRON 12%
EXCHANGES: 1 STARCH, 3 MEDIUM-FAT MEAT, 1 FAT
CARB. CHOICES: 1

CUTTING AND SHREDDING CHEESE

Cheese shreds and grates more easily right from the refrigerator or if frozen for about 30 minutes. For very soft cheese, use a grater with large holes, or finely chop or crumble instead.

Mold-ripened or blue-veined cheeses are crumbly. So cut them with dental floss or heavy thread, or freeze up to 30 minutes first.

Hash Brown Potato and Egg Bake

PREP: 20 min **COOK:** 10 min **BAKE:** 50 min ■
12 SERVINGS

1/2 lb bacon, chopped
1 medium onion, chopped (1/2 cup)
1 bag (30 oz) frozen shredded hash brown potatoes, thawed and drained
2 cups shredded Cheddar cheese (8 oz)
1/4 cup grated Parmesan cheese
9 large eggs
1 1/4 cups milk
1 container (8 oz) sour cream
1 teaspoon salt
1/4 teaspoon pepper
1 teaspoon ground mustard
1/2 cup cornflake crumbs
2 tablespoons butter or margarine, melted

1. Heat oven to 350°F. Spray 13 × 9-inch glass baking dish with cooking spray.

2. In 10-inch skillet, cook bacon and onion over medium-high heat about 10 minutes, stirring occasionally, until bacon is crisp and onion is tender; drain on paper towels.

3. In large bowl, toss bacon mixture, potatoes and cheeses. Spoon into baking dish. In same bowl, beat eggs, milk, sour cream, salt, pepper and mustard with fork or wire whisk until well mixed. Pour egg mixture over potato mixture.

4. Bake uncovered 35 minutes.

5. Meanwhile, in small bowl, toss cornflake crumbs and butter. Sprinkle cornflake mixture over partially baked casserole. Bake uncovered 10 to 15 minutes longer or until knife inserted in center comes out clean.

1 SERVING: CAL. 410 (CAL. FROM FAT 250); FAT 28g (SAT. FAT 12g); CHOL. 205mg; SODIUM 550mg; CARBS. 24g (FIBER 2g); PRO. 15g
% DAILY VALUE: VIT. A 14%; VIT. C 6%; CALC. 20%; IRON 8%
EXCHANGES: 1 1/2 STARCH, 1 1/2 HIGH-FAT MEAT, 3 FAT
CARB. CHOICES: 1 1/2

Impossibly Easy Breakfast Bake

PREP: 20 min **BAKE:** 47 min **COOL:** 5 min ▪ **12 SERVINGS**

2 packages (12 oz each) bulk pork sausage
1 medium bell pepper, chopped (1 cup)
1 medium onion, chopped (1/2 cup)
3 cups frozen hash brown potatoes
2 cups shredded Cheddar cheese (8 oz)
1 cup Original Bisquick® mix
2 cups milk
1/4 teaspoon pepper
4 large eggs

1. Heat oven to 400°F. Spray 13 × 9-inch glass baking dish with cooking spray.

2. In 10-inch skillet, cook sausage, bell pepper and onion over medium heat 8 to 10 minutes, stirring occasionally, until sausage is no longer pink; drain. Mix sausage mixture, potatoes and 1 1/2 cups of the cheese in baking dish.

3. In medium bowl, stir Bisquick® mix, milk, pepper and eggs with wire whisk or fork until blended. Pour into baking dish.

4. Bake uncovered 40 to 45 minutes or until knife inserted in center comes out clean. Sprinkle with remaining 1/2 cup cheese. Bake 1 to 2 minutes longer or just until cheese is melted. Cool 5 minutes.

1 SERVING: CAL. 310 (CAL. FROM FAT 170); FAT 19g (SAT. FAT 8g); CHOL. 115mg; SODIUM 660mg; CARBS. 20g (FIBER 1g); PRO. 15g
% DAILY VALUE: VIT. A 8%; VIT. C 12%; CALC. 18%; IRON 6%
EXCHANGES: 1 STARCH, 2 1/2 HIGH-FAT MEAT, **CARB. CHOICES:** 1

Apple, Bacon and Cheddar Bread Pudding

PREP: 25 min **CHILL:** 2 hr **BAKE:** 45 min **STAND:** 10 min ▪ **12 SERVINGS**

3 tablespoons butter or margarine
3 medium Granny Smith apples, peeled and coarsely chopped (3 cups)
3 tablespoons packed brown sugar
4 cups cubed firm bread
1 lb bacon, cooked, drained and chopped
2 cups shredded sharp Cheddar cheese (8 oz)
2 1/2 cups milk
1 teaspoon ground mustard
2 teaspoons Worcestershire sauce
1/4 teaspoon salt
1/8 teaspoon pepper
5 large eggs

1. Spray 2-quart casserole with cooking spray. In 10-inch skillet, melt butter over medium heat. Cook apples in butter 2 to 3 minutes, stirring occasionally, until crisp-tender. Stir in brown sugar; reduce heat to low. Cook 5 to 6 minutes, stirring occasionally, until apples are tender.

2. Layer half each of the bread, bacon, apples and cheese in casserole. Repeat with remaining bread, bacon, apples and cheese.

3. In medium bowl, beat remaining ingredients with fork or wire whisk; pour over cheese. Cover tightly and refrigerate at least 2 hours but no longer than 24 hours.

4. Heat oven to 350°F. Bake uncovered 40 to 45 minutes or until knife inserted in center comes out clean. Let stand 10 minutes before serving.

1 SERVING: CAL. 275 (CAL. FROM FAT 160); FAT 18g (SAT. FAT 9g); CHOL. 130mg; SODIUM 480mg; CARBS. 17g (FIBER 1g); PRO. 13g
% DAILY VALUE: VIT. A 10%; VIT. C 0%; CALC. 18%; IRON 6%
EXCHANGES: 1 STARCH, 1 MEDIUM-FAT MEAT, 3 FAT
CARB. CHOICES: 1

◀ **Apple, Bacon and Cheddar Bread Pudding**

Easy Mushroom Pizza Pie

PREP: 10 min **BAKE:** 40 min **STAND:** 5 min ■ **6 SERVINGS**

- 1 can (4 oz) mushroom pieces and stems, drained
- 2/3 cup chopped onion
- 1/3 cup grated Parmesan cheese
- 1 1/2 cups milk
- 3 large eggs
- 3/4 cup Original Bisquick® mix
- 1/2 cup pizza sauce
- 1/4 cup grated Parmesan cheese
- 1/3 cup chopped onion
- 1/2 cup chopped green bell pepper
- 1 to 1 1/2 cups shredded mozzarella cheese (4 to 6 oz)

1. Heat oven to 425°F. Spray 10-inch glass pie plate with cooking spray. Sprinkle mushrooms, 2/3 cup onion and 1/3 cup Parmesan cheese in pie plate.

2. In medium bowl, stir milk, eggs and Bisquick® mix with fork or wire whisk until blended. Pour over vegetable mixture in pie plate.

3. Bake 20 minutes. Spread pizza sauce over top. Top with remaining ingredients. Bake 15 to 20 minutes longer or until cheese is light brown. Let stand 5 minutes before cutting.

1 SERVING: CAL. 245 (CAL. FROM FAT 110); FAT 12g (SAT. FAT 6g); CHOL. 130mg; SODIUM 730mg; CARBS. 20g (FIBER 2g); PRO. 16g
% DAILY VALUE: VIT. A 12%; VIT. C 14%; CALC. 40%; IRON 6%
EXCHANGES: 1 STARCH, 2 MEDIUM-FAT MEAT, 1/2 FAT
CARB. CHOICES: 1

Ham and Swiss Pizza

PREP: 10 min **COOK:** 5 min **BAKE:** 12 min ■ **6 SERVINGS**

- 6 large eggs, beaten
- 1 package (10 oz) ready-to-serve thin Italian pizza crust or other 12-inch ready-to-serve pizza crust
- 1/4 cup mayonnaise or salad dressing
- 2 tablespoons Dijon mustard
- 1/2 cup diced fully cooked ham
- 4 medium green onions, sliced (1/4 cup)
- 1/4 cup chopped red bell pepper
- 1 cup shredded Swiss cheese (4 oz)

1. Heat oven to 400°F. Heat 10-inch nonstick skillet over medium heat.

2. Pour eggs into skillet. As mixture begins to set at bottom and side, gently lift cooked portions with spatula so that thin, uncooked portion can flow to bottom. Avoid constant stirring. Cook 3 to 4 minutes or until eggs are thickened throughout but still moist.

3. Place pizza crust on ungreased cookie sheet. In small bowl, mix mayonnaise and mustard; spread evenly over crust. Top with eggs, ham, onions, bell pepper and cheese.

4. Bake 10 to 12 minutes or until cheese is melted.

1 SERVING: CAL. 370 (CAL. FROM FAT 190); FAT 21g (SAT. FAT 7g); CHOL. 240mg; SODIUM 660mg; CARBS. 28g (FIBER 1g); PRO. 18g
% DAILY VALUE: VIT. A 18%; VIT. C 10%; CALC. 22%; IRON 14%
EXCHANGES: 2 STARCH, 2 MEDIUM-FAT MEAT, 1 1/2 FAT **CARB. CHOICES:** 2

LIGHTER HAM AND SWISS PIZZA

For 8 grams of fat and 250 calories per serving, substitute 1 1/2 cups fat-free cholesterol-free egg product for the eggs and 99% fat-free deli-style ham slices, diced, for the diced fully cooked ham; use fat-free mayonnaise and reduced-fat Swiss cheese.

Ham and Swiss Pizza ▶

Onion and Cheese Pie

PREP: 10 min **COOK:** 7 min **BAKE:** 45 min ▪ **6 SERVINGS**

Quickly and easily crush crackers into crumbs by sealing them in a plastic food-storage bag and pounding with your hand.

- 1 1/4 cups finely crushed saltine crackers (36 squares)
- 1/4 cup butter or margarine, melted
- 2 tablespoons butter or margarine
- 2 large onions, chopped (2 cups)
- 1 1/2 cups shredded sharp Cheddar cheese (6 oz)
- 1 cup milk
- 1/2 teaspoon salt
- 1/4 teaspoon pepper
- 3 large eggs
- Chopped seeded tomato and sliced green onion, if desired

1. Heat oven to 325°F. Spray 9-inch glass pie plate with cooking spray. In small bowl, mix cracker crumbs and 1/4 cup melted butter; press evenly in bottom and up side of pie plate.

2. In 10-inch skillet, melt 2 tablespoons butter over medium-high heat. Cook onions in butter 5 to 6 minutes, stirring frequently, until light brown. Spread onions in crust. Sprinkle with cheese.

3. In medium bowl, beat milk, salt, pepper and eggs with fork or wire whisk until blended; pour over cheese.

4. Bake 40 to 45 minutes or until knife inserted in center comes out clean. Garnish with tomato and onion. Serve immediately.

1 SERVING: CAL. 370 (CAL. FROM FAT 245); FAT 27g (SAT. FAT 15g); CHOL. 170mg; SODIUM 670mg; CARBS. 17g (FIBER 1g); PRO. 14g
% DAILY VALUE: VIT. A 20%; VIT. C 2%; CALC. 24%; IRON 6%
EXCHANGES: 1 STARCH, 1 1/2 HIGH-FAT MEAT, 3 FAT
CARB. CHOICES: 1

◀ **Onion and Cheese Pie**

Chiles Rellenos Bake

PREP: 10 min **BAKE:** 45 min ▪ **8 SERVINGS**

This version of the classic Mexican dish chiles rellenos *skips the extra work of stuffing and frying whole chiles.*

- 8 large eggs
- 1 cup sour cream
- 1/4 teaspoon salt
- 2 drops red pepper sauce
- 2 cups shredded Monterey Jack cheese (8 oz)
- 2 cups shredded Cheddar cheese (8 oz)
- 2 cans (4.5 oz each) chopped green chiles, undrained
- 2 cups salsa
- 2 tablespoons chopped fresh cilantro
- 1/2 cup black beans (from 15-oz can), rinsed and drained
- 1/2 cup frozen (thawed) or canned (drained) whole kernel corn

1. Heat oven to 350°F. Spray 13 × 9-inch glass baking dish with cooking spray.

2. In large bowl, beat eggs, sour cream, salt and pepper sauce with wire whisk. Stir in cheeses and chiles. Pour into baking dish.

3. Bake uncovered about 45 minutes or until golden brown and set in center.

4. Meanwhile, in small bowl, mix 1 cup of the salsa and the cilantro. In another small bowl, mix remaining 1 cup salsa, the beans and corn. Serve salsa mixtures with casserole.

1 SERVING: CAL. 400 (CAL. FROM FAT 260); FAT 29g (SAT. FAT 17g); CHOL. 285mg; SODIUM 870mg; CARB. 12g (FIBER 2g); PRO. 23g
% DAILY VALUE: VIT. A 30%; VIT. C 15%; CALC. 45%; IRON 10%
EXCHANGES: 1 STARCH, 3 HIGH-FAT MEAT, 1/2 FAT
CARB. CHOICES: 1

Classic Cheese Soufflé

PREP: 25 min **BAKE:** 1 hr ■ **4 SERVINGS**

Impress your friends! Wow them by bringing this golden, puffy cheese soufflé with its heavenly aroma hot out of the oven and straight to the table. Once it's cut, it loses its puffiness, but it still tastes incredibly delicious.

1/4 cup butter or margarine
1/4 cup all-purpose flour
1/2 teaspoon salt
1/4 teaspoon ground mustard
Dash of ground red pepper (cayenne)
1 cup milk
1 cup shredded Cheddar cheese (4 oz)
3 large eggs, separated
1/4 teaspoon cream of tartar

1. Heat oven to 350°F. Butter 1-quart soufflé dish or casserole. Make a 4-inch-wide band of triple-thickness foil 2 inches longer than circumference of dish. Butter one side of foil. Secure foil band, buttered side in, around top edge of dish.

2. In 2-quart saucepan, melt 1/4 cup butter over medium heat. Stir in flour, salt, mustard and red pepper. Cook over medium heat, stirring constantly, until smooth and bubbly; remove from heat. Stir in milk. Heat to boiling, stirring constantly. Boil and stir 1 minute. Stir in cheese until melted; remove from heat.

3. In medium bowl, beat egg whites and cream of tartar with electric mixer on high speed until stiff but not dry; set aside. In small bowl, beat egg yolks on high speed about 3 minutes or until very thick and lemon colored; stir into cheese mixture. Stir about one-fourth of the egg whites into cheese mixture. Fold cheese mixture into remaining egg whites. Carefully pour into soufflé dish.

4. Bake 50 to 60 minutes or until knife inserted halfway between center and edge comes out clean. Carefully remove foil band. Serve immediately by quickly dividing soufflé into sections with 2 forks.

1 SERVING: CAL. 335 (CAL. FROM FAT 235); FAT 26g (SAT. FAT 15g); CHOL. 225mg; SODIUM 620mg; CARBS. 10g (FIBER 0g); PRO. 15g
% DAILY VALUE: VIT. A 20%; VIT. C 0%; CALC. 24%; IRON 6%
EXCHANGES: 1/2 MILK, 1 1/2 HIGH-FAT MEAT, 3 FAT
CARB. CHOICES: 1/2

HOW TO MAKE A FOIL BAND FOR MAKING SOUFFLÉ

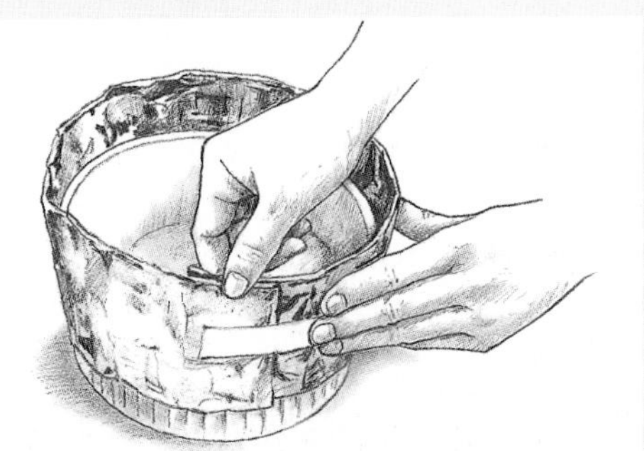

Make a 4-inch band of triple-thickness aluminum foil 2 inches longer than circumference of dish. Grease one side of band with butter. Extend dish by securing band, buttered side in, with masking tape around top outside edge.

Cheese Fondue

Cheese Fondue

PREP: 10 min **COOK:** 30 min ▪ **5 SERVINGS**

Fondue *is French for "melted." Be patient when making cheese fondue, and allow each addition of cheese to completely melt into the wine before adding more.*

- 2 cups shredded Swiss cheese (8 oz)
- 2 cups shredded Gruyère or Swiss cheese (8 oz)
- 2 tablespoons all-purpose flour
- 1 clove garlic, cut in half
- 1 cup dry white wine or nonalcoholic white wine
- 1 tablespoon lemon juice
- 3 tablespoons kirsch, dry sherry, brandy or nonalcoholic white wine
- 1 loaf (1 lb) French bread, cut into 1-inch pieces
- Apple and pear slices, if desired

1. In resealable plastic food-storage bag, place cheeses and flour. Shake until cheese is coated with flour.

2. Rub garlic on bottom and side of fondue pot, heavy saucepan or skillet; discard garlic. Add wine. Heat over simmer setting on fondue pot or over low heat just until bubbles rise to surface (do not boil). Stir in lemon juice.

3. Gradually add cheese mixture, about 1/2 cup at a time, stirring constantly with wire whisk over low heat, until melted. Stir in kirsch.

4. Keep warm over simmer setting. If prepared in saucepan or skillet, pour into a fondue pot or heatproof serving bowl and keep warm over low heat. Fondue must be served over heat to maintain its smooth, creamy texture.

5. Spear bread and fruit with fondue forks; dip and swirl in fondue with stirring motion. If fondue becomes too thick, stir in 1/4 to 1/2 cup heated wine.

1 SERVING: CAL. 610 (CAL. FROM FAT 270); FAT 30g (SAT. FAT 17g); CHOL. 90mg; SODIUM 800mg; CARBS. 50g (FIBER 3g); PRO. 35g
% DAILY VALUE: VIT. A 18%; VIT. C 0%; CALC. 96%; IRON 16%
EXCHANGES: 3 STARCH, 3 1/2 HIGH-FAT MEAT **CARB. CHOICES:** 3

CHAPTER 9
Fish & Shellfish

Fish

Shellfish

LOW-FAT = *3g or less, except main dishes with 10g or less* FAST = *Ready in 20 minutes or less* BREAD MACHINE = *Bread machine directions* SLOW COOKER = *Slow cooker directions* LIGHTER = *25% fewer calories or grams of fat*

◀ **Salmon with Honey-Mustard Glaze (page 247)**

Fish Basics

Fish is now more popular than ever! And it's no wonder. Fish is healthful and filled with flavor. You can cook it in so many ways. Thanks to the increased production of farm-raised fish, you can now buy many varieties almost anywhere, like catfish, salmon and trout. Fish is naturally rich in high-quality protein, yet most are low in fat, saturated fat, cholesterol and calories. Read on—and get in the swim of cooking fish today.

BUYING FISH

Seek out the best places in your area to buy the freshest fish. If you live near the ocean, visit the fish stores near the docks for the freshest "daily catch." Everywhere else, find a local seafood store or visit the fish counter in your local supermarket or gourmet food store.

Fresh Fillets, Steaks or Whole Fish

- Flesh should be shiny, firm, elastic and spring back when touched. Avoid fish with any darkening around the edges or brown or yellowish discoloration.
- Fish should smell fresh and mild, not fishy or like ammonia.
- Check the sell-by date and be sure to use by that date.
- Eyes should be bright, clear and slightly bulging; only a few fish, such as walleye, have naturally cloudy eyes.
- Gills should be bright pink to red—without any slime on them.
- Scales should bright, shiny and cling tightly to the skin.

Frozen Fish

- Only choose packages of frozen fish that are tightly wrapped and frozen solid with little or no ice crystals.
- Avoid packages with dark or dry spots, which indicate freezer burn.
- Buy only packages that are odor free.

Storing Fresh Fish

- Store fresh fish in its original wrapper or packaging in the meat compartment or coldest part of your refrigerator. Use within 1 to 2 days.
- To freeze, repackage fish wrapped in butcher paper tightly in foil or plastic freezer bags. Fish packaged in clear plastic wrap on a plastic or Styrofoam tray doesn't need to be repackaged. Freeze 3 to 6 months.

FISH POUNDS PER SERVING

The number of servings per pound varies depending on the form of fish.

Type of Fish	Pounds per Serving
Drawn (whole with head and tail; only the internal organs removed)	1/2 to 3/4
Fillets or Steaks	1/3 to 1/2
Pan-Dressed (often scaled with internal organs, head, tail and fins removed)	1/2
Whole (just as it comes from the water)	3/4 to 1

CLASSIFYING FISH

Fish can be classified by flavor and texture. To substitute, pick a fish with the same flavor and texture.

CLASSIFICATION OF FISH

Mild Flavor	Moderate Flavor	Full Flavor
DELICATE TO MEDIUM TEXTURE		
Alaska Pollock	Hake/Whiting	Herring/Sardines/ Smelt
Catfish	Lingcod	
Flounder	Walleye	
Orange Roughy	Whitefish	
Skate		
Sole		
MEDIUM-FIRM TEXTURE		
Cod	Amberjack	Bluefish/Snapper
Cusk	Black Sea Bass	Butterfish/Pompano
Haddock/ Scrod	Char	Mackerel (Ono, Wahoo)
Red Snapper	Chilean Sea Bass	Sablefish
Tilapia	Drum	Salmon (Atlantic, King, Sockeye)
Tilefish	Mahimahi	
	Perch (Lake, ocean)	
	Porgy/Scup	
	Redfish	
	Rainbow Trout	
	Rockfish	
	Sea Bass	
	Shad	
FIRM TEXTURE		
Grouper	Shark	Marlin
Halibut	Sturgeon	Swordfish
Monkfish		Tuna (Albacore, Bluefin, Yellowfin/Ahi)
Striped Bass		

COOKING FISH

Fish is so delicate and tender that overcooking makes it dry and tough. To avoid this, use the "10-minute rule." Then give it the "fork test" to see if the fish is done:

- *Measure fish at its thickest point.* If fish will be stuffed or rolled, measure it before stuffing or rolling.
- *"10 Minute Rule":* Cook fish for 10 minutes per inch of thickness. Turn over halfway through cooking time only if the recipe calls for this step. Fillets less than 1/2 inch thick usually do not need to be turned over. Cook unthawed frozen fish 20 minutes per inch. Add 5 minutes to the total cooking time if fish is cooked in foil or in a sauce.
- *"Fork Test":* To test if fish is done, insert a fork in the thickest part of the fish, then gently twist the fork. When the fish flakes, it's done. For food-safety reasons, cook fish to an internal temperature of 145°F for all cooking methods except the microwave oven. Because microwave ovens can cook unevenly, fish cooked in the microwave should reach an internal temperature of 170°F.

TIMETABLE FOR MICROWAVING FISH

1. Arrange fish fillets or steaks with thickest parts to outside edge in shallow microwavable dish that's large enough to hold fish in a single layer. (Fold thin ends of fillets under for more even thickness, or loosely roll up thin fillets.)
2. Cover with plastic wrap, folding one edge or corner back about 1/4 inch to vent steam.
3. Microwave on High (100%) as directed below, rotating dish once if microwave does not have turntable. When a thermometer inserted in thickest portion of fish reads 170°F and the fish flakes easily with fork, it's done.

Type	Approximate Weight	Microwave Time	Stand Time
Fillets	1 pound	5 to 7 minutes	2 minutes
	1 1/2 pounds	7 to 9 minutes	3 minutes
Steaks (1 inch thick)	1 pound	5 to 7 minutes	3 minutes
	1 1/2 pounds	8 to 10 minutes	3 minutes

Broiled Fish Steaks FAST

PREP: 5 min **BROIL:** 11 min ▪ **4 SERVINGS**

Here's one of the easiest and simplest ways to cook fresh fish. Simply broil it, then drizzle with just a squeeze of fresh lime or lemon juice.

- 4 small salmon, trout or other medium-firm fish steaks, about 3/4 inch thick (1 1/2 lb)
- Salt and pepper to taste
- 2 tablespoons butter or margarine, melted

1. Set oven control to broil.

2. Sprinkle both sides of fish with salt and pepper. Brush with half of the butter.

3. Place fish on rack in broiler pan. Broil with tops about 4 inches from heat 5 minutes. Brush with butter. Carefully turn fish; brush with butter. Broil 4 to 6 minutes longer or until fish flakes easily with fork.

1 SERVING: CAL. 280 (CAL. FROM FAT 135); FAT 15g (SAT. FAT 6g); CHOL. 125mg; SODIUM 340mg; CARBS. 0g (FIBER 0g); PRO. 36g
% DAILY VALUE: VIT. A 8%; VIT. C 2%; CALC. 2%; IRON 6%
EXCHANGES: 5 LEAN MEAT **CARB. CHOICES:** 0

BROILED FISH FILLETS Substitute 1 lb fish fillets, cut into 4 serving pieces, for the fish steaks. Broil with tops about 4 inches from heat 5 to 6 minutes or until fish flakes easily with fork (do not turn).

Pecan-Crusted Fish Fillets

PREP: 15 min **COOK:** 10 min ▪ **4 SERVINGS**

- 1 cup finely chopped pecans (not ground)
- 1/4 cup dry bread crumbs
- 2 teaspoons grated lemon peel
- 1 large egg
- 1 tablespoon milk
- 1 lb sole, orange roughy, walleye or other delicate- to medium-texture fish fillets, about 1/2 inch thick
- 1/2 teaspoon salt
- 1/4 teaspoon pepper
- 2 tablespoons vegetable oil
- Lemon wedges

1. In shallow dish, mix pecans, bread crumbs and lemon peel. In small bowl, beat egg and milk with fork or wire whisk until blended.

2. Cut fish into 4 serving pieces. Sprinkle both sides of fish with salt and pepper. Coat fish with egg mixture, then coat well with pecan mixture, pressing lightly into fish.

3. In 12-inch nonstick skillet, heat oil over medium heat. Add fish. Reduce heat to medium-low. Cook 6 to 10 minutes, carefully turning once with 2 pancake turners, until fish flakes easily with fork and is brown. Serve with lemon wedges.

1 SERVING: CAL. 350 (CAL. FROM FAT 225); FAT 25g (SAT. FAT 3g); CHOL. 105mg; SODIUM 450mg; CARBS. 9g (FIBER 3g); PRO. 24g
% DAILY VALUE: VIT. A 2%; VIT. C 0%; CALC. 6%; IRON 8%
EXCHANGES: 1/2 STARCH, 3 LEAN MEAT, 3 FAT **CARB. CHOICES:** 1/2

Beer Batter-Fried Fish

PREP: 15 min **COOK:** 4 min per batch ▪ **4 SERVINGS**

- Vegetable oil
- 1 lb walleye, sole or other delicate- to medium-texture fish fillets, about 3/4 inch thick
- 3 to 4 tablespoons Original Bisquick® mix
- 1 cup Original Bisquick® mix
- 1/2 cup regular or nonalcoholic beer
- 1 large egg
- 1/2 teaspoon salt
- Tartar Sauce (page 406), if desired

1. In 4-quart Dutch oven or deep fryer, heat oil (1 1/2 inches) to 350°F. Cut fish into 8 serving pieces. Lightly coat fish with 3 to 4 tablespoons Bisquick® mix.

2. In medium bowl, mix remaining ingredients except Tartar Sauce with hand beater until smooth. (If batter is too thick, stir in additional beer, 1 tablespoon at a time, until desired consistency.) Dip fish into batter, letting excess drip into bowl.

3. Fry batches of fish in oil about 4 minutes, turning once, until golden brown. Remove with slotted spoon; drain on paper towels. Serve hot with Tartar Sauce.

1 SERVING: CAL. 280 (CAL. FROM FAT 100); FAT 11g (SAT. FAT 2g); CHOL. 100mg; SODIUM 710mg; CARBS. 20g (FIBER 1g); PRO. 25g
% DAILY VALUE: VIT. A 2%; VIT. C 0%; CALC. 6%; IRON 6%
EXCHANGES: 1 STARCH, 3 LEAN MEAT, 1/2 FAT **CARB. CHOICES:** 1

HOW TO REMOVE BONES AND SKIN FROM FISH FILLETS

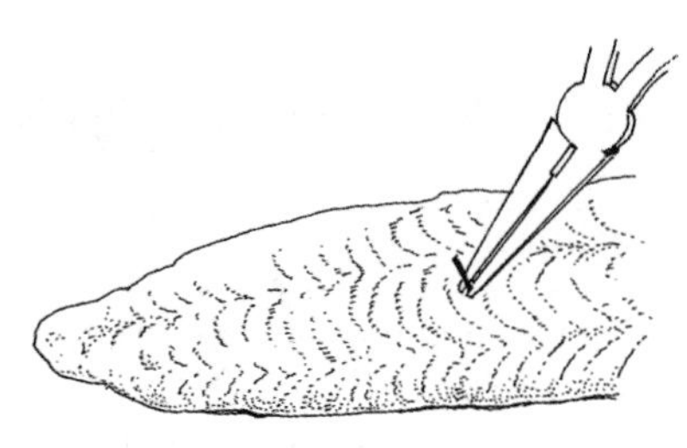

▲ **1.** Place fish fillet, skin side down, on cutting board. Run fingertips along surface of fillet to feel for bones. Remove any bones with needle-nose pliers or fingers.

2. Starting at tail end or shortest side of fillet, work the edge of a boning or carving knife between the flesh and skin to separate the flesh from the skin. Grasp end of skin with paper towel and pull on it as you run the knife in the opposite direction down the length of the fillet. Keep knife angled down slightly as close to the skin as possible, using a gentle sawing motion if necessary. Remove skin; discard. ▼

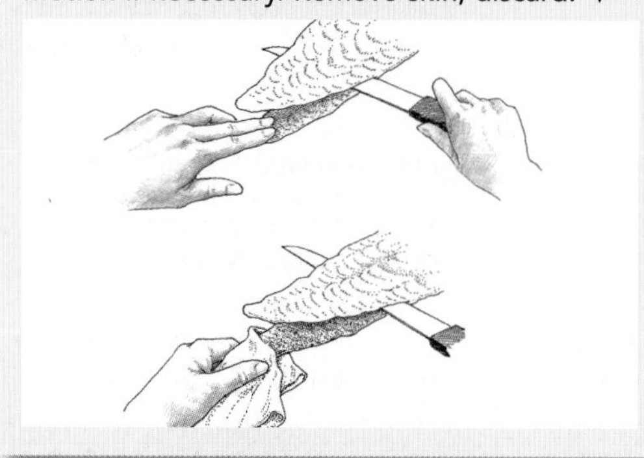

Orange-Almond Trout

PREP: 10 min **COOK:** 15 min ▪ **4 SERVINGS**

- 1 lb trout, salmon or other medium-firm fish fillets, about 3/4 inch thick
- 1/4 cup butter or margarine
- 1/4 cup sliced almonds
- 1 medium onion, sliced
- 1/2 cup all-purpose flour
- 1 teaspoon salt
- 1/2 teaspoon paprika
- 1/8 teaspoon pepper
- 2 oranges, peeled and sectioned (page 9)

1. If fish fillets are large, cut into 4 serving pieces.

2. In 10-inch skillet, melt butter over medium heat. Cook almonds and onion in butter, stirring occasionally, until onion is tender. Remove almonds and onion with slotted spoon; keep warm.

3. In shallow dish, mix flour, salt, paprika and pepper. Coat fish with flour mixture. Cook fish in same skillet over medium heat 6 to 10 minutes, turning once, until fish is brown and flakes easily with fork.

4. Top fish with almonds and onion. Garnish with orange sections.

1 SERVING: CAL. 380 (CAL. FROM FAT 180); FAT 20g (SAT. FAT 7g); CHOL. 85mg; SODIUM 710mg; CARBS. 23g (FIBER 3g); PRO. 27g
% DAILY VALUE: VIT. A 14%; VIT. C 60%; CALC. 10%; IRON 16%
EXCHANGES: 1 FRUIT, 1 VEGETABLE, 3 1/2 LEAN MEAT, 2 FAT
CARB. CHOICES: 1 1/2

Panfried Fish LOW-FAT

PREP: 10 min **COOK:** 10 min per batch ▪ **6 SERVINGS**

To keep the first batch of fried fish hot while frying the rest, place fish on a heatproof serving platter. Keep warm in a 250°F oven until ready to serve.

- Vegetable oil or shortening
- 1 1/2 lb perch, snapper or other medium-firm fish fillets, about 3/4 inch thick
- Salt and pepper to taste
- 1 large egg
- 1 tablespoon water
- 2/3 cup all-purpose flour, cornmeal or fine dry bread crumbs

1. In 10-inch skillet, heat oil (1/8 inch) over medium heat.

2. Cut fish into 6 serving pieces. Sprinkle both sides of fish with salt and pepper.

3. In small bowl, beat egg and water with fork or wire whisk until blended. Place flour in shallow dish. Dip fish into egg, then coat with flour.

4. Fry batches of fish in oil 6 to 10 minutes, turning once, until fish flakes easily with fork and is brown on both sides. Fish cooks very quickly; be careful not to overcook. Remove with slotted spoon; drain on paper towels.

1 SERVING: CAL. 205 (CAL. FROM FAT 65); FAT 7g (SAT. FAT 1g); CHOL. 95mg; SODIUM 230mg; CARBS. 11g (FIBER 0g); PRO. 24g **% DAILY VALUE:** VIT. A 2%; VIT. C 0%; CALC. 2%; IRON 6% **EXCHANGES:** 1 STARCH, 3 VERY LEAN MEAT, 1/2 FAT **CARB. CHOICES:** 1

Oven-Fried Fish

PREP: 15 min **BAKE:** 10 min ■ **4 SERVINGS**

- 1 lb cod, haddock or other medium-firm fish fillets, about 3/4 inch thick
- 1/4 cup cornmeal
- 1/4 cup dry bread crumbs
- 3/4 teaspoon chopped fresh or 1/4 teaspoon dried dill weed
- 1/2 teaspoon paprika
- 1/4 teaspoon salt
- 1/8 teaspoon pepper
- 1/4 cup milk
- 3 tablespoons butter or margarine, melted

1. Move oven rack to position slightly above middle of oven. Heat oven to 500°F.

2. Cut fish into 2 × 1 1/2-inch pieces. In shallow dish, mix cornmeal, bread crumbs, dill weed, paprika, salt and pepper. Place milk in another shallow dish. Dip fish into milk, then coat with cornmeal mixture.

3. Place fish in ungreased 13 × 9-inch pan. Drizzle melted butter over fish. Bake uncovered about 10 minutes or until fish flakes easily with fork.

1 SERVING: CAL. 245 (CAL. FROM FAT 100); FAT 11g (SAT. FAT 6g); CHOL. 85mg; SODIUM 360mg; CARBS. 12g (FIBER 1g); PRO. 24g **% DAILY VALUE:** VIT. A 8%; VIT. C 0%; CALC. 4%; IRON 6% **EXCHANGES:** 1 STARCH, 3 LEAN MEAT **CARB. CHOICES:** 1

Baked Fish Fillets LOW-FAT

PREP: 5 min **BAKE:** 20 min ■ **4 SERVINGS**

- 1 lb sole, orange roughy or other delicate- to medium-texture fish fillets, about 3/4 inch thick
- 2 tablespoons butter or margarine, melted
- 1 tablespoon lemon juice
- 1/4 teaspoon salt
- 1/4 teaspoon paprika

1. Heat oven to 375°F. Spray 13 × 9-inch pan with cooking spray.

2. Cut fish into 4 serving pieces; place in pan (if fish has skin, place skin sides down). Tuck under any thin ends for more even cooking.

3. In small bowl, mix remaining ingredients; drizzle over fish.

4. Bake uncovered 15 to 20 minutes or until fish flakes easily with fork. Remove skin from fish before serving if desired.

1 SERVING: CAL. 140 (CAL. FROM FAT 65); FAT 7g (SAT. FAT 4g); CHOL. 70mg; SODIUM 270mg; CARBS. 0g (FIBER 0g); PRO. 19g **% DAILY VALUE:** VIT. A 4%; VIT. C 0%; CALC. 2%; IRON 2% **EXCHANGES:** 2 1/2 LEAN MEAT **CARB. CHOICES:** 0

HOW TO CHECK FISH FOR DONENESS

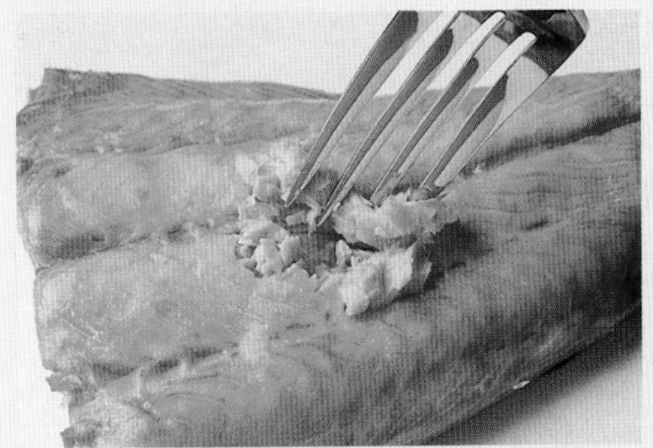

Check fish for doneness by placing a fork in the thickest part of the fish, then gently twisting the fork. When the fish flakes easily, it's done.

◀ **Oven-Fried Fish and Broccoli Sunshine Salad (page 384)**

Bass with Parmesan LOW-FAT

PREP: 10 min **COOK:** 10 min **BAKE:** 15 min ■ **4 SERVINGS**

- 1 1/2 lb sea bass, sole or pike fillets
- 1/4 cup all-purpose flour
- 2 tablespoons butter or margarine
- 2 medium green onions, thinly sliced (2 tablespoons)
- 1 cup dry white wine or chicken broth
- 2 tablespoons lemon juice
- 1/2 teaspoon salt
- 1/4 teaspoon pepper
- 1/4 cup freshly grated or shredded Parmesan cheese

1. Heat oven to 375°F. Coat fish fillets with flour; shake off excess flour. In 12-inch ovenproof skillet, melt butter over medium-low heat. Cook onions in butter about 5 minutes, stirring occasionally, until tender.

2. Add fish to skillet. Cook uncovered about 5 minutes or until light brown; carefully turn fish. Pour wine and lemon juice over fish. Sprinkle with salt, pepper and cheese.

3. Bake uncovered about 15 minutes or until cheese is melted and fish flakes easily with fork.

1 SERVING: CAL. 265 (CAL. FROM FAT 90); FAT 10g (SAT. FAT 5g); CHOL. 110mg; SODIUM 590mg; CARBS. 8g (FIBER 0g); PRO. 36g
% DAILY VALUE: VIT. A 8%; VIT. C 2%; CALC. 12%; IRON 6%
EXCHANGES: 1/2 STARCH, 5 VERY LEAN MEAT, 1 FAT **CARB. CHOICES:** 1/2

◀ Beer-Batter Fried Fish

BAKING FISH WITH SKIN ON

Baking fish with the skin on helps to hold delicate-texture fish fillets together. Removing the skin after the fish has been cooked is much easier than removing it before cooking. When fish is done, carefully insert a thin metal spatula between the skin and the flesh, starting at the tail end if the fillet has one. While holding on to a small piece of skin, slide the fish off the skin.

Sole Amandine

PREP: 15 min **BAKE:** 20 min ■ **6 SERVINGS**

A French term, amandine *means "garnished with almonds" and is often misspelled as "almondine." If you own a gratin dish, (a shallow oval-shaped ovenproof baking dish), use it to bake this classic dish.*

- 1 1/2 lb sole, orange roughy or other delicate- to medium-texture fish fillets, about 3/4 inch thick
- 1/2 cup sliced almonds
- 1/4 cup butter or margarine, softened
- 2 tablespoons grated lemon peel
- 1/2 teaspoon salt
- 1/2 teaspoon paprika
- 2 tablespoons lemon juice

1. Heat oven to 375°F. Spray 11 × 7-inch glass baking dish with cooking spray.

2. Cut fish into 6 serving pieces. Place in baking dish (if fish has skin, place skin sides down). Tuck under any thin ends for more even cooking

3. In small bowl, mix almonds, butter, lemon peel, salt and paprika; spoon over fish. Sprinkle with lemon juice.

4. Bake uncovered 15 to 20 minutes or until fish flakes easily with fork.

1 SERVING: CAL. 210 (CAL. FROM FAT 115); FAT 13g (SAT. FAT 5g); CHOL. 75mg; SODIUM 330mg; CARBS. 2g (FIBER 1g); PRO. 21g
% DAILY VALUE: VIT. A 6%; VIT. C 2%; CALC. 4%; IRON 4%
EXCHANGES: 3 LEAN MEAT, 1 FAT **CARB. CHOICES:** 0

LIGHTER SOLE AMANDINE

For 6 grams of fat and 140 calories per serving, decrease almonds to 2 tablespoons and butter to 2 tablespoons.

Asian Tuna with Wasabi Aioli

Asian Tuna with Wasabi Aioli

PREP: 10 min **MARINATE:** 2 hr **BROIL:** 15 min ▪ **8 SERVINGS**

Wasabi, also called Japanese horseradish, *has a sharp, pungent, fiery flavor. It comes in both a powder and paste form and is available in the Asian-foods aisle of large supermarkets. If you can't find it, use regular prepared horseradish instead.*

Tuna

2 lb tuna steaks, 3/4 to 1 inch thick
1/2 cup vegetable oil
1/3 cup soy sauce
2 tablespoons packed brown sugar
2 teaspoons sesame oil
2 teaspoons grated gingerroot
2 cloves garlic, finely chopped

Wasabi Aioli

1/2 cup mayonnaise or salad dressing
1 teaspoon wasabi powder or prepared horseradish

Garnish

2 teaspoons sesame seed, toasted if desired

1. If tuna steaks are large, cut into 8 serving pieces. In shallow glass or plastic dish or resealable plastic food-storage bag, mix vegetable oil, soy sauce, brown sugar, sesame oil, gingerroot and garlic. Add tuna; turn to coat with marinade. Cover dish or seal bag and refrigerate, turning once, at least 2 hours but no longer than 4 hours.

2. Meanwhile, in small bowl, mix aioli ingredients. Cover and refrigerate until serving.

3. Set oven control to broil. Remove tuna from marinade; reserve marinade. Place tuna on rack in broiler pan. Broil 4 to 6 inches from heat 10 to 15 minutes, brushing 2 to 3 times with marinade and turning once, until tuna flakes easily with fork. Discard any remaining marinade. Sprinkle sesame seed over tuna. Serve with aioli.

1 SERVING: CAL. 340 (CAL. FROM FAT 245); FAT 27g (SAT. FAT 5g); CHOL. 75mg; SODIUM 600mg; CARBS. 4g (FIBER 0g); PRO. 22g
% DAILY VALUE: VIT. A 2%; VIT. C 0%; CALC. 2%; IRON 6%
EXCHANGES: 3 MEDIUM-FAT MEAT, 2 1/2 FAT **CARB. CHOICES:** 0

Salmon with Honey-Mustard Glaze

PREP: 5 min **MARINATE:** 15 min **BROIL:** 15 min ▪ **4 SERVINGS**

Honey-Mustard Marinade

1 tablespoon packed brown sugar
1 tablespoon butter or margarine, melted
1 tablespoon olive or vegetable oil
1 tablespoon honey
1 tablespoon soy sauce
1 tablespoon Dijon mustard
1 clove garlic, finely chopped

Salmon

1 salmon fillet (1 lb)

1. In small bowl, mix all marinade ingredients.

2. Place salmon, skin side down, in shallow glass or plastic dish. Pour marinade over salmon. Cover and refrigerate at least 15 minutes but no longer than 1 hour.

3. Set oven control to broil. Remove salmon from marinade; reserve marinade. Place salmon, skin side down, on rack in broiler pan. Broil with top 4 to 6 inches from medium heat 10 to 15 minutes, brushing 2 or 3 times with marinade, until salmon flakes easily with fork. Discard any remaining marinade.

1 SERVING: CAL. 220 (CAL. FROM FAT 100); FAT 11g (SAT. FAT 4g); CHOL. 80mg; SODIUM 320mg; CARBS. 6g (FIBER 0g); PRO. 24g
% DAILY VALUE: VIT. A 4%; VIT. C 0%; CALC. 2%; IRON 4%
EXCHANGES: 1/2 STARCH, 3 LEAN MEAT **CARB. CHOICES:** 1/2

Cold Poached Salmon with Herb Mayonnaise

PREP: 25 min **COOK:** 19 min **CHILL:** 2 hr ■ **6 SERVINGS**

Salmon

2 cups water
1 cup dry white wine, nonalcoholic white wine or apple juice
1 teaspoon salt
1/4 teaspoon dried thyme leaves
1/4 teaspoon dried oregano leaves
1/8 teaspoon ground red pepper (cayenne)
1 small onion, sliced
4 black peppercorns
4 sprigs cilantro
2 lb salmon or other medium-firm fish fillets

Herb Mayonnaise

3/4 cup mayonnaise or salad dressing
1 1/2 tablespoons chopped fresh or 1 1/2 teaspoons dried dill weed or tarragon leaves
1 tablespoon chopped fresh chives
1 tablespoon chopped fresh parsley
1 tablespoon lemon juice
1 1/2 teaspoons Dijon mustard
Dash of ground red pepper (cayenne)

Garnish

Lemon wedges, if desired

1. In 12-inch skillet, heat all ingredients for the Salmon except salmon, Herb Mayonnaise and lemon wedges to boiling; reduce heat to low. Cover and simmer 5 minutes.

2. Cut salmon into 6 serving pieces. Place salmon in skillet; add water to cover if necessary. Heat to boiling; reduce heat to low. Simmer uncovered about 14 minutes or until salmon flakes easily with fork.

3. Carefully remove salmon with slotted spatula; drain on wire rack. Cover and refrigerate about 2 hours or until chilled.

4. Meanwhile, in small bowl, mix all Herb Mayonnaise ingredients; cover and refrigerate until serving. Serve salmon with Herb Mayonnaise and lemon wedges.

1 SERVING: CAL. 415 (CAL. FROM FAT 280); FAT 31g (SAT. FAT 6g); CHOL. 115mg; SODIUM 380mg; CARBS. 1g (FIBER 0g); PRO. 33g **% DAILY VALUE:** VIT. A 6%; VIT. C 2%; CALC. 2%; IRON 6% **EXCHANGES:** 4 MEDIUM-FAT MEAT, 2 1/2 FAT **CARB. CHOICES:** 0

Salmon Burgers with Sour Cream–Dill Sauce

PREP: 20 min **COOK:** 8 min ■ **4 SERVINGS**

Sour Cream–Dill Sauce

1/3 cup sour cream
3 tablespoons mayonnaise or salad dressing
3/4 teaspoon dried dill weed

Salmon Burgers

1 large egg
2 tablespoons milk
1 can (14 3/4 oz) red or pink salmon, drained, skin and bones removed and salmon flaked
2 medium green onions, chopped (2 tablespoons)
1 cup soft bread crumbs (about 1 1/2 slices bread)
1/4 teaspoon salt
1 tablespoon vegetable oil

1. In small bowl, stir all sauce ingredients until well mixed; refrigerate until serving.

2. In medium bowl, beat egg and milk with fork or wire whisk. Stir in remaining ingredients except oil. Shape mixture into 4 patties, about 4 inches in diameter.

3. In 10-inch nonstick skillet, heat oil over medium heat. Cook patties in oil about 8 minutes, turning once, until golden brown. Serve with sauce.

1 SERVING: CAL. 390 (CAL. FROM FAT 205); FAT 23g (SAT. FAT 6g); CHOL. 125mg; SODIUM 930mg; CARBS. 22g (FIBER 1g); PRO. 24g **% DAILY VALUE:** VIT. A 6%; VIT. C 0%; CALC. 30%; IRON 16% **EXCHANGES:** 1 1/2 STARCH, 3 MEDIUM-FAT MEAT, 1 FAT **CARB. CHOICES:** 1 1/2

Salmon Burgers with Sour Cream–Dill Sauce ▶

Shellfish Basics

Shellfish adds a taste of the sea to many wonderful dishes. Wherever you live, it's easy to find fresh and frozen shellfish any time of year. Check out the selection at your local supermarket or seafood market. Shellfish are usually grouped into two main categories:

Crustaceans have long bodies with soft, jointed shells and legs. Crabs, crayfish, lobster and shrimp are crustaceans.

Mollusks have soft bodies with no spinal column and are covered by a shell in one or more pieces. Mollusks are divided into three groups. Bivalves include clams, mussels, oysters and scallops. Cephalopods include octopus and squid, and gastropods include abalone and snails.

BUYING SHELLFISH

It's always smart to choose food carefully, but when buying shellfish it's especially important. If it's not fresh, don't buy it. Here are some things to look for:

Clams, mussels and oysters in shells should be purchased live. Look for tightly closed shells that are not cracked, chipped or broken. They should have a mild odor. The shell may open naturally but will close if lightly tapped, indicating it is still alive. Throw out any that are dead.

IMITATION SEAFOOD PRODUCTS

Imitation seafood products are less expensive than shellfish but provide a similar taste and texture in recipes. They come in various shapes like crab legs or pieces, lobster pieces and scallop pieces. Imitation seafood is usually made from pollock, a mild white-fleshed fish. To flavor it, real shellfish, a shellfish extract or artificial shellfish flavoring is added. Check labels carefully if you have a shellfish allergy.

Shucked clams, mussels and oysters (no shells) should be plump and surrounded by a clear, slightly milky or light gray liquid.

Shucked scallop varieties include *sea scallops,* which average 1 1/2 to 2 inches in diameter, and the tiny *bay scallops,* about 1/2 inch in diameter. Sweet and moist, scallops should look moist, have a mild, sweet odor and not be standing in liquid or in direct contact with ice. Scallops are usually creamy white and may be tinted light orange, light tan or pink.

Live crabs and lobsters will show some leg movement, and lobsters will curl their tails under when picked up. Crab and lobster must be cooked live or killed immediately before cooking; throw out any that are dead. Crabmeat is available in a pasteurized fresh form, and both crab and lobster meat are available frozen and canned.

Shrimp are sold either raw ("green") with the heads on; raw in the shell without the heads; raw and peeled and deveined ("cleaned"); cooked in the shell; or cooked, peeled and deveined. Shrimp should have a clean sea odor, if they smell like ammonia, don't purchase them. Fresh shrimp are sold by a descriptive size name like *jumbo* or *large,* and by "count," or number per pound. The larger the shrimp, the lower the count; the smaller the shrimp, the higher the count. Check the chart on page 250 for shrimp size and counts.

STORING SHELLFISH

- Live crabs (hard- or soft-shell) and lobster should be cooked the same day they are purchased. Before cooking, put them on a tray with sides, cover with a damp cloth and refrigerate.
- Scallops, shrimp, squid and shucked shellfish should be stored in a leakproof bag or plastic

container with a lid. Use scallops, shrimp and squid within 1 to 2 days. Shucked oysters should be used within seven days.

- Live clams, mussels and oysters should be refrigerated in containers covered with clean, damp cloths, **not with airtight lids or in plastic bags, which will cause suffocation**. Live clams, mussel and oysters may open their shells even when refrigerated. Give the shells a tap—they will close if alive; if not, throw them out. Use within 1 to 2 days.

Squid, also known as calamari, should be cream colored with reddish brown spots. As squid ages, the skin will turn pinkish. Buy fresh squid that's whole with clear eyes and a clean sea odor. It's also available cleaned. Cleaned squid should be in juices, and the meat should be firm.

Note: For more information about shellfish handling, safety and nutrition, call the FDA's Center for Food Safety and Applied Nutrition, 1-888-SAFEFOOD (723-3366). Recorded information is available 24 hours a day, or you can speak to an information specialist by calling Monday through Friday, 10 a.m. to 4 p.m. eastern standard time. Or check the FDA's Web site at www.fda.gov.

SHRIMP COUNT PER POUND

The following is an approximate guide to the number, or count, per pound of raw shrimp in shells, along with the common market names.

Shrimp Market Name	Count (Number) Per Pound
Colossal	Less than 10
Jumbo	11 to 15
Extra Large	16 to 20
Large	21 to 30
Medium	31 to 35
Small	36 to 45
Miniature to Tiny	About 100

SHELLFISH SERVINGS PER POUND

The number of servings per pound varies depending on the type and form of shellfish. Note that the serving amount for clams, mussels and oysters is given by number per serving.

Type of Shellfish	Servings per Pound (Numbers are per person)
Clams, Mussels, Oysters	
In shell	3 large hard-shell clams 6 small hard-shell clams 18 *razor* or *steamer clams* 18 mussels 6 oysters
Shucked	1/4 pound
Crab (hard-shell) or Lobster	1 1/4 pound live or 1/4 pound cooked
Crab, soft-shell	2 per person
Shrimp	
With head, unpeeled	1 pound
Headless, unpeeled	1/2 pound
Headless, peeled	1/4 pound
Squid	
Whole	1/2 pound
Cleaned	1/4 pound

COOKING SHELLFISH

Cooked shellfish should be moist and slightly chewy. Watch carefully; overcooking makes it tough and rubbery. Follow these guidelines to determine when shellfish is done:

- Crabs and lobsters will turn bright red.
- Scallops turn milky white or opaque and become firm. Cooking time depends on the size.
- Raw shrimp will turn pink and become firm. Cooking time depends on the size.
- Live clams, oysters and mussels will open their shells as they are done.
- Shucked clams, oysters and mussels will become plump, firm and opaque. Oyster edges will start to curl.

TIMETABLE FOR MICROWAVING SHELLFISH

1. Pat scallops dry with paper towels; cut large scallops in half. Rinse shrimp. Arrange shellfish in circle in shallow microwavable dish that's large enough to hold shellfish in a single layer.
2. Cover with plastic wrap, folding one edge or corner back about 1/4 inch to vent steam.
3. Microwave on High (100%) as directed in chart, rotating dish once if microwave does not have turntable, until shrimp are pink and firm or until scallops are white. Keep covered during standing time.

Type	Approximate Weight	Microwave Time	Stand Time
Scallops, bay or sea	1 pound	4 to 5 minutes	2 minutes
Shrimp, peeled and deveined	1 pound	6 to 8 minutes, stirring after 3 minutes	3 minutes
Shrimp in the shell	1 pound	5 to 7 minutes, stirring after 3 minutes	3 minutes

TIMETABLE FOR REHEATING COOKED CRAB LEGS

1. Cut crab legs to fit 8-inch square microwavable dish.
2. Cover with plastic wrap, folding one edge or corner back about 1/4 inch to vent steam.
3. Microwave on Medium-High (70%) as directed in chart below, rotating dish once if microwave does not have turntable, until hot.

Type	Approximate Weight	Microwave Time	Stand Time
Cooked crab legs in shell, thawed if frozen	2 pounds	5 to 6 minutes	5 minutes

Boiled Shrimp LOW-FAT

PREP: 30 min **COOK:** 5 min ■ **4 SERVINGS**

Cocktail Sauce

1 cup ketchup
4 teaspoons prepared horseradish
1 teaspoon Worcestershire sauce
2 or 3 drops red pepper sauce

Shrimp

4 cups water
1 lb uncooked medium shrimp in shells, thawed if frozen

1. In small bowl, mix all Cocktail Sauce ingredients. Stir in 1 to 2 teaspoons additional horseradish, if desired, until sauce has desired flavor. Cover and refrigerate until serving.

2. Heat water to boiling in 3-quart saucepan. Add shrimp. Cover and heat to boiling; reduce heat. Simmer uncovered 3 to 5 minutes or until shrimp are pink and firm; drain.

3. Peel shrimp, leaving tails on. Make a shallow cut lengthwise down back of each shrimp; wash out vein (see How to Devein Shrimp, page 253). Serve shrimp with sauce.

1 SERVING: CAL. 125 (CAL. FROM FAT 10); FAT 1g (SAT. FAT 0g); CHOL. 105mg; SODIUM 870mg; CARBS. 17g (FIBER 1g); PRO. 12g
% DAILY VALUE: VIT. A 18%; VIT. C 10%; CALC. 4%; IRON 12%
EXCHANGES: 1 OTHER CARB., 2 VERY-LEAN MEAT
CARB. CHOICES: 1

SHELLFISH

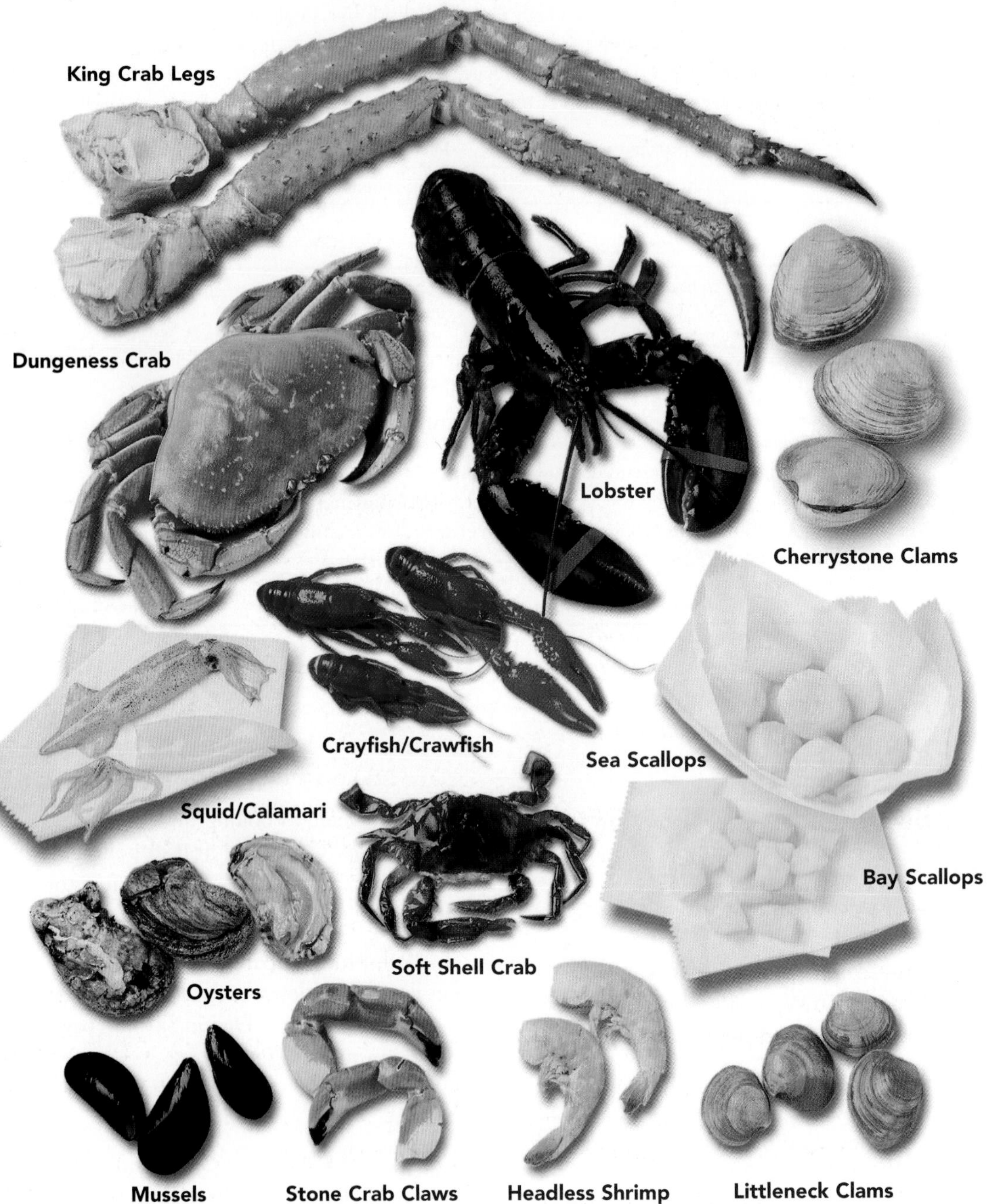
King Crab Legs
Dungeness Crab
Lobster
Cherrystone Clams
Crayfish/Crawfish
Sea Scallops
Squid/Calamari
Bay Scallops
Soft Shell Crab
Oysters
Mussels
Stone Crab Claws
Headless Shrimp
Littleneck Clams

HOW TO DEVEIN SHRIMP

Using a small, pointed knife or shrimp deveiner, make a shallow cut along the center back of each shrimp, and wash out vein.

Deep-Fried Shrimp

PREP: 35 min **COOK:** 1 min per batch ■ **4 SERVINGS**

When buying medium shrimp for this recipe, expect to get 31 to 35 per pound, though this number may vary slightly. Watch the temperature of the oil carefully during frying. If it starts to smoke, turn down the heat and wait a few minutes before putting in the next batch of shrimp.

- 1 lb uncooked medium shrimp in shells, thawed if frozen
- Vegetable oil
- 1/2 cup all-purpose flour
- 1 teaspoon salt
- 1/2 teaspoon pepper
- 2 large eggs
- 3/4 cup dry bread crumbs

1. Peel shrimp, leaving tails on. Make a shallow cut lengthwise down back of each shrimp; wash out vein (see How to Devein Shrimp above).

2. In deep fryer or 4-quart Dutch oven, heat oil (2 to 3 inches) to 350°F.

3. In shallow dish, mix flour, salt and pepper. In small bowl, beat eggs slightly with fork or wire whisk. Place bread crumbs in shallow dish. Coat shrimp with flour mixture. Dip shrimp into eggs, then coat with bread crumbs.

4. Fry 4 or 5 shrimp at a time in oil about 1 minute, turning once, until golden brown. Drain on paper towels.

1 SERVING: CAL. 310 (CAL. FROM FAT 125); FAT 14g (SAT. FAT 3g); CHOL. 210mg; SODIUM 920mg; CARBS. 27g (FIBER 1g); PRO. 19g
% DAILY VALUE: VIT. A 6%; VIT. C 0%; CALC. 8%; IRON 22%
EXCHANGES: 2 STARCH, 2 LEAN MEAT, 1 FAT **CARB. CHOICES:** 2

DEEP-FRIED OYSTERS OR CLAMS Substitute 3/4 lb shucked oysters or clams, drained, for the shrimp.

DEEP-FRIED SEA SCALLOPS Substitute 3/4 lb shucked sea scallops, drained, for the shrimp. Fry 3 to 4 minutes or until golden brown. Bay scallops, which are smaller, will cook more quickly.

Shrimp Scampi **LOW-FAT**

PREP: 30 min **COOK:** 3 min ■ **6 SERVINGS**

Serve these succulent shrimp over a bed of hot fettuccine or angel hair pasta and sprinkle with freshly chopped parsley.

- 1 1/2 lb uncooked medium shrimp in shells, thawed if frozen
- 2 tablespoons olive or vegetable oil
- 1 tablespoon chopped fresh parsley
- 2 tablespoons lemon juice
- 1/4 teaspoon salt
- 2 medium green onions, thinly sliced (2 tablespoons)
- 2 cloves garlic, finely chopped
- Grated Parmesan cheese, if desired

1. Peel shrimp. Make a shallow cut lengthwise down back of each shrimp; wash out vein (see How to Devein Shrimp above).

2. In 10-inch skillet, heat oil over medium heat. Cook shrimp and remaining ingredients except cheese in oil 2 to 3 minutes, stirring frequently, until shrimp are pink and firm; remove from heat. Sprinkle with cheese.

1 SERVING: CAL. 90 (CAL. FROM FAT 35); FAT 4g (SAT. FAT 1g); CHOL. 105mg; SODIUM 220mg; CARBS. 1g (FIBER 0g); PRO. 12g
% DAILY VALUE: VIT. A 4%; VIT. C 4%; CALC. 2%; IRON 10%
EXCHANGES: 2 VERY LEAN MEAT, 1/2 FAT **CARB. CHOICES:** 0

Shrimp Creole LOW-FAT

PREP: 30 min **COOK:** 30 min ▪ **6 SERVINGS**

- 2 lb uncooked medium shrimp in shells, thawed if frozen
- 1/4 cup butter or margarine
- 3 medium onions, chopped (1 1/2 cups)
- 2 medium green bell peppers, finely chopped (2 cups)
- 2 medium stalks celery, finely chopped (1 cup)
- 2 cloves garlic, finely chopped
- 1 cup water
- 2 teaspoons chopped fresh parsley
- 1 1/2 teaspoons salt
- 1/4 teaspoon ground red pepper (cayenne)
- 2 dried bay leaves
- 1 can (15 oz) tomato sauce
- 6 cups hot cooked rice (page 375)

1. Peel shrimp. Make a shallow cut lengthwise down back of each shrimp; wash out vein (see How to Devein Shrimp, page 253). Cover and refrigerate.

2. In 3-quart saucepan, melt butter over medium heat. Cook onions, bell peppers, celery and garlic in butter about 10 minutes, stirring occasionally, until onions are tender.

3. Stir in remaining ingredients except rice and shrimp. Heat to boiling; reduce heat to low. Simmer uncovered 10 minutes.

4. Stir in shrimp. Heat to boiling; reduce heat to medium. Cover and cook 4 to 6 minutes, stirring occasionally, until shrimp are pink and firm. Remove bay leaves. Serve shrimp mixture over rice.

1 SERVING: CAL. 380 (CAL. FROM FAT 80); FAT 9g (SAT. FAT 5g); CHOL. 160mg; SODIUM, 1280mg; CARBS. 54g (FIBER 3g); PRO. 21g
% DAILY VALUE: VIT. A 26%; VIT. C 42%; CALC. 6%; IRON 28%
EXCHANGES: 3 STARCH, 2 VEGETABLE, 1 LEAN MEAT, 1 FAT
CARB. CHOICES: 3 1/2

LIGHTER SHRIMP CREOLE

For 3 grams of fat and 335 calories per serving, decrease butter to 1 tablespoon and use nonstick saucepan.

Crab-Stuffed Shrimp

LOW-FAT

PREP: 45 min **COOK:** 2 min **BAKE:** 30 min ▪ **4 SERVINGS**

For an utterly decadent dinner, serve these shrimp with Hollandaise Sauce on page 410.

- 16 uncooked peeled deveined extra-large shrimp (about 1 lb), thawed if frozen and shells left on tails
- 1 tablespoon butter or margarine
- 2 tablespoons finely chopped onion
- 2 tablespoons finely chopped celery
- 1 clove garlic, finely chopped
- 2 tablespoons dry white wine or nonalcoholic white wine
- 1/2 cup soft bread crumbs (about 1 slice bread)
- 1/4 teaspoon salt
- 1 tablespoon chopped fresh parsley
- 2 tablespoons whipping (heavy) cream
- 1 can (6 oz) crabmeat, drained and rinsed
- 2 tablespoons grated Parmesan cheese
- 1/8 teaspoon paprika

◀ **Shrimp Creole**

1. Heat oven to 375°F.

2. Leaving the tail intact, cut a slit on the inside curve of each shrimp without cutting all the way through. Press open to butterfly.

3. In 10-inch skillet, melt butter over medium heat. Cook onion, celery and garlic in butter about 2 minutes, stirring occasionally, until softened. Stir in wine; cook about 30 seconds or until bubbly.

4. In medium bowl, stir vegetable mixture, bread crumbs, salt, parsley, whipping cream and crabmeat until well mixed.

5. Mound slightly less than 1 tablespoon of stuffing onto each butterflied shrimp, pressing to shape. In ungreased 15 × 10 × 1-inch pan, place shrimp with stuffing sides up. Sprinkle cheese and paprika over stuffing.

6. Bake about 30 minutes or until shrimp are pink and firm and stuffing is starting to brown.

1 SERVING: CAL. 195 (CAL. FROM FAT 70); FAT 8g (SAT. FAT 4g); CHOL. 135mg; SODIUM 80mg; CARBS. 11g (FIBER 1g); PRO. 20g **% DAILY VALUE:** VIT. A 8%; VIT. C 2%; CALC. 14%; IRON 14% **EXCHANGES:** 1 OTHER CARB., 3 VERY LEAN MEAT, 1/2 FAT **CARB. CHOICES:** 1

Almond-Crusted Shrimp

PREP: 20 min **BAKE:** 35 min ■ **4 SERVINGS**

Panko, or Japanese bread crumbs, are coarser in texture than those typically used in the United States, providing a very crunchy crust.

- 1/2 cup all-purpose flour
- 1 1/4 teaspoons salt
- 1 large egg
- 2 tablespoons water
- 1 cup panko or plain dry bread crumbs
- 1/2 cup sliced almonds
- 16 uncooked peeled deveined extra-large shrimp (about 1 lb), thawed if frozen and peel left on tails
- 1/4 cup butter or margarine, melted

1. Heat oven to 375°F. Generously spray 15 × 10 × 1-inch pan with cooking spray.

2. In shallow dish, mix flour and salt. In another shallow dish, beat egg and water with fork or wire whisk until well mixed. In third shallow dish, mix bread crumbs and almonds.

3. Coat shrimp with flour mixture. Dip shrimp into egg, coating well; finally, cover with bread crumb mixture, spooning mixture over shrimp and pressing to coat. Place coated shrimp in pan. Drizzle with butter.

4. Bake 30 to 35 minutes or until shrimp are pink and firm.

1 SERVING: CAL. 395 (CAL. FROM FAT 190); FAT 21g (SAT. FAT 9g); CHOL. 160mg; SODIUM 1150mg; CARBS. 34g (FIBER 2g); PRO. 18g **% DAILY VALUE:** VIT. A 12%; VIT. C 0%; CALC. 12%; IRON 24% **EXCHANGES:** 2 STARCH, 2 LEAN MEAT, 2 1/2 FAT **CARB. CHOICES:** 2

Almond-Crusted Shrimp

HOW TO OPEN RAW CLAMS

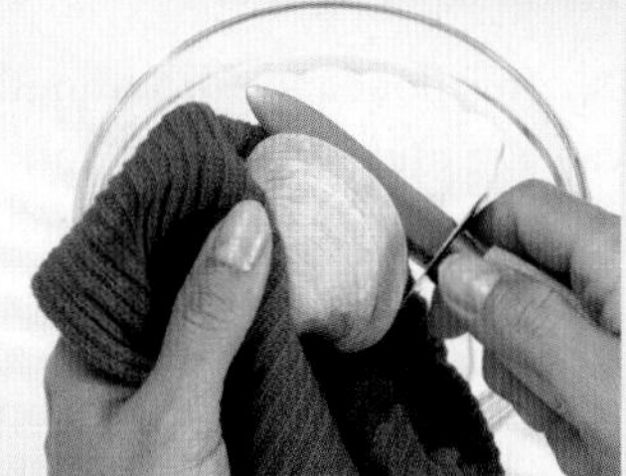

Hold a clam with the hinged side against a heavy cloth or oven mitt. Insert an oyster knife or blunt-tipped knife between shell halves.

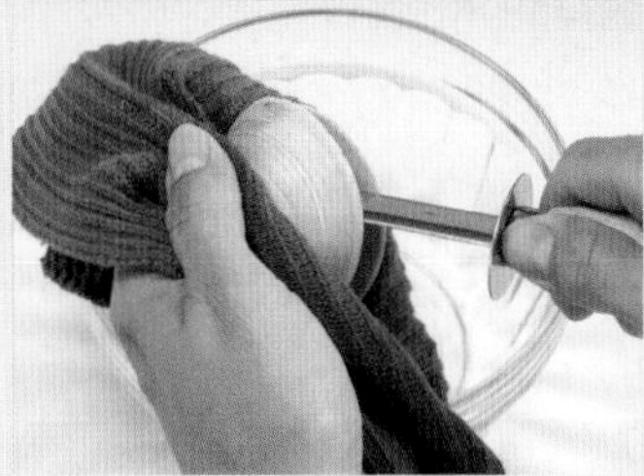

Gently twist the knife to pry open the shell and release juices. Be sure to work over a bowl or plate to catch juices.

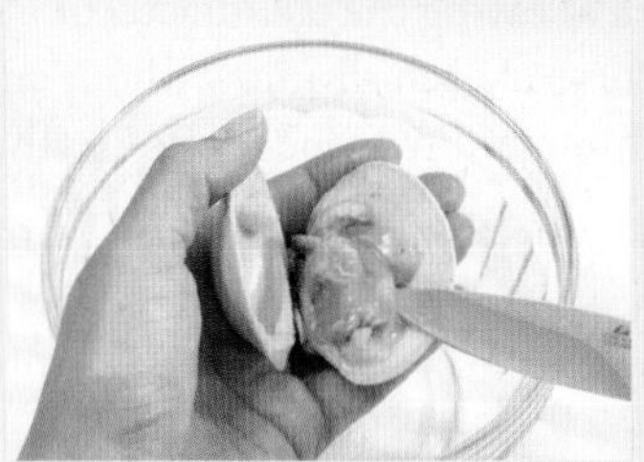

Holding the clam firmly, move a sharp knife around the clam, cutting the muscle at the hinge. Gently twist the knife to pry open the shell. Cut the clam meat from the shell.

Steamed Clams LOW-FAT

PREP: 10 min **STAND:** 30 min **COOK:** 8 min ■ **4 SERVINGS**

4 lb clams in shells
6 cups water
1/3 cup white vinegar
1/2 cup boiling water
Butter or margarine, melted, if desired

1. Discard any broken-shell or open (dead) clams. Place remaining clams in large container. Cover with 6 cups water and the vinegar. Let stand 30 minutes; drain. Scrub clams in cold water.

2. In steamer,* place clams and boiling water. Cover and steam 5 to 8 minutes or until clams open at least 1 inch, removing clams as they open. Discard any unopened clams.

3. Serve hot clams in shells with butter.

**If steamer is not available, place clams in 6-quart Dutch oven. Add 1 inch boiling water; cover tightly.*

1 SERVING: CAL. 55 (CAL. FROM FAT 10); FAT 1g (SAT. FAT 0g); CHOL. 25mg; SODIUM 40mg; CARBS. 2g (FIBER 0g); PRO. 9g
% DAILY VALUE: VIT. A 4%; VIT. C 6%; CALC. 2%; IRON 52%
EXCHANGES: 1 LEAN MEAT **CARB. CHOICES:** 0

Steamed Mussels LOW-FAT

PREP: 20 min **COOK:** 5 min per batch ■ **4 SERVINGS**

4 lb mussels in shells
1/2 cup boiling water
Butter or margarine, melted, if desired

1. Discard any broken-shell or open (dead) mussels. Scrub remaining mussels in cold water, removing any barnacles with a dull paring knife. Follow directions on page 257 to remove beards.

2. Place mussels in large container. Cover with cool water. Agitate water with hand, then drain and discard water. Repeat several times until water runs clear; drain.

3. In steamer,* place half of the mussels and the boiling water. Cover and steam 3 to 5 minutes, removing mussels as they open. Discard any unopened mussels. Repeat with remaining mussels.

4. Serve hot mussels in shells with butter.

◀ **Steamed Mussels**

**If steamer is not available, place mussels in 6-quart Dutch oven. Add 1 inch boiling water; cover tightly.*

1 SERVING: CAL. 90 (CAL. FROM FAT 10); FAT 1g (SAT. FAT 0g); CHOL. 45mg; SODIUM 370mg; CARBS. 3g (FIBER 0g); PRO. 17g
% DAILY VALUE: VIT. A 8%; VIT. C 14%; CALC. 6%; IRON 100%
EXCHANGES: 2 1/2 VERY LEAN MEAT **CARB. CHOICES:** 0

STEAMED OYSTERS Substitute oysters for the mussels. Clean as directed in Step 1 (oysters do not have beards). Omit Step 2. Continue as directed. Steam 5 to 8 minutes.

HOW TO REMOVE BEARDS FROM MUSSELS

Pull beard by giving it a tug (using a kitchen towel may help). If you have trouble removing it, use pliers to grip and pull gently.

Boiled Hard-Shell Blue Crabs LOW-FAT

PREP: 20 min **COOK:** 10 min per batch ▪ **4 SERVINGS**

Blue crab is the most familiar hard-shell crab. It is usually four to six inches in diameter and often has red claw tips.

4 quarts water
16 live hard-shell blue crabs
Cocktail Sauce (page 251), if desired

1. In stockpot or canner, heat water to boiling. Drop 4 crabs at a time into water. Cover and heat to boiling; reduce heat to low. Simmer 10 minutes; drain. Repeat with remaining crabs.

2. Follow directions below to remove meat. Serve with Cocktail Sauce.

1 SERVING: CAL. 100 (CAL. FROM FAT 20); FAT 2g (SAT. FAT 0g); CHOL. 105mg; SODIUM 290mg; CARBS. 0g (FIBER 0g); PRO. 21g
% DAILY VALUE: VIT. A 2%; VIT. C 2%; CALC. 10%; IRON 4%
EXCHANGES: 3 VERY LEAN MEAT **CARB. CHOICES:** 0

SOFT-SHELL CRABS

Soft-shell crabs are actually the same species as Atlantic hard-shell blue crabs, except the soft-shell crabs have been caught immediately after shedding their old hard shells. They stay soft for only a couple of hours. When their new shells harden, they are known as hard-shell blue crabs. Like all live crabs, they should be cooked the same day they're purchased.

HOW TO REMOVE CRABMEAT

Place crab on its back. Using thumb, pry up the tail flap, twist off and discard. Turn right side up; pry up top shell. Pull it away from the body and discard.

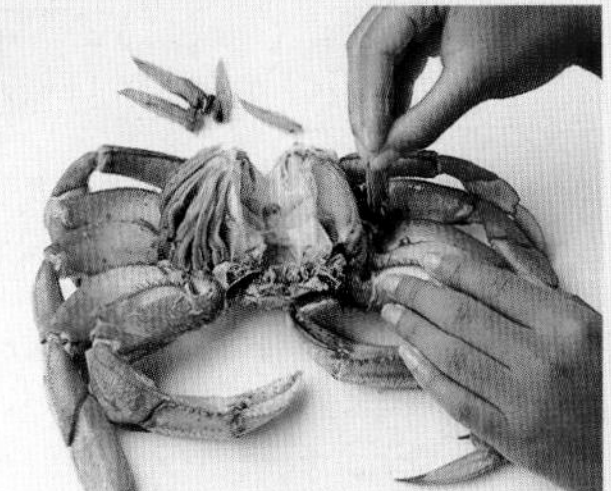

Using a small knife (or fingers), cut the gray-white gills from both sides of the crab. Discard gills and internal organs.

To remove meat, twist off claws and legs; use a nutcracker to crack shells at the joints. Remove meat with a small cocktail fork or nutpick. Break the body; remove any remaining meat.

Boiled Lobsters LOW-FAT

PREP: 20 min **COOK:** 12 min ▪ **2 SERVINGS**

2 to 4 quarts water
2 live lobsters (about 1 lb each)
Butter or margarine, melted, if desired
Lemon wedges, if desired

1. Fill 6-quart Dutch oven or stockpot one-third full of water. Heat to boiling. Plunge lobsters headfirst into water. Cover and heat to boiling; reduce heat to low. Simmer 10 to 12 minutes or until lobsters turn bright red; drain.

2. Follow directions below to remove meat. Serve with butter and lemon wedges.

1 SERVING: CAL. 100 (CAL. FROM FAT 10); FAT 1g (SAT. FAT 0g); CHOL. 85mg; SODIUM 450mg; CARBS. 1g (FIBER 0g); PRO. 21g
% DAILY VALUE: VIT. A 0%; VIT. C 0%; CALC. 6%; IRON 2%
EXCHANGES: 3 VERY LEAN MEAT **CARB. CHOICES:** 0

Lobster Newburg LOW-FAT

PREP: 10 min **COOK:** 15 min ▪ **6 SERVINGS**

1/4 cup butter or margarine
3 tablespoons all-purpose flour
1/2 teaspoon salt
1/2 teaspoon ground mustard
1/4 teaspoon pepper
2 cups milk
2 cups cut-up cooked lobster
2 tablespoons dry sherry or apple juice
6 cups hot cooked rice (page 375)

1. In 3-quart saucepan, melt butter over medium heat. Stir in flour, salt, mustard and pepper. Cook, stirring constantly, until smooth and bubbly; remove from heat.

2. Stir in milk. Heat to boiling, stirring constantly. Boil and stir 1 minute. Stir in lobster and sherry; heat through. Serve over rice.

1 SERVING: CAL. 365 (CAL. FROM FAT 90); FAT 10g (SAT. FAT 6g); CHOL. 60mg; SODIUM 470mg; CARBS. 52g (FIBER 1g); PRO. 17g
% DAILY VALUE: VIT. A 12%; VIT. C 0%; CALC. 14%; IRON 12%
EXCHANGES: 3 STARCH, 1/2 MILK, 1 LEAN MEAT, 1/2 FAT
CARB. CHOICES: 3 1/2

CRAB NEWBURG Substitute 2 cups chopped cooked crabmeat or imitation crabmeat for the lobster.

HOW TO REMOVE LOBSTER MEAT

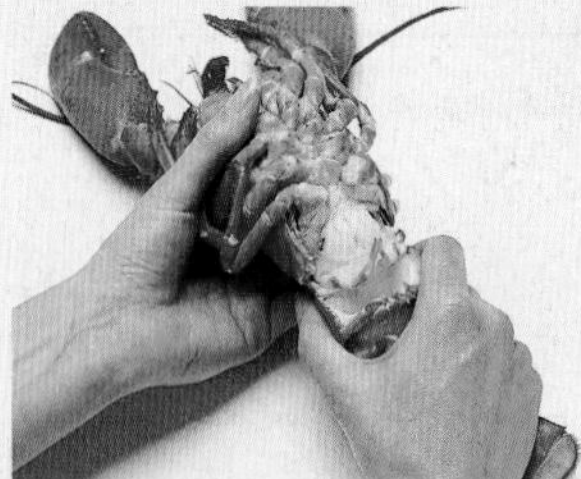

Separate tail from body by breaking shell in half where tail and body meet.

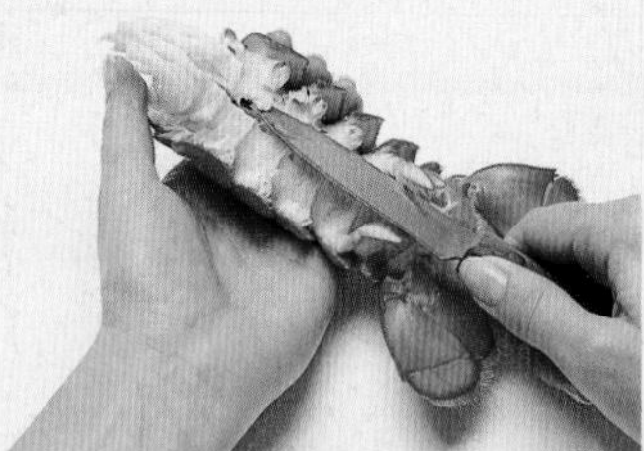

Cut away the membrane on the tail to expose meat. Discard the intestinal vein that runs through the tail and the small sac near the head of the lobster. Serve the green tomalley (liver) and coral roe (only in females) if desired.

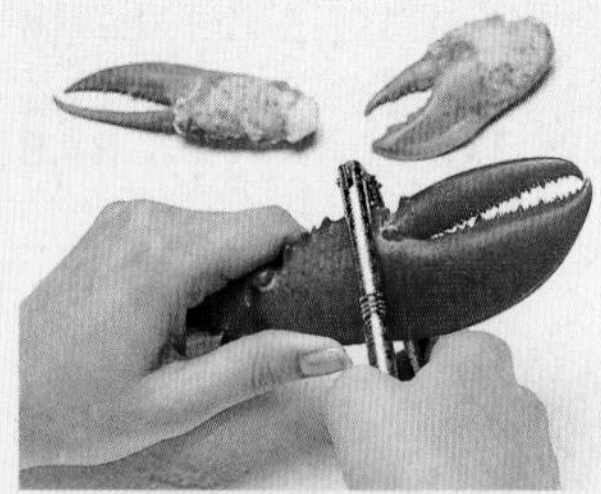

Twist the large claws away from the body of the lobster. Use a nutcracker to break open the claws. Remove meat from claws, tail and body.

Coquilles Saint Jacques

PREP: 45 min **COOK:** 15 min **BROIL:** 5 min ▪
6 SERVINGS

Coquilles *is French for "shell" or "scallop." Look for cleaned authentic or porcelain look-alike scallop shells in kitchenware or gourmet food shops; both can be used in the oven.*

- 1 1/2 lb bay scallops*
- 1 cup dry white wine, nonalcoholic white wine or chicken broth
- 1/4 cup chopped fresh parsley
- 1/2 teaspoon salt
- 2 tablespoons butter or margarine
- 6 oz mushrooms, sliced (2 cups)
- 2 shallots or green onions, chopped (2 to 3 tablespoons)
- 3 tablespoons butter or margarine
- 3 tablespoons all-purpose flour
- 1/2 cup half-and-half
- 1/2 cup shredded Swiss cheese (2 oz)
- 1 cup soft bread crumbs (about 1 1/2 slices bread)
- 2 tablespoons butter or margarine, melted

1. Lightly grease six 4-inch baking shells or ceramic ramekins** with butter. Place in 15 × 10 × 1-inch pan.

2. In 3-quart saucepan, place scallops, wine, parsley and salt. Add just enough water to cover scallops. Heat to boiling; reduce heat to low. Simmer uncovered about 6 minutes or until scallops are white.

3. Remove scallops with slotted spoon; reserve liquid. Heat reserved liquid to boiling. Boil until reduced to 1 cup. Strain and reserve.

4. In same saucepan, melt 2 tablespoons butter over medium heat. Cook mushrooms and shallots in butter 5 to 6 minutes, stirring occasionally, until mushrooms are tender. Remove from saucepan.

5. In same saucepan, melt 3 tablespoons butter over medium heat. Stir in flour. Cook, stirring constantly, until smooth and bubbly; remove from heat. Gradually stir in reserved liquid. Heat to boiling, stirring constantly; cook and stir 1 minute. Stir in half-and-half, scallops, mushroom mixture and 1/4 cup of the cheese; heat through.

6. In small bowl, toss bread crumbs and 2 tablespoons melted butter. Divide scallop mixture among baking shells. Sprinkle with remaining 1/4 cup cheese and the bread crumbs.

7. Set oven control to broil. Broil baking shells with tops 5 inches from heat 3 to 5 minutes or until crumbs are toasted.

**2 packages (12 oz each) frozen scallops, thawed, can be substituted for the fresh scallops.*

***Do not use glass custard cups or glass pie plates; they cannot withstand the heat from the broiler and may break.*

1 SERVING: CAL. 345 (CAL. FROM FAT 180); FAT 20g (SAT. FAT 12g); CHOL. 70mg; SODIUM 630mg; CARBS. 21g (FIBER 1g); PRO. 20g
% DAILY VALUE: VIT. A 20%; VIT. C 4%; CALC. 22%; IRON 20%
EXCHANGES: 1 STARCH, 1 VEGETABLE, 2 LEAN MEAT, 3 FAT
CARB. CHOICES: 1 1/2

Coquilles Saint Jacques ▶

Hearty Seafood Stew

LOW-FAT

PREP: 20 min **COOK:** 40 min ▪ **6 SERVINGS**

1/2 lb uncooked medium shrimp in shells, thawed if frozen
2 tablespoons vegetable oil
2 medium carrots, thinly sliced (1 cup)
2 medium stalks celery, sliced (1 cup)
1 large onion, chopped (1 cup)
1 clove garlic, finely chopped
1 can (14.5 oz) stewed tomatoes, undrained
2 cups water
1 tablespoon beef bouillon granules
1 medium potato, cut into 1/2-inch pieces (1 cup)
1 lb cod cod or other medium-firm fish fillets, cut into 1-inch pieces
1 can (15 to 16 oz) great northern beans, rinsed and drained
1 small zucchini, cut lengthwise in half, then cut crosswise into slices (1 cup)
1 teaspoon chopped fresh or 1/4 teaspoon dried thyme leaves
1/2 teaspoon pepper
Chopped fresh parsley, if desired

1. Peel shrimp. Make a shallow cut lengthwise down back of each shrimp; wash out vein (see How to Devein Shrimp, page 253). Cover and refrigerate.

2. In 4-quart Dutch oven, heat oil over medium-high heat. Cook carrots, celery, onion and garlic in oil, stirring frequently, until vegetables are tender. Stir in tomatoes, water, bouillon granules and potato. Heat to boiling; reduce heat. Cover and simmer 20 minutes, stirring occasionally.

3. Stir in shrimp, cod, beans, zucchini, thyme and pepper. Heat to boiling; reduce heat. Cover and simmer 6 to 10 minutes or until fish flakes easily with fork and shrimp are pink and firm. Serve topped with parsley.

1 SERVING: CAL. 250 (CAL. FROM FAT 55); FAT 6g (SAT. FAT 1g); CHOL. 75mg; SODIUM 950mg; CARBS. 27g (FIBER 5g); PRO. 25g **% DAILY VALUE:** VIT. A 80%; VIT. C 0%; CALC.10%; IRON 20% **EXCHANGES:** 1 1/2 STARCH, 1 VEGETABLE, 2 1/2 VERY LEAN MEAT, 1/2 FAT **CARB. CHOICES:** 1 1/2

CHAPTER 10
Grilling

LOW-FAT = *3g or less, except main dishes with 10g or less* FAST = *Ready in 20 minutes or less* BREAD MACHINE = *Bread machine directions* SLOW COOKER = *Slow cooker directions* LIGHTER = *25% fewer calories or grams of fat*

◀ **Pork Ribs with Smoky Barbecue Sauce (page 275)**

Grilling Basics

Grilling sizzles! And as it sizzles, if fills the air with irresistible aromas. Everyone seems to love delicious food, hot off the grill. And as family, friends and neighbors gather, mealtime turns into party time. So it's no wonder grilling is now more popular than ever, whatever the season. Here are some guidelines for making outdoor cooking fun, simple and safe.

FUELING THE FIRE

Gas Grilling

For gas grills, follow the manufacturer's directions for lighting and preheating for both direct- and indirect-heat grilling. Gas grills usually heat up in 5 to 10 minutes.

Electric Outdoor Grills

For electric outdoor grills, follow the manufacturer's directions. This type of grill is great for people living in apartments or condominiums where charcoal and gas grills are usually prohibited.

Charcoal Grilling

For charcoal grills, follow the manufacturer's directions. Generally, briquettes are mounded in a pyramid shape, sprayed with liquid lighter fluid and lit. There are other ways too, so check out Starting the Fire above right.

STARTING THE FIRE

Charcoal fires are not started by lighter fluid alone; that's just one option! Look for instant-lighting briquettes, electric coil starters, fire-starter gels and paraffin starters. Follow the package directions when using these products. Never use gasoline or kerosene to start a fire because they can ignite explosively and will give foods a very off flavor.

WHEN ARE COALS READY?

After lighting briquettes, leave them in the mounded shape until they are glowing red, which takes about 20 minutes, then spread them out into a single layer. In daylight, coals are ready when coated with a light gray ash; after dark, coals are ready when they have an even red glow.

Check the temperature of the coals by holding your hand, palm side down, near the grill rack and time how long you can comfortably keep it there.

2 seconds = High heat
3 seconds = Medium-High heat
4 seconds = Medium heat
5 seconds = Low heat

CONTROLLING THE HEAT

- *If the coals are too hot,* spread the coals apart or close the air vents halfway. For a gas or electric grill, adjust the burner to a lower setting.
- *If the coals are too cool,* move the coals closer together, knock ashes off coals by tapping them with long-handled tongs or open the air vents. For a gas or electric grill, adjust the burner to a higher setting.

CONTROLLING FLARE-UPS

Fats and liquids dripping through the grill rack can cause flare-ups and burn the food. The key is to keep flare-ups from forming—and control them if they do. Here are some helpful tips for keeping them under control:

- Don't line the inside of the bottom of the grill with foil. This prevents grease from draining properly into the grease catch pan.
- Keep the bottom of the grill and grease catch pan clean and free of debris.
- Trim excess fats from meats.
- Cover the grill.
- Move food to a different area of the grill rack.
- Brush on sugary or tomato-based sauces during the last 10 to 15 minutes to avoid burning.
- Spread coals farther apart, or if necessary, remove food from the grill and spritz the flames with water from a spray bottle. When flames are gone, return food to the grill.
- For a gas or electric grill, turn all burners off. **Never use water to extinguish flames on a gas grill.** When flames are gone, light the grill again.
- Clean grill rack with a brass bristle brush after each use.
- After cooking on a gas grill, turn the heat setting to high for 10 to 15 minutes with the lid closed. This burns off residue from the grill rack and lava rock or ceramic briquettes.

DIRECT- AND INDIRECT-HEAT GRILLING

- *Direct-Heat Grilling:* Food is cooked on the grill rack directly over the heat. This method is best for foods that cook in less than 25 minutes, like burgers and steaks. Follow grill manufacturer's directions for direct grilling.
- *Indirect-Heat Grilling:* Food is cooked on the grill rack but not directly over the heat; the heat comes from the sides. This method is best for foods that take longer than 25 minutes to cook, like whole chickens or turkeys and roasts. Follow grill manufacturer's directions for indirect grilling.

FOOD SAFETY TIPS FOR GRILLING

- *Use a long-handled brush* for adding sauces or marinades to food during grilling. To prevent spreading bacteria, don't use the same brush on raw meat that you use on cooked meat. Wash the brush in hot, soapy water before using again, or use a clean brush.
- *Before using a marinade* from raw meat, poultry, fish or seafood as a sauce with cooked food, be sure to heat the marinade to boiling and then boil 1 minute, stirring constantly, before serving.
- *Never serve cooked meat, poultry, fish or seafood on the same unwashed platter* used to carry it to the grill. Why? Bacteria can be present in juices of raw meat left on the platter and transfer to the cooked food.

Smoking Basics

Smoking creates unforgettable flavor in foods all the way through to that very last bite. And the best part, smoking is almost effortless! Just put on the foods and walk away. This type of outdoor cooking doesn't need frequent tending, turning or basting. All you need is a smoker, some tips you'll find here and the willingness to experiment with many different foods, again and again!

TYPES OF SMOKERS

Smokers are tall and cylinder shaped. They consist of a firebox, water pan, one or two grill racks and a dome-shaped cover. The most common smokers are:

- Electric water smokers (generally considered more reliable than charcoal water smokers for maintaining a consistent temperature inside)
- Charcoal water smokers

The food is placed on a grill rack high above the heat. A pan of water or other liquid (beer, fruit juice, wine, cola) rests between the heat source and the food. Aromatic wood chunks, chips or shreds, which have been soaked in water, are added for smoke and flavor. Foods cook very slowly in a dense cloud of smoke and steam, infusing the characteristic smoky flavor, moisture and tenderness. Follow smoker manufacturer's directions for smoking and use of wood chunks or chips. You'll find that foods best suited to smoking include ribs, beef brisket, roasts, poultry and fish.

IMPORTANT SAFETY TIPS FOR SMOKING

Smoking isn't an exact science. For best results, follow your manufacturer's directions—plus these basic safety tips:

- *Outdoor temperatures of 65°F* or higher with little or no wind are preferred for smoking. Do not use smokers when the outdoor air temperature is lower than 55°F because the smoker and food will not get hot enough. In fact, foods smoked at temperatures hovering around 55°F may require an additional 2 to 3 hours of cooking.
- *Use two thermometers* to ensure meat, poultry, fish and seafood are smoked safely. Use an ovenproof thermometer to monitor the air temperature inside the smoker to make sure the heat stays between 225°F and 300°F throughout the cooking process. Some smokers may have a built-in thermometer, but they may not be reliable or accurate, so it's best to use a separate thermometer.
- A *digital oven-cord thermometer* is preferred for reading the food temperature because it can stay in the food in the smoker, sounding an alarm when the food has reached the correct doneness temperature. Using a dial oven-safe thermometer is another option for the food; however, you must lift the cover to check for doneness (at the minimum time given in the recipe), which releases heat and increases the cooking time. Note that some smoked foods will remain pink even when fully cooked, so using a thermometer to determine doneness is very important. See The Facts on Food Thermometers, page 31, for more information.
- *Use only completely thawed meats, poultry, fish or seafood* because the heat inside a smoker is too low to thaw and cook frozen food safely.
- *Don't peek!* Each time the cover is removed to check the food, the cooking time will be increased by 15 to 20 minutes.

WOODS FOR SMOKING

Lingering, smoldering smoke infuses food inside a smoker, creating that delicious flavor of smoked foods. Soak wood chunks, chips or shreds in water for at least 30 minutes (and drain) before using so they smolder slowly instead of catching fire and burning quickly. Place wood in the smoker according to manufacturer's directions. In general, for every hour of cooking, you'll need two wood chunks or a generous handful of chips or shreds. Start with a small amount of wood to see how you like the flavor, then add more for greater smoky flavor. Don't add too much wood over long periods or foods may taste bitter. Experiment to find the type and amount of wood that gives you the desired results. You can buy bags of wood chips in hardware stores or stores that sell outdoor equipment.

WOODS FOR SMOKING

Type of Wood*	Description	Pair With
Alder	Delicate flavor	Fish, pork, poultry
Apple	Slightly sweet, fruity	Beef, fish, pork, poultry
Cherry	Slightly sweet, fruity	Pork, poultry
Grape Vines	Slightly sweet, slightly fruity	Beef, poultry
Hickory	Strong-smoky	Beef, fish, pork, poultry
Maple	Mild-smoky, slightly sweet	Ham, poultry, vegetables
Mesquite	Similar to hickory but more delicate and sweet	Beef, fish, pork, poultry, vegetables
Peach	Slightly sweet	Fish, pork, poultry
Pecan	Similar to hickory but slightly milder	Fish, lamb, pork, poultry

**Never use resin-based woods like pine and spruce, because they will give food a very bitter flavor.*

CREATING SMOKE IN A GAS OR CHARCOAL GRILL

Don't own a smoker? Here's how to turn your charcoal or gas grill into one. If your grill has a smoker box, go ahead and use that. If not, try this method:

- Cover 1 to 2 cups wood chips or shreds or 2 or 3 wood chunks with water, and soak at least 30 minutes; drain.
- Put soaked wood onto a piece of heavy-duty foil; seal tightly, forming a pouch. Poke 6 to 8 slits in top of pouch with a sharp knife.
- Put pouch on grill rack or follow manufacturer's directions for adding wood chips. Cover grill and let the pouch get hot enough to start smoking, about 10 minutes. Add the food, leaving the pouch in the grill during cooking. Keep an extra pouch handy for longer cooking items so smoke is maintained throughout the cooking time.

Turkey on the Grill

PREP: 30 min **MARINATE:** 8 hr **GRILL:** 4 hr
STAND: 15 min ■ **12 TO 14 SERVINGS**

Lemon-Garlic Marinade

1 cup chicken broth
1/4 cup olive or vegetable oil
2 tablespoons lemon juice
1/4 cup chopped fresh basil leaves
1/4 cup chopped fresh parsley or cilantro
1/2 teaspoon salt
1/4 teaspoon pepper
2 cloves garlic, finely chopped

Turkey

12-lb whole turkey, thawed if frozen
1 poultry or meat injector
2 tablespoons Cajun seasoning

1. In blender, place all marinade ingredients. Cover and blend until smooth. If turkey has plastic leg holder, remove and discard before grilling. Remove bag of giblets and neck if present. Rinse cavity; pat dry with paper towels. Inject marinade into turkey, following the directions that came with the injector. (Or pour marinade over turkey on large tray with 1-inch sides or in large glass dish.)

2. Sprinkle Cajun seasoning inside cavity and over outside of turkey. Fasten neck skin to back of turkey with skewer. Fold wings across back of turkey so tips are touching. Tuck legs under band of skin at tail. Place turkey on large tray with 1-inch sides or in large glass dish. Cover and refrigerate 8 hours but no longer than 24 hours.

3. If using charcoal grill, place drip pan directly under grilling area, and arrange coals around edge of firebox. Heat coals or gas grill for indirect heat (page 262).

4. Insert digital oven-cord thermometer in turkey so tip is in thickest part of inside thigh muscle and does not touch bone.

5. Place turkey, breast side up, over drip pan or over unheated side of gas grill. Cover and grill over medium heat 3 to 4 hours or until thermometer reads 180°F and leg moves easily when lifted or twisted. Let stand 15 minutes before carving.

1 SERVING: CAL. 415 (CAL. FROM FAT 190); FAT 21g (SAT. FAT 6g); CHOL. 155mg; SODIUM 340mg; CARBS. 1g (FIBER 0g); PRO. 56g
% DAILY VALUE: VIT. A 6%; VIT. C 2%; CALC. 4%; IRON 16%
EXCHANGES: 8 LEAN MEAT **CARB. CHOICES:** 0

Turkey on the Grill

Beer Can Chicken

PREP: 10 min **GRILL:** 1 hr 30 min **STAND:** 15 min ▪ **6 SERVINGS**

Basic Barbecue Rub
1 tablespoon paprika
2 teaspoons salt
1/2 teaspoon garlic powder
1/2 teaspoon onion powder
1/2 teaspoon pepper

Chicken
4-to 4 1/2-lb whole chicken
1 can (12 oz) beer or lemon-lime soda pop

1. If using charcoal grill, place drip pan directly under grilling area, and arrange coals around edge of firebox. Heat coals or gas grill for indirect heat (page 262).

2. In small bowl, mix all Basic Barbecue Rub ingredients. Fold wings of chicken across back with tips touching. Sprinkle rub inside cavity and all over outside of chicken; rub with fingers.

3. Pour 1/2 cup of beer from can. Holding chicken upright with larger opening of body cavity downward; insert beer can into larger cavity. Insert barbecue meat thermometer so tip is in thickest part of inside thigh muscle and does not touch bone.

4. Place chicken with beer can upright on grill rack over drip pan or over unheated side of gas grill. Cover and grill over medium heat 1 hour 15 minutes to 1 hour 30 minutes or until thermometer reads 180°F and leg moves easily when lifted or twisted.

5. Using tongs, carefully lift chicken to 13 × 9-inch pan, holding large metal spatula under beer can for support. Let stand 15 minutes before carving. Remove beer can; discard.

1 SERVING: CAL. 315 (CAL. FROM FAT 160); FAT 18g (SAT. FAT 5g); CHOL. 115mg; SODIUM 700mg; CARBS. 1g (FIBER 0g); PRO. 35g
% DAILY VALUE: VIT. A 12%; VIT. C 0%; CALC. 2%; IRON 10%
EXCHANGES: 5 LEAN MEAT, 1 FAT **CARB. CHOICES:** 0

Lemon Chicken with Grilled Fennel and Onions

PREP: 20 min **MARINATE:** 15 min **GRILL:** 25 min ▪ **6 SERVINGS**

Fresh fennel and chicken just seem to go together naturally—especially on the grill. It has a delicate, sweet flavor similar to anise but much more subtle. Look for fennel throughout the fall and spring months and use them either raw or cooked.

6 bone-in chicken breasts (about 3 lb)
1/3 cup olive or vegetable oil
1 teaspoon grated lemon peel
1/4 cup lemon juice
2 tablespoons chopped fresh or 2 teaspoons dried oregano leaves
1/2 teaspoon salt
2 medium bulbs fennel, cut into 1/2-inch slices
1 medium red onion, cut into 1/2-inch slices
Lemon slices, if desired
Fresh oregano sprigs, if desired

HOW TO MAKE BEER CAN CHICKEN ON THE GRILL

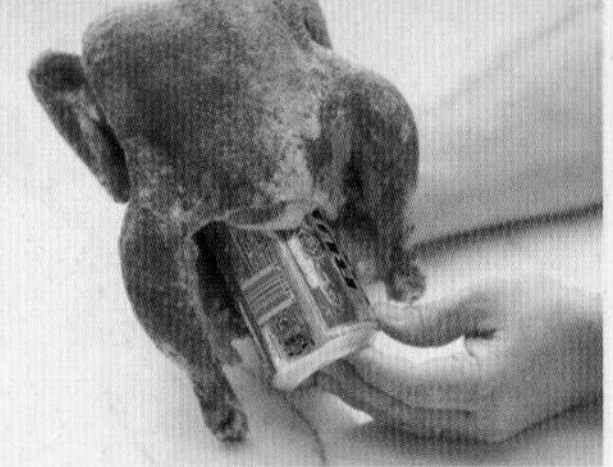

1. Insert opened beer can into cavity of chicken.

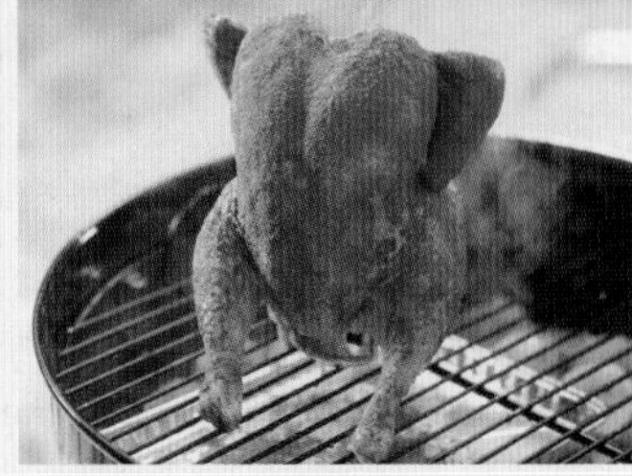

2. Place chicken with beer can upright on grill rack.

3. Using tongs, carefully lift chicken to pan, holding metal spatula under beer can for support.

1. Place chicken in shallow glass or plastic dish. In small bowl, mix oil, lemon peel, lemon juice, oregano and salt; pour over chicken. Cover and let stand 15 minutes.

2. Heat coals or gas grill for direct heat (page 262). Remove chicken from marinade. Brush fennel and onion with marinade. Cover and grill chicken (skin sides down), fennel and onion over medium heat 20 to 25 minutes, turning once and brushing frequently with marinade, until juice of chicken is clear when thickest part is cut to bone (170°F). Discard any remaining marinade. Garnish chicken with lemon slices and oregano sprigs.

1 SERVING: CAL. 265 (CAL. FROM FAT 135); FAT 15g (SAT. FAT 3g); CHOL. 75mg; SODIUM 240mg; CARBS. 8g (FIBER 3g); PRO. 28g
% DAILY VALUE: VIT. A 4%; VIT. C 10%; CALC. 6%; IRON 8%
EXCHANGES: 1 VEGETABLE, 4 LEAN MEAT, 1/2 FAT
CARB. CHOICES: 1/2

KEEPING GRILLED CHICKEN MOIST

For moist grilled chicken, use a pair of tongs instead of a fork to turn the pieces. A fork will pierce the flesh, letting too much of the juices run out and making the chicken drier.

Mediterranean Chicken Packets

PREP: 20 min **GRILL:** 25 min ■ **4 SERVINGS**

- 1 package (4 oz) crumbled basil-and-tomato feta cheese*
- 2 tablespoons grated lemon peel
- 1 teaspoon dried oregano leaves
- 4 boneless skinless chicken breasts (about 1 1/4 lb)
- 4 roma (plum) tomatoes, each cut into 3 slices
- 1 small red onion, finely chopped (1 cup)
- 20 pitted Kalamata olives

1. Heat coals or gas grill for direct heat (page 262). In small bowl, mix cheese, lemon peel and oregano.

2. Cut four 18 × 12-inch sheets of heavy-duty foil. Place 1 chicken breast, 3 tomato slices, 1/4 cup onion and 5 olives on one side of each sheet of foil. Spoon one-fourth of cheese mixture over chicken and vegetables on each sheet.

3. Fold foil over chicken and vegetables so edges meet. Seal edges, making tight 1/2-inch fold; fold again. Allow space on sides for circulation and expansion.

4. Cover and grill packets over medium heat 20 to 25 minutes or until juice of chicken is clear when thickest part is cut to bone (170°F). Place packets on plates. Cut large X across top of each packet; fold back foil.

**1 package (4 oz) regular crumbled feta cheese can be substituted for the flavored feta cheese.*

1 SERVING: CAL. 250 (CAL. FROM FAT 110); FAT 12g (SAT. FAT 6g); CHOL. 100mg; SODIUM 560mg; CARBS. 7g (FIBER 2g); PRO. 31g
% DAILY VALUE: VIT. A 12%; VIT. C 12%; CALC. 18%; IRON 10%
EXCHANGES: 1 VEGETABLE, 4 LEAN MEAT **CARB. CHOICES:** 1/2

Mediterranean Chicken Packets ▶

Pesto Chicken Packets

PREP: 15 min **GRILL:** 25 min ▪ **4 SERVINGS**

This is a perfect chance to try those heavy-duty foil bags made especially for grilling. Or make the packets yourself.

- 4 boneless skinless chicken breasts (about 1 1/4 lb)
- 8 roma (plum) tomatoes, cut into 1/2-inch slices
- 4 small zucchini, cut into 1/2-inch slices
- 1/2 cup Basil Pesto (page 405) or purchased basil pesto

1. Heat coals or gas grill for direct heat (page 262). Cut four 18 × 12-inch pieces of heavy-duty foil; spray with cooking spray.

2. Place 1 chicken breast, one-fourth of tomatoes and one-fourth of the zucchini on one side of each foil piece. Spoon 2 tablespoons Basil Pesto over chicken mixture on each sheet.

3. Fold foil over chicken and vegetables so edges meet. Seal edges, making tight 1/2-inch fold; fold again. Allow space on sides for circulation and expansion.

4. Cover and grill packets over medium heat 20 to 25 minutes or until juice of chicken is clear when thickest part is cut to bone (170°F). Place packets on plates. Cut large X across top of each packet; fold back foil.

1 SERVING: CAL. 350 (CAL. FROM FAT 190); FAT 21g (SAT. FAT 4g); CHOL. 80mg; SODIUM 350mg; CARBS. 10g (FIBER 3g); PRO. 32g
% DAILY VALUE: VIT. A 36%; VIT. C 26%; CALC. 16%; IRON 14%
EXCHANGES: 2 VEGETABLE, 4 LEAN MEAT, 2 FAT
CARB. CHOICES: 1/2

Cheddar Chicken Fillet Sandwiches

PREP: 20 min **GRILL:** 15 min ▪ **4 SANDWICHES**

Creamy mustard-mayonnaise sauce is great for grilled chicken. Look for it near the mayonnaise or mustard in the condiment aisle of your supermarket.

- 4 boneless skinless chicken breasts (about 1 1/4 lb)
- 1/2 teaspoon seasoned salt
- 1/4 teaspoon coarse pepper
- 1 medium Bermuda or other sweet onion, sliced
- 4 ounces fresh mushrooms, cut in half (1 1/2 cups)
- 1 tablespoon olive or vegetable oil
- 1/4 cup creamy mustard-mayonnaise sauce
- 4 slices sourdough bread
- 4 slices (3/4 oz each) sharp Cheddar cheese

1. Heat coals or gas grill for direct heat (page 262). Between sheets of plastic wrap or waxed paper, flatten each chicken breast to 1/4-inch thickness. Sprinkle with 1/4 teaspoon of the seasoned salt and the pepper.

2. In medium bowl, mix onion, mushrooms, remaining 1/4 teaspoon seasoned salt and the oil; toss to coat. Place in grill basket (grill "wok").

3. Place chicken and grill basket on grill. Cover and grill over medium heat 10 to 15 minutes, occasionally turning and brushing chicken with 2 tablespoons of the mustard-mayonnaise sauce and shaking grill basket to mix vegetables. Grill until chicken is clear when thickest part is cut to bone (170°F) and vegetables are tender. Add bread slices to grill for last 4 minutes of cooking, turning once, until crisp.

4. Top each cooked chicken breast with onion-mushroom mixture and cheese slice. Cover and grill until cheese is melted. Spread bread slices with remaining mustard-mayonnaise sauce. Top each bread slice with cheese-topped chicken breast.

1 SANDWICH: CAL. 550 (CAL. FROM FAT 250); FAT 28g (SAT. FAT 8g); CHOL. 100mg; SODIUM 845mg; CARBS. 36g (FIBER 2g); PRO. 39g
% DAILY VALUE: VIT. A 6%; VIT. C 0%; CALC. 15%; IRON 15%
EXCHANGES: 2 1/2 STARCH, 4 1/2 LEAN MEAT, 2 1/2 FAT
CARB. CHOICES: 2 1/2

Grilled Cranberry-Almond Chicken Salad

PREP: 20 min **GRILL:** 20 min ▪ **6 SERVINGS**

Creamy Poppy Seed Dressing*

3/4 cup mayonnaise or salad dressing
1/3 cup sugar
2 tablespoons cider vinegar
2 teaspoons poppy seed

Salad

6 boneless skinless chicken breasts (about 1 3/4 lb)
Cooking spray
1/2 teaspoon salt
3 cups bite-size pieces iceberg lettuce
3 cups bite-size pieces romaine lettuce
1/2 cup crumbled Gorgonzola cheese
1/2 cup dried cranberries
6 tablespoons slivered almonds, toasted (page 215)

1. Heat coals or gas grill for direct heat (page 262). In small bowl, mix all dressing ingredients with wire whisk. Reserve 3/4 cup dressing for the salad.

2. Spray chicken with cooking spray; sprinkle with salt. Cover and grill chicken over medium heat 15 to 20 minutes, turning once and brushing occasionally with remaining dressing, until juice is clear when thickest part is cut to bone (170°F). Discard any remaining dressing used for brushing. Cut chicken into 1/2-inch slices.

3. Divide lettuces among 6 individual serving plates. Top with chicken. Drizzle reserved 3/4 cup dressing over salads. Sprinkle with cheese, cranberries and almonds.

**1 cup purchased creamy poppy seed dressing or coleslaw dressing can be substituted for the dressing recipe.*

1 SERVING: CAL. 530 (CAL. FROM FAT 305); FAT 34g (SAT. FAT 7g); CHOL. 100mg; SODIUM 580mg; CARBS. 24g (FIBER 2g); PRO. 32g **% DAILY VALUE:** VIT. A 16%; VIT. C 16%; CALC. 12%; IRON 10% **EXCHANGES:** 1 OTHER CARB., 2 VEGETABLE, 4 LEAN MEAT, 4 1/2 FAT **CARB. CHOICES:** 1 1/2

Italian Mixed Grill

PREP: 15 min **STAND:** 1 hr **MICROWAVE:** 12 min **GRILL:** 21 min ▪ **8 SERVINGS**

Herbed Lemon Oil

1/2 cup olive or vegetable oil
3 tablespoons lemon juice
3 tablespoons chopped fresh parsley
1 tablespoon chopped fresh or 1 teaspoon dried rosemary leaves
2 teaspoons chopped fresh or 1/2 teaspoon dried thyme leaves
1/2 teaspoon salt
1/4 teaspoon pepper
2 large cloves garlic, finely chopped

Mixed Grill

4 fresh Italian sausages (about 1 lb)
1/2 cup water
1 small onion, chopped (1/4 cup)
4 boneless skinless chicken breasts or thighs (about 1 1/4 lb)
1-lb beef boneless top sirloin steak, about 1 inch thick

1. In small bowl, mix all Herbed Lemon Oil ingredients. Cover and let stand at least 1 hour to blend flavors.

2. In 2-quart microwavable casserole, place sausages, water and onion. Cover and microwave on High 5 minutes; rearrange sausages. Re-cover and microwave on Medium (50%) 5 to 7 minutes or until sausages are no longer pink in center. Remove sausages; discard onion and water.

3. Brush grill rack with vegetable oil. Heat coals or gas grill for direct heat (page 262). Brush all sides of chicken, beef and sausages with oil mixture.

4. Grill meats uncovered over medium heat, brushing frequently with oil mixture and turning occasionally, for the following times: Grill beef 5 minutes. Add chicken and continue grilling. Grill beef 12 to 16 minutes or to desired doneness. Grill chicken 15 to 20 minutes or until juice is clear when center of thickest part is cut (170°F). Add cooked sausages during the last 5 to 10 minutes of grilling to brown.

1 SERVING: CAL. 350 (CAL. FROM FAT 215); FAT 24g (SAT. FAT 6g); CHOL. 95mg; SODIUM 480mg; CARBS. 2g (FIBER 0g); PRO. 32g **% DAILY VALUE:** VIT. A 2%; VIT. C 2%; CALC. 2%; IRON 12% **EXCHANGES:** 4 1/2 MEDIUM-FAT MEAT **CARB. CHOICES:** 0

Texas T-Bones FAST

PREP: 10 min **GRILL:** 16 min ▪ **4 SERVINGS**

Crush the peppercorns in a heavy-duty resealable plastic bag using a rolling pin.

4 beef T-bone steaks, about 3/4 inch thick (10 to 12 oz each)
2 cloves garlic, cut in half
4 teaspoons black peppercorns, crushed
1/4 cup butter or margarine, softened
1 tablespoon Dijon mustard
1/2 teaspoon Worcestershire sauce
1/4 teaspoon lime juice
Salt and pepper to taste, if desired

1. Heat coals or gas grill for direct heat (page 262).

2. Trim fat on beef steaks to 1/4-inch thickness. Rub garlic on beef. Press peppercorns into beef. In small bowl, mix remaining ingredients except salt and pepper; set aside.

3. Cover and grill beef over medium heat 14 to 16 minutes for medium doneness, turning once. Sprinkle with salt and pepper. Serve with butter mixture.

1 SERVING: CAL. 390 (CAL. FROM FAT 225); FAT 25g (SAT. FAT 12g); CHOL. 140mg; SODIUM 270mg; CARBS. 1g (FIBER 0g); PRO. 40g
% DAILY VALUE: VIT. A 10%; VIT. C 0%; CALC. 0%; IRON 20%
EXCHANGES: 6 LEAN MEAT, 1 1/2 FAT **CARB. CHOICES:** 0

Strip Steaks with Chipotle-Peach Glaze

PREP: 15 min **GRILL:** 18 min ▪ **8 SERVINGS**

1/2 cup peach preserves
1/4 cup lime juice
1 chipotle chili in adobo sauce (from 7-oz can), seeded and chopped
1 teaspoon adobo sauce (from can of chilies)
2 tablespoons chopped fresh cilantro
8 beef boneless strip steaks, 1 inch thick (about 3 lb)
1 teaspoon garlic pepper*
1/2 teaspoon ground cumin
1/2 teaspoon salt
4 peaches, cut in half and pitted, if desired
Cilantro sprigs, if desired

1. Heat coals or gas grill for direct heat (page 262).

2. In 1-quart saucepan, heat preserves, lime juice, chili and adobo sauce over low heat, stirring occasionally, until preserves are melted. Stir in chopped cilantro; set aside. Sprinkle each beef steak with garlic pepper, cumin and salt.

3. Cover and grill beef over medium heat 15 to 18 minutes for medium doneness, turning once or twice and brushing top of beef with preserves mixture during last 2 minutes of grilling. Add peach halves to grill for last 2 to 3 minutes of grilling just until heated.

4. Heat any remaining preserves mixture to boiling; boil and stir 1 minute. Serve with beef and peaches. Garnish with cilantro sprigs.

LEARN WITH Betty — BEEF STEAK DONENESS GUIDE

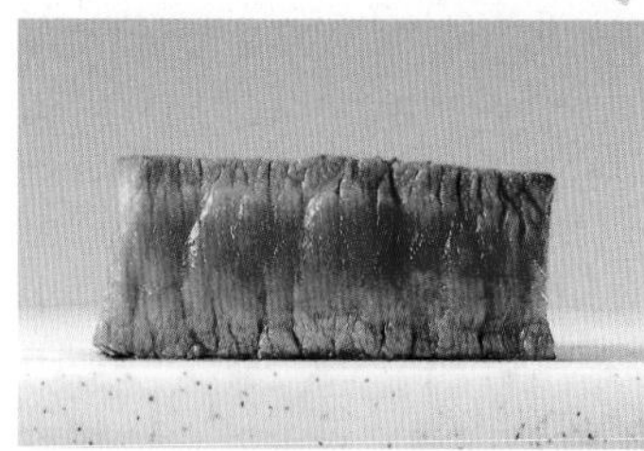

Medium rare (internal temperature 145°F). Steak will be very pink in the center and slightly brown toward the exterior.

Medium (internal temperature 160°F). Steak will be light pink in the center and brown toward the exterior.

Well done (internal temperature 170°F). Steak will be uniformly brown throughout.

**1/2 teaspoon garlic powder and 1/2 teaspoon coarsely ground black pepper can be substituted for the 1 teaspoon garlic pepper.*

1 SERVING: CAL. 315 (CAL. FROM FAT 110); FAT 12g (SAT. FAT 5g); CHOL. 95mg; SODIUM 240mg; CARBS. 14g (FIBER 0g); PRO. 37g **% DAILY VALUE:** VIT. A 0%; VIT. C 6%; CALC. 2%; IRON 18% **EXCHANGES:** 1 FRUIT, 5 LEAN MEAT **CARB. CHOICES:** 1

Fajitas

PREP: 30 min **MARINATE:** 8 hr **GRILL:** 26 min ■ **6 SERVINGS**

- Fajita Marinade (page 416)
- 1 1/2-lb beef boneless top sirloin steak, 1 1/2 inches thick
- 2 large onions, sliced
- 2 medium green or red bell peppers, cut into 1/4-inch strips
- 2 tablespoons vegetable oil
- 12 flour tortillas (8 to 10 inch)
- 1 jar (8 oz) picante sauce (1 cup)
- 1 cup shredded Cheddar or Monterey Jack cheese (4 oz)
- 1 1/2 cups Guacamole (page 46) or purchased guacamole
- 3/4 cup sour cream

1. In small bowl, make Fajita Marinade.

2. Remove fat from beef. Pierce beef with fork in several places. Place beef in resealable plastic food-storage bag or shallow glass or plastic dish. Pour marinade over beef; turn beef to coat with marinade. Cover and refrigerate at least 8 hours but no longer than 24 hours, turning beef occasionally.

3. Heat coals or gas grill for direct heat (page 262). Remove beef from marinade; reserve marinade. Cover and grill beef over medium heat 22 to 26 minutes for medium-rare to medium doneness, turning once and brushing occasionally with marinade. Discard any remaining marinade. Meanwhile, in large bowl, toss onions and bell peppers with oil; place in grill basket (grill "wok"). Cover and grill vegetables 6 to 8 minutes, shaking basket or stirring vegetables once or twice, until crisp-tender.

4. While beef and vegetables are grilling, heat oven to 325°F. Wrap tortillas in foil. Heat in oven about 15 minutes or until warm. Remove tortillas from oven; keep wrapped.

5. Cut beef across grain into very thin slices. For each fajita, place a few slices of beef, some of the onion mixture, 1 heaping tablespoonful each picante sauce and cheese, about 2 tablespoons Guacamole and 1 tablespoon sour cream on center of tortilla. Fold 1 end of tortilla up about 1 inch over filling; fold right and left sides over folded end, overlapping. Fold remaining end down.

1 SERVING: CAL. 745 (CAL. FROM FAT 325); FAT 35g (SAT. FAT 12g); CHOL. 100mg; SODIUM 1,070mg; CARBS. 66g (FIBER 8g); PRO. 39g **% DAILY VALUE:** VIT. A 24%; VIT. C 60%; CALC. 28%; IRON 36% **EXCHANGES:** 4 STARCH, 1 VEGETABLE, 4 MEDIUM-FAT MEAT, 2 FAT **CARB. CHOICES:** 4 1/2

LIGHTER FAJITAS

For 11 grams of fat and 520 calories per serving, omit vegetable oil; spray onions and bell peppers with cooking spray and toss before placing in grill basket. Use fat-free tortillas and reduced-fat cheese and sour cream. Omit Guacamole.

◀ **Strip Steaks with Chipotle-Peach Glaze**

Patty Melts with Smothered Onions

PREP: 20 min **GRILL:** 16 min ▪ **4 SERVINGS**

- 1 lb lean (at least 80%) ground beef or ground turkey*
- 1/4 teaspoon dried thyme leaves
- 1/4 teaspoon dried oregano leaves
- 2 teaspoons Dijon mustard
- 1/2 teaspoon salt
- 1/8 teaspoon pepper
- 1 clove garlic, finely chopped
- 1 teaspoon olive or vegetable oil
- 2 medium red onions, thinly sliced and separated into rings
- 1/8 teaspoon salt
- Dash of pepper
- 4 slices (3/4 oz each) Swiss cheese
- 8 slices rye bread

1. Heat coals or gas grill for direct heat (page 262). In medium bowl, mix beef, thyme, oregano, mustard, 1/2 teaspoon salt, 1/8 teaspoon pepper and the garlic. Shape mixture into 4 patties, about 3/4 inch thick; refrigerate until grilling.

2. In 8-inch skillet, heat oil over medium-high heat. Cook onions in oil, stirring frequently, until tender. Stir in 1/8 teaspoon salt and dash of pepper; keep warm.

3. Cover and grill beef patties over medium heat 13 to 15 minutes, turning once, until meat thermometer inserted in center reads 160°F and patties are no longer pink in center. Add bread slices to side of grill for last 5 minutes of grilling, turning once, until lightly toasted.

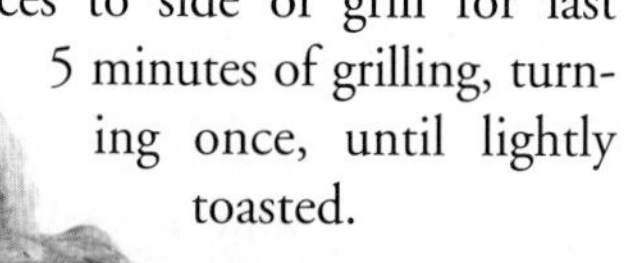

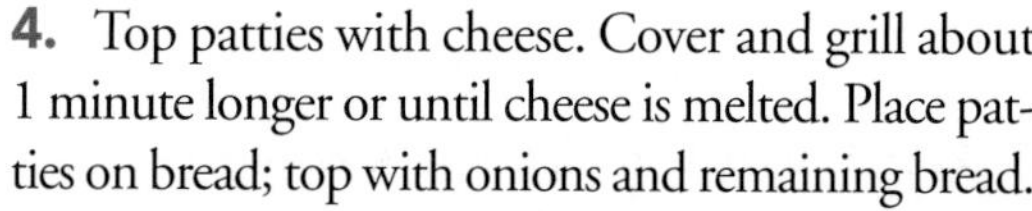

4. Top patties with cheese. Cover and grill about 1 minute longer or until cheese is melted. Place patties on bread; top with onions and remaining bread.

**If using ground turkey, brush grill rack with vegetable oil before lighting coals or turning on gas. Grill until meat thermometer inserted in center reads 165°F and patties are no longer pink in center.*

1 SERVING: CAL. 475 (CAL. FROM FAT 225); FAT 25g (SAT. FAT 11g); CHOL. 85mg; SODIUM 880mg; CARBS. 31g (FIBER 4g); PRO. 32g
% DAILY VALUE: VIT. A 6%; VIT. C 2%; CALC. 26%; IRON 18%
EXCHANGES: 2 STARCH, 4 MEDIUM-FAT MEAT, 1 FAT
CARB. CHOICES: 2

Onion-Topped Caesar Burgers

PREP: 15 min **GRILL:** 12 min ▪ **4 SANDWICHES**

- 1 lb lean (at least 80%) ground beef
- 2 tablespoons chopped fresh parsley
- 1/2 cup Caesar dressing
- 1/2 teaspoon peppered seasoned salt
- 1 small sweet onion (such as Bermuda, Maui, Spanish or Walla Walla), cut into 1/4- to 1/2-inch slices
- 1 1/2 cups shredded romaine lettuce
- 2 tablespoons freshly shredded Parmesan cheese
- 4 sandwich buns, split

1. Heat coals or gas grill for direct heat (page 262). In medium bowl, mix beef, parsley, 2 tablespoons of the dressing and the peppered seasoned salt. Shape mixture into 4 patties, about 1/2 inch thick.

2. Cover and grill patties over medium heat 10 to 12 minutes, turning once, until meat thermometer inserted in center reads 160°F and patties are no longer pink in center. Add onion slices for last 8 to 10 minutes of grilling, brushing with 2 tablespoons of the dressing and turning once, until crisp-tender.

3. In small bowl, toss romaine, remaining 1/4 cup dressing and the cheese. Layer romaine, burger and onion in each bun.

1 SANDWICH: CAL. 480 (CAL. FROM FAT 260); FAT 29g (SAT. FAT 9g); CHOL. 75mg; SODIUM 810mg; CARBS. 27g (FIBER 2g); PRO. 27g
% DAILY VALUE: VIT. A 14%; VIT. C 14%; CALC. 12%; IRON 20%
EXCHANGES: 1 1/2 STARCH, 1 VEGETABLE, 3 HIGH- FAT MEAT, 1 FAT **CARB. CHOICES:** 2

◀ **Onion-Topped Caesar Burgers**

Burger and Veggie Packets

PREP: 15 min **GRILL:** 30 min ▪ **4 SERVINGS**

- 1 lb extra-lean (at least 90% percent) ground beef
- 1 tablespoon Worcestershire sauce
- 1 teaspoon garlic pepper
- 1/2 teaspoon onion powder
- 2 cups (from 1-lb bag) frozen sugar snap peas, carrots, onions and mushrooms (or other combination)
- 32 frozen steak fries (from 28-oz bag)
- 4 frozen half-ears corn-on-the-cob
- 1/2 teaspoon garlic pepper

1. Heat coals or gas grill for direct heat (page 262). Cut four 18 × 12-inch sheets of foil.

2. In medium bowl, mix beef, Worcestershire sauce, 1 teaspoon garlic pepper and the onion powder. Shape mixture into 4 patties, about 1/4 inch thick.

3. Place 1 patty on center of each foil sheet. Top each with 1/2 cup vegetables and 8 steak fries. Place 1 piece of corn next to each patty. Sprinkle 1/2 teaspoon garlic pepper over vegetables. Fold foil over patties and vegetables. Seal edges at top, making tight 1/2-inch fold; fold again. Repeat folding at sides. Allow space on sides for circulation and expansion.

4. Cover and grill packets over medium heat 20 to 30 minutes or until vegetables are tender. Place packets on plates. Cut large X across top of each packet; fold back foil.

Burger and Veggie Packets

1 SERVING: CAL. 430 (CAL. FROM FAT 170); FAT 19g (SAT. FAT 6g); CHOL. 70mg; SODIUM 115mg; CARBS. 38g (FIBER 5g); PRO. 27g
% DAILY VALUE: VIT. A 30%; VIT. C 22%; CALC. 4%; IRON 20%
EXCHANGES: 2 STARCH, 1 VEGETABLE, 3 LEAN MEAT, 2 FAT
CARB. CHOICES: 2 1/2

TENDER, JUICY BURGERS!

It's all in the mixing and grilling! Too much handling of ground beef when forming patties makes burgers tough. Dampen your hands with water before forming the patties so the meat won't stick. This means you can shape the patties quicker, handle them less, and end up with tender burgers. For the juiciest burgers watch them closely as they grill—avoid overcooking and don't press them down with a spatula. You'll squeeze out too much of the great-tasting juices that make the burgers nice and moist!

LEARN WITH Betty — HAMBURGER DONENESS GUIDE

The center of this hamburger hasn't reached a safe temperature of 160°F; it is too pink and undercooked.

The center of this hamburger has reached a safe 160°F and is no longer pink.

This burger has been overcooked and is hard and dry.

Caribbean Pork Tenderloin

LOW-FAT

PREP: 25 min **MARINATE:** 15 min **GRILL:** 25 min ▪ **4 SERVINGS**

Dine as you would in the Caribbean islands, without leaving your home. Serve this dinner with grilled corn on the cob and melted cilantro-spiked butter. End the evening with sorbet or sherbet sprinkled with toasted coconut (page 215).

- 2 cups cut-up assorted fresh fruit, such as cantaloupe, honeydew melon, grapes, papaya and mango
- 1 tablespoon chopped fresh cilantro
- 1 to 2 teaspoons lime juice
- 1 tablespoon ground cinnamon
- 4 teaspoons ground nutmeg
- 4 teaspoons ground cumin
- 4 teaspoons garlic salt
- 1/4 to 1/2 teaspoon ground red pepper (cayenne)
- 1 pork tenderloin (about 1 1/4 lb)

1. In small bowl, mix fruit, cilantro and lime juice. Cover and refrigerate until serving.

2. In another small bowl, mix cinnamon, nutmeg, cumin, garlic salt and red pepper. Place pork in heavy-duty resealable plastic food-storage bag. Sprinkle cinnamon mixture over pork. Turn bag several times to coat pork. Seal bag; refrigerate 15 minutes.

3. Heat coals or gas grill for direct heat (page 262). Remove pork from bag. Cover and grill pork over medium heat 15 to 25 minutes, turning frequently, until no longer pink in center. Serve with fruit mixture.

1 SERVING: CAL. 235 (CAL. FROM FAT 55); FAT 6g (SAT. FAT 2g); CHOL. 90mg; SODIUM 550mg; CARBS. 13g (FIBER 2g); PRO. 33g
% DAILY VALUE: VIT. A 14%; VIT. C 18%; CALC. 4%; IRON 14%
EXCHANGES: 1 FRUIT, 5 VERY LEAN MEAT **CARB. CHOICES:** 1

◀ **Caribbean Pork Tenderloin**

Smoked Brown Sugar–Brined Pork Chops

LOW-FAT

PREP: 10 min **MARINATE:** 3 hr **SMOKE:** 1 hr 30 min ▪ **6 SERVINGS**

- 1/2 cup packed brown sugar
- 1/4 cup salt
- 2 dried bay leaves
- 1 clove garlic, crushed
- 1 teaspoon whole black peppercorns
- 4 cups water
- 6 bone-in center-cut pork loin chops, about 1 inch thick (4 to 5 lb)
- 4 to 6 chunks wood for smoking (hickory, mesquite or apple)*
- 2 tablespoons packed brown sugar
- 1/2 teaspoon garlic powder
- 1/2 teaspoon black pepper
- 1/4 teaspoon ground red pepper (cayenne)

1. In 2-gallon-size heavy-duty resealable plastic food-storage bag, mix 1/2 cup brown sugar, the salt, bay leaves, garlic, peppercorns and 4 cups water. Seal bag and squeeze to mix until sugar and salt have dissolved. Place pork chops in bag of brine; seal bag. Refrigerate at least 3 hours but no longer than 8 hours.

2. Cover wood chunks with water; soak at least 30 minutes.

3. Drain wood chunks. Prepare and heat smoker using wood chunks and adding water to water pan following manufacturer's directions.

4. Meanwhile, remove pork chops from brine; discard brine. Blot pork chops dry with paper towels. In small bowl, mix 2 tablespoons brown sugar, the garlic powder, black pepper and red pepper. Rub each side of pork chops with slightly less than 1 teaspoon brown sugar mixture.

5. Arrange pork chops 1 inch apart on top and bottom smoker racks. Cover and smoke about 1 hour 30 minutes or until meat thermometer inserted in center of pork reads 160°F (pork will remain pink when done). If smoking stops, add additional wood chunks through side door of smoker.

**2 cups hickory, mesquite or apple wood chips can be substituted.*

1 SERVING: CAL. 180 (CAL. FROM FAT 70); FAT 8g (SAT. FAT 3g); CHOL. 60mg; SODIUM 430mg; CARBS. 6g (FIBER 0g); PRO. 21g
% DAILY VALUE: VIT. A 0%; VIT. C 0%; CALC. 0%; IRON 4%
EXCHANGES: 1/2 OTHER CARB., 3 LEAN MEAT **CARB. CHOICES:** 1/2

ABOUT BRINING

Brining foods is now very trendy, but it's actually a centuries-old process. A brine is a marinade consisting of water and salt, with sugar, herbs or spices added for flavor. The concentration of salt in the water causes the food being brined (usually meat, poultry and fish) to absorb more of the water than if it were soaked in a traditional marinade containing a lot of acid ingredients like lemon juice or vinegar. The added moisture stays in the food during smoking or grilling, making it very moist but not too salty. Try these delicious brined recipes: Smoked Brined Salmon (page 276) and Smoked Brown Sugar–Brined Pork Chops (page 274).

Pork Ribs with Smoky Barbecue Sauce

PREP: 10 min **GRILL:** 1 hr 10 min **COOK:** 20 min ▪ **4 SERVINGS**

Because these smoky ribs are not precooked, they'll be winners for folks who like their ribs chewy and firm.

Ribs

4 lb pork loin back ribs (not cut into serving pieces)
1 tablespoon vegetable oil
4 teaspoons chopped fresh or 1 1/2 teaspoons dried thyme leaves

Smoky Barbecue Sauce

1/2 cup ketchup
1/4 cup water
3 tablespoons packed brown sugar
2 tablespoons white vinegar
1 teaspoon celery seed
1/4 teaspoon liquid smoke
1/4 teaspoon red pepper sauce

1. If using charcoal grill, place drip pan directly under grilling area, and arrange coals around edge of firebox. Brush grill rack with vegetable oil. Heat coals or gas grill for indirect heat (page 262).

2. Brush meaty sides of pork with oil. Sprinkle with thyme.

3. Place pork, meaty sides up, over drip pan or over unheated side of gas grill. Cover and grill over medium heat 1 hour to 1 hour 10 minutes, turning occasionally, or until tender.

4. While pork is grilling, in 1-quart saucepan, heat all sauce ingredients to boiling; reduce heat. Simmer uncovered 15 minutes, stirring occasionally. Brush sauce over pork 2 or 3 times during the last 15 minutes of grilling. Heat any remaining sauce to boiling; boil and stir 1 minute

5. To serve, cut pork into serving pieces. Serve with sauce.

1 SERVING: CAL. 910 (CAL. FROM FAT 605); FAT 67g (SAT. FAT 24g); CHOL. 265mg; SODIUM 560mg; CARBS. 13g (FIBER 0g); PRO. 64g
% DAILY VALUE: VIT. A 6%; VIT. C 4%; CALC. 10%; IRON 24%
EXCHANGES: 1 FRUIT, 8 1/2 HIGH-FAT MEAT **CARB. CHOICES:** 1

Country-Style Ribs with Hoisin Glaze

PREP: 10 min **BAKE:** 1 hr 30 min **GRILL:** 15 min ■ **6 SERVINGS**

Hoisin is a rich, reddish brown sauce with a sweet and spicy flavor. Also called Peking sauce, *it is a mixture of soybeans, garlic, chilies and spices. Look for it in the Asian section in your grocery store.*

Ribs

4 lb pork country-style ribs
1/2 teaspoon onion powder
1 tablespoon liquid smoke
1/4 cup water

Hoisin Glaze

1/2 cup chili sauce
1/4 cup hoisin sauce
2 tablespoons honey
1/8 teaspoon ground red pepper (cayenne)

1. Heat oven to 350°F. Place ribs in 13 × 9-inch pan. Sprinkle with onion powder; brush with liquid smoke. Add water to pan. Cover with foil and bake 1 hour 30 minutes.

2. While ribs are baking, in 1-quart saucepan, heat all glaze ingredients to boiling; reduce heat. Simmer uncovered 10 minutes, stirring occasionally.

3. Meanwhile, heat coals or gas grill for direct heat (page 262). Remove ribs from pan; place on grill. Cover and grill over medium heat 10 to 15 minutes, turning and brushing with glaze occasionally, until tender. Heat remaining glaze to boiling; boil 1 minute. Serve ribs with remaining glaze.

1 SERVING: CAL. 390 (CAL. FROM FAT 180); FAT 20g (SAT. FAT 7g); CHOL. 105mg; SODIUM 500mg; CARBS. 16g (FIBER 1g); PRO. 36g
% DAILY VALUE: VIT. A 8%; VIT. C 4%; CALC. 2%; IRON 8%
EXCHANGES: 1 STARCH, 4 1/2 LEAN MEAT, 1 FAT
CARB. CHOICES: 1

Smoked Brined Salmon

PREP: 10 min **MARINATE:** 3 hr **SMOKE:** 1 hr ■ **6 SERVINGS**

This deliciously moist salmon entree can also be served as an appetizer with crackers.

1/2 cup sugar
1/4 cup salt
1 tablespoon grated orange peel (from 1 small orange)
1 medium onion, sliced
1 teaspoon whole black peppercorns
4 cups water
2 1/2- to 3-lb skin-on salmon fillet
4 to 6 wood chunks for smoking (hickory, mesquite or apple)*
2 tablespoons vegetable oil
1/2 teaspoon paprika
1/4 teaspoon pepper

1. In large heavy-duty resealable plastic food-storage bag, mix sugar, salt, orange peel, onion, peppercorns and 4 cups water. Seal bag and squeeze to mix until sugar and salt have dissolved. Place salmon in bag of brine; seal bag. Refrigerate at least 3 hours but no longer than 4 hours.

2. Cover wood chunks with water; soak at least 30 minutes.

3. Drain wood chunks. Prepare and heat smoker using wood chunks and adding water to water pan following manufacturer's directions.

4. Meanwhile, remove salmon from brine; discard brine. Blot salmon dry with paper towels. Brush both sides of salmon with oil. Place salmon, skin side down. Sprinkle with paprika and pepper.

5. Place salmon, skin side down, on top grill rack in smoker. Cover and smoke about 1 hour or until salmon flakes easily with a fork. If smoking stops, add additional wood chunks through side door of smoker.

6. Place salmon, skin side up, on foil. Peel skin from fish and discard. Use foil to turn fish onto serving platter.

**2 cups hickory, mesquite or apple wood chips can be substituted.*

1 SERVING: CAL. 270 (CAL. FROM FAT 115); FAT 13g (SAT. FAT 3g); CHOL. 105mg; SODIUM 490mg; CARBS. 4g (FIBER 0g); PRO. 34g
% DAILY VALUE: VIT. A 2%; VIT. C 2%; CALC. 2%; IRON 6%
EXCHANGES: 5 LEAN MEAT **CARB. CHOICES:** 0

CHARCOAL CHIMNEY STARTERS

A charcoal chimney starter is a great grilling tool for starting coals quickly and evenly. It's a vented, cylinder-shaped canister with a large, easy-to-grasp handle. The canister is put on the bottom of the charcoal grill and crumpled newspaper is stuffed into the bottom; then briquettes go on top and it's lit. Remove the chimney and spread the hot coals before grilling food.

Planked Salmon with Peach-Mango Salsa

PREP: 20 min **CHILL:** 1 hr **GRILL:** 35 min ■ **8 SERVINGS**

Cooking foods on a wooden plank over a fire is an age-old technique, dating back to the days when the pilgrims learned "planking" from the Native Americans. Look for untreated cedar planks at cookware stores or lumber or large do-it-yourself warehouse stores. Treated lumber contains chemicals that are toxic, so if you're not buying the plank at a kitchen-type store, be absolutely certain the cedar plank is untreated.

Peach-Mango Salsa

1/4 cup lime juice
1 tablespoon honey
1/4 teaspoon salt
1 medium mango, cut lengthwise in half, pitted and chopped (1 cup)
2 cups chopped peeled peaches
1/4 cup chopped fresh cilantro
1 tablespoon finely chopped bell pepper

Salmon

1 untreated cedar plank, 16 × 6 × 2 inches
1 large salmon fillet (about 2 lb)
1/4 cup packed brown sugar

1. In medium bowl, mix lime juice, honey and salt; toss with remaining salsa ingredients. Cover and refrigerate at least 1 hour. Meanwhile, soak cedar plank in water at least 1 hour.

2. Heat coals or gas grill for direct heat (page 262). Place salmon, skin side down, on cedar plank. Make diagonal cuts in salmon every 2 inches, without cutting through the skin. Rub brown sugar over salmon.

3. Place cedar plank with salmon on grill. When cedar plank begins to smoke, cover grill. Cover and grill salmon over medium heat 30 to 35 minutes or until salmon flakes easily with fork. Serve salmon on plank, placing on a heatproof surface. Serve with salsa.

1 SERVING: CAL. 210 (CAL. FROM FAT 55); FAT 6g (SAT. FAT 2g); CHOL. 65mg; SODIUM 135mg; CARBS. 19g (FIBER 1g); PRO. 21g
% DAILY VALUE: VIT. A 8%; VIT. C 10%; CALC. 2%; IRON 4%
EXCHANGES: 1 FRUIT, 3 VERY LEAN MEAT, 1 FAT
CARB. CHOICES: 1

◀ **Smoked Brined Salmon**

Grilled Sea Bass with Citrus-Olive Butter

PREP: 10 min **CHILL:** 30 min **GRILL:** 13 min ■ **4 SERVINGS**

Sea bass isn't just one fish, but several varieties of saltwater fish of the drum or grouper family. It has firm, lean to moderately fat flesh. Grill it, bake it, poach it or even fry it. Anyway it's cooked, it's delicious with this olive butter.

Citrus-Olive Butter

2 tablespoons butter or margarine, softened
1 tablespoon finely chopped Kalamata olives
2 teaspoons chopped fresh parsley
1/2 teaspoon balsamic vinegar
1/4 teaspoon grated orange peel

Sea Bass

1-lb sea bass, salmon or snapper fillet, about 1 inch thick
1 tablespoon olive or vegetable oil
1/4 teaspoon salt
1/8 teaspoon pepper

1. In small bowl, mix all Citrus-Olive Butter ingredients. Refrigerate 30 minutes or until firm.

2. Heat coals or gas grill for direct heat (page 262). Brush all surfaces of fish with oil; sprinkle with salt and pepper.

3. Cover and grill fish over medium heat 10 to 13 minutes, turning fish after 5 minutes, until fish flakes easily with fork. Serve with Citrus-Olive Butter.

1 SERVING: CAL. 185 (CAL. FROM FAT 100); FAT 11g (SAT. FAT 4g); CHOL. 75mg; SODIUM 300mg; CARBS. 0g (FIBER 0g); PRO. 21g
% DAILY VALUE: VIT. A 6%; VIT. C 0%; CALC. 2%; IRON 2%
EXCHANGES: 3 LEAN MEAT, 1/2 FAT **CARB. CHOICES:** 0

Easy Grilled Fish FAST LOW-FAT

PREP: 5 min **GRILL:** 14 min ■ **4 SERVINGS**

Always leave the skin on when grilling fish because it helps keep the fish intact and moist. No need to turn it while it grills!

1 lb fish fillets or steaks, 3/4 to 1 inch thick
Salt and pepper to taste
2 tablespoons butter or margarine, melted

1. Brush grill rack with vegetable oil. Heat coals or gas grill for direct heat (page 262).

2. Cut fish into 4 serving pieces. Sprinkle both sides of fish with salt and pepper. Brush both sides with butter.

3. If fish has skin, place skin side down on grill. Cover and grill fish over medium heat 10 to 14 minutes or until fish flakes easily with fork.

1 SERVING: CAL. 140 (CAL. FROM FAT 65); FAT 7g (SAT. FAT 1g); CHOL. 50mg; SODIUM 160mg; CARBS. 0g (FIBER 0g); PRO. 19g
% DAILY VALUE: VIT. A 8%; VIT. C 0%; CALC. 2%; IRON 0%
EXCHANGES: 2 1/2 LEAN MEAT **CARB. CHOICES:** 0

Grilled Fish Tacos FAST LOW-FAT

PREP: 10 min **GRILL:** 7 min ■ **8 TACOS**

1 lb medium-firm white fish fillets, such as sea bass or red snapper
1 tablespoon olive or vegetable oil
1 teaspoon ground cumin or chili powder
1/2 teaspoon salt
1/4 teaspoon pepper
8 corn tortillas (6 inch)
1/4 cup sour cream
Toppers (shredded lettuce, chopped avocado, chopped tomatoes, chopped onion and chopped fresh cilantro), if desired
1/2 cup salsa
Fresh lime wedges, if desired

1. Brush grill rack with vegetable oil. Heat coals or gas grill for direct heat (page 262).

2. Brush fish with oil; sprinkle with cumin, salt and pepper. Cover and grill fish over medium heat 5 to 7 minutes, turning once, until fish flakes easily with fork.

3. Heat tortillas as directed on bag. Spread sour cream on tortillas. Add fish, Toppers and salsa. Squeeze juice from lime wedges over tacos.

1 TACO: CAL. 140 (CAL. FROM FAT 35); FAT 4g (SAT. FAT 1g); CHOL. 35mg; SODIUM 310mg; CARBS. 13g (FIBER 2g); PRO. 13g
% DAILY VALUE: VIT. A 4%; VIT. C 2%; CALC. 6%; IRON 4%
EXCHANGES: 1 STARCH, 1 1/2 LEAN MEAT **CARB. CHOICES:** 1

Grilled Shrimp Kabobs with Fresh Herbs LOW-FAT

PREP: 20 min **MARINATE:** 20 min **GRILL:** 12 min ▪ **6 SERVINGS**

Thick rosemary sprigs work best for these kabob "skewers" because they won't break when threaded. Trimming the ends of the rosemary stems to a point makes it easier to slip the shrimp and vegetables onto the stem. If you're finding that inserting the stem into the vegetables is difficult, poke an opening in the vegetable with a toothpick.

Rosemary-Lemon Marinade

24 sprigs rosemary, 6 inches long
1/4 cup fresh lemon juice
3 tablespoons olive or vegetable oil
1 tablespoon dry white wine or lemon juice
1/2 teaspoon salt
1/2 teaspoon pepper

Kabobs

24 fresh large basil leaves
24 uncooked peeled deveined extra-large shrimp (about 1 1/2 lb), with tails left on
12 small pattypan squash, cut in half*
24 cherry tomatoes
24 large cloves garlic

1. Strip leaves from rosemary sprigs, leaving 1 inch of leaves at top intact; set sprigs aside for kabobs. Measure 1 tablespoon rosemary leaves; chop. (Store remaining leaves for other uses.) In small bowl, mix chopped rosemary leaves and remaining marinade ingredients.

2. Wrap basil leaf around each shrimp. For each kabob, thread shrimp, squash half, tomato and garlic clove alternately on stem of rosemary sprig, leaving space between each piece. (Start threading at stem end, pulling it through to leaves at top.) Place kabobs in ungreased 13 × 9-inch glass baking dish. Pour marinade over kabobs. Cover and refrigerate at least 20 minutes but no longer than 2 hours.

3. Brush grill rack with olive or vegetable oil. Heat coals or gas grill for direct heat (page 262). Remove kabobs from marinade; reserve marinade. Cover and grill kabobs over medium heat about 12 minutes, turning and brushing with marinade 2 or 3 times, until shrimp are pink and firm. Discard any remaining marinade.

**1-inch slices of zucchini or yellow summer squash can be substituted for the pattypan squash.*

1 SERVING: CAL. 120 (CAL. FROM FAT 45); FAT 5g (SAT. FAT 1g); CHOL. 45mg; SODIUM 160mg; CARBS. 13g (FIBER 2g); PRO. 8g
% DAILY VALUE: VIT. A 20%; VIT. C 10%; CALC. 6%; IRON 10%
EXCHANGES: 1 VEGETABLE, 1 LEAN MEAT, 1 FAT
CARB. CHOICES: 1

Grilled Shrimp Kabobs with Fresh Herbs ▶

Herbed Seafood

PREP: 20 min **GRILL:** 10 min ▪ **4 SERVINGS**

- 1/2 lb sea or bay scallops
- 1/2 lb orange roughy fillets, cut into 1-inch pieces
- 1/2 lb uncooked fresh or frozen large shrimp, peeled and deveined (page 253)
- 2 tablespoons chopped fresh or 2 teaspoons dried marjoram leaves
- 1/2 teaspoon grated lemon peel
- 1/8 teaspoon white pepper
- 3 tablespoons butter or margarine, melted
- 2 tablespoons lemon juice
- 4 cups hot cooked pasta (page 376) or rice (page 375)

1. Heat coals or gas grill for direct heat (page 262). If using sea scallops, cut each in half.

2. Spray 18-inch square of heavy-duty foil with cooking spray. Arrange scallops, fish and shrimp on foil, placing shrimp on top. Sprinkle with marjoram, lemon peel and white pepper. Drizzle with butter and lemon juice. Bring corners of foil up to center and seal loosely.

3. Cover and grill foil packet over medium heat 8 to 10 minutes or until scallops are white, fish flakes easily with fork and shrimp are pink and firm. Serve seafood mixture over pasta.

1 SERVING: CAL. 395 (CAL. FROM FAT 100); FAT 11g (SAT. FAT 6g); CHOL. 145mg; SODIUM 270mg; CARBS. 41g (FIBER 2g); PRO. 33g
% DAILY VALUE: VIT. A 10%; VIT. C 2%; CALC. 6%; IRON 24%
EXCHANGES: 3 STARCH, 3 1/2 VERY LEAN MEAT, 1 FAT
CARB. CHOICES: 3

Grilled Portabella Mushroom Sandwiches

FAST

PREP: 10 min **GRILL:** 10 min ▪ **4 SANDWICHES**

Lemon-Herb Basting Sauce

- 1/2 cup olive or vegetable oil
- 1 tablespoon chopped fresh or 1 teaspoon dried thyme leaves
- 1 teaspoon grated lemon peel
- 2 tablespoons lemon juice
- 2 tablespoons Dijon mustard

Sandwiches

- 4 fresh large portabella mushroom caps
- 1 medium red onion, cut into 1/4-inch slices
- 4 whole wheat hamburger buns, split
- 4 lettuce leaves
- 4 tomato slices

1. Heat coals or gas grill for direct heat (page 262). In tightly covered container, shake all basting sauce ingredients.

2. Brush mushrooms and onion slices with basting sauce. Cover and grill mushrooms over medium heat 5 minutes. Add onions. Cover and grill about 5 minutes, turning and brushing mushrooms and onions with sauce occasionally, until vegetables are tender.

3. Brush cut sides of buns with remaining sauce. Fill each bun with lettuce, mushroom, tomato and onion.

1 SANDWICH: CAL. 305 (CAL. FROM FAT 190); FAT 21g (SAT. FAT 3g); CHOL. 0mg; SODIUM 370mg; CARBS. 27g (FIBER 4g); PRO. 6g
% DAILY VALUE: VIT. A 8%; VIT. C 8%; CALC. 6%; IRON 10%
EXCHANGES: 1 STARCH, 3 VEGETABLE, 3 FAT **CARB. CHOICES:** 2

Easy Grilled Vegetables

LOW-FAT

PREP: 10 min **MARINATE:** 1 hr **GRILL:** 15 min ▪ **6 SERVINGS**

- 12 pattypan squash, about 1 inch in diameter
- 2 medium red or green bell peppers, each cut into 6 pieces
- 1 large red onion, cut into 1/2-inch slices
- 1/3 cup Italian dressing
- Freshly ground pepper, if desired

◀ **Grilled Portabella Mushroom Sandwiches**

1. In 13 × 9-inch glass baking dish, place squash, bell peppers and onion. Pour dressing over vegetables. Cover and let stand 1 hour to blend flavors.

2. Heat coals or gas grill for direct heat (page 262).

3. Remove vegetables from marinade; reserve marinade. Place squash and bell peppers in grill basket (grill "wok"). Cover and grill squash and bell peppers over medium heat 5 minutes.

4. Add onion to grill basket. Cover and grill 5 to 10 minutes, turning and brushing vegetables with marinade 2 or 3 times, until tender. Sprinkle with pepper.

1 SERVING: CAL. 70 (CAL. FROM FAT 35); FAT 4g (SAT. FAT 1g); CHOL. 0mg; SODIUM 85mg; CARBS. 9g (FIBER 3g); PRO. 2g **% DAILY VALUE:** VIT. A 8%; VIT. C 44%; CALC. 6%; IRON 4% **EXCHANGES:** 2 VEGETABLE, 1/2 FAT **CARB. CHOICES:** 1/2

Smoky Cheddar Potatoes

PREP: 10 min **GRILL:** 1 hr ■ **4 SERVINGS**

- 4 medium potatoes, cut into 1-inch chunks
- 1/2 teaspoon salt
- 2 tablespoons butter or margarine
- 1 cup shredded smoked or regular Cheddar cheese (4 oz)
- 2 tablespoons bacon flavor bits or chips
- 2 medium green onions, sliced (2 tablespoons)

1. Heat coals or gas grill for direct heat (page 262).

2. Place potato chunks on 30 × 18-inch piece of heavy-duty foil. Sprinkle with salt. Cut butter into small pieces; sprinkle over potatoes. Sprinkle with cheese and bacon bits.

3. Wrap foil securely around potatoes; pierce top of foil once or twice with fork to vent steam. Cover and grill foil packet, seam side up, over medium heat 45 to 60 minutes or until potatoes are tender. Sprinkle with onions.

1 SERVING: CAL. 300 (CAL. FROM FAT 145); FAT 16g (SAT. FAT 10g); CHOL. 45mg; SODIUM 560mg; CARBS. 27g (FIBER 3g); PRO. 11g **% DAILY VALUE:** VIT. A 12%; VIT. C 10%; CALC. 18%; IRON 10% **EXCHANGES:** 2 STARCH, 1 VEGETABLE, 2 1/2 FAT **CARB. CHOICES:** 2

◀ **Easy Grilled Vegetables**

Grilled Baby Carrots and Green Beans

PREP: 15 min **GRILL:** 20 min ■ **4 SERVINGS**

When cooking vegetables in a grill basket, shake it often. This helps prevent burning and ensures the vegetables cook evenly.

- 1 cup baby-cut carrots, cut lengthwise in half
- 8 oz fresh green beans
- 1 tablespoon olive or vegetable oil
- 1/2 teaspoon dried marjoram leaves
- 1/2 teaspoon garlic pepper
- 1/4 teaspoon salt
- 1 medium red onion, cut into 1/2-inch wedges

1. Heat coals or gas grill for direct heat (page 262). In large bowl, toss all ingredients except onion. Place vegetables in grill basket (grill "wok"). Leave remaining oil mixture in bowl.

2. Cover and grill vegetables over medium heat 10 minutes. Add onion to oil mixture in bowl; toss to coat. Add onion to grill basket. Cover and grill 8 to 10 minutes longer, shaking basket or stirring vegetables occasionally, until vegetables are crisp-tender.

1 SERVING: CAL. 75 (CAL. FROM FAT 35); FAT 4g (SAT. FAT 0g); CHOL. 0mg; SODIUM 160mg; CARBS. 9g (FIBER 3g); PROTEIN 1g **% DAILY VALUE:** VIT. A 100%; VIT. C 4%; CALC. 4%; IRON 4% **EXCHANGES:** 1 1/2 VEGETABLE, 1 FAT **CARB. CHOICES:** 1/2

Tangy Onion Flowers

LOW-FAT

PREP: 20 min **GRILL:** 1 hr ■ **4 SERVINGS**

4 medium onions (4 to 5 oz each)
Vegetable oil
1/4 cup balsamic or cider vinegar
1 tablespoon chopped fresh or 1 teaspoon dried oregano leaves
1 tablespoon packed brown sugar
1/4 teaspoon salt
1/4 teaspoon pepper
1/3 cup seasoned croutons, crushed

1. Heat coals or gas grill for direct heat (page 262). Peel onions; cut 1/2-inch slice from top of each onion and leave root end. Cut each onion from top into 8 wedges to within 1/2 inch of root end. Gently pull wedges apart.

2. Cut four 12-inch squares of heavy-duty foil; brush with vegetable oil. Place 1 onion on each square; loosely shape foil around onion. Sprinkle onions with vinegar, oregano, brown sugar, salt and pepper. Wrap foil securely around onions.

3. Cover and grill onions over medium heat 50 to 60 minutes or until very tender. To serve, sprinkle croutons over onions.

1 SERVING: CAL. 85 (CAL. FROM FAT 20); FAT 2g (SAT. FAT 0g); CHOL. 0mg; SODIUM 190mg; CARBS. 16g (FIBER 2g); PRO. 2g
% DAILY VALUE: VIT. A 2%; VIT. C 2%; CALC. 2%; IRON 2%
EXCHANGES: 1/2 OTHER CARB., 1 VEGETABLE, 1/2 FAT
CARB. CHOICES: 1

Grilled Garlic Bread with Rosemary

PREP: 10 min **GRILL:** 15 min ■ **12 SERVINGS**

1 loaf (1 lb) unsliced French bread
1/2 cup butter or margarine, softened
2 tablespoons chopped fresh or 2 teaspoons dried rosemary leaves*
1 tablespoon chopped fresh parsley or 1 teaspoon parsley flakes
1/4 to 1/2 teaspoon garlic powder

1. Heat coals or gas grill for direct heat (page 262). Cut bread loaf into 1-inch slices without cutting through bottom of loaf. In small bowl, mix remaining ingredients; spread on both sides of bread slices.

2. Wrap bread in heavy-duty foil. Cover and grill bread over medium heat 10 to 15 minutes, turning once, until hot.

**2 tablespoons chopped fresh or 2 teaspoons dried basil leaves can be substituted for the rosemary.*

1 SERVING: CAL. 165 (CAL. FROM FAT 80); FAT 9g (SAT. FAT 5g); CHOL. 20mg; SODIUM 270mg; CARBS. 19g (FIBER 1g); PRO. 3g
% DAILY VALUE: VIT. A 6%; VIT. C 0%; CALC. 2%; IRON 6%
EXCHANGES: 1 STARCH, 1 FAT **CARB. CHOICES:** 1

Grilled Garlic Bread with Rosemary ▶

TIMETABLE FOR GRILLING MEAT WITH DIRECT HEAT

Heat coals or gas grill for direct heat (page 262).* Cover and grill over medium heat for the time listed until thermometer reaches the doneness temperature, turning once halfway through grilling (turn beef and pork tenderloins 2 or 3 times). See The Facts on Food Thermometers, page 31, for more information.

Meat Cut	Thickness (inches)	Approximate Total Grilling Time (minutes)	Doneness
BEEF			
Flank Steak *(best when marinated before cooking)*	1 to 1 1/2 pounds	17 to 21	145°F medium-rare to 160°F medium
Ground Patties *(4 per pound)*	3/4 inch thick (4 inch diameter)	10 to 12	160°F medium
(4 per 1 1/2 pounds)	1/2 inch thick (4 inch diameter)	12 to 15	160°F medium
Porterhouse/ T-Bone Steaks	3/4	10 to 12	145°F medium-rare to 160°F medium
	1	14 to 16	
	1 1/2	20 to 24	
Rib Eye Steak	3/4	6 to 8	145°F medium-rare to 160°F medium
	1	11 to 14	
	1 1/2	17 to 22	
Tenderloin	1	13 to 15	145°F medium-rare to 160°F medium
	1 1/2	14 to 16	
Top Loin Strip Steak	3/4	10 to 12	145°F medium-rare to 160°F medium
	1	15 to 18	
Top Round Steak *(best when marinated before cooking)*	3/4	8 to 9	145°F medium-rare to 160°F medium
	1	16 to 18	
	1 1/2	25 to 28	
Top Sirloin	3/4	13 to 16	145°F medium-rare to 160°F medium
	1	17 to 21	
	1 1/2	22 to 26	
LAMB			
Chop, Loin or Rib	1	10 to 15	160°F medium
Chop, Sirloin	1	12 to 15	160°F medium
PORK			
Chop *(bone-in or boneless)*	3/4 to 1	9 to 12	160°F medium
	1 1/2	12 to 16	160°F medium
Ground Patties	1/2	8 to 10	160°F medium
Loin Back Ribs or Spareribs *Use indirect heat*		1 1/2 to 2 hours	Tender
Tenderloin	1 to 1 1/2	15 to 25	160°F medium
VEAL			
Chop, Loin or Rib	3/4 to 1	14 to 16	160°F medium

**Use indirect heat for pork loin back or spareribs.*

TIMETABLE FOR GRILLING POULTRY WITH DIRECT HEAT

Heat coals or gas grill for direct heat (page 262). Cover and grill over medium heat for the time listed until thermometer reaches the doneness temperature or until juice is clear when thickest part is cut to bone (for bone-in pieces) or when center of thickest part of boneless pieces is cut. Turn poultry once halfway through grilling, but turn cut-up whole chicken pieces 2 or 3 times. See The Facts on Food Thermometers, page 31, for more information.

Type of Poultry	Weight (pounds)	Approximate Total Grilling Time (minutes)	Doneness
CHICKEN			
Bone-In Split Breasts *(Breast Halves)*	2 1/2 to 3	20 to 25	170°F
Boneless Skinless Breast Halves	1 1/4	15 to 20	170°F
Cut-Up Chicken	3 to 3 1/2	35 to 40	
Breasts			170°F
Thighs/Legs			180°F
Ground Chicken Patties *(1/2 inch thick)*	1	12 to 15	165°F
TURKEY			
Breast Slices	1 to 1 1/2	6 to 7	No longer pink in center
Ground Turkey Patties *(1/2 inch thick)*	1	12 to 15	165°F
Tenderloins	1 to 1 1/2	8 to 12	170°F

CHAPTER 11
Meats

LOW-FAT = *3g or less, except main dishes with 10g or less* FAST = *Ready in 20 minutes or less* BREAD MACHINE = *Bread machine directions* SLOW COOKER = *Slow cooker directions* LIGHTER = *25% fewer calories or grams of fat*

◀ **Roasted Beef Tenderloin (page 289)**

Meat Basics

Standing in front of the meat case at your local supermarket can be overwhelming. There are chops and cutlets, sirloin and ribeyes, short loin and top loin, roasts and ribs. And that's just the beginning, for each type of meat—from beef to veal, pork and lamb—seems to have their own lingo. Use this chapter to become more savvy about shopping for meat and cooking it like an expert.

BUYING FRESH MEATS

- Choose wrapped packages without any tears, holes or leaks. There should be little or no liquid in the bottom of the tray.
- Make sure the package is cold and feels firm. Avoid packages that are stacked too high in the meat case because they may not have been kept cold enough.
- Check the sell-by date and use within 2 days of the date.
- Put packages of meat in plastic bags before putting them in your grocery cart so that any bacteria in the juices doesn't drip on and contaminate other foods, especially those that won't be cooked.
- Don't buy or use meat that has turned gray, has an off odor or feels slimy.
- Refrigerate meat as soon as you get home from shopping. If it will take longer than 30 minutes to get it home, keep it cold in a cooler with ice packs.

READING A MEAT LABEL

A lot of information is squeezed onto the little meat label, so read it carefully. It'll help you choose the right meat for your recipe and even tell you how to cook it, step by step. Labels include the following information:

- The kind of meat: beef, pork, veal, lamb.
- The primal or wholesale cut (where it comes from on the animal): chuck, rib, loin, etc.

HOW MANY SERVINGS PER POUND?

The number of servings per pound varies depending on the type of meat and the amount of bone and fat. The average serving is based on 2¹/2 to 3¹/2 ounces per person of cooked meat, but you can always plan for more.

Type of Meat	Servings per Pound
Boneless cuts (ground, boneless chops, loin, tenderloin)	3 to 4
Bone-in cuts (rib roasts, pot roasts, country-style ribs)	2 to 3
Very bony cuts (back ribs, spareribs, short ribs, shanks)	1 to 1¹/2

- The retail cut (where it comes from on the primal cut): blade roast, loin chops, etc.
- The weight, price per pound, total price and sell-by date.

STORING MEAT

- Meat wrapped in butcher paper should be repackaged tightly in plastic wrap, foil or plastic freezer bags.
- Meat packaged in clear plastic wrap on a plastic or Styrofoam tray doesn't need to be repackaged.
- Store meat in the meat compartment or coldest part of your refrigerator, or freeze it as soon as possible. Ground meat is more perishable than other cuts, so use it within 2 days.
- Cook or freeze meat within 2 days of the sell-by date.
- If you purchased meat frozen or froze it right after purchasing, thaw it in the refrigerator as recommended in the Timetable for Thawing Meat on page 286. Then use it within the number of days listed in the refrigerator column in the timetable below. If you store the meat several days in the refrigerator before freezing, use it the same day you thaw it.

TIMETABLE FOR STORING MEAT

Cut of Meat	Refrigerator (36°F to 40°F)	Freezer (0°F or colder)
Cured, smoked and ready-to-serve meat products:		
Bacon	5 to 7 days	1 month
Corned beef	1 week	2 weeks
Hot dogs	3 to 5 days	1 month
Ground meats	1 to 2 days	3 to 4 months (beef) 2 to 3 months (veal) 1 to 3 months (pork)
Leftover cooked meats	3 to 4 days	2 to 3 months
Meat cuts: cubes, slices	2 to 3 days	6 to 12 months
Meat cuts: steaks and roasts		
Beef	3 to 4 days	6 to 12 months
Veal	1 to 2 days	6 to 9 months
Pork	2 to 4 days	3 to 6 months
Lamb	3 to 5 days	6 to 9 months

TIMETABLE FOR THAWING MEAT

Thaw meat slowly in the refrigerator. Don't thaw meat on the countertop because bacteria thrive at room temperature. Thaw meats in a dish or baking pan with sides or in a plastic bag to catch any drips during thawing. Thaw according to the following chart:

Amount of Frozen Meat	Thawing Time in Refrigerator
Ground beef or beef pieces (1 to 1 1/2-inch package)	24 hours
Ground beef patties (1/2 to 3/4 inch thick)	12 hours
Large roast (4 pounds or larger)	4 to 7 hours per pound
Small roast (under 4 pounds)	3 to 5 hours per pound
Steak or chops (1 inch thick)	12 to 14 hours total

HOW TO CARVE A BEEF RIB ROAST

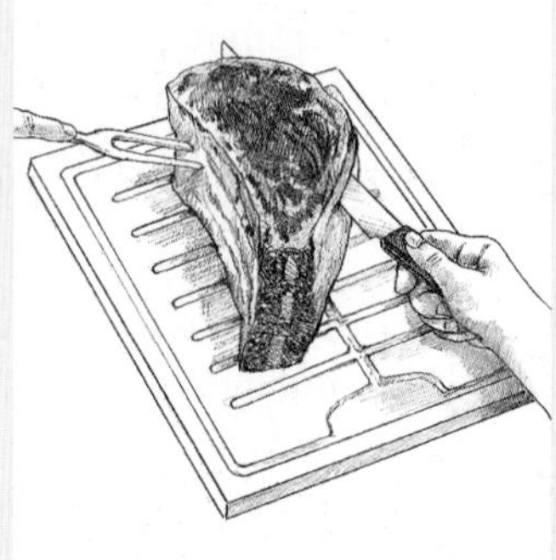

◀ **1.** With roast on carving board, remove slice from the large end so roast sits firmly. Then turn roast over, cut-side-down on board. Insert meat fork below top rib. Slice from outside of roast toward rib side.

2. After making several slices, cut along inner side of rib bone with tip of knife. As each slice is released, slide knife under and lift to plate. ▶

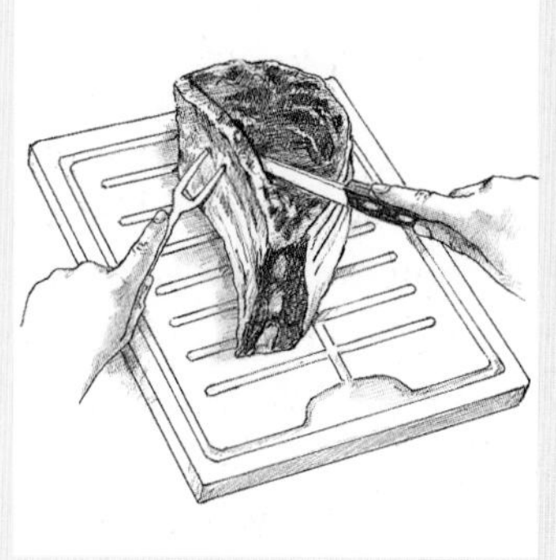

Beef Rib Roast with Yorkshire Pudding

PREP: 15 min **ROAST:** 2 hr 15 min **STAND/BAKE:** 25 min ▪ **8 SERVINGS**

Take a tip from the English—serve your next rib roast with Yorkshire Pudding. It resembles a little soufflé, puffs up like a popover and tastes like the drippings from the roast that it bakes in. When buying the roast, look for it under several names: beef rib roast, standing rib roast or prime rib roast.

Beef Roast

4- to 6-lb beef rib roast (small end)
1/2 teaspoon salt
1/4 teaspoon pepper

Yorkshire Pudding

Vegetable oil, if necessary
1 cup all-purpose flour
1 cup milk
1/2 teaspoon salt
2 large eggs

1. Heat oven to 350°F. For easy cleanup, line shallow roasting pan with foil. Place beef, fat side up, in roasting pan; sprinkle with salt and pepper. Insert ovenproof meat thermometer so tip is in center of the thickest part of beef and does not rest in fat or touch bone. (Do not add water.)

2. *For medium-rare,* roast 1 hour 45 minutes to 2 hours 15 minutes or until thermometer reads 135°F. Remove beef from pan onto carving board. Cover beef loosely with foil and let stand 15 to 20 minutes until thermometer reads 145°F. (Temperature will continue to rise about 10°F, and beef will be easier to carve.) *For medium,* roast uncovered 2 hours 15 minutes to 2 hours 45 minutes or until thermometer reads 150°F. Cover beef loosely with foil and let stand 15 to 20 minutes or until thermometer reads 160°F.

3. While beef is standing, make Yorkshire Pudding. Measure pan drippings, adding enough oil to drippings, if necessary, to measure 1/4 cup. Place hot drippings in 9-inch square pan; place pan in oven and heat until hot. Increase oven temperature to 450°F. In medium bowl, beat flour, milk, salt and eggs with wire whisk just until smooth. Pour batter into pan of drippings and oil. Bake 18 to 23 minutes or until puffy and golden brown (pudding will puff during baking but will deflate shortly after being removed from oven). Cut pudding into squares; serve immediately with beef.

1 SERVING: CAL. 340 (CAL. FROM FAT 155); FAT 17g (SAT. FAT 7g); CHOL. 135mg; SODIUM 390mg; CARBS. 14g (FIBER 0g); PRO. 32g **% DAILY VALUE:** VIT. A 4%; VIT. C 0%; CALC. 4%; IRON 20% **EXCHANGES:** 1 STARCH, 4 LEAN MEAT, 1 FAT **CARB. CHOICES:** 1

BEEF RIB ROAST WITH OVEN-BROWNED POTATOES Omit Yorkshire Pudding. About 1 1/2 hours before beef is done, prepare and boil 6 medium potatoes as directed on page 487. For decorative potatoes, make crosswise cuts almost through whole potatoes to make thin slices and decrease boiling time to 10 minutes. Place potatoes in beef drippings in pan, turning each potato to coat completely; or brush potatoes with melted butter or margarine and place on rack with beef. Continue cooking about 1 hour 15 minutes, turning potatoes once, until golden brown. Sprinkle with salt and pepper if desired.

HANDLING RAW MEAT

Cooking meat to the recommended doneness destroys any bacteria. To avoid food-borne illnesses and cross-contamination when preparing raw meat for cooking, follow the tips in Food Safety Basics, page 27.

Beef Rib Roast with Yorkshire Pudding ▶

Pot Roast

PREP: 30 min **COOK:** 3 hr 30 min ▪ **8 SERVINGS**

Spreading a layer of horseradish all over the outside of the meat is the secret to making this pot roast. Contrary to what you might think, the horseradish doesn't add a hot or spicy flavor. Instead, it mellows during cooking, leaving behind a delicious flavor you can't quite put your finger on.

- 4-lb beef chuck boneless arm, shoulder or blade pot roast*
- 1 to 2 teaspoons salt
- 1 teaspoon pepper
- 1 jar (8 oz) prepared horseradish
- 1 cup water
- 8 small potatoes, cut in half
- 8 medium peeled carrots, cut into fourths
- 8 small onions, skins removed
- 1/2 cup cold water
- 1/4 cup all-purpose flour

1. In 4-quart Dutch oven, cook beef over medium heat until brown on all sides; reduce heat to low.

2. Sprinkle beef with salt and pepper. Spread horseradish over all sides of beef. Add 1 cup water to Dutch oven. Heat to boiling; reduce heat. Cover and simmer 2 hours 30 minutes.

3. Add potatoes, carrots and onions to Dutch oven. Cover and simmer about 1 hour or until beef and vegetables are tender.

4. Remove beef and vegetables to warm platter; keep warm.

5. Skim excess fat from broth in Dutch oven. Add enough water to broth to measure 2 cups. In tightly covered container, shake 1/2 cup cold water and the flour; gradually stir into broth. Heat to boiling, stirring constantly. Boil and stir 1 minute. Serve gravy with beef and vegetables.

**3-lb beef bottom round, rolled rump, tip or chuck eye roast can be substituted; decrease salt to 3/4 teaspoon.*

1 SERVING: CAL. 365 (CAL. FROM FAT 100); FAT 11g (SAT. FAT 4g); CHOL. 85mg; SODIUM 470mg; CARBS. 32g (FIBER 5g); PRO. 35g
% DAILY VALUE: VIT. A 40%; VIT. C 20%; CALC. 6%; IRON 28%
EXCHANGES: 1 1/2 STARCH, 2 VEGETABLE, 4 VERY LEAN MEAT, 1 FAT **CARB. CHOICES:** 2

SLOW COOKER DIRECTIONS

In 12-inch skillet, cook beef over medium heat until brown on all sides. In 4- to 6-quart slow cooker, place potatoes, carrots and onions. Place beef on vegetables. In small bowl, mix horseradish, salt and pepper; spread evenly over beef. Pour water into slow cooker. Cover and cook on Low heat setting 8 to 10 hours.

BARBECUE POT ROAST Decrease pepper to 1/2 teaspoon. Omit horseradish and water. Make Smoky Barbecue Sauce (page 275). After browning beef in Step 1, pour Smoky Barbecue Sauce over beef. Omit 1/2 cup cold water and the flour. Skim fat from sauce after removing beef and vegetables in Step 4. Spoon sauce over beef and vegetables, or serve sauce with beef and vegetables.

CREAM GRAVY POT ROAST Substitute 1 can (10.5 oz) condensed beef broth for the 1 cup water. For the gravy in Step 5, add enough half-and-half or milk, instead of water, to the broth (from the roast) to measure 2 cups. Substitute 1/2 cup half-and-half or milk for the 1/2 cup cold water.

GARLIC-HERB POT ROAST Decrease pepper to 1/2 teaspoon. Omit horseradish. After browning beef in Step 1, sprinkle with 1 tablespoon chopped fresh or 1 teaspoon dried marjoram leaves, 1 tablespoon chopped fresh or 1 teaspoon dried thyme leaves, 2 teaspoons chopped fresh or 1/2 teaspoon dried oregano leaves and 4 cloves garlic, finely chopped. Substitute 1 can (10.5 oz) condensed beef broth for the 1 cup water.

CUTTING RAW MEAT

Need to cut raw meat into cubes, thin slices or strips? Put the meat in the freezer first! Leave the meat in the freezer until it's firm but not frozen, about 30 to 60 minutes, depending on the size of the piece. It'll be easy to slice, even paper thin!

Roasted Beef Tenderloin

PREP: 15 min **ROAST:** 40 min **STAND:** 20 min ▪ **6 SERVINGS**

For easy cleanup, line your shallow roasting pan with foil.

- 1 beef tenderloin roast (about 2 1/2 lb)
- 1 tablespoon olive or vegetable oil
- 1/2 teaspoon coarsely ground pepper
- 1/2 teaspoon dried marjoram leaves
- 1/4 teaspoon coarse kosher salt, coarse sea salt or regular salt

1. Heat oven to 425°F.

2. Turn small end of beef under about 6 inches. Tie turned-under portion of beef with string at about 1 1/2-inch intervals. Place in shallow roasting pan. Brush with oil. Sprinkle with pepper, marjoram and salt. Insert ovenproof meat thermometer so tip is in thickest part of beef.

3. *For medium-rare,* roast 35 to 40 minutes or until thermometer reads 135°F. Cover loosely with foil and let stand 15 to 20 minutes until thermometer reads 145°F. (Temperature will continue to rise about 10°F, and beef will be easier to carve.) *For medium,* roast uncovered 45 to 50 minutes or until thermometer reads 150°F. Cover beef loosely with foil and let stand 15 to 20 minutes until thermometer reads 160°F. Remove string from beef before carving.

1 SERVING: CAL. 310 (CAL. FROM FAT 145); FAT 16g (SAT. FAT 5g); CHOL. 105mg; SODIUM 190mg; CARBS. 0g (FIBER 0g); PRO. 41g
% DAILY VALUE: VIT. A 2%; VIT. C 0%; CALC. 0%; IRON 20%
EXCHANGES: 5 1/2 LEAN MEAT **CARB. CHOICES:** 0

Corned Beef and Cabbage

PREP: 20 min **COOK:** 3 hr 45 min ▪ **6 SERVINGS**

Corned beef is beef brisket that has been cured in a brine to give a distinct flavor. (Don't confuse it with the plain cut of meat called brisket.*) Corned beef is sold in a sealed plastic bag with the brine. Since the brine contains plenty of salt, none is called for in this recipe.*

- 2 1/2- to 3-lb well-trimmed beef corned brisket, undrained
- 1 medium onion, cut into 6 wedges
- 1 clove garlic, finely chopped
- 1 small head cabbage, cut into 6 wedges

1. Place beef in 4-quart Dutch oven; add juices and spices from package of corned beef. Add enough cold water just to cover beef. Add onion and garlic.

2. Heat to boiling; reduce heat to low. Cover and simmer 2 hours 30 minutes to 3 hours 30 minutes or until beef is tender.

3. Remove beef to warm platter; keep warm. Skim fat from broth. Add cabbage to broth. Heat to boiling; reduce heat. Simmer uncovered about 15 minutes or until cabbage is tender. Serve cabbage with beef.

1 SERVING: CAL. 375 (CAL. FROM FAT 235); FAT 26g (SAT. FAT 9g); CHOL. 130mg; SODIUM 1540mg; CARBS. 9g (FIBER 3g); PRO. 26g
% DAILY VALUE: VIT. A 4%; VIT. C 32%; CALC. 6%; IRON 18%
EXCHANGES: 2 VEGETABLE, 3 MEDIUM-FAT MEAT, 2 FAT
CARB. CHOICES: 1/2

SLOW COOKER DIRECTIONS

Place beef in 3 1/2- to 6-quart slow cooker; add juices and spices from package of corned beef. Add enough cold water just to cover beef. Add onion and garlic. Top with cabbage. Cover and cook on Low heat setting 7 to 8 hours.

NEW ENGLAND BOILED DINNER Omit 1 medium onion. Decrease simmer time of beef in Step 2 to 2 hours. Skim fat from broth. Add 6 small onions, 6 medium carrots (cut in half), 3 medium potatoes (cut in half) and, if desired, 3 turnips (cut into cubes) to broth. Cover and simmer 20 minutes. Remove beef to warm platter; keep warm. Add cabbage to broth. Heat to boiling; reduce heat. Simmer uncovered about 15 minutes or until vegetables are tender.

Swiss Steak LOW-FAT

PREP: 15 min **COOK:** 1 hr 50 min ■ **6 SERVINGS**

$1\frac{1}{2}$-lb beef boneless round, tip or chuck steak, about $\frac{3}{4}$ inch thick
3 tablespoons all-purpose flour
1 teaspoon ground mustard
$\frac{1}{2}$ teaspoon salt
2 tablespoons vegetable oil
1 can (14.5 oz) whole tomatoes, undrained
2 cloves garlic, finely chopped
1 cup water
1 large onion, sliced
1 large green bell pepper, sliced

1. Cut beef into 6 serving pieces. In small bowl, mix flour, mustard and salt. Sprinkle half of the flour mixture over 1 side of beef; pound in with meat mallet. Turn beef; pound in remaining flour mixture.

2. In 10-inch skillet, heat oil over medium heat. Cook beef in oil about 15 minutes, turning once, until brown.

3. Add tomatoes and garlic to skillet, breaking up tomatoes with a fork. Heat to boiling; reduce heat. Cover and simmer about 1 hour 15 minutes, spooning sauce occasionally over beef, until beef is tender.

4. Add water, onion and bell pepper to skillet. Heat to boiling; reduce heat. Cover and simmer 5 to 8 minutes or until vegetables are tender.

1 SERVING: CAL. 205 (CAL. FROM FAT 70); FAT 8g (SAT. FAT 2g); CHOL. 60mg; SODIUM 340mg; CARBS. 11g (FIBER 2g); PRO. 24g **% DAILY VALUE:** VIT. A 8%; VIT. C 30%; CALC. 2%; IRON 16% **EXCHANGES:** 2 VEGETABLE, 3 LEAN MEAT **CARB. CHOICES:** 1

SLOW COOKER DIRECTIONS

Omit water. Cut beef into 6 serving pieces. In small bowl, mix flour, mustard and salt; coat beef (do not pound in). In 10-inch skillet, heat oil over medium heat. Cook beef in oil about 15 minutes, turning once, until brown. Place beef in $3\frac{1}{2}$- to 6-quart slow cooker. Top with onion and bell pepper. Mix tomatoes and garlic; pour over beef and vegetables. Cover and cook on Low heat setting 7 to 9 hours.

Beef Stroganoff

PREP: 20 min **COOK:** 30 min ■ **6 SERVINGS**

Just for the fun and flavor, mix up your mushrooms! Instead of traditional white or button mushrooms, combine several fresh varieties such as baby portabella, shiitake and oyster mushrooms.

$1\frac{1}{2}$-lb beef tenderloin or boneless top loin steak, about $\frac{1}{2}$ inch thick
2 tablespoons butter or margarine
$1\frac{1}{2}$ cups beef broth
2 tablespoons ketchup
1 teaspoon salt
1 small clove garlic, finely chopped
3 cups sliced fresh mushrooms (8 oz)
1 medium onion, chopped ($\frac{1}{2}$ cup)
$\frac{1}{4}$ cup all-purpose flour
1 cup sour cream or plain yogurt
Hot cooked noodles or rice (page 376 or 375), if desired

1. Cut beef across grain into about $1\frac{1}{2} \times \frac{1}{2}$-inch strips. (Beef is easier to cut if partially frozen, 30 to 60 minutes.)

2. In 12-inch skillet, melt butter over medium-high heat. Cook beef in butter, stirring occasionally, until brown.

3. Reserve $\frac{1}{3}$ cup of the broth. Stir remaining broth, the ketchup, salt and garlic into beef. Heat to boiling; reduce heat. Cover and simmer about 10 minutes or until beef is tender.

4. Stir in mushrooms and onion. Heat to boiling; reduce heat. Cover and simmer about 5 minutes or until onion is tender.

5. In tightly covered container, shake reserved $\frac{1}{3}$ cup broth and the flour until mixed; gradually stir into beef mixture. Heat to boiling, stirring constantly. Boil and stir 1 minute; reduce heat to low.

6. Stir in sour cream; heat until hot. Serve over noodles.

1 SERVING (ABOUT 1 CUP): CAL. 330 (CAL. FROM FAT 180); FAT 20g (SAT. FAT 10g); CHOL. 100mg; SODIUM 810mg; CARBS. 10g (FIBER 1g); PRO. 28g **% DAILY VALUE:** VIT. A 10%; VIT. C 2%; CALC. 6%; IRON 16% **EXCHANGES:** 2 VEGETABLE, $3\frac{1}{2}$ LEAN MEAT, 1 FAT **CARB. CHOICES:** $\frac{1}{2}$

GROUND BEEF STROGANOFF Substitute 1 lb lean (at least 80%) ground beef for the steak; omit butter. Cook ground beef in 12-inch skillet, stirring occasionally, until brown; drain. Continue as directed.

SLOW COOKER DIRECTIONS

Substitute beef boneless bottom round steak for the beef tenderloin or boneless top loin steak; cut as directed in Step 1. Cook beef in butter as directed in Step 2. Reserve 1/3 cup of the broth. In 3- to 4-quart slow cooker, mix beef, remaining broth, ketchup, salt, garlic, mushrooms and onion. Cover and cook on Low heat setting 8 to 9 hours. In tightly covered container, shake reserved 1/3 cup broth and the flour until mixed; stir into beef mixture. Increase heat setting to High. Cover and cook 15 to 20 minutes or until thickened. Stir in sour cream; heat until hot. Serve over noodles.

Hungarian Goulash

PREP: 30 min **COOK:** 1 hr 40 min ■ **6 SERVINGS**

All paprika is made from ground sweet peppers and ranges in flavor from sweet to mild or hot. Look for Hungarian paprika for a fuller, sweet flavor or for hot if you prefer a bite.

- 1 tablespoon vegetable oil or bacon fat
- 1 1/2-lb beef boneless chuck, tip or round roast or pork boneless shoulder, cut into 3/4-inch cubes
- 1/2 cup beef broth
- 3 tablespoons paprika
- 1 1/2 teaspoons salt
- 1/2 teaspoon caraway seed
- 1/4 teaspoon pepper
- 3 large onions, chopped (3 cups)
- 2 cloves garlic, finely chopped
- 1 can (14.5 oz) whole tomatoes, undrained
- 1/4 cup cold water
- 2 tablespoons all-purpose flour
- 6 cups hot cooked noodles (page 376)

1. In 4-quart Dutch oven or 12-inch skillet, heat oil over medium heat. Cook beef in oil about 15 minutes, stirring occasionally, until beef is brown; drain.

2. Stir in remaining ingredients except water, flour and noodles, breaking up tomatoes with a fork. Heat to boiling; reduce heat. Cover and simmer about 1 hour 15 minutes, stirring occasionally, until beef is tender.

3. In tightly covered container, shake water and flour until mixed; gradually stir into beef mixture. Heat to boiling, stirring constantly. Boil and stir 1 minute. Serve over noodles.

1 SERVING (ABOUT 1 CUP): CAL. 495 (CAL. FROM FAT 160); FAT 18g (SAT. FAT 6g); CHOL. 120mg; SODIUM 850mg; CARBS. 54g (FIBER 5g); PRO. 33g **% DAILY VALUE:** VIT. A 54%; VIT. C 14%; CALC. 6%; IRON 36% **EXCHANGES:** 3 STARCH, 2 VEGETABLE, 3 MEDIUM-FAT MEAT **CARB. CHOICES:** 3 1/2

SLOW COOKER DIRECTIONS

In 12-inch skillet, cook beef in oil as directed in Step 1 for 5 to 7 minutes or just until beef is brown. In 2 1/2- to 3 1/2-quart slow cooker, mix beef and remaining ingredients except water, flour and noodles. Cover and cook on Low heat setting 8 to 9 hours. In tightly covered container, shake water and flour until mixed; stir into beef mixture. Increase heat setting to High. Cover and cook 10 to 20 minutes or until thickened. Serve over noodles.

LIGHTER HUNGARIAN GOULASH

For 7 grams of fat and 335 calories per serving, omit vegetable oil; spray Dutch oven with cooking spray before heating. Decrease beef to 1 lb. Use noodles made without egg yolks.

MEAT MARBLING

Ever examine a piece of meat and see the little specks and streaks of white fat throughout the lean? That's marbling, and it's an indicator of how juicy the meat will be when cooked. The more marbling, the more tender and juicy the meat, but also the more fat and calories per serving. The amount of marbling affects how you cook a cut of meat and for how long.

Pepper Steak

PREP: 15 min **COOK:** 30 min ■ **6 SERVINGS**

- 1 1/2-lb beef top round or sirloin steak, 3/4 to 1 inch thick
- 3 tablespoons vegetable oil
- 1 cup water
- 1 medium onion, cut into 1/4-inch slices
- 1 clove garlic, finely chopped
- 1/2 teaspoon finely chopped gingerroot or 1/4 teaspoon ground ginger
- 2 medium green bell peppers, cut into 3/4-inch strips
- 1 tablespoon cornstarch
- 2 teaspoons sugar, if desired
- 2 tablespoons soy sauce
- 2 medium tomatoes
- 6 cups hot cooked rice (page 375)

1. Remove fat from beef. Cut beef into 2 × 1/4-inch strips. (Beef is easier to cut if partially frozen, 30 to 60 minutes.)

2. In 12-inch skillet, heat oil over medium-high heat. Cook beef in oil about 5 minutes, turning frequently, until brown.

3. Stir in water, onion, garlic and gingerroot. Heat to boiling; reduce heat. Cover and simmer 12 to 15 minutes for round steak, 5 to 8 minutes for sirloin steak, adding bell peppers during last 5 minutes of simmering, until beef is tender and peppers are crisp-tender.

4. In small bowl, mix cornstarch, sugar and soy sauce; stir into beef mixture. Cook, stirring constantly, until mixture thickens and boils. Boil and stir 1 minute; reduce heat to low.

5. Cut each tomato into 8 wedges; place on beef mixture. Cover and cook over low heat about 3 minutes or just until tomatoes are heated through. Serve with rice.

1 SERVING (ABOUT 2 CUPS): CAL. 420 (CAL. FROM FAT 100); FAT 11g (SAT. FAT 2g); CHOL. 60mg; SODIUM 350mg; CARBS. 52g (FIBER 2g); PRO. 28g **% DAILY VALUE:** VIT. A 10%; VIT. C 36%; CALC. 2%; IRON 24% **EXCHANGES:** 3 STARCH, 1 VEGETABLE, 2 MEDIUM-FAT MEAT **CARB. CHOICES:** 3 1/2

LIGHTER PEPPER STEAK

For 4 grams of fat and 350 calories per serving, omit oil and use nonstick skillet. Spray skillet with cooking spray before heating in Step 2.

Savory Oven Beef Ribs

PREP: 25 min **COOK:** 8 min **BAKE:** 2 hr ■ **4 SERVINGS**

If you can't find the boneless beef ribs, buy double the amount of bone-in ribs instead. You may need a larger baking dish or shallow roasting pan and might need to increase the baking time.

- 1 cup beef broth
- 1/2 cup dry red wine or beef broth
- 1 can (15 oz) tomato sauce
- 1/2 teaspoon dried thyme leaves
- 1/2 teaspoon dried marjoram leaves
- 3 tablespoons all-purpose flour
- 1 teaspoon salt
- 1/4 teaspoon pepper
- 2 lb beef boneless country-style chuck ribs
- 2 tablespoons olive or vegetable oil
- 6 medium carrots, cut into 2-inch pieces
- 2 medium stalks celery, chopped (1 cup)
- 1 large onion, chopped (1 cup)
- 2 large cloves garlic, finely chopped

1. Heat oven to 350°F.

Savory Oven Beef Ribs ▶

2. In 13 × 9-inch glass baking dish, mix broth, wine, tomato sauce, thyme and marjoram.

3. In heavy-duty resealable plastic food-storage bag, place flour, salt and pepper; shake to mix. Add ribs; shake to coat. In baking dish, beat excess flour mixture (about 1 tablespoon) into tomato sauce mixture, using wire whisk.

4. In 12-inch nonstick skillet, heat 1 tablespoon of the oil over medium-high heat. Cook ribs in oil about 5 minutes, turning once, until brown. Place ribs in baking dish; turn to coat with sauce mixture. Add remaining 1 tablespoon oil to skillet; increase heat to high. Cook carrots, celery, onion and garlic in oil 3 minutes, stirring frequently.

5. Add carrot mixture to ribs and sauce. Cover tightly with foil. Bake 1 hour 30 minutes to 2 hours or until ribs are tender.

1 SERVING: CAL. 635 (CAL. FROM FAT 370); FAT 41g (SAT. FAT 14g); CHOL. 135mg; SODIUM 1670mg; CARBS. 19g; (FIBER 3g); PRO. 47g **% DAILY VALUE:** VIT. A 76%; VIT. C 16%; CALC. 6%; IRON 30% **EXCHANGES:** 1 STARCH, 1 VEGETABLE, 6 MEDIUM-FAT MEAT, 2 FAT **CARB. CHOICES:** 1

Beef Short Ribs Carbonnade

PREP: 30 min **COOK:** 10 min **BAKE:** 2 hr 30 min ■ **8 SERVINGS**

Popular beef short ribs combine with the classic flavors of "carbonnade à la flamande," which is the classic Belgian beef stew hailing from Flanders. Serve with creamy Mashed Potatoes on page 464.

- 3 tablespoons vegetable oil
- 4 lb beef chuck short ribs
- 2 large onions, sliced
- 3 tablespoons all-purpose flour
- 1 teaspoon dried thyme leaves
- 1 can (14 oz) beef broth
- 1 teaspoon balsamic vinegar
- 1 tablespoon packed brown sugar
- 1 teaspoon salt
- 1/4 teaspoon pepper
- 1 can or bottle (12 oz) beer or nonalcoholic beer

1. Heat oven to 325°F.

2. In 12-inch skillet, heat 1 tablespoon of the oil over high heat. Cook ribs in oil about 10 minutes, turning frequently, until brown on all sides. Discard drippings. Place ribs in large roasting pan. Cover and bake 1 hour; drain.

3. Meanwhile, in same skillet, heat remaining 2 tablespoons oil over medium-high heat. Cook onions in oil 10 to 15 minutes, stirring frequently, until tender and brown. Stir in flour, coating well. Stir in thyme, broth, vinegar, brown sugar, salt and pepper.

4. Pour onion mixture over beef ribs. Add beer. Cover and bake about 1 hour 30 minutes longer or until ribs are tender. Serve ribs with pan juices.

1 SERVING: CAL. 270 (CAL. FROM FAT 160); FAT 18g (SAT. FAT 6g); CHOL. 50mg; SODIUM 570mg; CARBS. 9g (FIBER 1g); PRO. 18g **% DAILY VALUE:** VIT. A 2%; VIT. C 2%; CALC. 2%; IRON 10% **EXCHANGES:** 1/2 STARCH, 2 1/2 MEDIUM-FAT MEAT, 1 FAT **CARB. CHOICES:** 1/2

Skillet Hash

PREP: 10 min **COOK:** 15 min ■ **4 SERVINGS**

For extra convenience, substitute 2 cups frozen diced hash browns, partially thawed, for the potatoes.

- 2 cups chopped cooked lean beef or corned beef
- 4 small potatoes, cooked and chopped (2 cups)
- 1 medium onion, chopped (1/2 cup)
- 1 tablespoon chopped fresh parsley
- 1/2 teaspoon salt
- 1/8 teaspoon pepper
- 2 to 3 tablespoons vegetable oil

1. In large bowl, mix beef, potatoes, onion, parsley, salt and pepper.

2. In 10-inch skillet, heat oil over medium heat. Spread beef mixture evenly in skillet. Cook 10 to 15 minutes, turning frequently, until brown.

1 SERVING (ABOUT 1 CUP): CAL. 310 (CAL. FROM FAT 115); FAT 13g (SAT. FAT 3g); CHOL. 50mg; SODIUM 340mg; CARBS. 27g (FIBER 3g); PRO. 22g **% DAILY VALUE:** VIT. A 4%; VIT. C 10%; CALC. 2%; IRON 12% **EXCHANGES:** 1 STARCH, 2 VEGETABLE, 2 MEDIUM-FAT MEAT, 1/2 FAT **CARB. CHOICES:** 2

OVEN HASH Heat oven to 350°F. Spray 8-inch square baking dish with cooking spray. Omit oil. Spread beef mixture evenly in baking dish. Bake uncovered about 20 minutes or until hot.

Meat Loaf

PREP: 20 min **BAKE:** 1 hr 15 min **STAND:** 5 min ■ **6 SERVINGS**

- 1 1/2-lb lean (at least 80%) ground beef
- 1 cup milk
- 1 tablespoon Worcestershire sauce
- 1 teaspoon chopped fresh or 1/4 teaspoon dried sage leaves
- 1/2 teaspoon salt
- 1/2 teaspoon ground mustard
- 1/4 teaspoon pepper
- 1 clove garlic, finely chopped, or 1/8 teaspoon garlic powder
- 1 large egg
- 3 slices bread, torn into small pieces*
- 1 small onion, chopped (1/4 cup)
- 1/2 cup ketchup, chili sauce or barbecue sauce

1. Heat oven to 350°F.

2. In large bowl, mix all ingredients except ketchup. Spread mixture in ungreased 8 × 4-inch or 9 × 5-inch loaf pan, or shape into 9 × 5-inch loaf in ungreased 13 × 9-inch pan. Spread ketchup over top.

3. Insert ovenproof meat thermometer so tip is in center of loaf. Bake uncovered 1 hour to 1 hour 15 minutes or until beef is no longer pink in center and thermometer reads at least 160°F.** (Also see Recommended Meat Doneness, page 307.) Drain meat loaf.

4. Let stand 5 minutes; remove from pan.

**1/2 cup dry bread crumbs or 3/4 cup quick-cooking oats can be substituted for the 3 slices bread.*

***Due to the natural nitrate content of certain ingredients often used in meat loaf such as onions, celery and bell peppers, meat loaf may remain pink even though beef is cooked to 160°F doneness. Always check meat loaf with a thermometer to make sure it has reached 160°F in the center.*

1 SERVING: CAL. 320 (CAL. FROM FAT 160); FAT 18g (SAT. FAT 7g); CHOL. 105mg; SODIUM 610mg; CARBS. 15g (FIBER 1g); PRO. 25g
% DAILY VALUE: VIT. A 8%; VIT. C 4%; CALC. 8%; IRON 14%
EXCHANGES: 1 STARCH, 3 MEDIUM-FAT MEAT, 1/2 FAT
CARB. CHOICES: 1

LIGHTER MEAT LOAF

For 7 grams of fat and 240 calories per serving, substitute ground turkey breast for the ground beef and 1/4 cup fat-free cholesterol-free egg product for the egg. Use fat-free (skim) milk. Bake uncovered 1 hour to 1 hour 15 minutes or until turkey is no longer pink in center and thermometer reads 165°F.

INDIVIDUAL MEAT LOAVES Spray 12 medium muffin cups with cooking spray. Divide beef mixture evenly among cups (cups will be very full). Brush tops with about 1/4 cup ketchup. Place muffin pan on cookie sheet to catch any spillover. Bake about 30 minutes or until loaves are no longer pink in center and thermometer reads 160°F when inserted in center of loaves in middle of muffin pan (outer loaves will be done sooner). Immediately remove from cups.

MEXICAN MEAT LOAF Omit sage. Substitute 2/3 cup milk and 1/3 cup salsa for the 1 cup milk. Stir in 1/2 cup shredded Colby-Monterey Jack cheese (2 oz) and 1 can (4.5 oz) chopped green chiles, drained, in Step 2. Substitute 2/3 cup salsa for the ketchup.

Mini Meatballs and Basil Pesto (page 405) ▶

Meatballs

PREP: 15 min **BAKE:** 25 min ■ **4 SERVINGS**

Shape meatballs fast by using an ice-cream scoop. Or instead of shaping balls at all, pat the mixture into a 9 × 3-inch rectangle in an ungreased 13 × 9-inch pan. Cut into 1½-inch squares, and separate slightly. Bake uncovered 25 to 30 minutes.

- 1 lb lean (at least 80%) ground beef
- ½ cup dry bread crumbs
- ¼ cup milk
- ½ teaspoon salt
- ½ teaspoon Worcestershire sauce
- ¼ teaspoon pepper
- 1 small onion, chopped (¼ cup)
- 1 large egg

1. Heat oven to 400°F.

2. In large bowl, mix all ingredients. Shape mixture into twenty 1½-inch meatballs. Place in ungreased 13 × 9-inch pan or on rack in broiler pan.

3. Bake uncovered 20 to 25 minutes or until no longer pink in center and thermometer inserted in center reads 160°F.

1 SERVING: CAL. 315 (CAL. FROM FAT 170); FAT 19g (SAT. FAT 7g); CHOL. 120mg; SODIUM 490mg; CARBS. 12g (FIBER 1g); PRO. 25g
% DAILY VALUE: VIT. A 4%; VIT. C 0%; CALC. 6%; IRON 16%
EXCHANGES: 1 STARCH, 3 MEDIUM-FAT MEAT **CARB. CHOICES:** 1

MINI MEATBALLS Shape beef mixture into 1-inch meatballs. Bake 15 to 20 minutes. 3 dozen appetizers.

SKILLET MEATBALLS In 10-inch skillet, cook meatballs over medium heat about 20 minutes, turning occasionally, until no longer pink in center and thermometer inserted in center reads 160°F.

TURKEY OR CHICKEN MEATBALLS Substitute 1 lb ground turkey or chicken for the ground beef. (If using ground chicken, decrease milk to 2 tablespoons.) To bake, spray rectangular pan with cooking spray; bake until no longer pink in center and thermometer inserted in center reads 165°F. To cook in skillet, heat 1 tablespoon vegetable oil over medium heat before adding meatballs; cook until no longer pink in center and thermometer inserted in center reads 165°F.

Impossibly Easy Cheeseburger Pie

PREP: 5 min **COOK:** 10 min **BAKE:** 25 min ■ **6 SERVINGS**

- 1 lb lean (at least 80%) ground beef
- 1 large onion, chopped (1 cup)
- ½ teaspoon salt
- 1 cup shredded Cheddar cheese (4 oz)
- ½ cup Original Bisquick® mix
- 1 cup milk
- 2 large eggs

1. Heat oven to 400°F. Spray 9-inch glass pie plate with cooking spray.

2. In 10-inch skillet, cook beef and onion over medium heat 8 to 10 minutes, stirring occasionally, until beef is brown; drain. Stir in salt. Spread in pie plate. Sprinkle with cheese.

3. In small bowl, stir remaining ingredients with fork or wire whisk until blended. Pour into pie plate.

4. Bake about 25 minutes or until knife inserted in center comes out clean.

1 SERVING: CAL. 310 (CAL. FROM FAT 180); FAT 20g (SAT. FAT 9g); CHOL. 100mg; SODIUM 520mg; CARBS. 11g (FIBER 1g); PRO. 22g
% DAILY VALUE: VIT. A 8%; VIT. C 0%; CALC. 18%; IRON 10%
EXCHANGES: 1 STARCH, 3 MEDIUM-FAT MEAT **CARB. CHOICES:** 1

Impossibly Easy Cheeseburger Pie ▶

Beef Enchiladas

PREP: 15 min **COOK:** 20 min **BAKE:** 20 min ■ **4 SERVINGS**

1 lb lean (at least 80%) ground beef
1 medium onion, chopped (1/2 cup)
1/2 cup sour cream
1 cup shredded Cheddar cheese (4 oz)
2 tablespoons chopped fresh parsley
1/4 teaspoon pepper
1/3 cup chopped green bell pepper
2/3 cup water
1 tablespoon chili powder
1 1/2 teaspoons chopped fresh or 1/2 teaspoon dried oregano leaves
1/4 teaspoon ground cumin
1 can (4.5 oz) chopped green chiles, drained
1 clove garlic, finely chopped
1 can (15 oz) tomato sauce
8 corn tortillas (5 or 6 inch)
Shredded cheese, sour cream and chopped onions, if desired

1. Heat oven to 350°F.

2. In 10-inch skillet, cook beef over medium heat 8 to 10 minutes, stirring occasionally, until brown; drain. Stir in onion, sour cream, 1 cup cheese, the parsley and pepper. Cover and remove from heat.

3. In 2-quart saucepan, heat bell pepper, water, chili powder, oregano, cumin, chiles, garlic and tomato sauce to boiling, stirring occasionally; reduce heat. Simmer uncovered 5 minutes. Pour into ungreased 9-inch pie plate.

4. Dip each tortilla into sauce in pie plate to coat both sides. Spoon about 1/4 cup beef mixture onto each tortilla; roll tortilla around filling. Place seam side down in ungreased 11 × 7-inch glass baking dish. Pour remaining sauce over enchiladas.

5. Bake uncovered about 20 minutes or until bubbly. Garnish with shredded cheese, sour cream and chopped onions.

1 SERVING: CAL. 590 (CAL. FROM FAT 295); FAT 33g (SAT. FAT 16g); CHOL. 115mg; SODIUM 1,570mg; CARBS. 40g (FIBER 7g); PRO. 34g
% DAILY VALUE: VIT. A 52%; VIT. C 20%; CALC. 30%; IRON 26%
EXCHANGES: 2 1/2 STARCH, 4 MEDIUM-FAT MEAT, 2 FAT
CARB. CHOICES: 2 1/2

LIGHTER ENCHILADAS

For 15 grams of fat and 420 calories per serving, substitute ground turkey breast for the ground beef; use fat-free flour tortillas and reduced-fat sour cream and cheese.

Stuffed Peppers

PREP: 15 min **COOK:** 20 min **BAKE:** 1 hr ■ **6 SERVINGS**

6 large bell peppers (any color)
1 lb lean (at least 80%) ground beef
2 tablespoons chopped onion
1 cup cooked rice (page 375)
1 teaspoon salt
1 clove garlic, finely chopped
1 can (15 oz) tomato sauce
3/4 cup shredded mozzarella cheese (3 oz)

1. Cut thin slice from stem end of each bell pepper to remove top of pepper. Remove seeds and membranes; rinse peppers. If necessary, cut thin slice from bottom of each pepper so they stand up straight. In 4-quart Dutch oven, add enough water to cover peppers. Heat to boiling; add peppers. Cook about 5 minutes; drain.

2. In 10-inch skillet, cook beef and onion over medium heat 8 to 10 minutes, stirring occasionally, until beef is brown; drain. Stir in rice, salt, garlic and 1 cup of the tomato sauce; cook until hot.

3. Heat oven to 350°F.

4. Stuff peppers with beef mixture. Stand peppers upright in ungreased 8-inch square glass baking dish. Pour remaining tomato sauce over peppers.

5. Cover tightly with foil. Bake 45 minutes. Uncover and bake about 15 minutes longer or until peppers are tender. Sprinkle with cheese.

1 SERVING: CAL. 290 (CAL. FROM FAT 125); FAT 14g (SAT. FAT 6g); CHOL. 50mg; SODIUM 970mg; CARBS. 24g (FIBER 4g); PRO. 21g
% DAILY VALUE: VIT. A 24%; VIT. C 100%; CALC. 14%; IRON 16%
EXCHANGES: 1 STARCH, 2 MEDIUM-FAT MEAT, 2 VEGETABLE
CARB. CHOICES: 1 1/2

LIGHTER STUFFED PEPPERS

For 3 grams of fat and 190 calories per serving, substitute ground turkey breast for the ground beef; use reduced-fat cheese.

VEGETARIAN STUFFED PEPPERS Substitute 1 package (12 oz) frozen veggie crumbles, thawed, for the ground beef; omit onion. Omit Step 2. In 10-inch nonstick skillet, cook veggie crumbles, rice, salt, garlic and 1 cup of the tomato sauce over medium heat, stirring occasionally, until hot. Continue as directed.

Veal Scallopini

PREP: 10 min **COOK:** 20 min ■ **4 SERVINGS**

- 1/2 cup all-purpose flour
- 2 teaspoons garlic salt
- 1 lb veal for scallopini*
- 1/4 cup vegetable oil
- 2 tablespoons butter or margarine
- 1/4 cup dry white wine, nonalcoholic white wine or chicken broth
- 2 tablespoons lemon juice
- 1/2 lemon, cut into 4 wedges

1. In shallow dish, mix flour and garlic salt. Coat veal with flour mixture.

2. In 10-inch skillet, heat 2 tablespoons of the oil over medium-high heat. Cook half of the veal in oil about 5 minutes, turning once, until brown. Remove veal; keep warm. Repeat with remaining oil and veal. Drain any remaining oil and overly browned particles from skillet.

3. Add butter, wine and lemon juice to skillet. Heat to boiling, scraping any remaining brown particles from skillet. Boil until liquid is reduced by about half and mixture has thickened slightly. Pour over veal. Serve with lemon wedges.

**1 lb veal round steak can be substituted for the veal for scallopini. Cut veal into 8 pieces. Place each piece between sheets of plastic wrap or waxed paper. Lightly pound with flat side of meat mallet until 1/4 inch thick.*

1 SERVING: CAL. 300 (CAL. FROM FAT 170); FAT 19g (SAT. FAT 7g); CHOL. 90mg; SODIUM 590mg; CARBS. 13g (FIBER 0g); PRO. 19g
% DAILY VALUE: VIT. A 4%; VIT. C 2%; CALC. 2%; IRON 8%
EXCHANGES: 1 STARCH, 2 MEDIUM-FAT MEAT, 2 FAT
CARB. CHOICES: 1

LIGHTER VEAL SCALLOPINI

For 14 grams of fat and 255 calories per serving, decrease oil to 2 tablespoons and cook half of the veal at a time in 1 tablespoon oil in nonstick skillet. Decrease butter to 1 tablespoon.

Veal Parmigiana

PREP: 1 hr 5 min **COOK:** 10 min **BAKE:** 25 min ■ **6 SERVINGS**

- 2 cups Italian Tomato Sauce (page 404) or purchased tomato pasta sauce
- 1 large egg
- 2 tablespoons water
- 2/3 cup dry bread crumbs
- 1/3 cup grated Parmesan cheese
- 1 1/2-lb veal for scallopini*
- 1/4 cup olive or vegetable oil
- 2 cups shredded mozzarella cheese (8 oz)

1. Make Italian Tomato Sauce.

2. Heat oven to 350°F.

3. In small bowl, beat egg and water. In shallow dish, mix bread crumbs and Parmesan cheese. Dip veal into egg mixture, then coat with bread crumb mixture.

4. In 12-inch skillet, heat oil over medium heat. Cook half of the veal at a time in oil about 5 minutes, turning once, until light brown; drain. Repeat with remaining veal, adding 1 or 2 tablespoons oil if necessary.

5. In ungreased 11 × 7-inch glass baking dish, place half of the veal, overlapping slices slightly. Spoon half of the sauce over veal. Sprinkle with 1 cup of the mozzarella cheese. Repeat with remaining veal, sauce and cheese.

6. Bake uncovered about 25 minutes or until sauce is bubbly and cheese is light brown.

**1 1/2 lb veal round steak can be substituted for the veal for scallopini. Cut veal into 12 pieces. Place each piece between sheets of plastic wrap or waxed paper. Lightly pound with flat side of meat mallet until 1/4 inch thick.*

1 SERVING: CAL. 440 (CAL. FROM FAT 205); FAT 23g (SAT. FAT 8g); CHOL. 120mg; SODIUM 890mg; CARBS. 26g (FIBER 1g); PRO. 33g
% DAILY VALUE: VIT. A 18%; VIT. C 10%; CALC. 42%; IRON 12%
EXCHANGES: 1 STARCH, 2 VEGETABLE, 4 MEDIUM-FAT MEAT
CARB. CHOICES: 2

CHICKEN PARMIGIANA Substitute 8 boneless skinless chicken breasts (about 2 lb) for the veal. Place each chicken breast between sheets of plastic wrap or waxed paper. Lightly pound with flat side of meat mallet until 1/4 inch thick. In Step 4, cook chicken until no longer pink in center.

Osso Buco

PREP: 40 min **COOK:** 2 hr 30 min ▪ **6 SERVINGS**

6 veal or beef shank cross cuts, 2 to 2 1/2 inches thick (3 to 3 1/2 lb)
1/2 teaspoon salt
1/4 teaspoon pepper
1/4 cup all-purpose flour
2 tablespoons olive or vegetable oil
1/3 cup dry white wine or apple juice
1 can (10.5 oz) condensed beef broth
1 clove garlic, finely chopped
1 dried bay leaf
2 tablespoons chopped fresh parsley
1 teaspoon grated lemon peel
6 cups hot cooked Mashed Potatoes (page 464) or spaghetti (page 376)
Grated Romano cheese, if desired

1. Sprinkle veal with salt and pepper; coat with flour.

2. In 4-quart Dutch oven, heat oil over medium heat. Cook veal in oil about 20 minutes, turning occasionally, until brown on all sides.

3. Stir in wine, broth, garlic and bay leaf. Heat to boiling; reduce heat. Cover and simmer 1 hour 30 minutes to 2 hours or until veal is tender.

4. Remove veal; place on serving platter. Skim fat from broth; remove bay leaf. Pour broth over veal; sprinkle with parsley and lemon peel. Serve with Mashed Potatoes and cheese.

1 SERVING: CAL. 650 (CAL. FROM FAT 240); FAT 27g (SAT. FAT 8g); CHOL. 210mg; SODIUM 1050mg; CARBS. 41g; (FIBER 3g); PRO. 56g **% DAILY VALUE:** VIT. A 15%; VIT. C 0%; CALC. 10%; IRON 15% **EXCHANGES:** 2 1/2 STARCH, 7 LEAN MEAT, 1 FAT **CARB. CHOICES:** 2 1/2

◀ **Osso Buco**

Pork Crown Roast with Fruited Stuffing Supreme

PREP: 20 min **COOK:** 15 min **ROAST:** 3 hr 20 min **STAND:** 20 min ▪ **16 SERVINGS**

When you want to make a big impression without much effort, plan to serve this pork crown roast. It's often available during the holidays, but call the meat department or your butcher ahead of time to reserve one. Those fancy paper frills usually come with the roast. If they don't, check a gourmet specialty shop.

Pork Roast

8- to 10-lb pork crown roast (about 16 to 18 ribs)*
2 teaspoons salt
1 teaspoon pepper

Fruited Stuffing Supreme

1 lb bulk pork sausage
1/4 cup butter or margarine
4 medium stalks celery, chopped (2 cups)
3/4 cup chopped onion (about 1 large)
1 cup chicken broth
1 teaspoon dried sage leaves, crumbled
1 teaspoon poultry seasoning
6 1/2 cups unseasoned stuffing cubes (16 oz)
1 can (8 oz) crushed pineapple, undrained
1 cup applesauce
1 cup orange marmalade

1. Heat oven to 325°F. Sprinkle pork with salt and pepper. On rack in shallow roasting pan, place pork with bone ends up. Wrap bone ends in foil to prevent excessive browning. Insert ovenproof meat thermometer so tip is in thickest part of pork and does not touch bone or rest in fat. Place small heatproof bowl or crumpled foil in crown to hold shape of roast evenly. Do not add water.

2. Roast uncovered 2 hours 40 minutes to 3 hours 20 minutes or until thermometer reads 155°F. (Also see Recommended Meat Doneness, page 308.)

3. Meanwhile, in 10-inch skillet, cook sausage over medium heat 8 to 10 minutes, stirring occasionally, until no longer pink; drain well and set aside. In same skillet, melt butter over medium-high heat. Cook celery and onion in butter about 5 minutes, stirring occasionally, until vegetables are crisp-tender. Stir in broth, sage and poultry seasoning. In very large bowl, mix stuffing cubes, sausage, pineapple, applesauce and marmalade. Add vegetable mixture; stir until well blended.

4. About 1 hour before pork is done, remove bowl and fill center of crown with stuffing. (Remaining stuffing can be baked in 1 1/2–quart covered casserole.) Cover stuffing with foil only for first 30 minutes. Remove foil and finish baking.

5. Remove pork from oven when thermometer reads 150°F, cover with tent of foil and let stand 15 to 20 minutes or until thermometer reads 160°F. (Temperature will continue to rise about 10°F, and pork will be easier to carve.)

6. Remove foil wrapping; place paper frills on bone ends. To serve, spoon stuffing into bowl and cut pork between ribs.

**A 4-lb pork boneless loin roast can be substituted. Roast uncovered in roasting pan about 1 hour 20 minutes. Remove pork from oven when thermometer reads 155°F, cover with tent of foil and let stand 15 to 20 minutes or until thermometer reads 160°F (temperature will continue to rise about 10°F, and pork will be easier to carve). Make stuffing as directed and bake in covered casserole.*

1 SERVING: CAL. 470 (CAL. FROM FAT 180); FAT 20g (SAT. FAT 8g); CHOL. 120mg; SODIUM 880mg; CARBS. 33g (FIBER 2g); PRO. 40g
% DAILY VALUE: VIT. A 2%; VIT. C 0%; CALC. 6%; IRON 10%
EXCHANGES: 2 STARCH, 5 LEAN MEAT, 1 FAT **CARB. CHOICES:** 2

HOW TO CARVE A PORK CROWN ROAST

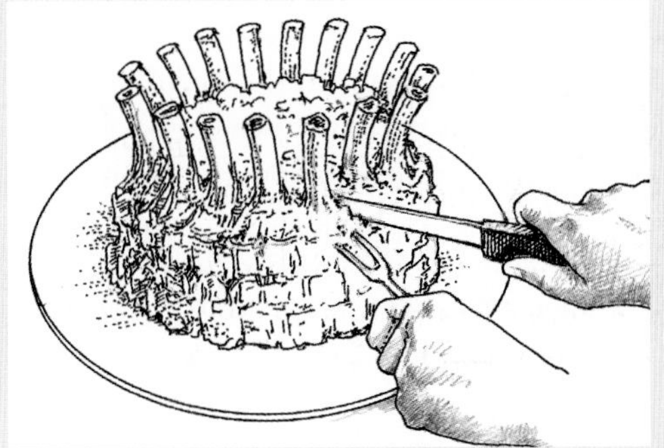

Place roast on carving board or serving platter. Insert meat fork into roast to keep it from moving; cut slices between ribs.

Glazed Baked Ham LOW-FAT

PREP: 10 min **BAKE:** 1 hr 30 min **STAND:** 10 min ■ **10 SERVINGS**

Ham

6-lb fully cooked smoked bone-in ham

Pineapple Glaze

1 cup packed brown sugar

1 tablespoon cornstarch

1/4 teaspoon salt

1 can (8 oz) crushed pineapple in syrup, undrained

2 tablespoons lemon juice

1 tablespoon yellow mustard

1. Heat oven to 325°F. Place ham on rack in shallow roasting pan. Insert ovenproof meat thermometer in thickest part of ham. Bake uncovered 1 hour 30 minutes or until thermometer reads 140°F.

2. Meanwhile, in 1-quart saucepan, mix brown sugar, cornstarch and salt. Stir in pineapple, lemon juice and mustard. Cook over medium heat, stirring constantly, until mixture thickens and boils. Boil and stir 1 minute. Brush glaze over ham during last 45 minutes of baking. (Also see Recommended Meat Doneness, page 308.)

3. Remove ham from oven, cover with tent with foil and let stand 10 to 15 minutes for easier carving.

1 SERVING: CAL. 290 (CAL. FROM FAT 65); FAT 7g (SAT. FAT 2g); CHOL. 70mg; SODIUM 1660mg; CARBS. 27g (FIBER 0g); PRO. 28g **% DAILY VALUE:** VIT. A 0%; VIT. C 0%; CALC. 2%; IRON 10% **EXCHANGES:** 1 OTHER CARB., 4 LEAN MEAT **CARB. CHOICES:** 1

HAM WITH BROWN SUGAR–ORANGE GLAZE Omit Pineapple Glaze. Bake ham as directed. In small bowl, mix 1/2 cup packed brown sugar, 2 tablespoons orange or pineapple juice and 1/2 teaspoon ground mustard. Brush glaze over ham during last 45 minutes of baking.

HOW TO CARVE A WHOLE HAM

▲ **1.** Place ham, fat side up, shank to your right, on carving board or platter. (Face shank to your left if you are left-handed.) Cut a few slices from one side.

2. Turn ham, cut side down, so it rests on flat cut side. Make vertical slices down the leg bone, then cut horizontally along bone to release slices. ▼

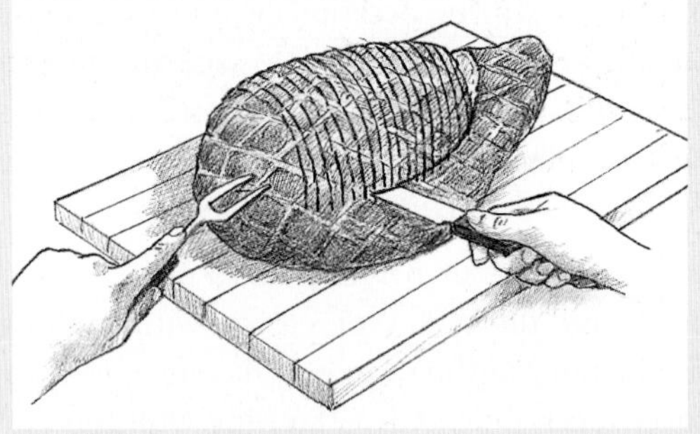

ALL ABOUT HAMS

Whatever kind of ham you choose, it all comes from cured pork leg meat. Curing gives ham its distinctive sweet-smoky and salty flavor. Hams are usually either wet- or dry-cured. Most supermarket hams, including the convenient spiral cut hams, are wet-cured, meaning they have been processed with a brine of water, salt, sugar and spices. Brining keeps the meat moist and tender. Dry-cured hams are rubbed with salt, sugar and spices, then aged several weeks to more than a year. These hams, referred to as country hams, are often named for the city where they are processed. Dry-cured hams are very salty, so follow package directions for using.

Herb-Crusted Pork Tenderloin

Herb-Crusted Pork Tenderloin LOW-FAT

PREP: 15 min **BAKE:** 35 min **STAND:** 15 min ■ **6 SERVINGS**

This is ideal for a dinner party, as tenderloins are quick to roast and easy to serve.

2 pork tenderloins (about 3/4 lb each)
1 cup soft bread crumbs (about 1 1/2 slices bread)
1/4 cup chopped fresh parsley
2 tablespoons chopped fresh or 1/2 teaspoon dried thyme leaves
1 tablespoon olive or vegetable oil
1/2 teaspoon salt
1/2 teaspoon fennel seed
1/4 teaspoon coarsely ground pepper
2 cloves garlic, finely chopped

1. Heat oven to 450°F. Spray shallow roasting pan and rack with cooking spray. Place pork tenderloins on rack in pan.

2. In small bowl, mix remaining ingredients. Spoon herb mixture evenly over pork. Insert ovenproof meat thermometer so tip is in the thickest part of pork. Cover pork loosely with foil.

3. Bake 20 minutes; remove foil. Bake uncovered 10 to 15 minutes longer or until thermometer reads 155°F. Cover pork loosely with foil and let stand 10 to 15 minutes or until thermometer reads 160°F. (Temperature will continue to rise about 5°F, and pork will be easier to carve.)

1 SERVING: CAL. 235 (CAL. FROM FAT 70); FAT 8g (SAT. FAT 2g); CHOL. 70mg; SODIUM 400mg; CARBS. 14g (FIBER 1g); PRO. 28g
% DAILY VALUE: VIT. A 4%; VIT. C 2%; CALC. 4%; IRON 14%
EXCHANGES: 1 STARCH, 3 1/2 VERY LEAN MEAT, 1 FAT
CARB. CHOICES: 1

Corn Bread– and Bacon-Stuffed Pork Chops

PREP: 20 min **COOK:** 13 min **BAKE:** 1 hr ▪ **6 SERVINGS**

6 pork rib or loin chops, 1 to 1 1/4 inches thick (about 4 lb)
4 slices bacon, cut into 1/2-inch pieces
1 medium onion, chopped (1/2 cup)
1 small green bell pepper, chopped (1/2 cup)
1 cup corn bread stuffing crumbs
1/2 cup water
1/2 cup shredded Cheddar cheese (2 oz)
1/2 teaspoon seasoned salt
1/2 teaspoon dried marjoram leaves
1/4 teaspoon pepper

1. Heat oven to 350°F.

2. Make a pocket in each pork chop by cutting into side of chop toward the bone.

3. In 12-inch skillet, cook bacon over medium heat 8 to 10 minutes, stirring occasionally, until crisp. Stir in onion and bell pepper. Cook 2 to 3 minutes, stirring occasionally, until vegetables are crisp-tender; remove from heat and drain. Stir in stuffing crumbs and water until well mixed. Stir in cheese.

4. Sprinkle both sides of pork with seasoned salt, marjoram and pepper. Fill pockets with about 1/3 cup corn bread mixture. In same skillet, cook pork over medium heat, turning once, until brown. Place pork in ungreased 13 × 9-inch pan. Cover tightly with foil.

5. Bake 45 minutes. Uncover and bake about 15 minutes longer or until pork is no longer pink when cut near bone.

HOW TO CUT A POCKET IN PORK CHOP

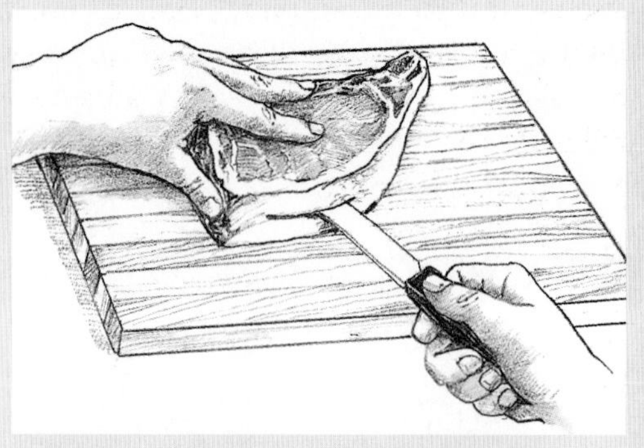

Make a pocket in each chop by cutting into side of chop toward the bone.

1 SERVING: CAL. 335 (CAL. FROM FAT 180); FAT 20g (SAT. FAT 7g); CHOL. 90mg; SODIUM 400mg; CARBS. 15g (FIBER 1g); PRO. 25g
% DAILY VALUE: VIT. A 4%; VIT. C 10%; CALC. 10%;IRON 8%
EXCHANGES: 1 STARCH, 3 MEDIUM-FAT MEAT, 1 FAT
CARB. CHOICES: 1

New-Style Pork Chops

PREP: 10 min **MARINATE:** 8 hr **COOK:** 40 min ▪ **6 SERVINGS**

6 pork loin or rib chops, about 1 inch thick (about 2 lb)
1 cup dry Marsala wine or beef broth
1 tablespoon balsamic vinegar
1 tablespoon fresh lemon juice
1 teaspoon honey
2 tablespoons olive or vegetable oil
1/2 cup chopped red onion
2 cloves garlic, finely chopped
1 cup Kalamata olives, pitted
1 tablespoon chopped fresh thyme leaves
1 tablespoon chopped fresh parsley
1/2 teaspoon salt
1/2 teaspoon pepper

1. Place pork in shallow glass or plastic dish. In small bowl, mix wine, vinegar, lemon juice and honey; pour over pork. Turn pork to coat both sides. Cover and refrigerate at least 8 hours but no longer than 24 hours, turning occasionally.

2. In 12-inch skillet, heat oil over medium-high heat. Cook remaining ingredients in oil about 5 minutes, stirring frequently, until onion is tender.

◀ **New-Style Pork Chops**

3. Remove pork from marinade; reserve marinade. Add pork to skillet. Cook about 10 minutes, turning pork once, until pork is brown. Add reserved marinade. Heat to boiling; reduce heat. Cover and simmer about 20 minutes or until pork is no longer pink when cut near bone. Serve pork with pan sauce.

1 SERVING: CAL. 260 (CAL. FROM FAT 135); FAT 15g (SAT. FAT 4g); CHOL. 65mg; SODIUM 460mg; CARBS. 9g (FIBER 1g); PRO. 23g
% DAILY VALUE: VIT. A 4%; VIT. C 2%; CALC. 2%; IRON 10%
EXCHANGES: 1/2 OTHER CARB., 3 MEDIUM-FAT MEAT
CARB. CHOICES: 1/2

Saucy Ribs

PREP: 20 min **BAKE:** 2 hr 15 min ■ **6 SERVINGS**

- 4 1/2 lb pork loin back ribs, pork spareribs or beef short ribs or 3 lb pork country-style ribs (choose one type of ribs)
- 1 recipe Spicy Barbecue Sauce, Molasses-Mustard Sauce or Sweet-Savory Sauce (right)

1. Heat oven to 350°F for all types of ribs. Cut ribs into serving pieces; place meaty sides up in pan listed for type of ribs below.

2. Make desired sauce; cover and refrigerate if not using immediately. Cook ribs as directed below.

PORK LOIN BACK RIBS Place ribs on rack in shallow roasting pan. Bake uncovered 1 hour 30 minutes; brush with sauce. Bake uncovered about 45 minutes longer, brushing frequently with sauce, until tender. Heat any remaining sauce to boiling, stirring constantly; boil and stir 1 minute. Serve sauce with ribs.

PORK SPARERIBS Place ribs on rack in shallow roasting pan. Bake uncovered 1 hour; brush with sauce. Bake uncovered about 45 minutes longer, brushing frequently with sauce, until tender. Heat any remaining sauce to boiling, stirring constantly; boil and stir 1 minute. Serve sauce with ribs.

PORK COUNTRY-STYLE RIBS Place ribs in 13 × 9-inch pan. Cover and bake about 2 hours or until tender; drain. Pour sauce over ribs. Bake uncovered 30 minutes longer. Spoon sauce from pan over ribs.

BEEF SHORT RIBS Place ribs in 13 × 9-inch pan. Pour sauce over ribs. Cover and bake about 2 hours 30 minutes or until tender. Spoon sauce from pan over ribs.

Spicy Barbecue Sauce

- 1/3 cup butter or margarine
- 2 tablespoons white or cider vinegar
- 2 tablespoons water
- 1 teaspoon sugar
- 1/2 teaspoon garlic powder
- 1/2 teaspoon onion powder
- 1/2 teaspoon pepper
- Dash of ground red pepper (cayenne)

In 1-quart saucepan, heat all ingredients over medium heat, stirring frequently, until butter is melted.

Molasses-Mustard Sauce

- 1/2 cup molasses
- 1/3 cup Dijon mustard
- 1/3 cup cider or white vinegar

In small bowl, mix molasses and mustard. Stir in vinegar.

Sweet-Savory Sauce

- 1 cup chili sauce
- 3/4 cup grape jelly
- 1 tablespoon plus 1 1/2 teaspoons dry red wine or beef broth
- 1 teaspoon Dijon mustard

In 1-quart saucepan, heat all ingredients over medium heat, stirring occasionally, until jelly is melted.

1 SERVING: CAL. 735 (CAL. FROM FAT 540); FAT 60g (SAT. FAT 25g); CHOL. 225mg; SODIUM 220mg; CARBS. 1g (FIBER 0g); PRO. 48g
% DAILY VALUE: VIT. A 8%; VIT. C 0%; CALC. 8%; IRON 16%
EXCHANGES: 7 HIGH-FAT MEAT, 1 FAT **CARB. CHOICES:** 0

SLOW COOKER DIRECTIONS

Use 3 1/2 lb ribs. Cut ribs into 2- or 3-rib portions. Place ribs in 5- to 6-quart slow cooker. Sprinkle with 1/2 teaspoon salt and 1/4 teaspoon pepper. Pour 1/2 cup water into slow cooker. Cover and cook on Low heat setting 8 to 9 hours. Remove ribs. Drain and discard liquid from slow cooker. Make desired sauce; pour into bowl. Dip ribs into sauce to coat. Place ribs in slow cooker. Pour any remaining sauce over ribs. Cover and cook on Low heat setting 1 hour.

Ham and Scalloped Potatoes

PREP: 20 min **BAKE:** 1 hr 40 min **STAND:** 5 min ▪ **6 SERVINGS**

- 3 tablespoons butter or margarine
- 1 small onion, finely chopped (1/4 cup)
- 3 tablespoons all-purpose flour
- 1 teaspoon salt
- 1/4 teaspoon pepper
- 2 1/2 cups milk
- 6 medium peeled or unpeeled potatoes, thinly sliced (6 cups)
- 1 1/2 cups cubed fully cooked ham
- 1 tablespoon butter or margarine

1. Heat oven to 350°F. Spray 2-quart casserole with cooking spray.

2. In 2-quart saucepan, melt 3 tablespoons butter over medium heat. Cook onion in butter about 2 minutes, stirring occasionally, until tender. Stir in flour, salt and pepper. Cook, stirring constantly, until smooth and bubbly; remove from heat. Stir in milk. Heat to boiling, stirring constantly. Boil and stir 1 minute.

3. Mix potatoes and ham in casserole; gently press down so surface is even. Pour sauce over potato mixture. Cut 1 tablespoon butter into small pieces; sprinkle over potatoes.

4. Cover and bake 30 minutes. Uncover and bake 1 hour to 1 hour 10 minutes longer or until potatoes are tender. Let stand 5 to 10 minutes before serving (sauce thickens as it stands).

1 SERVING: CAL. 305 (CAL. FROM FAT 115); FAT 13g (SAT. FAT 7g); CHOL. 50mg; SODIUM 1000mg; CARBS. 33g (FIBER 2g); PRO. 14g
% DAILY VALUE: VIT. A 10%; VIT. C 8%; CALC. 14%; IRON 6%
EXCHANGES: 1 1/2 STARCH, 1/2 MILK, 1 MEDIUM-FAT MEAT, 1 1/2 FAT **CARB. CHOICES:** 2

COOKING HAM

The most popular ham is fully cooked and ready to eat. To serve it hot, cook the ham until a meat thermometer inserted in center reads 140°F. Hams labeled "cook before eating" must be cooked to an internal temperature of 160°F. If you aren't sure which kind of ham you've bought, cook it to 160°F to be safe.

Greek Lamb Chops

PREP: 15 min **COOK:** 25 min ▪ **4 SERVINGS**

- 4 lamb shoulder, arm or loin chops, about 1/2 inch thick (about 6 oz each)
- 1 teaspoon dried oregano leaves
- 1/4 teaspoon salt
- 1/4 teaspoon pepper
- 4 cloves garlic, finely chopped (1 tablespoon)
- 1 tablespoon olive or vegetable oil
- 1/2 cup chicken broth
- 1 tablespoon lemon juice
- 1 tablespoon butter or margarine
- 1/4 cup sliced pitted Kalamata or ripe olives
- 2 tablespoons chopped fresh parsley
- 2 tablespoons crumbled feta cheese

1. Sprinkle both sides of lamb with oregano, salt and pepper. Press garlic into lamb.

2. In 12-inch skillet, heat oil over medium-high heat. Cook lamb in oil 4 to 6 minutes, turning once, until brown.

3. Add broth to skillet; reduce heat to medium-low. Cover and cook 8 to 10 minutes, turning once, until lamb is tender. Remove lamb from skillet; keep warm.

4. Heat broth in skillet to boiling. Boil 1 to 2 minutes or until slightly reduced. Stir in lemon juice and butter. Cook and stir just until slightly thickened. Stir in olives and parsley. Spoon sauce over lamb. Top with cheese.

1 SERVING: CAL. 265 (CAL. FROM FAT 150); FAT 17g (SAT. FAT 6g); CHOL. 95mg; SODIUM 480mg; CARBS. 2g (FIBER 1g); PRO. 27g
% DAILY VALUE: VIT. A 6%; VIT. C 2%; CALC. 4%; IRON 14%
EXCHANGES: 4 LEAN MEAT, 1 FAT **CARB. CHOICES:** 0

Herb and Garlic Roast Leg of Lamb

PREP: 15 min **ROAST:** 2 hr 15 hr **STAND:** 20 min ▪ **10 TO 12 SERVINGS**

Here's another perfect company dinner. Kosher salt is free of additives and is coarser grained than regular table salt. Table salt can be substituted.

1/4 cup finely chopped fresh parsley
1 tablespoon chopped fresh or 1 teaspoon dried rosemary leaves, crumbled
1 tablespoon chopped fresh or 1 teaspoon dried thyme leaves, crumbled
3 tablespoons olive or vegetable oil
2 teaspoons kosher salt
1/2 teaspoon pepper
2 cloves garlic, finely chopped
5- to 6-lb boneless leg of lamb

1. Heat oven to 325°F.

2. In small bowl, stir all ingredients except lamb until well mixed.

3. Place lamb in shallow roasting pan (keep netting or string on lamb). Spread herb mixture over entire surface of lamb. Insert meat thermometer so tip is in thickest part of lamb and does not rest in fat.

4. Roast uncovered 2 hours 5 minutes to 2 hours 15 minutes for medium-rare or until thermometer reads 140°F. (For medium doneness, bake until thermometer reads 155°F.)

5. Remove from oven; cover loosely with aluminum foil. Let stand 15 to 20 minutes or until thermometer reads 145°F (or 160°F for medium doneness). Remove netting or string before serving. Serve with pan juices if desired.

◀ **Herb and Garlic Roast Leg of Lamb**

1 SERVING: CAL. 370 (CAL. FROM FAT 180); FAT 20g (SAT. FAT 6g); CHOL. 160mg; SODIUM 590mg; CARBS. 0g (FIBER 0g); PRO. 48g
% DAILY VALUE: VIT. A 2%; VIT. C 2%; CALC. 2%; IRON 22%
EXCHANGES: 7 LEAN MEAT **CARB. CHOICES:** 0

Liver and Onions

PREP: 10 min **COOK:** 15 min ■ **4 SERVINGS**

Serve this favorite dish sprinkled with crumbled crisply cooked bacon, and add mashed potatoes on the side.

3 tablespoons butter or margarine
2 medium onions, thinly sliced
1 lb beef or veal liver, 1/2 to 3/4 inch thick
All-purpose flour
3 tablespoons vegetable oil or shortening
Salt and pepper to taste

1. In 10-inch skillet, melt butter over medium-high heat. Cook onions in butter 4 to 6 minutes, stirring frequently, until light brown. Remove onions from skillet; keep warm.

2. Coat liver with flour. In same skillet, heat oil over medium heat. Cook liver in oil 2 to 3 minutes on each side or until brown on outside and slightly pink in center, returning onions to skillet during last minute of cooking. Don't overcook or liver could become tough. Sprinkle with salt and pepper.

1 SERVING: CAL. 310 (CAL. FROM FAT 180); FAT 20g (SAT. FAT 8g); CHOL. 350mg; SODIUM 315mg; CARBS. 11g (FIBER 1g); PRO. 22g
% DAILY VALUE: VIT. A 100%; VIT. C 16%; CALC. 2%; IRON 32%
EXCHANGES: 2 VEGETABLE, 3 MEDIUM-FAT MEAT, 1 FAT
CARB. CHOICES: 1

LIGHTER LIVER AND ONIONS

For 8 grams of fat and 200 calories per serving, omit butter and decrease oil to 1 tablespoon. Use nonstick skillet. Spray skillet with cooking spray before cooking onions in Step 1.

Venison with Cranberry-Wine Sauce LOW-FAT

PREP: 20 min **MARINATE:** 2 hr **COOK:** 15 min ▪ **4 SERVINGS**

Venison is most often thought of as only deer meat, but the term also refers to meat from antelope, deer, caribou, elk and moose.

- 1/2 cup dry red wine or nonalcoholic red wine
- 1 tablespoon Dijon mustard
- 4 venison tenderloin steaks, about 1 inch thick (1 1/4 lb)
- 1/4 teaspoon salt
- 1/4 teaspoon coarsely ground pepper
- 1 tablespoon olive or vegetable oil
- 1/2 cup beef broth
- 1/2 cup dried cranberries
- 2 tablespoons currant or apple jelly
- 1 tablespoon butter or margarine
- 2 medium green onions, sliced (2 tablespoons)

1. In small bowl, mix wine and mustard until well blended. Place venison in resealable plastic food-storage bag or shallow glass or plastic dish. Pour wine mixture over venison; turn venison to coat with wine mixture. Seal bag or cover dish and refrigerate at least 2 hours but no longer than 4 hours, turning venison occasionally.

2. Remove venison from marinade; reserve marinade. Sprinkle venison with salt and pepper. In 12-inch nonstick skillet, heat oil over medium-high heat. Cook venison in oil about 4 minutes, turning once, until brown.

3. Add broth to skillet; reduce heat to low. Cover and cook about 10 minutes, turning venison once, until venison is tender and desired doneness. (Don't overcook or venison will become tough.)

4. Remove venison from skillet; keep warm. Stir marinade into skillet. Heat to boiling, scraping up any bits from bottom of skillet; reduce heat to medium. Cook about 5 minutes or until mixture is slightly reduced. Stir in cranberries, jelly, butter and onions. Cook 1 to 2 minutes, stirring occasionally, until butter is melted and mixture is hot. Serve sauce with venison.

1 SERVING: CAL. 300 (CAL. FROM FAT 90); FAT 10g (SAT. FAT 4g); CHOL. 125mg; SODIUM 450mg; CARBS. 20g (FIBER 1g); PRO. 33g
% DAILY VALUE: VIT. A 4%; VIT. C 4%; CALC. 2%; IRON 28%
EXCHANGES: 1 FRUIT, 4 1/2 LEAN MEAT **CARB. CHOICES:** 1

TIMETABLE FOR ROASTING MEAT

Place meat, directly from the refrigerator, fat side up, on a rack in a shallow roasting pan. (Bone-in roasts don't need a rack.) Insert ovenproof meat thermometer so tip is centered in thickest part of roast, not resting in fat or touching bone. Don't add water or liquid; don't cover. Roast at the oven temperature given in the chart for the time listed and until thermometer reaches the remove-from-oven temperature. Remove meat from oven; cover loosely with foil and let stand 15 to 20 minutes before carving. The temperature will rise 5°F to 10°F during standing to reach the Final Doneness Temperature.

Meat Cut	Weight (pounds)	Approximate Total Roasting Time (hours, unless noted otherwise)	Remove from Oven When Internal Temperature Reaches	Final Doneness Temperature (after standing 15 to 20 minutes)
BEEF				
Brisket, Corned *Roast at 325°F*	2 1/2 to 3 1/2 3 1/2 to 5	2 1/2 to 3 1/2 3 1/2 to 4 1/2	Follow package directions	170°F well done. Follow package directions
Brisket, Fresh *Roast at 325°F*	2 1/2 to 4	2 1/2 to 3	Must be cooked with liquid to partially cover	170°F well done
Round Roast, Eye *Roast at 325°F*	2 to 3	1 1/2 to 1 3/4	135°F	145°F medium-rare
Round Roast, Bottom *Roast at 325°F*	3 to 4	1 1/2 to 2	135°F	145°F medium-rare
Rib Roast (bone-in) *Roast at 350°F*	4 to 6 (2 ribs)	1 3/4 to 2 1/4 2 1/4 to 2 3/4	135°F 150°F	145°F medium-rare 160°F medium
	6 to 8 (2 to 4 ribs)	2 1/4 to 2 1/2 2 3/4 to 3	135°F 150°F	145°F medium-rare 160°F medium
	8 to 10 (4 to 5 ribs)	2 1/2 to 3 3 to 3 1/2	135°F 150°F	145°F medium-rare 160°F medium
Ribeye Roast (boneless) *Roast at 350°F*	3 to 4	1 1/2 to 1 3/4 1 3/4 to 2	135°F 150°F	145°F medium-rare 160°F medium
	4 to 6	1 3/4 to 2 2 to 2 1/2	135°F 150°F	145°F medium-rare 160°F medium
	6 to 8	2 to 2 1/4 2 1/2 to 2 3/4	135°F 150°F	145°F medium-rare 160°F medium
Round Tip Roast *Roast at 325°F*	3 to 4	1 3/4 to 2 2 1/4 to 2 1/2	140°F 155°F	145°F medium-rare 160°F medium
	4 to 6	2 to 2 1/2 2 1/2 to 3	140°F 155°F	145°F medium-rare 160°F medium
	6 to 8	2 1/2 to 3 3 to 3 1/2	140°F 155°F	145°F medium-rare 160°F medium
Rump Roast *Roast at 325°F*	3 to 4	1 1/2 to 2	135°F	145°F medium-rare
Tenderloin Roast *Roast at 425°F*	2 to 3	35 to 40 45 to 50	135°F 150°F	145°F medium-rare 160°F medium
	4 to 5	50 to 60 60 to 70	135°F 150°F	145°F medium-rare 160°F medium

TIMETABLE FOR ROASTING MEAT *(continued)*

Meat Cut	Weight (pounds)	Approximate Total Roasting Time (hours, unless noted otherwise)	Remove from Oven When Internal Temperature Reaches	Final Doneness Temperature (after standing 15 to 20 minutes)
Tri-Tip Roast *Roast at 425°F*	$1\frac{1}{2}$ to 2	30 to 40	135°F	145°F medium-rare
		40 to 45	150°F	160°F medium
VEAL				
Loin Roast (bone-in) *Roast at 325°F*	3 to 4	$1\frac{3}{4}$ to $2\frac{1}{4}$	155°F	160°F medium
Rib Roast (bone-in) *Roast at 325°F*	4 to 5	$1\frac{1}{2}$ to $2\frac{1}{4}$	155°F	160°F medium
PORK				
Crown Roast *Roast at 325°F*	6 to 10	20 minutes per pound	150°F	160°F medium
Ham, cook before eating (bone-in) *Roast at 325°F*	varies	15 to 20 minutes per pound	160°F	No standing time
Ham, fully cooked (bone-in or boneless) *Roast at 325°F*	varies	15 to 20 minutes per pound	140°F	No standing time
Loin Roast (bone-in or boneless) *Roast at 325°F*	2 to 5	20 minutes per pound	155°F	160°F medium
Ribs (Country-Style) *Roast at 350°F*	varies	$1\frac{1}{2}$ to 2	Tender	No standing time
Ribs (Loin Back or Spareribs) *Roast at 325°F*	varies, no specific weight	$1\frac{1}{2}$ to 2	Tender	No standing time
Shoulder Roast *Roast at 325°F*	3 to 6	20 minutes per pound	150°F	160°F medium
Tenderloin *Roast at 425°F to 450°F*	$\frac{3}{4}$ to 1	20 to 30 minutes	160°F	No standing time
LAMB				
Leg Roast (whole, boneless) *Roast at 325°F*	4 to 7	25 to 30 minutes per pound for medium-rare	140°F	145°F medium-rare
		30 to 35 minutes per pound for medium	155°F	160°F medium
Leg Roast (whole, bone-in) *Roast at 325°F*	5 to 7	20 to 25 minutes per pound for medium-rare	140°F	145°F medium-rare
		25 to 30 minutes per pound for medium	155° F	160°F medium
	7 to 9	15 to 20 minutes per pound for medium-rare	140° F	145°F medium-rare
		20 to 25 minutes per pound for medium	155°F	160°F medium
Shoulder Roast or Shank Leg Half (bone-in) *Roast at 325°F*	3 to 4	30 to 35 minutes per pound for medium-rare	140°F	145°F medium-rare
		40 to 45 minutes per pound for medium	155°F	160°F medium

TIMETABLE FOR COOKING MEAT ON STOVE-TOP

Cook meat directly from refrigerator. Use a heavy nonstick skillet, or lightly coat a regular skillet with vegetable oil or cooking spray. Heat the skillet over medium heat for 5 minutes. Add meat to skillet. Don't add water, liquids or fats; don't cover. Cook for the time listed and thermometer reaches the doneness temperature, turning once. If meat browns too quickly, reduce heat to medium-low. Season meat as desired.

Cut	Thickness (inches)	Approximate Cooking Time (minutes)	Doneness
BEEF			
Cubed Steak *Use medium-high heat*	varies	3 to 5	145°F medium-rare to 160°F medium
Ground Patties			
(4 per pound)	1/2 inch thick (4 inch diameter)	10 to 12	160°F medium
(4 per 1 1/2 pounds)	3/4 inch thick (4 inch diameter)	12 to 15	
Porterhouse/ T-Bone Steak	3/4	11 to 13	145°F medium-rare to 160°F medium
	1	14 to 17	
Rib Eye Steak	3/4	8 to 10	145°F medium-rare to 160°F medium
	1	12 to 15	
Tenderloin *Use medium-high heat for 1/2-inch thickness*	1/2	3 1/2 to 5 1/2	145°F medium-rare to 160°F medium
	3/4	7 to 9	
	1	10 to 13	
Top Loin Strip Steak	3/4	10 to 12	145° F medium-rare to 160°F medium
	1	12 to 15	
Top Round Steak *(best when marinated before cooking)*	3/4	11 to 12	145°F medium-rare to 160°F medium
	1	15 to 16	
Top Sirloin (boneless)	3/4	10 to 13	145°F medium-rare to 160°F medium
	1	15 to 20	
VEAL			
Chop, Loin or Rib *Use medium-high heat*	3/4 to 1	10 to 14	160°F medium
Cutlet *Use medium-high heat*	1/8	2 to 4	160°F medium
	1/4	4 to 6	160°F medium
Ground Patties *Use medium-high heat*	1/2	9 to 12	160°F medium
PORK			
Chop, Loin or Rib (bone-in or boneless)	3/4 to 1	8 to 12	160°F medium
Cutlets (bone-in or boneless)	1/4	3 to 4	Tender
Ground Patties	1/2	8 to 10	160°F medium
Ham Slice, cooked	1/2	6 to 8	160°F medium
Ham Steak, cooked	1	8 to 10	160°F medium
Tenderloin Medallions	1/4 to 1/2	4 to 8	Tender
	1/2	8 to 10	160°F medium
LAMB			
Chop, Loin or Rib	1	9 to 11	160°F medium
Ground Patties	1/2	9 to 12	160°F medium

TIMETABLE FOR BROILING MEAT

Cook meat directly from refrigerator. Set oven control to broil. Check oven's use-and-care manual for whether the oven door should be partially opened or closed during broiling. Place meat on rack in broiler pan. For cuts less than 1 inch thick, broil 2 to 3 inches from heat. For cuts 1 to 1 1/2 inches thick, broil 3 to 4 inches from heat unless chart gives different distance. Broil for the time listed, turning once.

Cut	Thickness	Approximate Cooking Time (minutes)	Doneness
BEEF			
Ground Patties			
(4 per pound)	1/2 inch thick (4 inch diameter)	10 to 12	160°F medium
(4 per 1 1/2 pounds)	3/4 inch thick (4 inch diameter)	12 to 14	
Porterhouse/T-Bone	3/4 inch	9 to 12	145°F medium-rare to 160°F medium
	1 inch	13 to 17	
	1 1/2 inches	24 to 31	
Rib Eye Steak	3/4 inch	8 to 12	145°F medium-rare to 160°F medium
	1 inch	14 to 18	
	1 1/2 inches	21 to 27	
Tenderloin	1 inch	13 to 16 (broil 2 to 3 inches from heat)	145°F medium-rare to 160°F medium
	1 1/2 inches	18 to 22	
Top Loin Strip Steak	3/4 inch	9 to 11	145°F medium-rare to 160°F medium
	1 inch	13 to 17	
	1 1/2 inches	19 to 23	
Top Sirloin Steak (boneless)	3/4 inch	9 to 12	145°F medium-rare to 160°F medium
	1 inch	16 to 21	
	1 1/2 inches	26 to 31	
	2 inches	34 to 39	
VEAL			
Chop, Loin or Rib	3/4 to 1 inch	14 to 16	160°F medium
PORK			
Chop (bone-in or boneless)	3/4 to 1 inch	9 to 12	160°F medium
	1 1/2 inches	12 to 16	160°F medium
Ground Patties	1/2 inch	8 to 10	160°F medium
LAMB			
Chop, Loin or Rib	1 inch	10 to 15	160°F medium
Chop, Sirloin	1 inch	12 to 15	160°F medium

Retail Beef Cuts...From the Meat Case to the Dinner Table

BEEF MADE EASY®

CHUCK 1

Chuck Arm Pot Roast, Boneless

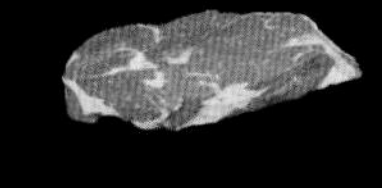

Chuck Shoulder Pot Roast, Boneless

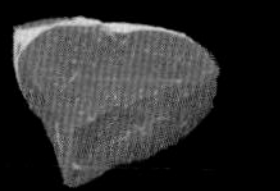

Chuck Shoulder Steak, Boneless

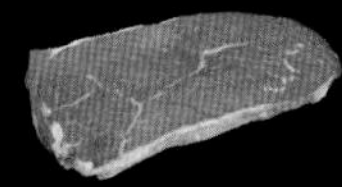

Chuck Eye Steak

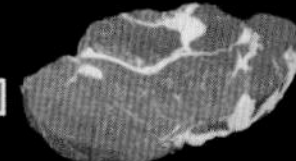

Chuck Top Blade Steak, Boneless

Chuck Mock Tender Steak

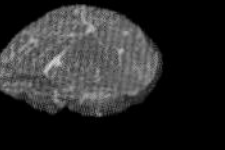

Chuck Blade Steak, Boneless

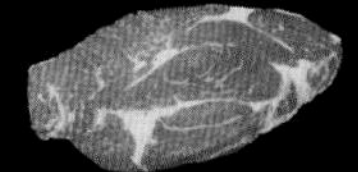

Chuck 7-Bone Pot Roast

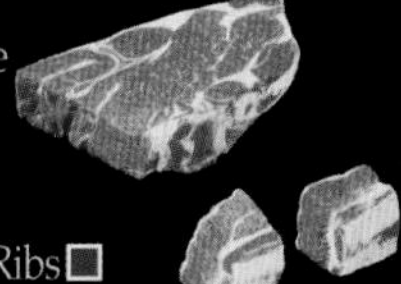

Chuck Short Ribs

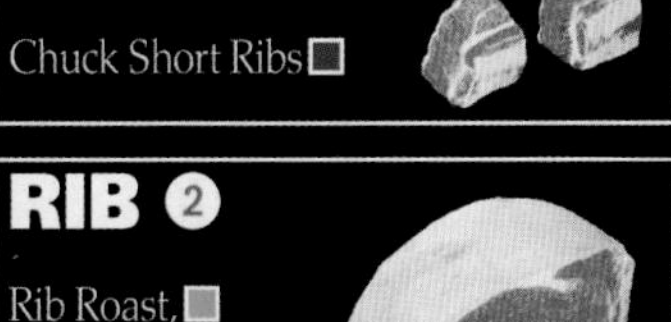

RIB 2

Rib Roast, Small End, Premium

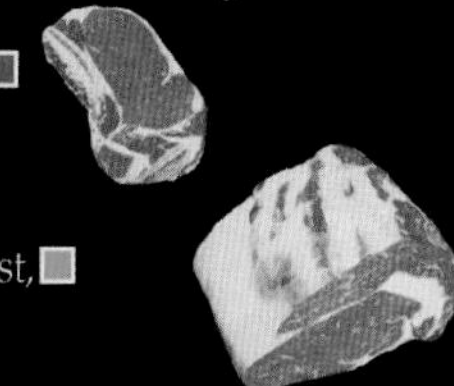

Rib Steak, Small End

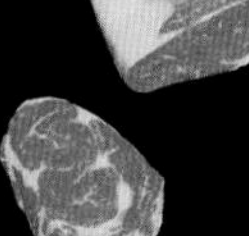

Ribeye Roast, Premium

Ribeye Steak

Back Ribs

Funded by America's Beef Producers.

SHORT LOIN 3

Top Loin (Strip) Steak, Boneless

T-Bone Steak

Porterhouse Steak

Tenderloin Roast, Premium

Tenderloin Steaks

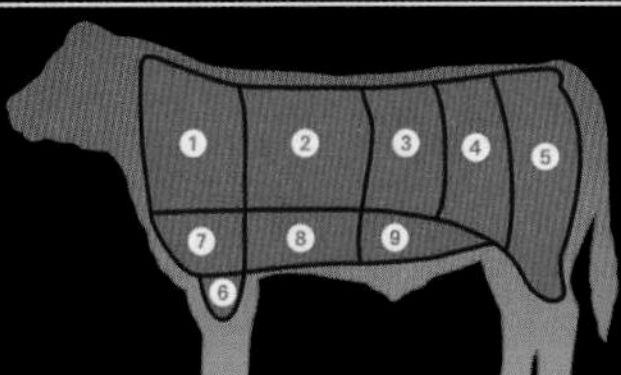

RECOMMENDED COOKING METHOD
- SKILLET
- GRILL/BROIL
- MARINATE & GRILL/MARINATE & BROIL
- STIR-FRY
- ROAST
- STEWING
- STEAKS FOR BRAISING
- POT ROAST

SHANK 6 & BRISKET 7

Shank Cross Cut

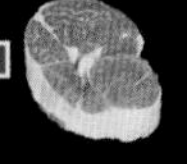

Brisket, Whole

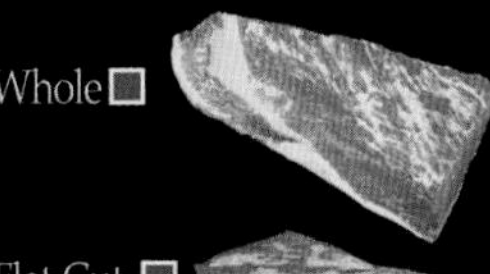

Brisket, Flat Cut, Boneless

PLATE 8 & FLANK 9

Skirt Steak

Flank Steak

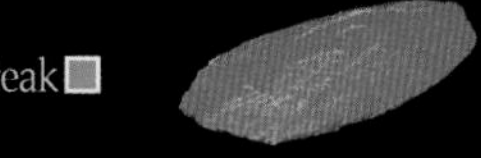

SIRLOIN 4

Top Sirloin Steak

Tri-Tip Roast

Tri-Tip Steak

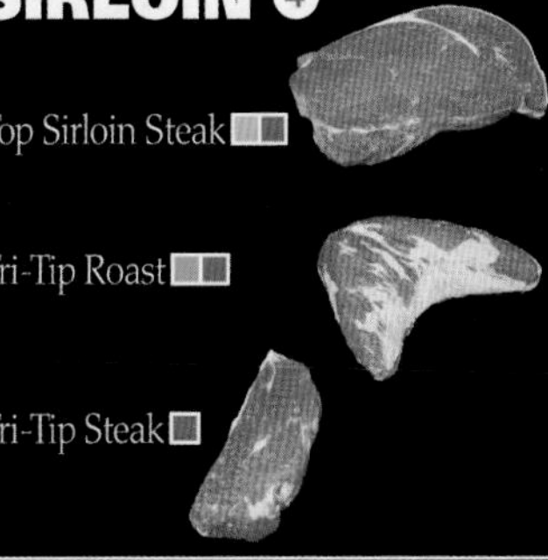

ROUND 5

Top Round Steak

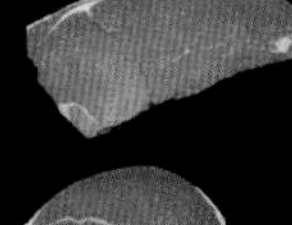

Round Tip Steak, Thin Cut

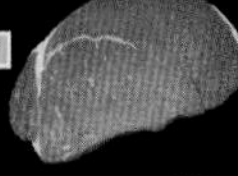

Round Tip Roast

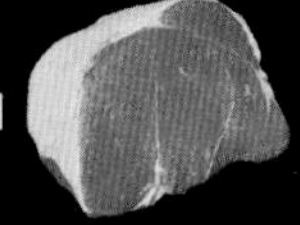

Bottom Round Roast

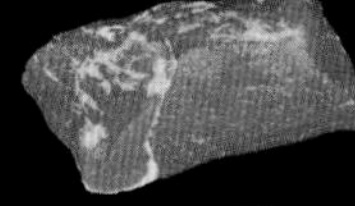

Eye Round Roast

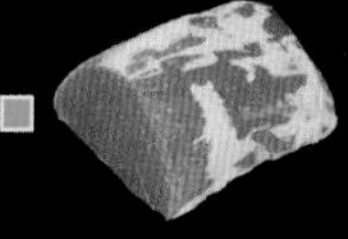

Eye Round Steak

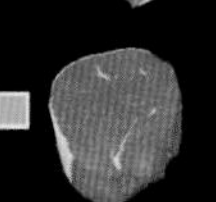

OTHER CUTS

Ground Beef

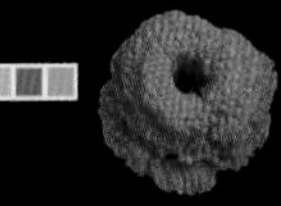

Cubed Steak

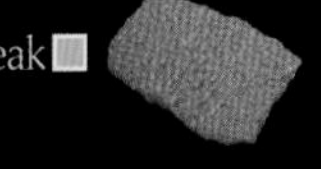

Beef for Kabobs

Beef for Stew

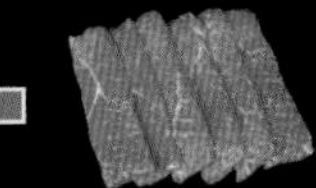

Beef for Stir-Fry

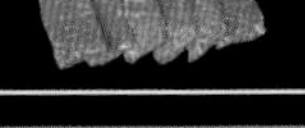

Veal

RETAIL CUTS

Where They Come From
How To Cook Them

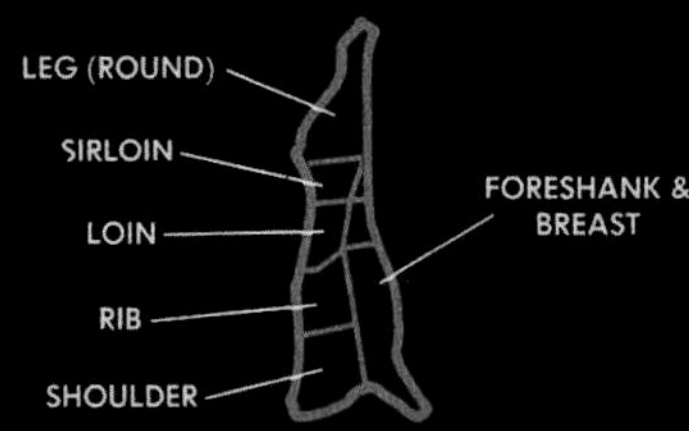

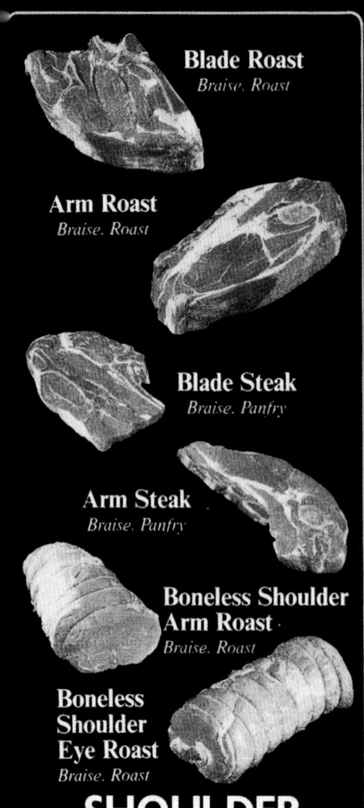

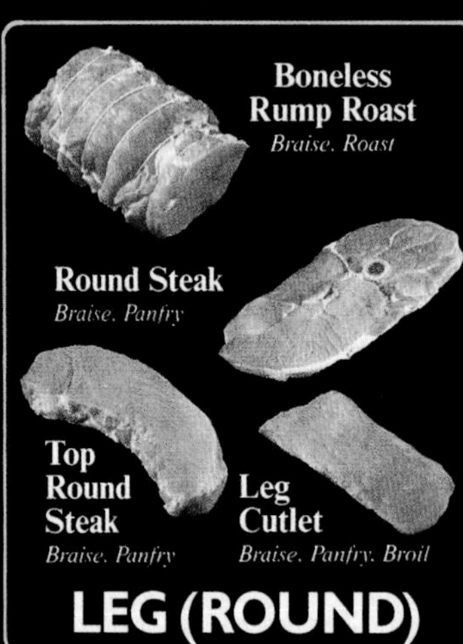

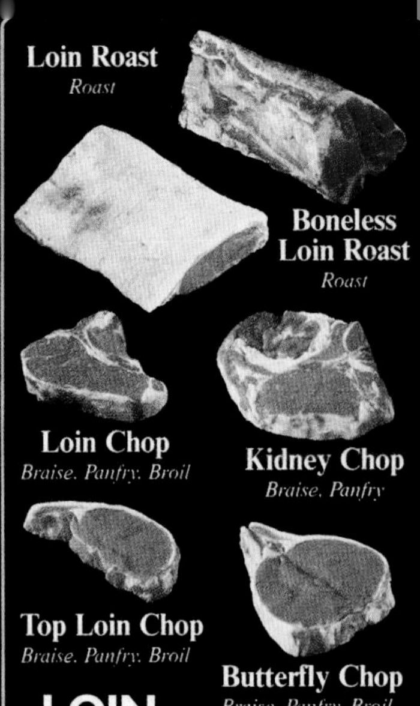

THIS CHART APPROVED BY
NATIONAL LIVE STOCK & MEAT BOARD

PURCHASING PORK

A Consumer Guide To Identifying Retail Pork Cuts.

Left: tenderloin
Right: Canadian-style bacon

CHOPS
Upper row (l-r): sirloin chop, rib chop, loin chop.
Lower row (l-r): boneless rib end chop, boneless center loin chop, butterfly chop.

ROASTS
Upper row (l-r): center rib roast (Rack of Pork), bone-in sirloin roast.
Middle: boneless center loin roast.
Lower row (l-r): boneless rib end roast, boneless sirloin roast.

RIBS Left: country-style ribs.
Right: back ribs.

BLADE BOSTON-STYLE SHOULDER
Upper row (l-r):
bone-in blade roast, boneless blade roast.
Lower row (l-r): ground pork, sausage, blade steak.

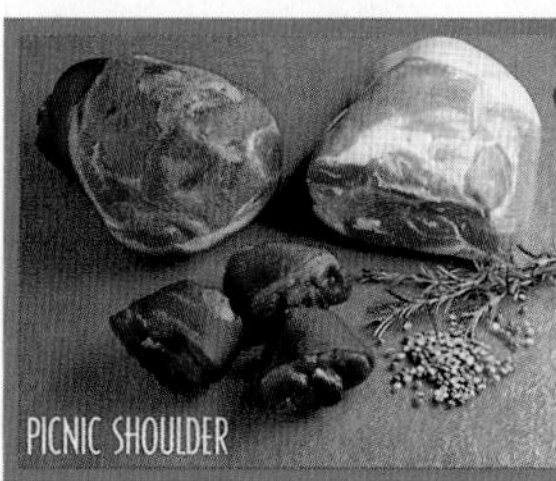

PICNIC SHOULDER
Upper row (l-r): smoked picnic, arm picnic roast.
Lower row: smoked hocks.

SIDE Top: spareribs.
Bottom: slab bacon, sliced bacon.

LEG
Upper row (l-r): bone-in fresh ham, smoked ham. Lower row (l-r): leg cutlets, fresh boneless ham roast.

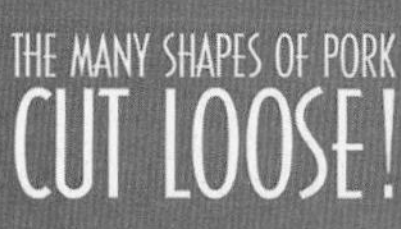

THE MANY SHAPES OF PORK
CUT LOOSE!

When shopping for pork, consider cutting traditional roasts into a variety of different shapes.

No-fuss family dinner, holiday favorite.

Dinner, backyard barbecue or gourmet entree.

Great for kabobs, stew and chili.

Super stir fry, fajitas and salads.

Delicious breakfast chops and sandwiches.

Lamb

RETAIL CUTS

Where They Come From
How To Cook Them

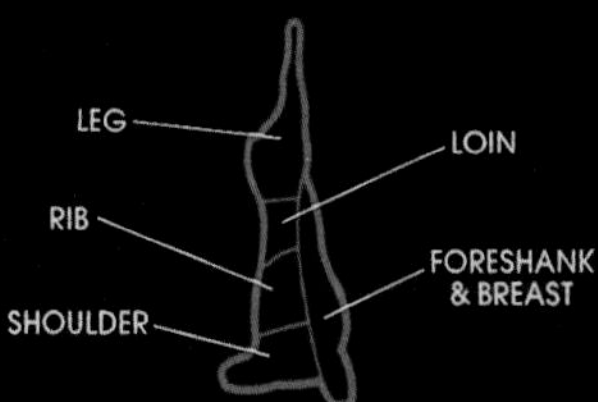

THIS CHART APPROVED BY
NATIONAL LIVE STOCK & MEAT BOARD

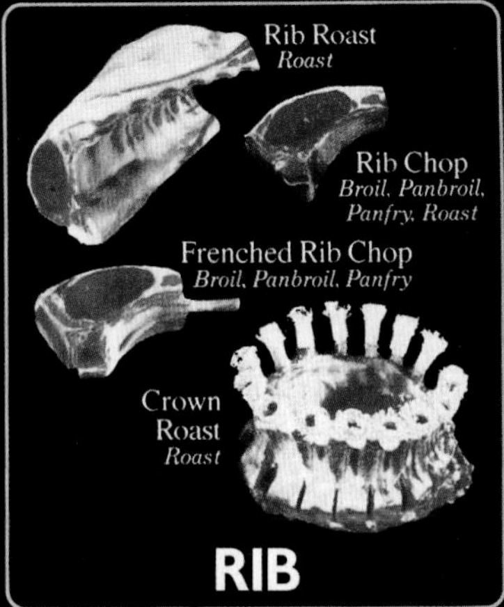

CHAPTER 12
Poultry

Turkey & Stuffing

Chicken

Game Fowl

Charts & Timetables

LOW-FAT = *3g or less, except main dishes with 10g or less* FAST = *Ready in 20 minutes or less* BREAD MACHINE = *Bread machine directions* SLOW COOKER = *Slow cooker directions* LIGHTER = *25% fewer calories or grams of fat*

◀ **Chicken Cacciatore (page 326)**

Poultry Basics

It's hard to go wrong when you serve chicken or turkey! From roasting to stir-fries, everyone has a favorite recipe.

BUYING FRESH POULTRY

Packaging

- Choose wrapped packages without any tears, holes or leaks. There should be little or no liquid in the bottom of the tray.
- Make sure the package is cold and feels firm. Avoid packages that are stacked too high in the meat case because they may not have been kept cold enough.
- Check the sell-by date and use within two days of the date.
- Put packages of poultry in plastic bags before putting them in your grocery cart so that any bacteria in the juices doesn't drip on and contaminate other foods, especially those that won't be cooked.
- Refrigerate poultry as soon as you get home from shopping. If it will take longer than 30 minutes to get it home, keep it cold in a cooler with ice packs.
- Frozen poultry should be hard to the touch and free of freezer burn and tears in the packaging.

Odor and Appearance

- Check for a fresh odor (odors can be smelled through the plastic). If it smells spoiled, don't buy it.
- Whole birds and cut-up pieces should be plump and meaty with smooth, moist-looking skin.
- Boneless skinless products should be plump and moist.
- Chicken skin color, ranging from yellow to white, doesn't indicate quality; it depends on what it was fed. Turkey skin, however, should have cream-colored skin.
- The cut ends of the poultry bones should be pink to red in color.
- Avoid poultry with traces of feathers.

STORING POULTRY

- Poultry wrapped in butcher paper should be repackaged tightly in plastic wrap, foil or plastic freezer bags.
- Poultry packaged in clear plastic wrap on a plastic or Styrofoam tray doesn't need to be repackaged.
- Store poultry in the meat compartment or coldest part of your refrigerator, or freeze it as soon as possible.
- Cook or freeze poultry within two days of the sell-by date.
- If poultry was purchased frozen or frozen right after purchasing it, thaw it in the refrigerator, then use it within the number of days listed in the Timetable for Storing Poultry, below. If the poultry was refrigerated several days before freezing, use it the same day you thaw it.

TIMETABLE FOR STORING POULTRY

Type of Poultry	Refrigerator (36°F to 40°F)	Freezer (0°F or colder)
Cooked	2 days	4 months
Ground	1 to 2 days	3 to 4 months
Whole Chicken and Turkey,	2 days	12 months
Whole Turkey Breasts, Chicken or Turkey Pieces		9 months

HOW TO GET A TURKEY READY FOR ROASTING

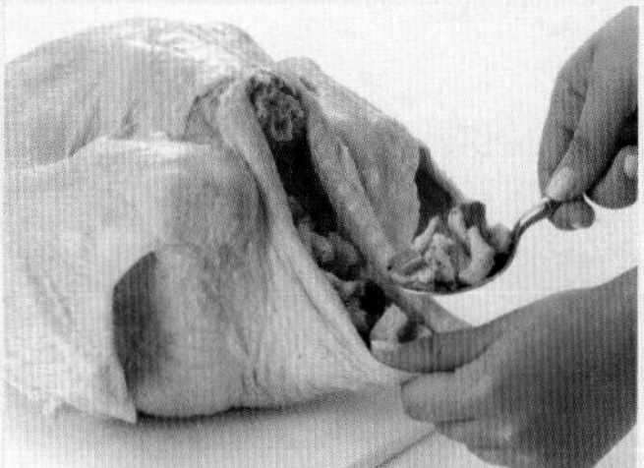

1. Turn turkey breast side down for easier filling of neck cavity. Fill neck cavity lightly with stuffing.

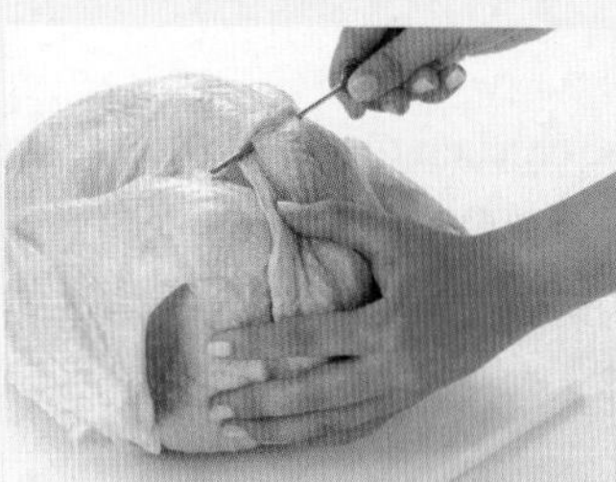

2. Fasten neck skin to back of turkey with skewer.

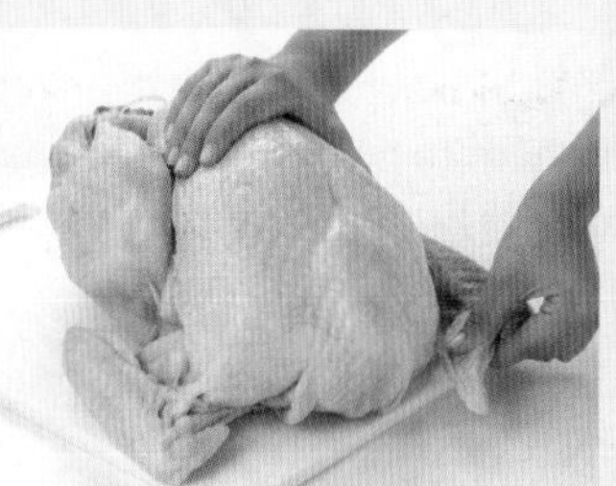

3. Turn turkey breast side up. Fold wings across back of turkey so tips are touching.

4. Fill body cavity lightly with stuffing.

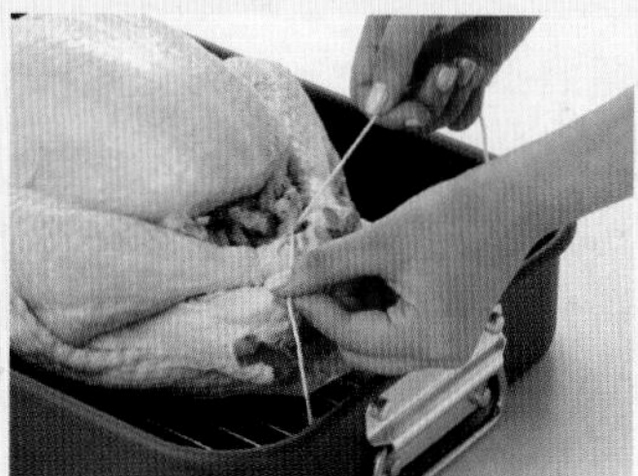

5. Tuck legs under band of skin at tail (if present), or tie together with heavy string, then tie to tail if desired.

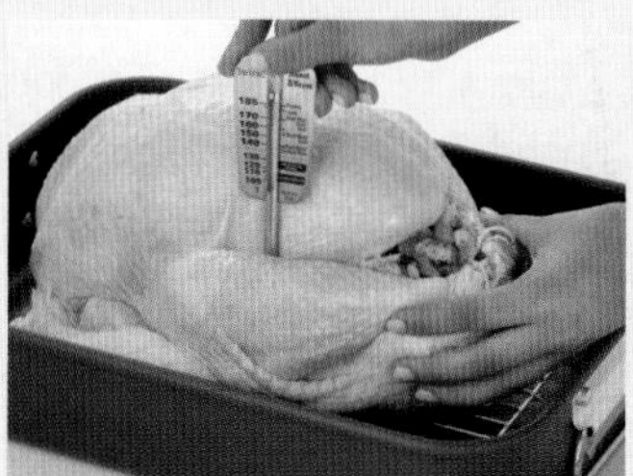

6. Insert ovenproof thermometer so tip is in thickest part of inside thigh and does not touch bone.

HOW TO CARVE ROAST TURKEY

Place turkey, breast up, on a cutting board. Remove ties or skewers. Remove stuffing. Let the bird stand for 15 to 20 minutes before cutting; this resting period allows the meat to become more firm, so carving smooth, uniform slices is easier. Use a sharp carving knife and meat fork for best results.

1. While gently pulling leg away from body, cut through joint between thigh and body. Separate drumstick and thigh by cutting through connecting joint.*

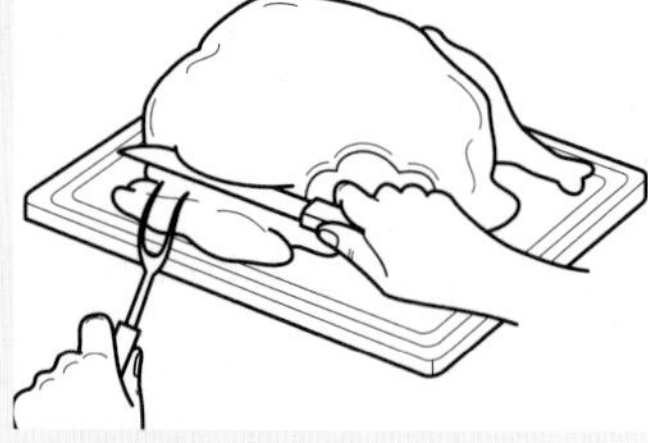

2. Make a deep horizontal cut into breast just above wing.

3. Insert fork in top of breast, and starting halfway up breast, carve thin slices down to the horizontal cut, working from outer edge of bird to the center. Remove wings by cutting through joint between wing and body.

**Serve drumsticks and thighs whole or carve them. To carve, remove meat from drumstick by slicing at an angle, and slice thigh by cutting even slices parallel to the bone.*

Roast Turkey

PREP: 20 min **ROAST:** 3 hr 45 min **STAND:** 15 min ■
12 TO 15 SERVINGS

Both fresh and frozen turkey are great. If using a frozen turkey, just remember to allow extra time to thaw it. To thaw a 12- to 15-pound whole turkey, place turkey (in its original wrap) in a baking pan in the refrigerator for two to three days.

- 12- to 15-lb whole turkey, thawed if frozen
- Bread Stuffing (right), if desired
- 3 tablespoons butter or margarine, melted

1. Heat oven to 325°F. Prepare turkey for roasting as directed on page 316.

2. Make Bread Stuffing. Stuff turkey just before roasting, not ahead of time. Turn turkey breast side down for easier filling of neck cavity. Fill neck cavity lightly with stuffing; fasten neck skin to back of turkey with skewer. Turn turkey breast side up. Fold wings across back of turkey so tips are touching. Fill body cavity lightly with stuffing. (Do not pack stuffing because it will expand during roasting). Place any remaining stuffing in a 1- or 2-quart casserole that has been greased with shortening or sprayed with cooking spray; cover and refrigerate. Bake stuffing in casserole with turkey for the last 35 to 40 minutes of baking or until heated through.

3. Tuck legs under band of skin at tail (if present), or tie together with heavy string, then tie to tail if desired. On rack in shallow roasting pan, place turkey, breast side up. Brush butter over turkey. Insert ovenproof meat thermometer so tip is in thickest part of inside thigh and does not touch bone. (Do not add water or cover turkey.)

4. Roast uncovered 3 hours to 3 hours 45 minutes. After roasting about 2 hours, place a tent of foil loosely over turkey when it begins to turn golden, and cut band of skin or remove tie holding legs to allow inside of thighs to cook through.

5. Turkey is done when thermometer reads 180°F and legs move easily when lifted or twisted. Thermometer placed in center of stuffing will read 165°F when done. If a meat thermometer is not used, begin testing for doneness after about 2 hours 30 minutes. When turkey is done, place on warm platter and cover with foil to keep warm. Let stand about 15 minutes for easiest carving. Cover and refrigerate any remaining turkey and stuffing separately.

1 SERVING: CAL. 400 (CAL. FROM FAT 230); FAT 25g (SAT. FAT 8g); CHOL. 150mg; SODIUM 150mg; CARBS. 0g (FIBER 0g); PRO. 45g **% DAILY VALUE:** VIT. A 8%; VIT. C 0%; CALC. 2%; IRON 10% **EXCHANGES:** 6 1/2 LEAN MEAT, 1 FAT **CARB. CHOICES:** 0

Bread Stuffing

PREP: 15 min **COOK:** 5 min **BAKE:** 40 min ■
10 SERVINGS, 1/2 CUP EACH

Do you prefer a soft, moist stuffing? Use a soft-textured bread. For a firmer, drier stuffing, choose a firm-textured bread.

- 3/4 cup butter or margarine
- 2 large stalks celery (with leaves), chopped (1 1/2 cups)
- 1 large onion, chopped (1 cup)
- 10 cups soft bread cubes (about 15 slices bread)
- 1 1/2 teaspoons chopped fresh or 1/2 teaspoon dried thyme leaves
- 1 teaspoon salt
- 1/2 teaspoon ground sage
- 1/4 teaspoon pepper

1. In 4-quart Dutch oven, melt butter over medium-high heat. Cook celery and onion in butter, stirring occasionally, until tender; remove from heat.

2. In large bowl, toss celery mixture and remaining ingredients. Use to stuff one 12- to 15-lb turkey. See Roasting Poultry (page 334), Timetable for Roasting Poultry (page 335) and Stuffing Tips (page 318) for specific directions. After stuffing turkey, place any remaining stuffing in a 1- or 2-quart casserole that has been greased with shortening or sprayed with cooking spray; cover and refrigerate. Bake stuffing in casserole with turkey for the last 35 to 40 minutes of baking or until heated through.

1 SERVING (ABOUT 1/2 CUP): CAL. 215 (CAL. FROM FAT 135); FAT 15g (SAT. FAT 9g); CHOL. 40mg; SODIUM 530mg; CARBS. 18g (FIBER 1g); PRO. 3g **% DAILY VALUE:** VIT. A 10%; VIT. C 2%; CALC. 4%; IRON 6% **EXCHANGES:** 1 STARCH, 3 FAT **CARB. CHOICES:** 1

STUFFING TIPS

- Just about any kind of bread makes great stuffing! Instead of white bread, try whole grain, sourdough, rye, herb or corn bread, or mix and match them. Short on time? Purchase stuffing cubes or a stuffing mix.
- Put stuffing (either the whole recipe or what's left after stuffing the bird) in a greased casserole; cover and bake it during the last 30 to 45 minutes of turkey roasting or until hot in the center. For a crisper, browned top, uncover the stuffing during the last 15 to 20 minutes.
- Always remove stuffing from the bird before carving it or it won't cool quickly enough, letting bacteria grow more easily.
- Stuff a chicken or turkey just before cooking. This helps prevent any bacteria from contaminating the stuffing. Never prestuff a chicken or turkey and then put it in the refrigerator or freezer for roasting later.
- Try stuffing the chicken or turkey with something besides bread. Add a couple of quartered onions and a clove or two of garlic to the cavity, or use wedges of fresh lemon and orange and fresh herbs.

LIGHTER BREAD STUFFING

For 6 grams of fat and 135 calories per serving, decrease butter to 1/4 cup. In 4-quart Dutch oven, heat butter and 1/2 cup chicken broth to boiling over medium-high heat. Cook celery and onion in broth mixture.

CORN BREAD STUFFING Substitute corn bread cubes for the soft bread cubes.

GIBLET STUFFING Place giblets (except liver*) and neck from turkey or chicken in 2-quart saucepan. Add enough water to cover; season with salt and pepper. Simmer over low heat 1 to 2 hours or until tender. Drain giblets. Remove meat from neck and finely chop with giblets; add with the remaining stuffing ingredients. 12 servings, 1/2 cup each.

OYSTER STUFFING Add 2 cans (8 oz each) oysters, drained and chopped, or 2 cups shucked oysters, drained and chopped, with the remaining stuffing ingredients. 12 servings, 1/2 cup each.

SAUSAGE STUFFING Omit salt. In 10-inch skillet, cook 1 lb bulk pork sausage over medium heat, stirring occasionally, until no longer pink; drain, reserving drippings. Substitute drippings for part of the butter. Add cooked sausage with the remaining stuffing ingredients. 12 servings, 1/2 cup each.

**The liver is very strongly flavored and should not be used to make the stuffing. Discard it, or reserve for another use.*

Cajun Deep-Fried Turkey

PREP: 1 hr 15 min **MARINATE:** 8 hr **COOK:** 42 min **STAND:** 20 min ■ **15 SERVINGS**

Cajun Spice Rub

2 tablespoons black pepper
1 tablespoon ground chipotle chilies or crushed red pepper
1 tablespoon white pepper
1 tablespoon ground cumin
1 tablespoon ground nutmeg
1 tablespoon salt

Cajun Marinade

1/2 cup vegetable oil
1/2 cup red wine vinegar
2 teaspoons sugar
2 teaspoons chili powder
1 teaspoon garlic powder
1 teaspoon salt
1/2 teaspoon ground pepper

Turkey

10- to 12-lb whole turkey, thawed if frozen
1 poultry or meat injector
1 turkey deep-fryer, consisting of 40- to 60-quart pot with basket, burner and propane tank
5 gallons peanut, canola or safflower oil

1. Read Turkey Deep-Frying Do's and Don'ts (page 319).

2. In small bowl, mix all Cajun Spice Rub ingredients. In another small bowl, mix all Cajun Marinade ingredients until salt is dissolved.

3. Dry inside of both turkey cavities because water added to hot oil can cause excessive bubbling. If turkey has plastic leg holder, remove and discard before deep-frying. To allow for

good oil circulation through the cavity, do not tie the legs together. Cut off wing tips and tail because they can get caught in the fryer basket. Place turkey in large pan.

4. Rub inside and outside of turkey with spice rub. Inject marinade into turkey, following the directions that came with injector. Cover turkey in pan with plastic wrap and place in refrigerator at least 8 hours but no longer than 24 hours.

5. Place the outdoor gas burner on a level dirt or grassy area or on concrete covered with cardboard. Add oil to cooking pot only to fill line. Clip deep-fry thermometer to edge of pot. At medium-high setting, heat oil to 375°F. (This can take 20 to 40 minutes depending on outside temperature, wind and weather conditions.) Place turkey, neck end down, on basket or rack. When deep-fry thermometer reaches 375°F, very slowly lower turkey into hot oil, wearing long oven mitts on both hands. (Level of oil will rise due to frothing caused by moisture from the turkey but will stabilize in about 1 minute.)

6. Immediately check oil temperature and increase flame so oil temperature is maintained at 350°F. (If temperature drops to 340°F or below, oil will begin to seep into turkey.)

7. Fry turkey about 3 to 4 minutes per pound, or about 35 to 42 minutes for a 10- to 12-pound turkey. Stay with the fryer at all times because the heat may need to be regulated throughout frying.

8. At the minimum frying time, carefully remove turkey to check for doneness. An instant-read meat thermometer inserted into thickest part of thigh should read 180°F and legs should move easily when lifted or twisted. If necessary, return turkey to oil and continue cooking. When turkey is done, let it drain a few minutes.

9. Remove turkey from basket or rack and place on serving platter. Cover with foil and let stand 15 minutes for easiest carving.

1 SERVING: CAL. 500 (CAL. FROM FAT 300); FAT 34g (SAT. FAT 8g); CHOL. 145mg; SODIUM 1,090mg; CARBS. 4g (FIBER 1g); PRO. 45g
% DAILY VALUE: VIT. A 10%; VIT. C 0%; CALC. 4%; IRON 20%
EXCHANGES: 6 1/2 LEAN MEAT, 3 FAT **CARB. CHOICES:** 0

TURKEY DEEP-FRYING DO'S AND DON'TS

For best results, use oils that can withstand high temperatures like peanut, canola or safflower. To learn more about deep-frying turkeys, visit the National Turkey Federation Web site at www.turkeyfed.org.

DO'S:

- Follow the use-and-care directions for your deep-fryer when deep-frying turkey, and review all safety tips.
- Place the fryer on a level dirt or grassy area away from the house or garage. Never fry a turkey indoors, including in a garage or any other structure attached to a building. If only concrete is available, place a large sheet of cardboard over area.
- Use only oils with high smoke points, such as peanut, canola or safflower oil. Before frying, a handy way to determine the correct amount of oil to use is to place the turkey in the basket and place in the pot. Add water until it reaches 1 to 2 inches above the turkey. Remove the turkey and note the water level, using a ruler to measure the distance from the top of the pot to the surface of the water. Pour out the water and dry the pot thoroughly. Be sure to measure for oil before breading or marinating turkey.
- Wear old shoes that you can slip out of easily and long pants just in case you do spill some oil on yourself.
- Wear long sleeves and oven mitts to protect from steam and oil spattering.
- Immediately wash hands, utensils, equipment and surfaces that have come in contact with the raw turkey.
- Have a fire extinguisher nearby for extra safety.
- Serve the turkey right after cooking, and store leftovers in the refrigerator within two hours of cooking.
- Allow the oil to cool completely before storing it or throwing it out.

DON'TS:

- Never fry on wooden decks or other structures that could catch fire.
- Never leave the hot oil unattended, and do not allow children or pets near the cooking area.
- Do not fry a stuffed turkey.

Herb Roast Chicken and Vegetables

PREP: 20 min **ROAST:** 1 hr 30 min **STAND:** 15 min ■ **6 SERVINGS**

If you don't have a roasting pan, you can use a broiler pan or a 13 × 9-inch baking dish.

- 1/4 cup olive or vegetable oil
- 2 tablespoons chopped fresh or 1 teaspoon dried thyme leaves
- 2 tablespoons chopped fresh or 1 teaspoon dried marjoram leaves
- 1/2 teaspoon salt
- 1/4 teaspoon coarsely ground pepper
- 1 lemon
- 4- to 5-lb whole chicken
- 6 small red potatoes, cut in half
- 1 cup baby-cut carrots
- 1/2 lb green beans

1. Heat oven to 375°F.

2. In small bowl, mix oil, thyme, marjoram, salt and pepper. Grate 1 teaspoon peel from lemon; stir peel into oil mixture. Cut lemon into fourths; place in cavity of chicken.

3. Fold wings of chicken across back so tips are touching. Tie or skewer legs to tail. On rack in shallow roasting pan, place chicken, breast side up. Brush some of the oil mixture on chicken. Insert ovenproof meat thermometer in chicken so tip is in thickest part of inside thigh and does not touch bone.

4. Roast uncovered 45 minutes. Arrange potatoes, carrots and green beans around chicken; brush oil mixture on chicken and vegetables. Roast uncovered 30 to 45 minutes longer or until thermometer reads 180°F and legs move easily when lifted or twisted. Let stand about 15 minutes for easiest carving. Remove lemon and discard.

5. Place chicken on platter; arrange vegetables around chicken. Serve with pan drippings.

1 SERVING: CAL. 475 (CAL. FROM FAT 225); FAT 25g (SAT. FAT 6g); CHOL. 110mg; SODIUM 320mg; CARBS. 27g; (FIBER 4g); PRO. 39g
% DAILY VALUE: VIT. A 72%; VIT. C 12%; CALC. 6%; IRON 20%
EXCHANGES: 1 STARCH, 2 VEGETABLE, 4 1/2 LEAN MEAT
CARB. CHOICES: 2

Skillet-Fried Chicken

PREP: 10 min **COOK:** 35 min ■ **6 SERVINGS**

- 1/2 cup all-purpose flour
- 1 tablespoon paprika
- 1 1/2 teaspoons salt
- 1/2 teaspoon pepper
- 3- to 3 1/2-lb cut-up whole chicken
- Vegetable oil

1. In shallow dish, mix flour, paprika, salt and pepper. Coat chicken with flour mixture.

2. In 12-inch nonstick skillet, heat oil (1/4 inch) over medium-high heat. Cook chicken in oil, skin sides down, about 10 minutes or until light brown on all sides; reduce heat to low. Turn chicken skin sides up.

3. Simmer uncovered about 20 minutes, without turning, until juice of chicken is clear when thickest part is cut to bone (170°F for breasts; 180°F for thighs and legs).

1 SERVING: CAL. 350 (CAL. FROM FAT 205); FAT 23g (SAT. FAT 5g); CHOL. 85mg; SODIUM 670mg; CARBS. 9g (FIBER 1g); PRO. 28g
% DAILY VALUE: VIT. A 16%; VIT. C 0%; CALC. 2%; IRON 10%
EXCHANGES: 1/2 STARCH, 4 MEDIUM-FAT MEAT **CARB. CHOICES:** 1/2

LIGHTER SKILLET-FRIED CHICKEN

For 11 grams of fat and 250 calories per serving, remove skin from chicken before cooking. Use 2 tablespoons oil in Step 2.

BUTTERMILK FRIED CHICKEN Increase flour to 1 cup. Dip chicken into 1 cup buttermilk before coating with flour mixture.

◄ **Herb Roast Chicken and Vegetables**

HOW TO CUT UP A WHOLE CHICKEN

1. Place chicken, breast up, on cutting board. Remove each wing from body by cutting into wing joint with sharp knife, rolling knife to let the blade follow through at the curve of the joint as shown.

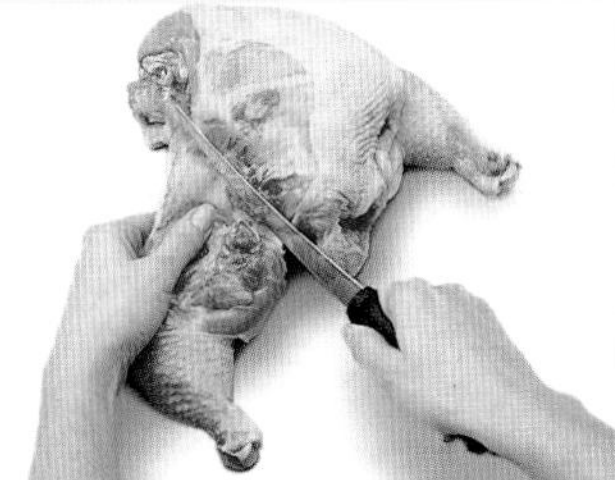

2. Cut off each leg by cutting skin between the thigh and body; continue cutting through the meat between the tail and hip joint, cutting as closely as possible to the backbone. Bend leg back until hip joint pops out as shown.

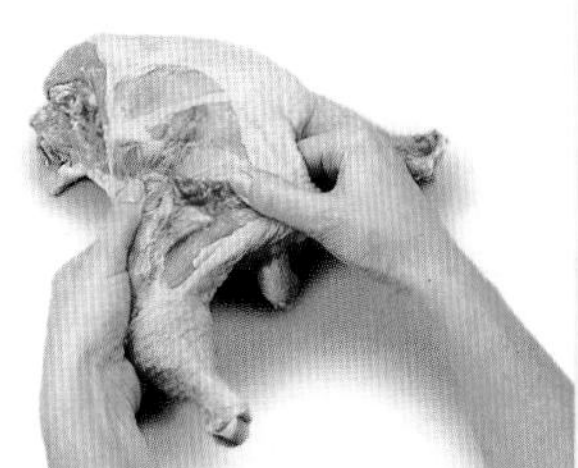

3. Continue cutting around bone and pulling leg from body until meat is separated from bone as shown. Cut through remaining skin.

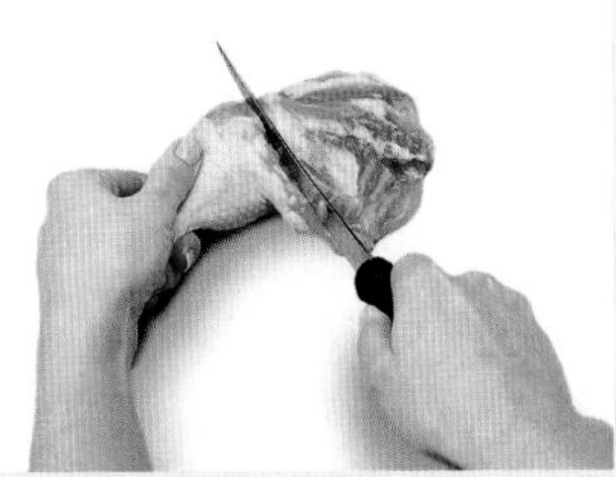

4. Separate thigh and drumstick by cutting about 1/8 inch from the fat line toward the drumstick as shown. (A thin white fat line runs crosswise at joint between drumstick and thigh.)

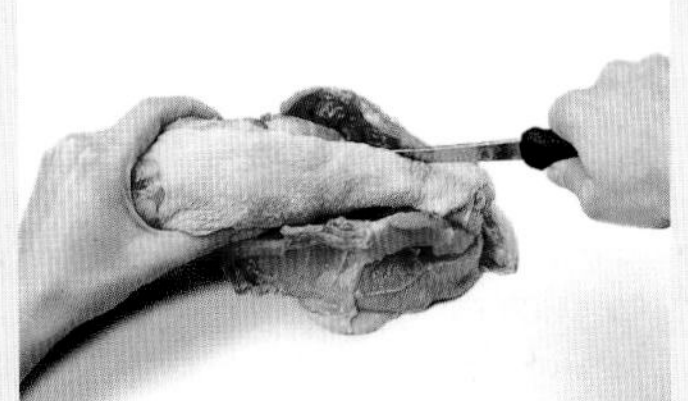

5. Separate back from breast by holding body, neck end down, and cutting downward along each side of backbone through the rib joints.

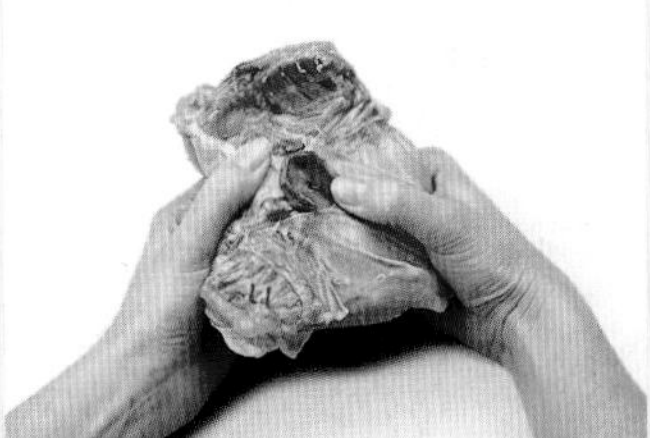

6. Bend breast halves back to pop out the keel bone. Remove keel bone, following directions in Step 3 below. Then using poultry scissors or chef's knife, cut breast in half through wishbone.

HOW TO BONE A CHICKEN BREAST

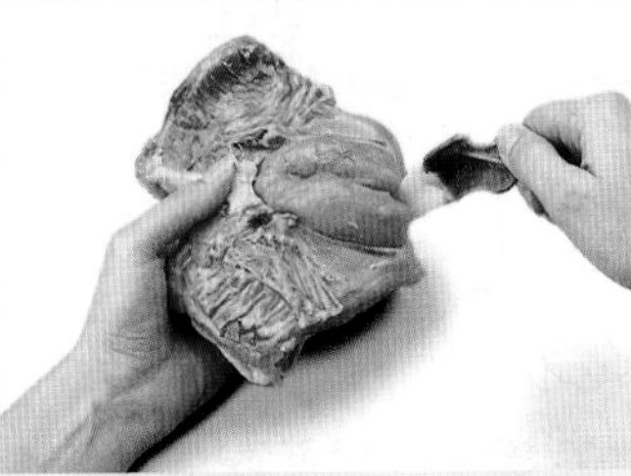

1. Loosen keel bone and white cartilage by running the tip of the index finger around both sides. Pull out bone in one or two pieces.

2. Insert tip of knife under long rib bone. Resting knife against bones, use steady and even pressure to gradually trim meat away from bones. Cut rib cage away from breast, cutting through shoulder joint to remove entire rib cage. Repeat on other side.

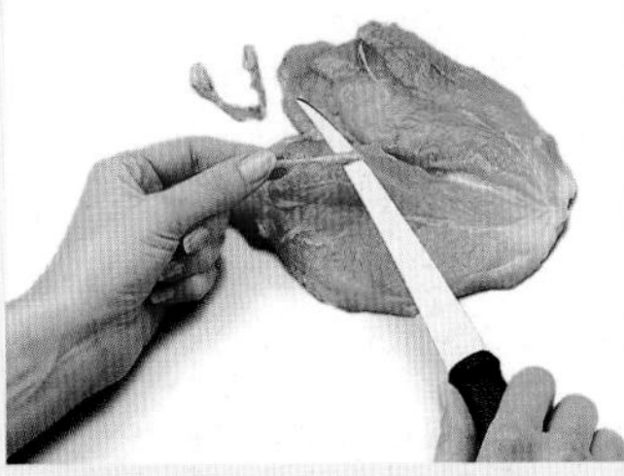

3. Cut away wishbone. Slip knife under white tendons on either side of breast; loosen and pull out tendons (grasp end of tendons with paper towel if tendons are slippery). Remove skin if desired. Cut breast lengthwise in half.

Oven-Fried Chicken

PREP: 10 min **BAKE:** 1 hr ▪ **6 SERVINGS**

- 1/4 cup butter or margarine
- 1/2 cup all-purpose flour
- 1 teaspoon paprika
- 1/2 teaspoon salt
- 1/4 teaspoon pepper
- 3- to 3 1/2-lb cut-up whole chicken

1. Heat oven to 425°F. Melt butter in 13 × 9-inch pan in oven.

2. In shallow dish, mix flour, paprika, salt and pepper. Coat chicken with flour mixture. Place chicken, skin sides down, in pan.

3. Bake uncovered 30 minutes. Turn chicken; bake about 30 minutes longer or until juice is clear when thickest part is cut to bone (170°F for breasts; 180°F for thighs and legs).

1 SERVING: CAL. 335 (CAL. FROM FAT 190); FAT 21g (SAT. FAT 8g); CHOL. 105mg; SODIUM 320mg; CARBS. 8g (FIBER 0g); PRO. 28g
% DAILY VALUE: VIT. A 10%; VIT. C 0%; CALC. 2%; IRON 10%
EXCHANGES: 1/2 STARCH, 4 MEDIUM-FAT MEAT **CARB. CHOICES:** 1/2

LIGHTER OVEN-FRIED CHICKEN

For 11 grams of fat and 240 calories per serving, remove skin from chicken before cooking. Do not melt butter in pan; spray pan with cooking spray. Decrease butter to 2 tablespoons; drizzle melted butter over chicken after turning in step 3.

CHICKEN FINGERS Substitute 1 1/2 lb boneless skinless chicken breasts, cut crosswise into 1 1/2-inch strips, for the cut-up whole chicken. Decrease butter to 2 tablespoons. After coating chicken with flour mixture in step 2, toss with melted butter in pan. Bake uncovered 15 minutes. Turn strips; bake 10 to 15 minutes longer or until no longer pink in center.

CRUNCHY OVEN-FRIED CHICKEN Substitute 1 cup cornflake crumbs for the 1/2 cup flour. Dip chicken into 1/4 cup butter or margarine, melted, before coating with crumb mixture.

Chicken and Dumplings

PREP: 20 min **COOK:** 2 hr 45 min ▪ **4 SERVINGS**

- 3- to 3 1/2-lb cut-up whole chicken
- 2 medium stalks celery (with leaves), cut up (about 1 cup)
- 1 medium carrot, sliced (1/2 cup)
- 1 small onion, sliced
- 2 tablespoons chopped fresh parsley or 2 teaspoons parsley flakes
- 1 teaspoon salt
- 1/8 teaspoon pepper
- 5 cups water
- 2 1/2 cups Original Bisquick® mix
- 2/3 cup milk

1. Remove excess fat from chicken. In 4-quart Dutch oven, place chicken, giblets (except liver*), neck, celery, carrot, onion, parsley, salt, pepper and water. Cover and heat to boiling; reduce heat. Simmer about 2 hours or until juice of chicken is clear when thickest part is cut to bone (170°F for breasts; 180°F for thighs and legs).

2. Remove chicken and vegetables from Dutch oven. Discard giblets and neck. Skim 1/2 cup fat from broth; reserve. Transfer broth to large bowl; reserve 4 cups (reserve remaining broth for another use).

3. In Dutch oven, heat reserved 1/2 cup fat over low heat. Stir in 1/2 cup of the Bisquick® mix. Cook, stirring constantly, until mixture is smooth and bubbly; remove from heat. Stir in reserved 4 cups broth. Heat to boiling, stirring constantly. Boil and stir 1 minute. Add chicken and vegetables; reduce heat to low. Heat about 20 minutes or until hot.

4. In medium bowl, stir remaining 2 cups Bisquick® and the milk with fork or wire whisk until soft dough forms. Drop dough by spoonfuls onto hot chicken mixture (do not drop directly into liquid). Cook uncovered over low heat 10 minutes. Cover and cook 10 minutes longer.

SUBSTITUTING CHICKEN PARTS

Use your favorite chicken pieces in any recipe that calls for a cut-up whole chicken. Just substitute 3 to 3 1/2 pounds breasts, thighs, legs or wings for the cut-up chicken. If you choose to use all breasts or thighs, which are thicker and meatier than other pieces, you may need to increase the cooking time.

**The liver is very strongly flavored and should not be used to make the broth. Discard it, or reserve for another use.*

1 SERVING: CAL. 810 (CAL. FROM FAT 485); FAT 54g (SAT. FAT 16g); CHOL. 115mg; SODIUM 1,780mg; CARBS. 48g (FIBER 1g); PRO. 34g **% DAILY VALUE:** VIT. A 8%; VIT. C 2%; CALC. 20%; IRON 22% **EXCHANGES:** 3 STARCH, 3 1/2 MEDIUM-FAT MEAT, 6 FAT **CARB. CHOICES:** 3

Coq au Vin

PREP: 10 min **COOK:** 1 hr 10 min ▪ **6 SERVINGS**

Here's a French classic—the beloved chicken-and-vegetable-stew that simmers in red wine. It uses small whole onions, also called pearl onions, which you can buy fresh or frozen. The frozen ones are super easy, because there are no skins to peel.

- 1/2 cup all-purpose flour
- 1 teaspoon salt
- 1/4 teaspoon pepper
- 3- to 3 1/2-lb cut-up whole chicken
- 8 slices bacon
- 3/4 cup frozen small whole onions (from 1-lb bag)
- 3 cups sliced fresh mushrooms (8 oz)
- 1 cup chicken broth
- 1 cup dry red wine or nonalcoholic red wine
- 1/2 teaspoon salt
- 4 medium carrots, cut into 2-inch pieces
- 1 clove garlic, finely chopped
- Bouquet garni*

1. In shallow dish, mix flour, 1 teaspoon salt and the pepper. Coat chicken with flour mixture.

2. In 12-inch skillet, cook bacon over medium heat 8 to 10 minutes, turning once, until crisp. Remove bacon with slotted spoon and drain on paper towels; set aside. Cook chicken in bacon fat over medium heat about 15 minutes, turning occasionally, until brown on all sides.

3. Move chicken to one side of skillet; add onions and mushrooms to other side. Cook over medium-high heat about 6 minutes, stirring occasionally, until mushrooms are tender. Drain fat from skillet.

4. Crumble bacon. Stir bacon and remaining ingredients into vegetables. Heat to boiling; reduce heat. Cover and simmer about 35 minutes or until juice of chicken is clear when thickest part is cut to bone (170°F for breasts; 180°F for thighs and legs). Remove bouquet garni; skim off excess fat.

**Tie 1/2 teaspoon dried thyme leaves, 2 large sprigs fresh parsley and 1 dried bay leaf in cheesecloth bag or place in tea ball. This classic trio of herbs hails from France and is used frequently in many types of recipes.*

1 SERVING: CAL. 380 (CAL. FROM FAT 160); FAT 18g (SAT. FAT 5g); CHOL. 90mg; SODIUM 980mg; CARBS. 23g (FIBER 3g); PRO. 34g **% DAILY VALUE:** VIT. A 26%; VIT. C 2%; CALC. 2%; IRON 14% **EXCHANGES:** 1 STARCH, 2 VEGETABLE, 4 LEAN MEAT, 1/2 FAT **CARB. CHOICES:** 1 1/2

SLOW COOKER DIRECTIONS

Remove skin from chicken. Decrease flour to 1/3 cup. Cut carrots into 1/2-inch slices. Cook, drain and crumble bacon; refrigerate. Brown chicken as directed. In 3 1/2- to 6-quart slow cooker, place carrots. Top with chicken. Mix remaining ingredients except mushrooms and bacon; pour over chicken. Cover and cook on Low heat setting 4 to 6 hours. Stir in mushrooms and bacon. Increase heat setting to High. Cover and cook 30 minutes. Remove bouquet garni; skim off excess fat.

Honey-Mustard Chicken

PREP: 5 min **BAKE:** 1 hr ▪ **6 SERVINGS**

- 3- to 3 1/2-lb cut-up whole chicken
- 1/3 cup country-style Dijon mustard
- 3 tablespoons honey
- 1 tablespoon mustard seed
- 1/2 teaspoon freshly ground pepper

1. Heat oven to 375°F.

2. In ungreased 13 × 9 inch pan, place chicken, skin sides down. In small bowl, mix remaining ingredients. Brush some of the mustard mixture on chicken.

3. Cover and bake 30 minutes. Turn chicken; brush with mustard mixture. Bake uncovered about 30 minutes longer or until juice of chicken is clear when thickest part is cut to bone (170°F for breasts; 180°F for thighs and legs). (If chicken begins to brown too quickly, cover with foil.)

1 SERVING: CAL. 285 (CAL. FROM FAT 135); FAT 15g (SAT. FAT 4g); CHOL. 85mg; SODIUM 410mg; CARBS. 10g (FIBER 0g); PRO. 28g **% DAILY VALUE:** VIT. A 2%; VIT. C 0%; CALC. 2%; IRON 8% **EXCHANGES:** 1/2 OTHER CARB., 4 LEAN MEAT, 1 FAT **CARB. CHOICES:** 1/2

Fiesta Chicken Breasts with Tomato-Avocado Salsa

Fiesta Chicken Breasts with Tomato-Avocado Salsa

PREP: 15 min **CHILL:** 1 hr **BAKE:** 1 hr **COOK:** 5 min ▪ **4 SERVINGS**

Tomato-Avocado Salsa*

2 medium tomatoes, seeded and chopped (1 1/2 cups)
1 medium avocado, pitted, peeled and chopped (1 cup)
4 medium green onions, sliced (1/4 cup)
1 to 2 tablespoons lime juice
1 1/2 teaspoons finely chopped jalapeño chili
1 clove garlic, finely chopped
1/4 teaspoon salt

Chicken

4 bone-in chicken breasts (about 2 lb)
1/4 cup lime juice
1/4 cup vegetable oil
1/2 teaspoon ground cumin
1/2 teaspoon salt
2 tablespoons vegetable oil
4 flour tortillas (8 inch), cut in half, then cut into 1/2-inch strips

1. In medium glass or plastic bowl, gently mix all salsa ingredients. Refrigerate until ready to serve.

2. Meanwhile, place chicken in shallow glass or plastic dish. In small bowl, mix 1/4 cup lime juice, 1/4 cup oil, the cumin and salt; pour over chicken. Cover and refrigerate 1 hour.

3. Heat oven to 375°F. Spray 9-inch square pan with cooking spray.

4. Place chicken, skin sides up, in pan. Pour marinade over chicken. Cover and bake 30 minutes. Uncover and bake 20 to 30 minutes longer, brushing occasionally with marinade, until juice of chicken is clear when thickest part is cut to bone (170°F).

5. In 10-inch skillet, heat 2 tablespoons oil over medium-high heat until hot. Cook tortilla strips in oil 3 to 5 minutes, stirring occasionally, until crisp and golden brown. Serve chicken topped with salsa. Serve with tortilla strips.

** 1 cup purchased thick-and-chunky salsa can be substituted for the Tomato-Avocado Salsa. Gently stir 1 cup chopped avocado into purchased salsa.*

1 SERVING: CAL. 505 (CAL. FROM FAT 245); FAT 27g (SAT. FAT 5g); CHOL. 75mg; SODIUM 580mg; CARBS. 32g (FIBER 5g); PRO. 32g
% DAILY VALUE: VIT. A 12%; VIT. C 18%; CALC. 8%; IRON 18%
EXCHANGES: 1 1/2 STARCH, 2 VEGETABLE, 3 MEDIUM-FAT MEAT, 2 1/2 FAT **CARB. CHOICES:** 2

Chicken Tagine

PREP: 15 min **COOK:** 45 min ■ **6 SERVINGS**

Sunny Morocco is famous for many varieties of stew called tagine. *Meat or poultry is simmered in a clay cooking vessel with broth, vegetables, olives and spices such as cinnamon, cumin, ginger and turmeric. Our version is cooked in a large skillet, as the traditional clay cooking vessels are hard to find.*

1 tablespoon vegetable oil
3- to 3 1/2-lb cut-up whole chicken
1 medium onion, sliced
2 cloves garlic, finely chopped
1/4 cup chopped fresh cilantro
1 teaspoon ground cumin
1 teaspoon ground turmeric
1 teaspoon ground ginger
1 teaspoon salt
1 cinnamon stick (2 inches long)
1 cup chicken broth
1 can (14.5 oz) diced tomatoes, undrained
1 cup dried plums, cut into bite-size pieces
1/2 cup pitted whole green olives
1 small lemon, cut into fourths
Hot cooked couscous or rice (page 375), if desired

1. In 4-quart Dutch oven, heat oil over medium-high heat. Place chicken, skin sides down, in hot oil; add onion and garlic. Cook 6 to 10 minutes, turning chicken occasionally, until chicken is brown on all sides.

2. Reduce heat to medium. Sprinkle cilantro, cumin, turmeric, ginger and salt over chicken. Add cinnamon stick; pour broth and tomatoes over chicken. Turn chicken several times to coat evenly. Add plums, olives and lemon, pressing into liquid around chicken. Reduce heat to low. Cover and simmer about 30 minutes or until juice of chicken is clear when thickest part is cut to bone (170°F for breasts; 180°F for thighs and legs).

3. Remove chicken to deep serving platter; cover to keep warm. Increase heat to high; boil sauce uncovered about 5 minutes, stirring occasionally, until thickened. Pour sauce over chicken. Garnish with additional chopped fresh cilantro if desired. Serve over couscous.

1 SERVING: CAL. 360 (CAL. FROM FAT 155); FAT 17g (SAT. FAT 4g); CHOL. 85mg; SODIUM 1,010mg; CARBS. 23g (FIBER 3g); PRO. 29g
% DAILY VALUE: VIT. A 8%; VIT. C 10%; CALC. 6%; IRON 14%
EXCHANGES: 1/2 FRUIT, 2 VEGETABLE, 3 1/2 MEDIUM-FAT MEAT, 1/2 FAT **CARB. CHOICES:** 1 1/2

THE SKINNY ON SKIN

Cooking chicken with the skin on adds to the flavor, not the fat. Research has found that the fat doesn't transfer to the meat during cooking. So go ahead and leave the skin on—it helps keep juices in, creates more moist and tender meat, and boosts the flavor. Then, once the chicken is cooked, remove the skin and throw it away to save on fat, calories and cholesterol.

Chicken Tagine ▶

Chicken Cacciatore

PREP: 20 min **COOK:** 1 hr ▪ **6 SERVINGS**

- 3- to 3 1/2-lb cut-up whole chicken
- 1/2 cup all-purpose flour
- 1/4 cup vegetable oil
- 1 medium green bell pepper
- 2 medium onions
- 1 can (14.5 oz) diced tomatoes, undrained
- 1 can (8 oz) tomato sauce
- 1 cup sliced fresh mushrooms (3 oz)
- 1 1/2 teaspoons chopped fresh or 1/2 teaspoon dried oregano leaves
- 1 teaspoon chopped fresh or 1/4 teaspoon dried basil leaves
- 1/2 teaspoon salt
- 2 cloves garlic, finely chopped
- Grated Parmesan cheese, if desired

1. Coat chicken with flour. In 12-inch skillet, heat oil over medium-high heat. Cook chicken in oil 15 to 20 minutes or until brown on all sides; drain.

2. Cut bell pepper and onions crosswise in half; cut each half into fourths.

3. Stir bell pepper, onions and remaining ingredients except cheese into chicken in skillet. Heat to boiling; reduce heat. Cover and simmer 30 to 40 minutes or until juice of chicken is clear when thickest part is cut to bone (170°F for breasts; 180°F for thighs and legs). Serve with cheese.

1 SERVING: CAL. 400 (CAL. FROM FAT 205); FAT 23g (SAT. FAT 5g); CHOL. 85mg; SODIUM 620mg; CARBS. 19g (FIBER 3g); PRO. 30g
% DAILY VALUE: VIT. A 14%; VIT. C 28%; CALC. 4%; IRON 14%
EXCHANGES: 3 VEGETABLE, 3 MEDIUM-FAT MEAT, 2 FAT
CARB. CHOICES: 1

SLOW COOKER DIRECTIONS

Remove skin from chicken. Decrease flour to 1/3 cup. Decrease oil to 2 tablespoons; omit tomato sauce. Use 1 jar (4.5 oz) sliced mushrooms, drained. Brown chicken as directed. Cut bell pepper and onions crosswise in half; cut each half into fourths. In 3 1/2- to 6-quart slow cooker, place half of the chicken. Mix bell pepper, onions and remaining ingredients except cheese; spoon half of mixture over chicken. Add remaining chicken; top with remaining vegetable mixture. Cover and cook on Low heat setting 4 to 6 hours. Serve with cheese.

Chicken Niçoise LOW-FAT

PREP: 10 min **COOK:** 25 min ▪ **4 SERVINGS**

Niçoise *comes from the French phrase meaning "as prepared in Nice," referring to dishes made in the Riviera part of France.*

- 1 1/4 cups dry white wine or chicken broth
- 4 boneless skinless chicken thighs (about 1 lb)
- 3 cloves garlic, finely chopped
- 1/2 cup frozen small whole onions (from 1-lb bag)
- 1 tablespoon Italian seasoning
- 2 medium bell peppers, sliced
- 6 Kalamata olives, pitted and chopped
- 2 cups hot cooked rice (page 375)

1. In 10-inch nonstick skillet, heat 1/4 cup of the wine to boiling. Cook chicken in wine about 5 minutes, turning once, until outside of chicken is white.

2. Add garlic, onions, Italian seasoning, bell peppers, olives and remaining 1 cup wine to skillet. Heat to boiling; boil 5 minutes.

Zesty Roasted Chicken and Potatoes ▶

3. Add chicken to skillet; reduce heat to medium. Cook 10 to 15 minutes or until juice of chicken is clear when center of thickest part is cut (180°F). Serve over rice.

1 SERVING: CAL. 330 (CAL. FROM FAT 90); FAT 10g (SAT. FAT 3g); CHOL. 70mg; SODIUM 125mg; CARBS. 30g (FIBER 2g); PRO. 27g **% DAILY VALUE:** VIT. A 8%; VIT. C 46%; CALC. 6%; IRON 22% **EXCHANGES:** 2 STARCH, 3 LEAN MEAT **CARB. CHOICES:** 2

Zesty Roasted Chicken and Potatoes

PREP: 10 min **BAKE:** 35 min ■ **6 SERVINGS**

6 boneless skinless chicken breasts (about 1 3/4 lb)
1 lb small red potatoes, cut into fourths
1/3 cup mayonnaise or salad dressing
3 tablespoons Dijon mustard
1/2 teaspoon pepper
2 cloves garlic, finely chopped
Chopped fresh chives, if desired

1. Heat oven to 350°F. Spray 15 × 10 × 1-inch pan with cooking spray.

2. Place chicken and potatoes in pan. In small bowl, mix remaining ingredients except chives; brush over chicken and potatoes.

3. Bake uncovered 30 to 35 minutes or until potatoes are tender and juice of chicken is clear when center of thickest part is cut (170°F). Sprinkle with chives.

1 SERVING: CAL. 300 (CAL. FROM FAT 125); FAT 14g (SAT. FAT 3g); CHOL. 80mg; SODIUM 330mg; CARBS. 14g (FIBER 1g); PRO. 29g **% DAILY VALUE:** VIT. A 0%; VIT. C 4%; CALC. 2%; IRON 10% **EXCHANGES:** 1 STARCH, 4 LEAN MEAT **CARB. CHOICES:** 1

Chicken Marsala LOW-FAT

PREP: 10 min **COOK:** 25 min ■ **4 SERVINGS**

4 boneless skinless chicken breasts (about 1 1/4 lb)
1/2 cup all-purpose flour
1/4 teaspoon salt
1/4 teaspoon pepper
2 tablespoons olive or vegetable oil
2 cloves garlic, finely chopped
1 cup sliced fresh mushrooms (3 oz)
1/4 cup chopped fresh parsley or 1 tablespoon parsley flakes
1/2 cup dry Marsala wine or chicken broth
Hot cooked pasta (page 376), if desired

1. Between sheets of plastic wrap or waxed paper, flatten each chicken breast to 1/4-inch thickness. In shallow dish, mix flour, salt and pepper. Coat chicken with flour mixture; shake off excess flour.

2. In 10-inch skillet, heat oil over medium-high heat. Cook garlic, mushrooms and parsley in oil 5 minutes, stirring frequently.

3. Add chicken to skillet. Cook about 8 minutes, turning once, until brown. Add wine. Cook 8 to 10 minutes or until chicken is no longer pink in center. Serve with pasta.

1 SERVING: CAL. 275 (CAL. FROM FAT 70); FAT 8g (SAT. FAT 2g); CHOL. 85mg; SODIUM 230mg; CARBS. 17g (FIBER 1g); PRO. 34g **% DAILY VALUE:** VIT. A 6%; VIT. C 4%; CALC. 2%; IRON 12% **EXCHANGES:** 1 STARCH, 4 VERY LEAN MEAT, 1 FAT **CARB. CHOICES:** 1

HOW TO FLATTEN CHICKEN BREASTS—TWO WAYS

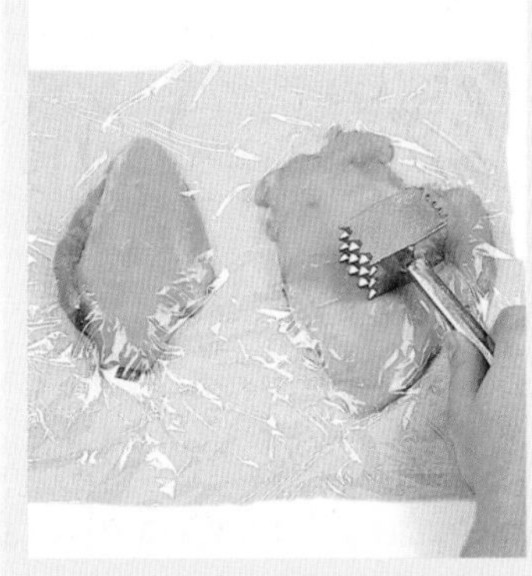

◀ **1.** Place chicken breast, smooth side up, between pieces of plastic wrap or waxed paper. Using flat side of meat mallet or rolling pin, gently pound chicken breasts, working from center out, until 1/4 inch thick.

2. Or using the heel of your hand, apply firm pressure (pounding lightly if necessary) to chicken breasts, pressing until 1/8 inch thick. ▶

Chicken in Brandy Cream Sauce

PREP: 10 min **COOK:** 22 min ▪ **4 SERVINGS**

- 1 tablespoon olive or vegetable oil
- 4 boneless skinless chicken breasts (about 1 1/4 lb)
- 1 package (8 oz) sliced fresh mushrooms (3 cups)
- 4 medium green onions, chopped (1/4 cup)
- 1/4 teaspoon salt
- 1/4 cup brandy or chicken broth
- 1/2 cup whipping (heavy) cream
- Hot cooked spinach fettuccine or regular fettuccine (page 376), if desired

1. In 10-inch skillet, heat oil over medium-high heat. Cook chicken in oil 10 to 15 minutes, turning once, until juice of chicken is clear when center of thickest part is cut (170°F).

2. Stir in mushrooms, onions, salt and brandy. Cook 4 to 5 minutes or until mushrooms are tender and most of the liquid has evaporated.

3. Gradually stir in whipping cream. Cook about 2 minutes or until hot. Serve over fettuccine.

1 SERVING: CAL. 305 (CAL. FROM FAT 155); FAT 17g (SAT. FAT 8g); CHOL. 120mg; SODIUM 240mg; CARBS. 5g (FIBER 1g); PRO. 34g
% DAILY VALUE: VIT. A 8%; VIT. C 2%; CALC. 4%; IRON 10%
EXCHANGES: 1 VEGETABLE, 4 1/2 LEAN MEAT, 1 FAT
CARB. CHOICES: 0

Cornmeal Chicken with Fresh Peach Salsa

PREP: 10 min **COOK:** 20 min ▪ **4 SERVINGS**

Fresh Peach Salsa

- 5 medium peaches, peeled and chopped (3 cups)*
- 1 large tomato, chopped (1 cup)
- 1/4 cup chopped fresh cilantro
- 3 tablespoons vegetable oil
- 2 tablespoons white vinegar
- 1/4 teaspoon salt

Chicken

- 1/2 cup yellow cornmeal
- 1/2 teaspoon salt
- 1/4 teaspoon pepper
- 4 boneless skinless chicken breasts (about 1 1/4 lb)
- 2 tablespoons vegetable oil

1. In large bowl, mix all salsa ingredients. Cover and refrigerate until serving.

2. In shallow dish, mix cornmeal, salt and pepper. Coat chicken with cornmeal mixture.

3. In 10-inch skillet, heat oil over medium-high heat. Cook chicken in oil 15 to 20 minutes, turning once, until juice is clear when center of thickest part is cut (170°F). Serve with salsa.

**3 cups chopped frozen (thawed) sliced peaches can be substituted for the fresh peaches.*

1 SERVING: CAL. 455 (CAL. FROM FAT 200); FAT 22g (SAT. FAT 4g); CHOL. 85mg; SODIUM 520mg; CARBS. 30g (FIBER 4g); PRO. 34g
% DAILY VALUE: VIT. A 12%; VIT. C 28%; CALC. 2%; IRON 12% **EXCHANGES:** 2 FRUIT, 5 LEAN MEAT, 1 FAT
CARB. CHOICES: 2

◄ **Cornmeal Chicken with Fresh Peach Salsa**

Moroccan Spiced Chicken

LOW-FAT

PREP: 10 min **COOK:** 20 min ■ **4 SERVINGS**

1 tablespoon paprika
1/2 teaspoon salt
1/2 teaspoon ground cumin
1/4 teaspoon ground allspice
1/4 teaspoon ground cinnamon
4 boneless skinless chicken breasts (about 1 1/4 lb)
1 tablespoon vegetable oil
1 small papaya, sliced
Hot cooked couscous, if desired

1. In small bowl, mix paprika, salt, cumin, allspice and cinnamon. Coat both sides of chicken with spice mixture.

2. In 10-inch skillet, heat oil over medium heat. Cook chicken in oil 15 to 20 minutes, turning once, until juice of chicken is clear when center of thickest part is cut (170°F). Serve chicken with papaya and couscous.

1 SERVING: CAL. 230 (CAL. FROM FAT 70); FAT 8g (SAT. FAT 2g); CHOL. 75mg; SODIUM 380mg; CARBS. 8g (FIBER 2g); PRO. 32g
% DAILY VALUE: VIT. A 38%; VIT. C 40%; CALC. 4%; IRON 8%
EXCHANGES: 1/2 FRUIT, 4 1/2 VERY LEAN MEAT, 1 FAT
CARB. CHOICES: 1/2

Indian Spiced Chicken and Chutney

LOW-FAT

PREP: 5 min **MARINATE:** 1 hr **COOK:** 20 min ■ **4 SERVINGS**

Entertain your friends with an Indian meal by serving this dish with traditional sides such as coconut, raisins, peanuts or cashews and fresh cilantro leaves.

Spicy Yogurt Marinade

1/2 cup plain yogurt
1 tablespoon lemon juice
2 teaspoons grated gingerroot
1/2 teaspoon paprika
1/2 teaspoon ground coriander
1/2 teaspoon salt
1/4 teaspoon ground red pepper (cayenne)
1/8 teaspoon ground cloves

Chicken and Chutney

4 boneless skinless chicken breasts (about 1 1/4 lb)
1/2 cup Golden Fruit Chutney (page 418) or purchased mango chutney
Hot cooked basmati rice or regular long-grain rice (page 375), if desired

1. In small bowl, mix all marinade ingredients.

2. Place chicken in resealable plastic food-storage bag or shallow glass or plastic dish. Pour marinade over chicken; turn chicken to coat with marinade. Seal bag or cover dish and refrigerate 1 hour.

3. In 12-inch skillet, cook chicken and marinade over medium-high heat 15 to 20 minutes, turning chicken once, until juice of chicken is clear when center of thickest part is cut (170°F). Top with chutney. Serve with rice.

1 SERVING: CAL. 235 (CAL. FROM FAT 45); FAT 5g (SAT. FAT 1g); CHOL. 75mg; SODIUM 410mg; CARBS. 14g (FIBER 0g); PRO. 33g
% DAILY VALUE: VIT. A 2%; VIT. C 6%; CALC. 6%; IRON 6%
EXCHANGES: 1 FRUIT, 4 1/2 VERY LEAN MEAT, 1/2 FAT
CARB. CHOICES: 1

Thai-Style Coconut Chicken

PREP: 25 min **COOK:** 7 min ■ **4 SERVINGS**

Make your favorite restaurant meal at home! Expect the dish to resemble a very flavorful broth, which is typical of many Thai dishes. Like your Thai food quite hot? Just add another chili or two.

- 1 tablespoon vegetable oil
- 1 lb boneless skinless chicken breasts, cut into bite-size pieces
- 1 teaspoon grated lime peel
- 1 teaspoon grated gingerroot
- 1 clove garlic, finely chopped
- 2 fresh serrano chilies or 1 jalapeño chili, seeded and finely chopped
- 1/4 cup finely chopped fresh cilantro
- 1 can (about 14 oz) coconut milk (not cream of coconut)
- 1 teaspoon packed brown sugar
- 1/2 teaspoon salt
- 1 tablespoon soy sauce
- 1 cup sugar snap pea pods
- 1 medium green bell pepper, cut into 1-inch cubes
- 1 medium tomato, chopped (3/4 cup)
- 1 tablespoon chopped fresh basil leaves
- Hot cooked jasmine rice (page 375), if desired

1. In nonstick wok or 12-inch nonstick skillet, heat oil over high heat. Add chicken; stir-fry 2 to 3 minutes or until chicken is no longer pink in center. Add lime peel, gingerroot, garlic, chilies and cilantro; stir-fry 1 minute.

2. Pour coconut milk over chicken. Stir in brown sugar, salt, soy sauce, pea pods and bell pepper. Reduce heat to medium. Simmer uncovered 3 to 5 minutes, stirring occasionally, until vegetables are crisp-tender. Stir into tomato.

3. Spoon into shallow serving bowls; top with basil. Serve with rice.

1 SERVING: CAL. 430 (CAL. FROM FAT 235); FAT 26g (SAT. FAT 17g); CHOL. 85mg; SODIUM 660mg; CARBS. 14g (FIBER 4g); PRO. 35g
% DAILY VALUE: VIT. A 10%; VIT. C 30%; CALC. 2%; IRON 12%
EXCHANGES: 1/2 STARCH, 1 VEGETABLE, 5 LEAN MEAT, 2 FAT
CARB. CHOICES: 1

Chicken Pot Pie

PREP: 40 min **BAKE:** 35 min ■ **6 SERVINGS**

Pot pie for dinner is possible, even if you're busy. Just pick up two ready-to-use pie crusts instead of making them yourself. You'll cut your preparation time in half.

- 1 box (10 oz) frozen peas and carrots
- 1/3 cup butter or margarine
- 1/3 cup all-purpose flour
- 1/3 cup chopped onion
- 1/2 teaspoon salt
- 1/4 teaspoon pepper
- 1 3/4 cups chicken broth
- 2/3 cup milk
- 2 1/2 to 3 cups cut-up cooked chicken or turkey
- Pastry for Two-Crust Pie (page 123)

1. Rinse frozen peas and carrots in cold water to separate; drain.

2. In 2-quart saucepan, melt butter over medium heat. Stir in flour, onion, salt and pepper. Cook, stirring constantly, until mixture is bubbly; remove from heat. Stir in broth and milk. Heat to boiling, stirring constantly. Boil and stir 1 minute. Stir in chicken and peas and carrots; remove from heat.

3. Heat oven to 425°F.

◄ **Thai-Style Coconut Chicken**

4. Make pastry. Roll two-thirds of the pastry into 13-inch square. Ease into ungreased 9-inch square pan. Pour chicken mixture into pastry-lined pan.

5. Roll remaining pastry into 11-inch square. Cut out designs with 1-inch cookie cutter. Place square over chicken mixture. Arrange cutouts on pastry. Turn edges of pastry under and flute. (See page 126 for Pastry Edges.)

6. Bake about 35 minutes or until golden brown.

1 SERVING (ABOUT 1 CUP): CAL. 665 (CAL. FROM FAT 385); FAT 43g (SAT. FAT 15g); CHOL. 80mg; SODIUM 1,050mg; CARBS. 45g (FIBER 3g); PRO. 25g **% DAILY VALUE:** VIT. A 100%; VIT. C 4%; CALC. 6%; IRON 20% **EXCHANGES:** 2 1/2 STARCH, 1 VEGETABLE, 2 MEDIUM-FAT MEAT, 6 1/2 FAT **CARB. CHOICES:** 3

LIGHTER CHICKEN POT PIE

For 22 grams of fat and 425 calories per serving, decrease butter to 2 tablespoons, increase flour to 1/2 cup, decrease broth to 1 1/2 cups and use fat-free (skim) milk. After melting butter in Step 2, stir in milk, onion, salt and pepper; stir in flour. Cook, stirring constantly, until mixture is bubbly; remove from heat. Stir in broth. Continue as directed—except use Pastry for One-Crust Pie instead of Pastry for Two-Crust Pie; use pastry for top crust in Step 5. Spray 9-inch square pan with cooking spray. Pour chicken mixture into pan (not pastry-lined). Bake 25 to 35 minutes or until golden brown.

TUNA POT PIE Substitute 1 can (12 oz) tuna, drained, for the chicken.

◀ **Chicken Pot Pie**

Turkey Divan

PREP: 35 min **BROIL:** 3 min ■ **6 SERVINGS**

1 1/2 lb broccoli*
1/4 cup butter or margarine
1/4 cup all-purpose flour
1/8 teaspoon ground nutmeg
1 1/2 cups chicken broth
1 cup grated Parmesan cheese
1/2 cup whipping (heavy) cream
2 tablespoons dry white wine or chicken broth
6 large slices cooked turkey or chicken breast, 1/4 inch thick (3/4 lb)

1. Cut broccoli lengthwise into 1/2-inch-wide spears. In 2-quart saucepan, heat 1 inch water (salted if desired) to boiling. Add broccoli. Heat to boiling. Boil uncovered 5 minutes; drain and keep warm.

2. In same saucepan, melt butter over medium heat. Stir in flour and nutmeg. Cook, stirring constantly, until smooth and bubbly; remove from heat. Stir in broth. Heat to boiling, stirring constantly. Boil and stir 1 minute; remove from heat. Stir in 1/2 cup of the cheese, the whipping cream and wine.

3. Place hot broccoli in ungreased 11 × 7-inch glass baking dish. Top with turkey. Pour cheese sauce over turkey. Sprinkle with remaining 1/2 cup cheese.

4. Set oven control to broil. Broil with top 3 to 5 inches from heat about 3 minutes or until cheese is bubbly and light brown.

**2 boxes (9 oz each) frozen broccoli spears, cooked and drained, can be substituted for the fresh broccoli.*

1 SERVING: CAL. 290 (CAL. FROM FAT 170); FAT 19g (SAT. FAT 11g); CHOL. 90mg; SODIUM 670mg; CARBS. 9g (FIBER 2g); PRO. 23g **% DAILY VALUE:** VIT. A 20%; VIT. C 54%; CALC. 24%; IRON 10% **EXCHANGES:** 2 VEGETABLE, 3 LEAN MEAT, 2 FAT **CARB. CHOICES:** 1/2

Orange-Roasted Pheasants

PREP: 20 min **ROAST:** 45 min **COOK:** 15 min ▪ **4 SERVINGS**

- 1/2 cup butter or margarine, softened
- 2 teaspoons grated orange peel
- 1 teaspoon salt
- 1/4 teaspoon pepper
- 2 tablespoons honey
- 4 medium green onions, sliced (1/4 cup)
- 2 pheasants (2 1/2 to 3 lb each)
- 1/2 cup orange liqueur or water
- 1 cup chicken broth

1. Heat oven to 350°F.

2. In small bowl, stir butter, orange peel, salt, pepper, honey and green onions until well mixed.

3. Place pheasants, breast sides up, in shallow roasting pan. For each pheasant, starting at the back opening, gently separate skin from breast, using fingers. Spread butter mixture on pheasant breast under skin. Secure skin to flesh with toothpick if necessary. Insert meat thermometer so tip is in thickest part of inside thigh and does not touch bone.

4. Roast uncovered about 45 minutes or until thermometer reads 180°F and legs move easily when lifted or twisted. Remove pheasants to serving platter; cover loosely with foil to keep warm.

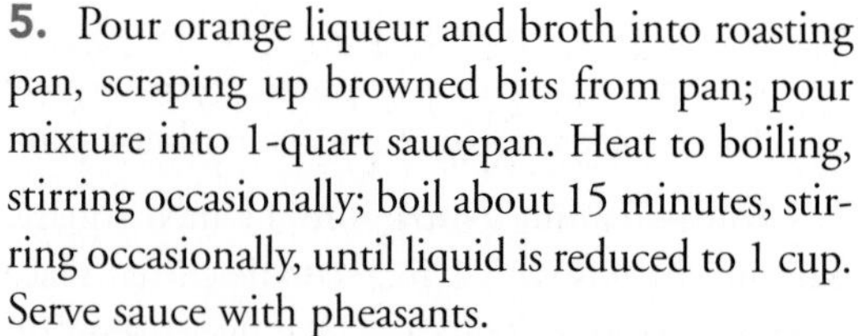

5. Pour orange liqueur and broth into roasting pan, scraping up browned bits from pan; pour mixture into 1-quart saucepan. Heat to boiling, stirring occasionally; boil about 15 minutes, stirring occasionally, until liquid is reduced to 1 cup. Serve sauce with pheasants.

1 SERVING: CAL. 670 (CAL. FROM FAT 405); FAT 45g (SAT. FAT 21g); CHOL. 220mg; SODIUM 1170mg; CARBS. 10g (FIBER 0g); PRO. 56g **% DAILY VALUE:** VIT. A 26%; VIT. C 4%; CALC. 10%; IRON 78% **EXCHANGES:** 1/2 STARCH, 8 MEDIUM-FAT MEAT **CARB. CHOICES:** 1/2

Duckling with Orange Sauce

PREP: 20 min **ROAST:** 2 hr 30 min **COOK:** 5 min **STAND:** 15 min ▪ **4 SERVINGS**

Piercing the duck skin is commonly done because it allows much of the unwanted fat to drain away. Using a fork, pierce the skin all over, especially at the breast, but don't pierce the flesh.

- 4- to 5-lb duckling, thawed if frozen
- 1/2 cup orange juice
- 2 teaspoons grated orange peel
- 1/4 cup currant jelly
- 1 tablespoon lemon juice
- 1/8 teaspoon ground mustard
- 1/8 teaspoon salt
- 1 tablespoon cold water
- 1 1/2 teaspoons cornstarch
- 1 medium orange, peeled and sectioned
- 1 tablespoon orange-flavored liqueur, if desired

1. Heat oven to 350°F.

2. Fasten neck skin to back of duckling with skewer. Fold wings across back of duckling so tips are touching. On rack in shallow roasting pan, place duckling, breast side up. Pierce skin all over with fork. Loosely tie legs to the tail, if desired, to better hold an even shape during cooking. Insert ovenproof meat thermometer so tip is in thickest part of inside thigh and does not touch bone.

◄ **Orange-Roasted Pheasants**

3. Roast uncovered about 2 hours 30 minutes or until thermometer reads 180°F and legs move easily when lifted or twisted. Place tent of foil loosely over breast during last hour to prevent excessive browning. Place duckling on heated platter. Let stand 15 minutes for easiest carving.

4. Meanwhile, in 1-quart saucepan, heat orange juice, orange peel, jelly, lemon juice, mustard and salt to boiling. In small bowl, mix water and cornstarch; stir into sauce. Cook over medium heat, stirring constantly, until mixture thickens and boils. Boil and stir 1 minute.

5. Stir orange sections and liqueur into sauce. Brush duckling with some of the sauce. Serve with remaining sauce.

1 SERVING: CAL. 490 (CAL. FROM FAT 215); FAT 24g (SAT. FAT 7g); CHOL. 155mg; SODIUM 230mg; CARBS. 20g (FIBER 1g); PRO. 49g
% DAILY VALUE: VIT. A 4%; VIT. C 24%; CALC. 4%; IRON 14%
EXCHANGES: 1 STARCH, 6 1/2 LEAN MEAT, 1 FAT **CARB. CHOICES:** 1

Roast Goose with Apple Stuffing

PREP: 1 hr 30 min **ROAST:** 3 hr 30 min **STAND:** 15 min
COOK: 10 min ■ **8 SERVINGS**

Celebrate the holidays in a new way by roasting a goose for dinner, in place of the traditional turkey. Save cleanup time by lining the roasting pan with foil before placing the goose on the rack.

- 8- to 10-lb goose, thawed if frozen
- 2 cups water
- 1 small onion, sliced
- 3/4 teaspoon salt
- 6 cups soft bread crumbs (about 9 slices bread)
- 1/4 cup butter or margarine, melted
- 1 1/2 teaspoons chopped fresh or 1/2 teaspoon dried sage leaves
- 3/4 teaspoon chopped fresh or 1/4 teaspoon dried thyme leaves
- 1/2 teaspoon salt
- 1/4 teaspoon pepper
- 3 medium tart apples, chopped (3 cups)
- 2 medium stalks celery (with leaves), chopped (about 1 cup)
- 1 medium onion, chopped (1/2 cup)
- 1/4 cup all-purpose flour

1. Remove excess fat from goose.

2. In 1-quart saucepan, heat giblets (except liver*) and neck from goose, water, sliced onion and 3/4 teaspoon salt to boiling; reduce heat. Cover and simmer about 1 hour or until giblets are tender. Strain broth; cover and refrigerate.

3. Remove meat from neck and finely chop with giblets. In large bowl, toss giblets and remaining ingredients except flour.

4. Heat oven to 350°F.

5. Fill wishbone area of goose with stuffing first. Fasten neck skin to back of goose with skewer. Fold wings across back of goose so tips are touching. Fill body cavity lightly. (Do not pack—stuffing will expand during roasting.) Fasten opening of cavity with skewers, and lace with string. Pierce skin all over with fork.

6. On rack in shallow roasting pan, place goose, breast side up. Insert ovenproof meat thermometer so tip is in thickest part of inside thigh and does not touch bone.

7. Roast uncovered 3 hours to 3 hours 30 minutes (if necessary, place tent of foil loosely over goose during last hour to prevent excessive browning), removing excess fat from pan occasionally, until thermometer reads 180°F and legs move easily when lifted or twisted. The center of the stuffing should be 165°F. Place goose on heated platter. Let stand 15 minutes for easiest carving.

8. Pour drippings from pan into bowl; skim off fat. Return 1/4 cup drippings to pan (discard remaining drippings). Stir in flour. Cook over medium heat, stirring constantly, until smooth and bubbly; remove from heat.

9. Add enough water to reserved broth, if necessary, to measure 2 cups. Stir into flour mixture. Heat to boiling, stirring constantly. Boil and stir 1 minute. Serve goose with apple stuffing and gravy.

**The liver is very strongly flavored and should not be used to make the broth. Discard it, or reserve for another use.*

1 SERVING: CAL. 800 (CAL. FROM FAT 485); FAT 54g (SAT. FAT 19g); CHOL. 210mg; SODIUM 630mg; CARBS. 25g (FIBER 3g); PRO. 57g
% DAILY VALUE: VIT. A 8%; VIT. C 4%; CALC. 6%; IRON 40%
EXCHANGES: 1 STARCH, 1/2 FRUIT, 8 MEDIUM-FAT MEAT, 2 FAT
CARB. CHOICES: 1 1/2

THAWING POULTRY—REFRIGERATOR AND COLD-WATER METHODS

Thaw poultry slowly in the refrigerator or in cold water. Don't thaw poultry on the countertop because bacteria thrive at room temperature. Thaw poultry in a dish or baking pan with sides or plastic bag to catch any drips during thawing.

Poultry Cut	Weight (pounds)	Thawing Time in Refrigerator	Thawing Time in Cold Water (Change water as needed to keep water cold.)
Chicken, Whole	3 to 4	24 hours	1½ to 2 hours
Turkey, Whole	8 to 12	1 to 2 days	4 to 6 hours
	12 to 16	2 to 3 days	6 to 8 hours
	16 to 20	3 to 4 days	8 to 10 hours
	20 to 24	4 to 5 days	10 to 12 hours
Chicken or Turkey, Cut-Up Pieces (cooked or uncooked)	Up to 4	3 to 9 hours	1½ to 2 hours Don't use cold-water method for cooked poultry.

Roasting Poultry

1. Remove bag of giblets and neck if present. Rinse cavity; pat dry with paper towels.

2. If stuffing poultry, stuff just before roasting, not ahead of time. (This prevents any bacteria in the raw poultry from contaminating the stuffing.) Do not stuff duck. Plan on using about ¾ cup stuffing per pound of poultry. Spoon in the stuffing without packing it in, because it expands during roasting. Lightly spoon some stuffing into the neck cavity (turn turkey breast side down for easier filling). For turkey, fasten the neck skin to the back of the turkey with a small skewer (this isn't necessary for chicken). Turn turkey breast side up. Fold the wings tips under the back of the turkey. Lightly spoon stuffing into cavity. For chicken, tie or skewer the legs to the tail. For turkey, tuck legs under the band of skin at the tail (if present), or tie together with heavy string, then tie to tail if desired.

3. Place breast side up on a rack in a shallow roasting pan. Brush with melted butter or margarine or vegetable oil. Insert ovenproof meat thermometer so tip is in thickest part of the inside thigh and does not touch bone. Do not add water or cover poultry. Use the following table for approximate roasting times, but use the temperature as the final doneness guide. For turkey, place a tent of foil loosely over the turkey when it begins to turn golden. When two-thirds done, cut band of skin or remove tie holding legs to allow inside of thighs to cook through.

4. Roast until thermometer reads 180°F and a leg moves easily when lifted or twisted. Thermometer placed in the center of stuffing will read 165°F when done. Remove from the oven; cover with foil to keep warm. Let stand about 15 minutes for easiest carving.

TIMETABLE FOR ROASTING POULTRY

Type of Bird and Weight	Oven Temperature	Roasting Time*
CHICKEN		
Whole Chicken** (stuffed)		
3 to 3 1/2 pounds	325°F	2 to 2 1/2 hours
Whole Chicken** (not stuffed)		
3 to 3 1/2 pounds	375°F	1 3/4 to 2 hours
TURKEY		
Whole Turkey (not stuffed)		
8 to 12 pounds	325°F	2 3/4 to 3 hours
12 to 14 pounds	325°F	3 to 3 3/4 hours
14 to 18 pounds	325°F	3 3/4 to 4 1/4 hours
18 to 20 pounds	325°F	4 1/4 to 4 1/2 hours
20 to 24 pounds	325°F	4 1/2 to 5 hours
Whole Turkey (stuffed)		
8 to 12 pounds	325°F	3 to 3 1/2 hours
12 to 14 pounds	325°F	3 1/2 to 4 hours
14 to 18 pounds	325°F	4 to 4 1/4 hours
18 to 20 pounds	325°F	4 1/4 to 4 3/4 hours
20 to 24 pounds	325°F	4 3/4 to 5 1/4 hours
Whole Turkey Breast (bone-in)		
2 to 4 pounds	325°F	1 1/2 to 2 hours
3 to 5 pounds	325°F	1 1/2 to 2 1/2 hours
5 to 7 pounds	325°F	2 to 2 1/2 hours
GAME		
Duck (do not stuff)		
3 1/2 to 4 pounds	350°F	2 hours
5 to 5 1/2 pounds	350°F	3 hours
Goose		
7 to 9 pounds	350°F	2 1/2 to 3 hours
9 to 11 pounds	350°F	3 to 3 1/2 hours
11 to 13 pounds	350° F	3 1/2 to 4 hours
Pheasant		
2 to 3 pounds	350°F	1 1/4 to 1 1/2 hours
Rock Cornish Hen		
1 to 1 1/2 pounds	350°F	1 to 1 1/4 hours

**Times given are for birds taken directly from the refrigerator. Times given are for unstuffed birds unless noted. Stuffed birds other than turkey require 15 to 30 minutes longer. Begin checking turkey doneness about 1 hour before end of recommended roasting time. For purchased prestuffed turkeys, follow package directions instead of this timetable.*

***May also be called* broiler-fryer chicken.

COOKED POULTRY YIELDS

If a recipe calls for 1 cup cubed cooked chicken, how much chicken or turkey should you cook?

Type of Poultry	Weight (pounds)	Yield of Chopped, Cubed or Shredded Cooked Poultry
CHICKEN		
Whole Chicken*	3 to 3½	2½ to 3 cups
Whole Breast, bone in	1½	2 cups
Boneless Skinless Breasts	1½	3 cups
Legs (Thighs and Drumsticks)	1½	1¾ cups
TURKEY		
Whole Turkey	6 to 8	7 to 10 cups
Whole Breast, bone in	1½	2½ cups
Tenderloins	1½	3 cups

**May also be called* broiler-fryer chicken.

TIMETABLE FOR BROILING POULTRY

Cook poultry directly from refrigerator. Set oven control to broil. Check your owner's manual for whether the oven door should be partially opened or closed during broiling. Place poultry on rack in broiler pan. Broil for the time listed, turning once, until thermometer reaches the doneness temperature or until juice is clear when thickest part is cut to bone (for bone-in pieces) or when center of thickest part of boneless pieces is cut.

Cut	Weight	Approximate Broiling Time	Doneness
CHICKEN			
Cut-Up Whole Chicken*	3 to 3½ pounds	Skin sides down 30 minutes; turn. Broil 15 to 25 minutes longer (7 to 9 inches from heat)	170°F breasts 180°F legs/thighs
Bone-In Breasts	2½ to 3 pounds	25 to 35 minutes (7to 9 inches from heat)	170°F
Boneless Skinless Breasts	1¼ pounds	15 to 20 minutes (4 to 6 inches from heat)	170°F
Wings	2 to 2½ pounds	10 minutes (5 to 7 inches from heat)	180°F
TURKEY			
Tenderloins	1 to 1½ pounds	8 to 12 minutes (4 to 6 inches from heat)	170°F
Breast Slices	1 to 1½ pounds	7 minutes (4 to 6 inches from heat)	Until no longer pink in center

**May also be called* cut-up broiler-fryer chicken.

CHAPTER 13

Rice, Grains, Beans & Pasta

LOW-FAT = *3g or less, except main dishes with 10g or less* FAST = *Ready in 20 minutes or less* BREAD MACHINE = *Bread machine directions* SLOW COOKER = *Slow cooker directions* LIGHTER = *25% fewer calories or grams of fat*

◀ **Wheat Berry Salad (page 343)**

Grains Basics

Grains have been around for centuries. So it's no wonder that every culture and cuisine depends upon them greatly in cooking—for creating classics like pilaf, risotto or polenta, mixing up vegetarian dishes or tossing into salads. They're not only versatile and economical, but they offer a wealth of nutrients and fiber too. And don't forget, they're low in fat and contain no cholesterol. Read on—you have all you need to know about grains right here in this chapter.

STORING UNCOOKED GRAINS

- Most uncooked grains can be stored up to 1 year at room temperature in a cool, dry location—and up to 2 years in the freezer.
- Store grains in tightly covered containers, label and date.
- Whole grains containing oil can become rancid and must be stored in the refrigerator or freezer up to 6 months. These include barley; brown rice; bulgur, kasha (roasted buckwheat groats/kernels); stone-ground or whole-grain cornmeal; wheat berries; wheat germ and whole wheat flour.

STORING AND REHEATING COOKED GRAINS

For the best ways to cook grain, check the Timetable for Cooking Grains on page 375. Store cooked grains tightly covered in the refrigerator up to 5 days or freeze up to 6 months.

Reheat grains using one of these methods:

- In a microwavable container, add 1 tablespoon water per cup of cooked grain, tightly cover and microwave on High for 1 to 2 minutes.
- In a covered saucepan, add 2 tablespoons water per cup of cooked grain, heat over low heat.
- Place grain in a colander, and pour boiling water over it until hot.

MAKING PERFECT RICE

- For perfect rice, measure the water and rice carefully.
- Rinse rice only if directed to on the package or in a recipe.
- Stirring makes rice sticky and starchy. The only exception is risotto, which relies on stirring to create its creamy texture.
- If rice is still wet after cooking, cook it uncovered over low heat for a few minutes.

LEARN WITH Betty — COOKING RICE

This rice was not cooked long enough and has hard, white centers.

There are no problems with this rice; the grains are fluffy and separate and are tender but still firm to the bite.

Cooking rice too long causes the grains to split open or fall apart, and the texture becomes mushy.

GRAINS AND RICE

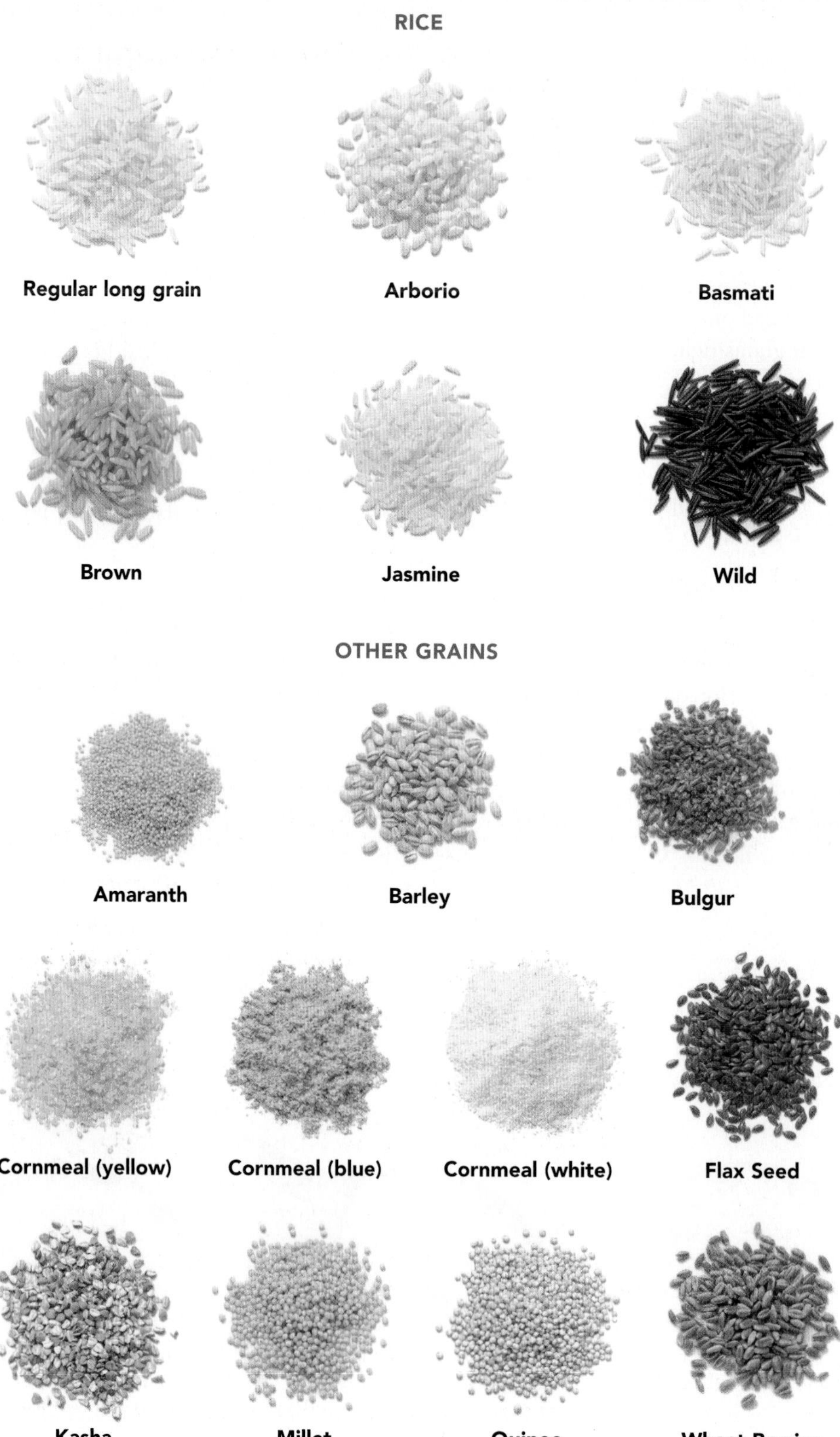

Rice Pilaf

PREP: 5 min **COOK:** 25 min **STAND:** 5 min ■ **4 SERVINGS**

- 2 tablespoons butter or margarine
- 1 small onion, chopped (1/4 cup)
- 1 cup uncooked regular long-grain rice
- 2 cups chicken broth
- 1/4 teaspoon salt

1. In 3-quart saucepan, melt butter over medium heat. Cook onion in butter about 3 minutes, stirring occasionally, until tender.

2. Stir in rice. Cook 5 minutes, stirring frequently. Stir in broth and salt.

3. Heat to boiling, stirring once or twice; reduce heat to low. Cover and simmer 16 minutes (do not lift cover or stir); remove from heat. Let stand covered 5 minutes.

1 SERVING (ABOUT 3/4 CUP): CAL. 260 (CAL. FROM FAT 65); FAT 7g (SAT. FAT 4g); CHOL. 15mg; SODIUM 1,250mg; CARBS. 42g (FIBER 1g); PRO. 7g **% DAILY VALUE:** VIT. A 4%; VIT. C 0%; CALC. 2%; IRON 10% **EXCHANGES:** 2 STARCH, 1 OTHER CARB., 1 FAT **CARB. CHOICES:** 3

CURRY PILAF Stir in 1/2 cup diced dried fruit and raisin mixture, 1/4 teaspoon ground allspice, 1/4 teaspoon ground turmeric and 1/4 teaspoon curry powder with the broth and salt in Step 2.

MUSHROOM PILAF Stir in 1 can (4 oz) mushroom pieces and stems, drained, with the broth and salt in Step 2.

Spanish Rice LOW-FAT

PREP: 10 min **COOK:** 30 min ■ **10 SERVINGS**

- 2 tablespoons vegetable oil
- 1 cup uncooked regular long-grain rice
- 1 medium onion, chopped (1/2 cup)
- 2 1/2 cups water
- 1 1/2 teaspoons salt
- 3/4 teaspoon chili powder
- 1/8 teaspoon garlic powder
- 1 small green bell pepper, chopped (1/2 cup)
- 1 can (8 oz) tomato sauce
- 1 large tomato, seeded and chopped (1 cup)

1. In 10-inch skillet, heat oil over medium heat. Cook rice and onion in oil about 5 minutes, stirring frequently, until rice is golden brown and onion is crisp-tender.

2. Stir in remaining ingredients except tomato. Heat to boiling; reduce heat. Cover and simmer 20 minutes, stirring occasionally. Stir in tomato. Cover and simmer about 5 minutes or until rice is tender.

1 SERVING (ABOUT 1/2 CUP): CAL. 100 (CAL. FROM FAT 25); FAT 3g (SAT. FAT 0g); CHOL. 0mg; SODIUM 510mg; CARBS. 20g (FIBER 1g); PRO. 2g **% DAILY VALUE:** VIT. A 6%; VIT. C 10%; CALC. 2%; IRON 6% **EXCHANGES:** 1 STARCH, 1/2 FAT **CARB. CHOICES:** 1

SPANISH RICE WITH BACON Omit oil. Cut 6 slices bacon into 1-inch pieces. In 10-inch skillet, cook bacon over medium heat, stirring occasionally, until crisp. Remove from skillet with slotted spoon and drain on paper towels. Drain all but 2 tablespoons bacon fat from skillet. Cook rice and onion in bacon fat over medium heat about 5 minutes, stirring frequently, until rice is golden brown and onion is crisp-tender. Continue as directed in Step 2. Stir in bacon just before serving.

FLAVOR-PACKED RICE AND GRAINS

Instead of water, substitute beef, chicken or vegetable broth for all of the water. Or try fruit juices like apple, orange or one of the many combinations. Vegetable juices and wine are other options to explore. If you choose fruit juice, vegetable juice or wine, be sure to use half water because if you replace all of the water with these high-acid ingredients, cooking times may increase significantly for longer-cooking rice or grains.

Classic Risotto

PREP: 10 min **COOK:** 25 min ■ **4 SERVINGS**

Here's the most classic of all risottos! It's called Risotto alla Milanese and is authentically made with saffron and veal marrow. This version is made with all basic ingredients—no marrow or saffron. Since you probably have the ingredients on-hand, stir up a batch anytime the mood strikes.

- 1 tablespoon butter or margarine
- 2 tablespoons olive or vegetable oil
- 1 small onion, thinly sliced
- 1 tablespoon chopped fresh parsley
- 1 cup uncooked Arborio or regular long-grain rice
- 1/2 cup dry white wine or chicken broth
- 3 cups chicken broth, warmed
- 1/2 cup freshly grated or shredded Parmesan cheese
- 1/4 teaspoon coarsely ground pepper

1. In nonstick 10-inch skillet or 3-quart saucepan, heat butter and oil over medium-high heat until butter is melted. Cook onion and parsley in oil mixture about 5 minutes, stirring frequently, until onion is tender.

2. Stir in rice. Cook, stirring occasionally, until edges of kernels are translucent. Stir in wine. Cook about 3 minutes, stirring constantly, until wine is absorbed.

3. Reduce heat to medium. Stir in 1 cup of the broth. Cook uncovered about 5 minutes, stirring frequently, until broth is absorbed. Repeat, adding another 1 cup of broth. Stir in remaining 1 cup broth. Cook about 8 minutes, stirring frequently, until rice is just tender and mixture is creamy.

4. Stir in cheese and pepper.

1 SERVING: CAL. 355 (CAL. FROM FAT 135); FAT 15g (SAT. FAT 5g); CHOL. 15mg; SODIUM 1,020mg; CARBS. 43g (FIBER 1g); PRO. 13g
% DAILY VALUE: VIT. A 6%; VIT. C 2%; CALC. 20%; IRON 12%
EXCHANGES: 3 STARCH, 2 1/2 FAT **CARB. CHOICES:** 3

CLASSIC RISOTTO WITH PEAS Just before serving, stir in 1 box (9 oz) frozen green peas, cooked and drained.

LEARN WITH Betty — COOKING RISOTTO

This risotto was not cooked long enough so stays soupy or watery instead of creamy.

There are no problems with this risotto; it is thickened and creamy.

This risotto was overcooked and is no longer creamy.

Cheesy Broccoli-Rice Bake

PREP: 15 min **BAKE:** 35 min ■ **8 SERVINGS**

1 tablespoon butter or margarine
1 large onion, chopped (1 cup)
1 package (1 lb) pasteurized prepared cheese product loaf, cut into cubes
1 can (10.75 oz) condensed cream of mushroom soup
2/3 cup milk
1/4 teaspoon pepper, if desired
2 cups 1/2-inch pieces broccoli flowerets
3 cups cooked rice (page 375)
1 cup fine soft bread crumbs (about 1 1/2 slices bread)
1 tablespoon butter or margarine, melted

1. Heat oven to 350°F. Spray 13 × 9-inch glass baking dish with cooking spray.

2. In 10-inch skillet, melt 1 tablespoon butter over medium-high heat. Cook onion in butter, stirring occasionally, until crisp-tender; reduce heat to medium. Stir in cheese, soup, milk and pepper. Cook, stirring frequently, until cheese is melted.

3. Stir in broccoli and rice. Spoon into baking dish. In small bowl, mix bread crumbs and 1 tablespoon melted butter; sprinkle over rice mixture.

4. Bake uncovered 30 to 35 minutes or until light brown on top and bubbly around edges.

1 SERVING: CAL. 415 (CAL. FROM FAT 245); FAT 27g (SAT. FAT 16g); CHOL. 70mg; SODIUM 1,150mg; CARBS. 26g (FIBER 1g); PRO. 17g **% DAILY VALUE:** VIT. A 24%; VIT. C 18%; CALC. 36%; IRON 8% **EXCHANGES:** 1 1/2 STARCH, 1 VEGETABLE, 1 1/2 MEDIUM-FAT MEAT, 3 1/2 FAT **CARB. CHOICES:** 2

LIGHTER CHEESY BROCCOLI-RICE BAKE

For 9 grams of fat and 275 calories per serving, omit 2 tablespoons butter; spray skillet with cooking spray. Use light pasteurized prepared cheese product loaf, condensed 98% fat-free cream of mushroom soup and fat-free (skim) milk. Omit bread crumbs.

Pork Fried Rice

PREP: 15 min **COOK:** 10 min ■ **4 SERVINGS**

Using cold day-old rice is best so the grains stay separate during frying.

1 cup bean sprouts
2 tablespoons vegetable oil
1 cup sliced fresh mushrooms (3 oz)
3 cups cold cooked regular long-grain rice (page 375)
1 cup cut-up cooked pork
2 medium green onions, sliced (2 tablespoons)
2 large eggs, slightly beaten
3 tablespoons soy sauce
Dash of white pepper

1. Rinse bean sprouts with cold water; drain.

2. In 10-inch skillet, heat 1 tablespoon of the oil over medium heat; rotate skillet until oil covers bottom. Cook mushrooms in oil about 1 minute, stirring frequently, until coated.

3. Add bean sprouts, rice, pork and onions to skillet. Cook over medium heat about 5 minutes, stirring and breaking up rice, until hot.

4. Move rice mixture to side of skillet. Add remaining 1 tablespoon oil to other side of skillet. Cook eggs in oil over medium heat, stirring constantly, until eggs are thickened throughout but still moist. Stir eggs into rice mixture. Stir in soy sauce and pepper.

1 SERVING (ABOUT 1 CUP): CAL. 350 (CAL. FROM FAT 125); FAT 14g (SAT. FAT 3g); CHOL. 135mg; SODIUM 740mg; CARBS. 37g (FIBER 1g); PRO. 20g **% DAILY VALUE:** VIT. A 4%; VIT. C 4%; CALC. 4%; IRON 16% **EXCHANGES:** 2 STARCH, 1 VEGETABLE, 2 MEDIUM-FAT MEAT, 1/2 FAT **CARB. CHOICES:** 2 1/2

LIGHTER PORK FRIED RICE

For 3 grams of fat and 240 calories per serving, decrease pork to 1/2 cup and finely chop. Use nonstick skillet and omit oil in Step 4. Substitute 1/2 cup fat-free cholesterol-free egg product for the eggs.

SHRIMP FRIED RICE Omit pork. Substitute 1 cup frozen cooked salad shrimp, thawed, for the pork.

Polenta LOW-FAT

PREP: 10 min **COOK:** 20 min ▪ **6 SERVINGS**

- 1 cup yellow cornmeal
- 3/4 cup water
- 3 1/4 cups boiling water
- 1 1/2 teaspoons salt

1. In 2-quart saucepan, mix cornmeal and 3/4 cup water. Stir in 3 1/4 cups boiling water and the salt. Cook over medium heat 8 to 10 minutes, stirring constantly, until mixture thickens and boils; reduce heat.

2. Cover and simmer about 10 minutes, stirring occasionally, until very thick; remove from heat. Stir until smooth.

1 SERVING (ABOUT 3/4 CUP): CAL. 80 (CAL. FROM FAT 0); FAT 0g (SAT. FAT 0g); CHOL. 0mg; SODIUM 590mg; CARBS. 18g (FIBER 2g); PRO. 2g **% DAILY VALUE:** VIT. A 0%; VIT. C 0%; CALC. 0%; IRON 4% **EXCHANGES:** 1 STARCH **CARB. CHOICES:** 1

FRIED POLENTA Spray 9 × 5-inch loaf pan with cooking spray. After simmering polenta 10 minutes in Step 2, spread in loaf pan. Cover and refrigerate at least 12 hours until firm. Turn pan upside down to unmold. Cut into 1/2-inch slices. Coat slices with flour. In 10-inch skillet, melt 2 tablespoons butter or margarine over low heat. Cook slices in butter about 5 minutes on each side or until brown. Serve with molasses, jam, maple syrup, sour cream or tomato pasta sauce if desired.

For Faster Fried Polenta, spread polenta in sprayed 13 × 9-inch pan; refrigerate uncovered about 3 hours or until firm. Cut into 6 squares. (Cut squares diagonally into triangles if desired.) Cook in butter as directed.

Cheese Grits

PREP: 20 min **BAKE:** 40 min **STAND:** 10 min ▪ **8 SERVINGS**

Down South, coarsely ground dried corn kernels called hominy grits are a treasured tradition. A bowl of this steaming hot favorite, topped with a pat of butter, often arrives with breakfast. This cheesy version frequently appears at buffets, patio luncheons and casual suppers.

- 2 cups milk
- 2 cups water
- 1/2 teaspoon salt
- 1/4 teaspoon pepper
- 1 cup uncooked white hominy quick grits
- 1 1/2 cups shredded Cheddar cheese (6 oz)
- 2 medium green onions, sliced (2 tablespoons)
- 2 large eggs, slightly beaten
- 1 tablespoon butter or margarine
- 1/4 teaspoon paprika

1. Heat oven to 350°F. Spray 1 1/2-quart casserole with cooking spray.

2. In 2-quart saucepan, heat milk, water, salt and pepper to boiling. Gradually add grits, stirring constantly; reduce heat. Simmer uncovered about 5 minutes, stirring frequently, until thickened. Stir in cheese and onions.

3. Stir 1 cup of the grits mixture into eggs, then stir back into remaining grits in saucepan. Pour into casserole. Cut butter into small pieces; sprinkle over grits. Sprinkle with paprika.

4. Bake uncovered 35 to 40 minutes or until set. Let stand 10 minutes before serving.

1 SERVING: CAL. 220 (CAL. FROM FAT 100); FAT 11g (SAT. FAT 7g); CHOL. 85mg; SODIUM 340mg; CARBS. 19g (FIBER 0g); PRO. 11g **% DAILY VALUE:** VIT. A 10%; VIT. C 0%; CALC. 20%; IRON 6% **EXCHANGES:** 1 STARCH, 1 HIGH-FAT MEAT, 1 FAT **CARB. CHOICES:** 1

LIGHTER CHEESE GRITS

For 1 gram of fat and 125 calories per serving, use fat-free (skim) milk, use reduced-fat Cheddar cheese and decrease amount to 1 cup, and substitute 1/2 cup fat-free cholesterol-free egg product for the eggs. Omit butter.

Barley-Vegetable Sauté

FAST **LOW-FAT**

PREP: 10 min **COOK:** 7 min ■ **4 SERVINGS**

Look for barley in two different varieties—regular and quick-cooking. Plan on 45 to 50 minutes for cooking regular barley. If you're in a hurry, choose the quick-cooking kind that takes just 10 to 12 minutes.

- 2 teaspoons butter or margarine
- 1 large onion, chopped (1 cup)
- 1 medium yellow or red bell pepper, chopped (1 cup)
- 1 clove garlic, finely chopped
- 4 cups cooked barley (page 375)
- 2 tablespoons chopped fresh or 2 teaspoons dried thyme leaves
- 1/2 teaspoon salt
- 1 bag (1 lb) frozen whole kernel corn, thawed
- 1 box (9 oz) frozen lima beans, thawed

1. In 10-inch skillet, melt butter over medium-high heat. Cook onion, bell pepper and garlic in butter about 2 minutes, stirring occasionally, until bell pepper is crisp-tender.

2. Stir in remaining ingredients. Cook about 5 minutes, stirring occasionally, until hot.

1 SERVING: CAL. 345 (CAL. FROM FAT 25); FAT 3g (SAT. FAT 1g); CHOL. 5mg; SODIUM 360mg; CARBS. 82g (FIBER 16g); PRO. 13g
% DAILY VALUE: VIT. A 12%; VIT. C 56%; CALC. 4%; IRON 16%
EXCHANGES: 3 1/2 STARCH, 1 OTHER CARB., 1 VEGETABLE
CARB. CHOICES: 5

Wheat Berry Salad

PREP: 10 min **SOAK:** 30 min **COOK:** 1 hr **CHILL:** 1 hr ■ **10 SERVINGS**

Wheat berries are whole, unprocessed kernels of wheat. Look for wheat berries in the cereal, self-serve bulk foods or natural-foods section of your supermarket.

Wheat Berries

- 3/4 cup uncooked wheat berries
- 3 cups water

Creamy Vinaigrette Dressing

- 1/3 cup vegetable oil
- 2 tablespoons mayonnaise or salad dressing
- 2 tablespoons red wine vinegar
- 1/2 teaspoon salt
- 1/4 teaspoon garlic powder
- 1/8 teaspoon pepper

Salad

- 1 cup chopped broccoli
- 1 cup chopped cauliflower
- 1 cup cherry tomatoes, cut in half
- 1 small green bell pepper, chopped (1/2 cup)
- 4 medium green onions, sliced (1/4 cup)
- 1/2 cup crumbled feta cheese

1. In 3-quart saucepan, soak wheat berries in water 30 minutes. Heat to boiling over high heat. Reduce heat to low. Partially cover and simmer 55 to 60 minutes or until wheat berries are tender. Drain and rinse with cold water.

2. In small bowl, stir all dressing ingredients until well mixed.

3. In large serving bowl, toss wheat berries, salad ingredients and dressing. Cover and refrigerate at least 1 hour.

1 SERVING: CAL. 155 (CAL. FROM FAT 100); FAT 11g (SAT. FAT 3g); CHOL. 10mg; SODIUM 230mg; CARBS. 11g (FIBER 3g); PRO. 3g
% DAILY VALUE: VIT. A 6%; VIT. C 40%; CALC. 4%; IRON 4%
EXCHANGES: 1/2 STARCH, 1 VEGETABLE, 2 FAT **CARB. CHOICES:** 1

Bulgur Pilaf

PREP: 15 min **COOK:** 25 min ▪ **6 SERVINGS**

2 tablespoons butter or margarine
1/2 cup slivered almonds
1 medium onion, chopped (1/2 cup)
1 medium carrot, chopped (1/2 cup)
1 can (14 oz) chicken broth
1 cup uncooked bulgur
1/4 teaspoon lemon pepper seasoning salt or regular pepper
1/4 cup chopped fresh parsley

1. In 12-inch skillet, melt 1 tablespoon of the butter over medium-high heat. Cook almonds in butter 2 to 3 minutes, stirring constantly, until golden brown. Remove almonds from skillet.

2. Add remaining 1 tablespoon butter, the onion and carrot to skillet. Cook about 3 minutes, stirring occasionally, until vegetables are crisp-tender.

3. Stir in broth, bulgur and lemon pepper seasoning salt. Heat to boiling; reduce heat. Cover and simmer about 15 minutes or until bulgur is tender and liquid is absorbed. Stir in almonds and parsley.

1 SERVING (ABOUT 1/2 CUP): CAL. 175 (CAL. FROM FAT 80); FAT 9g (SAT. FAT 3g); CHOL. 10mg; SODIUM 330mg; CARBS. 23g (FIBER 6g); PRO. 7g **% DAILY VALUE:** VIT. A 44%; VIT. C 4%; CALC. 4%; IRON 8% **EXCHANGES:** 1 STARCH, 1 VEGETABLE, 1 1/2 FAT **CARB. CHOICES:** 1 1/2

Lemon Millet Pilaf LOW-FAT

PREP: 10 min **COOK:** 25 min ▪ **6 SERVINGS**

1 can (14 oz) chicken broth
1/3 cup water
1/4 teaspoon onion powder
1/2 cup uncooked millet
1/2 cup uncooked regular long grain rice
1/2 cup frozen whole kernel corn (from 1-lb bag)
1/2 cup coarsely chopped fresh parsley
1 teaspoon grated lemon peel

1. In 2-quart saucepan, heat broth, water and onion powder to boiling. Stir in millet, rice and corn; reduce heat.

2. Cover and simmer 15 to 20 minutes or until millet and rice are tender and liquid is absorbed. Stir in parsley and lemon peel. Serve immediately.

1 SERVING: CAL. 145 (CAL. FROM FAT 10); FAT 1g (SAT. FAT 0g); CHOL. 0mg; SODIUM 300mg; CARBS. 29g (FIBER 2g); PRO. 5g **% DAILY VALUE:** VIT. A 8%; VIT. C 6%; CALC. 2%; IRON 8% **EXCHANGES:** 1 STARCH, 1 OTHER CARB. **CARB. CHOICES:** 2

Kasha and Bow-Tie Pilaf

PREP: 10 min **COOK:** 25 min ▪ **12 SERVINGS**

3 tablespoons butter or margarine
2 medium onions, coarsely chopped (1 cup)
1 medium red bell pepper, coarsely chopped (1 cup)
1 cup sliced fresh mushrooms (4 oz)
1 cup uncooked whole kasha (buckwheat groats)
1 egg, beaten
2 cups chicken broth
1/2 teaspoon salt
1/4 teaspoon pepper
1 cup uncooked farfalle (bow-tie) pasta (2 oz)
1/2 cup chopped fresh parsley

1. In 12-inch nonstick skillet, melt butter over medium heat. Cook onions, bell pepper and mushrooms in butter 3 to 4 minutes, stirring occasionally, until tender. Remove from skillet to plate.

2. In small bowl, stir kasha and egg, coating well. Cook kasha in same skillet over medium heat about 3 minutes, stirring constantly, until browned and dry.

3. Return vegetables to skillet with kasha; stir in broth, salt and pepper. Heat to boiling; reduce heat to low. Cover and simmer 10 to 15 minutes or until broth is absorbed and kasha is tender.

4. Meanwhile, cook and drain pasta as directed on package. Stir cooked pasta and parsley into kasha mixture.

1 SERVING: CAL. 105 (CAL. FROM FAT 35); FAT 4g (SAT. FAT 2g); CHOL. 25mg; SODIUM 300mg; CARBS. 13g (FIBER 2g); PRO. 4g **% DAILY VALUE:** VIT. A 18%; VIT. C 18%; CALC. 2%; IRON 4% **EXCHANGES:** 1 STARCH, 1/2 FAT **CARB. CHOICES:** 1

Kasha and Bow-Tie Pilaf ▶

Creamy Quinoa Primavera

Creamy Quinoa Primavera

PREP: 10 min **COOK:** 25 min ▪ **6 SERVINGS**

Quinoa, pronounced "KEEN-wa," was a staple grain of the Incas of Peru. It's very mild in flavor, and loaded with nutrients. Before cooking quinoa, rinse it thoroughly to remove its natural bitter coating.

1 1/2 cups uncooked quinoa
3 cups chicken broth
1 package (3 oz) cream cheese
1 tablespoon chopped fresh or 1 teaspoon dried basil leaves
2 teaspoons butter or margarine
2 cloves garlic, finely chopped
5 cups thinly sliced or bite-size pieces assorted uncooked vegetables (such as asparagus, broccoli, carrot or zucchini)
2 tablespoons grated Romano cheese

1. Rinse quinoa thoroughly; drain. In 2-quart saucepan, heat quinoa and broth to boiling; reduce heat. Cover and simmer 15 to 20 minutes or until all broth is absorbed. Stir in cream cheese and basil.

2. In 10-inch nonstick skillet, melt butter over medium-high heat. Cook garlic in butter about 30 seconds, stirring frequently, until golden. Stir in vegetables. Cook 2 to 4 minutes, stirring frequently, until vegetables are crisp-tender.

3. In skillet, toss vegetables and quinoa mixture. Sprinkle with Romano cheese.

1 SERVING: CAL. 265 (CAL. FROM FAT 90); FAT 10g (SAT. FAT 5g); CHOL. 20mg; SODIUM 630mg; CARBS. 36g (FIBER 5g); PRO. 12g **% DAILY VALUE:** VIT. A 90%; VIT. C 24%; CALC. 10%; IRON 26% **EXCHANGES:** 2 STARCH, 1 VEGETABLE, 1/2 MEDIUM-FAT MEAT, 1 FAT **CARB. CHOICES:** 2 1/2

Legumes Basics

Good things come in small packages—especially when you're talking about legumes (often referred to as beans). In spite of their tiny size, legumes are packed with protein, fiber, vitamins and minerals and are fat-free and cholesterol-free. Look for them dried, canned or frozen, in a colorful array of different varieties. You'll soon discover legumes are extremely versatile, have a mild flavor and make perfect partners with any herbs and spices. See Timetable for Cooking Legumes, page 376, for specific cooking directions.

STORING UNCOOKED AND COOKED LEGUMES

Uncooked: Most uncooked dried legumes can be stored up to one year at room temperature in a cool, dry location. Store in tightly covered containers, label and date.

Cooked: Cover and store cooked legumes in the refrigerator two to three days, or freeze in airtight containers up to six months.

SOAKING DRIED LEGUMES BEFORE COOKING

With the exception of black-eyed peas, lentils and split peas, dried legumes need to be soaked before cooking to soften and plump them. Soaking also makes legumes more digestible by dissolving sugars that cause intestinal gas. After soaking dried beans, drain the water and cook the legumes in fresh, cold water. Because legumes rehydrate to triple their dry size, choose a pot that's big enough.

There are two methods for soaking legumes. Choose the one that fits your time schedule best:

- **Quick-Soak Method:** Place dried legumes in a large saucepan; add enough water to cover them. Heat to boiling; boil 2 minutes. Remove from heat, cover and let stand for at least 1 hour before cooking. Drain, then cook in fresh, cold water.
- **Long-Soak Method:** Place dried legumes in a large saucepan or bowl; add enough cold water to cover them. Let stand 8 to 24 hours. Drain, then cook in fresh, cold water.

COOKING DRIED LEGUMES

- Use legumes of similar size and cooking times interchangeably in recipes.
- Reduce foaming and boilovers during cooking, by adding 1 tablespoon butter, margarine, olive oil or vegetable oil to the cooking water. Drain legumes and rinse. If the water does foam, skim it off once or twice.
- Salt and acidic ingredients like lemon juice, vinegar, tomatoes (whole, sauce, paste or juice) and wine toughen legumes, so add them only after legumes are soft and tender.
- If cooking legumes in high altitudes or hard water, you may need to increase the cooking time.
- Using a pressure cooker isn't recommended because foam can form during cooking and clog the pressure valve, causing a sudden release of pressure and possibly forcing the lid off.

DRIED BEAN YIELDS

When buying or cooking beans, use this chart as a guide.

This Amount	Equals
8 ounces dried beans	1 cup uncooked
1 pound dried beans	2 cups uncooked
1 cup dried beans	2 to 3 cups cooked
2 cups dried beans	4 to 6 cups cooked
1 can (15 to 16 ounces) cooked beans, drained	1 1/2 to 2 cups

LEGUMES

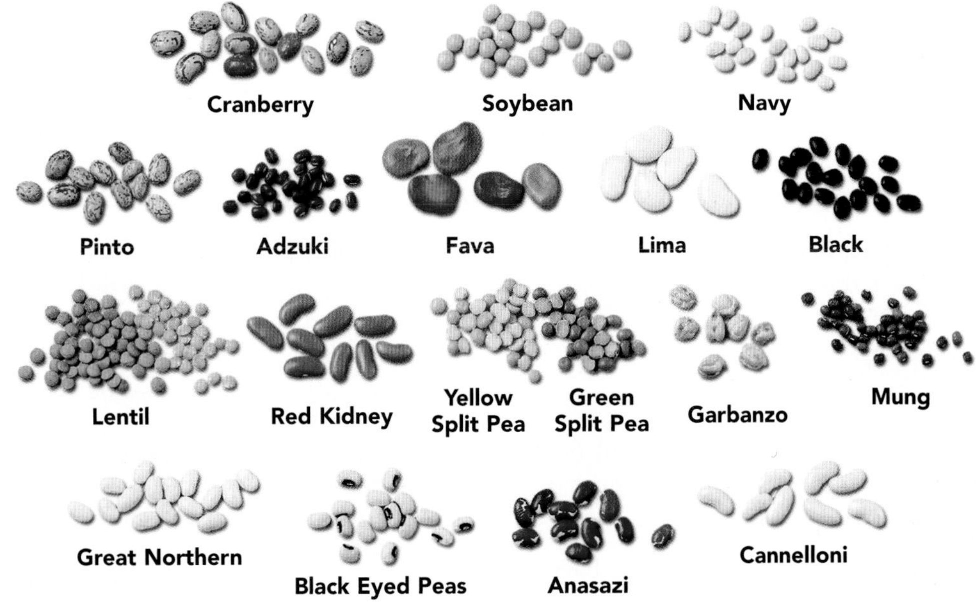

Old-Fashioned Baked Beans LOW-FAT

PREP: 20 min **BAKE:** 6 hr 15 min ▪ **10 SERVINGS**

Nothing's more comforting than a pot of Mom's baked beans. Start creating food memories for you and your family today with this old-fashioned favorite flavored with the spark of onion and the sweetness of molasses.

- 2 cups dried navy beans (1 lb), sorted and rinsed
- 10 cups water
- 1/2 cup packed brown sugar
- 1/4 cup molasses
- 1 teaspoon salt
- 6 slices bacon, crisply cooked and crumbled (about 1/3 cup)
- 1 medium onion, chopped (1/2 cup)
- 3 cups water

1. Heat oven to 350°F.

2. In ovenproof 4-quart Dutch oven, heat beans and 10 cups water to boiling. Boil uncovered 2 minutes. Stir in remaining ingredients except 3 cups water.

3. Cover and bake 4 hours, stirring occasionally.

4. Stir in 3 cups water. Bake uncovered 2 hours to 2 hours 15 minutes longer, stirring occasionally, until beans are tender and desired consistency.

1 SERVING (ABOUT 1/2 CUP): CAL. 200 (CAL. FROM FAT 20); FAT 2g (SAT. FAT 1g); CHOL. 5mg; SODIUM 300mg; CARBS. 42g (FIBER 6g); PRO. 10g **% DAILY VALUE:** VIT. A 0%; VIT. C 0%; CALC. 10%; IRON 16% **EXCHANGES:** 2 STARCH, 2 VEGETABLE **CARB. CHOICES:** 3

SLOW COOKER DIRECTIONS

In 3 1/2- to 6-quart slow cooker, place beans and 5 cups water. Cover and cook on High heat setting 2 hours. Turn off heat; let stand 8 to 24 hours. Stir in brown sugar, molasses, salt, bacon and onion. Cover and cook on Low heat setting 10 to 12 hours or until beans are very tender and most of liquid is absorbed.

Easy Skillet Baked Beans

PREP: 15 min **COOK:** 30 min ▪ **4 SERVINGS**

Chili sauce is a sweet and sassy condiment that looks just like ketchup but it's usually thicker and spicier, thanks to its chilies and flavorings. Look for it right next to the ketchup in your grocery store.

- 3 slices bacon, cut into 1-inch pieces
- 1 medium onion, chopped (1/2 cup)
- 2 cans (15 oz each) pork and beans
- 1/4 cup chili sauce
- 1 teaspoon yellow mustard

1. In 10-inch skillet, cook bacon and onion over medium heat 8 to 10 minutes, stirring occasionally, until bacon is crisp.

2. Stir in remaining ingredients. Heat to boiling; reduce heat. Simmer uncovered 15 to 20 minutes, stirring occasionally, until liquid is absorbed.

1 SERVING (ABOUT 1 CUP): CAL. 245 (CAL. FROM FAT 45); FAT 5g (SAT. FAT 2g); CHOL. 20mg; SODIUM 1,230mg; CARBS. 48g (FIBER 11g); PRO. 13g **% DAILY VALUE:** VIT. A 44%; VIT. C 8%; CALC. 12%; IRON 40% **EXCHANGES:** 3 STARCH **CARB. CHOICES:** 3

EASY OVEN BAKED BEANS Heat oven to 350°F. After boiling mixture in Step 2, pour into ungreased 1 1/2-quart casserole. Bake uncovered about 40 minutes.

Three-Bean Casserole

PREP: 10 min **COOK:** 10 **BAKE:** 45 min ▪ **8 SERVINGS**

You know you have a winning recipe when it shows up again and again, no matter where you are or whatever the occasion. And so it is with this terrific three-bean recipe that's perfect for potlucks and other gatherings.

- 1 lb bulk pork sausage
- 2 medium stalks celery, sliced (1 cup)
- 1 medium onion, chopped (1/2 cup)
- 1 large clove garlic, finely chopped
- 2 cans (21 oz each) baked beans (any variety)
- 1 can (15 to 16 oz) lima or butter beans, drained
- 1 can (15 to 16 oz) kidney beans, drained
- 1 can (8 oz) tomato sauce
- 1 tablespoon ground mustard
- 2 tablespoons honey or packed brown sugar
- 1 tablespoon white or cider vinegar
- 1/4 teaspoon red pepper sauce

1. Heat oven to 400°F.

2. In 10-inch skillet, cook sausage, celery, onion and garlic over medium heat 8 to 10 minutes, stirring occasionally, until sausage is no longer pink; drain.

3. Mix sausage mixture and remaining ingredients in ungreased 3-quart casserole. Bake uncovered about 45 minutes, stirring once, until hot and bubbly.

1 SERVING (ABOUT 1 1/3 CUPS): CAL. 365 (CAL. FROM FAT 90); FAT 10g (SAT. FAT 3g); CHOL. 20mg; SODIUM 1400mg; CARBS. 62g (FIBER 15g); PRO. 22g **% DAILY VALUE:** VIT. A 32%; VIT. C 8%; CALC. 12%; IRON 22% **EXCHANGES:** 4 STARCH, 1 FAT **CARB. CHOICES:** 4

SLOW COOKER DIRECTIONS

Substitute 1/2 cup ketchup for the tomato sauce. Decrease honey to 1 tablespoon. In 10-inch skillet, cook sausage, celery, onion and garlic over medium heat 8 to 10 minutes, stirring occasionally, until sausage is no longer pink; drain. In 3 1/2- to 6-quart slow cooker, mix sausage mixture and remaining ingredients. Cover and cook on High heat setting 2 hours to 2 hours 30 minutes to blend flavors.

BEEFY BARBECUE THREE-BEAN CASSEROLE Substitute 1 lb lean (at least 80%) ground beef for the pork sausage and 1 cup barbecue sauce for the tomato sauce.

Red Beans and Rice

PREP: 10 min **COOK:** 1 hr 45 min **STAND:** 5 min ■ **8 SERVINGS**

Simmer, don't boil, dried beans after they start cooking. Boiling beans too long can cause them to fall apart.

- 1 cup dried kidney beans (8 oz), sorted and rinsed*
- 3 cups water
- 2 oz salt pork (with rind), diced, or 3 slices bacon, cut up
- 1 medium onion, chopped (1/2 cup)
- 1 medium green bell pepper, chopped (1 cup)
- 1 cup uncooked regular long-grain rice
- 1 teaspoon salt

1. In 3-quart saucepan, heat beans and water to boiling. Boil uncovered 2 minutes; reduce heat. Cover and simmer 1 hour to 1 hour 15 minutes or until tender (do not boil or beans will fall apart).

2. Drain beans, reserving liquid. In 10-inch skillet, cook salt pork over medium heat, stirring occasionally, until crisp. Stir in onion and bell pepper. Cook, stirring occasionally, until onion is tender.

3. Add enough water to bean liquid, if necessary, to measure 2 cups. Add bean liquid, salt pork mixture, rice and salt to beans in 3-quart saucepan. Heat to boiling, stirring once or twice; reduce heat. Cover and simmer 14 minutes (do not lift cover or stir); remove from heat. Fluff with fork. Cover and let steam 5 to 10 minutes.

**1 can (15 to 16 oz) red kidney beans (drained and liquid reserved) can be substituted for the dried kidney beans. Omit water and Step 1.*

1 SERVING (ABOUT 3/4 CUP): CAL. 205 (CAL. FROM FAT 35); FAT 4g (SAT. FAT 2g); CHOL. 5mg; SODIUM 360mg; CARBS. 35g (FIBER 4g); PRO. 7g **% DAILY VALUE:** VIT. A 0%; VIT. C 12%; CALC. 2%; IRON 14% **EXCHANGES:** 2 STARCH, 1 VEGETABLE, 1/2 FAT **CARB. CHOICES:** 2

SLOW COOKER DIRECTIONS

Increase water to 3 1/4 cups. Use 1 1/3 cups uncooked instant rice. In 3 1/2- to 6-quart slow cooker, mix all ingredients except rice. Cover and cook on High heat setting 3 hours 30 minutes to 4 hours 30 minutes or until beans are tender. Stir in rice. Cover and cook on High heat setting 15 minutes. Stir well.

HOPPIN' JOHN Substitute 1 cup dried black-eyed peas for the kidney beans. Omit bell pepper.

Caribbean Black Beans

LOW-FAT

PREP: 15 min **COOK:** 55 min ■ **5 SERVINGS**

- 4 1/2 cups water
- 1 1/2 cups dried black beans*
- 2 teaspoons vegetable oil
- 1 medium papaya, peeled, seeded and diced (about 1 1/2 cups)
- 1 medium red bell pepper, finely chopped (1 cup)
- 1/2 cup finely chopped red onion (about 1/2 medium)
- 1/2 cup orange juice
- 1/4 cup lime juice
- 2 tablespoons chopped fresh cilantro
- 1/2 teaspoon ground red pepper (cayenne)
- 2 cloves garlic, finely chopped
- 5 cups hot cooked rice (page 375)

1. In 2-quart saucepan, heat water and beans to boiling. Boil uncovered 2 minutes; reduce heat. Cover and simmer about 45 minutes, stirring occasionally, until beans are tender; drain.

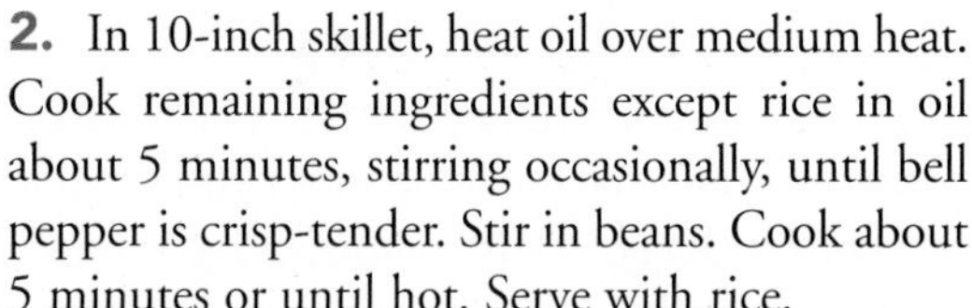

2. In 10-inch skillet, heat oil over medium heat. Cook remaining ingredients except rice in oil about 5 minutes, stirring occasionally, until bell pepper is crisp-tender. Stir in beans. Cook about 5 minutes or until hot. Serve with rice.

**2 cans (15 oz each) black beans, rinsed and drained, can be substituted for the dried black beans. Omit water and Step 1.*

1 SERVING: CAL. 425 (CAL. FROM FAT 25); FAT 3g (SAT. FAT 1g); CHOL. 0mg; SODIUM 10mg; CARBS. 93g (FIBER 11g); PRO. 17g
% DAILY VALUE: VIT. A 42%; VIT. C 80%; CALC. 14%; IRON 30%
EXCHANGES: 4 STARCH, 2 FRUIT **CARB. CHOICES:** 6

◀ **Caribbean Black Beans**

Spicy Split Peas

PREP: 10 min **COOK:** 40 min ■ **4 SERVINGS**

- 3 cups water
- 3/4 cup dried green or yellow split peas (6 oz), sorted and rinsed
- 2 tablespoons butter or margarine
- 1 teaspoon finely chopped gingerroot or 1/4 teaspoon ground ginger
- 1/2 teaspoon salt
- 1/2 teaspoon ground turmeric
- 1/2 teaspoon ground cumin
- 1 small onion, finely chopped (1/4 cup)

1. In 3-quart saucepan, heat water and peas to boiling. Boil uncovered 2 minutes; reduce heat to low. Cover and simmer about 25 minutes or until peas are tender but not mushy; drain.

2. In 10-inch skillet, melt butter over medium-high heat. Cook gingerroot, salt, turmeric, cumin and onion in butter about 3 minutes, stirring occasionally, until onion is tender. Stir in peas until evenly coated.

1 SERVING: CAL. 150 (CAL. FROM FAT 55); FAT 6g (SAT. FAT 4g); CHOL. 15mg; SODIUM 340mg; CARBS. 24g (FIBER 9g); PRO. 9g
% DAILY VALUE: VIT. A 6%; VIT. C 0%; CALC. 2%; IRON 8%
EXCHANGES: 1 1/2 STARCH, 1/2 FAT **CARB. CHOICES:** 1 1/2

LIGHTER SPICY SPLIT PEAS

For 3 grams of fat and 120 calories per serving, decrease butter to 1 tablespoon and use nonstick skillet.

Pasta Basics

Everyone loves pasta! Pasta's easy to find, fresh or dried, and simple to store. Keep pasta on-hand for quick meals at your fingertips. Stuff it, stir-fry it or just sauce it. Toss it into salads, layer it with cheese, or bake it in casseroles. However you serve it, the compliments are sure to come!

SELECTING PASTA

Dried Pasta: Look for unbroken pieces. Avoid dried pasta with a marbled surface (many fine lines); this indicates a drying problem, and the pasta may fall apart during cooking.

Fresh Pasta: Look for smooth, evenly colored, unbroken pieces. Fresh pasta may look dry, but it shouldn't be brittle or crumbly. Avoid packages with moisture droplets or liquid because the pasta may be moldy or mushy.

Frozen Pasta: Avoid packages with the pieces frozen together in a solid block, or those with ice crystals or freezer burn (dry, white spots).

STORING PASTA

Dried: Pasta can be stored up to 1 year at room temperature in a cool, dry location. Store in tightly covered containers, label and date.

Fresh: Refrigerate and use it by the "use by" date on the package. Store opened, uncooked pasta in a tightly covered container for no more than 3 days.

Frozen: Store unopened pasta in its original package in the freezer until ready to cook. Put unused amounts in airtight containers to avoid freezer burn. Freeze unopened pasta up to 9 months, opened pasta up to 3 months.

Homemade Pasta: If it's completely dried, store like dried pasta. Refrigerate freshly made pasta in a tightly covered container up to 3 days or freeze up to 1 month.

COOKING PASTA

- Pasta shapes can be substituted for one another, as long as they're similar in size.
- Use 1 quart (4 cups) water for every 4 ounces of pasta. The water should be boiling vigorously before adding the pasta. Add pasta gradually and stir frequently during cooking to prevent it from sticking together.
- Don't add oil to the cooking water. It isn't necessary, and sauces won't cling when tossed with oil-coated pasta.
- Salt isn't necessary for cooking, but it does add flavor. As a guide, use 1/2 teaspoon salt for every 8 ounces of pasta.
- Follow the package directions for cooking times. If using pasta in a baked dish or casserole, slightly undercook the pasta; it should be flexible but still firm. While the pasta bakes in the oven, it becomes more tender as it soaks up the sauce.
- Cooked pasta should be al dente, or tender but firm to the bite, without any raw flavor. Overcooked pasta is mushy and watery and loses its flavor.
- Do not rinse pasta after draining unless a recipe says to do so, or sauces won't cling. Pasta usually is rinsed only when it's used in cold salads.

PASTA YIELDS

When making pasta, plan on 1/2 to 3/4 cup cooked pasta per side-dish or appetizer serving. For main dishes, plan on 1 1/4 to 1 1/2 cups per serving.

Two ounces (2/3 cup) dried pasta will yield approximately 1 cup of cooked pasta. This will vary slightly depending on the shape, type and size of pasta.

To measure 4 ounces of spaghetti easily, make a circle with your thumb and index finger, about the size of a quarter, and fill it with pasta.

Uncooked	Cooked	Servings
SHORT PASTAS		
Penne, Rotini, Shells, Wagon Wheels, 6 to 7 ounces (2 cups)	4 cups	4 main dish to 6 side dish
LONG PASTAS		
Capellini, Linguine, Spaghetti, Vermicelli, 7 to 8 ounces	4 cups	4 main dish to 6 side dish
NOODLES		
8 ounces (cup amount varies for different noodle sizes)	4 to 5 cups	4 main dish to 6 side dish

STORING AND REHEATING COOKED PASTA

Toss cooked pasta with a small amount of vegetable or olive oil (1 to 2 teaspoons per pound of pasta) to prevent sticking during storage. Cover cooked pasta tightly and store in the refrigerator up to 5 days or freeze up to 2 months.

Reheat pasta using one of these methods:

- In microwavable container, cover and microwave on High for 1 to 2 minutes per 2 cups of pasta or until heated through.
- Heat water to boiling; remove from heat, immediately add cooked pasta and let stand 1 to 2 minutes (do not let water boil again or pasta will get too soft); drain.
- Place pasta in a colander, and pour boiling water over it until hot.

ASIAN NOODLES

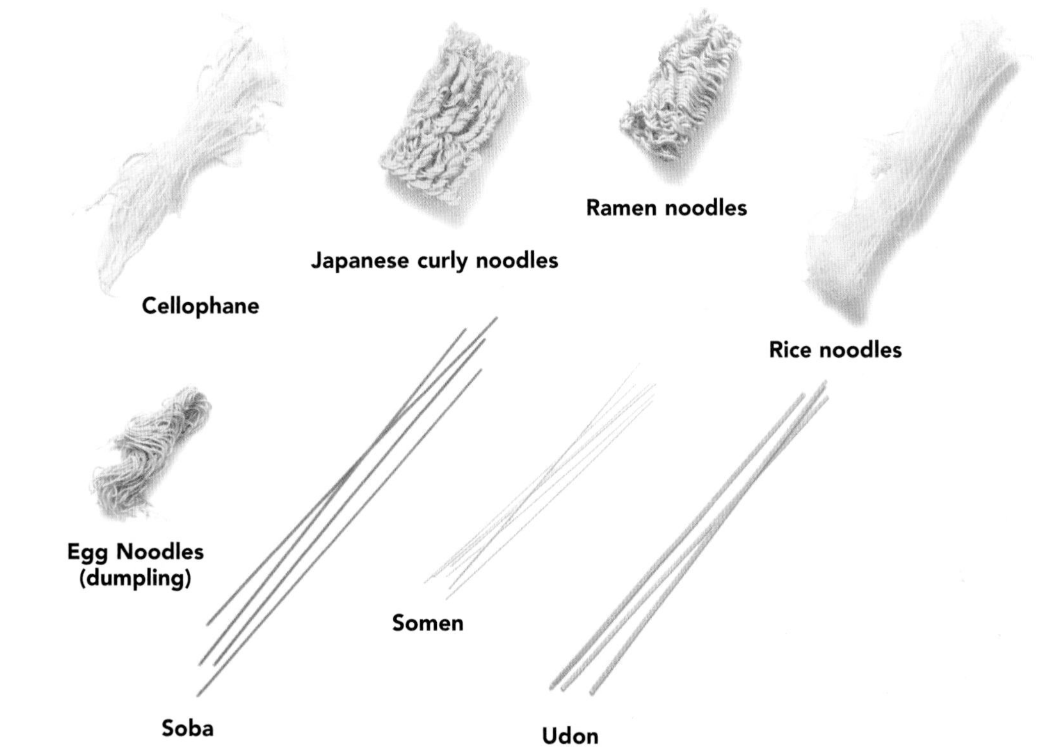

LONG AND LARGE PASTA SHAPES

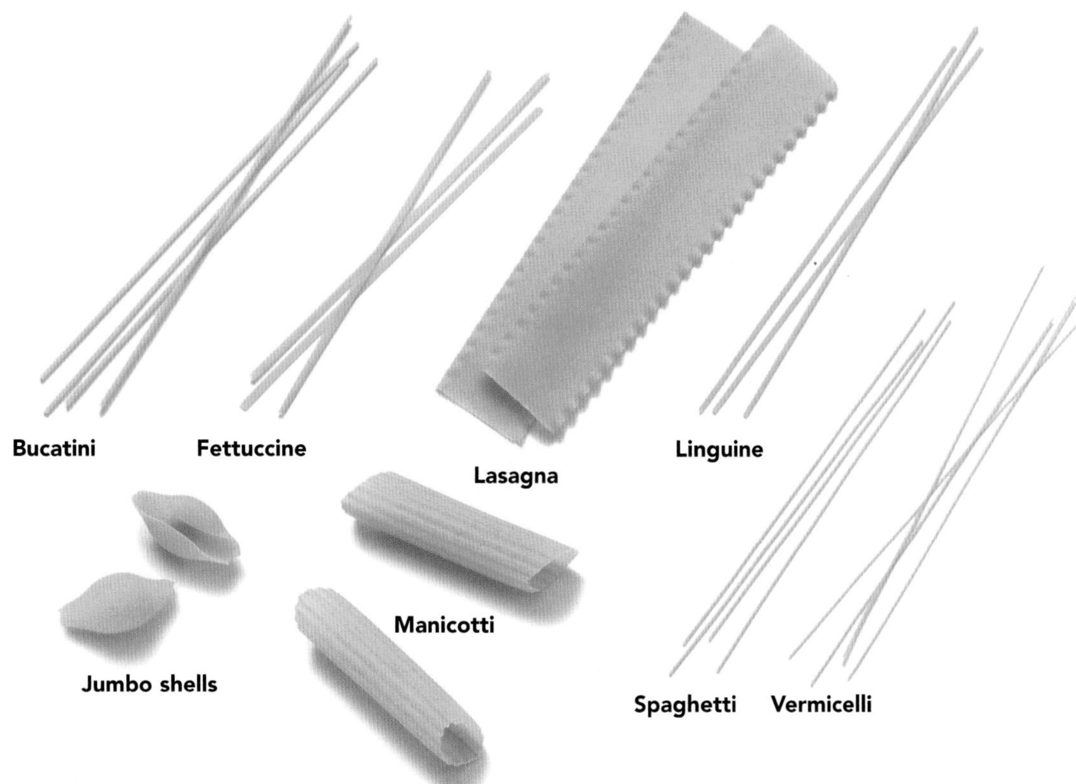

SHORT AND SMALL PASTA SHAPES

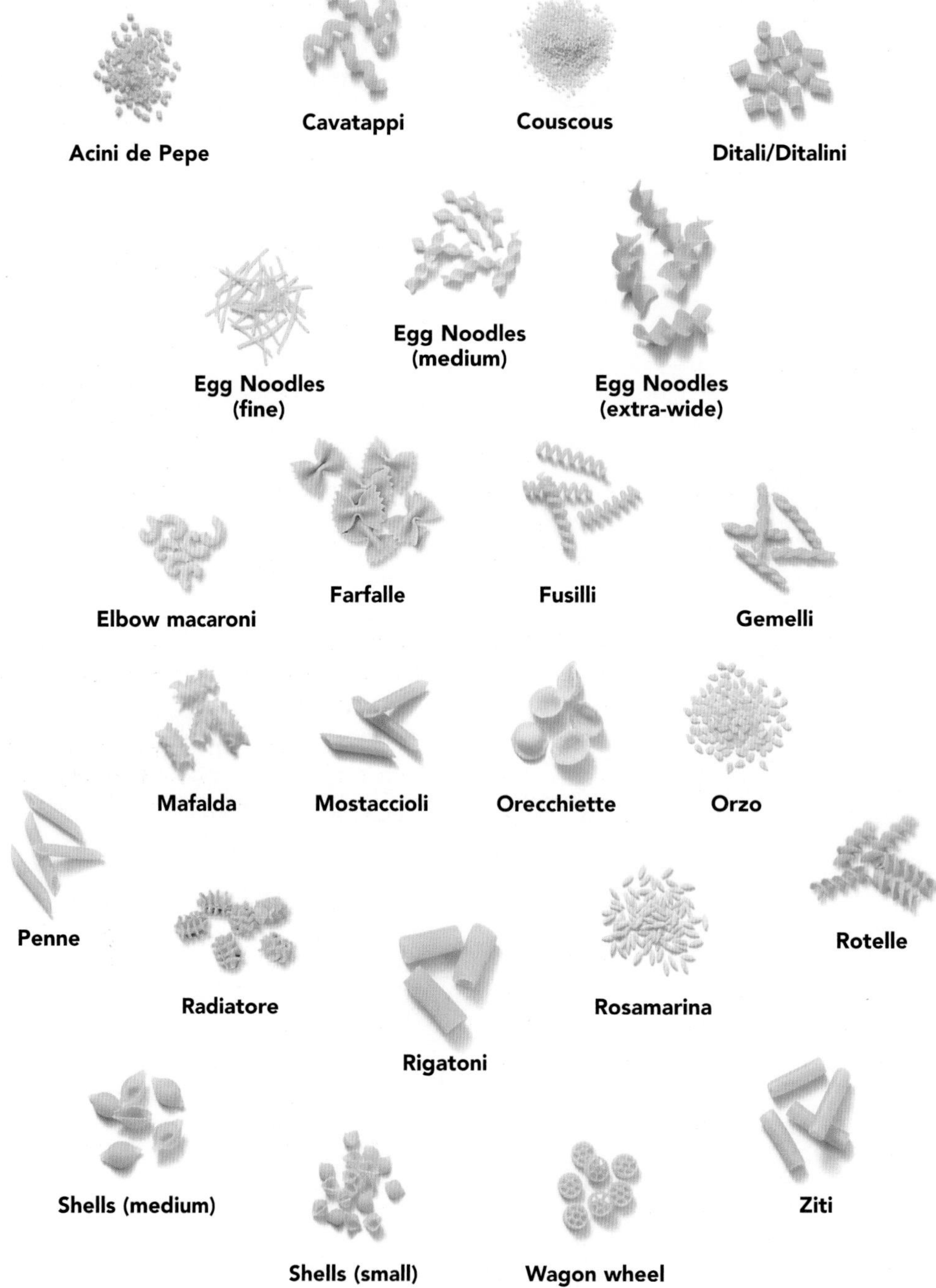

Homemade Pasta LOW-FAT

PREP: 30 min **ROLL/CUT:** 40 min **STAND:** 30 min
COOK: 15 min ■ **8 SERVINGS**

Use a large wooden board or laminated countertop for rolling out pasta dough. Cold surfaces, such as granite, metal or marble, do not work as well because the dough has a tendency to stick.

- 2 cups all-purpose flour*
- 1/2 teaspoon salt
- 2 large eggs
- 1/4 cup water
- 1 tablespoon olive or vegetable oil

1. In medium bowl, mix flour and salt. Make a well in center of flour mixture. Add eggs, water and oil to well; mix thoroughly. (If dough is too dry, mix in enough water to make dough easy to handle. If dough is too sticky, gradually add flour when kneading.)

2. Gather dough into a ball. On lightly floured surface, knead 5 to 10 minutes or until smooth and springy. Cover with plastic wrap or foil. Let stand 15 minutes.

3. Divide dough into 4 equal parts. On lightly floured surface, roll one-fourth of dough at a time into rectangle, 1/16 to 1/8 inch thick (keep remaining dough covered). Loosely fold rectangle lengthwise into thirds. Cut crosswise into 2-inch strips for lasagna, 1/4-inch strips for fettuccine or 1/8-inch strips for linguine. Unfold and gently shake out strips. Hang on pasta drying rack or arrange in single layer on lightly floured towels; let stand 30 minutes or until dry. (If using pasta machine, pass dough through machine until 1/16 inch thick.)

4. In 6- to 8-quart saucepan, heat 4 quarts water (salted if desired) to boiling; add pasta. Boil uncovered 2 to 5 minutes, stirring occasionally, until firm but tender. Begin testing for doneness when pasta rises to surface of water. Drain pasta.

**If using self-rising flour, omit salt.*

1 SERVING (ABOUT 3/4 CUP): CAL. 140 (CAL. FROM FAT 25); FAT 3g (SAT. FAT 1g); CHOL. 55mg; SODIUM 160mg; CARBS. 24g (FIBER 1g); PRO. 5g **% DAILY VALUE:** VIT. A 2%; VIT. C 0%; CALC. 0%; IRON 8% **EXCHANGES:** 1 1/2 STARCH, 1/2 FAT **CARB. CHOICES:** 1 1/2

HERB PASTA Add 1 tablespoon chopped fresh or 1 teaspoon dried herb leaves, crumbled, to the flour mixture before adding eggs.

HOW TO CUT HOMEMADE PASTA

▲ **1.** Cut pasta crosswise into 2-inch strips for lasagna, 1/4-inch strips for fettuccine or 1/8-inch strips for linguine.

2. Unfold and gently shake out strips. Hang strips on pasta drying rack or arrange in single layer on lightly floured towels. ▼

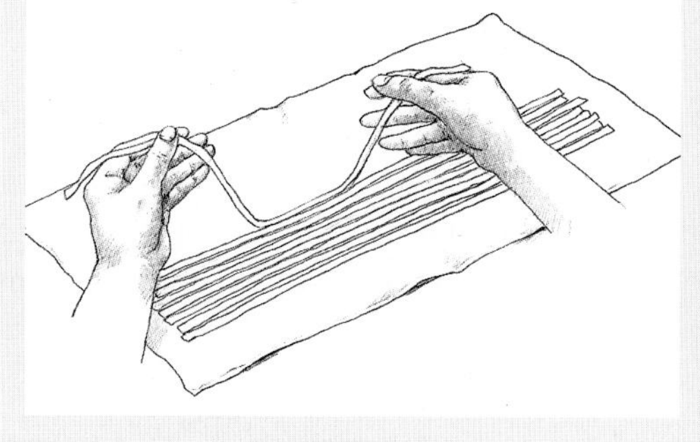

Egg Noodles

PREP: 15 min **ROLL/CUT:** 40 min **STAND:** 30 min
COOK: 15 min ▪ **6 SERVINGS**

2 cups all-purpose* or whole wheat flour
1 teaspoon salt
3 large egg yolks
1 large egg
1/3 to 1/2 cup water

1. In medium bowl, mix flour and salt. Make a well in center of flour mixture. Add egg yolks, whole egg and water to well; mix thoroughly. (If dough is too dry, mix in enough water to make dough easy to handle. If dough is too sticky, mix in enough flour to make dough easy to handle.)

2. Divide dough into 4 equal parts. On lightly floured surface, roll one-fourth of dough at a time into rectangle, 1/16 to 1/8 inch thick (keep remaining dough covered). Loosely fold rectangle lengthwise into thirds. Cut crosswise into 1/8-inch strips for narrow noodles, 1/4-inch strips for medium noodles or 1/2-inch strips for wide noodles. Unfold and gently shake out strips. Hang pasta on pasta drying rack or arrange in single layer on lightly floured towels; let stand 30 minutes or until dry. (If using pasta machine, pass dough through machine until 1/16 inch thick.)

3. Break strips into smaller pieces. In 6- to 8-quart saucepan, heat 4 quarts water (salted if desired) to boiling; add pasta. Boil uncovered 5 to 7 minutes, stirring occasionally, until firm but tender. Begin testing for doneness when pasta rises to surface of water. Drain pasta.

**If using self-rising flour, omit salt.*

1 SERVING (ABOUT 3/4 CUP): CAL. 190 (CAL. FROM FAT 35); FAT 4g (SAT. FAT 1g); CHOL. 140mg; SODIUM 410mg; CARBS. 32g (FIBER 1g); PRO. 7g **% DAILY VALUE:** VIT. A 4%; VIT. C 0%; CALC. 2%; IRON 12% **EXCHANGES:** 2 STARCH, 1/2 FAT **CARB. CHOICES:** 2

Spaetzle

PREP: 10 min **COOK:** 15 min ▪ **6 SERVINGS**

The name spaetzle *is German for "little sparrow," which is what the shape of these tiny noodles or dumplings resemble. Serve them as a side dish—tossed with a little melted butter like potatoes or rice, or topped with a creamy sauce or gravy. If you want to make them quickly, look for a spaetzle maker in your favorite kitchenware store.*

2 large eggs, beaten
1/4 cup milk or water
1 cup all-purpose flour*
1/4 teaspoon salt
Dash of pepper
1 tablespoon butter or margarine

1. In medium bowl, mix eggs, milk, flour, salt and pepper with fork (batter will be thick).

2. Fill 4-quart Dutch oven half full with water; heat to boiling.

3. Press a few tablespoons of the batter at a time through colander (preferably one with large holes) into boiling water. Stir once or twice to prevent sticking.

4. Cook about 5 minutes or until spaetzle rise to surface and are tender; drain. Toss with butter.

**Do not use self-rising flour.*

1 SERVING (ABOUT 1/2 CUP): CAL. 120 (CAL. FROM FAT 35); FAT 4g (SAT. FAT 2g); CHOL. 75mg; SODIUM 140mg; CARBS. 17g (FIBER 1g); PRO. 5g **% DAILY VALUE:** VIT. A 4%; VIT. C 0%; CALC. 2%; IRON 6% **EXCHANGES:** 1 STARCH, 1 FAT **CARB. CHOICES:** 1

LIGHTER SPAETZLE

For 2 grams of fat and 100 calories per serving, substitute 1/2 cup fat-free cholesterol-free egg product for the eggs.

CRACKING EGGS

If you find yourself always picking bits of eggshell out of the dish you're making, read on. Eggshells are less likely to splinter if they are cracked on a flat surface rather than on the edge of the mixing bowl. Try it the next time you need to crack open raw eggs.

Mediterranean Chicken with Rosemary Orzo

LOW-FAT

PREP: 10 min **COOK:** 20 min ▪ **4 SERVINGS**

- 1 lb chicken breast tenders (not breaded)*
- 1 can (14 oz) chicken broth
- $1\frac{1}{3}$ cups uncooked orzo or rosamarina pasta (about 8 oz)
- 2 cloves garlic, finely chopped
- 2 medium zucchini, cut lengthwise into fourths, then cut crosswise into slices ($1\frac{1}{2}$ cups)
- 3 roma (plum) tomatoes, cut into fourths and sliced ($1\frac{1}{2}$ cups)
- 1 medium bell pepper, chopped (1 cup)
- $\frac{1}{2}$ cup water
- 1 tablespoon chopped fresh or 1 teaspoon dried rosemary leaves
- $\frac{1}{2}$ teaspoon salt

1. Spray 10-inch skillet with cooking spray; heat over medium-high heat. Cook chicken in skillet about 5 minutes, turning occasionally, until brown.

2. Stir in broth, pasta and garlic. Heat to boiling; reduce heat. Cover and simmer about 8 minutes or until most of the liquid is absorbed.

3. Stir in remaining ingredients. Heat to boiling; reduce heat. Simmer uncovered about 5 minutes, stirring once, until bell pepper is crisp-tender and pasta is tender.

**1 lb boneless skinless chicken breasts, cut lengthwise into 1-inch strips, can be substituted for the chicken breast tenders.*

1 SERVING: CAL. 335 (CAL. FROM FAT 45); FAT 5g (SAT. FAT 1g); CHOL. 70mg; SODIUM 810mg; CARBS. 41g (FIBER 4g); PRO. 35g **% DAILY VALUE:** VIT. A 22%; VIT. C 34%; CALC. 4%; IRON 18% **EXCHANGES:** 2 STARCH, 2 VEGETABLE, 3 VERY LEAN MEAT **CARB. CHOICES:** 3

Spaghetti and Meatballs

PREP: 1 hr 45 min **COOK:** 30 min ▪ **6 SERVINGS**

- Italian Tomato Sauce (page 404)
- Meatballs (page 295)
- 4 cups hot cooked spaghetti (page 376)
- Grated Parmesan cheese, if desired

1. Make Italian Tomato Sauce.

2. Make Meatballs; drain.

3. Stir meatballs into sauce. Cover and simmer over low heat 30 minutes, stirring occasionally. Serve over spaghetti. Serve with cheese.

1 SERVING (ABOUT $1\frac{3}{4}$ CUPS): CAL. 380 (CAL. FROM FAT 145); FAT 16g (SAT. FAT 5g); CHOL. 80mg; SODIUM 490mg; CARBS. 40g (FIBER 3g); PRO. 22g **% DAILY VALUE:** VIT. A 8%; VIT. C 14%; CALC. 8%; IRON 20% **EXCHANGES:** 2 STARCH, 2 VEGETABLE, 2 MEDIUM-FAT MEAT, $\frac{1}{2}$ FAT **CARB. CHOICES:** $2\frac{1}{2}$

SPAGHETTI AND BEEF SAUCE Omit Meatballs. In 10-inch skillet, cook 1 lb lean (at least 80%) ground beef, 1 large onion, chopped (1 cup), and 2 cloves garlic, finely chopped, over medium heat 8 to 10 minutes, stirring occasionally, until beef is brown; drain. Stir beef mixture into sauce. Simmer as directed in Step 3.

Stir-Fried Asian Beef and Noodles LOW-FAT

PREP: 15 min **MARINATE:** 20 min **COOK:** 12 min ▪ **6 SERVINGS**

1 lb beef boneless sirloin or round steak, cut into 2 × 1/4-inch strips
1 tablespoon vegetable oil
1 teaspoon cornstarch
1/2 teaspoon soy sauce
1 package (6 or 7 oz) rice stick noodles
1 tablespoon vegetable oil
1 tablespoon finely chopped gingerroot
1 clove garlic, finely chopped
1 bag (1 lb) frozen broccoli, carrots and cauliflower (or other combination), thawed and drained
1 tablespoon vegetable oil
3/4 cup beef broth
1/3 cup rice or cider vinegar
1/3 cup honey
3 tablespoons soy sauce
1 teaspoon sesame oil
1/4 teaspoon crushed red pepper
4 medium green onions, sliced (1/4 cup)

1. In glass or plastic bowl, toss beef, 1 tablespoon vegetable oil, the cornstarch and 1/2 teaspoon soy sauce. Cover and refrigerate 20 minutes. Meanwhile, in large bowl, soak noodles in enough cold water to cover 5 minutes; drain.

2. Heat 12-inch skillet or wok over medium-high heat. Add 1 tablespoon vegetable oil; rotate skillet to coat with oil. Add gingerroot and garlic; stir-fry 30 seconds. Add vegetables; stir-fry until crisp-tender. Remove vegetables from skillet.

3. Add 1 tablespoon vegetable oil to skillet; rotate to coat. Add beef; stir-fry about 5 minutes or until brown. Remove beef from skillet.

4. Add broth, vinegar, honey, 3 tablespoons soy sauce, the sesame oil and red pepper to skillet. Stir in noodles; heat to boiling. Cook over medium heat about 2 minutes, stirring frequently, until noodles are tender. Stir in beef, vegetables and onions; cook and stir 1 minute.

1 SERVING (ABOUT 1 CUP): CAL. 350 (CAL. FROM FAT 90); FAT 10g (SAT. FAT 2g); CHOL. 40mg; SODIUM 700mg; CARBS. 46g (FIBER 3g); PRO. 19g **% DAILY VALUE:** VIT. A 42%; VIT. C 22%; CALC. 4%; IRON 14% **EXCHANGES:** 21/2 STARCH, 2 VEGETABLE, 1 LEAN MEAT, 1 FAT **CARB. CHOICES:** 3

Mexi Shells LOW-FAT

PREP: 20 min **COOK:** 22 min **BAKE:** 30 min **STAND:** 10 min ▪ **6 SERVINGS**

No-salt tomato sauce is used because the chili beans in sauce provides plenty of flavor.

18 uncooked jumbo pasta shells
4 cans (8 oz each) no-salt-added tomato sauce
2 tablespoons all-purpose flour
1 teaspoon chili powder
2 teaspoons ground cumin
3/4 lb extra-lean (at least 90%) ground beef
1 small onion, chopped (1/4 cup)
1 teaspoon ground cumin
1 tablespoon chopped fresh cilantro
1 can (4.5 oz) chopped green chiles, drained
1 can (15 or 16 oz) chili beans in sauce, undrained
1 cup shredded part-skim mozzarella cheese (4 oz)

1. Heat oven to 350°F. Cook pasta shells as directed on package.

2. Meanwhile, in medium bowl, mix tomato sauce, flour, chili powder and 2 teaspoons cumin; set aside.

3. In 2-quart saucepan, cook beef and onion over medium heat 8 to 10 minutes, stirring occasionally, until beef is brown; drain. Stir in 1 teaspoon cumin, the cilantro, green chiles and chili beans.

4. Drain pasta shells. In ungreased 13 × 9-inch glass baking dish, spread 1 cup of the tomato sauce mixture. Spoon about 11/2 tablespoons beef mixture into each pasta shell. Place filled-sides-up on sauce in dish. Pour remaining tomato sauce mixture over shells. Sprinkle with cheese.

Mexi Shells ▶

5. Cover with foil and bake 30 minutes. Uncover and let stand 10 minutes before serving.

1 SERVING: CAL. 340 (CAL. FROM FAT 80); FAT 9g (SAT. FAT 4g); CHOL. 65mg; SODIUM 1,050mg; CARBS. 45g (FIBER 7g); PRO. 27g
% DAILY VALUE: VIT. A 36%; VIT. C 26%; CALC. 20%; IRON 30%
EXCHANGES: 3 STARCH, 2 1/2 VERY LEAN MEAT, 1/2 FAT
CARB. CHOICES: 3

Kung Pao Pork Over Sesame Noodles

PREP: 15 min **COOK:** 20 min ■ **4 SERVINGS**

Chinese rice stick noodles are very thin and white and can be found in most large grocery stores in the Asian-foods aisle.

- 1 tablespoon vegetable oil
- 1 bag (1 lb) broccoli slaw mix*
- 1 lb pork boneless loin, cut into 1/2-inch pieces
- 1 medium red bell pepper, cut into 1/2-inch pieces
- 1/2 cup water
- 1/2 cup spicy Sichuan (Szechuan) stir-fry sauce
- 1 tablespoon honey
- 1 package (6 or 7 oz) rice stick noodles
- 2 teaspoons sesame or vegetable oil
- 2 tablespoons salted peanuts

1. Heat 12-inch nonstick skillet over medium-high heat. Add vegetable oil; rotate skillet to coat bottom. Add broccoli slaw; stir-fry 2 to 3 minutes or until crisp-tender. Remove broccoli slaw from skillet; keep warm.

2. Add pork to same skillet; stir-fry over medium-high heat 5 to 6 minutes or until brown. Stir in bell pepper and water. Cover and cook 3 to 4 minutes, stirring occasionally, until pork is tender. Stir in stir-fry sauce and honey; reduce heat. Simmer uncovered 1 to 2 minutes.

3. Meanwhile, in 4-quart Dutch oven, heat 3 quarts water to boiling. Add noodles. Boil 3 minutes; drain. In large bowl, toss noodles and sesame oil. Divide noodles among 4 individual serving bowls. Top with broccoli slaw and pork mixture. Sprinkle with peanuts.

**1 bag (1 lb) coleslaw mix can be substituted for the broccoli slaw mix.*

1 SERVING: CAL. 510 (CAL. FROM FAT 160); FAT 18g (SAT. FAT 4g); CHOL. 70mg; SODIUM 1,480mg; CARBS. 55g (FIBER 6g); PRO. 33g
% DAILY VALUE: VIT. A 64%; VIT. C 100%; CALC. 8%; IRON 16%
EXCHANGES: 3 STARCH, 2 VEGETABLE, 3 LEAN MEAT, 1 FAT
CARB. CHOICES: 3 1/2

Spanish Clams, Sausage and Linguine

PREP: 15 min **COOK:** 25 min ■ **6 SERVINGS**

Romano cheese, made from sheep's milk, has a sharper flavor than Parmesan made from cow's milk. Both are terrific toppers for this dish, but Romano gives you a bit more flavor.

- 1/2 lb bulk hot Italian sausage
- 3 medium onions, chopped (1 1/2 cups)
- 2 medium carrots, chopped (1 cup)
- 3 cloves garlic, finely chopped
- 1 can (28 oz) crushed tomatoes, undrained
- 2 cans (14.5 oz each) diced tomatoes with roasted garlic, undrained
- 1/2 cup dry red wine or clam juice
- 1 1/2 teaspoons ground cumin
- 1 teaspoon dried rosemary leaves, crumbled
- 1/2 cup small pimiento-stuffed olives, coarsely chopped
- 24 littleneck clams (about 2 lb), scrubbed*
- 12 oz uncooked linguine
- Grated Romano or Parmesan cheese, if desired

1. In 4-quart Dutch oven, cook sausage, onions, carrots and garlic over medium-high heat 5 to 7 minutes, stirring frequently, until sausage is no longer pink; drain.

2. Stir in remaining ingredients except clams, linguine and cheese. Heat to boiling; reduce heat to medium-low. Partially cover and simmer 10 minutes. Meanwhile, cook and drain linguine as directed on package; keep warm.

3. Add clams to sausage mixture. Cover and cook over medium-high heat 5 to 7 minutes or until clams open. Discard any unopened clams. Serve clam sauce over linguine. Serve with cheese.

**3 cans (10 oz each) whole clams, drained, can be substituted for the fresh clams.*

1 SERVING: CAL. 420 (CAL. FROM FAT 100); FAT 11g (SAT. FAT 3g); CHOL. 65mg; SODIUM 970mg; CARBS. 65g (FIBER 6g); PRO. 21g
% DAILY VALUE: VIT. A 40%; VIT. C 40%; CALC. 14%; IRON 52%
EXCHANGES: 3 STARCH, 4 VEGETABLE, 1/2 MEDIUM-FAT MEAT, 1 FAT **CARB. CHOICES:** 4

Straw and Hay Pasta

PREP: 15 min **COOK:** 25 min ▪ **4 SERVINGS**

In Italy, this dish is called paglia e fieno, *a toss of yellow and green pasta, often called straw and hay. In dishes like this one, serving long pasta can be tricky without the help of kitchen tongs, pasta servers or a wooden pasta fork. These handy, inexpensive items let you easily grab the pasta and transfer it onto your plate without taking more than you want.*

- 1 tablespoon butter or margarine
- 1 1/2 cups sliced fresh mushrooms (4 oz)
- 4 oz fully cooked ham, cut into 1 × 1/4-inch strips
- 2 tablespoons chopped fresh parsley
- 2 tablespoons chopped onion
- 1/4 cup brandy or chicken broth
- 1 cup whipping (heavy) cream
- 1/4 teaspoon salt
- 1/4 teaspoon pepper
- 1 package (9 oz) refrigerated plain fettuccine
- 1 package (9 oz) refrigerated spinach fettuccine
- 1/2 cup shredded Parmesan cheese
- Freshly ground pepper

1. In 10-inch skillet, melt butter over medium-high heat. Cook mushrooms, ham, parsley and onion in butter, stirring occasionally, until mushrooms are tender. Stir in brandy. Cook uncovered until liquid has evaporated.

2. Stir in whipping cream, salt and pepper. Heat to boiling; reduce heat. Simmer uncovered about 15 minutes, stirring frequently, until thickened.

3. Meanwhile, cook and drain fettuccines as directed on package; keep warm.

4. In large bowl, toss fettuccines and sauce. Sprinkle with cheese and pepper.

1 SERVING (ABOUT 1 1/4 CUPS): CAL. 755 (CAL. FROM FAT 290); FAT 32g (SAT. FAT 17g); CHOL. 210mg; SODIUM 860mg; CARBS. 86g (FIBER 4g); PRO. 30g **% DAILY VALUE:** VIT. A 24%; VIT. C 2%; CALC. 26%; IRON 34% **EXCHANGES:** 5 STARCH, 2 VEGETABLE, 1/2 HIGH-FAT MEAT, 3 FAT **CARB. CHOICES:** 6

Spaghetti Carbonara

PREP: 10 min **COOK:** 13 min ▪ **6 SERVINGS**

This recipe uses pasteurized fat-free cholesterol-free egg product instead of traditional raw eggs. This eliminates the risk of contracting salmonella from eating raw or undercooked eggs.

- 1 package (16 oz) spaghetti
- 1 clove garlic, finely chopped
- 6 slices bacon, cut into 1-inch pieces
- 3/4 cup fat-free cholesterol-free egg product
- 1 tablespoon olive or vegetable oil
- 1/2 cup freshly grated Parmesan cheese
- 1/2 cup freshly grated Romano cheese
- 2 tablespoons chopped fresh parsley
- 1/4 teaspoon pepper
- Additional freshly grated Parmesan cheese, if desired
- Freshly ground pepper, if desired

1. In 4-quart Dutch oven, cook spaghetti as directed on package.

2. Meanwhile, in 10-inch skillet, cook garlic and bacon over medium heat, stirring occasionally, until bacon is crisp; drain.

3. In small bowl, mix egg product, oil, 1/2 cup Parmesan cheese, the Romano cheese, parsley and 1/4 teaspoon pepper.

4. Drain spaghetti; return to Dutch oven. Add bacon mixture and egg product mixture. Cook over low heat, tossing mixture constantly, until egg product coats spaghetti; remove from heat. Serve with additional Parmesan cheese and freshly ground pepper.

1 SERVING (ABOUT 1 1/2 CUPS): CAL. 440 (CAL. FROM FAT 110); FAT 12g (SAT. FAT 5g); CHOL. 20mg; SODIUM 420mg; CARBS. 61g (FIBER 3g); PRO. 22g **% DAILY VALUE:** VIT. A 8%; VIT. C 0%; CALC. 24%; IRON 20% **EXCHANGES:** 4 STARCH, 1/2 MEDIUM-FAT MEAT **CARB. CHOICES:** 4

Linguine with Red Clam Sauce LOW-FAT

PREP: 30 min **COOK:** 30 min ■ **6 SERVINGS**

Red Clam Sauce

1 pint shucked fresh small clams, drained and liquor reserved*

1/4 cup olive or vegetable oil

3 cloves garlic, finely chopped

1 can (28 oz) Italian-style (plum) tomatoes, drained and chopped

1 small jalapeño chili, seeded and finely chopped

1 tablespoon chopped fresh parsley

1 teaspoon salt

Linguine

8 oz uncooked linguine

Garnish

Chopped fresh parsley

1. Chop clams; set aside. In 3-quart saucepan, heat oil over medium-high heat. Cook garlic in oil, stirring frequently, until golden. Stir in tomatoes and chili. Cook 3 minutes, stirring frequently. Stir in clam liquid. Heat to boiling; reduce heat. Simmer uncovered 10 minutes. Stir in clams, parsley and salt. Cover and simmer about 15 minutes, stirring occasionally, until clams are tender.

2. Meanwhile, cook and drain linguine as directed on package; keep warm.

3. In large bowl, toss linguine and sauce. Sprinkle with parsley.

**2 cans (6.5 oz each) minced clams, undrained, can be substituted for the fresh clams. Decrease simmer time to 5 minutes.*

1 SERVING (ABOUT 1 1/2 CUPS): CAL. 290 (CAL. FROM FAT 90); FAT 10g (SAT. FAT 1g); CHOL. 15mg; SODIUM 620mg; CARBS. 38g (FIBER 3g); PRO. 13g **% DAILY VALUE:** VIT. A 14%; VIT. C 22%; CALC. 6%; IRON 52% **EXCHANGES:** 2 STARCH, 1 VEGETABLE, 1 LEAN MEAT, 1 FAT **CARB. CHOICES:** 2 1/2

Spaghetti with White Clam Sauce

PREP: 10 min **COOK:** 15 min ■ **4 SERVINGS**

1 package (7 oz) spaghetti

1/4 cup butter or margarine

2 cloves garlic, finely chopped

2 tablespoons chopped fresh parsley

2 cans (6.5 oz each) minced clams, undrained

Additional chopped fresh parsley

1/2 cup grated Parmesan cheese

1. Cook spaghetti as directed on package.

2. Meanwhile, in 1 1/2-quart saucepan, melt butter over medium heat. Cook garlic in butter about 3 minutes, stirring occasionally, until light golden. Stir in 2 tablespoons parsley and the clams. Heat to boiling; reduce heat. Simmer uncovered 3 to 5 minutes.

3. Drain spaghetti. In large bowl, pour sauce over spaghetti; toss. Sprinkle with additional parsley and cheese.

1 SERVING (ABOUT 1 1/4 CUPS): CAL. 485 (CAL. FROM FAT 160); FAT 18g (SAT. FAT 10g); CHOL. 100mg; SODIUM 410mg; CARBS. 45g (FIBER 2g); PRO. 36g **% DAILY VALUE:** VIT. A 22%; VIT. C 18%; CALC. 26%; IRON 100% **EXCHANGES:** 3 STARCH, 3 MEDIUM-FAT MEAT, 1/2 FAT **CARB. CHOICES:** 3

Linguine with Red Clam Sauce ▶

Pad Thai with Shrimp

PREP: 35 min **COOK:** 5 min ▪ **4 SERVINGS**

Pad Thai is Thailand's most well known noodle dish, which you'll find on almost all Thai restaurant menus in America. A trip down the Asian-foods aisle in your supermarket should lead you to its traditional ingredients, such as rice noodles and fish sauce. *See photo on page 363.*

- 4 cups water
- 1 package (6 to 8 oz) linguine-style stir-fry rice noodles (rice stick noodles)*
- 1/3 cup fresh lime juice
- 1/3 cup water
- 3 tablespoons packed brown sugar
- 3 tablespoons fish sauce or soy sauce
- 3 tablespoons soy sauce
- 1 tablespoon rice vinegar or white vinegar
- 3/4 teaspoon ground red pepper (cayenne)
- 3 tablespoons vegetable oil
- 3 cloves garlic, finely chopped
- 1 medium shallot, finely chopped, or 1/4 cup finely chopped onion
- 2 eggs, beaten
- 12 oz frozen cooked peeled deveined medium shrimp, thawed
- 1/4 cup finely chopped dry-roasted peanuts
- 3 cups fresh bean sprouts
- 4 medium green onions, thinly sliced (1/4 cup)
- 1/4 cup firmly packed cilantro leaves

1. In 3-quart saucepan, heat 4 cups water to boiling. Remove from heat; add noodles (push noodles into water with back of spoon to cover completely with water if necessary). Soak noodles 3 to 5 minutes or until noodles are soft but firm. Drain noodles; rinse with cold water.

2. Meanwhile, in small bowl, stir lime juice, 1/3 cup water, the brown sugar, fish sauce, soy sauce, vinegar, red pepper and 1 tablespoon of the oil until well mixed; set aside.

3. In nonstick wok or 12-inch nonstick skillet, heat remaining 2 tablespoons vegetable oil over medium heat. Cook garlic and shallot in oil about 30 seconds, stirring constantly, until starting to brown. Add eggs. Cook about 2 minutes, stirring gently and constantly, until scrambled but still moist.

4. Stir in noodles and lime juice mixture. Increase heat to high. Cook about 1 minute, tossing constantly with 2 wooden spoons, until sauce begins to thicken. Add remaining ingredients except cilantro. Cook 2 to 3 minutes, tossing with 2 wooden spoons, until noodles are tender. Place on serving platter. Sprinkle with cilantro. Garnish with additional chopped dry-roasted peanuts and green onions if desired.

**Thin or thick rice stick noodles can be substituted for the linguine-style stir-fry rice noodles.*

1 SERVING: CAL. 540 (CAL. FROM FAT 205); FAT 23g (SAT. FAT 4g); CHOL. 240mg; SODIUM 1310mg; CARBS. 59g (FIBER 4g); PRO. 29g **% DAILY VALUE:** VIT. A 10%; VIT. C 14%; CALC. 12%; IRON 24% **EXCHANGES:** 3 STARCH, 1/2 OTHER CARB., 1 VEGETABLE, 2 1/2 LEAN MEAT, 2 1/2 FAT **CARB. CHOICES:** 4

PAD THAI WITH CHICKEN Substitute 2 cups chopped cooked chicken for the shrimp.

Pad Thai with Shrimp (page 362)

Fettuccine Alfredo

PREP: 10 min **COOK:** 15 min ▪ **4 SERVINGS**

This rich northern Italian dish is named after restaurateur Alfredo di Lello, who created it in 1914 at Alfredo's in Rome. When making this dish with freshly grated Parmesan cheese, expect the sauce to be a little thinner than if you used canned grated cheese. Fettuccine Alfredo is delicious, as a "side" for meat or on-its-own as a main dish.

Fettuccine

8 oz uncooked fettuccine

Alfredo Sauce

1/2 cup butter or margarine
1/2 cup whipping (heavy) cream
3/4 cup grated Parmesan cheese
1/2 teaspoon salt
Dash of pepper

Garnish

Chopped fresh parsley

1. Cook fettuccine as directed on package.

2. Meanwhile, in 10-inch skillet, heat butter and whipping cream over medium heat, stirring frequently, until butter is melted and mixture starts to bubble; reduce heat to low. Simmer 6 minutes, stirring frequently, until slightly thickened; remove from heat. Stir in cheese, salt and pepper.

3. Drain fettuccine; return to saucepan. Pour sauce over fettuccine; toss until fettuccine is well coated. Sprinkle with parsley.

1 SERVING (ABOUT 1 CUP): CAL. 550 (CAL. FROM FAT 350); FAT 39g (SAT. FAT 25g); CHOL. 160mg; SODIUM 810mg; CARBS. 38g (FIBER 2g); PRO. 15g **% DAILY VALUE:** VIT. A 28%; VIT. C 0%; CALC. 30%; IRON 14% **EXCHANGES:** 2 1/2 STARCH, 1 HIGH-FAT MEAT, 5 1/2 FAT **CARB. CHOICES:** 2 1/2

LIGHTER FETTUCCINE ALFREDO

For 17 grams of fat and 370 calories per serving, decrease butter to 1/4 cup and Parmesan cheese to 1/2 cup; substitute evaporated milk for the whipping cream.

Fettuccine with Wild Mushrooms

PREP: 5 min **STAND:** 30 min **COOK:** 22 min ▪ **4 SERVINGS**

- 1 cup hot water
- 1 package (about 1 oz) dried porcini or cèpe mushrooms
- 8 oz uncooked fettuccine
- 2 tablespoons olive or vegetable oil
- 1 small onion, chopped (1/4 cup)
- 2 cloves garlic, finely chopped
- 1 cup whipping (heavy) cream
- 1/2 teaspoon salt
- Coarsely ground pepper

1. In small bowl, pour water over mushrooms. Let stand 30 minutes; drain.* Coarsely chop mushrooms. Cook and drain fettuccine as directed on package; keep warm.

2. Meanwhile, in 10-inch skillet, heat oil over medium heat. Cook mushrooms, onion and garlic in oil, stirring occasionally, until onion is tender. Stir in whipping cream and salt. Heat to boiling; reduce heat to low. Simmer uncovered 3 to 5 minutes, stirring occasionally, until slightly thickened.

3. Return fettuccine to saucepan. Pour sauce over fettuccine; toss until fettuccine is well coated. Serve with pepper.

**If desired, strain the mushroom soaking liquid and use in soups, stews or gravies.*

1 SERVING: CAL. 445 (CAL. FROM FAT 245); FAT 27g (SAT. FAT 13g); CHOL. 115mg; SODIUM 330mg; CARBS. 41g; (FIBER 2g); PRO. 9g **% DAILY VALUE:** VIT. A 14%; VIT. C 2%; CALC. 6%; IRON 14% **EXCHANGES:** 3 STARCH, 4 1/2 FAT **CARB. CHOICES:** 3

KEEPING PASTA HOT

While pasta is cooking, fill the serving bowl with hot water and let it stand to warm up the bowl. Pour the water out just before adding pasta. Or put the pasta bowl and individual serving bowls or plates into a clean dishwasher and select the drying cycle to keep them toasty warm.

Gorgonzola Linguine with Toasted Walnuts

PREP: 10 min **COOK:** 15 min ▪ **4 SERVINGS**

How much is 8 ounces of linguine? All bundled up, 8 ounces of uncooked linguine is about 1 1/2 inches in diameter.

- 8 oz uncooked linguine
- 1 tablespoon butter or margarine
- 1 clove garlic, finely chopped
- 1 1/2 cups whipping (heavy) cream
- 1/4 cup dry white wine or chicken broth
- 1/4 teaspoon salt
- 1/2 cup crumbled Gorgonzola cheese (about 2 oz)
- 1/4 cup coarsely chopped walnuts, toasted (page 215)

1. Cook linguine as directed on package.

2. Meanwhile, in 10-inch skillet, melt butter over low heat. Cook garlic in butter, stirring occasionally, until garlic is golden. Stir in whipping cream, wine and salt. Simmer about 6 minutes, stirring constantly, until slightly thickened; remove from heat. Stir in cheese until melted.

3. Drain linguine; return to saucepan. Pour sauce over linguine; toss until linguine is well coated. Sprinkle with walnuts.

1 SERVING (ABOUT 1 1/2 CUPS): CAL. 615 (CAL. FROM FAT 370); FAT 41g (SAT. FAT 23g); CHOL. 120mg; SODIUM 440mg; CARBS. 50g (FIBER 2g); PRO. 14g **% DAILY VALUE:** VIT. A 24%; VIT. C 0%; CALC. 16%; IRON 14% **EXCHANGES:** 3 STARCH, 1/2 MILK, 7 FAT **CARB. CHOICES:** 3

LIGHTER GORGONZOLA LINGUINE WITH TOASTED WALNUTS

For 11 grams of fat and 400 calories per serving, substitute evaporated fat-free milk for the whipping cream; use 2 tablespoons finely chopped walnuts.

Asian Noodle Bowl

PREP: 10 min **COOK:** 20 min ■ **4 SERVINGS**

- 1/4 cup barbecue sauce
- 2 tablespoons hoisin sauce
- 1 tablespoon peanut butter
- Dash of ground red pepper (cayenne), if desired
- 1 tablespoon vegetable oil
- 1 small onion, cut into thin wedges
- 1/4 cup chopped red bell pepper
- 2 cups broccoli flowerets or 1 bag (14 oz) frozen broccoli flowerets, thawed
- 3/4 cup water
- 1/2 teaspoon salt, if desired
- 1 package (10 oz) Chinese curly noodles
- 1 can (14 oz) baby corn nuggets, drained
- 1/4 cup chopped peanuts

1. In medium bowl, mix barbecue sauce, hoisin sauce, peanut butter and ground red pepper; set aside.

2. In 12-inch skillet, heat oil over medium heat 1 to 2 minutes. Cook onion and bell pepper in oil 2 minutes, stirring frequently. Stir in broccoli and 3/4 cup water. Cover and cook 4 to 6 minutes, stirring occasionally, until broccoli is crisp-tender.

3. Meanwhile, fill 4-quart Dutch oven about half full with water; add salt. Cover and heat to boiling over high heat. Add noodles; heat to boiling. Boil uncovered 4 to 5 minutes, stirring frequently, until noodles are tender.

4. While noodles are cooking, stir corn and sauce mixture into vegetable mixture. Cook uncovered 3 to 4 minutes, stirring occasionally, until mixture is hot and bubbly.

5. Drain noodles. Divide noodles among 4 individual serving bowls. Spoon vegetable mixture over noodles. Sprinkle with peanuts.

1 SERVING: CAL. 470 (CAL. FROM FAT 110) FAT 12g (SAT. FAT 2g) CHOL. 0mg SODIUM 680mg CARBS. 80g (FIBER 7g) PRO. 17g
% DAILY VALUE: VIT. A 26% VIT. C 58% CALC. 6% IRON 26%
EXCHANGES: 5 STARCH, 1 VEGETABLE, 1 FAT **CARB. CHOICES:** 5

Asian Noodle Bowl ▶

Pasta Primavera

PREP: 15 min **COOK:** 20 min ▪ **4 SERVINGS**

8 oz uncooked fettuccine or linguine
1 tablespoon olive or vegetable oil
1 cup broccoli flowerets
1 cup cauliflowerets
2 medium carrots, thinly sliced (1 cup)
1 cup frozen green peas (from 1-lb bag), rinsed to separate
1 small onion, chopped (1/4 cup)
Alfredo Sauce (page 363)
1 tablespoon grated Parmesan cheese

1. Cook fettuccine as directed on package.

2. Meanwhile, in 12-inch skillet, heat oil over medium-high heat. Cook broccoli, cauliflower, carrots, peas and onion in oil 6 to 8 minutes, stirring frequently, until vegetables are crisp-tender. Remove from heat; keep warm.

3. Make Alfredo Sauce. Stir sauce into vegetable mixture.

4. Drain fettuccine. Stir fettuccine into sauce mixture; heat through. Sprinkle with cheese.

1 SERVING (ABOUT 13/4 CUPS): CAL. 500 (CAL. FROM FAT 270); FAT 30g (SAT. FAT 11g); CHOL. 130mg; SODIUM 420mg; CARBS. 48g (FIBER 5g); PRO. 15g **% DAILY VALUE:** VIT. A 46%; VIT. C 30%; CALC. 22%; IRON 18% **EXCHANGES:** 3 STARCH, 1 VEGETABLE, 1/2 HIGH-FAT MEAT, 4 FAT **CARB. CHOICES:** 3

KEEPING PASTA DISHES HOT

Because the ingredients in this recipe are uncooked, they'll stay warmer if you toss them with the pasta in a prewarmed bowl. To warm your serving bowl, fill it with hot water and let it stand while the pasta is cooking. Pour the water out just before you're ready to add the pasta.

Vermicelli with Fresh Herbs

FAST

PREP: 10 min **COOK:** 7 min ▪ **6 SERVINGS**

1 package (16 oz) vermicelli
1 tablespoon capers
1/4 cup olive or vegetable oil
2 tablespoons chopped pine nuts
1 tablespoon chopped fresh parsley
2 teaspoons chopped fresh rosemary leaves
2 teaspoons chopped fresh sage leaves
1 teaspoon chopped fresh basil leaves
1 pint (2 cups) cherry tomatoes, cut into fourths
Freshly ground pepper, if desired

1. Cook vermicelli as directed on package.

2. Meanwhile, coarsely chop capers if they are large. In medium bowl, mix capers and remaining ingredients except tomatoes and pepper. Stir in tomatoes.

3. Drain vermicelli. In large bowl, toss vermicelli and herb mixture. Sprinkle with pepper.

1 SERVING (ABOUT 11/2 CUPS): CAL. 390 (CAL. FROM FAT 110); FAT 12g (SAT. FAT 2g); CHOL. 0mg; SODIUM 50mg; CARBS. 64g (FIBER 4g); PRO. 11g **% DAILY VALUE:** VIT. A 10%; VIT. C 10%; CALC. 2%; IRON 20% **EXCHANGES:** 4 STARCH, 1 VEGETABLE, 1 FAT **CARB. CHOICES:** 4

Fresh Tomato and Garlic Penne LOW-FAT

PREP: 15 min **COOK:** 10 min ■ **4 SERVINGS**

$2^{1}/_{2}$ cups uncooked penne pasta (about 8 oz)
1 tablespoon olive or vegetable oil
3 cloves garlic, finely chopped
12 medium roma (plum) tomatoes (2 lb), coarsely chopped
2 tablespoons chopped fresh basil leaves
$^{1}/_{2}$ teaspoon salt
$^{1}/_{4}$ teaspoon freshly ground pepper

1. Cook and drain pasta as directed on package.

2. Meanwhile, in 10-inch skillet, heat oil over medium-high heat. Cook garlic in oil 30 seconds, stirring frequently. Stir in tomatoes. Cook 5 to 8 minutes, stirring frequently, until tomatoes are soft and sauce is slightly thickened.

3. Stir in basil, salt and pepper. Cook 1 minute. Serve sauce over pasta.

1 SERVING: CAL. 290 (CAL. FROM FAT 45); FAT 5g (SAT. FAT 1g); CHOL. 0mg; SODIUM 310mg; CARBS. 52g (FIBER 4g); PRO. 9g
% DAILY VALUE: VIT. A 26%; VIT. C 26%; CALC. 2%; IRON 16%
EXCHANGES: 3 STARCH, 1 VEGETABLE, 1/2 FAT **CARB. CHOICES:** $3^{1}/_{2}$

◀ **Sesame Noodle Salad**

Sesame Noodle Salad LOW-FAT

PREP: 15 min **COOK:** 8 min ■ **12 SERVINGS**

Sesame Dressing

3 tablespoons vegetable oil
3 tablespoons soy sauce
1 tablespoon balsamic or rice vinegar
1 tablespoon sesame oil
$4^{1}/_{2}$ teaspoons sugar
$1^{1}/_{2}$ teaspoons grated gingerroot
$^{1}/_{2}$ teaspoon garlic powder
$^{1}/_{8}$ teaspoon ground red pepper (cayenne)

Salad

8 to 9 oz uncooked soba (buckwheat) noodles or angel hair pasta
2 medium carrots, shredded (1 cup)
1 small cucumber, cut lengthwise in half, then cut crosswise into thin slices (1 cup)
2 medium green onions, thinly sliced (2 tablespoons)
1 tablespoon sesame seed, toasted (page 215)

1. In small bowl, stir all dressing ingredients until well mixed; set aside.

2. In 4-quart Dutch oven, heat 2 quarts water to boiling. Cook soba noodles in boiling water 6 to 8 minutes or until tender; drain and rinse with cold water. If using angel hair pasta, cook as directed on package; drain and rinse with cold water.

3. In large serving bowl, toss noodles, dressing and remaining salad ingredients. Cover and refrigerate until serving.

1 SERVING: CAL. 120 (CAL. FROM FAT 45); FAT 5g (SAT. FAT 1g); CHOL. 0mg; SODIUM 230mg; CARBS. 16g (FIBER 2g); PRO. 3g
% DAILY VALUE: VIT. A 6%; VIT. C 2%; CALC. 0%; IRON 4%
EXCHANGES: 1 STARCH, 1 FAT **CARB. CHOICES:** 1

Spicy Noodles and Cabbage Stir-Fry LOW-FAT

PREP: 25 min **COOK:** 12 min ▪ **12 SERVINGS**

Oyster sauce is a thick, dark brown sauce made from oysters, brine and soy sauce. It can be found in the Asian-foods section of most large supermarkets.

Stir-Fry Sauce

3 tablespoons soy sauce
1 tablespoon oyster sauce*
1 tablespoon rice vinegar or white vinegar
1 teaspoon sugar
1/2 teaspoon crushed red pepper
1/4 teaspoon sesame oil

Stir-Fry

8 oz uncooked fettuccine
1 tablespoon vegetable oil
2 cloves garlic, finely chopped
1 tablespoon finely chopped gingerroot
1 small onion, cut into 1/2-inch wedges
2 medium carrots, shredded (1 cup)
3 cups chopped Chinese (napa) cabbage
1 medium green onion, thinly sliced (1 tablespoon)
2 tablespoons chopped dry-roasted peanuts

1. In small bowl, stir all sauce ingredients until well mixed; set aside.

2. Cook fettuccine as directed on package. Drain and rinse in warm water.

3. Meanwhile, in nonstick wok or 12-inch nonstick skillet, heat vegetable oil over medium-high heat. Add garlic, gingerroot, onion and carrots to wok; stir-fry 2 minutes. Add cabbage; stir-fry 2 to 3 minutes or until cabbage is crisp-tender.

4. Add sauce and fettuccine to cabbage mixture; stir-fry about 2 minutes or until heated through. Spoon onto serving platter. Garnish with green onion and peanuts.

**Soy sauce can be substituted for the oyster sauce.*

1 SERVING: CAL. 105 (CAL. FROM FAT 25); FAT 3g (SAT. FAT 1g); CHOL. 15mg; SODIUM 290mg; CARBS. 16g (FIBER 1g); PRO. 3g **% DAILY VALUE:** VIT. A 6%; VIT. C 6%; CALC. 2%; IRON 6% **EXCHANGES:** 1 STARCH, 1/2 FAT **CARB. CHOICES:** 1

Mediterranean Couscous and Beans FAST LOW-FAT

PREP: 10 min **STAND:** 5 min ▪ **4 SERVINGS**

Couscous is a tiny pasta, but it's often shelved near the boxes of rice and grains in the supermarket. Several flavors of couscous, such as roasted garlic and sun-dried tomato, are available in addition to plain couscous.

3 cups vegetable or chicken broth
2 cups uncooked couscous
1/2 cup raisins or currants
1/4 teaspoon pepper
1/8 teaspoon ground red pepper (cayenne)
1 small tomato, chopped (1/2 cup)
1 can (15 to 16 oz) garbanzo beans, rinsed and drained
1/3 cup crumbled feta cheese

1. In 3-quart saucepan, heat broth to boiling. Stir in remaining ingredients except cheese; remove from heat.

2. Cover and let stand about 5 minutes or until liquid is absorbed; stir gently.

3. Sprinkle each serving with cheese.

1 SERVING: CAL. 550 (CAL. FROM FAT 55); FAT 6g (SAT. FAT 2g); CHOL. 10mg; SODIUM 1,050mg; CARBS. 115g (FIBER 14g); PRO. 23g **% DAILY VALUE:** VIT. A 14%; VIT. C 6%; CALC. 14%; IRON 26% **EXCHANGES:** 7 STARCH **CARB. CHOICES:** 7 1/2

Ravioli and Vegetables with Pesto Cream **FAST**

PREP: 10 min **COOK:** 8 min ■ **4 SERVINGS**

- 2 teaspoons olive or vegetable oil
- 8 oz green beans, cut into 1 1/2-inch pieces
- 1/2 medium yellow bell pepper, cut into 1/2-inch pieces (1/2 cup)
- 3 roma (plum) tomatoes, cut into 1/2-inch pieces (1 cup)
- 1/2 teaspoon salt
- 16 oz frozen cheese-filled ravioli (from 24-oz bag)
- 1/2 cup sour cream
- 3 tablespoons Basil Pesto (page 405) or purchased basil pesto
- 2 teaspoons grated lemon peel

1. In 12-inch nonstick skillet, heat oil over medium-high heat. Cook green beans and bell pepper in oil about 5 minutes, stirring frequently, until crisp-tender. Stir in tomatoes and salt. Cook 3 minutes.

2. Meanwhile, cook ravioli as directed on package. In small bowl, mix sour cream, Basil Pesto and lemon peel.

3. Drain ravioli; return to saucepan. Toss ravioli, vegetable mixture and sour cream mixture.

1 SERVING: CAL. 385 (CAL. FROM FAT 215); FAT 24g (SAT. FAT 9g); CHOL. 135mg; SODIUM 1,350mg; CARBS. 26g (FIBER 3g); PRO. 16g **% DAILY VALUE:** VIT. A 24%; VIT. C 30%; CALC. 32%; IRON 14% **EXCHANGES:** 1 1/2 STARCH, 1 1/2 HIGH-FAT MEAT, 1 VEGETABLE, 2 FAT **CARB. CHOICES:** 2

▲ **Ravioli and Vegetables with Pesto Cream**

GRAINS GLOSSARY

Rice

Arborio (Italian or Risotto) Rice: Is shorter, fatter and has a higher starch content than regular short-grain rice. Originally from northern Italy, Arborio is preferred for making risotto, a classic rice dish. As it cooks, the rice releases starch, providing its distinctive creamy texture.

Aromatic Rices: Contain a natural ingredient that gives a nutty or perfumy smell and taste. The quality of the fragrance can differ from year to year, and it intensifies with age. Aromatic rices include basmati, jasmine, texmati, Wehani and wild pecan rice.

Brown Rice: Unpolished rice with only the outer hull removed. It has a slightly firm texture and nutlike flavor, and it takes longer to cook than regular long-grain rice. Because the germ hasn't been removed, brown rice has more fiber and other nutrients.

Converted (Parboiled) Rice: Is steamed and pressure cooked before being milled and polished. This process retains more nutrients but hardens the grain, so it takes longer to cook than regular rice. It also removes excess starch, so the grains stay separate after cooking.

Instant Rice: Is partially cooked, rinsed and dehydrated before packaging, resulting in a very short cooking time. White, brown and wild rice all are available in this form.

Regular Long-Grain Rice: Has been milled to remove the hull, germ and most of the bran. About 90 percent of the rice produced in the United States is enriched. It's available in long, medium and short grains. The shorter the grain, the stickier the cooked rice will be; therefore, long grain is a better all-purpose rice.

Wild Rice: Not actually a rice, it is the seed of a grass that grows in marshes and rivers. Very dark greenish brown in color, it has a distinctive nutlike flavor and chewy texture. It's often found in rice mixtures with white or brown rice.

Other Grains

Barley: One of the first grains ever cultivated. Pearl barley, the most common variety, has been steamed and polished; it's good in soups, stews and served as a side dish like rice is. Barley is available in both regular and quick-cooking varieties.

Bulgur and Cracked Wheat: Made from whole wheat kernels. To make bulgur, wheat kernels are steamed, dried and crushed into coarse fragments. Cracked wheat is from kernels that are cleaned, then cracked or cut into fine fragments. Bulgur and cracked wheat are often used as breakfast cereals, and they appear in many Middle Eastern dishes.

Cornmeal: Crushed dried corn kernels that can be blue, yellow or white, depending on the variety of corn used. It may be either commercially or stone ground; stone ground is more nutritious because it still contains some of the hull and germ of the corn. Although cornmeal is available in fine, medium and coarse textures, only one type is generally available in most supermarkets. Grits is a very coarse-ground cornmeal.

Flaxseed: This tiny, shiny brown seed is booming in popularity because of its nutritional value. Packed inside are calcium, iron, niacin, phosphorous, vitamin E and omega-3 fatty acids. For its benefits to be reaped, the seed must be ground because whole seeds will pass through the digestive system without the body absorbing any nutrients. Flaxseed can be purchased ground, or it can be purchased whole and ground as needed in a coffee grinder, food processor or blender just before use. Sprinkle it on cereals and salads, blend it in smoothies, and look for recipes for cookies, muffins, quick breads and yeast breads that substitute ground flaxseed for a portion of the flour. Store tightly covered in the refrigerator up to 2 weeks or freeze up to 3 months.

Kasha: Also called *buckwheat groats*, it is the kernel inside the buckwheat seed. It's roasted for a toasty, nutty flavor, then coarsely ground.

Millet: A tiny, round, yellow seed that looks like whole mustard seed. Rich in protein, it has a chewy texture and mild flavor similar to brown rice. It's good whole as a hot cereal and is the base for dishes such as pilaf. It's also ground as a flour for puddings, cakes and breads.

Quinoa (KEEN-wa): An ancient grain native to South America where the Incas called it "the mother grain." Quinoa is higher in protein than any other grain. This creamy white, tiny, bead-shaped grain has a light texture and delicate flavor. Look for quinoa in larger supermarkets and health food stores.

Triticale: A cross between wheat and rye. It's more nutritious than either wheat or rye and is a blend of wheat's nutlike flavor and rye's chewy texture. It's available in berries, flakes and flour. Whole triticale can be cooked as cereal and used in casseroles and pilafs.

Wheat Berries: Hulled whole kernels of wheat. Presoaking is necessary to tenderize. Because they contain the entire wheat kernel, they take longer to cook and are high in nutritional value. They're eaten as a breakfast cereal and as a replacement for beans in chili, salads and baked dishes. They're also sprouted. Look for wheat berries in health food stores.

LEGUMES GLOSSARY

Adzuki Beans: Small, oval, reddish brown beans with a mild, nutty flavor. Originating in China and Japan, they taste similar to kidney beans and can replace them in recipes.

Anasazi Beans: Kidney-shaped, red-and-white speckled beans; the spots disappear when cooked. The name is Navajo, meaning "ancient ones." Their sweet, full flavor makes them excellent for Mexican dishes.

Black Beans: Also called *turtle beans,* black beans are found in the cuisines of Mexico, South and Central America as well as the Caribbean. Dark and full-flavored, they stand up well to bold seasonings.

Black-Eyed Peas: Also called *cowpeas* and *black-eyed suzies,* black-eyed peas are creamy colored with a small, dark brown to black spot on one side. They don't require presoaking and cook quickly. Found in traditional southern recipes, black-eyed peas pair well with strong-flavored greens such as spinach, chard and kale.

Butter Beans: Large, cream-colored lima beans with a smooth, buttery texture and mild flavor. They're often served as a vegetable side dish or added to soups, main dishes and salads for color and texture interest.

Cannellini Beans: Large white kidney beans that originated in South America. Adopted by Italy, they are often mixed with pasta and added to soups and salads.

Cranberry Beans: Pink with dark red streaks, the color fades during cooking but the nutty flavor is retained. They're a favorite in Italian cooking and are also known as *Roman beans.*

Fava Beans: Large flat beans with an earthy flavor that appear brown and wrinkled when dried. They are used in the Middle Eastern specialty *falafel.*

Garbanzo Beans: Tan, bumpy and round, garbanzo beans need long, slow cooking. Also called *chickpeas,* they are used in the popular Middle Eastern dip *hummus.* Their firm texture makes them a good addition to soups, stews, casseroles and salads.

Great Northern Beans: Kidney-shaped white beans that resemble lima beans, as well as their cousin, navy beans. Can be used in any dish calling for white beans, such as casseroles and soups. Cannellini beans are a good substitute, although they're smaller.

Kidney Beans: Available in dark and light red, they add color and texture to many dishes including chili or red beans and rice.

Lentils: The familiar small, grayish green lentil is only one of the hundreds of varieties and colors used around the world. Also available in white, yellow, red and black, dried lentils do not require presoaking, and they cook in a short time.

Lima Beans: Named for Lima, Peru, lima beans are pale green and plump and have a slight kidney-shaped curve. Usually available dried, frozen and canned (also see Butter Beans).

Marrow Beans: The largest and roundest of the white beans, marrow beans are typically served as a side dish.

Mung Beans: Called *grams,* or when hulled, *moong dal,* this sweet-flavored bean is native to India and is also popular in China. Americans know its sprouted form as bean sprouts. Use them in place of lentils or peas in recipes.

Navy Beans: Also known as *pea beans,* these small, white beans are so named because they have been a staple of sailors' diets since the early 1800s. You'll find navy beans in commercially canned pork and beans, and they're the beans of choice for homemade baked beans.

Pink Beans: Popular in the cooking of the western United States, these reddish brown beans are interchangeable with pinto beans in recipes.

Pinto Beans: Speckled pink and brown when dried, they lose their spots and fade to a pinkish brown when cooked. Their full-bodied, earthy flavor makes them a staple of southwestern and Mexican cooking.

Red Beans: A dark red bean that's popular in Mexican, southwestern United States and Caribbean cooking. Use them interchangeably with kidney beans.

Soybeans: Soybeans are a nutritional powerhouse! They're incorporated into energy and nutrition bars and salty-crunchy snacks and are being used just like any other bean in all sorts of recipes. Soybeans are also used to make miso, tofu, tempeh, soy sauce, soybean oil and many other products.

Split Peas: Available green or yellow, split peas are used mostly in soups. They don't need presoaking and cook in less time than beans. When cooked, they turn into a soft mush, making them perfect for soups and stews, as well as for *dal,* a spicy Indian dish.

PASTA GLOSSARY

Asian Noodles

- **Cellophane:** Also called *bean threads* or *glass noodles,* these noodles are made from the starch of mung beans. These dried, translucent noodles must be presoaked before using in most recipes unless they are added directly to soups or simmering liquids. The dry noodles also can be deep-fried; they puff up instantly and dramatically to a size many times larger than when dry. Rice sticks can be substituted.

- **Chinese Egg Noodles:** A type of wheat-egg noodle that closely resembles Italian pasta and is available either dried or fresh. Noodles range in thickness from very thin to thick and round. Narrow egg noodles, spaghetti or linguine can be substituted.

- **Japanese Curly Noodles:** Quick-cooking, wavy, thin, long noodles sold in rectangular "bricks." Toss in stir-fries, or top with stir-fried meat and vegetables.

- **Ramen Noodles:** These are instant, deep-fried noodles sold in cellophane packages with a seasoning packet and sometimes little bits of vegetables. The noodles can be cooked or used dry as a crunchy addition to salads. Some brands bake rather than deep-fry the noodles, so they are lower in fat.

- **Rice Noodles/Rice Sticks:** These noodles are opaque white in color and sold fresh or dried. Dried rice noodles are the most widely available and usually come in the form of very thin strands. Rice sticks are often fried, but when cooked, they have a creamy, soft texture. Angel hair or linguine can be substituted.

- **Soba:** Slightly wider than somen noodles, soba noodles are made from buckwheat flour. They have a chewy texture and nutty flavor and can be round or flat. They make a great addition to soups and stews or can be topped with a delicate sauce. Whole wheat spaghetti can be substituted.

- **Somen:** These noodles are made from wheat flour and formed into very thin strands. Vermicelli or angel hair pasta can be substituted.
- **Udon:** Fat and slippery noodles made from wheat flour. They can be flat, square or round and are available both dried and fresh. Fettuccine or linguine can be substituted.

Other Pasta

Acini de Pepe: Spaghetti cut to the size of peppercorns. Top with any sauce, or add to a casserole.

Anelli: Tiny rings of pasta. Excellent for soups, salads.

Bucatini: Long, hollow noodles that resemble drinking straws. Originating in Naples, the word *bucato* means "with a hole." Break into thirds, if desired, and serve with any sauce.

Capellini/Angel Hair: "Fine hairs" of pasta, the thinnest of spaghettis. Legend has it that Parmesan cheese clings to this pasta like gold clings to an angel's hair. Serve with more delicate sauces, or break in half for stir-fries.

Cappelletti: Small, stuffed pasta similar to tortellini but with the ends pinched together in the shape of "little hats."

Cavatappi: Corkscrew-shaped pasta with a hollow middle, making it perfect for thick and creamy vegetable, meat and seafood sauces.

Couscous: The tiniest pasta, it's made from granular semolina and is a staple of North African and some Middle Eastern cuisines. Often used as an alternative to rice. Available in regular, precooked (which cooks in just 5 minutes) and flavored varieties.

Ditali/Ditalini: Very tiny, very short tubes either grooved or smooth. In Italian, they're "little thimbles." Top with any sauce, toss into soup or bake in casseroles.

Egg Noodles: Flat or curly short pasta strips usually made with eggs or egg yolks. Top with sauces, or serve as a side dish.

Elbow Macaroni: Curved, short, hollow "elbows" of pasta. Perfect for soups, salads, casseroles and, of course, macaroni and cheese!

Farfalle: The bow-tie or butterfly pasta; its mini version is *tripolini.* This shape adds interest to soups and salads and is also wonderful with colorful sauces.

Fettuccine: Long, flat, narrow, "little ribbon" noodles. Perfect for heavier cheese and meat sauces. Available in many flavors, including plain and spinach.

Fusilli: A long or short spring-shaped pasta from southern Italy. Hailing originally from Naples, it is also known as *eliche,* or "propellers," for its quality of trapping some of the sauce and propelling the flavor.

Gemelli/Twist: A short, twisted pasta. Like fusilli, it adds interest to salads and also works well with sauces.

Gnocchi: "Little dumplings" made from potatoes, flour or farina; additions may include eggs, cheese or spinach. The dough is shaped into small balls or ovals. Gnocchi is served with butter and cheese or a variety of sauces.

Lasagna: Flat noodle, about two inches wide, with ruffled or straight edges. It's great for layering with sauces. Look for fresh, dried, frozen and precooked lasagna.

Linguine: Long, flat, thin noodle, usually $^{1}/_{8}$ inch wide. Italians call it "little tongues" because its original shape resembled the thickness of a songbird's tongue. A good shape for all sauces.

Mafalda: Mini lasagna noodles—short, flat with ruffled edges. Popular used with seafood sauces and for casseroles.

Manicotti/Cannelloni: A large, four-inch tubular noodle usually stuffed and baked. Comes from the word *canna,* meaning "hollow cane."

Mostaccioli: A short cut pasta about two inches long, either grooved or smooth. These tubular "mustaches" have slanted cuts at both ends.

Noodles: Noodles can be fresh, frozen or dried and are made with or without eggs. This flat pasta comes in a variety of lengths and widths, including extra-wide, wide, medium, fine, ribbons and dumpling.

Novelty Pasta Shapes: Unique, fun pasta in the shape of pumpkins, trees, rabbits, hearts, states, cars, birthday cakes, alphabets, grape clusters and garlic bulbs. Available in gourmet food stores and some large supermarkets.

Orecchiette: The name means "little ears." This tiny disk-shaped pasta is great with chunky vegetable or meat sauces.

Orzo: Tiny rice-shaped pasta. Terrific in salads, side dishes and soups and is a great substitute for rice. Orzo and rosamarina (see right) are very similar in shape, but traditional orzo is smaller than rosamarina. However, the size of each of these pastas varies depending on the brand. Both types can be used interchangeably.

Penne: A short cut pasta, about 1 1/4 inches long, either grooved or smooth. Tubular in shape with slanted cuts at both ends, it's narrower than mostaccioli. The word *penne* means "feather," indicating either the lightness of the noodle or the shape that resembles the wing of a bird. It is excellent with tomato and vegetable sauces.

Radiatore: Shaped like old-fashioned home-heating radiators or air conditioners; the ruffled edges help catch all the flavors in the sauce or dressing.

Ravioli: Pillow-shaped pasta, usually stuffed with cheese, chicken, meat or spinach, that's popular in several Italian regions. Ravioli also can be filled with less traditional ingredients like pumpkin or wild mushrooms. Typically served with butter or Parmesan, this pasta is delicious with tomato and meat sauces.

Rigatoni: Short cut, wide tubular pasta with lengthwise grooves, about one inch long. It suits most chunky sauces and meat sauces.

Rosamarina: Pumpkin seed-shaped pasta. Use in salads, side dishes and soups. Also see Orzo, left.

Rotelle: A wide, corkscrew-shaped pasta. Its curves are great for catching any kind of sauce.

Rotini: A skinny version of rotelle, it's plain or tricolored. Rotini is a favorite for pasta salads.

Shells: Shells are available in jumbo, medium and small sizes. Jumbo shells are great stuffed; medium and small shells are more suited to thick sauces, soups and salads. *Conchiglie* and *conchiglioni* are the Italian names for shells, or *conches.*

Spaghetti: Means "little strings" in Italian. These long, thin strands of pasta are round and solid.

Tortellini: Little rings of pasta filled with cheese, originating from Bologna, Italy. The fresh, refrigerated products are offered in many flavors with a variety of fillings such as Italian sausage and chicken. Tortellini usually is served with a tomato or cream sauce. It's also well-suited to soups and salads.

Vermicelli: A long, very thin pasta. "Little worms" is the original meaning of this word, named for the squirming motion the noodles make when being twirled around a fork. It was the original pasta for spaghetti and meatballs. Use vermicelli with lighter sauces and in soups.

Wagon Wheel: So named because its shape resembles a spoked wheel. A fun pasta to add to casseroles, soups and salads, especially when you want to boost the kid appeal. Some brands may also label this pasta *rotelle.*

Ziti: Medium-size tubular pasta that's perfect for chunky sauces and meat dishes. In Italian, it means "bridegrooms."

TIMETABLE FOR COOKING GRAINS

Type of Grain (1 cup)	Amount of Water (cups)	Cooking Directions	Approximate Yield (cups)
RICE			
Rice, long-grain white	2	Heat rice and water to boiling. Reduce heat to low. Cover and simmer 15 minutes.	3
Rice, converted white	2 1/2	Heat water to boiling. Stir in rice. Reduce heat to low. Cover and simmer 20 to 25 minutes. Remove from heat; let stand covered 5 minutes.	3 to 4
Rice, instant white	1	Heat water to boiling. Stir in rice. Cover and remove from heat; let stand covered 5 minutes.	2
Rice, long-grain brown	2 3/4	Heat rice and water to boiling. Reduce heat to low. Cover and simmer 45 to 50 minutes.	4
Rice, instant brown	1 1/4	Heat water to boiling. Stir in rice. Reduce heat to low. Cover and simmer 10 minutes.	2
Rice, basmati	1 1/2	Heat rice and water to boiling. Reduce heat to low. Cover and simmer 15 to 20 minutes.	3
Rice, jasmine	1 3/4	Heat rice and water to boiling. Reduce heat to low. Cover and simmer 15 to 20 minutes.	3
Rice, texmati	1 3/4	Heat rice and water to boiling. Reduce heat to low. Cover and simmer 15 to 20 minutes.	3
Rice, wild	2 1/2	Heat rice and water to boiling. Reduce heat to low. Cover and simmer 40 to 50 minutes.	3
OTHER GRAINS			
Barley, regular	4	Heat water to boiling. Stir in barley. Reduce heat to low. Cover and simmer 45 to 50 minutes.	4
Barley, quick-cooking	2	Heat water to boiling. Stir in barley. Reduce heat to low. Cover and simmer 10 to 12 minutes. Let stand covered 5 minutes.	3
Bulgur	3	Pour boiling water over bulgur. Cover and soak 30 to 60 minutes (do not cook). Drain if needed. Or cook as directed on package.	3
Kasha (roasted buckwheat groats/kernels)	2	Pour boiling water over kasha. Cover and soak 10 to 15 minutes (do not cook). Drain if needed. Or cook as directed on package.	4
Millet	2 1/2	Heat millet and water to boiling. Reduce heat to low. Cover and simmer 15 to 20 minutes.	4
Quinoa	2	Rinse well. Heat quinoa and water to boiling. Reduce heat to low. Cover and simmer 15 minutes.	3 to 4
Wheat Berries	2 1/2	Heat wheat berries and water to boiling. Reduce heat to low. Cover and simmer 50 to 60 minutes.	2 3/4 to 3

TIMETABLE FOR COOKING LEGUMES

Sort legumes to remove stones and shriveled, small or damaged legumes; rinse and drain. Place 1 cup uncooked legumes in 3- to 4-quart saucepan; add enough water to cover (black-eyed peas, lentils and split peas don't require soaking or pre-cooking). Heat to boiling; boil uncovered 2 minutes. Reduce heat to low. Cover and simmer (do not boil or legumes will burst), stirring occasionally, for amount of simmer time in chart or until tender.

Type of Legume	Approximate Simmer Time	Approximate Yield
Adzuki Beans Lentils	30 to 45 minutes	2 to 3 cups
Mung Beans Split Peas	45 to 60 minutes	2 to 2 1/4 cups
Black-Eyed Peas Butter Beans Cannellini Beans Great Northern Beans Lima Beans Navy Beans Pinto Beans	1 hour to 1 hour 30 minutes	2 to 2 1/2 cups
Anasazi Beans Black Beans Fava Beans Kidney Beans	1 to 2 hours	2 cups
Garbanzo Beans	2 hours to 2 hours 30 minutes	2 cups
Soybeans	3 to 4 hours	2 cups

Note: If legumes aren't quite tender but they've absorbed all the water, add a little more water and cook longer. Legumes continue to dry with age, so more water may be needed than a recipe calls for and they may take longer to cook. If the legumes are really old, they may never soften completely.

TIMETABLE FOR COOKING PASTA

You'll find cooking directions right on pasta packages, but if you've bought the pasta in bulk or stored it in a different container, this reference chart gives you approximate cooking times for the most popular types and shapes of pasta.

Type of Pasta	Cooking Time (minutes)
DRIED PASTA	
Acini de pepe	5 to 6
Capellini	5 to 6
Egg noodles, regular	8 to 10
Egg noodles, extra wide	10 to 12
Elbow macaroni	8 to 10
Farfalle	13 to 15
Fettuccine	11 to 13
Fusilli	11 to 13
Japanese curly noodles	4 to 5
Lasagna noodles	12 to 15
Linguine	9 to 13
Mafalda	8 to 10
Manicotti	10 to 12
Mostaccioli	12 to 14
Penne	9 to 13
Radiatore	9 to 11
Rigatoni	12 to 15
Rotelle	10 to 12
Rotini	8 to 10
Shells, jumbo	12 to 15
Shells, medium and small	9 to 11
Soba noodles	6 to 7
Spaghetti	8 to 10
Vermicelli	5 to 7
Wagon wheel	10 to 12
Ziti	14 to 15
REFRIGERATED PACKAGED FRESH PASTA	
Capellini	1 to 2
Farfalle	2 to 3
Fettuccine	1 to 2
Lasagna	2 to 3
Linguine	1 to 2
Ravioli	6 to 8
Tortellini	8 to 10

CHAPTER 14

Salads & Salad Dressings

Salads

Salad Dressings

LOW-FAT = *3g or less, except main dishes with 10g or less* FAST = *Ready in 20 minutes or less* BREAD MACHINE = *Bread machine directions* SLOW COOKER = *Slow cooker directions* LIGHTER = *25% fewer calories or grams of fat*

◀ **Gorgonzola and Toasted Walnut Salad (page 380)**

Salad Basics

Salads have become a mealtime standard. Toss up a starting course of some mixed greens, mix up a side dish of creamy potato salad or a hearty pasta salad for center stage. You'll find a spectacular collection of all kinds for every occasion, right here in this chapter. But first, brush up on your salad IQ with this helpful information.

SELECTING, STORING AND HANDLING SALAD GREENS

See Salad Greens Glossary (page 402) for more information.

- *Choose fresh, crisp greens* with no bruises, discoloration or wilting.
- *Remove roots and stems,* if necessary, and any brown or wilted spots.
- *To store,* line a plastic bag or tightly covered container with damp (not wet) paper towels. Place unwashed greens in bag, and refrigerate up to 5 days. Iceberg lettuce should be rinsed before storing; remove core and rinse core side up under cold water, then turn upside down to drain. Store as directed for other greens.
- *When ready to use greens,* rinse under cold water and shake off excess moisture.
- *Dry salad greens* as much as possible so dressings cling to the leaves and doesn't become watery. To dry greens, use a salad spinner or place them on a clean kitchen towel or several layers of paper towels and pat gently to dry. Once dry, greens can be stored gently rolled up in the towel or paper towels and placed in a plastic bag for up to 8 hours.

TIPS FOR TOSSED SALADS

- Mix mild-flavored greens with more assertive ones. Try tossing butterhead with mesclun, or red chard with romaine and iceberg lettuces. For little dashes of flavor, add fresh herbs!
- Tear greens with your fingers into bite-size pieces—don't cut them. Greens go limp and the edges darken if cut with a knife. If you do use a knife, cut up the greens just before serving or use a serrated plastic salad knife (sold in the utensils/gadgets section in large department or discount stores).
- Tomatoes are watery, so wait until just before tossing to add slices, or place them on top of a salad so they won't dilute the dressing or cause the greens to get soggy. Seeding the tomatoes first also helps.
- Add dressing to greens just before serving so they won't get soggy. When "dressing" greens, or tossing with a dressing, start with a small amount, using only enough to lightly coat the leaves, then toss. Or serve the dressing on the side so each person can dress their own. Salads that have been tossed with dressing don't make good leftovers because the salad will become soggy.
- As a rule, stronger greens need a stronger-flavored dressing and mild-tasting greens needs lighter-tasting dressings.

GREENS/LETTUCE

Arugula

Beet greens

Belgian endive

Boston

Collard greens

Curly endive

Frisée

Kale

Escarole

Mâche

Leaf lettuce (red)

Mesclun

Iceberg

Sorrel

Spinach

Radicchio

Romaine

Watercress

Swiss chard

Swiss chard (red)

Caesar Salad FAST

PREP: 15 min ■ **6 SERVINGS**

1 clove garlic, cut in half
8 anchovy fillets, cut up*
1/3 cup olive or vegetable oil
3 tablespoons lemon juice
1 teaspoon Worcestershire sauce
1/4 teaspoon salt
1/4 teaspoon ground mustard
Freshly ground pepper
1 large or 2 small bunches romaine lettuce, torn into bite-size pieces (10 cups)
1 cup garlic-flavored croutons
1/3 cup grated Parmesan cheese

1. Rub large wooden salad bowl with cut clove of garlic. Allow a few small pieces of garlic to remain in bowl if desired.

2. In salad bowl, mix anchovies, oil, lemon juice, Worcestershire sauce, salt, mustard and pepper.

3. Add romaine; toss until coated. Sprinkle with croutons and cheese; toss. Serve immediately.

**2 teaspoons anchovy paste can be substituted for the anchovy fillets.*

1 SERVING (ABOUT 1 3/4 CUPS): CAL. 195 (CAL. FROM FAT 145); FAT 16g (SAT. FAT 3g); CHOL. 10mg; SODIUM 500mg; CARBS. 7g (FIBER 2g); PRO. 6g **% DAILY VALUE:** VIT. A 40%; VIT. C 40%; CALC. 12%; IRON 8% **EXCHANGES:** 1 1/2 VEGETABLE, 1/2 HIGH-FAT MEAT, 2 1/2 FAT **CARB. CHOICES:** 1/2

CHICKEN CAESAR SALAD Broil or grill 6 boneless skinless chicken breast halves (page 321); slice diagonally and arrange on salads. Serve chicken warm or chilled.

SHRIMP CAESAR SALAD Broil or grill 1 lb peeled deveined large shrimp (page 253); arrange on salads. Serve shrimp warm or chilled.

Greek Salad FAST

PREP: 20 min ■ **8 SERVINGS**

Lemon Dressing

1/4 cup vegetable oil
2 tablespoons lemon juice
1/2 teaspoon sugar
1 1/2 teaspoons Dijon mustard
1/4 teaspoon salt
1/8 teaspoon pepper

Salad

7 oz washed fresh spinach leaves, torn into bite-size pieces (5 cups)
1 head Boston lettuce, torn into bite-size pieces (4 cups)
1 package (4 oz) crumbled feta cheese (1 cup)
4 medium green onions, sliced (1/4 cup)
24 pitted ripe olives*
3 medium tomatoes, cut into wedges
1 medium cucumber, sliced

1. In tightly covered container, shake all dressing ingredients.

2. In large bowl, toss salad ingredients and dressing. Serve immediately.

**Kalamata or Greek olives can be substituted.*

1 SERVING (ABOUT 1 3/4 CUPS): CAL. 140 (CAL. FROM FAT 100); FAT 11g (SAT. FAT 3g); CHOL. 5mg; SODIUM 680mg; CARBS. 6g (FIBER 2g); PRO. g **% DAILY VALUE:** VIT. A 60%; VIT. C 32%; CALC. 12%; IRON 8% **EXCHANGES:** 1 VEGETABLE, 2 1/2 FAT **CARB. CHOICES:** 1/2

HOW TO WASH SPINACH

To wash fresh spinach, remove and discard stems. Place leaves in a sink or bowl filled with cool water. Swish with your hands in the water to rinse the dirt off the spinach. Lift the leaves up to drain off excess water. Repeat until no dirt remains, changing water if necessary.

Bacon-Spinach Salad

PREP: 15 min **COOK:** 10 min ▪ **6 SERVINGS**

Save time by using bags of prewashed spinach.

- 4 slices bacon, cut into 1/2-inch pieces
- 3 tablespoons vegetable oil
- 5 medium green onions, chopped (1/3 cup)
- 2 teaspoons sugar
- 1/2 teaspoon salt
- 1/4 teaspoon pepper
- 2 tablespoons white or cider vinegar
- 8 oz washed fresh spinach leaves (9 cups)
- 2 Hard-Cooked Eggs (page 220), sliced

1. In 10-inch skillet, cook bacon over medium heat, stirring occasionally, until crisp. Remove bacon with slotted spoon; drain on paper towels. Drain all but 3 tablespoons bacon fat from skillet (if there aren't 3 tablespoons bacon fat remaining, add enough vegetable oil to bacon fat to equal 3 tablespoons).

2. Add oil, onions, sugar, salt and pepper to bacon fat in skillet. Cook over medium heat 2 to 3 minutes, stirring occasionally, until onions are slightly softened. Stir in vinegar.

3. Place spinach in very large bowl. Pour warm dressing over spinach; toss to coat. Arrange egg slices on top; sprinkle with bacon. Serve immediately.

1 SERVING (ABOUT 1 1/2 CUPS): CAL. 135 (CAL. FROM FAT 100); FAT 11g (SAT. FAT 2g); CHOL. 75mg; SODIUM 130mg; CARBS. 4g (FIBER 1g); PRO. 5g **% DAILY VALUE:** VIT. A 74%; VIT. C 22%; CALC. 6%; IRON 8% **EXCHANGES:** 1 VEGETABLE, 1/2 LEAN MEAT, 2 FAT **CARB. CHOICES:** 0

Gorgonzola and Toasted Walnut Salad **FAST**

PREP: 20 min ▪ **6 SERVINGS**

Toasted Walnut Dressing

- 1/3 cup olive or vegetable oil
- 1/3 cup coarsely chopped walnuts, toasted (page 215)
- 2 tablespoons lemon juice
- 1 clove garlic
- 1/8 teaspoon salt
- Dash of pepper

Salad

- 1 head radicchio, torn into bite-size pieces (4 cups)
- 1 head Bibb lettuce, torn into bite-size pieces (4 cups)
- 1/2 cup crumbled Gorgonzola or Roquefort cheese (2 oz)
- 1/2 cup 1/2-inch pieces fresh chives
- 1/3 cup coarsely chopped walnuts, toasted (page 215)

1. In blender or food processor, place all dressing ingredients. Cover and blend on high speed about 1 minute or until smooth.

2. In large bowl, toss salad ingredients and dressing. Serve immediately.

1 SERVING: CAL. 250 (CAL. FROM FAT 215); FAT 24g (SAT. FAT 4g); CHOL. 5mg; SODIUM 230mg; CARBS. 5g (FIBER 2g); PRO. 5g **% DAILY VALUE:** VIT. A 12%; VIT. C 66%; CALC. 12%; IRON 6% **EXCHANGES:** 1 VEGETABLE, 5 FAT **CARB. CHOICES:** 0

Mandarin Salad

PREP: 20 min **COOK:** 10 min ■ **6 SERVINGS**

Sugared Almonds

1/4 cup sliced almonds
1 tablespoon plus 1 teaspoon sugar

Sweet-Sour Dressing

1/4 cup vegetable oil
2 tablespoons sugar
2 tablespoons white or cider vinegar
1 tablespoon chopped fresh parsley
1/2 teaspoon salt
Dash of pepper
Dash of red pepper sauce

Salad

1/2 small head lettuce, torn into bite-size pieces (3 cups)
1/2 bunch romaine lettuce, torn into bite-size pieces (3 cups)
2 medium stalks celery, chopped (1 cup)
2 medium green onions, thinly sliced (2 tablespoons)
1 can (11 oz) mandarin orange segments, drained

1. In 1-quart saucepan, cook almonds and 1 tablespoon plus 1 teaspoon sugar over low heat about 10 minutes, stirring constantly, until sugar is melted and almonds are coated; cool and break apart.

2. In tightly covered container, shake all dressing ingredients. Refrigerate until serving.

3. In large bowl, toss salad ingredients, dressing and almonds. Serve immediately.

1 SERVING (ABOUT 1 1/3 CUPS): CAL. 170 (CAL. FROM FAT 110); FAT 12g (SAT. FAT 2g); CHOL. 0mg; SODIUM 220mg; CARBS. 16g (FIBER 3g); PRO. 2g **% DAILY VALUE:** VIT. A 20%; VIT. C 40%; CALC. 4%; IRON 4% **EXCHANGES:** 1/2 FRUIT, 2 VEGETABLE, 2 FAT **CARB. CHOICES:** 1

CRUNCHY CHICKEN MANDARIN SALAD Make salad as directed; divide among 6 individual serving plates. Top each serving with a grilled boneless skinless chicken breast, sliced (warm or cold). Sprinkle each salad with 2 tablespoons wide or regular chow mein noodles.

Italian Chopped Salad

PREP: 25 min ■ **4 SERVINGS**

Basil Vinaigrette

1/3 cup olive or vegetable oil
1/4 cup red wine vinegar
2 tablespoons chopped fresh or 2 teaspoons dried basil leaves
1 teaspoon sugar
1/4 teaspoon salt

Salad

6 cups chopped romaine lettuce
1 cup fresh basil leaves
1 cup cut-up cooked chicken
2 large tomatoes, chopped (2 cups)
2 medium cucumbers, chopped (1 1/2 cups)
1 package (3 oz) Italian salami, chopped
1 can (15 to 16 oz) cannellini beans, rinsed and drained

1. In tightly covered container, shake all vinaigrette ingredients.

2. In large bowl, place all salad ingredients. Pour vinaigrette over salad; toss until coated. Serve immediately.

1 SERVING: CAL. 480 (CAL. FROM FAT 260); FAT 29g (SAT. FAT 6g); CHOL. 45mg; SODIUM 740mg; CARBS. 38g (FIBER 10g); PRO. 27g **% DAILY VALUE:** VIT. A 72%; VIT. C 78%; CALC. 12%; IRON 32% **EXCHANGES:** 2 STARCH, 2 LEAN MEAT, 2 VEGETABLE, 4 FAT **CARB. CHOICES:** 2 1/2

Italian Chopped Salad ▶

Panzanella

PREP: 20 min **CHILL:** 1 hr ■ **6 SERVINGS**

Panzanella, or "bread salad," is an Italian classic. Buy a firm-textured bread so the pieces don't become soggy.

4 cups 1-inch pieces day-old Italian or other firm-textured bread
2 medium tomatoes, cut into bite-size pieces (2 cups)
2 cloves garlic, finely chopped
1 medium green bell pepper, coarsely chopped (1 cup)
1/3 cup chopped fresh basil leaves
2 tablespoons chopped fresh parsley
1/3 cup extra-virgin or regular olive oil
2 tablespoons red wine vinegar
1/2 teaspoon salt
1/8 teaspoon pepper

1. In large glass or plastic bowl, mix bread, tomatoes, garlic, bell pepper, basil and parsley.

2. In tightly covered container, shake remaining ingredients. Pour over bread mixture; toss gently until bread is evenly coated.

3. Cover and refrigerate at least 1 hour until bread is softened and flavors are blended but no longer than 8 hours. Toss before serving.

1 SERVING: CAL. 185 (CAL. FROM FAT 115); FAT 13g (SAT. FAT 2g); CHOL. 0mg; SODIUM 340mg; CARBS. 16g (FIBER 2g); PRO. 3g
% DAILY VALUE: VIT. A 4%; VIT. C 46%; CALC. 2%; IRON 6%
EXCHANGES: 1 STARCH, 2 FAT **CARB. CHOICES:** 1

Roasted Beet Salad

PREP: 15 min **ROAST:** 40 min **COOL:** 30 min ■ **4 SERVINGS**

1 1/2 lb small beets (1 1/2 to 2 inches in diameter)
4 cups bite-size pieces mixed salad greens
1 medium orange, peeled and sliced
1/2 cup walnut halves, toasted (page 215) and coarsely chopped
1/4 cup crumbled chèvre (goat) cheese
1/2 cup Fresh Herb Vinaigrette (page 399)

1. Heat oven to 425°F. Remove greens from beets, leaving about 1/2 inch of stem. Wash beets well; leave whole with root ends attached. Place beets in ungreased 13 × 9-inch pan; drizzle with oil. Bake uncovered about 40 minutes or until tender.

2. Remove skins from beets under running water. Let beets cool until easy to handle, about 30 minutes. Peel beets and cut off root ends; cut beets into slices. Cut each slice in half.

3. On 4 salad plates, arrange salad greens. Top with beets, orange slices, walnuts and cheese. Serve with Fresh Herb Vinaigrette.

1 SERVING: CAL. 320 (CAL. FROM FAT 250); FAT 28g (SAT. FAT 5g); CHOL. 5mg; SODIUM 280mg; CARBS. 16g (FIBER 5g); PROTEIN 7g
% DAILY VALUE: VIT. A 38%; VIT. C 24%; CALC. 8%; IRON 12%
EXCHANGES: 3 VEGETABLE, 5 1/2 FAT **CARB. CHOICES:** 1

◀ **Panzanella**

BEETS, NOT JUST RED ANYMORE!

The humble beet is emerging as one of the unsung heroes of the vegetable world, and rightly so. Sweet tasting and rich in nutrition, beets are not only tasty as a side dish but are also a beautiful addition to salads. They can range in color from deep red to white, with red and golden beets most widely available. Look for candy cane (Chioggia) beets with their stunning concentric rings of red and white. Explore your local farmers' market for the best variety.

Seven-Layer Salad

PREP: 25 min **CHILL:** 2 hr ■ **6 SERVINGS**

Comfort food never goes out of style!

- 1 box (9 oz) frozen green peas
- 6 cups bite-size pieces mixed salad greens
- 2 medium stalks celery, thinly sliced (1 cup)
- 1 cup thinly sliced radishes
- 8 medium green onions, sliced (1/2 cup)
- 12 slices bacon, crisply cooked and crumbled (3/4 cup)
- 1 1/2 cups mayonnaise or salad dressing
- 1/2 cup grated Parmesan cheese or shredded Cheddar cheese (2 oz)

1. Cook peas as directed on box; rinse with cold water and drain.

2. Place salad greens in large glass bowl. Layer celery, radishes, onions, bacon and peas on salad greens.

3. Spread mayonnaise over peas, covering top completely and sealing to edge of bowl. Sprinkle with cheese.

4. Cover and refrigerate at least 2 hours to blend flavors but no longer than 12 hours. Toss before serving if desired. Store covered in refrigerator.

1 SERVING (ABOUT 1 1/4 CUPS): CAL. 575 (CAL. FROM FAT 480); FAT 52g (SAT. FAT 10g); CHOL. 50mg; SODIUM 740mg; CARBS. 12g (FIBER 5g); PRO. 12g **% DAILY VALUE:** VIT. A 44%; VIT. C 38%; CALC. 18%; IRON 12% **EXCHANGES:** 2 VEGETABLE, 1 HIGH-FAT MEAT, 9 1/2 FAT **CARB. CHOICES:** 1

LIGHTER SEVEN-LAYER SALAD

For 12 grams of fat and 200 calories per serving, substitute 1/2 cup reduced-fat mayonnaise and 1 cup plain fat-free yogurt for the 1 1/2 cups mayonnaise. Decrease bacon to 6 slices and cheese to 1/4 cup.

Seven Layer Salad

Broccoli Sunshine Salad

FAST

PREP: 15 min ■ **6 SERVINGS**

Stir this salad just before serving to redistribute all the ingredients. If the dressing is too thick, thin it with a little milk.

- 1/2 cup mayonnaise or salad dressing
- 1 tablespoon sugar
- 2 tablespoons cider vinegar
- 3 cups broccoli flowerets (1/2 lb)
- 1/3 cup raisins
- 1/4 cup shredded Cheddar cheese (1 oz)
- 4 slices bacon, crisply cooked and crumbled (1/4 cup)
- 2 tablespoons chopped red onion

1. In large glass or plastic bowl, mix mayonnaise, sugar and vinegar.

2. Add remaining ingredients; toss until evenly coated. Store covered in refrigerator.

1 SERVING (ABOUT 1/2 CUP): CAL. 220 (CAL. FROM FAT 160); FAT 18g (SAT. FAT 4g); CHOL. 20mg; SODIUM 210mg; CARBS. 12g (FIBER 2g); PRO. 4g **% DAILY VALUE:** VIT. A 12%; VIT. C 68%; CALC. 4%; IRON 4% **EXCHANGES:** 2 VEGETABLE, 4 FAT **CARB. CHOICES:** 1

LIGHTER BROCCOLI SUNSHINE SALAD

For 8 grams of fat and 140 calories per serving, use reduced-fat mayonnaise and cheese. Decrease bacon to 2 slices.

HOW TO CUT BROCCOLI

To make spears, cut lengthwise into 1/2-inch stalks. For pieces, cut the 1/2-inch stalks crosswise into 1-inch pieces (or size desired).

Creamy Potato Salad

PREP: 15 min **COOK:** 40 min **CHILL:** 4 hr ■ **10 SERVINGS**

- 6 medium round red or white potatoes (2 lb), peeled
- 1 1/2 cups mayonnaise or salad dressing
- 1 tablespoon white or cider vinegar
- 1 tablespoon yellow mustard
- 1 teaspoon salt
- 1/4 teaspoon pepper
- 2 medium stalks celery, chopped (1 cup)
- 1 medium onion, chopped (1/2 cup)
- 4 Hard-Cooked Eggs (page 220), chopped
- Paprika, if desired

1. Place potatoes in 3-quart saucepan; add enough water just to cover potatoes. Cover and heat to boiling; reduce heat to low. Cook covered 30 to 35 minutes or until potatoes are tender; drain. Let stand until cool enough to handle. Cut potatoes into cubes.

2. In large glass or plastic bowl, mix mayonnaise, vinegar, mustard, salt and pepper. Add potatoes, celery and onion; toss. Stir in eggs. Sprinkle with paprika.

3. Cover and refrigerate at least 4 hours to blend flavors and chill. Store covered in refrigerator.

1 SERVING (ABOUT 3/4 CUP): CAL. 335 (CAL. FROM FAT 250); FAT 28g (SAT. FAT 5g); CHOL. 105mg; SODIUM 480mg; CARBS. 17g (FIBER 2g); PRO. 4g **% DAILY VALUE:** VIT. A 4%; VIT. C 10%; CALC. 2%; IRON 4% **EXCHANGES:** 1 STARCH, 5 1/2 FAT **CARB. CHOICES:** 1

LIGHTER CREAMY POTATO SALAD

For 13 grams of fat and 210 calories per serving, use reduced-fat mayonnaise and 2 eggs.

Hot German Potato Salad

LOW-FAT

PREP: 10 min **COOK:** 55 min ■ **6 SERVINGS**

- 4 medium round red or white potatoes ($1\frac{1}{3}$ lb)
- 3 slices bacon, cut into 1-inch pieces
- 1 medium onion, chopped (1/2 cup)
- 1 tablespoon all-purpose flour
- 1 tablespoon sugar
- 1/2 teaspoon salt
- 1/4 teaspoon celery seed
- Dash of pepper
- 1/2 cup water
- 1/4 cup white or cider vinegar

1. Place potatoes in 3-quart saucepan; add enough water just to cover potatoes. Cover and heat to boiling; reduce heat to low. Cook covered 30 to 35 minutes or until potatoes are tender; drain. Let stand until cool enough to handle. Cut potatoes into 1/4-inch slices.

2. In 10-inch skillet, cook bacon over medium heat 8 to 10 minutes, stirring occasionally, until crisp. Remove bacon from skillet with slotted spoon; drain on paper towels.

3. Cook onion in bacon fat in skillet over medium heat, stirring occasionally, until tender. Stir in flour, sugar, salt, celery seed and pepper. Cook over low heat, stirring constantly, until mixture is bubbly; remove from heat.

4. Stir water and vinegar into onion mixture. Heat to boiling, stirring constantly. Boil and stir 1 minute; remove from heat.

5. Stir in potatoes and bacon. Heat over medium heat, stirring gently to coat potato slices, until hot and bubbly. Serve warm.

1 SERVING (ABOUT 2/3 CUP): CAL. 120 (CAL. FROM FAT 20); FAT 2g (SAT. FAT 1g); CHOL. 5mg; SODIUM 250mg; CARBS. 22g (FIBER 3g); PRO. 3g **% DAILY VALUE:** VIT. A 0%; VIT. C 10%; CALC. 2%; IRON 10% **EXCHANGES:** 1 STARCH, 1 VEGETABLE, 1/2 FAT **CARB. CHOICES:** $1\frac{1}{2}$

SLOW COOKER DIRECTIONS

Increase flour to 2 tablespoons. Decrease water to 1/3 cup. Cut potatoes into 1/4-inch slices. Cook and drain bacon; refrigerate. In $3\frac{1}{2}$- to 6-quart slow cooker, mix all ingredients except bacon. Cover and cook on Low heat setting 8 to 10 hours or until potatoes are tender. Stir in bacon.

BEST POTATO SALAD POTATOES

Potato salad lovers know the secret to perfect potato salad—it starts with the potatoes! Round red or round white potatoes are best because they are a waxy variety, holding their shape after cooking. Starchy potatoes (long white), like Idaho and russets, have a fluffy texture after cooking so can become too soft and mushy for potato salad.

Cucumber Salad

LOW-FAT

PREP: 10 min **CHILL:** 3 hr ■ **6 SERVINGS**

Dress up the look of the "cukes" by running the tines of a fork down the length of each cucumber before slicing.

- 2 medium unpeeled cucumbers, thinly sliced
- 1/3 cup cider or white vinegar
- 1/3 cup water
- 2 tablespoons sugar
- 1/2 teaspoon salt
- 1/8 teaspoon pepper
- Chopped fresh dill weed or parsley, if desired

1. Place cucumbers in small glass or plastic bowl.

2. In tightly covered container, shake remaining ingredients except dill weed. Pour over cucumbers. Cover and refrigerate at least 3 hours to blend flavors.

3. Drain cucumbers. Sprinkle with dill weed. Store covered in refrigerator.

1 SERVING (ABOUT 1/2 CUP): CAL. 25 (CAL. FROM FAT 0); FAT 0g (SAT. FAT 0g); CHOL. 0mg; SODIUM 200mg; CARBS. 7g (FIBER 1g); PRO. 0g **% DAILY VALUE:** VIT. A 2%; VIT. C 6%; CALC. 0%; IRON 2% **EXCHANGES:** 1 VEGETABLE **CARB. CHOICES:** 1/2

CREAMY CUCUMBER SALAD After draining cucumbers, stir in 3/4 cup sour cream or plain yogurt. Store covered in refrigerator.

Chinese Cabbage Salad with Sesame Dressing

Chinese Cabbage Salad with Sesame Dressing

FAST LOW-FAT

PREP: 15 min ■ **4 SERVINGS**

Sesame Dressing

3 tablespoons rice or white wine vinegar
2 teaspoons sugar
2 teaspoons sesame seed, toasted (page 215)
2 teaspoons soy sauce
1 teaspoon sesame oil
1/8 teaspoon crushed red pepper

Salad

2 cups finely shredded napa (Chinese) cabbage (8 oz)
1/4 cup chopped jicama
1/4 cup chopped green bell pepper
1/4 cup coarsely shredded carrot

1. In tightly covered container, shake all dressing ingredients.

2. In medium glass or plastic bowl, toss salad ingredients and dressing. Cover and refrigerate until serving time.

1 SERVING: CAL. 60 (CAL. FROM FAT 20); FAT 2g (SAT. FAT 0g); CHOL. 0mg; SODIUM 170mg; CARBS. 9g (FIBER 2g); PRO. 1g
% DAILY VALUE: VIT. A 30%; VIT. C 48%; CALC. 2%; IRON 4%
EXCHANGES: 1 1/2 VEGETABLE, 1/2 FAT **CARB. CHOICES:** 1/2

HOW TO THINLY SLICE CABBAGE

To thinly slice cabbage, place a flat side of 1/4 head of cabbage on a cutting board. Cut into thin slices with a large sharp knife. Cut slices several times to make smaller pieces.

Creamy Coleslaw

PREP: 15 min **CHILL:** 1 hr ■ **8 SERVINGS**

- 1/2 cup mayonnaise or salad dressing
- 1/4 cup sour cream
- 1 tablespoon sugar
- 2 teaspoons lemon juice
- 2 teaspoons Dijon mustard
- 1/2 teaspoon celery seed
- 1/4 teaspoon salt
- 1/4 teaspoon pepper
- 1/2 medium head cabbage, thinly sliced or chopped (4 cups)
- 1 small carrot, shredded (1/2 cup)
- 1 small onion, chopped (1/4 cup)

1. In large glass or plastic bowl, mix all ingredients except cabbage, carrot and onion. Add remaining ingredients; toss until evenly coated.

2. Cover and refrigerate at least 1 hour to blend flavors. Store covered in refrigerator.

1 SERVING (ABOUT 2/3 CUP): CAL. 140 (CAL. FROM FAT 115); FAT 13g (SAT. FAT 3g); CHOL. 15mg; SODIUM 200mg; CARBS. 7g (FIBER 1g); PRO. 1g **% DAILY VALUE:** VIT. A 24%; VIT. C 26%; CALC. 2%; IRON 2% **EXCHANGES:** 1 VEGETABLE, 2 1/2 FAT **CARB. CHOICES:** 1/2

TROPICAL CREAMY COLESLAW Add 1 can (8 oz) pineapple tidbits or chunks, drained, with the cabbage, carrot and onion. Just before serving, sprinkle with 1/2 cup chopped macadamia nuts.

LIGHTER CREAMY COLESLAW

For 6 grams of fat and 85 calories per serving, use reduced-fat mayonnaise and sour cream.

Three-Bean Salad

PREP: 20 min **CHILL:** 3 hr ■ **6 SERVINGS**

You can almost always find three-bean salad at the deli counter—but you'll be amazed how much fresher it tastes when you make it at home.

- 1 cup Italian Dressing (page 398)
- 1 can (15 to 16 oz) cut green beans, drained
- 1 can (15 to 16 oz) wax beans, drained
- 1 can (15 to 16 oz) kidney, black or garbanzo beans, rinsed and drained
- 4 medium green onions, chopped (1/4 cup)
- 1/4 cup chopped fresh parsley
- 1 tablespoon sugar
- 2 cloves garlic, finely chopped

1. Make Italian Dressing.

2. In medium glass or plastic bowl, mix beans, onions and parsley.

3. In small bowl, mix dressing, sugar and garlic. Pour over salad; toss. Cover and refrigerate at least 3 hours to blend flavors, stirring occasionally.

4. Just before serving, spoon bean mixture into bowl with slotted spoon.

1 SERVING (ABOUT 3/4 CUP): CAL. 210 (CAL. FROM FAT 90); FAT 10g (SAT. FAT 1.5g); CHOL. 0mg; SODIUM 550mg; CARBS. 24g (FIBER 7g); PRO. 8g **% DAILY VALUE:** VIT. A 15%; VIT. C 20%; CALC. 6%; IRON 20% **EXCHANGES:** 1 STARCH, 2 VEGETABLE, 2 FAT **CARB. CHOICES:** 1 1/2

LIGHTER THREE-BEAN SALAD

For 1 gram of fat and 200 calories per serving, substitute purchased fat-free Italian dressing for the Italian Dressing.

Northern Italian White Bean Salad

PREP: 15 min **CHILL:** 2 hr ▪ **6 SERVINGS**

Cannellini beans are large white kidney beans originally from South America. The Italians have adopted them and, not surprisingly, they're now a delicious part of Italian cuisine.

2 cans (19 oz each) cannellini beans, rinsed and drained
1 large tomato, seeded and coarsely chopped (1 cup)
1 small red bell pepper, chopped ($^1/_2$ cup)
$^1/_2$ cup chopped red onion
$^1/_4$ cup chopped fresh parsley
$^1/_4$ cup olive or vegetable oil
2 tablespoons chopped fresh or 2 teaspoons dried basil leaves
2 tablespoons red wine vinegar
$^1/_2$ teaspoon salt
$^1/_8$ teaspoon pepper
12 lettuce leaves

1. In large glass or plastic bowl, carefully mix all ingredients except lettuce.

2. Cover and refrigerate at least 2 hours to blend flavors. Just before serving, spoon onto lettuce, using slotted spoon.

1 SERVING: CAL. 300 (CAL. FROM FAT 90); FAT 10g (SAT. FAT 1g); CHOL. 0mg; SODIUM 210mg; CARBS. 48g (FIBER 13g); PRO. 18g
% DAILY VALUE: VIT. A 14%; VIT. C 36%; CALC. 18%; IRON 40%
EXCHANGES: 3 STARCH, 1 VEGETABLE, 1 VERY LEAN MEAT
CARB. CHOICES: 3

◀ **Northern Italian White Bean Salad**

Strawberry Margarita Cups

LOW-FAT

PREP: 10 min **CHILL:** 4 hr ▪ **6 SERVINGS**

This recipe is an absolute "wow" and definitely not your 1950s-style gelatin mold! These soft-textured salads would also make a divine dessert.

- 1 package (6 oz) wild strawberry-flavored gelatin
- 1 1/2 cups boiling water
- 1 can (10 oz) frozen margarita mix concentrate, thawed
- 1 box (10 oz) frozen sweetened sliced strawberries, thawed and undrained
- 1/2 cup tequila or water
- Sweetened Whipped Cream (page 217), if desired
- Fresh strawberries, if desired
- Grated lime peel, if desired

1. In medium bowl, stir flavored gelatin (dry) and boiling water about 2 minutes or until mix is completely dissolved.

2. In blender or food processor, add margarita mix, sliced strawberries and tequila. Cover and blend on high speed until smooth.

3. Stir strawberry mixture into gelatin mixture. Spoon about 3/4 cup mixture into each of 6 margarita glasses or 10-ounce custard cups. Refrigerate about 4 hours or until firm.

4. Top with Sweetened Whipped Cream, fresh strawberries and lime peel.

1 SERVING: CAL. 250 (CAL. FROM FAT 0); FAT 0g (SAT. FAT 0g); CHOL. 0mg; SODIUM 75mg; CARBS. 60g (FIBER 1g); PRO. 2g
% DAILY VALUE: VIT. A 0%; VIT. C 0%; CALC. 0%; IRON 4%
EXCHANGES: 4 OTHER CARB. **CARB. CHOICES:** 4

Strawberry Margarita Cups ▶

Easy Cranberry-Orange Mold LOW-FAT

PREP: 5 min **COOK:** 5 min **CHILL:** 4 hr ▪ **8 SERVINGS**

- 1 can (11 oz) mandarin orange segments, drained and juice reserved
- 1 package (3 oz) orange-flavored gelatin
- 1 can (16 oz) whole berry cranberry sauce
- Salad greens, if desired

1. Add enough water to reserved mandarin orange juice to measure 1 1/4 cups. In 1-quart saucepan, heat juice mixture to boiling.

2. Place gelatin in medium bowl. Pour boiling mixture on gelatin; stir until gelatin is dissolved. Stir in cranberry sauce until sauce is melted. Stir in orange segments. Pour into 4-cup mold.

3. Refrigerate about 4 hours or until firm; unmold. Serve on salad greens.

1 SERVING: CAL. 145 (CAL. FROM FAT 0); FAT 0g (SAT. FAT 0g); CHOL. 0mg; SODIUM 40mg; CARBS. 35g (FIBER 1g); PRO. 1g **% DAILY VALUE:** VIT. A 2%; VIT. C 10%; CALC. 0%; IRON 0% **EXCHANGES:** 2 1/2 FRUIT **CARB. CHOICES:** 2

HOW TO UNMOLD GELATIN SALADS

Here's the secret for how to perfectly unmold a gelatin salad: Quickly dip the mold, almost to the top, into warm—not hot—water for several seconds. Loosen an edge of the salad with the tip of a knife, then tip the mold slightly to allow air in and to break the vacuum. Rotate the mold so all sides are loose. Place a serving plate brushed lightly with water upside down on top of the mold (the water will let you move the gelatin on the plate in case it doesn't come out in the center.) Holding both the mold and the plate firmly, turn the mold upside down and shake gently. Carefully lift the mold off the gelatin. If the gelatin doesn't come out, repeat the steps.

Tabbouleh

PREP: 10 min **STAND:** 30 min **CHILL:** 1 hr ▪ **6 SERVINGS**

- 3/4 cup uncooked bulgur
- 1 1/2 cups chopped fresh parsley
- 3 medium tomatoes, chopped (2 1/4 cups)
- 5 medium green onions, thinly sliced (1/3 cup)
- 2 tablespoons chopped fresh or 2 teaspoons crumbled dried mint leaves
- 1/4 cup olive or vegetable oil
- 1/4 cup lemon juice
- 3/4 teaspoon salt
- 1/4 teaspoon pepper
- Whole ripe olives, if desired

1. In small bowl, cover bulgur with cold water. Let stand 30 minutes; drain. Press out as much water as possible.

2. In medium glass or plastic bowl, place bulgur, parsley, tomatoes, onions and mint.

3. In tightly covered container, shake remaining ingredients except olives. Pour over bulgur mixture; toss. Cover and refrigerate at least 1 hour to blend flavors. Garnish with olives.

1 SERVING (ABOUT 3/4 CUP): CAL. 160 (CAL. FROM FAT 90); FAT 10g (SAT. FAT 1g); CHOL. 0mg; SODIUM 320mg; CARBS. 19g (FIBER 5g); PRO. 3g **% DAILY VALUE:** VIT. A 38%; VIT. C 60%; CALC. 4%; IRON 10% **EXCHANGES:** 1 STARCH, 1 VEGETABLE, 1 FAT **CARB. CHOICES:** 1

SOUTHWESTERN TABBOULEH Substitute 1 cup chopped fresh cilantro for the parsley. Decrease lemon juice to 2 tablespoons; increase salt to 1 teaspoon. Add 2 teaspoons ground cumin with the remaining ingredients in Step 3.

Chicken-Thyme Penne

PREP: 25 min **MARINATE:** 4 hr ■ **8 SERVINGS**

You'll need about 2 pounds of uncooked boneless skinless chicken breasts, which equals 4 cups cubed cooked chicken, to make this dish. Cook them however you wish—grill them, broil, poach or fry.

- 3 cups uncooked penne pasta (10 oz)
- 4 cups cubed cooked chicken
- 2 cups red grapes, cut in half
- 2 medium stalks celery, sliced (3/4 cup)
- 1/3 cup chopped onion
- 3 tablespoons olive or vegetable oil
- 2 tablespoons chopped fresh or 2 teaspoons dried thyme leaves, crumbled
- 1 1/4 cups mayonnaise or salad dressing
- 1 tablespoon milk
- 1 tablespoon honey
- 1 tablespoon coarse-ground mustard
- 1 teaspoon salt
- 1 cup chopped walnuts, toasted (page 215)

1. Cook and drain pasta as directed on package. Rinse with cold water; drain.

2. In very large (4-quart) bowl, mix pasta, chicken, grapes, celery and onion. In small bowl, mix oil and 1 tablespoon of the fresh thyme (or 1 teaspoon of the dried thyme). Pour oil mixture over chicken mixture; toss to coat.

3. In small bowl, mix mayonnaise, milk, honey, mustard, salt and remaining thyme. Cover chicken mixture and mayonnaise mixture separately and refrigerate at least 4 hours but no longer than 24 hours.

4. Up to 2 hours before serving, toss chicken mixture and mayonnaise mixture. Cover and refrigerate until serving time. Just before serving, stir in 3/4 cup of the walnuts. Sprinkle salad with remaining walnuts.

1 SERVING: CAL. 695 (CAL. FROM FAT 415); FAT 46g (SAT. FAT 7g); CHOL. 80mg; SODIUM 600mg; CARBS. 41g (FIBER 3g); PRO. 29g
% DAILY VALUE: VIT. A 2%; VIT. C 10%; CALC. 4%; IRON 16%
EXCHANGES: 2 STARCH, 1 FRUIT, 3 MEDIUM-FAT MEAT, 5 1/2 FAT
CARB. CHOICES: 3

Chicken-Thyme Penne ▶

Cobb Salad

PREP: 10 min **CHILL:** 1 hr ■ **4 SERVINGS**

Lemon Vinaigrette

- 1/2 cup vegetable oil
- 1/4 cup lemon juice
- 1 tablespoon red wine vinegar
- 2 teaspoons sugar
- 1/2 teaspoon salt
- 1/2 teaspoon ground mustard
- 1/2 teaspoon Worcestershire sauce
- 1/4 teaspoon pepper
- 1 clove garlic, finely chopped

Salad

- 1 small head lettuce, finely shredded (6 cups)
- 2 cups cut-up cooked chicken
- 3 Hard-Cooked Eggs (page 220), chopped
- 2 medium tomatoes, chopped (1 1/2 cups)
- 1 medium ripe avocado, pitted, peeled and chopped
- 1/4 cup crumbled blue cheese (1 oz)
- 4 slices bacon, crisply cooked and crumbled (1/4 cup)

1. In tightly covered container, shake all vinaigrette ingredients. Refrigerate at least 1 hour to blend flavors.

2. Divide lettuce among 4 salad plates or shallow bowls. Arrange remaining salad ingredients in rows on lettuce. Serve with vinaigrette.

1 SERVING (ABOUT 3 CUPS): CAL. 590 (CAL. FROM FAT 440); FAT 49g (SAT. FAT 10g); CHOL. 230mg; SODIUM 630mg; CARBS. 12g (FIBER 4g); PROTEIN 30g **% DAILY VALUE:** VIT. A 20%; VIT. C 36%; CALC. 8%; IRON 14% **EXCHANGES:** 2 VEGETABLE, 4 HIGH-FAT MEAT, 3 FAT **CARB. CHOICES:** 1

Primavera Pasta Salad

PREP: 25 min ■ **14 SERVINGS**

This colorful salad makes and excellent side dish for grilled chicken, steaks and chops. As a meatless main dish salad, it can serve up to 6 people.

- 3 1/2 cups uncooked farfalle (bow-tie) pasta (9 oz)
- 2 cups snow (Chinese) pea pods, strings removed (12 oz)
- 2 large red bell peppers, cut into 1-inch pieces (2 cups)
- 2 medium carrots, sliced (1 cup)
- 1/2 cup chopped fresh basil leaves
- 1/2 cup shredded Parmesan cheese (2 oz)
- 1 cup creamy Parmesan dressing
- 2 tablespoons milk

1. Cook and drain pasta as directed on package, adding pea pods for last minute of cooking. Rinse with cold water; drain.

2. In very large (4-quart) bowl, mix bell peppers, carrots, basil and cheese. In small bowl, mix dressing and milk with wire whisk. Add dressing mixture, pasta and pea pods to bell pepper mixture; toss to coat. Serve immediately or store covered in refrigerator until serving time.

1 SERVING: CAL. 175 (CAL. FROM FAT 80); FAT 9g (SAT. FAT 1g); CHOL. 6mg SODIUM 230mg; CARBS. 19g (FIBER 2g); PROTEIN 5g
% DAILY VALUE: VIT. A 36%; VIT. C 44%; CALC. 8%; IRON 6%
EXCHANGES: 1 STARCH, 1 VEGETABLE, 1 1/2 FAT
CARB. CHOICES: 1

Crunchy Oriental Chicken Salad

Crunchy Oriental Chicken Salad FAST

PREP: 10 min **COOK:** 5 min ▪ **6 SERVINGS**

- 2 tablespoons butter or margarine
- 1 package (3 oz) Oriental-flavor ramen noodle soup mix
- 2 tablespoons sesame seed
- 1/4 cup sugar
- 1/4 cup white vinegar
- 1 tablespoon sesame or vegetable oil
- 1/2 teaspoon pepper
- 2 cups cut-up cooked chicken
- 1/4 cup dry-roasted peanuts, if desired
- 4 medium green onions, sliced (1/4 cup)
- 1 bag (16 oz) coleslaw mix
- 1 can (11 oz) mandarin orange segments, drained

1. In 10-inch skillet, melt butter over medium heat. Stir in seasoning packet from soup mix. Break block of noodles into bite-size pieces over skillet; stir into butter mixture.

2. Cook noodles 2 minutes, stirring occasionally. Stir in sesame seed. Cook about 2 minutes longer, stirring occasionally, until noodles are golden brown; remove from heat.

3. In large glass or plastic bowl, mix sugar, vinegar, oil and pepper. Add noodle mixture and remaining ingredients; toss. Serve immediately.

1 SERVING (ABOUT 1 1/4 CUPS): CAL. 265 (CAL. FROM FAT 110); FAT 12g (SAT. FAT 4g); CHOL. 50mg; SODIUM 260mg; CARBS. 25g (FIBER 2g); PRO. 16g **% DAILY VALUE:** VIT. A 10%; VIT. C 68%; CALC. 6%; IRON 10% **EXCHANGES:** 1 STARCH, 2 VEGETABLE, 1 MEDIUM-FAT MEAT, 1 FAT **CARB. CHOICES:** 1 1/2

Taco Salad

PREP: 15 min **COOK:** 50 min **COOL:** 10 min ▪
8 SERVINGS

- Tortilla Shells* (right)
- 3/4 cup Thousand Island Dressing (page 399)
- 1 lb lean (at least 80%) ground beef
- 2/3 cup water
- 1 tablespoon chili powder
- 1/2 teaspoon salt
- 1/4 teaspoon garlic powder
- 1/4 teaspoon ground red pepper (cayenne)
- 1 can (15 to 16 oz) kidney beans, drained and can reserved
- 1 medium head lettuce, torn into bite-size pieces (10 cups)
- 1 cup shredded Cheddar cheese (4 oz)
- 2/3 cup sliced ripe olives
- 2 medium tomatoes, coarsely chopped (1 1/2 cups)
- 1 medium onion, chopped (1/2 cup)
- 1 medium ripe avocado, pitted, peeled and thinly sliced
- Sour cream, if desired

1. Make Tortilla Shells and Thousand Island Dressing.

2. In 10-inch skillet, cook beef over medium heat 8 to 10 minutes, stirring occasionally, until brown; drain. Stir in water, chili powder, salt, garlic powder, red pepper and beans. Heat to boiling; reduce heat. Simmer uncovered 15 minutes, stirring occasionally. Cool 10 minutes.

3. In large bowl, mix lettuce, cheese, olives, tomatoes and onion. Toss with dressing. Add beef mixture and toss. Divide among Tortilla Shells. Garnish with avocado and sour cream. Serve immediately.

Tortilla Shells

- Reserved empty kidney bean can
- Vegetable oil
- 8 flour tortillas (10 inch)

1. Remove label and both ends of kidney bean can. Wash can and dry thoroughly.

2. In 3-quart saucepan, heat oil (1 1/2 inches) to 375°F. (Diameter of saucepan should be at least 9 inches.)

3. Place 1 tortilla on top of oil in saucepan. Holding can with long-handled tongs, place can on center of tortilla. Push tortilla into oil by gently pushing can down.

4. Fry tortilla about 5 seconds or until set; remove can with tongs. Fry tortilla 1 to 2 minutes longer, turning tortilla in oil, until crisp and golden brown.

5. Carefully remove tortilla from oil, and drain excess oil from inside. Turn tortilla shell upside down on paper towels; cool.

6. Repeat with remaining tortillas.

**8 purchased taco shells can be substituted for the Tortilla Shells recipe.*

1 SERVING (ABOUT 2 CUPS): CAL. 690 (CAL. FROM FAT 385); FAT 43g (SAT. FAT 11g); CHOL. 50mg; SODIUM 1,060mg; CARBS. 58g (FIBER 9g); PRO. 27g **% DAILY VALUE:** VIT. A 20%; VIT. C 20%; CALC. 22%; IRON 34% **EXCHANGES:** 3 1/2 STARCH, 2 VEGETABLE, 2 HIGH-FAT MEAT, 3 1/2 FAT **CARB. CHOICES:** 4

LIGHTER TACO SALAD

For 14 grams of fat and 280 calories per serving, omit Tortilla Shells. Substitute ground turkey breast for the ground beef. Use reduced-fat Cheddar cheese, low-fat purchased Thousand Island dressing and light sour cream. Omit avocado. Serve salad on about 12 baked tortilla chips.

Tossed Chef's Salad

PREP: 25 min ■ **5 SERVINGS**

- 1/4 cup Classic French Dressing (page 398)*
- 1/2 cup julienne strips cooked meat (beef, pork or smoked ham)
- 1/2 cup julienne strips cooked chicken or turkey
- 1/2 cup julienne strips Swiss cheese
- 8 medium green onions, chopped (1/2 cup)
- 1 medium head lettuce, torn into bite-size pieces (10 cups)
- 1 small bunch romaine lettuce, torn into bite-size pieces (6 cups)
- 1 medium stalk celery, sliced (1/2 cup)
- 1/2 cup mayonnaise or salad dressing
- 2 Hard-Cooked Eggs (page 220), sliced
- 2 medium tomatoes, cut into wedges

1. Make Classic French Dressing.

2. Reserve a few strips of meat, chicken and cheese for topping salad. In large bowl, mix remaining meat, chicken and cheese, the onions, lettuce, romaine and celery.

3. In small bowl, mix mayonnaise and Classic French Dressing. Pour over lettuce mixture; toss. Top with reserved meat, chicken and cheese strips, the eggs and tomatoes. Serve immediately.

**1/4 cup purchased vinaigrette dressing can be substituted for the Classic French Dressing.*

1 SERVING (ABOUT 3 CUPS): CAL. 380 (CAL. FROM FAT 290); FAT 32g (SAT. FAT 6g); CHOL. 130mg; SODIUM 440mg; CARBS. 9g (FIBER 4g); PRO. 17g **% DAILY VALUE:** VIT. A 50%; VIT. C 56%; CALC. 20%; IRON 14% **EXCHANGES:** 2 VEGETABLE, 2 HIGH-FAT MEAT, 3 FAT **CARB. CHOICES:** 1/2

Salad Niçoise

PREP: 20 min **CHILL:** 1 hr ■ **4 SERVINGS**

- 2 cups frozen French-style green beans (from 1-lb bag)
- 3/4 cup Classic French Dressing (page 398)
- 1 head Bibb lettuce, torn into bite-size pieces (4 cups)
- 2 medium tomatoes, cut into sixths
- 2 Hard-Cooked Eggs (page 220), cut into fourths
- 1 can (6 oz) tuna in water, drained and flaked
- 2 tablespoons sliced ripe olives
- Chopped fresh parsley, if desired
- 6 anchovy fillets, if desired

1. Cook and drain green beans as directed on bag. Refrigerate at least 1 hour until chilled.

2. Make Classic French Dressing.

3. Place lettuce in deep platter or salad bowl. Arrange green beans, tomatoes and eggs around edge of lettuce. Mound tuna in center; sprinkle with olives. Sprinkle parsley over salad. Garnish with anchovies. Serve with dressing. Serve immediately or cover and refrigerate until serving time.

1 SERVING (ABOUT 2 CUPS): CAL. 345 (CAL. FROM FAT 225); FAT 26g (SAT. FAT 4g); CHOL. 120mg; SODIUM 310mg; CARBS. 12g (FIBER 4g); PRO. 16g **% DAILY VALUE:** VIT. A 36%; VIT. C 28%; CALC. 6%; IRON 12% **EXCHANGES:** 2 VEGETABLE, 2 LEAN MEAT, 4 FAT **CARB. CHOICES:** 1

Tuna-Macaroni Salad

PREP: 20 min **CHILL:** 1 hr ■ **6 SERVINGS**

1 package (7 oz) elbow macaroni
1/2 cup frozen green peas
1 can (9 oz) tuna, drained
1 cup mayonnaise or salad dressing
1 cup shredded Cheddar cheese (4 oz), if desired
1/4 cup sweet pickle relish, if desired
2 teaspoons lemon juice
3/4 teaspoon salt
1/4 teaspoon pepper
1 medium stalk celery, chopped (1/2 cup)
1 small onion, chopped (1/4 cup)

1. Cook macaroni as directed on package, adding peas for last 4 to 6 minutes of cooking; rinse with cold water and drain.

2. In large bowl, mix macaroni, peas and remaining ingredients. Cover and refrigerate at least 1 hour to blend flavors.

1 SERVING (ABOUT 1 CUP): CAL. 450 (CAL. FROM FAT 270); FAT 30g (SAT. FAT 5g); CHOL. 35mg; SODIUM 660mg; CARBS. 30g (FIBER 2g); PRO. 16g **% DAILY VALUE:** VIT. A 20%; VIT. C 4%; CALC. 2%; IRON 12% **EXCHANGES:** 2 STARCH, 1 1/2 MEDIUM-FAT MEAT, 4 FAT **CARB. CHOICES:** 2

LIGHTER TUNA-MACARONI SALAD

For 1 gram of fat and 210 calories per serving, use fat-free mayonnaise, reduced-fat Cheddar cheese and water-packed tuna.

◀ **Tuna-Macaroni Salad**

OILS FOR SALAD DRESSING

At a glance, this chart lists the many kinds of oils that are perfect for salad dressings and easily available at your supermarket or gourmet food shop. Most dressing recipes call for a specific type of oil that works well with the other dressing and salad ingredients, but feel free to experiment with different oils or oil combinations.

Type of Oil	Description
NUT OILS	**Nut oils are highly flavorful, so start with a smaller amount and add more as needed.**
Almond	Nutty, mildly sweet
Avocado	Nutty, sharp
Hazelnut	Nutty, rich
Walnut	Mildly nutty
OLIVE OILS	
Olive Oil (also called *pure olive oil*)	Delicate/neutral; golden color
Extra-Virgin Olive Oil	Fruity olive flavor that is stronger than Olive Oil; golden to green or bright green color
VEGETABLE OILS (also referred to as *salad oils*)	
Canola	Bland/neutral
Corn	Mildly buttery
Peanut	Mildly nutty
Safflower	Bland/neutral
Sunflower	Bland/neutral
Vegetable Oil (some oils are just labeled as *vegetable oil;* check label for oil source)	Bland/neutral
Sesame Oil	
Sesame Oil, light	Nutty, light color
Sesame Oil, dark (also called *Asian*)	Strong toasted sesame seed flavor; amber color

VINEGARS FOR SALAD DRESSING

Add zip and new flavors to salad dressings by using different vinegars. Start by trying some listed here. Most dressing recipes call for a specific type of vinegar that works well with the other dressing and salad ingredients, but feel free to experiment with different vinegars or vinegar combinations.

Type of Vinegar	Made From	Description
Balsamic	White grapes	Rich, sweet, dark brown
Cider	Fermented apple cider	Mild apple flavor, golden brown
Fruit	Blueberries, raspberries or strawberries most common (steeped in cider or white wine vinegar)	Flavor and color of berry used; mildly sweet
Herb	Basil, chive, dill weed or tarragon most common (steeped in white wine or cider vinegar)	Flavor of herb used
Rice (also called *rice wine vinegar*)	Fermented rice	Available in pure (plain) and sweetened forms; delicate, sweet flavor
White (distilled)	Grain alcohol	Strong, pungent
Wine	Champagne, sherry, red or white wine most common	Flavor of wine used; whites are milder, reds more robust

Italian Dressing FAST

PREP: 10 min ▪ **ABOUT 1 1/4 CUPS DRESSING**

- 1 cup olive or vegetable oil
- 1/4 cup white or cider vinegar
- 2 tablespoons finely chopped onion
- 1 tablespoon chopped fresh or 1 teaspoon dried basil leaves
- 1 teaspoon sugar
- 1 teaspoon ground mustard
- 1/2 teaspoon salt
- 1/2 teaspoon dried oregano leaves
- 1/4 teaspoon pepper
- 2 cloves garlic, finely chopped

In tightly covered container, shake all ingredients. Shake before serving. Store tightly covered in refrigerator.

1 TABLESPOON: CAL. 105 (CAL. FROM FAT 100); FAT 11g (SAT. FAT 1g); CHOL. 0mg; SODIUM 60mg; CARBS. 1g (FIBER 0g); PRO. 0g **% DAILY VALUE:** VIT. A 0%; VIT. C 0%; CALC. 0%; IRON 0% **EXCHANGES:** 2 FAT **CARB. CHOICES:** 0

LIGHTER ITALIAN DRESSING

For 5 grams of fat and 50 calories per serving, substitute 1/2 cup apple juice for 1/2 cup of the oil.

CREAMY ITALIAN DRESSING In small bowl, beat 1/2 cup Italian Dressing and 1/2 cup mayonnaise or salad dressing with hand beater or wire whisk until smooth. Store covered in refrigerator.

Classic French Dressing

FAST

PREP: 5 min ▪ **ABOUT 1 1/2 CUPS DRESSING**

- 1 cup olive or vegetable oil
- 1/4 cup white or cider vinegar
- 1/4 cup lemon juice
- 1/2 teaspoon salt
- 1/2 teaspoon ground mustard
- 1/2 teaspoon paprika

In tightly covered container, shake all ingredients. Shake before serving. Store tightly covered in refrigerator.

1 TABLESPOON: CAL. 80 (CAL. FROM FAT 80); FAT 9g (SAT. FAT 1g); CHOL. 0mg; SODIUM 50mg; CARBS. 0g (FIBER 0g); PRO. 0g **% DAILY VALUE:** VIT. A 0%; VIT. C 0%; CALC. 0%; IRON 0% **EXCHANGES:** 2 FAT **CARB. CHOICES:** 0

CLASSIC RED FRENCH DRESSING Mix 1/2 cup Classic French Dressing and 1/2 cup ketchup.

HOW MUCH JUICE IS IN A LEMON?

One fresh lemon yields about 2 to 3 tablespoons of juice. Room-temperature lemons (and limes) yield more juice. Before squeezing, roll the lemon back and forth on the counter several times with firm pressure, which helps to burst the cells holding the juice. Or try zapping whole lemons from the refrigerator in the microwave on High for about 20 seconds or so to warm them up.

Thousand Island Dressing

FAST

PREP: 15 min ■ **ABOUT 1 CUP DRESSING**

- 1 cup mayonnaise or salad dressing
- 1 tablespoon chopped fresh parsley
- 2 tablespoons chopped pimiento-stuffed olives or sweet pickle relish
- 2 tablespoons chili sauce or ketchup
- 1 teaspoon finely chopped onion
- 1/2 teaspoon paprika
- 1 Hard-Cooked Egg (page 220), finely chopped

In small bowl, mix all ingredients. Store tightly covered in refrigerator.

1 TABLESPOON: CAL. 105 (CAL. FROM FAT 100); FAT 11g (SAT. FAT 2g); CHOL. 20mg; SODIUM 135mg; CARBS. 1g (FIBER 0g); PRO. 1g **% DAILY VALUE:** VIT. A 2%; VIT. C 0%; CALC. 0%; IRON 0% **EXCHANGES:** 2 FAT **CARB. CHOICES:** 0

LIGHTER THOUSAND ISLAND DRESSING

For 5 grams of fat and 55 calories per serving, use reduced-fat mayonnaise; substitute 2 hard-cooked egg whites for the hard-cooked whole egg.

RUSSIAN DRESSING Omit parsley, olives and egg. Increase chili sauce to 1/4 cup. Add 1 teaspoon prepared horseradish.

Honey-Dijon Dressing

FAST

PREP: 5 min ■ **ABOUT 1 CUP DRESSING**

- 1/2 cup vegetable oil
- 1/3 cup honey
- 1/4 cup lemon juice
- 1 tablespoon Dijon mustard

In tightly covered container, shake all ingredients. Shake before serving. Store tightly covered in refrigerator.

1 TABLESPOON: CAL. 85 (CAL. FROM FAT 65); FAT 7g (SAT. FAT 1g); CHOL. 0mg; SODIUM 15mg; CARBS. 6g (FIBER 0g); PRO. 0g **% DAILY VALUE:** VIT. A 0%; VIT. C 2%; CALC. 0%; IRON 0% **EXCHANGES:** 1/2 FRUIT, 1 FAT **CARB. CHOICES:** 1/2

HONEY–POPPY SEED DRESSING Omit mustard. Add 1 tablespoon poppy seed.

Fresh Herb Vinaigrette

FAST

PREP: 10 min ■ **ABOUT 3/4 CUP VINAIGRETTE**

- 1/2 cup olive or vegetable oil
- 3 tablespoons red or white wine vinegar
- 1 tablespoon chopped fresh herb leaves (such as basil, marjoram, oregano, rosemary, tarragon or thyme)
- 1 tablespoon chopped fresh parsley
- 1 medium green onion, finely chopped (1 tablespoon)
- 3/4 teaspoon salt
- 1/4 teaspoon pepper

In tightly covered container, shake all ingredients. Shake before serving. Store tightly covered in refrigerator.

1 TABLESPOON: CAL. 80 (CAL. FROM FAT 80); FAT 9g (SAT. FAT 1g); CHOL. 0mg; SODIUM 55mg; CARBS. 0g (FIBER 0g); PRO. 0g **% DAILY VALUE:** VIT. A 0%; VIT. C 0%; CALC. 0%; IRON 0% **EXCHANGES:** 2 FAT **CARB. CHOICES:** 0

Raspberry Vinaigrette

FAST LOW-FAT

PREP: 10 min ■ **1 CUP VINAIGRETTE**

- 1/3 cup seedless raspberry jam
- 1/2 cup red wine vinegar
- 1/4 cup olive or vegetable oil
- 1/4 teaspoon salt

In small glass or plastic bowl, beat all ingredients with wire whisk until well blended. Store tightly covered in refrigerator.

1 TABLESPOON: CAL. 45 (CAL. FROM FAT 25); FAT 3g (SAT. FAT 0g); CHOL. 0mg; SODIUM 40mg; CARBS. 5g (FIBER 0g); PRO. 0g
% DAILY VALUE: VIT. A 0%; VIT. C 0%; CALC. 0%; IRON 0%
EXCHANGES: 1/2 FRUIT, 1/2 FAT **CARB. CHOICES:** 0

Oriental Dressing

FAST LOW-FAT

PREP: 5 min ■ **ABOUT 1 CUP DRESSING**

Toasting really brings out the flavor of sesame seed, so toast a whole 2-ounce package or jar of sesame seed (about 1/2 cup), then keep it in the freezer to use whenever you need some.

- 1/3 cup rice, white or cider vinegar
- 1/4 cup vegetable oil
- 3 tablespoons soy sauce
- 1 tablespoon sesame seed, toasted if desired (page 215)
- 2 tablespoons dry sherry or apple juice
- 1 teaspoon grated gingerroot or 1/4 teaspoon ground ginger
- 2 drops dark sesame oil, if desired

In tightly covered container, shake all ingredients. Shake before serving. Store tightly covered in refrigerator.

1 TABLESPOON: CAL. 30 (CAL. FROM FAT 25); FAT 3g (SAT. FAT 0g); CHOL. 0mg; SODIUM 170mg; CARBS. 1g (FIBER 0g); PRO. 0g
% DAILY VALUE: VIT. A 0%; VIT. C 0%; CALC. 0%; IRON 0%
EXCHANGES: 1/2 FAT **CARB. CHOICES:** 0

▲ Top row, from left to right: Italian (page 398) and Raspberry Vinaigrette (above) Dressings. Bottom row, from left to right: Honey-Dijon (page 399), Buttermilk Ranch (page 401) and Fresh Herb Vinaigrette (page 399) Dressings.

Buttermilk Ranch Dressing

PREP: 5 min **CHILL:** 2 hr ■ **ABOUT 1 1/4 CUPS DRESSING**

- 3/4 cup mayonnaise or salad dressing
- 1/2 cup buttermilk
- 1 teaspoon parsley flakes
- 1/2 teaspoon instant minced onion
- 1/2 teaspoon salt
- Dash of freshly ground pepper
- 1 clove garlic, finely chopped

1. In small bowl, mix all ingredients.

2. Cover and refrigerate at least 2 hours to blend flavors. Store tightly covered in refrigerator.

1 TABLESPOON: CAL. 70 (CAL. FROM FAT 70); FAT 8g (SAT. FAT 1g); CHOL. 5mg; SODIUM 140mg; CARBS. 1g (FIBER 0g); PRO. 0g
% DAILY VALUE: VIT. A 0%; VIT. C 0%; CALC. 0%; IRON 0%
EXCHANGES: 1 1/2 FAT **CARB. CHOICES:** 0

LIGHTER BUTTERMILK RANCH DRESSING

For 4 grams of fat and 45 calories per serving, use reduced-fat mayonnaise and buttermilk.

BUTTERMILK RANCH PARMESAN DRESSING

Add 1/3 cup grated Parmesan cheese and 1/2 teaspoon paprika.

Blue Cheese Dressing

PREP: 10 min **CHILL:** 3 hr ■ **ABOUT 1 2/3 CUPS DRESSING**

- 3/4 cup crumbled blue cheese (3 oz)
- 1 package (3 oz) cream cheese, softened
- 1/2 cup mayonnaise or salad dressing
- 1/3 cup half-and-half

1. Reserve 1/3 cup of the blue cheese. In small bowl, mix remaining blue cheese and the cream cheese until well blended.

2. Stir in mayonnaise and half-and-half until creamy. Stir in reserved 1/3 cup blue cheese. Cover and refrigerate at least 3 hours to blend flavors. Store tightly covered in refrigerator.

1 TABLESPOON: CAL. 60 (CAL. FROM FAT 55); FAT 6g (SAT. FAT 2g); CHOL. 10mg; SODIUM 80mg; CARBS. 0g (FIBER 0g); PRO. 1g
% DAILY VALUE: VIT. A 2%; VIT. C 0%; CALC. 2%; IRON 0%
EXCHANGES: 1 FAT **CARB. CHOICES:** 0

LIGHTER BLUE CHEESE DRESSING

For 3 grams of fat and 35 calories per serving, decrease blue cheese to 1/2 cup. Substitute 1/2 package (8-oz size) reduced-fat cream cheese (Neufchâtel) for the regular cream cheese and 1/4 cup fat-free (skim) milk for the half-and-half. Use reduced-fat mayonnaise.

SALAD GREENS GLOSSARY

Arugula (or Rocket): Has small, slender, dark green leaves similar to radish leaves and a slightly bitter, peppery mustard flavor. Choose smaller leaves for milder flavor.

Belgian Endive (or French): Has narrow, cupped, cream-colored leaves tinged with green and a slightly bitter flavor.

Butterhead Lettuce (Bibb or Boston): Bibb and Boston belong to the butterhead family and have small rounded heads of soft, tender, buttery leaves and a delicate flavor. Bibb is smaller in size than the other two but has the same delicate, mild flavor.

Cabbage: Comes in several varieties, each with its own distinct flavor. Green and red cabbage are most familiar and readily available; look for compact heads of waxy, tightly wrapped leaves. Savoy cabbage has crinkled leaves, and Chinese (or napa) cabbage has long, crisp leaves.

Curly Endive: Has frilly, narrow, somewhat prickly leaves with a slightly bitter taste.

Escarole: Another member of the endive family; has broad, wavy, medium green leaves and a slightly bitter flavor, although it's milder than Belgian or curly endive.

Frisée: A member of the chicory family; has slender, curly leaves ranging in color from yellow-white to yellow-green and a slightly bitter flavor.

Greens (beet, chard, collard, dandelion, mustard): All have a strong, biting flavor. Young greens are milder and more tender and can be tossed in salads; older greens are too bitter for salads and should be cooked for the best flavor.

Iceberg Lettuce (or Crisphead): Has a bland, mild flavor and very crisp texture. Look for solid, compact heads with tight leaves that range in color from medium green outer leaves to pale green inner ones.

Kale: Recognized by its sturdy but frilly leaves that usually are dark green and tinged with shades of blue and purple. A member of the cabbage family, it doesn't form a head, but it does have a mild cabbage taste. Choose young, small leaves for the best flavor.

Leaf Lettuce (green, red, oak leaf, salad bowl): Has tender but crisp leaves that don't form tight heads. These leafy bunches have a mild flavor that's more full-bodied than iceberg lettuce.

Mâche (Corn Salad): Spoon-shaped medium to dark green leaves with velvety texture. Mild, subtly sweet and nutty. Also called *field salad, field lettuce* and *lamb's lettuce.*

Mesclun (field or wild greens): A mixture of young, small greens often including arugula, chervil, chickweed, dandelion, frisée, mizuma and oak leaf lettuce.

Mixed Salad Greens (prepackaged): Already cleaned and ready to use, you'll find these in the produce section of your supermarket. Choose from a variety of mixes, each with its own combination of colors, flavors and textures.

Radicchio: Looks like a small, loose-leaf cabbage with smooth, tender leaves and a slightly bitter flavor. The two most common radicchios in the U.S. are a ruby red variety with broad, white veins and one with leaves speckled in shades of pink, red and green.

Romaine (or Cos): Has narrow, elongated, dark green, crisp leaves sometimes tinged with red on the tips. The broad white center rib is especially crunchy.

Sorrel (or Sourgrass): Looks much like spinach, but the leaves are smaller. Sorrel has a sharp, lemony flavor.

Spinach: Has smooth, tapered, dark green leaves, sometimes with crumpling at the edges, and a slightly bitter flavor.

Watercress: Has small, crisp, dark green, coin-size leaves and a strong peppery flavor.

CHAPTER 15

Sauces, Seasonings & Accompaniments

Sauces

Seasonings & Marinades

Condiments

Charts

LOW-FAT = *3g or less, except main dishes with 10g or less* FAST = *Ready in 20 minutes or less* BREAD MACHINE = *Bread machine directions* SLOW COOKER = *Slow cooker directions* LIGHTER = *25% fewer calories or grams of fat*

◀ **Tropical Fruit Salsa (page 416)**

Sauce Basics

Savory sauces make dishes sing and dance with flavor—whether they're rich and buttery, lively with tomato or sassy as in marinades. Sauces should enhance other ingredients, not mask their flavor. Learn more about sauces by reading on.

THICKENING SAUCES

Different sauces are thickened using different methods. Here are the four most common methods.

1. **Using a "roux,"** which is a mixture of flour and fat (usually butter) cooked over low to medium heat until smooth and bubbly before liquid is added. This step, along with additional cooking, prevents the finished sauce from tasting like raw flour. White Sauce (page 408) and Mornay Sauce (page 409) are examples.
2. **Using cornstarch,** which must be stirred into cold water or other liquid and thoroughly blended before heating so it doesn't form lumps. As they cook, cornstarch-based sauces become clear and almost shiny, making them perfect for sparkling fruit sauces. Raspberry Sauce (page 216) and Sweet-and-Sour Sauce (page 411) are examples.
3. **Using egg yolks (emulsion),** which must be cooked over low heat to avoid overcooking and curdling them. They must also be cooked thoroughly to kill salmonella bacteria. Hollandaise Sauce (page 410) and Whiskey Sauce (page 204) are examples.
4. **Using reduction,** which are liquids (usually savory broth, wine, vinegar or cream either by themselves or in various combinations) that are boiled or simmered to reduce volume, thicken and concentrate flavors by evaporation. Reducing liquids can be done faster by using a skillet with a large surface area instead of a saucepan.

SAUCE-MAKING TIPS

Make creamy, smooth sauces easily using these tips:

- To prevent lumping, use a wire whisk to mix sauces and stir constantly just until thickened.
- Before adding cornstarch or flour to thicken dishes like stew, mix it separately with an equal amount cold water to keep it from clumping.
- Cook sauces over low to medium heat unless a recipe specifies otherwise.

REHEATING SAUCES

Not all sauces can be reheated the same way. Use these guidelines for successful results:

- **Flour- or cornstarch-thickened sauces:** Use low or medium heat.
- **Egg-thickened sauces:** Use very low heat so they won't separate.

Italian Tomato Sauce

PREP: 15 min **COOK:** 50 min ▪ **ABOUT 4 CUPS SAUCE**

- 2 tablespoons olive or vegetable oil
- 1 large onion, chopped (1 cup)
- 1 small green bell pepper, chopped (1/2 cup)
- 2 large cloves garlic, finely chopped
- 2 cans (14.5 oz each) whole tomatoes, undrained
- 2 cans (8 oz each) tomato sauce
- 2 tablespoons chopped fresh or 2 teaspoons dried basil leaves
- 1 tablespoon chopped fresh or 1 teaspoon dried oregano leaves
- 1/2 teaspoon salt
- 1/2 teaspoon fennel seed
- 1/4 teaspoon pepper

1. In 3-quart saucepan, heat oil over medium heat. Cook onion, bell pepper and garlic in oil 2 minutes, stirring occasionally.

2. Stir in remaining ingredients, breaking up tomatoes with a fork. Heat to boiling; reduce heat. Simmer uncovered 45 minutes.

3. Use sauce immediately, or cover and refrigerate up to 2 weeks or freeze up to 1 year.

1/2 CUP: CAL. 80 (CAL. FROM FAT 35); FAT 4g (SAT. FAT 1g); CHOL. 0mg; SODIUM 660mg; CARBS. 12g (FIBER 3g); PRO. 2g
% DAILY VALUE: VIT. A 16%; VIT. C 26%; CALC. 4%; IRON 6%
EXCHANGES: 2 VEGETABLE, 1/2 FAT **CARB. CHOICES:** 1

SLOW COOKER DIRECTIONS

Use 1 medium onion. Substitute 1 can (28 oz) diced tomatoes, undrained, for the 2 cans whole tomatoes. Use 1 can (8 oz) tomato sauce. In 3 1/2- to 6-quart slow cooker, mix all ingredients. Cover and cook on Low heat setting 8 to 10 hours.

Marinara Sauce LOW-FAT

PREP: 15 min **COOK:** 35 min ▪ **ABOUT 12 CUPS SAUCE**

- 4 cans (14.5 oz each) diced tomatoes with Italian herbs, undrained
- 1 can (6 oz) tomato paste
- 1 large onion, chopped (1 cup)
- 8 cloves garlic, finely chopped
- 1 tablespoon olive or vegetable oil
- 2 teaspoons sugar
- 1 1/2 teaspoons dried basil leaves
- 1 teaspoon dried oregano leaves
- 1 teaspoon pepper
- 1/2 teaspoon salt

1. In 3-quart saucepan, stir all ingredients until well mixed.

2. Heat to boiling; reduce heat to low. Cover and simmer 30 minutes to blend flavors. Use sauce immediately, or cover and refrigerate up to 2 weeks or freeze up to 1 year.

1/2 CUP: CAL. 40 (CAL. FROM FAT 10); FAT 1g (SAT. FAT 0g); CHOL. 0mg; SODIUM 210mg; CARBS. 7g (FIBER 1g); PRO. 1g
% DAILY VALUE: VIT. A 6%; VIT. C 10%; CALC. 2%; IRON 2%
EXCHANGES: 1 1/2 VEGETABLE **CARB. CHOICES:** 1/2

Fresh Tomato Sauce FAST LOW-FAT

PREP: 20 min ▪ **ABOUT 4 CUPS SAUCE**

- 1 can (28 oz) Italian-style (plum) tomatoes, drained
- 2 cloves garlic, finely chopped
- 1 tablespoon chopped fresh or 1 teaspoon dried basil leaves
- 1 teaspoon chopped fresh parsley or 1 teaspoon parsley flakes
- 1 tablespoon grated Parmesan cheese
- 1 teaspoon olive or vegetable oil
- 1/2 teaspoon salt
- 1/2 teaspoon pepper
- 6 medium tomatoes, diced (about 4 1/2 cups)
- 3/4 cup pitted Kalamata or ripe olives, cut in half
- 1 tablespoon capers, if desired

1. In food processor or blender, place all ingredients except diced tomatoes, olives and capers. Cover and process until smooth. Pour into large glass or plastic bowl.

2. Stir in diced tomatoes, olives and capers.

3. Use sauce immediately, or cover and refrigerate up to 2 weeks or freeze up to 1 year.

1/2 CUP: CAL. 60 (CAL. FROM FAT 20); FAT 2g (SAT. FAT 0g); CHOL. 0mg; SODIUM 420mg; CARBS. 10g (FIBER 2g); PRO. 2g **% DAILY VALUE:** VIT. A 22%; VIT. C 26%; CALC. 4%; IRON 8% **EXCHANGES:** 2 VEGETABLE **CARB. CHOICES:** 1/2

Basil Pesto FAST

PREP: 10 min ■ **ABOUT 1 1/4 CUPS PESTO**

Pesto adds a powerhouse of flavor to any dish. Keep some on hand to toss with pasta, spread on sandwiches, add to salads or top off hot meats or vegetables.

- 2 cups firmly packed fresh basil leaves
- 3/4 cup grated Parmesan cheese
- 1/4 cup pine nuts
- 1/2 cup olive or vegetable oil
- 3 cloves garlic

1. In blender or food processor, place all ingredients. Cover and blend on medium speed about 3 minutes, stopping occasionally to scrape sides, until smooth.

2. Use pesto immediately, or cover tightly and refrigerate up to 5 days or freeze up to 1 month (color of pesto will darken as it stands).

2 TABLESPOONS: CAL. 150 (CAL. FROM FAT 135); FAT 15g (SAT. FAT 3g); CHOL. 5mg; SODIUM 140mg; CARBS. 2g (FIBER 1g); PRO. 3g **% DAILY VALUE:** VIT. A 14%; VIT. C 2%; CALC. 2%; IRON 4% **EXCHANGES:** 1/2 VEGETABLE, 3 FAT **CARB. CHOICES:** 0

CILANTRO PESTO Substitute 1 1/2 cups firmly packed fresh cilantro and 1/2 cup firmly packed fresh parsley for the basil.

SUN-DRIED TOMATO PESTO Use food processor. Omit basil. Decrease oil to 1/3 cup; add 1/2 cup oil-packed sun-dried tomatoes (undrained).

WINTER SPINACH PESTO Substitute 2 cups firmly packed fresh spinach and 1/2 cup firmly packed fresh basil leaves or 1/4 cup dried basil leaves for the fresh basil.

Peanut Sauce FAST

PREP: 5 min **COOK:** 5 min ■ **ABOUT 1 CUP SAUCE**

Turn peanut butter into this great sauce. It's perfect with grilled poultry and meats.

- 1/2 cup creamy peanut butter
- 1/2 cup water
- 2 tablespoons lime juice
- 1/2 teaspoon ground coriander
- 1/2 teaspoon ground cumin
- 1/8 teaspoon salt
- 1/8 teaspoon ground red pepper (cayenne) if desired
- 2 cloves garlic, finely chopped

1. In 1-quart saucepan, mix all ingredients with wire whisk. Heat over medium heat, stirring occasionally, until smooth and warm.

2. Use sauce immediately, or cover and refrigerate up to 3 days or freeze up to 2 months.

2 TABLESPOONS: CAL. 100 (CAL. FROM FAT 70); FAT 8g (SAT. FAT 2g); CHOL. 0mg; SODIUM 75mg; CARBS. 4g (FIBER 1g); PRO. 4g **% DAILY VALUE:** VIT. A 0%; VIT. C 2%; CALC. 0%; IRON 2% **EXCHANGES:** 1/2 HIGH-FAT MEAT, 1 FAT **CARB. CHOICES:** 0

◀ **Peanut Sauce**

Cucumbers and Tomatoes in Yogurt LOW-FAT

PREP: 10 min **STAND:** 10 min **CHILL:** 30 min ▪ **ABOUT 2 CUPS SAUCE**

Called raitas *in India, yogurt-based accompaniments cool the palate when spicy foods are eaten. Try it with Indian Spiced Chicken and Chutney (page 329). Or when friends are coming over, serve it as a dip with pita bread wedges or crackers.*

1 medium cucumber
1 medium green onion, chopped (1 tablespoon)
1/2 teaspoon salt
1 medium tomato, chopped (3/4 cup)
1 tablespoon chopped fresh cilantro or parsley
1/4 teaspoon ground cumin
Dash of pepper
1/2 clove garlic, finely chopped
1/2 cup plain yogurt

1. Cut cucumber lengthwise in half; scoop out seeds. Chop cucumber (about 1 1/4 cups).

2. In medium glass or plastic bowl, mix cucumber, onion and salt; let stand 10 minutes. Stir in tomato.

3. In small bowl, mix remaining ingredients except yogurt; toss with cucumber mixture. Cover and refrigerate at least 30 minutes to blend flavors.

4. Drain thoroughly. Just before serving, fold in yogurt. Store covered in refrigerator.

1/2 CUP: CAL. 30 (CAL. FROM FAT 10); FAT 1g (SAT. FAT 0g); CHOL. 0mg; SODIUM 320mg; CARBS. 5g (FIBER 1g); PRO. 2g **% DAILY VALUE:** VIT. A 8%; VIT. C 16%; CALC. 6%; IRON 2% **EXCHANGES:** 1 VEGETABLE **CARB. CHOICES:** 0

Tartar Sauce

PREP: 5 min **CHILL:** 1 hr ▪ **ABOUT 1 CUP SAUCE**

Creamy tartar sauce is easy to make at home! For a sweeter flavor, substitute pickle relish for the dill pickles.

1 cup mayonnaise or salad dressing
2 tablespoons finely chopped dill pickle or pickle relish
1 tablespoon chopped fresh parsley
2 teaspoons chopped pimiento
1 teaspoon grated onion

1. In small bowl, mix all ingredients.

2. Cover and refrigerate about 1 hour or until chilled.

1 TABLESPOON: CAL. 100 (CAL. FROM FAT 100); FAT 11g (SAT. FAT 2g); CHOL. 10mg; SODIUM 90mg; CARBS. 0g (FIBER 0g); PRO. 0g **% DAILY VALUE:** VIT. A 0%; VIT. C 0%; CALC. 0%; IRON 0% **EXCHANGES:** 2 FAT **CARB. CHOICES:** 0

LIGHTER TARTAR SAUCE

For 5 grams fat and 50 calories per serving, use reduced-fat mayonnaise.

Cucumbers and Tomatoes in Yogurt ▶

Whipped Horseradish Sauce FAST LOW-FAT

PREP: 10 min ▪ **ABOUT 1 1/3 CUPS SAUCE**

This sauce is sassy! It's perfect with beef and other meats.

- 1/4 cup sour cream
- 3 tablespoons grated fresh horseradish or prepared horseradish
- 1/4 teaspoon white pepper
- 1/2 cup whipping (heavy) cream

1. In small bowl, stir all ingredients except whipping cream until well mixed; set aside.

2. In chilled small bowl, beat whipping cream with electric mixer on high speed until stiff. Carefully fold into sour cream mixture.

3. Store sauce covered in refrigerator.

1 TABLESPOON: CAL. 20 (CAL. FROM FAT 20); FAT 2g (SAT. FAT 2g); CHOL. 0mg; SODIUM 10mg; CARBS. 1g (FIBER 0g); PRO. 0g **% DAILY VALUE:** VIT. A 2%; VIT. C 0%; CALC. 0%; IRON 0% **EXCHANGES:** 1 SERVING IS FREE **CARB. CHOICES:** 0

Herbed Butter Sauce FAST

PREP: 5 min **COOK:** 5 min ▪ **ABOUT 1/2 CUP SAUCE**

Sometimes simple is best—as with this easy butter sauce speckled with fresh herbs. It's sensational with fish, seafood, poultry and vegetables.

- 1/2 cup butter*
- 2 tablespoons chopped fresh or 1 teaspoon dried herb leaves (such as basil, chives, oregano, savory, tarragon or thyme)
- 2 teaspoons lemon juice

1. In heavy 1-quart saucepan or 8-inch skillet, melt butter over medium heat.

2. Stir in herbs and lemon juice.

**Do not use margarine or vegetable oil spreads.*

1 TABLESPOON: CAL. 110 (CAL. FROM FAT 110); FAT 12g (SAT. FAT 7g); CHOL. 30mg; SODIUM 75mg; CARBS. 0g (FIBER 0g); PRO. 0g **% DAILY VALUE:** VIT. A 10%; VIT. C 0%; CALC. 0%; IRON 0% **EXCHANGES:** 2 1/2 FAT **CARB. CHOICES:** 0

White Sauce FAST LOW-FAT

PREP: 5 min **COOK:** 5 min ▪ **ABOUT 1 CUP SAUCE**

Also known as Béchamel sauce, *it is versatile and has many uses. Pair it with vegetables, turn it into a creamy casserole or ladle it over seafood or sliced chicken. Serve "as is," make it into a cheese sauce or spice it up with mustard, dill or curry.*

- 2 tablespoons butter or margarine
- 2 tablespoons all-purpose flour
- 1/4 teaspoon salt
- 1/8 teaspoon pepper
- 1 cup milk

1. In 1 1/2-quart saucepan, melt butter over low heat. Stir in flour, salt and pepper. Cook over medium heat, stirring constantly, until mixture is smooth and bubbly; remove from heat.

2. Gradually stir in milk. Heat to boiling, stirring constantly; boil and stir 1 minute.

1 TABLESPOON: CAL. 25 (CAL. FROM FAT 20); FAT 2g (SAT. FAT 1g); CHOL. 5mg; SODIUM 55mg; CARBS. 1g (FIBER 0g); PRO. 1g
% DAILY VALUE: VIT. A 2%; VIT. C 0%; CALC. 2%; IRON 0%
EXCHANGES: 1 SERVING IS FREE **CARB. CHOICES:** 0

THICK WHITE SAUCE Increase butter to 1/4 cup and flour to 1/4 cup.

THIN WHITE SAUCE Decrease butter to 1 tablespoon and flour to 1 tablespoon.

CHEESE SAUCE Stir in 1/4 teaspoon ground mustard with the flour. After boiling and stirring sauce 1 minute, stir in 1/2 cup shredded Cheddar cheese (2 oz) until melted. Serve with eggs and vegetables or over toast for Welsh rabbit. About 1 1/3 cups sauce.

CURRY SAUCE Stir in 1/2 teaspoon curry powder with the flour. Serve with chicken, lamb and shrimp.

DILL SAUCE Stir in 1 teaspoon chopped fresh or 1/2 teaspoon dried dill weed and dash of ground nutmeg with the flour. Serve with fish.

MUSTARD SAUCE Decrease butter to 1 tablespoon and flour to 1 tablespoon. After boiling and stirring sauce 1 minute, stir in 3 tablespoons Dijon mustard. Serve with beef, veal, ham and vegetables.

HOW TO MAKE WHITE SAUCE

◀ **1.** Stir flour, salt and pepper into melted butter. Cook, stirring constantly, until mixture is smooth and bubbly.

2. Heat sauce to boiling, stirring constantly. Boil and stir 1 minute. ▶

Mornay Sauce FAST LOW-FAT

PREP: 5 min **COOK:** 5 min ■ **ABOUT 1 CUP SAUCE**

Here's the perfect sauce to serve with meat, fish, shellfish, eggs and vegetables.

2 tablespoons butter or margarine
2 tablespoons all-purpose flour
1/2 cup half-and-half
1/2 cup chicken broth
1/2 cup grated Parmesan cheese or shredded Swiss cheese
1/4 teaspoon salt
1/8 teaspoon ground red pepper (cayenne)

1. In 1 1/2-quart saucepan, melt butter over low heat. Stir in flour. Cook over low heat, stirring constantly, until mixture is smooth and bubbly; remove from heat.

2. Gradually stir in half-and-half and broth. Heat to boiling, stirring constantly. Boil and stir 1 minute. Stir in cheese, salt and red pepper; stir until cheese is melted.

1 TABLESPOON: CAL. 40 (CAL. FROM FAT 25); FAT 3g (SAT. FAT 2g); CHOL. 10mg; SODIUM 140mg; CARBS. 1g (FIBER 0g); PRO. 2g
% DAILY VALUE: VIT. A 2%; VIT. C 0%; CALC. 4%; IRON 0%
EXCHANGES: 1 FAT **CARB. CHOICES:** 0

VELOUTÉ SAUCE Omit half-and-half. Increase chicken broth to 1 cup. Add 1/8 teaspoon pepper and 1/8 teaspoon ground nutmeg. Omit cheese and ground red pepper (cayenne).

Bordelaise Sauce LOW-FAT

PREP: 10 min **COOK:** 15 min ■ **ABOUT 1 CUP SAUCE**

Bordelaise sauce is based on a classic brown sauce that involves roasting meat bones until very brown before being simmered in liquid. For a quicker variation, stir up this simplified version, which eliminates the bone-roasting step yet still provides great flavor. It's the perfect match for beef roasts, pork roasts, chops and even burgers.

2 tablespoons butter or margarine
1 thin slice onion
2 tablespoons all-purpose flour
1/2 cup beef broth
1/2 cup dry red wine
3/4 teaspoon chopped fresh or 1/4 teaspoon dried thyme leaves
1/2 teaspoon chopped fresh parsley
1/2 teaspoon finely chopped onion
1 dried bay leaf
1/4 teaspoon salt
1/8 teaspoon pepper

1. In 1 1/2-quart saucepan, melt butter over medium heat. Cook onion slice in butter, stirring constantly, until onion is brown; discard onion.

2. Stir flour into butter. Cook over medium heat, stirring constantly, until flour is bubbly and deep brown; remove from heat.

3. Gradually stir in broth and wine. Stir in thyme, parsley, finely chopped onion and bay leaf. Heat to boiling, stirring constantly; boil and stir 1 minute. Stir in salt and pepper. Remove bay leaf before serving.

1 TABLESPOON: CAL. 25 (CAL. FROM FAT 10); FAT 1g (SAT. FAT 1g); CHOL. 5mg; SODIUM 80mg; CARBS. 2g (FIBER 0g); PRO. 0g
% DAILY VALUE: VIT. A 2%; VIT. C 0%; CALC. 0%; IRON 0%
EXCHANGES: 1 SERVING IS FREE **CARB. CHOICES:** 0

Hollandaise Sauce FAST

PREP: 10 min **COOK:** 5 min ▪ **ABOUT 3/4 CUP SAUCE**

Here's the classic Hollandaise—lusciously rich, lemony and smooth. Spoon it over vegetables, eggs, fish and seafood for that heavenly touch.

3 large egg yolks
1 tablespoon lemon juice
1/2 cup firm butter*

1. In 1 1/2-quart saucepan, vigorously stir egg yolks and lemon juice with wire whisk. Add 1/4 cup of the butter. Heat over very low heat, stirring constantly with wire whisk, until butter is melted.

2. Add remaining 1/4 cup butter. Continue stirring vigorously until butter is melted and sauce is thickened. (Be sure butter melts slowly so eggs have time to cook and thicken sauce without curdling.) If the sauce curdles (mixture begins to separate), add about 1 tablespoon boiling water and beat vigorously with wire whisk or hand beater until it's smooth.

3. Serve immediately. Store covered in refrigerator. To serve refrigerated sauce, reheat over very low heat and stir in a small amount of water.

**Do not use margarine or vegetable oil spreads.*

1 TABLESPOON: CAL. 85 (CAL. FROM FAT 80); FAT 9g (SAT. FAT 5g); CHOL. 75mg; SODIUM 55mg; CARBS. 0g (FIBER 0g); PRO. 1g
% DAILY VALUE: VIT. A 6%; VIT. C 0%; CALC. 0%; IRON 0%
EXCHANGES: 2 FAT **CARB. CHOICES:** 0

BÉARNAISE SAUCE Stir in 1 tablespoon dry white wine with the lemon juice. After sauce thickens, stir in 1 tablespoon finely chopped onion, 1 1/2 teaspoons chopped fresh or 1/2 teaspoon dried tarragon leaves and 1 1/2 teaspoons chopped fresh or 1/4 teaspoon dried chervil leaves. Serve with fish and meat.

Pan Gravy FAST LOW-FAT

PREP: 5 min **COOK:** 5 min ▪ **ABOUT 1 CUP GRAVY**

The secret to perfect gravy is using equal amounts of fat and flour. Keep gravy warm in decorative insulated gravy and sauce containers available in kitchenware stores.

Drippings from cooked meat
2 tablespoons all-purpose flour
1 cup liquid* (meat juices, broth, water)
Browning sauce, if desired
Salt and pepper to taste

1. After removing meat from pan, pour drippings (meat juices and fat) into bowl or glass measuring cup, leaving brown particles in pan. Skim 2 tablespoons of fat from the top of the drippings and return fat to the pan. Discard any remaining fat; reserve remaining drippings.

2. Stir flour into fat in cooking pan. Cook over low heat, stirring constantly and scraping up brown particles, until mixture is smooth and bubbly; remove from heat.

LEARN WITH Betty — MAKING HOLLANDAISE SAUCE

This sauce was not cooked long enough and is too thin.

This sauce was cooked until thickened; there are no problems.

This sauce was cooked too long or over too high a heat and has curdled.

3. Gradually stir in reserved drippings plus enough broth or water to equal 1 cup. Heat to boiling, stirring constantly. Boil and stir 1 minute. Stir in a few drops browning sauce if a darker color is desired. Stir in salt and pepper.

1 TABLESPOON: CAL. 15 (CAL. FROM FAT 10); FAT 1g (SAT. FAT 0g); CHOL. 0mg; SODIUM 65mg; CARBS. 1g (FIBER 0g); PRO. 1g
% DAILY VALUE: VIT. A 0%; VIT. C 0%; CALC. 0%; IRON 0%
EXCHANGES: 1 SERVING IS FREE **CARB. CHOICES:** 0

CREAMY GRAVY Substitute milk for half of the liquid. Serve with turkey, chicken, pork and veal.

GIBLET GRAVY Place giblets (except liver**) and neck from turkey or chicken in 2-quart saucepan. Add 4 cups water; season with salt and pepper. Simmer over low heat 1 to 2 hours or until tender. Drain giblets, reserving 1 cup broth. Remove meat from neck and finely chop with giblets. Substitute broth from giblets for the liquid. Stir giblets into gravy. Heat until hot.

THIN GRAVY Decrease meat drippings to 1 tablespoon and flour to 1 tablespoon.

**Vegetable cooking water, consommé or tomato or vegetable juice can be substituted for part of the liquid.*

***The liver is very strongly flavored and should not be used to make the gravy. Discard it, or reserve for another use.*

Sweet-and-Sour Sauce

FAST LOW-FAT

PREP: 10 min **COOK:** 1 min ■ **ABOUT 1 1/2 CUPS SAUCE**

Use this sauce on pork, poultry and seafood.

- 1/2 cup packed brown sugar
- 1 tablespoon cornstarch
- 1 can (8 oz) crushed pineapple in juice, drained and juice reserved
- 1/3 cup white vinegar
- 1 tablespoon soy sauce
- 1/4 cup finely chopped green bell pepper

1. In 1-quart saucepan, mix brown sugar and cornstarch.

2. Add enough water to reserved pineapple juice to measure 1/2 cup; stir into sugar mixture. Stir in vinegar and soy sauce.

3. Heat to boiling over medium heat, stirring constantly. Boil and stir 1 minute. Stir in pineapple and bell pepper.

4. Use sauce immediately, or cover and refrigerate up to 2 weeks or freeze up to 1 year. Serve with pork, poultry and seafood.

1 TABLESPOON: CAL. 30 (CAL. FROM FAT 0); FAT 0g (SAT. FAT 0g); CHOL. 0mg; SODIUM 40mg; CARBS. 7g (FIBER 0g); PRO. 0g
% DAILY VALUE: VIT. A 0%; VIT. C 2%; CALC. 0%; IRON 0%
EXCHANGES: 1/2 FRUIT **CARB. CHOICES:** 1/2

Chimichurri Sauce

PREP: 10 min **CHILL:** 2 hr ■ **1 CUP SAUCE**

Chimichurri sauce is a standard condiment in Argentina—as popular as ketchup and mustard are in America. This herbed sauce tastes wonderful with grilled meat or poultry.

- 1 bunch parsley (about 1 cup firmly packed), chopped
- 2 cloves garlic, finely chopped
- 3/4 cup olive or vegetable oil
- 1/4 cup white vinegar
- 1/2 teaspoon salt
- 1/8 teaspoon pepper

In blender or food processor, place all ingredients. Cover and blend on high speed until well blended. Cover and refrigerate 2 hours.

2 TABLESPOONS: CAL. 185 (CAL. FROM FAT 180); FAT 20g (SAT. FAT 3g); CHOL. 0mg; SODIUM 150mg; CARBS. 1g (FIBER 0g); PRO. 0g **% DAILY VALUE:** VIT. A 14%; VIT. C 8%; CALC. 0%; IRON 2% **EXCHANGES:** 4 FAT **CARB. CHOICES:** 0

Chimichurri Sauce

Cranberry Sauce **LOW-FAT**

PREP: 15 min **COOK:** 15 min **CHILL:** 3 hr ■ **ABOUT 4 CUPS SAUCE**

Homemade cranberry sauce is a terrific treat! The natural pectin inside the cranberries thickens the sauce. Be sure to cook the cranberries until they pop so the pectin is released and the sauce gels as it cools.

- 4 cups fresh or frozen cranberries (1 lb)
- 2 cups sugar
- 2 cups water
- 1 tablespoon grated orange peel, if desired

1. Wash cranberries; remove any stems or blemished berries.

2. In 3-quart saucepan, heat sugar and water to boiling over medium heat, stirring occasionally. Boil 5 minutes.

3. Stir in cranberries. Heat to boiling; boil about 5 minutes or until cranberries pop. Stir in orange peel. Cover and refrigerate about 3 hours or until chilled. Store covered in refrigerator.

1/4 CUP: CAL. 110 (CAL. FROM FAT 0); FAT 0g (SAT. FAT 0g); CHOL. 0mg; SODIUM 0mg; CARBS. 29g (FIBER 1g); PRO. 0g **% DAILY VALUE:** VIT. A 0%; VIT. C 2%; CALC. 0%; IRON 0% **EXCHANGES:** 2 FRUIT **CARB. CHOICES:** 2

Seasoning Basics

For many cooks, seasoning food is a mystery. With a little practice—and experimenting—you can unlock the mystery and begin to look forward to combining "this and that" to put your own special signature on everything you cook. Herbs, spices, seeds and seasoning blends add salty, sour, spicy, sweet, cool, hot or slightly bitter flavor notes to food. There are so many ways to add flavor that it's really easy. The "good old standbys" are salt and pepper, but don't stop here. There are many other favorites in the U.S., such as basil, cinnamon, garlic powder, garlic salt, Italian seasoning, oregano and sesame seed. But these are just a fraction of the many ways to season food, start your taste adventure with the tips you'll find here.

STORING HERBS, SPICES, SEEDS AND SEASONING BLENDS

Dried herbs, spices, seeds and seasoning blends

Store in airtight containers away from heat, light and moisture. Whole spices and herbs keep up to 1 year and ground ones up to 6 months, but flavors become weaker over time. Refrigerate chili powder, ground red pepper (cayenne) and paprika to keep their color and flavor.

Fresh herbs

Basil, Cilantro, Parsley: Cut 1/2 inch off the bottoms of stems and place in jar of water. Cover tops with a loose-fitting plastic bag. Let basil stand at room temperature up to two days because refrigerator temperatures may cause it to turn black. Refrigerate cilantro and parsley up to 1 week.

Other Herbs

Wrap stems in a damp (not wet) paper towel, and place in resealable plastic bag. Refrigerate up to 2 weeks.

COOKING WITH HERBS

A snip of fresh herbs or a pinch of dried add oomph to an impressive array of foods. Take pesto, for example. The combination of fresh basil, olive oil, garlic and Parmesan can't be beat; it pairs well with pasta, chicken, fish, seafood and vegetables. Or how about fresh mint leaves? Adding a few crushed leaves to iced tea gives it a cool-sweet tang. Here are a few tips for using both fresh and dried herbs.

- Herbs range in flavor from delicate and sweet to strong and savory. Sometimes just a little bit goes a long way, especially for bolder herbs like oregano, rosemary, sage and tarragon. Because fresh herbs are milder than their dry counterparts, you generally need three times as much of the fresh herb. If you're using an herb for the first time, start out with 1 teaspoon of a strong-flavored fresh herb (rosemary) and 1 tablespoon of a milder fresh herb (basil) or 1/4 teaspoon of any type of dried herb for every four servings. Taste, then add more—a little at a time—until the flavor's just right. The "3-to-1" fresh to dried herb rule isn't written in stone, it's really a matter of personal preference!
- After measuring dried herbs, crumble them in your hand to release their flavor before adding to your recipe.

Southwestern Rub LOW-FAT

PREP: 10 min **MARINATE:** 30 min ■ **ABOUT 3 TABLESPOONS RUB**

Rubs are simple ways to season meats—just sprinkle or smear on the seasoning mixture and rub it into the meat with your fingers. Because this rub has oil in it, it's known as a "wet rub" *rather than a* "dry rub."

- 1 tablespoon chili powder
- 1 tablespoon vegetable oil
- 1 teaspoon ground cumin
- 1/4 teaspoon salt
- 1/4 teaspoon ground red pepper (cayenne)
- 1 large clove garlic, finely chopped

1. In small bowl, mix all ingredients.

2. Spread rub evenly on 1 pound boneless meat (chicken, pork or beef) or 2 1/2 pounds 1/2-inch-thick pork chops (about 8). Cover and refrigerate at least 30 minutes but no longer than 24 hours. Cook meat as desired.

1 TEASPOON: CAL. 20 (CAL. FROM FAT 20); FAT 2g (SAT. FAT 0g); CHOL. 0mg; SODIUM 75mg; CARBS. 1g (FIBER 0g); PRO. 0g
% DAILY VALUE: VIT. A 2%; VIT. C 0%; CALC. 0%; IRON 2%
EXCHANGES: 1 SERVING IS FREE **CARB. CHOICES:** 0

◄ **Southwestern Rub**

Teriyaki Marinade LOW-FAT

PREP: 5 min **MARINATE:** 1 hr ■ **ABOUT 1/2 CUP MARINADE**

- 1/4 cup water
- 1 tablespoon packed brown sugar
- 3 tablespoons soy sauce
- 1 tablespoon lemon juice
- 1 tablespoon vegetable oil
- 1/8 teaspoon coarsely ground pepper
- 1 clove garlic, finely chopped

1. In shallow glass or plastic dish or resealable plastic food-storage bag, mix all ingredients.

2. Add about 1 pound boneless or 2 to 3 pounds bone-in beef, pork or chicken, turning to coat with marinade. Cover dish or seal bag and refrigerate, turning meat occasionally, at least 1 hour but no longer than 24 hours.

3. Remove meat from marinade; reserve marinade. Cook meat as desired, brushing occasionally with marinade.

4. Remaining marinade must be boiled to be served as a sauce. In 1-quart saucepan, heat marinade to boiling, stirring constantly; boil and stir 1 minute.

1 TABLESPOON: CAL. 25 (CAL. FROM FAT 20); FAT 2g (SAT. FAT 0g); CHOL. 0mg; SODIUM 340mg; CARBS. 2g (FIBER 0g); PRO. 0g
% DAILY VALUE: VIT. A 0%; VIT. C 0%; CALC. 0%; IRON 0%
EXCHANGES: 1 SERVING IS FREE **CARB. CHOICES:** 0

MARINATING BASICS

Marinades add exciting flavor to meat, poultry, fish, seafood and vegetables! Mix marinades and marinate in glass or plastic containers or heavy plastic food-storage bags because these containers won't react with acid ingredients like vinegar, wine or lemon juice. Plan on using 1/4 to 1/2 cup marinade for each 1 to 2 pounds of food. You can marinate all foods except fish in the refrigerator up to 24 hours; if you let it marinate longer, food can become mushy. Marinate fish only 15 to 30 minutes or it will become mushy.

Garlic Marinade

PREP: 10 min **COOK:** 5 min **MARINATE:** 8 hr ■ **ABOUT 3/4 CUP MARINADE**

- 1/4 cup vegetable oil
- 4 cloves garlic, finely chopped
- 1 tablespoon chopped fresh or 1 teaspoon dried rosemary leaves, crumbled
- 1/2 teaspoon ground mustard
- 2 teaspoons soy sauce
- 1/4 cup red or white wine vinegar
- 1/4 cup dry sherry or apple juice

1. In 10-inch skillet, heat oil over medium-high heat. Cook garlic in oil, stirring frequently, until golden. Stir in rosemary, mustard and soy sauce; remove from heat. Stir in vinegar and sherry; cool.

2. Place 1 to 1 1/2 pounds boneless or 3 to 4 pounds bone-in beef, pork or lamb in shallow glass or plastic dish or resealable plastic food-storage bag. Pour marinade over meat. Cover dish or seal bag and refrigerate, turning meat occasionally, at least 8 hours but no longer than 24 hours.

3. Remove meat from marinade; reserve marinade. Cook meat as desired, brushing occasionally with marinade.

4. Remaining marinade must be boiled to be served as a sauce (if not boiled, discard marinade). In 1-quart saucepan, heat marinade to boiling, stirring constantly; boil and stir 1 minute.

1 TABLESPOON: CAL. 50 (CAL. FROM FAT 45); FAT 5g (SAT. FAT 1g); CHOL. 0mg; SODIUM 50mg; CARBS. 1g (FIBER 0g); PRO. 0g
% DAILY VALUE: VIT. A 0%; VIT. C 0%; CALC. 0%; IRON 0%
EXCHANGES: 1 FAT **CARB. CHOICES:** 0

Lemon-Herb Marinade

PREP: 10 min **MARINATE:** 4 hr ■ **ABOUT 2/3 CUP MARINADE**

- 1/3 cup vegetable oil
- 2/3 teaspoon grated lemon peel
- 2 tablespoons lemon juice
- 1 tablespoon dry vermouth, dry white wine or beef broth
- 1 teaspoon chopped fresh or 1/4 teaspoon crumbled dried sage leaves
- 1 teaspoon chopped fresh or 1/4 teaspoon dried oregano leaves
- 1/2 teaspoon salt
- 1/4 teaspoon coarsely ground pepper

1. In shallow glass or plastic dish or resealable plastic food-storage bag, mix all ingredients.

2. Add up to 2 pounds boneless beef, pork, chicken or turkey, turning to coat with marinade. Cover dish or seal bag and refrigerate, turning meat occasionally, at least 4 hours but no longer than 24 hours.

3. Remove meat from marinade; reserve marinade. Cook meat as desired, brushing occasionally with marinade.

4. Remaining marinade must be boiled to be served as a sauce (if not boiled, discard marinade). In 1-quart saucepan, heat marinade to boiling, stirring constantly; boil and stir 1 minute.

1 TABLESPOON: CAL. 65 (CAL. FROM FAT 65); FAT 7g (SAT. FAT 1g); CHOL. 0mg; SODIUM 110mg; CARBS. 0g (FIBER 0g); PRO. 0g
% DAILY VALUE: VIT. A 0%; VIT. C 0%; CALC. 0%; IRON 0%
EXCHANGES: 1 1/2 FAT **CARB. CHOICES:** 0

Fajita Marinade

PREP: 5 min **MARINATE:** 4 hr ▪ **ABOUT 1/2 CUP MARINADE**

- 1/4 cup vegetable oil
- 1/4 cup red wine vinegar
- 1 teaspoon sugar
- 1 teaspoon dried oregano leaves
- 1 teaspoon chili powder
- 1/2 teaspoon garlic powder
- 1/2 teaspoon salt
- 1/4 teaspoon pepper

1. In shallow glass or plastic dish or resealable plastic food-storage bag, mix all ingredients.

2. Add about 1 pound boneless or 2 to 3 pounds bone-in beef, pork or chicken, turning to coat with marinade. Cover dish or seal bag and refrigerate, turning meat occasionally, at least 4 hours but no longer than 24 hours.

3. Remove meat from marinade; reserve marinade. Cook meat as desired, brushing occasionally with marinade.

4. Remaining marinade must be boiled to be served as a sauce (if not boiled, discard marinade). In 1-quart saucepan, heat marinade to boiling, stirring constantly; boil and stir 1 minute.

1 TABLESPOON: CAL. 65 (CAL. FROM FAT 65); FAT 7g (SAT. FAT 1g); CHOL. 0mg; SODIUM 150mg; CARBS. 1g (FIBER 0g); PRO. 0g
% DAILY VALUE: VIT. A 2%; VIT. C 0%; CALC. 0%; IRON 0%
EXCHANGES: 1 1/2 FAT **CARB. CHOICES:** 0

Salsa LOW-FAT

PREP: 20 min **CHILL:** 1 hr ▪ **ABOUT 3 1/2 CUPS SALSA**

Salsa comes from the Mexican and Spanish words for "sauce"; some are fresh and others cooked. Many contain chilies, which give them that characteristic hot taste. Serve with tortilla chips, vegetables, meat, fish, chicken or eggs.

- 3 large tomatoes, seeded and chopped (3 cups)
- 1 small green bell pepper, chopped (1/2 cup)
- 8 medium green onions, sliced (1/2 cup)
- 3 cloves garlic, finely chopped
- 2 tablespoons chopped fresh cilantro
- 1 tablespoon finely chopped seeded jalapeño chilies
- 2 to 3 tablespoons lime juice
- 1/2 teaspoon salt

1. In medium glass or plastic bowl, mix all ingredients.

2. Cover and refrigerate at least 1 hour to blend flavors but no longer than 1 week.

2 TABLESPOONS: CAL. 10 (CAL. FROM FAT 0); FAT 0g (SAT. FAT 0g); CHOL. 0mg; SODIUM 5mg; CARBS. 2g (FIBER 0g); PRO. 0g
% DAILY VALUE: VIT. A 4%; VIT. C 12%; CALC. 0%; IRON 0%
EXCHANGES: 1 SERVING IS FREE **CARB. CHOICES:** 0

BLACK BEAN SALSA Stir in 1 can (15 oz) black beans, rinsed and drained. About 5 cups salsa.

Tropical Fruit Salsa LOW-FAT

PREP: 15 min **CHILL:** 1 hr ▪ **ABOUT 2 CUPS SALSA**

Serve this salsa at room temperature for the fullest flavor. If mangoes and papayas are not available, try substituting a combination of peaches, nectarines, plums and apricots.

- 2 medium kiwifruit, peeled and chopped
- 1 medium mango, peeled, pitted and chopped
- 1 medium papaya, peeled, seeded and chopped
- 1 jalapeño chili, seeded and finely chopped
- 1 cup pineapple chunks
- 1 tablespoon finely chopped red onion
- 1 tablespoon chopped fresh cilantro
- 2 tablespoons lime juice

1. In medium glass or plastic bowl, mix all ingredients. Cover and refrigerate 1 to 2 hours to blend flavors.

2. Serve with grilled poultry, pork and seafood.

1/4 CUP: CAL. 50 (CAL. FROM FAT 0); FAT 0g (SAT. FAT 0g); CHOL. 0mg; SODIUM 5mg; CARBS. 14g (FIBER 2g); PRO. 1g
% DAILY VALUE: VIT. A 12%; VIT. C 90%; CALC. 2%; IRON 0%
EXCHANGES: 1 FRUIT **CARB. CHOICES:** 1

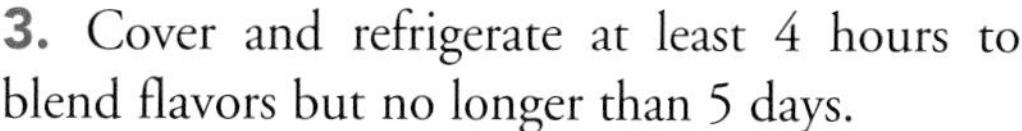

Corn Relish LOW-FAT

PREP: 10 min **COOK:** 5 min **CHILL:** 4 hr ■ **ABOUT 2 CUPS RELISH**

What's a hot dog without its relish? And this corn relish is a favorite. Try it on brats, sausages and hamburgers too.

- 2 cups frozen whole kernel corn (from 1-lb bag), thawed and drained, or 1 can (15.25 oz) whole kernel corn, drained
- 2 tablespoons chopped green bell pepper
- 1 tablespoon finely chopped onion
- 1 jar (2 oz) diced pimientos, drained
- $\frac{1}{2}$ cup sugar
- $\frac{1}{2}$ cup cider vinegar or white vinegar
- $\frac{1}{2}$ teaspoon celery seed
- $\frac{1}{4}$ teaspoon salt
- $\frac{1}{4}$ teaspoon mustard seed
- $\frac{1}{4}$ teaspoon red pepper sauce

1. In medium heatproof glass or plastic bowl, mix corn, bell pepper, onion and pimientos.

2. In 1-quart saucepan, heat remaining ingredients to boiling, stirring occasionally. Boil 2 minutes. Pour over corn mixture; stir.

3. Cover and refrigerate at least 4 hours to blend flavors but no longer than 5 days.

2 TABLESPOONS: CAL. 45 (CAL. FROM FAT 0); FAT 0g (SAT. FAT 0g); CHOL. 0mg; SODIUM 40mg; CARBS. 11g (FIBER 1g); PRO. 1g
% DAILY VALUE: VIT. A 2%; VIT. C 8%; CALC. 0%; IRON 0%
EXCHANGES: 2 VEGETABLE **CARB. CHOICES:** 1

▲ **Corn Relish (top) and Black Bean Salsa (left and bottom)**

Easy Refrigerator Pickles

LOW-FAT

PREP: 10 min **CHILL:** 24 hr ■ **6 CUPS PICKLES**

When choosing cucumbers for pickles, pick out the smaller ones and pickle them soon after buying or harvesting the cucumbers.

- 6 cups thinly sliced unpeeled cucumbers
- 2 small onions, sliced
- 1 medium carrot, thinly sliced ($\frac{1}{2}$ cup)
- $1\frac{3}{4}$ cups sugar
- 1 cup white or cider vinegar
- 2 tablespoons salt
- 1 tablespoon chopped fresh or 1 teaspoon dried dill weed*

1. In $2\frac{1}{2}$- or 3-quart glass container, layer cucumbers, onions and carrot.

2. In medium bowl, stir remaining ingredients until sugar is dissolved; pour over cucumbers.

3. Cover and refrigerate at least 24 hours but no longer than 2 weeks.

**1 teaspoon celery seed can be substituted for the dill weed.*

1/4 CUP: CAL. 65 (CAL. FROM FAT 0); FAT 0g (SAT. FAT 0g); CHOL. 0mg; SODIUM 590mg; CARBS. 16g (FIBER 0g); PRO. 0g
% DAILY VALUE: VIT. A 2%; VIT. C 2%; CALC. 0%; IRON 0%
EXCHANGES: 1 OTHER CARB. **CARB. CHOICES:** 1

EASY BELL PEPPER–GARLIC REFRIGERATOR PICKLES Cut 1 small red bell pepper into thin strips; layer with cucumbers, onions and carrot in container. Add 1 whole clove of garlic with remaining ingredients.

Golden Fruit Chutney

LOW-FAT

PREP: 20 min **COOK:** 45 min **COOL:** 2 hr ▪ **ABOUT 4 1/2 CUPS CHUTNEY**

Chutney is both a little sweet and a little sour. It's perfect for spooning onto turkey, grilled pork chops, ham and steak.

- 1 cup golden raisins
- 1/2 cup packed brown sugar
- 3/4 cup pineapple or apple juice
- 1/2 cup cider vinegar
- 1 1/2 teaspoons ground ginger
- 1 teaspoon ground mustard
- 1/8 teaspoon ground red pepper (cayenne)
- 1 can (20 oz) pineapple chunks in juice or syrup, undrained
- 2 packages (6 oz each) dried apricots, coarsely chopped (2 cups)

1. In 3-quart saucepan or 4-quart Dutch oven, heat all ingredients to boiling, stirring occasionally; reduce heat. Cover and simmer 30 minutes.

2. Uncover and simmer about 15 minutes longer, stirring occasionally, until mixture is very thick. Cool about 2 hours. Cover and refrigerate up to 2 weeks or freeze up to 2 months.

1 TABLESPOON: CAL. 30 (CAL. FROM FAT 0); FAT 0g (SAT. FAT 0g); CHOL. 0mg; SODIUM 0mg; CARBS. 8g (FIBER 1g); PRO. 0g
% DAILY VALUE: VIT. A 4%; VIT. C 2%; CALC. 0%; IRON 0%
EXCHANGES: 1/2 FRUIT **CARB. CHOICES:** 1/2

SLOW COOKER DIRECTIONS

Drain pineapple. In 3 1/2- to 6-quart slow cooker, mix all ingredients. Cover and cook on Low heat setting 6 to 7 hours or until very thick.

Cranberry-Orange Relish

LOW-FAT

PREP: 20 min **CHILL:** 24 hr ▪ **ABOUT 2 1/2 CUPS RELISH**

Save time by using a food processor to chop the cranberries and oranges for this relish. Choose a fine blade for a velvety texture; a coarse blade, for a rougher texture. You'll find this relish is a natural with pork, ham and poultry.

- 1 cup sugar
- 1 tablespoon finely chopped crystallized ginger, if desired
- 1 bag (12 oz) fresh or frozen cranberries (3 cups)
- 1 unpeeled orange

1. Place sugar and ginger in medium bowl.

2. Wash and dry cranberries; remove any stems or blemished berries.

3. Wash and dry orange; cut into 1-inch pieces (with peel) and remove seeds.

4. In food processor, place half of the cranberries and orange pieces. Cover and process, using short on-and-off motions, about 15 seconds or until evenly chopped. Stir cranberry mixture into sugar mixture. Repeat with remaining cranberries and orange pieces.

5. Cover and refrigerate at least 24 hours to blend flavors but no longer than 1 week.

2 TABLESPOONS: CAL. 50 (CAL. FROM FAT 0); FAT 0g (SAT. FAT 0g); CHOL. 0mg; SODIUM 0mg; CARBS. 13g (FIBER 1g); PRO. 0g
% DAILY VALUE: VIT. A 0%; VIT. C 12%; CALC. 0%; IRON 0%
EXCHANGES: 1 FRUIT **CARB. CHOICES:** 1

Savory Butters FAST

PREP: 5 min ▪ **ABOUT 1/2 CUP BUTTER**

Add flavor fast with a dollop of one of these easy butters. Top grilled or broiled beef or fish steaks, pork chops or chicken breasts. Or toss with hot pasta, rice or vegetables. And of course, these butters are also great to spread on bread.

In small bowl, beat butter and ingredients for one of the flavor variations below, with electric mixer on medium speed until light and fluffy. If desired, chill about 1 hour to blend flavors.

1 TEASPOON: CAL. 35 (CAL. FROM FAT 35); FAT 4g (SAT. FAT 2g); CHOL. 10mg; SODIUM 25mg; CARBS. 0g (FIBER 0g); PRO. 0g
% DAILY VALUE: VIT. A 2%; VIT. C 0%; CALC. 0%; IRON 0%
EXCHANGES: 1 FAT **CARB. CHOICES:** 0

GARLIC BUTTER 1/2 cup softened butter, 1 to 2 cloves garlic, finely chopped, or 1/4 to 1/2 teaspoon garlic powder.

HERB BUTTER 1/2 cup softened butter, 2 tablespoons to 1/4 cup chopped fresh or 1 to 2 teaspoons dried herb leaves (basil, chives, oregano, savory, tarragon or thyme), 2 teaspoons lemon juice and 1/2 teaspoon salt.

ITALIAN PARMESAN BUTTER 1/2 cup softened butter, 2 tablespoons grated Parmesan cheese and 1/2 teaspoon Italian seasoning.

LEMON-PEPPER BUTTER 1/2 cup softened butter, 2 tablespoons finely shredded lemon peel, 1 teaspoon lemon juice and 1/8 to 1/4 teaspoon pepper.

Sweet Butters FAST

PREP: 5 min ■ **ABOUT 1/2 CUP BUTTER**

You'll especially enjoy the aroma of these butters when they're served on warm breads, rolls and biscuits.

In small bowl, beat butter with electric mixer on medium speed until light and fluffy; stir in ingredients for one of the flavor variations, below, with spoon. If desired, chill about 1 hour to blend flavors.

1 TEASPOON: CAL. 45 (CAL. FROM FAT 35); FAT 4g (SAT. FAT 2g); CHOL. 10mg; SODIUM 25mg; CARBS. 2g (FIBER 0g); PRO. 0g
% DAILY VALUE: VIT. A 2%; VIT. C 0%; CALC. 0%; IRON 0%
EXCHANGES: 1 FAT **CARB. CHOICES:** 0

ALMOND BUTTER 1/2 cup softened butter, 1 tablespoon finely chopped almonds and 1/2 teaspoon almond extract.

HONEY BUTTER 1/2 cup softened butter, 1/2 cup honey.

ORANGE BUTTER 1/2 cup softened butter, 1 teaspoon grated orange peel and 1 tablespoon orange juice.

PECAN BUTTER 1/2 cup softened butter, 1/4 cup chopped pecans and 2 tablespoons packed brown sugar.

RASPBERRY BUTTER 1/2 cup softened butter, 1/2 cup raspberries, crushed, and 1 tablespoon sugar. Or 1/2 cup softened butter and 1/4 cup raspberry jam.

Cream Cheese Spreads FAST

PREP: 5 min ■ **ABOUT 2/3 TO 1 CUP SPREAD**

In small bowl, stir cream cheese and ingredients for one of the flavor variations, below, with spoon.

1 TABLESPOON: CAL. 45 (CAL. FROM FAT 35); FAT 4g (SAT. FAT 2g); CHOL. 10mg; SODIUM 35mg; CARBS. 0g (FIBER 0g); PRO. 2g
% DAILY VALUE: VIT. A 2%; VIT. C 0%; CALC. 4%; IRON 0%
EXCHANGES: 1 FAT **CARB. CHOICES:** 0

BACON-CHIVE-CHEDDAR CREAM CHEESE SPREAD Stir 1 package (3 oz) cream cheese, softened, and 2 tablespoons milk until blended. Stir in 1/4 cup shredded Cheddar cheese, 2 tablespoons crumbled crisply cooked bacon (2 slices) and 1 tablespoon chopped fresh chives.

MAPLE-CINNAMON CREAM CHEESE SPREAD Stir 1 package (3 oz) cream cheese, softened, 2 tablespoons maple-flavored syrup and 1/4 teaspoon ground cinnamon until blended.

OLIVE-WALNUT CREAM CHEESE SPREAD Stir 1 package (3 oz) cream cheese, softened, and 2 tablespoons milk until blended. Stir in 1/2 cup finely chopped walnuts and 1/4 cup finely chopped pitted Kalamata or pimiento-stuffed olives.

PEANUT BUTTER–HONEY CREAM CHEESE SPREAD Stir 1 package (3 oz) cream cheese, softened, and 2 tablespoons milk until blended. Stir in 1/4 cup crunchy peanut butter and 1 tablespoon honey.

Cream Cheese Spreads: Maple-Cinnamon (top), Peanut Butter–Honey (middle), Olive-Walnut (bottom left), Bacon-Chive-Cheddar (bottom right) ▶

Blueberry Freezer Jam

LOW-FAT

PREP: 30 min **COOK:** 6 min **STAND:** 24 hr ■
ABOUT 5 HALF-PINTS JAM

- 2 pints (4 cups) blueberries, crushed ($2^1/_2$ cups)
- 3 cups sugar
- 1 teaspoon grated orange peel, if desired
- $^1/_2$ cup water
- 1 package ($1^3/_4$ oz) powdered fruit pectin

1. In large bowl, mix blueberries, sugar and orange peel. Let stand 20 minutes, stirring occasionally, until sugar is dissolved.

2. In 1-quart saucepan, mix water and pectin. Heat to boiling, stirring constantly. Boil and stir 1 minute. Pour hot pectin mixture over blueberry mixture; stir constantly 3 minutes.

3. Immediately spoon mixture into freezer containers, leaving $^1/_2$-inch headspace. Wipe rims of containers; seal. Let stand at room temperature about 24 hours or until set.

4. Store in freezer up to 6 months or in refrigerator up to 3 weeks. Thaw frozen jam and stir before serving.

1 TABLESPOON: CAL. 70 (CAL. FROM FAT 0); FAT 0g (SAT. FAT 0g); CHOL. 0mg; SODIUM 0mg; CARBS. 18g (FIBER 1g); PRO. 0g
% DAILY VALUE: VIT. A 0%; VIT. C 2%; CALC. 0%; IRON 0%
EXCHANGES: 1 FRUIT **CARB. CHOICES:** 1

Strawberry Freezer Jam

LOW-FAT

PREP: 15 min **COOK:** 5 min **STAND:** 24 hr ■
ABOUT 5 HALF-PINTS JAM

- 1 quart strawberries (4 cups), cut in half
- 4 cups sugar
- $^3/_4$ cup water
- 1 package ($1^3/_4$ oz) powdered fruit pectin

1. In large bowl, mash strawberries with potato masher (or process in food processor) until slightly chunky (not pureed) to make 2 cups crushed strawberries. Stir sugar into strawberries in large bowl. Let stand at room temperature 10 minutes, stirring occasionally.

2. In 1-quart saucepan, mix water and pectin. Heat to boiling, stirring constantly. Boil and stir 1 minute. Pour hot pectin mixture over strawberry mixture; stir constantly 3 minutes.

3. Immediately spoon mixture into freezer containers, leaving $^1/_2$-inch headspace. Wipe rims of containers; seal. Let stand at room temperature about 24 hours or until set.

4. Store in freezer up to 6 months or in refrigerator up to 3 weeks. Thaw frozen jam and stir before serving.

1 TABLESPOON: CAL. 90 (CAL. FROM FAT 0); FAT 0g (SAT. FAT 0g); CHOL. 0mg; SODIUM 0mg; CARBS. 22g (FIBER 1g); PRO. 0g
% DAILY VALUE: VIT. A 0%; VIT. C 14%; CALC. 0%; IRON 0%
EXCHANGES: $1^1/_2$ FRUIT **CARB. CHOICES:** $1^1/_2$

RASPBERRY FREEZER JAM Substitute 3 pints (6 cups) raspberries (3 cups crushed) for the strawberries. Increase sugar to $5^1/_4$ cups.

Apple Butter

LOW-FAT

PREP: 30 min **COOK:** 2 hr **COOL:** 2 hr ■
ABOUT 4 CUPS APPLE BUTTER

- 12 medium Granny Smith or other cooking apples (4 lb), peeled and cut into fourths
- $1^1/_2$ cups packed brown sugar
- $1^1/_4$ cups apple juice
- 1 tablespoon ground cinnamon
- 1 tablespoon lemon juice
- 1 teaspoon ground allspice
- 1 teaspoon ground nutmeg
- $^1/_2$ teaspoon ground cloves

1. In 4-quart Dutch oven, heat all ingredients to boiling, stirring occasionally; reduce heat. Cover and simmer 1 hour.

2. Mash apples with potato masher or large fork.

3. Simmer uncovered about 1 hour longer, stirring occasionally, until mixture is very thick. Cool about 2 hours.

4. Spoon apple butter into container. Store covered in refrigerator up to 3 weeks.

1 TABLESPOON: CAL. 35 (CAL. FROM FAT 0); FAT 0g (SAT. FAT 0g); CHOL. 0mg; SODIUM 0mg; CARBS. 9g (FIBER 1g); PRO. 0g
% DAILY VALUE: VIT. A 0%; VIT. C 2%; CALC. 0%; IRON 0%
EXCHANGES: $^1/_2$ FRUIT **CARB. CHOICES:** $^1/_2$

SLOW COOKER DIRECTIONS

Decrease apple juice to 1/2 cup. In 5- to 6-quart slow cooker, mix all ingredients. Cover and cook on Low heat setting 8 to 10 hours or until apples are very tender. Mash apples with potato masher or large fork. Cook uncovered on Low heat setting 1 to 2 hours longer, stirring occasionally, until very thick.

Lemon Curd FAST LOW-FAT

PREP: 15 min **COOK:** 8 min ■ **ABOUT 2 CUPS CURD**

This is a tart, refreshing custard that makes a tasty spread for Scones (page 74) or filling Silver White Cake (page 105).

- 1 cup sugar
- 1 tablespoon finely shredded lemon peel
- 1 cup lemon juice (5 large lemons)
- 3 tablespoons firm butter or margarine, cut up
- 3 large eggs, slightly beaten

1. In heavy 1 1/2-quart saucepan, mix sugar, lemon peel and lemon juice with wire whisk.

◀ **Lemon Curd**

2. Stir in butter and eggs. Cook over medium heat about 8 minutes, stirring constantly, until mixture thickens and coats back of spoon (do not boil). Immediately pour into one 1-pint container or two 1-cup containers.

3. Store covered in refrigerator up to 2 months.

1 TABLESPOON: CAL. 50 (CAL. FROM FAT 20); FAT 2g (SAT. FAT 1g); CHOL. 20mg; SODIUM 15mg; CARBS. 7g (FIBER 0g); PRO. 1g
% DAILY VALUE: VIT. A 0%; VIT. C 2%; CALC. 0%; IRON 0%
EXCHANGES: 1/2 FRUIT, 1/2 FAT **CARB. CHOICES:** 1/2

KEY LIME CURD Substitute lime peel for the lemon peel and Key lime juice for the lemon juice.

Herb Vinegar LOW-FAT

PREP: 10 min **STAND:** 10 days ■ **ABOUT 2 CUPS VINEGAR**

Flavored vinegars add distinctive taste to your favorite recipes. Making them yourself not only gives satisfaction but also can be less costly than buying them.

- 2 cups white wine vinegar or white vinegar
- 1/2 cup firmly packed fresh herb leaves (such as basil, chives, dill weed, mint, oregano, rosemary or tarragon)

1. In tightly covered glass jar or bottle, shake vinegar and herb leaves. Let stand in cool, dry place 10 days.

2. Strain vinegar; discard herbs. Place 1 sprig of fresh herb in jar to identify flavor if desired. Store covered at room temperature up to 6 months.

1 TABLESPOON: CAL. 5 (CAL. FROM FAT 0); FAT 0g (SAT. FAT 0g); CHOL. 0mg; SODIUM 0mg; CARBS. 0g (FIBER 0g); PRO. 0g
% DAILY VALUE: VIT. A 0%; VIT. C 0%; CALC. 0%; IRON 0%
EXCHANGES: 1 SERVING IS FREE **CARB. CHOICES:** 0

BERRY VINEGAR Substitute 2 cups berries, crushed, for the herb.

GARLIC VINEGAR Substitute 6 cloves garlic, cut in half, for the herb.

LEMON VINEGAR Substitute peel from 2 lemons for the herb.

Guide to Using Herbs, Spices, Seeds, Seasoning Blends

These charts provide an overview of herbs, spices, seeds and seasoning blends—their form, flavor and how they can be used. Explore and enjoy!

HERBS: FORMS, FLAVORS AND USES

Herbs are leaves of plants without woody stems that have distinctive fragrances and flavors—from savory to sweet—which they infuse in the foods they're used in.

Herb and Form	Flavor	Use
Basil (fresh and dried leaves, ground)	Sweet and spicy; a cross between cloves and black licorice; key ingredient in pesto	Eggs, meats, pesto, salads, soups, stews, tomato dishes
Bay Leaves (dried leaves)	Earthy, grassy, slightly piney	Meats, soups, stews, vegetables
Chervil (fresh and dried leaves)	Delicate, slightly peppery; tastes a bit like black licorice	Eggs, fish, salads, sauces, soups, stuffings
Chives (fresh, freeze-dried)	Tastes like mild green onions	Appetizers, cream soups, eggs, garnish, salads
Cilantro (fresh; also called *Chinese parsley*)	Lively, pungent flavor some describe as slightly soapy; key ingredient in pico de gallo (salsa)	Indian, Indonesian and Mexican dishes, garnish, pasta salads, pesto
Dill Weed (fresh, dried)	Fresh, peppery and tangy; tastes like dill pickles	Breads, dips, fish, salads, sauces, vegetables
Lemongrass (fresh)	Sour lemon flavor	Thai and Vietnamese dishes, tea
Marjoram (fresh and dried leaves, ground)	Mild, sweet oregano flavor	Fish, lamb, poultry, soups, stews, stuffings, vegetables
Mint (fresh, dried)	Strong, cool, fresh and sweet	Beverages, desserts, fish, lamb, sauces, soups
Oregano (fresh and dried leaves, ground)	Stronger than marjoram, slightly bitter	Fish, Italian dishes, meats, poultry, sauces, soups, vegetables
Parsley (fresh curly leaf, fresh Italian flat leaf, flakes)	Slightly peppery; Italian parsley has a slightly stronger flavor	Garnish, herb mixtures, sauces, soups, stews
Rosemary (fresh and dried leaves)	Sweet, hints of pine and lemon	Breads, casseroles, fish, lamb, salads, seafood, vegetables
Sage (fresh and dried leaves, rubbed, ground)	Slightly bitter with subtle musty-mint flavor	Fish, meats, poultry, salads, sausages, soups, stuffings
Savory (fresh, ground)	A cross between mint and thyme	Bean dishes, fish, meats, poultry, soups, vegetables
Tarragon (fresh and dried leaves)	Mild black licorice flavor; key ingredient in béarnaise sauce	Fish, poultry, sauces, vegetables
Thyme (fresh and dried leaves, ground)	Peppery, minty, light lemon flavor	Fish, meats, poultry, sauces, soups, stuffings, vegetables

SPICES: FORMS, FLAVORS AND USES

Spices add specific flavors to foods—from fragrant to spicy. Use them grated, ground, powdered, in stick form, or whole. Add spices sparingly, as they're usually highly concentrated in flavor. Spices come from various parts of plants and trees: the bark, buds, fruits, roots, seeds and stems.

Spice and Form	Flavor	Use
Allspice (whole, ground; a single spice, not a blend)	A cross between cinnamon, cloves and nutmeg	Cakes, cookies, fruits, jerk seasoning, pickling, pies, poaching fish, spinach, stews
Cinnamon (stick, ground)	Sweet and woodsy	Cakes, cappuccino, cookies, fruit desserts, hot chocolate, maple syrup, pies, pickling, puddings, savory dishes, winter hot drinks
Cloves (whole, ground)	Sweet, peppery	Baked beans, desserts, fruits, gravies, ham, meats, pickling, pork, stews, syrups, tea, vegetables
Garlic (minced, powdered, dehydrated, flaked, fresh, paste, juice)	Slightly musty	Appetizers, bread, fish, meats, poultry, salads, sauces, soups, vegetables
Ginger (whole, cracked bits, ground, crystallized, fresh)	Spicy-hot, sweet	Beverages, baked goods, fish, fruits, meats, poultry, sauces, soups, stir-fries, tea, vegetables
Nutmeg (whole, ground;) *mace* is the covering of the nutmeg seed and can be used the same way	Sweet, spicy; key ingredient in eggnog	Baked goods, beverages, custard, sauces, vegetables
Paprika (ground; made from dried sweet red peppers)	Ranges from sweet to hot, slightly bitter; smoked paprika is also available	Casseroles, eggs, fish, garnish, meats, salads, soups, vegetables
Pepper, black, white and green (whole, ground, cracked; green sold packed in brine or dried)	Slightly hot with a hint of sweetness; black pepper is the strongest, green is the mildest	Savory foods of all kinds
Pepper, red (ground; also known as *cayenne*)	Very hot and peppery	Chili, corn bread, eggs, fish, gravies, guacamole, meats, sauces, vegetables
Saffron (strands, powdered)	Distinctive flavor, softly bitter; key ingredient in paella	Indian and Spanish dishes
Turmeric (ground)	Fragrant, woodsy; key ingredient in store-bought curry powder	Curry powder, eggs, food color, pickling, poultry, rice, seafood

SEEDS: FORMS, FLAVORS AND USES

Seeds are little kernels of seasoning that you can sprinkle on top of dishes or mix into food to give flavor, texture and eye appeal.

Seed and Form	Flavor	Use
Anise Seed (whole)	Tastes like black licorice	Baked goods, candy, Italian and Southeast Asian dishes
Caraway Seed (whole)	Nutty, delicate black licorice flavor	Austrian, German and Hungarian dishes; breads, cabbage, meats, pickling, sauerkraut, stews, vegetables
Cardamom (whole pod, seeds, ground)	Strongly fragrant with a slight lemony-sweet flavor and a touch of pepper and ginger	Scandinavian and East Indian dishes, breads, chai, stews
Celery Seed (whole, ground)	Slightly bitter, tastes like strong celery	Meats, pickling, salads, sauces, soups, stuffings, tomato juice-based drinks
Coriander (whole, ground)	Mildly fragrant, a cross between caraway, lemon and sage	Mexican and Spanish dishes, curry powder, marinades, pastries, pickling, soups
Cumin (whole, ground)	Strongly fragrant, slightly smoky, warm flavor; key ingredient in chili powder	Asian, Mediterranean, Mexican and Middle Eastern dishes; chili, curries
Dill Seed (whole, ground)	Fresh, peppery and tangy; stronger than dill weed	Breads, fish, meats, pickling, processed meats, salads, sauces, soups
Fennel Seed (whole, ground)	Sweet with a delicate black licorice flavor	Italian dishes, breads, sauces, soups, sweet pickles
Fenugreek Seed (whole)	Pleasantly bitter and slightly sweet	Curry powders, spice blends, tea
Mustard Seed (whole, ground)	Yellow seed has a more mild mustard flavor than brown seed, which is more pungent; key ingredient in mustard	Indian dishes, meats, pickling, poultry, relishes, salads, sauces, vegetables
Poppy Seed (whole)	Sweet, nutty and crunchy	Baked goods, noodles, salad dressings, savory dishes, sweet fillings
Sesame Seed (whole)	Oily with a nutty, slightly sweet flavor	Baked goods, dips, salad dressings, savory dishes

SEASONING BLENDS: FORMS, FLAVORS AND USES

Seasoning blends are nifty shortcuts for adding lots of flavor to food. They include blends of dry herbs, spices and salt as well as liquid blends such as red pepper sauce, Worcestershire sauce and marinades. Pick them up at the supermarket, or create your own seasoning collection at home.

Seasoning Blend and Form	Flavor	Use
Apple Pie Spice (ground blend of cinnamon, cloves, nutmeg or mace, allspice and ginger)	Spicy, sweet	Fruit pies, fruit sauces, pastries
Barbecue Spice (ground blend of chili peppers, cumin, garlic, cloves, paprika, salt and sugar)	Savory, spicy and slightly sweet	Barbecue sauce, meat, poultry, Texas toast
Chili Powder (ground blend of dried chili peppers, cloves, coriander, cumin, garlic and oregano)	From mild to hot, depending on the variety	Mexican dishes, soups, stews
Cinnamon-Sugar (blend of ground cinnamon and granulated sugar)	Sweet and fragrant	Baked goods, fruit desserts, toast
Crab Boil (blend of whole allspice, bay leaves, cloves, crushed red peppers, gingerroot, mustard seed and peppercorns)	Savory, slightly sweet	Add to water when boiling seafood or poaching fish
Curry Powder (ground blend of as many as twenty spices—ginger, turmeric, fenugreek seed, cloves, cinnamon, cumin seed, black pepper and red pepper are typical)	Strongly fragrant, mild to hot depending on variety	Appetizers, curries, eggs, fish, pork, poultry, salads, seafood, sauces, vegetables
Fines Herbes (blend of chervil, chives, parsley and tarragon)	Delicate, yet tangy	French dishes, dips, eggs, fish, poultry, salad dressings, salads, sauces, veal, vegetable
Five-Spice Powder (blend of cinnamon, cloves, fennel seed, star anise and Sichuan peppercorns)	Pungent, slightly sweet, a little goes a long way	Asian dishes, marinades, meats, poultry, sauces
Grill Seasoning (salt-based with varied herbs and spices)	Mild to spicy	Fish, meats, poultry, seafood, vegetables
Herb Seasoning (varied blends of mild dried herb leaves such as marjoram, oregano, basil and chervil)	Mild and savory	Casseroles, meat loaves, salad dressings, salads, sauces, vegetables
Herbes de Provence (blend of basil, fennel seed, lavender, marjoram, rosemary, sage, summer savory and thyme)	Savory	Fish, meats, poultry, vegetables
Italian Seasoning (blend of basil, marjoram, oregano, rosemary, sage, savory and thyme)	Savory	Italian dishes, pasta, pizza
Lemon-Pepper Seasoning Salt (ground blend of salt, pepper, onion, garlic, sugar, lemon oil and celery seed)	Spicy, tangy	Fish, poultry, seafood, vegetables
Poultry Seasoning (ground blend of sage, rosemary and other spices)	Savory, pungent, a little goes a long way	Meat loaves, poultry, stuffings
Pumpkin Pie Spice (ground blend of cinnamon, nutmeg, cloves and ginger)	Spicy, sweet	Baked goods, sweet potatoes, winter squash

HERBS

Marjoram
Parsley—Curly
Parsley—Flat
Basil
Mint
Cilantro
Rosemary
Oregano
Sage
Chives
Thyme
Savory
Dill Weed
Lemongrass
Chervil
Tarragon

SPICES AND SEEDS

SEASONING BLENDS

CHAPTER 16
Soups, Sandwiches & Pizza

Stews

Broths

Soups

Pizzas & Calzones

Sandwiches

LOW-FAT = *3g or less, except main dishes with 10g or less* FAST = *Ready in 20 minutes or less* BREAD MACHINE = *Bread machine directions* SLOW COOKER = *Slow cooker directions* LIGHTER = *25% fewer calories or grams of fat*

◀ Tomato-Basil Soup (page 437); American Grilled Cheese (page 450)

Soup, Stew and Chili Basics

When the weather cools down outside, heat it up inside with a soup, stew or chili. These soul-satisfying dishes can be the whole meal in one-bowl or its light beginning. Soups can be clear or creamy, hot or cold, quickly cooked or slowly simmered. Stews, on the other hand, are stick-to-your-ribs chunky concoctions of meat, poultry, fish and vegetables. And chili? It depends on where you live! Usually tomato-based, chili either contains beans and meat or, in some southern states, just the meat. Green and white chilies are popular, too. Get out the ladle and starting simmering!

SOUP, STEW AND CHILI TIPS

- *Be sure to use the size of pan specified* in the recipe. Recipes cooked in pans that are too small can boil over or the mixture heats so slowly that some vegetables and meats overcook.
- *Cut ingredients the same size* so they'll get done at the same time.
- *Heat soups made with dairy products slowly.* Creamy or cheesy soups may separate and curdle if they are boiled.
- *To remove fat,* refrigerate broth or soup 6 to 8 hours, or overnight, until the fat hardens on the surface, then lift it off with a spoon.

BROTH TIPS

- *Wash vegetables,* then cut into large pieces; no peeling or trimming is necessary.
- *Customize the salt and seasonings* in a broth to meet the tastes of your family. Follow the recipe, then adjust salt and seasonings, keeping in mind that as broths evaporate, flavors intensify.

HOMEMADE BROTH SUBSTITUTES

If you don't have time to make homemade broth, try one of these quick substitutions:

Ready-to-serve broth: 1 can (14 oz) chicken, beef or vegetable broth equals about 1 3/4 cups broth.

Condensed broth: 1 can (10.5 oz) condensed chicken or beef broth diluted with 1 soup can water equals 2 2/3 cups broth.

Bouillon: 1 chicken, beef or vegetable bouillon cube or 1 teaspoon bouillon granules mixed with 1 cup water equals 1 cup broth.

Broth or Stock Base: Follow directions on container; each brand is different.

STORING AND REHEATING SOUPS, STEWS AND CHILIES

Refrigerate

Refrigerate soups, stews and chilies in shallow containers so they cool down rapidly. Once completely cooled, cover tightly. Refrigerate most soups, stews and chilies up to 3 days; refrigerate those made with fish and shellfish for 1 day.

Freeze

Soups and chilies usually freeze very well, making them the perfect recipe to double and freeze, so you'll always have a quick meal on hand. Some stews, however, may not freeze well; see tips below.

- Pour soup, stew or chili into freezer containers, leaving 1/4- to 1/2-inch headspace because it will expand as it freezes.

- Pour broth into freezer containers, leaving 1/4- to 1/2-inch headspace because it will expand as it freezes. Or freeze in ice-cube trays. Once frozen, put the broth cubes into a resealable plastic freezer bag.
- Stews thickened with flour or cornstarch may separate after freezing. To freeze this type of stew, save the thickening step until reheating it.
- Freezing potatoes makes them soft and grainy, so add cooked potatoes when reheating.
- Freeze soups, stews and chilies up to 3 months.

Reheat

Freezing may affect the flavor and texture of soups, stews and chilies, so keep these tips in mind.

- Thaw in the refrigerator and use right away.
- Heat broth-based soups over medium heat, stirring occasionally, until hot. Or reheat in the microwave following manufacturer's directions.
- Heat thick purees or soups containing milk, cream, eggs or cheese over low heat, stirring frequently. Don't let them boil or the ingredients may curdle or separate.
- The flavor of green bell pepper intensifies, and onion gradually loses its flavor, so the seasoning may need to be adjusted to taste during reheating.
- Thick soups tend to become thicker during storage. While reheating, add a little broth, milk or half-and-half until the soup reaches the desired consistency.

Beef Stew LOW-FAT

PREP: 15 min **COOK:** 3 hr 30 min ■ **8 SERVINGS**

1 lb beef stew meat, cut into 1/2-inch pieces
1 medium onion, cut into eighths
1 bag (8 oz) baby-cut carrots (about 30)
1 can (14.5 oz) diced tomatoes, undrained
1 can (10.5 oz) condensed beef broth
1 can (8 oz) tomato sauce
1/3 cup all-purpose flour
1 tablespoon Worcestershire sauce
1 teaspoon salt
1 teaspoon sugar
1 teaspoon dried marjoram leaves
1/4 teaspoon pepper
12 small red potatoes (1 1/2 lb), cut into fourths
2 cups sliced fresh mushrooms (about 5 oz) or 1 package (3.4 oz) fresh shiitake mushrooms, sliced

1. Heat oven to 325°F.
2. In ovenproof 4-quart Dutch oven, mix all ingredients except potatoes and mushrooms. Cover and bake 2 hours, stirring once.
3. Stir in potatoes and mushrooms. Cover and bake 1 hour to 1 hour 30 minutes longer or until beef and vegetables are tender.

1 SERVING (ABOUT 1 1/4 CUPS): CAL. 305 (CAL. FROM FAT 65); FAT 7g (SAT. FAT 3g); CHOL. 35mg; SODIUM 820mg; CARBS. 43g (FIBER 6g); PRO. 18g **% DAILY VALUE:** VIT. A 100%; VIT. C 28%; CALC. 6%; IRON 28% **EXCHANGES:** 2 STARCH, 2 VEGETABLE, 1 MEDIUM-FAT MEAT, 1/2 FAT **CARB. CHOICES:** 3

SLOW COOKER DIRECTIONS

Chop onion (1/2 cup). Omit tomato sauce. Increase flour to 1/2 cup. In 3 1/2- to 6-quart slow cooker, mix all ingredients except beef. Add beef (do not stir). Cover and cook on Low heat setting 8 to 9 hours. Stir well.

▲ **Beef Stew**

Chili

PREP: 25 min **COOK:** 1 hr 10 min ■ **4 SERVINGS**

This recipe is sometimes called chili con carne, Spanish for "chili with meat." Everyone has a favorite chili; if you like yours "on the hot side," add 1/2 teaspoon red pepper sauce or a seeded and chopped jalapeño chili.

- 1 lb lean (at least 80%) ground beef
- 1 medium onion, chopped (1/2 cup)
- 1 clove garlic, finely chopped
- 1 can (14.5 oz) diced tomatoes, undrained
- 1 can (8 oz) tomato sauce
- 1 tablespoon chili powder
- 3/4 teaspoon ground cumin
- 1/4 teaspoon salt
- 1/4 teaspoon pepper
- 1 can (15 to 16 oz) kidney or pinto beans, rinsed and drained, if desired

1. In 3-quart saucepan, cook beef, onion and garlic over medium heat 8 to 10 minutes, stirring occasionally, until beef is brown; drain.

2. Stir in remaining ingredients except beans. Heat to boiling; reduce heat. Cover and simmer 1 hour, stirring occasionally.

3. Stir in beans. Heat to boiling; reduce heat. Simmer uncovered about 10 minutes, stirring occasionally, until desired thickness.

1 SERVING: CAL. 395 (CAL. FROM FAT 155); FAT 17g (SAT. FAT 7g); CHOL. 65mg; SODIUM 970mg; CARBS. 37g (FIBER 10g); PRO. 33g **% DAILY VALUE:** VIT. A 30%; VIT. C 22%; CALC. 8%; IRON 34% **EXCHANGES:** 2 STARCH, 1 VEGETABLE, 3 LEAN MEAT, 1 FAT **CARB. CHOICES:** 2 1/2

CINCINNATI-STYLE CHILI For each serving, spoon about 3/4 cup beef mixture over 1 cup hot cooked spaghetti (page 376). Sprinkle each serving with 1/4 cup shredded Cheddar cheese and 2 tablespoons chopped onion. Top with sour cream if desired.

White Chili LOW-FAT

PREP: 10 min **COOK:** 35 min ▪ **6 SERVINGS**

"Accessorizing" your chili is half the fun. Serve it with several bowls of toppings, including shredded cheese, crushed tortilla chips, chopped green onions, diced tomatoes, chopped fresh cilantro, sliced avocado or sour cream.

- 1 tablespoon vegetable oil
- 2 medium onions, chopped (1 cup)
- 2 cloves garlic, finely chopped
- 3 cups chicken broth
- 2 tablespoons chopped fresh cilantro
- 2 tablespoons lime juice
- 1 teaspoon ground cumin
- 1/2 teaspoon dried oregano leaves
- 1/4 teaspoon red pepper sauce
- 1/4 teaspoon salt
- 1 can (11 oz) white shoepeg corn or whole kernel corn, drained
- 1 can (15 to 16 oz) great northern beans, drained
- 1 can (15 to 16 oz) butter beans, drained
- 2 cups chopped cooked chicken breast

1. In 4-quart Dutch oven, heat oil over medium heat. Cook onions and garlic in oil 4 to 6 minutes, stirring occasionally, until onions are tender.

2. Stir in remaining ingredients except chicken. Heat to boiling; reduce heat. Simmer uncovered 20 minutes. Stir in chicken; simmer about 5 minutes or until hot.

1 SERVING (ABOUT 1 1/3 CUPS): CAL. 320 (CAL. FROM FAT 55); FAT 6g (SAT. FAT 1g); CHOL. 40mg; SODIUM 940mg; CARBS. 46g (FIBER 11g); PRO. 31g **% DAILY VALUE:** VIT. A 2%; VIT. C 4%; CALC. 12%; IRON 42% **EXCHANGES:** 2 STARCH, 3 VEGETABLE, 2 LEAN MEAT **CARB. CHOICES:** 3

Shrimp Gumbo LOW-FAT

PREP: 10 min **COOK:** 25 min ▪ **6 SERVINGS**

- 1/4 cup butter or margarine
- 2 medium onions, sliced
- 1 medium green bell pepper, cut into thin strips
- 2 cloves garlic, finely chopped
- 2 tablespoons all-purpose flour
- 3 cups beef broth
- 1/2 teaspoon red pepper sauce
- 1/4 teaspoon salt
- 1/4 teaspoon pepper
- 1 dried bay leaf
- 1 box (10 oz) frozen cut okra, thawed and drained
- 1 can (14.5 oz) whole tomatoes, undrained
- 1 can (6 oz) tomato paste
- 1 lb uncooked peeled deveined medium shrimp, thawed if frozen and tails peeled
- 3 cups hot cooked rice (page 375)
- 1/4 cup chopped fresh parsley

1. In 4-quart Dutch oven, melt butter over medium heat. Cook onions, bell pepper and garlic in butter 5 minutes, stirring occasionally. Stir in flour. Cook over medium heat, stirring constantly, until bubbly; remove from heat.

2. Stir in remaining ingredients except shrimp, rice and parsley, breaking up tomatoes with a fork. Heat to boiling; reduce heat. Simmer uncovered 10 minutes, stirring occasionally.

3. Stir shrimp into gumbo. Cover and simmer about 5 minutes or until shrimp are pink and firm. Remove bay leaf. Serve soup in bowls over rice. Sprinkle with parsley.

1 SERVING (ABOUT 1 1/2 CUPS): CAL. 295 (CAL. from FAT 80); FAT 9g (Sat. 5g); CHOL. 130mg; SODIUM 1,230mg; CARBS. 40g (FIBER 5g); PRO. 19g **% DAILY VALUE:** VIT. A 34%; VIT. C 42%; CALC. 12%; IRON 24% **EXCHANGES:** 2 STARCH, 2 VEGETABLE, 1 LEAN MEAT, 1 FAT **CARB. CHOICES:** 2

Quick Jambalaya

PREP: 15 min **COOK:** 15 min ▪ **4 SERVINGS**

1 package (7 to 8 oz) frozen brown-and-serve sausage links
1 1/2 cups uncooked instant rice
1 1/2 cups chicken broth
1 teaspoon chopped fresh or 1/4 teaspoon dried thyme leaves
1/4 teaspoon chili powder
1/8 teaspoon ground red pepper (cayenne)
1 small green bell pepper, chopped (1/2 cup)
1 small onion, chopped (1/4 cup)
1 can (14.5 oz) stewed tomatoes, undrained
1 package (10 oz) frozen quick-cooking cleaned shrimp

1. Cut sausages diagonally into 1-inch slices. In deep 10-inch skillet, cook as directed on package; drain.

2. Stir in remaining ingredients. Heat to boiling, stirring occasionally; reduce heat. Simmer uncovered 10 minutes, stirring occasionally.

1 SERVING: CAL. 500 (CAL. FROM FAT 200); FAT 22g (SAT. FAT 8g); CHOL. 190mg; SODIUM 1,360mg; CARBS. 45g (FIBER 2g); PRO. 30g **% DAILY VALUE:** VIT. A 10%; VIT. C 26%; CALC. 10%; IRON 26% **EXCHANGES:** 2 1/2 STARCH, 2 VEGETABLE, 2 1/2 MEDIUM-FAT MEAT, 2 1/2 FAT **CARB. CHOICES:** 3

LIGHTER QUICK JAMBALAYA

For 2 grams of fat and 280 calories per serving, omit sausage links.

Oyster Stew FAST

PREP: 10 min **COOK:** 10 min ▪ **4 SERVINGS**

1/4 cup butter or margarine
1 pint (2 cups) shucked oysters, undrained
2 cups milk
1/2 cup half-and-half
1/2 teaspoon salt
Dash of pepper

1. In 1 1/2-quart saucepan, melt butter over low heat. Stir in oysters. Cook 2 to 4 minutes, stirring occasionally, just until edges curl.

2. In 2-quart saucepan, heat milk and half-and-half over medium-low heat until hot. Stir in salt, pepper and oyster mixture; heat until hot.

1 SERVING (ABOUT 1 CUP): CAL. 285 (CAL. FROM FAT 180); FAT 20g (SAT. FAT 12g); CHOL. 115mg; SODIUM 710mg; CARBS. 12g (FIBER 0g); PRO. 14g **% DAILY VALUE:** VIT. A 20%; VIT. C 4%; CALC. 24%; IRON 46% **EXCHANGES:** 1 MILK, 1 MEDIUM-FAT MEAT, 3 FAT **CARB. CHOICES:** 1

BOWLED OVER

Instead of serving soup, stew or chili in soup bowls, bowl them over by serving it in a fun, new way:

- Extra-large coffee mugs
- Hollowed-out hard rolls or kaiser rolls, leaving 1/4-inch-thick shell (best for very thick mixtures)
- Hollowed-out pumpkin for whole recipe or baby pumpkins for individual servings
- Line individual serving bowls with flour tortillas
- Mini casserole or gratin dishes
- Soup plates

Cioppino

PREP: 15 min **COOK:** 35 min ■ **6 SERVINGS**

- 1 tablespoon vegetable oil
- 3 medium onions, chopped (1 1/2 cups)
- 6 cloves garlic, finely chopped
- 1 cup chopped fresh parsley
- 1 can (28 oz) whole tomatoes, undrained
- 1 can (14.5 oz) stewed tomatoes, undrained
- 1 can (8 oz) no-salt-added tomato sauce
- 3/4 cup dry white wine or fish broth
- 2 teaspoons dried basil leaves
- 1/4 teaspoon pepper
- 12 small clams in the shell, washed
- 1 lb fresh halibut or cod, cut into 1 1/2-inch pieces
- 1 lb uncooked peeled deveined medium shrimp, thawed if frozen and tails peeled
- 6 oz chopped cooked crabmeat, cartilage removed
- French bread slices, if desired

1. In 5-quart Dutch oven, heat oil over medium-high heat. Cook onions, garlic and parsley in oil 3 to 5 minutes, stirring occasionally, until onions are crisp-tender.

2. Stir in whole and stewed tomatoes, tomato sauce, wine, basil and pepper, breaking up tomatoes with a fork. Heat to boiling; reduce heat to low. Simmer uncovered 10 minutes, stirring occasionally.

3. Return to boiling. Stir in clams and halibut; cover and simmer over medium heat 4 to 6 minutes or until clam shells open and fish flakes easily with a fork. Stir in shrimp; cover and simmer until shrimp are pink and firm.

4. Stir in crabmeat. Simmer uncovered about 5 minutes or until thoroughly heated. Serve with bread to dip into broth.

1 SERVING: CAL. 270 (CAL. FROM FAT 45); FAT 5g (SAT. FAT 1g); CHOL. 180mg; SODIUM 670mg; CARBS. 20g (FIBER 4g); PRO. 37g
% DAILY VALUE: VIT. A 40%; VIT. C 45%; CALC. 15%; IRON 40%
EXCHANGES: 4 VEGETABLE, 4 VERY LEAN MEAT, 1 FAT
CARB. CHOICES: 1

Chicken and Broth LOW-FAT

PREP: 25 min **COOK:** 1 hr ■ **ABOUT 4 CUPS BROTH AND 2 1/2 TO 3 CUPS COOKED CHICKEN**

- 3- to 3 1/2-lb cut-up whole chicken*
- 4 1/2 cups cold water
- 1 teaspoon salt
- 1/2 teaspoon pepper
- 1 medium stalk celery with leaves, cut up
- 1 medium carrot, cut up
- 1 small onion, cut up
- 1 sprig parsley

1. Remove any excess fat from chicken. In 4-quart Dutch oven or stockpot, place chicken, giblets (except liver**) and neck. Add remaining ingredients; heat to boiling. Skim foam from broth; reduce heat. Cover and simmer about 45 minutes or until juice of chicken is clear when thickest part is cut to bone (170°F for breasts, 180°F for thighs and legs).

2. Remove chicken from broth. Cool chicken about 10 minutes or just until cool enough to handle. Strain broth through cheesecloth-lined sieve; discard vegetables.

3. Remove skin and bones from chicken. Cut chicken into 1/2-inch pieces. Skim fat from broth. Use broth and chicken immediately, or cover and refrigerate broth and chicken in separate containers up to 24 hours or freeze up to 6 months.

1 CUP: CAL. 155 (CAL. FROM FAT 55); FAT 6g (SAT. FAT 2g); CHOL. 65mg; SODIUM 700mg; CARBS. 1g (FIBER 0g); PRO. 24g
% DAILY VALUE: VIT. A 0%; VIT. C 0%; CALC. 2%; IRON 6%
EXCHANGES: 3 VERY LEAN MEAT, 1 FAT **CARB. CHOICES:** 0

SLOW COOKER DIRECTIONS

Decrease water to 3 cups. Increase salt to 1 1/4 teaspoons. In 3 1/2- to 6-quart slow cooker, mix all ingredients including giblets (except liver**) and neck. Cover and cook on Low heat setting 8 to 10 hours. Continue as directed in Step 2.

3 to 3 1/2 lb chicken necks, backs and giblets (except liver) can be used to make broth.*

***The liver is very strongly flavored and should not be used to make the broth. Discard it, or reserve for another use.*

Beef and Broth LOW-FAT

PREP: 30 min **COOK:** 3 hr 15 min ■ **ABOUT 6 CUPS BROTH AND 1 CUP COOKED BEEF**

2 lb beef shank cross-cuts or soup bones
2 tablespoons vegetable oil, if desired
6 cups cold water
1 teaspoon salt
1/4 teaspoon dried thyme leaves
1 medium carrot, cut up
1 medium stalk celery with leaves, cut up
1 small onion, cut up
5 peppercorns
3 whole cloves
3 sprigs parsley
1 dried bay leaf

1. Remove marrow from centers of bones. In 4-quart Dutch oven, melt marrow over low heat until hot, or heat 2 tablespoons vegetable oil until hot. Cook beef shanks in marrow or oil over medium heat until brown on both sides.

2. Add water; heat to boiling. Skim foam from broth. Stir in remaining ingredients; heat to boiling. Skim foam from broth; reduce heat. Cover and simmer 3 hours.

3. Remove beef from broth. Cool beef about 10 minutes or just until cool enough to handle. Strain broth through cheesecloth-lined sieve; discard vegetables and seasonings.

4. Remove beef from bones. Cut beef into 1/2-inch pieces. Skim fat from broth. Use broth and beef immediately, or cover and refrigerate broth and beef in separate containers up to 24 hours or freeze up to 6 months.

1 CUP: CAL. 130 (CAL. FROM FAT 45); FAT 5g (SAT. FAT 1g); CHOL. 40mg; SODIUM 580mg; CARBS. 2g (FIBER 0g); PRO. 21g
% DAILY VALUE: VIT. A 0%; VIT. C 0%; CALC. 0%; IRON 10%
EXCHANGES: 3 VERY LEAN MEAT, 1/2 FAT **CARB. CHOICES:** 0

SLOW COOKER DIRECTIONS

Decrease water to 5 cups. Increase salt to 1 1/4 teaspoons. In 10-inch skillet, heat marrow or 2 tablespoons vegetable oil over medium heat. Cook beef in marrow or oil until brown on both sides. In 3 1/2- to 6-quart slow cooker, mix remaining ingredients; add beef. Cover and cook on Low heat setting 8 to 10 hours. Continue as directed in Step 3.

Vegetable Broth LOW-FAT

PREP: 20 min **COOK:** 1 hr 10 min ■ **ABOUT 8 CUPS BROTH**

6 cups coarsely chopped mild vegetables (such as bell peppers, carrots, celery, leeks, mushroom stems, potatoes, spinach or zucchini)
1 medium onion, coarsely chopped (1/2 cup)
1/2 cup parsley sprigs
8 cups cold water
2 tablespoons chopped fresh or 2 teaspoons dried basil leaves
2 tablespoons chopped fresh or 2 teaspoons dried thyme leaves
1 teaspoon salt
1/4 teaspoon cracked black pepper
4 cloves garlic, finely chopped
2 dried bay leaves

1. In 4-quart Dutch oven or stockpot, heat all ingredients to boiling; reduce heat. Cover and simmer 1 hour, stirring occasionally.

2. Cool about 10 minutes. Strain broth through cheesecloth-lined sieve; discard vegetables and seasonings. Use broth immediately, or cover and refrigerate up to 24 hours or freeze up to 6 months. Stir before measuring.

1 CUP: CAL. 5 (CAL. FROM FAT 0); FAT 0g (SAT. FAT 0g); CHOL. 0mg; SODIUM 270mg; CARBS. 2g (FIBER 0g); PRO. 0g
% DAILY VALUE: VIT. A 0%; VIT. C 0%; CALC. 0%; IRON 0%
EXCHANGES: 1 SERVING IS FREE **CARB. CHOICES:** 0

Fish Broth LOW-FAT

PREP: 20 min **COOK:** 40 min ▪ **ABOUT 6 CUPS BROTH**

- $1\frac{1}{2}$ lb fish bones and trimmings
- 4 cups cold water
- 2 cups dry white wine or clam juice
- 1 tablespoon lemon juice
- 1 teaspoon salt
- $\frac{1}{2}$ teaspoon dried thyme leaves
- 1 large celery stalk with leaves, chopped
- 1 small onion, sliced
- 3 medium mushrooms, chopped
- 3 sprigs parsley
- 1 dried bay leaf

1. Rinse fish bones and trimmings with cold water; drain. In 4-quart Dutch oven or stockpot, mix bones, trimmings, 4 cups cold water and remaining ingredients; heat to boiling. Skim foam from broth; reduce heat. Cover and simmer 30 minutes.

2. Cool about 10 minutes. Strain broth through cheesecloth-lined sieve; discard skin, bones, vegetables and seasonings. Use broth immediately, or cover and refrigerate up to 24 hours or freeze up to 6 months.

1 CUP: CAL. 40 (CAL. FROM FAT 10); FAT 1g (SAT. FAT 0g); CHOL. 0mg; SODIUM 360mg; CARBS. 1g (FIBER 0g); PRO. 3g **% DAILY VALUE:** VIT. A 0%; VIT. C 0%; CALC. 0%; IRON 0% **EXCHANGES:** 1 SERVING IS FREE **CARB. CHOICES:** 0

Chicken Noodle Soup

LOW-FAT

PREP: 1 hr 25 min **COOK:** 30 min ▪ **6 SERVINGS**

- Chicken and Broth (page 434)
- 2 medium carrots, sliced (1 cup)
- 2 medium stalks celery, sliced (1 cup)
- 1 small onion, chopped ($\frac{1}{4}$ cup)
- 1 tablespoon chicken bouillon granules
- 1 cup uncooked medium noodles (2 oz)
- Chopped fresh parsley, if desired

1. Make Chicken and Broth. Refrigerate cut-up chicken. Add enough water to broth to measure 5 cups.

2. In 4-quart Dutch oven, heat broth, carrots, celery, onion and bouillon granules to boiling; reduce heat. Cover and simmer about 15 minutes or until carrots are tender.

3. Stir in noodles and chicken. Heat to boiling; reduce heat. Simmer uncovered 7 to 10 minutes or until noodles are tender. Sprinkle with parsley.

1 SERVING (ABOUT 1 CUP): CAL. 110 (CAL. FROM FAT 25); FAT 3g (SAT. FAT 1g); CHOL. 30mg; SODIUM 1,000mg; CARBS. 9g (FIBER 1g); PRO. 13g **% DAILY VALUE:** VIT. A 70%; VIT. C 2%; CALC. 2%; IRON 6% **EXCHANGES:** 1/2 STARCH, $1\frac{1}{2}$ VERY LEAN MEAT **CARB. CHOICES:** 1/2

CHICKEN RICE SOUP Substitute $\frac{1}{2}$ cup uncooked regular long-grain rice for the uncooked noodles. Stir in rice with the vegetables. Cover and simmer about 15 minutes or until rice is tender. Stir in chicken; heat until chicken is hot.

QUICK CHICKEN SOUP Make as directed—except substitute 3 cans (14 oz each) chicken broth and 2 cups cut-up cooked chicken or turkey for the Chicken and Broth. Omit chicken bouillon granules.

Vegetable-Beef Soup

LOW-FAT

PREP: 3 hr 45 min **COOK:** 45 min ■ **7 SERVINGS**

- Beef and Broth (page 435)
- 1 ear corn or 1/2 cup frozen whole kernel corn
- 2 medium potatoes, cubed (2 cups)
- 2 medium tomatoes, chopped (1 1/2 cups)
- 1 medium carrot, thinly sliced (1/2 cup)
- 1 medium stalk celery, sliced (1/2 cup)
- 1 medium onion, chopped (1/2 cup)
- 1 cup 1-inch pieces green beans
- 1 cup shelled green peas or 1 cup frozen green peas
- 1/4 teaspoon pepper

1. Make Beef and Broth. If necessary add enough water to broth to measure 5 cups. Return strained beef and broth to 4-quart Dutch oven.

2. Cut kernels from corn cob. Stir corn and remaining ingredients into broth. Heat to boiling; reduce heat. Cover and simmer about 30 minutes or until vegetables are tender.

1 SERVING (ABOUT 1 1/2 CUPS): CAL. 235 (CAL. FROM FAT 90); FAT 10g (SAT. FAT 4g); CHOL. 45mg; SODIUM 660mg; CARBS. 20g (FIBER 4g); PRO. 20g **% DAILY VALUE:** VIT. A 44%; VIT. C 18%; CALC. 4%; IRON 18% **EXCHANGES:** 1 STARCH, 1 VEGETABLE, 2 LEAN MEAT, 1/2 FAT **CARB. CHOICES:** 1

Tomato-Basil Soup

LOW-FAT

PREP: 30 min **COOK:** 30 min ■ **4 SERVINGS**

Fully ripe, juicy tomatoes provide the best flavor in this soup. If your tomatoes aren't completely ripe, you may need to increase the salt and sugar just a bit.

- 2 tablespoons olive or vegetable oil
- 2 medium carrots, finely chopped (1/2 cup)
- 1 small onion, finely chopped (1/2 cup)
- 1 clove garlic, finely chopped
- 6 large tomatoes, peeled, seeded and chopped (6 cups)*
- 1 can (8 oz) tomato sauce
- 1/4 cup thinly sliced fresh basil leaves or 2 teaspoons dried basil leaves
- 1/2 teaspoon sugar
- 1/4 teaspoon salt
- Dash of pepper

1. In 3-quart saucepan, heat oil over medium heat. Cook carrots, onion and garlic in oil about 10 minutes, stirring occasionally, until tender but not browned.

2. Stir in tomatoes. Cook uncovered about 10 minutes, stirring occasionally, until heated through.

3. Stir in remaining ingredients. Cook uncovered about 10 minutes, stirring occasionally, until hot.

**3 cans (14.5 oz each) diced tomatoes, undrained, can be substituted for the fresh tomatoes. Omit salt; increase sugar to 1 teaspoon.*

1 SERVING: CAL. 155 (CAL. FROM FAT 70); FAT 8g (SAT. FAT 1g); CHOL. 0mg; SODIUM 550mg; CARBS. 22g (FIBER 5g); PRO. 4g **% DAILY VALUE:** VIT. A 100%; VIT. C 54%; CALC. 4%; IRON 10% **EXCHANGES:** 4 VEGETABLE, 1 FAT **CARB. CHOICES:** 1 1/2

Gazpacho

LOW-FAT

PREP: 20 min **CHILL:** 1 hr ■ **8 SERVINGS**

- 1 can (28 oz) whole tomatoes, undrained
- 1 medium green bell pepper, finely chopped (1 cup)
- 1 cup finely chopped cucumber
- 1 cup croutons
- 1 medium onion, chopped (1/2 cup)
- 2 tablespoons dry white wine or chicken broth
- 2 tablespoons olive or vegetable oil
- 1 tablespoon ground cumin
- 1 tablespoon white vinegar
- 1/2 teaspoon salt
- 1/4 teaspoon pepper

1. In blender or food processor, place tomatoes, 1/2 cup of the bell pepper, 1/2 cup of the cucumbers, 1/2 cup of the croutons, 1/4 cup of the onion and the remaining ingredients. Cover and blend on medium speed until smooth. Pour into large bowl.

2. Cover and refrigerate at least 1 hour. Serve remaining vegetables and croutons as accompaniments.

1 SERVING (ABOUT 1/2 CUP): CAL. 75 (CAL. FROM FAT 35); FAT 4g (SAT. FAT 1g); CHOL. 0mg; SODIUM 320mg; CARBS. 10g (FIBER 2g); PRO. 2g **% DAILY VALUE:** VIT. A 8%; VIT. C 48%; CALC. 4%; IRON 4% **EXCHANGES:** 2 VEGETABLE, 1/2 FAT **CARB. CHOICES:** 1/2

French Onion Soup

PREP: 20 min **COOK:** 1 hr 5 min **BROIL:** 2 min ▪ **4 SERVINGS**

The long, slow cooking of the onions gives this soup its rich flavor and color. Gruyère cheese is a rich, nutty, buttery-tasting form of Swiss, without the holes.

- 2 tablespoons butter or margarine
- 4 medium onions, sliced
- 2 cans (10.5 oz each) condensed beef broth
- 1 1/2 cups water
- 1/8 teaspoon pepper
- 1/8 teaspoon dried thyme leaves
- 1 dried bay leaf
- 4 slices French bread, 3/4 to 1 inch thick, toasted
- 1 cup shredded Gruyère, Swiss or mozzarella cheese (4 oz)
- 1/4 cup grated Parmesan cheese

1. In 4-quart nonstick Dutch oven, melt butter over medium-high heat. Stir in onions to coat with butter. Cook uncovered 10 minutes, stirring every 3 to 4 minutes.

2. Reduce heat to medium-low. Cook 35 to 40 minutes longer, stirring well every 5 minutes, until onions are light golden brown (onions will shrink during cooking).

3. Stir in broth, water, pepper, thyme and bay leaf. Heat to boiling; reduce heat. Cover and simmer 15 minutes. Remove bay leaf.

4. Set oven control to broil. Place toasted bread in 4 ovenproof bowls or individual ceramic casseroles.* Add onion soup. Top with Gruyère cheese. Sprinkle with Parmesan cheese. Place bowls on cookie sheet or in pan with shallow sides.

5. Broil with cheese about 5 inches from heat 1 to 2 minutes or just until cheese is melted and golden brown. Watch carefully so cheese does not burn. Serve with additional French bread if desired.

**Do not use glass containers; they cannot withstand the heat from the broiler and may break.*

1 SERVING: CAL. 360 (CAL. FROM FAT 160); FAT 18g (SAT. FAT 10g); CHOL. 50mg; SODIUM 1,210mg; CARBS. 28g (FIBER 3g); PRO. 22g **% DAILY VALUE:** VIT. A 14%; VIT. C 6%; CALC. 42%; IRON 10% **EXCHANGES:** 2 STARCH, 2 HIGH-FAT MEAT **CARB. CHOICES:** 2

GOLDEN ONION SOUP Omit French bread and cheeses; do not broil.

Borscht

PREP: 25 min **COOK:** 3 hr 40 min ▪ **6 SERVINGS**

This hearty soup, traditionally made with fresh beets, originally hales from Russia. To save on measuring time, it is seasoned with pickling spice. Though the blend can vary among brands, it often contains a fragrant mix of coarse pieces of allspice, bay leaves, cardamom, cinnamon, cloves, coriander, ginger, mustard seed and peppercorns.

- 3/4 lb beef boneless chuck, tip or round, cut into 1/2-inch cubes
- 1 smoked pork hock
- 4 cups water
- 1 can (10.5 oz) condensed beef broth
- 1 teaspoon salt
- 1/4 teaspoon pepper
- 4 medium beets, cooked (page 481), or 1 can (15 oz) sliced beets, drained
- 1 large onion, sliced
- 2 cloves garlic, finely chopped
- 2 medium potatoes, cubed (2 cups)
- 3 cups shredded cabbage
- 2 teaspoons dill seed or 1 sprig dill weed
- 1 tablespoon pickling spice
- 1/4 cup red wine vinegar
- 3/4 cup sour cream
- Chopped fresh dill weed, if desired

1. In 4-quart Dutch oven, heat beef, pork hock, water, broth, salt and pepper to boiling; reduce heat. Cover and simmer 1 hour to 1 hour 30 minutes or until beef is tender.

Borscht

2. Shred beets, or cut into 1/4-inch strips. Remove pork from soup; let stand until cool enough to handle. Remove pork from bone; cut pork into bite-size pieces.

3. Stir pork, beets, onion, garlic, potatoes and cabbage into soup. Tie dill seed and pickling spice in cheesecloth bag or place in tea ball; add to soup. Cover and simmer 2 hours.

4. Stir in vinegar. Simmer uncovered 10 minutes. Remove spice bag. Serve sour cream with soup. Sprinkle with chopped dill weed.

1 SERVING: CAL. 275 (CAL. FROM FAT 115); FAT 13g (SAT. FAT 6g); CHOL. 60mg; SODIUM 800mg; CARBS. 22g (FIBER 3g); PRO. 20g
% DAILY VALUE: VIT. A 6%; VIT. C 14%; CALC. 8%; IRON 12%
EXCHANGES: 4 VEGETABLE, 2 MEDIUM-FAT MEAT, 1/2 FAT
CARB. CHOICES: 1 1/2

SLOW COOKER DIRECTIONS

Decrease water to 3 cups. In 4- to 6-quart slow cooker, mix all ingredients except vinegar, sour cream and chopped dill weed. Cover and cook on Low heat setting 8 to 10 hours. Remove pork hock; let stand until cool enough to handle. Remove pork from bone; cut into bite-size pieces. Stir pork and vinegar into soup. Cover and cook on Low heat setting 10 minutes. Serve sour cream with soup. Sprinkle with chopped dill weed.

THICKEN WITHOUT FAT

To make soups thicker—without using cream, cream cheese, sour cream or even flour—try this:

In a blender or food processor, puree one or more of the cooked vegetables from the recipe with a little of the soup or stew liquid. Stir the thick puree back into the soup or stew.

Beer-Cheese Soup

PREP: 15 min **COOK:** 10 min ▪ **4 SERVINGS**

2 tablespoons butter or margarine
1 small onion, chopped (1/4 cup)
1 medium stalk celery, thinly sliced (1/2 cup)
2 tablespoons all-purpose flour
1/4 teaspoon pepper
1/4 teaspoon ground mustard
1 can or bottle (12 oz) regular or nonalcoholic beer
1 cup milk
2 cups shredded Cheddar cheese (8 oz)
Popped popcorn, if desired

1. In 2-quart saucepan, melt butter over medium heat. Cook onion and celery in butter about 2 minutes, stirring occasionally, until tender.

2. Stir in flour, pepper and mustard. Stir in beer and milk. Heat to boiling over medium heat, stirring constantly. Boil and stir 1 minute; reduce heat to low.

3. Gradually stir in cheese. Heat over low heat, stirring constantly, just until cheese is melted. Sprinkle each serving with popcorn.

1 SERVING: CAL. 345 (CAL. FROM FAT 235); FAT 26g (SAT. FAT 16g); CHOL. 80mg; SODIUM 440mg; CARBS. 12g (FIBER 1g); PRO. 17g **% DAILY VALUE:** VIT. A 20%; VIT. C 2%; CALC. 38%; IRON 4% **EXCHANGES:** 1 STARCH, 2 MEDIUM-FAT MEAT, 2 1/2 FAT **CARB. CHOICES:** 1

CHEESE SOUP Substitute 1 can (10.5 oz) condensed chicken broth for the beer. Serve topped with paprika if desired.

Wild Rice Soup

PREP: 35 min **COOK:** 35 min ▪ **7 SERVINGS**

The next time you serve wild rice as a side dish, cook more than you need and freeze the leftovers. Use later to make this delicious creamy soup.

1/4 cup butter or margarine
4 medium stalks celery, sliced (2 cups)
2 medium carrots, coarsely shredded (2 cups)
1 large onion, chopped (1 cup)
1 medium green bell pepper, chopped (1 cup)
1/4 cup plus 2 tablespoons all-purpose flour
1 teaspoon salt
1/2 teaspoon pepper
3 cups cooked wild rice (page 375)
2 cups water
2 cans (10.5 oz each) condensed chicken broth
3 cups half-and-half
2/3 cup slivered almonds, toasted (page 215), if desired
1/2 cup chopped fresh parsley

1. In 4-quart saucepan or Dutch oven, melt butter over medium-high heat. Cook celery, carrots, onion and bell pepper in butter about 10 minutes, stirring frequently, until crisp-tender.

2. Stir in flour, salt and pepper. Stir in wild rice, water and broth. Heat to boiling; reduce heat. Cover and simmer 15 minutes, stirring occasionally.

3. Stir in half-and-half, almonds and parsley. Heat just until hot (do not boil or soup may curdle).

1 SERVING: CAL. 345 (CAL. FROM FAT 180); FAT 20g (SAT. FAT 12g); CHOL. 55mg; SODIUM 440mg; CARBS. 31g (FIBER 3g); PRO. 11g **% DAILY VALUE:** VIT. A 88%; VIT. C 22%; CALC. 14%; IRON 10% **EXCHANGES:** 1 STARCH, 1 MILK, 1 VEGETABLE, 3 FAT **CARB. CHOICES:** 2

LIGHTER WILD RICE SOUP

For 3 gram of fat and 215 calories per serving, omit butter; spray saucepan with cooking spray before heating. Use 3 cups fat-free half-and-half.

CHICKEN–WILD RICE SOUP Stir in 4 cups cubed cooked chicken or turkey with the half-and-half.

▲ **Wild Rice Soup**

Corn Chowder LOW-FAT

PREP: 15 min **COOK:** 20 min ■ **6 SERVINGS**

- 1/2 lb bacon, cut up
- 1 medium onion, chopped (1/2 cup)
- 2 medium stalks celery, chopped (1 cup)
- 2 tablespoons all-purpose flour
- 4 cups milk
- 1/8 teaspoon pepper
- 1 can (14.75 oz) cream-style corn
- 1 can (15 oz) tiny whole potatoes, drained and diced
- Chopped fresh parsley, if desired
- Paprika, if desired

1. In 3-quart saucepan, cook bacon over medium heat 8 to 10 minutes, stirring occasionally, until crisp. Drain fat, reserving 3 tablespoons in saucepan. Drain bacon on paper towels; set aside.

2. Cook onion and celery in bacon fat over medium heat about 5 minutes, stirring occasionally, until tender. Stir in flour. Cook over medium heat, stirring constantly, until mixture is bubbly; remove from heat.

3. Gradually stir in milk. Heat to boiling, stirring constantly. Boil and stir 1 minute.

4. Stir in pepper, corn and potatoes. Heat until hot. Stir in bacon. Sprinkle each serving with parsley and paprika.

1 SERVING (ABOUT 1 CUP): CAL. 255 (CAL. FROM FAT 80); FAT 9g (SAT. FAT 4g); CHOL. 20mg; SODIUM 570mg; CARBS. 35g (FIBER 4g); PRO. 12g **% DAILY VALUE:** VIT. A 8%; VIT. C 10%; CALC. 22%; IRON 10% **EXCHANGES:** 1 STARCH, 1 MILK, 1 VEGETABLE, 1 FAT **CARB. CHOICES:** 2

Cream of Mushroom Soup

PREP: 15 min **COOK:** 15 min ▪ **4 SERVINGS**

1 lb fresh mushrooms
1/4 cup butter or margarine
3 tablespoons all-purpose flour
1/2 teaspoon salt
1 cup whipping (heavy) cream
1 can (14 oz) chicken broth
1 tablespoon dry sherry, if desired
Freshly ground pepper

1. Slice enough mushrooms to measure 1 cup. Chop remaining mushrooms.

2. In 3-quart saucepan, melt butter over medium heat. Cook sliced and chopped mushrooms in butter about 10 minutes, stirring occasionally, until mushrooms are golden brown. Sprinkle with flour and salt. Cook, stirring constantly, until thickened.

3. Gradually stir in whipping cream and broth; heat until hot. Stir in sherry. Sprinkle with pepper.

1 SERVING: CAL. 350 (CAL. FROM FAT 280); FAT 31g (SAT. FAT 19g); CHOL. 95mg; SODIUM 840mg; CARBS. 11g (FIBER 1g); PRO. 7g
% DAILY VALUE: VIT. A 22%; VIT. C 2%; CALC. 6%; IRON 8%
EXCHANGES: 3 VEGETABLE, 6 FAT **CARB. CHOICES:** 1

LIGHTER CREAM OF MUSHROOM SOUP

For 7 grams of fat and 145 calories per serving, decrease butter to 2 tablespoons and substitute 1 cup fat-free half-and-half for the whipping cream.

Cream of Broccoli Soup

LOW-FAT

PREP: 35 min **COOK:** 10 min ▪ **8 SERVINGS**

1 1/2 lb broccoli
2 cups water
1 large stalk celery, chopped (3/4 cup)
1 medium onion, chopped (1/2 cup)
2 tablespoons butter or margarine
2 tablespoons all-purpose flour
2 1/2 cups chicken broth
1/2 teaspoon salt
1/8 teaspoon pepper
Dash of ground nutmeg
1/2 cup whipping (heavy) cream
Shredded cheese, if desired

1. Remove flowerets from broccoli; set aside. Cut stalks into 1-inch pieces, discarding any leaves.

2. In 3-quart saucepan, heat water to boiling. Add broccoli flowerets and stalk pieces, celery and onion. Cover and heat to boiling; reduce heat. Simmer about 10 minutes or until broccoli is tender (do not drain).

3. Carefully place broccoli mixture in blender. Cover and blend on medium speed until smooth.

4. In 3-quart saucepan, melt butter over medium heat. Stir in flour. Cook, stirring constantly, until mixture is smooth and bubbly; remove from heat. Stir in broth. Heat to boiling, stirring constantly. Boil and stir 1 minute.

5. Stir in broccoli mixture, salt, pepper and nutmeg. Heat just to boiling. Stir in whipping cream. Heat just until hot (do not boil or soup may curdle). Serve soup topped with cheese.

1 SERVING (ABOUT 1 CUP): CAL. 110 (CAL. FROM FAT 70); FAT 8g (SAT. FAT 5g); CHOL. 25mg; SODIUM 510mg; CARBS. 6g (FIBER 2g); PRO. 4g **% DAILY VALUE:** VIT. A 20%; VIT. C 40%; CALC. 4%; IRON 4% **EXCHANGES:** 2 VEGETABLE, 1 FAT **CARB. CHOICES:** 1/2

CREAM OF CAULIFLOWER SOUP Substitute 1 head cauliflower (about 2 lb), separated into flowerets, for the broccoli. Add 1 tablespoon lemon juice with the onion in Step 2.

Manhattan Clam Chowder

LOW-FAT

PREP: 15 min **COOK:** 25 min ■ **4 SERVINGS**

Cooks in Rhode Island in the late 1800s liked to throw tomatoes into clam chowder. Sometime around the mid-twentieth century, their creation became known as Manhattan clam chowder. It resembles New England clam chowder except tomatoes are used instead of milk or cream.

- 1/4 cup finely chopped bacon or salt pork
- 1 small onion, finely chopped (1/4 cup)
- 2 cans (6.5 oz each) minced or whole clams, undrained*
- 2 medium potatoes, diced (2 cups)
- 1/3 cup chopped celery
- 1 cup water
- 2 teaspoons chopped fresh parsley
- 1 teaspoon chopped fresh or 1/4 teaspoon dried thyme leaves
- 1/4 teaspoon salt
- 1/8 teaspoon pepper
- 1 can (14.5 oz) whole tomatoes, undrained

1. In 4-quart Dutch oven, cook bacon and onion over medium heat 8 to 10 minutes, stirring occasionally, until bacon is crisp and onion is tender; drain off fat.

2. Stir in clams, potatoes, celery and water. Heat to boiling; reduce heat. Cover and simmer about 10 minutes or until potatoes are tender.

3. Stir in remaining ingredients, breaking up tomatoes with a fork. Heat to boiling, stirring occasionally.

**1 pint shucked fresh clams with their liquid can be substituted for the canned clams. Chop clams and stir in with the potatoes in Step 2.*

1 SERVING: CAL. 225 (CAL. FROM FAT 25); FAT 3g (SAT. FAT 1g); CHOL. 65mg; SODIUM 450mg; CARBS. 23g (FIBER 3g); PRO. 26g **% DAILY VALUE:** VIT. A 16%; VIT. C 34%; CALC. 12%; IRON 100% **EXCHANGES:** 1 STARCH, 2 VEGETABLE, 3 VERY LEAN MEAT **CARB. CHOICES:** 1 1/2

SLOW COOKER DIRECTIONS

In 10-inch skillet, cook bacon (without onion) as directed in Step 1. In 2- to 3 1/2 -quart slow cooker, mix bacon, onion and remaining ingredients except clams and thyme. Cover and cook on Low heat setting 9 to 10 hours. Stir in undrained clams and thyme. Increase heat setting to High. Cover and cook 10 to 20 minutes or until hot.

New England Clam Chowder

LOW-FAT

PREP: 10 min **COOK:** 25 min ■ **4 SERVINGS**

This favorite chowder from colonial days is a white chowder made with milk or cream.

- 1/4 cup cut-up bacon or salt pork
- 1 medium onion, chopped (1/2 cup)
- 2 cans (6.5 oz each) minced or whole clams*
- 1 medium potato, diced (1 cup)
- 1/2 teaspoon salt
- Dash of pepper
- 2 cups milk

1. In 2-quart saucepan, cook bacon and onion over medium heat, stirring occasionally, until bacon is crisp and onion is tender; drain off fat.

2. Drain clams, reserving liquid. Add enough water, if necessary, to clam liquid to measure 1 cup.

3. Stir clams, clam liquid, potato, salt and pepper into bacon and onion. Heat to boiling; reduce heat. Cover and simmer about 15 minutes or until potato is tender.

4. Stir in milk. Heat, stirring occasionally, just until hot (do not boil or soup may curdle).

**1 pint shucked fresh clams with their liquid can be substituted for the canned clams. Chop clams and stir in with the potato in Step 3.*

1 SERVING (ABOUT 1 CUP): CAL. 245 (CAL. FROM FAT 55); FAT 6g (SAT. FAT 2g); CHOL. 70mg; SODIUM 480mg; CARBS. 19g (FIBER 1g); PRO. 29g **% DAILY VALUE:** VIT. A 14%; VIT. C 20%; CALC. 24%; IRON 100% **EXCHANGES:** 1/2 STARCH, 1/2 MILK, 1 VEGETABLE, 3 VERY LEAN MEAT, 1 FAT **CARB. CHOICES:** 1

Cuban Black Bean Soup

LOW-FAT

PREP: 20 min **COOK:** 2 hr 15 min ■ **8 SERVINGS**

2 tablespoons vegetable oil
1 large onion, chopped (1 cup)
3 cloves garlic, finely chopped
2 2/3 cups dried black beans (1 lb), sorted and rinsed
1 cup finely chopped cooked ham
3 cups beef broth
3 cups water
1/4 cup dark rum or apple cider
1 1/2 teaspoons ground cumin
1 1/2 teaspoons dried oregano leaves
1 medium green bell pepper, chopped (1 cup)
1 large tomato, chopped (1 cup)
Chopped Hard-Cooked Eggs (page 220), if desired
Additional chopped onions, if desired

1. In 4-quart Dutch oven, heat oil over medium heat. Cook 1 cup chopped onion and the garlic in oil 4 to 6 minutes, stirring occasionally, until onion is tender.

2. Stir in remaining ingredients except eggs and additional chopped onions; heat to boiling. Boil 2 minutes; reduce heat. Cover and simmer about 2 hours or until beans are tender.

3. Serve soup topped with eggs and onions.

1 SERVING (ABOUT 1 1/2 CUPS): CAL. 245 (CAL. FROM FAT 55); FAT 6g (SAT. FAT 1g); CHOL. 10mg; SODIUM 610mg; CARBS. 44g (FIBER 11g); PRO. 19g **% DAILY VALUE:** VIT. A 4%; VIT. C 16%; CALC. 12%; IRON 24% **EXCHANGES:** 2 STARCH, 2 VEGETABLE, 1 VERY LEAN MEAT **CARB. CHOICES:** 3

SLOW COOKER DIRECTIONS

Decrease water to 1 3/4 cups. In 3 1/2- to 6-quart slow cooker, mix all ingredients except eggs and additional chopped onions. Cover and cook on High heat setting 6 to 8 hours or until beans are tender. Serve soup topped with eggs and onions.

◀ **Cuban Black Bean Soup**

Senate Bean Soup LOW-FAT

PREP: 20 min **STAND:** 1 hr **COOK:** 3 hr 15 min ▪ **8 SERVINGS**

- 2 cups dried navy beans (1 lb), sorted and rinsed
- 12 cups water
- 1 ham bone, 2 lb ham shanks or 2 lb smoked pork hocks
- $2^1/2$ cups Mashed Potatoes (page 464)
- 2 teaspoons salt
- $^1/4$ teaspoon pepper
- 1 large onion, chopped (1 cup)
- 2 medium stalks celery, chopped (1 cup)
- 1 clove garlic, finely chopped

1. In 4-quart Dutch oven, heat beans and water to boiling. Boil uncovered 2 minutes; remove from heat. Cover and let stand 1 hour.

2. Add ham bone. Heat to boiling; reduce heat. Cover and simmer about 2 hours or until beans are tender.

3. Stir in remaining ingredients. Cover and simmer 1 hour.

4. Remove ham bone; let stand until cool enough to handle. Remove ham from bone. Remove excess fat from ham; cut ham into $^1/2$-inch pieces. Stir ham into soup.

1 SERVING: CAL. 285 (CAL. FROM FAT 80); FAT 9g (SAT. FAT 3g); CHOL. 15mg; SODIUM 960mg; CARBS. 45g (FIBER 9g); PRO. 15g **% DAILY VALUE:** VIT. A 4%; VIT. C 6%; CALC. 10%; IRON 18% **EXCHANGES:** 3 STARCH, 1 VERY LEAN MEAT **CARB. CHOICES:** 3

SLOW COOKER DIRECTIONS

Decrease water to 8 cups and salt to $1^1/2$ teaspoons. In 4- to 6-quart slow cooker, mix all ingredients except mashed potatoes. Cover and cook on Low heat setting 8 to 9 hours or until beans are tender. Remove ham bone; let stand until cool enough to handle. Remove excess fat from ham; cut ham into $^1/2$-inch pieces. Stir ham and mashed potatoes into soup. Increase heat setting to High. Cover and cook 15 minutes.

SOUTHWESTERN BEAN SOUP Add 1 can (4.5 oz) chopped green chiles, 1 tablespoon chili powder and 1 teaspoon ground cumin with remaining ingredients in Step 3. Top soup with salsa if desired.

Split Pea Soup LOW-FAT

PREP: 20 min **COOK:** 2 hr ▪ **8 SERVINGS**

Split peas are a variety of legume grown specifically for drying. They are found with dried beans and lentils in the supermarket.

- $2^1/4$ cups dried split peas (1 lb), sorted and rinsed
- 8 cups water
- $^1/4$ teaspoon pepper
- 1 large onion, chopped (1 cup)
- 2 medium stalks celery, finely chopped (1 cup)
- 1 ham bone, 2 lb ham shanks or 2 lb smoked pork hocks
- 3 medium carrots, cut into $^1/4$-inch slices ($1^1/2$ cups)

1. In 4-quart Dutch oven, heat all ingredients except carrots to boiling, stirring occasionally; reduce heat. Cover and simmer 1 hour to 1 hour 30 minutes.

2. Remove ham bone; let stand until cool enough to handle. Remove ham from bone. Remove excess fat from ham; cut ham into $^1/2$-inch pieces.

3. Stir ham and carrots into soup. Heat to boiling; reduce heat. Cover and simmer about 30 minutes or until carrots are tender and soup is desired consistency.

1 SERVING: CAL. 195 (CAL. FROM FAT 45); FAT 5g (SAT. FAT 2g); CHOL. 15mg; SODIUM 250mg; CARBS. 34g (FIBER 12g); PRO. 16g **% DAILY VALUE:** VIT. A 50%; VIT. C 4%; CALC. 2%; IRON 12% **EXCHANGES:** 2 STARCH, 1 VEGETABLE, 1 VERY LEAN MEAT **CARB. CHOICES:** 2

SLOW COOKER DIRECTIONS

Decrease water to 7 cups. In 4- to 6-quart slow cooker, mix all ingredients. Cover and cook on Low heat setting 3 to 4 hours or until peas are tender. Remove ham bone; let stand until cool enough to handle. Remove excess fat from ham; cut ham into $^1/2$-inch pieces. Stir ham into soup.

Pizza LOW-FAT

PREP: 45 min **REST:** 30 min **BAKE:** 20 min ■
2 PIZZAS, 8 SLICES EACH

Have pizza your way! This recipe includes several options for some of the ingredients. Choose your favorite ones, or add a few of your own, to create your own pizza.

- Pizza Crust (below) or 2 ready-to-serve pizza crusts (12 inch)
- 1 lb lean (at least 80%) ground beef, ground pork, ground lamb or ground turkey
- 1 large onion or 1 medium green bell pepper, chopped (1 cup)
- 1 teaspoon Italian seasoning
- 2 cloves garlic, finely chopped
- 1 can (8 oz) pizza sauce
- 1 jar (4.5 oz) sliced mushrooms, drained, or 1 can (4.5 oz) chopped green chiles, drained
- 2 cups shredded mozzarella, Cheddar, Monterey Jack or brick cheese (8 oz)
- 1/4 cup grated Parmesan or Romano cheese

1. Make dough for Pizza Crust; let rest 30 minutes. Partially bake as directed for thin crusts or thick crusts.

2. Meanwhile, in 10-inch skillet, cook beef, onion, Italian seasoning and garlic over medium heat 8 to 10 minutes, stirring occasionally, until beef is brown and onion is tender; drain.

3. Spread pizza sauce over partially baked crusts. Top with beef mixture, mushrooms and cheeses.

4. Bake thin-crust pizzas at 425°F for 8 to 10 minutes, thick-crust pizzas at 375°F about 20 minutes, or until cheese is melted.

Pizza Crust

- 2 1/2 to 3 cups all-purpose* or bread flour
- 1 tablespoon sugar
- 1 teaspoon salt
- 1 package regular or quick active dry yeast (2 1/4 teaspoons)
- 3 tablespoons olive or vegetable oil
- 1 cup very warm water (120°F to 130°F)

In large bowl, mix 1 cup of the flour, the sugar, salt and yeast. Add oil and warm water. Beat with electric mixer on medium speed 3 minutes, scraping bowl frequently. Stir in enough remaining flour until dough is soft and leaves sides of bowl. Place dough on lightly floured surface. Knead 5 to 8 minutes or until dough is smooth and springy. Cover loosely with plastic wrap and let rest 30 minutes. Continue as directed below for thin crusts or thick crusts.

For Thin Crusts: Heat oven to 425°F. Grease 2 cookie sheets or 12-inch pizza pans with oil. Divide dough in half. Pat each half into 12-inch circle on cookie sheets. Partially bake 7 to 8 minutes or until crust just begins to brown. Add toppings and bake as directed in Step 4.

For Thick Crusts: Grease two 8-inch square pans or 9-inch round pans with oil. Sprinkle with cornmeal. Divide dough in half. Pat each half in bottom of pan. Cover loosely with plastic wrap and let rise in warm place 30 to 45 minutes or until almost doubled in size. Move oven rack to lowest position. Heat oven to 375°F. Partially bake 20 to 22 minutes or until crust just begins to brown. Add toppings and bake as directed in Step 4.

**Do not use self-rising flour.*

1 SLICE: CAL. 195 (CAL. FROM FAT 80); FAT 9g (SAT. FAT 4g); CHOL. 25mg; SODIUM 340mg; CARBS. 18g (FIBER 1g); PRO. 12g
% DAILY VALUE: VIT. A 4%; VIT. C 2%; CALC. 14%; IRON 8%
EXCHANGES: 1 STARCH, 1 VEGETABLE, 1 HIGH-FAT MEAT
CARB. CHOICES: 1

CHEESE PIZZA Omit beef, onion, Italian seasoning and garlic. Increase shredded cheese to 3 cups.

MEAT LOVER'S PIZZA Substitute bulk Italian sausage for the beef. Add 1 cup sliced pepperoni on top of Italian sausage in Step 3.

FRESH MOZZARELLA CHEESE

Fresh mozzarella is very different than the familiar blocks of mozzarella or shredded mozzarella. The fresh version is usually made with whole milk, is white colored and has a delicate, sweet, milky flavor and much softer texture. Some cheese shops, delis and large supermarkets may carry an Italian import called *"buffalo mozzarella,"* which is made with water buffalo milk or a combination of cow's and water buffalo milk. Fresh mozzarella is packed in water or whey and is often formed into balls or slices.

Fresh Mozzarella and Tomato Pizza

Fresh Mozzarella and Tomato Pizza LOW-FAT

PREP: 35 min **RISE:** 20 min **CHILL:** 2 hr **BAKE:** 20 min ■ **1 PIZZA, 8 SLICES**

The fresh mozzarella on this pizza melts beautifully, covering the entire top as it bakes.

- Italian-Style Pizza Dough (right)
- 4 oz fresh mozzarella cheese, well drained
- 2 roma (plum) tomatoes, thinly sliced
- 1/4 teaspoon salt
- Fresh cracked pepper to taste
- 1/4 cup thin strips fresh basil leaves
- 1 tablespoon chopped fresh oregano leaves
- 1 tablespoon small capers, if desired
- 1 tablespoon extra-virgin or regular olive oil

1. Make Italian-Style Pizza Dough.

2. Move oven rack to lowest position. Heat oven to 425°F. Grease cookie sheet or 12-inch pizza pan with oil. Press dough into 12-inch circle on cookie sheet or pat in pizza pan, using floured fingers. Press dough from center to edge so edge is slightly thicker than center.

3. Cut cheese into 1/4-inch slices. Place cheese on dough to within 1/2 inch of edge. Arrange tomatoes on cheese. Sprinkle with salt, pepper, 2 tablespoons of the basil, the oregano and capers. Drizzle with oil.

4. Bake about 20 minutes or until crust is golden brown and cheese is melted. Sprinkle with remaining 2 tablespoons basil.

Italian-Style Pizza Dough

- 1 package regular or quick active dry yeast (2 1/4 teaspoons)
- 1/2 cup warm water (105°F to 115°F)
- 1 1/4 to 1 1/2 cups all-purpose flour
- 1 teaspoon extra-virgin or regular olive oil
- 1/2 teaspoon salt
- 1/2 teaspoon sugar

In large bowl, dissolve yeast in warm water. Stir in half of the flour, the oil, salt and sugar. Stir in enough of the remaining flour to make dough easy to handle. Place dough on lightly floured surface. Knead about 10 minutes or until smooth and springy. Grease large bowl with shortening. Place dough in bowl, turning dough to grease all sides. Cover and let rise in warm place 20 minutes. Gently push fist into dough to deflate. Cover and refrigerate at least 2 hours but no longer than 48 hours. (If dough should double in size during refrigeration, gently push fist into dough to deflate.)

1 SLICE: CAL. 130 (CAL. FROM FAT 45); FAT 5g (SAT. FAT 2g); CHOL. 5mg; SODIUM 300mg; CARBS. 16g (FIBER 1g); PRO. 6g
% DAILY VALUE: VIT. A 6%; VIT. C 2%; CALC. 10%; IRON 6%
EXCHANGES: 1 STARCH, 1 FAT **CARB. CHOICES:** 1

SHREDDED MOZZARELLA AND TOMATO PIZZA Substitute 2 cups shredded mozzarella cheese (8 oz) for the fresh mozzarella. Sprinkle 1 cup of the cheese over dough. Add remaining ingredients as directed—except sprinkle with remaining 1 cup cheese before drizzling with oil.

Calzone

PREP: 45 min **REST:** 30 min **BAKE:** 25 min ▪ **6 SERVINGS**

A calzone is a stuffed pizza that looks like a big turnover.

- Pizza Crust (page 446)
- 2 cups shredded mozzarella cheese (8 oz)
- 1/4 lb salami, cut into thin strips
- 1/2 cup ricotta cheese
- 1/4 cup chopped fresh basil leaves
- 2 roma (plum) tomatoes, chopped
- Freshly ground pepper
- 1 large egg, slightly beaten

1. Make dough for Pizza Crust; let rest 30 minutes.

2. Heat oven to 375°F. Grease 2 cookie sheets with shortening or spray with cooking spray.

3. Divide dough into 6 equal parts. On lightly floured surface, roll each part into 7-inch circle with floured rolling pin.

4. Top half of each dough circle with mozzarella cheese, salami, ricotta cheese, basil and tomatoes to within 1 inch of edge. Sprinkle with pepper. Carefully fold dough over filling; pinch edges or press with fork to seal securely.

5. Place calzones on cookie sheets. Brush with egg. Bake about 25 minutes or until golden brown.

1 SERVING: CAL. 460 (CAL. FROM FAT 200); FAT 22g (SAT. FAT 9g); CHOL. 80mg; SODIUM 970mg; CARBS. 44g (FIBER 2g); PRO. 24g
% DAILY VALUE: VIT. A 14%; VIT. C 2%; CALC. 34%; IRON 18%
EXCHANGES: 3 STARCH, 2 HIGH-FAT MEAT, 1/2 FAT **CARB. CHOICES:** 3

LIGHTER CALZONE

For 8 grams of fat and 350 calories per serving, use reduced-fat mozzarella cheese and fat-free ricotta cheese; substitute cooked chicken for the salami.

HOW TO MAKE A CALZONE

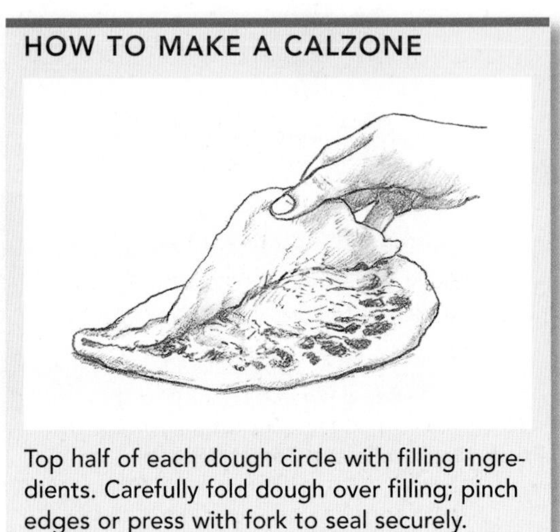

Top half of each dough circle with filling ingredients. Carefully fold dough over filling; pinch edges or press with fork to seal securely.

Sloppy Joes

PREP: 10 min **COOK:** 25 min ▪ **6 SANDWICHES**

- 1 lb lean (at least 80%) ground beef
- 1 medium onion, chopped (1/2 cup)
- 1/4 cup chopped celery
- 1 cup ketchup
- 1 tablespoon Worcestershire sauce
- 1 teaspoon ground mustard
- 1/8 teaspoon pepper
- 6 hamburger buns, split

1. In 10-inch skillet, cook beef, onion and celery over medium heat 8 to 10 minutes, stirring occasionally, until beef is brown; drain.

2. Stir in remaining ingredients except buns. Heat to boiling; reduce heat. Simmer uncovered 10 to 15 minutes, stirring occasionally, until vegetables are tender.

3. Fill buns with beef mixture.

1 SANDWICH: CAL. 325 (CAL. FROM FAT 115); FAT 13g (SAT. FAT 5g); CHOL. 45mg; SODIUM 780mg; CARBS. 35g (FIBER 2g); PRO. 19g
% DAILY VALUE: VIT. A12%; VIT. C 6%; CALC. 8%; IRON 16%
EXCHANGES: 2 STARCH, 1 VEGETABLE, 1 1/2 HIGH-FAT MEAT
CARB. CHOICES: 2

LIGHTER SLOPPY JOES

For 3 grams of fat and 235 calories per serving, substitute ground turkey breast for the ground beef; spray skillet with cooking spray before heating.

Barbecued Roast Beef Sandwiches

PREP: 15 min **COOK:** 15 min ■ **6 SANDWICHES**

Zesty Barbecue Sauce

1/2 cup ketchup
3 tablespoons white vinegar
2 tablespoons chopped onion
1 tablespoon Worcestershire sauce
2 teaspoons packed brown sugar
1/4 teaspoon ground mustard
1 clove garlic, finely chopped

Sandwiches

1 lb thinly sliced cooked roast beef, cut into 1-inch strips (3 cups)
6 hamburger buns, split

1. In 1-quart saucepan, heat all sauce ingredients to boiling over medium heat, stirring constantly; reduce heat. Simmer uncovered 10 minutes, stirring occasionally.

2. Stir beef into sauce. Cover and simmer about 5 minutes or until beef is hot.

3. Fill buns with beef mixture.

1 SANDWICH: CAL. 335 (CAL. FROM FAT 115); FAT 13g (SAT. FAT 5g); CHOL. 60mg; SODIUM 550mg; CARBS. 30g (FIBER 1g); PRO. 25g
% DAILY VALUE: VIT. A 6%; VIT. C 2%; CALC. 6%; IRON 22%
EXCHANGES: 2 STARCH, 3 LEAN MEAT **CARB. CHOICES:** 2

Reuben Sandwiches

PREP: 20 min **COOK:** 20 min ■ **6 SANDWICHES**

Although the traditional Reuben sandwich is served grilled, it also is delicious served cold without grilling. If you decide to skip the grilling, omit the 1/4 cup butter or margarine and Step 2.

6 tablespoons Thousand Island Dressing (page 399)*
12 slices rye bread
6 slices (1 oz each) Swiss cheese
1 can (16 oz) sauerkraut, drained
3/4 lb thinly sliced cooked corned beef
1/4 cup butter or margarine, softened

1. Spread 1 tablespoon Thousand Island Dressing over each of 6 slices bread. Top with cheese, sauerkraut and corned beef. Top with remaining bread slices.

2. Spread 1 teaspoon butter over each top slice of bread. Place sandwiches, butter sides down, in skillet. Spread remaining butter over top slices of bread. Cook uncovered over low heat about 10 minutes or until bottoms are golden brown. Turn; cook about 8 minutes longer or until bottoms are golden brown and cheese is melted.

**Purchased Thousand Island dressing can be substituted.*

1 SANDWICH: CAL. 510 (CAL. FROM FAT 295); FAT 33g (SAT. FAT 15g); CHOL. 105mg; SODIUM 1,700mg; CARBS. 30g (FIBER 5g); PRO. 24g
% DAILY VALUE: VIT. A 12%; VIT. C 18%; CALC. 34%; IRON 20%
EXCHANGES: 2 STARCH, 2 1/2 MEDIUM-FAT MEAT, 3 1/2 FAT
CARB. CHOICES: 2

LIGHTER REUBEN SANDWICHES

For 11 grams of fat and 335 calories per serving, use purchased fat-free Thousand Island dressing; substitute thinly sliced turkey or chicken for the corned beef. Omit butter; spray skillet with cooking spray before heating.

RACHEL SANDWICHES Substitute thinly sliced cooked deli turkey breast for the corned beef.

Reuben Sandwiches ▶

American Grilled Cheese

PREP: 10 min **COOK:** 15 min ▪ **4 SANDWICHES**

Dunk these sandwiches into bowls of steaming tomato soup.

- 12 slices process American cheese (about 8 oz)
- 8 slices white or whole wheat bread
- 1/3 cup butter or margarine, softened

1. Place 3 slices cheese on each of 4 slices bread. Top with remaining bread slices. Spread 2 teaspoons butter over each top slice of bread.

2. Place sandwiches, butter sides down, in skillet. Spread remaining butter over top slices of bread. Cook uncovered over medium heat about 5 minutes or until bottoms are golden brown. Turn and cook 2 to 3 minutes longer or until bottoms are golden brown and cheese is melted.

1 SANDWICH: CAL. 470 (CAL. FROM FAT 295); FAT 33g (SAT. FAT 21g); CHOL. 90mg; SODIUM 1,180mg; CARBS. 26g (FIBER 1g); PRO. 18g
% DAILY VALUE: VIT. A 24%; VIT. C 0%; CALC. 34%; IRON 10%
EXCHANGES: 2 STARCH, 2 HIGH-FAT MEAT, 2 1/2 FAT
CARB. CHOICES: 2

PESTO-PARMESAN GRILLED CHEESE Spread Basil Pesto (page 405) or purchased basil pesto lightly over each bread slice before adding cheese in Step 1. Sprinkle butter-topped slices with Parmesan cheese before grilling.

Beef Burritos

PREP: 25 min **COOK:** 5 min ▪ **8 SERVINGS**

- 2 cups shredded cooked beef
- 1 cup canned refried beans
- 8 flour tortillas (10 inch)
- 2 cups shredded lettuce
- 2 medium tomatoes, chopped (1 1/2 cups)
- 1 cup shredded Cheddar cheese (4 oz)

1. In two 1-quart saucepans, heat beef and refried beans separately over medium heat 2 to 5 minutes, stirring occasionally, until hot. Warm tortillas as directed on bag.

2. Place about 1/4 cup of the beef on center of each tortilla. Spoon about 2 tablespoons beans onto beef. Top with 1/4 cup of the lettuce, 3 tablespoons tomatoes and 2 tablespoons cheese.

3. Fold one end of tortilla up about 1 inch over filling; fold right and left sides over folded end, overlapping. Fold remaining end down.

1 BURRITO: CAL. 390 (CAL. FROM FAT 135); FAT 15g (SAT. FAT 6g); CHOL. 45mg; SODIUM 520mg; CARBS. 44g (FIBER 4g); PRO. 20g
% DAILY VALUE: VIT. A 8%; VIT. C 6%; CALC. 16%; IRON 22%
EXCHANGES: 3 STARCH, 1 1/2 MEDIUM-FAT MEAT, 1 FAT
CARB. CHOICES: 3

HOW TO FOLD A BURRITO

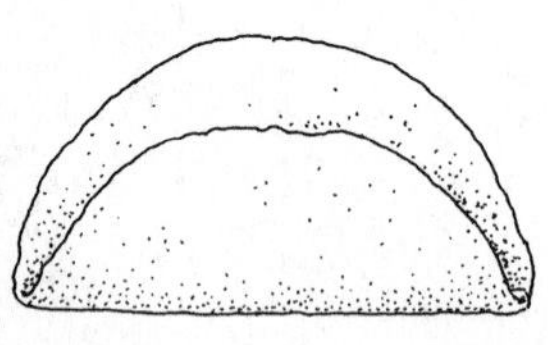

1. Fold one end of tortilla up about 1 inch over filling.

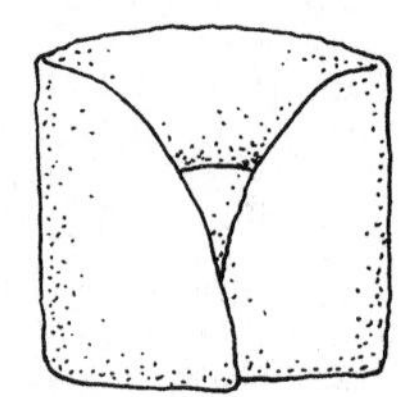

2. Fold right and left sides over folded end, overlapping.

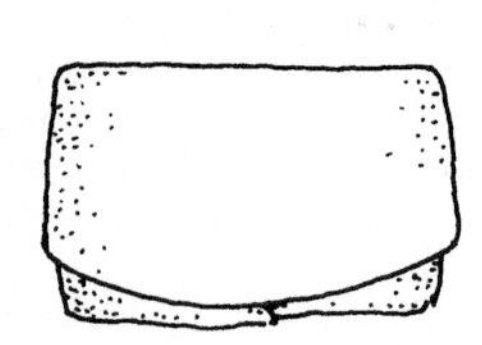

3. Fold remaining end down.

Cuban Pork Sandwiches

FAST

PREP: 10 min **COOK:** 6 min ▪ **4 SANDWICHES**

Florida restaurants introduced the simple, delicious flavors of this Cuban favorite to the United States. If you don't have leftover roast pork, just pick up some from the deli.

- 4 white hamburger buns, split
- 2 teaspoons yellow mustard
- 4 teaspoons mayonnaise or salad dressing
- 4 oz thinly sliced cooked roast pork
- 4 oz thinly sliced cooked ham
- 4 oz sliced Swiss cheese
- 12 slices dill pickles
- 3 tablespoons butter or margarine, melted

1. For each sandwich, spread one cut side of each bun with 1/2 teaspoon mustard and the other side with 1 teaspoon mayonnaise. Layer pork, ham, cheese and 3 pickle slices in each bun, folding meats or cheese to fit if necessary. Press sandwiches firmly with palm of hand to flatten to about 1-inch thickness.

2. Heat 12-inch nonstick skillet over medium-high heat. Brush tops of sandwiches with melted butter. Place sandwiches, buttered sides down, in skillet. Brush bottoms with remaining butter. Cook about 6 minutes, turning once, until crisp and brown on both sides.

1 SANDWICH: CAL. 455 (CAL. FROM FAT 250); FAT 28g (SAT. FAT 13g); CHOL. 90mg; SODIUM 1140mg; CARBS. 24g (FIBER 2g); PRO. 27g
% DAILY VALUE: VIT. A 12%; VIT. C 0%; CALC. 34%; IRON 12%
EXCHANGES: 1 1/2 STARCH, 3 1/2 MEDIUM-FAT MEAT, 1 1/2 FAT
CARB. CHOICES: 1 1/2

Cuban Pork Sandwiches ▶

Chicken Salad Sandwiches

FAST

PREP: 15 min ▪ **4 SANDWICHES**

- 1 1/2 cups chopped cooked chicken or turkey
- 1/2 cup mayonnaise or salad dressing
- 1/4 teaspoon salt
- 1/4 teaspoon pepper
- 1 medium stalk celery, chopped (1/2 cup)
- 1 small onion, chopped (1/4 cup)
- 8 slices bread

1. In medium bowl, mix all ingredients except bread.

2. Spread chicken mixture on each of 4 slices bread. Top with remaining bread.

1 SANDWICH: CAL. 435 (CAL. FROM FAT 245); FAT 27g (Sat. 5g); CHOL. 60mg; SODIUM 630mg; CARBS. 28g (FIBER 2g); PRO. 19g
% DAILY VALUE: VIT. A 2%; VIT. C 4%; CALC. 8%; IRON 12%
EXCHANGES: 2 STARCH, 2 MEDIUM-FAT MEAT, 3 FAT
CARB. CHOICES: 2

LIGHTER CHICKEN SALAD SANDWICHES

For 6 grams of fat and 260 calories per serving, use fat-free mayonnaise.

EGG SALAD SANDWICHES Substitute 6 Hard-Cooked Eggs (page 220), chopped, for the chicken.

HAM SALAD SANDWICHES Substitute 1 1/2 cups chopped cooked ham for the chicken. Omit salt and pepper. Stir in 1 teaspoon yellow mustard.

TUNA SALAD SANDWICHES Substitute 2 cans (6 oz each) tuna in water, drained, for the chicken. Stir in 1 teaspoon lemon juice.

Garden Vegetable Wraps

FAST

PREP: 15 min ▪ **4 SERVINGS**

Here are some fun totable sandwiches with endless filling possibilities. Try different flavors of cream cheese, chopped fresh broccoli, sliced green onions or shredded zucchini. Or add your favorite cheeses and deli meats. Anything goes!

- 1/2 cup cream cheese (about 4 oz)
- 4 flour tortillas (8 to 10 inch)
- 1 cup lightly packed spinach leaves
- 1 large tomato, thinly sliced
- 3/4 cup shredded carrot
- 8 slices (1 oz each) Muenster or Monterey Jack cheese
- 1 small yellow bell pepper, chopped (1/2 cup)

1. Spread 2 tablespoons of the cream cheese over each tortilla. Top with spinach and tomato to within 1 inch of edge. Sprinkle with carrot. Top with cheese slices. Sprinkle with bell pepper.

2. Roll up tortillas tightly. Serve immediately, or wrap securely with plastic wrap and refrigerate up to 24 hours.

1 WRAP: CAL. 460 (CAL. FROM FAT 270); FAT 30g (SAT. FAT 18g); CHOL. 35mg; SODIUM 660mg; CARBS. 31g (FIBER 3g); PRO. 20g
% DAILY VALUE: VIT. A 100%; VIT. C 78%; CALC. 50%; IRON 14%
EXCHANGES: 2 STARCH, 2 HIGH-FAT MEAT, 2 FAT
CARB. CHOICES: 2

HOW TO MAKE A WRAP

Top tortilla with filling ingredients to within 1 inch of edge. Roll up tortilla tightly.

CHAPTER 17

Vegetables & Fruits

Vegetables

Vegetable Basics, 453

Fruit

Fruit Basics, 468

Charts & Glossaries

LOW-FAT = *3g or less, except main dishes with 10g or less* FAST = *Ready in 20 minutes or less* BREAD MACHINE = *Bread machine directions* SLOW COOKER = *Slow cooker directions* LIGHTER = *25% fewer calories or grams of fat*

◀ **Roasted Vegetables (page 465)**

Vegetable Basics

A fabulous bounty of vegetables is just waiting to be picked at your local grocery store, supermarket or farmers' market—any time of year. It's a cornucopia of familiar favorites and exotic newcomers, from carrots to lemongrass or green beans to longbeans. Vegetables bring vivid color, texture and flavor to our plates, and they also add something more—a wealth of healthy nutrients. To learn more, take a look at the New and Specialty Vegetables Glossary on pages 471–475 and New and Specialty Vegetables photo on page 490.

SELECTING AND COOKING FRESH VEGETABLES

Look up a specific vegetable in the Guidelines for Buying, Preparing and Cooking Fresh Vegetables chart (pages 480–488) to find guidelines on selection, storage, preparation and cooking. Cooking times are approximate; ripeness, age, size, moisture content and storage method all can affect cooking times.

Asparagus with Maple-Mustard Sauce FAST

PREP: 5 min **COOK:** 5 min ■ **8 SERVINGS**

- 2 lb asparagus
- 2 tablespoons real maple syrup, maple-flavored syrup or honey
- 2 tablespoons Dijon mustard
- 2 tablespoons olive or vegetable oil

1. Snap off tough ends of asparagus spears. In 12-inch skillet or 4-quart Dutch oven, heat 1 inch water (salted if desired) to boiling. Add asparagus. Heat to boiling; reduce heat to medium. Cover and cook 4 to 5 minutes or until asparagus is crisp-tender; drain.

2. In small bowl, mix maple syrup, mustard and oil. Drizzle over asparagus.

1 SERVING: CAL. 65 (CAL. FROM FAT 35); FAT 4g (SAT. FAT 1g); CHOL. 0mg; SODIUM 95mg; CARBS. 6g (FIBER 1g); PRO. 2g
% DAILY VALUE: VIT. A 10%; VIT. C 10%; CALC. 2%; IRON 2%
EXCHANGES: 1 VEGETABLE, 1 FAT **CARB. CHOICES:** 1/2

Asparagus with Maple-Mustard Sauce ▶

Favorite Green Bean Casserole

PREP: 20 min **BAKE:** 40 min ■ **6 SERVINGS**

1 can (10.75 oz) condensed cream of mushroom, cream of celery or cream of chicken soup
1/2 cup milk
1/8 teaspoon pepper
2 cans (14.5 oz each) French-style green beans, drained*
1 can (2.8 oz) French-fried onions

1. Heat oven to 350°F.

2. In 2-quart casserole or 8-inch square glass baking dish, mix soup, milk and pepper. Stir in beans. Sprinkle with onions.

3. Bake uncovered 30 to 40 minutes or until hot in center.

**2 bags (1 lb each) frozen cut green beans can be substituted for the canned beans. Cook as directed on bag for minimum time; drain.*

1 SERVING (ABOUT 3/4 CUP): CAL. 160 (CAL. FROM FAT 90); FAT 10g (SAT. FAT 3g); CHOL. 5mg; SODIUM 830mg; CARBS. 16g (FIBER 3g); PRO. 4g **% DAILY VALUE:** VIT. A 20%; VIT. C 6%; CALC. 8%; IRON 10% **EXCHANGES:** 1/2 STARCH, 2 VEGETABLE, 1 1/2 FAT **CARB. CHOICES:** 1

▲ **Green Beans with Bacon, Onion and Tomato**

Green Beans with Bacon, Onion and Tomato LOW-FAT

PREP: 10 min **COOK:** 30 min ■ **4 SERVINGS**

1 lb green beans, cut into 1-inch pieces*
4 slices bacon, cut up
1 medium onion, chopped (1/2 cup)
1 medium tomato, chopped (3/4 cup)
1 clove garlic, finely chopped
1 teaspoon chopped fresh or 1/2 teaspoon dried oregano leaves
1/2 teaspoon salt
Dash of pepper
2 tablespoons lemon or lime juice

1. Place beans in 1 inch water in 2-quart saucepan. Heat to boiling; reduce heat. Simmer uncovered 6 to 8 minutes or until crisp-tender; drain. Immediately rinse with cold water; drain.

2. In 10-inch skillet, cook bacon over medium heat 8 to 10 minutes, stirring occasionally, until crisp. Remove bacon from skillet, reserving 1 tablespoon fat in skillet. Drain bacon on paper towels.

3. Cook onion in bacon fat in skillet over medium heat 3 to 4 minutes, stirring occasionally, until tender. Stir in tomato, garlic, oregano, salt and pepper. Simmer uncovered 5 minutes. Stir in beans; heat through. Drizzle with lemon juice. Garnish with bacon.

**A 1-lb bag of frozen cut green beans can be substituted for the fresh beans. Cook as directed in Step 1.*

1 SERVING: CAL. 70 (CAL. FROM FAT 25); FAT 3g (SAT. FAT 1g); CHOL. 5mg; SODIUM 410mg; CARBS. 11g (FIBER 4g); PRO. 4g **% DAILY VALUE:** VIT. A 16%; VIT. C 10%; CALC. 6%; IRON 6% **EXCHANGES:** 2 VEGETABLE, 1/2 FAT **CARB. CHOICES:** 1

Green Beans with Shiitake Mushrooms

PREP: 15 min **COOK:** 25 min ■ **6 SERVINGS**

Once grown only in Japan and Korea, shiitake mushrooms are now cultivated in the United States. Their meaty flesh has a full-bodied, some even say steak-like, flavor. The stems are tough but add a wonderful flavor to stocks and sauces. (Don't forget to discard the stems before serving.)

1 1/2 lb fresh green beans*
1/4 cup slivered almonds
6 oz fresh shiitake mushrooms
1 tablespoon olive or vegetable oil
1 tablespoon sesame oil
3 cloves garlic, finely chopped
2 tablespoons soy sauce

1. Remove ends of beans. Leave beans whole, or cut into 1-inch pieces. Place steamer basket in 1/2 inch water in saucepan or skillet (water should not touch bottom of basket). Place green beans in steamer basket. Cover tightly and heat to boiling; reduce heat. Steam 10 to 12 minutes or until crisp-tender.

2. Meanwhile, in ungreased heavy 8-inch skillet, cook almonds over medium-low heat 5 to 7 minutes, stirring frequently until browning begins, then stirring constantly until golden brown and fragrant; remove from heat.

3. Remove tough stems of mushrooms; cut mushrooms into 1/4-inch slices. In 12-inch skillet, heat olive and sesame oils over medium heat. Cook mushrooms and garlic in oil 3 minutes, stirring occasionally. Stir in soy sauce and green beans. Cook 2 to 3 minutes or until green beans are heated through. Sprinkle with almonds.

**2 bags (14 oz each) frozen whole green beans can be substituted for the fresh green beans.*

1 SERVING: CAL. 95 (CAL. FROM FAT 65); FAT 7g (SAT. FAT 1g); CHOL. 0mg; SODIUM 310mg; CARBS. 9g (FIBER 4g); PRO. 3g
% DAILY VALUE: VIT. A 12%; VIT. C 4%; CALC. 6%; IRON 8%
EXCHANGES: 2 VEGETABLE, 1 FAT **CARB. CHOICES:** 1/2

Roasted Beets

PREP: 10 min **ROAST:** 40 min **COOL:** 30 min ■ **6 SERVINGS**

2 lb small beets (1 1/2 to 2 inches in diameter)
1/2 teaspoon salt
1/4 teaspoon coarsely ground pepper
2 tablespoons extra-virgin or regular olive oil
2 tablespoons chopped fresh basil leaves
1 tablespoon balsamic vinegar

1. Heat oven to 425°F. Cut off all but 2 inches of beet tops. Wash beets; leave whole with root ends attached.

2. Place beets in ungreased 13 × 9-inch pan. Sprinkle with salt and pepper. Drizzle with oil.

3. Roast uncovered about 40 minutes or until beets are tender. Let beets cool until easy to handle, about 30 minutes. Peel beets and cut off root ends; cut beets into 1/2-inch slices.

4. In medium bowl, toss beets, basil and vinegar. Serve warm or at room temperature.

1 SERVING: CAL. 90 (CAL. FROM FAT 45); FAT 5g (SAT. FAT 1g); CHOL. 0mg; SODIUM 270mg; CARBS. 10g (FIBER 2g); PRO. 2g
% DAILY VALUE: VIT. A 0%; VIT. C 2%; CALC. 2%; IRON 4%
EXCHANGES: 2 VEGETABLE, 1 FAT **CARB. CHOICES:** 1/2

▲ **Roasted Beets**

Sesame Buttered Broccoli

FAST

PREP: 10 min **COOK:** 4 min ▪ **4 SERVINGS**

- 1 1/2 lb broccoli, cut into 1 1/2-inch pieces (about 4 cups)
- 2 tablespoons butter or margarine, melted
- 2 teaspoons soy sauce
- 1 teaspoon sesame seed, toasted (page 215)
- 1/2 teaspoon sesame oil

1. In 2-quart saucepan, heat 1 inch water to boiling. Add broccoli. Heat to boiling. Boil uncovered 4 to 6 minutes or until crisp-tender; drain well. Return broccoli to saucepan.

2. Meanwhile, in small bowl, stir remaining ingredients until well mixed. Pour butter mixture over hot broccoli; toss to coat.

1 SERVING: CAL. 100 (CAL. FROM FAT 65); FAT 7g (SAT. FAT 4g); CHOL. 15mg; SODIUM 220mg; CARBS. 6g (FIBER 3g); PRO. 4g
% DAILY VALUE: VIT. A 30%; VIT. C 80%; CALC. 4%; IRON 6%
EXCHANGES: 1 VEGETABLE, 1 1/2 FAT **CARB. CHOICES:** 1/2

▲ **Sesame Buttered Broccoli**

Sweet-Sour Red Cabbage

LOW-FAT

PREP: 20 min **COOK:** 30 min ▪ **8 SERVINGS**

Some like this classic cabbage dish sweeter and some prefer it more sour; it's all a matter of personal preference. For a sweeter touch, add another tablespoon of brown sugar; for a more sour taste, add an extra tablespoon of vinegar.

- 1 medium head red cabbage (1 1/2 lb), thinly sliced
- 4 slices bacon, diced
- 1 small onion, sliced
- 1/4 cup packed brown sugar
- 2 tablespoons all-purpose flour
- 1/4 cup water
- 3 tablespoons white vinegar
- 1/4 teaspoon salt
- 1/8 teaspoon pepper

1. In 10-inch skillet, heat 1 inch water to boiling. Add cabbage; heat to boiling. Boil uncovered about 15 minutes, stirring occasionally, until tender; drain and set aside. Wipe out and dry skillet with paper towel.

2. In same skillet, cook bacon over medium heat 4 minutes, stirring occasionally. Stir in onion. Cook 2 to 4 minutes, stirring occasionally, until bacon is crisp. Remove bacon and onion with slotted spoon; drain on paper towels. Drain fat, reserving 1 tablespoon in skillet.

3. Stir sugar and flour into bacon fat in skillet. Stir in water, vinegar, salt and pepper until well mixed.

4. Stir in cabbage, bacon and onion. Cook over medium heat 1 to 2 minutes, stirring occasionally, until hot.

1 SERVING: CAL. 95 (CAL. FROM FAT 20); FAT 2g (SAT. FAT 1g); CHOL. 5mg; SODIUM 140mg; CARBS. 16g (FIBER 2g); PRO. 3g
% DAILY VALUE: VIT. A 0%; VIT. C 50%; CALC. 6%; IRON 4%
EXCHANGES: 2 VEGETABLE, 1/2 OTHER CARB. **CARB. CHOICES:** 1

SLOW COOKER DIRECTIONS

Omit Step 1. Cook bacon (without onion) as directed in Step 2; reserve 1 tablespoon fat. Refrigerate bacon. Increase water to 1/3 cup. In 3 1/2- to 4-quart slow cooker, mix 1 tablespoon bacon fat, the brown sugar, flour, water, vinegar, salt and pepper. Stir in cabbage and onion. Cover and cook on Low heat setting 6 to 7 hours. Crumble bacon; stir into cabbage.

Glazed Carrots

PREP: 20 min **COOK:** 15 min ■ **6 SERVINGS**

- 1 1/2 lb carrots, cut into julienne strips* (page 8)
- 1/3 cup packed brown sugar
- 2 tablespoons butter or margarine
- 1/2 teaspoon salt
- 1/2 teaspoon grated orange peel

1. In 2-quart saucepan, heat 1 inch water to boiling. Add carrots. Heat to boiling; reduce heat. Simmer uncovered 6 to 9 minutes or until crisp-tender. Drain and reserve.

2. In 12-inch skillet, cook remaining ingredients over medium heat, stirring constantly, until bubbly.

3. Stir in carrots. Cook over low heat about 5 minutes, stirring occasionally, until carrots are glazed and hot.

**1 1/4 bags (1-lb size) frozen sliced carrots, cooked as directed on bag, or fresh baby-cut carrots can be substituted for the 1 1/2 lb julienne carrots.*

1 SERVING: CAL. 130 (CAL. FROM FAT 35); FAT 4g (SAT. FAT 2g); CHOL. 10mg; SODIUM 260mg; CARBS. 22g (FIBER 3g); PRO. 1g
% DAILY VALUE: VIT. A 100%; VIT. C 8%; CALC. 4%; IRON 4%
EXCHANGES: 1 OTHER CARB., 1 VEGETABLE, 1 FAT
CARB. CHOICES: 1 1/2

Spicy Collard Greens with Bacon

PREP: 25 min **COOK:** 1 hr 5 min ■ **4 SERVINGS**

For that true southern flavor, offer cider vinegar on the side for those who want to add a splash.

- 2 lb collard greens, ribs and stems removed and leaves coarsely chopped (about 8 cups)
- 6 cups water
- 6 slices bacon, chopped
- 1 medium onion, chopped (1/2 cup)
- 1 jalapeño chili, seeded and finely chopped
- 1/2 teaspoon dried thyme leaves
- 1/2 teaspoon seasoned salt
- 1/2 teaspoon pepper

1. In 4-quart Dutch oven, heat water to boiling. Add collard greens to water; heat to boiling. Boil 30 minutes; drain.

2. Meanwhile, in 12-inch skillet, cook bacon over medium-high heat, stirring occasionally, until crisp. Remove bacon with slotted spoon, reserving 1 tablespoon bacon fat in skillet. Drain bacon on paper towels.

3. In same skillet, heat reserved bacon fat over medium heat. Cook remaining ingredients in bacon fat 5 minutes, stirring frequently. Stir in collard greens and bacon; reduce heat to low. Cover and cook about 15 minutes longer, stirring occasionally, until collard greens are very tender.

1 SERVING: CAL. 95 (CAL. FROM FAT 45); FAT 5g (SAT. FAT 2g); CHOL. 10mg; SODIUM 360mg; CARBS. 12g (FIBER 7g); PRO. 7g
% DAILY VALUE: VIT. A 100%; VIT. C 52%; CALC. 24%; IRON 2%
EXCHANGES: 2 VEGETABLE, 1/2 HIGH-FAT MEAT
CARB. CHOICES: 1

COLLARD GREENS WITH BLACK-EYED PEAS During last 5 minutes of cooking, stir in 1 can (15 to 16 oz) black-eyed peas, rinsed and drained.

Scalloped Corn

PREP: 10 min **COOK:** 8 min **BAKE:** 35 min ■ **8 SERVINGS**

2 tablespoons butter or margarine
1 small onion, finely chopped (1/4 cup)
1/4 cup finely chopped green bell pepper
2 tablespoons all-purpose flour
1/2 teaspoon salt
1/2 teaspoon paprika
1/4 teaspoon ground mustard
Dash of pepper
3/4 cup milk
1 can (15.25 oz) whole kernel corn, drained*
1 large egg, slightly beaten
1 cup cornflakes cereal
1 tablespoon butter or margarine, melted

1. Heat oven to 350°F.

2. In 10-inch skillet, melt 2 tablespoons butter over medium heat. Cook onion and bell pepper in butter 2 to 4 minutes, stirring occasionally, until crisp-tender. Stir in flour, salt, paprika, mustard and pepper. Cook, stirring constantly, until smooth and bubbly; remove from heat.

3. Stir in milk. Heat to boiling, stirring constantly. Boil and stir 1 minute; remove from heat. Stir in corn and egg. Pour into ungreased 1-quart casserole.

4. In small bowl, mix cereal and 1 tablespoon butter; sprinkle over corn mixture. Bake uncovered 30 to 35 minutes or until center is set.

**2 cups frozen whole kernel corn, thawed, can be substituted for the canned corn.*

1 SERVING: CAL. 135 (CAL. FROM FAT 55); FAT 6g (SAT. FAT 3g); CHOL. 40mg; SODIUM 450mg; CARBS. 17g (FIBER 1g); PRO. 4g
% DAILY VALUE: VIT. A 6%; VIT. C 8%; CALC. 4%; IRON 10%
EXCHANGES: 1 STARCH, 1 FAT **CARB. CHOICES:** 1

Zesty Corn Combo FAST

LOW-FAT

PREP: 10 min **COOK:** 10 min ■ **8 SERVINGS**

Simplify! Chop bell peppers, jalapeño chili and herbs ahead of time and store in individual plastic food-storage bags in the refrigerator.

1 tablespoon butter or margarine
1 medium red bell pepper, coarsely chopped (1 cup)
1 medium green bell pepper, coarsely chopped (1 cup)
1 medium jalapeño chili, seeded and finely chopped
2 bags (1 lb each) frozen whole kernel corn
2 teaspoons chopped fresh or 1/2 teaspoon dried oregano leaves
1/2 teaspoon salt
1/4 cup chopped fresh cilantro

1. In 12-inch nonstick skillet, melt butter over medium heat. Cook bell peppers and chili in butter 2 to 3 minutes, stirring occasionally, until bell peppers are crisp-tender.

2. Stir in frozen corn, oregano and salt. Cover and cook 5 to 6 minutes, stirring occasionally, until corn is tender. Stir in cilantro.

1 SERVING: CAL. 120 (CAL. FROM FAT 20); FAT 2g (SAT. FAT 0g); CHOL. 0mg; SODIUM 160mg; CARBS. 23g (FIBER 3g); PRO. 3g
% DAILY VALUE: VIT. A 24%; VIT. C 38%; CALC. 0%; IRON 2%
EXCHANGES: 1 STARCH, 1/2 OTHER CARB.
CARB. CHOICES: 1 1/2

Zesty Corn Combo ▶

Sautéed Mushrooms

PREP: 15 min **COOK:** 7 min ■ **4 SERVINGS**

Slice fresh mushrooms the fast and easy way—with a hard-cooked egg slicer. Look for one at grocery stores, in specialty cookware stores or in the cookware sections of department store.

2 tablespoons butter or margarine
2 tablespoons olive or vegetable oil
2 cloves garlic, finely chopped
1/2 teaspoon salt
1/4 teaspoon pepper
1 lb mushrooms, sliced (6 cups)
Chopped fresh parsley, if desired

1. In 12-inch skillet, heat all ingredients except mushrooms and parsley over medium-high heat until butter is melted. Stir in mushrooms.

2. Cook 4 to 6 minutes, stirring frequently, until mushrooms are light brown. Sprinkle with parsley.

1 SERVING: CAL. 140 (CAL. FROM FAT 115); FAT 13g (SAT. FAT 5g); CHOL. 15mg; SODIUM 340mg; CARBS. 5g (FIBER 1g); PRO. 3g
% DAILY VALUE: VIT. A 4%; VIT. C 2%; CALC. 0%; IRON 8%
EXCHANGES: 1 VEGETABLE, 2 1/2 FAT **CARB. CHOICES:** 0

LIGHTER SAUTÉED MUSHROOMS

For 3 grams of fat and 55 calories per serving, omit oil and decrease butter to 1 tablespoon; use nonstick skillet.

WHOLE SAUTÉED MUSHROOMS Substitute 2 packages (8 oz each) whole mushrooms (about 3 cups) for the sliced mushrooms. Cook as directed except increase cooking time in Step 2 to 4 to 8 minutes.

Caramelized Onions

LOW-FAT

PREP: 5 min **COOK:** 50 min ■ **7 SERVINGS**

Onions of the sweet variety contain more sugar than other onions, and it is the sugar that caramelizes, giving a deep golden brown color and rich flavor. If you can't find sweet onions for this recipe, regular yellow onions can be used—just sprinkle about 1 tablespoon of brown sugar over the onions and cook as directed.

2 tablespoons butter*
3 large sweet onions (such as Bermuda, Maui, Spanish or Walla Walla), sliced (8 cups)
1/4 teaspoon salt

1. In 12-inch nonstick skillet, melt butter over medium-high heat. Stir in onions to coat with butter. Cook uncovered 10 minutes, stirring every 3 to 4 minutes.

2. Reduce heat to medium-low. Sprinkle salt over onions. Cook 35 to 40 minutes longer, stirring well every 5 minutes, until onions are deep golden brown (onions will shrink during cooking).

**Do not use margarine or vegetable oil spreads.*

1 SERVING: CAL. 55 (CAL. FROM FAT 25); FAT 3g (SAT. FAT 2g); CHOL. 10mg; SODIUM 110mg; CARBS. 6g (FIBER 1g); PRO. 1g
% DAILY VALUE: VIT. A 4%; VIT. C 2%; CALC. 0%; IRON 0%
EXCHANGES: 1 VEGETABLE, 1/2 FAT **CARB. CHOICES:** 1/2

LEARN WITH Betty — MAKING CARAMELIZED ONIONS

These onions were not cooked long enough so are too light in color and will not have a caramelized flavor.

There are no problems with these onions; they are deep golden brown in color and will taste caramelized.

These onions were cooked too long so are too dark with charred edges and will taste burned.

Fresh Peas and Prosciutto

PREP: 25 min **COOK:** 15 min ▪ **4 SERVINGS**

- 1/4 cup olive or vegetable oil
- 1/3 lb prosciutto or deli-style ham slices, chopped (1/3 cup)
- 1 small onion, chopped (1/4 cup)
- 2 lb fresh green peas, shelled*
- 1/2 cup chicken broth
- 1 tablespoon sugar
- 1 tablespoon chopped fresh parsley
- 1/4 teaspoon salt

1. In 10-inch skillet, heat oil over medium-high heat. Cook prosciutto and onion in oil, stirring frequently, until onion is tender.

2. Reduce heat to medium. Stir in remaining ingredients. Cover and cook about 10 minutes or until peas are tender.

**2 1/2 cups frozen green peas (from 1-lb bag) can be substituted for the fresh peas. After stirring in remaining ingredients in Step 2, cover and cook 3 to 5 minutes or until peas are hot.*

1 SERVING: CAL. 25 (CAL. FROM FAT 155); FAT 17g (SAT. FAT 3g); CHOL. 20mg; SODIUM 830mg; CARBS. 16g (FIBER 5g); PRO. 12g
% DAILY VALUE: VIT. A 16%; VIT. C 30%; CALC. 2%; IRON 10%
EXCHANGES: 1 STARCH, 1/2 MEDIUM-FAT MEAT, 1 1/2 FAT
CARB. CHOICES: 1

Twice-Baked Potatoes

PREP: 15 min **BAKE:** 1 hr 35 min ▪ **8 SERVINGS**

Here's an all-American favorite way to serve baked potatoes. Bake them once, scoop them out, whip them up, them pile them back into their shells. They can then be baked right away— or wrapped up tightly and put in the fridge or freezer before being baked the second time. Bake refrigerated potatoes 30 minutes, frozen potatoes about 40 minutes.

- 4 large unpeeled Idaho or russet baking potatoes (8 to 10 oz each)
- 1/4 to 1/2 cup milk
- 1/4 cup butter or margarine, softened
- 1/4 teaspoon salt
- Dash of pepper
- 1 cup shredded Cheddar cheese (4 oz)
- 1 tablespoon chopped fresh chives

1. Heat oven to 375°F. Gently scrub potatoes, but do not peel. Pierce potatoes several times with a fork to allow steam to escape while potatoes bake.

2. Bake 1 hour to 1 hour 15 minutes or until potatoes are tender when pierced in center with a fork.

3. When potatoes are cool enough to handle, cut lengthwise in half; scoop out inside, leaving a thin shell. In medium bowl, mash potatoes with potato masher or electric mixer on low speed until no lumps remain. Add milk in small amounts, beating after each addition with potato masher or electric mixer on low speed (amount of milk needed to make potatoes smooth and fluffy depends on kind of potatoes used).

4. Add butter, salt and pepper; beat vigorously until potatoes are light and fluffy. Stir in cheese and chives. Fill potato shells with mashed potato mixture. Place on ungreased cookie sheet.

5. Increase oven temperature to 400°F. Bake about 20 minutes or until hot.

1 SERVING: CAL. 180 (CAL. FROM FAT 100); FAT 11g (SAT. FAT 7g); CHOL. 30mg; SODIUM 210mg; CARBS. 16g (FIBER 1g); PRO. 5g
% DAILY VALUE: VIT. A 8%; VIT. C 8%; CALC. 8%; IRON 2%
EXCHANGES: 1 STARCH, 2 FAT **CARB. CHOICES:** 1

BACON AND PEPPER TWICE-BAKED POTATOES Stir in 1/2 cup crumbled crisply cooked bacon (8 slices) and 1/2 cup diced red bell pepper with the cheese and chives in Step 4.

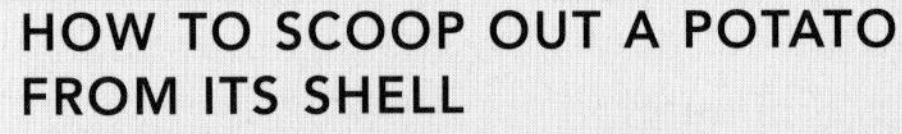

HOW TO SCOOP OUT A POTATO FROM ITS SHELL

Scoop out potatoes from shells using a soup spoon. Carefully scoop out the inside of each potato half, leaving about a 1/4-inch shell.

Scalloped Potatoes

PREP: 20 min **BAKE:** 1 hr 40 min **STAND:** 5 min ■ **6 SERVINGS**

- 3 tablespoons butter or margarine
- 1 small onion, finely chopped (1/4 cup)
- 3 tablespoons all-purpose flour
- 1 teaspoon salt
- 1/4 teaspoon pepper
- 2 1/2 cups milk
- 6 medium peeled or unpeeled potatoes, thinly sliced (6 cups)
- 1 tablespoon butter or margarine

1. Heat oven to 350°F. Grease 2-quart casserole with shortening or spray with cooking spray.

2. In 2-quart saucepan, melt 3 tablespoons butter over medium heat. Cook onion in butter about 2 minutes, stirring occasionally, until tender. Stir in flour, salt and pepper. Cook, stirring constantly, until smooth and bubbly; remove from heat.

3. Stir in milk. Heat to boiling, stirring constantly. Boil and stir 1 minute.

4. Spread potatoes in casserole. Pour sauce over potatoes. Cut 1 tablespoon butter into small pieces; sprinkle over potatoes.

5. Cover and bake 30 minutes. Uncover and bake 1 hour to 1 hour 10 minutes longer or until potatoes are tender. Let stand 5 to 10 minutes before serving (sauce thickens as it stands).

1 SERVING: CAL. 325 (CAL. FROM FAT 90); FAT 10g (SAT. FAT 6g); CHOL. 30mg; SODIUM 500mg; CARBS. 30g (FIBER 2g); PRO. 6g
% DAILY VALUE: VIT. A 10%; VIT. C 8%; CALC. 14%; IRON 4%
EXCHANGES: 1 STARCH, 1/2 MILK, 1/2 OTHER CARB.
CARB. CHOICES: 2

▲ **Au Gratin Potatoes**

Au Gratin Potatoes

PREP: 25 min **BAKE:** 1 hr 20 min ■ **6 SERVINGS**

- 2 tablespoons butter or margarine
- 1 small onion, chopped (1/4 cup)
- 1 tablespoon all-purpose flour
- 1/2 teaspoon salt
- 1/4 teaspoon pepper
- 2 cups milk
- 2 cups shredded sharp Cheddar cheese (8 oz)
- 6 medium potatoes, peeled and thinly sliced (6 cups)
- 1/4 cup dry bread crumbs
- Paprika, if desired

1. Heat oven to 375°F. Grease 1 1/2-quart casserole with shortening or spray with cooking spray.

2. In 2-quart saucepan, melt butter over medium heat. Cook onion in butter about 2 minutes, stirring occasionally, until tender. Stir in flour, salt and pepper. Cook, stirring constantly, until bubbly; remove from heat.

3. Stir in milk. Heat to boiling, stirring constantly. Boil and stir 1 minute; remove from heat. Stir in 1 1/2 cups of the cheese until melted.

4. Spread potatoes in casserole. Pour cheese sauce over potatoes. Bake uncovered 1 hour.

5. In small bowl, mix remaining 1/2 cup cheese and the bread crumbs; sprinkle over potatoes. Sprinkle with paprika. Bake uncovered 15 to 20 minutes or until top is brown and bubbly and potatoes are tender.

1 SERVING: CAL. 355 (CAL. FROM FAT 160); FAT 18g (SAT. FAT 11g); CHOL. 55mg; SODIUM 540mg; CARBS. 34g (FIBER 3g); PRO. 15g
% DAILY VALUE: VIT. A 14%; VIT. C 8%; CALC. 32%; IRON 6%
EXCHANGES: 2 STARCH, 1/2 MILK, 1/2 HIGH-FAT MEAT, 2 FAT
CARB. CHOICES: 2

Roasted Rosemary-Onion Potatoes

PREP: 15 min **ROAST:** 25 min ■ **4 SERVINGS**

- 4 medium peeled or unpeeled potatoes (1 1/3 lb)
- 1 small onion, finely chopped (1/4 cup)
- 2 tablespoons olive or vegetable oil
- 2 tablespoons chopped fresh or 2 teaspoons dried rosemary leaves
- 1 teaspoon chopped fresh or 1/4 teaspoon dried thyme leaves
- 1/4 teaspoon salt
- 1/8 teaspoon pepper

1. Heat oven to 450°F. Spray 15 × 10 × 1-inch pan with cooking spray.

2. Cut potatoes into 1-inch chunks. In large bowl, mix remaining ingredients. Add potatoes; toss to coat. Spread potatoes in single layer in pan.

3. Roast uncovered 20 to 25 minutes, turning occasionally, until potatoes are light brown and tender when pierced with a fork.

1 SERVING: CAL. 175 (CAL. FROM FAT 65); FAT 7g (SAT. FAT 1g); CHOL. 0mg; SODIUM 160mg; CARBS. 26g (FIBER 3g); PRO. 2g
% DAILY VALUE: VIT. A 0%; VIT. C 8%; CALC. 0%; IRON 2%
EXCHANGES: 2 STARCH, 1 OTHER CARB., 1 FAT **CARB. CHOICES:** 2

Fried Potatoes

PREP: 10 min **COOK:** 20 min ■ **4 SERVINGS**

Slice the potatoes up to a day ahead of time, and cover them completely with cold water so they don't turn brown or black. Drain and pat dry with paper towels before cooking, so water won't make the hot fat spatter.

- 2 tablespoons vegetable oil
- 4 medium peeled or unpeeled potatoes, thinly sliced (4 cups)
- 1 medium onion, thinly sliced, if desired
- 1 1/2 teaspoons salt
- 1/4 teaspoon pepper

1. In 10-inch nonstick skillet, heat oil over medium heat. Add potatoes and onion to skillet; sprinkle with salt and pepper.

2. Cover and cook over medium heat 10 minutes, stirring occasionally. Uncover and cook 10 minutes longer, stirring occasionally, until potatoes are brown and tender.

1 SERVING: CAL. 180 (CAL. FROM FAT 65); FAT 7g (SAT. FAT 1g); CHOL. 0mg; SODIUM 890mg; CARBS. 27g (FIBER 2g); PRO. 2g
% DAILY VALUE: VIT. A 0%; VIT. C 8%; CALC. 2%; IRON 2%
EXCHANGES: 1 STARCH, 1 OTHER CARB., 1 FAT
CARB. CHOICES: 2

Oven-Fried Potato Wedges

LOW-FAT

PREP: 10 min **BAKE:** 30 min ■ **4 SERVINGS**

If you love seasoned French fries but not the fat, then you'll love this recipe for making them from scratch, especially since it's so easy! Simply mist wedges of potatoes with cooking spray, sprinkle with seasonings and bake in the oven instead of deep-frying.

- 3/4 teaspoon salt
- 1/2 teaspoon sugar
- 1/2 teaspoon paprika
- 1/4 teaspoon ground mustard
- 1/4 teaspoon garlic powder
- 3 medium unpeeled Idaho or russet baking potatoes (8 to 10 oz each)
- Cooking spray

1. Heat oven to 425°F. In small bowl, mix salt, sugar, paprika, mustard and garlic powder.

2. Gently scrub potatoes, but do not peel. Cut each potato lengthwise in half; cut each half lengthwise into 4 wedges. Place potato wedges, skin sides down, in ungreased 13 × 9-inch pan.

3. Spray potatoes with cooking spray until lightly coated. Sprinkle with salt mixture.

4. Bake uncovered 25 to 30 minutes or until potatoes are tender when pierced with a fork. (Baking time will vary depending on the size and type of potato used.)

1 SERVING: CAL. 90 (CAL. FROM FAT 0); FAT 0g (SAT. FAT 0g); CHOL. 0mg; SODIUM 450mg; CARBS. 20g (FIBER 2g); PRO. 2g
% DAILY VALUE: VIT. A 0%; VIT. C 6%; CALC. 0%; IRON 6%
EXCHANGES: 1 STARCH **CARB. CHOICES:** 1

HOW TO CUT A POTATO INTO WEDGES

To cut potatoes into wedges, cut each potato lengthwise in half. Turn potatoes cut sides down, and cut each half lengthwise into 4 wedges.

Hash Brown Potatoes

PREP: 15 min **COOK:** 30 min ■ **4 SERVINGS**

- 4 medium peeled or unpeeled Idaho or russet baking potatoes ($1\frac{1}{2}$ lb)
- 2 tablespoons finely chopped onion
- $\frac{1}{2}$ teaspoon salt
- $\frac{1}{8}$ teaspoon pepper
- 2 tablespoons vegetable oil

1. Shred enough potatoes to measure 4 cups. Rinse well; drain and pat dry.

2. In large bowl, mix potatoes, onion, salt and pepper. In 10-inch nonstick skillet, heat 1 tablespoon of the oil over medium heat. Pack potato mixture firmly in skillet, leaving $\frac{1}{2}$-inch space around edge.

3. Reduce heat to medium-low. Cook about 15 minutes or until bottom is brown. Drizzle oil evenly over potatoes. Cut potato mixture into fourths; turn over. Cook about 12 minutes longer or until bottom is brown.

1 SERVING: CAL. 160 (CAL. FROM FAT 65); FAT 7g (SAT. FAT 1g); CHOL. 0mg; SODIUM 300mg; CARBS. 22g (FIBER 2g); PRO. 2g
% DAILY VALUE: VIT. A 0%; VIT. C 10%; CALC. 0%; IRON 2%
EXCHANGES: 1 STARCH, $\frac{1}{2}$ OTHER CARB.,1 FAT **CARB. CHOICES:** $1\frac{1}{2}$

Potato Pancakes

PREP: 15 min **COOK:** 20 min ■ **16 PANCAKES**

These pancakes are a favorite in German and Jewish homes and restaurants. Traditionally they're served with sour cream or applesauce. Try them with sliced green onions or maple syrup too.

- 4 medium Idaho or russet baking potatoes ($1\frac{1}{2}$ lb), peeled
- 4 large eggs, beaten
- 1 small onion, finely chopped ($\frac{1}{4}$ cup), if desired
- $\frac{1}{4}$ cup all-purpose flour
- 1 teaspoon salt
- $\frac{1}{4}$ cup vegetable oil

1. Shred enough potatoes to measure 4 cups. Rinse well; drain and pat dry.

2. In large bowl, mix potatoes, eggs, onion, flour and salt. In 12-inch skillet, heat 2 tablespoons of the oil over medium heat. Using $\frac{1}{4}$ cup potato mixture for each pancake, place 4 mounds into skillet. Flatten each with spatula to about 4 inches in diameter.

3. Cook pancakes about 2 minutes on each side or until golden brown. Cover to keep warm while cooking remaining pancakes.

4. Repeat with remaining potato mixture; as mixture stands, liquid and potatoes will separate, so stir to mix as necessary. Add remaining oil as needed to prevent sticking.

1 PANCAKE: CAL. 80 (CAL. FROM FAT 45); FAT 5g (SAT. FAT 1g); CHOL. 55mg; SODIUM 160mg; CARBS. 7g (FIBER 0g); PRO. 2g
% DAILY VALUE: VIT. A 0%; VIT. C 2%; CALC. 0%; IRON 0%
EXCHANGES: $\frac{1}{2}$ STARCH, 1 FAT **CARB. CHOICES:** $\frac{1}{2}$

Mashed Potatoes

PREP: 10 min **COOK:** 30 min ▪ **6 SERVINGS**

6 medium peeled or unpeeled round red or white potatoes (2 lb)
1/3 to 1/2 cup milk
1/4 cup butter or margarine, softened
1/2 teaspoon salt
Dash of pepper

1. Place potatoes in 2-quart saucepan; add enough water just to cover potatoes. Heat to boiling; reduce heat. Cover and simmer 20 to 30 minutes or until potatoes are tender when pierced with a fork; drain. Shake pan with potatoes over low heat to dry (this will help mashed potatoes be fluffier).

2. Mash potatoes in pan with potato masher until no lumps remain. Add milk in small amounts, mashing after each addition (amount of milk needed to make potatoes smooth and fluffy depends on kind of potatoes used).

3. Add butter, salt and pepper. Mash vigorously until potatoes are light and fluffy. If desired, sprinkle with small pieces of butter or sprinkle with paprika, chopped fresh parsley or chives.

1 SERVING: CAL. 185 (CAL. FROM FAT 70); FAT 8g (SAT. FAT 5g); CHOL. 20mg; SODIUM 260mg; CARBS. 25g (FIBER 3g); PRO. 3g
% DAILY VALUE: VIT. A 6%; VIT. C 6%; CALC. 2%; IRON 2%
EXCHANGES: 1 STARCH, 1/2 OTHER CARB., 1 1/2 FAT
CARB. CHOICES: 1 1/2

LIGHTER MASHED POTATOES

For 4 grams of fat and 145 calories per serving, use fat-free (skim) milk and decrease butter to 2 tablespoons.

BUTTERMILK MASHED POTATOES Substitute buttermilk for the milk.

GARLIC MASHED POTATOES Cook 6 cloves garlic, peeled, with the potatoes. Mash garlic with potatoes.

HORSERADISH MASHED POTATOES Add 2 tablespoons prepared mild or hot horseradish with the butter, salt and pepper in Step 3.

BEATING UP MIXER POTATOES

Here's how to mash potatoes with an electric mixer:

- For unlined stainless steel or glass saucepans, beat potatoes in saucepan with electric mixer on low speed as directed above.
- For nonstick saucepans or saucepans that are not shiny inside (such as saucepans made of anodized steel, which are dark gray in color), transfer potatoes to medium bowl after step 1. Beat potatoes with electric mixer on low speed as directed above.

Potato Casserole Supreme

PREP: 15 min **BAKE:** 50 min ▪ **8 SERVINGS**

1 can (10.75 oz) condensed cream of mushroom soup
1 can (10.75 oz) condensed cream of chicken soup
1 container (8 oz) sour cream
1/2 cup milk
1/4 teaspoon pepper
1 package (30 oz) frozen shredded hash brown potatoes
8 medium green onions, sliced (1/2 cup)
1 cup shredded Cheddar cheese (4 oz)

1. Heat oven to 350°F. Spray 13 × 9-inch glass baking dish with cooking spray.

2. In very large bowl, stir soups, sour cream, milk and pepper until well mixed. Stir in potatoes and onions. Spoon into baking dish.

3. Bake uncovered 30 minutes. Sprinkle with cheese. Bake uncovered 15 to 20 minutes longer or until golden brown on top and bubbly around edges.

1 SERVING: CAL. 325 (CAL. FROM FAT 135); FAT 15g (SAT. FAT 8g); CHOL. 40mg; SODIUM 1,060mg; CARBS. 39g (FIBER 3g); PRO. 9g
% DAILY VALUE: VIT. A 12%; VIT. C 12%; CALC. 16%; IRON 6%
EXCHANGES: 2 STARCH, 1/2 OTHER CARB., 2 FAT
CARB. CHOICES: 2 1/2

LIGHTER POTATO CASSEROLE SUPREME

For 4 grams of fat and 240 calories per serving, use condensed 98% fat-free cream of mushroom and cream of chicken soups, fat-free sour cream, fat-free (skim) milk and reduced-fat Cheddar cheese.

Roasted Vegetables

PREP: 15 min **ROAST:** 25 min ■ **10 SERVINGS**

Pick packaged baby-cut carrots that are all about the same size so they cook evenly and are done at the same time.

- 3 tablespoons olive or vegetable oil
- 1/2 teaspoon salt
- 1/8 teaspoon pepper
- 1 clove garlic, finely chopped
- 1 cup baby-cut carrots
- 6 small red potatoes, cut into fourths
- 2 small onions, cut into 1/2-inch wedges
- 1 small red bell pepper, cut into 1-inch pieces
- 1 medium zucchini, cut lengthwise in half, then cut crosswise into 1-inch slices
- 1 cup grape tomatoes or cherry tomatoes

1. Heat oven to 450°F.

2. In small bowl, stir oil, salt, pepper and garlic until well mixed. In 15 × 10 × 1-inch pan, toss carrots, potatoes, onions, bell pepper and zucchini with oil mixture until coated.

3. Roast uncovered 20 minutes, stirring once.

4. Stir in tomatoes. Bake about 5 minutes longer or until vegetables are tender and starting to brown.

1 SERVING: CAL. 110 (CAL. FROM FAT 35); FAT 4g (SAT. FAT 1g); CHOL. 0mg; SODIUM 130mg; CARBS. 16g(FIBER 3g); PRO. 2g
% DAILY VALUE: VIT. A 70%; VIT. C 24%; CALC. 2%; IRON 8%
EXCHANGES: 1/2 STARCH, 2 VEGETABLE, 1/2 FAT
CARB. CHOICES: 1

Candied Sweet Potatoes

PREP: 5 min **COOK:** 30 min ■ **6 SERVINGS**

- 6 medium sweet potatoes (2 lb)*
- 1/3 cup packed brown sugar
- 3 tablespoons butter or margarine
- 3 tablespoons water
- 1/2 teaspoon salt

1. Place sweet potatoes in 2-quart saucepan; add enough water just to cover potatoes. Heat to boiling; reduce heat. Cover and simmer 20 to 25 minutes or until tender when pierced with a fork; drain. When potatoes are cool enough to handle, slip off skins; cut potatoes into 1/2-inch slices.

2. In 10-inch skillet, heat remaining ingredients over medium heat, stirring constantly, until smooth and bubbly. Add potatoes. Gently stir until glazed and hot.

**1 can (23 oz) sweet potatoes, drained and cut into 1/2-inch slices, can be substituted for the fresh sweet potatoes; omit Step 1.*

1 SERVING: CAL. 210 (CAL. FROM FAT 55); FAT 6g (SAT. FAT 4g); CHOL. 15mg; SODIUM 250mg; CARBS. 40g (FIBER 3g); PRO. 2g
% DAILY VALUE: VIT. A 100%; VIT. C 24%; CALC. 4%; IRON 4%
EXCHANGES: 1 STARCH, 1 1/2 OTHER CARB., 1 FAT
CARB. CHOICES: 2 1/2

LIGHTER CANDIED SWEET POTATOES

For 2 grams of fat and 185 calories per serving, decrease butter to 1 tablespoon; use nonstick skillet.

MASHED SWEET POTATOES Cook potatoes as directed in Step 1—except do not cut into slices. Omit 1/3 cup brown sugar, 3 tablespoons butter and 3 tablespoons water. Add 2 tablespoons butter or margarine and 1/2 teaspoon salt to cooked, skinned potatoes. Mash potatoes in saucepan with potato masher until no lumps remain.

ORANGE SWEET POTATOES Substitute orange juice for the water. Add 1 tablespoon grated orange peel with the brown sugar.

PINEAPPLE SWEET POTATOES Omit water. Add 1 can (8 oz) crushed pineapple in syrup, undrained, with the brown sugar.

Caribbean Crunch Squash

Wilted Spinach

PREP: 20 min **COOK:** 10 min ▪ **4 SERVINGS**

2 tablespoons olive or vegetable oil
1 medium onion, chopped (1/2 cup)
1 slice bacon, cut up
1 clove garlic, finely chopped
1/2 teaspoon salt
1/4 teaspoon pepper
1/4 teaspoon ground nutmeg
1 lb washed fresh spinach leaves
2 tablespoons lime juice

1. In 4-quart Dutch oven, heat oil over medium heat. Cook onion, bacon and garlic in oil 8 to 10 minutes, stirring occasionally, until bacon is crisp; reduce heat to low.

2. Stir in salt, pepper and nutmeg. Gradually add spinach. Toss just until spinach is wilted. Drizzle with lime juice.

1 SERVING (ABOUT 1/2 CUP): CAL. 115 (CAL. FROM FAT 70); FAT 8g (SAT. FAT 1g); CHOL. 0mg; SODIUM 410mg; CARBS. 7g (FIBER 3g); PRO. 4g **% DAILY VALUE:** VIT. A 100%; VIT. C 28%; CALC. 12%; IRON 18% **EXCHANGES:** 1 1/2 VEGETABLE, 1 1/2 FAT **CARB. CHOICES:** 1/2

Caribbean Crunch Squash

PREP: 15 min **BAKE:** 1 hr ▪ **4 SERVINGS**

Grilled pork chops, pork roast and pork tenderloin are excellent choices to serve with this sweetly spiced squash.

1 buttercup squash (2 to 2 1/2 lb)*
2 tablespoons butter or margarine, melted
2 tablespoons peach or apricot preserves
2 tablespoons graham cracker crumbs
2 tablespoons shredded coconut
1/4 teaspoon ground ginger
1/8 teaspoon ground allspice
1/8 teaspoon pepper

1. Heat oven to 350°F. Cut squash into fourths; remove seeds and fibers. Place squash, cut sides up, in ungreased 13 × 9-inch pan.

2. In small bowl, mix butter and preserves. Brush about half of preserves mixture over cut sides of squash pieces. In another small bowl, mix remaining ingredients; sprinkle over squash. Drizzle with remaining preserves mixture.

3. Bake uncovered 45 to 60 minutes or until tender.

**Two acorn squash (1 to 1 1/2 lb each) can be substituted for the buttercup squash.*

1 SERVING: CAL. 160 (CAL. FROM FAT 70); FAT 8g (SAT. FAT 5g); CHOL. 15mg; SODIUM 65mg; CARBS. 25g (FIBER 5g); PRO. 2g
% DAILY VALUE: VIT. A 100%; VIT. C 14%; CALC. 2%; IRON 4%
EXCHANGES: 1/2 STARCH, 1 OTHER CARB., 1 1/2 FAT
CARB. CHOICES: 1 1/2

Glazed Acorn Squash

PREP: 10 min **BAKE:** 1 hr ▪ **4 SERVINGS**

- 2 acorn squash (1 to 1 1/2 lb each)
- 4 tablespoons maple-flavored syrup
- 4 tablespoons whipping (heavy) cream, butter or margarine

1. Heat oven to 350°F. Cut each squash lengthwise in half; remove seeds and fibers. In ungreased 13 × 9-inch pan, place squash, cut sides up. Spoon 1 tablespoon maple syrup and 1 tablespoon whipping cream into each half.

2. Bake uncovered about 1 hour or until tender.

1 SERVING: CAL. 210 (CAL. FROM FAT 45); FAT 5g (SAT. FAT 3g); CHOL. 15mg; SODIUM 35mg; CARBS. 47g (FIBER 9g); PRO. 3g
% DAILY VALUE: VIT. A 18%; VIT. C 18%; CALC. 10%; IRON 10%
EXCHANGES: 2 STARCH, 1 OTHER CARB., 1 FAT **CARB. CHOICES:** 3

SLOW COOKER DIRECTIONS

Use squash that are 3/4 to 1 lb each. Cut squash crosswise in half; remove seeds and fibers. Pour 1/4 cup water into 5- to 6-quart slow cooker. Place squash halves, cut sides up, in cooker. (Stacking squash halves in cooker may be necessary.) Spoon 1 tablespoon maple syrup and 1 tablespoon whipping cream into each half. Cover and cook on High heat setting 3 to 4 hours or until tender.

APPLE-STUFFED ACORN SQUASH Omit maple syrup and whipping cream. Bake squash halves 30 minutes. In small bowl, mix 1 large tart red apple, diced, 2 tablespoons chopped nuts, 2 tablespoons packed brown sugar and 1 tablespoon butter or margarine, melted. Spoon apple mixture into squash halves. Bake about 30 minutes longer or until tender.

Garden Patch Sauté FAST

LOW-FAT

PREP: 10 min **COOK:** 8 min ▪ **6 SERVINGS**

All of the vegetables and the chives can be cut up one day ahead and kept covered in the refrigerator.

- 1 tablespoon olive or vegetable oil
- 1 medium zucchini, cut into 1/4-inch slices (1 cup)
- 1 medium yellow summer squash, cut into 1/4-inch slices (1 cup)
- 1 cup sliced mushrooms
- 1 cup grape tomatoes or cherry tomatoes, cut in half
- 2 tablespoons chopped fresh chives*
- 1/2 teaspoon garlic salt

1. In 10-inch nonstick skillet, heat oil over medium-high heat. Cook zucchini, yellow squash and mushrooms in oil 4 to 5 minutes, stirring frequently, until vegetables are crisp-tender.

2. Stir in tomatoes. Sprinkle vegetables with chives and garlic salt. Cook 2 to 3 minutes, stirring frequently, just until tomatoes begin to soften.

**Fresh basil, oregano, marjoram or even lemon balm can be substituted for the fresh chives.*

1 SERVING: CAL. 45 (CAL. FROM FAT 25); FAT 3g (SAT. FAT 0g); CHOL. 0mg; SODIUM 85mg; CARBS. 4g (FIBER 1g); PRO. 1g
% DAILY VALUE: VIT. A 10%; VIT. C 12%; CALC. 2%; IRON 2%
EXCHANGES: 1 VEGETABLE, 1/2 FAT **CARB. CHOICES:** 0

Garden Patch Sauté ▶

Fruit Basics

Fresh fruit, whether juicy, crisp, sweet or tart, is available year-round. The choices are truly amazing, from Granny Smith apples to limequats and many, many more. To learn more, take a look at the Tropical and Specialty Fruits Glossary, pages 475–479 and Tropical and Specialty Fruits photo, page 489.

TIPS FOR BUYING AND STORING FRESH FRUIT

- Look for fruit that is plump, heavy for its size and free from bruises, cuts, mildew and mold.
- Many fruits are shipped to grocery stores while still unripe and firm. Unfortunately, there isn't one rule for determining when a fruit is ripe—it varies from fruit to fruit. Produce departments often have information near the fruit that describes how to tell when each type of fruit is ripe; if your store doesn't provide that information, ask to speak to the produce manager, or browse the Internet for helpful Web sites.
- To ripen most fruits, place in a small paper bag. Don't use plastic bags because fruit can't breathe and moisture builds up, causing mold. Close the bag loosely and let stand at room temperature, checking daily until fruit is ripe. Eat ripe fruit right away, or refrigerate and eat within 2 days.
- Fruits have different storage recommendations and many are described in the Tropical and Specialty Fruits Glossary, pages 475–479. In general, all fruits should be stored unwashed. For more information, browse the Internet.
- Some fruit, such as blackberries, cherries, grapes, pineapples and watermelon, don't ripen any more after they've been picked. Other fruit, including peaches, cantaloupe and blueberries, ripen in color, texture and juiciness after picking. Kiwifruit, pears and papayas ripen in flavor, too.
- To learn more about apple varieties for eating, baking and salads, take a look at the Picking Apples chart, page 218.

Applesauce FAST LOW-FAT

PREP: 5 min **COOK:** 15 min ▪ **6 SERVINGS**

4 medium cooking apples (1 1/3 lb), peeled, cut into fourths and cored
1/2 cup water
1/4 cup packed brown sugar or 3 to 4 tablespoons granulated sugar
1/4 teaspoon ground cinnamon
1/8 teaspoon ground nutmeg

1. In 2-quart saucepan, heat apples and water to boiling over medium heat, stirring occasionally; reduce heat. Simmer uncovered 5 to 10 minutes, stirring occasionally to break up apples, until tender.

2. Stir in remaining ingredients. Heat to boiling. Boil and stir 1 minute. Cover and refrigerate until serving. Store covered in refrigerator.

1 SERVING (ABOUT 1/2 CUP): CAL. 90 (CAL. FROM FAT 0); FAT 0g (SAT. FAT 0g); CHOL. 0mg; SODIUM 5mg; CARBS. 22g (FIBER 2g); PRO. 0g **% DAILY VALUE:** VIT. A 0%; VIT. C 2%; CALC. 2%; IRON 2% **EXCHANGES:** 1 1/2 FRUIT **CARB. CHOICES:** 1 1/2

SLOW COOKER DIRECTIONS

Decrease water to 1/4 cup. In 3 1/2- to 6-quart slow cooker, mix all ingredients. Cover and cook on High heat setting 1 hour 30 minutes to 2 hours or until apples are tender; stir.

Apple-Pear Salad

PREP: 25 min ▪ **8 SERVINGS**

- 1 large red apple, cut into fourths, then cut crosswise into thin slices
- 1 large pear, cut into fourths, then cut crosswise into thin slices
- 1 medium stalk celery, cut diagonally into thin slices (1/2 cup)
- 4 oz Havarti cheese, cut into julienne strips
- 3 tablespoons olive or vegetable oil
- 2 tablespoons frozen (thawed) apple juice concentrate
- 3 tablespoons coarsely chopped honey-roasted peanuts

1. In medium salad bowl, mix apple, pear, celery and cheese.

2. In small bowl, thoroughly mix oil and juice concentrate. Pour over apple mixture; toss to coat. Sprinkle with peanuts.

1 SERVING: CAL. 150 (CAL. FROM FAT 100); FAT 11g (SAT. FAT 4g); CHOL. 15mg; SODIUM 110mg; CARBS. 10g (FIBER 1g); PRO. 3g
% DAILY VALUE: VIT. A 4%; VIT. C 4%; CALC. 8%; IRON 0%
EXCHANGES: 1/2 FRUIT, 1/2 HIGH-FAT MEAT, 1 1/2 FAT
CARB. CHOICES: 1/2

Peach and Plum Salad FAST

PREP: 10 min ▪ **6 SERVINGS**

- 3 medium plums, sliced
- 3 medium peaches, sliced
- 1/2 cup coarsely chopped walnuts, toasted (page 215)
- 1/4 cup raspberry preserves
- 2 tablespoons red wine vinegar or white vinegar
- 1 tablespoon vegetable oil

1. Arrange plums and peaches on serving plate. Sprinkle with walnuts.

2. In small bowl, mix remaining ingredients; drizzle over fruit.

1 SERVING: CAL. 170 (CAL. FROM FAT 80); FAT 9g (SAT. FAT 1g); CHOL. 0mg; SODIUM 5mg; CARBS. 21g (FIBER 2g); PRO. 2g
% DAILY VALUE: VIT. A 2%; VIT. C 12%; CALC. 2%; IRON 2%
EXCHANGES: 1 1/2 FRUIT, 2 FAT **CARB. CHOICES:** 1 1/2

Key West Fruit Salad

LOW-FAT

PREP: 20 min **COOK:** 5 min **CHILL:** 2 hr ▪ **28 SERVINGS**

This salad makes about 14 cups, so it's perfect for potlucks, open houses, graduations and showers.

- 3/4 cup sugar
- 1/4 cup water
- 1/4 cup fresh or bottled Key lime juice or regular lime juice
- 2 to 3 tablespoons tequila or Key lime juice
- 1 teaspoon grated Key lime peel or regular lime peel
- 14 cups cut-up fresh fruit (such as pineapple, strawberries, kiwifruit or grapes)

1. In 1 1/2-quart saucepan, heat sugar and water to boiling; reduce heat. Simmer uncovered about 2 minutes, stirring constantly, until sugar is dissolved; remove from heat. Stir in lime juice and tequila.

2. Let lime dressing stand until room temperature. Cover and refrigerate about 2 hours or until cool.

3. Stir lime peel into dressing. In very large bowl, carefully toss fruit and dressing. Serve immediately.

1 SERVING: CAL. 65 (CAL. FROM FAT 0); FAT 0g (SAT. FAT 0g); CHOL. 0mg; SODIUM 5g; CARBS. 16 (FIBER 2g); PRO. 1g
% DAILY VALUE: VIT. A 6; VIT. C 62; CALC. 0%; IRON 2%
EXCHANGES: 1 FRUIT **CARB. CHOICES:** 1

Apple-Pear Salad ▶

Rhubarb Sauce LOW-FAT

PREP: 10 min **COOK:** 15 min ▪ **6 SERVINGS**

Rhubarb varies in sweetness, so add sugar to taste. Besides making a great side to meats and poultry, this sauce also can be served for dessert, either by itself or over pound cake or ice cream.

- 1/2 to 3/4 cup sugar
- 1/2 cup water
- 1 lb rhubarb, cut into 1-inch pieces (4 cups)
- Ground cinnamon, if desired

1. In 2-quart saucepan, heat sugar and water to boiling, stirring occasionally. Stir in rhubarb; reduce heat. Simmer uncovered about 10 minutes, stirring occasionally, until rhubarb is tender and slightly transparent.

2. Stir in cinnamon. Serve sauce warm or chilled.

1 SERVING (ABOUT 1/2 CUP): CAL. 75 (CAL. FROM FAT 0); FAT 0g (SAT. FAT 0g); CHOL. 0mg; SODIUM 0mg; CARBS. 18g (FIBER 1g); PRO. 1g **% DAILY VALUE:** VIT. A 2%; VIT. C 2%; CALC. 14%; IRON 0% **EXCHANGES:** 1 FRUIT **CARB. CHOICES:** 1

STRAWBERRY-RHUBARB SAUCE Substitute 1 cup strawberries, cut in half, for 1 cup of the rhubarb. After simmering rhubarb, stir in strawberries; heat just to boiling.

Caramel Apples

PREP: 10 min **COOK:** 20 min ▪ **6 SERVINGS**

Nothing beats the old-fashioned flavor of caramel apples—especially when you make the caramel from scratch!

- 6 medium apples
- 6 wooden skewers
- 1 cup sugar
- 1/2 cup light corn syrup
- 1 can (14 oz) sweetened condensed milk
- 1/8 teaspoon salt
- 1 teaspoon vanilla
- Candy sprinkles, chopped candy or chopped peanuts, if desired

1. Wash apples and dry thoroughly. Insert a wooden skewer in stem end of each apple. Spray plate with cooking spray.

2. In 2-quart saucepan, mix sugar, corn syrup, milk and salt. Cook over low heat, stirring constantly, to 230°F on candy thermometer or until a few drops of syrup dropped into cup of cold water forms a soft ball that flattens when removed from water. Remove from heat; stir in vanilla. Cool slightly.

3. Quickly dip apples into caramel, swirling until completely covered. Dip bottoms in candy sprinkles. Place apples on plate until caramel is set.

1 SERVING: CAL. 585 (CAL. FROM FAT 70); FAT 8g (SAT. FAT 5g); CHOL. 30mg; SODIUM 200mg; CARBS. 124g (FIBER 4g); PRO. 7g **% DAILY VALUE:** VIT. A 8%; VIT. C 8%; CALC. 26%; IRON 2% **EXCHANGES:** 1 FRUIT, 7 OTHER CARB., 1 1/2 FAT **CARB. CHOICES:** 8

◄ **Caramel Apples**

NEW AND SPECIALTY VEGETABLES GLOSSARY

Asian Vegetables:

- **Daikon:** A large black or white radish of Asian origin. It ranges from 6 to 15 inches in length and 2 to 3 inches or more in diameter. Its flesh is crisp, juicy and white with a sweet, fresh flavor. Serve raw in salads, in stir-fries or as a garnish. Refrigerate unwashed in plastic bag up to 7 days. Available year-round.
- **Eggplant (Chinese, Japanese, Thai):** Botanically, eggplant is actually a fruit but is generally thought of and used as a vegetable. Chinese and Japanese eggplants have purple skin and are longer and smaller than the common deep purple eggplant. Thai eggplant ranges in color from green to white and is 1 to 2 inches in diameter. See storage directions in Guidelines for Buying, Preparing and Cooking Fresh Vegetables chart, page 483.
- **Gai Lan (Chinese Kale, Chinese Broccoli):** This long, leafy green is more sharply flavored than common broccoli. Broccoli rabe can be substituted. Refrigerate unwashed in plastic bag up to 1 week.
- **Lemongrass:** Sold by the stalk that resembles a woody green onion. Imparts lemony flavor to Thai and Vietnamese dishes. Use the white base portion of the stalk only to where the leaves begin to branch. Remove lemongrass pieces from a dish before serving. Refrigerate unwashed in plastic bag up to 2 weeks.
- **Lo Bok (Chinese Radish):** Shorter and fatter than daikon, it has a crisp texture and sharp flavor. Use chopped or grated in salads or serve with fried food. Refrigerate unwashed in plastic bag up to 1 week.
- **Longbean (Asparagus Bean, Chinese Longbean, Yard-Long Bean):** Although this looks like a long version of the common green bean, it is actually from the same plant family as the black-eyed pea. The flavor is similar to green beans but is milder and not as sweet. They are normally harvested when about a foot long but sometimes can grow to three feet. Usually they are cut in half or into smaller pieces and sautéed or stir-fried. If overcooked, they become mushy. Refrigerate unwashed in a plastic bag up to 5 days. Available year-round.
- **Lotus Root:** The porous vegetable is the root of the water lily. It is sweet and crunchy and can be steamed, stir-fried or battered and tempura-fried. Refrigerate unwashed and uncut up to 2 weeks; peel before using.

Baby Vegetables: A few vegetables, including broccoli, carrots, corn, eggplant, potatoes and summer squash, are available in some markets as "small," "tiny," "new" or "baby." They look like miniature versions of the larger vegetables, but the skin may be thinner and the flesh more delicate. See storage directions in Guidelines for Buying, Preparing and Cooking Fresh Vegetables chart, pages 480–488. Baby vegetables don't keep as long as mature vegetables.

Broccoli Rabe (Broccoletta, Broccoli Raab, Brocoletti di Rape, Rapini): Although this vegetable is related to the cabbage and turnip families, the look and flavor isn't similar. Long, slender, dark green stalks have small clusters of broccoli-like buds and lots of leafy greens. Entirely edible, it has a pungent, bitter flavor. Refrigerate unwashed in a plastic bag up to 5 days. Available year-round.

Cardoon: This stalk is a member of the thistle family and is popular in France and Italy. The flavor is a cross between artichoke, celery and salsify. Cut-up stalks can be cooked, pan-fried or used in soups and stews. Refrigerate unwashed in plastic bag up to 1 week.

Celeriac (Celeri-Rave, Celery Knob, Celery Root, Turnip-Rooted Celery): This large, knobby root ranges in size from that of an apple to a small cantaloupe. The stems and leaves are inedible and often removed before being shipped. Peel the heavy brown skin from the root; the interior is creamy white. The mild flavor tastes like a combination of cauliflower and celery. Cook or serve raw, grated or chopped, in salads. Refrigerate unwashed in a plastic bag up to 1 week. Available October through April.

Elephant Garlic: A large, white-skinned member of the leek family with bulbs the size of a small grapefruit and very large cloves that average 1 ounce each. It has a milder flavor than common garlic with no strong aftertaste or odor. Store in a cool, dry place. Available year-round.

Fennel (Sweet Anise): The licorice-flavored white bulb can be sliced and eaten raw or be cooked numerous ways. The delicate fronds are used like an herb to flavor soups and stews. Refrigerate unwashed in a plastic bag up to 1 week.

Jicama (Ahipa, Mexican Potato, Yam Bean): A crunchy, juicy root vegetable with a sweet, nutty flavor. Peel before using. The ivory flesh doesn't turn brown and can be served raw in salads or on a vegetable platter or cooked in stir-fries. When cooked, it stays crisp. Refrigerate unwashed up to 2 weeks. Available year-round.

Kohlrabi: A member of the turnip family, this mild-flavored bulb can be peeled and eaten raw or cooked like potatoes. The leaves can be cooked like collard greens. Refrigerate unwashed, tightly wrapped in plastic wrap, up to 4 days.

Mushrooms: Specialty mushrooms may be available fresh but are often sold in dried form. Dried mushrooms are more concentrated in flavor than fresh and can be stored in a cool, dry location for up to 1 year. Rehydrate dried mushrooms as directed on the package. After rehydrating, 1 ounce of dried mushrooms equals about 4 ounces of fresh mushrooms. There are literally thousands of varieties of mushrooms; following are some of the most popular. See storage directions in the Guidelines for Buying, Preparing and Cooking Fresh Vegetables chart, page 484.

- **Chanterelle:** A trumpet-shaped wild mushroom often sold dried. It has a delicate, nutty flavor and a chewy texture. Cook as a side dish or add to soups, sauces and stir-fries. Available in dried form year-round.
- **Crimini (Brown, Cremini):** A dark brown, slightly firmer version of the cultivated white mushroom but with a slightly stronger flavor. The full-size version is the portabella mushroom. Available year-round.
- **Enoki:** Grown in clumps from a single base, this fresh mushroom has a long, thin stem and tiny, snow-white cap. They are prized for their delicate size and fresh, grapelike flavor. Cut them away from the base and trim 1 or 2 inches from the stems before using. Eat raw or add to cooked dishes at the last minute to prevent overcooking. Usually available year-round.
- **Morel:** A ruffled, cone-shaped wild mushroom that looks like a sponge on a stalk. It may be 2 to 4 inches long and range in color from tan to dark brown. The smoky, earthy, nutty flavor can be enjoyed by simply sautéing them in butter. Fresh wild morels are usually available April through June; cultivated morels may be available at other times during the year. Dried are available year-round.
- **Oyster:** A fan-shaped mushroom that grows both wild and cultivated on rotting tree trunks. They have a robust, earthy flavor and very tender texture. Fresh and dried oyster mushrooms are normally available year-round.
- **Padi Straw (Straw):** Especially popular in Asian cooking, this mushroom is so named because it is grown on straw that has been used in a rice paddy. Most often available dried, the flavor is mild and the texture silky.
- **Porcini:** This mushroom has an earthy flavor and firm texture popular in French and Italian cooking. Fresh, they range from 1 to 10 inches in diameter. Most often available dried and found year-round.

- **Portabella (Portobello):** A dark brown, very large mushroom, often up to 6 inches in diameter, that has a dense, meaty texture. Grill for sandwiches, sauté as a side dish or slice for a salad or main dish. The crimini mushroom is a younger version of the portabella. Available year-round.
- **Shiitake (Golden Oak):** Originally from Japan and Korea, this mushroom is now grown in the U.S. The average shiitake mushroom is 3 to 6 inches in diameter and has a full-bodied, almost steaklike flavor. Discard the tough, woody stems. Do not use raw. Available fresh in the spring and fall; dried are available year-round.
- **Wood Ear:** The slightly chewy texture of this mushroom makes it an excellent substitute for meat in stir-fry dishes. It is mild in flavor and absorbs the flavor of the ingredients cooked with it. Dried are available year-round.

Onions:

- **Boiler Onion:** A small onion, 1 inch in diameter, available in white, gold, red or purple. Boilers have a mild onion flavor and are often used as a side dish or roasted with meat or poultry. They can also be added to stews. Store in a cool, dry place up to 1 month. Available year-round.
- **Cipolline:** A sweet, delicately flavored onion originally grown in Italy. It can be baked, broiled, stuffed or used in the same way as other onions. Store in a cool, dry place up to 2 weeks. Peak season is September through February.
- **Sweet Onions:** Sweet onions contain more sugar, are juicier and are more mildly flavored than other varieties. Some of the most popular varieties are Maui (Hawaiian), Oso Sweet, Rio Sweet, Vidalia® and Walla Walla. Sweet onions are good for making caramelized onions and adding to sandwiches and salads as well as using in the same way as other onions. Store in a cool, dark place, or refrigerate in plastic wrap up to 2 weeks. Seasonal by variety.

Parsley Root (Hamburg Parsley, Rooted Parsley, Turnip-Rooted Parsley): Originally popular only in Europe, it is now grown in the United States. Although the leaves can be used like regular parsley, it is grown mostly for its root. It is often used in soups and stews and tastes like a combination of carrot and celery. Refrigerate unwashed in a plastic bag up to 1 week. Available year-round.

Potatoes:
(See storage directions in the Guidelines for Buying, Preparing and Cooking Fresh Vegetables chart, pages 486–487, unless otherwise noted.)

- **Fingerling:** These slender little potatoes average about 4 inches long and have a very thin skin ranging in color from light tan to yellow or rose. Varieties include Finnish, Yellow Russian Banana, Ruby Crescent and French. All have a fine texture and mild flavor. Store in a cool (45°F to 60°F), dry, dark place with good ventilation up to 1 month.
- **Purple:** Minerals in the soil cause this potato to have its vibrant color. This small potato has a dense texture similar to russet potatoes that is good for boiling, frying, mashing or potato salad. Most of the purple color fades during cooking. Store in a cool (45°F to 60°F), dry, dark place with good ventilation up to 1 month.
- **Yellow (Yellow Finnish, Yukon Gold):** The skin and flesh of this potato ranges from buttery yellow to golden. It has a mild butterlike flavor, is good for boiling and makes excellent mashed potatoes. The yellow color fades just slightly during cooking. Store in a cool (45°F to 60°F), dry, dark place with good ventilation up to 1 month.

Salsify (Oyster Plant): A long, narrow root with the texture of a carrot and a subtle oyster flavor. The white interior can be eaten raw in salads, added to soups and meats or sautéed as a side dish. Refrigerate unwashed in a plastic bag up to 2 weeks. Available June through February.

Squash: Many varieties of winter squash are available all year, but peak season is usually late summer, fall and sometimes into the winter. See storage directions in the Guidelines for Buying, Preparing and Cooking Fresh Vegetables chart, page 488.

- **Carnival:** A small, pumpkin-shaped squash with cream, orange and green coloring. The delicate yellow flesh can be baked or steamed and tastes a bit like sweet potatoes or butternut squash.
- **Delicata (Sweet Potato Squash):** This oblong squash ranges from 5 to 9 inches long and 2 to 3 inches in diameter. It has pale yellow skin with green stripes. The seed cavity is small, so the squash yields a lot of edible flesh. It can be baked or steamed and has a sweet, buttered corn flavor.
- **Golden Nugget:** A round squash about the size of a softball with a ridged, bright orange shell. The orange flesh is moist and sweet but slightly bland. It can be baked or steamed.
- **Kabocha (Delica, Edisu, Haka):** Forest green skin with light striations; ranges from 9 to 12 inches in diameter. The moist, golden flesh is almost fiberless with a rich, sweet flavor similar to a sweet potato or pumpkin. It is usually baked or steamed.
- **Sugar Loaf (Orange Delicata):** A shorter, more squat squash than the Delicata with orange or tan skin and green stripes. Its flesh is moist and creamy and has a sweet, buttered-corn flavor.
- **Sweet Dumpling:** This small, softball-size squash has green and white stripes. It is naturally sweet and is good stuffed with rice or stuffing.

Taro Root (Dasheen): This starchy potato-like root has a nutty flavor when cooked. It ranges in length from 5 to over 12 inches. The flesh is usually creamy white or pale pink and sometimes becomes tinged with purple when cooked. It is used like a potato and can be boiled, fried or baked; the edible leaves can be steamed and served like spinach. In Hawaii, it is used to make *poi*. Store unwashed in a single layer in a cool, dry location. Available year-round.

Tomatoes, Heirloom: Although actually classified as fruit, most of us think of tomatoes as vegetables, so that is why they are listed here. Heirloom tomatoes are making a resurgence due to demand and the devotion to seed preservation. There are two major categories: *commercial,* which are open-pollinated varieties introduced before 1940; and *family,* which are seeds that have been passed down in families for many generations. Literally hundreds of heirloom varieties can be ordered through seed catalogs, and some can be purchased at farmers' markets. To find out more information, browse the Internet. Some popular varieties are listed below.

- **Amish Paste:** Similar in size and shape to a roma tomato, this tomato is meaty and juicy with full flavor. Use in pastes and sauces.
- **Arkansas Traveler:** This pink, medium-size tomato is a great all-purpose tomato.
- **Aunt Ruby's German Green:** One of the only green beefsteak-type tomatoes, this fruit weighs in at 1 pound or more. It is sweet, juicy and slightly spicy. Use in sandwiches, salads and sauces.
- **Big Rainbow:** Very large beefsteak tomato that is gold and red when mature. The sweet flavor makes it ideal for slicing and salads.
- **Brandywine:** One of the most popular heirloom varieties, this is a large, pink beefsteak tomato with rich, intense tomato flavor. Use in salads and sandwiches and for slicing.
- **Broad Ripple Yellow Currant:** Small, yellow cranberry-shaped tomato that is tasty in salads, eating out of hand and for garnishes.
- **Green Grape:** Full-flavored, 1-inch tomato that is yellowish green when mature. Use in salads, eating out of hand and for garnishes.
- **Purple Russian:** Dark red to purple flesh and skin make this plum tomato interesting. The flavor is sweet, and the texture is meaty. Use in sauces and salads and for slicing.

- **Rose de Berne:** This large pink tomato is very sweet and juicy. Use in sandwiches and for slicing.
- **White Beauty:** This slightly flattened round tomato boasts creamy white skin and flesh. It is a high-acid tomato. Use for slicing and in salads and sandwiches.
- **Yellow Pear:** Usually about 1 1/2 inches long, these colorful pear-shaped tomatoes are sweet and tasty in salads, for eating out of hand and for garnishes.

Water Chestnut (fresh): A common Asian ingredient that is now cultivated in the U.S. It's an aquatic plant that grows in shallow waters. Under the brownish black skin is white, crunchy flesh that is bland with a hint of sweetness. It can be served raw or cooked. Although available fresh, it is most often sold in cans. Refrigerate fresh water chestnuts in water up to 1 week. Available year-round.

Yuca Root (Cassava, Manioc): A tuber native to South America that is also grown in Asia and Africa. There are two types of yuca—bitter and sweet. Yuca has tough, brown skin and flesh that is hard, dense and white. The bitter variety must be cooked before eating. It is usually prepared like potatoes and has a starchy, slightly sweet flavor. Store unwashed in a cool, dry place up to 3 days. Available year-round.

TROPICAL AND SPECIALTY FRUITS GLOSSARY

Asian Pear: Over 100 varieties exist of this crunchy, sweet and very juicy fruit that has the texture of a pear and the crispness of an apple. Ranges from large and golden brown to tiny and yellow-green. Peak season is late summer through early fall. Fruit is sold ripe; store unwashed in the refrigerator up to 4 weeks.

Babáco: Resembling a star when cut crosswise, this extremely juicy five-sided fruit is related to the papaya and often called "mountain papaya." When mature, the fruit is soft with golden yellow skin with the aroma of strawberries, pineapples and papayas. Peak season is usually October through November. Store unwashed at room temperature until soft and skin turns slightly yellow.

Baby Kiwi: Bite-size berries are the size of grapes with smooth green skin and no fuzz. The flesh is sweet, soft and creamy with edible tiny black seeds. Fruit is delicate; refrigerate unwashed up to 3 days. Limited season from early to mid-autumn.

Baby Pineapple: Miniature, sweet pineapple with an edible core weighing about 1 pound. If bought refrigerated, keep refrigerated; if bought at room temperature, store at room temperature up to 1 week.

Bananas/Plantains:

- **Baby Banana (Niño):** A short, chubby banana with a rich, sweet flavor and a soft, creamy texture. Ripe baby bananas are yellow with some black spots. Store unwashed at room temperature until soft. Available year-round.
- **Burro Banana:** Squat and square in shape, this banana has a tangy lemon-banana flavor. When ripe, the peel is yellow with black spots and the flesh is creamy. Store unwashed room temperature until soft. Available year-round.
- **Manzano:** Short and chubby in shape, this banana has a mild flavor combination of apples and strawberries. When peel is fully black, manzanos are at their peak flavor. Store unwashed room temperature until soft. Available year-round.
- **Plantain:** Large and long with thick skin and pointed ends, this fruit is most often served as a vegetable because of its lower sugar content. Cooked when the skin is green, the fruit is starchy with no banana taste; cooked when the skin is yellow or brown and the fruit is ripe, it has a sweet banana taste and a slightly chewy texture. Do not refrigerate until plantains have reached desired ripeness. Available year-round.

- **Red Banana:** Heavier and chunkier than yellow bananas, the flavor is sweeter with a hint of raspberry. When ripe, the skin is purplish and the flesh is creamy with a touch of pink or orange. Store at room temperature until soft. Available year-round.

Cactus (Prickly) Pear: The pear-shaped fruit of cactus plants has medium green to dark magenta skin. The flesh ranges from pale green to ruby red with small edible seeds. Peak season is from September through April. Store unwashed at room temperature until fruit yields to slight pressure, then refrigerate up to 3 days.

Cape Gooseberry (Golden Berry): These sweet-tart berries are light green to orange-red and are enclosed in a papery husk. They have small, soft edible seeds. When ripe, they smell a bit like pineapple. Peak season is February to July. Refrigerate unwashed up to 1 month.

Champagne Grapes: These tiny, reddish purple, seedless grapes are crunchy, sweet and juicy. Select fragrant, unblemished fruit with fresh stems. Peak season is July through October. Refrigerate unwashed in a plastic bag up to 1 week.

Cherimoya (Custard Apple): Heart-shaped fruit with thin green skin that resembles a closed pine cone. Pulp is creamy white with large black almond-shaped seeds and a sweet custard taste. Select firm fruit; ripen unwashed at room temperature until fruit yields to gentle pressure, then refrigerate briefly to chill before serving. Available year-round.

Citrus:

- **Blood Orange (Moro Orange):** Deep red flesh that is sweet and juicy is characteristic of this orange. The peel is smooth or pitted with a red blush. Select fruit that is firm and has a sweet fragrance. Peak season is December through May. Refrigerate unwashed up to 8 weeks.
- **Key Lime:** The Florida Keys are the primary growing area for this yellowish lime that is smaller and rounder than a green Persian lime. The flesh is yellow, less acidic and full of seeds. Refrigerate unwashed in plastic bag up to one week. Available year-round. Look for bottled Key lime juice in the grocery store.
- **Kumquat:** Resembling a miniature orange football, this 1- to 2-inch fruit is entirely edible. The skin is sweet, and the orange pulp is tart. Select firm fruit with a fresh scent that have no soft spots. Peak season is December through May. Store unwashed at room temperature up to two days or refrigerate up to 2 weeks.
- **Lavender Gem:** Crossing a grapefruit with a Sampson tangelo produced this hybrid fruit. It resembles a miniature grapefruit with bright yellow peel. The flesh is pinkish with small seeds and has a delicate, sweet grapefruit taste. Peak season is December through February. Select fruit that is heavy for its size. Store unwashed in the refrigerator.
- **Limequat:** A cross between a kumquat and a lime, it has a sweet, edible rind and acidic lime flavor. Select firm and glossy fruit. Store unwashed fruit at room temperature up to two days or refrigerate up to 2 weeks.
- **Meyer Lemon:** Sweeter than common lemons, they're favored for their mild, juicy flesh. Some cooks use the entire lemon because the smooth, bright yellow rind doesn't have the bitter flavor of common lemons. Peak season is November through May. Refrigerate unwashed in a plastic bag up to 2 weeks.
- **Oro Blanco:** Crossing a pummelo with a grapefruit created this fruit with a thick, yellow peel. The name means "white gold" in Spanish. The flesh is sweet and juicy with a grapefruit flavor and no bitterness or acidity. Peak season is November through February. Refrigerate unwashed up to 1 month.
- **Pummelo:** The largest of all citrus, it ranges in size from a small cantaloupe to a basketball. The thick peel is green to yellow, and the sweet-tart flesh ranges from white to pink or

rose red. Fruit is sweeter, firmer and less juicy than a grapefruit. Peak season is November to March. Select fruit that yields to gentle pressure. Refrigerate unwashed up to 1 week.

- **Tangelo:** Tangelos are a cross between a grapefruit and a tangerine. Tangelos can range in size from that of a tiny orange to a small grapefruit. The skin can be rough to smooth and range in color from yellow-orange to deep orange. They are juicy, sweet-tart and contain few seeds. The most common variety is the Minneola. Peak season is November through March. Refrigerate unwashed up to 2 weeks.
- **Uniq Fruit (Ugli® Fruit):** A hybrid of a tangerine and grapefruit. The uneven, bumpy, loose green skin gives it an unattractive appearance., hence its name. The fruit is large like a grapefruit and easy to peel. The flesh is sweet and very juicy. Peak season occurs winter to spring with limited availability. Select fruit that yields to gentle pressure and has a fragrant aroma. Refrigerate unwashed up to 1 month.

Coconut: The fruit of the coconut palm has a thick, fibrous, brown, oval husk surrounding a thin, hard shell that encloses white flesh. The center is hollow and filled with coconut milk. Select coconuts that are heavy for their size and sound full of liquid. Store unwashed at room temperature up to six months. When opened, store flesh in refrigerator up to 4 days or freeze up to 6 months. Available year-round.

Coquito Nuts: Nuts are the size and shape of marbles and resemble miniature smooth, brown coconuts. They have a hollow center with white flesh that is hard, crunchy and sweet like coconut. The nuts come from a Chilean palm that takes up to 50 years to produce and remains productive for hundreds of years. Store unwashed in an airtight container in the refrigerator up to 2 weeks. Available year-round.

Donut® Peach: A peach that has rounded sides that pull into the center, creating the look of a doughnut. The sweet, juicy fruit has light yellow skin with a red blush and a white to pale orange flesh. Peak season is mid-August. Select fruit free of brown spots. Store unwashed at room temperature until soft to the touch, then refrigerate up to 3 days.

Feijoa: This small, egg-shaped fruit has a thin, slightly bumpy, lime green to olive green skin. Flesh has a granular texture with a creamy color. Taste is a unique blend of pineapple, eucalyptus and spearmint. New Zealand fruit is available from spring to early summer, and California fruit from fall to early winter. Ripen fruit at room temperature. It is ready to eat when it yields slightly to gentle pressure and has a sweet smell. Store unwashed at room temperature until soft to the touch, then refrigerate up to three days; peel bitter skin before eating.

Fig: Over 600 varieties of this teardrop-shaped fruit exist. Common varieties in the U.S. include Adriatic, Brown, Calimyrna, Kadota, Mission and Turkey. The peel can be purple, green or red, and the very sweet flesh ranges from creamy to purplish in color. Peak season is July to August. Refrigerate unwashed 2 to 3 days.

Horned Melon: The name comes from the spikes covering this yellow to orange melon. The bright lime green pulp is jellylike in texture with edible seeds that resemble those in a cucumber. The flavor is a blend of cucumber and lime. The melon is at its peak ripeness when it is golden orange. Store unwashed at room temperature up to 2 weeks. Available year-round.

Gold Kiwifruit: Egg-shaped fruit with thin, smooth, brown skin. The sweet flavor is a combination of banana, strawberry and papaya with tiny edible black seeds. Look for firm fruit. Store unwashed at room temperature up to 7 days or refrigerate up to 3 weeks.

Loquat: Originating in China, this pear-shaped fruit was introduced into the United States as a Japanese plum. It is the size of an apricot with yellowish orange skin. The creamy flesh is orange, juicy and tender with one or more inedible seeds. It has a sweet and slightly acid flavor with a hint of cherries, plums and grapes. Peak season occurs sporadically during the spring months. Ripen unwashed at room temperature until flesh yields to gentle pressure.

Lychee: Chinese evergreen trees produce this small fruit the size of a large grape that has a tough, reddish brown, bumpy peel. It has a grapelike texture with a single black seed and a flavor resembling a melon. Fruit comes from trees up to 40 feet tall that take up to 15 years to mature. Peak season is June and July. Refrigerate unwashed up to 2 weeks.

Mango: Sporting over 500 varieties, those available in the U.S. are yellowish red, oblong fruit with a leathery rind. The golden flesh is juicy and tangy-sweet with a single large seed. Mangoes are the most consumed fruit in the world and have been cultivated for over 6,000 years. Store unwashed at room temperature until flesh yields to gentle pressure, then refrigerate up to 1 week. Available year-round.

Papaya: Large, oblong, yellowish green fruit that contains black seeds that are usually thrown away. The flesh of Hawaiian fruit is bright yellow to orange, and the flesh of Mexican fruit is bright orange to salmon red. Store unwashed at room temperature until fruit yields to gentle pressure, then refrigerate up to 1 week. Available year-round.

- **Golden Sunrise Papaya:** This yellow papaya with a red blush is heavier, meatier and sweeter than the more common variety. Peak season is January through June. Ripen unwashed at room temperature until flesh gives to gentle pressure, then refrigerate.
- **Maradol Papaya:** The average weight of this long, round papaya with yellow to green peel is 3 to 5 pounds. The sweet and juicy flesh is salmon red and contains black seeds that need to be removed before eating. Select fruit that is soft to the touch. Refrigerate unwashed up to 3 days. Available year-round.

Passion Fruit: Egg-shaped fruit of the passionflower family with purplish, leathery skin. The flesh is golden and jellylike with a tart lemony flavor and small, black, edible seeds. New Zealand fruit is available March through June, and California fruit from July through May. Ripen unwashed at room temperature until the skin is almost black and very wrinkled, then refrigerate up to 1 week.

Pepino Melon (Mellowfruit, Tree Melon, Sweet Cucumber): Teardrop-shaped melon has smooth, green skin and flesh that is golden yellow and fragrant. The flavor is a slightly sweet combination of cantaloupe and cucumber. Available from late fall to mid-spring. As the fruit ripens, the skin will turn yellow and develop purple stripes. Ripen unwashed at room temperature until soft to the touch, then refrigerate up to 3 days.

Persimmon:

- **Fuyu:** Persimmon shaped like a flattened ball that has skin ranging in color from pale orange to brilliant red-orange. The flesh is coreless with few seeds and has a sweet flavor. Peak season is September through mid-December. Store in a cool place. Fruit can be eaten when firm or soft. The Sharon variety is almost identical to the Fuyu but is nearly seedless. Store unwashed in a cool, dry location up to 1 month.
- **Hachiya:** Somewhat heart-shaped, this persimmon has smooth, brilliant reddish orange skin and flesh. The taste is extremely astringent when immature, and sweet and spicy when ripe. Peak season is September through mid-December. Ripen unwashed at room temperature, and eat fruit when very soft.

Pomegranate: Leathery red rind covers this round fruit that is filled with tiny seeds encased in red juicy pulp. The seeds have a sweet and tangy taste and are sectioned between shiny, tough, white membranes. Although available September through December, peak season is October. Refrigerate unwashed up to 2 months.

Quince: One of the earliest known fruits; is apple shaped and ranges from apple to grapefruit size. The golden skin usually has a woolly surface, and the white flesh is firm and somewhat dry with an acidic pineapple taste. In ancient times, this fruit was called "golden apple" and was considered an emblem of love and happiness. Peak season is September through December. Select large, smooth fruit. Refrigerate unwashed up to 1 month.

Rambutan: Growing in clusters on ornamental-type trees, this fruit has soft hairy spines protruding from reddish brown, leathery skin. Its name comes from the Malay word *rambut,* meaning "hair." When peeled, pale flesh with a single seed is revealed. The fruit is sweet with a texture similar to grapes. A small crop is available in June and July and a large crop November through January. Refrigerate unwashed up to 2 weeks.

Sapote: Coreless, juicy fruit the size and shape of an apple has delicate, thin green skin that bruises easily. The flesh is yellowish, and the mild flavor is a combination of peaches, lemons and mangoes. Peak season is August through November. Select fruit that is hard, and ripen unwashed at room temperature about 3 days. Refrigerate ripe fruit.

Starfruit (Carambola): When sliced crosswise, this fruit resembles a star. The skin and flesh are yellow, and the taste is sweet with a lemon tartness. Store unwashed at room temperature until a few brown spots appear on the ridges, then refrigerate in covered container. Available year-round.

Tamarillo: This egg-shaped fruit with a stem is related to the tomato and potato. Available in gold and red varieties, they have smooth, glossy skin and are similar to an apricot in texture with tiny edible seeds. They have a slightly bitter tomato taste. Peak season is May through August. Ripen unwashed at room temperature until flesh yields to slight pressure and becomes fragrant. Refrigerate up to 1 week.

Tamarind (Tamarindos): Also known as an Indian date, these brownish, barklike pods, about 5 inches long, are filled with a tart apricot-lemon-flavored pulp that is very sticky. The pulp is sour-sweet and becomes very sour when dried. East Indian and Middle Eastern cuisines use tamarind in many dishes similar to how lemon juice is used in the U.S. Store unwashed pods in refrigerator up to 1 month, or remove pulp and freeze. Available year-round.

GUIDELINES FOR BUYING, PREPARING AND COOKING FRESH VEGETABLES

Use the following chart for buying, preparing and cooking vegetables. Several cooking options are available for each vegetable.

Conventional Directions

To Bake: Heat the oven. Place vegetables in baking pan (place vegetables in skin, like baking potatoes, directly on oven rack). Bake for amount of time in chart.

To Boil: In saucepan, heat 1 inch water (salted, if desired) to boiling, unless stated otherwise. Add vegetables. Heat to boiling; reduce heat to low. Simmer (boil gently) for amount of time in chart; drain.

To Steam: In saucepan or skillet, place steamer basket in 1/2 inch water (water should not touch bottom of basket). Place vegetables in steamer basket. Cover tightly and heat to boiling; reduce heat to low. Steam for amount of time in chart.

Microwave Directions

Microwave on High, unless stated otherwise, for amount of cooking time in chart; drain. To vent plastic wrap, fold back one edge or corner of plastic 1/4 inch to release steam. Many vegetables call for a stand time after cooking, which completes the cooking and equalizes the temperature throughout the food.

Vegetable with Selection, Storage and Amounts for 4 Servings	Preparation	Conventional Directions (above)	Microwave Directions (above)
ARTICHOKES, GLOBE (4 medium; 1 lb) Choose plump firm globes that are heavy for their size, with soft green color. Refrigerate in plastic bag up to 1 week.	Remove discolored leaves; trim stem even with base. Cut 1 inch off top and discard. Snip tips off remaining leaves with scissors. Rinse with cold water. To prevent discoloration, dip into cold water mixed with small amount of lemon juice (1 tablespoon lemon juice per 1 quart water). To fill and bake, remove center leaves and the choke before cooking. (*Choke* is the fuzzy growth covering artichoke heart.)	**Boil:** Use 6 quarts water and 2 tablespoons lemon juice. Boil uncovered 20 to 30 minutes, rotating occasionally, until leaves pull out easily and bottom is tender when pierced with knife. **Steam:** Covered 20 to 25 minutes or until bottoms are tender when pierced with knife.	*1 medium:* Place in 4-cup glass measuring cup; add 1/4 cup water. Cover with vented plastic wrap. Microwave 5 to 7 minutes or until leaves pull out easily. *2 medium:* Place in 8 × 4-inch loaf pan; add 1/4 cup water. Cover with vented plastic wrap. Microwave 9 to 11 minutes or until leaves pull out easily.
ARTICHOKES, JERUSALEM (Sunchokes) (4 medium; 1 lb) Choose artichokes that are hard with fairly smooth skins and no soft spots. Refrigerate unwashed in plastic bag up to 1 week.	Scrub artichokes; peel thinly if desired. Leave whole, or cut into 1/4-inch slices or 1/2-inch cubes. To prevent discoloration, toss with cold water mixed with small amount of lemon juice (1 tablespoon lemon juice per 1 quart water).	**Boil:** Whole—covered 20 to 25 minutes. Slices or cubes—covered 7 to 9 minutes or until crisp-tender. **Steam:** Covered 15 to 20 minutes or until crisp-tender. **Note:** Can also be fried; see Fried Potatoes (page 462) for directions.	*Slices or cubes*—Place in 1-quart casserole; add 2 tablespoons water. Cover. Microwave 5 to 7 minutes, stirring once, until crisp-tender. Let stand covered 2 minutes.

(continues)

GUIDELINES FOR BUYING, PREPARING AND COOKING FRESH VEGETABLES *(continued)*

Vegetable with Selection, Storage and Amounts for 4 Servings	Preparation	Conventional Directions (page 480)	Microwave Directions (page 480)
ASPARAGUS (1 1/2 lb) Choose firm, round stalks with closed, compact tips. Wrap ends in damp paper towel. Refrigerate unwashed in plastic bag up to 4 days.	Break off tough ends as far down as stalks snap easily. Wash asparagus; remove scales if sandy or tough. For spears, tie whole stalks in bundles with string, or hold together with band of foil. Or cut stalks into 1-inch pieces.	**Boil:** Spears—Place stalks upright in deep, narrow pan. Boil uncovered 6 to 8 minutes or until crisp-tender. *Pieces*—Boil uncovered 4 to 6 minutes or until crisp-tender. **Steam:** Covered 6 to 8 minutes or until crisp-tender.	Place spears in 8 × 4-inch loaf pan or pieces in 1-quart casserole; add 2 tablespoons water. Cover with vented plastic wrap. Microwave 4 to 6 minutes or until crisp-tender. Let stand 2 covered minutes.
BEANS, GREEN, PURPLE WAX AND YELLOW WAX (1 lb) Choose bright, smooth, crisp pods. Purple wax beans will turn dark green when cooked. Refrigerate unwashed in plastic bag up to 4 days.	Wash beans; remove ends. Leave beans whole, or cut into 1-inch pieces.	**Boil:** Uncovered 6 to 8 minutes or until crisp-tender. **Steam:** Covered 10 to 12 minutes or until crisp-tender.	Place pieces in 1-quart casserole; add 1 cup water. Cover. Microwave 10 to 12 minutes or until crisp-tender. Let stand covered 5 minutes; drain.
BEANS, LIMA (3 lb unshelled; 3 cups shelled) Choose broad, thick, shiny pods that are plump with large seeds. Refrigerate unwashed in plastic bag up to 4 days.	Wash beans. Shell just before cooking. To shell beans, remove thin outer edge of pod with sharp knife or scissors. Slip out beans.	**Boil:** Uncovered 5 minutes. Cover and boil 15 to 20 minutes longer or until tender.	Place in 1-quart casserole; add 1 cup water. Cover. Microwave on High 4 to 5 minutes or until boiling. Microwave on Medium-Low (30%) 20 to 25 minutes or until tender. Let stand covered 5 minutes; drain.
BEETS (5 medium; 1 1/4 lb) Choose firm, round, smooth, purple-red beets with fresh, unwilted tops. Golden-colored beets are also available. Refrigerate unwashed in plastic bag up to 1 week.	Cut off all but 1 inch of beet tops. Wash beets; leave whole with root ends attached.	**Boil:** Use 6 cups water, 1 tablespoon white vinegar (to keep color) and salt if desired. Boil covered 40 to 50 minutes or until tender. **Steam:** Covered 45 to 50 minutes or until tender. Add boiling water during steaming if necessary.	Place in 1 1/2-quart casserole; add 2 cups water. Cover. Microwave 18 to 20 minutes, rearranging once, until tender. Let stand covered 5 minutes; drain.

(continues)

GUIDELINES FOR BUYING, PREPARING AND COOKING FRESH VEGETABLES *(continued)*

Vegetable with Selection, Storage and Amounts for 4 Servings	Preparation	Conventional Directions (page 480)	Microwave Directions (page 480)
BROCCOLI (1 1/2 lb) Choose firm, compact, dark green clusters; avoid thick, tough stems. Refrigerate unwashed in plastic bag up to 5 days.	Trim off large leaves; remove tough ends of lower stems. Wash broccoli; peel if desired. For spears, cut lengthwise into 1/2-inch-wide stalks. For pieces, cut lengthwise into 1/2-inch-wide stalks, then cut stalks crosswise into 1-inch pieces. If desired, cut flowerets into bite-size pieces.	**Boil:** *Spears*—uncovered 5 to 7 minutes or until stems are crisp-tender. *Flowerets*—uncovered 3 to 5 minutes or until crisp-tender. **Steam:** Covered 10 to 11 minutes or until stems are crisp-tender.	*Spears*—Place with just the water that clings to spears in 8-inch square dish in spoke pattern with flowerets in the center. Cover with vented plastic wrap. Microwave 6 to 8 minutes or until stems are crisp-tender. Let stand 2 minutes *Pieces*—Place with just the water that clings to pieces in 2-quart casserole. Cover. Microwave 5 to 7 minutes or until crisp-tender. Let stand covered 2 minutes.
BRUSSELS SPROUTS (1 lb) Choose firm, unblemished, bright green sprouts with compact leaves. Refrigerate unwashed in plastic bag up to 3 days.	Remove any discolored leaves; cut off stem ends. Wash sprouts; cut large sprouts in half.	**Boil:** Uncovered 8 to 12 minutes or until tender. **Steam:** Covered 8 to 12 minutes or until tender.	Place in 1-quart casserole; add 2 tablespoons water. Cover. Microwave 5 to 6 minutes or until tender. Let stand covered 2 minutes; drain.
CARROTS (1 lb; 6 to 7 medium) Choose firm, nicely shaped carrots with good color. Refrigerate unwashed in plastic bag up to 2 weeks.	Peel carrots thinly; cut off ends. Leave baby-cut carrots whole or cut carrots lengthwise into julienne strips. Or cut carrots crosswise into 1/4-inch slices or shred.	**Boil:** *Baby-cut whole*—covered 7 to 10 minutes. *Julienne strips*—covered 6 to 10 minutes. *Slices*—covered 6 to 10 minutes. *Shredded*—covered 5 minutes or until tender. **Steam:** *Baby-cut whole*—covered 8 to 10 minutes. *Slices*—covered 6 to 9 minutes or until tender.	*Baby-cut whole or julienne strips*—Place in 1-quart casserole; add 2 tablespoons water. Cover. Microwave 5 to 7 minutes, stirring once, until crisp-tender. (Baby-cut carrots may take 2 to 3 minutes longer to cook.) Let stand covered 5 minutes; drain.
CAULIFLOWER (2 lb; 1 medium head) Choose creamy white, compact heads with bright green, fresh, firmly attached leaves. Refrigerate unwashed in plastic bag up to 1 week.	Remove outer leaves and stalk; cut off any discoloration. Wash cauliflower. Leave whole, cutting cone-shaped center to remove core, or separate into flowerets.	**Boil:** *Whole*—uncovered 10 to 12 minutes. *Flowerets*—uncovered 5 to 7 minutes or until tender. **Steam:** *Whole*—covered 18 to 22 minutes. *Flowerets*—covered 6 to 8 minutes or until tender.	Place flowerets in 2-quart casserole; add 2 tablespoons water. Cover. Microwave 8 to 10 minutes or until tender. Let stand covered 2 minutes; drain.

(continues)

GUIDELINES FOR BUYING, PREPARING AND COOKING FRESH VEGETABLES *(continued)*

Vegetable with Selection, Storage and Amounts for 4 Servings	Preparation	Conventional Directions (page 480)	Microwave Directions (page 480)
CORN (4 ears) Choose bright green, tight-fitting husks, fresh-looking silk, with plump consistently sized kernels. Wrap unhusked ears in damp paper towels and refrigerate up to 2 days.	Corn is sweetest and most tender when eaten as soon after picking as possible. Husk ears and remove silk just before cooking.	**Boil:** Heat 1 gallon unsalted water and 1 tablespoon sugar to boiling. Add corn; return to boiling. Boil uncovered 5 to 7 minutes. **Steam:** Covered 5 to 7 minutes or until tender.	Wrap ears in microwavable plastic wrap, or place in 8-inch square dish and add 1 tablespoon water. Cover with vented plastic wrap. Microwave for times below, turning once: *1 ear:* 2 to 3 minutes *2 ears:* 3 to 4 minutes *4 ears:* 6 to 8 minutes Let stand covered 2 minutes.
EGGPLANT (1½ lb; 1 medium) Choose firm, even-colored eggplants that are heavy for their size and free of blemishes. Caps and stems should be intact with no mold. Refrigerate unwashed in plastic bag up to 5 days.	Just before cooking, wash eggplant; peel if desired. Cut into ½-inch cubes or ¼-inch slices.	**Boil:** Covered 5 to 8 minutes or until tender. **Sauté:** In 10-inch skillet, melt 3 to 4 tablespoons butter or margarine over medium-high heat. Cook eggplant in butter uncovered 5 to 10 minutes, stirring frequently, until tender. **Steam:** Covered 5 to 7 minutes or until tender.	*Cubes*—Place in 1½-quart casserole; add 2 tablespoons water. Cover. Microwave 7 to 9 minutes, stirring twice, until tender. Let stand covered 5 minutes. *Slices*—Arrange slices, overlapping, in a circle around edge of 9-inch pie plate; add 2 tablespoons water. Cover with vented plastic wrap. Microwave 5 to 7 minutes or until tender. Let stand covered 5 minutes.
FENNEL (1 lb; 3 to 4 medium) Choose fairly large, squat bulbs with a pearl-like sheen without cracks, dried or brown spots. Tops should be fresh and feathery. Refrigerate unwashed in plastic bag up to 1 week.	Remove feathery tops (chop to use as a seasoning; it has a mild licorice flavor) and tough or discolored outer ribs; trim base. Cut bulbs lengthwise into fourths	**Boil:** Covered 8 to 11 minutes or until tender. **Steam:** Covered 12 to 15 minutes or until tender.	Place in 1-quart casserole; add 2 tablespoons water. Cover. Microwave 4½ to 5½ minutes or until crisp-tender. Let stand covered 2 minutes.
GREENS: BEET, CHICORY, COLLARDS, ESCAROLE, KALE, MUSTARD, SPINACH, SWISS CHARD, TURNIP (1 lb) Choose tender, young, unblemished leaves with bright green color. Refrigerate unwashed. Wrap in paper towel and place in plastic bag up to 4 days (greens toughen as they age).	Remove root ends and imperfect leaves. Wash several times in water, lifting out each time; drain.	**Cook:** For greens except spinach, cover and cook with just the water that clings to leaves over medium-high heat 8 to 10 minutes or until tender. For spinach, cover and cook with just the water that clings to the leaves over medium-high heat 3 to 5 minutes or until tender.	For beet tops, chicory or escarole, place in 2-quart casserole; add 2 tablespoons water. Cover. Microwave 8 to 10 minutes, stirring once, until tender. For collards, kale, mustard, spinach, Swiss chard or turnip, place in 2-quart casserole; add 2 tablespoons water. Cover. Microwave 4 to 6 minutes, stirring once, until tender. *(continues)*

GUIDELINES FOR BUYING, PREPARING AND COOKING FRESH VEGETABLES *(continued)*

Vegetable with Selection, Storage and Amounts for 4 Servings	Preparation	Conventional Directions (page 480)	Microwave Directions (page 480)
KOHLRABI (1 lb; 4 medium) Choose firm, purple-tinged white bulbs with no soft spots, cracks or yellowing leaf tips. Those less than 3 inches in diameter are most tender. Refrigerate unwashed in plastic bag up to 1 week.	Cut off root ends and tops. Wash; peel thinly. Cut into 1/2-inch pieces or cubes.	**Boil:** Covered 15 to 20 minutes or until tender **Steam:** Covered 8 to 12 minutes or until tender.	Place in 1-quart casserole; add 2 tablespoons water. Cover. Microwave 3 1/2 to 5 minutes, stirring once, until tender. Let stand covered 2 minutes.
LEEKS (2 lb; 6 medium) Choose white bulbs with pliable, crisp, green tops. Bulbs less than 1 1/2 inches in diameter are most tender. Refrigerate unwashed in plastic bag up to 1 week.	Remove green tops to within 2 inches of white part (reserve greens for soup or stew). Peel outside layer of bulbs. Wash leeks several times in cold water; drain. Cut large leeks lengthwise into fourths.	**Boil:** Covered 10 to 12 minutes or until tender. **Steam:** Covered 10 to 12 minutes or until tender.	Place in 1-quart casserole; add 2 tablespoons water. Cover. Microwave 4 to 5 minutes, stirring once, until tender. Let stand covered 2 minutes.
MUSHROOMS (1 lb) Choose creamy white to light brown caps, closed around the stems; if slightly open, gills should be light pink or tan. Refrigerate unwashed. Wrap in paper towel and place in plastic or paper bag up to 4 days.	Wipe clean with damp paper towel or rinse if necessary. Trim off stem ends; do not peel. Leave whole, or cut into 1/4-inch slices.	**Sauté:** Whole or slices—In 12-inch skillet, melt 1/4 cup butter or margarine over medium-high heat. Cook mushrooms in butter uncovered 4 to 6 minutes, stirring frequently, until tender. Also see Sautéed Mushrooms, page 459. **Steam:** Covered 4 to 5 minutes or until tender.	*Whole or slices*—Place in 1-quart casserole; add 1 tablespoon butter, margarine or vegetable oil. Cover with microwavable paper towel. Microwave 3 to 4 minutes or until tender.
OKRA (1 lb) Choose tender, unblemished, bright green pods, less than 4 inches long. Refrigerate unwashed in plastic bag up to 3 days.	Wash okra; remove ends. Leave whole, or cut into 1/2-inch slices.	**Boil:** Uncovered about 10 minutes or until tender. **Steam:** Covered 6 to 8 minutes or until tender.	*Whole*—Place in 1-quart casserole; add 1/4 cup water. Cover. Microwave 5 to 6 minutes, stirring once, until tender. Let stand covered 2 minutes.

(continues)

GUIDELINES FOR BUYING, PREPARING AND COOKING FRESH VEGETABLES *(continued)*

Vegetable with Selection, Storage and Amounts for 4 Servings	Preparation	Conventional Directions (page 480)	Microwave Directions (page 480)
ONIONS, WHITE, YELLOW OR RED (1 1/2 lb; 8 to 10 small) Choose firm, well-shaped onions with unblemished, papery skins and no sign of mold or sprouting. Store whole onions in mesh bag or basket in a cool (45°F–60°F), dry, dark place with good ventilation up to 2 months. Refrigerate peeled, cut onions in plastic wrap up to 4 days.	Peel onions in cold water to prevent eyes from watering. See cooking directions for piece size.	**Bake:** Place large onions in ungreased baking dish. Pour water into dish until 1/4 inch deep. Cover and bake in 350°F oven 40 to 50 minutes or until tender. **Boil:** *Small*—covered 15 to 20 minutes. *Large*—covered 30 to 35 minutes or until tender. **Sauté:** Cut onions into 1/4-inch slices. In 10-inch skillet, melt 3 to 4 tablespoons butter or margarine or heat olive or vegetable oil over medium-high heat. Cook onions in butter uncovered 6 to 9 minutes, stirring frequently, until tender. **Steam:** *Small*—covered 15 to 20 minutes. *Large*—covered 30 to 35 minutes or until tender.	*Whole*—Place in 1 1/2-quart casserole; add 1/4 cup water. Cover. Microwave 7 to 9 minutes or until tender. Let stand covered 2 minutes.
PARSNIPS (1 1/2 lb; 6 to 8 medium) Choose firm, nicely shaped, unblemished parsnips that are not too wide and have smooth white skins. Avoid those with cracks. Refrigerate unwashed in plastic bag up to 10 days.	Scrape or peel. Leave whole, or cut into halves or fourths or 1/4-inch slices or strips.	**Boil:** *Whole or halves*—covered 10 to 15 minutes. *Slices or strips*—covered 7 to 9 minutes or until tender. **Steam:** *Whole or halves*—covered 15 to 20 minutes. *Slices or strips*—covered 8 to10 minutes or until tender.	*Slices or strips*—Place in 1-quart casserole; add 2 tablespoons water. Cover. Microwave 5 to 6 minutes, stirring once, until tender. Let stand covered 2 minutes.
PEA PODS, SNOW (CHINESE) (1 lb) Choose flat, crisp and evenly green pods with a velvety feel. Refrigerate unwashed in plastic bag up to 3 days.	Wash pods; remove tips and strings.	**Boil:** Uncovered 2 to 3 minutes, stirring occasionally, until crisp-tender. **Steam:** Covered 3 to 5 minutes or until crisp-tender.	Place in 1-quart casserole with just the water that clings to the pea pods. Cover. Microwave 6 to 7 minutes, stirring once, until crisp-tender. Let stand covered 2 minutes.
PEAS, GREEN (2 lb) Choose plump, tender, bright green pods. Refrigerate unwashed in plastic bag up to 3 days.	Wash and shell peas just before cooking.	**Boil:** Uncovered 5 to 10 minutes or until tender. **Steam:** Covered 8 to 10 minutes or until tender.	Place peas with just the water that clings to them in 1-quart casserole. Cover. Microwave 4 to 6 minutes, stirring once, until tender. Let stand covered 2 minutes.

(continues)

GUIDELINES FOR BUYING, PREPARING AND COOKING FRESH VEGETABLES *(continued)*

Vegetable with Selection, Storage and Amounts for 4 Servings	Preparation	Conventional Directions (page 480)	Microwave Directions (page 480)
PEAS, SUGAR SNAP (1 lb) Choose bright-green, plump, well-filled pods. Refrigerate unwashed in plastic bag up to 3 days.	Snip off stem ends and remove strings if present.	**Boil:** Uncovered 4 to 5 minutes, stirring occasionally, until crisp-tender. **Steam:** Covered 6 to 7 minutes or until crisp-tender.	Place in 1-quart casserole with just the water that clings to the pea pods. Cover. Microwave 6 to 7 minutes, stirring once, until crisp-tender.
PEPPERS, BELL (2 medium; 1/2 lb) Choose well-shaped, shiny, bright-colored, unblemished peppers with firm sides. Refrigerate unwashed in plastic bag up to 5 days.	Wash peppers; remove stems, seeds and membranes. Leave whole to stuff and bake, or cut into thin slices or rings.	**Sauté:** *Slices or rings*—In 10-inch skillet, melt 1 to 2 tablespoons butter or margarine over medium-high heat. Cook peppers in butter uncovered 3 to 5 minutes, stirring frequently, until crisp-tender. **Steam:** *Slices or rings*—covered 4 to 6 minutes or until crisp-tender.	Place peppers with just the water that clings to them in 1-quart casserole. Cover. Microwave 3 to 4 minutes, stirring once, until crisp-tender. Let stand covered 2 minutes.
POTATOES, SMALL NEW (RED OR WHITE) (1 1/2 lb; 10 to 12) Choose nicely shaped, smooth, firm potatoes with unblemished skins (some are very delicate). Choose potatoes of similar size, about 1 1/2 inches in diameter. Store in a cool (45°F–60°F), dry, dark place with good ventilation up to 2 weeks. A bitter-tasting green tinge forms on potatoes when exposed to bright light; cut or scrape off before cooking. Refrigerating potatoes causes them to taste sweet and turn dark when cooked.	Scrub potatoes.	**Boil:** Place potatoes in 2-quart saucepan. Add water just to cover. Heat to boiling; reduce heat to low. Simmer covered 15 to 20 minutes or until tender. **Steam:** Covered 18 to 22 minutes or until tender.	Place in 1 1/2-quart casserole; add 1/4 cup water. Cover. Microwave 9 to 11 minutes, stirring once, until tender. Let stand covered 5 minutes.
POTATOES, SWEET (4 medium; 1 1/2 lb) Choose nicely shaped, smooth, firm potatoes with even-colored skins. (See varieties of potatoes, page 493.) Choose potatoes of similar size. Store in a cool (45°F–60°F), dry, dark place with good ventilation up to 2 months.	Scrub potatoes, but do not peel. *To bake*—Pierce potatoes to allow steam to escape. *To boil or steam*—Leave whole, or cut into large pieces.	**Bake:** Uncovered in 375°F oven about 45 minutes, in 350°F oven about 1 hour, in 325°F oven about 1 1/4 hours or until tender. **Boil:** Place potatoes in 2-quart saucepan. Add water just to cover. Heat to boiling; reduce heat to low. Simmer covered: *Whole*—20 to 25 minutes or until tender. *Pieces*—10 to 15 minutes or until tender. **Steam:** Whole—covered 15 to 20 minutes or until tender.	*Whole:* Pierce potatoes to allow steam to escape. Arrange on microwavable paper towel in spoke pattern with narrow ends in center. Microwave 9 to 11 minutes, turning once, until tender. Cover and let stand covered 5 minutes.

(continues)

GUIDELINES FOR BUYING, PREPARING AND COOKING FRESH VEGETABLES *(continued)*

Vegetable with Selection, Storage and Amounts for 4 Servings	Preparation	Conventional Directions (page 480)	Microwave Directions (page 480)
POTATOES, WHITE AND RED (6 medium; 2 lb) Choose nicely shaped, smooth, firm potatoes with unblemished skins, free from discoloration. Store in a cool (45°F–60°F), dry, dark place with good ventilation up to 2 weeks. A bitter-tasting green tinge forms on potatoes when exposed to bright light; cut or scrape off before cooking. Refrigerating potatoes causes them to taste sweet and turn dark when cooked.	*To bake*—Choose potatoes of similar size. Scrub potatoes, but do not peel; if desired, rub with oil for softer skins. Pierce potatoes to allow steam to escape. *To boil or steam*—Scrub potatoes. Leave skins on whenever possible, or peel thinly and remove eyes. Leave whole, or cut into large pieces.	**Bake:** Uncovered in 375°F oven 1 to 1 1/4 hours, in 350°F oven 1 1/4 to 1 1/2 hours, in 325°F oven about 1 1/2 hours or until tender. **Boil:** Place potatoes in 2-quart saucepan. Add water just to cover. Heat to boiling; reduce heat to low. Simmer covered: *Whole or pieces*—20 to 30 minutes or until tender. **Steam:** Covered 30 to 35 minutes or until tender.	*Whole*—Pierce potatoes to allow steam to escape. Place on microwavable paper towels. *1 potato:* Microwave 4 to 5 minutes, turning once, until tender. Cover; let stand covered 5 minutes. *2 potatoes:* Microwave 6 to 8 minutes, turning once, until tender. Cover; let stand covered 5 minutes. *3 potatoes:* Arrange in spoke pattern with narrow ends in center. Microwave 8 to 10 minutes, turning once, until tender. Cover; let stand covered 5 minutes. *4 potatoes:* Arrange in spoke pattern with narrow ends in center. Microwave 12 to 14 minutes, turning once, until tender. Cover; let stand covered 5 minutes.
RUTABAGAS (1 1/2 lb; 2 medium) Choose rutabagas that are clean, heavy for their size, well shaped (round or elongated) and fairly smooth. Store in a cool (45°F–60°F), dry, dark place with good ventilation up to 2 months or unwrapped at room temperature or in the refrigerator up to 1 week.	Wash rutabagas; peel thinly. Cut into 1/2-inch cubes or 2-inch pieces.	**Boil:** Covered 20 to 25 minutes or until tender. **Steam:** Covered 20 to 25 minutes or until tender.	Place in 2-quart casserole; add 1/4 cup water. Cover. Microwave 13 to 15 minutes, stirring twice, until tender. Let stand covered 5 minutes.

(continues)

GUIDELINES FOR BUYING, PREPARING AND COOKING FRESH VEGETABLES *(continued)*

Vegetable with Selection, Storage and Amounts for 4 Servings	Preparation	Conventional Directions (page 480)	Microwave Directions (page 480)
SQUASH, SUMMER (CHAYOTE, CROOKNECK, GREEN ZUCCHINI, PATTYPAN, STRAIGHTNECK, YELLOW ZUCCHINI) (1 1/2 lb) Choose firm squash with shiny, tender rinds. Refrigerate unwashed in plastic bag up to 5 days.	Wash squash; remove stem and blossom ends, but do not peel. Cut small squash in half. Cut large squash into 1/2-inch slices or cubes.	**Boil:** *Slices*—uncovered 5 to 10 minutes. *Cubes*—uncovered 3 to 6 minutes or until tender. **Steam:** Covered 5 to 7 minutes or until tender.	Place in 1 1/2-quart casserole; add 1 tablespoon water. Cover. Microwave 4 to 6 minutes, stirring once, until almost tender. Let stand covered 2 minutes.
SQUASH, WINTER (ACORN, BUTTERCUP, BUTTERNUT, SPAGHETTI) AND PUMPKIN (2 lb) Choose squash that are heavy for their size with a dull-colored hard rind with no soft spots. Store whole squash in a cool (45°F–60°F), dry, dark place with good ventilation up to 2 months. Refrigerate peeled, cut squash in plastic wrap up to 5 days.	Wash squash. To bake, carefully cut each squash lengthwise in half; remove seeds and fibers. To boil, carefully peel squash if desired. Cut into 1-inch slices or cubes.	**Bake:** Place squash halves, cut sides up, in ungreased 13 × 9-inch baking dish. Sprinkle cut sides with salt and pepper. Dot with butter or margarine. Pour water into dish until 1/4 inch deep. Cover and bake in 400°F oven 30 to 40 minutes, in 350°F oven about 40 minutes, in 325°F oven about 45 minutes or until tender. **Boil:** *Slices or cubes*—covered 10 to 15 minutes or until tender. **Steam:** *Slices*—covered 12 to 15 minutes. *Cubes*—covered 7 to 10 minutes or until tender.	*For whole squash except spaghetti*—Pierce with knife in several places to allow steam to escape. Place on microwavable paper towel. Microwave uncovered 5 minutes or until squash feels warm to the touch. Cut in half; remove seeds. Arrange halves, cut sides down, in shallow dish. Microwave 5 to 8 minutes or until tender. Let stand covered 5 minutes. *For whole spaghetti*—Pierce with knife in several places to allow steam to escape. Place on microwavable paper towel. Microwave uncovered 18 to 23 minutes, turning once, until tender. Let stand covered 10 minutes. Cut in half; remove seeds and fibers.
TURNIPS (1 lb; 4 medium) Choose turnips that are smooth, round and firm, with fresh tops. Refrigerate unwashed in plastic bag up to 1 week.	Cut off tops. Wash turnips; peel thinly. Leave whole, or cut into 1/2-inch pieces.	**Boil:** *Whole*—covered 25 to 30 minutes. *Pieces*—covered 15 to 20 minutes or until tender. **Steam:** *Pieces*—covered 15 to 20 minutes or until tender.	*Pieces*—Place in 1-quart casserole; add 2 tablespoons water. Cover. Microwave 6 to 8 minutes, stirring once, until tender. Let stand covered 2 minutes.

TROPICAL AND SPECIALTY FRUITS

NEW AND SPECIALTY VEGETABLES

Eggplant (Chinese)

Daikon

Eggplant (Japanese)

LoBok (Chinese radish)

Gai Lan (Chinese kale/ Chinese broccoli)

Lemongrass

Lotus Root

Longbean

Kohlrabi

Celeriac

Salsify (oyster plant)

Fennel (bulbs and fronds)

Yuca Root

Parsley Root

Taro root

TOMATOES

MUSHROOMS

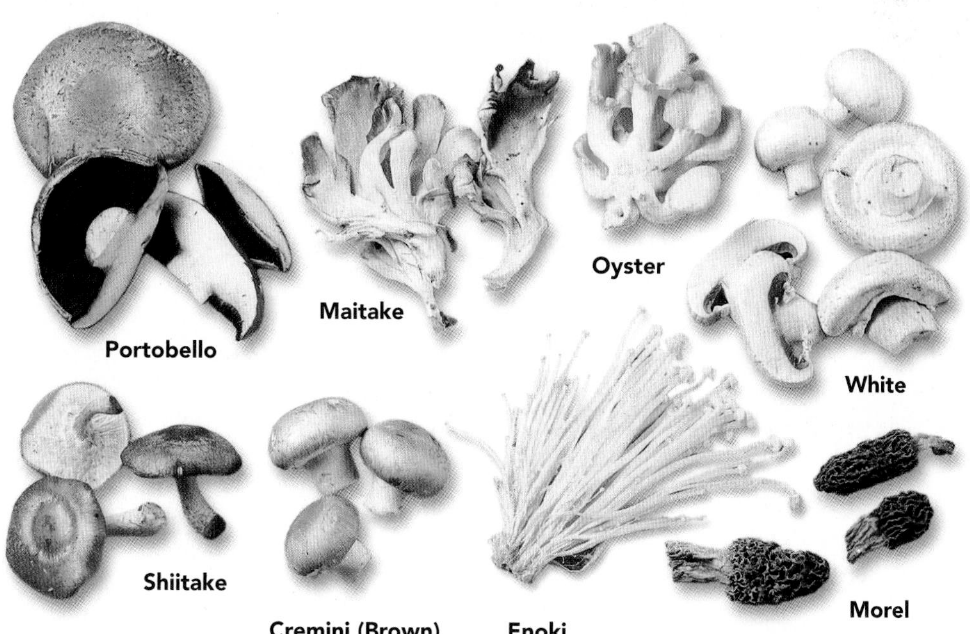

ONIONS

Yellow
Green
Boiler
Red
Cipolline
Shallots
Pearl
Vidalia
Maui
Walla Walla

POTATOES

Fingerling
Purple
Yellow/
Yukon Gold
Sweet
Yam
Round White
Round Red
Russet/Idaho
New Red

SQUASH

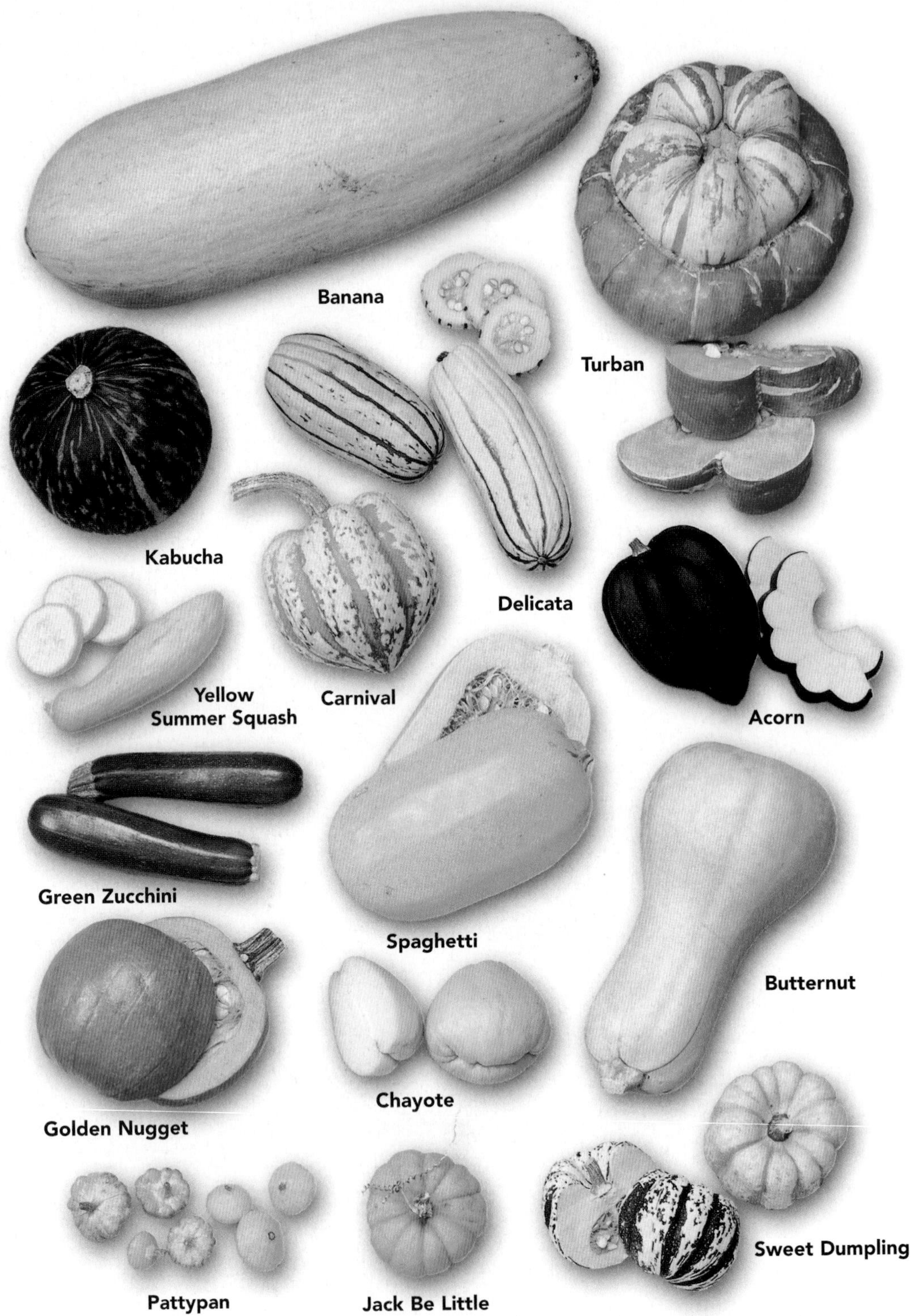
Banana
Turban
Kabucha
Delicata
Yellow Summer Squash
Carnival
Acorn
Green Zucchini
Spaghetti
Butternut
Chayote
Golden Nugget
Sweet Dumpling
Pattypan
Jack Be Little

CHAPTER 18
Vegetarian

Chart

LOW-FAT = *3g or less, except main dishes with 10g or less* FAST = *Ready in 20 minutes or less* BREAD MACHINE = *Bread machine directions* SLOW COOKER = *Slow cooker directions* LIGHTER = *25% fewer calories or grams of fat*

◀ **Hearty Soybean and Cheddar Pasta Salad (page 507)**

Vegetarian Basics

Vegetarianism—and eating more meatless meals—is here to stay. It's no longer a trend; for many people it's a way of life. By definition, vegetarians don't include beef, pork, chicken, fish or seafood in their diets. Can't imagine not eating animal-based proteins? There are actually many delicious alternatives to choose from, including legumes, grains, pasta, vegetables and fruits. In many families, different types of eaters pull a chair up to the supper table, so here's a lot of information and great recipes to get you on your way!

TOFU AND TEMPEH

Tofu and tempeh are protein-packed alternatives to animal-based proteins. Read on to learn more about them.

Tofu

Tofu, also called bean curd, is made with soybeans that are soaked, cooked, ground and then mixed with a curdling ingredient. The curds are drained and then pressed into a solid block. When cooked or marinated, tofu acts like a sponge, absorbing flavors from other ingredients. Look for tofu in the produce, dairy, deli or vegetarian section of the supermarket. Tofu is sold in water-filled tubs, vacuum packs or aseptic packages. Check package labels for Web sites and recipes.

Types of Tofu

Extra-Firm or Firm: Solid, dense and holds its shape. It is higher in protein, fat and calcium than other types of tofu. Use it in casseroles, salads, stir-fries, on the grill or in any dish where you want to keep the shape of the tofu.

Flavored: Also known as baked tofu, it is very firm with a chewy, meaty texture. Flavors will vary by brand but may include familiar favorites like barbecue and teriyaki. Use it in casseroles, salads, stir-fries, on the grill or in any dish where you want to keep the shape of the tofu.

Reduced-fat or Lite: Similar in texture to soft tofu. Use it in dips, dressings, desserts, smoothies and spreads.

Silken: Comes in soft, regular and firm varieties. It's processed in a slightly different way from other types of tofu to give it a creamy, smooth, custard-like texture. Use it in dips, dressings, desserts, sauces, smoothies and spreads.

Soft: Soft in texture and doesn't hold its shape. Use it in dips, dressings, desserts, sauces, smoothies and spreads.

TYPES OF VEGETARIANS

Vegetarian diets differ based on the foods vegetarians choose to eliminate. The types of vegetarians are identified in this chart, along with a checklist of foods each type doesn't eat.

THIS TYPE OF VEGETARIAN . . .	DOES NOT EAT . . .						
	Animal-Based Broth	Animal-Based Products (gelatin, honey, lard)	Eggs	Dairy Products	Fish/ Seafood	Meat	Poultry
Lacto	x	x			x	x	x
Ovo-Lacto	x	x			x	x	x
Semi						x	
Vegan	x	x	x	x	x	x	x

Tempeh

Tempeh, a chunky soybean cake, is made from fermented whole soybeans and has a nutty-yeasty flavor. It can be crumbled and used like ground meat, marinated and grilled, or added to soups, stews, casseroles and chili. Flavored tempeh also is available. Look for tempeh in the produce, dairy, deli, vegetarian or freezer section of the supermarket.

Storing Tofu and Tempeh

- Tofu and tempeh are perishable, so check the "sell-by" date on the package.
- Store tofu in the refrigerator unless it's in an aseptic package. Once opened, refrigerate tofu covered with water for up to one week, changing water daily. Tofu can also be frozen for up to 5 months (see Freezing Tofu, below).
- Once tofu is opened, refrigerate, covered with fresh water and changing water daily, up to 1 week.
- Throw out tofu that smells sour.
- Store refrigerated tempeh in the refrigerator and frozen tempeh in the freezer. Tempeh can be refrigerated up to 2 weeks and frozen up to 3 months.

A WORLD OF SOY!

Soy has burst into popularity due to its wonderful versatility and impressive health benefits. Soy products are excellent sources of high-quality protein, and they have a fair amount of fiber, omega-3 fatty acids and calcium. The fat content varies among products. Soy products also contain isoflavones, hormone-like substances that may have heart-protective and cancer-preventive effects. Tofu and tempeh are just two of the many, many soy products available. Here is a list of more great soy products you may want to try:

- Soy cheese
- Soy flour
- Soy ice cream
- Soy margarine
- Soy mayonnaise
- Soy meat analogs (substitutes for animal-based protein, such as veggie burgers and veggie crumbles)
- Soy milk
- Soy nuts
- Soy sauce
- Soy sour cream
- Soy sprouts
- Soy yogurt
- Soybean oil

FREEZING TOFU

Freezing tofu makes it meatier and chewier, and it absorbs flavors more easily. When frozen, the color may change from white to beige, yellow or caramel; however, it may become white again as it thaws. Freeze up to 5 months.

To freeze whole blocks: Drain; wrap tightly in plastic wrap or put in resealable plastic freezer bag.

To freeze pieces: Drain; cut into slices, chunks or cubes. Arrange pieces—not touching—on cookie sheet; freeze until hard. Put frozen pieces in resealable plastic freezer bag.

To thaw: Thaw in refrigerator; press or squeeze out excess liquid before using.

SOY PRODUCTS

Chunky Vegetable Lasagna

PREP: 35 min **BAKE:** 40 min **STAND:** 10 min ▪ **8 SERVINGS**

- 12 uncooked lasagna noodles
- 3 cups frozen broccoli flowerets (from 1-lb bag), thawed
- 3 large carrots, coarsely shredded (2 cups)
- 1 can (14.5 oz) diced tomatoes, drained
- 1 medium red bell pepper, cut into thin strips
- 1 medium green bell pepper, cut into thin strips
- 3/4 cup Basil Pesto (page 405) or purchased basil pesto
- 1/4 teaspoon salt
- 1 container (15 oz) ricotta cheese
- 1/2 cup grated Parmesan cheese
- 1/4 cup chopped fresh parsley
- 1 large egg
- 3 tablespoons butter or margarine
- 1 clove garlic, finely chopped
- 3 tablespoons all-purpose flour
- 2 cups milk
- 3 cups shredded mozzarella cheese (12 oz)

1. Heat oven to 350°F.

2. Cook and drain noodles as directed on package.

3. In large bowl, mix broccoli, carrots, tomatoes, bell peppers, Basil Pesto and salt. In medium bowl, mix ricotta cheese, Parmesan cheese, parsley and egg.

4. In 2-quart saucepan, melt butter over medium heat. Cook garlic in butter about 2 minutes, stirring frequently, until garlic is golden. Stir in flour. Cook over medium heat, stirring constantly, until mixture is smooth and bubbly; remove from heat. Stir in milk. Heat to boiling, stirring constantly. Boil and stir 1 minute.

5. Place 3 noodles in ungreased 13 × 9-inch pan. Spread half of the cheese mixture over noodles. Top with 3 noodles; spread with half of the vegetable mixture. Sprinkle with 1 cup of the mozzarella cheese. Top with 3 noodles; spread with remaining cheese mixture. Top with 3 noodles; spread with remaining vegetable mixture. Pour sauce evenly over top. Sprinkle with remaining 2 cups mozzarella cheese.

6. Bake uncovered 35 to 40 minutes or until hot in center. Let stand 10 minutes before cutting.

1 SERVING: CAL. 560 (CAL. FROM FAT 280); FAT 31g (SAT. FAT 14g); CHOL. 85mg; SODIUM 820mg; CARBS. 40g (FIBER 5g); PRO. 30g
% DAILY VALUE: VIT. A 100%; VIT. C 68%; CALC. 68%; IRON 18%
EXCHANGES: 2 STARCH, 2 VEGETABLE, 3 HIGH-FAT MEAT, 1 FAT
CARB. CHOICES: 2 1/2

Spaghetti Torte LOW-FAT

PREP: 10 min **COOK:** 10 min **BAKE:** 30 min **STAND:** 15 min ▪ **8 SERVINGS**

- 1 package (16 oz) spaghetti
- 1/2 cup grated Parmesan cheese
- 1/2 cup ricotta cheese
- 1 tablespoon Italian seasoning
- 2 large eggs, beaten
- 1/4 cup finely chopped fresh or 1 1/2 teaspoons dried basil leaves
- 2 medium tomatoes, each cut into 5 slices
- 4 slices (1 oz each) provolone cheese, cut in half

1. Heat oven to 350°F. Spray 9-inch springform pan with cooking spray.

2. Cook and drain spaghetti as directed on package. Rinse with cold water; drain.

3. In large bowl, toss spaghetti, Parmesan cheese, ricotta cheese, Italian seasoning and eggs until spaghetti is well coated.

4. Press half of the spaghetti mixture in bottom of pan. Sprinkle with half of the basil. Layer with half of the tomato and cheese slices. Press remaining spaghetti mixture on top. Layer with remaining tomato and cheese slices.

5. Bake 30 minutes. Let stand 15 minutes. Remove side of pan. Sprinkle torte with remaining basil. Cut into wedges to serve.

1 SERVING: CAL. 345 (CAL. FROM FAT 80); FAT 9g (SAT. FAT 5g); CHOL. 70mg; SODIUM 280mg; CARBS. 49g (FIBER 3); PRO. 17g
% DAILY VALUE: VIT. A 12%; VIT. C 4%; CALC. 26%; IRON 16%
EXCHANGES: 3 STARCH, 1 VEGETABLE, 1 MEDIUM-FAT MEAT
CARB. CHOICES: 3

Garden Vegetable Spaghetti LOW-FAT

PREP: 10 min **COOK:** 15 min ■ **6 SERVINGS**

- 1 package (16 oz) spaghetti
- 2 tablespoons olive or vegetable oil
- 2 medium carrots, sliced (1 cup)
- 1 medium onion, diced (1/2 cup)
- 2 medium zucchini, cut into 1/2-inch slices (4 cups)*
- 2 cloves garlic, finely chopped
- 3 medium tomatoes, cut into 1-inch pieces
- 1/2 cup frozen green peas (from 1-lb bag), cooked and drained
- 1 tablespoon chopped fresh or 1 teaspoon dried basil leaves
- 1/2 teaspoon salt
- 1/4 teaspoon pepper
- 2/3 cup grated Parmesan cheese

1. Cook and drain spaghetti as directed on package.

2. Meanwhile, in 10-inch skillet, heat oil over medium-high heat. Cook carrots, onion, zucchini and garlic in oil, stirring frequently, until vegetables are crisp-tender.

3. Stir in remaining ingredients except cheese; cook until hot. Serve vegetable mixture over spaghetti. Sprinkle with cheese.

**1 small eggplant (about 12 oz), peeled and diced (3 1/2 cups), can be substituted for the zucchini.*

1 SERVING: CAL. 440 (CAL. FROM FAT 90); FAT 10g (SAT. FAT 3g); CHOL. 15mg; SODIUM 430mg; CARBS. 71g (FIBER 6g); PRO. 17g
% DAILY VALUE: VIT. A 96%; VIT. C 18%; CALC. 18%; IRON 22%
EXCHANGES: 4 STARCH, 2 VEGETABLE, 1 1/2 FAT
CARB. CHOICES: 5

Fettuccine with Ricotta, Tomato and Basil FAST

PREP: 10 min **COOK:** 5 min ■ **6 SERVINGS**

Many Italian dishes have one thing in common—they contain ricotta. It's the white, moist, subtly sweet cheese with a slightly grainy texture that's easy to find in most supermarkets.

- 2 packages (9 oz each) refrigerated fettuccine
- 6 tablespoons butter or margarine, melted
- 1 1/2 cups ricotta cheese
- 1 cup grated Parmesan cheese
- 2 large tomatoes, seeded and chopped (2 cups)
- 1/4 cup coarsely chopped fresh basil leaves

1. Cook and drain fettuccine as directed on package, using 4-quart saucepan. Return to saucepan.

2. In small bowl, mix butter, ricotta cheese and 3/4 cup of the Parmesan cheese; toss with fettuccine.

3. Serve fettuccine topped with tomatoes, basil and remaining 1/4 cup Parmesan cheese.

1 SERVING: CAL. 575 (CAL. FROM FAT 225); FAT 25g (SAT. FAT 14g); CHOL. 135mg; SODIUM 480mg; CARBS. 62g (FIBER 3g); PRO. 25g
% DAILY VALUE: VIT. A 30%; VIT. C 10%; CALC. 42%; IRON 24%
EXCHANGES: 3 1/2 STARCH, 2 VEGETABLE, 1 1/2 HIGH-FAT MEAT, 1 FAT **CARB. CHOICES:** 4

◀ **Garden Vegetable Spaghetti**

Rice Noodles with Peanut Sauce

PREP: 15 min **COOK:** 1 min ▪ **4 SERVINGS**

Rice stick noodles are white and translucent and have a very delicate flavor and texture, making them perfect for soaking up whatever flavors they're mixed with. Look for them in the Asian-foods section of the supermarket.

- 8 oz rice stick noodles
- 1/2 cup creamy peanut butter
- 2 tablespoons soy sauce
- 1 teaspoon grated gingerroot
- 1/2 teaspoon crushed red pepper
- 1/2 cup vegetable or chicken broth
- 1 cup shredded carrots (1 1/2 medium)
- 1 small red bell pepper, cut into 1/4-inch strips
- 2 medium green onions, sliced (2 tablespoons)
- 2 tablespoons chopped fresh cilantro, if desired

1. In 3-quart saucepan, heat 2 quarts water to boiling. Break noodles in half and pull apart slightly; drop into boiling water. Cook uncovered 1 minute; drain. Rinse with cold water; drain.

2. In small bowl, beat peanut butter, soy sauce, gingerroot and crushed red pepper with wire whisk until smooth. Gradually beat in broth.

3. Place noodles in large bowl. Add peanut butter mixture, carrots, bell pepper and onions; toss. Sprinkle with cilantro.

1 SERVING (1 CUP): CAL. 425 (CAL. FROM FAT 155); FAT 17g (SAT. FAT 3g); CHOL. 0mg; SODIUM 770mg; CARBS. 60g (FIBER 5g); PRO. 11g **% DAILY VALUE:** VIT. A 125%; VIT. C 30%; CALC. 4%; IRON 8% **EXCHANGES:** 3 1/2 STARCH, 1 VEGETABLE, 3 FAT **CARB. CHOICES:** 3 1/2

Teriyaki Noodles LOW-FAT

PREP: 20 min **COOK:** 16 min ▪ **4 SERVINGS**

- 1 cup hot water
- 6 dried Chinese black or shiitake mushrooms (1/2 oz)
- 8 oz uncooked soba (buckwheat) noodles or whole wheat spaghetti
- 1 tablespoon vegetable oil
- 1 large onion, sliced
- 1 package (8 oz) sliced mushrooms (3 cups)
- 8 oz fresh shiitake, crimini or baby portabella mushrooms, sliced
- 1/3 cup teriyaki sauce
- 1/4 cup chopped fresh cilantro
- 1 tablespoon sesame seed, toasted (page 215), if desired

1. In small bowl, pour hot water over dried mushrooms. Let stand about 20 minutes or until soft; drain. Rinse with warm water; drain. Squeeze out excess moisture from mushrooms. Remove and discard stems; cut caps into 1/2-inch strips.

2. Meanwhile, cook and drain noodles as directed on package.

3. In 12-inch skillet, heat oil over medium-high heat. Cook onion in oil 3 minutes, stirring frequently. Stir in all mushrooms; cook 3 minutes, stirring frequently. Stir in teriyaki sauce; reduce heat. Partially cover and simmer about 2 minutes or until vegetables are tender. Stir in noodles, cilantro and sesame seed.

1 SERVING (ABOUT 2 CUPS): CAL. 285 (CAL. FROM FAT 45); FAT 5g (SAT. FAT 1g); CHOL. 0mg; SODIUM 930mg; CARBS. 51g (FIBER 7g); PRO. 13g **% DAILY VALUE:** VIT. A 2%; VIT. C 4%; CALC. 4%; IRON 18% **EXCHANGES:** 3 STARCH, 1 VEGETABLE, 1/2 FAT **CARB. CHOICES:** 3 1/2

TOFU TERIYAKI NOODLES Cut 1-lb block of extra-firm tofu into 1/4-inch pieces; add with mushrooms in Step 3.

Spicy Chipotle-Peanut Noodle Bowls

Spicy Chipotle-Peanut Noodle Bowls

PREP: 15 min **COOK:** 15 min ■ **4 SERVINGS**

Chipotle chilies are dried jalapeño chilies. Look for them either as loose dried chilies, ground powder or in a spicy tomato, or "adobo," *sauce.*

- 1/2 cup creamy peanut butter
- 1/2 cup apple juice
- 2 tablespoons soy sauce
- 2 chipotle chilies in adobo sauce (from 7-oz can), seeded and chopped
- 1 teaspoon adobo sauce from can of chilies
- 1/4 cup chopped fresh cilantro
- 4 cups water
- 2 medium carrots, cut into julienne strips (1 1/2 × 1/4 × 1/4 inch)
- 1 medium red bell pepper, cut into julienne strips (1 1/2 × 1/4 × 1/4 inch)
- 1 package (8 to 10 oz) Chinese curly noodles
- 2 tablespoons chopped peanuts

1. In small bowl, mix peanut butter, apple juice, soy sauce, chilies and adobo sauce until smooth. Stir in cilantro.

2. In 2-quart saucepan, heat water to boiling. Add carrots and bell pepper; cook 1 minute. Remove carrots and bell pepper from water with slotted spoon. Add noodles to water; cook and drain as directed on package.

3. Toss noodles with peanut butter mixture; divide noodles among 4 bowls. Top with carrots and bell pepper. Sprinkle with peanuts.

1 SERVING: CAL. 500 (CAL. FROM FAT 180); FAT 20g (SAT. FAT 4g); CHOL. 0mg; SODIUM 800mg; CARBS. 62g (FIBER 6g); PRO. 18g
% DAILY VALUE: VIT. A 100%; VIT. C 50%; CALC. 4%; IRON 20%
EXCHANGES: 3 1/2 STARCH, 2 VEGETABLE, 1/2 HIGH FAT MEAT, 3 FAT **CARB. CHOICES:** 4

Southwest Fettuccine Bowl

LOW-FAT

PREP: 15 min **COOK:** 25 min ▪ **4 SERVINGS**

- 8 oz uncooked fettuccine
- Olive oil-flavored cooking spray
- 1 cup salsa
- 1/3 cup frozen whole kernel corn (from 1-lb bag)
- 1/4 cup water
- 2 tablespoons chili sauce
- 1/2 teaspoon ground cumin
- 1 can (15 oz) black beans, rinsed and drained
- 1/4 cup chopped fresh cilantro

1. Cook and drain fettuccine as directed on package. Place fettuccine in medium bowl. Spray fettuccine 2 or 3 times with cooking spray, tossing after each spray. Cover to keep warm.

2. In same saucepan used to cook fettuccine, mix remaining ingredients except cilantro. Cook over medium heat 4 to 6 minutes, stirring occasionally, until corn is tender.

3. Divide fettuccine among 4 individual bowls. Top each with about 3/4 cup sauce mixture. Sprinkle with cilantro.

1 SERVING: CAL. 355 (CAL. FROM FAT 25); FAT 3g (SAT. FAT 1g); CHOL. 50mg; SODIUM 800mg; CARBS. 74g (FIBER 10g); PRO. 18g **% DAILY VALUE:** VIT. A 14%; VIT. C 10%; CALC. 10%; IRON 32% **EXCHANGES:** 4 1/2 STARCH **CARB. CHOICES:** 5

Pasta and Bean Skillet

LOW-FAT

PREP: 10 min **COOK:** 18 min ▪ **4 SERVINGS**

- 1 cup salsa
- 2/3 cup uncooked elbow macaroni (2 oz)
- 3/4 cup water
- 2 teaspoons chili powder
- 1 can (15 to 16 oz) kidney beans, rinsed and drained
- 1 can (8 oz) tomato sauce
- 1/2 cup shredded Cheddar cheese (2 oz)

1. In 10-inch nonstick skillet, heat all ingredients except cheese to boiling; reduce heat to low.

2. Cover and simmer about 15 minutes, stirring frequently, just until macaroni is tender. Sprinkle with cheese.

1 SERVING: CAL. 270 (CAL. FROM FAT 55); FAT 6g (SAT. FAT 3g); CHOL. 15mg; SODIUM 1,000mg; CARBS. 45g (FIBER 9g); PRO. 16g **% DAILY VALUE:** VIT. A 20%; VIT. C 6%; CALC. 14%; IRON 28% **EXCHANGES:** 3 STARCH, 1 MEDIUM-FAT MEAT **CARB. CHOICES:** 3

Roasted Vegetable Stew

LOW-FAT

PREP: 15 min **BROIL:** 15 min **COOK:** 20 min ▪ **6 SERVINGS**

Loading up a soup or stew with vegetables and pasta turns it into a very substantial meatless meal. Easy Garlic-Cheese Biscuits (page 74) and Mandarin Salad (page 381) are perfect to round out the menu.

- 5 small red potatoes (3/4 lb), cut into fourths
- 1 large onion, cut into fourths
- 1 medium red bell pepper, cut into fourths and seeded
- 1 medium green bell pepper, cut into fourths and seeded
- 1 medium carrot, cut into 1/4-inch diagonal slices
- 1 small zucchini, cut into 1/2-inch slices
- 4 oz medium whole mushrooms
- 2 cloves garlic, finely chopped
- 2 tablespoons olive or vegetable oil
- 1 can (14 oz) vegetable or chicken broth
- 2 cans (14.5 oz each) Italian-style stewed tomatoes, undrained
- 1 1/4 cups uncooked rotini pasta (4 oz)
- 2 tablespoons chopped fresh parsley
- Freshly ground pepper, if desired

1. Set oven control to broil. In large bowl, toss potatoes, onion, bell peppers, carrot, zucchini, mushrooms, garlic and oil. In ungreased 15 × 10 × 1-inch pan, spread vegetable mixture, skin sides up.

2. Broil with tops 4 to 6 inches from heat 10 to 15 minutes or until roasted. Remove vegetables as they become soft; cool. Remove skins from peppers. Coarsely chop potatoes, onion and peppers.

3. In 4-quart Dutch oven, mix vegetables, broth, tomatoes and pasta. Heat to boiling; reduce heat. Cover and simmer about 15 minutes, stirring occasionally, until pasta is tender. Sprinkle with parsley and pepper.

1 SERVING (ABOUT 1 1/2 CUPS): CAL. 245 (CAL. FROM FAT 45); FAT 5g (SAT. FAT 1g); CHOL. 0mg; SODIUM 680mg; CARBS. 49g (FIBER 6g); PRO. 7g **% DAILY VALUE:** VIT. A 78%; VIT. C 48%; CALC. 8%; IRON 18% **EXCHANGES:** 2 STARCH, 3 VEGETABLE **CARB. CHOICES:** 3

Lemon-Pepper Pasta and Asparagus

PREP: 10 min **COOK:** 15 min ■ **4 SERVINGS**

2 cups uncooked farfalle (bow-tie) pasta (4 oz)
1/4 cup olive or vegetable oil
1 medium red bell pepper, chopped (1 cup)
1 lb asparagus, cut into 1-inch pieces
1 teaspoon grated lemon peel
1/2 teaspoon salt
1/2 teaspoon freshly ground pepper
3 tablespoons lemon juice
1 can (15 to 16 oz) navy beans, rinsed and drained
Freshly ground pepper, if desired

1. Cook and drain pasta as directed on package.

2. Meanwhile, in 12-inch skillet, heat oil over medium-high heat. Cook bell pepper, asparagus, lemon peel, salt and 1/2 teaspoon pepper in oil, stirring occasionally, until vegetables are crisp-tender.

3. Stir lemon juice and beans into vegetable mixture. Cook until beans are hot. Add pasta; toss. Sprinkle with pepper.

1 SERVING: CAL. 380 (CAL. FROM FAT 135); FAT 15g (SAT. FAT 2g); CHOL. 0mg; SODIUM 710mg; CARBS. 55g (FIBER 9g); PRO. 15g **% DAILY VALUE:** VIT. A 44%; VIT. C 40%; CALC. 10%; IRON 24% **EXCHANGES:** 3 STARCH, 2 VEGETABLE, 2 FAT **CARB. CHOICES:** 3 1/2

Gazpacho Pasta Salad with Tomato-Lime Dressing

Gazpacho Pasta Salad with Tomato-Lime Dressing

PREP: 10 min **COOK:** 15 min ■ **4 SERVINGS**

Tomato-Lime Dressing

1/4 cup tomato juice
2 tablespoons olive or vegetable oil
2 tablespoons lime juice
1/4 teaspoon salt
1/8 teaspoon pepper
1 clove garlic, finely chopped

Salad

1 package (8 oz) farfalle (bow-tie) pasta
1 large tomato, seeded and coarsely chopped (1 cup)
1 small cucumber, coarsely chopped (3/4 cup)
1 small bell pepper, coarsely chopped (1/2 cup)
4 medium green onions, sliced (1/4 cup)
1/2 green Anaheim chili, seeded and chopped
1 can (2 1/4 oz) sliced ripe olives, drained
1/4 cup chopped fresh cilantro

1. In tightly covered container, shake all dressing ingredients.

2. Cook and drain pasta as directed on package.

3. In large bowl, mix pasta and remaining salad ingredients. Pour dressing over mixture; toss. Serve immediately, or cover and refrigerate until serving.

1 SERVING: CAL. 320 (CAL. FROM FAT 90); FAT 10g (SAT. FAT 1g); CHOL. 0mg; SODIUM 350mg; CARBS. 52g (FIBER 4g); PRO. 9g **% DAILY VALUE:** VIT. A 18%; VIT. C 32%; CALC. 4%; IRON 20% **EXCHANGES:** 3 STARCH; 2 VEGETABLE; 1 FAT **CARB. CHOICES:** 3 1/2

Veggie and Bean Burgers

PREP: 10 min **COOK:** 12 min ▪ **4 SANDWICHES**

- 1/4 cup uncooked instant rice
- 1/4 cup boiling water
- 1/2 cup broccoli flowerets
- 2 oz fresh mushrooms (about 4 medium)
- 1/2 small red bell pepper, cut up
- 1 can (15 to 16 oz) garbanzo beans, rinsed and drained
- 1 large egg
- 1 clove garlic
- 1/2 teaspoon seasoned salt
- 1 teaspoon instant chopped onion
- 1/3 cup Italian-style dry bread crumbs
- 3 tablespoons vegetable oil
- 4 whole wheat hamburger buns, split
- Toppings (Cheddar cheese slices, lettuce, sliced tomato, sliced onion and mayonnaise), if desired

1. In medium bowl, stir rice and boiling water. Cover and let stand 5 minutes. Drain if necessary.

2. Meanwhile, in food processor, place broccoli, mushrooms and bell pepper. Cover and process, using quick on-and-off motions, to finely chop vegetables (do not puree). Stir vegetables into rice.

3. Add beans, egg, garlic and seasoned salt to food processor. Cover and process until smooth. Stir bean mixture, onion and bread crumbs into vegetable mixture.

4. Using about 1/2 cup vegetable mixture for each patty, shape into 1/2-inch-thick patties.

5. In 10-inch nonstick skillet, heat oil over medium-high heat. Cook patties in oil 8 to 10 minutes, turning once, until brown and crisp. Serve on buns with toppings.

1 SANDWICH: CAL. 410 (CAL. FROM FAT 145); FAT 16g (SAT. FAT 2g); CHOL. 55mg; SODIUM540mg; CARBS. 61g (FIBER 11g); PRO. 17g
% DAILY VALUE: VIT. A 14%; VIT. C 24%; CALC. 12%; IRON 30%
EXCHANGES: 3 1/2 STARCH, 2 VEGETABLE, 2 FAT **CARB. CHOICES:** 4

VEGGIE AND BEAN "MEATBALLS" Heat oven to 400°F. Generously spray 15 × 10 × 1-inch pan with cooking spray. Shape vegetable mixture into 16 balls; place in pan. Generously spray tops of balls with cooking spray. Bake about 20 minutes or until crisp. Serve with pasta sauce (any flavor) or cheese sauce.

California Black Bean Burgers

PREP: 15 min **COOK:** 10 min ▪ **6 SANDWICHES**

Coating the patties with cornmeal gives them a delicious crispy coating.

- 1 can (15 oz) black beans, undrained
- 1 can (4.5 oz) chopped green chiles, undrained
- 1 cup plain dry bread crumbs
- 1 teaspoon chili powder
- 1 large egg, beaten
- 1/4 cup yellow cornmeal
- 2 tablespoons vegetable oil
- 6 hamburger buns, toasted
- 2 tablespoons mayonnaise or salad dressing
- 1 1/4 cups shredded lettuce
- 3 tablespoons thick-and-chunky salsa

◀ **Veggie and Bean Burgers**

1. In food processor or blender, place beans. Cover and process until slightly mashed; remove from food processor to medium bowl. Stir chilies, bread crumbs, chili powder and egg into beans. Shape mixture into 6 patties, each about 1/2 inch thick. Coat each patty with cornmeal.

2. In 10-inch skillet, heat oil over medium heat. Cook patties in oil 5 to 10 minutes, turning once, until crisp and thoroughly cooked on both sides.

3. Spread bottom halves of buns with mayonnaise. Top with lettuce, patties, salsa and tops of buns.

1 SANDWICH: CAL. 365 (CAL. FROM FAT 100); FAT 11g (SAT. FAT 2g); CHOL. 35mg; SODIUM 1,090mg; CARBS. 60g (FIBER 8g); PRO. 14g
% DAILY VALUE: VIT. A 10%; VIT. C 14%; CALC. 16%; IRON 26%
EXCHANGES: 4 STARCH, 1 FAT **CARB. CHOICES:** 4

Garbanzo Bean Sandwich

FAST

PREP: 15 min ■ **4 SERVINGS**

- 1 can (15 to 16 oz) garbanzo beans, rinsed and drained
- 1/2 cup water
- 2 tablespoons chopped fresh parsley
- 2 tablespoons chopped walnuts
- 1 tablespoon finely chopped onion
- 1 clove garlic, finely chopped
- 4 whole wheat pita breads (6 inch)
- Lettuce leaves
- 1 medium tomato, seeded and chopped (3/4 cup)
- 1/2 medium cucumber, sliced and slices cut into fourths
- 1/2 cup cucumber-ranch dressing

1. In food processor or blender, place beans, water, parsley, walnuts, onion and garlic. Cover and process until smooth.

2. Cut each pita bread in half to form 2 pockets; line with lettuce. Spoon 2 tablespoons bean spread into each pita half. Add tomato, cucumber and dressing.

1 SERVING: CAL. 490 (CAL. FROM FAT 190); FAT 21g (SAT. FAT 2g); CHOL. 10mg; SODIUM 790mg; CARBS. 69g (FIBER 14g); PRO. 18g
% DAILY VALUE: VIT. A 10%; VIT. C 20%; CALC. 12%; IRON 30%
EXCHANGES: 4 STARCH, 2 VEGETABLE, 2 1/2 FAT
CARB. CHOICES: 4 1/2

South-of-the-Border Burritos

FAST

PREP: 10 min **COOK:** 10 min ■ **4 SERVINGS**

Use a garlic press to quickly crush the garlic instead of chopping it. Look for the self-cleaning type; it presses all the garlic through the holes instead of leaving the pieces behind.

- 2 tablespoons vegetable oil
- 1 large onion, chopped (1 cup)
- 6 cloves garlic, finely chopped
- 1 can (15 oz) black beans, rinsed, drained and mashed
- 1 to 2 teaspoons finely chopped drained chipotle chilies in adobo sauce (from 7-oz can)
- 4 flour tortillas (8 or 10 inch)
- 1 cup shredded mozzarella cheese (4 oz)
- 1 large tomato, chopped (1 cup)

1. In 10-inch nonstick skillet, heat oil over medium-high heat. Cook onion and garlic in oil 6 to 8 minutes, stirring occasionally, until onion is tender. Stir in beans and chilies. Cook, stirring frequently, until hot.

2. Place one-fourth of the bean mixture on center of each tortilla. Top with cheese and tomato.

3. Fold one end of tortilla up about 1 inch over filling; fold right and left sides over folded end, overlapping. Fold remaining end down. Place seam side down on serving platter or plate.

1 SERVING: CAL. 430 (CAL. FROM FAT 145); FAT 16g (SAT. FAT 5g); CHOL. 15mg; SODIUM 780mg; CARBS. 60g (FIBER 10g); PRO. 22g
% DAILY VALUE: VIT. A 12%; VIT. C 10%; CALC. 34%; IRON 24%
EXCHANGES: 3 1/2 STARCH, 2 VEGETABLE, 1 HIGH-FAT MEAT
CARB. CHOICES: 4

Middle East Vegetable Tacos

PREP: 10 min **COOK:** 12 min ■ **6 SERVINGS**

The vegetable mixture also tastes great served over strands of spaghetti squash or pasta.

- 1 tablespoon olive or vegetable oil
- 1 medium eggplant (1 lb), peeled and cut into 1/2-inch cubes
- 1 medium red bell pepper, cut into 1/2-inch strips
- 1 medium onion, cut into 1/2-inch wedges
- 1 can (14.5 oz) diced tomatoes with roasted garlic, onion and oregano (or other variety), undrained
- 1/4 teaspoon salt
- 1 container (8 oz) refrigerated hummus
- 12 taco shells
- Plain yogurt or sour cream, if desired

1. In 10-inch nonstick skillet, heat oil over medium-high heat. Cook eggplant, bell pepper and onion in oil 5 to 7 minutes, stirring occasionally, until vegetables are crisp-tender.

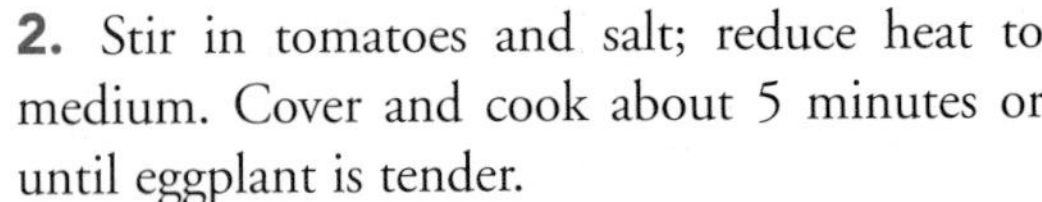

2. Stir in tomatoes and salt; reduce heat to medium. Cover and cook about 5 minutes or until eggplant is tender.

3. Spread scant 2 tablespoons hummus inside each taco shell. Spoon about 1/2 cup vegetable mixture over hummus in each shell. Serve with yogurt.

1 SERVING: CAL. 260 (CAL. FROM FAT 110); FAT 12g (SAT. FAT 2g); CHOL. 0mg; SODIUM 430mg; CARBS. 38g (FIBER 8g); PRO. 7g
% DAILY VALUE: VIT. A 30%; VIT. C 42%; CALC. 10%; IRON 14%
EXCHANGES: 2 STARCH, 2 VEGETABLE, 1 FAT **CARB. CHOICES:** 2 1/2

Spiced Skillet Vegetables

LOW-FAT

PREP: 15 min **COOK:** 10 min ■ **5 SERVINGS**

- 2 teaspoons vegetable oil
- 2 medium carrots, sliced (1 cup)
- 1 large onion, chopped (1 cup)
- 1 large red bell pepper, cut into 3/4-inch pieces (1 cup)
- 2 cloves garlic, finely chopped
- 1 can (15 to 16 oz) garbanzo beans, rinsed and drained
- 1 small zucchini, sliced (1 cup)
- 1/2 cup raisins
- 1 teaspoon ground cumin
- 1/2 teaspoon salt
- 1/4 teaspoon ground turmeric
- 1/4 teaspoon ground cinnamon
- 1/8 teaspoon pepper
- 2 tablespoons chopped fresh parsley

1. In 12-inch nonstick skillet, heat oil over medium-high heat. Cook carrots, onion, bell pepper and garlic in oil about 4 minutes, stirring frequently, until onion is tender.

2. Stir in remaining ingredients except parsley. Cook about 5 minutes, stirring frequently, until zucchini is tender. Serve topped with parsley.

1 SERVING: CAL. 210 (CAL. FROM FAT 35); FAT 4g (SAT. FAT 1g); CHOL. 0mg; SODIUM 470mg; CARBS. 44g (FIBER 9g); PRO. 9g
% DAILY VALUE: VIT. A 98%; VIT. C 32%; CALC. 6%; IRON 20%
EXCHANGES: 2 STARCH, 2 VEGETABLE **CARB. CHOICES:** 3

◀ **Middle East Vegetable Tacos**

Pepper and Soybean Stir-Fry FAST

PREP: 5 min **COOK:** 8 min ▪ **4 SERVINGS**

1 tablespoon vegetable oil
1 tablespoon curry powder
1 bag (1 lb) frozen stir-fry bell peppers and onions
1 bag (12 oz) frozen soybeans*
4 cloves garlic, finely chopped
1 cup unsweetened coconut milk (not cream of coconut)
2 cups hot cooked jasmine or brown rice (page 375)
1/2 cup salted roasted cashews
Chopped fresh cilantro or parsley, if desired

1. In 12-inch nonstick skillet, heat oil over medium-high heat. Cook curry powder in oil 1 minute, stirring frequently. Stir in bell peppers and onions, soybeans and garlic. Cook 2 minutes, stirring frequently. Cover and cook about 3 minutes longer or until vegetables are tender.

2. Stir in coconut milk; reduce heat. Simmer uncovered 2 minutes, stirring occasionally.

3. Serve mixture over rice. Sprinkle with cashews and cilantro.

**1 box (9 oz) frozen green peas can be substituted for the soybeans.*

1 SERVING: CAL. 520 (CAL. FROM FAT 270); FAT 30g (SAT. FAT 12g); CHOL. 0mg; SODIUM 280mg; CARBS. 50g (FIBER 10g); PRO. 22g
% DAILY VALUE: VIT. A 6%; VIT. C 28%; CALC. 12%; IRON 42%
EXCHANGES: 3 STARCH, 1 VEGETABLE, 1 1/2 MEDIUM-FAT MEAT, 3 FAT **CARB. CHOICES:** 3

Hearty Soybean and Cheddar Pasta Salad

PREP: 20 min **COOK:** 12 min **CHILL:** 1 hr ▪ **4 SERVINGS**

Dressing

1/3 cup vegetable oil
1/4 cup red wine vinegar
1 teaspoon Italian seasoning
1/2 teaspoon salt
1/4 teaspoon pepper
1/4 teaspoon garlic powder

Salad

1 cup uncooked penne pasta (3 oz)
1 box (10 oz) frozen soybeans (about 2 cups)
1 large tomato, coarsely chopped (1 cup)
1/2 medium cucumber, coarsely chopped (1/2 cup)
1 small yellow bell pepper, coarsely chopped (1/2 cup)
6 oz Cheddar cheese, cut into 1/2-inch cubes (1 1/2 cups)

1. In small bowl, beat all dressing ingredients with wire whisk until well mixed.

2. Cook and drain pasta as directed on package. Rinse with cold water; drain.

3. Meanwhile, cook soybeans as directed on package. Rinse with cold water; drain.

4. In large bowl, toss pasta, soybeans, remaining salad ingredients and dressing. Cover and refrigerate at least 1 hour.

1 SERVING: CAL. 580 (CAL. FROM FAT 370); FAT 41g (SAT. FAT 13g); CHOL. 45mg; SODIUM 770mg; CARBS. 31g (FIBER 7g); PRO. 28g
% DAILY VALUE: VIT. A 18%; VIT. C 32%; CALC. 32%; IRON 24%
EXCHANGES: 2 STARCH, 3 HIGH-FAT MEAT, 2 1/2 FAT
CARB. CHOICES: 2

EDAMAME

Edamame is the Japanese name for fresh green soybeans, tasty little, bright green gems that are high in protein and easily digested. The soybeans are picked before they are completely mature and are often sold in their fuzzy green pods. Fresh edamame is available spring through fall in raw or ready-to-eat forms at co-ops, natural-foods stores or large supermarkets. Raw beans should be steamed 20 minutes before eating and are usually served chilled. They're also available frozen in boxes or bags. Once cooked, edamame can be served right in the pods as a fun appetizer or snack, and it can be shelled and used in salads or other cold or hot side dishes.

Brown Rice and Lentils

LOW-FAT

PREP: 15 min **COOK:** 55 min ■ **4 SERVINGS**

- 2 tablespoons butter or margarine
- 1 small onion, chopped (1/4 cup)
- 1 clove garlic, finely chopped
- 1/2 cup dried lentils (4 oz), sorted and rinsed
- 1/2 cup uncooked brown rice
- 1 can (14 oz) vegetable or chicken broth
- 1/4 cup water
- 1/4 teaspoon red pepper sauce
- 1 medium green bell pepper, coarsely chopped (1 cup)
- 1/2 cup shredded mozzarella cheese (2 oz)

1. In 2-quart saucepan, melt butter over medium heat. Cook onion and garlic in butter about 3 minutes, stirring occasionally, until onion is tender.

2. Stir in lentils, rice, broth, water and pepper sauce. Heat to boiling; reduce heat. Cover and simmer about 50 minutes, adding water if necessary, until rice is tender and liquid is absorbed.

3. Stir in bell pepper. Sprinkle with cheese.

1 SERVING (ABOUT 1 CUP): CAL. 260 (CAL. FROM FAT 80); FAT 9g (SAT. FAT 5g); CHOL. 25mg; SODIUM 560mg; CARBS. 39g (FIBER 8g); PRO. 14g **% DAILY VALUE:** VIT. A 14%; VIT. C 24%; CALC. 14%; IRON 18% **EXCHANGES:** 2 STARCH, 2 VEGETABLE, 1 LEAN MEAT **CARB. CHOICES:** 2 1/2

Vegetables and Tofu Skillet Supper

LOW-FAT

PREP: 15 min **COOK:** 27 min ■ **4 SERVINGS**

- 2 tablespoons olive or vegetable oil
- 1/2 cup coarsely chopped red onion
- 4 or 5 small red potatoes, sliced (2 cups)
- 1 cup frozen cut green beans (from 1-lb bag)
- 1/2 teaspoon Italian seasoning
- 1/2 teaspoon garlic salt
- 1/2 package (14-oz size) firm tofu, cut into 1/2-inch cubes
- 2 roma (plum) tomatoes, thinly sliced
- 1 Hard-Cooked Egg (page 220), chopped

1. In 12-inch skillet, heat oil over medium-high heat. Cook onion in oil 2 minutes, stirring frequently. Stir in potatoes; reduce heat to medium-low. Cover and cook 10 to 12 minutes, stirring occasionally, until potatoes are tender.

2. Stir in green beans, Italian seasoning and garlic salt. Cover and cook 6 to 8 minutes, stirring occasionally, until beans are tender and potatoes are light golden brown.

3. Stir in tofu and tomatoes. Cook 3 to 5 minutes, stirring occasionally and gently, just until hot. Sprinkle each serving with egg.

1 SERVING: CAL. 105 (CAL. FROM FAT 80); FAT 9g (SAT. FAT 1g); CHOL. 55mg; SODIUM 320mg; CARBS. 31g (FIBER 5g); PRO. 6g **% DAILY VALUE:** VIT. A 18%; VIT. C 6%; CALC. 10%; IRON 20% **EXCHANGES:** 2 STARCH, 1 FAT **CARB. CHOICES:** 2

◀ **Vegetables and Tofu Skillet Supper**

Tempeh Stir-Fry with Yogurt-Peanut Sauce

PREP: 20 min **COOK:** 20 min ■ **4 SERVINGS**

Tempeh, pronounced "TEHM-pay" and also spelled "tempe," is a fermented, high-protein soybean cake with a chewy texture and slightly nutty flavor.

- 1/4 cup creamy peanut butter
- 1/4 cup vanilla yogurt
- 3 tablespoons teriyaki marinade
- 1 tablespoon honey
- 2 tablespoons vegetable oil
- 1 package (8 oz) tempeh, cut into 2 × 1/4 × 1/4-inch strips
- 1 medium onion, cut into thin wedges
- 3 medium carrots, cut into 2 × 1/4 × 1/4-inch strips (1 1/2 cups)
- 8 oz green beans, cut in half (1 1/2 cups)
- 1/4 cup water
- 1 medium red bell pepper, cut into thin strips
- 1/4 cup chopped fresh cilantro

1. In small bowl, beat peanut butter, yogurt, teriyaki marinade and honey with wire whisk until smooth; set aside.

2. In 12-inch skillet, heat 1 tablespoon of the oil over medium heat. Cook tempeh in oil 5 to 6 minutes, turning frequently, until light golden brown. Remove tempeh from skillet; set aside.

3. Add remaining 1 tablespoon oil and the onion to skillet. Cook 1 minute, stirring occasionally. Stir in carrots, green beans and water. Cover and cook 5 minutes. Stir in bell pepper. Cook 2 to 3 minutes, stirring occasionally, until vegetables are crisp-tender.

4. Stir in tempeh and peanut butter mixture until well mixed. Cook 1 to 2 minutes, stirring occasionally, until heated through. Sprinkle with cilantro.

1 SERVING: CAL. 345 (CAL. FROM FAT 180); FAT 20g (SAT. FAT 3g); CHOL. 0mg; SODIUM 460mg; CARBS. 30g (FIBER 7g); PRO. 18g
% DAILY VALUE: VIT. A 100%; VIT. C 54%; CALC. 14%; IRON 16%
EXCHANGES: 2 STARCH, 2 MEDIUM-FAT MEAT, 1 FAT
CARB. CHOICES: 2

Baked "Veggie-Burger" Stew LOW-FAT

PREP: 15 min **BAKE:** 1 hr ■ **4 SERVINGS**

Check out your supermarket's freezer case for all of the new meatless burgers that are becoming available. Many are made from vegetables and grains and have the texture of ground beef but less fat and usually no cholesterol.

- 2 medium potatoes, cubed (2 cups)
- 2 small turnips, peeled and cubed*
- 1/2 medium rutabaga, peeled and cubed
- 2 medium stalks celery, sliced (1 cup)
- 2 medium carrots, sliced (1 cup)
- 1/2 cup all-purpose flour
- 2 cups beef broth
- 3 small onions, cut into fourths
- 1 can (14.5 oz) whole tomatoes, undrained
- 2 tablespoons chopped fresh or 3/4 teaspoon dried thyme leaves
- 2 tablespoons chopped fresh or 3/4 teaspoon dried marjoram leaves
- 1/4 teaspoon salt
- 1/4 teaspoon pepper
- 1 dried bay leaf
- 4 frozen soy-protein vegetable burgers, thawed and cut into 1-inch pieces
- Fresh thyme, if desired

1. Heat oven to 350°F.

2. In ovenproof 4-quart Dutch oven, mix potatoes, turnips, rutabaga, celery and carrots.

3. In medium bowl, stir flour and broth until smooth. Stir broth mixture and remaining ingredients except burger pieces into vegetable mixture, breaking up tomatoes with a fork. Heat to boiling over medium-high heat. Stir in burger pieces.

4. Cover and bake 50 to 60 minutes, stirring occasionally, until vegetables are tender. Remove bay leaf. Garnish with thyme.

**Parsnips can be substituted for the turnips.*

1 SERVING: CAL. 260 (CAL. FROM FAT 25); FAT 3g (SAT. FAT 1g); CHOL. 0mg; SODIUM 1220mg; CARBS. 45g (FIBER 7g); PRO. 18g
% DAILY VALUE: VIT. A 100%; VIT. C 32%; CALC. 12%; IRON 26%
EXCHANGES: 2 1/2 STARCH, 2 VEGETABLE, 1/2 VERY LEAN MEAT
CARB. CHOICES: 3

Barley-Vegetable Casserole

LOW-FAT

PREP: 15 min **COOK:** 5 min **BAKE:** 1 hr 20 min ■ **4 SERVINGS**

- 2 teaspoons olive or vegetable oil
- 1 medium onion, chopped (1/2 cup)
- 1 cup water
- 1 cube vegetable bouillon
- 2/3 cup uncooked barley
- 2 teaspoons chopped fresh or 1/2 teaspoon dried oregano leaves
- 1/4 teaspoon salt
- 1/4 teaspoon pepper
- 1 can (14.5 oz) whole tomatoes, undrained
- 1 can (8 oz) sliced water chestnuts, undrained
- 1 bag (1 lb) frozen mixed vegetables

1. Heat oven to 350°F.

2. In 8-inch nonstick skillet, heat oil over medium-high heat. Cook onion in oil 4 to 5 minutes, stirring occasionally, until crisp-tender.

3. In small microwavable bowl, microwave water and bouillon uncovered on High about 2 minutes or until boiling and bouillon is dissolved.

4. In 3-quart casserole, mix onion, bouillon mixture and remaining ingredients except frozen vegetables, breaking up tomatoes with a fork. Cover and bake about 40 minutes or until bubbly around edge.

5. Stir in frozen vegetables. Cover and bake 30 to 40 minutes longer or until barley is tender.

1 SERVING: CAL. 205 (CAL. FROM FAT 24); FAT 3g (SAT. FAT 0g); CHOL. 0mg; SODIUM 630mg; CARBS. 46g (FIBER 10g); PRO. 8g
% DAILY VALUE: VIT. A 68%; VIT. C 42%; CALC. 10%; IRON 12%
EXCHANGES: 21/2 STARCH, 1 VEGETABLE **CARB. CHOICES:** 3

Deluxe Stuffed-Crust Pizza

PREP: 25 min **BAKE:** 17 min ■ **6 SERVINGS**

- Yellow cornmeal
- 1 loaf (1 lb) frozen whole wheat bread dough, thawed
- 4 sticks (1 oz each) string cheese, cut lengthwise in half
- 1/4 cup Italian-style tomato paste
- 1 small onion, cut lengthwise in half, then thinly sliced
- 1 medium bell pepper, thinly sliced
- 1 can (4 oz) mushroom pieces and stems, drained
- 1 oz sliced soy-protein pepperoni-style slices, coarsely chopped (1/4 cup)*
- 12 pitted Kalamata or Greek olives, coarsely chopped (1/3 cup)
- 2 cups shredded mozzarella cheese (8 oz)

1. Heat oven to 400°F. Grease large cookie sheet with shortening or spray with cooking spray. Sprinkle cornmeal over cookie sheet.

2. Pat or roll dough into 13-inch circle on cookie sheet. Arrange string cheese sticks in circle around edge of dough. Carefully roll edge of dough up over cheese; seal well.

Deluxe Stuffed-Crust Pizza ▶

3. Spread tomato paste evenly over dough. Top with onion, bell pepper, mushrooms, pepperoni and olives. Sprinkle with cheese.

4. Bake 15 to 17 minutes or until crust is golden brown and cheese is melted.

**2 frozen (thawed) soy-protein vegetable burgers, cut into 1/4-inch pieces, or 1/2 cup frozen (thawed) soy-protein burger crumbles can be substituted for the pepperoni-style slices.*

1 SERVING: CAL. 375 (CAL. FROM FAT 125); FAT 14g (SAT. FAT 7g); CHOL. 35mg; SODIUM 960mg; CARBS. 44g (FIBER 7g); PRO. 25g
% DAILY VALUE: VIT. A 14%; VIT. C 18%; CALC. 48%; IRON 20%
EXCHANGES: 3 STARCH, 2 LEAN MEAT, 1/2 FAT **CARB. CHOICES:** 3

Cheese Enchiladas

PREP: 15 min **COOK:** 8 min **BAKE:** 20 min ■
4 SERVINGS

If you like, use reduced-fat or fat-free cheese and sour cream.

- 2 cups shredded Monterey Jack cheese (8 oz)
- 1 cup shredded Cheddar cheese (4 oz)
- 1/2 cup sour cream
- 1 medium onion, chopped (1/2 cup)
- 2 tablespoons chopped fresh parsley
- 1/4 teaspoon pepper
- 1 can (15 oz) tomato sauce
- 1 small green bell pepper, chopped (1/2 cup)
- 1 can (4.5 oz) chopped green chiles, drained
- 1 clove garlic, finely chopped
- 2/3 cup water
- 1 tablespoon chili powder
- 1 1/2 teaspoons chopped fresh or 1/2 teaspoon dried oregano leaves
- 1/4 teaspoon ground cumin
- 8 corn tortillas (5 or 6 inch)
- Additional shredded cheese, sour cream and chopped onion, if desired

1. Heat oven to 350°F.

2. In medium bowl, mix cheeses, sour cream, onion, parsley and pepper; set aside.

3. In 2-quart saucepan, heat tomato sauce, bell pepper, chiles, garlic, water, chili powder, oregano and cumin to boiling, stirring occasionally; reduce heat. Simmer uncovered 5 minutes. Pour into ungreased 9-inch glass pie plate.

4. Dip each tortilla into sauce to coat both sides. Spoon about 1/4 cup cheese mixture onto each tortilla; roll tortilla around filling. Place seam side down in ungreased 11 × 7-inch glass baking dish. Pour remaining sauce over enchiladas.

5. Bake uncovered about 20 minutes or until bubbly. Garnish with additional shredded cheese, sour cream and chopped onion.

1 SERVING: CAL. 545 (CAL. FROM FAT 305); FAT 34g (SAT. FAT 20g); CHOL. 100mg; SODIUM 1,410mg; CARBS. 37g (FIBER 6g); PRO. 27g
% DAILY VALUE: VIT. A 60%; VIT. C 40%; CALC. 70%; IRON 16%
EXCHANGES: 2 STARCH, 1 VEGETABLE, 2 HIGH-FAT MEAT, 3 1/2 FAT **CARB. CHOICES:** 2 1/2

Vegetable Curry with Couscous LOW-FAT

PREP: 10 min **COOK:** 12 min ■ **4 SERVINGS**

1 tablespoon vegetable oil
1 medium red bell pepper, cut into thin strips
1/4 cup vegetable or chicken broth
1 tablespoon curry powder
1 teaspoon salt
1 bag (1 lb) frozen broccoli, carrots and cauliflower (or other combination)
1/2 cup raisins
1/3 cup chutney
2 cups hot cooked couscous or rice (page 375)
1/4 cup chopped peanuts

1. In 12-inch skillet, heat oil over medium-high heat. Cook bell pepper in oil 4 to 5 minutes, stirring frequently, until tender.

2. Stir in broth, curry powder, salt and vegetables. Heat to boiling. Boil about 4 minutes, stirring frequently, until vegetables are crisp-tender.

3. Stir in raisins and chutney. Serve over couscous. Sprinkle with peanuts.

1 SERVING: CAL. 305 (CAL. FROM FAT 80); FAT 9g (SAT. FAT 2g); CHOL. 0mg; SODIUM 740mg; CARBS. 53g (FIBER 7g); PRO. 10g **% DAILY VALUE:** VIT. A 98%; VIT. C 80%; CALC. 8%; IRON 12% **EXCHANGES:** 3 STARCH, 2 VEGETABLE, 1/2 FAT **CARB. CHOICES:** 3 1/2

Twice-Baked Cheese Potatoes

PREP: 15 min **BAKE:** 1 hr 35 min ■ **4 SERVINGS**

If you're in a hurry, microwave the potatoes on High for 12 to 14 minutes, and finish the stuffed potato shells in the oven. Did you know? Bacon flavor bits are made from soy and don't contain any animal products.

4 medium unpeeled Idaho or russet baking potatoes (1 1/2 lb)
1/2 can (15- to 16-oz size) great northern or cannellini beans, rinsed and drained
1/3 cup sour cream
1/4 cup chopped fresh chives
3 cups chopped fresh spinach (4 oz)
1 cup ricotta cheese
1/2 cup shredded Cheddar cheese (2 oz)
3/4 cup chopped onions (1 1/2 medium)
2 teaspoons butter or margarine, softened
2 large eggs
1 tablespoon bacon flavor bits or chips, if desired

1. Heat oven to 375°F. Gently scrub potatoes, but do not peel. Pierce potatoes several times with fork to allow steam to escape while potatoes bake. Bake 1 hour to 1 hour 15 minutes or until potatoes are tender when pierced in center with fork.

2. When potatoes are cool enough to handle, cut lengthwise in half; scoop out inside, leaving a thin shell.

3. In medium bowl, mash potatoes and beans with potato masher or electric mixer on low speed until no lumps remain. Stir in 2 tablespoons of the sour cream, 2 tablespoons of the chives and remaining ingredients except bacon bits. Fill shells with potato mixture. Place in ungreased 13 × 9-inch pan.

4. Bake uncovered 15 to 20 minutes or until hot and light brown. Top with remaining sour cream, chives and the bacon bits.

1 SERVING: CAL. 390 (CAL. FROM FAT 165); FAT 18g (SAT. FAT 10g); CHOL. 160mg; SODIUM 240mg; CARBS. 38g (FIBER 5g); PRO. 21g **% DAILY VALUE:** VIT. A 60%; VIT. C 10%; CALC. 30%; IRON 15% **EXCHANGES:** 2 STARCH, 1 VEGETABLE, 2 MEDIUM-FAT MEAT, 1 FAT **CARB. CHOICES:** 2

◀ **Vegetable Curry with Couscous**

Eggplant Parmigiana

PREP: 1 hr 5 min **COOK:** 10 min **BAKE:** 25 min ▪
6 SERVINGS

- 2 cups Italian Tomato Sauce (page 404) or purchased tomato pasta sauce
- 2 small unpeeled eggplants (about 1 lb each)
- 1 large egg
- 2 tablespoons water
- 2/3 cup dry bread crumbs
- 1/3 cup grated Parmesan cheese
- 1/4 cup olive or vegetable oil
- 2 cups shredded mozzarella cheese (8 oz)

1. Make Italian Tomato Sauce.

2. Heat oven to 350°F.

3. Cut eggplants into 1/4-inch slices. In shallow dish, mix egg and water. In another shallow dish, mix bread crumbs and Parmesan cheese. Dip eggplant into egg mixture, then coat with bread crumb mixture.

4. In 12-inch skillet, heat oil over medium heat. Cook half of the eggplant at a time in oil about 5 minutes, turning once, until light brown; drain on paper towels. Repeat with remaining eggplant, adding 1 or 2 tablespoons oil if necessary.

5. In ungreased 11 × 7-inch glass baking dish, place half of the eggplant, overlapping slices slightly. Spoon half of the sauce over eggplant. Sprinkle with 1 cup of the mozzarella cheese. Repeat with remaining eggplant, sauce and cheese.

6. Bake uncovered about 25 minutes or until sauce is bubbly and cheese is light brown.

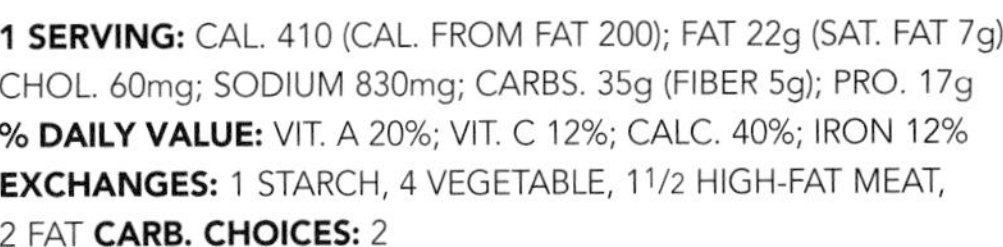

1 SERVING: CAL. 410 (CAL. FROM FAT 200); FAT 22g (SAT. FAT 7g); CHOL. 60mg; SODIUM 830mg; CARBS. 35g (FIBER 5g); PRO. 17g **% DAILY VALUE:** VIT. A 20%; VIT. C 12%; CALC. 40%; IRON 12% **EXCHANGES:** 1 STARCH, 4 VEGETABLE, 1 1/2 HIGH-FAT MEAT, 2 FAT **CARB. CHOICES:** 2

Mozzarella and Pesto Strata

PREP: 15 min **CHILL:** 2 hr **BAKE:** 1 hr **STAND:** 5 min ▪
8 SERVINGS

French bread loaves can vary in length and width. If you use a 1-pound loaf of French bread, you will need only about 11 slices of bread.

- 16 slices (3/4 inch thick) French bread (1/2-lb loaf)
- 1/2 cup Basil Pesto (page 405) or purchased basil pesto
- 1/2 cup sliced ripe olives
- 1 jar (12 oz) roasted red bell peppers, drained and sliced (1 cup)
- 2 cups shredded mozzarella cheese (8 oz)
- 8 large eggs
- 2 cups milk
- 1/4 teaspoon salt
- 1/8 teaspoon pepper
- 2 tablespoons freshly shredded Parmesan cheese

1. Spray 13 × 9-inch glass baking dish with cooking spray. Spread one side of each bread slice with Basil Pesto. Arrange bread, pesto sides up, in bottom of baking dish, cutting slices to fit if necessary. Sprinkle with olives, bell peppers and mozzarella cheese.

2. In medium bowl, beat eggs, milk, salt and pepper with fork or wire whisk until well blended. Pour evenly over cheese in dish. Sprinkle with Parmesan cheese. Cover and refrigerate at least 2 hours but no longer than 24 hours.

3. Heat oven to 325°F. Bake uncovered 55 to 60 minutes or until knife inserted in center comes out clean and top is golden brown. Let stand 5 minutes before cutting.

1 SERVING: CAL. 360 (CAL. FROM FAT 190); FAT 21g (SAT. FAT 8g); CHOL. 235mg; SODIUM 720mg; CARBS. 21g (FIBER 2g); PRO. 21g **% DAILY VALUE:** VIT. A 34%; VIT. C 24%; CALC. 42%; IRON 12% **EXCHANGES:** 1 STARCH, 1 VEGETABLE, 2 HIGH-FAT MEAT, 1 FAT **CARB. CHOICES:** 1 1/2

◀ **Mozzarella and Pesto Strata**

Skillet Nachos

PREP: 15 min **COOK:** 10 min ▪ **4 SERVINGS**

- 1 tablespoon olive or vegetable oil
- 1 medium green bell pepper, chopped (1 cup)
- 1 small zucchini, chopped (1 cup)
- 1 cup thick-and-chunky salsa
- 1 cup chili beans in chili sauce (from 15-oz can)
- 4 oz tortilla chips (about 50)
- 1 1/2 cups shredded Monterey Jack cheese (6 oz)
- Sliced ripe olives, if desired

1. In 12-inch skillet, heat oil over medium-high heat. Cook bell pepper and zucchini in oil about 2 minutes, stirring frequently, until vegetables are crisp-tender.

2. Stir in 1/2 cup of the salsa and the beans. Cook, stirring frequently, until hot. Remove mixture from skillet.

3. Wipe skillet clean. Arrange tortilla chips in single layer in skillet. Spoon vegetable mixture onto chips. Sprinkle with cheese.

4. Cover and cook over medium-high heat about 5 minutes or until cheese is melted. Sprinkle with olives. Serve with remaining 1/2 cup salsa.

1 SERVING: CAL. 400 (CAL. FROM FAT 220); FAT 24g (SAT. FAT 9g); CHOL. 40mg; SODIUM 1,140mg; CARBS. 34g (FIBER 6g); PRO. 17g
% DAILY VALUE: VIT. A 28%; VIT. C 28%; CALC. 36%; IRON 18%
EXCHANGES: 2 STARCH, 1 VEGETABLE, 1 1/2 HIGH-FAT MEAT, 1 1/2 FAT **CARB. CHOICES:** 2

Pizza Soup LOW-FAT

PREP: 25 min **COOK:** 20 min **BROIL:** 2 min ▪ **6 SERVINGS**

- 1 tablespoon olive or vegetable oil
- 1 medium onion, sliced
- 1 large red bell pepper, cut into 1-inch pieces
- 1 large green bell pepper, cut into 1-inch pieces
- 2 cloves garlic, finely chopped
- 2 cups water
- 2 cans (14.5 oz each) diced tomatoes in olive oil, garlic and spices (or other variety), undrained
- 1 can (6 oz) tomato paste
- 1 cup sliced fresh mushrooms (3 oz)
- 1 1/2 teaspoons Italian seasoning, crumbled
- 1 teaspoon fennel seed
- 1 can (15 to 16 oz) kidney beans, rinsed and drained
- 1 can (15 to 16 oz) cannellini beans, rinsed and drained
- 6 slices French bread, 1/2 inch thick
- 1 1/2 cups shredded mozzarella cheese (6 oz)

1. Heat oven to 425°F. In 4-quart Dutch oven, heat oil over medium heat. Cook onion, bell peppers and garlic in oil 6 to 8 minutes, stirring occasionally, until onion is tender. Stir in water, tomatoes and tomato paste until blended.

2. Stir in remaining ingredients except bread and cheese. Heat to boiling; reduce heat. Cover and simmer 10 minutes, stirring occasionally.

3. Place bread on ungreased cookie sheet. Toast bread in oven about 6 minutes, turning once, until golden brown.

4. Set oven control to broil. Pour hot soup into 6 ovenproof soup bowls or casseroles. Top each with 1 slice toast. Sprinkle with cheese. Broil with tops 3 to 4 inches from heat 1 to 2 minutes or until cheese is melted.

1 SERVING: CAL. 420 (CAL. FROM FAT 80); FAT 9g (SAT. FAT 4g); CHOL. 15mg; SODIUM 1100mg; CARBS. 72g (FIBER 14g); PRO. 27g
% DAILY VALUE: VIT. A 26%; VIT. C 66%; CALC. 36%; IRON 40%
EXCHANGES: 4 STARCH, 2 VEGETABLE, 1 LEAN MEAT
CARB. CHOICES: 5

Marinated Ratatouille Heroes

PREP: 15 min **STAND:** 20 min **COOK:** 10 min ■ **4 SERVINGS**

- 3 cups cubed peeled eggplant (1/2 lb)
- 1 medium green bell pepper, chopped (1 cup)
- 1 medium zucchini or yellow summer squash, cut lengthwise in half, then sliced (1 cup)
- 1 small red onion, sliced
- 1/3 cup balsamic vinaigrette dressing
- 4 crusty Italian or French rolls, split horizontally
- 4 oz soft chèvre (goat) cheese with herbs*
- 1 large tomato, thinly sliced

1. In large bowl, mix eggplant, bell pepper, zucchini and onion. Toss with dressing. Let stand 20 minutes.

2. Transfer vegetables with dressing into 3-quart saucepan. Cook over medium-high heat about 10 minutes, stirring frequently, until vegetables are tender.

3. Spread bottom halves of rolls with cheese. Top with tomato slices and eggplant mixture. Top with top halves of rolls; secure with toothpicks.

**Soft cream cheese with chives and onions can be substituted for the chèvre cheese.*

1 SERVING: CAL. 315 (CAL. FROM FAT 145); FAT 16g (SAT. FAT 6g); CHOL. 30mg; SODIUM 770mg; CARBS. 37g (FIBER 4g); PRO. 10g **% DAILY VALUE:** VIT. A 20%; VIT. C 34%; CALC. 22%; IRON 12% **EXCHANGES:** 2 STARCH, 1 VEGETABLE, 3 FAT **CARB. CHOICES:** 2 1/2

Mediterranean Salad FAST LOW-FAT

PREP: 15 min ■ **4 SERVINGS**

Give this salad a great flavor twist—sprinkle with crumbled feta cheese, blue cheese or Gorgonzola cheese. Serve with crusty rolls and iced tea.

- 2 medium oranges, peeled and cut into 1-inch pieces
- 2/3 cup finely chopped red bell pepper
- 1/2 cup thinly sliced fresh spinach
- 2 tablespoons halved pitted Kalamata or ripe olives
- 1 can (15 to 16 oz) great northern beans, rinsed and drained
- 3 tablespoons red wine vinegar
- 2 tablespoons olive or vegetable oil
- 1/8 teaspoon pepper
- 1 clove garlic, finely chopped

1. In medium bowl, mix oranges, bell pepper, spinach, olives and beans.

2. In tightly covered container, shake remaining ingredients. Pour over orange mixture; toss.

1 SERVING: CAL. 235 (CAL. FROM FAT 70); FAT 8g (SAT. FAT 1g); CHOL. 0mg; SODIUM 45mg; CARBS. 37g (FIBER 7g); PRO. 11g **% DAILY VALUE:** VIT. A 38%; VIT. C 100%; CALC. 12%; IRON 24% **EXCHANGES:** 1 1/2 STARCH, 1/2 FRUIT, 1 VEGETABLE, 1/2 HIGH-FAT MEAT **CARB. CHOICES:** 2 1/2

Broiled Portabella Mushroom Salad

Broiled Portabella Mushroom Salad FAST

PREP: 10 min **BROIL:** 7 min ▪ **4 SERVINGS**

During the summer, cook the portabella mushrooms on an outdoor grill for extra flavor. If goat cheese isn't your favorite, use 1/2 cup garden-vegetable or soft cream cheese with chives and onions instead.

- 1/2 cup Italian dressing
- 3/4 lb sliced fresh portabella mushrooms
- 4 cups bite-size pieces mixed salad greens
- 1/2 cup crumbled herbed or plain chèvre (goat) cheese (2 oz)
- 1/2 cup shredded mozzarella cheese (2 oz)
- 4 slices French bread, toasted and cut in half
- 4 roma (plum) tomatoes, sliced

1. Set oven control to broil. Spray broiler pan rack with cooking spray. Brush dressing on both sides of mushrooms; reserve remaining dressing. Place mushrooms on rack in broiler pan. Broil with tops 2 to 4 inches from heat 4 minutes; turn. Broil about 3 minutes longer or just until mushrooms are tender.

2. Meanwhile, divide salad greens among 4 plates. In small bowl, mix cheeses; spread on toast.

3. Place mushrooms on salad greens. Top with tomatoes. Drizzle with remaining dressing. Serve with toast.

1 SERVING: CAL. 425 (CAL. FROM FAT 190); FAT 21g (SAT. FAT 5g); CHOL. 25mg; SODIUM 890mg; CARBS. 43g (FIBER 4g); PRO. 16g **% DAILY VALUE:** VIT. A 44%; VIT. C 36%; CALC. 28%; IRON 20% **EXCHANGES:** 2 STARCH, 2 VEGETABLE, 1 HIGH-FAT MEAT, 2 1/2 FAT **CARB. CHOICES:** 3

CHAPTER 19

20 Minutes or Less

LOW-FAT = *3g or less, except main dishes with 10g or less* FAST = *Ready in 20 minutes or less* BREAD MACHINE = *Bread machine directions* SLOW COOKER = *Slow cooker directions* LIGHTER = *25% fewer calories or grams of fat*

◀ **Asian Chicken Roll-ups (page 524)**

20 Minutes or Less Cooking Basics

Is getting dinner on the table fast your greatest cooking challenge? If so, you're not alone. Everyone is busy these days, trying to do as much as possible, especially during the week. That's when easy speedy meals are essential. Look no further; the solutions are right here! The recipes in this chapter taste great, go together easily, and take just 20 minutes or less, start to finish. You'll find simple shortcuts that shave kitchen time, like using convenience products and time-saving cooking techniques. Check out all of the handy tips and recipes on the following pages to help get you out of the kitchen fast.

20-MINUTE MEAL TIPS

Do It Ahead!

Why not chop another onion or two or brown up an extra pound of ground beef while you're already in the kitchen? Just taking that extra bit of time to make some things ahead really saves you time in the future. And on those nights when you'd rather get in and out of the kitchen fast, you'll have a great head start! Here are some handy do-ahead ideas that work:

Bread

- Make bread crumbs, either plain or seasoned with your favorite herbs, spices or seasoning blend, from extra or stale bread. Put desired amounts in resealable plastic freezer bags or containers with lids; label and date. Freeze up to 3 months.

Grains and Pasta

- Cook grains and pasta ahead so you can fix supper fast. Be sure to store them right; check out Storing and Reheating Cooked Grains on page 337 and Storing and Reheating Cooked Pasta on page 352.

Meat and Poultry

- Cut uncooked meat and poultry into cubes or slices. Arrange in single layer on foil-lined baking pan or cookie sheet; freeze. Remove from baking pan. Put the amount you'll use at one time in separate resealable plastic freezer bags or containers with lids; label and date. Freeze up to 6 months. Use in casseroles, skillet meals, soups, stews and stir-fries.
- Make extra uncooked hamburger patties. Place waxed paper between each patty, then wrap tightly; label and date. Freeze up to 4 months. To use patties, thaw in refrigerator before cooking.
- Make extra uncooked or cooked meatballs. Arrange in single layer on foil-lined baking pan or cookie sheet; freeze. Remove from baking pan. Put the number you'll use at one time in separate resealable plastic freezer bags or containers with lids; label and date. Freeze uncooked meatballs up to 4 months and cooked meatballs up to 3 months. Use cooked meatballs directly from freezer in cooked recipes. If using uncooked meatballs, cook until no longer pink in center and thermometer inserted in center reads 160°F.
- Cook ground beef plain or with seasonings and diced onions or other diced vegetables; drain. Spoon the amount you'll use at one time into resealable plastic freezer bags or containers with lids; label and date. Freeze up to 3 months. Use in casseroles, chilies, skillet meals, sloppy joes, soups, spaghetti or tacos.

Produce

- Chop bell peppers, carrots, celery and onions. Arrange in single layer on foil-lined baking pan or cookie sheet; freeze. Remove from baking pan. Put the amounts you usually need at a time in resealable plastic freezer bags or containers with lids; label and date. Freeze up to 1 month. To use, add unthawed vegetables directly to the dish being cooked. Or to sauté, thaw slightly just to break apart pieces. Use in casseroles, skillet meals, soups, stews and stir-fries.

FIX-IT-FAST PANTRY

Keep your cupboard stocked with these quick dinner basics. Convenience foods are a little more expensive, but the trade-off is the time you save getting dinner on the table in less than half an hour.

Bakery/Bread

- French bread
- Pita bread
- Pizza crust (ready-to-eat)
- Sandwich buns
- Tortillas, flour

Dairy

- Cheeses (cubed, shredded, sliced)
- Cheese spreads
- Cream cheese
- Eggs
- Refrigerated pasta
- Refrigerated pasta sauces
- Refrigerated potatoes
- Sour cream
- Yogurt

Fish/Meat/Poultry

- Chicken breasts (boneless skinless)
- Deli meats
- Fish (fillets, steaks)
- Ground beef
- Pork (boneless chops, tenderloin)
- Precooked shredded meats and poultry in barbecue sauce
- Preseasoned meats and poultry (ready-to-cook)
- Turkey (slices, tenderloins)

Frozen

- Filled pasta
- Fish products (breaded, unbreaded)
- Noodles
- Potatoes
- Seafood
- Vegetables (combinations, plain)

Grocery

- Beans (canned plain, flavored)
- Bisquick® mix
- Bread crumbs (plain, flavored)
- Broth (beef, chicken, vegetable)
- Chicken (canned)
- Couscous
- Dried herbs
- Olives
- Pasta
- Pasta sauces
- Rice (instant)
- Roasted red bell peppers
- Salmon, Shrimp (canned)
- Seasoning packets (Alfredo, gravy, meat loaf, sloppy joe, spaghetti)
- Sun-dried tomatoes
- Tomato products (plain, seasoned)
- Tuna (canned, in pouches)
- Vegetables

Produce

- Bagged lettuce (complete kits, lettuce mixtures, plain lettuce)
- Carrots (baby-cut, shredded)
- Fruit (fresh precut)
- Garlic (minced in jars)
- Vegetables (fresh precut)
- Vegetables (mixtures in bags)

Condiments/Sauces/ Seasonings

- Barbecue sauce
- Marinades
- Mustard
- Salsa
- Seasoning blends, dried
- Stir-fry sauces
- Teriyaki sauces

Pecan-Maple Chicken **FAST**

PREP: 5 min **COOK:** 12 min ■ **4 SERVINGS**

4 boneless skinless chicken breasts (about 1 1/4 lb)
2 tablespoons butter or margarine
1/2 teaspoon salt
2 tablespoons maple-flavored syrup
1/2 cup pecan halves

1. Between sheets of plastic wrap or waxed paper, flatten each chicken breast to 1/4-inch thickness (see page 327).

2. In 12-inch nonstick skillet, melt butter with salt over medium heat. Cook chicken in butter 1 to 2 minutes, turning once, until brown.

3. Stir in maple syrup and pecans. Cook 8 to 10 minutes, turning chicken once and stirring pecans once or twice, until chicken is no longer pink in center.

1 SERVING: CAL. 320 (CAL. FROM FAT 170); FAT 19g (SAT. FAT 6g); CHOL. 90mg; SODIUM 410mg; CARBS. 9g (FIBER 1g); PRO. 28g
% DAILY VALUE: VIT. A 4%; VIT. C 0%; CALC. 2%; IRON 6%
EXCHANGES: 1/2 OTHER CARB., 4 LEAN MEAT, 1 1/2 FAT
CARB. CHOICES: 1/2

◀ **Quick 'n Crunchy Potato Chip Chicken**

Quick 'n Crunchy Potato Chip Chicken **FAST**

PREP: 5 min **COOK:** 12 min ■ **4 SERVINGS**

Add great crunch and flavor to chicken. Choose your favorite flavor of potato chips, like Cheddar or barbecue, and crush them into a tasty coating. In fact, why not use the crumbs in the bottom of the bag? To quickly crush chips, place them in a tightly sealed plastic food-storage bag and crush with a rolling pin.

4 cups sour cream and onion-flavored potato chips, crushed (1 cup)
1 tablespoon parsley flakes
1 large egg
2 teaspoons Worcestershire sauce
2 tablespoons vegetable oil
4 boneless skinless chicken breasts (about 1 1/4 lb)

1. In shallow bowl, mix crushed potato chips and parsley. In another shallow bowl, beat egg and Worcestershire sauce.

2. In 10-inch nonstick skillet, heat oil over medium-low heat. Dip chicken into egg mixture, then coat with potato chip mixture.

3. Cook chicken in oil 10 to 12 minutes, turning once, until deep golden brown and juice of chicken is clear when center at thickest part is cut (170°F).

1 SERVING: CAL. 305 (CAL. FROM FAT 155); FAT 17g (SAT. FAT 3g); CHOL. 125mg; SODIUM 200mg; CARBS. 9g (FIBER 1g); PRO. 29g **% DAILY VALUE:** VIT. A 2%; VIT. C 2%; CALC. 2%; IRON 8% **EXCHANGES:** 1/2 STARCH, 4 LEAN MEAT, 1 FAT **CARB. CHOICES:** 1/2

Spicy Skillet Chicken FAST LOW-FAT

PREP: 5 min **COOK:** 15 min ▪ **4 SERVINGS**

1 to 2 teaspoons chili powder
1/2 teaspoon salt
1/4 teaspoon pepper
4 boneless skinless chicken breasts (about 1 1/4 lb)
1 tablespoon vegetable oil
1 can (15 oz) black beans, rinsed and drained
1 cup (11 oz) whole kernel corn with red and green peppers, undrained
1/3 cup salsa
2 cups hot cooked rice (page 375)

1. In small bowl, mix chili powder, salt and pepper. Sprinkle evenly over both sides of chicken.

2. In 10-inch nonstick skillet, heat oil over medium heat. Cook chicken in oil 8 to 10 minutes, turning once, until juice is clear when center of thickest part is cut (170°F).

3. Stir in beans, corn and salsa. Heat to boiling; reduce heat. Cover and simmer 3 to 5 minutes or until vegetables are hot. Serve with rice.

1 SERVING: CAL. 460 (CAL. FROM FAT 70); FAT 8g (SAT. FAT 2g); CHOL. 75mg; SODIUM 870mg; CARBS. 66g (FIBER 9g); PRO. 40g
% DAILY VALUE: VIT. A 6%; VIT. C 10%; CALC. 10%; IRON 28%
EXCHANGES: 4 STARCH, 4 VERY LEAN MEAT, 1 VEGETABLE
CARB. CHOICES: 4 1/2

Pasta with Turkey and Asian Vegetables FAST LOW-FAT

PREP: 10 min **COOK:** 10 min ▪ **4 SERVINGS**

8 oz uncooked capellini (angel hair) pasta
1 box (9 oz) frozen sugar snap pea pods
12 oz turkey breast tenderloins, cut into thin strips
1 large red bell pepper, cut into thin strips (1 1/2 cups)
2 cloves garlic, finely chopped
1 tablespoon grated gingerroot
4 medium green onions, sliced (1/4 cup)
1 tablespoon sesame seed, toasted (page 215)

1. Cook pasta as directed on package, adding frozen pea pods to the cooking water with the pasta. Drain well; transfer to large serving bowl.

2. Meanwhile, spray 12-inch skillet with cooking spray; heat over medium-high heat. In skillet, cook turkey, bell pepper, garlic and gingerroot 5 to 10 minutes, stirring constantly, until turkey is no longer pink in center and bell pepper is crisp-tender.

3. Toss turkey mixture, pasta and pea pods. Sprinkle with onions and sesame seed.

1 SERVING: CAL. 355 (CAL. FROM FAT 25); FAT 3g (SAT. FAT 1g); CHOL. 55mg; SODIUM 45mg; CARBS. 54g (FIBER 5g); PRO. 31g
% DAILY VALUE: VIT. A 54%; VIT. C 90%; CALC. 6%; IRON 28%
EXCHANGES: 3 STARCH, 2 1/2 VERY LEAN MEAT, 2 VEGETABLE
CARB. CHOICES: 3 1/2

Thai Chicken with Basil FAST

PREP: 10 min **COOK:** 10 min ▪ **4 SERVINGS**

4 boneless skinless chicken breasts (about 1 1/4 lb)
2 tablespoons vegetable oil
3 cloves garlic, finely chopped
2 red or green jalapeño chilies, seeded and finely chopped
1 tablespoon fish sauce or soy sauce
1 teaspoon sugar
1/4 cup chopped fresh basil leaves
1 tablespoon chopped fresh mint leaves
1 tablespoon chopped unsalted roasted peanuts

1. Cut each chicken breast into 4 pieces.

2. In 12-inch skillet, heat oil over medium-high heat. Cook chicken, garlic and chilies in oil 8 to 10 minutes, stirring occasionally, until chicken is no longer pink in center. Stir in fish sauce and sugar. Sprinkle with basil, mint and peanuts.

1 SERVING: CAL. 230 (CAL. FROM FAT 110); FAT 12g (SAT. FAT 2g); CHOL. 75mg; SODIUM 300mg; CARBS. 3g (FIBER 1g); PRO. 28g
% DAILY VALUE: VIT. A 6%; VIT. C 2%; CALC. 2%; IRON 6%
EXCHANGES: 4 LEAN MEAT **CARB. CHOICES:** 0

Fettuccine with Chicken and Vegetables FAST

PREP: 5 min **COOK:** 15 min ▪ **4 SERVINGS**

Fresh fettuccine and packaged broccoli flowerets from the produce department help you get this dish to the table faster.

1 package (9 oz) refrigerated fettuccine
2 cups small broccoli flowerets
1/2 cup Italian dressing
1 lb chicken breast strips for stir-fry
1 medium red onion, cut into thin wedges
1/4 teaspoon garlic pepper*
1/2 cup sliced drained roasted red bell peppers (from 7-oz jar)
Shredded Parmesan cheese, if desired

1. Cook and drain fettuccine and broccoli together as directed on fettuccine package. Toss with 2 tablespoons of the dressing. Cover to keep warm.

2. Meanwhile, in 12-inch nonstick skillet, heat 2 tablespoons of the dressing over medium-high heat. Cook chicken, onion and garlic pepper in dressing 4 to 6 minutes, stirring occasionally, until chicken is no longer pink in center.

3. Stir bell peppers and remaining 1/4 cup dressing into chicken mixture. Cook 2 to 3 minutes, stirring occasionally, until warm. Serve chicken mixture over fettuccine and broccoli. Serve with cheese.

**1/8 teaspoon each garlic powder and pepper can be substituted for the garlic pepper.*

1 SERVING: CAL. 470 (CAL. FROM FAT 135); FAT 15g (SAT. FAT 2g); CHOL. 125mg; SODIUM 260mg; CARBS. 49g (FIBER 4g); PRO. 35g
% DAILY VALUE: VIT. A 32%; VIT. C 58%; CALC. 8%; IRON 22%
EXCHANGES: 3 STARCH, 1 VEGETABLE, 31/2 LEAN MEAT
CARB. CHOICES: 3

TIME-SAVING SECRET FOR COOKING VEGETABLES WITH PASTA

When making a pasta dish that cooks fresh or frozen vegetables, add the vegetables to the saucepan of boiling pasta and water during the last 3 to 5 minutes of cooking for crisp-tender vegetables. Drain pasta and vegetables in a colander, and continue with the recipe.

Cheesy Chicken Strips

Cheesy Chicken Strips FAST

PREP: 5 min **BAKE:** 12 min ▪ **4 SERVINGS**

2 cups cheese-flavored crackers, crushed (1 cup)
1/2 cup finely shredded Cheddar cheese (2 oz)
1 large egg
1 lb chicken breast tenders (not breaded)
Barbecue sauce, ketchup or ranch dressing, if desired

1. Heat oven to 400°F. Spray 15 × 10 × 1-inch pan with cooking spray.

2. In large resealable plastic food-storage bag, mix crushed crackers and cheese. In large bowl, beat egg.

3. Add chicken to egg; toss to coat. Remove chicken from egg, allowing excess to drip into bowl, then place in bag of cracker mixture. Seal bag and shake to coat chicken evenly with cracker mixture. Place chicken in single layer in pan.

4. Bake uncovered 10 to 12 minutes or until no longer pink in center. Serve with barbecue sauce.

1 SERVING: CAL. 300 (CAL. FROM FAT 130); FAT 14g (SAT. FAT 6g); CHOL. 140mg; SODIUM 340mg; CARBS. 11g (FIBER 0g); PRO. 32g
% DAILY VALUE: VIT. A 6%; VIT. C 0%; CALC. 10%; IRON 10%
EXCHANGES: 1 STARCH, 4 LEAN MEAT **CARB. CHOICES:** 1

Chicken-Rice Skillet FAST

PREP: 5 min **COOK:** 10 min **STAND:** 5 min ■ **4 SERVINGS**

- 1 tablespoon vegetable oil
- 1 1/4 lb boneless skinless chicken breasts, cut into 1-inch pieces
- 2 cups water
- 1 tablespoon butter or margarine
- 1 bag (1 lb) frozen broccoli, red peppers, onions and mushrooms (or other combination), thawed and drained
- 2 cups uncooked instant rice
- 1 teaspoon salt
- 1/4 teaspoon pepper
- 1 cup shredded Cheddar cheese (4 oz)

1. In 12-inch skillet, heat oil over medium-high heat. Cook chicken in oil 3 to 4 minutes, stirring occasionally, until no longer pink in center.

2. Add water and butter; heat to boiling. Stir in vegetables, rice, salt and pepper. Sprinkle with cheese; remove from heat.

3. Cover and let stand about 5 minutes or until water is absorbed.

1 SERVING: CAL. 585 (CAL. FROM FAT 190); FAT 21g (SAT. FAT 10g); CHOL. 125mg; SODIUM 870mg; CARBS. 54g (FIBER 3g); PRO. 45g **% DAILY VALUE:** VIT. A 50%; VIT. C 54%; CALC. 20%; IRON 22% **EXCHANGES:** 3 STARCH, 2 VEGETABLE, 4 1/2 LEAN MEAT, 1 FAT **CARB. CHOICES:** 3 1/2

◀ Chicken-Rice Skillet

Turkey Soft Tacos FAST LOW-FAT

PREP: 10 min **COOK:** 10 min ■ **4 SERVINGS**

Speed preparation time by using already-chopped garlic in jars, and look for bags of frozen chopped onions—no tears!

- 1/2 cup chicken broth
- 1 medium onion, chopped (1/2 cup)
- 1 small red or green bell pepper, diced (1/2 cup)
- 1/2 cup frozen whole kernel corn (from 1-lb bag)
- 1/2 lb ground turkey breast
- 4 cloves garlic, finely chopped
- 1/2 cup salsa
- 1/4 cup chopped fresh cilantro
- 8 flour tortillas (8 to 10 inch), warmed*
- Sour cream, if desired

1. In 10-inch nonstick skillet, heat broth to boiling over high heat. Cook onion, bell pepper and corn in broth 2 to 3 minutes, stirring occasionally, until vegetables are crisp-tender. Reduce heat to medium-high.

2. Stir in turkey and garlic. Cook 2 minutes, stirring occasionally. Stir in salsa. Cook about 5 minutes, stirring occasionally, until turkey is no longer pink. Stir in cilantro.

3. Spoon slightly less than 1/2 cup turkey mixture down center of each tortilla; roll up tortilla. Serve with sour cream.

**To warm tortillas, heat them in a hot ungreased skillet or griddle for 30 seconds to 1 minute. Or wrap desired number of tortillas tightly in foil and heat in 250°F oven for 15 minutes. Or place 2 tortillas at a time between dampened microwavable paper towels or sheets of microwavable plastic wrap and microwave on High for 15 to 20 seconds until warm.*

1 SERVING: CAL. 370 (CAL. FROM FAT 65); FAT 7g (SAT. FAT 2g); CHOL. 40mg; SODIUM 710mg; CARBS. 58g (FIBER 5g); PRO. 23g **% DAILY VALUE:** VIT. A 28%; VIT. C 36%; CALC. 14%; IRON 22% **EXCHANGES:** 4 STARCH, 1 1/2 VERY LEAN MEAT **CARB. CHOICES:** 4

Italian White Beans with Chicken FAST

PREP: 10 min **COOK:** 10 min ▪ **4 SERVINGS**

1 tablespoon olive or vegetable oil
1 tablespoon chopped fresh or 1 teaspoon dried basil leaves
1 clove garlic, finely chopped
2 cups cut-up cooked chicken or turkey
1/2 cup chopped drained oil-packed sun-dried tomatoes
1/4 cup sliced ripe olives
2 cans (15 to 16 oz each) great northern beans, rinsed and drained

1. In 10-inch skillet, heat oil over medium heat. Cook basil and garlic in oil 3 minutes, stirring frequently.

2. Stir in remaining ingredients. Cook 5 to 7 minutes, stirring frequently, until hot.

1 SERVING: CAL. 445 (CAL. FROM FAT 110); FAT 12g (SAT. FAT 2g); CHOL. 60mg; SODIUM 180mg; CARBS. 57g (FIBER 14g); PRO. 41g **% DAILY VALUE:** VIT. A 6%; VIT. C 12%; CALC. 22%; IRON 52% **EXCHANGES:** 4 STARCH, 4 VERY LEAN MEAT **CARB. CHOICES:** 4

QUICK-COOKING CUT-UPS

"No matter how you cut it" doesn't apply to quick-cooking techniques. How about a bowl of creamy fresh mashed potatoes in 10 minutes instead of the usual 20? How food is cut up before it's cooked affects cooking time. Cutting meat, poultry or vegetables into smaller or thinner pieces shortens cooking. Another speedy shortcut is to flatten boneless skinless chicken breasts to a thickness of 1/4 inch.

Double-Cheese, Spinach and Chicken Pizza FAST

PREP: 5 min **BAKE:** 10 min ▪ **6 SERVINGS**

Why not buy bags of fresh spinach and shredded cheese? All the hard work of washing and shredding is already done.

1 package (14 oz) ready-to-serve original Italian pizza crust or other 12-inch ready-to-serve pizza crust
1 cup shredded Havarti cheese (4 oz)
2 cups washed fresh baby spinach leaves (from 10-oz bag)
1 cup diced cooked chicken
1/4 cup chopped drained roasted red bell peppers (from 7-oz jar)
1/2 teaspoon garlic salt
1 cup shredded Cheddar cheese (4 oz)

1. Heat oven to 425°F. Place pizza crust on ungreased pizza pan.

2. Top with Havarti cheese, spinach, chicken, bell peppers, garlic salt and Cheddar cheese.

3. Bake 8 to 10 minutes or until crust is golden brown.

1 SERVING: CAL. 385 (CAL. FROM FAT 160); FAT 18g (SAT. FAT 9g); CHOL. 60mg; SODIUM 660mg; CARBS. 36g (FIBER 2g); PRO. 20g **% DAILY VALUE:** VIT. A 36%; VIT. C 12%; CALC. 22%; IRON 16% **EXCHANGES:** 2 STARCH, 1 VEGETABLE, 2 MEDIUM-FAT MEAT, 1 FAT **CARB. CHOICES:** 2 1/2

Asian Chicken Roll-Ups

FAST

PREP: 15 min ▪ **4 SERVINGS**

Look for bags of shredded lettuce and carrots in the produce case. Or, use 3 cups broccoli slaw instead.

- 2 tablespoons crunchy peanut butter
- 2 tablespoons teriyaki baste and glaze (from 12-oz bottle)*
- 1 tablespoon packed brown sugar
- 1 tablespoon hot water
- 1 teaspoon sesame oil or vegetable oil
- 4 flour tortillas (8 to 10 inch)
- 8 slices sliced cooked deli chicken breast
- 1 1/2 cups shredded iceberg lettuce
- 1 1/2 cups shredded carrots
- 1/2 cup chopped fresh cilantro

1. In small bowl, beat peanut butter, teriyaki baste and glaze, brown sugar, water and oil with wire whisk until smooth.

2. Spread about 2 tablespoons peanut butter mixture over each tortilla. Top each with 2 slices chicken, about 1/3 cup lettuce, about 1/3 cup carrots and 2 tablespoons cilantro. Roll up tortillas.

**Stir-fry sauce can be substituted for the teriyaki baste and glaze.*

1 ROLL-UP: CAL. 280 (CAL. FROM FAT 90); FAT 10g (SAT. FAT 2g); CHOL. 25mg; SODIUM 540mg; CARBS. 35g (FIBER 4g); PRO. 16g
% DAILY VALUE: VIT. A 100%; VIT. C 8%; CALC. 8%; IRON 12%
EXCHANGES: 2 STARCH, 1 LEAN MEAT, 1 VEGETABLE, 1 FAT
CARB. CHOICES: 2

Savory Beef Tenderloin

FAST

PREP: 10 min **COOK:** 10 min ▪ **4 SERVINGS**

Slice prep time by purchasing pre-sliced mushrooms; just measure and start cooking!

- 1 lb beef tenderloin
- 2 teaspoons chopped fresh or 1/2 teaspoon dried marjoram leaves
- 2 teaspoons sugar
- 1 teaspoon coarsely ground pepper
- 1 tablespoon vegetable oil
- 1 cup sliced fresh mushrooms (3 oz)
- 1 small onion, thinly sliced
- 3/4 cup beef broth
- 1/4 cup dry red wine or nonalcoholic wine
- 1 tablespoon cornstarch

1. Cut beef into four 3/4-inch slices. In small bowl, mix marjoram, sugar and pepper; rub on both sides of beef slices.

2. In 10-inch skillet, heat oil over medium-high heat. Cook beef in oil 3 to 5 minutes, turning once, until brown. Remove beef to serving platter; keep warm.

3. In drippings in skillet, cook mushrooms and onion over medium-high heat about 2 minutes, stirring occasionally, until onion is crisp-tender.

4. In small bowl, mix broth, wine and cornstarch; stir into mushroom mixture. Cook over medium-high heat about 2 minutes, stirring constantly, until mixture thickens and boils. Boil and stir 1 minute. Pour over beef.

1 SERVING: CAL. 240 (CAL. FROM FAT 110); FAT 12g (SAT. FAT 4g); CHOL. 65mg; SODIUM 250mg; CARBS. 6g (FIBER 1g); PRO. 26g
% DAILY VALUE: VIT. A 2%; VIT. C 0%; CALC. 2%; IRON 14%
EXCHANGES: 1 VEGETABLE, 3 LEAN MEAT, 1 FAT
CARB. CHOICES: 1/2

Skillet Calzone

Skillet Calzone FAST

PREP: 5 min **BROIL:** 2 min **COOK:** 9 min ■ **4 SERVINGS**

- 8 diagonally cut slices French bread, 1/2 inch thick
- Cooking spray
- 2 tablespoons grated Parmesan cheese
- 1 lb lean (at least 80%) ground beef
- 1 small green bell pepper, sliced
- 1 or 2 cloves garlic, finely chopped
- 1 can (14.5 oz) diced tomatoes with Italian-style herbs (or other variety), undrained
- 1 can (8 oz) pizza sauce
- 1 jar (4.5 oz) sliced mushrooms, drained

1. Set oven control to broil. Place bread slices on ungreased cookie sheet. Spray bread with cooking spray; sprinkle with cheese. Broil with tops 4 to 6 inches from heat 1 to 2 minutes or until light brown; set aside.

2. In 10-inch skillet, cook beef, bell pepper and garlic over medium-high heat 5 to 7 minutes, stirring occasionally, until beef is brown; drain. Stir in tomatoes, pizza sauce and mushrooms. Cook 1 to 2 minutes or until hot.

3. Place 2 toasted bread slices on each of 4 serving plates; top with beef mixture.

1 SERVING: CAL. 495 (CAL. FROM FAT 200); FAT 22g (SAT. FAT 8g); CHOL. 65mg; SODIUM 1,040mg; CARBS. 44g (FIBER 5g); PRO. 30g **% DAILY VALUE:** VIT. A 14%; VIT. C 36%; CALC. 14%; IRON 28 **EXCHANGES:** 2 STARCH, 2 VEGETABLE, 3 MEDIUM-FAT MEAT, 1 1/2 FAT **CARB. CHOICES:** 3

Bow-Tie Pasta with Beef and Tomatoes FAST

PREP: 5 min **COOK:** 15 min ▪ **4 SERVINGS**

- 2 cups uncooked farfalle (bow-tie) pasta (5 oz)
- 1 tablespoon olive or vegetable oil
- 1 cup frozen stir-fry bell peppers and onions (from 1-lb bag)
- 1 lb thinly sliced beef for stir-fry
- 1 can (14.5 oz) Italian-style stewed tomatoes, undrained
- 1 teaspoon garlic salt
- 1/4 teaspoon pepper
- Fresh basil leaves, if desired
- Freshly shredded Parmesan cheese, if desired

1. Cook and drain pasta as directed on package.

2. Meanwhile, in 12-inch skillet, heat oil over medium-high heat. Cook frozen stir-fry vegetables in oil 3 minutes, stirring frequently. Stir in beef. Cook 5 to 6 minutes, stirring frequently, until beef is no longer pink.

3. Stir in tomatoes, garlic salt and pepper. Cook 2 to 3 minutes, stirring frequently and breaking up tomatoes slightly with spoon, until mixture is hot. Stir in pasta. Cook 1 to 2 minutes, stirring constantly, until pasta is well coated and hot. Garnish with basil. Serve with cheese.

1 SERVING: CAL. 350 (CAL. FROM FAT 110); FAT 12g (SAT. FAT 4g); CHOL. 125mg; SODIUM 300mg; CARBS. 31g (FIBER 2g); PRO. 29g **% DAILY VALUE:** VIT. A 2%; VIT. C 14%; CALC. 2%; IRON 20% **EXCHANGES:** 2 STARCH, 3 LEAN MEAT, 1/2 FAT **CARB. CHOICES:** 2

Orange Teriyaki Beef with Noodles FAST LOW-FAT

PREP: 5 min **COOK:** 15 min ▪ **4 SERVINGS**

Check out the Asian-foods section in your grocery store—you'll find many teriyaki stir-fry sauces. Some are thick and others, a bit thinner. Try several until you find the one that you like best.

- 1 lb beef boneless sirloin, cut into thin strips
- 1 can (14 oz) beef broth
- 1/4 cup teriyaki stir-fry sauce
- 2 tablespoons orange marmalade
- Dash of ground red pepper (cayenne)
- 1 1/2 cups frozen snap pea pods (from 1-lb bag)
- 1 1/2 cups uncooked fine egg noodles (3 oz)

1. Spray 12-inch skillet with cooking spray. Cook beef in skillet over medium-high heat 2 to 4 minutes, stirring occasionally, until brown. Remove beef from skillet; keep warm.

2. In same skillet, mix broth, stir-fry sauce, marmalade and red pepper. Heat to boiling. Stir in pea pods and noodles; reduce heat to medium. Cover and cook about 5 minutes or until noodles are tender.

3. Stir in beef. Cook uncovered 2 to 3 minutes or until sauce is slightly thickened.

1 SERVING: CAL. 260 (CAL. FROM FAT 45); FAT 5g (SAT. FAT 2g); CHOL. 80mg; SODIUM 1,190mg; CARBS. 27g (FIBER 2g); PRO. 29g **% DAILY VALUE:** VIT. A 4%; VIT. C 20%; CALC. 4%; IRON 24% **EXCHANGES:** 1 STARCH, 3 VERY LEAN MEAT, 2 VEGETABLE, 1/2 FAT **CARB. CHOICES:** 2

Orange Teriyaki Beef with Noodles ▶

Cheesy Hamburger Hash

FAST

PREP: 5 min **COOK:** 15 min ■ **4 SERVINGS**

1 lb lean (at least 80%) ground beef
1 tablespoon butter or margarine
1 bag (1 lb 4 oz) refrigerated diced potatoes with onions
1 can (14.5 oz) diced tomatoes with Italian herbs (or other variety), undrained
1 tablespoon pizza seasoning or Italian seasoning
1 1/2 cups shredded pizza cheese blend (mozzarella and Cheddar cheeses 6 oz)
2 tablespoons chopped fresh parsley

1. In 12-inch nonstick skillet, cook beef over medium-high heat 8 to 10 minutes, stirring occasionally, until brown; drain. Remove beef from skillet.

2. Melt butter in same skillet. Add potatoes. Cover and cook over medium heat about 5 minutes, stirring occasionally, until almost tender. Stir in beef, tomatoes and pizza seasoning. Cook about 5 minutes, stirring occasionally, until thoroughly heated.

3. Sprinkle with cheese and parsley. Cover and heat until cheese is melted.

1 SERVING: CAL. 515 (CAL. FROM FAT 245); FAT 27g (SAT. FAT 13g); CHOL. 115mg; SODIUM 480mg; CARBS. 31g (FIBER 4g); PRO. 37g
% DAILY VALUE: VIT. A 22%; VIT. C 22%; CALC. 32%; IRON 24%
EXCHANGES: 2 STARCH, 4 1/2 MEDIUM-FAT MEAT, 1/2 FAT
CARB. CHOICES: 2

Chili Beef 'n Pasta

FAST

PREP: 10 min **COOK:** 10 min ■ **4 SERVINGS**

2 1/2 cups uncooked rotini pasta (8 oz)
1 lb lean (at least 80%) ground beef
1 medium onion, chopped (1/2 cup)
1 can (11.25 oz) condensed fiesta chili beef with beans soup
1 jar (8 oz) salsa (1 cup)
1/2 cup water
1 cup shredded Cheddar cheese (4 oz)

1. Cook and drain pasta as directed on package.

2. Meanwhile, in 12-inch skillet, cook beef and onion over medium-high heat, stirring occasionally, until beef is brown; drain. Reduce heat to medium. Stir soup, salsa and water into beef. Cook until thoroughly heated.

3. Serve beef mixture over pasta. Sprinkle with cheese.

1 SERVING: CAL. 400 (CAL. FROM FAT 180); FAT 20g (SAT. FAT 9g); CHOL. 95mg; SODIUM 650mg; CARBS. 32g (FIBER 3g); PRO. 26g
% DAILY VALUE: VIT. A 10%; VIT. C 10%; CALC. 14%; IRON 20%
EXCHANGES: 2 STARCH, 3 MEDIUM-FAT MEAT **CARB. CHOICES:** 2

Chili Beef 'n Pasta ▶

Pizza Burgers FAST

PREP: 5 min **COOK:** 14 min ■ **6 SANDWICHES**

- 1 lb lean (at least 80%) ground beef
- 1 medium onion, chopped (1/2 cup)
- 1 small green bell pepper, chopped (1/2 cup)
- 1 jar (14 oz) or 1 can (15 oz) pepperoni-flavored or regular pizza sauce
- 1/2 cup sliced ripe olives, if desired
- 6 sandwich buns, split
- 3/4 cup shredded pizza cheese blend (mozzarella and Cheddar cheeses 3 oz)

1. In 10-inch skillet, cook beef, onion and bell pepper over medium heat 8 to 10 minutes, stirring occasionally, until beef is brown; drain.

2. Stir in pizza sauce and olives. Heat to boiling, stirring occasionally.

3. Spoon about 1/2 cup beef mixture on bottom half of each bun. Immediately sprinkle each with 2 tablespoons of the cheese; add tops of bun. Serve immediately, or let stand about 2 minutes until cheese is melted.

1 SANDWICH: CAL. 365 (CAL. FROM FAT 155); FAT 17g (SAT. FAT 6g); CHOL. 60mg; SODIUM 670mg; CARBS. 29g (FIBER 3g); PRO. 24g
% DAILY VALUE: VIT. A 12%; VIT. C 20%; CALC. 18%; IRON 16%
EXCHANGES: 2 STARCH, 2 1/2 MEDIUM-FAT MEAT, 1/2 FAT
CARB. CHOICES: 2

Ranchero Beef Pizza FAST

PREP: 5 min **BAKE:** 15 min ■ **6 SERVINGS**

- 1 package (14 oz) ready-to-serve original Italian pizza crust or other 12-inch ready-to-serve pizza crust
- 2 cups shredded smoked or regular Cheddar cheese (8 oz)
- 2 cups shredded or sliced cooked beef in barbecue sauce (from 20- or 24-oz container)
- 4 slices red onion, separated into rings

1. Heat oven to 400°F.

2. Place pizza crust on ungreased cookie sheet. Sprinkle with 1 cup of the cheese. Top with beef and onion. Sprinkle with remaining 1 cup cheese.

3. Bake about 15 minutes or until hot.

1 SERVING: CAL. 475 (CAL. FROM FAT 190); FAT 21g (SAT. FAT 12g); CHOL. 70mg; SODIUM 970mg; CARBS. 52g (FIBER 2g); PRO. 20g
% DAILY VALUE: VIT. A 10%; VIT. C 2%; CALC. 22%; IRON 18%
EXCHANGES: 3 STARCH, 1 VEGETABLE, 1 HIGH-FAT MEAT, 3 FAT
CARB. CHOICES: 3 1/2

Beef and Artichoke Fettuccine **FAST**

PREP: 5 min **COOK:** 15 min ■ **6 SERVINGS**

- 8 oz uncooked spinach fettuccine
- 1 jar (6 to 7 oz) marinated artichoke hearts, cut in half and 1 tablespoon marinade reserved
- 1 small onion, finely chopped (1/4 cup)
- 1 cup half-and-half
- 1/2 cup grated Parmesan cheese
- 2 cups cut-up cooked roast beef
- Pepper, if desired

1. Cook and drain fettuccine as directed on package.

2. Meanwhile, in 12-inch skillet, heat 1 tablespoon reserved artichoke marinade to boiling over medium-high heat. Cook onion in marinade about 2 minutes, stirring occasionally, until crisp-tender.

3. Stir in half-and-half; heat until hot. Stir in cheese, artichoke hearts and beef; heat until hot.

4. Add fettuccine; toss. Sprinkle with pepper.

1 SERVING: CAL. 355 (CAL. FROM FAT 145); FAT 16g (SAT. FAT 7g); CHOL. 90mg; SODIUM 300mg; CARBS. 31g (FIBER 3g); PRO. 22g
% DAILY VALUE: VIT. A 6%; VIT. C 2%; CALC. 18%; IRON 18%
EXCHANGES: 2 STARCH, 2 MEDIUM-FAT MEAT, 1 FAT
CARB. CHOICES: 2

Speedy Cassoulet **FAST**

LOW-FAT

PREP: 5 min **COOK:** 10 min ■ **4 SERVINGS**

Traditional French cassoulet is a slow-cooking white bean stew made with a variety of meats, such as sausage, pork, duck or goose. This one still tastes great—but it's ready to serve in just fifteen minutes! And the best part—it cuts back on fat and calories, too.

- 1 can (15 to 16 oz) cannellini or great northern beans, rinsed and drained
- 1 can (14.5 oz) diced tomatoes with roasted garlic (or other variety), undrained
- 1 can (14 oz) chicken broth
- 1/2 lb fully cooked turkey kielbasa (turkey Polish sausage), cut into 1/2-inch slices (1 1/2 cups)
- 1 1/2 cups frozen chopped green bell peppers (from 10-oz bag), thawed*
- Seasoned bread crumbs, if desired

1. In 3-quart saucepan, heat beans, tomatoes, broth and kielbasa to boiling, stirring occasionally; reduce heat.

2. Stir in bell peppers. Simmer uncovered 5 minutes, stirring occasionally. Sprinkle with bread crumbs.

**1 1/2 cups frozen stir-fry bell peppers and onions (from 1-lb bag), thawed, can be substituted for the frozen chopped bell peppers.*

1 SERVING: CAL. 250 (CAL. FROM FAT 55); FAT 6g (SAT. FAT 2g); CHOL. 30mg; SODIUM 1170mg; CARBS. 35g (FIBER 9g); PRO. 22g
% DAILY VALUE: VIT. A 10%; VIT. C 52%; CALC. 14%; IRON 30%
EXCHANGES: 2 STARCH, 1 VEGETABLE, 2 VERY LEAN MEAT
CARB. CHOICES: 2

Breaded Pork Chops FAST

PREP: 5 min **COOK:** 10 min ▪ **8 SERVINGS**

1/2 cup Original Bisquick® mix
12 saltine crackers, crushed (1/2 cup)
1 teaspoon seasoned salt
1/4 teaspoon pepper
1 large egg or 1/4 cup fat-free cholesterol-free egg product
2 tablespoons water
8 pork boneless loin chops, 1/2 inch thick (about 2 lb)
3 tablespoons vegetable oil

1. In shallow bowl, mix Bisquick® mix, cracker crumbs, seasoned salt and pepper. In another shallow bowl, mix egg and water.

2. Dip pork into egg mixture, then coat with Bisquick® mixture.

3. In 12-inch nonstick skillet, heat oil over medium-high heat. Cook pork in oil 10 to 12 minutes, turning once, until no longer pink in center.

1 SERVING: CAL. 265 (CAL. FROM FAT 135); FAT 15g (SAT. FAT 4g); CHOL. 90mg; SODIUM 380mg; CARBS. 8g; (FIBER 0g); PRO. 24g
% DAILY VALUE: VIT. A 0%; VIT. C 0%; CALC. 2%; IRON 6%
EXCHANGES: 1/2 STARCH; 3 LEAN MEAT, 1 1/2 FAT
CARB. CHOICES: 1/2

Nut-Crusted Pork Medallions FAST

PREP: 10 min **COOK:** 8 min ▪ **4 SERVINGS**

You'll think you're in the Deep South when you taste this dish. The honey, cornmeal and pecans give these medallions of pork that traditional Southern flavor.

1 large egg
1/4 cup honey
3/4 to 1 lb pork tenderloin, cut into 1/2-inch slices
1 cup chopped pecans (4 oz)
1/2 cup yellow cornmeal
1 teaspoon salt
1/2 teaspoon pepper
2 tablespoons vegetable oil

1. In large bowl, mix egg and honey. Add pork slices; toss to coat.

2. In food processor, place pecans, cornmeal, salt and pepper. Cover and process until finely chopped. Place pecan mixture in resealable plastic food-storage bag. Add pork slices; seal bag and shake to coat.

3. In 10-inch nonstick skillet, heat oil over medium-high heat. Cook pork in oil 6 to 8 minutes, turning once, until golden brown on outside and no longer pink in center.

1 SERVING: CAL. 530 (CAL. FROM FAT 290); FAT 32g (SAT. FAT 4g); CHOL. 105mg; SODIUM 640mg; CARBS. 35g (FIBER 4g); PRO. 25g
% DAILY VALUE: VIT. A 2%; VIT. C 0%: CALC. 2%; IRON 14%
EXCHANGES: 2 STARCH, 2 LEAN MEAT, 4 FAT **CARB. CHOICES:** 2

◀ **Breaded Pork Chops**

Sesame Pork with Garlic Cream Sauce FAST

PREP: 5 min **COOK:** 4 min **BROIL:** 11 min ■ **6 SERVINGS**

- 1 1/2 lb pork tenderloin
- 2 tablespoons vegetable oil
- 1/4 cup sesame seed
- 1 tablespoon butter or margarine
- 2 cloves garlic, finely chopped
- 1 package (3 oz) cream cheese, cut into cubes and softened
- 1/3 cup milk
- 1 tablespoon chopped fresh chives or 1 teaspoon freeze-dried chives

1. Cut pork crosswise into 12 slices. Between sheets of plastic wrap or waxed paper, flatten slices to 1/2-inch thickness by pounding with heel of hand.

2. Set oven control to broil. Brush oil on both sides of pork. Place pork on rack in broiler pan. Sprinkle with half of the sesame seed. Broil pork with tops 4 to 6 inches from heat 6 minutes; turn. Sprinkle with remaining sesame seed. Broil about 5 minutes longer or until pork is no longer pink in center.

3. Meanwhile, in 10-inch skillet, melt butter over medium heat. Cook garlic in butter about 1 minute, stirring occasionally; reduce heat. Add cream cheese and milk. Cook 2 to 3 minutes, stirring constantly, until smooth and hot. Stir in chives. Serve sauce with pork.

1 SERVING: CAL. 295 (CAL. FROM FAT 170); FAT 19g (SAT. FAT 7g); CHOL. 95mg; SODIUM 120mg; CARBS. 2g (FIBER 1g); PRO. 29g
% DAILY VALUE: VIT. A 8%; VIT. C 0%; CALC. 4%; IRON 10%
EXCHANGES: 4 LEAN MEAT, 1 1/2 FAT **CARB. CHOICES:** 0

Pasta with Prosciutto and Asiago Cheese FAST

PREP: 10 min **COOK:** 10 min ■ **4 SERVINGS**

It may taste like Parmesan and Romano, but it's really Asiago. This rich, nutty Italian cheese goes perfect with pasta.

- 2 cups uncooked fusilli (corkscrew) pasta (6 oz)
- 2 tablespoons olive or vegetable oil
- 1 package (8 oz) sliced fresh mushrooms (3 cups)
- 6 medium green onions, cut into 1/2-inch pieces
- 1 medium red bell pepper, coarsely chopped (1 cup)
- 1 clove garlic, finely chopped
- 1 package (3 oz) sliced prosciutto ham or fully cooked ham, cut into thin strips
- 1 tablespoon chopped fresh or 1/2 teaspoon dried basil leaves
- 2 teaspoons chopped fresh or 1/4 teaspoon dried oregano leaves
- 1/4 teaspoon salt
- 1/4 cup shredded Asiago cheese

1. Cook and drain pasta as directed on package.

2. Meanwhile, in 10-inch nonstick skillet, heat 1 tablespoon of the oil over medium-high heat. Cook mushrooms, onions, bell pepper and garlic in oil 2 to 3 minutes, stirring occasionally, until vegetables are tender.

3. Stir in prosciutto, basil, oregano and salt. Stir in pasta and remaining 1 tablespoon oil; toss. Sprinkle each serving with cheese.

1 SERVING: CAL. 230 (CAL. FROM FAT 110); FAT 12g (SAT. FAT 3g); CHOL. 20mg; SODIUM 560mg; CARBS. 40g (FIBER 3g); PRO. 15g
% DAILY VALUE: VIT. A 40%; VIT. C 52%; CALC. 10%; IRON 16%
EXCHANGES: 2 STARCH, 1 LEAN MEAT, 2 VEGETABLE, 1 1/2 FAT
CARB. CHOICES: 2 1/2

Creamy Ham and Fettuccine FAST

PREP: 10 min **COOK:** 6 min ▪ **4 SERVINGS**

- 1 package (9 oz) refrigerated fettuccine
- 1 tablespoon vegetable oil
- 4 medium green onions, sliced (1/4 cup)
- 6 oz thinly sliced fully cooked ham, cut into 1/4-inch strips
- 1 cup frozen green peas, thawed (from 1-lb bag)
- 1/3 cup sour cream
- 1/4 cup ranch dressing
- 2 tablespoons milk

1. Cook and drain fettuccine as directed on package.

2. Meanwhile, in 12-inch skillet, heat oil over medium-high heat. Cook onions in oil 1 minute, stirring frequently. Stir in ham and peas. Cook 1 to 2 minutes, stirring frequently, until hot; reduce heat to low.

3. Stir in sour cream, dressing and milk. Add fettuccine. Cook 2 to 3 minutes, stirring constantly, until hot.

1 SERVING: CAL. 470 (CAL. FROM FAT 190); FAT 21g (SAT. FAT 5g); CHOL. 100mg; SODIUM 840mg; CARBS. 49g (FIBER 4g); PRO. 21g **% DAILY VALUE:** VIT. A 10%; VIT. C 4%; CALC. 8%; IRON 22% **EXCHANGES:** 3 STARCH, 1 1/2 MEDIUM-FAT MEAT, 2 1/2 FAT **CARB. CHOICES:** 3

LIGHTER CREAMY HAM AND FETTUCCINE

For 10 grams of fat and 380 calories per serving, omit oil; spray skillet with cooking spray. Use Canadian-style bacon instead of the ham. Use reduced-fat sour cream, reduced-fat ranch dressing and fat-free (skim) milk.

Countryside Pasta Toss

FAST LOW-FAT

PREP: 10 min **COOK:** 10 min ▪ **4 SERVINGS**

- 1 cup uncooked rotini pasta (3 oz)
- 3/4 lb new potatoes, cut into 1/2-inch wedges
- 1 cup baby-cut carrots
- 1 cup broccoli flowerets
- 1/2 cup sugar snap pea pods
- 1 tablespoon butter or margarine
- 2 tablespoons chopped fresh parsley
- 1 teaspoon dried dill weed
- 1/2 teaspoon salt
- 4 oz fully cooked ham, cut into thin strips

1. Cook and drain pasta as directed on package.

2. Meanwhile, place steamer basket in 1/2 inch water in 3-quart saucepan (water should not touch bottom of basket). Place potatoes and carrots in basket. Cover tightly and heat to boiling; reduce heat to medium-low. Steam 5 minutes. Add broccoli and pea pods. Cover and steam about 2 minutes longer or until potatoes are tender.

3. Place vegetables in medium bowl. Add butter, parsley, dill weed and salt; toss. Add ham and pasta; toss.

1 SERVING: CAL. 250 (CAL. FROM FAT 55); FAT 6g (SAT. FAT 3g); CHOL. 25mg; SODIUM 760mg; CARBS. 37g (FIBER 5g); PRO. 12g **% DAILY VALUE:** VIT. A 100%; VIT. C 32%; CALC. 4%; IRON 18% **EXCHANGES:** 2 STARCH, 1 VEGETABLE, 1/2 MEDIUM-FAT MEAT, 1/2 FAT **CARB. CHOICES:** 2 1/2

Orange and Dill Pan-Seared Tuna FAST LOW-FAT

PREP: 5 min **COOK:** 15 min ■ **4 SERVINGS**

- 4 tuna, swordfish or other firm fish steaks, 3/4 inch thick (4 oz each)
- 1/2 teaspoon peppered seasoned salt
- 1 small red onion, thinly sliced
- 3/4 cup orange juice
- 1 tablespoon chopped fresh or 1/4 teaspoon dried dill weed
- 1 tablespoon butter or margarine
- 1 teaspoon grated orange peel, if desired

1. Heat 10-inch nonstick skillet over medium-high heat. Sprinkle both sides of tuna with peppered seasoned salt. Add tuna to skillet; reduce heat to medium-low. Cover and cook 6 to 8 minutes, turning once, until tuna is slightly pink in center. Remove tuna from skillet; keep warm.

2. Add onion to skillet. Cook over medium-high heat 2 minutes, stirring occasionally. Stir in orange juice; cook 2 minutes. Stir in dill weed, butter and orange peel. Cook 1 to 2 minutes or until slightly thickened. Serve sauce over fish.

1 SERVING: CAL. 215 (CAL. FROM FAT 80); FAT 9g (SAT. FAT 3g); CHOL. 50mg; SODIUM 240mg; CARBS. 6g (FIBER 0g); PRO. 27g
% DAILY VALUE: VIT. A 74%; VIT. C 14%; CALC. 2%; IRON 8%
EXCHANGES: 4 LEAN MEAT **CARB. CHOICES:** 1/2

Snapper with Sautéed Tomato-Pepper Sauce

FAST LOW-FAT

PREP: 8 min **COOK:** 12 min ■ **4 SERVINGS**

For a slightly sweeter-tasting sauce, use a red, yellow or orange bell pepper.

- 1 lb red snapper, cod or other medium-firm fish fillets (1/2 inch thick)
- 1 large tomato, chopped (1 cup)
- 1 small green bell pepper, chopped (1/2 cup)
- 1 small onion, sliced
- 2 tablespoons finely chopped fresh cilantro or parsley
- 1/4 teaspoon salt
- 1/4 cup dry white wine or chicken broth

1. If fish fillets are large, cut into 4 serving pieces. Heat 10-inch nonstick skillet over medium heat.

2. Arrange fish, skin sides down, in single layer in skillet. Cook uncovered 4 to 6 minutes, turning once, until fish flakes easily with fork. Remove fish to warm platter; keep warm.

3. In same skillet, cook remaining ingredients except wine over medium heat 3 to 5 minutes, stirring frequently, until bell pepper and onion are crisp-tender. Stir in wine; cook about 1 minute or until hot. Spoon tomato mixture over fish.

1 SERVING: CAL. 125 (CAL. FROM FAT 20); FAT 2g (SAT. FAT 0g); CHOL. 60mg; SODIUM 250mg; CARBS. 5g (FIBER 1g); PRO. 22g
% DAILY VALUE: VIT. A 10%; VIT. C 22%; CALC. 2%; IRON 4%
EXCHANGES: 1 VEGETABLE, 3 VERY LEAN MEAT
CARB. CHOICES: 0

Ramen Shrimp and Vegetables **FAST** **LOW-FAT**

PREP: 5 min **COOK:** 15 min ■ **4 SERVINGS**

Look for bags of fresh stir-fry vegetables in the produce aisle. The mixture of vegetables will vary but usually have carrots, celery, bok choy, bean sprouts and broccoli.

- 1 lb uncooked peeled deveined medium shrimp, thawed if frozen and tails peeled
- 2 cups water
- 1 package (3 oz) Oriental-flavor ramen noodle soup mix
- 1 bag (1 lb) fresh stir-fry vegetables
- 1/4 cup stir-fry sauce

1. Heat 12-inch nonstick skillet over medium-high heat. Cook shrimp in skillet 2 to 4 minutes, stirring occasionally, until pink and firm. Remove shrimp from skillet; keep warm.

2. Heat water to boiling in same skillet. Break up noodles from soup mix into water; stir until slightly softened. Stir in vegetables.

3. Heat to boiling. Boil 4 to 6 minutes, stirring occasionally, until vegetables are crisp-tender. Stir in seasoning packet from soup mix and stir-fry sauce. Cook 3 to 5 minutes, stirring frequently, until hot. Stir in shrimp.

▲ **Ramen Shrimp and Vegetables**

1 SERVING: CAL. 210 (CAL. FROM FAT 35); FAT 4g (SAT. FAT 1g); CHOL. 160mg; SODIUM 1160mg; CARBS. 21g (FIBER 3g); PRO. 22g **% DAILY VALUE:** VIT. A 100%; VIT. C 30%; CALC. 6%; IRON 24% **EXCHANGES:** 1 STARCH, 1 VEGETABLE, 2 1/2 VERY LEAN MEAT, 1/2 FAT **CARB. CHOICES:** 1 1/2

RAMEN BEEF AND VEGETABLES Substitute 1 lb beef sirloin or tenderloin strips for stir-fry for the shrimp. Cook beef in sprayed and heated skillet 3 to 5 minutes, stirring occasionally, until brown.

Garlic Shrimp **FAST** **LOW-FAT**

PREP: 15 min **COOK:** 5 min ■ **4 SERVINGS**

- 1 tablespoon vegetable oil
- 3 large cloves garlic, finely chopped
- 1 lb uncooked peeled deveined medium shrimp, thawed if frozen and tails peeled
- 1 large carrot, cut into julienne strips (1 1/2 × 1/4 × 1/4 inch)
- 2 tablespoons chopped fresh cilantro
- Hot cooked noodles or rice (page 376), if desired

1. In 12-inch skillet, heat oil over medium-high heat. Cook garlic in oil 1 minute, stirring frequently. Add shrimp. Cook 1 minute, stirring frequently.

2. Stir in carrot. Cook about 3 minutes, stirring frequently, until shrimp are pink and firm and carrot is crisp-tender. Stir in cilantro.

3. Serve shrimp mixture over noodles.

1 SERVING: CAL. 120 (CAL. FROM FAT 35); FAT 4g (SAT. FAT 1g); CHOL. 160mg; SODIUM 190mg; CARBS. 3g (FIBER 1g); PRO. 18g **% DAILY VALUE:** VIT. A 70%; VIT. C 2%; CALC. 4%; IRON 14% **EXCHANGES:** 1 VEGETABLE, 2 VERY LEAN MEAT, 1/2 FAT **CARB. CHOICES:** 0

Corn and Crab Quesadillas

FAST

PREP: 5 min **COOK:** 10 min ■ **6 SERVINGS**

1 package (8 oz) cream cheese, softened
1 can (11 oz) whole kernel corn, drained
1/2 cup chopped fresh cilantro or parsley
1/3 cup sliced green onions (5 medium)
1 jar (2 oz) diced pimientos, drained
1/2 teaspoon pepper
1/4 teaspoon ground red pepper (cayenne)
1 lb chopped cooked crabmeat or imitation crabmeat (2 cups)
6 sun-dried tomato or spinach-cilantro flavored flour tortillas (8 to 10 inch)
1 tablespoon butter or margarine, melted
Sour cream and chopped fresh cilantro, if desired

1. In medium bowl, mix cream cheese, corn, cilantro, onions, pimientos, pepper and red pepper. Fold in crabmeat. Spread 2/3 cup of the crabmeat mixture over each tortilla; fold tortilla in half, pressing lightly. Brush both sides of each tortilla with butter.

2. In 12-inch skillet, cook 3 tortillas at a time over medium-high heat about 5 minutes, turning once, until light brown. Garnish with sour cream and cilantro.

1 SERVING: CAL. 420 (CAL. FROM FAT 180); FAT 20g (SAT. FAT 10g); CHOL. 120mg; SODIUM 660mg; CARBS. 36g (FIBER 3g); PRO. 24g
% DAILY VALUE: VIT. A 30%; VIT. C 20%; CALC. 8%; IRON 20%
EXCHANGES: 2 STARCH, 1 VEGETABLE, 2 LEAN MEAT
CARB. CHOICES: 2 1/2

Penne with Vegetables in Tomato-Basil Sauce

FAST

LOW-FAT

PREP: 5 min **COOK:** 15 min ■ **4 SERVINGS**

Fresh can be fast! Look for already-shredded carrots in the produce aisle, and chop the onion in a food processor using short pulses.

2 cups uncooked penne pasta (6 oz)
1 tablespoon olive or vegetable oil
1 medium onion, chopped (1/2 cup)
1/2 cup shredded carrot
1 can (14.5 oz) diced tomatoes with basil, garlic and oregano (or other variety), undrained
1 can (8 oz) tomato sauce
1 small zucchini, thinly sliced (1 cup)
1/2 teaspoon dried basil leaves
2 tablespoons chopped fresh parsley
1/4 cup sh redded Parmesan cheese

1. Cook and drain pasta as directed on package.

2. Meanwhile, in 10-inch nonstick skillet, heat oil over medium-high heat. Cook onion and carrot in oil 2 to 3 minutes, stirring occasionally, until crisp-tender. Stir in tomatoes and tomato sauce. Cook 5 minutes.

3. Stir in zucchini and basil; reduce heat to medium. Cook about 5 minutes, stirring occasionally, until sauce is desired consistency. Stir in parsley. Serve over pasta. Sprinkle with cheese.

1 SERVING: CAL. 265 (CAL. FROM FAT 55); FAT 6g (SAT. 2g); CHOL. 5mg; SODIUM 650mg; CARBS. 47g (FIBER 5g); PRO. 11g
% DAILY VALUE: VIT. A 74%; VIT. C 24%; CALC. 14%; IRON 16%
EXCHANGES: 2 1/2 STARCH, 2 VEGETABLE, 1/2 FAT **CARB. CHOICES:** 3

Corn and Crab Quesadillas ▶

Three-Pepper Pasta FAST LOW-FAT

PREP: 5 min **COOK:** 15 min ▪ **4 SERVINGS**

- 3 cups uncooked farfalle (bow-tie) pasta (6 oz)
- 1 tablespoon olive or vegetable oil
- 1 small green bell pepper, cut into 1/4-inch strips
- 1 small red bell pepper, cut into 1/4-inch strips
- 1 small yellow bell pepper, cut into 1/4-inch strips
- 1 cup tomato pasta sauce (any variety)
- Chopped fresh basil leaves, if desired
- Shredded Parmesan cheese, if desired

1. Cook and drain pasta as directed on package.

2. Meanwhile, in 10-inch nonstick skillet, heat oil over medium heat. Cook bell peppers in oil about 5 minutes, stirring occasionally, until crisp-tender.

3. Stir in pasta sauce. Cook 2 to 3 minutes or until hot. Serve sauce over pasta. Top each serving with basil and cheese.

1 SERVING: CAL. 260 (CAL. FROM FAT 55); FAT 6g (SAT. FAT 1g); CHOL. 0mg; SODIUM 310mg; CARBS. 48g (FIBER 3g); PRO. 7g **% DAILY VALUE:** VIT. A 32%; VIT. C 78%; CALC. 2%; IRON 12% **EXCHANGES:** 3 STARCH, 1/2 FAT **CARB. CHOICES:** 3

Spring Vegetable Fettuccine FAST

PREP: 5 min **COOK:** 12 min ▪ **4 SERVINGS**

- 1 package (9 oz) refrigerated fettuccine
- 1 cup half-and-half
- 1 container (5 oz) garlic-and-herb spreadable cheese
- 1/2 teaspoon garlic salt
- 1 bag (1 lb) frozen baby peas, carrots, pea pods and corn (or other combination), thawed and drained
- Freshly ground pepper, if desired

1. Cook and drain fettuccine as directed on package.

2. Meanwhile, in 12-inch nonstick skillet, heat half-and-half to boiling over medium heat. Stir in cheese and garlic salt. Cook, stirring constantly, until cheese is melted and mixture is smooth.

3. Stir in vegetables. Cook about 7 minutes, stirring occasionally, until vegetables are tender. Serve over fettuccine. Sprinkle with pepper.

1 SERVING: CAL. 460 (CAL. FROM FAT 200); FAT 22g (SAT. FAT 13g); CHOL. 115mg; SODIUM 290mg; CARBS. 51g (FIBER 5g); PRO. 15g **% DAILY VALUE:** VIT. A 100%; VIT. C 30%; CALC. 14%; IRON 20% **EXCHANGES:** 3 STARCH, 1 VEGETABLE, 1/2 HIGH-FAT MEAT, 3 1/2 FAT **CARB. CHOICES:** 3 1/2

SHRIMP VEGETABLE FETTUCCINE Add 1/2 lb cooked peeled shrimp, thawed if frozen, with the vegetables in Step 3.

Shrimp Vegetable Fettuccine ▶

Mostaccioli with Sun-Dried Tomato Pesto FAST

LOW-FAT

PREP: 5 min **COOK:** 15 min ▪ **6 SERVINGS**

- 3 cups uncooked mostaccioli pasta (9 oz)
- 1/3 cup oil-packed sun-dried tomatoes, drained
- 1/4 cup firmly packed fresh mint leaves or 4 teaspoons dried mint leaves
- 2 tablespoons chopped walnuts
- 2 tablespoons tomato paste
- 1 tablespoon olive or vegetable oil
- 1 teaspoon lemon juice
- 1/2 teaspoon pepper
- 1 clove garlic
- 1/2 cup crumbled feta cheese

1. Cook and drain pasta as directed on package.

2. Meanwhile, in food processor or blender, place remaining ingredients except cheese. Cover and process until mixture is almost smooth.

3. In large bowl, toss pasta, tomato mixture and cheese.

1 SERVING: CAL. 250 (CAL. FROM FAT 70); FAT 8g (SAT. FAT 3g); CHOL. 10mg; SODIUM 200mg; CARBS. 37g (FIBER 2g); PRO. 8g
% DAILY VALUE: VIT. A 8%; VIT. C 6%; CALC. 8%; IRON 12%
EXCHANGES: 2 STARCH, 1 VEGETABLE, 1 1/2 FAT
CARB. CHOICES: 2 1/2

BOIL WATER FASTER

Need boiling water in a hurry? Start with hot water and cover the saucepan with a lid; it will boil faster!

Rustic Vegetable Baguette with Smashed Avocado

FAST

PREP: 15 min **BROIL:** 3 min ▪ **4 SANDWICHES**

- 1 loaf (1 lb) rustic sourdough baguette bread
- 1/3 cup Italian dressing
- 6 oz sliced Cheddar cheese
- 2 small ripe avocados, pitted and peeled
- 4 small tomatoes, sliced

1. Set oven control to broil. Cut bread horizontally in half. Drizzle dressing on cut side of top half of bread. Arrange cheese on bottom half. Place both halves on large cookie sheet. Broil with tops 4 to 6 inches from heat 2 to 3 minutes or until cheese is melted and bread is slightly golden brown.

2. In small bowl, mash avocados with fork until slightly smooth. Spread avocado over cheese; top with tomato slices and top half of bread. Cut loaf into 4 pieces.

1 SERVING: CAL. 675 (CAL. FROM FAT 335); FAT 37g (SAT. FAT 12g); CHOL. 45mg; SODIUM 1,120mg; CARBS. 68g (FIBER 7g); PRO. 23g
% DAILY VALUE: VIT. A 24%; VIT. C 38%; CALC. 34%; IRON 26%
EXCHANGES: 4 STARCH, 1 VEGETABLE, 1 1/2 HIGH-FAT MEAT, 4 FAT
CARB. CHOICES: 4 1/2

Middle Eastern Pita Pizzas

Middle Eastern Pita Pizzas

FAST LOW-FAT

PREP: 10 min **BAKE:** 10 min ▪ **4 SERVINGS**

- 4 pita breads (6 inch)
- 1/2 cup roasted garlic-flavored or regular hummus
- 1 cup crumbled feta cheese (4 oz)
- 1 small onion, sliced
- 2 cups thinly sliced fresh spinach
- 1 large tomato, seeded and chopped (1 cup)
- 1/4 cup sliced ripe or Kalamata olives

1. Heat oven to 400°F.

2. Place pita breads in ungreased 15 × 10 × 1-inch pan. Spread hummus on pita breads. Sprinkle with cheese.

3. Bake 8 to 10 minutes or until cheese is melted. Top each pizza with onion, spinach, tomato and olives.

1 SERVING: CAL. 300 (CAL. FROM FAT 90); FAT 10g (SAT. FAT 5g); CHOL. 25mg; SODIUM 790mg; CARBS. 41g (FIBER 5g); PRO. 12g **% DAILY VALUE:** VIT. A 38%; VIT. C 12%; CALC. 24%; IRON 18% **EXCHANGES:** 2 STARCH, 2 VEGETABLE, 2 FAT **CARB. CHOICES:** 3

MIDDLE EASTERN CHICKEN PITA PIZZAS Sprinkle 1 to 2 tablespoons chopped cooked chicken over hummus on each pita bread. Continue as directed.

Helpful Nutrition and Cooking Information

NUTRITION GUIDELINES

We provide nutrition information for each recipe that includes calories, fat, cholesterol, sodium, carbohydrate, fiber and protein. Individual food choices can be based on this information.

RECOMMENDED INTAKE FOR A DAILY DIET OF 2,000 CALORIES AS SET BY THE FOOD AND DRUG ADMINISTRATION

Total Fat	**Less than 65g**
Saturated Fat	Less than 20g
Cholesterol	Less than 300mg
Sodium	Less than 2,400mg
Total Carbohydrate	300g
Dietary Fiber	25g

Criteria Used for Calculating Nutrition Information

- The first ingredient was used wherever a choice is given (such as 1/3 cup sour cream or plain yogurt).
- The first ingredient amount was used wherever a range is given (such as 3- to 3 1/2–pound cut-up whole chicken).
- The first serving number was used wherever a range is given (such as 4 to 6 servings).
- "If desired" ingredients and recipe variations were not included (such as sprinkle with brown sugar, if desired).
- Only the amount of a marinade or frying oil that is estimated to be absorbed by the food during preparation or cooking was calculated.

Ingredients Used in Recipe Testing and Nutrition Calculations

- Ingredients used for testing represent those that the majority of consumers use in their homes: large eggs, 2% milk, 80%-lean ground beef, canned ready-to-use chicken broth and vegetable oil spread containing not less than 65 percent fat.
- Fat-free, low-fat or low-sodium products were not used, unless otherwise indicated.
- Solid vegetable shortening (not butter, margarine, nonstick cooking sprays or vegetable oil spread as they can cause sticking problems) was used to grease pans, unless otherwise indicated.

Equipment Used in Recipe Testing

We use equipment for testing that the majority of consumers use in their homes. If a specific piece of equipment (such as a wire whisk) is necessary for recipe success, it is listed in the recipe.

- Cookware and bakeware without nonstick coatings were used, unless otherwise indicated.
- No dark-colored, black or insulated bakeware was used.
- When a pan is specified in a recipe, a metal pan was used; a baking dish or pie plate means ovenproof glass was used.
- An electric hand mixer was used for mixing only when mixer speeds are specified in the recipe directions. When a mixer speed is not given, a spoon or fork was used.

EQUIVALENT MEASURES

3 teaspoons	=	1 tablespoon
4 tablespoons	=	1/4 cup
5 tablespoons + 1 teaspoon	=	1/3 cup
8 tablespoons	=	1/2 cup
12 tablespoons	=	3/4 cup
16 tablespoons	=	1 cup (8 ounces)
2 cups	=	1 pint (16 ounces)
4 cups (2 pints)	=	1 quart (32 ounces)
8 cups (4 pints)	=	1/2 gallon (64 ounces)
4 quarts	=	1 gallon (128 ounces)

COMMON ABBREVIATIONS

degree	° (or dg)	package	pkg
dozen	doz	pint	pt
gallon	gal	pound	lb (or #)
hour	hr	quart	qt
inch	(or in.)	second	sec
minute	min	tablespoon	Tbsp (or T)
ounce	oz	teaspoon	tsp (or t)

Metric Conversion Chart

VOLUME

U.S. Units	Canadian Metric	Australian Metric
1/4 teaspoon	1 mL	1 ml
1/2 teaspoon	2 mL	2 ml
1 teaspoon	5 mL	5 ml
1 tablespoon	15 mL	20 ml
1/4 cup	50 mL	60 ml
1/3 cup	75 mL	80 ml
1/2 cup	125 mL	125 ml
2/3 cup	150 mL	170 ml
3/4 cup	175 mL	190 ml
1 cup	250 mL	250 ml
1 quart	1 liter	1 liter
1 1/2 quarts	1.5 liters	1.5 liters
2 quarts	2 liters	2 liters
2 1/2 quarts	2.5 liters	2.5 liters
3 quarts	3 liters	3 liters
4 quarts	4 liters	4 liters

WEIGHT

U.S. Units	Canadian Metric	Australian Metric
1 ounce	30 grams	30 grams
2 ounces	55 grams	60 grams
3 ounces	85 grams	90 grams
4 ounces (1/4 pound)	115 grams	125 grams
8 ounces (1/2 pound)	225 grams	225 grams
16 ounces (1 pound)	455 grams	500 grams
1 pound	455 grams	1/2 kilogram

MEASUREMENTS

Inches	Centimeters
1	2.5
2	5.0
3	7.5
4	10.0
5	12.5
6	15.0
7	17.5
8	20.5
9	23.0
10	25.5
11	28.0
12	30.5
13	33.0

TEMPERATURES

Fahrenheit	Celsius
32°	0°
212°	100°
250°	120°
275°	140°
300°	150°
325°	160°
350°	180°
375°	190°
400°	200°
425°	220°
450°	230°
475°	240°
500°	260°

Note: The recipes in this cookbook have not been developed or tested using metric measures. When converting recipes to metric, some variations in quality may be noted.

Index

Note: *Italicized page references* indicate photographs or illustrations

A

B

C

D

G

P

S

T

W

Y

Z

Complete your cookbook library with these *Betty Crocker* titles

Betty Crocker's Best Bread Machine Cookbook
Betty Crocker's Best Chicken Cookbook
Betty Crocker's Best Christmas Cookbook
Betty Crocker's Best of Baking
Betty Crocker's Best of Healthy and Hearty Cooking
Betty Crocker's Best-Loved Recipes
Betty Crocker's Bisquick® Cookbook
Betty Crocker Bisquick® II Cookbook
Betty Crocker Bisquick® Impossibly Easy Pies
Betty Crocker Celebrate!
Betty Crocker's Complete Thanksgiving Cookbook
Betty Crocker's Cook Book for Boys and Girls
Betty Crocker's Cook It Quick
Betty Crocker's Cookbook, Bridal Edition
Betty Crocker's Cookie Book
Betty Crocker's Cooking Basics
Betty Crocker's Cooking for Two
Betty Crocker's Cooky Book, Facsimile Edition
Betty Crocker's Diabetes Cookbook
Betty Crocker Dinner Made Easy with Rotisserie Chicken
Betty Crocker Easy Family Dinners
Betty Crocker's Easy Slow Cooker Dinners
Betty Crocker's Eat and Lose Weight
Betty Crocker's Entertaining Basics
Betty Crocker's Flavors of Home
Betty Crocker's 4-Ingredient Dinners
Betty Crocker's Great Grilling
Betty Crocker's Healthy New Choices
Betty Crocker's Indian Home Cooking
Betty Crocker's Italian Cooking
Betty Crocker's Kids Cook!
Betty Crocker's Kitchen Library
Betty Crocker's Living with Cancer Cookbook
Betty Crocker Low-Carb Lifestyle Cookbook
Betty Crocker's Low-Fat Low-Cholesterol Cooking Today
Betty Crocker More Slow Cooker Recipes
Betty Crocker's New Cake Decorating
Betty Crocker's New Chinese Cookbook
Betty Crocker's A Passion for Pasta
Betty Crocker's Picture Cook Book, Facsimile Edition
Betty Crocker's Quick & Easy Cookbook
Betty Crocker's Slow Cooker Cookbook
Betty Crocker's Ultimate Cake Mix Cookbook
Betty Crocker's Vegetarian Cooking
Cocina Betty Crocker (Bilingual—Spanish and English)